Scheduling and Load Balancing in Parallel and Distributed Systems

Scheduling and Load Balancing in Parallel and Distributed Systems

Behrooz A. Shirazi
Ali R. Hurson
Krishna M. Kavi

IEEE Computer Society Press
Los Alamitos, California

Washington   •   Brussels   •   Tokyo

Library of Congress Cataloging-in-Publication Data

Shirazi, Behrooz A.
    Scheduling and load balancing in parallel and distributed systems
    / Behrooz A. Shirazi, Ali R. Hurson, Krishna M. Kavi
       p.   cm.
    Includes bibliographical references.
    ISBN 0-8186-6587-4
    1. Parallel processing (Electronic computers)   2. Electronic data processing—Distributed
processing.   3. Computer capacity—Management.   I. Hurson, A.R.   II. Kavi, Krishna M.
III. Title.
QA76.58.S55   1995
005.4'3—dc20

                                                  95-3159
                                                    CIP

Published by the
IEEE Computer Society Press
10662 Los Vaqueros Circle
P.O. Box 3014
Los Alamitos, CA 90720-1264

IEEE Computer Society Press Order Number BP06587
IEEE Catalog Number EH0417-6
Library of Congress Number 95-3159
ISBN 0-8186-6587-4

Additional copies can be ordered from

| IEEE Computer Society Press Customer Service Center 10662 Los Vaqueros Circle P.O. Box 3014 Los Alamitos, CA 90720-1264 Tel: (714) 821-8380 Fax: (714) 821-4641 Email: cs.books@computer.org | IEEE Service Center 445 Hoes Lane P.O. Box 1331 Piscataway, NJ 08855-1331 Tel: (908) 981-1393 Fax: (908) 981-9667 mis.custserv@computer.org | IEEE Computer Society 13, avenue de l'Aquilon B-1200 Brussels BELGIUM Tel: +32-2-770-2198 Fax: +32-2-770-8505 euro.ofc@computer.org | IEEE Computer Society Ooshima Building 2-19-1 Minami-Aoyama Minato-ku, Tokyo 107 JAPAN Tel: +81-3-3408-3118 Fax: +81-3-3408-3553 tokyo.ofc@computer.org |

Technical Editor: Mukesh Singhal
Production Editor: Lisa O'Conner
Cover Art: Norall Design
Printed in the United States of America by KNI, Incorporated

99 98 97 96   6 5 4 3

The Institute of Electrical and Electronics Engineers, Inc.

Contents

Preface

Our motivation for the publication of this tutorial comes from the profound importance and impact of scheduling and load balancing methods on parallel and distributed systems. Concurrent processing in general, and scheduling and load balancing in particular, have been the subjects of research and development during the past two decades. Since the late 1980s, newly available commercial concurrent systems have heightened interest in the areas of scheduling and load balancing. For example, the number of papers published in this area, both in journals and conference proceedings, has increased continually over the past few years. In addition, several workshops and special issues of journals have recently been dedicated to the topic of scheduling and load balancing in parallel systems. Some examples include:

- a special issue of the *Journal of Parallel and Distributed Computing*, on "Scheduling and Load Balancing," co-edited by Behrooz Shirazi and A. R. Hurson, December 1992;
- a workshop on "Scheduling," in the Supercomputing Conference, coordinated by John Feo and Behrooz Shirazi, November 1992;
- a dedicated track on "Scheduling and Load Balancing," in the Hawaii International Conference on Systems Sciences, coordinated by Behrooz Shirazi and A. R. Hurson, January 1993;
- a dedicated track on "Program Partitioning and Scheduling in Parallel and Distributed Systems," in the Hawaii International Conference on Systems Sciences, coordinated by Min-You Wu, January 1994;
- a dedicated track on "Partitioning and Scheduling for Parallel and Distributed Systems," in the Hawaii International Conference on Systems Sciences, coordinated by Apostolos Gerasoulis and Tao Yang, January 1995.

Many of the international conferences in the areas of parallel or distributed processing have allocated several sessions to both static and dynamic scheduling topics in recent years. Examples of such conferences include the IEEE Symposium on Parallel and Distributed Processing, the International Conference on Parallel Processing, the International Parallel Processing Symposium, and the International Conference on Distributed Computing Systems.

Finally, many journals, such as *IEEE Transactions on Parallel and Distributed Systems*, *Journal of Parallel and Distributed Computing*, *IEEE Transactions on Software Engineering*, and *IEEE Parallel and Distributed Technology,* routinely publish papers in the areas of static scheduling and dynamic load balancing.

The central goal of this book is to provide an overview, a detailed discussion, and a prognosis of future directions of the static scheduling and dynamic load balancing methods in parallel and distributed systems. The book covers a wide range of topics, from theoretical background to practical state-of-the-art scheduling and load balancing techniques. However, as scheduling and load balancing can potentially cover a very broad range of topics, we limit our coverage to the following specific subject matters:

- static task scheduling,
- partitioning and task granularity issues,
- scheduling tools,
- load balancing and load sharing,
- task migration, and
- load indices measurement techniques.

It should be noted that there are some important topics, relevant to the subject of this tutorial, that are not covered here, including system (architecture) partitioning, data partitioning, trace scheduling, loop scheduling, user-level threads, and real-time scheduling. It should be noted that real-time scheduling is already covered in another IEEE book (*Tutorial on Hard Real-Time Systems,* by John A. Stankovic and Krithi Ramamritham, 1988.).

This book is intended to be useful to a large number of readers working on different aspects of parallel and distributed systems, including industry professionals, academic professors, and students, who are involved in research or development in the following areas:

- parallel processing applications;
- compilers and operating systems for parallel or distributed systems;
- software tools for parallel program development; and
- system design for parallel and distributed systems, in general.

The readers are expected to have a basic background in the field of parallel or distributed processing. Therefore, the level of the material presented in this tutorial is in the *intermediate to advanced* range.

To the best of our knowledge, there are no books in the market today that specifically address the topic of scheduling and load balancing in parallel and distributed systems. Some closely related books include *Introduction to Parallel Computing*, by Ted G. Lewis and Hesham El-Rewini, Prentice Hall, 1992, *Partitioning and Scheduling Parallel Programs for Multiprocessors*, by Vivek Sarkar, MIT Press, 1989, *Parallel Programming and Compilers*, by Constantine D. Polychronopoulos, Kluwer Academic Publishers, 1988, *Assignment Problems in Parallel and Distributed Computing*, by Shahid Bokhari, Kluwer Academic Publishers, 1987, and *Distributed Operating Systems*, by Andrzej Goscinski, Addison-Wesley, 1992.

Thus, we strongly feel that it is time to publish a comprehensive tutorial to address the important topic of scheduling and load balancing in parallel and distributed systems.

There is a large body of literature on the subject of scheduling and load balancing. This has made the preparation of this manuscript rather difficult since many outstanding and important papers could not be included due to space limitations. To compensate for this problem and provide a more comprehensive coverage of the topic, we have included an extensive bibliography in the introduction section of each chapter. We hope such sections will help interested readers to identify more easily the important papers in their areas of endeavor.

Behrooz A. Shirazi
The University of Texas at Arlington
Ali R. Hurson
Pennsylvania State University
Krishna M. Kavi
The University of Texas at Arlington

Acknowledgments

The editors would like to express their appreciation to Hsing-Bung Chen, a PhD student in the Department of Computer Science and Engineering at The University of Texas at Arlington, who unselfishly helped the editors in the collection of the papers and participated in the technical discussions leading to this work. The editors' deepest gratitude goes to the anonymous reviewers of the outline of the tutorial and its first draft. The reviewers' insightful comments have helped improve the quality of this work. Finally, the editors are thankful to Mary C. Shirazi for her work in editing the original contributions in this book.

Chapter 1

Introduction to Scheduling and Load Balancing

Advances in hardware and software technologies have led to increased interest in the use of large-scale parallel and distributed systems for database, real-time, defense, and large-scale commercial applications. The operating system and management of the concurrent processes constitute integral parts of the parallel and distributed environments. One of the biggest issues in such systems is the development of effective techniques for the distribution of the processes of a parallel program on multiple processors. The problem is how to distribute (or schedule) the processes among processing elements to achieve some performance goal(s), such as minimizing execution time, minimizing communication delays, and/or maximizing resource utilization [Casavant 1988, Polychronopoulos 1987]. From a system's point of view, this distribution choice becomes a resource management problem and should be considered an important factor during the design phases of multiprocessor systems.

Process scheduling methods are typically classified into several subcategories as depicted in Figure 1.1 [Casavant 1988]. (It should be noted that throughout this manuscript the terms "job," "process," and "task" are used interchangeably.) Local scheduling performed by the operating system of a processor consists of the assignment of processes to the time-slices of the processor. Global scheduling, on the other hand, is the process of deciding where to execute a process in a multiprocessor system. Global scheduling may be carried out by a single central authority, or it may be distributed among the processing elements. In this tutorial, our focus will be on global scheduling methods, which are classified into two major groups: static scheduling and dynamic scheduling (often referred to as dynamic load balancing).

1.1 Static scheduling

In static scheduling, the assignment of tasks to processors is done before program execution begins. Information regarding task execution times and processing resources is assumed to be known at compile time. A task is always executed on the processor to which it is assigned; that is, static scheduling methods are processor nonpreemptive. Typically, the goal of static scheduling methods is to minimize the overall execution time of a concurrent program while minimizing the communication delays. With this goal in mind, static scheduling methods [Lo 1988, Sarkar 1986, Shirazi 1990, Stone 1977] attempt to:

- predict the program execution behavior at compile time (that is, estimate the process or task, execution times, and communication delays);
- perform a partitioning of smaller tasks into coarser-grain processes in an attempt to reduce the communication costs; and,
- allocate processes to processors.

The major advantage of static scheduling methods is that all the overhead of the scheduling process is incurred at compile time, resulting in a more efficient execution time environment compared to dynamic scheduling methods. However, static scheduling suffers from many disadvantages, as discussed shortly.

Static scheduling methods can be classified into optimal and suboptimal. Perhaps one of the most critical shortcomings of static scheduling is that, in general, generating optimal schedules is an NP-complete problem. It is only possible to generate optimal solutions in restricted cases (for example, when the execution time of all of the tasks is the same and only two processors are used). NP-completeness of optimal static scheduling, with or without communication cost considerations, has been proven in the literature [Chretienne 1989, Papadimitriou 1990, Sarkar 1989]. Here, we give a simple example to demonstrate the difficulties in attaining general optimal schedules.

Assume we have n processes, with different execution times, which are to be scheduled on two processing elements, PE_1 and PE_2. Since the goal of a scheduling method is to minimize the completion time of a set of processes, the scheduler must decide which process should be assigned to (or scheduled on) which PE so

1

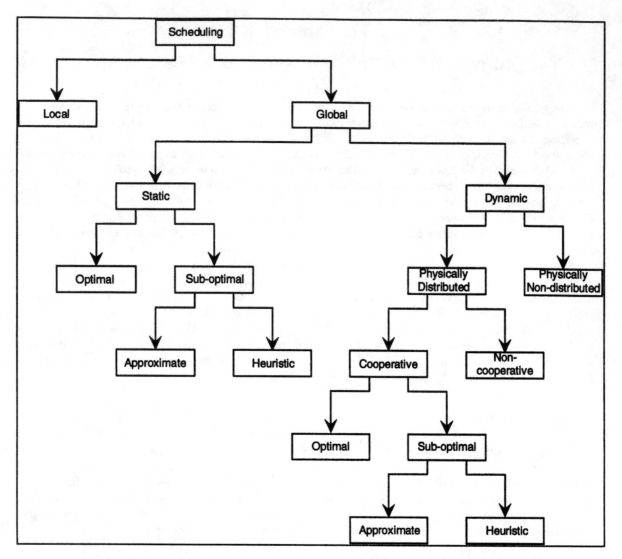

Figure 1.1. Classification of scheduling methods [Casavant 1988].

that the overall completion time is minimized. In this case, the optimum schedule will ensure that the processing loads assigned PE_1 and PE_2 are equal (with no unnecessary delay periods). However, this problem is NP-complete since it can be easily mapped to the well-known, NP-complete "set-partitioning" problem. The set-partitioning problem is as follows:

Let Z be the set of integers. Given a finite set A and a "size" $s(a) \in Z$ for each $a \in A$, find a subset of A (that is , A') such that

$$\sum_{a \in A'} s(a) = \sum_{b \in (A-A')} s(b).$$

Because reaching optimal static schedules is an NP-complete problem, most of the research and development in this area has been focused on suboptimal solutions. These methods are classified into approximate and heuristic approaches. In approximate suboptimal static scheduling methods, the solution space is searched in either a depth-first or a breadth-first fashion. However, instead of searching the entire solution space for an optimal solution, the algorithm stops when a "good" (or acceptable) solution is reached.

Heuristic methods, as the name indicates, rely on rules-of-thumb to guide the scheduling process in the right direction to reach a "near" optimal solution. For example, the length of a critical path for a task is defined as the length of one of several possible longest paths from that task, through several intermediate and dependent tasks, to the end of the program. No concurrent program can complete its execution in a time period less than the length of its critical path. A heuristic scheduling method may take advantage of this fact by giving a higher priority in the scheduling of tasks with longer critical path lengths. The idea is that by scheduling the tasks on the critical path first, we have an opportunity to schedule other tasks around them, thus avoiding the lengthening of the critical path.

It should be noted that there is no universally accepted figure or standard for defining a "good" solution or a degree of "nearness" to an optimal solution. The researchers often use a loose lower-bound on the execution time of a concurrent program (for example, the length of a critical path), and show that their method can always achieve schedules with execution times within a factor of this lower-bound.

In addition to the NP-completeness of optimal general scheduling algorithms, static scheduling suffers from a wide range of problems, most notable of which are the following:

- The insufficiency of efficient and accurate methods for estimating task execution times and communication delays can cause unpredictable performance degradations [Lee 1991, Wang 1991]. The compile-time estimation of the execution time of a program's tasks (or functions) is often difficult to find due to conditional and loop constructs, whose condition values or iteration counts are unknown before execution. Estimating communication delays at compile time is not practical because of the run-time network contention delays.
- Existing task/function scheduling methods often ignore the data distribution issue. This omission causes performance degradations due to run-time communication delays for accessing data at remote sites.
- Finally, static scheduling schemes should be augmented with a tool to provide a performance profile of the predicted execution of the scheduled program on a given architecture. The user can then utilize this tool to improve the schedule or to experiment with a different architecture.

The above shortcomings, as well as the existing and possible solutions to them, will be discussed in detail in the introduction section of the relevant chapters throughout this book.

1.2 Prognosis and future directions in static scheduling

Until now the focus of research in this area has been on the efficiency of scheduling algorithms. By "efficiency" we refer to both the efficiency of the scheduling algorithm itself and the efficiency of the schedule it generates. Based on our experience and evaluations [Shirazi 1990], our contention is that most of the existing heuristic-based static scheduling algorithms perform comparably. Thus, the likelihood is low of finding a scheduling method that can achieve orders-of-magnitude (or even significant) improvements in performance over the existing methods. As a result, we believe that, while this research direction must continue, efforts should be focused on the practical applications of the developed static scheduling methods to the existing parallel systems. This recommendation implies that we may need a whole new set of tools to support the practical application of theoretic scheduling algorithms.

One such tool is a directed acyclic graph (DAG) generator. The input to a DAG generator will be a parallel program, written in the user's choice of language, and its output will be the DAG equivalent of the program (with proper functional dependencies, and execution-time and communication-delay estimations). A more general question in this regard is, if we cannot estimate the execution times and communication delays accurately, can we still get performance via static scheduling? Preliminary results with PYRROS [Yang 1992] show that as long as the task graph is coarse-grain and we use asynchronous communication, we can get good performance. Another supporting tool for static scheduling is a *performance profiler*. The function of a performance profiler tool is to read in the schedule of a parallel program on a given architecture and produce a graphical profile of the expected performance of the input program. The tool should also provide an *ideal parallelism profile* of the application, giving the user an idea of the inherent parallelism in the program.

1.3 Dynamic scheduling

Dynamic scheduling is based on the redistribution of processes among the processors during execution time. This redistribution is performed by transferring tasks from the heavily loaded processors to the lightly loaded processors (called load balancing) with the aim of improving the performance of the application [Eager 1986, Lin 1987, Shivaratri 1992, Wang 1985]. A typical load balancing algorithm is defined by three inherent policies:

- information policy, which specifies the amount of load information made available to job placement decision-makers;
- transfer policy, which determines the conditions under which a job should be transferred, that is, the current load of the host and the size of the job under consideration (the transfer policy may or may not include task migration, that is, suspending an executing task and transferring it to another processor to resume its execution); and
- placement policy, which identifies the processing element to which a job should be transferred.

The load balancing operations may be centralized in a single processor or distributed among all the processing elements that participate in the load balancing process. Many combined policies may also exist. For example, the information policy may be centralized but the transfer and placement policies may be distributed. In that case, all processors send their load information to a central processor and receive system load information from that processor. However, the decisions regarding when and where a job should be transferred are made locally by each processor. If a distributed information policy is employed, each processing element keeps its own local image of the system load. This cooperative policy is often achieved by a gradient distribution of load information among the processing elements [Lin 1987]. Each processor passes its current load information to its neighbors at preset time intervals, resulting in the dispersement of load information among all the processing elements in a short period of time. A distributed-information policy can also be noncooperative. Random scheduling is an example of noncooperative scheduling, in which a heavily loaded processor randomly chooses another processor to which to transfer a job. Random load balancing works rather well when the loads of all the processors are relatively high, that is, when it does not make much difference where a job is executed.

The advantage of dynamic load balancing over static scheduling is that the system need not be aware of the run-time behavior of the applications before execution. The flexibility inherent in dynamic load balancing allows for adaptation to the unforeseen application requirements at run-time. Dynamic load balancing is particularly useful in a system consisting of a network of workstations in which the primary performance goal is maximizing utilization of the processing power instead of minimizing execution time of the applications. The major disadvantage of dynamic load balancing schemes is the run-time overhead due to:

- the load information transfer among processors,
- the decision-making process for the selection of processes and processors for job transfers, and
- the communication delays due to task relocation itself.

1.4 Prognosis and future directions in dynamic load balancing

Up until now research and development in the dynamic load balancing area have been focused on the identification and evaluation of efficient policies for information distribution, job transfers, and placement decision-making. In the future, a greater exchange of information among programmer, compiler, and operating system is needed. In particular, we feel the emphasis will be on the development of efficient policies for load information distribution and placement decision-making, because these two areas cause most of the overhead of dynamic load balancing. Although dynamic load balancing incurs overhead due to task transfer operations, a task transfer will not take place unless the benefits of the relocation outweigh its overhead. Thus, it is our contention that in the future research and development in this area will emphasize:

- hybrid dynamic/static scheduling;
- effective load index measures;
- hierarchical system organizations with local load information distribution and local load balancing policies; and
- incorporation of a set of primitive tools at the distributed operating system level, used to implement different load balancing policies depending on the system architecture and application requirements.

1.5 Chapter organization and overview

The three papers in this chapter provide a general overview of the fields of static scheduling and dynamic load balancing. The first paper, by Casavant and Kuhl, presents a comprehensive taxonomy of scheduling in general-purpose concurrent systems. The proposed taxonomy provides the common terminology and classification mechanism necessary in addressing the scheduling problem in concurrent systems. The second paper, by Stone, is included for its historical significance in that it was one of the first papers to address the issue of multiprocessor scheduling. The paper makes use of the modified Ford-Fulkerson algorithm for finding maximum flows in commodity networks to assign a program's modules in a multiprocessor system. The solutions are discussed to the two-processor problem and its extensions to three- and n-processor problems. The last paper by Shivaratri, Krueger, and Singhal, focuses on the problem of the redistribution of the load of the system among its processors so that overall performance is maximized. The paper provides a good introduction and overview of dynamic scheduling, since it presents the motivations and design trade-offs for several load distribution algorithms; several load balancing algorithms are compared and their performances evaluated.

Bibliography

Bokhari, S. H., *Assignment Problems in Parallel and Distributed Computing*, Kluwer Academic Publishers, Norwell, Mass., 1987.

Bokhari, S. H., "Partitioning Problems in Parallel, Pipelined, and Distributed Computing," *IEEE Trans. Computers*, Vol. C-37, No. 1, Jan. 1988, pp. 48–57.

Casavant, T. L., and J. G. Kuhl, "A Taxonomy of Scheduling in General-Purpose Distributed Computing Systems," *IEEE Trans. Software Eng.*, Vol. 14, No. 2, Feb. 1988, pp. 141–154; reprinted here.

Chretienne, P., "Task Scheduling Over Distributed Memory Machines," *Proc. Int'l Workshop Parallel and Distributed Algorithms*, North Holland Publishers, Amsterdam, 1989.

Eager, D. L., E. D. Lazowska, and J. Zahorjan, "Adaptive Load Sharing in Homogeneous Distributed Systems," *IEEE Trans. Software Eng.*, Vol. SE-12, No. 5, May 1986, pp. 662–675.

Goscinski, A., *Distributed Operating Systems*, Addison-Wesley, Reading, Mass., 1992.

Hummel, S. F., E. Schonberg, and L. E. Flynn, "Factoring: A Method for Scheduling Parallel Loops," *Comm. ACM*, Vol. 35, No. 8, Aug. 1992, pp. 90–101.

Lee, B., A. R. Hurson, and T.-Y. Feng, "A Vertically Layered Allocation Scheme for Data Flow Systems," *J. Parallel and Distributed Computing*, Vol. 11, No. 3, 1991, pp. 175–187.

Lewis, T. G., and H. El-Rewini, *Introduction to Parallel Computing*, Prentice Hall, Englewood Cliffs, N.J., 1992.

Lin, F. C. H., and R. M. Keller, "The Gradient Model Load Balancing Method," *IEEE Trans. Software Eng.*, Vol. SE-13, No. 1, Jan. 1987, pp. 32–38.

Lo, V. M., "Heuristic Algorithms for Task Assignment in Distributed Systems," *IEEE Trans. Computers*, Vol. C-37, No. 11, Nov. 1988, pp. 1384–1397.

Papadimitriou, C., and M. Yannakakis, "Towards an Architecture-Independent Analysis of Parallel Algorithms," *SIAM J. Comput.*, Vol. 19, 1990, pp. 322–328.

Polychronopoulos, C. D., and D. J. Kuck, "Guided Self-Scheduling: A Practical Scheduling Scheme for Parallel Supercomputers," *IEEE Trans. Computers*, Vol. C-36, No. 12, Dec. 1987, pp. 1425–1439.

Polychronopoulos, C. D., *Parallel Programming and Compilers*, Kluwer Academic Publishers, Norwell, Mass., 1988.

Sarkar, V., and J. Hennessy, "Compile-Time Partitioning and Scheduling of Parallel Programs," *Symp. Compiler Construction*, ACM Press, New York, N.Y., 1986, pp. 17–26.

Sarkar, V., *Partitioning and Scheduling Parallel Programs for Multiprocessors*, MIT Press, Cambridge, Mass., 1989.

Shirazi, B., M. Wang, and G. Pathak, "Analysis and Evaluation of Heuristic Methods for Static Task Scheduling," *J. Parallel and Distributed Computing*, Vol. 10, 1990, pp. 222–232.

Shirazi, B., and A. R. Hurson, eds., *Proc. Hawaii Intl Conf. Systems Sciences*, Special Software Track on "Scheduling and Load Balancing," Vol. 2, IEEE CS Press, Los Alamitos, Calif., 1993, pp. 484–486.

Shirazi, B., and A. R. Hurson,, eds., *J. Parallel and Distributed Computing*, Special Issue on "Scheduling and Load Balancing," Vol. 16, No. 4, Dec. 1992.

Shivaratri, N. G., P. Kreuger, and M. Singhal, "Load Distributing for Locally Distributed Systems," *Computer*, Vol. 25, No. 12, Dec. 1992, pp. 33–44; reprinted here.

Stone, H. S.,"Multiprocessor Scheduling with the Aid of Network Flow Algorithms," *IEEE Trans. Software Eng.*, Vol. SE-3, No. 1, Jan. 1977, pp. 85–93; reprinted here.

Wang, M., et al., "Accurate Communication Cost Estimation in Static Task Scheduling," *Proc. 24th Ann. Hawaii Int'l Conf. System Sciences*, Vol. I, IEEE CS Press, Los Alamitos, Calif., 1991, pp. 10–16.

Wang, Y.-T., and R. J. T. Morris, "Load Sharing in Distributed Systems," *IEEE Trans. Computers*, Vol. C-34, No. 3, Mar. 1985, pp. 204–217.

Xu, J., and K. Hwang, "Dynamic Load Balancing for Parallel Program Execution on a Message-Passing Multicomputer," *Proc. 2nd IEEE Symp. Parallel and Distributed Processing*, IEEE CS Press, Los Alamitos, Calif., 1990, pp. 402–406.

Yang, T., and A. Gerasoulis, "PYRROS: Static Task Scheduling and Code Generation for Message Passing Multiprocessors," *Proc. 6th ACM Int'l Conf. Supercomputing* (ICS92), ACM Press, New York, N.Y., 1992, pp. 428–437.

A Taxonomy of Scheduling in General-Purpose Distributed Computing Systems

THOMAS L. CASAVANT, MEMBER, IEEE, AND JON G. KUHL, MEMBER, IEEE

Abstract—One measure of usefulness of a general-purpose distributed computing system is the system's ability to provide a level of performance commensurate to the degree of multiplicity of resources present in the system. Many different approaches and metrics of performance have been proposed in an attempt to achieve this goal in existing systems. In addition, analogous problem formulations exist in other fields such as control theory, operations research, and production management. However, due to the wide variety of approaches to this problem, it is difficult to meaningfully compare different systems since there is no uniform means for qualitatively or quantitatively evaluating them. It is difficult to successfully build upon existing work or identify areas worthy of additional effort without some understanding of the relationships between past efforts. In this paper, a taxonomy of approaches to the resource management problem is presented in an attempt to provide a common terminology and classification mechanism necessary in addressing this problem. The taxonomy, while presented and discussed in terms of *distributed scheduling*, is also applicable to most types of resource management. As an illustration of the usefulness of the taxonomy an annotated bibliography is given which classifies a large number of distributed scheduling approaches according to the taxonomy.

Index Terms—Distributed operating systems, distributed resource management, general-purpose distributed computing systems, scheduling, task allocation, taxonomy.

I. INTRODUCTION

THE study of distributed computing has grown to include a large range of applications [16], [17], [31], [32], [37], [54], [55]. However, at the core of all the efforts to exploit the potential power of distributed computation are issues related to the management and allocation of system resources relative to the computational load of the system. This is particularly true of attempts to construct large *general-purpose* multiprocessors [3], [8], [25], [26], [44]–[46], [50], [61], [67].

The notion that a loosely coupled collection of processors could function as a more powerful general-purpose computing facility has existed for quite some time. A large body of work has focused on the problem of managing the resources of a system in such a way as to effectively exploit this power. The result of this effort has been the pro-

posal of a variety of widely differing techniques and methodologies for distributed resource management. Along with these competing proposals has come the inevitable proliferation of inconsistent and even contradictory terminology, as well as a number of slightly differing problem formulations, assumptions, etc. Thus, it is difficult to analyze the relative merits of alternative schemes in a meaningful fashion. It is also difficult to focus common effort on approaches and areas of study which seem most likely to prove fruitful.

This paper attempts to tie the area of distributed scheduling together under a common, uniform set of terminology. In addition, a taxonomy is given which allows the classification of distributed scheduling algorithms according to a reasonably small set of salient features. This allows a convenient means of quickly describing the central aspects of a particular approach, as well as a basis for comparison of commonly classified schemes.

Earlier work has attempted to classify certain aspects of the scheduling problem. In [9], Casey gives the basis of a hierarchical categorization. The taxonomy presented here agrees with the nature of Casey's categorization. However, a large number of additional fundamental distinguishing features are included which differentiate between existing approaches. Hence, the taxonomy given here provides a more detailed and complete look at the basic issues addressed in that work. Such detail is deemed necessary to allow meaningful comparisons of different approaches. In contrast to the taxonomy of Casey, Wang [65] provides a taxonomy of load-sharing schemes. Wang's taxonomy succinctly describes the range of approaches to the load-sharing problem. The categorization presented describes solutions as being either *source initiative* or *server initiative*. In addition, solutions are characterized along a continuous range according to the degree of information dependency involved. The taxonomy presented here takes a much broader view of the distributed scheduling problem in which load-sharing is only one of several possible *basic* strategies available to a system designer. Thus the classifications discussed by Wang describe only a narrow category within the taxonomy.

Among existing taxonomies, one can find examples of flat and hierarchical classification schemes. The taxonomy proposed here is a hybrid of these two—hierarchical as long as possible in order to reduce the total number of classes, and flat when the descriptors of the system may be chosen in an arbitrary order. The levels in the hier-

Manuscript received August 30, 1985.

T. L. Casavant was with the Department of Electrical and Computer Engineering, University of Iowa, Iowa City, IA 52242. He is now with the School of Electrical Engineering, Purdue University, West Lafayette, IN 47907.

J. G. Kuhl is with the Department of Electrical and Computer Engineering, University of Iowa, Iowa City, IA 52242.

IEEE Log Number 8718386.

Reprinted from *IEEE Trans. on Software Eng.*, vol. 14, no. 2, Feb. 1988, pp. 141–154.

archy have been chosen in order to keep the description of the taxonomy itself small, and do not necessarily reflect any ordering of importance among characteristics. In other words, the descriptors comprising the taxonomy do not attempt to hierarchically order the characteristics of scheduling systems from more to less general. This point should be stressed especially with respect to the positioning of the flat portion of the taxonomy near the bottom of the hierarchy. For example, load balancing is a characteristic which pervades a large number of distributed scheduling systems, yet for the sake of reducing the size of the description of the taxonomy, it has been placed in the flat portion of the taxonomy and, for the sake of brevity, the flat portion has been placed near the bottom of the hierarchy.

The remainder of the paper is organized as follows. In Section II, the scheduling problem is defined as it applies to distributed resource management. In addition, a taxonomy is presented which serves to allow *qualitative* description and comparison of distributed scheduling systems. Section III will present examples from the literature to demonstrate the use of the taxonomy in qualitatively describing and comparing existing systems. Section IV presents a discussion of issues raised by the taxonomy and also suggests areas in need of additional work.

In addition to the work discussed in the text of the paper, an extensive annotated bibliography is given in an Appendix. This Appendix further demonstrates the effectiveness of the taxonomy in allowing standardized description of existing systems.

II. The Scheduling Problem and Describing Its Solutions

The *general scheduling* problem has been described a number of times and in a number of different ways in the literature [12], [22], [63] and is usually a restatement of the classical notions of job sequencing [13] in the study of production management [7]. For the purposes of distributed process scheduling, we take a broader view of the scheduling function as a *resource management resource*. This management resource is basically a mechanism or policy used to efficiently and effectively manage the access to and use of a resource by its various consumers. Hence, we may view every instance of the scheduling problem as consisting of three main components.

1) Consumer(s).
2) Resource(s).
3) Policy.

Like other management or control problems, understanding the functioning of a scheduler may best be done by observing the effect it has on its environment. In this case, one can observe the behavior of the scheduler in terms of how the *policy* affects the *resources* and *consumers*. Note that although there is only one policy, the scheduler may be viewed in terms of how it affects either or both resources and consumers. This relationship between the scheduler, policies, consumers, and resources is shown in Fig. 1.

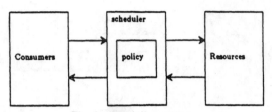

Fig. 1. Scheduling system.

In light of this description of the scheduling problem, there are two properties which must be considered in evaluating any scheduling system 1) the satisfaction of the consumers with how well the scheduler manages the resource in question (performance), and 2) the satisfaction of the consumers in terms of how difficult or costly it is to access the management resource itself (efficiency). In other words, the consumers want to be able to quickly and efficiently access the actual resource in question, but do not desire to be hindered by overhead problems associated with using the management function itself.

One by-product of this statement of the general scheduling problem is the unification of two terms in common use in the literature. There is often an implicit distinction between the terms *scheduling* and *allocation*. However, it can be argued that these are merely alternative formulations of the same problem, with allocation posed in terms of *resource allocation* (from the resources' point of view), and *scheduling* viewed from the consumer's point of view. In this sense, allocation and scheduling are merely two terms describing the same general mechanism, but described from different viewpoints.

A. The Classification Scheme

The usefulness of the four-category taxonomy of computer architecture presented by Flynn [20] has been well demonstrated by the ability to compare systems through their relation to that taxonomy. The goal of the taxonomy given here is to provide a commonly accepted set of terms and to provide a mechanism to allow comparison of past work in the area of distributed scheduling in a qualitative way. In addition, it is hoped that the categories and their relationships to each other have been chosen carefully enough to indicate areas in need of future work as well as to help classify future work.

The taxonomy will be kept as small as possible by proceeding in a hierarchical fashion for as long as possible, but some choices of characteristics may be made independent of previous design choices, and thus will be specified as a set of descriptors from which a subset may be chosen. The taxonomy, while discussed and presented in terms of distributed process scheduling, is applicable to a larger set of resources. In fact, the taxonomy could usefully be employed to classify any set of resource management systems. However, we will focus our attention on the area of process management since it is in this area which we hope to derive relationships useful in determining potential areas for future work.

1) Hierarchical Classification: The structure of the hierarchical portion of the taxonomy is shown in Fig. 2. A discussion of the hierarchical portion then follows.

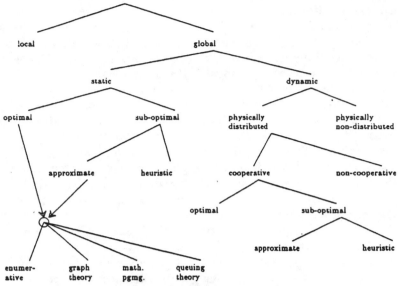

Fig. 2. Task scheduling characteristics.

a) Local Versus Global: At the highest level, we may distinguish between *local* and *global* scheduling. Local scheduling is involved with the assignment of processes to the time-slices of a single processor. Since the area of scheduling on single-processor systems [12], [62] as well as the area of sequencing or job-shop scheduling [13], [18] has been actively studied for a number of years, this taxonomy will focus on global scheduling. Global scheduling is the problem of deciding *where* to execute a process, and the job of local scheduling is left to the operating system of the processor to which the process is ultimately allocated. This allows the processors in a multiprocessor increased autonomy while reducing the responsibility (and consequently overhead) of the global scheduling mechanism. Note that this does not imply that global scheduling must be done by a single central authority, but rather, we view the problems of local and global scheduling as separate issues, and (at least logically) separate mechanisms are at work solving each.

b) Static Versus Dynamic: The next level in the hierarchy (beneath global scheduling) is a choice between *static* and *dynamic* scheduling. This choice indicates the time at which the scheduling or assignment decisions are made.

In the case of static scheduling, information regarding the total mix of processes in the system as well as all the independent subtasks involved in a job or task force [26], [44] is assumed to be available by the time the program object modules are linked into load modules. Hence, each executable image in a system has a static assignment to a particular processor, and each time that process image is submitted for execution, it is assigned to that processor. A more relaxed definition of static scheduling may include algorithms that schedule task forces for a particular hardware configuration. Over a period of time, the topology of the system may change, but characteristics describing the task force remain the same. Hence, the scheduler may generate a new assignment of processes to processors to serve as the schedule until the topology changes again.

Note here that the term *static scheduling* as used in this paper has the same meaning as *deterministic scheduling* in [22] and *task scheduling* in [56]. These alternative terms will not be used, however, in an attempt to develop a consistent set of terms and taxonomy.

c) Optimal Versus Suboptimal: In the case that all information regarding the state of the system as well as the resource needs of a process are known, an *optimal* assignment can be made based on some criterion function [5], [14], [21], [35], [40], [48]. Examples of optimization measures are minimizing total process completion time, maximizing utilization of resources in the system, or maximizing system throughput. In the event that these problems are computationally infeasible, *suboptimal* solutions may be tried [2], [34], [47]. Within the realm of suboptimal solutions to the scheduling problem, we may think of two general categories.

d) Approximate Versus Heuristic: The first is to use the same formal computational model for the algorithm, but instead of searching the entire solution space for an optimal solution, we are satisfied when we find a "good" one. We will categorize these solutions as *suboptimal-approximate*. The assumption that a *good* solution can be recognized may not be so insignificant, but in the cases where a metric is available for evaluating a solution, this technique can be used to decrease the time taken to find an acceptable solution (schedule). The factors which determine whether this approach is worthy of pursuit include:

1) Availability of a function to evaluate a solution.

2) The time required to evaluate a solution.

3) The ability to judge according to some metric the value of an optimal solution.

4) Availability of a mechanism for intelligently pruning the solution space.

The second branch beneath the suboptimal category is

labeled *heuristic* [15], [30], [66]. This branch represents the category of static algorithms which make the most realistic assumptions about *a priori* knowledge concerning process and system loading characteristics. It also represents the solutions to the static scheduling problem which require the most reasonable amount of time and other system resources to perform their function. The most distinguishing feature of heuristic schedulers is that they make use of special parameters which affect the system in indirect ways. Often, the parameter being monitored is correlated to system performance in an indirect instead of a direct way, and this alternate parameter is much simpler to monitor or calculate. For example, clustering groups of processes which communicate heavily on the same processor and physically separating processes which would benefit from parallelism [52] directly decreases the overhead involved in passing information between processors, while reducing the interference among processes which may run without synchronization with one another. This result has an impact on the overall service that users receive, but cannot be *directly* related (in a quantitative way) to system performance as the user sees it. Hence, our intuition, if nothing else, leads us to believe that taking the aforementioned actions when possible will improve system performance. However, we may not be able to *prove* that a first-order relationship between the mechanism employed and the desired result exists.

e) Optimal and Suboptimal Approximate Techniques: Regardless of whether a static solution is optimal or suboptimal-approximate, there are four basic categories of task allocation algorithms which can be used to arrive at an assignment of processes to processors.

1) Solution space enumeration and search [48].
2) Graph theoretic [4], [57], [58].
3) Mathematical programming [5], [14], [21], [35], [40].
4) Queueing theoretic [10], [28], [29].

f) Dynamic Solutions: In the dynamic scheduling problem, the more realistic assumption is made that very little *a priori* knowledge is available about the resource needs of a process. It is also unknown in what environment the process will execute during its lifetime. In the static case, a decision is made for a process image before it is ever executed, while in the dynamic case no decision is made until a process begins its life in the dynamic environment of the system. Since it is the responsibility of the running system to decide where a process is to execute, it is only natural to next ask where the decision itself is to be made.

g) Distributed Versus Nondistributed: The next issue (beneath dynamic solutions) involves whether the responsibility for the task of global dynamic scheduling should physically reside in a single processor [44] (*physically nondistributed*) or whether the work involved in making decisions should be *physically distributed* among the processors [17]. Here the concern is with the logical *authority* of the decision-making process.

h) Cooperative Versus Noncooperative: Within the realm of distributed dynamic global scheduling, we may also distinguish between those mechanisms which involve cooperation between the distributed components (*cooperative*) and those in which the individual processors make decisions independent of the actions of the other processors (*noncooperative*). The question here is one of the degree of *autonomy* which each processor has in determining how its own resources should be used. In the noncooperative case individual processors act alone as autonomous entities and arrive at decisions regarding the use of their resources independent of the effect of their decision on the rest of the system. In the cooperative case each processor has the responsibility to carry out its own portion of the scheduling task, but all processors are working toward a common system-wide goal. In other words, each processor's local operating system is concerned with making decisions in concert with the other processors in the system in order to achieve some global goal, instead of making decisions based on the way in which the decision will affect local performance only. As in the static case, the taxonomy tree has reached a point where we may consider optimal, suboptimal-approximate, and suboptimal-heuristic solutions. The same discussion as was presented for the static case applies here as well.

In addition to the hierarchical portion of the taxonomy already discussed, there are a number of other distinguishing characteristics which scheduling systems may have. The following sections will deal with characteristics which do not fit uniquely under any particular branch of the tree-structured taxonomy given thus far, but are still important in the way that they describe the behavior of a scheduler. In other words, the following could be branches beneath several of the leaves shown in Fig. 2 and in the interest of clarity are not repeated under each leaf, but are presented here as a flat extension to the scheme presented thus far. It should be noted that these attributes represent a *set* of characteristics, and any particular scheduling subsystem may possess some subset of this set. Finally, the placement of these characteristics near the bottom of the tree is not intended to be an indication of their relative importance or any other relation to other categories of the hierarchical portion. Their position was determined primarily to reduce the size of the description of the taxonomy.

2) Flat Classification Characteristics:

a) Adaptive Versus Nonadaptive: An adaptive solution to the scheduling problem is one in which the algorithms and parameters used to implement the scheduling policy change dynamically according to the previous and current behavior of the system in response to previous decisions made by the scheduling system. An example of such an adaptive scheduler would be one which takes many parameters into consideration in making its decisions [52]. In response to the behavior of the system, the scheduler may start to ignore one parameter or reduce the importance of that parameter if it believes that parameter is either providing information which is inconsistent with the rest of the inputs or is not providing any information regarding the change in system state in relation to the values of the other parameters being observed. A second example of adaptive scheduling would be one which is based on the stochastic learning automata model [39]. An analogy may be drawn here between the notion of an adaptive scheduler and adaptive control [38], although the usefulness of such an analogy for purposes of performance analysis and implementation are questionable [51]. In contrast to an adaptive scheduler, a nonadaptive scheduler would be one which does not necessarily modify its basic control mechanism on the basis of the history of system activity. An example would be a scheduler which always weighs its inputs in the same way regardless of the history of the system's behavior.

b) Load Balancing: This category of policies, which has received a great deal of attention recently [10], [11], [36], [40]–[42], [46], [53], approaches the problem with the philosophy that being fair to the hardware resources of the system is good for the users of that system. The basic idea is to attempt to balance (in some sense) the load on all processors in such a way as to allow progress by all processes on all nodes to proceed at approximately the same rate. This solution is most effective when the nodes of a system are homogeneous since this allows all nodes to know a great deal about the structure of the other nodes. Normally, information would be passed about the network periodically or on demand [1], [60] in order to allow all nodes to obtain a local estimate concerning the global state of the system. Then the nodes act together in order to remove work from heavily loaded nodes and place it at lightly loaded nodes. This is a class of solutions which relies heavily on the assumption that the information at each node is quite accurate in order to prevent processes from endlessly being circulated about the system without making much progress. Another concern here is deciding on the basic unit used to measure the load on individual nodes.

As was pointed out in Section I, the placement of this characteristic near the bottom of the hierarchy in the flat portion of the taxonomy is not related to its relative importance or generality compared with characteristics at higher levels. In fact, it might be observed that at the point that a choice is made between optimal and suboptimal characteristics, that a specific objective or cost function must have already been made. However, the purpose of the hierarchy is not so much to describe relationships between classes of the taxonomy, but to reduce the size of the overall description of the taxonomy so as to make it more useful in comparing different approaches to solving the scheduling problem.

c) Bidding: In this class of policy mechanisms, a basic protocol framework exists which describes the way in which processes are assigned to processors. The resulting scheduler is one which is usually cooperative in the sense that enough information is exchanged (between nodes with tasks to execute and nodes which may be able to execute tasks) so that an assignment of tasks to processors can be made which is beneficial to all nodes in the system as a whole.

To illustrate the basic mechanism of bidding, the framework and terminology of [49] will be used. Each node in the network is responsible for two roles with respect to the bidding process: *manager* and *contractor*. The manager represents the task in need of a location to execute, and the contractor represents a node which is able to do work for other nodes. Note that a single node takes on both of these roles, and that there are no nodes which are strictly managers or contractors alone. The manager announces the existence of a task in need of execution by a *task announcement*, then receives *bids* from the other nodes (contractors). A wide variety of possibilities exist concerning the type and amount of information exchanged in order to make decisions [53], [59]. The amount and type of information exchanged are the major factors in determining the effectiveness and performance of a scheduler employing the notion of bidding. A very important feature of this class of schedulers is that all nodes generally have full autonomy in the sense that the manager ultimately has the power to decide where to send a task from among those nodes which respond with bids. In addition, the contractors are also autonomous since they are never forced to accept work if they do not choose to do so.

d) Probabilistic: This classification has existed in scheduling systems for some time [13]. The basic idea for this scheme is motivated by the fact that in many assignment problems the number of permutations of the available work and the number of mappings to processors so large, that in order to analytically examine the entire solution space would require a prohibitive amount of time.

Instead, the idea of randomly (according to some known distribution) choosing some process as the next to assign is used. Repeatedly using this method, a number of different schedules may be generated, and then this set is analyzed to choose the best from among those randomly generated. The fact that an important attribute is used to bias the random choosing process would lead one to expect that the schedule would be better than one chosen entirely at random. The argument that this method actually produces a good selection is based on the expectation that enough variation is introduced by the random choosing to allow a *good* solution to get into the randomly chosen set.

An alternative view of probabilistic schedulers are those which employ the principles of decision theory in the form of team theory [24]. These would be classified as probabilistic since suboptimal decisions are influenced by prior probabilities derived from *best-guesses* to the actual states of nature. In addition, these prior probabilities are used to determine (utilizing some random experiment) the next action (or scheduling decision).

e) One-Time Assignment Versus Dynamic Reassignment: In this classification, we consider the entities to be scheduled. If the entities are *jobs* in the traditional batch processing sense of the term [19], [23], then we consider the single point in time in which a decision is made as to where and when the job is to execute. While this technique technically corresponds to a dynamic approach, it is static in the sense that once a decision is made to place and execute a job, no further decisions are made concerning the job. We would characterize this class as one-time assignments. Notice that in this mechanism, the only information usable by the scheduler to make its decision is the information given it by the user or submitter of the job. This information might include estimated execution time or other system resource demands. One critical point here is the fact that once users of a system understand the underlying scheduling mechanism, they may present false information to the system in order to receive better response. This point fringes on the area of psychological behavior, but human interaction is an important design factor to consider in this case since the behavior of the scheduler itself is trying to mimic a general philosophy. Hence, the interaction of this philosophy with the system's users must be considered.

In contrast, solutions in the dynamic reassignment class try to improve on earlier decisions by using information on smaller computation units—the executing subtasks of jobs or task forces. This category represents the set of systems which 1) do not trust their users to provide accurate descriptive information, and 2) use dynamically created information to adapt to changing demands of user processes. This adaptation takes the form of migrating processes (including current process state information). There is clearly a price to be paid in terms of overhead, and this price must be carefully weighed against possible benefits.

An interesting analogy exists between the differentiation made here and the question of preemption versus nonpreemption in uniprocessor scheduling systems. Here, the difference lies in whether to move a process from one place to another once an assignment has been made, while in the uniprocessor case the question is whether to remove the running process from the processor once a decision has been made to let it run.

III. EXAMPLES

In this section, examples will be taken from the published literature to demonstrate their relationships to one another with respect to the taxonomy detailed in Section II. The purpose of this section is twofold. The first is to show that many different scheduling algorithms can fit into the taxonomy and the second is to show that the categories of the taxonomy actually correspond, in most cases, to methods which have been examined.

A. Global Static

In [48], we see an example of an optimal, enumerative approach to the task assignment problem. The criterion function is defined in terms of optimizing the amount of time a task will require for all interprocess communication and execution, where the tasks submitted by users are assumed to be broken into suitable modules before execution. The cost function is called a *minimax criterion* since it is intended to minimize the maximum execution and communication time required by any single processor involved in the assignment. Graphs are then used to represent the module to processor assignments and the as-

signments are then transformed to a type of graph matching known as weak homomorphisms. The optimal search of this solution space can then be done using the *A** algorithm from artificial intelligence [43]. The solution also achieves a certain degree of processor load balancing as well.

Reference [4] gives a good demonstration of the usefulness of the taxonomy in that the paper describes the algorithm given as a solution to the optimal dynamic assignment problem for a two processor system. However, in attempting to make an objective comparison of this paper with other *dynamic* systems, we see that the algorithm proposed is actually a static one. In terms of the taxonomy of Section II, we would categorize this as a static, optimal, graph theoretical approach in which the *a priori* assumptions are expanded to include more information about the set of tasks to be executed. The way in which reassignment of tasks is performed during process execution is decided upon before any of the program modules begin execution. Instead of making reassignment *decisions* during execution, the stronger assumption is simply made that all information about the dynamic needs of a collection of program modules is available *a priori*. This assumption says that if a collection of modules possess a certain communication pattern at the beginning of their execution, and this pattern is completely predictable, that this pattern may change over the course of execution and that these variations are predictable as well. Costs of relocation are also assumed to be available, and this assumption appears to be quite reasonable.

The model presented in [35] represents an example of an optimum mathematical programming formulation employing a branch and bound technique to search the solution space. The goals of the solution are to minimize interprocessor communications, balance the utilization of all processors, and satisfy all other engineering application requirements. The model given defines a cost function which includes interprocessor communication costs and processor execution costs. The assignment is then represented by a set of zero-one variables, and the total execution cost is then represented by a summation of all costs incurred in the assignment. In addition to the above, the problem is subject to constraints which allow the solution to satisfy the load balancing and engineering application requirements. The algorithm then used to search the solution space (consisting of all potential assignments) is derived from the basic branch and bound technique.

Again, in [10], we see an example of the use of the taxonomy in comparing the proposed system to other approaches. The title of the paper—"Load Balancing in Distributed Systems"—indicates that the goal of the solution is to balance the load among the processors in the system in some way. However, the solution actually fits into the static, optimal, queueing theoretical class. The goal of the solution is to minimize the execution time of the entire program to maximize performance and the algorithm is derived from results in Markov decision theory. In contrast to the definition of load balancing given in Section II, where the goal was to even the load and utilization of system resources, the approach in this paper is consumer oriented.

An interesting approximate mathematical programming solution, motivated from the viewpoint of fault-tolerance, is presented in [2]. The algorithm is suggested by the computational complexity of the optimal solution to the same problem. In the basic solution to a mathematical programming problem, the state space is either implicitly or explicitly enumerated and searched. One approximation method mentioned in this paper [64] involves first removing the integer constraint, solving the continuous optimization problem, discretizing the continuous solution, and obtaining a bound on the discretization error. Whereas this bound is with respect to the continuous optimum, the algorithm proposed in this paper directly uses an approximation to solve the discrete problem and bound its performance with respect to the discrete optimum.

The last static example to be given here appears in [66]. This paper gives a heuristic-based approach to the problem by using extractable data and synchronization requirements of the different subtasks. The three primary heuristics used are:

1) loss of parallelism,
2) synchronization,
3) data sources.

The way in which loss of parallelism is used is to assign tasks to nodes one at a time in order to affect the least loss of parallelism based on the number of units required for execution by the task currently under consideration. The synchronization constraints are phrased in terms of *firing conditions* which are used to describe precedence relationships between subtasks. Finally, data source information is used in much the same way a functional program uses precedence relations between parallel portions of a computation which take the roles of varying classes of suppliers of variables to other subtasks. The final heuristic algorithm involves weighting each of the previous heuristics, and combining them. A distinguishing feature of the algorithm is its use of a greedy approach to find a solution, when at the time decisions are made, there can be no guarantee that a decision is optimal. Hence, an optimal solution would more carefully search the solution space using a back track or branch and bound method, as well as using exact optimization criterion instead of the heuristics suggested.

B. Global Dynamic

Among the dynamic solutions presented in the literature, the majority fit into the general category of physically distributed, cooperative, suboptimal, heuristic. There are, however, examples for some of the other classes.

First, in the category of physically nondistributed, one of the best examples is the experimental system developed for the Cm* architecture—Medusa [44]. In this system, the functions of the operating system (e.g., file system,

scheduler) are physically partitioned and placed at different places in the system. Hence, the scheduling function is placed at a particular place and is accessed by all users at that location.

Another rare example exists in the physically distributed *noncooperative class*. In this example [27], random level-order scheduling is employed at all nodes independently in a tightly coupled MIMD machine. Hence, the overhead involved in this algorithm is minimized since no information need be exchanged to make random decisions. The mechanism suggested is thought to work best in moderate to heavily loaded systems since in these cases, a random policy is thought to give a reasonably balanced load on all processors. In contrast to a cooperative solution, this algorithm does not detect or try to avoid system overloading by sharing loading information among processors, but makes the assumption that it will be under heavy load most of the time and bases all of its decisions on that assumption. Clearly, here, the processors are not necessarily concerned with the utilization of their own resources, but neither are they concerned with the effect their individual decisions will have on the other processors in the system.

It should be pointed out that although the above two algorithms (and many others) are given in terms relating to general-purpose distributed processing systems, that they do not strictly adhere to the definition of distributed data processing system as given in [17].

In [57], another rare example exists in the form of a physically distributed, cooperative, *optimal* solution in a dynamic environment. The solution is given for the two-processor case in which critical load factors are calculated prior to program execution. The method employed is to use a graph theoretical approach to solving for load factors for each process on each processor. These load factors are then used at run time to determine when a task could run better if placed on the other processor.

The final class (and largest in terms of amount of existing work) is the class of physically distributed, cooperative, suboptimal, heuristic solutions.

In [53] a solution is given which is adaptive, load balancing, and makes one-time assignments of *jobs* to processors. No *a priori* assumptions are made about the characteristics of the jobs to be scheduled. One major restriction of these algorithms is the fact that they only consider assignment of jobs to processors and once a job becomes an active process, no reassignment of processes is considered regardless of the possible benefit. This is very defensible, though, if the overhead involved in moving a process is very high (which may be the case in many circumstances). Whereas this solution cannot exactly be considered as a bidding approach, exchange of information occurs between processes in order for the algorithms to function. The first algorithm (a copy of which resides at each host) compares its own *busyness* with its estimate of the busyness of the least busy host. If the difference exceeds the bias (or threshold) designated at the current time, one job is moved from the job queue of the busier host to the less busy one. The second algorithm allows each host to compare itself with all other hosts and involves two biases. If the difference exceeds bias1 but not bias2, then one job is moved. If the difference exceeds bias2, then two jobs are moved. There is also an upper limit set on the number of jobs which can move at once in the entire system. The third algorithm is the same as algorithm one except that an antithrashing mechanism is added to account for the fact that a delay is present between the time a decision is made to move a job, and the time it arrives at the destination. All three algorithms had an adaptive feature added which would turn off all parts of the respective algorithm except the monitoring of load when system load was below a particular minimum threshold. This had the effect of stopping *processor thrashing* whenever it was practically impossible to balance the system load due to lack of work to balance. In the high load case, the algorithm was turned off to reduce extraneous overhead when the algorithm could not affect any improvment in the system under any redistribution of jobs. This last feature also supports the notion in the noncooperative example given earlier that the load is usually automatically balanced as a side effect of heavy loading. The remainder of the paper focuses on simulation results to reveal the impact of modifying the biasing parameters.

The work reported in [6] is an example of an algorithm which employs the heuristic of load-balancing, and probabilistically estimates the remaining processing times of processes in the system. The remaining processing time for a process was estimated by one of the following methods:

memoryless: $Re(t) = E\{S\}$

pastrepeats: $Re(t) = t$

distribution: $Re(t) = E\{S - t \mid S > t\}$

optimal: $Re(t) = R(t)$

where $R(t)$ is the remaining time needed given that t seconds have already elapsed, S is the service time random variable, and $Re(t)$ is the scheduler's estimate of $R(t)$. The algorithm then basically uses the first three methods to predict response times in order to obtain an expected delay measure which in turn is used by pairs of processors to balance their load on a pairwise basis. This mechanism is adopted by all pairs on a dynamic basis to balance the system load.

Another adaptive algorithm is discussed in [52] and is based on the bidding concept. The heuristic mentioned here utilizes prior information concerning the known characteristics of processes such as resource requirements, process priority, special resource needs, precedence constraints, and the need for clustering and distributed groups. The basic algorithm periodically evaluates each process at a current node to decide whether to transmit bid requests for a particular process. The bid requests include information needed for contractor nodes to make decisions regarding how well they may be able to execute

the process in question. The manager receives bids and compares them to the local evaluation and will transfer the process if the difference between the best bid and the local estimate is above a certain threshold. The key to the algorithm is the formulation of a function to be used in a modified McCulloch–Pitts neuron. The neuron (implemented as a subroutine) evaluates the current performance of individual processes. Several different functions were proposed, simulated, and discussed in this paper. The adaptive nature of this algorithm is in the fact that it dynamically modifies the number of hops that a bid request is allowed to travel depending on current conditions. The most significant result was that the information regarding process clustering and distributed groups seems to have had little impact on the overall performance of the system.

The final example to be discussed here [55] is based on a heuristic derived from the area of Bayesian decision theory [33]. The algorithm uses no *a priori* knowledge regarding task characteristics, and is dynamic in the sense that the probability distributions which allow maximizing decisions to be made based on the most likely current state of nature are updated dynamically. Monitor nodes make observations every p seconds and update probabilities. Every d seconds the scheduler itself is invoked to approximate the current state of nature and make the appropriate maximizing action. It was found that the parameters p and d could be tuned to obtain maximum performance for a minimum cost.

IV. DISCUSSION

In this section, we will attempt to demonstrate the application of the qualitative description tool presented earlier to a role beyond that of classifying existing systems. In particular, we will utilize two behavior characteristics—*performance* and *efficiency*, in conjunction with the classification mechanism presented in the taxonomy, to identify general qualities of scheduling systems which will lend themselves to managing large numbers of processors. In addition, the uniform terminology presented will be employed to show that some earlier-thought-to-be-synonymous notions are actually distinct, and to show that the distinctions are valuable. Also, in at least one case, two earlier-thought-to-be-different notions will be shown to be much the same.

A. Decentralized Versus Distributed Scheduling

When considering the decision-making policy of a scheduling system, there are two fundamental components—responsibility and authority. When responsibility for making and carrying out policy decisions is shared among the entities in a distributed system, we say that the scheduler is *distributed*. When authority is distributed to the entities of a resource management system, we call this *decentralized*. This differentiation exists in many other organizational structures. Any system which possesses decentralized authority must have distributed responsibility, but it is possible to allocate responsibility for gathering information and carrying out policy decisions, without giving the authority to change past or make future decisions.

B. Dynamic Versus Adaptive Scheduling

The terms *dynamic scheduling* and *adaptive scheduling* are quite often attached to various proposed algorithms in the literature, but there appears to be some confusion as to the actual difference between these two concepts. The more common property to find in a scheduler (or resource management subsystem) is the dynamic property. In a dynamic situation, the scheduler takes into account the current state of affairs as it perceives them in the system. This is done during the normal operation of the system under a dynamic and unpredictable load. In an adaptive system, the scheduling policy itself reflects changes in its environment—the running system. Notice that the difference here is one of level in the hierarchical solution to the scheduling problem. Whereas a dynamic solution takes environmental inputs into account when making its decisions, an adaptive solution takes environmental stimuli into account to modify the scheduling policy itself.

C. The Resource/Consumer Dichotomy in Performance Analysis

As is the case in describing the actions or qualitative behavior of a resource management subsystem, the performance of the scheduling mechanisms employed may be viewed from either the resource or consumer point of view. When considering performance from the consumer (or user) point of view, the metric involved is often one of minimizing individual program completion times—*response*. Alternately, the resource point of view also considers the rate of process execution in evaluating performance, but from the view of total system throughput. In contrast to response, *throughput* is concerned with seeing that *all* users are treated fairly and that *all* are making progress. Notice that the resource view of maximizing resource utilization is compatible with the desire for maximum system throughput. Another way of stating this, however, is that all users, when considered as a single collective user, are treated best in this environment of maximizing system throughput or maximizing resource utilization. This is the basic philosophy of load-balancing mechanisms. There is an inherent conflict, though, in trying to optimize both response and throughput.

D. Focusing on Future Directions

In this section, the earlier presented taxonomy, in conjunction with two terms used to quantitatively describe system behavior, will be used to discuss possibilities for distributed scheduling in the environment of a large system of loosely coupled processors.

In previous work related to the scheduling problem, the basic notion of performance has been concerned with evaluating the way in which users' individual needs are being satisfied. The metrics most commonly applied are

response and *throughput* [23]. While these terms accurately characterize the goals of the system in terms of how well users are served, they are difficult to measure during the normal operation of a system. In addition to this problem, the metrics do not lend themselves well to direct interpretation as to the action to be performed to increase performance when it is not at an acceptable level.

These metrics are also difficult to apply when analysis or simulation of such systems is attempted. The reason for this is that two important aspects of scheduling are necessarily intertwined. These two aspects are *performance* and *efficiency*. Performance is the part of a system's behavior that encompasses how well the resource to be managed is being used to the benefit of all users of the system. Efficiency, though, is concerned with the added cost (or overhead) associated with the resource management facility itself. In terms of these two criteria, we may think of desirable system behavior as that which has the highest level of performance possible, while incurring the least overhead in doing it. Clearly, the exact combination of these two which brings about the most desirable behavior is dependent on many factors and in many ways resembles the space/time tradeoff present in common algorithm design. The point to be made here is that simultaneous evaluation of efficiency and performance is very difficult due to this inherent entanglement. What we suggest is a methodology for designing scheduling systems in which efficiency and performance are separately observable.

Current and future investigations will involve studies to better understand the relationships between performance, efficiency, and their components as they effect quantitative behavior. It is hoped that a much better understanding can be gained regarding the costs and benefits of alternative distributed scheduling strategies.

V. Conclusion

This paper has sought to bring together the ideas and work in the area of resource management generated in the last 10 to 15 years. The intention has been to provide a suitable framework for comparing past work in the area of resource management, while providing a tool for classifying and discussing future work. This has been done through the presentation of common terminology and a taxonomy on the mechanisms employed in computer system resource management. While the taxonomy could be used to discuss many different types of resource management, the attention of the paper and included examples have been on the application of the taxonomy to the processing resource. Finally, recommendations regarding possible fruitful areas for future research in the area of scheduling in large scale general-purpose distributed computer systems have been discussed.

As is the case in any survey, there are many pieces of work to be considered. It is hoped that the examples presented fairly represent the true state of research in this area, while it is acknowledged that not *all* such examples have been discussed. In addition to the references at the end of this paper, the Appendix contains an annotated bibliography for work not explicitly mentioned in the text but which have aided in the construction of this taxonomy through the support of additional examples. The exclusion of any particular results has not been intentional nor should it be construed as a judgment of the merit of that work. Decisions as to which papers to use as examples were made purely on the basis of their applicability to the context of the discussion in which they appear.

APPENDIX
ANNOTATED BIBLIOGRAPHY

Application of Taxonomy to Examples from Literature

This Appendix contains references to additional examples not included in Section III as well as abbreviated descriptions of those examples discussed in detail in the text of the paper. The purpose is to demonstrate the use of the taxonomy of Section II in classifying a large number of examples from the literature.

[1] G. R. Andrews, D. P. Dobkin, and P. J. Downey, "Distributed allocation with pools of servers," in *ACM SIGACT-SIGOPS Symp. Principles of Distributed Computing*, Aug. 1982, pp. 73–83.
Global, dynamic, distributed (however in a limited sense), cooperative, suboptimal, heuristic, bidding, nonadaptive, dynamic reassignment.

[2] J. A. Bannister and K. S. Trivedi, "Task allocation in fault-tolerant distributed systems," *Acta Inform.*, vol. 20, pp. 261–281, 1983.
Global, static, suboptimal, approximate, mathematical programming.

[3] F. Berman and L. Snyder, "On mapping parallel algorithms into parallel architectures," in *1984 Int. Conf. Parallel Proc.*, Aug. 1984, pp. 307–309.
Global, static, optimal, graph theory.

[4] S. H. Bokhari, "Dual processor scheduling with dynamic reassignment," *IEEE Trans. Software Eng.*, vol. SE-5, no. 4, pp. 326–334, July 1979.
Global, static, optimal, graph theoretic.

[5] ——, "A shortest tree algorithm for optimal assignments across space and time in a distributed processor system," *IEEE Trans. Software Eng.*, vol. SE-7, no. 6, pp. 335–341, Nov. 1981.
Global, static, optimal, mathematical programming, intended for tree-structured applications.

[6] R. M. Bryant and R. A. Finkel, "A stable distributed scheduling algorithm," in *Proc. 2nd Int. Conf. Dist. Comp.*, Apr. 1981, pp. 314–323.
Global, dynamic, physically distributed, cooperative, suboptimal, heuristic, probabilistic, load-balancing.

[7] T. L. Casavant and J. G. Kuhl, "Design of a loosely-coupled distributed multiprocessing network," in *1984 Int. Conf. Parallel Proc.*, Aug. 1984, pp. 42–45.
Global, dynamic, physically distributed, cooper-

ative, suboptimal, heuristic, load-balancing, bidding, dynamic reassignment.

[8] L. M. Casey, "Decentralized scheduling," *Australian Comput. J.*, vol. 13, pp. 58–63, May 1981.
Global, dynamic, physically distributed, cooperative, suboptimal, heuristic, load-balancing.

[9] T. C. K. Chou and J. A. Abraham, "Load balancing in distributed systems," *IEEE Trans. Software Eng.*, vol. SE-8, no. 4, pp. 401–412, July 1982.
Global, static, optimal, queueing theoretical.

[10] T. C. K. Chou and J. A. Abraham, "Load redistribution under failure in distributed systems," *IEEE Trans. Comput.*, vol. C-32, no. 9, pp. 799–808, Sept. 1983.
Global, dynamic (but with static parings of supporting and supported processors), distributed, cooperative, suboptimal, provides 3 separate heuristic mechanisms, motivated from fault recovery aspect.

[11] Y. C. Chow and W. H. Kohler, "Models for dynamic load balancing in a heterogeneous multiple processor system," *IEEE Trans. Comput.*, vol. C-28, no. 5, pp. 354–361, May 1979.
Global, dynamic, physically distributed, cooperative, suboptimal, heuristic, load-balancing, (part of the heuristic approach is based on results from queueing theory).

[12] W. W. Chu *et al.*, "Task allocation in distributed data processing," *Computer*, vol. 13, no. 11, pp. 57–69, Nov. 1980.
Global, static, optimal, suboptimal, heuristic, heuristic approached based on graph theory and mathematical programming are discussed.

[13] K. W. Doty, P. L. McEntire, and J. G. O'Reilly, "Task allocation in a distributed computer system," in *IEEE InfoCom*, 1982, pp. 33–38.
Global, static, optimal, mathematical programming (nonlinear spatial dynamic programming).

[14] K. Efe, "Heuristic models of task assignment scheduling in distributed systems," *Computer*, vol. 15, pp. 50–56, June 1982.
Global, static, suboptimal, heuristic, load-balancing.

[15] J. A. B. Fortes and F. Parisi-Presicce, "Optimal linear schedules for the parallel execution of algorithms," in *1984 Int. Conf. Parallel Proc.*, Aug. 1984, pp. 322–329.
Global, static, optimal, uses results from mathematical programming for a large class of data-dependency driven applications.

[16] A. Gabrielian and D. B. Tyler, "Optimal object allocation in distributed computer systems," in *Proc. 4th Int. Conf. Dist. Comp. Systems*, May 1984, pp. 84–95.
Global, static, optimal, mathematical programming, uses a heuristic to obtain a solution close to optimal, employs backtracking to find optimal one from that.

[17] C. Gao, J. W. S. Liu, and M. Railey, "Load bal-

ancing algorithms in homogeneous distributed systems," in *1984 Int. Conf. Parallel Proc.*, Aug. 1984, pp. 302–306.

Global, dynamic, distributed, cooperative, suboptimal, heuristic, probabilistic.

[18] W. Huen *et al.*, "TECHNEC, A network computer for distributed task control," in *Proc. 1st Rocky Mountain Symp. Microcomputers*, Aug. 1977, pp. 233–237.

Global, static, suboptimal, heuristic.

[19] K. Hwang *et al.*, "A Unix-based local computer network with load balancing," *Computer*, vol. 15, no. 4, pp. 55–65, Apr. 1982.

Global, dynamic, physically distributed, cooperative, suboptimal, heuristic, load-balancing.

[20] D. Klappholz and H. C. Park, "Parallelized process scheduling for a tightly-coupled MIMD machine," in *1984 Int. Conf. Parallel Proc.*, Aug. 1984, pp. 315–321.

Global, dynamic, physically distributed, noncooperative.

[21] C. P. Kruskal and A. Weiss, "Allocating independent subtasks on parallel processors extended abstract," in *1984 Int. Conf. Parallel Proc.*, Aug. 1984, pp. 236–240.

Global, static, suboptimal, but optimal for a set of optimistic assumptions, heuristic, problem stated in terms of queuing theory.

[22] V. M. Lo, "Heuristic algorithms for task assignment in distributed systems," in *Proc. 4th Int. Conf. Dist. Comp. Systems*, May 1984, pp. 30–39.

Global, static, suboptimal, approximate, graph theoretic.

[23] ——, "Task assignment to minimize completion time," in *5th Int. Conf. Distributed Computing Systems*, May 1985, pp. 329–336.

Global, static, optimal, mathematical programming for some special cases, but in general is suboptimal, heuristic using the LPT algorithm.

[24] P. Y. R. Ma, E. Y. S. Lee, and J. Tsuchiya, "A task allocation model for distributed computing systems," *IEEE Trans. Comput.*, vol. C-31, no. 1, pp. 41–47, Jan. 1982.

Global, static, optimal, mathematical programming (branch and bound).

[25] S. Majumdar and M. L. Green, "A distributed real time resource manager," in *Proc. IEEE Symp. Distributed Data Acquisition, Computing and Control*, 1980, pp. 185–193.

Global, dynamic, distributed, cooperative, suboptimal, heuristic, load balancing, nonadaptive.

[26] R. Manner, "Hardware task/processor scheduling in a polyprocessor environment," *IEEE Trans. Comput.*, vol. C-33, no. 7, pp. 626–636, July 1984.

Global, dynamic, distributed control and responsibility, but centralized information in hardware on bus lines. Cooperative, optimal, (priority) load balancing.

[27] L. M. Ni and K. Hwang, "Optimal load balancing for a multiple processor system," in *Proc. Int. Conf. Parallel Proc.*, 1981, pp. 352–357.

Global, static, optimal, mathematical programming.

[28] L. M. Ni and K. Abani, "Nonpreemptive load balancing in a class of local area networks," in *Proc. Comp. Networking Symp.*, Dec. 1981, pp. 113–118.

Global, dynamic, distributed, cooperative, optimal and suboptimal solutions given—mathematical programming, and adaptive load balancing, respectively.

[29] J. Ousterhout, D. Scelza, and P. Sindhu, "Medusa: An experiment in distributed operating system structure," *Commun. ACM*, vol. 23, no. 2, pp. 92–105, Feb. 1980.

Global, dynamic, physically nondistributed.

[30] M. L. Powell and B. P. Miller, "Process migration in DEMOS/MP," in *Proc. 9th Symp. Operating Systems Principles* (OS Review), vol. 17, no. 5, pp. 110–119, Oct. 1983.

Global, dynamic, distributed, cooperative, suboptimal, heuristic, load balancing but no specific decision rule given.

[31] C. C. Price and S. Krishnaprasad, "Software allocation models for distributed computing systems," in *Proc. 4th Int. Conf. Dist. Comp. Systems*, May 1984, pp. 40–48.

Global, static, optimal, mathematical programming, but also suggest heuristics.

[32] C. V. Ramamoorthy *et al.*, "Optimal scheduling strategies in a multiprocessor system," *IEEE Trans. Comput.*, vol. C-21, no. 2, pp. 137–146, Feb. 1972.

Global, static, optimal solution presented for comparison with the heuristic one also presented. Graph theory is employed in the sense that it uses task precedence graphs.

[33] K. Ramamritham and J. A. Stankovic, "Dynamic task scheduling in distributed hard real-time systems," in *Proc. 4th Int. Conf. Dist. Comp. Systems*, May 1984, pp. 96–107.

Global, dynamic, distributed, cooperative, suboptimal, heuristic, bidding, one-time assignments (a real time guarantee is applied before migration).

[34] J. Reif and P. Spirakis, "Real-time resource allocation in a distributed system," in *ACM SIGACT-SIGOPS Symp. Principles of Distributed Computing*, Aug. 1982, pp. 84–94.

Global, dynamic, distributed, noncooperative, probabilistic.

[35] S. Sahni, "Scheduling multipipeline and multiprocessor computers," in *1984 Int. Conf. Parallel Processing*, Aug. 1984, pp. 333–337.

Global, static, suboptimal, heuristic.

[36] T. G. Saponis and P. L. Crews, "A model for decentralized control in a fully distributed processing system," in *Fall COMPCON*, 1980, pp. 307–312.

Global, static, suboptimal, heuristic based on load

balancing. Also intended for applications of the nature of coupled recurrence systems.

[37] C. C. Shen and W. H. Tsai, "A graph matching approach to optimal task assignment in distributed computing systems using a minimax criterion," *IEEE Trans. Comput.*, vol. C-34, no. 3, pp. 197–203, Mar. 1985.

Global, static, optimal, enumerative.

[38] J. A. Stankovic, "The analysis of a decentralized control algorithm for job scheduling utilizing Bayesian decision theory," in *Proc. Int. Conf. Parallel Proc.*, 1981, pp. 333–337.

Global, dynamic, distributed, cooperative, suboptimal, heuristic, one-time assignment, probabilistic.

[39] ——, "A heuristic for cooperation among decentralized controllers," in *IEEE INFOCOM 1983*, Apr. 1983, pp. 331–339.

Global, dynamic, distributed, cooperative, suboptimal, heuristic, one-time assignment, probabilistic.

[40] J. A. Stankovic and I. S. Sidhu, "An adaptive bidding algorithm for processes, clusters and distributed groups," in *Proc. 4th Int. Conf. Dist. Comp. Systems*, May 1984, pp. 49–59.

Global, dynamic, physically distributed, cooperative, suboptimal, heuristic, adaptive, bidding, additional heuristics regarding clusters and distributed groups.

[41] J. A. Stankovic, "Simulations of three adaptive, decentralized controlled, job scheduling algorithms," *Comput. Networks*, vol. 8, no. 3, pp. 199–217, June 1984.

Global, dynamic, physically distributed, cooperative, suboptimal, heuristic, adaptive, load-balancing, one-time assignment. Three variants of this basic approach given.

[42] ——, "An application of Bayesian decision theory to decentralized control of job scheduling," *IEEE Trans. Comput.*, vol. C-34, no. 2, pp. 117–130, Feb. 1985.

Global, dynamic, physically distributed, cooperative, suboptimal, heuristic based on results from Bayesian decision theory.

[43] ——, "Stability and distributed scheduling algorithms," in *Proc. ACM Nat. Conf.*, New Orleans, Mar. 1985.

Here there are two separate algorithms specified. The first is a Global, dynamic, physically distributed, cooperative, heuristic, adaptive, dynamic reassignment example based on stochastic learning automata. The second is a Global, dynamic, physically distributed, cooperative, heuristic, bidding, one-time assignment approach.

[44] H. S. Stone, "Critical load factors in two-processor distributed systems," *IEEE Trans. Software Eng.*, vol. SE-4, no. 3, pp. 254–258, May 1978.

Global, dynamic, physically distributed, cooperative, optimal, (graph theory based).

[45] H. S. Stone and S. H. Bokhari, "Control of distributed processes," *Computer*, vol. 11, pp. 97–106, July 1978.

Global, static, optimal, graph theoretical.

[46] H. Sullivan and T. Bashkow, "A large-scale homogeneous, fully distributed machine—I," in *Proc. 4th Symp. Computer Architecture*, Mar. 1977, pp. 105–117.

Global, dynamic, physically distributed, cooperative, suboptimal, heuristic, bidding.

[47] A. M. VanTilborg and L. D. Wittie, "Wave scheduling—Decentralized scheduling of task forces in multicomputers," *IEEE Trans. Comput.*, vol. C-33, no. 9, pp. 835–844, Sept. 1984.

Global, dynamic, distributed, cooperative, suboptimal, heuristic, probabilistic, adaptive. Assumes tree-structured (logically) task-forces.

[48] R. A. Wagner and K. S. Trivedi, "Hardware configuration selection through discretizing a continuous variable solution," in *Proc. 7th IFIP Symp. Comp. Performance Modeling, Measurement and Evaluation*, Toronto, Canada, 1980, pp. 127–142.

Global, static, suboptimal, approximate, mathematical programming.

[49] Y. T. Wang and R. J. T. Morris, "Load sharing in distributed systems," *IEEE Trans. Comput.*, vol. C-34, no. 3, pp. 204–217, Mar. 1985.

Global, dynamic, physically distributed, cooperative, suboptimal, heuristic, one-time assignment, load-balancing.

[50] M. O. Ward and D. J. Romero, "Assigning parallel-executable, intercommunicating subtasks to processors," in *1984 Int. Conf. Parallel Proc.*, Aug. 1984, pp. 392–394.

Global, static, suboptimal, heuristic.

[51] L. D. Wittie and A. M. Van Tilborg, "MICROS, a distributed operating system for MICRONET, a reconfigurable network computer," *IEEE Trans. Comput.*, vol. C-29, no. 12, pp. 1133–1144, Dec. 1980.

Global, dynamic, physically distributed, cooperative, suboptimal, heuristic, load-balancing (also with respect to message traffic).

REFERENCES

[1] A. K. Agrawala, S. K. Tripathi, and G. Ricart, "Adaptive routing using a virtual waiting time technique," *IEEE Trans. Software Eng.*, vol. SE-8, no. 1, pp. 76–81, Jan. 1982.

[2] J. A. Bannister and K. S. Trivedi, "Task allocation in fault-tolerant distributed systems," *Acta Inform.*, vol. 20, pp. 261–281, 1983.

[3] J. F. Bartlett, "A nonstop kernel," in *Proc. 8th Symp. Operating Systems Principles*, Dec. 1981, pp. 22–29.

[4] S. H. Bokhari, "Dual processor scheduling with dynamic reassignment," *IEEE Trans. Software Eng.*, vol. SE-5, no. 4, pp. 326–334, July 1979.

[5] S. H. Bokhari, "A shortest tree algorithm for optimal assignments across space and time in a distributed processor system," *IEEE Trans. Software Eng.*, vol. SE-7, no. 6, pp. 335–341, Nov. 1981.

[6] R. M. Bryant and R. A. Finkel, "A stable distributed scheduling algorithm," in *Proc. 2nd Int. Conf. Dist. Comp.*, Apr. 1981, pp. 314–323.

[7] E. S. Buffa, *Modern Production Management*, 5th ed. New York: Wiley, 1977.

[8] T. L. Casavant and J. G. Kuhl, "Design of a loosely-coupled distributed multiprocessing network," in *1984 Int. Conf. Parallel Proc.*, Aug. 1984, pp. 42–45.

[9] L. M. Casey, "Decentralized scheduling," *Australian Comput. J.*, vol. 13, pp. 58–63, May 1981.

[10] T. C. K. Chou and J. A. Abraham, "Load balancing in distributed systems," *IEEE Trans. Software Eng.*, vol. SE-8, no. 4, pp. 401–412, July 1982.

[11] Y. C. Chow and W. H. Kohler, "Models for dynamic load balancing in a heterogeneous multiple processor system," *IEEE Trans. Comput.*, vol. C-28, no. 5, pp. 354–361, May 1979.

[12] E. G. Coffman and P. J. Denning, *Operating Systems Theory*. Englewood Cliffs, NJ: Prentice-Hall, 1973.

[13] R. W. Conway, W. L. Maxwell, and L. W. Miller, *Theory of Scheduling*. Reading, MA: Addison-Wesley, 1967.

[14] K. W. Doty, P. L. McEntire, and J. G. O'Reilly, "Task allocation in a distributed computer system," in *IEEE InfoCom*, 1982, pp. 33–38.

[15] K. Efe, "Heuristic models of task assignment scheduling in distributed systems," *Computer*, vol. 15, pp. 50–56, June 1982.

[16] C. S. Ellis, J. A. Feldman, and J. E. Heliotis, "Language constructs and support systems for distributed computing," in *ACM SIGACT-SIGOPS Symp. Principles of Distributed Computing*, Aug. 1982, pp. 1–9.

[17] P. H. Enslow Jr., "What is a "distributed" data processing system," *Computer*, vol. 11, no. 1, pp. 13–21, Jan. 1978.

[18] J. R. Evans *et al.*, *Applied Production and Operations Management*. St. Paul, MN: West, 1984.

[19] I. Flores, *OSMVT*. Boston, MA: Allyn and Bacon, 1973.

[20] M. J. Flynn, "Very high-speed computing systems," *Proc. IEEE*, vol. 54, pp. 1901–1909, Dec. 1966.

[21] A. Gabrielian and D. B. Tyler, "Optimal object allocation in distributed computer systems," in *Proc. 4th Int. Conf. Dist. Comp. Systems*, May 1984, pp. 84–95.

[22] M. J. Gonzalez, "Deterministic processor scheduling," *ACM Comput. Surveys*, vol. 9, no. 3, pp. 173–204, Sept. 1977.

[23] H. Hellerman and T. F. Conroy, *Computer System Performance*. New York: McGraw-Hill, 1975.

[24] Y. Ho, "Team decision theory and information structures," *Proc. IEEE*, vol. 68, no. 6, pp. 644–654, June 1980.

[25] E. D. Jensen, "The Honeywell experimental distributed processor—An overview," *Computer*, vol. 11, pp. 28–38, Jan. 1978.

[26] A. K. Jones *et al.*, "StarOS, a multiprocessor operating system for the support of task forces," in *Proc. 7th Symp. Operating System Prin.*, Dec. 1979, pp. 117–127.

[27] D. Klappholz and H. C. Park, "Parallelized process scheduling for a tightly-coupled MIMD machine," in *1984 Int. Conf. Parallel Proc.*, Aug. 1984, pp. 315–321.

[28] L. Kleinrock, *Queuing Systems, Vol. 2: Computer Applications*. New York: Wiley, 1976.

[29] L. Kleinrock and A. Nilsson, "On optimal scheduling algorithms for time-shared systems," *J. ACM*, vol. 28, no. 3, pp. 477–486, July 1981.

[30] C. P. Kruskal and A. Weiss, "Allocating independent subtasks on parallel processors extended abstract," in *1984 Int. Conf. Parallel Proc.*, Aug. 1984, pp. 236–240.

[31] R. E. Larsen, *Tutorial: Distributed Control*. New York: IEEE Press, 1979.

[32] G. Le Lann, *Motivations, Objectives and Characterizations of Distributed Systems* (Lecture *Notes in Computer Science*, Vol. 105). New York: Springer-Verlag, 1981, pp. 1–9.

[33] B. W. Lindgren, *Elements of Decision Theory*. New York: MacMillan, 1971.

[34] V. M. Lo, "Heuristic algorithms for task assignment in distributed systems," in *Proc. 4th Int. Conf. Dist. Comp. Systems*, May 1984, pp. 30–39.

[35] P. Y. R. Ma, E. Y. S. Lee, and J. Tsuchiya, "A task allocation model for distributed computing systems," *IEEE Trans. Comput.*, vol. C-31, no. 1, pp. 41–47, Jan. 1982.

[36] R. Manner, "Hardware task/processor scheduling in a polyprocessor environment," *IEEE Trans. Comput.*, vol. C-33, no. 7, pp. 626–636, July 1984.

[37] P. L. McEntire, J. G. O'Reilly, and R. E. Larson, *Distributed Computing: Concepts and Implementations*. New York: IEEE Press, 1984.

[38] E. Mishkin and L. Braun Jr., *Adaptive Control Systems*. New York: McGraw-Hill, 1961.

[39] K. Narendra, "Learning automata—A survey," *IEEE Trans. Syst., Man, Cybern.*, vol. SMC-4, no. 4, pp. 323–334, July 1974.

[40] L. M. Ni and K. Hwang, "Optimal load balancing strategies for a multiple processor system," in *Proc. Int. Conf. Parallel Proc.*, 1981, pp. 352–357.

[41] L. M. Ni and K. Abani, "Nonpreemptive load balancing in a class of local area networks," in *Proc. Comp. Networking Symp.*, Dec. 1981, pp. 113–118.

[42] L. M. Ni, K. Hwang, "Optimal load balancing in a multiple processor system with many job classes," *IEEE Trans. Software Eng.*, vol. SE-11, no. 5, pp. 491–496, May 1985.

[43] N. J. Nilsson, *Principles of Artificial Intelligence*. Palo Alto, CA: Tioga, 1980.

[44] J. Ousterhout, D. Scelza, and P. Sindhu, "Medusa: An experiment in distributed operating system structure," *Commun. ACM*, vol. 23, no. 2, pp. 92–105, Feb. 1980.

[45] G. Popek *et al.*, "LOCUS: A network transparent, high reliability distributed system," in *Proc. 8th Symp. O.S. Principles*, Dec. 1981, pp. 169–177.

[46] M. L. Powell and B. P. Miller, "Process migration in DEMOS/MP," in *Proc. 9th Symp. Operating Systems Principles* (OS Review), vol. 17, no. 5, pp. 110–119, Oct. 1983.

[47] C. C. Price and S. Krishnaprasad, "Software allocation models for distributed computing systems," in *Proc. 4th Int. Conf. Dist. Comp. Systems*, May 1984, pp. 40–48.

[48] C. Shen and W. Tsai, "A graph matching approach to optimal task assignment in distributed computing systems using a minimax criterion," *IEEE Trans. Comput.*, vol. C-34, no. 3, pp. 197–203, Mar. 1985.

[49] R. G. Smith, "The contract net protocol: High-level communication and control in a distributed problem solver," *IEEE Trans. Comput.*, vol. C-29, no. 12, pp. 1104–1113, Dec. 1980.

[50] M. H. Solomon and R. A. Finkel, "The ROSCOE distributed operating system," in *Proc. 7th Symp. O.S. Principles*, Dec. 1979, pp. 108–114.

[51] J. A. Stankovic *et al.*, "An evaluation of the applicability of different mathematical approaches to the analysis of decentralized control algorithms," in *Proc. IEEE COMPSAC 82*, Nov. 1982, pp. 62–69.

[52] J. A. Stankovic and I. S. Sidhu, "An adaptive bidding algorithm for processes, clusters and distributed groups," in *Proc. 4th Int. Conf. Dist. Comp. Systems*, May 1984, pp. 49–59.

[53] J. A. Stankovic, "Simulations of three adaptive, decentralized controlled, job scheduling algorithms," *Comput. Networks*, vol. 8, no. 3, pp. 199–217, June 1984.

[54] ——, "A perspective on distributed computer systems," *IEEE Trans. Comput.*, vol. C-33, no. 12, pp. 1102–1115, Dec. 1984.

[55] J. A. Stankovic, "An application of Bayesian decision theory to decentralized control of job scheduling," *IEEE Trans. Comput.*, vol. C-34, no. 2, pp. 117–130, Feb. 1985.

[56] J. A. Stankovic *et al.*, "A review of current research and critical issues in distributed system software," *IEEE Comput. Soc. Distributed Processing Tech. Committee Newslett.*, vol. 7, no. 1, pp. 14–47, Mar. 1985.

[57] H. S. Stone, "Critical load factors in two-processor distributed systems," *IEEE Trans. Software Eng.*, vol. SE-4, no. 3, pp. 254–258, May 1978.

[58] H. S. Stone and S. H. Bokhari, "Control of distributed processes," *Computer*, vol. 11, pp. 97–106, July 1978.

[59] H. Sullivan and T. Bashkow, "A large-scale homogeneous, fully distributed machine—II," in *Proc. 4th Symp. Computer Architecture*, Mar. 1977, pp. 118–124.

[60] A. S. Tanenbaum, *Computer Networks*. Englewood Cliffs, NJ: Prentice-Hall, 1981.

[61] D. P. Tsay and M. T. Liu, "MIKE: A network operating system for the distributed double-loop computer network," *IEEE Trans. Software Eng.*, vol. SE-9, no. 2, pp. 143–154, Mar. 1983.

[62] D. C. Tsichritzis and P. A. Bernstein, *Operating Systems*. New York: Academic, 1974.

[63] K. Vairavan and R. A. DeMillo, "On the computational complexity of a generalized scheduling problem," *IEEE Trans. Comput.*, vol. C-25, no. 11, pp. 1067–1073, Nov. 1976.

[64] R. A. Wagner and K. S. Trivedi, "Hardware configuration selection through discretizing a continuous variable solution," in *Proc. 7th IFIP Symp. Comp. Performance Modeling, Measurement and Evaluation*, Toronto, Canada, 1980, pp. 127–142.

[65] Y. T. Wang and R. J. T. Morris, "Load sharing in distributed systems," *IEEE Trans. Comput.*, vol. C-34, no. 3, pp. 204–217, Mar. 1985.

[66] M. O. Ward and D. J. Romero, "Assigning parallel-executable, intercommunicating subtasks to processors," in *1984 Int. Conf. Parallel Proc.*, Aug. 1984, pp. 392–394.

[67] L. D. Wittie and A. M. Van Tilborg, "MICROS: A distributed operating system for MICRONET, a reconfigurable network computer," *IEEE Trans. Comput.*, vol C-29, no. 12, pp. 1133–1144, Dec. 1980.

Thomas L. Casavant (S'85–'86) received the B.S. degree in computer science and the M.S. and Ph.D. degrees in electrical and computer engineering from the University of Iowa, Iowa City, in 1982, 1983, and 1986, respectively.

He is currently an Assistant Professor of Electrical Engineering at Purdue University, West Lafayette, IN. His research interests include computer architecture, operating systems, distributed systems, and performance analysis.

Dr. Casavant is a member of the IEEE Computer Society and the Association for Computing Machinery.

Jon G. Kuhl (S'76–M'79) received the M.S. degree in electrical and computer engineering and the Ph.D. degree in computer science from the University of Iowa, Iowa City, in 1977 and 1980, respectively.

He is an Associate Professor in the Department of Electrical and Computer Engineering at the University of Iowa. His primary research interests are in distributed systems, parallel processing, and fault-tolerant computing. His other research interests include computer architecture, graph theory, and computer communications.

Multiprocessor Scheduling with the Aid of Network Flow Algorithms

HAROLD S. STONE, MEMBER, IEEE

Abstract—In a distributed computing system a modular program must have its modules assigned among the processors so as to avoid excessive interprocessor communication while taking advantage of specific efficiencies of some processors in executing some program modules. In this paper we show that this program module assignment problem can be solved efficiently by making use of the well-known Ford–Fulkerson algorithm for finding maximum flows in commodity networks as modified by Edmonds and Karp, Dinic, and Karzanov. A solution to the two-processor problem is given, and extensions to three and *n*-processors are considered with partial results given without a complete efficient solution.

Index Terms—Computer networks, cutsets, distributed computers, Ford–Fulkerson algorithm, load balancing, maximum flows.

I. INTRODUCTION

DISTRIBUTED processing has been a subject of recent interest due to the availability of computer networks such as the Advanced Research Projects Agency Network (ARPANET), and to the availability of microprocessors for use in inexpensive distributed computers. Fuller and Siewiorek [8] characterize distributed computer systems in terms of a coupling parameter such that array computers and multiprocessors are tightly coupled, and computers linked through ARPANET are loosely coupled. In loosely coupled systems the cost of interprocessor communication is sufficiently high to discourage the execution of a single program distributed across several computers in the network. Nevertheless, this has been considered for ARPANET by Thomas and Henderson [17], Kahn [12], and Thomas [16].

In this paper we focus on the type of distributed system that Fuller and Siewiorek treat as systems with intermediate coupling. A primary example of this type of system is the multiprocessor interface message processor for ARPANET designed by Bolt, Beranek, and Newman (Heart *et al.* [10]). Two-processor distributed systems are widely used in the form of a powerful central processor connected to a terminal-oriented satellite processor. Van Dam [18] and Foley *et al.* [7] describe two-processor systems in which program modules may float from processor to processor at load time or during the execution of a program. The ability to reassign program modules to different processors in a distributed system is essential to make the best use of system resources as programs change from one computation phase to another or as system load changes.

Manuscript received November 7, 1975; revised July 9, 1976. This work was supported in part by the National Science Foundation under Grant DCR 74-20025.

The author is with the Department of Electrical and Computer Engineering, University of Massachusetts, Amherst, MA 01002.

In this paper we treat the problem of assigning program modules to processors in a distributed system. There are two kinds of costs that must be considered in such an assignment. In order to reduce the cost of interprocessor communication, the program modules in a working set should be coresident in a single processor during execution of that working set. To reduce the computational cost of a program, program modules should be assigned to processors on which they run fastest. The two kinds of assignments can be incompatible. The problem is to find an assignment of program modules to processors that minimizes the collective costs due to interprocessor communication and to computation. We show how to make such an assignment efficiently by using methods of Ford and Fulkerson [6], Dinic [3], Edmonds and Karp [4], and Karzanov [13] that have been developed for maximizing flows in commodity networks. The two-processor assignment problem can be stated as a commodity flow problem with suitable modifications. We show how to construct a graph for the *n*-processor problem for which a minimal cost cut is a minimal cost partition of the graph into *n* disjoint subgraphs. We give partial results for finding the minimal cost cut but, unfortunately, an efficient solution has not yet been obtained.

In Section II of this paper we discuss the computer model in more detail. Section III reviews the essential aspects of commodity flow problems. The main results of this paper appear in Section IV, in which we show how to solve the two-processor problem, and in Section V, in which we consider the *n*-processor problem. A brief summary with an enumeration of several questions for future research appears in the final section.

II. THE MULTIPROCESSOR MODEL

We use a model of a multiprocessor based on the multiprocessor system at Brown University [18], [15]. In this model, each processor is an independent computer with full memory, control, and arithmetic capability. Two or more processors are connected through a data link or high-speed bus to create a multiprocessor system. The processors need not be identical; in fact, the system cited above has a System/360 computer linked to a microprogrammable minicomputer. This much of the description of the model fits many systems. The distinguishing feature of the multiprocessor under discussion is the manner in which a program executes. In essence, each program in this model is a serial program, for which execution can shift dynamically from processor to processor. The two processors may both be multiprogrammed, and may execute concurrently on different programs, but may not execute concurrently on the same program.

A program is partitioned into functional modules some of

Reprinted from *IEEE Trans. on Software Eng.*, vol. SE-3, no. 1, Jan. 1977, pp. 85–93.

21

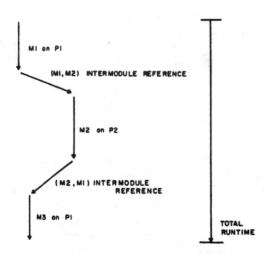

Fig. 1. Module $M1$ calls module $M2$ on a distributed computer system.

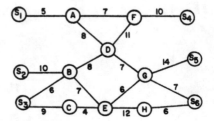

Fig. 2. Commodity flow network.

which are assigned to particular processors, the remainder of which are permitted to "float" from processor to processor during program execution. Some modules have a fixed assignment because these modules depend on facilitites within their assigned processor. The facilities might be high-speed arithmetic capability, access to a particular data base, the need for a large high-speed memory, access to a specific peripheral device, or the need for any other facility that might be associated with some processor and not with every processor.

When program execution begins, the floating modules are given temporary assignments to processors, assignments that reflect the best guess as to where they should reside for maximum computation speed. As execution progresses, the floating modules are free to be reassigned so as to improve execution speed and to reflect the changing activity of the program. Here we presume that interprocessor communication incurs relatively high overhead, whereas computations that make no calls to other processors incur zero additional overhead. Fig. 1 shows the sequence of events that occur when module $M1$ on processor $P1$ calls module $M2$ on processor $P2$. The program state shifts from processor $P1$ to processor $P2$, and returns to processor $P1$ when module $M2$ returns control to $M1$. Instead of transferring state to $P2$, it may be better to colocate $M1$ and $M2$ on the same computer. The choice depends on the number of calls between $M1$ and $M2$, and on the relationship of $M2$ and $M1$ to other modules.

The advantage of this type of approach over other forms of multiprocessing is that it takes advantage of program locality. When activity within a program is within one locality, in ideal circumstances all the activity can be forced to reside within one processor, thereby eliminating conflicts due to excessive use of shared resources. The locality need not be known beforehand, because program modules tend to float to processors in which their activity is highest. Another type of multiprocessor is exemplified by C.mmp (Wulf and Bell [19]) in which up to 16 minicomputers and 16 memories are linked together through a crossbar. The coupling among processors in this system is very tight because potentially every memory fetch accesses memory through the crossbar. Conflicts are potentially high because two or more processors may attempt

to access the same memory module simultaneously for an extended period of time.

In the present model, we eliminate the costly crossbar, the degradation on every memory access due to delays through the crossbar, and the potential for conflicts on every memory access to further degrade memory access. If this model is more effective than the crossbar architecture of C.mmp, it is because the costly interprocessor calls incurred in practice occur rarely due to the ability to assign program working sets to a single processor. Whether or not this is the case has not been settled. The question of the relative effectiveness of this architecture and the crossbar architecture has barely been investigated at this writing. The memory assignment algorithm described in the following sections indicates that it is possible to control a distributed computer of the type under study here reasonably efficiently, thereby opening the door to further and deeper studies of this idea.

III. MAXIMUM NETWORK FLOWS AND MINIMUM CUTSETS

In this section we review the commodity flow problem for which Ford and Fulkerson formulated a widely used algorithm [6]. The algorithm is reasonably fast in practice, but the original formulation of the algorithm is subject to rather inefficient behavior in pathological cases. Edmonds and Karp [4] have suggested several different modifications to the Ford-Fulkerson algorithm so as to eliminate many of the inefficiencies, at least for the pathological examples, and to obtain improved worst-case bounds on the complexity of the algorithm. Dinic [3] and Karzanov [13] have derived other ways to increase speed.

In this section we shall describe the problem solved by the Ford-Fulkerson algorithm as modified by Edmonds and Karp, but we shall refer the reader to the literature for descriptions of the various implementations of the algorithm. The important idea is that we can treat an algorithm for the solution of the maximum flow problem as a "black box" to solve the module assignment problem. We need not know exactly what algorithm is contained in the black box, provided that we know the implementation is computationally efficient for our purposes.

The maximum flow problem is a problem involving a commodity network graph. Fig. 2 shows the graph of such a network.

The nodes labeled S_1, S_2, and S_3 are source nodes, and the nodes labeled S_4, S_5, and S_6 are sink nodes. Between these subsets of nodes lie several interior nodes with the entire collection of nodes linked by weighted branches. Source nodes represent production centers, each theoretically capable

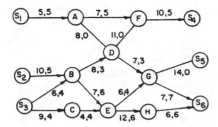

Fig. 3. Flow in a commodity flow network.

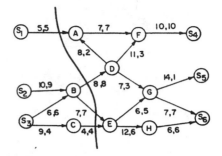

Fig. 4. Maximum flow and minimum cut in a commodity flow network.

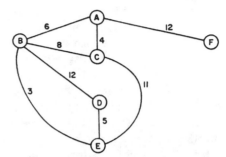

Fig. 5. Intermodule-connection graph.

of producing an infinite amount of a specific commodity. Sink nodes represent demand centers, each of which can absorb an infinite amount of the commodity. The branches represent commodity transport linkages, with the weight of a branch indicating the capacity of the corresponding link.

A *commodity flow* in this network is represented by weighted directed arrows along the branches of the network, with the weight of the arrow indicating the amount of the flow on that branch, and the direction of the arrow indicating the direction of the commodity flow. Fig. 3 shows a commodity flow for the graph in Fig. 2. Each arrow in Fig. 3 carries a pair of numbers, the first of which is the capacity of that branch and the second of which is the actual flow on that branch. A *feasible* commodity flow in this network is a commodity flow originating from the source nodes and ending at the sink nodes such that: 1) at each intermediate node, the sum of the flows into the node is equal to the sum of the flows out of the node; 2) at each sink node the net flow into the nodes is nonnegative, and at each source node the net flow directed out of the node is nonnegative; and 3) the net flow in any branch in the network does not exceed the capacity of that branch. Note that the flow in Fig. 3 is a feasible flow according to this definition. The three constraints in this definition guarantee that interior nodes are neither sources nor sinks, that source nodes and sink nodes are indeed sources and sinks, respectively, and that each branch is capable of supporting the portion of the flow assigned to it.

The *value* of a commodity flow is the sum of the net flows out of the source nodes of the network. Because the net flow into the network must equal the net flow out of the network, the value of a commodity flow is equal to the sum of net flows into the sink nodes. The value of the flow in Fig. 3 is 18. A *maximum flow* is a feasible flow whose value is maximum among all feasible flows. Fig. 4 shows a maximum flow for the network in Fig. 2.

The maximum flow in Fig. 4 is related to a cutset of the network. A *cutset* of a commodity network is a set of edges which when removed disconnects the source nodes from the sink nodes. No proper subset of a cutset is a cutset. Note that branches (S_1, A), (B, E), (B, D), and (C, E) form a cutset of the graph in Fig. 4. The *weight* of a cutset is equal to the sum of the capacities of the branches in the cutset. The weight of the above cutset is 24, which is equal to the value of the maximum flow. This is not a coincidence, because central to the Ford–Fulkerson algorithm is the following theorem.

Max-flow, Min-cut Theorem (Ford and Fulkerson [6]): The value of a maximum flow in a commodity network is equal to the weight of a minimum weight cutset of that network.

The proof of this theorem and a good tutorial description of algorithms for finding a maximum flow and minimum weight cutset appear in Ford and Fulkerson [6]. A very clear treatment of both the Ford–Fulkerson algorithm and the Edmonds–Karp modifications appear in Even [5]. At this point we note that the commodity flow problem as described can be solved in a time bounded from above by the fifth power of the number of nodes in the graph. All of the variations of the maximum flow algorithm of interest compute both a maximum flow in the graph and find a minimum weight cutset. We shall make use of this fact in solving the module assignment problem because each possible assignment corresponds to a cutset of a commodity graph, and the optimum assignment corresponds to a minimum weight cutset.

IV. THE SOLUTION TO THE TWO-PROCESSOR ASSIGNMENT PROBLEM

In this section we show how the maximum-flow algorithm finds an optimal partition of a modular program that runs on a two-processor system. In the following section we show how this algorithm generalizes to systems with three or more processors.

To use the maximum flow algorithm we develop a graphical model of a modular program. Fig. 5 shows a typical example in which each node of the graph represents a module and the branches of the graph represent intermodule linkages. The modules should be viewed as program segments which either contain executable instructions plus local data or contain global data accessible to other segments. The weights on the

TABLE I

Module	P_1 Run Time	P_2 Run Time
A	5	10
B	2	∞
C	4	4
D	6	3
E	5	2
F	∞	4

branches indicate the cost of intermodule references when the modules are assigned to different computers. We assume that the cost of an intermodule reference is zero when the reference is made between two modules assigned to the same computer.

The cost function used to compute the branch weights may vary depending on the nature of the system. Initially we choose to minimize the absolute running time of a program, without permitting dynamic reassignments. We modify the constraints later. The weight of a branch under this assumption is the total time charged to the intermodule references represented by the branch. Thus if k references between two modules occur during the running of a program and each reference takes t seconds when the modules are assigned to different computers, then the weight of the branch representing these references is kt.

The graph in Fig. 5 captures the notion of the costs for crossing boundaries between processors. This is only part of the assignment problem. We must also consider the relative running time of a module on different processors. One processor may have a fast floating-point unit, or a faster memory than another processor, and this may bias the assignment of modules. Table I gives the cost of running the modules of the program in Fig. 5 on each of two processors. The symbol ∞ in the table indicates an infinite cost, which is an artifice to indicate that the module cannot be assigned to the processor. Since our objective in this part of the discussion is to minimize the total absolute running time of a program, the costs indicated in Table I give the total running time of each module on each processor.

In this model of a distributed computing system, there is no parallelism or multitasking of module execution within a program. Thus the total running time of a program consists of the total running time of the modules on their assigned processors as given in Table I plus the cost of intermodule references between modules assigned to different processors. Note that an optimum assignment must take into consideration both the intermodule reference costs and the costs of running the modules themselves. For the running example, if we assume that B must be assigned to P_1, and F must be assigned to P_2, then the optimum way of minimizing the intermodule costs alone is to view B and F as source and sink, respectively, of a commodity-flow network. The minimum cut is the minimum intermodule cost cut, and this assigns B, C, D, and E to P_1, and A and F to P_2. On the other

hand, an optimum way to minimize only the running time of the individual modules is to assign A, B, and C to P_1 and D, E, and F to P_2. But neither of these assignments minimize the total running time.

To minimize the total running time, we modify the module interconnection graph so that each cutset in the modified graph corresponds in a one-to-one fashion to a module assignment and the weight of the cutset is the total cost for that assignment. With this modification, we can solve a maximum flow problem on the modified graph. The minimum weight cutset obtained from this solution determines the module assignment, and this module assignment is optimal in terms of total cost.

We modify the module interconnection graph as follows.

1) Add nodes labeled S_1 and S_2 that represent processors P_1 and P_2, respectively. S_1 is the unique source node and S_2 is the unique sink node.

2) For each node other than S_1 and S_2, add a branch from that node to each of S_1 and S_2. The weight of the branch to S_1 carries the cost of executing the corresponding module on P_2, and the weight of the branch to S_2 carries the cost of executing the module on P_1. (The reversal of the subscripts is intentional.)

The modified graph is a commodity flow network of the general type exemplified by the graph in Fig. 2. Each cutset of the commodity flow graph partitions the nodes of the graph into two disjoint subsets, with S_1 and S_2 in distinct subsets. We associate a module assignment with each cutset such that if the cutset partitions a node into the subset containing S_1, then the corresponding module is assigned to processor P_1. Thus the cut shown in Fig. 6 corresponds to the assignment of A, B, and C to P_1 and D, E, and F to P_2.

With this association of cutsets to module assignments it is not difficult to see that module assignments and cutsets of the commodity flow graph are in one-to-one correspondence. (The one-to-one correspondence depends on the fact that each interior node is connected directly to a source and sink, for otherwise, a module assignment might correspond to a subset of edges that properly contains a cutset.) The following theorem enables us to use a maximum flow algorithm to find a minimum cost assignment.

Theorem: The weight of a cutset of the modified graph is equal to the cost of the corresponding module assignment.

Proof: A module assignment incurs two types of costs. One cost is from intermodule references from processor to processor. The other cost incurred is the cost of running each module on a specific processor. The cutset corresponding to a module assignment contains two types of branches. One type of branch represents the cost of intermodule references for modules in different processors, and a particular assignment. All costs due to such references contribute to the weight of the corresponding cutset, and no other intermodule references contribute to the weight of the cutset.

The second type of branch in a cutset is a branch from an internal node to a source or sink node. If an assignment places a module in processor P_1, then the branch between that node and S_2 is in the cutset, and this contributes a cost equal to the cost of running that module on P_1, because the

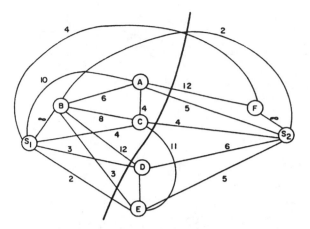

Fig. 6. Modified module-interconnection graph and a cut that determines a module assignment.

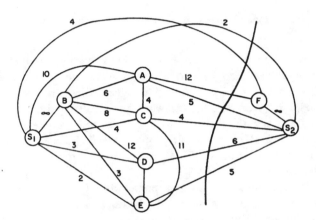

Fig. 7. Minimum cost cut.

branch to S_2 carries the P_1 running time cost. Similarly, the cost of assigning a module to P_2 is reflected by adding the cost of running that module on P_2 to the weight of the cutset.

Thus the weight of a cutset accounts for all costs due to its corresponding assignment, and no other costs contribute to the weight. This proves the theorem.

The theorem indicates that an optimal assignment can be found by running a maximum flow algorithm on the modified graph. A maximum flow algorithm applied to the graph shown in Fig. 6 produces the minimum weight cutset shown in Fig. 7. The corresponding module assignment is different from the assignment that minimizes the cost of intermodule references and the assignment that minimizes the individual running time costs, and its total cost is lower than the total cost of either of the two other assignments.

At this point the basic essentials for treating the module assignment problem as a maximum flow problem are clear. There remain a number of details concerning the practical implementation of the algorithm that merit discussion.

The running example indicates how to select an optimum *static* assignment that minimizes total running time. We mentioned earlier that it makes sense to change assignments dynamically to take advantage of local behavior of programs and the relatively infrequent changes in program locality. To solve the dynamic assignment problem we essentially have to solve a maximum flow problem at each point in time during which the working set of a program changes. Fortunately, the dynamic problem is no harder than the static one, except for the need to solve several maximum flow problems instead of a single one. The only additional difficulty in dynamic assignments is detecting a change in the working set of a program. Since a control program must intervene to perform intermodule transfers across processor boundaries, it should monitor such transfers, and use changes in the rate and nature of such transfers as a signal that the working set has changed. Thus we can reasonably expect to solve the dynamic assignment problem if it is possible to solve a static assignment problem for each working set.

The major difficulty in solving a static assignment problem is obtaining the requisite data for driving the maximum flow algorithm. It is not usually practical to force the user to supply these data, nor is it completely acceptable to use compiler generated estimates. Some of the data can be gathered during program execution. The cost of each invocation of a module on a particular processor can be measured by a control program, and it usually measures this anyway as part of the system accounting. However, we need to know the cost of running a module on each processor to compute an optimal assignment, and we certainly cannot ship a module to every other processor in a system for a time trial to determine its relative running time.

A reasonable approximation is to assume that the running time of a module on processor P_1 is a fixed constant times the running time of that module on processor P_2 where the constant is determined in advance as a measure of the relative power of the processors without taking into consideration the precise nature of the program to be executed. Under these assumptions if we can gather data about intermodule references, we can obtain sufficient data to drive the maximum flow algorithm. If after making one or more assignments a module is executed on different computers, sufficient additional information can be obtained to refine initial estimates of relative processor performance. The refined data should be used in determining new assignments as the data are collected.

How do we collect data concerning intermodule references? Here the collection of data follows a similar philosophy as for running time measurements. Initially an analysis of the static program should reveal where the intermodule references exist, and these in turn can be assumed to be of equal weight to determine an initial assignment. We assume that we automatically measure the intermodule references across processor boundaries because all such references require control program assistance. In measuring these references we obtain new data that refine the original estimates. If as a result of the refinement of these data we reassign modules, then we obtain new data about intermodule links that further refine the data, which in turn permit a more accurate appraisal of a minimum cost assignment.

At this writing the control methodology described here has been implemented by J. Michel and R. Burns on the system described by Stabler [15] and van Dam [18]. That system gathers the requisite statistics in real time in a suitable form

Fig. 8. Module-interconnection graph.

TABLE II

Module	P_1 Time	P_2 Time	P_3 Time
A	4	∞	∞
B	∞	6	∞
C	∞	∞	7
D	10	7	5
E	4	7	3

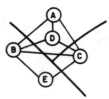

Fig. 9. Cut representing a module assignment to three processors.

for input to the algorithm. It is too early to say how effective the statistics gathering and automatic reassignment processes are in performing load balancing, but it is safe to say that the ability to gather suitable statistics automatically has been demonstrated.

In closing this section we take up one last subject, that of considering objective functions other than total running time. There are many suitable cost functions one may wish to use. For example, instead of absolute time, one may choose to minimize dollars expended. For this objective function, the intermodule reference costs are measured in dollars per transfer, and the running time costs of each module are measured in dollars for computation time on each processor, taking into account the relative processor speeds and the relative costs per computation on each processor. Many other useful objective functions can be met by choosing the cost function appropriately. We should also point out that generalizations of the maximum flow algorithm are applicable to module assignment problems under more complex cost measures. The most notable maximum flow problem generalization is the selection of a maximum flow with minimum cost. For this problem each flow is associated with both a flow value and a cost. The algorithm selects among several possible maximum flows to return the one of minimum cost. The equivalent problem for the module assignment problem is to find an assignment that achieves fastest computation time and incurs the least dollar cost of all such assignments.

The fact that the two-processor assignment problem is mapped into a commodity flow problem for solution suggests that the flow maximized in the commodity flow problem corresponds to some physical entity flowing between the two-processors in the two-processor assignment problem. There is no such correspondence, however, since the maximal flow value corresponds to time in a two-processor assignment, and not to information flow.

V. Extension to Three or More Processors

In this section we show how the module assignments to three or more processors can be accomplished by using the principles described in the previous section. We first obtain a suitable generalization of the notion of cutset. Then we describe a procedure to construct a modified graph of a program such that its cutsets are in one-to-one correspondence with the multiprocessor cutsets, and the value of each cutset is equal to the cost of the corresponding assignment. Finally we consider how to solve the generalized multiprocessor flow problem, and obtain partial results but no efficient solution.

Let us take as a running example the three-processor program shown in Fig. 8 with the running times for each pro-

cessor given in Table II. Since we have to assign the nodes to three rather than to two processors, we need to generalize the notion of cutset. Let us designate the source and sink nodes of a commodity network to be distinguished nodes, and we say they are distinguished of type *source* or type *sink*. For the *n*-processor problem we shall have *n* types of distinguished nodes. This leads naturally to the following definition.

Definition: A *cutset* in a commodity flow graph with *n* types of nodes is a subset of edges that partitions the nodes of the graph into *n* disjoint subsets, each of which contains all of the distinguished nodes of a single type plus a possibly empty collection of interior nodes. No proper subset of a cutset is also a cutset.

A cutset for the network of Fig. 8 appears in Fig. 9. We shall deal with networks in which there is a single distinguished node of each type, and this node represents the processor to which the interior nodes associated with it are assigned.

Proceeding as before we modify the intermodule reference graph of a program to incorporate the relative running time costs of each module on each processor. Again we add a branch from each interior node to each distinguished node as in the two-processor case. The weight on each such branch is computed by a formula explained below and exemplified in Fig. 10. The weights are selected so that, as in the two-processor case, the value of a cutset is equal to total running time.

For simplicity Fig. 10 does not show the branches from nodes *A*, *B*, and *C* to nodes to which they are not assigned. Suppose that module *D* runs in time T_i on processor P_i, $i = 1, 2, 3$. Then the branch from node *D* to distinguished node S_1 carries the weight $(T_2 + T_3 - T_1)/2$, and likewise the branches to nodes S_2 and S_3 carry the weights $(T_1 + T_3 - T_2)/2$, and $(T_1 + T_2 - T_3)/2$, respectively. Under this weight assignment, if *D* is assigned to processor P_1, the arcs to S_2 and S_3 are cut, and their weights total to T_1, the running time of *D* on P_1.

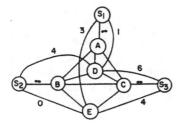

Fig. 10. Modified module-interconnection graph for a three-processor assignment.

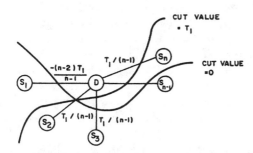

Fig. 11. Two possible assignments of module D in an n-processor system.

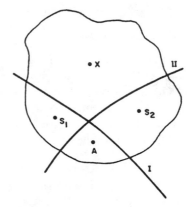

Fig. 12. Two cutsets in a graph.

This idea generalizes naturally to n-processors. The running time of D on P_1 contributes to the weight of the branches from D to every distinguished node S_i, $i = 1, 2, \cdots, n$. Its contribution to the branch to S_1 is $-(n-2)T_1/(n-1)$. Its contribution to the branch to S_i, $i \neq 1$, is $T_1/(n-1)$. If D is assigned to S_1, then $n-1$ branches are cut, each of which contributes $T_1/(n-1)$ to the cutset, giving a net contribution of T_1. If D is assigned to S_i, $i \neq 1$, then $n-2$ branches contribute $T_1/(n-1)$ to the cutset weight and the branch to S_1 contributes $-(n-2)T_1/(n-1)$ for a net contribution of zero. This is shown graphically in Fig. 11. Consequently, under the graph modification scheme described here, we obtain the desired property that the weight of a cutset is equal to the cost of the corresponding module assignment.

One problem with this scheme is that some individual edges of the graph may have a negative capacity, and this cannot be treated by maximum flow algorithms. This problem can easily be overcome, however. Suppose that among the branches added to node D is an arc with negative weight $-W$, and this is the most negative of the weights of the branches added to node D. Then increase the weights of all branches added to D by the amount $W + 1$, and we claim that no branch has negative weight after this change. Moreover, every cut that isolates D from a distinguished node breaks precisely $(n-1)$ of the branches added to D, contributing a value to the cutset of $(n-1)(W+1)$ plus the run time of D on the processor corresponding to the cut. The term $(n-1)(W+1)$ is a constant independent of the assignment so that an assignment that minimizes the cutset weight in the present graph is an assignment that finds a minimum time solution of the original problem.

At this point we come to the question of finding a minimum cutset in an n-processor graph. The solution can be found by exhaustive enumeration but the computational complexity of such an approach is quite unattractive. It seems natural that the n-processor problem can be reduced to several two-processor flow problems, and can be attacked efficiently in this way. In the remainder of this section we show that a two-processor flow can give information about the minimal cut in an n-processor graph, but we are unable to produce a complete efficient algorithm.

Specifically, consider what happens when we run a two-processor flow from S_1 to the subset $\{S_i: 2 \leqslant i \leqslant n\}$, where the nodes in the subset are all sink nodes for the flow. This two-processor flow produces a cutset that associates some nodes with S_1, and the remainder of the nodes in the graph to the subset of $n-1$ distinguished nodes. Does this flow give any information about the minimum cut in the n-processor graph? Indeed it does, as is shown by the following theorem. The proof technique is similar to the proof technique used by Gomory and Hu [9] and Hu [11].

Theorem: Let node A be associated with distinguished node S_1 by a two-processor flow algorithm. Then A is associated with S_1 in a minimum cost partition of the n-processor graph.

Proof: Without loss of generality, suppose that A is associated with S_1 by the two-processor flow algorithm, and that it must be associated with S_2 in a minimum cost partition. We prove the theorem by showing that A can be moved from S_2 to S_1 in the minimum cost partition without altering the cost of the partition. Fig. 12 shows the cutset I that associates A with S_1 when the two-processor flow is run, and the cutset II that associates A with S_2 in the minimum cost partition. These cutsets cross each other, thus dividing the graph into four disjoint regions. Let us denote the four regions as S_1, S_2, A, and X according to the nodes appearing in these regions in Fig. 12. (Region X may be empty, but this will not upset the proof.) Let $c(U, V)$ denote the sum of the weights of all branches between two regions U and V.

Since II is a minimal cut the value of II does not exceed the value of a cut that fails to include A with S_2. Thus,

$$c(S_2, X) + c(S_2, S_1) + c(A, X) + c(A, S_1) \leqslant c(S_2, X)$$
$$+ c(S_2, S_1) + c(S_2, A). \tag{1}$$

From this we find that $c(A, S_1) \leqslant c(S_2, A) - c(A, X)$, and since all costs are nonnegative we may add $2c(A, X)$ to the right-hand side of the inequality and obtain

$$c(A, S_1) \leqslant c(S_2, A) + c(A, X). \tag{2}$$

By hypothesis the algorithm associates node A with S_1, with a cost for cut I equal to $c(S_1, X) + c(S_1, S_2) + c(A, X) + c(S_2, A)$. However, if cut I veers slightly to exclude node A, and otherwise remains the same, the cost of the new cut is $c(S_1, X) + c(S_1, S_2) + c(A, S_1)$. Since I is a minimal cost cut, we must have

$$c(A, S_1) \geqslant c(S_2, A) + c(A, X). \tag{3}$$

From (2) and (3) we find that the inequality in (3) can be changed to equality. Since (3) holds with equality, by substituting (3) into (1) we find $2c(A, X) \leqslant 0$, which must hold with equality since all costs are nonnegative. Then (1) holds with equality. Thus cut II can be altered to exclude node A from S_2's subset and include A with S_1's subset without changing the cost of partition. This proves the theorem.

The previous theorem suggests that a two-processor algorithm may be used several times to find a minimum n-processor cutset. There are some difficulties in extending the theorem, however, that have left the n-processor problem still unsolved. Among the difficulties are the following.

1) The theorem states that a node associated with a distinguished node by a two-processor flow belongs with that node in the minimum n-processor cutset. Unfortunately, it is easy to construct examples in which a node that belongs with a particular distinguished node in a minimum n-processor cutset fails to be associated with that node by a two-processor flow.

2) Suppose a two-processor flow is run that results in the assignment of one or more nodes to a particular distinguished node. Let these nodes and the corresponding distinguished node be removed from the graph, and run a new two-processor flow from some other distinguished node S_l to all of the other distinguished nodes. In the cut found by this algorithm the nodes associated with S_l need not be associated with S_l in a minimum cost n-processor partition. In other words, the theorem does not apply when graph reduction is performed.

We conjecture that at most n^2 two-processor flows are necessary to find the minimum cost partition for n-processor problems, since there are only $n(n-1)/2$ different flows from one distinguished node to another distinguished node. These flows should somehow contain all the information required to find a minimal cost n-processor partition. It is possible that only n two-processor flows are required to solve the problem since Gomory and Hu [9] have shown that there are only $n-1$ independent two-terminal flows in an n-terminal network. This problem remains open at present.

VI. Summary and Conclusions

The two algorithms presented here provide for the assignment of program modules to two processors to minimize the cost of a computation on a distributed computer system. The algorithm uses a maximum flow algorithm as a subroutine so the complexity of the module assignment is dependent upon the implementation of the maximum flow algorithm used. Fortunately, the maximum flow algorithm is generally effi-

cient and there are various modifications of the algorithm that take advantage of special characteristics of the module to obtain increased efficiency (see Dinic [3], Karzanov [13]). To obtain truly optimal assignments, the costs for intermodule transfers and relative running times have to be known. However, if good estimates are available, these can be used to obtain near-optimal assignments that are satisfactory in a pragmatic sense.

One may choose to use the assignment algorithm in a static sense, that is, to find one assignment that holds for the lifetime of a program, and incurs least cost. We believe it is more reasonable to reassign modules dynamically during a computation at the points where working sets change. Each dynamic assignment then is chosen to be optimal for a given working set. Dynamic identification of working sets and the identification of times at which a working set changes is still a subject of much controversy with proposals favoring particular schemes [2] or disfavoring those schemes [14]. Progress in this area will in turn lead to progress in the ability to make dynamic module assignments in a distributed processor system.

The model presented here is highly simplified and idealized, but it is useful in real systems. Foley *et al.* [7] can use our algorithms in place of their backtracking algorithms to do module reassignment in their distributed computer systems. We suspect that the maximum flow approach is more efficient than backtracking because worst-case performance of backtracking has a much greater complexity than maximum flow algorithm complexity. However, the actual performance of their algorithm may be quite different from worst-case performance, and could have a small average complexity, perhaps lower than the average complexity of maximum flow algorithms. No data on actual running times appears in Foley's report, so there is no information on which to base estimates of relative running times.

There are a number of open problems related to the research reported here. We mention just a few of them here.

1) If the minimum cost module assignment is not unique, then what additional criteria are useful in selecting the most desirable minimum cost assignment? Given such criteria, this form of the problem can be solved by using efficient algorithms to find a maximum flow of minimal cost. Such algorithms are described by Ford and Fulkerson [6] and Edmonds and Karp [4].

2) If a program is divided into tasks that can execute simultaneously under various precedence constraints, how can modules be assigned so as to minimize the cost of computation? This differs from the multiprocessor scheduling problem studied by Coffman and Graham [1] and by others in that there is no cost incurred in that model for interprocessor references.

3) If the various processors in distributed computer systems are each multiprogrammed, and queue lengths become excessive at individual processors, how might modules be reassigned to minimize costs of computation over several programs?

4) Given that a module reassignment incurs a processor-to-processor communication cost, how might the cost of

reassigning a module be factored into the module assignment problem?

Since distributed computer systems are still in early stages of development it is not clear which one of the research questions listed here will emerge to become important questions to solve for distributed computer systems as they come of age. The implementation of the methodology described here on the system at Brown University suggests that automatic load balancing among different processors can be done. We hope that the present and future research will show not only the possibility of load balancing but that it can be done efficiently and that load balancing is an efficient method for tapping the power of a distributed computer system.

ACKNOWLEDGMENT

The author is deeply indebted to Professor Andries van Dam for providing the inspiration and motivation for the research, and to J. Michel and R. Burns for implementing the ideas described here on the ICOPS system at Brown University. Discussions with Professor W. Kohler, S. Bokhari, and P. Jones provided additional stimulation that contributed to the research.

REFERENCES

[1] E. G. Coffman, Jr., and R. L. Graham, "Optimal scheduling for two-processor systems," *Acta Informatica*, vol. 1, pp. 200–213, 1972.

[2] P. J. Denning, "Properties of the working set mode," *Commun. Ass. Comput. Mach.*, vol. 11, pp. 323–333, May 1968.

[3] E. A. Dinic, "Algorithm for solution of a problem of maximum flow in a network with power estimation," *Soviet Math. Doklady*, vol. 11, no. 5, pp. 1277–1280, 1970.

[4] J. Edmonds and R. M. Karp, "Theoretical improvements in algorithm efficiency for network flow problems," *J. Ass. Comput. Mach.*, vol. 19, pp. 248–264, Apr. 1972.

[5] S. Even, *Algorithmic Combinatorics*. New York: Macmillan, 1973.

[6] L. R. Ford, Jr., and D. R. Fulkerson, *Flows in Networks*. Princeton, NJ: Princeton Univ. Press, 1962.

[7] J. D. Foley *et al.*, "Graphics system modeling," Rome Air Development Center, Final Rep. Contract F30602-73-C-0249, Rep. RADC-TR-211, Aug. 1974.

[8] S. H. Fuller and D. P. Siewiorek, "Some observations on semiconductor technology and the architecture of large digital modules," *Computer*, vol. 6, pp. 14–21, Oct. 1973.

[9] R. E. Gomory and T. C. Hu, "Multiterminal network flows," *J. SIAM*, vol. 9, pp. 551–570, Dec. 1961.

[10] F. E. Heart *et al.*, "A new minicomputer/multiprocessor for the ARPA network," in *Proc. 1973 Nat. Comput. Conf., AFIPS Conf. Proc.*, vol. 42. Montvale, NJ: AFIPS Press, 1973.

[11] T. C. Hu, *Integer Programming and Network Flows*. Reading, MA: Addison-Wesley, 1970.

[12] R. E. Kahn, "Resource-sharing computer communications networks," *Proc. IEEE*, vol. 60, pp. 1397–1407, Nov. 1972.

[13] A. V. Karzanov, "Determining the maximal flow in a network by the method of preflows," *Soviet Math. Doklady*, vol. 15 no. 2, pp. 434–437, 1974.

[14] B. G. Prieve, "Using page residency to select the working set parameter," *Commun. Ass. Comput. Mach.*, vol. 16, pp. 619–620, Oct. 1973.

[15] G. M. Stabler, "A system for interconnected processing," Ph.D. dissertation, Brown Univ., Providence, RI, Oct. 1974.

[16] R. H. Thomas, "A resource sharing executive for the ARPANET," in *Proc. 1973 Nat. Comput. Conf., AFIPS Conf. Proc.*, vol. 42. Montvale, NJ: AFIPS Press, 1973.

[17] R. H. Thomas and D. Henderson, "McRoss—A multi-computer programming system," in *Proc. 1972 Spring Joint Comput. Conf., AFIPS Conf. Proc.*, vol. 40. Montvale, NJ: AFIPS Press, 1972.

[18] A. van Dam, "Computer graphics and its applications," Final Report, NSF Grant GJ-28401X, Brown University, May 1974.

[19] W. A. Wulf and C. G. Bell, "C.mmp—A multi-miniprocessor," in *Proc. 1972 Fall Joint Comput. Conf., AFIPS Conf. Proc.*, vol. 41, Part II. Montvale, NJ: AFIPS Press, 1972, pp. 765–777.

Harold S. Stone (S'61–M'63) received the B.S. degree from Princeton University, Princeton, NJ, in 1960 and the M.S. and Ph.D. degrees from the University of California, Berkeley, in 1961 and 1963, respectively.

While at the University of California he was a National Science Foundation Fellow and Research Assistant in the Digital Computer Laboratory. From 1963 until 1968 he was with Stanford Research Institute, and from 1968 until 1974 he was Associate Professor of Electrical and Computer Science at Stanford University. He is currently Professor of Electrical and Computer Engineering at the University of Massachusetts, Amherst. He has recently been engaged in research in parallel computation, computer architecture, and advanced memory system organization. In the past he has performed research in several areas including combinatorial algorithms, operating systems, and switching theory. He has authored over thirty technical publications, and is an author, coauthor, or editor of five text books in computer science. He has also been a Visiting Lecturer at the University of Chile, the Technical University of Berlin, and the University of Sao Paulo, and has held a NASA Research Fellowship at NASA Ames Research Center.

Dr. Stone is a member of Sigma Xi and Phi Beta Kappa. He has served as Technical Editor of *Computer*, and as a member of the Governing Board of the IEEE Computer Society.

Load Distributing for Locally Distributed Systems

Niranjan G. Shivaratri, Phillip Krueger, and Mukesh Singhal
Ohio State University

Load-distributing algorithms can improve a distributed system's performance by judiciously redistributing the workload among its nodes. This article describes load-distributing algorithms and compares their performance.

The availability of low-cost microprocessors and advances in communication technologies has spurred considerable interest in locally distributed systems. The primary advantages of these systems are high performance, availability, and extensibility at low cost. To realize these benefits, however, system designers must overcome the problem of allocating the considerable processing capacity available in a locally distributed system so that it is used to its fullest advantage.

This article focuses on the problem of judiciously and transparently redistributing the load of the system among its nodes so that overall performance is maximized. We discuss several key issues in load distributing for general-purpose systems, including the motivations and design trade-offs for load-distributing algorithms. In addition, we describe several load-distributing algorithms and compare their performance. We also survey load-distributing policies used in existing systems and draw conclusions about which algorithm might help in realizing the most benefits of load distributing.

Issues in load distributing

We first discuss several load-distributing issues central to understanding its intricacies. In this article, we use the terms computer, processor, machine, workstation, and node interchangeably.

Motivation. A *locally distributed system* consists of a collection of autonomous computers connected by a local area communication network. Users submit tasks at their host computers for processing. As Figure 1 shows, the random arrival of tasks in such an environment can cause some computers to be heavily loaded while other computers are idle or only lightly loaded. Load distributing improves performance by transferring tasks from heavily loaded computers, where service is poor, to lightly loaded computers, where the tasks can take advantage of

Reprinted from *Computer*, vol. 25, no. 12, Dec. 1992, pp. 33–44.

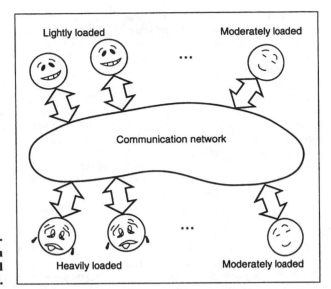

Figure 1. Distributed system without load distributing.

computing capacity that would otherwise go unused.

If workloads at some computers are typically heavier than at others, or if some processors execute tasks more slowly than others, the situation shown in Figure 1 is likely to occur often. The usefulness of load distributing is not so obvious in systems in which all processors are equally powerful and have equally heavy workloads over the long term. However, Livny and Melman[1] have shown that even in such a homogeneous distributed system, at least one computer is likely to be idle while other computers are heavily loaded because of statistical fluctuations in the arrival of tasks to computers and task-service-time requirements. Therefore, even in a homogeneous distributed system, system performance can potentially be improved by appropriate transfers of workload from heavily loaded computers (senders) to idle or lightly loaded computers (receivers).

What do we mean by performance? A widely used performance metric is the *average response time* of tasks. The response time of a task is the time elapsed between its initiation and its completion. Minimizing the average response time is often the goal of load distributing.

Dynamic, static, and adaptive algorithms. Load-distributing algorithms can be broadly characterized as dynamic, static, or adaptive. *Dynamic* load-distributing algorithms use system-state information (the loads at nodes), at least in part, to make load-distributing decisions, while *static* algorithms make no use of such information.

Decisions are hardwired in static load-distributing algorithms using a priori knowledge of the system. For example, under a simple "cyclic splitting" algorithm, each node assigns the ith task it initiates to node $i \bmod N$, where N is the number of nodes in the system. Alternatively, a probabilistic algorithm assigns a task to node i with probability p_i, where the probabilities are determined statically according to factors such as the average task-initiation rate and execution rate for each node. Each of these algorithms can potentially make poor assignment decisions. Because they do not consider node states when making such decisions, they can transfer a task initiated at an otherwise idle node to a node having a serious backlog of tasks.

Dynamic algorithms have the potential to outperform static algorithms by using system-state information to improve the quality of their decisions. For example, a simple dynamic algorithm might be identical to a static algorithm, except that it would not transfer an arriving task if the node where it arrived was idle. A more sophisticated dynamic algorithm might also take the state of the receiving node into account, possibly transferring a task to a node only if the receiving node was idle. A still more sophisticated dynamic algorithm might transfer an executing task if it was shar-

ing a node with another task and some other node became idle. Essentially, dynamic algorithms improve performance by exploiting short-term fluctuations in the system state. Because they must collect, store, and analyze state information, dynamic algorithms incur more overhead than their static counterparts, but this overhead is often well spent. Most recent load-distributing research has concentrated on dynamic algorithms, and they will be our focus for the remainder of this article.

Adaptive load-distributing algorithms are a special class of dynamic algorithms. They adapt their activities by dynamically changing their parameters, or even their policies, to suit the changing system state. For example, if some load-distributing policy performs better than others under certain conditions, while another policy performs better under other conditions, a simple adaptive algorithm might choose between these policies based on observations of the system state. Even when the system is uniformly so heavily loaded that no performance advantage can be gained by transferring tasks, a nonadaptive dynamic algorithm might continue operating (and incurring overhead). To avoid overloading such a system, an adaptive algorithm might instead curtail its load-distributing activity when it observes this condition.

Load. A key issue in the design of dynamic load-distributing algorithms is identifying a suitable *load index*. A load index predicts the performance of a task if it is executed at some particular node. To be effective, load index readings taken when tasks initiate should correlate well with task-response times. Load indexes that have been studied and used include the length of the CPU queue, the average CPU queue length over some period, the amount of available memory, the context-switch rate, the system call rate, and CPU utilization. Researchers have consistently found significant differences in the effectiveness of such load indexes — and that simple load indexes are particularly effective. For example, Kunz[2] found that the choice of a load index has considerable effect on performance, and that the most effective of the indexes we have mentioned is the CPU queue length. Furthermore, Kunz found no performance improvement over this simple measure when combinations of these load indexes were used. It is crucial that the mechanism used to measure load be efficient and impose minimal overhead.

Preemptive versus nonpreemptive transfers. *Preemptive* task transfers involve transferring a partially executed task. This operation is generally expensive, since collecting a task's state (which can be quite large or complex) is often difficult. Typically, a task state consists of a virtual memory image, a process control block, unread I/O buffers and messages, file pointers, timers that have been set, and so on. *Nonpreemptive* task transfers, on the other hand, involve only tasks that have not begun execution and hence do not require transferring the task's state. In both types of transfers, information about the environment in which the task will execute must be transferred to the remote node. This information may include the user's current working directory and the privileges inherited by the task. Nonpreemptive task transfers are also called *task placements*. Artsy and Finkel[3] and Douglis and Ousterhout[4] contain detailed discussions of issues in preemptive task transfer.

Centralization. Dynamic load-distributing algorithms differ in their degree of centralization. Algorithms can be centralized, hierarchical, fully decentralized, or some combination of these. Algorithms with some centralized components are potentially less reliable than fully decentralized algorithms, since the failure of a central component may cause the entire system to fail. A solution to this problem is to maintain redundant components, which can become active when the previously active component fails. A second weakness of centralized algorithms is not so easily remedied: A central component is potentially a bottleneck, limiting load distribution. While hierarchical algorithms can alleviate both problems, the complete solution lies in fully decentralized algorithms.

Components of a load-distributing algorithm. Typically, a dynamic load-distributing algorithm has four components: a *transfer policy*, a *selection policy*, a *location policy*, and an *information policy*.

Transfer policy. A transfer policy determines whether a node is in a suitable state to participate in a task transfer, either as a sender or a receiver. Many proposed transfer policies are *threshold* policies.[1,5-7] Thresholds are expressed in units of load. When a new task originates at a node, the transfer policy decides that the node is a *sender* if the load at that node exceeds a threshold T_1. On the other hand, if the load at a node falls below T_2, the transfer policy decides that the node can be a *receiver* for a remote task. Depending on the algorithm, T_1 and T_2 may or may not have the same value.

Alternatives to threshold transfer policies include *relative* transfer policies. Relative policies consider the load of a node in relation to loads at other system nodes. For example, a relative policy might consider a node to be a suitable receiver if its load is lower than that of some other node by at least some fixed δ. Alternatively, a node might be considered a receiver if its load is among the lowest in the system.

Selection policy. Once the transfer policy decides that a node is a sender, a selection policy selects a task for transfer. Should the selection policy fail to find a suitable task to transfer, the node is no longer considered a sender.

The simplest approach is to select one of the newly originated tasks that caused the node to become a sender. Such a task is relatively cheap to transfer, since the transfer is nonpreemptive.

A selection policy considers several factors in selecting a task:

(1) The overhead incurred by the transfer should be minimal. For example, a small task carries less overhead.

Load sharing versus load balancing

Dynamic load-distributing algorithms can be further classified as being load-sharing or load-balancing algorithms. The goal of a *load-sharing algorithm* is to maximize the rate at which a distributed system performs work when work is available. To do so, load-sharing algorithms strive to avoid *unshared states*[1]: states in which some computer lies idle while tasks contend for service at some other computer.

If task transfers were instantaneous, unshared states could be avoided by transferring tasks only to idle computers. Because of the time required to collect and package a task's state and because of communication delays, transfers are not instantaneous. The lengthy unshared states that would otherwise result from these delays can be partially avoided through *anticipatory transfers*,[1] which are transfers from overloaded to lightly loaded computers, under the assumption that lightly loaded computers are likely to become idle soon. The potential performance gain of these anticipatory transfers must be weighed against the additional overhead they incur.

Load-balancing algorithms also strive to avoid unshared states, but go a step beyond load sharing by attempting to equalize the loads at all computers. Krueger and Livny[2] have shown that load balancing can potentially reduce the mean and standard deviation of task response times, relative to load-sharing algorithms. Because load balancing requires a higher transfer rate than load sharing, however, the higher overhead incurred may outweigh this potential performance improvement.

References

1. M. Livny and M. Melman, "Load Balancing in Homogeneous Broadcast Distributed Systems," *Proc. ACM Computer Network Performance Symp.*, 1982, pp. 47-55. Proceedings printed as a special issue of *ACM Performance Evaluation Rev.*, Vol. 11, No. 1, 1982, pp. 47-55.

2. P. Krueger and M. Livny, "The Diverse Objectives of Distributed Scheduling Policies," *Proc. Seventh Int'l Conf. Distributed Computing Systems*, IEEE CS Press, Los Alamitos, Calif., Order No. 801 (microfiche only), 1987, pp. 242-249.

(2) The selected task should be long lived so that it is worthwhile to incur the transfer overhead.

(3) The number of *location-dependent* system calls made by the selected task should be minimal. Location-dependent calls are system calls that must be executed on the node where the task originated, because they use resources such as windows, the clock, or the mouse that are only at that node.[4,8]

Location policy. The location policy's responsibility is to find a suitable "transfer partner" (sender or receiver) for a node, once the transfer policy has decided that the node is a sender or receiver.

A widely used decentralized policy finds a suitable node through *polling:* A node polls another node to find out whether it is suitable for load sharing. Nodes can be polled either serially or in parallel (for example, multicast). A node can be selected for polling on a random basis,[5,6] on the basis of the information collected during the previous polls,[1,7] or on a nearest neighbor basis. An alternative to polling is to broadcast a query seeking any node available for load sharing.

In a centralized policy, a node contacts one specified node called a *coordinator* to locate a suitable node for load sharing. The coordinator collects information about the system (which is the responsibility of the information policy), and the transfer policy uses this information at the coordinator to select receivers.

Information policy. The information policy decides when information about the states of other nodes in the system is to be collected, from where it is to be collected, and what information is collected. There are three types of information policies:

(1) *Demand-driven policies.* Under these decentralized policies, a node collects the state of other nodes only when it becomes either a sender or a receiver, making it a suitable candidate to initiate load sharing. A demand-driven information policy is inherently a dynamic policy, as its actions depend on the system state. Demand-driven policies may be sender, receiver, or symmetrically initiated. In *sender-initiated* policies, senders look for receivers to

which they can transfer their load. In *receiver-initiated* policies, receivers solicit loads from senders. A *symmetrically initiated* policy is a combination of both: Load-sharing actions are triggered by the demand for extra processing power or extra work.

(2) *Periodic policies.* These policies, which may be either centralized or decentralized, collect information periodically. Depending on the information collected, the transfer policy may decide to transfer tasks. Periodic information policies generally do not adapt their rate of activity to the system state. For example, the benefits resulting from load distributing are minimal at high system loads because most nodes in the system are busy. Nevertheless, overheads due to periodic information collection continue to increase the system load and thus worsen the situation.

(3) *State-change-driven policies.* Under state-change-driven policies, nodes disseminate information about their states whenever their states change by a certain degree. A state-change-driven policy differs from a demand-driven policy in that it disseminates information about the state of a node, rather than collecting information about other nodes. Under centralized state-change-driven policies, nodes send state information to a centralized collection point. Under decentralized state-change-driven policies, nodes send information to peers.

Stability: We first informally describe two views of stability: the queuing theoretic perspective and the algorithmic perspective. According to the *queuing theoretic perspective,* when the long-term arrival rate of work to a system is greater than the rate at which the system can perform work, the CPU queues grow without bound. Such a system is termed unstable. For example, consider a load-distributing algorithm performing excessive message exchanges to collect state information. The sum of the load

> ## Using detailed state information does not always significantly aid system performance.

due to the external work arriving and the load due to the overhead imposed by the algorithm can become higher than the service capacity of the system, causing system instability.

On the other hand, an algorithm can be stable but still cause a system to perform worse than the same system without the algorithm. Hence, we need a more restrictive criterion for evaluating algorithms — the *effectiveness* of an algorithm. A load-distributing algorithm is effective under a given set of conditions if it improves performance relative to a system not using load distributing. An effective algorithm cannot be unstable, but a stable algorithm can be ineffective.

According to the *algorithmic perspective,* if an algorithm can perform fruitless actions indefinitely with nonzero probability, the algorithm is unstable. For example, consider *processor thrashing:* The transfer of a task to a receiver may increase the receiver's queue length to the point of overloading it, necessitating the transfer of that task to yet another node. This process may repeat indefinitely. In this case, a task moves from one node to another in search of a lightly loaded node without ever receiving any service. Casavant and Kuhl[9] discuss algorithmic instability in detail.

Example algorithms

During the past decade, many load-distributing algorithms have been proposed. In the following sections, we describe several representative algorithms that have appeared in the literature. They illustrate how the components of load-distributing algorithms fit together and show how the choice of components affects system stability. We discuss the performance of these algorithms in the "Performance comparison" section.

Sender-initiated algorithms

Under sender-initiated algorithms, load-distributing activity is initiated by an overloaded node (sender) trying to send a task to an underloaded node (receiver). Eager, Lazowska, and Zahorjan[6] studied three simple, yet effective, fully distributed sender-initiated algorithms.

Transfer policy. Each of the algorithms uses the same transfer policy, a threshold policy based on the CPU queue length. A node is identified as a sender if a new task originating at the node makes the queue length exceed a threshold T. A node identifies itself as a suitable receiver for a task transfer if accepting the task will not cause the node's queue length to exceed T.

Selection policy. All three algorithms have the same selection policy, considering only newly arrived tasks for transfer.

Location policy. The algorithms differ only in their location policies, which we review in the following subsections.

Random. One algorithm has a simple dynamic location policy called random, which uses no remote state information. A task is simply transferred to a node selected at random, with no information exchange between the nodes to aid in making the decision. Useless task transfers can occur when a task is transferred to a node that is already heavily loaded (its queue length exceeds T).

An issue is how a node should treat a transferred task. If a transferred task is treated as a new arrival, then it can again be transferred to another node, providing the local queue length exceeds T. If such is the case, then irrespective of the average load of the system, the system will eventually enter a state in which the nodes are spending all their time transferring tasks, with no time spent executing them. A simple solution is to limit the number of times a task can be transferred. Despite its simplicity, this random location policy provides substantial performance improvements over systems not using load distributing.[6] The "Performance comparison" section contains examples of this ability to improve performance.

Threshold. A location policy can avoid useless task transfers by polling a node (selected at random) to determine whether transferring a task would make its queue length exceed T (see Figure 2). If not, the task is transferred to the selected node, which must execute the task regardless of its state when the task actually arrives. Otherwise, another node is selected at random and is polled. To keep the overhead low, the number of polls is limited by a parameter called

the *poll limit*. If no suitable receiver node is found within the poll limit polls, then the node at which the task originated must execute the task. By avoiding useless task transfers, the threshold policy provides a substantial performance improvement over the random location policy.[6] Again, we will examine this improvement in the "Performance comparison" section.

Shortest. The two previous approaches make no effort to choose the best destination node for a task. Under the shortest location policy, a number of nodes (poll limit) are selected at random and polled to determine their queue length. The node with the shortest queue is selected as the destination for task transfer, unless its queue length is greater than or equal to T. The destination node will execute the task regardless of its queue length when the transferred task arrives. The performance improvement obtained by using the shortest location policy over the threshold policy was found to be marginal, indicating that using more detailed state information does not necessarily improve system performance significantly.[6]

Information policy. When either the shortest or the threshold location policy is used, polling starts when the transfer policy identifies a node as the sender of a task. Hence, the information policy is demand driven.

Stability. Sender-initiated algorithms using any of the three location policies cause system instability at high system loads. At such loads, no node is likely to be lightly loaded, so a sender is unlikely to find a suitable destination node. However, the polling activity in sender-initiated algorithms increases as the task arrival rate increases, eventually reaching a point where the cost of load sharing is greater than its benefit. At a more extreme point, the workload that cannot be offloaded from a node, together with the overhead incurred by polling, exceeds the node's CPU capacity and instability results. Thus, the actions of sender-initiated algorithms are not effective at high system loads and cause system instability, because the algorithms fail to adapt to the system state.

Receiver-initiated algorithms

In receiver-initiated algorithms, load-distributing activity is initiated from an underloaded node (receiver), which tries to get a task from an overloaded node (sender). In this section, we describe an algorithm studied by Livny and Melman,[1] and Eager, Lazowska, and Zahorjan[5] (see Figure 3).

Transfer policy. The algorithm's threshold transfer policy bases its decision on the CPU queue length. The policy is triggered when a task departs. If the local queue length falls below the threshold T, then the node is identified as a receiver for obtaining a task from a

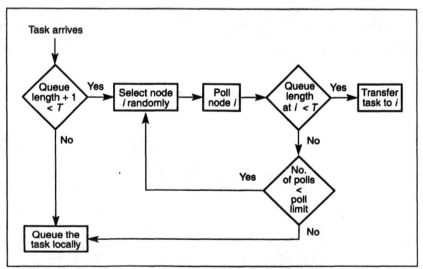

Figure 2. Sender-initiated load sharing using a threshold location policy.

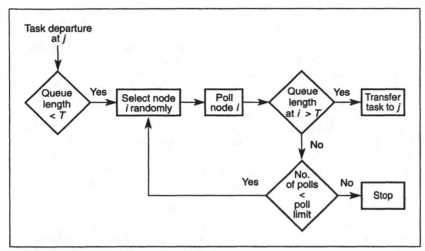

Figure 3. Receiver-initiated load sharing.

node (sender) to be determined by the location policy. A node is identified to be a sender if its queue length exceeds the threshold T.

Selection policy. The algorithm considers all tasks for load distributing, and can use any of the approaches discussed under "Selection policy" in the "Issues in load distributing" section.

Location policy. The location policy selects a node at random and polls it to determine whether transferring a task would place its queue length below the threshold level. If not, then the polled node transfers a task. Otherwise, another node is selected at random, and the procedure is repeated until either a node that can transfer a task (a sender) is found or a static poll limit number of tries has failed to find a sender.

A problem with the location policy is that if all polls fail to find a sender, then the processing power available at a receiver is completely lost by the system until another task originates locally at the receiver (which may not happen for a long time). The problem severely affects performance in systems where only a few nodes generate most of the system workload and random polling by receivers can easily miss them. The remedy is simple: If all the polls fail to find a sender, then the node waits until another task departs or for a predetermined period before reinitiating the load-distributing activity, provided the node is still a receiver.[7]

Information policy. The information

policy is demand driven, since polling starts only after a node becomes a receiver.

Stability. Receiver-initiated algorithms do not cause system instability because, at high system loads, a receiver is likely to find a suitable sender within a few polls. Consequently, polls are increasingly effective with increasing system load, and little waste of CPU capacity results.

A drawback. Under the most widely used CPU scheduling disciplines (such as round-robin and its variants), a newly arrived task is quickly provided a quantum of service. In receiver-initiated algorithms, the polling starts when a node becomes a receiver. However, these polls seldom arrive at senders just after new tasks have arrived at the senders but before these tasks have begun executing. Consequently, most transfers are preemptive and therefore expensive. Sender-initiated algorithms, on the other hand, make greater use of nonpreemptive transfers, since they can initiate load-distributing activity as soon as a new task arrives.

An alternative to this receiver-initiated algorithm is the reservation algorithm proposed by Eager, Lazowska, and Zahorjan.[5] Rather than negotiate an immediate transfer, a receiver requests that the next task to arrive be nonpreemptively transferred. Upon arrival, the "reserved" task is transferred to the receiver if the receiver is still a receiver at that time. While this algorithm does not require preemptive task

transfers, it was found to perform significantly worse than the sender-initiated algorithms.

Symmetrically initiated algorithms

Under symmetrically initiated algorithms,[10] both senders and receivers initiate load-distributing activities for task transfers. These algorithms have the advantages of both sender- and receiver-initiated algorithms. At low system loads, the sender-initiated component is more successful at finding underloaded nodes. At high system loads, the receiver-initiated component is more successful at finding overloaded nodes. However, these algorithms may also have the disadvantages of both sender- and receiver-initiated algorithms. As with sender-initiated algorithms, polling at high system loads may result in system instability. As with receiver-initiated algorithms, a preemptive task transfer facility is necessary.

A simple symmetrically initiated algorithm can be constructed by combining the transfer and location policies described for sender-initiated and receiver-initiated algorithms.

Adaptive algorithms

A stable symmetrically initiated adaptive algorithm. The *main cause* of system instability due to load sharing in the previously reviewed algorithms is indiscriminate polling by the sender's negotiation component. The stable symmetrically initiated algorithm[7] uses the information gathered during polling (instead of discarding it, as the previous algorithms do) to classify the nodes in the system as *sender/overloaded, receiver/underloaded*, or *OK* (nodes having manageable load). The knowledge about the state of nodes is maintained at each node by a data structure composed of a senders list, a receivers list, and an OK list. These lists are maintained using an efficient scheme: List-manipulative actions, such as moving a node from one list to another or determining to which list a node belongs, impose a small and constant overhead, irrespective of the number of nodes in the system. Consequently, this algorithm scales well to large distributed systems.

Initially, each node assumes that every other node is a receiver. This state is represented at each node by a receivers list containing all nodes (except the node itself), and an empty senders list and OK list.

Transfer policy. The threshold transfer policy makes decisions based on the CPU queue length. The transfer policy is triggered when a new task originates or when a task departs. The policy uses two threshold values — a lower threshold and an upper threshold — to classify the nodes. A node is a sender if its queue length is greater than its upper threshold, a receiver if its queue length is less than its lower threshold, and OK otherwise.

Location policy. The location policy has two components: the *sender-initiated component* and the *receiver-initiated component*. The sender-initiated component is triggered at a node when it becomes a sender. The sender polls the node at the head of the receivers list to determine whether it is still a receiver. The polled node removes the sender node ID from the list it is presently in, puts it at the head of its senders list, and informs the sender whether it is currently a receiver, sender, or OK. On receipt of this reply, the sender transfers the new task if the polled node has indicated that it is a receiver. Otherwise, the polled node's ID is removed from the receivers list and is put at the head of the OK list or the senders list based on its reply.

Polling stops if a suitable receiver is found for the newly arrived task, if the number of polls reaches a poll limit (a parameter of the algorithm), or if the receivers list at the sender node becomes empty. If polling fails to find a receiver, the task is processed locally, though it may later be preemptively transferred as a result of receiver-initiated load sharing.

The goal of the receiver-initiated component is to obtain tasks from a sender node. The nodes polled are selected in the following order:

(1) *Head to tail in the senders list.* The most up-to-date information is used first.

(2) *Tail to head in the OK list.* The most out-of-date information is used first in the hope that the node has become a sender.

(3) *Tail to head in the receivers list.* Again, the most out-of-date information is used first.

The receiver-initiated component is triggered at a node when the node becomes a receiver. The receiver polls the selected node to determine whether it is a sender. On receipt of the message, the polled node, if it is a sender, transfers a task to the polling node and informs it of its state after the task transfer. If the polled node is not a sender, it removes the receiver node ID from the list it is presently in, puts it at the head of the receivers list, and informs the receiver whether the polled node is a receiver or OK. On receipt of this reply, the receiver node removes the polled node ID from whatever list it is presently in and puts it at the head of its receivers list or OK list, based on its reply.

Polling stops if a sender is found, if the receiver is no longer a receiver, or if the number of polls reaches a static poll limit.

Selection policy. The sender-initiated component considers only newly arrived tasks for transfer. The receiver-initiated component can use any of the approaches discussed under "Selection policy" in the "Issues in load distributing" section.

Information policy. The information policy is demand driven, as polling starts when a node becomes either a sender or a receiver.

Discussion. At high system loads, the probability of a node's being underloaded is negligible, resulting in unsuccessful polls by the sender-initiated component. Unsuccessful polls result in the removal of polled node IDs from receivers lists. Unless receiver-initiated polls to these nodes fail to find senders, which is unlikely at high system loads, the receivers lists remain empty. This scheme prevents future sender-initiated polls at high system loads (which are most likely to fail). Hence, the sender-initiated component is deactivated at high system loads, leaving only receiver-initiated load sharing (which is effective at such loads).

At low system loads, receiver-initiated polls are frequent and generally fail. These failures do not adversely affect performance, since extra processing capacity is available at low system loads.

In addition, these polls have the positive effect of updating the receivers lists. With the receivers lists accurately reflecting the system's state, future sender-initiated load sharing will generally succeed within a few polls. Thus, by using sender-initiated load sharing at low system loads, receiver-initiated load sharing at high loads, and symmetrically initiated load sharing at moderate loads, the stable symmetrically initiated algorithm achieves improved performance over a wide range of system loads and preserves system stability.

A stable sender-initiated adaptive algorithm. This algorithm[7] uses the sender-initiated load-sharing component of the previous approach but has a modified receiver-initiated component to attract future nonpreemptive task transfers from sender nodes. An important feature is that the algorithm performs load sharing only with nonpreemptive transfers, which are cheaper than preemptive transfers. The stable sender-initiated algorithm is very similar to the stable symmetrically initiated algorithm. In the following, we point out only the differences.

In the stable sender-initiated algorithm, the data structure (at each node) of the stable symmetrically initiated algorithm is augmented by an array called the *state vector*. Each node uses the state vector to keep track of which list (senders, receivers, or OK) it belongs to at all the other nodes in the system. For example, *statevector$_i$[nodeid]* says to which list node i belongs at the node indicated by *nodeid*. As in the stable symmetrically initiated algorithm, the overhead for maintaining this data structure is small and constant, irrespective of the number of nodes in the system.

The sender-initiated load sharing is augmented with the following step: When a sender polls a selected node, the sender's state vector is updated to show that the sender now belongs to the senders list at the selected node. Likewise, the polled node updates its state vector based on the reply it sent to the sender node to reflect which list it will belong to at the sender.

The receiver-initiated component is replaced by the following protocol: When a node becomes a receiver, it informs only those nodes that are misinformed about its current state. The misinformed nodes are those nodes whose receivers lists do not contain the receiver's ID. This information is available in the state vector at the receiver. The state vector at the receiver is then updated to reflect that it now belongs to the receivers list at all those nodes that were misinformed about its current state.

There are no preemptive transfers of partly executed tasks here. The sender-initiated load-sharing component will do any task transfers, if possible, on the arrival of a new task. The reasons for this algorithm's stability are the same as for the stable symmetrically initiated algorithm.

Performance comparison

In this section, we discuss the general performance trends of some of the example algorithms described in the pre-

Example systems

Here we review several working load-distributing algorithms.

V-system. The V-system[1] uses a state-change-driven information policy. Each node broadcasts (or publishes) its state whenever its state changes significantly. State information consists of expected CPU and memory utilization and particulars about the machine itself, such as its processor type and whether it has a floating-point coprocessor. The broadcast state information is cached by all the nodes. If the distributed system is large, each machine can cache information about only the best N nodes (for example, only those nodes having unused or underused CPU and memory).

The V-system's selection policy selects only newly arrived tasks for transfer. Its relative transfer policy defines a node as a receiver if it is one of the M most lightly loaded nodes in the system, and as a sender if it is not. The decentralized location policy locates receivers as follows: When a task arrives at a machine, it consults the local cache and constructs the set containing the M most lightly loaded machines that can satisfy the task's requirements. If the local machine is one of the M machines, then the task is scheduled locally. Otherwise, a machine is chosen randomly from the set and is polled to verify the correctness of the cached data. This random selection reduces the chance that multiple machines will select the same remote machine for task execution. If the cached data matches the machine's state (within a degree of accuracy), the polled machine is selected for executing the task. Otherwise, the entry for the polled machine is updated and the selection procedure is repeated. In practice, the cache entries are quite accurate, and more than three polls are rarely required.[1]

The V-system's load index is the CPU utilization at a node. To measure CPU utilization, a background process that periodically increments a counter is run at the lowest priority possible. The counter is then polled to see what proportion of the CPU has been idle.

Sprite. The Sprite system[2] is targeted toward a workstation environment. Sprite uses a centralized state-change-driven information policy. Each workstation, on becoming a receiver, notifies a central coordinator process. The location policy is also centralized: To locate a receiver, a workstation contacts the central coordinator process.

Sprite's selection policy is primarily manual. Tasks must be chosen by users for remote execution, and the workstation on which these tasks reside is identified as a sender. Since the Sprite system is targeted for an environment in which workstations are individually owned, it must guarantee the availability of the workstation's resources to the workstation owner. To do so, it evicts foreign tasks from a workstation whenever the owner wishes to use the workstation. During eviction, the selection policy is automatic, and Sprite selects only foreign tasks for eviction. The evicted tasks are returned to their home workstations.

In keeping with its selection policy, the transfer policy used in Sprite is not completely automated:

(1) A workstation is automatically identified as a sender only when foreign tasks executing at that workstation must be evicted. For normal transfers, a node is identified as a sender manually and implicitly when the transfer is requested.

(2) Workstations are identified as receivers only for transfers of tasks chosen by the users. A threshold-based policy decides that a workstation is a receiver when the workstation has had no keyboard or mouse input for at least 30 seconds and the number of active tasks is less than the number of processors at the workstation.

The Sprite system designers used semiautomated selection and transfer policies because they felt that the benefits of completely automated policies would not outweigh the implementation difficulties.

To promote fair allocation of computing resources, Sprite can evict a foreign process from a workstation to allow the workstation to be allocated to another foreign process under the following conditions: If the central coordinator cannot find an idle workstation for a remote execution request and it finds that a user has been allocated more than his fair share of workstations, then one of the heavy user's processes is evicted from a workstation. The freed workstation is then allocated to the process that had received less than its fair share. The evicted process may be automatically transferred elsewhere if idle workstations become available.

For a parallelized version of Unix "make," Sprite's designers have observed a speedup factor of five for a system containing 12 workstations.

Condor. Condor[3] is concerned with scheduling long-running CPU-intensive tasks (background tasks) only. Condor is designed for a workstation environment in which the total availability of a workstation's resources is guaranteed to the user logged in at the workstation console (the owner).

Condor's selection and transfer policies are similar to Sprite's in that most transfers are manually initiated by users. Unlike Sprite, however, Condor is centralized, with a workstation designated as the controller. To transfer a task,

vious sections. In addition, we compare their performance with that of a system that performs no load distributing (a system composed of n independent M/M/1 systems) and that of an ideal system that performs perfect load distributing (no unshared states) without incurring any overhead in doing so (an M/M/K system). The results we present are from simulations of a distributed system containing 40 nodes, interconnected by a 10-megabit-per-second token ring communication network.

For the simulation we made the following assumptions: Task interarrival times and service demands are independently exponentially distributed, and the average task CPU service demand is one time unit. The size of a polling message is 16 bytes, and the CPU overhead to either send or receive a polling

a user links it with a special system-call library and places it in a local queue of background tasks. The controller's duty is to find idle workstations for these tasks. To accomplish this, Condor uses a periodic information policy. The controller polls each workstation at two-minute intervals to find idle workstations and workstations with background tasks waiting. A workstation is considered idle only when the owner has not been active for at least 12.5 minutes. The controller queues information about background tasks. If it finds an idle workstation, it transfers a background task to that workstation.

If a foreign background task is being served at a workstation, a local scheduler at that workstation checks for local activity from the owner every 30 seconds. If the owner has been active since the previous check, the local scheduler preempts the foreign task and saves its state. If the workstation owner remains active for five minutes or more, the foreign task is preemptively transferred back to the workstation at which it originated. The task may be transferred later to an idle workstation if one is located by the controller.

Condor's scheduling scheme provides fair access to computing resources for both heavy and light users. Fair allocation is managed by the "up-down" algorithm, under which the controller maintains an index for each workstation. Initially the indexes are set to zero. They are updated periodically in the following manner: Whenever a task submitted by a workstation is assigned to an idle workstation, the index of the submitting workstation is increased. If, on the other hand, the task is not assigned to an idle workstation, the index is decreased. The controller periodically checks to see if any new foreign task is waiting for an idle workstation. If a task is waiting, but no idle workstation is available and some foreign task from the lowest priority (highest index value) workstation is running, then that foreign task is preempted and the freed workstation is assigned to the new foreign task. The preempted foreign task is transferred back to the workstation at which it originated.

Stealth. The Stealth Distributed Scheduler[4] differs from V-system, Sprite, and Condor in the degree of cooperation that occurs between load distributing and local resource allocation at individual nodes. Like Condor and Sprite, Stealth is targeted for workstation environments in which the availability of a workstation's resources must be guaranteed to its owner. While Condor and Sprite rely on preemptive transfers to guarantee availability, Stealth accomplishes this task through preemptive allocation of local CPU, memory, and file-system resources.

A number of researchers and practitioners have noted that even when workstations are being used by their owners, they are often only lightly utilized, leaving large portions of their processing capacities available. The designers of Stealth[4] observed that over a network of workstations, this unused capacity represents a considerable portion of the total unused capacity in the system — often well over half.

To exploit this capacity, Stealth allows foreign tasks to execute at workstations even while those workstations are used by their owners. Owners are insulated from these foreign tasks through prioritized local resource allocation. Stealth includes a prioritized CPU scheduler, a unique prioritized virtual memory system, and a prioritized file-system cache. Through these means, owners' tasks get the resources they need, while foreign tasks get only the leftover resources (which are generally substantial). In effect, Stealth replaces an expensive global operation (preemptive transfer) with a cheap local operation (prioritized allocation). By doing so, Stealth can simultaneously increase the accessibility of unused computing capacity (by exploiting underused workstations, as well as idle workstations) and reduce the overhead of load distributing.

Under Stealth, task selection is fully automated. It takes into account the availability of CPU and memory resources, as well as past successes and failures with transferring similar tasks under similar resource-availability conditions. The remainder of Stealth's load-distributing policy is identical to the stable sender-initiated adaptive policy discussed in the "Example algorithms" section of the main text. Because it does not need preemptive transfers to assure the availability of workstation resources to their owners, Stealth can use relatively cheap nonpreemptive transfers almost exclusively. Preemptive transfers are necessary only to prevent starvation of foreign tasks.

References

1. M. Stumm, "The Design and Implementation of a Decentralized Scheduling Facility for a Workstation Cluster," *Proc. Second Conf. Computer Workstations*, IEEE CS Press, Los Alamitos, Calif., Order No. 810, 1988, pp. 12-22.

2. F. Douglis and J. Ousterhout, "Transparent Process Migration: Design Alternatives and the Sprite Implementation," *Software — Practice and Experience*, Vol. 21, No. 8, Aug. 1991, pp. 757-785.

3. M.J. Litzkow, M. Livny, and M.W. Mutka, "Condor — A Hunter of Idle Workstations," *Proc. Eighth Int'l Conf. Distributed Computing Systems*, IEEE CS Press, Los Alamitos, Calif., Order No. 865, 1988, pp. 104-111.

4. P. Krueger and R. Chawla, "The Stealth Distributed Scheduler," *Proc. 11th Int'l Conf. Distributed Computing Systems*, IEEE CS Press, Los Alamitos, Calif., Order No. 2144, 1991, pp. 336-343.

message is 0.003 time units. A nonpreemptive task transfer incurs a CPU overhead of 0.02 time units, and a preemptive transfer incurs a 0.1 time unit overhead. Transfer overhead is divided evenly between the sending and the receiving nodes. The amount of information that must be communicated for a nonpreemptive transfer is 8 Kbytes, while a preemptive transfer requires 200 Kbytes.

While the specific performance values we present are sensitive to these assumptions, the performance trends we observe are far less sensitive and endure across a wide range of distributed systems. Errors in the results we present are less than 5 percent at the 90 percent confidence level.

Figure 4 plots the performance of the following:

- M/M/1, a distributed system that performs no load distributing;
- a sender-initiated algorithm with a random location policy, assuming that a task can be transferred at most once;
- a sender-initiated algorithm with a threshold location policy;
- a symmetrically initiated algorithm (sender- and receiver-initiated algorithms combined);
- a stable sender-initiated algorithm;
- a receiver-initiated algorithm;
- a stable symmetrically initiated algorithm; and
- M/M/K, a distributed system that performs ideal load distributing without incurring overhead for load distributing.

A fixed threshold of T = upper threshold = lower threshold = 1 was used for each algorithm.

For these comparisons, we assumed a small fixed poll limit (5). A small limit is sufficient: If P is the probability that a particular node is below threshold, then the probability that a node below threshold is first encountered on the ith poll is $P(1 - P)^{i-1}$.[6] (This result assumes that nodes are independent, a valid assumption if the poll limit is small relative to the number of nodes in the system.) For large P, this expression decreases rapidly with increasing i. The probability of succeeding on the first few polls is high. For small P, the quantity decreases more slowly. However, since most nodes are

above threshold, the improvement in systemwide response time that will result from locating a node below threshold is small. Quitting the search after the first few polls does not carry a substantial penalty.

Main result. The ability of load distributing to improve performance is intuitively obvious when work arrives at some nodes at a greater rate than at others, or when some nodes have faster processors than others. Performance advantages are not so obvious when all nodes are equally powerful and have equal workloads over the long term. Figure 4a plots the average task response time versus offered system load for such a homogeneous system under each load-distributing algorithm. Comparing M/M/1 with the sender-initiated algorithm (random location policy), we see that even this simple load-distributing scheme provides a substantial performance improvement over a system that does not use load distributing. Considerable further improvement in performance can be gained through simple sender-initiated (threshold location policy) and receiver-initiated load-

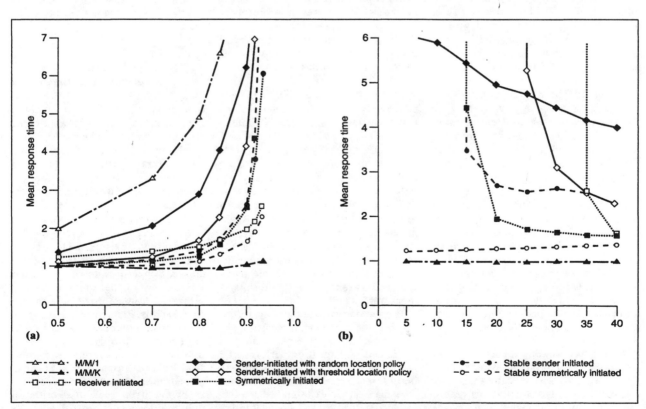

Figure 4. Average response time versus system load (a) and number of load-generating machines (b).

sharing schemes. The performance of the best algorithm — the stable symmetrically initiated algorithm — approaches that of M/M/K, though this optimistic lower bound can never be reached, since it assumes no load-distribution overhead.

Receiver- versus sender-initiated load sharing. Figure 4a shows that the sender-initiated algorithm with a threshold location policy performs marginally better than the receiver-initiated algorithm at light to moderate system loads, while the receiver-initiated algorithm performs substantially better at high system loads (even though the preemptive transfers it uses are much more expensive than the nonpreemptive transfers used by the sender-initiated algorithm). Receiver-initiated load sharing is less effective at low system loads because load sharing is not initiated at the time that one of the few nodes becomes a sender, and thus load sharing often occurs late.

In robustness, the receiver-initiated policy has an edge over the sender-initiated policy. The receiver-initiated policy performs acceptably over the entire system load spectrum, whereas the sender-initiated policy causes system instability at high loads. At such loads, the receiver-initiated policy maintains system stability because its polls generally find busy nodes, while polls due to the sender-initiated policy are generally ineffective and waste resources in efforts to find underloaded nodes.

Symmetrically initiated load sharing. This policy takes advantage of its sender-initiated load-sharing component at low system loads, its receiver-initiated component at high system loads, and both at moderate system loads. Hence, its performance is better than or matches that of the sender-initiated algorithm with threshold location policy at all levels of system load, and is better than that of the receiver-initiated policy at low to moderate system loads. Nevertheless, this policy also causes system instability at high system loads because of the ineffective polling by its sender-initiated component at such loads.

Stable load-sharing algorithms. The performance of the stable symmetrically initiated algorithm matches that of the best of the algorithms at low system loads and offers substantial improve-

ments at high loads (greater than 0.85) over all the nonadaptive algorithms. This performance improvement results from its judicious use of the knowledge gained by polling. Furthermore, this algorithm does not cause system instability.

The stable sender-initiated algorithm yields as good or better performance than the sender-initiated algorithm with threshold location policy, with marked improvement at loads greater than 0.6, and yields better performance than the receiver-initiated policy for system loads less than 0.85. And it does not cause system instability. While it is not as good as the stable symmetrically initiated algorithm, it does not require expensive preemptive task transfers.

Heterogeneous workload. Heterogeneous workloads are common in distributed systems.[8] Figure 4b plots mean response time against the number of load-generating nodes in the system. All system workload is assumed to initiate at this subset of nodes, with none originating at the remaining nodes. A smaller subset of load-generating nodes indicates a higher degree of heterogeneity.

We assume a system load of 0.85. Without load distributing, the system becomes unstable even at low levels of heterogeneity under this load. While we do not plot these results, instability occurs for M/M/1 when the number of load-generating nodes is less than or equal to 33.

Among the load-distributing algorithms, Figure 4b shows that the receiver-initiated algorithm becomes unstable at a much lower degree of heterogeneity than any other algorithm. The instability occurs because random polling is unlikely to find a sender when only a few nodes are senders. The sender-initiated algorithm with a threshold location policy also becomes unstable at relatively low levels of heterogeneity. As fewer nodes receive all the system load, they must quickly transfer tasks. But the senders become overwhelmed as random polling results in many wasted polls.

The symmetrically initiated algorithm also becomes unstable, though at higher levels of heterogeneity, because of ineffective polling. It outperforms the receiver- and sender-initiated algorithms because it can transfer tasks at a higher rate than either. The stable sender-initiated algorithm remains stable for

higher levels of heterogeneity than the sender-initiated algorithm with a threshold location policy because it is able to poll more effectively. Its eventual instability results from the absence of preemptive transfers, which prevents senders from transferring existing tasks even after they learn about receivers. Thus senders become overwhelmed.

The sender-initiated algorithm with a random location policy, the simplest algorithm of all, performs better than most algorithms at extreme levels of heterogeneity. By simply transferring tasks from the load-generating nodes to randomly selected nodes without any regard to their status, it essentially balances the load across all nodes in the system, thus avoiding instability.

Only the stable symmetrically initiated algorithm remains stable for all levels of heterogeneity. Interestingly, it performs better with increasing heterogeneity. As heterogeneity increases, senders rarely change their states and will generally be in the senders lists at the nonload-generating nodes. The nonload-generating nodes will alternate between the OK and receiver states and appear in the OK or receivers lists at the load-generating nodes. With the lists accurately representing the system state, nodes are often successful in finding partners.

O ver the past decade, the mode of computing has shifted from mainframes to networks of computers, which are often engineering workstations. Such a network promises higher performance, better reliability, and improved extensibility over mainframe systems. The total computing capacity of such a network can be enormous. However, to realize the performance potential, a good load-distributing scheme is essential.

We have seen that even the simplest load-distributing algorithms have a great deal of potential to improve performance. Simply transferring tasks that arrive at busy nodes to randomly chosen nodes can improve performance considerably. Performance is improved still more if potential receiving nodes are first polled to determine whether they are suitable as receivers. Another significant performance benefit can be gained, with little additional complexity, by modifying such an algorithm to poll only the nodes most likely to be suitable receivers. Each of these algorithms can be designed to use nonpreemptive transfers exclusively. As a result, all carry relatively low overhead in software development time, maintenance time, and execution overhead. Among these algorithms, an algorithm such as the stable sender-initiated algorithm plotted in Figure 4 provides good performance over a wide range of conditions for all but the most "extreme" systems.

By extreme systems we mean systems that may experience periods during which a few nodes generate very heavy workloads. Under such conditions, a load-distributing algorithm that uses preemptive transfers may be necessary. We recommend an algorithm such as the stable symmetrically initiated algorithm, which can initiate transfers from either potential sending or potential receiving nodes, and targets its polls to nodes most likely to be suitable partners in a transfer. Such an algorithm provides larger performance improvements — over a considerably wider range of conditions — than any other algorithm discussed in this article. ∎

Acknowledgments

We are deeply grateful to the referees, whose comments helped to improve the presentation. Portions of this material are based on work supported by the National Science Foundation under Grant No. CCR-8909072.

References

1. M. Livny and M. Melman, "Load Balancing in Homogeneous Broadcast Distributed Systems," *Proc. ACM Computer Network Performance Symp.*, 1982, pp. 47-55. Proceedings printed as a special issue of *ACM Performance Evaluation Rev.*, Vol. 11, No. 1, 1982, pp. 47-55.

2. T. Kunz, "The Influence of Different Workload Descriptions on a Heuristic Load Balancing Scheme," *IEEE Trans. Software Eng.*, Vol. 17, No. 7, July 1991, pp. 725-730.

3. Y. Artsy and R. Finkel, "Designing a Process Migration Facility: The Charlotte Experience," *Computer*, Vol. 22, No. 9, Sept. 1989, pp. 47-56.

4. F. Douglis and J. Ousterhout, "Transparent Process Migration: Design Alternatives and the Sprite Implementation," *Software — Practice and Experience*, Vol. 21, No. 8, Aug. 1991, pp. 757-785.

5. D.L. Eager, E.D. Lazowska, and J. Zahorjan, "A Comparison of Receiver-Initiated and Sender-Initiated Adaptive Load Sharing," *Performance Evaluation*, Vol. 6, No. 1, Mar. 1986, pp. 53-68.

6. D.L. Eager, E.D. Lazowska, and J. Zahorjan, "Adaptive Load Sharing in Homogeneous Distributed Systems," *IEEE Trans. Software Eng.*, Vol. 12, No. 5, May 1986, pp. 662-675.

7. N.G. Shivaratri and P. Krueger, "Two Adaptive Location Policies for Global Scheduling," *Proc. 10th Int'l Conf. Distributed Computing Systems*, IEEE CS Press, Los Alamitos, Calif., Order No. 2048, 1990, pp. 502-509.

8. P. Krueger and R. Chawla, "The Stealth Distributed Scheduler," *Proc. 11th Int'l Conf. Distributed Computing Systems*, IEEE CS Press, Los Alamitos, Calif., Order No. 2144, 1991, pp. 336-343.

9. T.L. Casavant and J.G. Kuhl, "Effects of Response and Stability on Scheduling in Distributed Computing Systems," *IEEE Trans. Software Eng.*, Vol. 14, No. 11, Nov. 1988, pp. 1,578-1,587.

10. P. Krueger and M. Livny, "The Diverse Objectives of Distributed Scheduling Policies," *Proc. Seventh Int'l Conf. Distributed Computing Systems*, IEEE CS Press, Los Alamitos, Calif., Order No. 801 (microfiche only), 1987, pp. 242-249.

Niranjan G. Shivaratri is a PhD student in the Department of Computer and Information Science at Ohio State University. From 1983 to 1987, he worked as a systems programmer for the Unisys Corporation, concentrating on network and operating systems software development. His research interests include distributed systems and performance modeling. He and Mukesh Singhal coauthored *Advanced Concepts in Operating Systems*, to be published by McGraw-Hill.

Shivaratri received a BS degree in electrical engineering from Mysore University, India, in 1979, and an MS degree in computer science from Villanova University in 1983. He is a member of the IEEE Computer Society.

Phillip Krueger is an assistant professor of computer science at Ohio State University. He directs the Stealth Distributed Scheduler Project at Ohio State, focusing on the design and construction of a distributed scheduler targeted for workstation-based distributed systems. His research interests include operating systems, concurrent and distributed systems, real-time systems, simulation, and performance analysis.

Krueger received his BS degree in physics, and his MS and PhD degrees in computer science from the University of Wisconsin - Madison. He is a member of the IEEE Computer Society and the ACM.

Mukesh Singhal has been a member of the faculty of the Department of Computer and Information Science at Ohio State University since 1986 and is currently an associate professor. His research interests include distributed systems, distributed databases, and performance modeling. He and Niranjan Shivaratri coauthored *Advanced Concepts in Operating Systems*, to be published by McGraw-Hill. He also served as co-guest editor of the August 1991 special issue of *Computer* on distributed computing systems.

Singhal received a bachelor of engineering degree in electronics and communication engineering with high distinction from the University of Roorkee, India, in 1980, and a PhD in computer science from the University of Maryland in 1986.

Readers can contact the authors at the Dept. of Computer and Information Science, Ohio State University, Columbus, OH 43210. Their e-mail addresses are {niran philk singhal}@cis.ohio-state.edu.

Chapter 2
Static Scheduling

2.1 Introduction

In static scheduling, the assignment of processes of a parallel program to the processing elements is done at compile time with the goal of minimizing the overall execution time (completion time) of the program, while minimizing the communication delays. The terms "scheduling," "allocation," and "assignment" are used interchangeably in this chapter. In general, all of these terms refer to the process of the placement of a program's functions on the processors of a multiprocessor system. The terms "scheduling" and "assignment" are often used from a user's point of view, while the term "allocation" is used from a system manager's point of view as a resource management operation. In the literature, these terms may have been used differently in different contexts. For example, while "task assignment" has been used to refer to the initial placement of tasks on processors, "task scheduling" has been used to describe local CPU scheduling of individual tasks.

Static scheduling methods often assume that a concurrent program's processes, with parallelism and dependencies among them, are defined before the scheduling operations begin. The issue of the partitioning of finer grain tasks into coarser ones will be covered more specifically in Chapter 3. In addition, in static scheduling, the information regarding execution time and communication delays of a process is assumed to be known before run-time. Static scheduling methods are almost always non-preemptive; that is, a task is executed on the processor to which it is assigned.

In static scheduling, the two predominant models for representation of a concurrent program are static task graphs (STG) [Bokhari 1988, Berman 1987, Fernandez-Baca 1989, Lo 1988, and Stone 1977] and directed acyclic graphs (DAG) [Hurson 1990, Polychronopoulos 1987, Sarkar 1986, Shirazi 1990]. In a static task graph model, a concurrent program is represented by an undirected, connected graph G, the vertices of which are the tasks, or functions, of the program and the edges of which indicate that the corresponding tasks communicate. Figure 2.1 depicts an example of a STG in which S_1, S_2, and S_3 are the source nodes and S_4, S_5, S_6 are the sink nodes. Source nodes represent starting nodes, where the program can begin its execution. Similarly, sink nodes represent ending nodes, where program execution terminates. Between the source nodes and sink nodes lie several interior nodes with the entire set of nodes linked by weighted edges. The weight of an edge represents the communication delay for message-passing between the program tasks.

In a DAG model a concurrent program is identified by a DAG, in which the nodes represent the program tasks and the directed edges represent both the precedence (dependency) relationship and the communication among the tasks. Let $G(T,E)$ be a DAG representation of a program such that:

T = Set of DAG nodes representing program tasks (such as functions or modules) and

E = Set of directed edges among T nodes.

E represents a partial ordering ($<$) among the tasks, such that $T_i < T_j$ implies T_i must complete its execution and pass some information to T_j before T_j can initiate its execution. In addition, there is a function $W : T \longrightarrow R$, which gives the weight or execution time of a task, and a function $C : E \longrightarrow R$, which gives the communication delay for message-passing on an edge, where R is the set of non-negative real numbers. Figure 2.2a depicts an example DAG. Nodes A through M represent the program's tasks, the numbers inside each node represent the execution time of the nodes, and the numbers on each edge represent the communication delay for message-passing between the corresponding nodes.

Recently a hybrid graph model of parallel computation, that is, a temporal communication graph (TCG), was introduced in [Lo 1992]. The TCG model integrates the DAG and static task graph models of computation and provides the ability to identify logically synchronous phases of communication and computation. In addition, TCGs can be used to describe the temporal behavior of parallel algorithms.

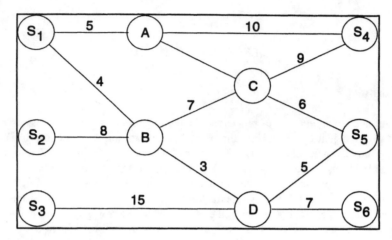

Figure 2.1. An example static task graph.

In static scheduling, a multiprocessor system is represented by a processor graph *PG(PE,LK)*, where:

PE = Set of processing elements and

LK = Set of links connecting the processing elements.

Figure 2.2b shows an example of a processor graph (a 4-processor mesh or hypercube).

Thus, given a program graph *G* and a processor graph *PG*, static scheduling becomes a mapping from *G* to *PG* with the goal of minimizing the execution time of the program. Figure 2.2c shows such a mapping of the DAG of Figure 2.2a on the processor graph of Figure 2.2b. The Gantt chart of Figure 2.2c shows the placement of the tasks on the PEs to be executed at the specified times. The hashed areas are used to indicate the processors' idle time periods.

2.2 Classification of static scheduling methods

In general, the optimal static scheduling problem, with or without communication delays, has been proven to be NP-complete [Fernandez-Baca 1989, Veltman 1990, Chretienne 1989, Papadimitriou 1990, Sarkar 1989]. Thus, research efforts in this area have focused on the development of:

- special-case optimal scheduling,
- locally optimal solutions, and
- suboptimal methods.

By imposing restrictions on the program graph structure and/or the underlying multiprocessor architecture, optimal schedules can be obtained. An example of optimal scheduling on a two-processor system can be found in [Stone 1977]. Other typical restrictions for attaining optimal schedules include tree-organized DAGs, a fully connected sets of PEs, and limited number of tasks and PEs.

2.2.1 Locally optimal solutions

The locally optimal scheduling methods rely on efficient search techniques to identify the optimal schedule in the solution space of a problem. Since these methods often do not guarantee a globally optimal solution, they are called *locally optimal methods*. The algorithms in this group can be classified as:

- simulated annealing methods,
- mathematical programming methods, and
- state-space search methods.

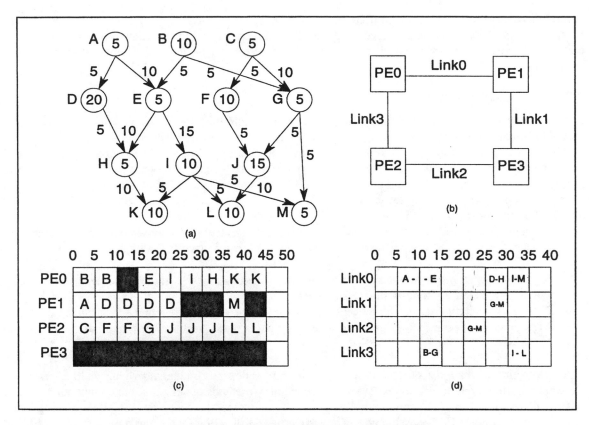

Figure 2.2. An example of static scheduling.

The simulated annealing methods use the properties of the physical annealing process as a way to conduct a sequential search for an optimal scheduling solution [Talbi 1993, Lee 1992]. The process consists of 1) making small random changes to an initial schedule, 2) evaluating the new schedule, and 3) continuing this process iteratively until no improvements in the scheduling time can be obtained. As variations of this method, genetic algorithms [Mitra 1993] and mean field annealing [Bultan 1992] have also been applied to the scheduling problem.

Mathematical programming methods typically rely on integer, linear, or nonlinear programming techniques to resolve task scheduling problems [Gabrielian 1984, Prakash 1992, Price 1984]. The process consists of:

- the definition of an objective function to be minimized, which is often the program execution time as an aggregate of task execution times and communication delays;
- the definition of a set of constraints to preserve properties, such as tasks precedence relations, communication delay constraints, memory constraints, and guarantees that each task is assigned only once; and
- the application of a method for solving complex constrained optimization problems, such as dynamic programming or heuristic techniques.

The state-space search methods rely on branch- and bound-search techniques to conduct a search of the solution space for the scheduling of an application on a given architecture [Greenblatt 1987, Kasahara 1984]. The process consists of building a search tree of possible schedules, defining a cost evaluation function, and searching the tree for the best schedule, while pruning unacceptable solution paths.

Even though it is argued that the above-mentioned optimal and locally optimal methods provide high-quality scheduling solutions, they suffer from a major disadvantage. Because of their complexity, these methods are extremely computation-intensive and time-consuming. For larger DAGs and multiprocessor systems, several days, or even weeks, may be necessary to obtain the required solutions. In order to overcome these computational difficulties, it is proposed that some of the system constraints or search methods be relaxed. In that case, the quality of the solutions is affected and similar results can be obtained through suboptimal, faster techniques.

2.2.2 Suboptimal solutions

Because of the difficulties in obtaining optimal scheduling solutions, the research in this area has been focused on heuristic methods in achieving suboptimal solutions. As the name indicates, these methods rely on heuristics and rules-of-thumb to guide the scheduling process to an acceptable solution. Among general heuristic methods, list scheduling is by far the most widely used technique, even though it could perform poorly in the presence of high communication costs. List scheduling consists of two simple steps: 1) provide a priority list of tasks to be assigned to the PEs, and 2) repeatedly remove the top task on the priority list and allocate it to the most suitable PE for execution.

The scheduling methods differ in how they prioritize the tasks and how they select the most suitable PE for the task assignment. Different heuristics can be used to prioritize tasks, for example:

- Precedence relationship and the execution time of the tasks—the tasks at the higher levels of the DAG with longer execution times will receive higher priority;
- Critical path length—tasks with longer critical path lengths will receive a higher priority; and
- Aggregates of several factors such as critical path length, task execution time, and number of successor tasks.

The selection of the most suitable PE for task assignment depends on the underlying multiprocessor architecture and the communication delays. Some scheduling methods assume that the computation time of tasks is much higher than the communication costs. In such cases, the communication delays are ignored. Thus, the most suitable PE for assignment of a task at time T will be the PE that has the least amount of load already assigned to it up to time T; that is, it is the PE that can execute this task at the earliest possible time.

If communication delays are considered to be significant, then the scheduling method must identify a PE that can execute the given task as soon as possible, taking into account the communication delays. In such a case, all, or a subset of the PEs must be investigated to see which can accommodate the current assignment. The scheduling example of Figure 2.2 takes the effect of communication delay into account. In this example, not only processes are assigned to the processors (Figure 2.2c), but the communication messages are assigned to communication links (Figure 2.2d) as well. The advantage of such a link assignment is that one can consider the effect of the link contention during the scheduling. For example, note that *link0* of the system is in use during the 25–35 time period because of message-passing between process pairs (D-H) and (I-M). Thus, if during the scheduling process another message requires the use of *link0* during this time period, that message should be delayed till time 35. Also, having such information is quite useful during the scheduling process, because one may be able to identify an alternate route that can complete the message transmission with a shorter delay.

2.3 Prognosis and future directions in static scheduling

As discussed in Chapter 1, it is our contention that there already is a large number of high-quality scheduling methods available in the literature. What is sorely missing is practical application of the theoretical work in the field. This gap implies that we may need a whole new set of tools and techniques to bridge the gap between current research results in this area and their practical applications. Some of the currently active areas as well as future research and development directions in static scheduling include:

- *Development of a "DAG generator" tool*: The input to a DAG generator will be a parallel program, written in the user's choice of language, and its output will be the DAG equivalent of the program. Currently, the existing scheduling tools either use specialized code for DAG generation or rely on functional languages, such as SISAL, for easy conversion of the programs to a DAG form (see scheduling tools in

Chapter 4). However, the majority of industry and commercial applications are developed in either C, Fortran, or a close variation of such languages. Thus, for the practical success of scheduling methods, it is imperative to develop a tool that can generate the DAG equivalent of C or Fortran code.

- *Development of an "execution time estimation" tool*: One of the most important characteristics of static scheduling is the assumption that the task execution times are known before the actual execution of the tasks. This assumption is often unrealistic since the execution times of the tasks may vary, due to conditional and loop constructs and variations in input values. Also, accurate estimations of communication delays are difficult, due to the dynamic behavior of the network subsystems. Thus, a DAG generator tool should be augmented with a tool that can provide reasonably accurate estimates of the execution times of the tasks and the communication delays at compile-time. Several directions can be investigated in this regard:

  - *User estimates*: The programmers are expected to annotate the program with their estimates of the execution times. In a related method, the programmers may be required to specify the probability of taking a condition, or estimate the number of iterations of a loop. Such information can then be used to produce a probabilistic estimate of the execution times of the tasks.

  - *Simulation-based estimates*: The runtime program behavior can be simulated, at compile-time, by executing those instructions that affect the program control flow. For the remaining instructions, the simulated time is advanced accordingly. The statistics regarding the frequency of the execution of instructions and their estimated execution delays can be gathered in this manner.

  - *Profile-based estimations*: The idea is to monitor previous runs of the program, or sequentially execute the program, and collect the execution time delays and frequency of the execution of the tasks.

- *Development of a "performance profiler" tool*: The function of a performance profiler tool is to read-in the schedule of a parallel program on a given architecture and produce a graphical profile of the expected performance of the input program. The tool should also provide an "ideal parallelism profile" of the application, giving the user an idea of the inherent parallelism in the program. Many of the scheduling tools discussed in Chapter 4 contain such a performance tool.

- *Development of a "data distribution" tool*: The existing scheduling methods are based simply on function distribution (scheduling), ignoring the data distribution issue. This omission causes performance degradations, due to the runtime communication delays for accessing data at remote sites. Any functional scheduling method should be augmented with a data distribution tool so that the data needed by the scheduled program partitions can be accessed locally most of the time.

2.4 Chapter organization and overview

Since one of the goals of this tutorial is to cover more practical scheduling and load balancing techniques, the papers presented in this chapter mainly describe heuristic scheduling methods. Based on the classification presented in Section 2.1, the papers in this chapter are classified into three categories: scheduling methods based on the DAG model of computation, scheduling methods based on the STG model of computation, and scheduling methods based on dataflow graphs.

1. *DAG-based papers*: To provide an overview of the heuristic-based scheduling methods, we have included the paper by Shirazi, Wang, and Pathak. It presents a comparative study of three different scheduling heuristics: heavy-node-first, critical-path, and weighted-length methods. It shows that simple and fast heuristic algorithms can yield the same high-quality schedules as more complex schemes. The next two papers, one by Sarkar and Hennessy, and one by Polychronopoulos and Kuck, are included because they represent widely cited pioneering work in this area. Sarkar and Hennessey describe a three-step process scheduling method. First, the program graph is expanded, for example, by unrolling the loops to expose sufficient parallelism and to keep all processors busy. Second, an internalization step is performed to decide which tasks must be scheduled on the same processor. Through this step, tasks that would require communication are scheduled on the same processor, thus eliminating communication overhead. The partitioned tasks are then assigned to the processing elements. Polychronopoulos and Kuck address the problem of scheduling arbitrarily nested parallel program loops on shared memory multiprocessor

systems. The proposed guided self-scheduling method can achieve minimal overhead and optimal schedules for certain types of loops. The parameterized nature of the scheme allows its tuning for different systems. Finally, the paper by Veltman, Lageweg, and Lenstra proposes a scheduling model that allows for communication delays between precedence-related tasks. This paper also provides an overview of several existing optimal and approximate algorithms, along with their complexities.

2. *STG-based papers*: The paper by Lo is one of the most comprehensive papers in the STG-based scheduling methods. It proposes a family of heuristic algorithms for Stone's (see Chapter 1) classic scheduling model. In addition, this paper shows how to augment Stone's model to include interference costs that reflect the degree of incompatibility between two tasks. This cost is designed to compensate for overly sequentializing the tasks, due to communication costs. Although the paper by Fernández-Baca is a theoretical one, it is included in this chapter to establish the background and foundation in this area. It shows the NP-completeness of the scheduling problem and proves that a local-search algorithm cannot exist that requires polynomial time per iteration and yields an optimum assignment. The paper also outlines the conditions under which it is possible to achieve optimal solutions.

3. *Dataflow papers*: The last two papers included in this chapter present aspects of the scheduling methods based on dataflow graph model. Ha and Lee address the problem of scheduling dataflow graphs onto parallel processors. Four scheduling strategies are presented and analyzed: fully dynamic, static assignment, self-timed, and fully static. The paper proposes compile-time decisions regarding assignment, ordering, and timing of dataflow actors that eliminate the need for dynamic scheduling. Hurson et al. propose a vertically layered allocation scheme of the dataflow graphs that relies on the critical path heuristic to form sequential partitions in the program graph. These partitions, called vertical layers, are then assigned to the processing elements.

Bibliography

Baxter, J., and J. H. Patel, "The LAST Algorithm: A Heuristic-Based Static Task Allocation Algorithm," *Proc. Int'l Conf. Parallel Processing*, Vol. 2, Pennsylvania State Univ., University Park, Penn., 1989, pp. 217–222.

Berman, F., and L. Snyder, "On Mapping Parallel Algorithms into Parallel Architectures," *J. Parallel and Distributed Computing*, Vol. 4, No. 5, Oct. 1987, pp. 439–458.

Bokhari, S. H., "Partitioning Problems in Parallel, Pipelined, and Distributed Computing," *IEEE Trans. Computers*, Vol. 37, No. 1, 1988, pp. 48–57.

Bowen, N. S., C. N. Nikolaou, and A. Ghafoor, "On the Assignment Problem of Arbitrary Process Systems to Heterogeneous Distributed Computer Systems," *IEEE Trans. Computers*, Vol. 41, No. 3, Mar. 1992, pp. 257–273.

Bultan, T., and C. Aykanat, "A New Mapping Heuristic Based on Mean Field Annealing," *J. Parallel and Distributed Computing*, Vol. 16, No. 4, Dec. 1992, pp. 292–305.

Chretienne, P., "Task Scheduling Over Distributed Memory Machines," *Proc. Int'l Workshop Parallel and Distributed Algorithms*, North Holland Publishers, Amsterdam, 1989.

Fernández-Baca, D., "Allocating Modules to Processors in a Distributed System," *IEEE Trans. Software Eng.*, Vol. SE-15, No. 11, Nov. 1989, pp. 1427–1436; reprinted here.

Gabrielian, A., and D. Tyler, "Optimal Object Allocation in Distributed Computer Systems," *Proc. Int'l Conf. Distributed Computing Systems*, IEEE CS Press, Los Alamitos, Calif., 1984, pp. 88–99.

Greenblatt, B., and C. J. Linn, "Branch and Bound Style Algorithms for Scheduling Communicating Tasks in a Distributed System," *Proc. IEEE Spring CompCon Conf.*, IEEE CS Press, Los Alamitos, Calif., 1987, pp. 12–17.

Ha, S., and E. A. Lee, "Compile-Time Scheduling and Assignment of Data-Flow Program Graphs with Data-Dependent Iteration," *IEEE Trans. Computers*, Vol. C-40, No. 11, Nov. 1991, pp. 1225–1238; reprinted here.

Hurson, A. R., et al., "A Program Allocation Scheme for Data Flow Computers," *Proc. Int'l Conf. Parallel Processing*, Vol. 1, Pennsylvania State Univ., University Park, Penn., 1990, pp. 415–422; reprinted here.

Hwang, J.-J., et al., "Scheduling Precedence Graphs in Systems with Interprocessor Communication Times," *SIAM J. Computing*, Vol. 18, No. 2, Apr. 1989, pp. 244–257.

Kasahara, H., and S. Narita, "Practical Multiprocessor Scheduling Algorithms for Efficient Parallel Processing," *IEEE Trans. Computers*, Vol. C-33, No. 11, Nov. 1984, pp. 1023–1029.

Kramer, O., and H. Muhlenbein, "Mapping Strategies in Message-Based Multiprocessor Systems," *Parallel Computing*, Vol. 9, 1988/1989, pp. 213–225.

Kruskal, C. P., and A. Weiss, "Allocating Independent Subtasks on Parallel Processors," *IEEE Trans. Software Eng.*, Vol. SE-11, No. 10, Oct. 1985, pp. 1001–1016.

Lee, B., A. R. Hurson, and T.-Y. Feng, "A Vertically Layered Allocation Scheme for Data Flow Systems," *J. Parallel and Distributed Computing*, Vol. 11, No. 3, 1991, pp. 175–187.

Lee, K.-G., and S.-Y. Lee, "Efficient Parallelization of Simulated Annealing Using Multiple Markov Chains: An Application to Graph Partitioning," *Proc. Int'l Conf. Parallel Processing, Vol. 3,* CRC Press, Boca Raton, Fla., 1992, pp. 177–180.

Lee, S.-Y., and J. K. Aggarwal, "A Mapping Strategy for Parallel Processing," *IEEE Trans. Computers,* Vol. C-36, No. 4, Apr. 1987, pp. 433–441.

Lo, V. M., "Heuristic Algorithms for Task Assignment in Distributed Systems," *IEEE Trans. Computers,* Vol. C-37, No. 11, Nov. 1988, pp. 1384–1397; reprinted here.

Lo, V. M., "Temporal Communication Graphs: Lamport's Process-Time Graphs Augmented for the Purpose of Mapping and Scheduling," *J. Parallel and Distributed Computing,* Vol. 16, Dec. 1992, pp. 378–384.

Milutinovic, V. M., J. J. Crnkovic, and C. E. Houstis, "A Simulation Study of Two Distributed Task Allocation Procedures," *IEEE Trans. Software Eng.,* Vol. SE-14, No. 1, Jan. 1988, pp. 54–61.

Mitra, H., and P. Ramanathan, "A Genetic Approach for Scheduling Non-preemptive Tasks with Precedence and Deadline Constraints," *Proc. 26th Hawaii Int'l Conf. System Sciences,* Vol. 2, IEEE CS Press, Los Alamitos, Calif., 1993, pp. 556–564.

Papadimitriou, C., and M. Yannakakis, "Towards an Architecture-Independent Analysis of Parallel Algorithms," *SIAM J. Comput.,* Vol. 19, 1990, pp. 322-328.

Polychronopoulos, C. D., and D. J. Kuck, "Guided Self-Scheduling: A Practical Scheduling Scheme for Parallel Supercomputers," *IEEE Trans. Computers,* Vol. C-36, No. 12, Dec. 1987, pp. 1425–1439; reprinted here.

Prakash, S., and A. Parker, "SOS: Synthesis of Application-Specific Heterogeneous Multiprocessor Systems," *J. Parallel and Distributed Computing,* Vol. 16, No. 4, Dec. 1992, pp. 338–351.

Price, C., and S. Krishnaprasad, "Software Allocation Models for Distributed Computing Systems," *Proc. Int'l Conf. Distributed Computing Systems,* IEEE CS Press, Los Alamitos, Calif., 1984, pp. 40–48.

Sarkar, V., and J. Hennessy, "Compile-Time Partitioning and Scheduling of Parallel Programs," *Symp. Compiler Construction,* ACM Press, New York, N.Y., 1986, pp. 17–26; reprinted here.

Sarkar, V., *Partitioning and Scheduling Parallel Programs for Multiprocessors,* MIT Press, Cambridge, Mass., 1989.

Sheu, J.-P., and T.-H. Tai, "Partitioning and Mapping Nested Loops on Multiprocessor Systems," *IEEE Trans. Parallel and Distributed Systems,* Vol. 2, No. 4, Oct. 1991, pp. 430–439.

Shirazi, B., M. Wang, and G. Pathak, "Analysis and Evaluation of Heuristic Methods for Static Task Scheduling," *J. Parallel and Distributed Computing,* Vol. 10, 1990, pp. 222–232; reprinted here.

Sih, G. C., and E. A. Lee, "Dynamic-Level Scheduling for Heterogeneous Processor Networks," *Proc. 2nd IEEE Symp. Parallel and Distributed Processing,* IEEE CS Press, Los Alamitos, Calif., 1990, pp. 42–49.

Stone, H. S., "Multiprocessor Scheduling with the Aid of Network Flow Algorithms," *IEEE Trans. Software Eng.,* Vol. SE-3, No. 1, Jan. 1977, pp. 85–93; reprinted here.

Talbi, E. G., and T. Muntean, "Hill-climbing, Simulated Annealing and Genetic Algorithms: A Comparative Study and Application to the Mapping Problem," *Proc. 26th Hawaii Int'l Conf. System Sciences,* Vol. 2, IEEE CS Press, Los Alamitos, Calif., 1993, pp. 565–573.

Veltman, B., B. J. Lageweg, and J. K. Lenstra, "Multiprocessor Scheduling with Communication Delays," *Parallel Computing,* Vol. 16, 1990, pp. 173–182; reprinted here.

Wang, M., et al., "Accurate Communication Cost Estimation in Static Task Scheduling," *Proc. 24th Hawaii Int'l Conf. System Sciences,* Vol. 1, IEEE CS Press, Los Alamitos, Calif., 1991, pp. 10–16.

Analysis and Evaluation of Heuristic Methods for Static Task Scheduling*

BEHROOZ SHIRAZI[†] AND MINGFANG WANG

Department of Computer Science and Engineering, Southern Methodist University, Dallas, Texas 75275

AND

GIRISH PATHAK

Xerox Corporation, 4 Cambridge Center, 4th floor, Cambridge, Massachusetts 02142-1494

Optimal task scheduling in a multiprocessor environment is known to be an NP-hard problem. The research efforts in this area have focused on heuristic methods for efficient distribution of tasks. This paper introduces two static task scheduling algorithms. The first algorithm, called Heavy Node First (HNF), is based on a local analysis of program graph nodes at each level. The second algorithm, called Weighted Length (WL), considers a more global view of the program graph and takes into account the relationship among the nodes at different levels. The two algorithms are compared to the classical Critical Path Method (CPM). For a given Directed Acyclic Graph of n nodes representing a program, it is shown that HNF requires $O(n \log(n))$ steps while WL and CPM require $O(n^2)$ steps to accomplish the allocation. The nontrivial worst case performances of the three algorithms are analytically evaluated and their average case performances are evaluated through a simulation study. It is shown that the performance of the three algorithms, which is measured in terms of program execution time and processors' idle time, is almost the same. Therefore, taking into account the time complexity of the task distribution itself, we conclude that a simple and fast heuristic algorithm, such as HNF, may be sufficient to achieve adequate performance. © 1990 Academic Press, Inc.

1. INTRODUCTION

Recent real-time and fifth generation applications have created a computation gap between the performance capabilities of the existing machines and the performance required by these applications. The attempts to close this gap on the basis of technology improvements alone have failed due to physical laws and limitations. The universally acceptable solution is through parallel processing. However, one of the most important issues in a parallel environment is that of the operating system and the management of the parallel tasks. The major question is how to distribute the tasks among several processing elements to achieve minimal execution time. The task distribution is important not only for the execution of application programs on multicomputer systems but also for the design stage of multicomputer systems to determine a computer architecture which will perform better for a type of application [7].

The task allocation can be performed either dynamically during the execution or statically at compile time. Dynamic task allocation is based on the redistribution of tasks among the processors during the execution, with the aim of balancing the load among the idle and the busy processors. The approach is especially beneficial if the program behavior cannot be determined before the execution. However, the redistribution process creates additional overheads which often cause a system performance degradation.

On the other hand, the static task allocation (scheduling) methods attempt to foresee the program execution behavior at compile time and to distribute program tasks among the processors accordingly. Although this eliminates the additional execution overhead, the approach can be applied to only a subset of problems whose run-time behavior is predictable. Examples of such applications include matrix multiplication, sorting, Towers of Hanoi, Sieve of Eratosthenes, and adaptive method of solving partial differential equations [2, 15, 16].

In a static task scheduling approach, a program is represented by a Directed Acyclic Graph (DAG) [9, 12, 15]. A node of a DAG represents an operation or a task, while a directed edge represents the precedence among the nodes. Each node is associated with a weight which represents the amount of computation of the node. The task scheduling problem focuses on the distribution of the DAG nodes among the Processing Elements (PE) so that the maximum number of parallel operations or the minimal execution delay is achieved. Of course, most programs contain constructs such

* This research is supported in part by the DARPA under Contract 5-25089 and by the Texas Instruments under Contract 5-27708.

† Current address: University of Texas at Arlington, Department of Computer Science Engineering, P.O. Box 19015, Arlington, Texas 76019–0015.

as loops and conditionals. In general, these constructs do introduce uncertainty in the program behavior. However, in the case of the programs suitable for static task scheduling, the loops can be unfolded. The conditionals such as the If-Then-Else construct introduce two exclusive solutions to a problem. These two solutions can be represented by two DAGs and both solutions can be distributed to the same set of PEs. A detailed treatment of the extraction of time information from application programs is available in [7].

An optimal solution to the task scheduling problem is proven to be computationally hard (NP-complete) [6, 8, 11]. Thus, obtaining optimal schedules is not practical. As a result, some of the research efforts in this area have focused on heuristic methods and AI techniques to obtain near optimal solutions [9, 12, 14]. It should be noted that it is important to specify the upper-bound limit for the generated schedules. Even though the schedules obtained by heuristic methods may not be optimum, this boundary information would be useful in the handling of real-time applications which are best suited for static task allocation. Therefore, in our analysis of the proposed algorithms, their worst case behavior is studied, showing their upper-bound limits.

There are several static task scheduling methods, including graph reduction, preemptive scheduling, max-flow min-cut, domain decomposition, and priority list scheduling [4-6, 9-16]. In this paper we concentrate on the priority list scheduling methods [6, 9, 11]. Here, all the schedulable nodes of a DAG are put into a list according to some priority assigned

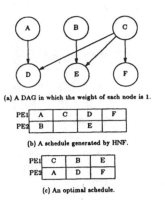

(a) A DAG in which the weight of each node is 1.

PE1	A	C		D	F
PE2	B			E	

(b) A schedule generated by HNF.

PE1	C	B	E
PE2	A	D	F

(c) An optimal schedule.

FIG. 2.   An example of an allocation using HNF.

to each node. The priority is determined on the basis of the heuristic function(s) used. The node with the highest priority is then assigned to a PE which is thought to be the most appropriate to carry out the task.

This paper introduces two new static task scheduling algorithms and compares them to the classical Critical Path Method (CPM). The first algorithm, Heavy Node First (HNF), is based on a simple local analysis of the DAG nodes at each level. The second algorithm, Weighted Length (WL), considers a global view of a DAG by taking into account the relationship among the nodes at different levels. The three algorithms are analyzed for their nontrivial worst case behavior and their average performances are evaluated through a simulation study.

Section 2 defines the framework of the research by covering our basic assumptions and definitions. Section 3 describes various task scheduling algorithms and their analyses. Section 4 discusses the simulation results for a number of applications. And finally, Section 5 presents concluding remarks as well as directions for future research work.

2. DEFINITIONS AND ASSUMPTIONS

In order to set up a framework for our discussions, we first introduce a set of assumptions and definitions. It is assumed that we have a multiprocessor environment in which each processor has its own local memory. The PEs are connected through some interconnection network and the distributed tasks communicate with eachother through a packet switching protocol. In addition, we assume that the number of processors is not enough to cope with the parallelism inherent in the programs (e.g., order of 10's of processors). Another assumption is that a program is represented by a DAG whose nodes are labeled by a weight which represents the length of time to execute the node. In addition, the ratio of computation to communication is assumed to be high.

We now introduce a set of definitions which are used in the description and analysis of the algorithms:

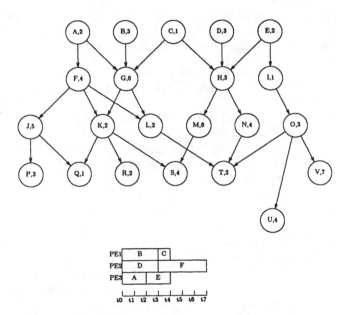

Mature nodes at different moments:
  t0:{A, B, C, D, E}
  t1:{C, E}
  t2:{C, E, F}
  t3:{C, F}
  t4:{G, H, I}

FIG. 1.   An example of a DAG and its partial assignment.

DEFINITION 1. The accumulate time of PE_i, $AT(PE_i)$, for $1 \leq i \leq m$ (where m is the number of PEs), is the total time needed for PE_i to finish all the tasks assigned to it up to current time.

DEFINITION 2. A node is said to be a "mature" node if it is ready to be assigned to a PE. The maturity condition for a node at time t_a is satisfied if the node has no parent or if all of its parent nodes are already assigned to some $PE(PE_k)$, and $AT(PE_k) \leq t_a$ (for all k). The last condition is required to ensure that a task is not assigned before its predecessors are completed.

DEFINITION 3. The level of a DAG node is recursively defined as follows. All the mature nodes at time 0 are at level 0. All the nodes that mature when all the nodes at level i are distributed are at level $i + 1$.

DEFINITION 4. $LAST(PE_i)$ at time t is the level of the last node assigned to PE_i before t. If no nodes have been assigned to PE_i then $LAST(PE_i) = -1$.

DEFINITION 5. An "exit path" of a node P is a path from P to an exit point of the DAG whose length is the longest path among all possible paths from P to any exit point. A node may have several different maximal paths. Any one of these paths can be an exit path.

Figure 1 pictorially depicts some of the above definitions. In Fig. 1, we use a capitalized character to identify a particular node (ID). The number following the node ID is the weight of the node. Here, $AT(PE_1) = 4$ while $AT(PE_2) = 7$. The mature nodes at time t_2 are in the set $\{C, E, F\}$. The level of node M is 2, $LAST(PE_2) = 1$, and an exit path of node A is $\{A, F, J, P\}$. In the following sections we use $WT(P)$ to indicate the weight of the node P.

3. THE HEURISTIC ALGORITHM

This section presents three heuristic algorithms: Heavy Node First algorithm, which is based on giving priority to

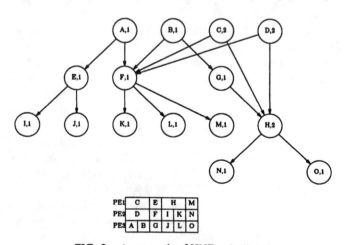

FIG. 3. An example of HNF task allocation.

heavy nodes; Critical Path Method, which depends on traditional critical path analysis; and Weighted Length algorithm, which uses a complex heuristic on the basis of a global view of the task graph.

3.1. Heavy Node First Algorithm

The general idea behind this heuristic is to use a simple and localized analysis of the tasks for their allocation to the PEs. For this purpose, we assign the tasks level by level and at each level assign the heaviest nodes first. The algorithm is as follows:

The HNF Algorithm

Input: A DAG with n nodes and with no redundant transitive arcs.

Output: A task schedule of nodes on the PEs.

1. Let j indicate the current level. Initially, $j=0$. Two lists, *CURRENT* and *NEXT*, are used. Initially, both lists are empty.
2. Let $S=\{PE_i | AT(PE_i)$ is the smallest at current time$\}$.
3. For each PE_i, repeat steps 3.1–3.3.
    3.1 Let node P be the last node assigned to PE_i, remove all the edges from P to its children.
    3.2 If $LAST(PE_i)<j$, add all the nodes matured by P to *CURRENT*.
    3.3 If $LAST(PE_i)=j$, add all the nodes matured by P to *NEXT*.
4. If *CURRENT* is empty, assign a dummy node to all the PEs in S. The weight of the dummy node is equal to $AT(PE_j)-AT(PE_i)$ where PE_j is the node with $AT(PE_j)$ strictly larger than $AT(PE_i)$. If no such PE_j can be found, stop the algorithm, otherwise goto step 2.
5. Assign a node with heaviest weight in *CURRENT* to a PE in S. Remove this PE from S. Remove the assigned node from *CURRENT*. If *CURRENT* is empty goto step 6. If S is empty goto step 2. Otherwise, repeat step 5.

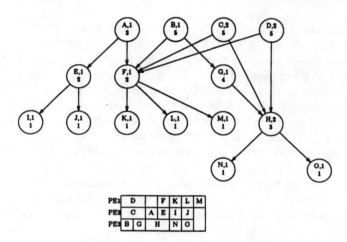

FIG. 4. An example of CPM task allocation.

6. Let *CURRENT:=NEXT, NEXT:=*empty, and increment *j* by 1. Goto step 2.

In this algorithm, load balancing is achieved through (i) assigning the mature nodes to the PEs with smallest accumulated time first and (ii) assigning the heaviest nodes first. A similar version of this heuristic was introduced in [12].

The HNF algorithm requires *n* repetitions to complete, where *n* is the number of nodes. If we use a heap to store the nodes in the *CURRENT* list, one repetition of step 5 requires $\log(n)$ time units. Therefore, the time complexity of this algorithm is $O(n \log(n))$.

Using the HNF algorithm, we may face the situation in which the last node assigned in a level can introduce $m - 1$ dummy (idle) nodes, one in each of $m - 1$ remaining PEs. The weight of each dummy node is equal to the weight of this node. Figure 2 shows an example of such a case. Assigning C to PE_1 causes two dummy nodes to be assigned to PE_2. If the dummy nodes occur at each level and the DAG nodes have the same weights, we have the worst case behavior of the HNF algorithm. Let *n* be the number of nodes in the DAG, *m* be the number of PEs, *s* be the number of DAG levels, and *w* be the weight of each node. The total execution delay under worst case condition is

$$T1 = w\left(\frac{n}{m} + s\left(1 - \frac{1}{m}\right)\right). \quad (1)$$

Assuming that there is enough parallelism in the program, we have $s \leqslant n/m$. Then $T1$ becomes

$$T1 \leqslant w\frac{n}{m}\left(2 - \frac{1}{m}\right). \quad (2)$$

Since $s \leqslant n/m$, we can define a loose lower bound for the execution as

$$T_{low} = w\frac{n}{m}. \quad (3)$$

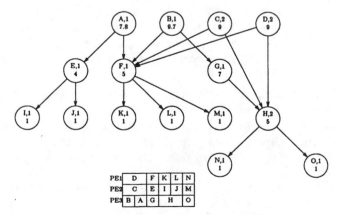

FIG. 5.   An example of WL task allocation.

TABLE I
The Execution Times in Different Experiments

No. of PEs	Execution times		
	HNF	CPM	WL
1	125,719	125,719	125,719
2	63,702	63,598	63,588
3	43,642	43,310	43,279
4	34,125	33,583	33,547
5	28,835	23,206	28,159
6	25,818	25,074	25,025
7	23,901	23,288	23,264
8	22,740	22,212	22,210
9	22,063	21,691	21,681

This loose lower bound is valid only if there exists at least one arrangement which guarantees that at any moment there are always at least *m* mature nodes for the *m* PEs to execute. Comparing $T1$ and T_{low} we have

$$\frac{T1}{T_{low}} \leqslant \left(2 - \frac{1}{m}\right). \quad (4)$$

Equation (4) gives the behavior of the HNF under the worst case situation. Under these conditions, the execution time of a schedule that HNF generates is almost twice as long as that of the optimal schedule. The additional delay T_{dly} introduced in the worst case becomes

$$T_{dly} = T1 - T_{low} \leqslant w\frac{n}{m}\left(1 - \frac{1}{m}\right). \quad (5)$$

If $m = 1$ then $T_{dly} = 0$, which is the case when the program is executed on a uniprocessor. However, if *m* increases (up to *n*), then T_{low} decreases (up to *w*), and thus, T_{dly} approaches T_{low}.

In Fig. 3, another example of the use of HNF is shown. The sum of the weights of all the nodes is 18 time units. For a three-PE system, the total execution time of any optimal schedule can be no less than 6 time units. Here HNF gives an optimal schedule.

3.2. Critical Path Method Algorithm

Many of the earlier and classical task allocation schemes are based on a critical path heuristic. The idea is that the tasks on the critical path determine the shortest possible execution delay for the whole program. Furthermore, the tasks on the critical path have to be executed in sequence. Therefore, one may identify the length of a critical path for each graph node, rank the nodes accordingly, and assign the nodes to the PEs on the basis of the priority list scheduling method. In order to be able to complete this process we first need to identify the length of the critical path for each node of the program graph. It should be noted that finding the length of the critical path is equivalent to finding an "exit path" for a node. The following algorithm finds the length of an exit path for each node of a graph.

Exit Path Algorithm

Input: A DAG.
Output: The length of an exist path for each node.
Variables: Let n be number of nodes in the DAG. For $1 \leq i \leq n$, let N_i be the outdegree (number of chilren) of node P_i, and L_i be the length of exit path for node P_i. Let CL be a list. Initially, $L_i = 0$, CL is empty, and $N_i = 0$ for all the exit nodes.

1. For all P_k being an exit node, assign the weight of P_k to L_k. Add all the exit nodes to CL.
2. Let P_i be a node in CL. Repeat steps 2.1–2.3 until CL is empty:
    2.1 For each parent node P_j of node P_i do:
        2.1.1 $N_j = N_j - 1$
        2.1.2 If $L_j < WT(P_j) + L_i$, then $L_j = WT(P_j) + L_i$.
    2.2 If $N_j = 0$ and P_j is not an entry node, add P_j to CL.
    2.3 Remove P_i from CL.

In this algorithm, each node is processed only once in step 2. Since steps 2.1–2.3 can be repeated a maximum of n times, the time complexity of the algorithm is $O(n^2)$.

We now present the Critical Path algorithm for task assignment based on using the length of an exit path for each node.

The CPM Algorithm

Input: A DAG with n nodes and with no redundant transitive arcs.
Output: A distribution of DAG nodes among the PEs.

1. Call the Exit Path Algorithm to get the length of exit path for each node.

TABLE II

The Processor Idle Times in Different Experiments

No. of PEs	Processor idle times		
	HNF	CPM	WL
1	0	0	0
2	1,685	1,477	1,457
3	5,207	4,211	4,118
4	10,781	8,613	8,469
5	18,456	15,311	15,076
6	29,189	24,725	24,431
7	41,588	37,297	37,127
8	56,055	51,819	51,803
9	72,607	69,189	69,155

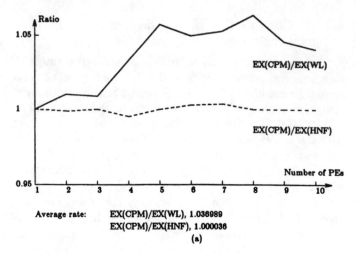

Average rate: EX(CPM)/EX(WL), 1.036989
                EX(CPM)/EX(HNF), 1.000036
(a)

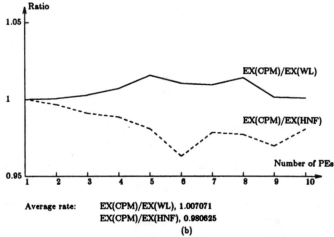

Average rate: EX(CPM)/EX(WL), 1.007071
                EX(CPM)/EX(HNF), 0.980625
(b)

FIG. 6.   The relative behavior of the three methods.

2. Repeat steps 2.1–2.4 until the accumulate time of all the PEs is the same and there are no *mature* nodes available:
    2.1 Choose PE_i such that $AT(PE_i)$ is the smallest.
    2.2 Find a *mature* node with the largest exit path length.
    2.3 If found, assign the node to PE_i.
    2.4 If there are no *mature* nodes available, assign a dummy node to PE_i. The weight of the dummy node is equal to the difference between $AT(PE_i)$ and $AT(PE_j)$ where $AT(PE_j)$ is strictly larger than (PE_i).

Assume that the information regarding the length of an exit path is kept as a heap. Step 1 requires $O(n^2)$ iterations, while step 2 requires n times to complete. Step 2.2 requires $O(\log n)$ times to complete. Therefore, the total time complexity of the CPM algorithm is about $(n^2 + n \log n)$, which is $O(n^2)$.

Figure 4 depicts an example of the application of the CPM algorithm to the same DAG used in Fig. 3, given three PEs. In Fig. 4, the length of the exit path of a node is given under the node IDs. The principle behind this algorithm is to assign the nodes with the longest exit path lengths first. Thus, critical paths of a graph, which represent the minimal execution time requirements, are assigned first. Load balancing is achieved by assigning the nodes to the PE with the smallest accumulation time at each step and using the noncritical nodes to fill the empty slots. Note that compared to HNF, the CPM algorithm resulted in a nonoptimal solution for this particular DAG.

For our analytical analysis of the CPM algorithm, we need to identify the worst case behavior of the algorithm. Let $MT(t_i)$ be the set of mature nodes at time t_i and $CHILD(t_i)$ be the set of child nodes of all the nodes in $MT(t_i)$. P is said to be a *control node* if P is a parent node of all the nodes in $CHILD(t_i)$. If there are more than one such node, the weight of P is the smallest among all these nodes. P is called a control node since none of the children of the mature nodes in $MT(t_i)$ can become mature until P is carried out.

Let PE_i be the PE to which the heaviest node in $MT(t_i)$ is assigned. Also, let $PE_1, PE_2, \ldots, PE_{m'}$ be the processing elements whose accumulated time is less than $AT(PE_i)$ at time t_i. Then, the total idle time due to P at time t_i is

$$T_{idle} = \sum_{j=1}^{m'} AT(PE_i) - AT(PE_j). \qquad (6)$$

The average delay caused by P is

$$T_{av\_dly} = \frac{T_{idle}}{m}. \qquad (7)$$

This average delay is maximized if the weight of the nodes in $MT(t_i)$ is the same (e.g., w) and $m' = m - 1$. In this case, we have

$$T_{av\_dly} = \left(1 - \frac{1}{m}\right)w. \qquad (8)$$

If s is the number of the DAG's levels, then in the worst case, the total delay is

$$T_{dly} = ws\left(1 - \frac{1}{m}\right). \qquad (9)$$

TABLE III
Optimality Rate of the HNF Algorithm

Graphs	Optimality rate of HNF	Optimality rate of random schedule
10-node with varying weights	0.93	0.73
10-node with unit weight	1	0.98
13-node with varying weights	0.76	0.43
13-node with unit weight	0.90	0.86

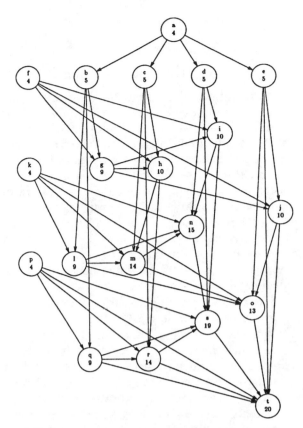

FIG. 7. The DAG for the LU decomposition algorithm.

For a control node P, the idle set of P is defined as the set $MT(t_i) - \{P\}$. Let $D_1, D_2, \ldots, D_v$ be v idle sets and let Pc_i be the control node for D_i ($1 \leq i \leq v$). The CPM algorithm's worst case behavior occurs when Pc_1 is an entry node, Pc_i is a child of Pc_{i-1} (for $2 \leq i \leq v$), all the children nodes of Pc_v are exit nodes, and $v = s$.

Let $|D_i|$ be the cardinality of the set D_i and let the weight of each node in the DAG be w. Then, the worst case execution time is

$$T2 = w\left(s + \frac{\sum_{i=1}^{s}(|D_i| - 1)}{m}\right). \qquad (10)$$

Since $\sum |D_i| = n$, we have

$$T2 = w\left(s - \frac{s}{m} + \frac{n}{m}\right), \qquad (11)$$

or equivalently,

$$T2 = w\left(\frac{n}{m} + s\left(1 - \frac{1}{m}\right)\right). \qquad (12)$$

It is obvious that the worst case execution times ((1) and (12)) and the worst case additional delay times ((5) and

55

(9)) for the HNF and CPM algorithms are respectively equivalent.

3.3. Weighted Length Algorithm

The major problem with the CPM algorithm is that it does not consider the weight of the nodes in the subtrees of the nodes. In other words, the number of nodes (or subgraphs) dependent on a node are not taken into account. This is especially evident in the case of control nodes. For example, in CPM, if a heavy node is assigned to a PE, then several other nodes must be assigned to other PEs in order to balance the load among the processing elements. But if this node is a control node, all other PEs must remain idle until the node is completed. In this case, it may be advantageous to assign the control node first (instead of last as in the CPM algorithm) and use the other nodes in the idle set to balance the load among the PEs.

In order to assign a control node earlier, it must be assigned a priority number which is greater than that of the other nodes. Therefore, we propose an extension to the CPM algorithm in which the rank of a node depends on the length of an exit path, the branching factor, the number of children, and the weights of the children and their descendants. The heuristic assigns each node a number which we call the weighted length. The weighted length singles out the control node more effectively and is expected to compensate the shortcomings of CPM. Let $WL(P)$ be the weighted length of node P, $U(P)$ be the maximum weighted length of the children of P, and $V(P)$ be the summation of the weighted lengths of the children of P. Then, the weighted length of node P is defined as

$$WL(P) = WT(P) + U(P) + \frac{V(P)}{U(P)}, \quad (13)$$

where $WT(P)$ is the weight of node P. Note that the sum of the weighted length of the children of P are normalized over $U(P)$. In order to complete the Weighted Length method, we first need an algorithm for calculating the weighted lengths of the nodes of a DAG:

Weighted Length Calculation

Input: A DAG.
Output: The weighted length of each node.

1. Set $WL(P_i)=WT(P_i)$ for all P_is being an exit node.
2. Repeat steps 2.1–2.3 for every node (P) whose $WL(P)$ is unknown, but the weighted lengths of its children are already calculated:
   2.1 Find $U(P)$.
   2.2 Calculate $V(P)$.
   2.3 Set $WL(P)=WT(P)+U(P)+\dfrac{V(P)}{U(P)}$.

The time complexity of this algorithm is $O(n^2)$ since step 2 is repeated n times and for each iteration, steps 2.1 and 2.2 may require up to n operations. Here, n is the number of nodes in the DAG.

The Weighted Length algorithm is exactly the same as the CPM algorithm with two exceptions. First, in step 1 we need to call the Weighted Length Calculation to find the weighted length of the DAG nodes. Second, in step 2.2, instead of finding a mature node with the largest exit path length, we need to find a mature node with the largest weighted length.

Figure 5 depicts an example of the WL task allocation scheme. The DAG used in this example is the same as that used in the HNF and CPM examples except that the length of exit path is replaced by the weighted length. It is notable that the total execution time is reduced compared to the CPM allocation and that no dummy nodes are introduced.

In the WL algorithm, the small exit path length of the important control nodes is compensated by considering the weight of its children. This gives the control nodes a better chance of being allocated first with good opportunities for using the other nodes at that same level for load balancing.

The time complexity of the WL algorithm is the same as that of the CPM algorithm, i.e., $O(n^2)$. The worst case occurs when at each step of the algorithm all the mature nodes are

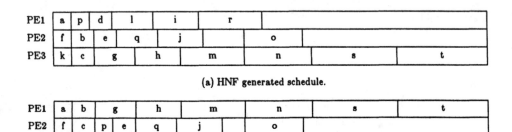

(a) HNF generated schedule.

(b) CPM and WL generated schedule.

FIG. 8.   The LU decomposition algorithm schedules with three PEs.

56

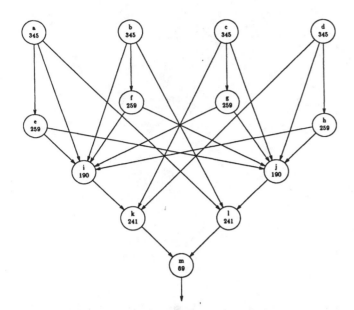

FIG. 9. The computation DAG of the dynamic scene analysis algorithm.

also control nodes. In that case, the execution time of the tasks will be the same as that of the CPM schedule. However, the possibility of the occurrence of the worst case in the WL is very small.

4. PERFORMANCE EVALUATION

So far, we have presented an analysis of the worst case behavior of the three heuristic-based task allocation schemes, i.e., HNF, CPM, and WL. However, the analytical evaluation of these algorithms provides little information for their comparison. The three algorithms behave the same under their own worst case behavior. It must be noted that the difference in the execution times between a schedule generated by a heuristic algorithm and an optimal schedule is maximized when a DAG represents a worst case for the heuristic algorithm. The worst case analytical models that we presented here show the situation where a heuristic algorithm unnecessarily generates many idle tasks. For example, if a control node is executed earlier, the PEs will not be idle before the execution of all the nodes in one level is finished. Such unnecessary idle tasks eventually extend the total execution time.

In order to be able to evaluate the performance of the three methods on the basis of the average cases, we conducted

three simulation studies. The three algorithms were tested by their application to randomly generated DAGs using a varying number of PEs. In the first study, 110 different DAGs are randomly generated. Each DAG has 40 nodes and the weight of each node is randomly chosen between 1 and 50. The generated DAGs are then distributed between 1 and 9 processors using HNF, CPM, and WL algorithms. In each experiment, the total execution times and idle times are measured. Table I depicts the execution times in different cases, while Table II shows the total processor idle times in each experiment. From the simulation result we can see that the WL heuristic has resulted in a slightly better distribution than the CPM, and the CPM distributes the tasks a bit more efficiently than the HNF. However, the differences in the execution times and the idle times for the three cases do not seem to be significant.

In the second study, we experimented with the range of the weights for each node. In these experiments, 40 40-node random graphs were used and the number of processors ranged from 1 to 10. We first used a fixed weight of 10 units of time for each node and present the relative behavior of the three methods in Fig. 6a. Then, we randomly chose the weight of the nodes in the range of 10 to 20 time units. Figure 6b depicts the relative behavior of the three methods. In Fig. 6 the relative behavior of WL and HNF algorithms are compared to that of CPM. Here, EX(K) indicates the execution time resulting from application of heuristic K. As shown in Fig. 6, when uniform weights are used, both HNF and WL methods outperform CPM, although HNF is only slightly better. However, for a random distribution of weights in the range of 10 to 20 time units, WL is still performing better than CPM but CPM becomes better than HNF. Again, the differences in the execution times for different algorithms are not significant. In other words, the average relative behavior of HNF and WL over CPM ranges from 0.98 to 1.03, which is essentially the same due to the assumed 10% margin of error.

In the third study, we tried to find out how close the results from the HNF algorithm are to the optimal results. Unfortunately, this was a very time consuming experiment. We could only afford to run some example DAGs with few nodes. We generated 100 10-node DAGs and 100 13-node DAGs. For each such DAG, there were two versions, one with unit weight nodes and the other with the node weight varying between 1 and 20. Each time a DAG was generated, the exhaustive search method was used to find out the optimal

PE1	a	d	h	i	k	m
PE2	b	f	e		j	l	
PE3	c	g				

FIG. 10. A schedule for the dynamic scene analysis algorithm on three PEs.

57

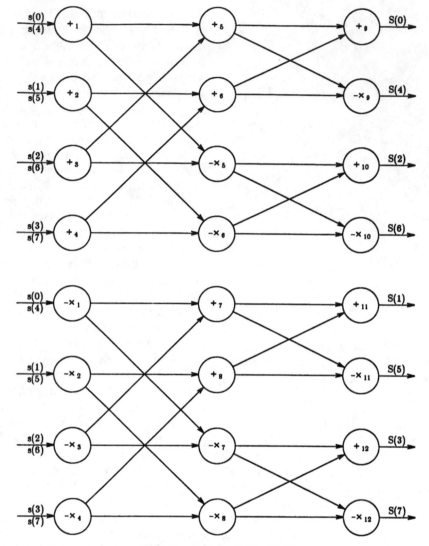

FIG. 11. Program DAG of FFT.

solution. Then HNF algorithm was applied and the results from the two methods were compared. Table III gives the result of the experiments. The schedules are based on a three-PE system. We did not try DAGs with more nodes or use more PEs because the simulation time increases drastically. It is interesting to note that the HNF always generated an optimal solution when a unit weight was used for the tasks and the number of nodes was limited to a small number (10).

According to the above performance studies WL method is seemingly better than the other two. But the differences are very small. It is generally true that the more information used by a heuristic, the better the results should be. But, it is also interesting to see how the efforts that are spent on collecting information compare to the improvement of the results. In the task scheduling situation, the Critical Path algorithm and the Weighted Length algorithm include more information about the DAG to make the scheduling decision. However, the improvements in their results do not match the efforts spent to collect the information. The HNF, even though very simple, gives results of the same quality as the other two heuristics. To emphasize this point, we applied these algorithms to several real applications and the results are presented in the following subsections:

LU Decomposition

The problem of solving linear systems of equations is encountered in many scientific applications. One of the most common ways of solving this problem is by the LU decomposition method [12]. VLSI computing structures such as systolic arrays have often been proposed for solving such problems. Figure 7 shows the computation DAG for the LU

PE1	$-\times_4$		$-\times_1$		$-\times_7$	$+_5$	$-\times_9$		$+_{12}$	$+_{11}$	$+_9$
PE2	$-\times_3$	$+_4$	$+_2$	$-\times_8$		$-\times_5$		$-\times_{12}$		$+_{10}$	
PE3	$-\times_2$	$+_3$	$+_1$	$-\times_6$	$+_8$	$+_7$	$+_6$	$+_{11}$		$+_{10}$	

FIG. 12. Schedule for FFT as generated by heuristic algorithms.

decomposition algorithm. The weight of each node is indicated by the number shown in the node. The lowercase letters are used to label the nodes.

Figure 8 shows the schedules generated by the three heuristic algorithms. A three-PE computer system is assumed. The schedule in Fig. 8a is generated by HNF algorithm. CPM and WL algorithms generate the same schedule as that shown in Figure 8b. Although these two schedules are different, they yield the same execution time.

Dynamic Scene Analysis

Dynamic scene analysis is an algorithm for extracting images of moving objects. Many details of the algorithm are introduced in [12]. The computation DAG of the algorithm is shown in Fig. 9. Again, the lowercase letters are used to label the nodes and the weight of each node is given by the number in each node.

Given the DAG in Fig. 9, the three scheduling algorithms generate the same schedule, shown in Fig. 10. The schedule is optimal and the total execution is the length of the critical path of the DAG.

Fast Fourier Transformation (FFT)

The DAG in Fig. 11 represents an FFT algorithm designed to perform an 8-point FFT transformation. The basic operations are addition ("+") and subtraction and multiplication ("$-\times$"). A "+" node simply adds the two input data together, while a "$-\times$" node performs $(I_1 - I_2) \times W^k$, where I_1 and I_2 are two input data, $W = e^{2\pi i/8}$, and $0 \leqslant k \leqslant 7$. We assume that the weight of each "+" node is 1 time unit and that of each "$-\times$" node is 5 time units. Figure 12 shows a schedule generated by all three algorithms. This time, the scheduling algorithms do not give the optimal solution. An optimal solution is shown in Fig. 13.

5. CONCLUSION

This paper presented three different heuristic functions for static task allocation in a distributed multiprocessor environment. The first heuristic function (HNF) uses local, level by level information to distribute the tasks from a DAG. The second heuristic function (CPM) takes advantage of the length of critical path for each node to achieve the allocation. Finally, the third heuristic (WL) extends CPM to include more global information for each node, such as the weight of the nodes in the subgraphs which are dependent on that node.

The three algorithms behave similarly under worst case conditions as demonstrated by analytical results. But intuitively we believe that the worst cases for different methods occur with different probabilities. The worst case for WL occurs with the least probability. This can be verified by the simulation results which indicate that WL is slightly better than the other two methods. The simulation results show the average behavior of the three methods. In our study, the time complexity of HNF allocation algorithm is $O(n \log n)$, while time complexity of the CPM and the WL is $O(n^2)$. Table IV shows the execution time of these algorithms on DAGs of different sizes. The delays presented depict the time required for the generation of the node priorities and the task assignment. The experiments were conducted as individual jobs on a PC-AT compatible machine. Each execution delay is the average of applying the method to 10 DAGs of a given size. It is notable that HNF not only has a lower asymptotic complexity but also has a sufficiently low overhead that its running time is lower than that of the other two methods. Judging the algorithms by their time complexity and the results they produce, HNF algorithm is obviously a very promising scheduling method.

In addition, since HNF algorithm uses local information from a given DAG, the DAG can be partitioned into small levels and each level can be processed independently. In other words, only part of the precedence relation among the nodes is needed to make the assignment. The same is also true for the CPM algorithm, whereas the WL algorithm cannot be used in a partitioned graph because it needs more complete information than HNF and CPM; i.e., the whole DAG has to be used in the decision-making process.

PE1	$-\times_4$		$-\times_1$		$-\times_7$	$+_5$	$-\times_9$		$+_{12}$	$+_{11}$	$+_9$
PE2	$-\times_3$	$+_4$	$+_2$	$-\times_8$	$+_8$	$-\times_5$		$-\times_{12}$		$+_{10}$	
PE3	$-\times_2$	$+_3$	$+_1$	$-\times_6$	$+_7$	$+_6$	$+_{11}$		$+_{10}$		

FIG. 13. Optimal schedule for FFT.

TABLE IV
Run-Time Delay Information for the Three Methods

No. of DAG nodes	Execution delays (in seconds)		
	HNF	CPM	WL
20	0.20	0.24	0.26
40	0.57	0.75	0.80
60	1.00	1.37	1.51
80	1.47	2.11	2.35
100	1.98	2.96	3.33
120	2.51	3.91	4.43
140	3.06	4.95	5.67

ACKNOWLEDGMENTS

The authors express their appreciation to the anonymous reviewers of this manuscript for their constructive suggestions.

REFERENCES

1. Agrawal, D. P., Janakiram, V. K., and Pathak G. Evaluating the performance of multicomputer configurations. *IEEE Comput.* (May 1986), 23.

2. Berger, M. J., and Bokhari S. H. A partition strategy for nonuniform problems on multiprocessors. *IEEE Trans. Comput.* C-36 5 (May 1987), 570.

3. Bokhari, S. H. Multiprocessing the sieve of eratosthenes. *IEEE Comput.* (Apr. 1987), 50.

4. Chu, W. W. *et al.* Task allocation and precedence relations for distributed real-time systems. *IEEE Trans. Comput.* (June 1987), 667.

5. Chu, W. W. *et al.* Task allocation in distributed data processing. *IEEE Comput.* (Nov. 1980), 57.

6. Coffman, E. G. *et al. Computer and Jop-shop Scheduling Theory.* Wiley-Interscience, New York, 1976.

7. Covington, R. C. *et al.* The rice parallel processing testbed. *Proc. 1988 Sigmetrics Conf. on Measurement and Modeling of Computer Systems,* Santa Fe, NM, May 1988. p. 4.

8. Garey, M. R., and Johnson, D. S. Computers and intractability: A guide to the theory of NP-completeness. Bell Laboratories Tech. Rep., Murray Hill, NJ.

9. Kasahara, H. *et al.* Practical multiprocessor scheduling algorithms for efficient parallel processing. *IEEE Trans. Comput.* C-33 (Nov. 1984), 1023.

10. Lee, S. Y., and Aggarwal, J. K. A mapping strategy for parallel processing. *IEEE Trans. Comput.* (Apr. 1987), 433.

11. Miklosko, J., and Kotov, V. E. *Algorithms, Software and Hardware of Parallel Computers.* VEDA, Publishing House of the Slovak Academy of Sciences, Bratislava, 1984.

12. Pathak, G., and Agrawal, D. P. Task division and multicomputer system. *Proc. 5th Int. Conf. on Distributed Computing System,* Denver, CO, May 1985, p. 273.

13. Polychronopoulos, C. D., and Banerjee, U. Processor allocation for horizontal and vertical parallelism and related speedup bounds. *IEEE Trans. Comput.* (Apr. 1987), 410.

14. Ravi, T. M. *et al.* Static allocation for a data flow multiprocessor system. *Proc. 2nd Int. Conf. on Supercomputing,* May 1987.

15. Sarkar, V., and Hennessy, J. Compile-time partitioning and scheduling of parallel programs. *Proc. SIGPLAN '86 Symp. on Compiler Construction,* 1986, p. 17.

16. Shen, C. C., and Tsai, W. H. A graph matching approach to optimal task assignment in distributed computing system using a minimax criterion. *IEEE Trans. Comput.* (Mar. 1985), 197.

BEHROOZ SHIRAZI received his M.S. and Ph.D. degrees in computer science from the University of Oklahoma in 1980 and 1985, respectively. Since then, he has joined the Department of Computer Science and Engineering at Southern Methodist University as an assistant professor. His research interests encompass distributed processing, computer architecture, dataflow computation, and parallel processing. Dr. Shirazi has been the Chair of the Dallas Chapter of IEEE Computer Society, IEEE Region 5 Area Activities Board Chair, and General Chair of the First as well as the Co-program Chair of the Second IEEE Symposium on Parallel and Distributed Processing. He is a member of IEEE, IEEE Computer Society, ACM, and Sigma XI.

MINGFANG WANG received his M.S. degree in computer science from Shanghai Jiao Tong University in 1983. He joined the Department of Computer Science at the University of Maryland as a visiting scholar during the 1985–1986 academic year. He is currently a Ph.D. candidate at the Department of Computer Science and Engineering at Southern Methodist University. Mr. Wang's research interests include distributed systems, parallel architectures, database systems, and prolog machines. He is a member of IEEE.

GIRISH PATHAK received his Ph.D. in electrical and computer engineering from North Carolina State University, Raleigh, in 1984. Since July 1989 he has been a senior researcher at Xerox Advanced Information Technology at Cambridge, where he is engaged in research and development activity in Engineering Information System (EIS) technology and in Real-Time Active Database Systems. From 1984 to 1989 Dr. Pathak was a member of the Technical Staff at Information Technologies Laboratory of Texas Instruments Incorporated. At Texas Instruments he was one of the key technical members responsible for the design and development of a distributed object-oriented database system, Zeitgeist. Dr. Pathak is a senior member of IEEE, IEEE Computer Society, a member of ACM, and a member of OODB Task Group for ANSI's Database Systems Study Group. He has published about 24 articles in various books, journals, conferences, and technical reports, and has a U.S. patent pending. He was conference Chairperson of the second annual regional conference on "New directions in database and knowledge management systems." In 1988, IEEE Dallas Section awarded him for outstanding service to computers.

Received September 14, 1988; revised October 30, 1989; accepted July 19, 1989

Compile-time Partitioning and Scheduling
of Parallel Programs

Vivek Sarkar and John Hennessy
Computer Systems Laboratory
Stanford University

Abstract

Partitioning and scheduling techniques are necessary to implement parallel languages on multiprocessors. Multiprocessor performance is maximized when parallelism between tasks is optimally traded off with communication and synchronization overhead. We present compile-time partitioning and scheduling techniques to achieve this trade-off.

1. Introduction

One of the biggest challenges facing compiler writers is to efficiently implement programming languages on multiprocessors. We need to find compilation techniques for general-purpose parallel languages; these techniques should be adaptable to a wide range of multiprocessor architectures.

There are three fundamental problems to be solved when compiling a program for parallel execution on a multiprocessor:

1. Identifying potential parallelism.
2. Partitioning the program into sequential tasks.
3. Scheduling the concurrent execution of these tasks.

We address the latter two problems and suggest that they be solved at compile-time instead of run-time for applications with fairly predictable execution times. In these cases the benefits are tremendous. A global, compile-time analysis

This work has been supported by the National Science Foundation under grant # DCR8351269 and by the Defense Research Projects Agency under contract # MDA 903-83-C-0335.

reduces communication overhead for the entire program; such an analysis cannot be done on the fly at run-time. Compile-time partitioning and scheduling also eliminates task scheduling overhead and load balancing overhead at run-time.

A compile-time partitioner-cum-scheduler has been implemented to process program graphs in the intermediate language, IF1 [21]. IF1 represents computation as dataflow graphs, as described later in Section 6. A list of target parameters (e.g. number of processors, communication overhead, inter-processor distances) drives the partitioning for a given multiprocessor architecture. Using a front-end from SISAL [15] to IF1, we apply this system to different benchmark programs written in the single-assignment language SISAL. Like other functional languages, SISAL is implicitly parallel; this eliminates the need to extract parallelism from the program. However, our approach is applicable to any environment where a program graph representation can be obtained.

2. Overview of our approach

Our approach is to expose enough parallelism in the "main program" function graph and then assign computations to processors so as to minimize the parallel execution time, while considering communication overhead. As shown in Figure 2-1, there are four basic steps in this process:

1. Cost Assignment: Traverse the program graph and assign execution time costs to nodes and communication size costs to edges.
2. Graph Expansion: Expand the graph so that the main function contains sufficient parallelism to keep all processors busy. Nodes in the expanded program graph are mapped to tasks.
3. Internalization: Decide which tasks must go together on the same processor, even if other processors are available. This internalizes their communication and eliminates its overhead, at the expense of sequentializing the tasks.
4. Processor Assignment: Assign tasks to processors so as to minimize parallel execution time. Tasks in the

Reprinted with permission from *Proc. of the SIGPLAN 86 Symp. on Compiler Construction,* ACM Press, New York, N.Y., 1986, pp. 17–26.
©1986 Association for Computing Machinery.

same block of the internalized partition must be assigned to the same processor.

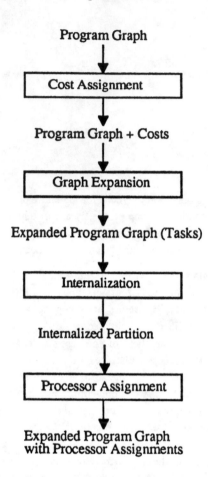

Program Graph

↓

Cost Assignment

↓

Program Graph + Costs

↓

Graph Expansion

↓

Expanded Program Graph (Tasks)

↓

Internalization

↓

Internalized Partition

↓

Processor Assignment

↓

Expanded Program Graph
with Processor Assignments

Figure 2-1: Overview

Note that we rely heavily on compile-time estimates of communication and computation costs. These costs drive the expansion, internalization and scheduling of parallel tasks. We have found that our cost estimates yield good partitions for a range of programs and input data.

These four phases for compile-time partitioning and scheduling are described in later sections. We begin with a discussion of multiprocessor models and real multiprocessors.

3. Multiprocessor Scheduling Theory

Let's start by examining the traditional model for multiprocessor scheduling, which consists of:

- P identical, independent processors.
- A set of N tasks, $T = \{T_1, ..., T_N\}$ with execution times $t_1, ..., t_N$.
- A partial order → on T.

The partial order describes precedence constraints on the tasks, so that $T_i \rightarrow T_j$ forces T_j to start only after T_i has completed execution.

The problem is to find a valid schedule with the smallest completion time. This problem (along with several restricted versions) has been shown to be NP-complete [14]. However, there exist efficient scheduling algorithms that generate schedules with a worst-case performance bound of 2, relative to an optimal schedule [11]. Thus the NP-completeness of the scheduling problem is not an impediment to achieving linear speed-up in multiprocessors.

This model is inadequate for our purpose because it ignores the overhead of inter-processor synchronization and communication. Most schemes for considering communication overhead do so by separately maximizing parallelism and minimizing communication. We believe that these parameters should be combined into a single objective function. The next section shows how we extend this model to incorporate communication costs.

4. Modelling Communication Costs

Communication costs are represented by a communication matrix. $C[i,j]$ is the size of communication (in bytes, say) from task T_i to T_j. For simplicity, we assume that communication only occurs along precedence edges, though all precedence edges need not have an associated communication. The data along a communication edge is only available to the consumer after the producer has completed execution. We also define an inter-processor distance matrix; $D[k,l]$ gives the communication distance (number of hops) between processors k and l. This is a property of the multiprocessor rather than the tasks.

Communication overhead in a multiprocessor has two components:

1. *Processor component* - the duration for which a processor participates in its communication.
2. *Delay component* - the fraction of communication time during which the producer and consumer processors are free to execute other tasks.

Let $\pi(i)$ be the processor to which task T_i is assigned. The communication overhead for each non-local edge from T_i to T_j (i.e. $\pi(i) \neq \pi(j)$) is modeled as:

1. *Processor component* - add $\omega(C[i,j], D[\pi(i),\pi(j)])$ to the execution time of task T_i, and $\rho(C[i,j], D[\pi(i),\pi(j)])$ to the execution time of T_j.
2. *Delay component* - require that T_j not be able to start till $\delta(C[i,j], D[\pi(i),\pi(j)])$ time has elapsed after T_i completed execution.

ρ, ω and σ are simple functions for the costs of reading inputs, writing outputs and communication delay respectively.

They convert communication size to execution time units for the target multiprocessor. So far, we have used functions of the form $K_1 + K_2 \times C[i,j] \times D[\pi(i), \pi(j)]$, where K_1 and K_2 are constants.

We ignore the effect of communication demand on communication overhead in this model. This is valid when the demand is less than the available bandwidth. If contention for communication resources is to be considered, it can be approximated by using average overhead values.

Synchronization between tasks is modeled by a synchronization relation (boolean matrix) S. The pair $<i,j>$ is in S if task T_j must synchronize and wait for task T_i's completion. It would be safe to make S the same as the precedence relation $\rightarrow$, but would be inefficient because $\rightarrow$ is a partial order and contains transitive edges which lead to unnecessary synchronizations. The communication matrix does not entirely determine the synchronization relation, because some synchronizations are due to control dependencies. Besides, the communication matrix can also have transitive edges. So, for efficiency and generality, we represent synchronization by a separate relation.

Each pair $<i,j>$ in S adds to the execution times of tasks T_i and T_j due to *signal* and *wait* operations respectively. The execution cost used for a *wait* is actually the cost of a <u>successful</u> *wait*. Time spent spinning in a busy-wait loop is considered to be idle time and is not added to the task's execution time.

5. Real Multiprocessors

Multiprocessors are general-purpose, asynchronous, MIMD parallel machines. They can be classified as being "tightly coupled" or "loosely coupled". Tightly coupled multiprocessors (e.g. Sequent [19], Encore [8], Ultracomputer [10], Cm* [12]) communicate through a shared memory. Loosely coupled multiprocessors (e.g. the Cosmic Cube [18]) communicate by exchanging messages. Our model is designed to be tractable on this wide class of architectures and we discuss how some of these machines are modeled in our system.

Machines like the Sequent and Encore communicate through a single bus connected to a shared memory and individual processor caches. The communication overhead consists entirely of its processor component, since the processors are directly involved in accessing the shared memory. Also, the distance matrix is uniform, so that $D[k,l] = 1$ for all pairs of processors. Functions ρ and ω for the processor component represent the time taken to respectively read from or write to the shared memory. Both machines use write-through caches and invalidating snoopy caches.

Because they use invalidation, the value of ρ is the cost of a cache miss (i.e. a main memory access - on the order of 5-10 cycles). Because writes are buffered and a write-through cache is used, writes will cost one cycle when there is no contention. Thus, the value of ω depends primarily on bus and main memory traffic. Bus contention increases the cost to read shared memory because cache misses take longer to satisfy; it increases the cost to write shared memory, because delays may cause write stalls.

Synchronization costs differ on these machines because they use different hardware mechanisms for synchronization. The Sequent has 64 hardware "gates" that can be used to ensure mutual exclusion, making synchronization cheap. The Encore has a test-and-set instruction. The difficulty in accurately modeling such machines is that the cost of various operations (reading and writing shared data and synchronization) depends on the amount of contention for shared resources.

A single bus architecture is feasible for only a small number of processors. Interconnection networks are used to support more processors in shared-memory machines like the Ultracomputer. Communication and synchronization overhead is modeled in basically the same way as single bus architectures. There are two important differences: the time to access shared memory increases with the processor count (because of the interconnection network delay), and the communication costs are less affected by contention.

Another important class of machines are those using point-to-point communication. These include the Cosmic Cube, the Intel Advanced Scientific Processor and the NCube machine. All of these machines use a boolean N-cube interconnect, which defines the distance matrix. Since these machines use a "message passing" approach we can easily model their communication properties. Assuming that communication contention is negligible, the following table summarizes the properties of the Cosmic Cube and Intel cube. The processor component is for the initiating processor and is given as X + Y, where X is the start-up and Y is the cost per 100 bytes, both in milliseconds. The delay component is in milliseconds per hop for each 100 bytes. Packetization introduces a nonlinearity in communication costs, but we ignore this effect.

Machine	Processor Component	Delay Component
Cosmic Cube	1.5 + 0.4	0.4
Intel Cube	6.0 + 0.08	0.08

As we have indicated, the primary limitation of this model is its inability to deal with contention for communication or synchronization resources. As we measure more problems running on real machines, we believe that we can refine the model to realistically accommodate such issues.

Having discussed the target architectures, let's now examine the intermediate language used in our system.

6. IF1 Program Graphs

Our compilation system operates on a graphical representation of programs, namely IF1 [21]. IF1 is an intermediate form for applicative languages. It is strongly based on the features of single-assignment languages SISAL [15] and VAL [1].

An IF1 program is a hierarchy of acyclic dataflow graphs [7]; the nodes denote operations and the edges carry data. Nodes are either *simple* or *compound*. A simple node's outputs are direct functions of its inputs. IF1 has about 50 simple nodes, e.g. Plus, ArrayCatenate, FunctionCall. A compound node contains subgraphs and its outputs depend on the interaction between these subgraphs. The following table lists the five compound nodes available in IF1. These compound nodes obviate the need for labels, goto's and cycles in the program graph.

Compound Node	Subgraphs
Select	Selector, Alternatives
TagCase	Alternatives (for Union)
Forall	Generator, Body, Results
While, Until	Init, Test, Body, Returns

Nodes have numbered ports connected by edges. An edge contains the node and port numbers of its producer and consumer. It also contains an optional type number, which is used for strongly typed languages like SISAL. Literals are special edges used for constant values. A literal has no producer - its value is given by a string. All data is carried by edges. No variables or memory locations are used.

Basic types include boolean, character, integer, real and double. Arrays, streams, records and unions are used to construct more complex types. Arrays are dynamically extendible. Nodes and edges in IF1 can use pragmas to carry additional information. We use pragmas to store profile-based frequency counts, communication and computation costs, graph partitions and processor assignments.

This program graph representation is well suited for compile-time partitioning and scheduling. However, generation of sequential machine code is more complicated than from traditional, sequential intermediate languages. It is imperative to avoid unnecessary copying when an update-in-place is possible. This effectively coalesces data on input and output edges to be the same "variable". A few research projects are under way to address this problem. The SISAL [15] project includes code generation from IF1 for the VAX 780 and Cray-2 architectures. A project is under way at Stanford to translate SAL [6] graphs (similar to IF1) to U-code [20]. Our partitioner will benefit from all advances in this field, as sequential code generation and optimization techniques can be applied to intra-task computations.

7. Cost Assignment

The first step in compile-time partitioning and scheduling is to estimate computation and communication costs in the program. Communication costs are determined by examining the data type of an edge and assessing its size in an appropriate unit (e.g. bytes). Estimation of node execution times is more difficult and is undecidable in general. The unknown parameters are:

- The frequency distribution of subgraphs in a compound node (e.g. number of iterations for a While Body, probability distribution of Alternatives in a Select)
- Array size for nodes that operate on entire arrays.
- Recursion depth for recursive function calls.

Average node execution times are determined by using average values for these frequency parameters. These frequency values can be estimated using simple rules of thumb, can be provided by the programmer through pragmas, or can be derived from profile information. Our current implementation uses profile data.

Given these parameters, it is a straightforward task to compute the cost of a node from the cost of its components via a depth-first traversal of the program graph. The cost of a function call is determined by the cost assigned to the callee. The strongly connected components (SCC's) in the call graph reveal groups of mutually recursive functions. The recursion depth estimate is used to evaluate the costs of functions in the same SCC. The reduced inter-SCC graph is acyclic and is traversed in topological order so that the callee's costs are assigned before processing the caller.

8. Graph Expansion

Given execution time costs, the next step is to create a set of parallel tasks. This phase begins by considering the body of the "main program" function to be a single task and proceeds by recursively expanding the current tasks to reveal more parallelism. A task containing an entire acyclic dataflow graph can be replaced by a set of new tasks - one for each node in the graph. A task corresponding to a function call node can be replaced by tasks for nodes in the callee's function body, as in conventional procedure integration.

A Forall node is special because we know that all its iterations can be executed in parallel. Thus a task for a Forall node can be replaced by S+2 new tasks - a Scatter task, S sub-Forall tasks and a Gather task. The value of S is determined in part by F, the number of iterations in the original Forall. Assuming that all iterations take the same time, the smallest S that yields an optimal completion time on P processors is $\lceil F / \lceil F/P \rceil \rceil$. This makes S = P for large F.

A task for a non-Forall compound node is replaced by a task for each of its subgraphs. These subgraphs are totally ordered by control dependencies, according to the semantics of the compound node. This ordering avoids the possibility of wasted work through eager evaluation of (say) Alternative subgraphs in a Select node. Instead, the Alternative will only start after the Selector has been evaluated, at which time it is known which Alternative should be evaluated. It's possible to perform a Parafrase-style [13] dependency analysis on While expressions and try to convert them to Forall's. This would be a compatible pre-pass to our partitioning system. We have not pursued that approach because we assume that the programs were written with a view to parallelism, and leave it to the programmer to use Forall's where appropriate.

We'd like the final task system to:

- Contain sufficient parallelism for the given number of processors,
- Not have an impractically large number of tasks (e.g. one task per instruction is too many!).

Both objectives can be conveniently quantified using costs. The task system will have sufficient parallelism if no task is a *bottleneck*. Task T_i is a bottleneck when all tasks that can be executed in parallel with it together contain insufficient work to keep P-1 processors busy during T_i's execution, i.e.

$$\Sigma_{T_j \text{ parallel to } T_i} \text{cost}(T_j) < (P-1) \times \text{cost}(T_i)$$

Only bottleneck nodes are considered for further expansion.

The problem of determining parallel tasks is equivalent to finding the transitive closure of the graph's adjacency matrix. Transitive closure algorithms have a worst-case execution time between $O(N^{2.5})$ and $O(N^3)$, making them impractical for large programs [5]. We use a divide-and-conquer approach on the hierarchical structure of IF1 program graphs to compute the path relation more efficiently. It is only necessary to use the $O(N^3)$ algorithm on dataflow graphs at each level. Their path relations are then efficiently combined in a depth-first traversal of the entire hierarchy. This corresponds to the notion of path-preserving homomorphic graph structures [17], and makes it practical to determine the path relation for a large program graph.

To enforce a reasonable limit on the number of tasks, we employ a Granularity Threshold Factor, ε. Any computation with execution time less than $\varepsilon \times$ (Total Program Cost) / P is considered not worthwhile for further expansion. This threshold value controls task granularity - 0.001 is a typical value for ε. A smaller value of ε usually increases the number of tasks and hence the execution time for compile-time partitioning. Programs with sufficient coarse-grain parallelism are unaffected by ε; a few expansions remove all bottleneck nodes causing the expansion process to terminate before tasks reach the granularity threshold size.

After task expansion, there is scope for further economy on the number of tasks by merging small tasks when their total cost is less than the threshold value. These small tasks are usually simple nodes (e.g. Plus, ArrayBuild) that were exposed along with larger computations during task expansion. By merging tasks, we map a set of IF1 nodes to a single task. This set must:

- Have a total execution time that's smaller than the threshold value.
- Form a convex subgraph of the original precedence graph so that the reduced precedence graph with the single merged task will still be acyclic. A simple way to form convex subgraphs is by picking intervals on any linear completion of the precedence graph.
- Form a connected subgraph so that it does not destroy any parallelism outside the merged task.

Task expansion and task merging partition the program graph nodes into tasks. Each task should either be a non-bottleneck or have a smaller execution time than the threshold value. A task that satisfies neither property is expanded, if possible. Tasks are merged if their total cost is still less than the threshold value. Both expansion and merging can be incorporated in a single depth-first traversal of the program graph. At each level, all subcomputations are first recursively processed, which determines the expanded nodes. A second pass at the same level performs the merging, and then returns to the parent level.

9. Internalization Pre-pass

Once the task boundaries have been established, the problem is represented in terms of our model for multiprocessor scheduling with communication. We have tasks with execution times and communication edges. A single pass scheduling algorithm is unsuitable for handling communication costs. For example, in Figure 9-1, if tasks A and B are assigned to different processors, a single pass algorithm is later on forced to make one of C_1 or C_2 non-local, and incur its overhead. This is inevitable no matter how large C_1 or C_2 may be. It could be avoided by backtracking on previous assignments, but that would be too inefficient. Instead, we first perform an Internalization pass that partitions tasks into blocks, so that all tasks in the same block must be assigned to the same processor. After Internalization, a single pass Processor Assignment algorithm can be used to assign internalized task blocks to processors.

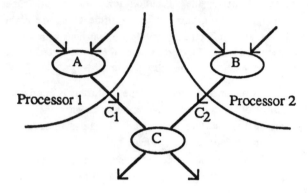

Figure 9-1: Counter-example for one-pass scheduling

The Internalization problem is to find a partition that minimizes the critical path length of the task system, i.e. minimizes the completion time of the task system on an unbounded number of processors. If we ignore communication overhead, this optimal completion time can be simply achieved by assigning each task to a different processor. This is not so with communication costs, since the optimal critical path may only occur when some parallel tasks are assigned to the same processor. It is a harder problem and is in fact NP-complete.

So, we designed a greedy approximation algorithm to solve this problem. It begins with the trivial partition that places each task in a separate block. It also maintains a table DeltaCPL[i,j], which represents the decrease in the critical path length obtained by merging blocks i and j. The algorithm then iteratively merges the best pair of blocks - the pair that yields the largest decrease in the critical path length - and terminates when no remaining merger could possibly reduce the critical path length (i.e. all entries in DeltaCPL are negative).

In computing the critical path length, we force all tasks in the same block to execute sequentially since they will be assigned to the same processor. There could be several possible task sequences consistent with the precedence constraints, and it's for that very reason that the problem is NP-complete. An algorithm that tries all possible sequences will have a worst-case exponential time. Instead we just use an arbitrary topological order (priority list) to provide a sequence for tasks in the same block. Figure 9-2 outlines the body of procedure DetermineCompletionTime, used to compute the completion time for a given partition. Because

of step 3, it has an $O(N+E)$ worst-case execution time, for N tasks and E synchronization and communication edges.

<u>Inputs:</u> Tasks, costs, partition, priority list.

<u>Output:</u> Completion time.

<u>Algorithm:</u>

1. **for each task T_i do**
   Add non-local synchronization and communication costs to T_i's execution time. (Use processor component for communication)
   end for

2. **for each block B do**
   BlockTime[B] $\leftarrow$ 0
   end for

3. **for each task T_j in priority list order do**
   StartTime $\leftarrow$
   max(BlockTime[Block(T_j)],
        CompletionTime[i] $\forall$ <i,j> $\in$ S,
        CompletionTime[i] + delay component of C[i,j]
        $\forall$ non-local input communication C[i,j])
   CompletionTime[j] $\leftarrow$ StartTime + ExecutionTime[j]
   BlockTime[Block(T_j)] $\leftarrow$ CompletionTime[j]
   end for

4. **return** max(CompletionTime[j] $\forall$ tasks T_j)

Figure 9-2: Procedure DetermineCompletionTime

The internalization algorithm has an $O(N^2 \times (N+E))$ execution time because there are $O(N^2)$ entries in DeltaCPL. In the worst case, $E = O(N^2)$, making this an $O(N^4)$ algorithm. Just like the path relation in the previous section, the critical path can be obtained by combining critical path values of subgraphs. The algorithm incurs an $O(N^4)$ worst-case execution time at each level, but is practical for large programs. Most programs have a small number (< 100) of tasks at each level. We have seen programs with over 5000 nodes containing fewer than 20 tasks per level. This is because there's not much computation that can be expressed without using compound nodes. Even if there are several simple nodes at the same level, they often get merged into a small number of tasks, due to the granularity threshold value.

Though this is an approximation algorithm, we have shown that it finds the optimal partition for a restricted class of communication graphs, namely series-parallel graphs. Further, we have shown that this algorithm has a worst-case performance bound of 2, relative to the optimal critical path. The proofs of these results are beyond the scope of this paper.

10. Processor Assignment

With the internalization pre-pass completed, the ground is finally set for the actual assignment of tasks to processors. Tasks in the same internalized block must be assigned to the

66

same processor. We use a modified Priority List scheduling algorithm [11] to perform the processor assignment. An outline of this algorithm is given in Figure 10-1.

Inputs: Tasks, costs, internalized partition, priority list.

Output: Processor assignment for each task.

Algorithm:

1. **for each** task T_i **do**
   Processor[i] $\leftarrow$ 0
   end for

2. **for** proc $\leftarrow$ 1 to P **do**
   ProcessorBlock[proc] $\leftarrow$ 0
   end for

3. **for each** task T_j in priority list order **do**
   if Processor[j] = 0 **then**

   a. **for** proc $\leftarrow$ 1 to P **do**
      Call procedure DetermineCompletionTime for partition that merges blocks Block(T_j) and ProcessorBlock[proc].
      Set BestProc to the value of proc with the smallest completion time.
      end for

   b. Merge blocks Block(T_j) and ProcessorBlock[BestProc].

   c. ProcessorBlock[BestProc] $\leftarrow$ Block(T_j)

   d. **for each** task T_i with Block(T_i) = Block(T_j) **do**
      Processor[i] $\leftarrow$ BestProc
      end for

   end if
   end for

4. **return** Processor

Figure 10-1: Procedure Schedule

The algorithm visits tasks in priority list order, so that a task is only scheduled after all its predecessors have been scheduled. Processor[i] stores the processor number for task T_i. It is initialized to zero and is set when visiting the first task in T_i's block. Like the Internalization algorithm, Processor Assignment proceeds by merging blocks in the partition. It terminates when there are at most as many blocks as processors. At that time, all tasks T_i in ProcessorBlock[*proc*] will have Processor[i] set to *proc*. Once again, we use Procedure DetermineCompletionTime to compute the completion time for a given partition.

This algorithm has a worst-case $O(B \times (N+E))$ execution time, where B is the number of internalized blocks. The scheduling problem does not lend itself to an efficient divide-and-conquer algorithm, as the path relation and critical path problems, because all sub-computations share the same set of processors. Instead, its efficiency lies in being able to assign an entire block of tasks to a processor at a time.

11. Code Generation Issues

The output of the processor assignment phase consists of P task sequences for P processors. Each task's computation is translated to sequential code, as in uniprocessor compilation. However, synchronization primitives and communication code for any non-local synchronizations and communications must be appropriately placed in a prologue and epilogue for each task. These non-local synchronizations and communications are barriers that must not be crossed when optimizing and reordering instructions. Their rearrangement could form a cycle in inter-processor synchronization and lead to deadlock during execution. Even if it avoided deadlock, the schedule would be different from the one chosen by our algorithm, and could have a larger parallel execution time. However, the code generator is free to reorder and optimize instructions that do not cross an external synchronization or communication. There should be a large scope for such conventional code optimizations, since we exploit outer-level parallelism and each task can have a lot of computation buried inside it.

12. Preliminary Results

As mentioned earlier, a partitioner-cum-scheduler based on these techniques has been implemented to process IF1 program graphs. We have instrumented the Livermore IF1 interpreter to provide statistics for a multiprocessor simulation. The simulation uses processor assignments generated by the partitioner. Execution time values are based on actual run-time frequencies and data sizes.

Figure 12-1 shows the speed-up obtained for the following SISAL programs:

1. Towers of Hanoi. A program to solve the puzzle for a tower of height 10. Graph expansion unwound the recursive function calls to get a binary tree with $\lceil \lg P \rceil$ levels. Hence the non-linearity when the number of processors is a power of 2.

2. Batcher's iterative merge-exchange sorting algorithm [4] on 100 integers. This is an excellent algorithm for parallel sorting. It consists of two nested While loops, each with log N iterations, and an inner Forall with N iterations. Graph expansion successively expanded the While bodies and finally the Forall, which contains the parallelism.

3. Eight Queens - a recursive program to generate all solutions to the 8 queens problem. A recursion depth value of 8 directed the graph expansion algorithm to expand the recursive call to 8 levels. The Forall at each level was then expanded.

4. Multi-precision multiplication. A divide-and-conquer solution to the problem of multiplying two N-bit numbers [2]. The algorithm breaks each number into halves, recursively finds 3 sub-products and combines them to get the full product. Using 3 (instead of 4)

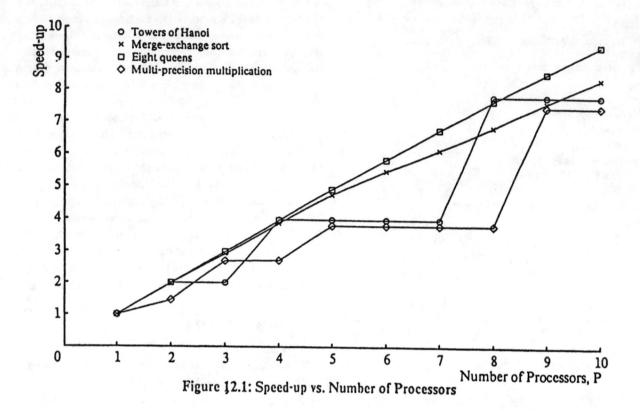

Figure 12.1: Speed-up vs. Number of Processors

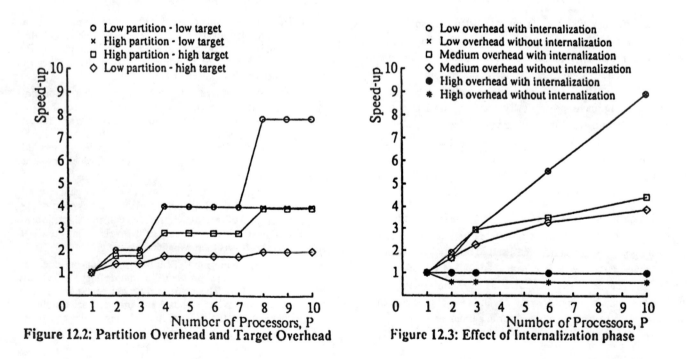

Figure 12.2: Partition Overhead and Target Overhead

Figure 12.3: Effect of Internalization phase

recursive multiplications makes this an $O(N^{lg\ 3}) = O(N^{1.59})$ algorithm (instead of N^2).

These speed-up curves show that compile-time processor assignment can be successfully used to exploit parallelism. We'd like to make similar speed-up measurements on real machines, e.g. Sequent, Encore, iPSC. That will be possible when the translator from IF1 to U-code is ready. Another approach is to translate IF1 to C. We have already hand-coded the partitioned merge-exchange sort program in C and observed linear speed-up on the Sequent (12 processors) and Encore (20 processors).

Figure 12-2 illustrates the match between a partition and its target multiprocessor parameters. These measurements were taken for the Towers of Hanoi program, using two sets of target parameters that represent low and high communication overhead. The four curves show all four combinations of the two partitions with the two targets. Naturally, the low overhead target curves show a better speed-up than the high overhead target. But, for a given target, the partition that was generated for it performed better than the other partition.

Figure 12-3 shows the effect of the Internalization phase on partitioning. The SISAL program used was a simple matrix multiplication of two 20×20 integer matrices. The program was partitioned and simulated for three sets of target parameters representing low, medium and high communication overhead. Two partitions were generated in each case - one with and one without using the Internalization phase. As seen in the figure, the partition with Internalization performed better, especially for high communication overhead.

13. Related Work

As mentioned in the introduction, a compiler system for parallel machines must deal with the problems of extracting parallelism, partitioning the program into tasks and scheduling tasks. The major effort so far has been in solving the first problem. Kuck's Parafrase [13], [16] and the Rice vectorizer [3] have been successful in extracting parallelism from Fortran programs. They have been used for vector machines, where partitioning and scheduling is not an issue. This parallelism is typically local, since global parallelism (say between subroutines) is difficult to automatically extract from a sequential language. Both these systems could be used to produce an IF1-like graph representation that serves as input to our partitioner. Whether such an approach would be effective depends on the ability of these systems to recognize larger-grain parallelism.

The Bulldog compiler [9] extracts local parallelism and schedules operations for VLIW (Very Long Instruction Word)

architectures. Loop unrolling and trace scheduling are among the techniques used to get more parallelism than that available within basic blocks. This is similar in spirit to our task expansion, except that we start at the outermost level and move inwards looking for parallelism at the macro level. The Bulldog approach attempts to generate a set of synchronous, fine-grained parallel operations that can be "packed" into a single wide instruction word. The primary technique used to find parallelism is local expansion of basic blocks. Our partitioner is targeted to asynchronous multiprocessors, which perform most efficiently with coarse-grain parallelism.

In the Hughes Data Flow Machine compiler [5], dataflow nodes (actors) are statically allocated to processing elements. The allocation is based on heuristics to minimize communication and maximize parallelism. The heuristic functions use inter-processor distances and a count of parallel actors; they do not consider the frequency count of individual actors or the communication size of data. Static allocation of an actor causes all its invocations to be sequential, since they are executed on the same processing element. This can reduce parallelism for an actor in the body of a Forall or in a function called more than once in parallel. We address the problem by task expansion, so that different sub-Forall's or different calls to the same function can be executed on different processors. It is necessary to do a transitive closure of the dataflow graph to determine parallel actors. Their "local allocator" uses an $O(N^3)$ transitive closure algorithm and took 3 VAX CPU hours to schedule 415 actors. Because of this high cost, they use a "global allocator" to approximate the heuristics by partitioning the graph and set of processing elements into separate pieces that can be individually handled by the local allocator. Transitive closure is done more efficiently in our partitioner, because we exploit the program graph hierarchy to determine the path relation, e.g. it took only 10 VAX CPU seconds for a program graph with over 1500 nodes.

14. Conclusions

We have demonstrated that the problem of partitioning and scheduling parallel programs can be solved at compile-time. Our techniques are practical and have been implemented to process IF1 program graphs. They rely on estimates of frequency parameters, which we obtain from execution profile data.

These techniques do not assume any particular multiprocessor architecture. Instead, they are driven by a table of parameters that describe the target multiprocessor.

The central issue in partitioning and scheduling is the trade-off between parallelism and the overhead of synchronization and communication. We use costs to incorporate these overheads in our model for multiprocessor scheduling.

The implementation has already been used to partition many benchmark programs, and the simulation results are very encouraging. As more multiprocessors become available, we will use this implementation as a basis to compare alternative architectures and their interaction with different application programs.

References

1. Ackerman, W. B. & Dennis, J. B. VAL -- a value-oriented algorithmic language. Preliminary reference manual. MIT/LCS/TR-218, Laboratory for Computer Science, MIT, June, 1979.

2. Aho, A. V., Hopcroft, J. E., Ullman, J. D.. *The Design and Analysis of Computer Algorithms.* Addison-Wesley, 1974.

3. Allen, J. R. & Kennedy, K. PFC: A Program to Convert Fortran to Parallel Form. The Proceedings of the IBM Conference on Parallel Computers and Scientific Computations, March, 1982.

4. Batcher, K. E. "Sorting networks and their applications". *1968 Spring Joint Computer Conf., AFIPS Proc. 32* (1968), 307-314.

5. Campbell, M. L. Static Allocation for a Dataflow Multiprocessor. Proc. 1985 Int. Conf. Parallel Processing, 1985, pp. 511-517.

6. Celoni, J. R. & Hennessy, J. L. SAL: A Single-Assignment Language for Parallel Algorithms. ClaSSiC-83-01, Center for Large Scale Scientific Computation, Stanford University, Sept., 1983.

7. Davis, A. L. & Keller, R. M. "Data Flow Program Graphs". *IEEE Computer 15*, 2 (Feb. 1982).

8. *Using the Encore Multimax.* Argonne National Laboratory, Mathematics and Computer Science Division, ANL/MCS-TM-65, 1986.

9. Fisher, J. A. *et al.* "Parallel Processing: A Smart Compiler and a Dumb Machine". *SIGPLAN Notices 19*, 6 (June 1984).

10. Gottlieb, A. *et al.* "The NYU Ultracomputer - Designing an MIMD Shared Memory Parallel Computer". *IEEE Trans. Computers C-32*, 2 (Feb. 1983).

11. Graham, R. L. "Bounds on Multiprocessing Timing Anomalies". *SIAM J. Appl. Math. 17*, 2 (March 1969).

12. Jones, A. K., Gehringer, E. F. The Cm* Multiprocessor Project: A Research Review. CMU-CS-80-131, Computer Science Department, Carnegie-Mellon University, 1980.

13. Kuck, D. J. *et al.* Dependence Graphs and Compiler Optimizations. Proc. 8th ACM Symp Principles Programming Languages, Jan., 1981, pp. 207-218.

14. Lenstra, J. K. & Rinnooy Kan, A. H. G. "Complexity of Scheduling under Precedence Constraints". *Operations Research 26*, 1 (Jan-Feb 1978).

15. McGraw, J. *et al.* SISAL: Streams and Iteration in a Single Assignment Language, Language Reference Manual, Version 1.2. M-146, LLNL, March, 1985.

16. Padua, D. A., Kuck, D. J. & Lawrie, D. H. "High-Speed Multiprocessors and Compilation Techniques". *IEEE Trans. Computers C-29*, 9 (1980).

17. Pfaltz, J. L.. *Computer Data Structures.* McGraw-Hill, Inc., 1977.

18. Seitz, C. L. "The Cosmic Cube". *CACM 28*, 1 (Jan. 1985).

19. *Using the Sequent Balance 8000.* Argonne National Laboratory, Mathematics and Computer Science Division, ANL/MCS-TM-66, 1986.

20. Sites, R. *et al.* Machine-independent Pascal Optimizer Project: Final Report. UCSD/CS-79/038, University of California at San Diego, Nov., 1979.

21. Skedzielewski, S. & Glauert, J. IF1 -- An Intermediate Form for Applicative Languages, Version 1.0. M-170, LLNL, July, 1985.

Guided Self-Scheduling: A Practical Scheduling Scheme for Parallel Supercomputers

CONSTANTINE D. POLYCHRONOPOULOS, MEMBER, IEEE, AND DAVID J. KUCK, FELLOW, IEEE

Abstract—This paper proposes *guided self-scheduling*, a new approach for scheduling arbitrarily nested parallel program loops on shared memory multiprocessor systems. Utilizing loop parallelism is clearly most crucial in achieving high system and program performance. Because of its simplicity, guided self-scheduling is particularly suited for implementation on real parallel machines. This method achieves simultaneously the two most important objectives: load balancing and very low synchronization overhead. For certain types of loops we show analytically that guided self-scheduling uses minimal overhead and achieves optimal schedules. Two other interesting properties of this method are its insensitivity to the initial processor configuration (in time) and its parameterized nature which allows us to tune it for different systems. Finally we discuss experimental results that clearly show the advantage of guided self-scheduling over the most widely known dynamic methods.

Index Terms—Parallel Fortran programs, parallel loops, parallel supercomputers, run-time overhead, self-scheduling, synchronization.

I. INTRODUCTION

AS technology approaches physical limitations, parallel processor systems offer a promising and powerful alternative for high performance computing. In principle, parallelism offers performance that can increase without bounds and depends only on the application at hand. In reality, however, parallelism does have its limitations [6], [19], [27]. Technology is still unable to support the realization of parallel machines with large numbers of general purpose processors. An even greater obstacle is our inability to efficiently utilize such massively parallel systems. Problems such as specifying parallelism, mapping or scheduling parallel programs on a given architecture, synchronizing the execution of a parallel program, memory management in parallel processing environments, and compiling for parallel machines remain areas for much future work.

In this paper we propose a practical method that can be used to obtain very efficient schedules of parallel loops on shared memory parallel machines. The problem of mapping or assigning different tasks of the same program to different processors (otherwise known as "scheduling") has only recently attracted considerable attention with the introduction

of many parallel machines in the market. Although scheduling is an old, notorious problem with numerous versions and has attracted the attention of many researchers in the past [4], [5], [9], [12], [24], the results known to date offer little help when dealing with real parallel machines.

Existing methods are not adequate because they consider an idealized form of the problem where task execution times are fixed and known in advance, and they ignore "side-effects" (interprocessor communication and synchronization) [21], [23]. In reality, however, branching statements in programs, memory access interference, random processor latencies, and other "random events" make task execution times impossible to predict accurately in general. Furthermore, side-effects have a very important impact on scheduling.

The complexity of the scheduling problem has led the computing community to adopt heuristic approaches for each new machine. In many cases [6] the problem is entirely left to the user, and it is well known that hand-coding and manually inserting system calls in a program are necessary to achieve maximum performance. Worse yet this manual approach is different from machine to machine and is highly empirical. One could say that programming parallel machines is anything but "user friendly." Unless a systematic solution to the problem is found, only experts will be able to code for the parallel machines of the future, or these machines will be confined to a few processors and simple architectures.

On the other hand, it is difficult or impossible to find a universal solution for problems such as scheduling, minimization of interprocessor communication, and synchronization. This is so because these problems are often architecture dependent. Thus, a solution which is efficient for one machine organization may be inefficient for another. We believe, however, that more general solutions can be found for large classes of machine architectures. It is also clear that such problems must be solved automatically by the compiler, the operating system, or by the hardware.

This paper proposes guided self-scheduling (GSS), a new method for executing parallel loops on parallel processor systems. Even though we use Fortran loops in this presentation, the concepts and the proposed method are valid for parallel loops coded in any other language. The GSS method not only generates efficient (load balanced) schedules, but it also reduces substantially (and often minimizes) the number of synchronized accesses to loop indexes, an expensive operation on many shared memory parallel machines [30]. As shown later, GSS can be easily automated and should be efficient for most shared memory parallel processor systems.

The rest of the paper is organized as follows. Section II

Manuscript received January 30, 1987; revised May 29, 1987. This work was supported in part by the National Science Foundation under Grants NSF DCR84-10110 and NSF DCR84-06916, the U.S. Department of Energy under Grant DOE DE-FG02-85ER25001, and the IBM Donation.

The authors are with the Center for Supercomputing Research and Development, University of Illinois at Urbana-Champaign, Urbana, IL 61801.

IEEE Log Number 8717030.

Reprinted from *IEEE Trans. on Computers*, vol. C-36, no. 12, Dec. 1987, pp. 1425–1439.

gives some background information and the necessary definitions. Section III discusses alternatives for the parallel execution of programs and identifies the main advantages and disadvantages of each scheme. Section IV presents the guided self-scheduling method in detail and its application to a simple parallel loop. Different versions of GSS are discussed in Section IV-B. The results of experimental work that was performed with GSS are presented in Section V. Finally, the conclusion is given in Section VI.

II. BACKGROUND

The machine model used for this paper is a *shared memory parallel processor* system. It consists of p homogeneous and autonomous processors connected through an interconnection network to a set of memory modules, such that each memory module is accessible by all p processors. Commercial systems such as the Cray X-MP, Alliant FX/8, IBM 3090, and experimental machines such as the Cedar and the RP3 fit this model. High performance on shared memory parallel processor machines is achieved by executing a single program on more than one processor concurrently. During parallel execution, the data dependences must be observed in order for the semantics of the program to be preserved.

Data dependences [3], [13], [16], define a partial order·or precedence relation on the statements of a program. There are three major types of data dependences, flow, anti, and output dependences. A *flow* dependence is defined between two (not necessarily different) program statements s_1 and s_2 (denoted $s_1 \delta s_2$), if a scalar or array variable assigned by s_1 is used in s_2. An *antidependence* $s_1 \bar{\delta} s_2$ between the two statements occurs if a variable used in s_1 is assigned by s_2, and s_1 lexically precedes s_2. If s_1 and s_2 assign values to the same variable, an *output* dependence $s_1 \delta^0 s_2$ is defined between the two statements. Dependences are also represented by arcs between nodes that represent statements. In the above definitions, arcs originating from s_1 and pointing to s_2 can be used to mark the corresponding dependences. A *forward* dependence is one whose arc points lexically forward. Similarly we define *backward* dependences.

The definition of dependences in Fortran loops is similar and requires the use of statement *instances*. A statement s_l that belongs to a loop of the form DO $I = 1, N$, has N different instances, one for each iteration of the loop. Statement instances are denoted by $s_i(I)$, $(1 \leq I \leq N)$. For two statements s_l and s_j that belong to a DO loop, a dependence $s_i \delta^* s_j$ is defined if and only if there are instances $s_i(I_1)$ and $s_j(I_2)$, such that $1 \leq I_1 \leq I_2 \leq N$ and $s_i(I_1)\delta^* s_j(I_2)$, where δ^* denotes any of the three types of data dependencies defined earlier. Such a dependence is called a *cross-iteration* dependence if the two statement instances involved in the dependence correspond to two different values of the loop index, i.e., $I_1 \neq I_2$. The difference $I_1 - I_2$ is called the *dependence distance*. The statement $s_i(I_1)$ is called the *dependence source* and the statement $s_j(I_2)$ the *dependence sink*.

A Fortran DO loop is of the form

DO $I = M, N, d$
    $\{B\}$
ENDO

where M and N are the lower and upper index bounds, d is the loop stride, and B is the loop body which can be straightline code or a loop itself. A DO loop can always be *normalized* to have $M = 1$ and $d = 1$ [29]. A DOALL loop is a DO loop without cross-iteration dependences. Obviously the iterations of DOALL loops are data independent. Thus, each iteration of a DOALL can be executed independently of the others. DO loops with cross-iteration dependences that are forward are called FORALL. FORALL loops can also be executed as DOALL's if synchronization is used to assure the correct order of execution of statements involved in a dependence. Index alignment can be used to convert some FORALL loops to DOALL's. Finally, we may have DO loops that also contain cross-iteration backward dependences. Such loops are called DOACR and they constitute the most complex case of parallel loops [7]. The DOACR loop covers the entire spectrum by determining the maximum amount of overlap between successive iterations. If total overlap is possible, then we have the DOALL case; in the zero overlap case, the DOACR loop is a serial or DOSERIAL loop.

Another type of parallelism arises from the concurrent execution of lexically disjoint program fragments (e.g., the parallel execution of two different subroutine calls). The act of allocating different program fragments to different processors is called *spreading*. Spreading can be done at the operation or statement level and is called *low-level spreading* (fine granularity), or it can be done at the loop and subroutine level and is called *high-level spreading* (coarse granularity).

In this paper we are primarily concerned with DOALL and FORALL loops. Since synchronization makes FORALL's appear as DOALL's we consider both types of loops to be DOALL's. A *one-way* nested loop with nest depth k, denoted by $L = (N_1, \cdots, N_k)$, has exactly one loop at each nest level, where N_i, $(i = 1, \cdots, k)$ is the number of iterations of the loop at the ith level. A *multiway* nested loop has at least two loops at some nest level. Nested loops that contain combinations of DOALL, DOACR, and DOSERIAL loops are called *hybrid*.

A compiler transformation called *loop coalescing* can be used to transform multiple one-way nested loops into singly nested loops. This transformation is useful for self-scheduling of parallel loops. The overhead associated with the access of loop indexes is reduced sharply in many cases when loop coalescing is applied. Coalescing transforms a multidimensional space into a linear space. All array indexes inside the loop code can now be expressed in terms of a single index. Another transformation that can be useful in our case is *loop distribution* [13], [18]. Loop distribution distributes a loop around each statement in its body, or around code modules inside the loop that form strongly connected components of the data dependence graph [18]. It is useful for transforming multiway nested loops to one-way nested. Thus, when coalescing is applied in conjunction with loop distribution, multiway nested loops can also be transformed into single loops. Another source transformation used in this paper is *loop interchange* [29]. Loop interchange permutes a pair of nested loops so that the outer becomes innerloop and vice versa. This transformation can be applied to improve in many aspects the parallel execution of Fortran loops on a particular machine. A detailed description of loop coalescing, loop distribution, and loop interchange can be found in the sources referenced above.

A program can be *partitioned* into a number of data dependent or independent tasks. A *task* is defined to be a program module that executes on one or more processors. Tasks can be *serial* or *parallel* depending on whether they can execute on one or more processors. A parallel task consists of a set of *processes* that can be defined by the compiler before execution, or dynamically during program execution. For example, a DOALL loop with N iterations is a task that can spawn up to N processes. Processes are serial and their execution is *nonpreemptive*. A *program task graph* is a directed graph whose nodes are tasks and arcs represent dependences between tasks. The program task graph can be constructed by the compiler.

The schemes used to schedule the tasks of a program on a parallel system can be broadly distinguished into two classes: *static* and *dynamic*. (In this paper the terms *scheduling*, *processor allocation*, and *processor assignment* are used interchangeably.) In static scheduling, processors are assigned tasks before execution starts. When program execution starts, each processor knows exactly which tasks to execute. A scheduling scheme is called *dynamic* when the actual processor allocation is performed by hardware or software mechanisms during program execution. Therefore, during dynamic scheduling, decisions for allocating processors are taken on-the-fly for different parts of the program, as the program executes. Dynamic scheduling can be performed through a *central* control unit or it can be *distributed*. A special case of scheduling through distributed control units is *self-scheduling* (SS) [26]. As implied by the term, there is no single control unit that makes global decisions for allocating processors, but rather the processors themselves are responsible for determining what task to execute next.

There are several factors (such as communication time and task granularity) that must be taken into account during scheduling. Implementations of pure versions of dynamic or self-scheduling that look at the instruction level for parallelism could be very inefficient and involve enormous overhead. There is no method that allows us to have some knowledge about the topology of the program at run time unless compiler support of some form is provided. Hybrid forms of dynamic or self-scheduling are possible by having the compiler help the control unit or the processors in making a scheduling decision. Guided self-scheduling is such a hybrid scheme that we discuss in this paper.

III. Design Rules for Run-Time Scheduling Schemes

When static scheduling is used, the run-time overhead is minimal. With dynamic scheduling, however, the run-time overhead becomes a critical factor and may account for a significant portion of the total execution time of a program. This is a logical consequence of dynamic scheduling. While at compile time the compiler or an intelligent preprocessor is responsible for making the scheduling decisions, at run time this decision must be made in a case-by-case fashion, and the time spent for this decision-making process is reflected in the program's execution time.

One way to alleviate this problem is to have the scheduler make scheduling decisions for a chunk of the program while other parts of the program are already executing on the processors. This, however, implies advance knowledge about the structure of the program which cannot be available at run time. For example, we must know how to partition the program into a series of task sets so that during execution of a task set, decisions for the scheduling of the next task set can be overlapped. The execution time of the tasks in each task set should thus be long enough to allow the scheduler the necessary time to make the next decision. Moreover, if the scheduler is the operating system, the above overlapped scheduling is impossible since one or more processors must be "wasted" to execute the operating system itself. If a global control unit (GCU) is used and if the compiler is used to generate a substantial amount of scheduling information, we can decide on the number of processors for each specific task at run time. This can be done in many cases without additional overhead assuming the GCU can make decisions about a subset of tasks while the computational processors are working on another subset. In this case overlapped scheduling implies that the GCU is a stand-alone unit (a superprocessor) and, therefore, more costly than a traditional control unit which is essentially a sequencer. With parallel loops the problem is less complex since the structure of the loop is known as described later.

A. Complete Program Graphs

It has been shown [4] that, in certain cases of random task graphs, optimal schedules can be achieved by deliberately keeping one or more processors idle in order to better utilize them at a later point. This and other scheduling "anomalies" are reported in [12]. Detecting such anomalies, however, requires processing of the entire task graph in advance. Since this is not possible at run time, the luxury of deliberately keeping processors idle (with the *hope* that we may better utilize them later) should not be permitted. Even if we had a way of processing the task graph in its entirety at run time, the scheduling overhead of an intelligent heuristic could be enormous in many cases.

We believe that the following guideline for any run-time scheduling scheme should always be applied: make simple and fast scheduling decisions at run time. This principle implicitly forbids asking (and answering) questions of the form: "How many processors should we allocate to this task?" Answering such a question means, in general, that we are willing to hold up idle processors until they become as many as the number of processors requested by that task. This is true assuming that a task cannot start execution unless all processors allocated to it are available (and thus they all start executing that task at the same time). As explained later, the concept of processor allocation is very useful when it is used in a different context.

Since we want to avoid deliberate idling of processors as much as possible, any run-time scheduling scheme should rather be designed to ask (and answer) questions of the following type: "How much work should we give to this processor?" In other words, when a processor becomes idle, try to assign to it a new task as soon as possible making the best possible selection. As shown in [4] and [21], this policy is guaranteed to generate a schedule length (i.e., an execution time) which is at most twice as long as the optimal. Therefore, in our case, the entity of importance is the individual processor rather than the individual task.

More precisely, our approach to the scheduling problem can be outlined as follows. The program task graph (as defined in Section II) is constructed at compile time and contains two kinds of tasks (nodes): serial and parallel. (During execution, parallel tasks may be executed by more than one physical processor, while serial tasks are always executed by a single processor.) Parallel tasks are always composed of parallel loops. Note that very low granularity parallelism inside a serial task can be exploited by the different functional units of a single processor (if applicable). The next activity that occurs at compile time is the evaluation of the optimal number of *virtual* processors for each task. (Virtual processors are the processors *requested* by (but not necessarily granted to) each task.) This activity involves compile-time analysis of the anticipated run-time overhead incurred by the parallel execution of tasks. Therefore, only parallel tasks are considered during this phase. The optimal number of virtual processors gives an upper bound on the number of physical processors assigned to that task during execution. Methods for computing the optimal number of virtual processors and for performing compile-time overhead analysis are out of the scope of this paper [7], [20], [21]. During program execution, the request by a given task for the optimal number of processors may or may not be honored. In any case the number of physical processors used to concurrently execute a specific task is restricted to be less than or equal to the virtual processors attributed to that task at compile time.

Let us consider what happens during execution where the program is represented by the program task graph (with each node pointing to the appropriate fragment of code). Each node has as an attribute the number of virtual processors allocated to it. We assume that there is some kind of mechanism (e.g., in the operating system) that performs the bookkeeping, that is, determines which tasks have completed and which are ready to execute (based on the data dependence or precedence relations). Tasks ready to execute are queued in a shared pool of ready-to-execute tasks. When execution starts, individual processors (rather than tasks) become the central entity. During the execution phase, our approach is to consider each processor as it becomes idle, and decide the amount of work to be given to that processor. When an idle processor checks the first available task in the shared pool, it dispatches the entire task (if it is serial) or part of it (if it is parallel). The rest of this paper presents practical schemes for solving the scheduling problem for a very important class of parallel tasks, namely, arbitrarily nested parallel loops. Note that high-level spreading can be performed by organizing the queue of ready tasks appropriately, but again this is out of the scope of this work.

B. Parallel Loops

Because of the well-defined structure of loop tasks, scheduling of such constructs is less complicated. Furthermore, it has been shown that parallel loops account for the greatest percentage of program parallelism [17]. Therefore, designing low-overhead methods for the efficient allocation of parallel loops is crucial to machine performance.

Very little work has been done on this topic so far. This is partly due to the fact that one level (single loop) parallelism is enough to fully utilize the processors of most of the existing parallel machines. Also due to high run-time overhead, the first parallel processor machines (e.g., Cray X-MP with multitasking) looked for parallelism at the subroutine level; parallelism at the loop level was too expensive to exploit. Soon thereafter Cray systems employed microtasking [23] that now can be used to utilize parallelism at the loop level. The microtasking library is a tool supplied to the user, but how to use it effectively is again the user's responsibility. One of the few commercial systems that can schedule parallel loops automatically is the Alliant FX/8 multiprocessor. The machine consists of a set of computational processors each with pipelined arithmetic units. Thus, parallel loops with vector statements can fully utilize the concurrency features of this system. Different iterations of parallel loops are assigned to different processors. Below we show why this scheme is inefficient. Again up to two levels of parallelism can be utilized by the Alliant FX/8. On future systems with large numbers of processors, it will be necessary to exploit multidimensional parallelism, i.e., execute several nested loops concurrently.

A straightforward practice that has been widely discussed by users and system designers is exploiting the parallelism in DOALL loops by allocating successive iterations to successive processors. Depending on the implementation, this scheme can be anywhere from suboptimal to very inefficient. Thus, in a system with p processors it is common to execute a DOALL loop with $N > p$ iterations in the following way: iteration 1 is assigned to processor 1, iteration 2 to processor 2, $\cdots$, iteration p to processor p, iteration $p + 1$ to processor 1 and so on. Therefore, processor i will execute iterations $i, i + p, i + 2p, \cdots$. However, it is more efficient to make the assignment so that a block of successive iterations is allocated to the same processor. For example, in the above case it would be more wise to assign iterations $1, 2, \cdots, \lceil N/p \rceil$ to the first processor, iterations $\lceil N/p \rceil + 1, \lceil N/p \rceil + 2, \cdots, 2\lceil N/p \rceil$ to the second processor, and so on. Memory interleaving cannot be brought up as an argument against the latter approach since memory allocation can be done to best facilitate scheduling in either case.

There are several advantages that favor the second approach of assigning iterations to processors. When iterations of a parallel loop are assigned to processors by blocks of successive iterations, each processor does not have to check the value of the loop index each time it executes an iteration. Recall that the loop index is a shared variable and each processor must lock and unlock a semaphore in order to be granted access to it and get the next iteration. In case all processors finish simultaneously they will all access the loop index serially going through a time-consuming process. In the worst case, a time delay equivalent to the time required for N accesses to a shared variable will be added to at least one processor. If the assignment of blocks of iterations is performed instead, this worst case delay will be equivalent to only p accesses to the shared loop index. For a large N and a small p this will result in substantial savings, considering the fact that each access to the loop index will have to go through the processor-to-memory network. Note that the number of accesses to the loop index is independent of N in our case. Another advantage of this scheme is that when we execute FORALL loops in parallel, the block assignment can be done so that the cross-iteration dependences are contained within one block and the dependences are therefore satisfied by virtue of the assignment. Thus, synchronization needs to be used only selectively which, in certain cases, may result in shorter execution times. In what follows the second method is used, that is, whenever a parallel loop (excluding DOACR's) is executed on several processors, the allocation will be done so that each processor is assigned a block of successive iterations.

IV. SELF-SCHEDULING THROUGH IMPLICIT COALESCING

Most of the schemes that have been proposed so far [15], [28], implement self-scheduling by making extensive use of synchronization instructions. For example in [28] a barrier synchronization is associated with each loop in the construct. In addition all accesses to loop indexes are, by necessity, synchronized. Another common characteristic of these schemes is that they assign only one loop iteration to each incoming idle processor. Our scheme differs in all aspects discussed above. Only one barrier per serial loop is used. Furthermore, independently of the nest pattern and the number of loops involved we need synchronized access to only a single loop index. In contrast, the above schemes need synchronized access to a number of indexes which is equal to the number of loops in the construct.

Self-scheduling can become more effective by using loop coalescing [22]. The key characteristic of this transformation which is useful here, is its ability to express all indexes in a loop nest as a function of a single index. This makes it clear why synchronized access to each loop index is wasteful. We can always use a single index. If the loop bounds are known at run time just before we enter the loop, we may decide exactly how many iterations each processor will receive. Thus, when a processor accesses the single loop index to dispatch a range of consecutive iterations, it goes through a single synchronization point. Since the range of iterations is determined beforehand, each processor will dispatch all the work it is responsible for, the very first time it accesses the corresponding loop index. Therefore, only a total of p synchronization instructions will be executed. As a matter of comparison, in the schemes mentioned above, each processor executes a synchronization instruction for each loop in the nest, and each time it dispatches a new iteration. In a nested loop that consists of m separate loops we would then have a total of $m\Pi_{i=1}^{m} N_i$ synchronization instructions that will execute before the loop completes. The difference between p and $m\Pi_{i=1}^{m} N_i$ can obviously be tremendous. The schemes in [28] and [15] for example, involve an overhead which is unbounded on p. In the general case, however, where loops contain conditional statements, the assignment of $\lceil N/p \rceil$ iterations to each processor will compromise load balancing. Therefore, we need something in between which will involve less overhead than self-scheduling, but it will also achieve load balancing.

A. The Guided Self-Scheduling (GSS(k)) Algorithm

In this section we present a simple, yet powerful algorithm for dynamic scheduling. The idea is to implement *guided self-scheduling* with bound k (GSS(k)), by "guiding" the processors on the amount of work they choose. The *bound* is defined to be the minimum number of loop iterations assigned to a given processor by GSS. The algorithm is discussed below in great detail and is summarized for $k = 1$ in Fig. 3. First we present the case of $k = 1$, GSS(1) or GSS for short, and later we discuss the general case for $k > 1$. The GSS algorithm achieves optimal execution times in many cases. Actually optimality is achieved in two dimensions. First, assuming that synchronization overhead is counted as part of a loop's execution time, GSS obtains optimal load balancing between processors and thus optimal execution time. At the same time GSS uses the minimum number of synchronization instructions that are needed to guarantee optimal load balancing.

1) Implicit Loop Coalescing and Interchange: Let us describe in more detail how self-scheduling through implicit loop coalescing works. First, assume that we have a perfectly (one-way) nested loop $L = (N_1, \cdots, N_m)$. Loop coalescing coalesces all m loops into a single loop $L' = (N = \Pi_{i=1}^{m} N_i)$ through a set of transformations f_i that map the index I of the coalesced loop L' to the indexes I_i, ($i = 1, 2, \cdots, m$) of the original loop L such that $I_i = f_i(I)$, ($i = 1, 2, \cdots, m$). This transformation is needed to express indexes of array subscripts, (that occur in the original loop body) as functions of the index I of the coalesced loop. This index transformation is universal, i.e., it is the same for all loops, perfectly nested or not and it is given by

$$I_k = f_k(I) = \left\lceil \frac{I}{\prod_{i=m}^{k-1} N_i} \right\rceil - N_k \left\lfloor \frac{I-1}{\prod_{i=m}^{k} N_i} \right\rfloor ,$$

$$(k = 1, 2, \cdots, m). \quad (1)$$

Thus, a reference to an array element of the form $A(I_1, I_2, \cdots, I_m)$ in L can be uniquely expressed as $A(f_1(I), f_2(I), \cdots, f_m(I))$ in L' using the above transformation. (The introduction of complicated index expressions does not pose any performance "threat" since they are computed only once per processor or, in a different implementation, they may be completely ignored [21].) Therefore, each processor can compute locally f_i for a given I. Better yet, each processor can compute locally a range of values $f(x:y)$ for a range of $x \leq I \leq y$. The global index I is then kept in global memory as a shared variable. Each processor accesses I in a synchronized way and dispatches the next set of consecutive iterations of L along with a pointer to its code. Then inside each processor, mappings f_i as defined by (1) are used to compute the corresponding range for each index I_i of the original loop. After the index ranges are computed for each processor, execution proceeds in the normal mode. In case all loops in L are parallel and in the absence of conditional statements, no

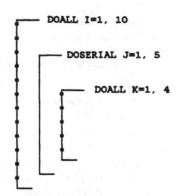

Fig. 1. Example loop for the application of GSS.

processor will ever go back to dispatch another range of iterations of I. This is obviously the minimum possible amount of synchronization that is needed with any self-scheduling scheme.

The process is more complicated with self-scheduling of hybrid loops. Let us look at the case of hybrid loops that consist of DOALL's and DOSERIAL loops, and in particular consider the example of Fig. 1. In this example the innermost and outermost loops are DOALL's and the second is a serial loop. Let us denote this loop with $L = (N_1, N_2, N_3) = (10, 5, 4)$. We have a total of $N = 200$ iterations. On a machine with an unlimited number of processors (200 in this case) each processor would execute five iterations of L, and this is the best possible that we can achieve. On a system with p processors, self-scheduling should be done such that iterations of L are evenly distributed among the p processors (assuming an equal execution time for all iterations). The presence of the serial loop in L, however, limits our ability to do this. It is noteworthy that the approach of assigning consecutive iterations of I to each processor would fail here. (This is true because after coalescing we have a single iteration space and assignments are done in blocks of consecutive iterations.) At most four successive iterations may be assigned at once. If all four are given to the same processor, the loop is executed serially. If each processor receives one iteration on the other hand, we can use only up to four processors.

This problem can be eliminated by permuting the indexes of the original loop, or equivalently, by applying implicit loop interchange [29]. Our goal is to permute the indexes so that the longest possible set of parallel iterations corresponds to successive values of the index I of L'. This can be done by permuting the indexes I and J so that the serial loop becomes the outermost loop or by permuting J and K so that the serial becomes the innermost loop. In general a serial loop can be interchanged with any DOALL that surrounds it, but it cannot be interchanged with a loop surrounded by it. Therefore, in the case of our example, we implicitly interchange loops I and J.

The interchange can be implemented trivially using implicit coalescing as follows. The mappings of I and J are permuted such that I is defined by the mapping of J and vice versa. No physical loop interchange takes place (neither physical coalescing). More specifically, if I_c is the global index of the coalesced loop for the example loop of Fig. 1, then the original indexes I, J, and K are mapped to I_c by (1) as follows.

$$I = \left\lceil \frac{I_c}{20} \right\rceil - 10 \left\lfloor \frac{I_c - 1}{200} \right\rfloor$$

$$J = \left\lceil \frac{I_c}{4} \right\rceil - 5 \left\lfloor \frac{I_c - 1}{20} \right\rfloor$$

$$K = I_c - 4 \left\lfloor \frac{I_c - 1}{4} \right\rfloor .$$

After implicit loop interchange, the mappings become

$$I = \left\lceil \frac{I_c}{4} \right\rceil - 10 \left\lfloor \frac{I_c - 1}{40} \right\rfloor$$

$$J = \left\lceil \frac{I_c}{40} \right\rceil - 5 \left\lfloor \frac{I_c - 1}{200} \right\rfloor$$

$$K = I_c - \left\lfloor \frac{I_c - 1}{4} \right\rfloor .$$

The result is that the first 40 successive values of I_c correspond now to 40 parallel iterations (instead of four iterations as previously). Therefore, up to 40 processors can be used in parallel. Extra synchronization is still needed, however. Each serial loop in L needs a barrier synchronization to enforce its seriality. The following proposition tells us when it is legal to apply loop interchange in order to maximize the number of consecutive parallel iterations.

Proposition 1: In a hybrid perfectly nested loop, any DOALL can be interchanged with any serial or DOACR loop that is in a deeper nest level. This loop interchange can be applied repeatedly and independently for any pair of (DOALL, DOSERIAL/DOACR) loops.

Proof: The proof is clear for the case of two loops. The general case follows by induction on the number of loops interchanged. ∎

The only case that remains to be discussed is nonperfectly (multiway) nested loops. This is identical to the one-way nested loop case, unless one of the following two conditions is met. 1) Loops at the same nest level have different loop bounds. 2) High-level spreading is to be applied to loops at the same nest level (i.e., loops at the same nest level are executed in parallel). In the first case, if k loops $N_{I+1}, N_{I+2}, \cdots, N_{I+k}$ happen to be at the ith nest level, the global index I_c is computed with N_i iterations for the ith level, which is given by

$$N_i = \max_{1 \le j \le k} \{N_{I+j}\}.$$

Then during execution, loop N_{I+j} at the ith level will have $N_i - N_{I+j}$ null iterations (which are not actually computed). Therefore, some of the processors execute only part of the code at level i. This corresponds to computing slices of each loop on the same processor. Thus, slices of the two loops corresponding to the same index values will be assigned to each idle processor. In general, if loops at the same nest level are independent or involve dependencies in only one direction, outer loops can be distributed [13] around them and each loop is considered separately (i.e., we coalesce each of them and consider them as separate tasks). When there are bidirectional dependences across loops at the same nest level, barrier synchronization can be used as mentioned above. If high-level spreading is to be applied, then implicit loop coalescing and a global index I_c will be computed for each loop that is spread.

2) The Scheduling Algorithm: So far we have seen how GSS coalesces the loops and assigns blocks of iterations to incoming (idle) processors. We have not mentioned, however, how the algorithm decides the number of iterations to be assigned to each idle processor. The schemes that have been proposed so far [2], [15], [26], [28] assign a single iteration at a time. For nested loops with many iterations, this approach involves a tremendous amount of overhead since several critical regions must be accessed each time a single iteration is dispatched. The GSS algorithm follows another approach by assigning several iterations (or an *iteration block*) to each processor. The size of each block varies and is determined by using a simple but powerful rule that is described below. Before we describe how block sizes are computed let us state our constraints.

Suppose that a parallel loop L (e.g., a DOALL) is to be executed on p processors. We assume that each of the p processors starts executing some iteration(s) of L at different times (i.e., not all p processors start computing L simultaneously). This is clearly a valid and practical assumption. If L, for example, is not the first loop in the program, the processors will be busy executing other parts of the program before they start on L. Therefore, in general, they will start executing L at different times which may vary significantly. (Of course one could force all p processors to start on L at the same time by enforcing a join (or barrier) operation before L; this would clearly be very inefficient.) Given now the assumption that the p processors will start executing L at arbitrary times, our goal is to dispatch a block of consecutive iterations of L to each incoming processor such that all processors terminate at approximately the same time. This is a very desirable property. If L_d, for example, is nested inside a serial loop L_s, then a barrier synchronization must be performed each time L_d completes (i.e., for each iteration of L_s). If the processors working on L_d do not terminate at the same time, a very significant amount of idle processor time (overhead) may be accumulated by the time L_s completes.

In general the best possible solution is that which guarantees that all p processors will terminate with at most B units of time difference from each other; where B is the execution time of the loop body of L. This goal can be achieved if blocks of iterations are assigned to idle processors following the next principle. An incoming processor p_i^x will dispatch a number of iterations x_i considering that the remaining $p - 1$ processors will also be scheduled at this (same) time. In other words p_i^x should leave enough iterations to keep the remaining $p - 1$ processors busy (in case they all decide to start simultaneously) while it will be executing its x_i iterations. If N is the total number of iterations, this can be easily done as follows. Since GSS coalesces loops, there will be a single index $I_c = 1 \cdots N$, from which idle processors will dispatch blocks of

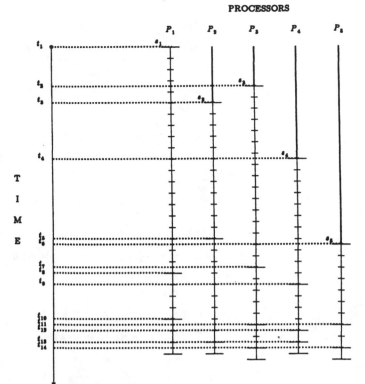

Fig. 2. An example of the application of the GSS algorithm for $N = 100$, $p = 5$.

iterations. Therefore, the assignment of iteration blocks is done by having each idle processor p_i perform the following operations:

$$x_i = \left\lceil \frac{R_i}{p} \right\rceil \; ; \qquad R_{i+1} \leftarrow R_i - x_i, \qquad (2)$$

and the range of iterations assigned to the ith processor is given by $[N - R_i + 1, \cdots, N - R_i + x_i]$, where $R_1 = N$. The detailed algorithm is described in Fig. 3.

As an example, consider the case of a DOALL L with $N = 100$ iterations that executes on five processors. All five processors start on L at different times. Each idle processor is assigned a block of consecutive iterations using the rule described above. The resulting execution profile is shown in Fig. 2. Even though the results presented in this section hold for the general case where different iterations of the same loop have different execution times, for this example we assume that all 100 iterations have equal execution times. Each vertical line segment in Fig. 2 represents the execution time of a loop iteration. The thick lines represent the execution of previous (unrelated to L) tasks on processors P_2, P_3, P_4, and P_5. The wider horizontal line segments mark the time when iteration blocks are actually dispatched by idle processors. For example, at time t_1 processor P_1 dispatches $\lceil 100/5 \rceil = 20$ iterations. The next processor to become available is P_3 which at time t_2 dispatches $\lceil (100 - 20)/5 \rceil = 16$ iterations. Processor P_1 will receive its next assignment at time t_8. The detailed assignment of iterations to processors for this example is shown in Table I. The events in the table are ordered by

Input An arbitrarily nested loop L, and p processors.

Output The optimal dynamic schedule of L on the p processors. The schedule is reproducible if the execution time of the loop bodies and the initial processor configuration (of the p processors) are known.

- Distribute the loops in L wherever possible.

- For each ordered pair of (DOALL, DOSERIAL/DOACR) loops, (where the DOALL is the outer loop) perform loop interchange.

- Apply implicit loop coalescing, and let I_c be the index of the coalesced iteration space.

- For each index i_k of the original loop define the index mapping as in (1),

$$i_k = f_{i_k}(I_c)$$

- If R_i is the number of remaining iterations at step i, then set $R_1 = N$, $i=1$, and for each idle processor do.

REPEAT

- Each idle processor (scheduled at step i) receives

$$z_i = \left\lceil \frac{R_i}{p} \right\rceil$$

iterations.

- $R_{i+1} = R_i - z_i$

- The range of the global index is $I_c \in [N-R_i+1,....,N-R_i+z_i] \equiv [l_i, ..., u_i]$

- The range of each original loop index for that processor is given by

$$i_k \in [f_{i_k}(l_i),...,f_{i_k}(u_i)]$$

- $i = i+1$

UNTIL $(R_i = 0)$

Fig. 3. The GSS algorithm.

TABLE I
THE DETAILED SCHEDULING EVENTS OF THE EXAMPLE OF FIG. 2
ORDERED BY TIME

Time	No. of unused iterations (I)	Next processor to be scheduled	No. of iterations assigned to this processor
t_1	100	P_1	20
t_2	80	P_3	16
t_3	64	P_2	13
t_4	51	P_4	11
t_5	40	P_5	8
t_6	32	P_3	7
t_7	25	P_5	5
t_8	20	P_1	4
t_9	16	P_4	4
t_{10}	12	P_1	3
t_{11}	9	P_3	2
t_{12}	7	P_5	2
t_{13}	5	P_4	1
t_{14}	4	P_4	1
t_{15}	3	P_3	1
t_{16}	2	P_5	1
t_{17}	1	P_4	1
			TOTAL= 100

virtual time. From Fig. 2 we observe that although the five processors start executing L at different times, they all terminate within B units of time difference from each other. In general if p processors are assigned to a DOALL with N iterations using the above scheme, we have the following.

Lemma 1: Each of the *last $p - 1$* processors to be scheduled under the GSS algorithm is assigned exactly one iteration of L. These $p - 1$ processors are not necessarily physically distinct.

Proof: First we will show that there exists an i such that

R_i [as defined by (2)] is

$$R_i = p+1 \quad \text{or} \quad R_i = p \qquad (3)$$

where p is the number of processors. Suppose that such an i does not exist. Then there exists an i for which

$$R_i \geq p+2 \quad \text{and} \quad R_{i+1} \leq p-1.$$

But $R_{i+1} = R_i - \lceil R_i/p \rceil$ by definition. Thus, $\lceil R_i/p \rceil = R_i - R_{i+1} \geq p + 2 - (p - 1) = 3$, hence $R_i > 2p$.

Let $R_i = kp + r$ where $k \geq 2$ and $r > 1$. But $R_{i+1} = R_i - \lceil R_i/p \rceil < p$, or $kp + r - (k + 1) < p$, and since $r > 1$, $(k - 1)p - k < 0$ or finally $p < k/(k - 1)$. But since $k \geq 2$, it follows that $p < 2$ which contradicts the initial hypothesis that $p > 1$. Hence, (3) is true.

From (2) and (3) it follows directly that at least the last $p - 1$ and at most the last p assignments will involve iteration blocks of size 1. ∎

Theorem 1: Independently of the initial configuration (startup time) of the p processors that are scheduled under GSS, all processors finish executing L within B units of time difference from each other.

Proof: We will prove the theorem for the case where all p processors start executing L simultaneously. The proof for the general case is similar. By Lemma 1, at least the last $p - 1$, and at most the last p assignments will involve single iterations. Let us consider the latter case. The are two possible scenarios during the scheduling of L under GSS. In the first case each of the last p iterations is assigned to a different processor. Then by virtue of GSS it is easy to see that if t_i, t_j are the termination times for processors p_i, p_j, $i, j \in [1 \cdots p]$, respectively, we have $|t_i - t_j| < B$.

The second case is when the last p iterations of L are assigned to at most $p - 1$ different processors. Let p_i^x denote a processor whose last assignment was an iteration block of size x, and p_j^1 denote a processor that is assigned one or more of the last p iterations. Let t_i^x and t_j^1 be their corresponding completion times. Using the same argument as above we can show that all processors that received one of the last p iterations finish within B units of time apart from each other. It remains to show that any p_i^x and any p_j^1 terminate within B units of time from each other. We consider the case for $x = 2$. The general case is similar. We will prove that for any p_i^x and any p_j^1, $|t_i^x - t_j^1| \le B$.

Case 1: $t_i^x > t_j^1$, and suppose that $t_i^x - t_j^1 > B$ or equivalently, $t_i^x - 2B > t_j^1 - B$. The last inequality implies that p_j^1 was assigned a single iteration before the iteration block of size $x = 2$ was assigned to p_i^x. Clearly this contradicts the basic steps of the GSS algorithm. Therefore $t_i^x - t_j^1 \le B$.

Case 2: $t_i^x < t_j^1$ and suppose $t_j^1 - t_i^x > B$ or, $t_j^1 - B > t_i^x$ but the last inequality can never be true since p_i^x would have been assigned the last iteration instead of p_j^1. Therefore, $t_j^1 - t_i^x \le B$ and thus the statement of the theorem is true.

Note that if the p processors start executing L at different times $s_1 \le s_2 \le \cdots \le s_p$, the theorem still holds true under the following condition:

$$N > \frac{1}{B} \sum_{i=1}^{p} (s_p - s_i). \qquad \blacksquare$$

In reality B varies for different iterations (due to the presence of conditional statements) and $B \in \{b_1, b_2, \cdots, b_k\}$, where b_i, $(i = 1, \cdots, k)$ are all possible values of B. Suppose that B can assume any of its possible values with the same probability, i.e., $P[B = b_i] = 1/k$, $(i = 1, 2, \cdots, k)$. Then Lemma 1 and Theorem 1 are still valid. Of course a uniform distribution is not always a valid assumption. For example, in numerical software we often have exit IF's inside loops that test for some error condition. The loop is exited if the error condition arises. In such cases we can safely ignore the conditional statements. If the user or the compiler cannot make any assertion about the distribution of true/false branches, other heuristic tunnings can be used in GSS. For example, if we know that the probability of clustered true (false) branches (of a conditional statement inside a loop) is high, then we can make p artificially large to decrease the size of the iteration blocks assigned to each processor by GSS. Even though simulation results show that even in such cases GSS is still superior to self-scheduling, we can no longer prove that GSS is optimal. Under the above assumptions we also have the following.

Theorem 2: If iterations have constant execution time, the GSS algorithm obtains an optimal schedule under any initial processor configuration. GSS also uses the minimum possible number of synchronization points necessary to achieve optimal load balancing.

By synchronization points we mean the number of times processors enter critical regions (i.e., loop indexing). An implementation of GSS can be done so that when q (out of the p) processors become simultaneously available at step i, the first $q - 1$ receive $\lceil R_i/p \rceil$ iterations and the qth processor receives $\min (\lceil (R_i - (q - 1)\lceil R_i/p \rceil)/p \rceil, \lceil R_i/p \rceil)$ iterations, where R_i is the number of unassigned iterations at the ith step of GSS. In general, when GSS is applied using (2) the number of synchronized accesses to loop indexes is given by the following theorem.

Theorem 3: The number of synchronization points required by GSS is p in the best case, and $O(pH_{\lceil N/p \rceil})$ in the worst case, where H_n denotes the nth harmonic number and $H_n \approx \ln (n) + \gamma + 1/2n$ (γ is Euler's constant).

Proof: The best case is obvious from the above discussion. In general it is clear that the number of iterations assigned to each processor will be (possibly multiple) occurrences of (some of) the integers

$$\left\lceil \frac{N}{p} \right\rceil, \left\lceil \frac{N}{p} \right\rceil - 1, \left\lceil \frac{N}{p} \right\rceil - 2, \cdots, 1$$

in this order. Obviously there will be at least $p - 1$ and at most p assignments of exactly one iteration. It can be also observed that the number of different assignments of iteration blocks of size $\lceil N/p \rceil - k$, $(k = 1, 2, \cdots, \lceil N/p \rceil - 2)$ depend on the relative values of p and $\lceil N/p \rceil - k$. More precisely, we can have at most

$$\left\lceil \frac{p}{\lceil N/p \rceil - k} \right\rceil, \qquad (k = 1, 2, \cdots, \lceil N/p \rceil - 2)$$

different assignments of iteration blocks of size $\lceil N/p \rceil - k$. Therefore, the total number of different assignments and thus the total number σ of synchronization points in the worst case is given by

$$\sigma \le p + \sum_{i=2}^{\lceil N/p \rceil} \left\lceil \frac{p}{i} \right\rceil = \sum_{i=1}^{\lceil N/p \rceil} \left\lceil \frac{p}{i} \right\rceil .$$

For computing the order of magnitude we can ignore the ceiling and finally have

$$\sigma \approx \sum_{i=1}^{\lceil N/p \rceil} \frac{p}{i} = p \sum_{i=1}^{\lceil N/p \rceil} \frac{1}{i} = pH_{\lceil N/p \rceil}$$

Therefore, the number of synchronization points in the worst case is $\sigma = O(pH_{\lceil N/p \rceil})$. $\blacksquare$

Thus, GSS goes through $O(p \ln (N/p))$ synchronization points in the worst case compared to $O(mN)$ synchronization points used by the schemes in [15] and [28]. Note that if barriers are used, GSS can coalesce all loops, serial and parallel. Consider for example a DOALL loop with $\Pi_{i=1}^{m} N_i$ iterations which is the result of coalescing m DOALL's. Suppose now that this DOALL is nested inside a serial loop with M iterations. GSS works fine on this doubly nested loop but it still must access two shared variables (loop indexes) for each assignment. The other alternative is to implicitly coalesce the serial and parallel loops into a single *block-parallel* loop or BDOALL with MN iterations. To do this a barrier synchronization must be executed every N iterations. If $I_c = 1 \cdots MN$, the number of remaining iterations R_i [in (2)] still assumes an initial value N. The difference here is that each time ($I_c \bmod N = 0$) a barrier synchronization is executed and R is reinitialized to N. This happens M times before the entire loop completes execution.

It should be noted that since GSS is a dynamic scheme the assumption that loop bounds are known is a realistic one. The index bounds of DO loops must be known just before we enter the loop.

B. Further Reduction of Synchronization Operations

Another interesting feature of the GSS algorithm is that it can be tuned to further reduce the number of synchronization operations that are required during scheduling. As mentioned above, the last $p - 1$ allocations performed by GSS assigned exactly one iteration to each processor. The synchronization overhead involved in these $p - 1$ allocations may still be very high, especially when p is very large and the loop body is small.

We shall see now how to eliminate the last $p - 1$ assignments of single iterations of GSS. In fact we can eliminate all assignments of iteration blocks of size k ($< \lceil N/p \rceil$) or less. Let us discuss first the problem of eliminating assignments of single iterations from GSS. We show how this can be done by means of an example. Consider the application of GSS to a DOALL with $N = 14$ iterations on $p = 4$ processors. The assignment of iterations to processors [using (2)] is shown below in detail.

$$\lceil 14/4 \rceil = 4, \ \lceil 10/4 \rceil = 3, \ \lceil 7/4 \rceil = 2, \ \lceil 5/4 \rceil = 2,$$
$$\lceil 3/4 \rceil = 1, \ \lceil 2/4 \rceil = 1, \ \lceil 1/4 \rceil = 1.$$

The seven successive assignments were done with iteration blocks of size 4, 3, 2, 2, 1, 1, 1. In this case the single iteration assignments account for almost half of the total assignments. We can eliminate the single iteration assignments by increasing the block size of the first $p - 1$ assignments by 1. The successive assignments in that case would be 5, 4, 3, and 2. Therefore, the total number of scheduling decisions (and thus synchronization operations) is reduced by $p - 1$. This reduction can be performed automatically by setting $R_1 = N + p$ in (2). Thus, the first assignment will dispatch $x_1 = \lceil (N + p)/p \rceil$ iterations. Otherwise, GSS is applied in precisely the same way. However, now it terminates not when the iterations are exhausted, but when for some i, $x_i < 2$. For the above example the application of GSS will generate the following assignments ($R_1 = \lceil (N + p)/p \rceil$).

$$\lceil 18/4 \rceil = 5, \ \lceil 13/4 \rceil = 4, \ \lceil 9/4 \rceil = 3, \ \lceil 6/4 \rceil = 2.$$

When the ratio N/p is rather small, GSS(k) for $k = 2$ may result in considerable savings. There is still a drawback, however, since the rule of making all the assignments of iteration blocks of size two or more is now always accurate. Consider again the previous example but now let $N = 15$. The

assignments generated by GSS(2) will now be

$$\lceil 19/4 \rceil = 5, \ \lceil 14/4 \rceil = 4, \ \lceil 10/4 \rceil = 3, \ \lceil 7/4 \rceil = 2, \ \lceil 5/4 \rceil = 2.$$

But $5 + 4 + 3 + 2 + 2 = 16 > N = 15$, i.e., the number of iterations assigned by GSS(2) is more than the iterations of the loop. Fortunately the number of superfluous iterations in such cases cannot be more than one, and the termination problem can be easily corrected. The solution is given by the following theorem.

Theorem 4: Let k be the step in (2) such that $x_k = 2$ and $x_{k+1} = 1$. If $R_{k+1} = p$ then

$$\sum_{i=1}^{k} x_i = N$$

else, if $R_{k+1} = p - 1$ then

$$1 + \sum_{i=1}^{k-1} x_i = N.$$

Proof: The algorithm starts with a total of $N + p$ iterations, and it must assign a total of N iterations in blocks of size ranging from $\lceil (N + p)/p \rceil$ to 2. Since (for $p \geq 2$) at least one iteration block will be of size 2, and all assignments of iteration blocks of size 2 must be performed, it follows that the last assignment of GSS(2) will involve $R_k = p + 1$ or $R_k = p + 2$. In the latter case the last assignment will dispatch two iterations and the algorithm will terminate assigning, therefore, a total of $N + p - R_{k+1} = N$ iterations. If $R_k = p + 1$, the last assignment will also dispatch two iterations. In that case, however, the total number of iterations assigned will be $N + p - (p - 1) = N + 1$. Thus, $1 + \Sigma_{i=1}^{k-1} x_i = N$. ∎

Theorem 4 supplies the test for detecting and correcting superfluous assignments. The assignment and termination condition for GSS(2) is now given by

$$x_i = \left\lceil \frac{R_i}{p} \right\rceil ; \ R_{i+1} \leftarrow R_i - x_i$$

if $(R_{i+1} \leq p)$ then
{stop;
   if $(R_{i+1} < p)$ then $x_i = 1$}.   (4)

Using (4) now, the last assignment of GSS(2) for the last example will dispatch a single iteration. The same process can be applied to derive GSS(k) for any $2 < k < \lceil N/p \rceil$. The best value of k is machine and application dependent.

It should be emphasized that the GSS scheme can be implemented in hardware, it can be incorporated in the compiler, or it can be explicitly coded by the programmer. In the latter case the programmer may compute the iteration block size for each assignment, and force the assignment of such blocks by coding the corresponding loop appropriately. Consider for example the loop of Fig. 4(a). If array B holds the block size and S holds the starting iteration for each assignment, the loop of Fig. 4(a) can be coded as in Fig. 4(b).

```
      DOALL 1 I = 1, N
          . . .
          . . .
          . . .
      ENDOALL
                    (a)


      DOALL 1 I = 1, K
          DOSERIAL 2 J = S(I), S(I)+B(I)
              . . .
              . . .
          ENDOSERIAL
      ENDOALL
                    (b)
```

Fig. 4.   Example of the application of GSS at the program level.

V. SIMULATION RESULTS

A simulator was implemented to study the performance of self-scheduling (SS) and GSS (GSS(1)). In the SS scheme, loop scheduling was done by assigning a single iteration to each idle processor [2], [6], [28]. Idle processors access each loop index in a loop nest by using appropriate synchronization instructions. The simulator was designed to accept program traces generated by Parafrase, and it can be extended easily to implement other scheduling strategies. The experiments conducted for this work, however, used four representative loops which are shown in Fig. 5.

A. The Simulator

The simulator input consists of a set of tuples, where each tuple represents a single loop or a block of straight-line code [1]. Each tuple includes information such as number of iterations, execution time of basic blocks inside the loop, branching frequencies for the branches of each conditional statement inside a loop, dependence information, type of loop, etc. In the presence of conditional statements the conditions are "evaluated" separately for each iteration of the loop and the appropriate branch is selected. The user supplies the expected frequency with which each branch is selected. Otherwise, the simulator considers each branch equally probable. For this purpose a random number generator is used with a period of $2^{31} - 1$ [14]. Random numbers are generated using a uniform distribution and are normalized (in [0 $\cdots$ 1]). For each conditional statement in the loop, the interval [0 $\cdots$ 1] is partitioned into a number of subintervals equal to the number of counted paths in that statement. The size of each subinterval is proportional to the expected frequency of that branch. For each iteration of the loop, a random number is generated and the subinterval to which it belongs is determined. Then the branch corresponding to that subinterval is taken.

The execution of arbitrary loops on multiprocessor systems with 2–4096 processors can be simulated. Processors can start on a loop at random times. The simulator also takes into

```
        DOALL 1 I1 = 1, 100
          DOALL 2 I2 = 1, 50
            DOALL 3 I3 = 1, 4
L1:             {20}
                [if C then {10}]
            ENDOALL
          ENDOALL
        ENDOALL
                    (a)


        DOALL 1 I1 = 1, 50
          {5}
          [if C then {10}]
          DOALL 2 I2 = 1, 40
            {5}
            DOALL 3 I3 = 1, 4
L2:             {10}
                [if C then {20}]
            ENDOALL
          ENDOALL
        ENDOALL
                    (b)


        DOSERIAL 1 I1 = 1, 40
          DOALL 2 I2 = 1, 500
L3:         {100}
            [if C then {50}]
          ENDOALL
        ENDOSERIAL
                    (c)


        DOSERIAL 1 I1 = 1, 50

          DOALL 2 I2 = 1, 10
            DOALL 3 I3 = 1, 10
              DOALL 4 I4 = 1, 4
                {10}
                [if C then {50}]
              ENDOALL
            ENDOALL
          ENDOALL

                    |
                    V

          DOALL 5 I5 = 1, 100
            {50}
L4:         DOALL 6 I6 = 1, 5
              {100}
              [if C then {30}]
            ENDOALL
          ENDOALL

                    |
                    V

          DOALL 7 I7 = 1, 20
            DOALL 8 I8 = 1, 4
              {30}
            ENDOALL
          ENDOALL

        ENDSERIAL
                    (d)
```

Fig. 5.   Loops $L1$, $L2$, $L3$, and $L4$ used for the experiments.

account overhead incurred with operations on shared variables. For our purposes shared variables are considered to be only loop indexes. Although the current version of the simulator assumes a fixed memory access time, it can be easily extended to take into account random delays (due to network contention in shared memory systems). For each memory access, a random delay may be computed to fall within given upper and lower bounds. These bounds may be readjusted each time the number of processors (and thus the number of stages of the network) grows.

B. Experiments

The four loops $L1$, $L2$, $L3$, and $L4$ of Fig. 5 were used to conduct the experiments for this work. These loops are representative of those found in production numerical software. Serial and parallel loops are specified by the programmer, or are created by a restructuring compiler (e.g., Parafrase). The loops of Fig. 5 cover most cases since they include loops that are 1) all parallel and perfectly nested ($L1$), 2) hybrid and perfectly nested ($L3$), 3) all parallel and nonperfectly nested ($L2$), 4) hybrid nonperfectly nested ($L4$), 5) and finally one-way ($L2$), and multiway nested ($L4$). The arrows in $L4$ indicate flow dependences between adjacent loops. The numbers enclosed in brackets give the execution times of straight-line code in the corresponding positions.

Two sets of experiments were conducted, E_1 and E_2. The first set used the four loops of Fig. 5 ignoring the conditional statements which are enclosed in square brackets. Therefore, for E_1 all iterations of a particular loop had equal execution times. For E_2 the conditional statements were taken into account as well. Thus, in E_2 different iterations of a given loop had different execution times. The next step will be to consider loops with multiple and nested conditionals which were not included in these experiments.

Earlier in this paper we discussed the various types of overhead that are incurred during dynamic scheduling. One type of overhead is the time spent accessing and operating on a shared variable; in our case loop indexes. This time is not constant in practice and it depends on several factors such as network traffic, number of simultaneous requests for a particular index, and so on. For our experiments we chose this overhead to be constant and independent of the loop size or the number of processors. Since the purpose of our experiments is to study the relative (rather than the absolute) performance of GSS(1) and SS, the above assumption is not very restricting. For each scheduling decision the overhead is assumed to be a constant which represents, for instance, the number of clock cycles spent operating on a shared variable. Let o denote the overhead constant. We conducted the simulations for a best case (o_b), and a "worst" case (o_w) overhead. For the best case $o_b = 2$ since at least two clock cycles are needed to operate on a shared variable. For the worst case we chose $o_w = 10$. The value of 10 was chosen arbitrarily. In real parallel processor machines o_b and o_w can be much greater, but we are more interested in the difference $o_b - o_w$ rather than in their absolute values. E_1^b and E_1^w denote the set of experiments that ignored IF statements for $o_b = 2$ and $o_w = 10$, respectively. Similarly, E_2^b and E_2^w denote the set of experiments using $L1$, $L2$, $L3$, and $L4$ with IF statements, for $o_b = 2$ and $o_w = 10$, respectively.

The plots of Figs. 6 and 7 show the speedup of the four loops $L1$–$L4$ of Fig. 5, for different numbers of processors, for the experiment E_1 (E_1^b and E_1^w). There are four curves in each plot. Solid lines plot the speedup curves for GSS(1), and dashed lines plot the speedup curves for SS. More specifically the plot of Fig. 6(a) corresponds to loop $L1$. The upper and lower solid lines are the speedup curves resulting from the schedule of $L1$ under GSS(1) and for $o_b = 2$, $o_w = 10$, respectively. The upper and lower dashed lines are the

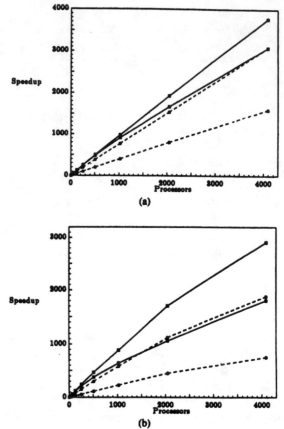

Fig. 6. GSS and SS speedups for (a) $L1$, and (b) $L2$ without IF's.

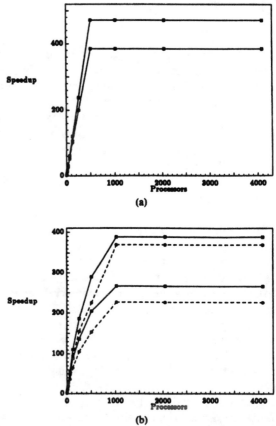

Fig. 7. GSS and SS speedups for (a) $L3$, and (b) $L4$ without IF's.

82

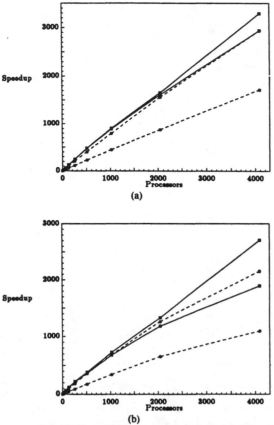

(a)

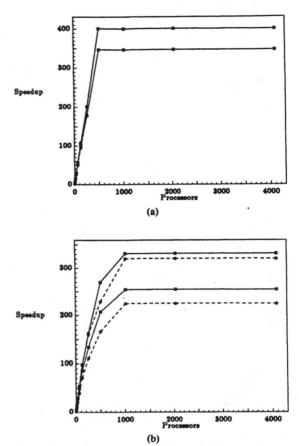

(a)

Fig. 8.   GSS and SS speedups for (a) $L1$, and (b) $L2$ with IF's.

(b)

Fig. 9.   GSS and SS speedups for (a) $L3$, and (b) $L4$ with IF's.

speedup curves of $L1$ under SS for $o_b = 2$, and $o_w = 10$. The plot of Fig. 6(b) shows the performance of GSS(1) and SS for $L2$ in E_1. Similarly Fig. 7(a) and (b) corresponds to $L3$ and $L4$ for E_1. In all plots, the upper solid and dashed lines correspond to GSS(1) and SS for $o_b = 2$, respectively. The lower solid and dashed lines correspond to GSS(1) and SS for $o_w = 10$.

In the same way Figs. 8 and 9 correspond to $L1$, $L2$, and $L3$, $L4$ respectively, for the E_2 experiments, i.e., with the IF statements taken into account. Therefore, in each plot we can see the relative performance of GSS(1), $o_b = 2$ versus GSS(1), $o_w = 10$; SS, $o_b = 2$ versus SS, $o_w = 10$; GSS(1), $o_b = 2$ versus SS, $o_b = 2$; and GSS(1) $o_w = 10$ versus SS, $o_w = 10$, for E_1 and E_2.

Except in the case of $L3$ where both GSS(1) and SS perform almost identically, we observe that in all other cases GSS(1) is better than SS by almost a factor of two in E_1 and E_2. In $L3$ for $p \geq 500$ we have the case of unlimited processors where each processor is assigned one iteration by both schemes. It is also clear from the plots that the difference in performance between GSS(1) and SS grows as the overhead grows. As it should be expected GSS(1) is less sensitive to scheduling overhead than SS.

The plots in Figs. 10, 11, 12, and 13 correspond to Figs. 6, 7, 8, and 9, respectively, and illustrate the speedup ratio GSS(1)/SS for each case for E_1 and E_2. The horizontal axis shows the log of the number of processors. In each plot there are two curves. The upper curve plots the speedup ratio GSS/SS for $o_b = 10$. The lower curve plots the same ratio for $o_w =$

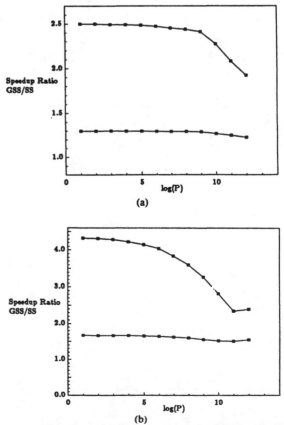

(a)

(b)

Fig. 10.   Speedup ratio of GSS/SS for (a) $L1$, and (b) $L2$ without IF's.

83

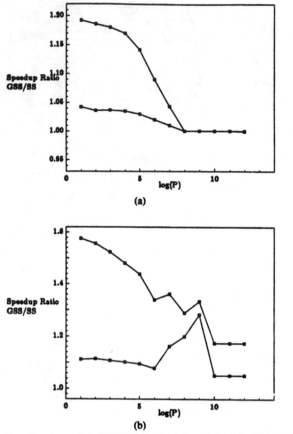

(a)

(b)

Fig. 11. Speedup ratio of GSS/SS for (a) $L3$, and (b) $L4$ without IF's.

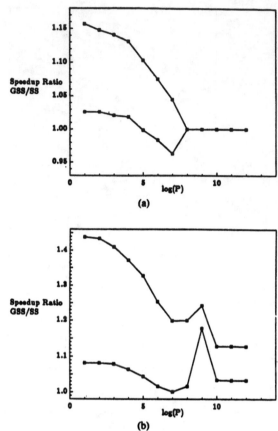

(a)

(b)

Fig. 13. Speedup ratio of GSS/SS for (a) $L3$, and (b) $L4$ with IF's.

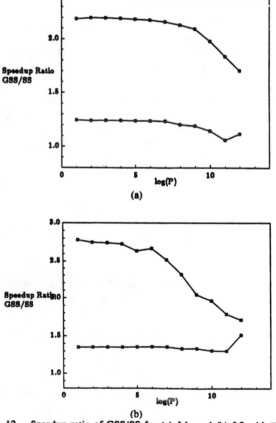

(a)

(b)

Fig. 12. Speedup ratio of GSS/SS for (a) $L1$, and (b) $L2$ with IF's.

2. The common characteristic of all ratio plots is that as the number of processors grows very large, the performance difference between GSS and SS becomes less significant. The large perturbations in the ratio curves can be explained by the fact that GSS is "logarithmically sensitive" while SS is "linearly sensitive" to scheduling overhead. Thus, the performance of SS tends to saturate much earlier (as the number of processors grows) than that of GSS. As the overhead grows the improvement offered by GSS becomes more significant. This is apparent in the plots of Figs. 10–13 where the ratio GSS(1)/SS is significantly larger for $o_w = 10$.

VI. CONCLUSIONS

Since parallel loops account for the greatest percentage of parallelism in numerical programs, the efficient scheduling of such loops is vital to program and system performance. In this paper we presented an efficient dynamic approach to solve the loop scheduling problem. The proposed method is general and can be easily incorporated into the compiler or the hardware.

Two important objectives are automatically satisfied: low overhead and load balancing. By guiding the amount of work given to each processor, very good (and often optimal) load balancing is achieved. The assignment of large iteration blocks, on the other hand, reduces the number of accesses to loop indexes and thus the run-time overhead.

If the GSS scheme is coupled with loop coalescing, the overhead can be further reduced, and by choosing the minimum unit of allocation, guided self-scheduling can be

84

tuned to perform optimally for any given loop–system combination. Finally we showed that for certain types of loops the GSS scheme is optimal. Simulation results indicate that in general GSS is better than any other known dynamic method. Its simplicity and low overhead make it a good candidate for implementation on existing and future parallel processor machines.

ACKNOWLEDGMENT

We would like to thank the referees for their comments and suggestions that greatly enhanced the quality of the presentation of this work.

REFERENCES

[1] A. V. Aho and J. D. Ullman, *Principles of Compiler Design.* Reading, MA: Addison-Wesley, 1977.

[2] Alliant Computer Systems Corp., *FX/Series Architecture Manual*, Acton, MA, 1985.

[3] U. Banerjee, "Speedup of ordinary programs," Ph.D. dissertation, Univ. Illinois, Urbana-Champaign, DCS Rep. UIUCDCS-R-79-989, Oct. 1979.

[4] E. G. Coffman, Jr., Ed., *Computer and Job-Shop Scheduling Theory.* New York: Wiley, 1976.

[5] E. G. Coffman and R. L. Graham, "Optimal scheduling on two processor systems," *Acta Informatica*, vol. 1, no. 3, 1972.

[6] "Multitasking user guide," Cray Comput. Syst. Tech. Note SN-0222, Jan. 1985.

[7] R. G. Cytron, "Doacross: Beyond vectorization for multiprocessors," extended abstract, in *Proc. 1986 Int. Conf. Parallel Processing*, St. Charles, IL, Aug. 1986, pp. 836–844.

[8] J. R. Beckman Davies, "Parallel loop constructs for multiprocessors," M.S. Thesis, Univ. Illinois, Urbana-Champaign, DCS Rep. UIUCDCS-R-81-1070, May 1981.

[9] M. R. Garey and D. S. Johnson, *Computers and Intractability, A Guide to the Theory of NP-Completeness.* San Francisco, CA: Freeman, 1979.

[10] A. Gottlieb, R. Grishman, C. P. Kruskal, K. P. McAuliffe, L. Rudolph, and M. Snir, "The NYU Ultracomputer—Designing an MIMD shared-memory parallel machine," *IEEE Trans. Comput.*, vol. C-32, pp. 175–189, Feb. 1983.

[11] D. J. Kuck, E. S. Davidson, D. H. Lawrie, and A. H. Sameh, "Parallel supercomputing today and the cedar approach," *Science*, vol. 231, pp. 967–974, Feb. 28, 1986.

[12] R. L. Graham, "Bounds on multiprocessor scheduling anomalies and related packing algorithms," in *Proc. Spring Joint Comput. Conf.*, 1972.

[13] D. J. Kuck, R. Kuhn, D. Padua, B. Leasure, and M. Wolfe, "Dependence graphs and compiler optimizations," in *Proc. 8th ACM Symp. Principles Programming Languages*, Jan. 1981, pp. 207–218.

[14] H. Kobayashi, *Modeling and Analysis*, 2nd ed. Reading, MA: Addison-Wesley, 1981.

[15] C. Kruskal and A. Weiss, "Allocating independent subtasks on parallel processors," *IEEE Trans. Software Eng.*, vol. SE-11, Oct. 1985.

[16] D. J. Kuck, *The Structure of Computers and Computations, Vol. 1.* New York: Wiley, 1978.

[17] D. J. Kuck et al., "The effects of program restructuring, algorithm change and architecture choice on program performance," in *Proc. Int. Conf. Parallel Processing*, Aug. 1984.

[18] D. A. Padua Haiek, "Multiprocessors: Discussions of some theoretical and practical problems," Ph.D. dissertation, Univ. Illinois, Urbana-Champaign, DCS Rep. UIUCDCS-R-79-990, Nov. 1979.

[19] C. D. Polychronopoulos and U. Banerjee, "Processor allocation for horizontal and vertical parallelism and related speedup bounds," *IEEE Trans. Comput.*, vol. C-36, Apr. 1987.

[20] C. D. Polychronopoulos, D. J. Kuck, and D. A. Padua, "Execution of parallel loops on parallel processor systems," in *Proc. 1986 Int. Conf. Parallel Processing*, St. Charles, IL, Aug. 1986, pp. 519–527.

[21] C. D. Polychronopoulos, "On program restructuring scheduling and communication for parallel processor systems," Ph.D. dissertation, Rep. 595, Center Supercomput. Res. Development, Univ. Illinois, Aug. 1986.

[22] ——, "Loop coalescing: A compiler transformation for parallel machines," in *Proc. 1987 Int. Conf. Parallel Processing*, St. Charles, IL, Aug. 1987.

[23] S. Reinhardt, "A data-flow approach to multitasking on CRAY X-MP computers," in *Proc. 10th ACM Symp. Oper. Syst. Principles*, Dec. 1985.

[24] S. Sahni, "Scheduling multipipeline and multiprocessor computers," *IEEE Trans. Compt.*, vol. C-33, July 1984.

[25] K. Schwan and C. Gaimon, "Automatic resource allocation for the Cm* multiprocessor," in *Proc. 1985 Int. Conf. Distributed Comput. Syst.*, 1985.

[26] B. Smith, "Architecture and applications of the HEP multiprocessor computer system," in *Real Time Processing IV, Proc. SPIE*, 1981, pp. 241–248.

[27] H. S. Stone, "Multiprocessor scheduling with the aid of network flow algorithms," *IEEE Trans. Software Eng.*, vol. SE-3, Jan. 1977.

[28] P. Tang and P. C. Yew, "Processor self-scheduling for multiple-nested parallel loops," in *Proc. 1986 Int. Conf. Parallel Processing*, Aug. 1986.

[29] M. J. Wolfe, "Optimizing supercompilers for supercomputers," Ph.D. dissertation, Univ. Illinois, Urbana-Champaign, DCS Rep. UIUC-CDCS-R-82-1105, 1982.

[30] C. Q. Zhu, P. C. Yew, and D. H. Lawrie, "Cedar synchronization primitives," Lab. Advanced Supercomput. Cedar Doc. 18, Sept. 1983.

Constantine D. Polychronopoulos (S'85–M'86) was born on April 5, 1958, in Patras, Greece. He received the Dipl. degree in mathematics from the University of Athens, Athens, Greece, in 1980, the M.S. degree in computer science from Vanderbilt University, Nashville, TN, in 1982, and the Ph.D. degree in computer science from the University of Illinois, Urbana-Champaign in 1986.

From 1982 to 1986 he was a Research Assistant in the Department of Computer Science and the Center for Supercomputing Research and Development at the University of Illinois. Since July 1986, he has been a Senior Software Engineer at the Center for Supercomuting Research and Development, and a Visiting Assistant Professor in the Department of Electrical and Computer Engineering at the University of Illinois. At CSRD he participates in the design of the Cedar compiler and the Parafrase II project. His primary research interests are in the areas of parallel processing, program restructuring, scheduling, synchronization, and interprocessor communication, and he has published a number of papers in these topics. He was a Fulbright Scholar in 1981–1982.

Dr. Polychronopoulos served on the program committee for the International Conference on Supercomuting, and he was coeditor of the proceedings. He is a member of the ACM and the IEEE Computer Society.

David J. Kuck (S'59–M'69–SM'83–F'85), was born in Muskegon, MI, on October 3, 1937. He received the B.S.E.E. degree from the University of Michigan, Ann Arbor, in 1959, and the M.S. and Ph.D. degrees from Northwestern University, Evanston, IL, in 1960 and 1963, respectively.

From 1963 to 1965, he was a Ford Postdoctoral Fellow and Assistant Professor of Electrical Engineering at the Massachusetts Institute of Technology, Cambridge. In 1965, he joined the Faculty of the University of Illinois, Urbana. He is now a Professor of Computer Science and of Electrical and Computer Engineering and the Director of the Center for Supercomuting Research and Development, which he organized in 1984. He is currently engaged in the development of the Cedar parallel processing system. His research interests are in the coherent design of hardware and software systems, including the development of the Parafrase system, a program transformation facility for array and multiprocessor machines. He was a principal designer of the Burroughs Scientific Processor and Illiac IV. In addition to serving as a consultant to a number of government and industrial organizations including Alliant Computer Systems, he was a founder of Kuck and Associates, Inc., which produces software that restructures programs for parallel and vector machines, as well as numerical software for such machines. Among his publications is *The Structure of Computers and Computations, Vol. 1.*

Dr. Kuck has served as an Editor for a number of professional journals, including the *IEEE Transactions on Computers* and the *Journal of the Association for Computing Machinery.*

Multiprocessor scheduling with communication delays

B. VELTMAN and B.J. LAGEWEG

Centre for Mathematics and Computer Science, P.O. Box 4079, 1009 AB Amsterdam, The Netherlands

J.K. LENSTRA

Department of Mathematics and Computer Science, Eindhoven University of Technology, P.O. Box 513, 5600 MB Eindhoven, The Netherlands, and Centre for Mathematics and Computer Science, P.O. Box 4079, 1009 AB Amsterdam, The Netherlands

Received 25 June 1990

Abstract. This paper adresses certain types of scheduling problems that arise when a parallel computation is to be executed on a multiprocessor. We define a model that allows for communication delays between precedence-related tasks, and propose a classification of various submodels. We also review complexity results and optimization and approximation algorithms that have been presented in the literature.

Keywords. Scheduling, Parallel processors, Communication delays, Algorithms, Complexity.

1. Introduction

Over the past decade, distributed memory architectures passed from the state of theoretical models to that of real machines. To take advantage of the inherent parallelism of these architectures, new allocation and scheduling problems have to be solved. These problems differ from their classical variants mainly in that interprocessor communication delays have to be taken into account.

In this paper, we address such problems in the context of deterministic machine scheduling theory. Scheduling theory in general is concerned with the optimal allocation of scarce resources to activities over time. A *processor*, or machine, is a resource that can perform at most one activity at any time. The activities are commonly referred to as *tasks*, or jobs. The problems we consider are *deterministic* in the sense that all the information that defines an instance is known with certainty in advance.

We will assume that there are *data dependencies* among the tasks. That is, some tasks produce output that is required by other tasks as input. Such dependencies define a *precedence relation* on the task set. Whenever the two tasks of a (predecessor, successor) pair are assigned to different processors, a *communication delay* occurs. For this class of problems, we formulate a model, we propose a classification that extends the scheme of Graham, et al. [12] and we review the available literature. We also briefly mention a practical project that motivated this research.

In the literature, we distinguish two basically different approaches to handle communication delays. The first approach formulates the problem in graph theoretic terms and is called the *mapping* problem [3]. The program graph is regarded as an undirected graph, where the vertices correspond to program modules and an (undirected) edge indicates that the adjacent modules interact, that is, communicate with each other. The multiprocessor architecture is also regarded as an undirected graph, with nodes corresponding to processors. Processors are assigned to program modules. A mapping aims at reducing the total interprocessor communication time and balancing the workload of the processors, thus attempting to find an allocation that minimizes the overall completion time.

The second approach considers the allocation problem as a pure *scheduling* problem. It regards the program graph as an acyclic directed graph. Again, the vertices represent the program modules, but a (directed) arc indicates a one-way communication between a (predecessor, successor) pair of modules. A *schedule* is an allocation of each task (module) to a time interval on one or more processors, such that, among others, precedence constraints and communication delays are taken into account. It aims at minimizing the completion time.

In this paper we take the second approach. Eventually, it may be desirable to combine the two approaches in allocating a parallel program to a multiprocessor. In that case, a first step would schedule the program modules on a virtual architecture graph, and a second step would find a mapping of the virtual architecture graph onto the physical architecture of the multiprocessor [15].

2. The processor model

The multiprocessor chosen consists of a collection of *m processors*, each provided with a *local memory* and mutually connected by an *intercommunication network*. The multiprocessor architecture can be represented by an undirected graph. The nodes of this graph correspond to the processors of the architecture. Transmitting data from one processor to another is considered as an independent event, which does not influence the availability of the processors on the transmittal path. In case of a shared memory, the assumption of having local memory only overestimates the communication delays.

3. The program model

A parallel program is represented by means of an acyclic directed graph. The nodes of this program graph correspond to the modules in which the program is decomposed; they are called *tasks*. Each task produces *information*, which is in whole or in part required by one or more other tasks. These data dependencies impose a *precedence relation* on the task set; that is, whenever a task requires information, it has to succeed the tasks that deliver this information. The arcs of the graph represent these precedence constraints. The transmittal of information may induce several sorts of *communication delays*, which will be discussed in the next section. *Task duplication*, that is, the creation of copies of a task, might reduce such communication delays.

In general, a task can be processed on various subgraphs of the multiprocessor graph. We assume that, for each task, a collection of subgraphs on which it can be processed is specified and that, for each task and each of its feasible subgraphs, a corresponding processing time is given. If the processors of the architecture are identical, then for each task the processing times related to isomorphic subgraphs are equal. For instance, one may think of a collection of subhypercubes of a hypercube system of processors. Another possibility occurs when each task can be processed on any subgraph of a given task-dependent size.

If *preemption* is allowed, then the processing of any operation may be interrupted and resumed at a later time. Although task splitting may induce communication delays, it may also decrease the cost of a schedule with respect to one or more criteria. We will not explore the aspect of communication delays that are induced by preemption in detail, but concentrate on communication delays in between precedence-related tasks.

4. Communication

The information a task needs (or produces) has to be (or becomes) available on all the processors handling this task. The size of this data determines the communication times.

If two tasks J_k and J_l both succeed a task J_j, then they might partly use the same information form task J_j. Under the condition that the memory capacity of a processor is adequate, only on transmission of this common information is needed if J_k and J_l are scheduled on the same subgraph of the multiprocessor graph. It is therefore important to determine the *data set* a task needs from each of its predecessors. The transfer of data between J_j and J_k can be represented by associating a data set with the arc (J_j, J_k) of the transitive closure of the program graph. This would generally lead to the specification of $\Theta(n^2)$ sets, if there are n tasks. Another possibility is to associate two sets $IN(j)$ and $OUT(j)$ with each task J_j, representing the data that this task requires and delivers, respectively. This requires $\Theta(n)$ sets. The intersection $OUT(j) \cap IN(k)$ gives the data dependency of tasks J_j and J_k.

Each information set has a *weight*, which is specified by a function $c : 2^D \to \mathbb{N}$, where D is the set containing all information. This function gives the time needed to transmit data from one processor to another, regarded as independent of the processors involved. Let $U \in 2^D$ be a data set and let $\{U_1, U_2, \ldots, U_u\}$ be a partition of U. We assume that U can be transmitted in such a way that $\bigcup_{i=1}^{t} U_i$ is available when a time period of length at most $c(\bigcup_{i=1}^{t} U_i)$ has elapsed, for each t with $1 \leqslant t \leqslant u$. We also assume that $c(\emptyset) = 0$ and that $c(U) \leqslant c(W)$ for all $U \subset W \in 2^D$. These conditions state that a data set U can be transmitted in such a way that a subset of U becomes available no later than when this subset would be transmitted on its own.

Interprocessor *communication* occurs when a task J_k needs information from a predecessor J_j and makes use of at least one processor that is not used by J_j. Let M_i be such a processor. Let $F(j)$ denote the set of successors of J_j and, given a schedule, let $P(k, i)$ denote the set of tasks scheduled on M_i before and including J_k. Prior to the execution of J_k, the data set $U(i, j, k) = \bigcup_{l \in F(j) \cap P(k,i)} (OUT(j) \cap (IN(l)))$ has to be transmitted to M_i, since not only J_k but also each successor of J_j that precedes J_k on M_i requires its own data set. The time gap in between the completion of J_j (at time C_j) and the start of J_k (at time S_k) has to allow for the transmission of $U(i, j, k)$. The communication time is given by $c(U(i, j, k))$. For feasibility it is required that $S_k - C_j \geqslant c(U(i, j, k))$. At the risk of laboring the obvious, let it be mentioned that the communication time is schedule-dependent.

Sometimes one wishes to disregard the data sets and simply to associate a communication delay with each pair of tasks. That is, a (predecessor, successor) pair of tasks (J_j, J_k) assigned to different processors needs a communication time of a given duration c_{jk}. The communication time is of length c_{j*} if it depends on the broadcasting task only, it is of length c_{*k} if it depends on the receiving task only. Finally, it may be of constant length c, independent of the tasks.

5. Classification

In general, m processors M_i ($i = 1, \ldots, m$) have to process n tasks J_j ($j = 1, \ldots, n$). A schedule is an allocation of each task to a time interval on one or more processors. A schedule is *feasible* if no two of these time intervals on the same processor overlap and if, in addition, it meets a number of specific requirements concerning the processor environment and the task characteristics (e.g. precedence constraints and communication delays). A schedule is *optimal* if it minimizes a given optimality criterion. The processor environment, the task characteristics and the optimality criterion that together define a problem type, are specified in terms of a threefield classification $\alpha \mid \beta \mid \gamma$, which is specified below. Let $\circ$ denote the empty symbol.

5.1 Processor environment

The first field $\alpha = \alpha_1 \alpha_2$ specifies the processor environment. The characterization $\alpha_1 = P$ indicates that the processors are *identical parallel processors*. The characterization $\overline{P}$ indicates that, in addition, the number of processors is at least equal to the number of tasks: $m \geqslant n$.

If α_2 is a positive integer, then m is a constant, equal to α_2; it is specified as part of the problem type. If $\alpha_2 = \circ$, then m is a variable, the value of which is specified as part of the problem instance.

5.2 Task characteristics

The second field $\beta \subset \{\beta_1, \ldots, \beta_7\}$ indicates a number of task characteristics, which are defined as follows.

1. $\beta_1 \in \{$ *prec, tree, chain,* $\circ$ $\}$.

   $\beta_1 = prec$: A *precedence relation* $\rightarrow$ is imposed on the task set due to data dependencies. It is denoted by an acyclic directed graph G with vertex set $\{1, \ldots, n\}$. If G contains a directed path from j to k, then we write $J_j \rightarrow J_k$ and require that J_j has been completed before J_k can start.

   $\beta_1 = tree$: G is a *rooted tree* with either outdegree at most one for each vertex or indegree at most one for each vertex.

   $\beta_1 = chain$: G is a collection of vertex-disjoint chains.

   $\beta_1 = \circ$: No data dependencies occur, so that the precedence relation is empty.

2. $\beta_2 \in \{$ *com,* $c_{jk}, c_{j*}, c_{*k}, c, c = 1, \circ$ $\}$

   This characteristic concerns the communication delays that occur due to data dependencies. To indicate this, one has to write β_2 directly after β_1.

   $\beta_2 = com$: Communication delays are derived from given data sets and a given weight function, as described in Section 4. In all the other cases, the communication delays are directly specified.

   $\beta_2 = c_{jk}$: Whenever $J_j \rightarrow J_k$ and J_j and J_k are assigned to different processors, a communication delay of a given duration c_{jk} occurs.

   $\beta_2 = c_{j*}$: The communication delays depend on the broadcasting task only.

   $\beta_2 = c_{*k}$: The communication delays depend on the receiving task only.

   $\beta_2 = c$: The communication delays are equal.

   $\beta_2 = c = 1$: Each communication delay takes unit time.

   $\beta_2 = \circ$: No communication delays occur (which does not imply that no data dependencies occur).

3. $\beta_3 \in \{$ *dup,* $\circ$ $\}$.

   $\beta_3 = dup$: Task duplication is allowed.

   $\beta_3 = \circ$: Task duplication is not allowed.

4. $\beta_4 \in \{$ *any, set$_j$, size$_j$, cube$_j$, fix$_j$,* $\circ$ $\}$.

   $\beta_4 = any$: Each task can be processed on any subgraph of the multiprocessor graph.

   $\beta_4 = set_j$: Each task has its own collection of subgraphs of the multiprocessor graph on which it can be processed.

   $\beta_4 = size_j$: Each task can be processed on any subgraph of a given task-dependent size.

$\beta_4 = cube_j$: Each task can be processed on a subhypercube of given task-dependent dimension.

$\beta_4 = fix_j$: Each task can be processed on exactly one subgraph.

$\beta_4 = \circ$: Each task can be processed on any single processor.

5. $\beta_5 \in \{ \circ , p_j = 1\}$.

$\beta_5 = \circ$: For each task and each subgraph on which it can be processed, a processing time is specified.

$\beta_5 = p_j = 1$: Each task has a unit processing requirement.

6. $\beta_6 \in \{ pmtn, \circ \}$.

$\beta_6 = pmtn$: Preemption of tasks is allowed.

$\beta_6 = \circ$: Preemption is not allowed.

7. $\beta_7 \in \{c, c = 1, \circ \}$.

This characteristic concerns the communication delays that occur due to preemption. To indicate this, one has to write β_7 directly after β_6.

$\beta_7 = c$: When a task is preempted and resumed on a different processor, a communication delay of constant length occurs.

$\beta_7 = c = 1$: Each communication delay takes unit time.

$\beta_7 = \circ$: No communication delays occur.

5.3 Optimality criterion

The third field γ refers to the optimality criterion. In any schedule, each task J_j has a *completion time* C_j. A traditional optimality criterion involves the minimization of the *maximum completion time* or *makespan* $C_{\max} = \max_{1 \leq j \leq n} C_j$. Another popular criterion is the *total completion time* $\Sigma C_j = \Sigma_{j=1}^n C_j$.

The optimal value of γ will be denoted by γ^*, and the value produced by an (approximation) algorithm A by $\gamma(A)$. If $\gamma(A) \leq \rho \gamma^*$ for all instances of a problem, then we say that A is a ρ-approximation algorithm for the problem.

6. Literature review

Practical experience makes it clear that some computational problems are easier to solve than others. Complexity theory provides a mathematical framework in which computational problems can be classified as being *solvable in polynomial time* or $\mathcal{NP}$-*hard*. The reader is referred to the book by Garey and Johnson [10] for a detailed treatment of the subject. In reviewing the literature, we will assume that the reader is familiar with the basic concepts of complexity theory. As a general reference on sequencing and scheduling, we mention the survey of deterministic machine scheduling theory by Lawler et al. [16], which updates the previous survey by Graham et al. [12].

6.1 Single-processor tasks and communication delays

Colin and Chrétienne [8] address a problem that arises in the case of scheduling tasks on an idealized distributed multiprocessor system. They investigate $\overline{P} \mid prec, c_{jk}, dup \mid C_{\max}$ where the communication delays are small in the sense that for all J_k we have $\min\{ p_j \mid J_k \in F(j)\} \geq \max\{ c_{jk} \mid J_k \in F(j)\}$. A *critical path*-like algorithm is presented, which is shown to construct an optimal schedule in polynomial time. First, a lower bound b_j on the starting time is computed for each task J_j. Tasks without predecessors get a zero lower bound. For each task J_k that has no lower bound yet but whose predecessors do have lower bounds, let i be such that

$b_i + p_i + c_{ik} = \max\{b_j + p_j + c_{jk} \mid J_j \to J_k\}$ and define $b_k = \max\{b_i + p_i, \max\{b_j + p_j + c_{jk} \mid J_j \to J_k, J_j \neq J_i\}\}$. In the second step of the algorithm, a schedule is built such that each task and its duplications are scheduled to start at their lower bound. An arc $J_j \to J_k$ is *critical* if $b_j + p_j + c_{jk} > b_k$. The subgraph of the precedence graph consisting of all critical arcs is shown to be a spanning forest. Therefore, the assignment of each path of this subgraph to a distinct processor leads to an optimal schedule. The algorithm runs in $O(n^2)$ time.

This work extends the paper by Chrétienne [7], who studies $\overline{P} \mid tree, c_{jk} \mid C_{max}$. He shows that, if the maximum communication delay is at most equal to the minimum processing time of any task, the scheduling problem is solvable in polynomial time. He gives an $O(n)$ algorithm for problem instances with a rooted tree as a precedence relation, in which each vertex has outdegree at most one. Due to the restriction on communication times, there exist an optimal schedule such that for any task J_j the tasks immediately preceding J_j are assigned to distinct processors, and one immediate predecessor is assigned to the same processor to which J_j itself is assigned. The algorithm has a recursive structure. Leaves are assigned to distinct processors, and each root J_j of a subtree is assigned to a processor that executes one of its immediate predecessors, such that the partial schedule itself is optimal.

Papadimitriou and Yannakakis [19] show by a reduction from the CLIQUE problem that $\overline{P} \mid prec, c, p_j = 1 \mid C_{max}$ is $\mathcal{NP}$-hard. They also present a polynomial-time 2-approximation algorithm for $P \mid prec, c_{j*}, dup \mid C_{max}$. This rather complicated algorithm starts by assigning a lower bound b_j on the starting time to each task J_j, as follows. Zero lower bounds are assigned to source tasks. For any task J_k other than a source, consider its predecessors, and for each predecessor J_j compute $f_j = b_j + p_j + c_{j*}$. Sort the predecessors in nonincreasing order of f_j. Next, determine the smallest integer λ satisfying $f_{j_i} \geq \lambda \geq f_{j_{i+1}}$ with $f_{j_i} > f_{j_{i+1}}$ and such that a subset of $\{J_{j_1}, \ldots, J_{j_i}\}$ of *critical* tasks can be scheduled within a makespan of λ on one processor with their starting times at least equal to their lower bounds. These tasks are critical in the sense that copies of them have to precede any duplicate of J_k on the processor on which this duplicate is executed. The lower bound b_k will be equal to λ. Once the information of all the critical tasks that precede J_k is available, this task itself can be executed after a time b_k has elapsed. It is observed that the information for the critical tasks becomes available no later than time b_k, so that J_k can start no later than $2b_k$.

Rayward-Smith [20] allows preemption and studies $\overline{P} \mid pmtn, c \mid C_{max}$. He observes that the communication delays increase C_{max}^* by at most $c - 1$. Thus, $P \mid pmtn, c = 1 \mid C_{max}$ is solvable in polynomial time by McNaughton's *wrap-around rule* [18]. Surprisingly, for any fixed $x \geq 2$, the problem is $\mathcal{NP}$-hard, which is proved by a reduction from 3-PARTITION. For the special case that all processing times are at most $C_{max}^* - c$, the wrap-around algorithm will also yield a valid c-delay schedule.

Rayward-Smith [21] shows by a reduction from $P \mid prec, p_j = 1 \mid C_{max}$ that $P \mid prec, c = 1, p_j = 1 \mid C_{max}$ is $\mathcal{NP}$-hard. The quality of *greedy* schedules (G) is analyzed. A schedule is said to be greedy if no processor remains idle if there is a task available; list scheduling, for example, produces greedy schedules. It is proved that $C_{max}(G)/C_{max}^* \leq 3 - 2/m$. To this end, various concepts are introduced. The *depth* of a node is defined as the number of nodes on a longest path from any source to that node. A *layer* of a digraph comprises all nodes of equal depth. A digraph is *layered* if every node that is not a source has all of its parents in the same layer. A layered digraph is (n, m)-*layered* if it has n layers, all terminal nodes are in the nth layer, and m layers are such that all of their nodes have more than one parent. A precedence relation is (n, m)-*layered* if the corresponding directed graph is (n, m)-layered. It takes at least time $n + m$ to schedule tasks with (n, m)-layered precedence constraints. Given a greedy schedule, let t be a point in time when one or more processors are idle. The tasks processed after t have at least one predecessor processed at $t - 1$ or t. Moreover, if all processors are idle at t, then every task processed after t must have at least two predecessors processed at $t - 1$. Therefore, from a greedy schedule, a layered digraph can be extracted. Some computations then yield the above result.

Lee et al. [17] consider a variant of $P \mid prec, c_{jk} \mid C_{\max}$. A *distance* is given for each pair of processors. Each communication delay is the product of the distance in between the processors to which two precedence-related tasks J_j and J_k are assigned, and the number c_{jk}. A simple worst-case bound is obtained for their *earliest ready task* heuristic (ERT): $C_{\max}(ERT) \leqslant (2 - 1/m)C_{\max} + C_{\mathrm{com}}$, where $C_{\max}$ is the optimal makespan without considering communication delays and C_{com} is the maximum communication delay in any chain of tasks. The ERT algorithm recursively chooses among the available tasks one that can be processed earliest. Hwang et al. [14] is a rewritten version of this paper.

Kim [15] also studies $P \mid prec, c_{jk} \mid C_{\max}$. His approach starts by reducing the program graph, by merging nodes with high internode communication cost through the iterative use of a *critical path* algorithm. This (undirected) graph is then mapped to a multiprocessor graph by mapping algorithms. Numerical results are given.

Sarkar [22] defines a graphical representation for parallel programs and a cost model for multiprocessors. Together with frequency information obtained from execution profiles, these models give rise to a scheme for compile-time cost assignment of execution times and communication sizes in a program. Most attention is payed to the partitioning of a parallel program, which is outside the scope of this paper. As to scheduling, Sarkar shows for a *runtime scheduling* algorithm (RS) with restriction to $P \mid prec \mid C_{\max}$ that $C_{\max}(RS)/C_{\max}^* \leqslant 2 - 1/m$. He also proves that $P \mid prec, c_{jk} \mid C_{\max}$ is $\mathcal{NP}$-hard in the strong sense. Not surprisingly, since this result is dominated by Rayward-Smith [21].

6.2 Multiprocessor tasks

The problems and algorithms mentioned above deal with tasks that are processed on a single processor and focus on communication delays. The following papers disregard the notion of communication and concentrate on tasks that require a subgraph of the multiprocessor graph.

Chen and Lai [5] present a worst-case analysis of *largest dimension, largest processing time list scheduling (LDLPT)* for $P \mid cube_j \mid C_{\max}$. They show that $C_{\max}(LDLPT)/C_{\max}^* \leqslant 2 - 1/m$. LDLPT scheduling is an extension of Graham's *largest processing time scheduling* algorithm (*LPT*) [11]. It considers the given tasks one at a time in lexicographical order of nonincreasing dimension of the subcubes and processing times, with each task assigned to a subcube that is earliest available.

For the preemptive problem $P \mid cube_j, pmtn \mid C_{\max}$, Chen and Lai [6] give an $O(n^2)$ algorithm that produces a schedule in which each task meets a given deadline, if such a schedule exists. The algorithm considers the tasks one at a time in order of nonincreasing dimension. It builds up a *stairlike* schedule. A schedule is stairlike if a nonincreasing function $f: \{1, \ldots, m\} \to \mathbf{N}$ exists such that each processor M_i is busy up to time $f(i)$ and idle afterwards. The number of preemptions is at most $n(n-1)/2$. By binary search over the deadline values, an optimal schedule is obtained in $O(n^2(\log n + \log \max_j p_j))$ time.

Van Hoesel [13] also studies $P \mid cube_j, pmtn \mid C_{\max}$ and presents an $O(n \log n)$ algorithm to decide whether the tasks can be scheduled within a given deadline T. Instead of building up stairlike schedules, this algorithm produces *pseudo-stairlike* schedules. Given a schedule, let t_i be such that processor M_i is busy for $[0, t_i]$ and free for $[t_i, T]$. A schedule is pseudo-stairlike if $t_i < t_h < T$ implies $h < i$, for any two processors M_h and M_i. Again, the tasks are ordered according to nonincreasing dimension. Dealing with J_j, the algorithm recursively searches for the highest i such that $p_j > T - t_i$. It schedules J_j on processors $M_{i-(2^{d_j}-1)}, \ldots, M_i$ in the time slot $[t_i, T]$, and on $M_{i+1}, \ldots, M_{i+2^{d_j}-1}$ in the time slot $[t_{i+1}, p_j - (T - t_i)]$. By a combination of this algorithm and *binary search* $C_{\max}^*$ can be determined in $O(n \log n \log(n + \max_j p_j))$

time. Furthermore, since each task except the first is preempted at most once, the algorithm creates no more than $n - 1$ preemptions, and this bound is tight.

Blazewicz, Weglarz and Drabowski [2] propose an $O(n \log n)$ algorithm for solving $P \mid size_j, pmtn \mid C_{\max}$, where the tasks require either one or two processors for processing. An initial step computes $C_{\max}^*$ without giving an optimal schedule. Subsequently, the 2-processor tasks are scheduled using McNaughton's *wrap-around rule* [18]. A modification of this rule schedules the single-processor tasks one at a time in order of nonincreasing processing times. The following paper extends this result.

Blazewicz, Drabowski and Weglarz [1] present an $O(n)$ algorithm for solving $P \mid size_j, p_j = 1 \mid C_{\max}$, where the tasks require either one or k processors. After calculating the optimal makespan, it schedules the k-processor tasks and next the single-processor tasks. For the problem with sizes belonging to $\{1, 2, \ldots, k\}$, an *integer programming* formulation leads to the observation that for fixed k the problem is solvable in polynomial time. However, if k is specified as part of the problem instance, then the problem is strongly $\mathcal{NP}$-complete. For the preemptive case $P \mid size_j, pmtn \mid C_{\max}$, where the tasks require either one or k processors, a modification of McNaughton's *wrap-around rule* [18] leads to an $O(n \log n)$ algorithm. Similar to Blazewicz, Weglarz and Drabowski [2], an initial step computes $C_{\max}^*$. A *linear programming* formulation shows that for any fixed number of processors the problem $Pm \mid size_j, pmtn \mid C_{\max}$ with sizes belonging to $\{1, 2, \ldots, k\}$ is solvable in polynomial time.

Bozoki and Richard [4] study $P \mid fix_j \mid C_{\max}$. They concentrate on *incompatibility*, where two tasks are said to be incompatible if they have at least one processor in common. A *branch and bound* algorithm is presented. Lower bounds for the optimal makespan are the maximum amount of processing time that is required by a single processor, and the maximum amount of processing time required by tasks that are mutually incompatible. Upper bounds are obtained by list scheduling according to priority rules such as *shortest processing time (SPT)* and *maximum degree of competition (MDC)*. The degree of competition of a task represents the number of tasks incompatible with it. *MDC* gives tasks with large degree of competition priority over tasks with low degree, breaking ties by use of *SPT*. In branching, an *acceptable* subset of tasks that yield smallest lower bounds is selected at each decision moment t. A set of tasks is acceptable if the tasks are mutually compatible, each task of the set is compatible with each task that is in process at time t, and each task is incompatible with at least one task terminating at t.

Du and Leung [9] show that $P2 \mid chain, size_j \mid C_{\max}$ and $P5 \mid size_j \mid C_{\max}$ with sizes belonging to $\{1, 2, 3\}$ are strongly $\mathcal{NP}$-complete. A *dynamic programming* approach leads to the observation that $P2 \mid any \mid C_{\max}$ and $P3 \mid any \mid C_{\max}$ are solvable in pseudopolynomial time. Arbitrary schedules for instances of these problems can be transformed into so called *canonical schedules*. A canonical schedule for the machine environment with two processors is one that first processes the tasks using both processors. Such a canonical schedule for two processors is completely determined by three numbers: the total execution times of the single-processor tasks on processor M_1 and M_2 respectively, and the total execution time of the 2-processor tasks. In case of three processors, similar observations are made. These characterizations are the basis for the development of the pseudopolynomial algorithms. The problem $P4 \mid any \mid C_{\max}$ remains open; no pseudopolynomial algorithm is given. For the preemptive case, they prove that $P \mid any, pmtn \mid C_{\max}$ is strongly $\mathcal{NP}$-complete by a reduction from 3-PARTITION. With restriction to two processors, $P2 \mid any, pmtn \mid C_{\max}$ is still $\mathcal{NP}$-complete, as is shown by a reduction from PARTITION. Using a result of Blazewicz, Drabowski and Weglarz [1], Du and Leung show that for any fixed number of processors $Pm \mid any, pmtn \mid C_{\max}$ is also solvable in pseudopolynomial time. The basic idea of the algorithm is as follows. To each schedule S of $Pm \mid any, pmtn \mid C_{\max}$, there is a corresponding instance of $P \mid size_j, pmtn \mid C_{\max}$ with sizes belonging to $\{1, \ldots, k\}$, in which a task J_j is an l-processor task if it uses l processors with respect to S. An optimal schedule for the latter problem can be found in polynomial time. All that is needed is to generate optimal schedules for all instances of $P\,|\,size_j,\ pmtn\,|\,C_{max}$ that correspond to schedules of $Pm\,|\,any,\ pmtn\,|\,C_{max}$, and choose the shortest among all. It is shown by a dynamic programming approach that the number of schedules generated can be bounded from above by a pseudopolynomial function of the size of $Pm\,|\,any,\ pmtn\,|\,C_{max}$.

7 ScheduLink

The work presented here has been carried out at the CWI in Amsterdam as part of the *ScheduLink* subproject within the *ParTool* project. The latter project aims at the creation of a parallel development environment, which is a set of integrated methods and tools that enable the development of programs for parallel processors, with a strong emphasis on programs for scientific and technical computations. The subproject ScheduLink will provide in one of these tools. It concerns the design and analysis of methods for the scheduling of a given computation graph on a given processor model, allowing for communication delays. Below we will specify the scheduling problems we are studying.

The multiprocessor chosen consists of a collection of m identical parallel processors, each provided with a local memory and mutually connected by an intercommunication network. The multiprocessor architecture is represented by an undirected graph.

Transmitting data does not influence the availability of the processors but is an independent event. One can therefore regard the multiprocessor graph as a complete graph. Yet, by assuming the processor graph to be complete, one disregards routing problems that may occur during the transmission of data. If, for instance, three processors M_1, M_2, M_3 are linearly connected (e.g. $\{M_1, M_2\}$ and $\{M_2, M_3\}$ are edges), then the simultaneous transmission of data from M_1 and M_2 to M_3 will influence each other. In general, it will take more than the time represented by the model. However, in the type of application under consideration several good routes are usually available, so that the communication time between two processors is practically independent of the chosen route.

The memory size of a processor is large enough to handle each of its tasks. The decomposition of a parallel program has to satisfy this property. It is also desirable that information which is available on a certain processor remains available throughout the entire process. Otherwise the unnecessary transmission of data might cause a delay. If, for instance, tasks J_2 and J_3 need the same information from task J_1 and are scheduled on the same processor, then one transmission of data would be sufficient if the local memory size of the processor is large enough. It remains to be seen whether this assumption is realistic. In case of a shared memory, our assumption of having local memory only overestimates the communication delays.

We assume that the multiprocessor is represented by a complete graph of identical processors. Hence, it suffices to concentrate on the sizes of the subgraphs of the multiprocessor graph and to make no distinction concerning the identities of the processors belonging to a subgraph. In the most general case we consider, each task can be processed on all subgraphs of a predetermined size. These sizes tend to be small with respect to the total number of processors available. Execution times on the subgraphs do not differ, because all the processors are identical, so that each task J_j requires a given processing time p_j.

Preemption of a task produces high communication costs and will therefore not be allowed. A task, once started, has to be processed without interruption until it is finished.

With the notation defined and used in the previous sections, the problem we consider in its most general form is denoted by $P\,|\,prec,\ com,\ dup,\ size_j\,|\,C_{max}$. This model is different and more general than the models that have been considered in the literature. In the first place, by the combination of communication delays and multiprocessor tasks and, secondly, by the specification of communication delays by means of data sets.

Acknowledgement

The Partool project is partially supported by SPIN, a Dutch computer science stimulation program.

References

[1] J. Blazewicz, M. Drabowski and J. Weglarz, Scheduling multiprocessor tasks to minimize schedule length, *IEEE Trans. Comput.* C-35 (1986) 389–393.

[2] J. Blazewicz, J. Weglarz and M. Drabowski, Scheduling independent 2-processor tasks to minimize schedule length, *Inform. Process. Lett.* 18 (1984) 267–273.

[3] S.H. Bokhari, On the mapping problem, *IEEE Trans. Comput.* C-30 (1981) 207–214.

[4] G. Bozoki and J.P. Richard, A branch-and-bound algorithm for the continuous-process task shop scheduling problem, *AIIE Trans.* 2 (1970) 246–252.

[5] G.I. Chen and T.H. Lai, Scheduling independent jobs on hypercubes, *Proc. Conf. Theoretical Aspects of Computer Science* (1988) 273–280.

[6] G.I. Chen and T.H. Lai, Preemptive scheduling of independent jobs on a hypercube, *Inform. Process. Lett.* 28 (1988) 201–206.

[7] P. Chrétienne, A polynomial algorithm to optimally schedule tasks on a virtual distributed system under tree-like precedence constraints, *European J. Oper. Res.* 43 (1989) 225–230.

[8] J.Y. Colin and P. Chrétienne, C.P.M. scheduling with small communication delays and task duplication, *Oper. Res.* (1990) to appear.

[9] J. Du and J.Y.-T. Leung, Complexity of scheduling parallel task systems, *SIAM J. Discrete Math.* 2 (1989) 473–487.

[10] M.R. Garey and D.S. Johnson, *Computers and Intractability: a Guide to the Theory of NP-Completeness* (Freeman, San Francisco, 1979).

[11] R.L. Graham, Bounds for certain multiprocessing anomalies, *Bell System Tech. J.* 45 (1966) 1563–1581.

[12] R.L. Graham, E.L. Lawler, J.K. Lenstra and A.H.G. Rinnooy Kan, Optimization and approximation in deterministic sequencing and scheduling: a survey, *Ann. Discrete Math.* 5 (1979) 287–326.

[13] C.P.M. van Hoesel, Preemptive scheduling on a hypercube (1990).

[14] J.J. Hwang, Y.C. Chow, F.D. Anger and C.Y. Lee, Scheduling precedence graphs in systems with interprocessor communication times, *SIAM J. Comput.* 18 (1989) 244–257.

[15] S.J. Kim, A General Approach to Multiprocessor Scheduling, Dissertation TR-88-04, University of Texas at Austin, 1988.

[16] E.L. Lawler, J.K. Lenstra, A.H.G. Rinnooy Kan and D.B. Shmoys, Sequencing and scheduling: algorithms and complexity, in: S.C. Graves, A.H.G. Rinnooy Kan and P. Zipkin, eds., *Handbooks in Operations Research and Management Science, Volume 4: Logistics of Production and Inventory* (North-Holland, Amsterdam, 1989).

[17] C.Y. Lee, J.J. Hwang, Y.C. Chow and F.D. Anger, Multiprocessor scheduling with interprocessor communication delays, *Discrete Appl. Math.* 20 (1988) 141–147.

[18] R. McNaughton, Scheduling with deadlines and loss functions, *Management Sci.* 6 (1959) 1–12.

[19] C.H. Papadimitriou and M. Yannakakis, Towards an architecture-independent analysis of parallel algorithms, *Proc. 20th Annual ACM Symp. Theory of Computing* (1988) 510–513.

[20] V.J. Rayward-Smith, The complexity of preemptive scheduling given interprocessor communication delays, *Inform. Process. Lett.* 25 (1987) 123–125.

[21] V.J. Rayward-Smith, UET scheduling with unit interprocessor communication delays, *Discrete Appl. Math.* 18 (1987) 55–71.

[22] V. Sarkar, *Partitioning and Scheduling Parallel Programs for Multiprocessors* (Pitman, London, 1989).

Heuristic Algorithms for Task Assignment in Distributed Systems

VIRGINIA MARY LO, MEMBER, IEEE

Abstract—In this paper, we investigate the problem of static task assignment in distributed computing systems, i.e., given a set of k communicating tasks to be executed on a distributed system of n processors, to which processor should each task be assigned? We propose a family of heuristic algorithms for Stone's classic model of communicating tasks whose goal is the minimization of the total execution and communication costs incurred by an assignment. In addition, we augment this model to include *interference costs* which reflect the degree of incompatibility between two tasks. Whereas high communication costs serve as a force of attraction between tasks, causing them to be assigned to the same processor, interference costs serve as a force of repulsion between tasks, causing them to be distributed over many processors. The inclusion of interference costs in the model yields assignments with greater concurrency, thus overcoming the tendency of Stone's model to assign all tasks to one or a few processors. Simulation results show that our algorithms perform well and in particular, that the highly efficient Simple Greedy Algorithm performs almost as well as more complex heuristic algorithms.

Index Terms—Distributed systems, load balancing, resource allocation, scheduling, task assignment, task scheduling.

I. INTRODUCTION

IN THE distributed computing environment, a job to be executed on the distributed system consists of a set of communicating tasks which we shall refer to as a *task force*. We define a *distributed system* as any configuration of two or more processors each with private memory. A systemwide operating system provides a message-passing mechanism among the processors, and it is assumed that the cost of transporting messages between processors is nonnegligible. During the lifetime of the task force in the distributed system, task management modules guide the task force through several clearly identifiable phases:

- *task definition*—the specification of the identity and characteristics of the task force by the user, the compiler, and based on monitoring of the task force during execution.
- *task assignment*—the initial placement of tasks on processors
- *task scheduling*—local CPU scheduling of the individual tasks in the task force with consideration of the overall progress of the task force as a whole

Manuscript received December 18, 1985; revised December 28, 1987. This work was supported in part by the U.S. Office of Naval Research under Contract N00014-79-C09775 and by the U.S. Department of Energy under Contract DE-AC02-76ER02383.A003.

The author is with the Department of Computer and Information Science, University of Oregon, Eugene, OR 97403.

IEEE Log Number 8820887.

- *task migration*—dynamic reassignment of tasks to processors in response to changing loads on the processors and communication network.

In this paper, we focus on the problem of *task assignment*. We use this term to describe an initial assignment of tasks to processors which neither requires nor precludes subsequent dynamic migration of tasks. In particular, we are concerned with centralized task assignment algorithms that have global knowledge of the characteristics of the task force and of the distributed system. These task assignment algorithms seek to assign tasks to processors in order to achieve goals such as minimization of interprocess communication costs (IPC), good load balancing among the processors, quick turnaround time for the task force, a high degree of parallelism, and efficient utilization of system resources in general.

Our work is an extension of the graph theoretic approach to the task assignment problem begun by Stone [22] in which the definition of the task force is limited to 1) the execution cost of each task on each of the (heterogeneous) processors and 2) communication costs (IPC) incurred between tasks when they are assigned to different processors. In Stone's work, a Max Flow/Min Cut Algorithm can be utilized to find assignments which minimize total execution and communication costs. In this paper, we use Stone's model to develop a heuristic algorithm which combines recursive invocation of Max Flow/Min Cut Algorithms with a greedy-type algorithm to find suboptimal assignments of tasks to processors. We present simulation results that show the performance of this heuristic to be very good.

We also discuss a serious deficiency in Stone's model in that it makes no direct effort to achieve concurrency, yielding assignments which utilize only one or a few of the processors. We therefore propose an extension of Stone's model to include an additional factor called *interference costs* which are incurred when tasks are assigned to the same processor. Interference costs reflect the degree of incompatibility between two tasks. For example, a pair of tasks that are both highly CPU bound would have greater interference costs than a pair in which one task is CPU bound and the other is I/O bound. Similarly, if two tasks were involved in pipelining, it would be undesirable that they be assigned to the same processor; this incompatibility would be expressed in a high interference cost for that pair of tasks. Simulations show that addition of interference costs as a factor greatly improves the degree of concurrency in task assignments. We also show that network flow algorithms can be successfully applied to the extended model to find task assignments which minimize total

Reprinted from *IEEE Trans. on Computers*, vol. 37, no. 11, Nov. 1988, pp. 1384–1397.

execution, communication, and interference costs in certain restricted cases and near minimal cost assignments in more general cases.

Finally, we look at several versions of our algorithm which vary in their degree of complexity. We show that the more efficient algorithms perform almost as well as more complex versions. Thus, if initial assignment is followed by later dynamic task migration, it would be more cost effective to use a simpler task assignment algorithm. This choice is also justified by the imprecise nature of task definition which can only make approximations of task characteristics such as IPC, interference cost, and execution costs. However, if task assignment modules make a permanent assignment of tasks to processors, the increased overhead of a more complex algorithm is justified for the incremental improvement in the assignment.

Section II gives background information on the task assignment problem. Sections III and V discuss the two models for this problem, heuristic algorithms for task assignment, and simulation results. Section IV compares the efficiency of these algorithms and Section VI discusses conclusions and directions for further research in this area.

II. Background on the Task Assignment Problem

The task assignment problem has received quite a lot of attention in the past decade. One approach to this problem has been through the development of centralized algorithms whose purpose is minimization/maximization of a clearly defined objective function that reflects the goals mentioned in Section I. Stone and Bokhari [1]–[3], [22]–[24] conducted numerous studies of the task assignment problem for nonprecedence-constrained task systems with the objective of minimizing total execution and communication costs. Other researchers have looked at task assignment to minimize interprocess communications costs (IPC) with constraints on the degree to which the processors' loads are balanced [8]; minimization of the number of tasks per processor [14]; minimization of completion time [7], [14], [15], [19]. There is general agreement about the desire to minimize IPC as well as to achieve load balancing and to maximize parallelism, and the fact that these goals often come into conflict with each other.

In these many formulations of the task assignment problem, the problem of finding an optimal assignment of tasks to processors is found to be NP-hard [11], [14] in all but very restricted cases. Thus, research has focused on the development of heuristic algorithms to find suboptimal assignments. Many of these heuristic algorithms use a graphical representation of the task-processor system such that a Max Flow/Min Cut Algorithm [10] can be utilized to find assignments of tasks to processors which minimize total execution and communication costs [14], [22], [23], [24]. This is the approach we shall take in this paper.

Before proceeding, we briefly mention some additional approaches to the task assignment problem. One such approach that is in contrast to the use of centralized algorithms involves decentralized negotiation between the individual processors and a manager working on behalf of the task force. In [20], a contract bidding protocol is used in a hierarchically structured processor system to establish the assignment of tasks to processors. In the MICROS operating system for MICRONET [25], a scheme called *wave scheduling* is used to assign tasks on a distributed system that has an underlying hierarchical virtual machine which reflects the management structure of the system. In this scheme, a task force manager requests a set of processors for its tasks and that request is transmitted in waves to lower levels of the management hierarchy. This technique is used to achieve simultaneous, decentralized task assignment for several task forces at the same time.

Some problems that occur in both these negotiation methods are that they do not adequately address the problem of minimization of IPC, and they incur significant overhead during the negotiation process. In addition, there is no concept of optimal assignment associated with this approach and thus it is difficult to evaluate a particular assignment over other possible assignments. However, the negotiation approach takes into account many more factors than the theoretically oriented algorithms described earlier.

Other techniques that have been used to study the task assignment problem include 0–1 quadratic programming [5], [18], clustering analysis [12], and queueing theory [4], [16]. A good overview of the task assignment problem can be found in [5].

III. Task Assignment to Minimize Total Execution and Communication Costs

We begin with the following model of task-processor systems and look at task assignment to minimize total execution and communication costs. Formally, we define a task force as a set of k tasks $T = \{t_1, t_2, \cdots, t_k\}$. In a distributed system containing n processors $P = \{p_1, p_2, \cdots, p_n\}$, x_{iq} denotes the execution cost of task t_i when it is assigned to and executed on processor p_q, $1 \leq i \leq k$, $1 \leq q \leq n$. The execution cost of task t_i on processor p_q depends on the work to be performed by that task and on the attributes of the processor, such as its clock rate, instruction set, existence of floating point hardware, cache memory, etc. Let c_{ij} denote the communication cost between two tasks t_i and t_j if they are assigned to different processors. Throughout our discussion, we will assume that the communication cost between two tasks executed on the same processor is negligible. These execution and communication costs are derived from an appraisal of the characteristics of the task force and of the distributed system. They may be specified explicitly by the programmer, deduced automatically by the compiler, queried from the operating system, or refined by dynamic monitoring of previous executions of the task force. For this study, we presume that the data about the execution and communication costs are somehow available and that these costs are expressible in some common unit of measurement. For tractability we ignore other attributes of the task-processor system such as memory requirements, deadlines, precedence constraints, and we assume that communication costs are independent of the communication link upon which they occur.

An assignment of tasks to processors can formally be described by a function from the set of tasks to the set of

Execution Costs			
	p_1	p_2	p_3
t_1	31	4	14
t_2	1	5	6
t_3	2	4	24
t_4	3	28	10

Communication Costs			
	t_1	t_2	t_3	t_4
t_1	0	35	3	8
t_2	35	0	6	4
t_3	3	6	0	23
t_4	8	4	23	0

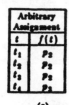

Arbitrary Assignment	
t	$f(t)$
t_1	p_2
t_2	p_2
t_3	p_2
t_4	p_2

(a)

Optimal Assignment	
t	$f(t)$
t_1	p_2
t_2	p_2
t_3	p_1
t_4	p_1

(b)

Fig. 1. Example of task assignment problem. (a) Cost of arbitrary assignment (total execution and communication costs) $= x_{12} + x_{22} + x_{32} + x_{42} + c_{14} + c_{24} + c_{34} = 4 + 5 + 4 + 10 + 8 + 4 + 23 = 58$. (b) Cost of optimal assignment (total execution and communication costs) $= x_{12} + x_{22} + x_{31} + x_{41} + c_{13} + c_{23} + c_{14} + c_{24} = 4 + 5 + 2 + 3 + 3 + 3 + 6 + 8 + 4 = 38$.

processors, $f:T \to P$. In a system of k tasks and n processors there are n^k possible assignments of tasks to processors. An optimal assignment is defined as one which minimizes the total sum of execution and communication costs incurred by that assignment. For example, consider the task processor system depicted in Fig. 1. This system is made up of four tasks and three processors. The execution costs x_{iq} and the communication costs c_{ij} are represented in tabular form. Fig. 1(a) shows the total execution and communication costs incurred by an arbitrary assignment and Fig. 1(b) shows the cost incurred by an optimal assignment (one which minimizes total execution and communication costs).

The problem of finding an assignment of tasks to processors which minimizes total execution and communication costs was elegantly analyzed using a network flow model and network flow algorithms by Stone [22], [23] and by a number of other researchers [9], [14], [15], [17], [24], [26]. Using this approach, a system of k tasks and n processors is modeled as a network in which each processor is a distinguished node and each task is an ordinary node. An edge is drawn between each pair of task nodes t_i and t_j and is given the weight c_{ij}, the communication costs between the two tasks. There is an edge from each task node t_i to each processor node p_q with the weight

$$w_{iq} = \frac{1}{n-1} \sum_{r \neq q} x_{ir} - \frac{n-2}{n-1} x_{iq}. \qquad (1)$$

An n-way cut in such a network is defined to be a set of edges which partitions the nodes of the network into n disjoint subsets with exactly one processor node in each subset and thus corresponds naturally to an assignment of tasks to

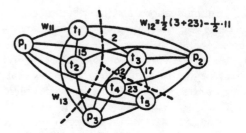

Fig. 2. n-processor network.

processors. The cost of an n-way cut is defined to be the sum of the weights on the edges in the cut. Because of the judicious choice of weights according to (1), the cost of the n-way cut is exactly equal to the total sum of execution and communication costs incurred by the corresponding assignment. This construction is illustrated in Fig. 2. In a two-processor system, an optimal assignment can be found in polynomial time utilizing Max Flow/Min Cut Algorithms [10]. However, for arbitrary n, the problem is known to be NP-hard [11]. Thus, it is necessary to turn to heuristic algorithms which are computationally efficient but which may yield suboptimal assignments.

A. Algorithm A

Our algorithm, which we shall refer to as Algorithm A consists of three parts: I) Grab, II) Lump, and III) Greedy. We first describe Algorithm A informally and then give a formal treatment of each portion of the algorithm.

The first part of Algorithm A, Grab, produces a partial (possibly complete) assignment of tasks to processors by having each processor "grab" those tasks that are strongly attracted to it (i.e., the weight is large on the edges connecting those tasks to this processor). This process is accomplished as follows.

1) For a given processor p_l we convert the n-processor network described above into a two-processor network consisting of p_l and a supernode $\bar{p}_l$ which represents the other $n - 1$ processors. (The details of this construction are described later.)

2) We then apply a Max Flow/Min Cut Algorithm to this two-processor network to find those tasks that would be assigned to p_l in the two-processor network.

3) Steps 1) and 2) are repeated for each processor, yielding a partial assignment of tasks to processors. This repeated application of the Max Flow/Min Cut Algorithm, once for each processor, constitutes *one pass* of Grab.

4) The n-processor network is then reconfigured by eliminating the tasks assigned in the previous pass and by recalculating the edge weights to reflect the partial assignment. Grab continues iteratively with the next pass using the reconfigured network.

5) Grab halts when no further assignment of tasks to processors occurs.

If the assignment is complete, it is optimal. However, it is possible that some tasks may remain unassigned. In that case, Lump tries to find a quick and dirty assignment by assigning all remaining tasks to one processor if it can be done "cheaply enough." The precise meaning of "cheaply enough" is a tunable parameter and is described later. Finally, if Lump

98

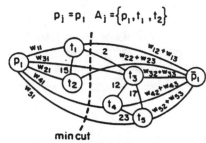

$p_j = p_1 \quad A_j = \{p_1, t_1, t_2\}$

Fig. 3. Reduced network.

cannot complete the assignment, Greedy is invoked. Greedy identifies clusters of tasks between which communication costs are "large." Greedy merges such clusters of tasks and assigns all tasks in the same cluster to the cheapest processor for that cluster. The resultant assignment may be suboptimal.

1) Details of Grab: In this section, we describe Grab in detail and prove that if Grab produces a total assignment of tasks to processors, that assignment is optimal.

Definition: Let $\Pi = \{S_1, S_2, \cdots, S_n, S'\}$ be a partition of the tasks T in an n-processor system into $n + 1$ disjoint subsets, with S' possibly empty. Let f_Π be the (partial) assignment of tasks to processors in which tasks in S_i are assigned to processor p_i, $i = 1, \cdots, n$ and tasks in S' are not assigned to any processor. The (partial) assignment f_Π is said to be a *prefix* of an optimal assignment if there exists an optimal assignment for which tasks in S_i are assigned to processor p_i, $i = 1, \cdots, n$.

Theorem 3.1: Let p_j be an arbitrary processor in an n-processor system. Consider the network G_j obtained from the network G in Fig. 2 by the following construction: the set of processor nodes $P - \{p_j\}$ are merged into a single supernode $\bar{p}_j$. For each task node t_i, $i = 1, \cdots, k$, the edges from node t_i to processor nodes p_q in the set $P - \{p_j\}$ are replaced with one edge with weight equal to the combined sum of the weights on the original edges (see Fig. 3). The minimum cut in the network G_j with p_j and $\bar{p}_j$ as source and sink, respectively, induces a partition of nodes in G_j into two disjoint subsets, A_j containing p_j and $\bar{A}_j$ containing $\bar{p}_j$. The (partial) assignment in which tasks in A_j are assigned to processor p_j is a prefix of all optimal assignments for G. A similar theorem was proved by Stone [22]. Our proof can be found in [14].[1]

Lemma 3.1: Let G be a network as described in Theorem 3.1 and let p_{j_1} and p_{j_2} be two distinct processor nodes in G. Let A_{j_1} be the set of tasks assigned to processor p_{j_1} and let A_{j_2} be the set of tasks assigned to processor p_{j_2} by the application of Theorem 3.1 to G. Then $A_{j_1} \cap A_{j_2} = \phi$. In other words, no two processors will try to grab the same task.

Proof: By Theorem 3.1, the partial assignment in which tasks in A_{j_1} are assigned to p_{j_1} is a prefix of all optimal assignments for G and the partial assignment in which tasks in

---

[1] Theorem 3.1 as stated above was shown to be incorrect by Abraham and Davidson in [27]. The last sentence of the theorem should be reworded to read "The (partial) assignment which corresponds to *a minimum cut with minimum node cardinality* in which tasks in A_j are assigned to processor p_j is a prefix of all optimal assignments for G." The corrected proof for Theorem 3.1 can be found in the Abraham and Davidson paper. Fortunately, the error in Theorem 3.1 above does not affect the operation of Algorithm A if a Max Flow/Min Cut Algorithm which finds the minimum cut of minimum cardinality (such as the Ford-Fulkerson Algorithm) is utilized.

A_{j_2} are assigned to p_{j_2} is also a prefix of all optimal assignments for G. If $A_{j_1} \cap A_{j_2} \neq \phi$, then there exists a task which is assigned to both p_{j_1} and to p_{j_2} in every optimal assignment. This result is impossible. Q.E.D.

Algorithm Grab:

- Initially, we begin with network $G^1 = G$ as defined above.
- $m = 0$ /* m is the pass number */
- Repeat until all tasks are assigned or no new tasks are assigned in a given pass.

  /* **begin pass** */
  •• $m = m + 1$
  •• For $j = 1$ to n do /* for each processor j do */

    Convert network G^m into a two-processor network with processor node p_j as source and the set $P - \{p_j\}$ as the sink (as described in Theorem 3.1) and apply the Max Flow/Min Cut Algorithm to determine the subset of tasks assigned to p_j.

    /* Note that by Lemma 3.1 no task will be assigned to more than one processor by this procedure. The resultant assignment may be partial in that there may be tasks which remain unassigned. */

  •• Let T^m denote the set of tasks which remain unassigned after m passes. Construct a network G^{m+1} from the network G^m used in the mth pass by deleting from G^m all task nodes not in T^m and by redefining the execution cost for t_i in T^m on processor p_q as

$$x_{iq}^{m+1} \triangleq x_{iq} + \sum_{r \neq q} \sum_{t_j \in S_r^m} c_{ij} \qquad (2)$$

  where S_r^m is the set of tasks assigned to processor p_r by the first m passes of Grab.

  /* In other words, x_{iq}^{m+1} is equal to the original execution cost x_{iq} plus the sum of communication costs between t_i and all tasks already assigned to processors other than p_q. */

  •• Recalculate the weight on each edge from t_i to p_q according to (1) with the new values of execution cost for all tasks in T^m.

  /* end of pass */

Theorem 3.2: An assignment produced by Algorithm Grab is a prefix of all optimal assignments for G.

Proof: The proof is by induction on the number of passes m in Algorithm Grab and can be found in the Appendix.

Lemma 3.2: If the assignment produced by Grab is complete, that assignment is optimal.

Proof: By Theorem 3.2, the assignment f produced by Grab is a prefix of all optimal assignments for G^1. Since f is a prefix of itself, it is therefore an optimal assignment. Q.E.D.

2) Details of Lump: If Grab halts with unassigned tasks remaining, Part II of Algorithm A, Lump, tests the possibility of assigning all the remaining tasks to one processor. Lump is applied to a reduced network containing the subset of tasks T^m not assigned by Grab. In the reduced network, the processor nodes are eliminated and we only look at the task nodes with edges between communicating tasks labeled with weight c_{ij}. Lump computes a lower bound L on the cost of an optimal n-way cut for the reduced network under the constraint that more than one processor be utilized in the corresponding assignment. We defined the lower bound to be

$$L = \sum_{t_i \in T^m} \min_p (x_{ip}) + \min_{l \neq r} c(t_r, t_l)$$

where $c(t_r, t_l)$ is the cost of the minimum cut for some arbitrarily chosen task t_r and task t_l.

L then is the sum of two quantities. The first term is a lower bound on the *execution* costs in the optimal n-way cut. This term is simply the execution costs incurred if each task in T^m is assigned to its cheapest processor. The second term is a lower bound on the *communication* costs incurred in an optimal n-way cut. This lower bound is computed by arbitrarily choosing some task t_r and computing all the minimum cuts between t_r and the other tasks in T^m. We then find the minimum of these mincuts and this quantity serves as a lower bound on the communication costs incurred in an optimal n-way cut because in such a cut, t_r must be separated from some other task. Based on this lower bound, the algorithm then checks to see if it would be cheaper to assign all remaining tasks to one processor. If so, the tasks in T^m are all assigned to the one processor yielding minimum total execution cost for those tasks. In this case, the resultant assignment in combination with the assignment from Part I is optimal. Otherwise, Part III is invoked to complete the assignment.

3) Details of Greedy: Part III, Algorithm Simple Greedy, locates clusters of tasks between which communication costs are "large." Tasks in a cluster are then assigned to the same processor, and the resultant assignment may be suboptimal. Let $T^m = \{t_1, t_2, \cdots, t_\gamma\}$ be the set of unassigned tasks remaining after Lump. Let G be a graph in which each task t_i is represented by a node and in which there is an edge between each pair of communicating tasks with weight c_{ij}. Greedy uses two tunable parameters: C, a cutoff value for communication costs, and X, a cutoff value for execution costs. For this implementation of Simple Greedy we defined

$C = $ the average communication costs over all pairs of tasks

$$= \sum_{1 \leq i \leq j \leq k} \frac{c_{ij}}{\binom{k}{2}}$$

and

$$X = \infty \text{ (i.e., clusters are always merged).}$$

Algorithm Simple Greedy:
- Initially, each task in T^m is in a task group by itself.
- Compute the average communication cost C as defined above.
- Mark all edges between tasks $t_1, t_2, \cdots, t_\gamma$ for which $c_{ij} \leq C$.

- While there are unmarked edges remaining
  - •• Find an unmarked edge $e = (t_i, t_j)$. Mark it. G_i is the task group containing t_i. G_j is the task group containing t_j.
  - •• If there is some processor p_q for which

    $$\sum_{t_i \sim G_i \cup G_j} x_{iq} < X \quad \text{then}$$

    - ••• Merge the two groups: $G = G_i \cup G_j$
    - ••• Mark all the edges between tasks in G_i and tasks in G_j
  - •• Else do not merge G_i and G_j
- Assign each task group to a processor which minimizes the total execution cost of the group.

Simulations

In order to evaluate the performance of Algorithm A in finding suboptimal task assignments which minimize total execution and communication costs, simulation runs were performed on a variety of typical task forces. Altogether, 536 task forces were simulated with the number of tasks ranging from 4 to 35 and the number of processors ranging from 3 to 6. The simulations were performed under the UNIX operating system running on a VAX 11/780. Optimal assignments were computed using a branch and bound backtracking algorithm.

The data used in the simulations are organized into four categories. Dataset 1 *(clustered)* consists of randomly generated task-processor systems in which tasks form clusters. Communication costs between tasks within the same cluster are on the average larger than communication costs between tasks in different clusters. Dataset 2 *(sparse)* consists of randomly generated task-processor configurations in which the communication matrix is sparse. In particular, the communication costs are nonzero for only 1/6 of the $\binom{k}{2}$ possible pairs of tasks. Dataset 3 *(actual)* consists of data representing actual task forces derived from numerical algorithms, operating systems programs, and general applications programs. In this dataset, specific information about the number of tasks and/or about which pairs of tasks communicate with each other was available in the literature. Estimates of execution and communication costs were made from information such as the number and type of messages passed between tasks, from the function of the tasks, and from raw data on these costs. Dataset 4 *(structured)* consists of task forces whose task graphs have the structure of a ring, a pipe, a tree, or a lattice. Details about these data sets can be found in [14].

The results of these simulations show Algorithm A to be very successful in finding suboptimal assignments. Fig. 4 summarizes this information by showing the distribution of the ratio T_A/T_O, where T_A is the total sum of execution and communication costs for assignments produced by Algorithm A, and T_O is the total sum of execution and communication costs for an optimal assignment. For all datasets combined, Algorithm A found an optimal assignment in 33.4 percent of the cases, and for data sets 1 and 2 Algorithm A found an optimal assignment in 46.9 percent and 47.3 percent of the cases, respectively. In 92.7 percent of the cases, the cost of the

Table 1: Distribution of T_A/T_O by Dataset							
Dataset	Total No. of Simulations	Percent of Simulations					
		(Optimal) = 1.00	≤ 1.10	≤ 1.20	≤ 1.30	≤ 1.40	≤ 1.50
All Data	536	33.4%	57.8%	74.1%	84.3%	89.9%	92.7%
(1) Clustered	228	46.9%	69.3%	80.3%	85.6%	90.9%	93.5%
(2) Sparse	55	47.3%	70.9%	85.4%	94.5%	96.3%	96.3%
(3) Actual	168	23.8%	53.0%	71.5%	84.0%	90.5%	91.7%
(4) Structured	85	7.1%	28.2%	55.3%	75.3%	82.4%	90.6%

Distribution of T_A/T_O							
Dataset	Total No. of Simulations	Percent of Simulations					
		(Optimal) = 1.00	≤ 1.10	≤ 1.20	≤ 1.30	≤ 1.40	≤ 1.50
Algorithm A	82	23.1%	62.2%	84.1%	90.2%	93.9%	96.3%
Simple Greedy	68	20.5%	52.8%	73.3%	77.7%	89.4%	93.8%
Complex Greedy	68	17.6%	55.8%	70.5%	82.2%	89.5%	93.9%
Sort Greedy	68	20.5%	54.3%	76.3%	83.6%	90.9%	92.3%

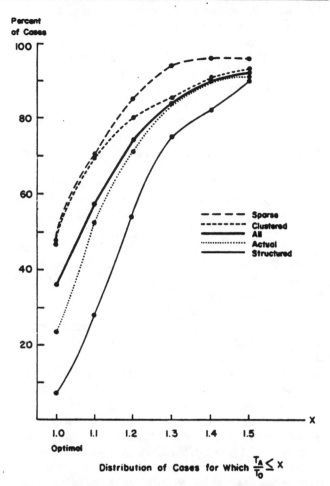

Fig. 4. Performance of Algorithm A for several data sets.

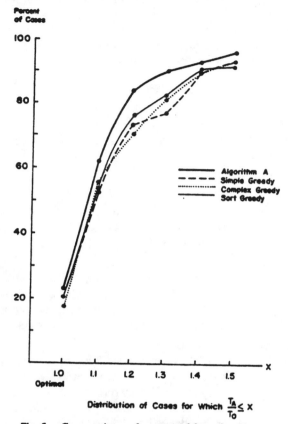

Fig. 5. Comparative performance of four algorithms.

assignment produced by Algorithm A was less than 1.5 times greater than the cost of an optimal assignment. Ratios greater than 2.0 were found in only three cases of the 536 cases. The worst ratio T_A/T_O was 2.7. Algorithm A did not perform as well on the *actual* and *structured* data sets because Greedy presumes some clustering of tasks while the data sets did not exhibit this feature.

The Simple Greedy phase of Algorithm A was initially designed to "finish up" assignments that were not completed by Grab and Lump. However, because of the efficiency of Simple Greedy, we decided to investigate its performance alone. Fig. 5 compares the performance of the phases of Algorithm A to that of Simple Greedy and two augmented versions of Simple Greedy which we shall call Complex Greedy and Sort Greedy.

Simple Greedy is the Greedy algorithm of Algorithm A.

Complex Greedy is an augmented version of Simple Greedy in which an estimate is made of the cost of assigning

two task groups to different processors. Complex Greedy merges the two groups if and only if there exists a processor for which the cost of assigning all tasks in the two groups is smaller than the estimate.

Sort Greedy is an augmented version of Simple Greedy in which communication edges are examined in order of nonincreasing cost. (In Simple Greedy, these edges are examined in random order.) The sorting of communication edges adds a factor of $O(e \log e)$ to the complexity of the algorithm, where e is the number of communication edges with nonzero cost.

From Fig. 5, we see that the performance of Simple Greedy was close to that of the more complex Algorithm A. For example, Algorithm A found an optimal assignment in 23.1 percent of the cases while Simple Greedy found an optimal assignment in 20.5 percent of the cases. We conclude that when an assignment is subject to further adjustment through dynamic task migration, efficient algorithms like Simple Greedy are more useful for a quick initial assignment of tasks to processors. If the assignment is permanent, the better performance of Algorithm A is worth the increased overhead.

From the table we also see that there was no significant difference in the performance of the three Greedy Algorithms. It is surprising that Sort Greedy did not yield better results.

One would expect that elimination of communication edges in the order most expensive to least expensive would be more effective in the identification of communicating clusters and thus yield better assignments. One possible explanation for this phenomenon is the fact that in both Simple Greedy and Sort Greedy, communication edges whose costs are less than the average communication cost are eliminated from consideration. As a result, primarily intercluster edges remain, reducing the probability that tasks from two different clusters will be merged. The order in which the communication edges are examined would thus be less crucial.

IV. Complexity of Algorithms

The complexity of each of the parts of Algorithm A is discussed below. *Let e be the number of edges in the network representation of a task–processor system with k tasks and n processors.*

Grab: $O(nk^2e \log k)$

There exist Max Flow/Min Cut Algorithms of complexity $O(ke \log k)$ [10] and there will be at most k total iterations with n min cuts per iteration.

Lump: $O(k^2e \log k)$

Computation of the lower bound L on the cost of an n-way cut when tasks are assigned to more than one processor involves finding $k - 1$ min cuts in a network with task nodes only.

Simple Greedy: $O(e)$ or $O(nk^2)$

If $X = \infty$, then Simple Greedy simply examines each communication edge. If $X < \infty$, Simple Greedy must check to see if there is a processor to which all the tasks in the groups to be merged can be assigned.

V. Task Assignment with Interference Costs

A major flaw in the use of total execution and communication costs as the performance criteria to be optimized is that no explicit advantage is given to concurrency. In other words, no explicit effort is made to utilize many processors in order to reduce the completion time of the set of tasks. Some degree of parallelism is introduced into task assignments as a byproduct of the goal of avoiding high total costs, but concurrency is not sought as a goal itself. Thus, the use of total execution and communication costs as the performance measure often yields assignments which utilize only a few of the available processors.

For example, in the two-processor task system shown in Fig. 6, an assignment which minimizes total execution and communication costs is shown with solid lines (task t_1 assigned to processor p_1 and tasks t_2 through t_6 assigned to processor p_2). The assignment shown with dotted lines (t_1 through t_3 on p_1 and t_4 through t_6 on p_2) has the same cost. We note that the latter assignment yields a higher degree of parallelism. Use of total execution and communication costs as the performance criterion fails to discriminate between these two assignments, and the Max Flow/Min Cut Algorithm will select the former assignment. In systems with n identical processors, the use of total execution and communication costs as the criteria for optimality is even more undesirable since an optimal assignment always assigns all tasks to one processor (thereby eliminating all communication costs).

For this reason, we present the concept of interference costs which are incurred when two tasks are assigned to the same processor. Interference costs reflect the degree of incompatibility between two tasks based on characteristics of the two tasks and the processors to which they may be mutually assigned. For example, a pair of tasks that are both highly CPU bound could have greater interference cost than a pair in which one task is CPU bound and the other performs a lot of I/O. Interference costs serve as forces of repulsion between tasks to counterbalance the forces of attraction due to (high) communication costs. We assume interference costs are derived somehow from user specifications, compiler analyses, and dynamic monitoring of the task force; and that a common unit of measure can be found for execution, communication, and interference costs.

In particular, let $T = \{t_1, \cdots, t_k\}$ be the set of tasks, $P = \{p_1, \cdots, p_n\}$ be the set of processors, and let x_{ij}, $1 \leq i \leq k$, $1 \leq j \leq n$ and c_{ij}, $1 \leq i, j \leq k$ be the execution costs and communication costs, respectively, as defined before. Let $I_q(i, j)$, $1 \leq i, j \leq k$, $1 \leq q \leq n$ be the interference cost incurred if tasks t_i and t_j are assigned to the same processor p_q. We assume that $I_q(i, j) = I_q(j, i)$. We define an optimal assignment as one which minimizes the total sum of execution, communication, and interference costs.

Interference costs can be attributed to two main factors. The first factor affects every pair of tasks that are assigned to the same processor and involves contention between tasks for the resources of the processor to which the tasks are both assigned. In particular, when several tasks execute on the same processor, they incur overhead due to process switching in a multiprogrammed environment and overhead due to synchronization for access to shared resources such as memory, I/O devices, CPU time, etc. We shall refer to the portion of interference costs attributable to contention for resources as *processor-based interference costs*. The second factor which contributes to interference cost involves only those tasks which communicate with each other. When two communicating tasks are assigned to the same processor, they may utilize the interprocess communication services provided by that processor in order to send and receive messages. Thus, communicating tasks incur an interference cost due to contention for messages buffers and synchronization for message passing. We shall refer to the portion of interference costs attributable to contention for these latter resources as *communication-based interference costs*. We note that the communication-based interference costs which are incurred when two communicating tasks are assigned to the same processor are always smaller in magnitude than the communication costs incurred when the two tasks are assigned to different processors. In both cases, the communicating tasks incur costs because they utilize the interprocess communication facilities. However, if the tasks reside on different processors, communication costs include, in addition, transit delay incurred by sending messages through the communication subnetwork.

Thus, the interference cost between two tasks t_i and t_j which

Execution Costs		
	p_1	p_2
t_1	20	50
t_2	25	10
t_3	5	20
t_4	10	20
t_5	10	20
t_6	50	10

Communication Costs						
	t_1	t_2	t_3	t_4	t_5	t_6
t_1	0	15	0	0	0	0
t_2	0	0	50	0	0	0
t_3	0	0	0	15	0	0
t_4	0	0	0	0	50	0
t_5	0	0	0	0	0	15
t_6	0	0	0	0	0	0

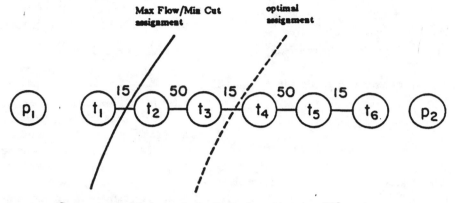

$$\text{Cost} = z_{11} + z_{22} + z_{32} + z_{42} + z_{52} + z_{62} + c_{12} = 115$$

$$\text{Cost} = z_{11} + z_{21} + z_{31} + z_{42} + z_{52} + z_{62} + z_{34} = 115$$

(a)

Interference Costs						
	t_1	t_2	t_3	t_4	t_5	t_6
t_1	0	10	10	10	10	10
t_2	10	0	10	10	10	10
t_3	10	10	0	10	10	10
t_4	10	10	10	0	10	10
t_5	10	10	10	10	0	10
t_6	10	10	10	10	10	0

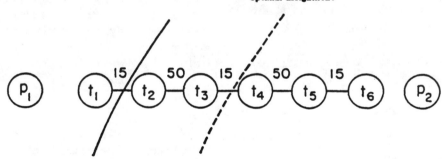

$$\text{Cost} = z_{11} + z_{22} + z_{32} + z_{42} + z_{52} + z_{62} + c_{12}$$
$$+ I_{23} + I_{24} + I_{25} + I_{26} + I_{34} + I_{35} + I_{36}$$
$$+ I_{45} + I_{46} + I_{56}$$
$$= 115 + \binom{5}{2} \cdot 10$$
$$= 215$$

$$\text{Cost} = z_{11} + z_{21} + z_{31} + z_{42} + z_{52} + z_{62} + c_{34}$$
$$+ I_{12} + I_{13} + I_{23} + I_{45} + I_{46} + I_{56}$$
$$= 115 + \binom{3}{2} \cdot 10 + \binom{3}{2} \cdot 10$$
$$= 175$$

(b)

Fig. 6. (a) Poor assignment without interference costs. (b) Better assignment with interference costs.

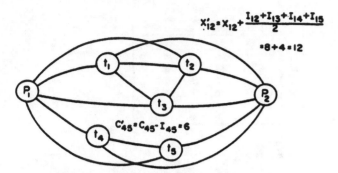

$$x'_{12} = x_{12} + \frac{I_{12} + I_{13} + I_{14} + I_{15}}{2}$$

$$= 8 + 4 = 12$$

$$c_{45} = C_{45} - I_{45} = 6.$$

Fig. 7. Processor-independent interference costs.

arises when they are both assigned to processor p_q can be expressed as the sum of two components:

$$I_q(i, j) = I_q^P(i, j) + I_q^C(i, j)$$

where $I_q^P(i, j)$ is the processor-based component of interference cost and $I_q^C(i, j)$ is the communication-based component. The communication-based component satisfies the inequality

$$I_q^C(i, j) \le c_{ij}.$$

In the next three sections, we show that the network flow model can be successfully extended to several interesting cases which consider execution, communication, and interference costs. Simulation results show that the addition of interference cost to the model does indeed yield assignments with greater concurrency.

A. Interference Costs which are Independent of Processor

In this section, we consider task-processor systems for which interference cost is independent of the processor to which the two tasks t_i and t_j are assigned. That is, $I_p(i, j) = I_{ij}$. An n-processor system can be modeled as a network in which an n-way cut corresponds to an assignment of tasks to processors. Let the edge from each task node t_i to each processor node p_q have the weight

$$w_{iq} = \frac{1}{n-1} \sum_{r \ne q} x_{ir} - \frac{n-2}{n-1} x_{iq} + \frac{1}{2(n-1)} \sum_{1 \le l \le k} I_{il}.$$

Let the edge between two task nodes t_i and t_j have the weight

$$c'_{ij} = c_{ij} - I_{ij}.$$

This construction is illustrated in Fig. 7.

Theorem 4.1: An n-way cut in such a network has cost equal to the total sum of execution, communication, and interference costs for the assignment corresponding to that cut. (Thus, a minimum cut yields an assignment which minimizes the total sum of execution, communication, and interference costs.) The proof of this theorem can be found in the Appendix.

It is known that the problem of finding an optimal n-way cut in a network is NP-complete and thus the problem of finding an optimal assignment is also NP-complete. However, because an optimal assignment is equivalent to an n-way cut, Algorithm A of Section III can be applied to find suboptimal assignments with near minimal values for total execution, communication, and interference costs.

If we further assume that $I_{ij} \le c_{ij}$, $1 \le i, j \le k$, then $c'_{ij} = I_{ij} - c_{ij} > 0$ and the Max Flow/Min Cut Algorithm can be applied to find optimal assignments for two-processor systems. For n-processor systems, Algorithm A described above can be applied to find suboptimal assignments. For arbitrary I_{ij}, the Max Flow/Min Cut Algorithm cannot be invoked because there may be edges with negative weights in the network representation of the task-processor system. However, in this case, the Simple Greedy Algorithm of Algorithm A can be applied to find suboptimal assignments.

B. Simulations

Simulations were performed 1) to demonstrate that the use of interference costs does indeed yield assignments with greater parallelism and 2) to examine the performance of Algorithm A in finding assignments which minimize the total sum of execution, communication, and interference costs. The simulations used data representing typical task-processor configurations generated from the four datasets described in Section III. For each configuration, interference costs were generated from the uniform distributions over the intervals [1, $2\bar{c}$], [1, $(3/2)\bar{c}$], [1, $(\bar{c}/2)$], and [1, $(\bar{c}/10)$], where $\bar{c}$ is the average communication cost for a particular task-processor system.

For each task-processor configuration, we measured optimal and suboptimal values of *total costs* for the configuration with execution, communication, and interference costs and also for the same configuration without interference costs (execution and communication costs only). In order to assess the degree of parallelism attained by assignments, we also measured optimal and suboptimal values of *completion time* for each task-processor configuration, both with and without interference costs. Our definition of *completion time* is a natural extension to the classical definition of *latest finishing time* used in deterministic scheduling theory for multiprocessor systems with execution costs only [6]. In the model with execution and communication costs, we define *completion time* as

$$\omega_f = \max_{1 \le q \le n} \left(\sum_{f(t_i) = p_q} x_i + \sum_{\substack{f(t_i) = p_q \\ f(t_j) \ne p_q}} c_{ij} \right)$$

i.e., the total execution and communication costs incurred on the processor for which these costs are maximal over all processors. Similarly, in the model with execution, communication, and interference costs, *completion time* is defined as

$$\omega_f = \max_{1 \le q \le n} \left(\sum_{f(t_i) = p_q} x_i + \sum_{\substack{f(t_i) = p_q \\ f(t_j) \ne p_q}} c_{ij} + \sum_{\substack{f(t_i) = p_q \\ f(t_j) = p_q}} I_{ij} \right)$$

i.e., the total sum of execution, communication, and interference costs incurred on the processor for which this total is maximal over all the processors. The concept of *completion time* is illustrated in Fig. 8 using a Gantt diagram. In this figure, the communication costs are depicted as occurring in one lump, but is should be kept in mind that these costs are actually dispersed in time throughout the execution of the tasks.

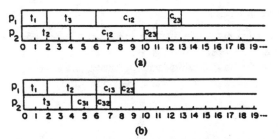

Fig. 8. Completion time (execution and communication costs). (a) One assignment $\omega_f = 13$. (b) Optimal assignment $\omega_f = 9$.

		Distribution of ω_T/ω_0					
Model	Total No. of Simulations	Percent of Simulations					
		(Optimal) = 1.00	≤ 1.10	≤1.20	≤1.50	≤ 2.00	≤ 2.75
With l_u	130	22.0%	61.0%	84.7%	98.3%	100.0%	100.0%
No l_u	130	3.4%	10.1%	18.6%	49.1%	83.0%	100.0%

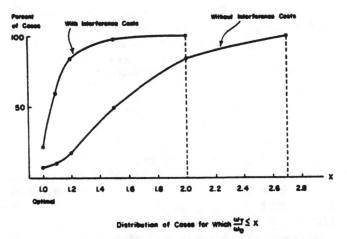

Fig. 9. Degree of concurrency attained by assignments that are optimal w.r.t. total costs.

The five values that we measured are listed below. The interpretation of the terms *total cost* and *completion time* depend on whether the configuration includes interference costs or not.

T_A, the total cost of an assignment by Algorithm A;
T_O, the optimal value of total cost;
ω_A, the completion time of an assignment by Algorithm A;
ω_O, the optimal value of completion time;
ω_T, the completion time of an assignment which optimizes total cost.

In each of the figures to be discussed below, we compare the ratio of suboptimal costs to optimal costs. For example, the ratio ω_A/ω_O reflects the performance of Algorithm A in finding assignments with minimal completion time. If the ratio is 1.0, Algorithm A's assignment is optimal. If the ratio is 1.10, Algorithm A's assignment is 10 percent greater than optimal, and so on. In each figure, results are presented both in table form and graphically.

Figs. 9 and 10 demonstrate empirically that addition of interference costs to the model yields assignments with a high

		Distribution of ω_A/ω_O					
Model	Total No. of Simulations	Percent of Simulations					
		(Optimal) = 1.00	≤ 1.10	≤1.20	≤1.50	≤ 2.00	≤ 2.75
With l_u	130	6.7%	18.6%	45.7%	93.2%	100.0%	100.0%
No l_u	130	1.6%	5.0%	10.1%	42.3%	86.4%	100.0%

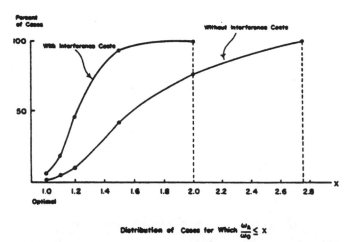

Distribution of Cases for Which $\frac{\omega_A}{\omega_O} \leq x$

Fig. 10. Degree of concurrency attained by assignments that are suboptimal w.r.t. total costs.

degree of concurrency. Fig. 9 shows this is true for assignments which have optimal values for total costs while Fig. 10 shows this is also true for suboptimal assignments found by Algorithm A. Figs. 9 and 10 also compare the degree of concurrency attained in assignments for the interference cost model to the degree of concurrency attained in assignments in the model without interference costs. While the improvement is as expected, the magnitude of the improvement is significant.

Fig. 9 shows the distribution of the ratio ω_T/ω_O for systems which include interference costs and for systems without interference costs. Recall that ω_T is the completion time of an assignment which is optimal with respect to total costs while ω_O is the optimal value of completion time. Thus, the ratio ω_T/ω_O reflects the degree of concurrency attained by assignments with an optimal value for total costs. From the percentage figures in the first row of the table in Fig. 9, we see that assignments with an optimal value for total costs also have excellent values for completion time. For example, 22 percent of the assignments were also optimal with respect to completion time, 61.0 percent of the assignments are less than 1.1 times the optimal value, and 98.3 percent of the assignments were less than 1.5 times the optimal value. We also see that use of interference costs yields a marked improvement in the distribution of the ratio ω_T/ω_O. For example, when interference costs are included, 98.3 percent of the assignments that are optimal with respect to total costs also have completion times that are less than 1.5 times the optimal completion time. However, without interference costs, that figure is only 49.1 percent. While this difference is as expected, the magnitude of the difference is notable.

Fig. 10 shows the distribution of the ratio ω_A/ω_O for systems with interference costs and for systems without interference costs. Recall that ω_A is the completion time of an assignment

		Distribution of T_A/T_o					
Model	Total No. of Simulations	Percent of Simulations					
		(Optimal) = 1.00	≤ 1.10	≤ 1.20	≤ 1.30	≤ 1.40	≤ 1.50
With I_s	130	3.0%	12.3%	27.9%	46.1%	67.6%	78.4%
No I_s	356	25.0%	50.6%	68.5%	80.3%	87.6%	91.3%

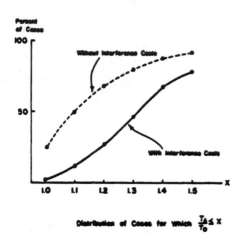

Fig. 11. Performance of Algorithm A on the interference cost model.

found by Algorithm A while ω_O is the optimal value of completion time. This ratio demonstrates the degree of concurrency attained by suboptimal assignments found by Algorithm A. The results from this table show that Algorithm A finds assignments with a good degree of concurrency when interference costs are included in the model. For example, when interference costs are included, 93.2 percent of assignments found by Algorithm A have completion times that are less than 1.5 times the optimal completion time. However, in the model without interference costs, only 42.3 percent of the assignments found by Algorithm A have a completion time that is less than 1.5 times the optimal value.

Fig. 11 demonstrates the performance of Algorithm A in finding suboptimal assignments which minimize total execution, communication, and interference costs. (In other words, we now ignore the issue of concurrency and just look at the performance of Algorithm A in finding suboptimal assignments in the interference cost model.) The table shows the distribution of the ratio T_A/T_O for Algorithm A with and without interference costs. It is clear that Algorithm A does perform better for Stone's model than for the model with interference costs added. For example, without interference costs, Algorithm A found an optimal assignment in 25 percent of the cases. However, with interference costs, Algorithm A found an optimal assignment in only 3 percent of the cases. Similarly, the cost of 91.3 percent of the assignments were less than 1.5 times the cost of an optimal assignment without interference costs, but this figure fell to only 78.4 percent with interference costs. Thus, Algorithm A is not well suited for minimizing total costs when interference costs are added to the model. This result is not surprising since Algorithm A was designed for Stone's model and thus considers interference costs only during the Grab part of the algorithm.

To summarize,

1) In the model with interference costs, an assignment with optimal total costs also has excellent values of completion time. In the model without interference costs, an assignment with optimal total costs often has poor values of completion time.

2) This same trend holds for suboptimal assignments found by Algorithm A.

3) Algorithm A is not as well suited as a heuristic for the model with interference costs and we should investigate other heuristics for this model.

Thus, we have shown that it is desirable to augment Stone's model with interference costs and that heuristics designed to minimize total execution, communication, and interference costs will also yield assignments with a high degree of concurrency. However, Algorithm A is not a useful heuristic for this purpose.

C. Arbitrary Interference Costs

In this section, we consider the general cost when interference cost is dependent on both the processor and the tasks involved. Let $I_q(i, j)$ be the interference cost incurred when tasks t_i and t_j are both assigned to processor p_q. We will show that for task-processor systems with two processors and under the assumption that

$$\frac{I_1(i, j) + I_2(i, j)}{2} \le c_{ij} \qquad (3)$$

an optimal assignment of tasks to processors can be found using network flow algorithms. This assumption states that the average interference cost between two tasks over the two processors be less than or equal to the communication costs between the two tasks. Again, if we consider interference costs as arising from the memory contention and synchronization overhead between communicating tasks, it is reasonable to make an even stronger assumption that

$$I_q(i, j) \le c_{ij}; \qquad q = 1, 2$$

and thus (3) certainly holds true.

We represent the task-processor system as a network as usual. The edge from task node t_i to processor node p_q is given the weight

$$x'_{iq} = x_{iq} + \sum_{1 \le l \le k} \frac{I_q(i, l)}{2}$$

and the edge between task nodes t_i and t_j is given the weight

$$c'_{ij} = c_{ij} - \frac{I_1(i, j) + I_2(i, j)}{2}.$$

This construction is illustrated in Fig. 12.

Theorem 4.2: A cut in such a network has cost equal to the total sum of execution, communication, and interference costs for the assignment corresponding to that cut. (Thus, a minimum cut yields an assignment which minimizes the total sum of execution, communication, and interference costs.)

106

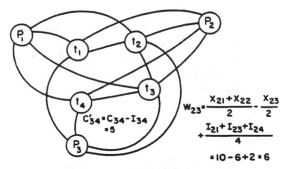

$$W_{23} = \frac{x_{21}+x_{22}}{2} - \frac{x_{23}}{2}$$
$$+ \frac{I_{21}+I_{23}+I_{24}}{4}$$
$$= 10 - 6 + 2 = 6$$

$C'_{34} = C_{34} - I_{34}$
$= 5$

Fig. 12. Arbitrary interference costs.

The proof is analogous to the proof of Theorem 4.1 (see Appendix) and can be found in [14]. Again, the Max Flow/Min Cut Algorithm can be applied to find optimal assignments for the two-processor case.

For the n-processor case, a suitable model has not yet been found.

VI. Conclusions and Areas for Further Research

Our investigation of the static task assignment problem has resulted in the development of several heuristic algorithms for Stone's model which considers execution and communication costs only, and for our model which introduces the concept of interference costs. Simulation results indicate that these algorithms perform well on a variety of task–processor systems. In addition, we have shown that highly efficient algorithms perform almost as well as more complex ones and thus are feasible for use in practical applications.

One current research continues to look at the task assignment problem. An obvious extension to this research is to increase the complexity of the model to include such factors as memory requirements, deadlines, precedence constraints, and communication link loads. It will be interesting to see how much complexity we can include in the model before we are forced to move from elegant graph theoretic algorithms to increasingly empirical techniques. We are also interested in characteristics of the algorithms themselves. In particular, a task assignment algorithm should incorporate qualities such as

monotonicity—as the resources of the distributed system increase (e.g., more processors available), the cost of the assignment produced by the algorithm should not increase. In other words, the algorithm should not display anomalous behavior such as the FIFO page replacement algorithm.

sensitivity—since execution, communication, and interference costs will always be approximations, the algorithm should not be overly sensitive to small variations in these quantities.

robustness (fault tolerance)—the algorithm should adapt to failures in the system such as removal of nodes, failure of communication links, etc.

In addition, we are looking more closely at the relationship between the two goals of achieving load balancing among processors and the minimization of interprocess communication (IPC). There is general agreement that these two goals are often in conflict with one another, but there are no data

available about the degree and circumstances for this conflict. Experiments are underway to determine parameters of the task force that may affect the degree of conflict between these two goals. In addition, while there is a quantifiable measure for IPC, a precise definition of load balancing does not exist. Completion time is often used as a measure of the degree to which an algorithm achieves load balancing, but this metric can yield fairly unbalanced assignments. We are looking into new ways to measure load balancing within the context of the task assignment problem.

Task assignment thus continues to offer a wide variety of challenging problems. While much work has focused on this problem by itself, it is also time to integrate our view of task assignment into the overall picture of task management (task definition, task assignment, task scheduling, and task migration)—to see its place in the total life cycle of the task force in the distributed system.

Appendix

Below are the proofs for Theorems 3.2 and 4.1.

Theorem 3.2: An assignment produced by Algorithm Grab is a prefix of all optimal assignments for G.

Proof: We prove the theorem by induction on the number of passes m in Algorithm Grab.

a) Suppose Grab halts after one pass. In one pass of Algorithm Grab, the Max Flow/Min Cut Algorithm is applied for each processor node as described in Theorem 3.1 to assign tasks to each processor. Let S_i^1 be the set of tasks assigned to processor p_i in pass 1 of Grab, $i = 1, \cdots, n$. By Theorem 3.1, each of the n individual assignments which assigns S_i^1 to one processor p_i is a prefix of every optimal assignment. The assignment produced by pass 1 of Grab can be represented as the union of these n individual assignments and thus is also a prefix of every optimal assignment.

b) We now prove the theorem for $m + 1$ passes of Algorithm Grab. Let Grab be applied to network G^1. Suppose that after m passes it produces a partial assignment f^m represented by a partition Π^m of the tasks of G^1:

$$\Pi^m = \{S_1^m, \cdots, S_n^m, T^m\}$$

where S_i^m is the set of tasks assigned to processor p_i and T^m is the set of tasks which remain unassigned. By our induction hypothesis, we know that the (partial) assignment f^m forms a prefix of every optimal assignment for G^1. The cost of any optimal assignment f_{OPT} is

$$C(f_{OPT}) = \sum_{\substack{f_{OPT}(t_i)=p_q \\ t_i \in T}} x_{iq} + \sum_{\substack{f_{OPT}(t_i) \neq f_{OPT}(t_j) \\ t_i, t_j \in T}} c_{ij}$$

$$= \sum_{\substack{f_{OPT}(t_i)=p_q \\ t_i \in T-T^m}} x_{iq} + \sum_{\substack{f_{OPT}(t_i)=p_q \\ t_i \in T^m}} x_{iq} + \sum_{\substack{f_{OPT}(t_i) \neq f_{OPT}(t_j) \\ t_i, t_j \in T-T^m}} c_{ij}$$

$$+ \sum_{\substack{f_{OPT}(t_i) \neq f_{OPT}(t_j) \\ t_i, t_j \in T^m}} c_{ij} + \sum_{\substack{f_{OPT}(t_i) \neq f_{OPT}(t_j) \\ t_i \in T-T^m \\ t_j \in T^m}} c_{ij}.$$

By rearranging terms, we have

$$C(f_{OPT}) = C(f^m) + C[T^m]$$

where

$$C(f^m) = \sum_{\substack{f_{OPT}(t_i) = p_q \\ t_i \in T - T^m}} x_{iq} + \sum_{\substack{f_{OPT}(t_i) \neq f_{OPT}(t_j) \\ t_i, t_j \in T - T^m}} c_{ij}$$

$$C[T^m] = \sum_{\substack{f_{OPT}(t_i) = p_q \\ t_i \in T^m}} x_{iq} + \sum_{\substack{f_{OPT}(t_i) \neq f_{OPT}(t_j) \\ t_i, t_j \in T^m}} c_{ij} + \sum_{\substack{f_{OPT}(t_j) \neq f^m(t_i) \\ t_i \in T - T^m \\ t_j \in T^m}} c_{ij}.$$

In other words, the cost of any optimal assignment for G^1 can be broken down into two components: 1) the cost $C(f^m)$ of first assigning tasks in $T - T^m$ according to m passes of Grab and 2) the cost $C[T^m]$ of *subsequently* assigning tasks in T^m. Since tasks in $T - T^m$ must be assigned according to f^m in every optimal assignment for G^1, $C(f^m)$ is fixed and thus an optimal assignment for G^1 is one which minimizes $C[T^m]$.

Now consider the network G^{m+1} constructed for the $(m + 1)$st pass of Grab. By definition of Grab, $m + 1$ passes on G^1 can be viewed as m passes on G^1 followed by one pass on G^{m+1}. Thus, in order to prove that the (partial) assignment resulting from $m + 1$ passes on G^1 is a prefix of all optimal assignments for G^1, we need to show that the assignment produced by one pass on G^{m+1} is a prefix of all assignments of tasks in T^m which minimize $C[T^m]$. By construction of G^{m+1}, we know that an optimal assignment $f_{OPT'}$ for G^{m+1} minimizes $C[T^m]$ as shown below:

$$C(f_{OPT'}) = \sum_{\substack{f_{OPT'}(t_i) = p_q \\ t_i \in T^m}} x_{iq}^{m+1} + \sum_{\substack{f_{OPT'}(t_i) \neq f_{OPT'}(t_j) \\ t_i \in T^m}} c_{ij}$$

which by (2)

$$= \sum_{\substack{f_{OPT'}(t_i) = p_q \\ t_i \in T^m}} x_{iq} + \sum_{\substack{f_{OPT'}(t_i) \neq f^m(t_i) \\ t_i \in T - T^m \\ t_j \in T^m}} c_{ij} + \sum_{\substack{f_{OPT'}(t_i) \neq f_{OPT'}(t_j) \\ t_i \in T^m}} c_{ij}$$

$$= c[T^m].$$

Also, by our base induction hypothesis a), the (partial) assignment produced by one pass of Grab on G^{m+1} is a prefix of all optimal assignments $f_{OPT'}$ for G^{m+1}. Thus, the (partial) assignment produced by m passes on G^1 followed by one pass on G^{m+1} is a prefix of all optimal assignments for G^1. Or equivalently, the (partial) assignment produced by $m + 1$ passes on G^1 is a prefix of all optimal assignments for G^1.   Q.E.D.

Theorem 4.1: An n-way cut in such a network has cost equal to the total sum of execution, communication, and interference costs for the assignment corresponding to that cut.

(Thus, a minimum cut yields an assignment which minimizes the total sum of execution, communication, and interference costs.)

Proof: For a given assignment, if two tasks, t_i and t_j, are assigned to the same processor, say p_1, then tasks nodes t_i and t_j are cut off from all processor nodes other than p_1. Thus, the $n - 1$ edges from t_i to the processor nodes other than p_1 are cut, incurring a cost of

$$\sum_{r \neq 1} w_{ir} = x_{i1} + (n-1) \times \frac{1}{2(n-1)} \sum_{1 \leq l \leq k} I_{il}.$$

Similarly, the $n - 1$ edges from t_j to the processor nodes other than p_1 are cut, incurring a cost of

$$\sum_{r \neq 1} w_{jr} = x_{j1} + (n-1) \times \frac{1}{2(n-1)} \sum_{1 \leq l \leq k} I_{jl}.$$

Considering only the interference costs between t_i and t_j, we see that the combined cost is equal to

$$x_{i1} + x_{j1} + I_{ij}.$$

Hence, when two tasks are assigned to the same processor, the incurred cost is equal to the sum of execution and interference costs.

If t_i and t_j are assigned to different processors, e.g., t_i to p_1 and t_j to p_2, the edges from t_i to all processor nodes other than p_1 are cut, and the edges from t_j to all processor nodes other than p_2 are cut. Moreover, the edges between t_i and t_j are cut, incurring the costs

$$\sum_{r \neq 1} w_{ir} = x_{i1} + \frac{1}{2} \sum_{1 \leq l \leq k} I_{il}$$

$$\sum_{r \neq 2} w_{jr} = x_{j2} + \frac{1}{2} \sum_{1 \leq l \leq k} I_{jl}$$

and

$$c_{ij} - I_{ij},$$

respectively. Again, considering only the interference costs between t_i and t_j, we see that the incurred cost is equal to

$$x_{i1} + \frac{I_{ij}}{2} + x_{j2} + \frac{I_{ij}}{2} + c_{ij} - I_{ij} = x_{i1} + x_{j2} + c_{ij}.$$

Thus, when two tasks are assigned to different processors, the total cost incurred is equal to the sum of execution and communication costs but no interference costs. This reasoning may be extended to all possible pairs of tasks. Hence, the cost of an n-way cut is equal to the total sum of execution, communication, and interference costs incurred by the corresponding assignment. The cost of an assignment f is given by

$$c_f = \sum_{q=1}^{n} \left(\sum_{f(t_i)=p_q} \sum_{r \neq q} w_{ir} \right) + \sum_{f(t_i) \neq f(t_j)} c'_{ij}$$

$$= \sum_{q=1}^{n} \sum_{f(t_i)=p_q} \left(\sum_{r \neq q} \left(\frac{1}{n-1} \sum_{s \neq r} x_{is} - \frac{n-2}{n-1} x_{ir} \right) \right. \\ \left. + \frac{1}{2(n-1)} \sum_{1 \leq j \leq k} I_{ij} \right) + \sum_{f(t_i) \neq f(t_j)} c'_{ij}$$

$$= \sum_{q=1}^{n} \sum_{f(t_i)=p_q} \left(x_{iq} + \sum_{r \neq q} \frac{1}{2(n-1)} \sum_{1 \leq j \leq k} I_{ij} \right) + \sum_{f(t_i) \neq f(t_j)} c'_{ij}$$

$$= \sum_{q=1}^{n} \sum_{f(t_i)=p_q} \left(x_{iq} + (n-1) \times \frac{1}{2(n-1)} \sum_{1 \leq j \leq k} I_{ij} \right) \\ + \sum_{f(t_i) \neq f(t_j)} c'_{ij}$$

$$= \sum_{q=1}^{n} \sum_{f(t_i)=p_q} \left(x_{iq} + \sum_{1 \leq j \leq k} \frac{I_{ij}}{2} \right) + \sum_{f(t_i) \neq f(t_j)} c'_{ij}$$

$$= \sum_{q=1}^{n} \sum_{f(t_i)=p_q} x_{iq} + \sum_{q=1}^{n} \sum_{f(t_i)=p_q} \sum_{1 \leq j \leq k} \frac{I_{ij}}{2} \\ + \left(\sum_{f(t_i) \neq f(t_j)} c_{ij} - \sum_{f(t_i) \neq f(t_j)} I_{ij} \right)$$

$$= \sum_{q=1}^{n} \sum_{f(t_i)=p_q} x_{iq} + \sum_{f(t_i) \neq f(t_j)} c_{ij} + 2 \times \left(\sum_{f(t_i)=f(t_j)} \frac{I_{ij}}{2} \right) \\ + 2 \times \left(\sum_{f(t_i) \neq f(t_j)} \frac{I_{ij}}{2} \right) - \sum_{f(t_i) \neq f(t_j)} I_{ij}$$

$$= \sum_{q=1}^{n} \sum_{f(t_i)=p_q} x_{iq} + \sum_{f(t_i) \neq f(t_j)} c_{ij} + \sum_{q=1}^{n} \sum_{f(t_i)=f(t_j)=p_q} I_{ij}$$

= total execution, communication, and
interference costs incurred by f.   Q.E.D.

REFERENCES

[1] S. H. Bokhari, "Dual processor scheduling with dynamic reassignment," *IEEE Trans. Software Eng.*, vol. SE-5, pp. 341-349, July 1979.

[2] ——, "Optimal assignments in dual-processor distributed systems under varying load conditions," ICASE Rep. 79-14, July 1979.

[3] ——, "A shortest tree algorithm for optimal assignments across space and time in a distributed processor system," *IEEE Trans. Software Eng.*, vol. SE-7, pp. 583-589, Nov. 1981.

[4] Y. C. Chow and W. H. Kohler, "Models of dynamic load balancing in a heterogeneous multiple processor system," *IEEE Trans. Comput.*, pp. 354-361, May 1979.

[5] W. W. Chu, L. J. Holloway, M. T. Lan, and Kemal Efe, "Task allocation in distributed data processing," *IEEE Computer*, pp. 57-69, Nov. 1980.

[6] E. G. Coffman and P. J. Denning, *Operating Systems Theory*. Englewood Cliffs, NJ: Prentice-Hall, 1973.

[7] D. H. Cornett and M. A. Franklin, "Scheduling independent tasks with communications," Washington Univ., Dept. Elec. Eng., Tech. Rep., 1979.

[8] K. Efe, "Heuristic models of task assignment scheduling in distributed systems," *IEEE Computer*, pp. 50-56, June 1982.

[9] O. J. El-Dessouki, "Program partitioning and load balancing in network computers," Ph.D. dissertation, Illinois Instit. Technol., Dec. 1978.

[10] Z. Galil, S. Micali, and H. Gabow, "Priority queues with variable priority and an $O(EV \log V)$ algorithm for finding a maximal weighted matching in general graphs," in *Proc. 23rd Annu. Symp. Foundations Comput. Sci.*, Nov. 3-5, 1982, pp. 255-261.

[11] M. Gursky, "Some complexity results for a multi-processor scheduling problem," private communication from H. S. Stone, 1981.

[12] V. B. Gylys and J. A. Edwards, "Optimal partitioning of workload for distributed systems," in *Dig. Papers COMPCON*, Fall 1976, pp. 353-357.

[13] V. M. Lo, "Task assignment in distributed multiprocessor systems," in *Proc. IEEE Conf. Parallel Processing*, 1981, pp. 358-360.

[14] ——, "Task assignment in distributed systems," Ph.D. dissertation, Dep. Comput. Sci., Univ. Illinois, Oct. 1983.

[15] ——, "Heuristic algorithms for task assignment in distributed systems," in *Proc. IEEE 4th Int. Conf. Distributed Comput. Syst.*

[16] L. M. Ni and K. Hwang, "Optimal load balancing strategies for a multiple processor operating system," in *Proc. IEEE Conf. Parallel Processing*, 1981, pp. 352-357.

[17] C. C. Price, "Search techniques for a nonlinear multiprocessor scheduling problem," *Naval Res. Logist. Quarterly*, June 1982, pp. 213-233.

[18] C. C. Price and S. Krishnaprasad, "Software allocation models for distributed computing systems," in *Proc. 4th Int. Conf. Distributed Comput. Syst.*, May 1984, pp. 40-48.

[19] C. C. Shen and W. H. Tsai, "A graph matching approach to optimal task assignment in distributed computing systems using a minimax criterion," *IEEE Trans. Comput.*, vol. C-34, pp. 197-203, Mar. 1985.

[20] R. G. Smith, "The contract bid protocol: High-level communication and control in a distributed problem-solver," *IEEE Trans. Comput.*, vol. C-29, pp. 1104-1113, Dec. 1980.

[21] H. S. Stone and S. H. Bokhari, "Control of distributed processes," *IEEE Computer.*, pp. 97-106, July 1978.

[22] H. S. Stone, "Multiprocessor scheduling with the aid of network flow algorithms," *IEEE Trans. Software Eng.*, vol. SE-3, pp. 85-93, Jan. 1977.

[23] ——, "Program assignment in three-processor systems and tricutset partitioning of graphs," Tech. Rep. ECE-CS-77-7, Dep. Elec. Eng., Univ. Massachusetts, Amherst, 1977.

[24] ——, "Critical load factors in two-processors distributed systems," *IEEE Trans. Software Eng.*, vol. SE-4, pp. 254-258, May 1978.

[25] A. M. Van Tilborg and L. D. Wittie, "Wave scheduling—Decentralized scheduling of task forces in multicomputers," *IEEE Trans. Comput.*, vol. C-33, pp. 835-844, Sept. 1984.

[26] C. S. Wu and M. T. Liu, "Assignment of tasks and resources for distributed processing," in *IEEE COMPCON Fall 1980, Proc. Distributed Processing*, pp. 655-662.

[27] S. G. Abraham and E. S. Davidson, "Task assignment using network flow methods for minimizing communication in n-processor systems," Center for Supercomput. Res. Develop., Tech. Rep. 598, Sept. 1986.

Virginia Mary Lo (A'85) received the A.B. degree from the University of Michigan, Ann Arbor, in 1969, the M.S. degree in computer science from the Pennsylvania State University, University Park, in 1978, and the Ph.D. degree in computer science from the University of Illinois at Urbana-Champaign in 1983.

She has been on the faculty of the Department of Computer and Information Science at the University of Oregon since January 1985. Her research interests include scheduling and load balancing in distributed and real-time distributed systems.

Dr. Lo is a member of the Association for Computing Machinery and the IEEE Computer Society.

Allocating Modules to Processors in a Distributed System

DAVID FERNÁNDEZ-BACA

Abstract—We study the complexity of the problem of allocating modules to processors in a distributed system to minimize total communication and execution costs. We show that, unless P = NP, there can be no polynomial-time ϵ-approximate algorithm for the problem nor can there exist a local search algorithm that requires polynomial time per iteration and yields an optimum assignment. Both results hold even if the communication graph is planar and bipartite. On the positive side, we show that if the communication graph is a partial k-tree or an almost tree with parameter k, the module allocation problem can be solved in polynomial time.

Index Terms—Computer networks, distributed systems, dynamic programming, scheduling, task allocation.

I. INTRODUCTION

THE following problem arises in the allocation of tasks to processors in a distributed system [8], [28]. We are given a program with m modules each of which must be assigned to one of p processors. Unless stated otherwise, we assume that modules are numbered from 1 to m and processors are numbered from 1 to p. Together with the set of modules we have an undirected, connected graph G, called the *communication graph* of the system, whose vertices are the modules of the program and such that there is an edge between two vertices if the corresponding modules communicate. As assignment of modules to processors is represented by a vector $X = (x_1, \cdots, x_m) \in \{1, \cdots, p\}^m$, where $x_i = k$ if module i is assigned to processor k. The cost of executing module i on processor x_i is denoted by $e_i(x_i)$. If modules i and j communicate, then $c_{i,j}(x_i, x_j)$ denotes the communication cost between modules i and j when i is assigned to processor x_i and j is assigned to processor x_j. If $x_i = x_j$, $c_{i,j}(x_i, x_j)$ can be viewed as an interference cost, which may result, for instance, from tasks i and j competing for the same resource. The costs can be obtained analytically, from knowledge of the underlying software and hardware, experimentally, by monitoring the system over a sufficiently long period of time, or using simulation. Some parameters, such as interference costs, can be specified by the system manager, in order, for instance, to achieve a more balanced loading [18]. Regardless of how they are obtained, we shall assume that the e_i's and the c_{ij}'s are available in tables. The *cost* of assignment X is given by[1]

$$C(X) = \sum_{i \in V(G)} e_i(x_i) + \sum_{(i,j) \in E(G)} c_{i,j}(x_i, x_j).$$

The *module allocation problem* (MA) is to find an assignment of minimum cost. Module allocation is an important aspect of all phases of the development of a distributed system. Algorithms for the problem are useful during the design stage, where they can aid in determining a configuration that achieves a certain performance level; during the operational stage, where they can provide a strategy for optimum use of the available resources; and during reconfiguration, where tasks may have to be reassigned due to changes in the system [10].

MA has been studied extensively (see, e.g., [25], [26], [8], [10], [28], [24], [16], [18], [13]), and the problem is known to be NP-hard in general [8]. Communication costs are said to be *uniform* when the communication cost between any two modules is equal to zero if the modules are coresident and, if modules are assigned to different processors, is not a function of the processors to which they are assigned (i.e., $c_{ij}(a, b)$, $a \neq b$, is independent of a and b). For $p = 2$ and arbitrary G, MA with uniform costs can be solved in polynomial time using maximum-flow algorithms [25]. Polynomial-time algorithms have been developed for the cases where the communication graph is either a tree or a series-parallel graph and p is arbitrary. The algorithm for trees, due to Bokhari [8], runs in $O(mp^2)$ time, while the algorithm for series-parallel graphs, due to Towsley [28], runs in $O(mp^3)$ time. Both methods apply even if costs are not uniform.

This paper is divided into two parts. In the first, we consider the complexity of finding an assignment that is approximately optimum and of finding an optimum assignment through local search. Our main results are proofs of the nonexistence (unless P = NP) of either a polynomial-time ϵ-approximate algorithm for MA or an exact local search algorithm that takes polynomial time per iteration. (Definitions of these terms can be found in [14], [21], and in Sections III and IV of this paper.) These results hold even if the communication graph is planar and bipartite and the execution costs are zero.

In the second part, we show that despite these negative results, it is possible to extend the work of Bokhari and

Manuscript received July 15, 1988; revised January 3, 1989. Recommended by P. A. Ng.

The author is with the Department of Computer Science, Iowa State University, Ames, IA 50011.

IEEE Log Number 8930505.

[1] Throughout this paper $V(G)$ and $E(G)$ denote, respectively, the vertex and edge sets of graph G.

Reprinted from *IEEE Trans. on Software Eng.*, vol. 15, no. 11, Nov. 1989, pp. 1427–1436.

110

Towsley to much wider classes of graphs by exploiting the connection between MA and *nonserial dynamic programming* [9], [22]. We provide polynomial-time algorithms for problems where the communication graph is a *partial k-tree* [2], [6] or an *almost tree with parameter k* [15]. Each of these algorithms extends previous work in a different way. The running time of the algorithm for partial k-trees is $O(mp^{k+1})$, which allows us to find optimal assignments for several families of graphs that are known to be partial k-trees for fixed k (see Section VI). In particular, it is well known [2] that trees are partial 1-trees and series-parallel graphs are partial 2-trees. Thus, the running time of the algorithm for partial k-trees matches that of Bokhari's algorithm and that of Towsley's algorithm when it is applied to each class of graph.

Almost trees with parameter k are partial $(k + 1)$-trees [6]; hence, using the algorithm for k-trees an optimum assignment can be found in $O(mp^{k+2})$ time. We use a technique from [15] to obtain a faster $O(mp^{\lceil k/2 \rceil +2})$ algorithm. Since a tree is an almost tree with parameter 0, the running time of our algorithm matches that of Bokhari's method when the communication graph is a tree.

A. Organization of the Paper

In Section II we prove the NP-completeness of a restricted version of MA. This result is used in Sections III and IV. In Section III we study the complexity of finding an approximate assignment. In Section IV we study the complexity of local search for MA. Section V discusses the relationship between MA and nonserial dynamic programming and introduces the concept of variable elimination, which is used in the algorithms of the next two sections. In Section VI we provide a polynomial-time algorithm for communication graphs that are partial k-trees. In Section VII, we present a polynomial-time algorithm for almost trees with parameter k. Section VIII contains some concluding remarks.

II. NP-Completeness of 0-1 MA

Here we prove a result that shall be used in the next two sections. It concerns *0-1 MA*, the problem of determining whether an instance of MA where the e_i's are zero and the c_{ij}'s are zero-one functions has a zero-cost assignment. We assume familiarity with the theory of NP-completeness, as treated, for example, in [14].

Lemma 2.1: 0-1 MA is NP-complete for $p \geq 3$ even if G is planar and bipartite.

Proof: Membership of this problem in NP is immediate. We prove that it is NP-complete by exhibiting a reduction from *planar 3-SAT*, which is known to be NP-complete [17].

Planar 3-SAT is defined as follows. Let φ be a boolean formula in conjunctive normal form with variables $y_1, \cdots, y_n$, and clauses $C_1, \cdots, C_q$. φ is said to be a 3CNF formula if each clause has three literals (a literal is either a negated or unnegated variable) and it is said to be *planar* if the bipartite graph G_φ, obtained from φ as described below, is planar. $V(G_\varphi)$ consists of $n + q$ vertices, one

for each clause and variable in φ. Two vertices are adjacent if and only if one is a variable y_i, the other is a clause C_j, and y_i appears negated or unnegated in C_j. *Planar 3-SAT* is the problem of determining whether a planar 3CNF formula is satisfiable.

From φ define an instance M of 0-1 MA as follows. M has $m = n + q$ modules, one for each variable and clause of φ; $p = 3$ processors; and communication graph $G = G_\varphi$. To distinguish between modules that correspond to clauses and modules that correspond to truth variables, we shall label modules with their corresponding clause or truth variable. The assignment variables in M corresponding to truth variables in φ are $z_1, \cdots, z_n$ and those corresponding to clauses are $D_1, \cdots, D_q$. An assignment is represented by a vector $X = (z_1, \cdots, z_n, D_1, \cdots, D_q)$. The execution costs are zero, and the function to be minimized is

$$C(X) = \sum_{(y_i, C_j) \in E(G_\varphi)} c_{y_i, C_j}(z_i, D_j).$$

For $k = 1, 2, 3$, the communication cost c_{y_i, C_j} is defined as follows. Let $l_j[k]$ denote the kth literal of C_j.
- If $l_j[k] = y_i$, then $c_{y_i, C_j}(1, k) = 0$ and $c_{y_i, C_j}(2, k) = c_{y_i, C_j}(3, k) = 1$.
- If $l_j[k] = \neg y_i$, then $c_{y_i, C_j}(1, k) = c_{y_i, C_j}(3, k) = 1$ and $c_{y_i, C_j}(2, k) = 0$.
- If $l_j[k]$ is neither y_i nor $\neg y_i$, then $c_{y_i, C_j}(z_i, k) = 0$ for $z_i = 1, 2, 3$.

We claim that M has a zero-cost assignment if and only if φ is satisfiable. Reexpress the objective function of M as

$$C(X) = \sum_{j=1}^{q} F_j(X_j),$$

where $F_j(X_j) = \sum_{i \in A_j} c_{y_i, C_j}(z_i, D_j)$, $A_j = \{i \mid (y_i, C_j) \in E(G_\varphi)\}$, and $X_j = \{D_j\} \cup \{z_i \mid i \in A_j\}$. By the definition of the $c_{y, C}$'s, for any choice of values for the variables in X_j, $F_j(X_j)$ equals either zero or 1.

We first show that to every zero-cost assignment X for M there corresponds a satisfying truth assignment Y for φ. Y is constructed by setting $y_i =$ true if $z_i = 1$, $y_i =$ false if $z_i = 2$ or 3. Y must be a satisfying truth assignment, for, if it were otherwise, there would be a false clause C_j, in which case $F_j(X_j) = 1$ and hence $C(X) > 0$, a contradiction.

To complete the proof, we show that for every satisfying truth assignment Y for φ there is a zero-cost assignment for M. For $i = 1, \cdots, n$, set z_i to 1 or 2 according to whether y_i is true or false. For $j = 1, \cdots, q$, set D_j equal to k, where $l_j[k]$ is any true literal in C_j. Thus, for $j = 1, \cdots, m$, $F_j(X_j) = 0$.] $\square$

For $p = 2$, 0-1 MA can be solved in polynomial time by a method similar to the algorithm for 2-SAT presented in [12]. Given Lemma 2.1, the following corollary is easy to prove.

Corollary 2.1: MA is NP-hard for $p \geq 3$, even if the e_i's are all zero and the interaction graph is planar and bipartite.

III. Complexity of Finding an Approximate Solution

Since MA is, in general, NP-hard, it would be desirable to have a polynomial algorithm that yields a near-optimum solution. Let A^* be the cost of an optimum solution to a minimization problem. An ϵ-*approximate algorithm* for the problem is an algorithm that produces a feasible solution of cost A such that $A \leq (1 + \epsilon) A^*$. Here we prove the following.

Theorem 3.1: Unless P = NP, there is no ϵ-approximate polynomial-time algorithm for MA with $p \geq 3$ for any $\epsilon > 0$, even if G is planar and bipartite and the e_i's are all zero.

Proof: The proof is along the lines of [27] and amounts to showing that the existence of a polynomial-time ϵ-approximate solution to MA for *any* fixed $\epsilon > 0$ would imply that 0-1 MA can be solved in polynomial time. By Lemma 2.1, the latter cannot be true unless P = NP.

Given an instance M of 0-1 MA, we construct an instance M' of MA with zero execution costs and the same communication graph G as follows. Let the communication costs c'_{ij} of M' be given by

$$c'_{ij}(a, b) = \begin{cases} 1 & \text{if } c_{ij}(a, b) = 0 \\ 2 + \epsilon |E(G)| & \text{otherwise,} \end{cases}$$

and let C' be the objective function for M'. Suppose we have an ϵ-approximate algorithm for MA and let X be the assignment obtained by this algorithm. We shall show that $C'(X) = |E(G)|$ if and only if M has a zero-cost assignment. For the "only if" part, observe that if $C'(X) = |E(G)|$, X is a zero-cost assignment for M. We prove the "if" part by contradiction. Suppose $C'(X) > |E(G)|$, but there exists a zero-cost assignment for M. If X^* is an optimum assignment for M' then $C'(X^*) \geq |E(G)|$, but since M has a zero-cost assignment, $C'(X^*) = |E(G)|$. On the other hand, $C'(X) \geq |E(G)| - 1 + (2 + \epsilon |E(G)|) = 1 + (1 + \epsilon) |E(G)|$. But then $C'(X) \geq (1 + \epsilon) |E(G)| = (1 + \epsilon) C'(X^*)$, which contradicts the assumption that the algorithm is ϵ-approximate. Hence, if M has a zero-cost assignment, $C'(X) = |E(G)|$. Therefore, having a polynomial-time ϵ-approximate algorithm for MA for *any* fixed $\epsilon > 0$ allows us to solve 0-1 MA in polynomial time. $\square$

IV. Complexity of Exact Local Search

Another approach for dealing with hard optimization problems is *local search*. The idea is as follows. Start with any feasible solution to the problem and try to find an improved solution in its neighborhood, where the neighborhood is defined in some problem-dependent way. If such a solution exists, repeat the process; otherwise, stop. A solution that is best possible in its neighborhood is called a *local optimum* [21, Ch. 19]. A local optimum is not, in general, a global optimum, yet local search is often a valuable heuristic [21], [24]. A local search al-

gorithm that is guaranteed to terminate with a global optimum, regardless of whether or not the number of iterations is polynomial in the input size, is said to be *exact*.

A necessary condition for local search to be exact is that the algorithm I that finds an improved solution in the neighborhood be able to tell whether the current solution is globally optimal. We shall show that the problem of determining whether an assignment is suboptimal, subsequently referred to as *MA suboptimality*, is NP-complete. It will follow that no local search algorithm where each call to I takes polynomial time can be exact unless P = NP.

Theorem 4.1: MA suboptimality is NP-complete for $p \geq 4$, even if G is planar and bipartite and the e_i's are all zero.

Proof: The approach is similar to that in [20]. We leave the proof of membership in NP to the reader. As a preliminary step, we show that the problem of determining whether an instance of 0-1 MA with $p \geq 4$ has a zero-cost assignment is NP-complete even if, as part of the input, we are given an assignment of cost one. We call this problem *restricted MA* and prove its NP-completeness by reduction from 0-1 MA.

Given an instance M of 0-1 MA with $p \geq 3$, construct an instance M' of restricted MA with the same communication graph G and $p' = p + 1$ processors. The execution costs of M' are zero, and its communication costs are as follows. For all $(i, j) \in E(G)$, $c'_{i,j}(a, b) = c_{i,j}(a, b)$ and $c'_{i,j}(a, p') = 1$, $1 \leq a, b \leq p$. For all $(i, j) \in E(G) - \{(u, v)\}$, where (u, v) is an edge in $E(G)$ chosen arbitrarily, make $c'_{i,j}(p', p') = 0$. For (u, v), make $c_{u,v}(p', p') = 1$. M' has an assignment of cost one, obtained by making $x_i = p'$ for all i, and it has a zero-cost assignment if and only if M does. Thus, restricted MA is NP-hard, and since, as the reader can check, it is in NP, it is also NP-complete.

We now reduce restricted MA to MA suboptimality. Let M be an instance of restricted MA whose given unit-cost assignment is X. We construct an instance $\tilde{M}$ of MA suboptimality as follows. $\tilde{M}$ has the same communication graph G as M and the assignment whose suboptimality we wish to test is X. The execution costs of $\tilde{M}$ are zero, and its communication costs are given by

$$\bar{c}_{ij}(a, b) = \begin{cases} 1 & \text{if } c_{ij}(a, b) = 0 \\ 2 & \text{otherwise.} \end{cases}$$

Denote by C and $\bar{C}$, respectively, the objective functions for M and $\tilde{M}$. Then $\bar{C}(X) = |E(G)| + 1$. Let X^* be the optimum assignment for $\tilde{M}$. Then $\bar{C}(X^*) \geq |E(G)|$ and, if $\bar{C}(X^*) = |E(G)|$, X^* is a zero-cost assignment for M. Thus, X is suboptimal for $\tilde{M}$ if and only if there is a zero-cost assignment for M. $\square$

An argument similar to one presented in [20] shows that testing whether a solution to MA is more than $1 + \epsilon$ times the optimum is NP-complete for any $\epsilon > 0$. Theorem 4.1, together with the discussion preceding it, yields the following corollary.

Corollary 4.1: Unless P = NP, there can be no exact local search algorithm with polynomial time per iteration for MA with $p \geq 4$.

V. RELATIONSHIP WITH NONSERIAL DYNAMIC PROGRAMMING

In the next two sections, we extend the class of polynomial-time solvable instances of MA by using the relationship between MA and *nonserial dynamic programming* [9] [22]. In nonserial dynamic programming we are asked to minimize (or maximize)

$$f(y_1, \cdots, y_n) = \sum_{i \in T} f_i(Y_i), \qquad (1)$$

where T is an index set, and each *term* f_i is a function of a subset Y_i of the variables. Each variable y_i is allowed to take on values from a finite set $\{1, \cdots, d_i\}$, and the values of the terms for different values of their arguments are provided in tables. Associated with (1) there is an *interaction graph G* whose vertices are integers i such that y_i is a variable, and such that there is an edge between nodes i and j if and only if y_i and y_j appear together in some term. Clearly MA is a special case of nonserial dynamic programming, although this fact was apparently not observed before. The communication graph of an instance of MA is simply the interaction graph of the objective function $C(X)$. From this observation, it follows that if the communication graph is planar (in which case, by Corollary 2.1, the problem remains NP-hard), MA can be solved in $p^{O(\sqrt{m})}$ time using the planar separator theorem of Lipton and Tarjan [19]. This is an asymptotic improvement over the $O(p^m)$ time required for exhaustive enumeration, but is still far from being practical.

A well-known technique for solving nonserial dynamic programming problems is *variable elimination* [9]. Consider the problem of minimizing (1). Our goal is to replace this problem by another one with fewer variables but such that the minimum for the new problem is the same as that of the original problem. Assume, without loss of generality, that the variables to be eliminated are $y_1, \cdots, y_l$. Let D be the set of all i such that f_i is a function of at least one variable in $\{y_1, \cdots, y_l\}$ and let Y_D be the set of variables that appear together with one of $\{y_1, \cdots, y_l\}$ in some term; i.e., $Y_D = (\cup_{i \in D} Y_i) - \{y_1, \cdots, y_l\}$. Define

$$f_a(y_1, \cdots, y_l, Y_D) = \sum_{i \in D} f_i(Y_i)$$

and let

$$f_b(Y_D) = \min f_a(y_1, \cdots, y_l, Y_D),$$

where the minimum is taken over all possible choices of values for the variables $y_1, \cdots, y_l$. Then it can be shown [9] that

$$f'(y_{l+1}, \cdots, y_n) = f_b(Y_D) + \sum_{i \in T-D} f_i(Y_i) \qquad (2)$$

has the same minimum as f. The new term f_b captures all the information about the eliminated variables and terms

that is needed for minimization. The interaction graph of the new problem can be obtained from that of the original problem by removing the nodes corresponding to eliminated variables, along with their incident edges, and by completely connecting the nodes corresponding to variables in Y_D. Since there is such a close correspondence between variable elimination and the removal of nodes from the interaction graph, we shall talk interchangeably about variable and vertex (or module) elimination. The elimination process is continued until either all variables are removed or the number of variables is sufficiently small to solve the problem directly by exhaustive enumeration. Once we have a choice of $y_{l+1}, \cdots, y_n$ that minimizes f', an assignment $(y_1, \cdots, y_n)$ that minimizes f can be obtained using the standard "back pointer" technique employed in many dynamic programming algorithms [3]. I.e., when constructing f_b from f_a we store, together with each entry in the table for f_b, the values of $y_1, \cdots, y_l$ that minimized f_a.

Bokhari's algorithm for trees [8] and Towsley's algorithm for series-parallel graphs [28] can be viewed as methods whereby the original problem is successively reduced by eliminating assignment variables one at a time. In Bokhari's algorithm, for instance, the assignment variables are eliminated by fixing one module as the root of the tree, and then carrying out a series of steps, at each of which a variable corresponding to a leaf module is eliminated. As we shall see, variable elimination can be used for a much wider class of communication graphs. The algorithms presented in the next two sections use the technique in different ways. The first solves MA for partial k-trees by eliminating variables one at a time. The second solves MA for almost trees by eliminating variables in blocks.

VI. COMMUNICATION GRAPHS THAT ARE PARTIAL k-TREES

In this section we present an algorithm that finds an optimum assignment in $O(mp^{k+1})$ time when the communication graph is a *partial k-tree*. As mentioned in the Introduction, trees and series-parallel graphs are partial k-trees with $k = 1$ and $k = 2$, respectively, and our algorithm is as efficient as the methods in [8] and [28] for these kinds of graphs. Other families of graphs are also partial k-trees. For instance, *Halin* graphs are partial 3-trees [7], Δ-*Y-reducible* graphs are partial 4-trees [11], *bandwidth-r* graphs are partial r-trees [6], and *r-outerplanar* graphs are partial $(3r-1)$-trees [7]. The running times of our algorithm on these graphs are, respectively, $O(mp^4)$, $O(mp^5)$, $O(mp^{r+1})$, and $O(mp^{3r})$. The above bounds assume knowledge of a suitable decomposition of the communication graph (see Section VI-C).

A. Definitions

A *k-clique* is a set of k pairwise adjacent vertices. A *k-leaf* is a vertex of degree k such that its neighbors form a k-clique. A graph is a *k-tree* if and only if

113

1) it is K_k, the complete graph on k vertices, or

2) it has a k-leaf v such that the graph obtained by removing v together with its incident edges is a k-tree.

From the above definition, it is easy to check that an m-vertex k-tree has $k(m - k) + k(k - 1)/2$ edges and $k(m - k) + 1$ k-cliques. Furthermore, if G is a k-tree, it has a vertex elimination ordering that allows us to reduce it to a single k-clique, such that at the time when a vertex is eliminated it is a k-leaf. We call an ordering with these properties *natural*. All trees are 1-trees, since any tree can be reduced to a single vertex (a 1-clique) by successively removing vertices of degree 1 (1-leaves, or, in ordinary tree terminology [3], leaves). Fig. 1 shows a 3-tree. By removing vertices 1, 2, and 3, we are left with a 3-clique on vertices 4, 5, and 6. If 1, 2, and 3 are eliminated in sequence, each vertex will be a 3-leaf at the time of deletion; thus, 1, 2, 3 is a natural elimination ordering.

A *partial k-tree* is a subgraph of a k-tree. If G is a partial k-tree, there exists a k-tree H, called an *embedding k-tree* of G, such that $V(G) = V(H)$ and $E(G) \subseteq E(H)$ [12].

B. The Algorithm

Our algorithm is a straightforward application of the technique of variable elimination described in Section V, together with other ideas introduced in [1] and [5]. Suppose we have an instance of MA with communication graph G. To simplify matters, we shall assume that G is a k-tree. If G is only a partial k-tree, we first find an embedding k-tree H [2]. Next, we create a new instance of MA with the same execution costs and where the communication cost between modules i and j, $(i, j) \in E(H)$, is the same as in the original problem if $(i, j) \in E(G)$, and equal to zero, regardless of the assignments for i and j, if $(i, j) \notin E(G)$. Clearly, the optima for both problems are the same.

We shall assume that the algorithm is provided with a natural elimination ordering for G and, without loss of generality, that the vertices in this ordering are numbered $1, 2, \cdots, m - k$. Our algorithm eliminates variables x_1, $x_2, \cdots, x_{m-k}$ in sequence. To accomplish this, we shall need the following information about the k-cliques in G. Associated with the lth vertex in the elimination ordering there is a k-clique $K(l)$ that contains the neighbors of vertex l at the time it is removed. For each vertex $j \in K(l)$ there is a k-clique $K_j(l)$ formed by the vertices in $(K(l) - \{j\}) \cup \{l\}$. The procedure must be provided, for vertex l in the order, with $K(l)$ and $K_j(l)$ for all $j \in K(l)$. For the 3-tree in Fig. 1, for instance, $K(2) = \{3, 5, 6\}$, $K_3(2) = \{3, 5, 6\}$, $K_5(2) = \{2, 3, 6\}$, and $K_6(2) = \{2, 3, 5\}$. Methods for finding a natural elimination ordering and the information about k-cliques are presented in [4] and [2]. The running time of these methods is discussed in the next section.

To each k-clique K in G we associate a function $h_K(X_K)$, where X_K is the set of all variables that correspond to vertices in K. Initially, we set h_K to 0 for all

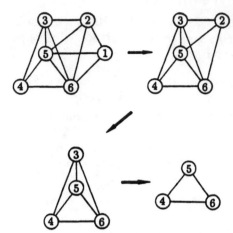

Fig. 1. A 3-tree is shown in the upper left. The numbering of the vertices corresponds to a natural elimination ordering.

possible assignments to the variables in X_K. We thus have

$$
C(x_1, \cdots, x_m) = \sum_{i \in V(G)} e_i(x_i) + \sum_{(i,j) \in E(G)} c_{i,j}(x_i, x_j) \\
+ \sum_{K \in G} h_K(X_K),
$$

where "$K \in G$" is shorthand for "K is a k-clique in G." The algorithm carries out $m - k$ iterations, at the lth of which vertex l is removed from the graph and the corresponding variable x_l is eliminated from the objective function. The information about the eliminated variable will be retained by updating $h_{K(l)}(X_{K(l)})$.

Let $G_0 = G$ and $C_0 = C$. Let G_l be the communication graph at iteration l and let $C_l(x_{l+1}, \cdots, x_m)$ be the objective function for the instance of MA at this stage. Before l is eliminated we have

$$
C_{l-1}(x_l, \cdots, x_m) = \sum_{i=l}^{m} e_i(x_i) + \sum_{(i,j) \in E(G_{l-1})} c_{i,j}(x_i, x_j) \\
+ \sum_{K \in G_{l-1}} h_K(X_K).
$$

To eliminate x_l for $l = 1, \cdots, m - k$, we proceed in the same way that led from (1) to (2) in Section V. First, collect all the terms that are a function of x_l by constructing the table for function

$$
h_l(x_l, X_{K(l)}) = e_l(x_l) + \sum_{j \in K(l)} c_{l,j}(x_l, x_j) + h_{K(l)}(X_{K(l)}) \\
+ \sum_{j \in K(l)} h_{K_j(l)}(X_{K_j(l)}). \tag{3}
$$

Next, we store all the information about x_l that is needed for minimization. In Section V, this was accomplished by defining a new function that is the minimum of (3) over all assignments for x_l. Since in the present case the new function would depend only on the variables in $X_{K(l)}$, instead of defining a new function, we simply update $h_{K(l)}$ by setting

$$
h_{K(l)}(X_{K(l)}) \leftarrow \min_{x_l} h_l(x_l, X_{K(l)}). \tag{4}
$$

The new objective function is

$$C_l(x_{l+1}, \cdots, x_m) = \sum_{i=l+1}^{m} e_i(x_i) + \sum_{(i,j)\in E(G_l)} c_{i,j}(x_i, x_j) + \sum_{K\in G_l} h_K(X_K),$$

which, by the discussion in Section V, has the same optimum as C_{l-1}. After eliminating modules 1 through $m - k$, the objective function is C_{m-k}, which has only k variables. We minimize C_{m-k} by exhaustive enumeration of all possible p^k-assignments for the remaining modules.

C. Run Time Analysis

The first step in the procedure is to find an embedding k-tree for G, a natural elimination ordering, and the information about the k-cliques. If $k = 1$ or 2, all this can be found in $O(m)$ time, while for $k = 3$, it can be found in $O(m \log m)$ time [4]. For $k > 3$, obtaining the information appears to be a more difficult problem. Efficient algorithms are known for certain special kinds of k-trees, such as r-outerplanar graphs [7], while, for the general problem, Arnborg et al. [2] have designed an algorithm that runs in $O(m^{k+2})$ time. Robertson and Seymour have shown that there exists an $O(m^2)$ time algorithm for recognizing partial k-trees [23]; their proof, however, is nonconstructive and provides no way of obtaining an algorithm with the claimed time bound. Furthermore, even though the running time of this recognition procedure looks appealing, the constant of proportionality associated with it is enormously high. It is, of course, conceivable that a practical algorithm will eventually be found, at least for small values of k.

We now turn our attention to the variable elimination process. At the beginning of the lth step, we construct h_l, given by (3). The terms in (3) are readily available, since, by assumption, we have all the needed information about the k-cliques. Since h_l is a function of $k + 1$ variables, the table for h_l has p^{k+1} entries. The time needed to compute each entry is $O(k)$, because there are that many terms in (3). Thus, if k is fixed, (3) is obtained in $O(p^{k+1})$ time. To carry out (4), the updating of $h_{K(l)}$, for each of the p^k possible assignments to the arguments of $h_{K(l)}$, we need to find, by trying all p possibilities, the choice of assignment for module l that minimizes h_l. This requires $O(p^{k+1})$ time. Since there are $m - k$ iterations, the total work in variable elimination is $O(mp^{k+1})$. Finally, solving C_{m-k} enumeratively takes $O(p^k)$ time. Thus, the total running time is $O(mp^{k+1})$, not counting the time needed to obtain the elimination order. Clearly, it is always to our advantage to find the smallest value of k such that G is a partial k-tree; unfortunately, this problem is NP-hard [2].

VII. Communication Graphs That Are Almost Trees

In this section, we present a polynomial time algorithm for *almost trees with parameter k*, a class of graphs introduced by Gurevich, Stockmeyer, and Vishkin [15]. It was shown by Bodlaender [6] that every almost tree with parameter k is a partial $(k + 1)$-tree. Thus, the algorithm given in the previous section takes $O(mp^{k+2})$ time on almost trees with parameter k, provided we are given an appropriate elimination order. In this section we describe a faster algorithm, based on techniques discussed in [15], that finds an optimum assignment in $O(mp^{\lceil k/2 \rceil + 2})$ time and does not need to be provided with an elimination ordering for the graph.

A. Definitions

An undirected graph G is said to be *biconnected* if G remains connected after the removal of any vertex along with its incident edges. A *biconnected component* of G is a maximal biconnected subgraph of G. If G is not biconnected, it will contain at least one vertex whose removal disconnects G. Such a vertex is called an *articulation point* [3]. Fig. 2 shows a graph G with five biconnected components, $C_1, \cdots, C_5$, whose articulation points are vertices 4, 6, and 9.

Let $C_1, C_2, \cdots, C_t$ and $s_1, s_2, \cdots, s_q$ denote, respectively, the biconnected components and the articulation points of G. For each C_i, let k_i equal the number of edges that must be deleted from C_i to obtain a tree (i.e., $k_i = |E(C_i)| - |V(C_i)| + 1$) and let $k(G)$ denote the maximum of k_i for $1 \le i \le t$. The set of graphs G with $k(G) = k$ is referred to as the class of *almost trees with parameter k*. If $k(G) = 0$, the biconnected components contain no cycles, and thus G is a tree. The 3-tree of Fig. 1 is biconnected; thus, since it has 6 vertices and 12 edges, it is an almost tree with parameter 7. The reader can verify that for the graph in Fig. 2, $k_1 = 2$, $k_2 = k_3 = 1$, and $k_4 = k_5 = 0$, and thus $k(G) = 2$.

B. The Algorithm

Our algorithm centers on a recursive procedure ASSIGN (M, G, s, h), which, given an instance M of MA with communication graph G and a special vertex $s \in V(G)$, constructs the function

$$h(x_s) = e_s(x_s) + \min \left\{ \sum_{i\in V(G)-\{s\}} e_i(x_i) + \sum_{(i,j)\in E(G)} c_{i,j}(x_i, x_j) \right\}, \qquad (5)$$

where the minimum is taken over all possible assignments for variables x_i, $i \in V(G) - \{s\}$. ASSIGN eliminates all the terms in M and all vertices in G except s. In effect, by calling ASSIGN, we reduce M to a problem with one module s whose execution cost function is h. This is because the min in (5) contains all the terms that depend on variables x_i, $i \in V(G) - \{s\}$, and it follows from the discussion in Section V that $\min C(x_1, \cdots, x_m) = \min h(x_s)$.

Of course, we could take the min in (5) over *all* variables, including x_s, and obtain, once and for all, the cost of the optimum assignment. We do not do this for the following reason. For the initial call to ASSIGN, the spe-

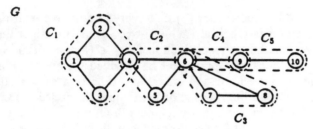

Fig. 2. A graph that is not biconnected.

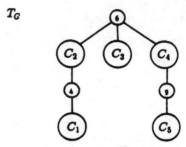

Fig. 3. The superstructure of the graph in Fig. 2.

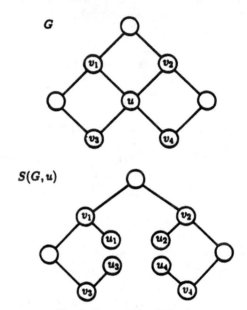

Fig. 4. Constructing $S(G, u)$.

cial vertex s is chosen arbitrarily; in subsequent recursive calls, however, G will not be the entire communication graph, but only a graph derived from one of its biconnected components. The articulation point that connects G to the rest of the communication graph will be s (see Case 2 below). We cannot eliminate x_s, since we do not know what effect its removal will have on the assignments to variables corresponding to the rest of the graph.

The first step of the algorithm is to obtain a suitable representation of the connectivity structure of the graph. The biconnected components of G yield a tree-like structure where each vertex that belongs to more than one component is an articulation point. We may thus associate with G a tree T_G, called the *superstructure* of G, where

$$V(T_G) = \{C_1, \cdots, C_t, s_1, \cdots, s_q\}$$

and

$$E(T_G) = \{(C_i, s_j) \mid s_j \text{ is a vertex of } C_i\}.$$

See Fig. 3. We shall assume as in [15] that we have available a procedure SEP(G, v, T_G) that given a graph G and a vertex $v \in V(G)$, returns the superstructure of G as a rooted tree T_G such that if v is an articulation point, then v is the root of T_G and if v is not an articulation point, the root of T_G is the unique component C that contains v. By suitably modifying the biconnectivity algorithm of Tarjan (see, e.g., [3]) it is possible to produce T_G in $O(|E(G)|)$ time. Observe that the superstructure tree of Fig. 3 has been drawn with the articulation point 6 as its root, which is what would result from a call to SEP(G, 6, T_G), where G is the graph of Fig. 2. A call to SEP(G, 5, T_G) would result in the same superstructure, except that C_2, the component that contains 5, would be the root. The first step of ASSIGN is to call SEP(G, s, T_G). The way the algorithm proceeds from this point depends on whether G is biconnected or not.

Case 1: G is biconnected.
If G is an edge (s, w), then

$$h(x_s) = e_s(x_s) + \min_{a \in \{1, \cdots, p\}} \{e_w(a) + c_{s,w}(x_s, a)\},$$

and, after deleting w from G and removing e_s, e_w, and $c_{s,w}$ from M, we are done. If G is not an edge, then pick a vertex $u \in V(G) - \{s\}$. For reasons that will soon become apparent, we call u the *splitting vertex*. To compute (5), we consider a constrained version of the original problem in which we eliminate the variables in $V(G) - \{s\}$ subject to the requirement that $x_u = d$, $d \in \{1,$

$\cdots, p\}$. To be more precise, we are interested in obtaining

$$h_d(x_s) = e_s(x_s) + \min \left\{ \sum_{i \in V(G) - \{s\}} e_i(x_i) \right.$$
$$\left. + \sum_{(i,j) \in E(G)} c_{i,j}(x_i, x_j) \right\},$$

where the minimum is taken over all assignments for variables x_i, $i \in V(G) - \{s\}$ such that $x_u = d$. Given $h_d(x_s)$ for each $d \in \{1, \cdots, p\}$, we can obtain $h(x_s)$ by making

$$h(x_s) = \min_{1 \leq d \leq p} \{h_d(x_s)\}.$$

To obtain h_d, we use the following idea. Let δ be the degree of u and let $\{v_1, \cdots, v_\delta\}$ be the set of all vertices that are adjacent to u. From G, construct a graph $S(G, u)$ by "splitting" vertex u. More formally, $S(G, u)$ consists of the subgraph of G induced by $V(G) - \{u\}$, together with vertices $u_1, \cdots, u_\delta$, and edges (v_i, u_i), for $i = 1, \cdots, \delta$ (see Fig. 4). We construct an instance $M_d(u)$ of MA whose communication graph is $S(G, u)$, where $e_{u_i}(x_{u_i}) = 0$ for all x_{u_i} and $c_{u_i, v_i}(x_{u_i}, x_{v_i}) = c_{u, v_i}(d, x_{v_i})$ for all x_{u_i} and x_{v_i}. If we now call ASSIGN($M_d(u)$, $S(G, u)$, s, g_d), we will have $h_d(x_s) = g_d(x_s) + e_u(d)$. Once h_s is computed, we eliminate all terms in M and all vertices in G except s.

116

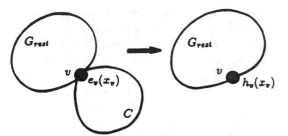

Fig. 5. Processing a biconnected component.

We have left the choice of splitting vertex open up to now. It turns out to be convenient to choose u to be of maximum degree. This selection does not affect in any way the variable elimination process described above, but as will become clear later, it improves the worst-case running time.

Case 2: G is not biconnected.

The algorithm proceeds to traverse T_G from the leaves up. Consider the situation depicted in Fig. 5. Here we are processing component C such that C is a leaf in T_G, which is connected via vertex v to the rest of the graph, denoted G_{rest}. Let $M(C)$ denote the instance M of MA restricted to C. Since C interacts with G_{rest} only through v, we can eliminate all vertices in $V(C) - \{v\}$, together with the corresponding variables by calling ASSIGN $(M(C), C, v, h_v)$. We now obtain a new instance of MA with the same optimum as the original one by replacing $e_v(x_v)$ with $h_v(x_v)$. If, after this is done, there is another leaf component, we repeat the process; otherwise, we stop. The details of the algorithm are provided in Fig. 6.

Given the communication graph of Fig. 2, a call to AS-SIGN $(M, G, 6, h)$ would first construct the superstructure T_G given in Fig. 3. Since G is not biconnected, T_G will be processed bottom up. A possible sequence of eliminations is as follows. Call ASSIGN $(M(C_1), C_1, 4, h)$, replace e_4 by h; call ASSIGN $(M(C_5), C_5, 9, h)$, replace e_9 by h; call ASSIGN $(M(C_2), C_2, 6, h)$, replace e_6 by h; call ASSIGN $(M(C_3), C_3, 6, h)$, replace e_6 by h; finally, call ASSIGN $(M(C_4), C_4, 6, h)$ and replace e_6 by h. Details of how each recursive call is processed are left to the reader. After the final call to ASSIGN, the cost of an optimum assignment is simply $\min_{x_6 \in \{1, \cdots, p\}} h(x_6)$.

C. Run Time Analysis

Let G be a graph with $E \geq 1$ edges and $k(G) = k$. For a given number of processors p, denote by $T_N(E, k)$ the running time of ASSIGN on G if G is not biconnected and by $T_B(E, k)$ the running time if G is biconnected. The worst-case running time over all graphs is therefore max $\{T_N(E, k), T_B(E, k)\}$. In what follows, we assume c to be a constant sufficiently large to account for the various overheads of the algorithm. If G is not biconnected, we have

$$T_N(E, k) \leq \max \left\{ \Sigma \, T_B(E_i, k_i) \middle| \Sigma \, E_i \right.$$

$$= E \text{ and } \max k_i = k \right\} + cE.$$

If G is biconnected, we consider three possibilities, depending on the value of k. If $k = 0$, then G is an edge (E

```
procedure ASSIGN(M, G, s, h);

begin
    SEP(G, s, T_G);
    if G is biconnected then begin
        if G is an edge (s, w) then
            for each d ∈ {1, ..., p} do
                h(d) ← e_s(d) + min_{a∈{1,...,p}}{e_w(a) + c_{s,w}(d, a)} ;
        else begin
            Find a vertex u ≠ s of maximum degree;
            Construct S(G, u);
            for d ← 1 to p do begin
                Construct M_d(u);
                ASSIGN (M_d(u), S(G, u), s, g_d)
            end;
            for a ← 1 to p do
                h(a) ← min_{d∈{1,...,p}}{g_d(a) + e_u(d)};
        end;
        Remove all vertices in V(G) − {s}, along with their incident edges;
        Remove all terms from M;
    end
    else begin
        while T_G is nonempty do begin
            Pick any leaf in T_G;
            if the leaf is an articulation point then delete it from T_G
            else begin
                let the leaf be a component C;
                if C is the root of T_G then v ← s
                else v ← father of C in T_G;
                ASSIGN(M(C), C, v, h);
                e_v ← h;
                Delete C from T_G
            end
        end
    end
end
```

Fig. 6. The algorithm for almost trees.

$= 1$) and

$$T_B(1, 0) \leq c \cdot p^2.$$

If $k = 1$, then G is a cycle and $S(G, u)$ is a tree rooted at s that has two subtrees, each of which is a path (see Fig. 7). There will be p recursive calls to ASSIGN and each call will take at most cEp^2 time, since the biconnected components of $S(G, u)$ are edges and applying ASSIGN to an edge takes time proportional to p^2. Thus,

$$T_B(E, 1) \leq cE \cdot p^3.$$

For $k \geq 2$, we use the following two lemmas, which are proved in [15]. Let δ denote the degree of u.

Lemma 7.1: $k(S(G, u)) \leq k(G) - \delta + 1$.

Lemma 7.2: If $k(G) \geq 2$, then $\delta \geq 3$.

Thus, for $k \geq 2$,

$$T_B(E, k) \leq \max \left\{ p \cdot \left(T_N(E, k') + cp^2\delta \right) \middle| \delta \right.$$

$$\geq 3 \text{ and } k' \leq k - \delta + 1, \delta \geq 3 \right\} + cE,$$

where the $cp^2\delta$ term accounts for the time needed to create $M_d(u)$ from M (i.e., it is necessary to define δ new communication cost functions, each consisting of p^2 entries, and δ new execution cost functions). Lemmas 7.1 and 7.2 justify choosing u to be of maximum degree.

It straightforward to verify that

$$T_B(E, k) \leq A \cdot Ep^{\lceil k/2 \rceil + 2} - A_B \cdot E$$

and

$$T_N(E, k) \leq A \cdot Ep^{\lceil k/2 \rceil + 2} - A_N \cdot E,$$

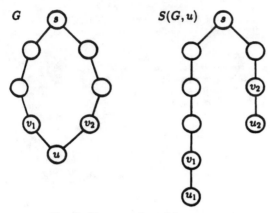

Fig. 7. The case where G is a cycle.

where

$$A = \left(\frac{2p^3 - p^2 + p + 1}{p^3 - p^2} \right) c,$$

$$A_B = \left(\frac{p^3 + p + 1}{p - 1} \right) c,$$

and

$$A_N = \left(\frac{p^3 + 2}{p - 1} \right) c.$$

Thus, the running time of ASSIGN is $O(Ep^{\lceil k/2 \rceil + 2})$. A partial $(k + 1)$-tree has $E \leq (k + 1)(m - k - 1) + (k + 1)k/2$ (see Section VI-A); thus, $E = O(m)$ for fixed k. Since every almost tree with parameter k is a partial $(k + 1)$-tree, the running time of ASSIGN is $O(mp^{\lceil k/2 \rceil + 2})$ are claimed.

VIII. DISCUSSION

We have presented both negative and positive results regarding the complexity of the module allocation problem. We showed that (unless P = NP) it is impossible to find certain kinds of approximation and local search algorithms. In our proofs, however, we have assumed that communication costs are unrestricted. Thus, our results do not rule out the possibility of obtaining fast approximation algorithms or good local search algorithms for MA with uniform costs.

We have also shown that the class of polynomial-time solvable instances of MA is considerably larger than was known before. The algorithm for k-trees is reasonably efficient for small values of k, and is quite effective if the number of processors is bounded. Its main disadvantage is that its efficiency hinges on the speed with which an embedding k-tree can be found, and this may be the dominating factor in the running time, especially if k is larger than 3. As we pointed out in Section VI, this situation may improve since, at least in theory, it is possible to compute the needed information efficiently. Furthermore, the algorithm for almost trees shows that there is a subclass of k-trees where this information does not have to be comptuted at all. It would be interesting to know if other such classes exist.

A problem that seems harder to avoid is that our algorithms are exponential in k and hence could be unacceptably slow, even for relatively small k. It has been pointed out [5] that many graphs that arise in reliability problems are partial 4-trees. Whether or not a similar situation holds for communication graphs of real-life programs is a question that appears to merit further study.

The utility of our allocation algorithms will ultimately depend on how well they can be incorporated into the overall task of designing and managing a distributed system. We should note that in this paper we have focused on only one aspect of the general module allocation problem, namely, minimizing total execution and communication costs. In a real system, other issues must be taken into account, including memory restrictions, load balancing, and queueing delays. How to integrate these various factors into a model of task allocation that is both realistic and (at least in some cases) tractable remains a challenging problem.

ACKNOWLEDGMENT

I wish to thank C. Martel for introducing me to this problem long ago, M. Langston for bringing [23] to my attention, S. Arnborg for providing valuable references, and the referees for their valuable comments on the presentation of this paper.

REFERENCES

[1] S. Arnborg, "Efficient algorithms for combinatorial problems on graphs with bounded decomposability—A survey," *BIT*, vol. 25, pp. 305–314, 1985.
[2] S. Arnborg, D. G. Corneil, and A. Proskurowski, "Complexity of finding embeddings in a k-tree," *SIAM J. Alg. Discr. Methods*, vol. 8, no. 2, pp. 277–284, 1987.
[3] A. V. Aho, J. E. Hopcroft, and J. D. Ullman, *The Design and Analysis of Computer Algorithms*. Reading, MA: Addison-Wesley, 1974.
[4] S. Arnborg and A. Proskurowski, "Characterization and recognition of partial 3-trees," *SIAM J. Alg. Discr. Methods*, vol. 7, pp. 305–314, 1986.
[5] ——, "Linear-time algorithms for NP-hard problems restricted to partial k-trees," manuscript.
[6] H. L. Bodlaender, "Classes of graphs with bounded tree-width," Dep. Comput. Sci., Univ. Utrecht, The Netherlands, Tech. Rep. RUU-CS-86-22, Dec. 1986.
[7] ——, "Some classes of graphs with bounded tree-width," *Bull. EATCS*, vol. 36, pp. 116–126, 1988.
[8] S. Bokhari, "A shortest tree algorithm for optimal assignments across space and time in a distributed processor system," *IEEE Trans. Software Eng.*, vol. SE-7, no. 6, pp. 583–589, 1981.
[9] U. Bertelè and F. Brioschi, *Nonserial Dynamic Programming*. New York: Academic, 1972.
[10] W. W. Chu, L. J. Holloway, M. Lan, and K. Efe, "Task allocation in distributed data processing," *Computer*, pp. 57–69, Nov. 1980.
[11] E. S. Elmallah and C. J. Colbourn, "Reliability of Δ-Y networks," *Congressus Numerantium*, vol. 48, pp. 49–54, 1985.
[12] S. Even, A. Itai, and A. Shamir, "On the complexity of multicommodity flow problems," *SIAM J. Comput.*, vol. 5, no. 4, pp. 691–703, 1976.
[13] D. Fernández-Baca and G. Slutzki, "Solving parametric problems on trees," Dep. Comput. Sci., Iowa State Univ., Tech. Rep. 87-12, 1987, to appear in *J. Algorithms*.
[14] M. Garey and D. Johnson, *Computers and Intractability: A Guide to the Theory of NP-Completeness*. San Francisco, CA: Freeman, 1979.
[15] Y. Gurevich, L. Stockmeyer, and U. Vishkin, "Solving NP-hard problems on graphs that are almost trees and an application to facility location problems," *J. ACM*, vol. 31, no. 3, pp. 459–473, 1984.
[16] D. Gusfield, "Parametric combinatorial computing and a problem in module distribution," *J. ACM*, 1983.

[17] D. Lichtenstein, "Planar formulae and their uses," *SIAM J. Comput.*, vol. 11, no. 2, pp. 329–343, 1982.

[18] V. M. Lo, "Heuristic algorithms for task assignment in distributed systems," *IEEE Trans. Comput.*, vol. C-37, no. 11, pp. 1384–1397, 1988.

[19] R. Lipton and R. Tarjan, "Applications of a planar separator theorem," *SIAM J. Comput.*, vol. 9, no. 3, pp. 615–627, 1980.

[20] C. H. Papadimitriou and K. Steiglitz, "The complexity of local search for the traveling salesman problem," *SIAM J. Comput.*, vol. 6, no. 1, pp. 76–83, 1977.

[21] ——, *Combinatorial Optimization: Algorithms and Complexity.* Englewood Cliffs, NJ: Prentice-Hall, 1982.

[22] A. Rosenthal, "Dynamic programming is optimal for nonserial optimization problems," *SIAM J. Comput.*, vol. 11, no. 1, pp. 47–59, 1982.

[23] N. Robertson and P. D. Seymour, "Graph minors XIII: The disjoint paths problem," Manuscript, Sept. 1986.

[24] J. B. Sinclair, "Efficient computation of optimal assignments for distributed tasks," *J. Parallel Distributed Comput.*, vol. 4, no. 4, pp. 342–362, 1987.

[25] H. Stone, "Multiprocessor scheduling with the aid of network flow algorithms," *IEEE Trans. Software Eng.*, vol. SE-3, pp. 85–94, 1977.

[26] ——, "Critical load factors in two-processor distributed systems," *IEEE Trans. Software Eng.*, vol. SE-4, pp. 254–258, 1978.

[27] S. Sahni and T. Gonzalez, "P-complete approximation problems," *J. ACM*, vol. 23, pp. 555–565, 1976.

[28] D. Towsley, "Allocating programs containing branches and loops within a multiple processor system," *IEEE Trans. Software Eng.*, vol. SE-12, no. 10, pp. 1018–1024, 1986.

David Fernández-Baca received the B.S. degree in engineering from the National Autonomous University of Mexico, Mexico City, in 1980, and the M.S. degree in electrical engineering and the Ph.D. degree in computer science from the University of California, Davis, in 1983 and 1986, respectively.

Before attending U.C. Davis, he worked as a research associate at the Instituto de Investigaciones Eléctricas in Cuernavaca, Mexico. Since 1986, he has been on the faculty of the Department of Computer Science, Iowa State University, Ames. His research interests include the design and analysis of algorithms, combinatorial optimization, and scheduling.

Dr. Fernández-Baca is a member of the Association for Computing Machinery and the European Association for Theoretical Computer Science.

Compile-Time Scheduling and Assignment of Data-Flow Program Graphs with Data-Dependent Iteration

Soonhoi Ha, *Student Member, IEEE,* and Edward A. Lee, *Member, IEEE*

Abstract— Scheduling of data-flow graphs onto parallel processors consists in assigning actors to processors, ordering the execution of actors within each processor, and firing the actors at particular times. Many scheduling strategies do at least one of these operations at compile time to reduce run-time cost. In this paper, we classify four scheduling strategies: 1) fully dynamic, 2) static-assignment, 3) self-timed, and 4) fully static. These are ordered in decreasing run-time cost. Optimal or near-optimal compile-time decisions require deterministic, data-independent program behavior known to the compiler. Thus, moving from strategy 1) toward 4) either sacrifices optimality, decreases generality by excluding certain program constructs, or both. This paper proposes scheduling techniques valid for strategies 2), 3), and 4). In particular, we focus on data-flow graphs representing data-dependent iteration; for such graphs, although it is impossible to deterministically optimize the schedule at compile time, reasonable decisions can be made. For many applications, good compile-time decisions remove the need for dynamic scheduling or load balancing. We assume a known probability mass function for the number of cycles in the data-dependent iteration and show how a compile-time decision about assignment and/or ordering as well as timing can be made. The criterion we use is to minimize the expected total idle time caused by the iteration; in certain cases, this will also minimize the expected makespan of the schedule. We will also show how to determine the number of processors that should be assigned to the data-dependent iteration. The method is illustrated with a practical programming example, yielding preliminary results that are very promising.

Index Terms— Data flow, data-dependent iteration, parallel processors, parallelizing compilers, quasi-static scheduling, scheduling.

I. INTRODUCTION

A data-flow representation is suitable for programming multiprocessors because parallelism can be extracted automatically from the representation [1], [2]. Each node, or actor, in a data-flow graph represents a task to be executed according to the precedence constraints represented by arcs, which also represent the flow of data. Nodes in a data-flow graph are to be scheduled in such a way as to achieve the fastest execution from a given multiprocessor architecture. We make no assumption here about the granularity of the data-flow graph. The proposed techniques are valid both for fine-grain and large-grain.

Manuscript received May 15, 1989; revised February 6, 1990. This work was supported by the Defense Advanced Research Projects Agency.

The authors are with the Department of Electrical Engineering and Computer Sciences, University of California at Berkeley, Berkeley, CA 94720.

IEEE Log Number 9102631.

Scheduling of parallel computations consists in assigning actors to processors, ordering the actors on each processor, and specifying their firing time, each of which can be done either at compile time or at run time. Depending on when a particular operation is done, we define four classes of scheduling. The first is *fully dynamic*, where actors are scheduled at run-time only. When all input operands for a given actor are available, the actor is assigned to an idle processor at run time. The second type is *static allocation*, where an actor is assigned to a processor at compile time and a local run-time scheduler invokes actors assigned to the processor. In the third type of scheduling, the compiler determines the order in which actors fire as well as assigning them to the processors. At run-time, the processor waits for data to be available for the next actor in its ordered list and then fires that actor. We call this *self-timed* scheduling because of its similarity to self-timed circuits. The fourth type of scheduling is *fully static;* here the compiler determines the exact firing time of actors, as well as their assignment and ordering. This is analogous to synchronous circuits. As with most taxonomies, the boundaries between these categories are not rigid.

We can give familiar examples of each of the four strategies applied in practice. Fully dynamic scheduling has been applied in the MIT static data-flow architecture [10], the LAU system, from the Department of Computer Science, ONERA/CERT, France [35], and the DDM1 [9]. It has also been applied in a digital signal processing context for coding vector processors, where the parallelism is of a fundamentally different nature than that in data-flow machines [23]. A machine that has a mixture of fully dynamic and static assignment scheduling is the Manchester data-flow machine [39]. Here, 15 processing elements are collected in a ring. Actors are assigned to a ring at compile time, but to a PE within the ring at run time. Thus, assignment is dynamic within rings, but static across rings.

Examples of static-assignment scheduling include many data-flow machines [37]. Data-flow machines evaluate data-flow graphs at run time, but a commonly adopted practical compromise is to allocate the actors to processors at compile time. Many implementations are based on the tagged-token concept [2] for example TI's data-driven processor (DDP) executes Fortran programs that are translated into data-flow graphs by a compiler [8] using static assignment. Another example (targeted at digital signal processing) is the NEC uPD7281 [5]. The cost of implementing tagged-token architectures has

Reprinted from *IEEE Trans. on Computers,* vol. 40, no. 11, Nov. 1991, pp. 1225–1238.

120

recently been dramatically reduced using an "explicit token store" [34]. Another example of an architecture that assumes static assignment is the proposed "argument-fetching data-flow architecture" [15], which is based on the argument-fetching data-driven principle of Dennis and Gao [11].

When there is no hardware support for scheduling (except synchronization primitives), then self-timed scheduling is usually used. Hence, most applications of today's general-purpose multiprocessor systems use some form of self-timed scheduling, using for example CSP principles [19] for synchronization. In these cases, it is often up to the programmer, with meager help from a compiler, to perform the scheduling. A more automated class of self-timed schedulers targets wavefront arrays [24]. Another automated example is a data-flow programming system for digital signal processing called Gabriel that targets multiprocessor systems made with programmable DSP's [28]. Taking a broad view of the meaning of parallel computation asynchronous digital circuits can also be said to use self-timed scheduling.

Systolic arrays, SIMD (single instruction, multiple data), and VLIW (very large instruction word) computations [13] are fully statically scheduled. Again taking a broad view of the meaning of parallel computation, synchronous digital circuits can also be said to be fully statically scheduled.

As we move from strategy 1 to strategy 4, the compiler requires increasing information about the actors in order to construct good schedules. However, assuming that information is available, the ability to construct deterministically optimal schedules increases. To construct an optimal fully static schedule, the execution time of each actor has to be known; this requires that a program have only deterministic and data-independent behavior [25], [26]. Constructs such as conditionals and data-dependent iteration make this impossible and realistic I/O behavior makes it impractical. The concept of static scheduling has been extended to solve some of these problems, using a technique called *quasi-static scheduling* [27]. In quasi-static scheduling, some firing decisions are made at run time, but only where absolutely necessary.

Self-timed scheduling in its pure form is effective for only the subclass of applications where there is no data-dependent firing of actors and the execution times of actors do not vary greatly. Signal processing algorithms, for example, generally fit this model [25], [26]. The run-time overhead is very low, consisting only of simple handshaking mechanisms. Furthermore, provably optimal (or close to optimal) schedules are viable. As with fully static scheduling, data-dependent behavior is excluded if the resulting schedule is to be optimal. Again, quasi-static scheduling solves some of the problems, but data-dependent iteration has been out of reach except for certain special cases.

Static-assignment scheduling is a compromise that admits data dependencies, although all hope of optimality must be abandoned in most cases. Although static-assignment scheduling is commonly used, compiler strategies for accomplishing the assignment are not satisfactory. Numerous authors have proposed techniques that compromise between interprocessor communication cost and load balance [33], [6], [40], [31], [12], [30]. But none of these consider precedence relations between

actors. To compensate for ignoring the precedence relations, some researchers propose a dynamic load balancing scheme at run time [22], [4], [21]. Unfortunately, the cost can be nearly as high as fully dynamic scheduling. Others have attempted with limited success to incorporate precedence information in heuristic scheduling strategies. For instance, Chu and Lan use very simple stochastic computation models to derive some principles that can guide heuristic assignment for more general computations [7].

Fully dynamic scheduling is most able to utilize the resources and fully exploit the concurrency of a data-flow representation of an algorithm. However it requires too much hardware and/or software run-time overhead. For instance, the MIT static data-flow machine [10] proposes an expensive broad-band packet switch for instruction delivery and scheduling. Furthermore, it is not usually practical to make globally optimal scheduling decisions at run time. One attempt to do this by using static (compile-time) information to assign priorities to actors to assist a dynamic scheduler was rejected by Granski *et al.*, who conclude that there is not enough performance improvement to justify the cost of the technique [18].

In view of the high cost of fully dynamic scheduling, static-assignment and self-timed are attractive alternatives. Self-timed is more attractive for scientific computation and digital signal processing, while static-assignment is more attractive where there is more data dependency. Consequently, it is appropriate to concentrate on finding good compile-time techniques for these strategies. In this paper we propose a way to schedule a data-dependent iteration for general cases with the assumption that the probability distribution of the number of cycles of the iteration is known or can be approximated at compile time. The technique is not optimal except in certain special cases, but it is intuitively appealing and computationally tractable.

In the next section, we set the context by explaining what we mean by data-dependent iteration, and explaining precisely the problem we are solving. A complete compiler using this solution also needs other scheduling techniques from the literature, as explained. In Section III, we introduce the notion of "assumed" execution time for a data-dependent iteration. Once the scheduler "assumes" an execution time for the iteration, it can construct a static schedule containing the iteration. The question addressed in this section is, what should the assumed execution time be? The answer is *not* the expected execution time, as one might expect. Instead, the answer depends on the number of processors devoted to the iteration relative to the total number of processors. In Section IV we explain how to decide how many processors to devote to the iteration. Section V describes the technique applied to a real programming example from graphics. Section VI explains precisely why the proposed technique is not optimal, except under unrealistic assumptions, but also why we should expect good performance. Through Section VI we have assumed "quasi-static" execution, which requires global synchronization of the processors. In Section VII, we show that the method applies much more broadly to self-timed and static-assignment scheduling.

II. DATA-DEPENDENT ITERATION

In data-dependent iteration, the number of iteration cycles is determined at run time and cannot be known at compile time. Two possible data-flow representations for data-dependent iteration are shown in Fig. 1 [27]. The numbers adjacent to the arcs indicate the number of tokens produced or consumed when an actor fires [25]. In Fig. 1(a), since the up-sample actor produces X tokens each time it fires and the iteration body consumes only one token when it fires, the iteration body must fire X times for each firing of the up-sample actor. In Fig. 1(b), the number of iterations need not be known prior to the commencement of the iteration. Here, a token coming in from above is routed through a "select" actor into the iteration body. The "D" on the arc connected to the control input of the "select" actor indicates an initial token on that arc with value "false." This ensures that the data coming into the "F" input will be consumed the first time the "select" actor fires. After this first input token is consumed, the control input to the "select" actor will have value "true" until the function $t(\cdot)$ indicates that the iteration is finished by producing a token with value "false." During the iteration, the output of the iteration function $f(\cdot)$ will be routed around by the "switch" actor, again until the test function $t(\cdot)$ produces a token with value "false." There are many variations on these two basic models for data-dependent iteration.

For simplicity, we will group the body of a data-dependent iteration into one node, and call it a data-dependent iteration actor. In other words, we assume a hierarchical data-flow graph. In Fig. 1(a), the "iteration body" actor consists of the up-sample, data-dependent iteration, and down-sample actors. The data-dependent iteration actor may consist of a subgraph of arbitrary complexity and may itself contain data-dependent iterations. In Fig. 1(b), everything between the "select" and the "switch," inclusive, is the data-dependent iteration actor. In both cases, the data-dependent iteration actor can be viewed as an actor with a stochastic run time, but unlike atomic actors, it can be scheduled onto several processors. Although our proposed strategy can handle multiple and nested iteration, for simplicity all our examples will have only one iteration actor in the data-flow graph.

The method given in this paper can be applied to both kinds of iteration in Fig. 1 identically. There is, however, an important difference between them. In Fig. 1(b), each cycle of the iteration depends on the previous cycle. There is a recurrence that prevents simultaneous execution of successive cycles. In Fig. 1(a), there is no such restriction, unless the iteration body itself contains a recurrence. For the purposes of this paper, we will simply assume that successive cycles of the iteration must be executed sequentially. An extension that handles overlapped cycles will be reported in a separate paper.

The proposed scheme has two components. First, the compiler must determine which processors to allocate to the data-dependent iteration actor. These will be called the iteration processors, and the rest will be called noniteration processors. Second, the data-dependent iteration actor is optimally assigned an *assumed execution time,* to be used by the scheduler. In other words, although its run time will actually be random,

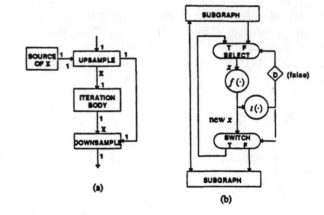

Fig. 1. Data-dependent iteration can be represented using the either of the data-flow graphs shown. The graph in (a) is used when the number of iterations is known prior to the commencement of the iteration, and (b) is used otherwise.

the scheduler will assume a carefully chosen deterministic run time and construct the schedule accordingly. The assumed run time is chosen so that the expected total idle time caused by the difference between the assumed and actual run times is minimal. It is well known that locally minimizing idle time fails to minimize expected makespan, except in certain special cases. (The makespan of the schedule is defined to be the time from the start of the computation to when the last processor finishes.) We will discuss these special cases and argue that the strategy is nonetheless promising, particularly when combined with other heuristics.

Using the assumed execution time, a fully static schedule is constructed. When the program is run, the execution time of data-dependent actors will probably differ from the assumption, so processors must be synchronized. If all processors are synchronized together, using for example a global "enable" line, then we say the execution is quasi-static. It is not fully static because absolute firing times depend on the data. If processors are pairwise synchronized, then the execution is self-timed or static-assignment, depending on whether ordering changes are permitted.

The assumed execution time and the number of processors devoted to the iteration together give the scheduler the information it needs to schedule all actors around the data-dependent iteration. It does not address, however, how to schedule the data-dependent iteration itself. We will not concentrate on this issue because it is the standard problem of statically scheduling a periodic data-flow graph onto a set of processors [25]. Nonetheless, it is worth mentioning techniques that can be used. To reduce the computational complexity of scheduling and to allow any number of nested iterations without difficulty, *blocked scheduling* can be used. In blocked scheduling, all iteration processors are synchronized after each cycle of the iteration so that the pattern of processor availability is flat before and after each cycle (meaning that all processors become available for the next cycle at the same time). If the scheduling is fully static, then this can be accomplished by padding with no-ops so that each processor finishes a cycle at the same time. The wasted computation can be reduced using advanced techniques such as *retiming*

122

or *loop winding*[1] [29], [17]. In these techniques, several cycles of an iteration are executed in parallel to increase the overall throughput. For blocked scheduling, the objective is to minimize the makespan of one cycle. Throughput can also be improved using optimal periodic scheduling strategies, such as cyclostatic scheduling [36]. The proposal below applies regardless of the method used, but in all our illustrations we assume blocked scheduling. We similarly avoid specifics about how the scheduling of the overall data-flow graph is performed. Our method is consistent with simple heuristic scheduling algorithms, such as Hu-level scheduling [20], as well as more elaborate methods that attempt, for example, to reduce interprocessor communication costs. Broadly, our method can be used to extend any deterministic scheduling algorithm (based on execution times of actors) to include data-dependent iteration.

III. THE ASSUMED EXECUTION TIME

To schedule the actors around the data-dependent iteration actor at compile time, it is necessary to assign some fixed execution time to the data-dependent iteration actor. Since the number of cycles of the iteration to be executed is not known at compile time, we have to assume a number. The first guess might be to simply assume the *expected* execution time, which can be approximated using methods proposed by Martin and Estrin [32], but this will often be far from optimal. In fact, the assumed number should depend on the ratio of the number of iteration processors to the total number of processors. When the actual execution time differs from the assumed run time, some processors will be idled as a consequence. Our strategy is to find the assumed run time that minimizes the expected value of this idle time. We make the bold assumption that the probability distribution of the number of cycles of the iteration actor is known or can be approximated at compile time.

Let the number of cycles of an iteration be a random variable I with known probability mass function $p(i)$. Denote the minimum possible value of I by MIN and the maximum by MAX. MAX need not be finite. In this section, we assume that we have already allocated somehow the number N of processors to the data-dependent iteration actor. How to allocate the number of processors will be addressed in the next section. If the total number of the processors is T, the number of noniteration processors is $T - N$.

Let the assumed execution time of the data-dependent iteration actor be t. For the time being we restrict t to multiples of the execution time of one cycle of the iteration. If the execution time of a cycle is τ, then $x = t/\tau$ denotes the assumed number of cycles of the iteration. At run time, for each invocation of the iteration actor, there are three possible outcomes: the actual number i of cycles of the iteration is equal to, greater than, or less than x. These cases are displayed in Fig. 2. In order for the scheduler to resume static scheduling after the iteration is complete, it must know the "pattern of processor availability." As indicated in Fig. 2, this

pattern simply defines the relative times at which processors become free after the iteration. For now, assume this pattern is strictly enforced by some global synchronization mechanism, regardless of the number of iteration cycles actually executed at run time. This will force either the iteration processors or the noniteration processors to be idle, depending on whether the iteration finishes early or late. This constraint is precisely what we mean by "quasi-static" scheduling of data-dependent iterations. It is not strictly static, in that exact firing times are not given at compile time, but relative firing times *are* enforced.

Consider the case where the assumed number x is exactly correct. Then no idle time exists on any processor (Fig. 2(a)). Otherwise, the noniteration processors will be idled if the iteration takes more than x cycles (Fig. 2(b)), or else the iteration processors will be idled (Fig. 2(c)). Our strategy is to select x to minimize the expected idle time on all processors for a given number of iteration processors.

Let $p(i)$ be the probability mass function of the number of iteration cycles confined within MIN and MAX. For a fixed assumed x the expected idle time $t_1(x)$ on the iteration processors is

$$t_1(x) = N\tau \sum_{i=\text{MIN}}^{x} p(i)(x - i). \tag{1}$$

The expected idle time $t_2(x)$ on the noniteration processors is

$$t_2(x) = (T - N)\tau \sum_{i=x+1}^{\text{MAX}} p(i)(i - x). \tag{2}$$

The total expected idle time $t(x)$ is $t(x) = t_1(x) + t_2(x)$. The optimal value of x minimizes this quantity. From this we can get that

$$t(x) - t(x + 1) = -N\tau \sum_{i=\text{MIN}}^{x} p(i) + (T - N)\tau \sum_{i=x+1}^{\text{MAX}} p(i)$$

$$= -N\tau + T\tau \sum_{i=x+1}^{\text{MAX}} p(i). \tag{3}$$

Similarly,

$$t(x) - t(x - 1) = N\tau - T\tau \sum_{i=x}^{\text{MAX}} p(i). \tag{4}$$

The optimal x will satisfy the following two inequalities: $t(x) - t(x+1) \leq 0$ and $t(x) - t(x-1) \leq 0$. Since τ is positive, from (3) and (4),

$$\sum_{i=x+1}^{\text{MAX}} p(i) \leq \frac{N}{T} \leq \sum_{i=x}^{\text{MAX}} p(i). \tag{5}$$

All quantities in this inequality are between 0 and 1. The left and right sides are decreasing function of x. Furthermore, for all possible x, the intervals

$$\left[\sum_{i=x+1}^{\text{MAX}} p(i), \sum_{i=x}^{\text{MAX}} p(i) \right] \tag{6}$$

---

[1] As a possibly interesting side issue, it does not appear to have been pointed out in the literature that retiming is simply a data-flow perspective on loop winding, so the techniques are in fact equivalent.

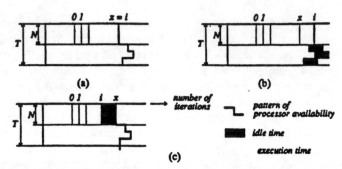

Fig. 2. A static schedule is constructed using a fixed assumed number x of cycles in the iteration. The idle time caused by the difference between x and the actual number of cycles i is shown for 3 cases: (a) i is equal to, (b) less than, or (c) greater than the assumed number, x.

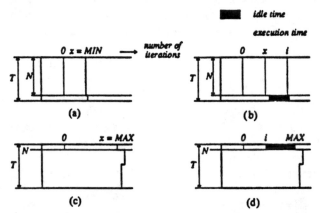

Fig. 3. When the number of iteration processors N approaches the total number T, x approaches MIN and the iteration processors will not be idled for any actual number of iterations ((a) and (b)). On the other hand, when N is small, x tends toward MAX so that the noniteration processors will not be idled ((c) and (d)).

are nonoverlapping and cover the interval $[0, 1]$. Hence, either there is exactly one integer x for which N/T falls in the interval, or N/T falls on the boundary between two intervals. Consequently, (5) uniquely defines the one optimal value for x or two adjacent optimal values.

This choice of x is intuitive. As the number of iteration processors approaches the total number, T, of processors, N/T goes to 1 and x tends towards MIN. Thus even if an iteration finishes unexpectedly early, the iteration processors will not be idled. Instead the noniteration processors (if there are any) will be idled (Fig. 3(a) and (b)). On the other hand, x will be close to MAX if N is small. In this case, unless the iteration runs through nearly MAX cycles, the iteration processors, of which there are few, will be idled while the noniteration processors need not be idled (Fig. 3(c) and (d)). In both cases, the processors that are more likely to be idled at run time are the lesser of the iteration or noniteration processors.

Consider the special case where $N/T = 1/2$. Then from (5),

$$\sum_{i=x+1}^{\text{MAX}} p(i) = 1 - \sum_{\text{MIN}}^{x} p(i) \leq 1/2 \qquad (7)$$

which implies that

$$\sum_{\text{MIN}}^{x} p(i) \geq 1/2. \qquad (8)$$

Furthermore,

$$\sum_{i=x}^{\text{MAX}} p(i) \geq 1/2. \qquad (9)$$

Taken together, (8) and (9) imply that x is the *median* of the random variable I (not the mean, as one might expect). In retrospect, this result is obvious because, for any random variable I, the value of x that minimizes $E|I - x|$ is the median. Note that for a discrete-valued random variable, the median is not always uniquely defined, in that there can be two equally good candidate values. This is precisely the situation where x falls on the boundary between two intervals in (6).

Up to now, we have implicitly assumed that the optimal x is an integer, corresponding to an integer number of cycles of the iteration. For noninteger x, the total expected idle time is restated as

$$t(x) = N\tau \sum_{i=\text{MIN}}^{\lfloor x \rfloor} p(i)(x - i)$$
$$+ (T - N)\tau \sum_{i=\lfloor x \rfloor + 1}^{\text{MAX}} p(i)(i - x). \qquad (10)$$

Define $\delta_x = x - \lfloor x \rfloor$, so $0 \leq \delta_x < 1$. Then (10) becomes

$$t(x) = N\tau \sum_{i=\text{MIN}}^{\lfloor x \rfloor} p(i)(\lfloor x \rfloor - i + \delta_x)$$

124

$$+(T-N)\tau \sum_{i=\lfloor x\rfloor+1}^{MAX} p(i)(i-\lfloor x\rfloor-\delta_x)$$

$$=t(\lfloor x\rfloor)+N\tau \sum_{i=MIN}^{\lfloor x\rfloor} p(i)\delta_x -(T-N)\tau \sum_{i=\lfloor x\rfloor+1}^{MAX} p(i)\delta_x$$

$$=t(\lfloor x\rfloor)+\tau\delta_x\left(N-T\sum_{i=\lfloor x\rfloor+1}^{MAX} p(i)\right). \tag{11}$$

This tells us that between $\lfloor x\rfloor$ and $\lfloor x\rfloor+1, t(x)$ is an affine function of δ_x, so it must have its minimum at $\delta_x = 0$ or $\delta_x \to 1$, depending on the sign of the slope. Either of these results is an integer, so inequality (5) is sufficient to find the optimal value of x.

As an example, assume $p(i)$ is a uniform distribution over the range MIN to MAX. In other words,

$$p(i) = \begin{cases} \dfrac{1}{MAX - MIN + 1}; & MIN \le i \le MAX \\ 0, & \text{otherwise.} \end{cases} \tag{12}$$

Then the optimal number x satisfies

$$\frac{(MAX - x)}{(MAX - MIN + 1)} < \frac{N}{T} < \frac{(MAX - x + 1)}{(MAX - MIN + 1)}, \tag{13}$$

from inequality (5). From this,

$$x > MAX - \frac{N}{T}(MAX - MIN + 1),$$

$$x < MAX + 1 - \frac{N}{T}(MAX - MIN + 1). \tag{14}$$

Together these imply that

$$x = MAX - \left\lfloor \frac{N}{T}(MAX - MIN + 1)\right\rfloor. \tag{15}$$

In the special case where exactly half of the processors are devoted to the iteration, x becomes the *expected* number of cycles of the iteration, which for this distribution is the same as the median. Also, as N gets small, x tends toward MAX, and as N approaches T, x tends towards MIN, just as expected.

A uniform probability mass function $p(i)$ is not a good model for many types of iteration. In situations involving convergence, a geometric probability mass function may be a better approximation. At each cycle of the iteration, we proceed to the next cycle with probability q and stop with probability $1 - q$.

For generality, we still allow an arbitrary minimum number MIN of cycles of iteration. The maximum number, MAX, is infinite. Let $j = i - MIN$, where i is the number of cycles of the iteration. Then, the geometric probability mass function means that for any nonnegative integer r,

$$P[j \ge r] = q^r \tag{16}$$

and

$$P[j = r] = p(r) = q^r(1 - q). \tag{17}$$

To use inequality (5), we find

$$\sum_{i=x+1}^{MAX} p(i) = \sum_{i=x+1}^{\infty} p(i) = P[j \ge x + 1 - MIN]$$
$$= q^{x+1-MIN}. \tag{18}$$

Similarly,

$$\sum_{i=x}^{MAX} p(i) = q^{x-MIN}. \tag{19}$$

Therefore, from inequality (5), x satisfies

$$x+1 - MIN > \log_q \frac{N}{T}$$
$$x - MIN < \log_q \frac{N}{T}. \tag{20}$$

Combining these, we get that

$$x = MIN + \left\lfloor \log_q \frac{N}{T}\right\rfloor. \tag{21}$$

To gain intuition about this expression, consider the special case where $q = 0.5$, meaning that after each cycle of iteration we are as likely to proceed as to stop. Further specializing, when exactly half of the processors are devoted to the iteration, x becomes $MIN + 1$, which is the expected number of iteration cycles, as well as the median. Note that practical applications are likely to have a larger value for q, in which case the median will be smaller than the mean.

The expressions for x, the assumed number of iteration cycles, are simple enough to be of practical use in a parallelizing compiler that assumes a geometric or uniform probability mass function. However, there remains the question of determining how many processors to devote to an iteration.

IV. PROCESSOR PARTITIONING

In the previous discussion, we assumed that we can somehow allocate the optimal number N of processors to the data-dependent iteration. Now we give a strategy determining this number. Unfortunately, in practical situations, the detailed structure of the data-flow graph has an impact on the optimal choice of N. To keep the scheduler simple, our preference is to adopt suboptimal policies that are optimal for a subset of graphs and reasonable for the rest. In particular, we can apply a principle similar to that used in Section III. We will discuss the limitations of our method in Section VI.

Recall that our scheduling strategy is to assume that the iteration runs for x cycles exactly and to construct a static schedule accordingly. When the actual number of cycles differs from x (as it often will), global synchronization is used to idle either the iteration processors (if the iteration finishes early) or the noniteration processors (if the iteration finishes late). From this, we can conclude that the total cost of the data-dependent iteration in quasi-static scheduling is the execution time spent on the iteration plus the idle time caused by it. This is an approximation, as discussed in the next section, because it ignores the effect that the data-dependent iteration may have on other computations. Nonetheless, we propose to select N to minimize this cost.

As before, i is the number of iterations, τ_N is the run time per iteration cycle (with N iteration processors), and x_N is the assumed number of iteration cycles from the previous section (with N iteration processors). Note that τ_N and x_N are both nonincreasing in N.

If i is smaller than x_N, the iteration processors will be idled and the total cost will be $Nx_N\tau_N$ (Fig. 2(c)). On the other hand, if i is greater than x_N, the cost of the iteration consists of execution time on the iteration processors plus idle time on the noniteration processors. In this case, the total cost becomes $Ni\tau_N + (T - N)(i - x_N)\tau_N$ (Fig. 2(b)). As a result, the expected value of the cost of the iteration for a fixed N is

$$t_o(N) = \sum_{i=\text{MIN}}^{x_N-1} p(i)Nx_N\tau_N$$
$$+ \sum_{i=x_N}^{\text{MAX}} p(i)(Ni\tau_N + (T-N)(i-x_N)\tau_N). \quad (22)$$

After a few manipulations, (22) becomes

$$t_o(N) = Nx_N\tau_N + T\tau_N \sum_{i=x_N}^{\text{MAX}} p(i)(i - x_N). \quad (23)$$

Our proposal is to minimize this quantity. This can be done for specific distributions $p(i)$.

First, let us again consider a geometric distribution on the number of cycles of the iteration. Since

$$\sum_{i=x_N}^{\text{MAX}} p(i)(i - x_N) = \frac{q}{1-q} q^{x_N-\text{MIN}}, \quad (24)$$

we get

$$t_o(N) = N\tau_N x_N + T\tau_N \frac{q}{1-q} q^{x_N-\text{MIN}}. \quad (25)$$

Since both x_N and τ_N are functions of N, dependency of $t_o(N)$ on N cannot be clearly defined. If we replace x_N using (21), we get

$$t_o(N) = N\tau_N \left(\text{MIN} + \left\lfloor \log_q \frac{N}{T} \right\rfloor \right) + T\tau_N \frac{q}{1-q} q^{\lfloor \log_q \frac{N}{T} \rfloor}, \quad (26)$$

which is a complicated transcendental that looks as if it has to be minimized numerically. Fortunately, we can draw some intuitive conclusions for certain interesting special cases.

Consider the case where linear speedup of the iteration actor is possible. In other words, $\tau_N N = K$, where K is the total amount of computation in one cycle of the iteration. The (26) simplifies slightly to

$$t_o(N) = K(\text{MIN}) + K \left\lfloor \log_q \frac{N}{T} \right\rfloor + T \frac{K}{N} \frac{q}{1-q} q^{\lfloor \log_q \frac{N}{T} \rfloor}. \quad (27)$$

The first term is constant in N and the second term is decreasing in N. We will now show that the third term is

approximately constant in N, suggesting that $t_o(N)$ is minimized by selecting the largest possible value, $N = T$. This is intuitively appealing, since, with linear speedup, applying more processors to the problem would seem to make sense. To show that the third term is approximately constant, note that

$$\frac{N}{qT} = q^{(\log_q \frac{N}{T} - 1)} > q^{\lfloor \log_q \frac{N}{T} \rfloor} \geq \frac{N}{T}. \quad (28)$$

Consequently, the third term is bounded as follows:

$$\frac{K}{1-q} > T \frac{K}{N} \frac{q}{1-q} q^{\lfloor \log_q \frac{N}{T} \rfloor} \geq \frac{Kq}{1-q}. \quad (29)$$

These bounds do not depend on N. Note, however, that when $N = T$, this third term is at its minimum, $Kq/(1-q)$. It may also be at this minimum for other values of N, but since the middle term in (26) decreases as N increases, the conclusion is that N should be made as large as possible, namely $N = T$.

Consider another extreme situation, when no speedup of the iteration is possible. In this case, $\tau_N = K$, independent of N. For the third term in (26), we use similar bounding arguments and find that both upper and lower bounds on the third term increase linearly in N. The first term also increases linearly in N. The second term is

$$N\tau \left\lfloor \log_q \frac{N}{T} \right\rfloor \quad (30)$$

which also increases in N, so the conclusion is that if no speedup is possible, we should use as few processors as possible, or $N = 1$. This is a reassuring conclusion.

For general speedup characteristics, we cannot draw general conclusions. This suggests that a compiler implementing this technique may need to solve (26) numerically for the optimal N. If the total number of processors T is modest, then this task should not be too onerous, although we would certainly prefer not to have to do it. The task can be somewhat simplified, perhaps, by the observation that we can shrink the range of N to be examined by looking into the range of $t_o(N)$. From (20),

$$q^{x_N+1-\text{MIN}} \leq \frac{N}{T} \leq q^{x_N-\text{MIN}} \quad (31)$$

which implies that

$$\tau_N N \left(x_N + \frac{q}{1-q} \right) \leq t_o(N) \leq \tau_N N \left(x_N + \frac{1}{1-q} \right). \quad (32)$$

For some values of N, the upper bound is smaller than the lower bound for some other value of N, so we can ignore the latter N's.

As another example, consider the case where $p(i)$ is a uniform distribution. Then (23) becomes

$$t_o(N) = N\tau_N x_N + T\tau_N \frac{(\text{MAX} - x_N)(\text{MAX} - x_N + 1)}{2(\text{MAX} - \text{MIN} + 1)}. \quad (33)$$

We can replace x_N with the value given by (15). Observe that if we define $R = \text{MAX} - \text{MIN} + 1$, then

$$\left\lfloor \frac{N}{T} (\text{MAX} - \text{MIN} + 1) \right\rfloor \approx \frac{N}{T} R \quad (34)$$

when $R.V/T$ is large. This crude approximation simplifies the analysis compared with a bounding argument such as that above, which can be carried out and leads to the same conclusion. If in addition we assume linear speedup, so that $N\tau_N = K$, then (33) simplifies to

$$t_o(N) = K(\text{MAX}) + \frac{K}{2}\left[1 - \frac{N}{T}R\right]. \qquad (35)$$

We see that this function is decreasing linearly in N, suggesting again that we should select the maximum $N = T$.

To summarize, we have derived a general cost function that depends on the speedup attainable for the iteration as more processors are devoted to it. The cost function was given for the special cases where the probability mass function for the number of cycles of the iteration is geometric or uniform. Furthermore, simple special situations lead to intuitive results. Namely, if linear speedup is attainable, then we should devote all the processors to the iteration. If no speedup is possible, then we should devote no more than one processor to the iteration. For more general situations, finding the optimal number of processors requires numerically solving a complicated transcendental.

V. An Example

We can illustrate our method with an application from graphics, in which a geometric shape is displayed and rotated in three dimensions, with perspective. This is an attractive application because the program is simple and can be written with or without iteration, and the iteration can be data-dependent or not. We can compare quite a variety of realizations. Not surprisingly, we find that using data-dependent iteration considerably decreases the total amount of computation compared with programs that avoid data-dependent iteration. Furthermore, when we use data-dependent iteration, our scheduling method results in a program that is only 3% slower than the best that can be expected from dynamic scheduling, for this example. We are comparing against a hopelessly optimistic model of dynamic scheduling, so with a realistic model, our method would yield a program that is considerably faster. The target architecture is a shared-memory multiprocessor with four programmable DSP microcomputers (Motorola DSP56001's).

The data-flow graph for the program using data-dependent iteration is shown in Fig. 4. This graph is similar to an implementation we have constructed using the Gabriel signal processing environment [28], with the major difference that it uses data-dependent iteration. It works as follows: two table-lookup actors supply the x and y coordinates of the vertices of the geometric shape. A z coordinate could also be supplied, but our example assumes this is constant. Constants are supplied by the actors labeled dc. The x, y, and z coordinates are rotated along two axes by multiplying pairwise by two complex exponentials, generated by computing sines and cosines. Next, perspective is added by using the z coordinate to modify the x and y coordinates according to a set of parameters that indicate the location of the vanishing point. The result is two coordinates only, since the image has now been mapped

onto two dimensions. The last step is to draw a line between two successive vertices. This is done by first computing the length of the line and then using this length to determine how many points to draw. The length is the output of the magnitude actor in the upper right of Fig. 4(a). Since the number of points drawn depends on the length of the line, we need data-dependent iteration. The length, scaled by an empirically determined constant, serves as the control input for two "repeat" actors, which are special cases of the "up-sample" actors in Fig. 1(a). These actors simply repeat the tokens at their data inputs a number of times given by the control input. The upper repeat actor has a vector input giving the direction of the line to be drawn. The input to the lower repeat actor is the location of the position of the start of the line. In our lab, the D/A drives a vector display with an analog signal, but a bit-mapped display could easily replace this. The overall data-flow graph is repeated in an infinite iteration, thus refreshing the display continually.

A key observation is that without data-dependent iteration, the implementation requires applying the rotation and perspective operators to every point, rather than just the vertices. Since most of the computation is in these transformations, the cost is high. For a particular test shape (a blocklettered G), we determined that the implementation that avoided iteration required an average of 2581 instruction cycles (on four processors) to draw one line. This is the first entry in Fig. 5. Programs using iteration are much less expensive.

In Fig. 4(b), the execution time of each actor is given in Motorola 56000 instruction cycles (currently 75 ns). These are not ideal implementations of these actors, but they are working implementations in the Gabriel system. Suppose that we have four processors. Then, we may assign $1 \leq N \leq 4$ processors to the data-dependent iteration actor. To make the best decision on how many processors are assigned to the actor, we check the total cost of the iteration as a function of the number of assigned processors, as explained in Section IV. For each N, we calculate x_N and the corresponding $t_o(N)$ assuming a given probability mass function of the length of line segment. The cost of iteration, shown in Fig. 4(c), and the schedule, shown in Fig. 4(d), assume a geometric distribution with MIN $= 0$ and $q = 0.95$. In the actual scheduling process, the number N greater than 3 is not considered at all since the makespan of the subgraph within the iteration actor is not shortened with more than two processors. Thus, the search space for N can often be reduced significantly. From the numbers in Fig. 4(c), we choose to assign $N = 2$ processors to the iteration. After the decision is made, we can construct the global schedule (Fig. 4(d)). This Gantt chart shows the assumed length of the iteration as a shaded region.

To make the program more parallelizable, we retimed the graph in front of the data-dependent iteration actor. This is perfectly reasonable for this application, and can be automated [29]. With the specific example we used, we achieved reasonably high processor utilization (82.6%) and low makespan (429 cycles). Of course, at execution time, the number of cycles of the iteration will vary, so the performance will vary. Since there is idle time right at the end of noniteration processors owing to the iteration actor, from the reasoning in Section VI

127

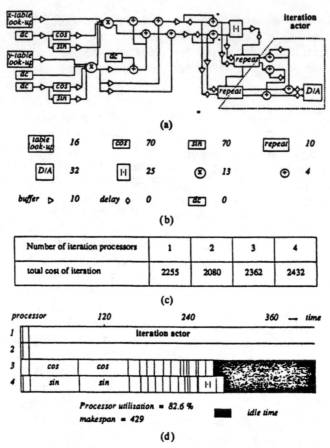

(a)

table look-up	16	cos	70	sin	70	repeat	10
D/A	32	|·|	25	⊗	13	⊕	4
buffer ▷	10	delay ◇	0	dc	0		

(b)

Number of iteration processors	1	2	3	4
total cost of iteration	2255	2080	2362	2432

(c)

(d)

Fig. 4. (a) A data-flow graph of a program that will display a rotating geometric shape in three dimensions with perspective. (b) The execution time of each actor is given in Motorola 56000 instruction cycles (currently 75 ns). (c) The total cost of the iteration as a function of the number of processors assigned to the iteration. (d) One of the schedules produced by the method given in this paper.

below, we expect that the schedule is not optimal. However, it is certainly near optimal in this case.

The major question that remains unanswered is how to determine the stochastic model that best fits an iteration. Our choice here of a geometric model with $q = 0.95$ (the probability of continuing is 0.95) is probably not very accurate. We applied the program to simple geometric shape (letter "G") in order to compare the run-time performance with several scheduling decisions (see Fig. 5). The performance is measured by the average number of cycles to draw one line and depends on the specific shape being drawn. As discussed earlier, fully static scheduling without iteration gives the worst result. Another method that can use fully static scheduling is to perform the maximum number of iteration cycles every time, which gives the second worst result, as shown in the second row of Fig. 5. Next we approximate the run-time statistics using geometric distribution with two different parameters: $q = 0.9$ and $q = 0.95$. The first value grossly underestimates the average length of the lines drawn. The second value results is a probability mass function with the appropriate mean but the wrong shape. For the fifth experiment shown in Fig. 5, we use exactly the correct probability mass function, computed by histograming the lengths of the lines in the geometric shape being drawn. In the sixth experiment, we calculate the performance for fully-dynamic scheduling, ignoring overhead.

The results are remarkable. Using the exact probability mass function, we are within 3% of the best that can be expected

from fully dynamic scheduling, for this program (fifth line, Fig. 5). Using a function with the right mean but the wrong shape, the result is identical (fourth line). Using a function with the wrong mean and the wrong shape, we are still within 12% of the best that can be expected from fully dynamic scheduling (third line).

These results are particularly promising because we are making comparisons with a fully dynamic scheduling strategy that is far more sophisticated than what would be practical, and we are ignoring the scheduling overhead. Specifically, we assume the dynamic scheduler somehow knows how many cycles of the iteration will be executed before each cycle of the overall program begins. It then uses a critical path method (Hu-level scheduling) to construct a schedule for this number of cycles. Since practical dynamic scheduling algorithms are much more primitive, we view the performance of this algorithm as a bound on the performance of all dynamic schedulers. When we count the run-time overhead, the fully dynamic scheduling will be abandoned without hesitation for this example.

The promising results for this program should be viewed only as promising results based on one program. We are developing a programming environment that will permit much more extensive experimentation with practical programs; only after those experiments are complete will we know just how general this method is. Nonetheless, the experiments we have done show that with a good stochastic model for the iteration,

	Average # of cycles to draw 1 line
Fully-static without iteration	2581
Fully static with worst case iteration	1293
Qausi-static (geometric, q = 0.9 : x = 6)	735
Quasi-static (geometric, q = 0.95 : x = 13)	672
Quasi-static (exact distribution : x = 20)	672
Fully dynamic (ideal without overhead)	657

Fig. 5. Performance comparison of several scheduling decisions. The performance is measured by the average number of cycles to draw one line.

at least some programs will get schedules that are about as good as can be expected in practice. They also show that the scheduling method depends on the validity of the stochastic model for the iteration. However, we make the very preliminary postulate that the performance of the technique will not be highly sensitive to the stochastic model since even a crude model might give a near-optimal number for the iteration cycles. This can only be verified by trying many examples, something that requires first developing much more infrastructure. Should the sensitivity prove to be greater, we can then envision successive refinements of the schedule based on observations of the executing program.

VI. OPTIMALITY

The solution we have given is the optimal solution to a simple, but unrealistic problem. Observe that the makespan of a schedule can be given as follows:

$$\text{makespan} = \frac{1}{T}(IN\tau_N + Y + A) \quad (36)$$

where $IN\tau_N$ is the total computation time devoted to the iteration (lightly shaded in Fig. 2), Y is the idle time caused by our quasi-static synchronization strategy (dark shading in Fig. 2), and A is the rest of the computation, including all idle time that may result both within the schedule and at the end. Our solution minimizes the makespan under the bold (and unrealistic) assumption that A is independent of our decisions for N and x_N. For fixed N, the first term in (36) is independent of x_N, so our choice of x_N, which minimizes the second term, is optimal. For variable N, our strategy is to minimize the sum of the first two terms.

The key assumption is unreasonable when precedence constraints make A dependent on our choices. Consider, for example, the situation where there are more processors than we can effectively use, and the data-dependent iteration is in the critical path for all possible outcomes of I. In this case, it may be helpful to devote more processors to the iteration than the optimal number predicted in Section IV. On the other hand, suppose there are no precedence constraints. Then the key assumption is not bad as long as the execution times of all actors are small relative to the makespan. Realistic situations

are likely to fall between these two extremes. Perhaps the best solution is to use our policy, but permit the programmer to indicate a different preference through annotation of the program.

VII. STATIC ASSIGNMENT AND SELF-TIMED SCHEDULING

Once the number of iteration processors and the assumed number of iteration cycles are decided, we can construct a static schedule accordingly. Quasi-static scheduling means global synchronization that makes the pattern of processor availability after the iteration consistent with the scheduled one, as shown in Fig. 2. This implies hardware for global synchronization, which may be less expensive than the handshaking required for self-timed execution (a simple wired-OR circuit would suffice). However, some idle time compulsorily inserted may be unnecessary in reality. Furthermore, if handshaking is omitted, then the system is intolerant of run-time fluctuations, caused for example by interrupts of I/O operations. Hence the quasi-static scheduling strategy is regarded as impractical. Nonetheless, it suggests a good strategy for static-assignment or self-timed scheduling. First we use the techniques of the previous sections to construct a quasi-static schedule. To get a self-timed execution, we insert handshaking at run time and ignore the firing times dictated by the quasi-static schedule. To get static-assignment execution, we discard all information from the quasi-static schedule except the assignment of actors to processors.

A. Static-Assignment Scheduling

In static-assignment scheduling, actors are assigned to processors without defining the execution order. In contrast to dynamic load balancing or techniques that compromise between interprocessor communication cost and load balance, our proposed strategy considers arbitrary precedence relations at compile time. If the actual computation times are similar to those assumed by the scheduler, then our technique can get close to the minimal makespan.

An example of static-assignment scheduling is shown in Fig. 6. A data-flow program consists of six actors with precedence relationships shown in Fig. 6(a). Actor D represents a data-dependent iteration. Suppose that the program is statically scheduled using our technique, and the resulting assignment puts actors D, C, and F onto the first processor and the rest onto the second processor. The ordering and timing information is discarded. Assuming D has a data-dependent execution time, the run-time schedule depends on its outcome. Two possible schedules are shown in Fig. 6(b) and (c). By inspection, we can see in Fig. 6 that the schedules shown are optimal in the sense of minimizing makespan. However, designing a run-time scheduler that reliably produces these schedules is not easy. Assume that when a processor becomes free, if there is an actor ready to be fired, then the run-time scheduler will fire it. This is not necessarily optimal, but in deterministic processor scheduling it can be shown to be reasonable. Then the only decision to be made by the scheduler occurs when there is more than one actor ready to fire. In Fig. 6(b), the run-time scheduler never faces this

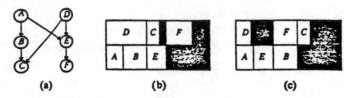

Fig. 6. An example of static-assignment scheduling. The precedence relations are shown in (a), and two possible schedules, which depend on the execution time of actor D, are shown in (b) and (c).

decision, so a very simple strategy will yield the schedule shown. In Fig. 6(c), however, after the completion of actor A, the second processor must decide between firing B or E. E is the better choice, but it is not clear at all how the scheduler might know this. An immediate idea is to use some of the static information that was discarded: specifically the ordering information. However, this does not guarantee the right choice, because the static information is based on an assumption about the data-dependent execution time, and the outcome may be far from this. The alternative of stochastic modeling of the program is not very promising either, because only the most grossly oversimplified stochastic models yield to optimization.

The above observations lead to an interesting conclusion. In static-assignment scheduling, the run-time scheduler on each processor faces an ambiguous decision only if more than one of the actors assigned to it are ready to fire when the last actor completes. If this situation arises rarely, then a naive scheduler will work well. However, under the same conditions, a self-timed strategy would work just as well, and the cost would be lower. On the other hand, if the situation arises frequently, then we do not know how to make the decision. Practical proposals are to make the decision arbitrarily, subject to a "fairness" principle, in which no actor will be tried twice before all other actors have been tried [4]. It may be profitable to augment this strategy by using information discarded from the static schedule, but as argued before, this is not guaranteed to lead to an optimal schedule.

A comparison with the Granski *et al.* proposal [18] is in order. In fully dynamic scheduling, assignment is easy, assuming the target architecture is homogeneous. It does not matter which free processor gets an actor, once the decision has been made to fire that actor. So the decisions to be made by the scheduler are simply which of the actors that are ready to be fired should be fired. If the number of actors that are ready to be fired is smaller than the number of available processors, then there is no decision to be made, and the scheduler will not be helped by static information. It is only if the number of ready actors is large that static information can help. In [18] the authors report that the improvement brought about by the use of static information in a dynamic scheduler degrades to no improvement for large numbers of processors. We just stated the reason for this.

B. Self-Timed Scheduling

In self-timed scheduling, we define the execution order of actors at compile time, thus avoiding the difficulty of designing the local controller. In the example of Fig. 6, suppose

that actors are constrained to execute in the order given by Fig. 6(b). In this case, we sacrifice some freedom to optimize at execution time. However, if the variability in execution time is small enough, then there is little justification for paying the run-time cost of static-assignment scheduling. Of course, if the explicit token store mechanism of Papadopoulos [34] proves to be truly low cost, then the additional adaptability of static-assignment scheduling makes it more attractive. As pointed out earlier, however, tractable static-assignment scheduling is *not* guaranteed to outperform self-timed. It is easy to construct demonstration examples where, for example, an iteration finishes well before expected, causing an order change that results in a *larger* makespan than if there were no order change.

The difference between quasi-static and self-timed scheduling is shown in Fig. 7. In quasi-static scheduling, actors A and B are executed after the iteration even if actor A is independent of the iteration, assuming the scheduler places A after the assumed end of the iteration. We also have to synchronize the processors of actors by inserting idle time compulsorily. However, in self-timed scheduling, actor A is executed independently of the completion of the iteration when its data are available. Idle time may be automatically inserted after A while the next actor waits for data. Similarly, actor B is executed as soon as it is runnable; that is, all input data are available and the assigned processor is available. Since all actors are executed before or at the same synchronized time from the quasi-static scheduling case, the self-timed scheduling strategy always gives a result better than or equal to the quasi-static scheduling strategy, assuming overhead for synchronization is comparable. In addition, it does not need a global synchronization mechanism, but only local handshaking. As a result, we believe that self-timed scheduling is more attractive.

Self-timed scheduling overcomes a difficulty of quasi-static scheduling illustrated in Fig. 8. In the precedence graph shown in Fig. 8(a), assume the iteration actor E is equally likely to run for 0, 1, or 2 iterations of unit length and one of two processors is to be devoted to the iteration. Then our proposed strategy yields the quasi-static schedule in (b). However, suppose the actual number of iterations i exceeds the assumed number x. A strict quasi-static schedule, in which global synchronization enforces the pattern of processor availability after the iteration, would execute as shown in Fig. 8(c) while a self-timed schedule would execute as shown in (d). In this case, our proposed schedule is no more optimal than that in (d), because we considered only the idle time before the completion of the iteration actor when deciding the value x. In other words, our choice of x is only locally optimal. In this example, the idle time after the iteration depends on x. Self-timed execution can sometimes compensate for this deficiency in the scheduling strategy. Idle time immediately after the completion of the iteration has no effect on the performance since there is no compulsory idle time. In other words, for self-timed execution, the schedules in Fig. 8(b) and (d) are equivalent.

This does not lead us to the conclusion that the strategy we propose is optimal under self-timed execution. Consider

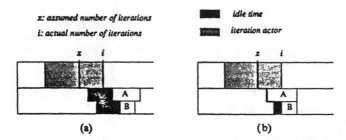

Fig. 7. Comparison between (a) quasi-static scheduling and (b) self-timed scheduling. In quasi-static scheduling, the pattern of processor availability after the iteration is enforced by global synchronization. In self-timed scheduling, the pattern is only enforced if the precedences require it. Here we have assumed that actor B is dependent on the iteration but actor A not.

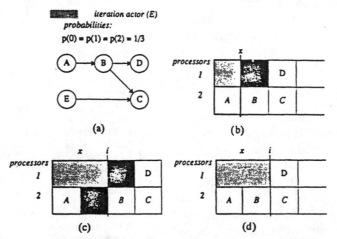

Fig. 8. An example showing that a difficulty in quasi-static scheduling is overcome in self-timed scheduling. According to the precedence graph in (a), the proposed quasi-static schedule is shown in (b). Assume now that the actual number of iterations is 2. Static execution of the schedule results in the schedule shown in (c), while self-timed execution results in the schedule shown in (d).

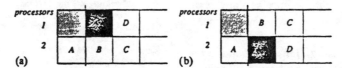

Fig. 9. For the same precedence graph as in Fig. 8, two static schedules ((a) optimal scheduling and (b) bad scheduling) with the same makespan are shown. However, if the actual number of iterations turns out to be 2, the schedule in (a) is better than that in (b).

the two schedules in Fig. 9, which assume the same precedence graph from Fig. 8(a). Under self-timed scheduling, the schedule in Fig. 9(a) is clearly preferable to that in Fig. 9(b), because even if the iteration runs twice as long as the assumed number x, the makespan will not be affected. Our scheduling strategy thus far imposes no constraints that would prefer the schedule in Fig. 9(a). Intuitively, care should be taken to schedule actors after the iteration actor in static-assignment or self-timed scheduling. For examples of this type, the problem can be largely avoided by the following heuristic: all else being equal, actors independent of the iteration should be assigned to the noniteration processors after the iteration. This heuristic may be easily incorporated in the original static scheduling without significant cost.

VIII. CONCLUSION

Static-assignment and self-timed scheduling strategies look like the most promising compromises between hardware cost/performance and flexibility. The choice should depend on the amount of data-dependent behavior in the expected applications. Both strategies require compile-time decisions; they require that tasks be assigned to processors at compile time; in addition, self-timed scheduling requires that the order of execution of the tasks be specified. If there is no data dependency in the application, then these decisions can be made optimally (or nearly so, to avoid complexity problems). When there is data dependency, however, optimal or near optimal compile-time strategies become intractable. Most previously proposed solutions include random choices, clustering (to minimize communication overhead), and load balancing. These solutions either ignore precedence relationships in the data-flow graph or use heuristics based on oversimplified stochastic models. This is justifiable if there is so much data dependency that the precedence relationships are constantly changing. However, there is a large class of applications, including scientific computations and digital signal processing, where this is not true.

131

Nearly all applications of parallel computers involve *some* data-dependent behavior. Consequently, there is a clear need for compile-time strategies that can use precedence information in these cases. Quasi-static scheduling strategies have previously been proposed that can handle conditionals and some forms of iteration [27]. The main contribution of this paper is to extend these techniques to handle data-dependent iterations and to propose that the resulting static schedules give the information needed by a compiler in self-timed and static-assignment situations. The resulting technique can be used to enhance many scheduling algorithms, including those that try to reduce interprocessor communication together with reducing makespan. The proposed method should work well when the amount of data dependency is small, but we admittedly cannot quantify at what level the technique breaks down.

The probability mass function of the number of iteration cycles must be known or estimated at compile time for each iterative construct in the program. Using these probabilities, we find an "assumed" number x of iterations that the scheduler can use to construct a static schedule. This number is selected to minimize the expected idle time on all processors at run time caused by the difference between x and the actual number of iteration cycles executed. This idle time is computed by assuming that the processors are globally synchronized. When half the processors are devoted to the iteration, the resulting choice for x is the *median* number of iterations (not the mean). It is shown that if the execution is self-timed, then the performance can only improve over the quasi-static case, and that the information generated by the quasi-static schedule can be used at very low cost. For static-assignment scheduling, tractable run-time scheduling algorithms may actually lead to *worse* schedules than the quasi-static case, although most of the time the schedules will be better.

The technique is illustrated using one programming example. These results are only a very preliminary indication of the potential practical impact, but they are very promising. For this one program, we found that the resulting quasi-static schedule could be as little as 3% slower than an ideal (and highly unrealistic) fully dynamic schedule. This performance depends on a reasonable (but not exact) stochastic model of the iteration, assumed by the compiler. For the particular program we selected, the performance does not degrade rapidly as the stochastic model gets further from actual program behavior, suggesting that a compiler can use fairly simple techniques to estimate the model. We are developing a programming environment that will permit much more extensive experimentation with the technique.

We are also currently working on natural extensions to the methods described here and will report on these in a subsequent paper. These extensions include the ability to overlap successive cycles of an iteration and to support conditionals and recursion using the same principles.

REFERENCES

[1] W. B. Ackerman, "Data flow languages," *IEEE Computer*, vol. 15, no. 2, pp. 15–25, Feb. 1982.

[2] Arvind and K. P. Gostelow, "The U-Interpreter," *IEEE Computer*, vol. 15, no. 2, Feb. 1982.

[3] J. Backus, "Can programming be liberated from the von Neumann style? A functional style and its algebra of programs," *Commun. Assoc. Comput. Mach.*, vol. 21, no. 8, pp. 613–641, Aug. 1982.

[4] F. W. Burton and M. R. Sleep, "Executing functional programs on a virtual tree of processors," in *Proc. ACM Conf. Functional Programming Lang. Comput. Arch.* 1981, pp. 187–194.

[5] M. Chase, "A pipelined data flow architecture for signal processing: the NEC uPd7281," in *VLSI Signal Processing*, New York, IEEE Press, (1984).

[6] W. W. Chu, L. J. Holloway, L. M.-T. Lan, and K. Efe, "Task allocation in distributed data processing," *IEEE Computer*, pp. 57–69, Nov. 1980.

[7] W. W. Chu and L. M.-T. Lan, "Task allocation and precedence relations for distributed real-time systems," *IEEE Trans. Comput.*, vol. C-36, pp. 667–679, June 1987.

[8] M. Cornish, D. W. Hogan, and J. C. Jensen, "The Texas Instruments distributed data processor," in *Proc. Louisiana Computer Exposition* Lafayette, LA, Mar. 1979, pp. 189–193.

[9] A. L. Davis, "The architecture and system method of DDM1: A recursively structured data driven machine," in *Proc. Fifth Annu. Symp. Comput. Architecture*, Apr. 1978, pp. 210–215.

[10] J. B. Dennis, "Data flow supercomputers," *IEEE Computer*, vol. 13, no. 11, Nov. 1980.

[11] J. B. Dennis and G. R. Gao, "An efficient pipelined dataflow processor architecture," in *Proc. ACM SIGARCH Conf. Supercomputing*, Nov. 1988.

[12] K. Efe, "Heuristic models of task assignment scheduling in distributed systems," *IEEE Computer*, pp. 50–56, June 1982.

[13] J. A. Fisher, "The VLIW machine: A multiprocessor for compiling scientific code," *IEEE Computer*, vol. 17, no. 7, July 1984.

[14] G. R. Gao, "A pipeline code mapping scheme for static dataflow computers," Ph.D. dissertation, Laboratory for Computer Science, MIT, Cambridge, MA, (1983).

[15] G. R. Gao, R. Tio, and H. H. J. Hum, "Design of an efficient dataflow architecture without data flow," in *Proc. Int. Conf. Fifth Generation Comput. Syst.*, 1988.

[16] J. L. Gaudiot, "Data-driven multicomputers in digital signal processing," *Proc. IEEE*, vol. 75, pp. 1220–1234, Sept. 1987.

[17] E. F. Girczyc, "Loop winding—A data flow approach to functional pipelining," in *ISCAS*, 1987, pp. 382–385.

[18] M. Granski, I. Korn, and G. M. Silberman, "The effect of operation scheduling on the performance of a data flow computer," *IEEE Trans. Comput.* vol. C-36, Sept. 1987.

[19] C. A. R. Hoare, "Communicating sequential processes," *Commun. Assoc. Comput. Mach.*, vol. 21, no. 8, Aug. 1978.

[20] T. C. Hu, "Parallel sequencing and assembly line problems," *Oper. Res.*, vol. 9, no. 6, pp. 841–848.

[21] M. A. Iqbal, J. H. Saltz, and S. H. Bokhari, "A comparative analysis of static and dynamic load balancing strategies," in *Proc. Int. Conf. Parallel Processing*, 1986, pp. 1040–1045.

[22] R. M. Keller, F. C. H. Lin, and J. Tanaka, "Rediflow multiprocessing," in *Proc. IEEE COMPCON*, Feb. 1984, pp. 410–417.

[23] J. Kunkel, "Parallelism in COSSAP," *Internal Memorandum*, Aachen University of Technology, Fed. Rep. of Germany, 1987.

[24] S. Y. Kung, *VLSI Array Processors*. Englewood Cliffs, NJ: Prentice-Hall, 1988.

[25] E. A. Lee and D. G. Messerschmitt, "Static scheduling of synchronous data flow graph for digital signal processing," *IEEE Trans. Comput.*, Jan. 1987.

[26] E. A. Lee and D. G. Messerschmitt, "Synchronous data flow," *Proc. IEEE*, vol. 75, Sept. 1987.

[27] E. A. Lee, "Recurrences, iteration, and conditionals in statically scheduled data flow," submitted to *IEEE Trans. Comput.*

[28] E. A. Lee, W.-H. Ho, E. Goei, J. Bier, and S. Bhattacharyya, "Gabriel: A design environment for DSP," *IEEE Trans. Acoust., Speech, Signal Processing*, vol. 37, Nov. 1989.

[29] C. E. Leiserson, "Optimizing synchronous circuitry by retiming," presented at Third Caltech Conf. VLSI, Pasadena, CA, Mar. 1983.

[30] H. Lu and M. J. Carey, "Load-balanced task allocation in locally distributed computer systems," in *Proc. Int. Conf. Parallel Processing*, 1986, pp. 1037–1039.

[31] P. R. Ma, E. Y. S. Lee, and M. Tsuchiya, "A task allocation model for distributed computing systems," *IEEE Trans. Comput.*, vol. C-31, pp. 41–47, Jan. 1982.

[32] D. F. Martin and G. Estrin, "Path length computations on graph models of computations," *IEEE Trans. Comput.* vol. C-18, pp. 530–536, June 1969.

[33] H. Muhlenbeim, M. Gorges-Schleuter, and O. Kramer, "New solutions

to the mapping problem of parallel systems: The evolution approach," *Parallel Comput.*, vol. 4, pp. 269–279, 1987.

[34] G. M. Papadopoulos, "Implementation of a general purpose dataflow multiprocessor," Dep. Elec. Eng. and Comput. Sci., MIT, Ph.D. thesis, Aug. 1988.

[35] A. Plas *et al.*, "LAU system architecture: A parallel data-driven processor based on single assignment," in *Proc. 1976 Int. Conf. Parallel Processing*, pp. 293–302.

[36] D. A. Schwartz and T. P. Barnwell III, "Cyclo-static solutions: Optimal multiprocessor realizations of recursive algorithms," in *VLSI Signal Processing*, New York: IEEE Press, 1986.

[37] V. P. Srini, in "An architectural comparison of dataflow systems," *IEEE Computer*, pp. 68–88, Mar. 1986.

[38] S. R. Vegdahl, "A survey of proposed architectures for the execution of functional languages," *IEEE Trans. Comput.*, vol. C-33, pp. 1050–1071, Dec. 1984.

[39] I. Watson and J. Gurd, "A practical data flow computer," *IEEE Computer*, vol. 15, Feb. 1982.

[40] M. A. Zissman and G. G. O'Leary, "A block diagram compiler for a digital signal processing MIMD computer," in *Proc. IEEE Int. Conf. ASSP*, 1987, pp. 1867–1870.

Soonhoi Ha (S'91) received the B.S. (honors) and M.S. degrees in electrical and electronics engineering from Seoul National University, Seoul, Korea, in 1985 and 1987, respectively.

He is currently a Ph.D. degree candidate in the Electrical Engineering and Computer Sciences Department at the University of California at Berkeley. His research interests include parallel computation, multiprocessor scheduling algorithms, and mixed paradigm simulation.

Edward A. Lee (S'80–M'86) received the B.S. degree from the Yale University in 1979, the S.M. degree from the Massachusetts Institute of Technology in 1981, and the Ph.D. degree from the University of California at Berkeley in 1986.

From 1979 to 1982 he was a member of technical staff at Bell Telephone Laboratories, Holmdel, NJ, in the Advanced Data Communications Laboratory, where he did extensive work with early programmable DSP's and exploratory work on voice-band data modem techniques and simultaneous voice and data transmission. He is now an associate professor in the Electrical Engineering and Computer Sciences Department at the University of California at Berkeley. His research activities include parallel computation, architecture and software techniques for programmable DSP's, design environments for the development of real-time software, and digital communication.

Dr. Lee was a recipient of a 1987 NSF Presidential Young Investigator award and IBM faculty development award, the 1986 Sakrison prize at U.C. Berkeley for the best thesis in electrical engineering, and a paper award from the IEEE Signal Processing Society. He is coauthor of *Digital Communication* (with D.G. Messerschmitt, Kluwer Academic, 1988) and *Digital Signal Processing Experiments* (with Alan Kamas, Prentice Hall, 1989) and has published numerous technical papers.

A Program Allocation Scheme for Data Flow Computers

A. R. Hurson and B. Lee
Department of Electrical Engineering,
The Pennsylvania State University
University Park, PA 16802

B. Shirazi and M. Wang
Department of Computer Science,
Southern Methodist University
Dallas, TX 75275

ABSTRACT

The asynchronous nature of data flow model of computation allows the exploitation of maximum inherent parallelism in many application programs. However, one of the major hurdles facing designers of data flow computers is the issue of program allocation. Finding an allocation algorithm which exploits maximum parallelism while minimizing communication overhead belongs to the class of NP-complete. This paper proposes a method called the Vertically Layered allocation scheme which utilizes heuristic rules in finding a compromise between computation and communication costs.

I INTRODUCTION

In recent years, several computer architectures based on the concept of data flow have been proposed [2, 20]. The data flow model of computation deviates from the conventional control flow model in that data flow operations are asynchronous. That is, the execution of an instruction is based upon the *availability* of its operands. A data flow program is represented as a directed graph $G = G(N, A)$ where the nodes in N represent the instructions and the arcs in A represent the data dependencies between the nodes. The operands are conveyed from one node to another in data packets called *tokens*. Therefore, instructions in the data flow model do not impose any constraints on sequencing except the data dependencies in the program. For high speed computations, the advantage of the data flow approach over the conventional control flow method, stems from the inherent parallelism embedded at the instruction level. This allows efficient exploitation of the fine-grain parallelism in an application program.

The data flow model of computation, due to this implicit parallelism, offers promising performance improvement over the conventional model of computation, which is sequential by nature [8, 17]. However, before data flow computers can become a viable alternative to their conventional control flow counterparts, several major drawbacks must be overcome [14]. This paper addresses the problem of *program allocation* for data flow systems.

II DATA FLOW COMPUTERS AND THE ALLOCATION PROBLEM

To illustrate the problem of allocating data flow graphs, we will consider three data flow architectures: MIT's Static Data Flow Machine (SDFM) [4], the Manchester Data Flow Machine (MDFM) [10], and MIT's Tagged-Token Data Flow Machine (TTDFM) [2]. These architectures can be classified as either *static* or *dynamic* data-driven architectures [20]. Static architectures allow at most one instance of a node to be enabled for firing. An acknowledge scheme is used to detect enabled nodes that are ready for execution. On the other hand, the characteristics of dynamic architectures permit firing of several instances of a node at a time. To distinguish between different instances of a node, a *tag* is associated with each token. A tag identifies the context in which a particular token was generated. The detection of an enabled node is done by comparing the tags of its operands for a match. The SDFM is an example of a static organization while the TTDFM and the MDFM are classified as dynamic architectures.

Data flow architectures can also be classified as *centralized* or *distributed* systems based on the organization of their instruction memories. In a centralized memory organization, the communication cost of conveying a token from one node to another is independent of the actual allocation of nodes in the memory. The SDFM and the MDFM are examples of architectures that utilize a centralized instruction memory. In a data flow multiprocessor system such as the TTDFM, the instruction memory is distributed among the processing elements (PEs). Therefore, inter-PE communication costs are higher than intra-PE communication costs.

MIT's SDFM, proposed by Dennis [4], contains a centralized memory section consisting of physically independent Cell Blocks (CBs). One problem with the group Cell Block organization is the degradation in performance due to an unfortunate distribution of instructions over the Cell Blocks. Tokens destined for concurrently executable instructions residing in the same Cell Block will compete for the same input port since a Cell Block can only access one token at a time from the Distribution Network. The contention problem for the Cell Block organization can be remedied if concurrently executable instructions are distributed over distinct or separate Cell Blocks.

The basic organization of the MDFM, developed by Watson and Gurd at the University of Manchester, contains a Switch Unit, a Token Queue, a Matching Unit, a Node Store, and a Processing Unit connected in a ring network [10]. Similar to the SDFM discussed previously, the Node Store (NS) contains program instructions and is also organized as a centralized memory. Due to its dynamic nature, the execution of nodes are initiated by collecting input tokens with matching tags and destination addresses. These operations are performed in the Matching Unit (MU).

In recent performance studies of the MDFM, it was observed that the Matching Unit and the Node Store were the main sources of a bottleneck [7]. It has been proposed that the overall performance of the MDFM can be improved by utilizing multiple Matching Units and Node Stores. However, the introduction of multiple Node Stores must be accompanied by an appropriate allocation scheme which minimizes contention for these units.

The TTDFM was proposed by Arvind, *et al.* [2]. As mentioned before, the main conceptual difference between the two MIT proposals is that the TTDFM allows multiple tokens to coexist on a single arc to provide greater concurrency in the execution of data flow graphs (i.e., dynamic parallelism). The TTDFM consists of N identical processing elements (PEs) connected by an NxN packet communication network. A single PE constitutes a simple data flow computer consisting of a Program Memory to store codes associated with a program, a data memory called I-structure Store for storing arrays, a Waiting-Matching Store for matching tokens, and a Service Section which contains an arithmetic logic unit (ALU).

The TTDFM is a data flow multiprocessor where executable instructions are executed by their individually associated PE's. Tokens generated by a PE can be routed locally within the PE or to other PEs through the communication network. In general, the costs are higher for inter-PE communications than for intra-PE communications. In this system, therefore, the allocation problem is more severe than in the two centralized memory architectures discussed previously.

Despite the architectural differences of the three machines discussed, it is apparent that they all share a common goal in the allocation of programs: maximizing the inherent concurrency in a program graph by minimizing contention for processing resources. It has been shown that obtaining an optimal allocation of a graph with precedences is NP-complete [18]. Therefore, heuristic solutions are the only possible approach to solving the allocation problem suboptimally in polynomial time.

A number of heuristic algorithms have been developed for the allocation problem based on *critical path list schedules* [1, 12 , 18]. The basic idea behind the critical path list scheduling is to assign each node of a directed graph a weight that equals the maximum execution time from that node to an exit node (i.e. critical path). An ordered list of nodes is constructed according to their weights, which is then used to dynamically assign nodes with highest weights to processors as they become idle. However, the major problem with these heuristic schemes is the lack of consideration for communication delays among the

nodes. Enforcing only critical path scheduling without considering the communication overhead associated with the predecessor-successor nodes assigned to different processors, will not necessarily minimize the overall execution time.

In response to this shortcoming, Ravi, *et al.* [19], have proposed a static allocation scheme, which is a variation of the critical path list scheduling. In this method, several top *candidates* whose critical paths fall within a certain range are considered for allocation, rather than simply choosing the topmost node on the list. From this set of candidates, a node is selected which maximizes savings in communication time.

The allocation scheme just mentioned succeeds in including the communication costs. However, the effectiveness of the scheme depends primarily on the range chosen for selection of a node. It has been shown that, when the deviation is chosen to be very large, the scheduling of nodes no longer conforms to the critical path and the nodes are allocated based only on the minimization of communication delays. On the other hand, when the set of candidates is chosen to be very small, the effectiveness of minimizing the communication costs diminishes [19]. Therefore, the success of this algorithm relies on a parameter which is difficult to generalize for arbitrary program graphs and their implementations on different underlying architectures.

In light of the discussion presented above, we propose an alternative scheme which allocates data flow graphs to data flow computers.

III THE PROPOSED ALLOCATION SCHEME

The proposed allocation scheme will be based on two general philosophies: (i) assign concurrently executable nodes to separate processing elements and (ii) assign nodes connected serially to the same processing element. That is, total execution time and contention is minimized by distributing nodes of a data flow graph on all available processors while total communication time is minimized by clustering nodes in as few processing elements as possible. These are two conflicting objectives, and to provide a compromise, we present the *Vertically Layered* (VL) allocation scheme which utilizes a set of heuristics for determining the appropriate partitioning strategy.

III.1 VERTICALLY LAYERED ALLOCATION SCHEME

The heart of the VL allocation scheme is layered directed graphs. To construct such a graph, consider an arbitrary data flow graph $G = G(N, A)$, shown in Figure 1, where N represents the set of instructions and A represents the partial ordering <• between the instructions. A directed path from node n_i to node n_j implies that n_i precedes n_j (i.e., $n_i <• n_j$). Also included with each node in Figure 1 is the execution time t_i in bold letters. Before a directed graph G can be layered, it must be transformed into an acyclic graph. This is only necessary for the layering process. Once the layering is complete, the actual data flow graph is executed. To perform such a transformation, we employ a method similar to the ones presented in [9, 18]. The algorithm performs a depth-first traversal marking all backward-pointing arcs which close the loops. A modified topological sort, which ignores these markings, is then performed to partition the data flow graph G into disjoint *horizontal* layers H such that the nodes in each layer H_l ($l = 1, 2, ..., k$) can be performed in parallel and the layers are linearly ordered with respect to their precedence constraints (i.e., $H_l < \bullet H_{l+1}$, $1 \leq l \leq k-1$). Such a layered graph can be constructed as follows: Initially, the root node in G is labeled as the horizontal layer $l=1$. If no root node exists, a *dummy* root node is introduced. In succeeding steps, all edges (arcs) originating from the labeled nodes are removed. Find all unlabeled nodes with zero in-degree and label these nodes as layer $l+1$. This process is repeated until all the nodes in G have been assigned a label. An example of a horizontally layered data flow graph of Figure 1 is shown in Figure 2.

Once a program graph has been horizontally layered, the actual allocation is done in two phases: the *separation* and the *optimization* phase. In the separation phase, a data flow graph is initially partitioned into distinct program modules based only on the execution times T. Each program module consists of a serially connected set of nodes which is considered for assignment to a processing element. This is done by rearranging the nodes in G into *vertical* layers where nodes constituting a single vertical layer can be allocated to a processing element. In the second phase, the inter-processor communication costs are considered to optimize the overall execution time of the data flow graphs.

To determine the appropriate vertical layers, the separation phase starts by first identifying the critical path of a directed graph G. The critical path defines all the critical nodes; therefore, by assigning the nodes that lie on the critical path to a single vertical layer, the communication overhead associated with critical nodes is minimized. However, before the critical path of an arbitrary directed graph G can be determined, special provisions must be taken to handle conditional nodes and loops. Due to space limitations, the handling of conditional nodes and loops will not be discussed. The interested reader is referred to [14] for details.

Once the critical path is identified, the nodes in each horizontal layer H_l, for $l = 1, 2, ..., k$, are rearranged so that nodes which lie on the critical path form a single vertical layer. These nodes will be defined as belonging to the vertical layer V_{CP}. At the same time the set of nodes V_{CP} is queued in a First In First Out (FIFO) queue Q according to their precedence relationship. For data flow graphs with vertical layers V_m (for $m = 1, 2, ..., p$), the set of nodes V_{CP} is assigned to the vertical layer $m = \lceil p/2 \rceil$. All other nodes $n_i \notin V_{CP}$ are also rearranged in an iterative manner as follows: Let V^{s-1} represent the set of nodes which have already been rearranged into vertical layers at the $s-1^{\text{th}}$ step (initially we have $V^0 = V_{CP}$). We remove a node n_i from the queue Q and then find a set of nodes V^s_{LDP} that forms the longest directed path (LDP) for every output arc emanating from n_i such that

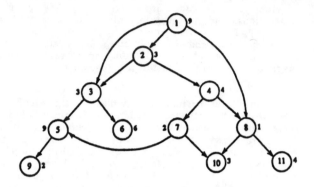

Figure 1: An example of a data flow graph.

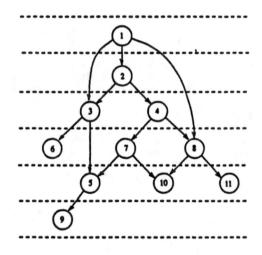

Figure 2: Horizontally layered graph of Figure 1.

$$V^s_{LDP} \cap V^{s-1} = \{ \} \qquad \text{and} \qquad V^s_{LDP} \cup V^{s-1} = V^s.$$

Note that finding the longest directed path emanating from an arc in node n_i involves the same procedure as determining the critical path with the nodes in the set V^{s-1} removed. To implement this, each node in V^s_{LDP}, as it is inserted into the queue, is marked to indicate that it has already been considered for allocation.

Each set of nodes V^s_{LDP} is then assigned to the first available vertical layer. The procedure used to determine whether a vertical layer is available for allocation is based on how densely the nodes can be assigned to a vertical layer. For a given number of processors p, a density factor, D, keeps track of largest number of nodes assigned to a particular horizontal/vertical intersection. When a set of nodes is considered for allocation to a particular vertical layer, the number of nodes already assigned to each horizontal/vertical intersection must be less than the

136

density factor D for all $n_i \in V^s_{LDP}$. If the search process fails for all the vertical layers, the density factor D is incremented by 1 and the process is repeated. This ensures that all of the layers will be arranged as densely as possible. It is important to note that nodes are rearranged only within the assigned horizontal layer. Therefore, the precedence constraints among the nodes defined by the horizontal layers are still observed. The separation phase is completed when the queue is empty and all the nodes in G are rearranged into vertical layers. An example of a vertically layered graph of Figure 2 is shown in Figure 3.

The effectiveness of the vertically layered allocation scheme with the CP and the LDP heuristics can be represented by the *lower* (T^L_{EXE}) and the *upper* (T^U_{EXE}) bound on total execution times

$$T^L_{EXE} = \sum_{n_i \in V_{CP}} t_i \qquad \text{and}$$

$$T^U_{EXE} = \sum_{l=1}^{k} \max_{n_i \in H_l} \{t_i\} + \sum_{l=1}^{k-1} c_l,$$

where c_l refers to the communication cost from horizontal layer l to horizontal layer $l+1$. Note that the execution time component of T^U_{EXE} is a special case of the lower bound where execution times of all nodes in a horizontal layer are equal.

It is apparent from the equations presented above that there is a large gap between lower and upper bounds using only the CP and LDP heuristics. This gap is mainly due to the inter-PE communication delays that may occur between pairs of nodes in two successive horizontal layers which are not assigned to the same processing element. This gap can be minimized by also considering the inter-PE communication costs.

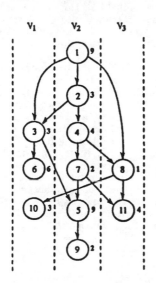

$v_1 \qquad v_2 \qquad v_3$

Figure 3: Vertically layered graph of Figure 2.

The *communication to execution time ratio* (CTR) heuristic algorithm considers two types of inter-PE communication behavior for optimization: Type A and Type B. Type A is associated with the transitory relationship between two subsets of nodes in G that are arranged in two distinct vertical layers. For example, consider two subsets of nodes N_α and N_β which are assigned to vertical layers V_α and V_β, respectively. If $(n_i \in V_\alpha) <\bullet (n_j \in V_\beta)$ and $(n_j \in V_\beta) <\bullet (n_k \in V_\alpha)$, then there will be inter-PE communication costs associated with the execution of the two vertical layers which may delay the execution time of the vertical layer V_α. Type B, on the other hand, is a more general case of Type A behavior.

Consider an example of Type A inter-PE communication behavior as shown in Figure 4. Assume T_α and T_β are the total execution costs associated with N_α and N_β, respectively, where

$$T_\alpha = \sum_{n_i \in N_\alpha} t_i \qquad \text{and} \qquad T_\beta = \sum_{n_i \in N_\beta} t_i$$

If there is a transitory relation between N_α and N_β, we can associate with it a communication cost, $C_{\alpha\beta}$, where

$$C_{\alpha\beta} = c_{\alpha\beta} + c_{\beta\alpha} = 2c_{\alpha\beta}.$$

With these parameters three cases are possible:

Case 1: $T_\beta + C_{\alpha\beta} < T_\alpha$

Case 2: $T_\alpha < T_\beta + C_{\alpha\beta} < T_\beta + T_\alpha$

Case 3: $T_\beta + T_\alpha < T_\beta + C_{\alpha\beta}$

In Case 1, the execution time T_α is greater than the execution time T_β plus the communication cost $C_{\alpha\beta}$ incurred during the transmission of tokens between the vertical layers. Therefore, the initial assignment of the vertical layers to two distinct PEs will not affect the overall execution time. In Case 2, the execution time T_β and the communication cost $C_{\alpha\beta}$ are significant enough to affect the execution time T_α and, therefore, the overall execution time. This will result in a new critical path through the subset of nodes N_β. In order to improve the overall execution time, we can consider combining the subset of nodes N_α and N_β into a single vertical layer. This eliminates the communication cost $C_{\alpha\beta}$ and results in an overall execution time of $T_\beta + T_\alpha$. However, if by combining N_α and N_β into a single vertical layer, the overall execution time $T_\beta + T_\alpha$ results in a larger delay than would result by executing them in two separate vertical layers, then the two subsets are assigned to different PEs.

In Case 3, the execution of N_α and N_β in a single PE results in superior performance. Therefore, if the ratio of communication to execution cost, $C_{\alpha\beta}/(T_\alpha + T_\beta)$, is greater than $1 - T_\beta/(T_\alpha + T_\beta)$, an improved total execution time can be obtained by combining N_α and N_β and executing them on a single PE.

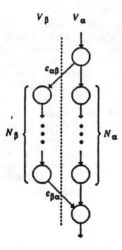

Figure 4: Type A inter-PE communicational behavior.

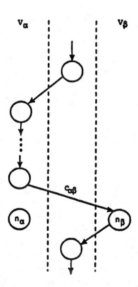

Figure 5: Type B inter-PE communicational behavior.

Consider an example of Type B behavior depicted in Figure 5. One of the major causes of delay for the new critical path is a function of the relative assignment of node n_β. As can be seen, the assignment of n_β to the vertical layer V_β has increased the total execution time. To reduce the inter-PE communication costs, we can consider combining nodes n_β and n_α into a single vertical layer V_α. Then we have either $c_{\alpha\beta} < t_\alpha$ or $t_\beta < c_{\alpha\beta}$. If the communication to execution time ratio, $c_{\alpha\beta}/t_\alpha$, is less than unity, no improvement in performance will be gained by reassigning the node n_β to the vertical layer V_α. However, if $c_{\alpha\beta}/t_\alpha$ is greater than unity, then an incremental improvement $c_{\alpha\beta} - t_\beta$ in total execution time results by combining the nodes into the vertical layer V_α.

To apply the CTR heuristic algorithm, we consider the execution time T_{CP} of a new critical path which includes the effects of inter-PE communication costs. Hence, T_{CP} corresponds to the total execution time T_{EXE} after the program graph G has been vertically layered in the separation phase. We then consider the type of communication behavior which resulted in T_{CP}. If an improvement in T_{CP} results after applying the CTR heuristic, the nodes are combined into a single PE. Since combining two parallel subsets of nodes into a single processing element forces them to be executed sequentially, a new critical path may emerge from the optimization process. Therefore, this process is repeated in an iterative manner until no improvement in performance can be obtained by combining two subsets of nodes associated with T_{CP}.

In certain cases, there may exist multiple critical paths which will not result in an improved performance with a single iteration. This is due to the fact that the CTR heuristic algorithm only considers communication behavior of the nodes that lie on a single critical path. Thus, improving the communication behavior in one critical path may not affect the communication behavior in another. A log, therefore, is kept for each iteration until no multiple critical paths exist and no further improvement in the total execution time can be obtained. The log is then "rolled-back" to the state which resulted in the best total execution time. A formal description of the VL allocation scheme is given in Algorithm 1.

The final allocation of program graphs is influenced by the machine's interconnection network topology and the physical characteristics of each processing element. For example, in data flow machines with a centralized memory organization, each vertical layer can be assigned to a Cell Block (CB). The actual assignment of the vertical layers to the CBs can be done arbitrarily, since each node is equally accessible to result tokens generated by all other instructions and the optimization phase can, therefore, be omitted. Nodes in each layer represent the sequential execution of a sub-graph in G, and the separation phase of the VL allocation scheme minimizes the CB contention.

In data flow multiprocessors, the inter-PE communication cost is generally higher than intra-PE communication costs. Thus, the VL allocation scheme initially attempts to minimize the inter-PE communication costs by identifying as many longest directed paths as possible for allocation to PEs. Unfortunately, the separation phase attempts this process with very little information about the communications overhead. Once the initial allocation is completed, more information regarding the relative assignment of predecessor-successor nodes and its inter-PE communication costs are known. The CTR heuristic algorithm utilizes this information to optimize the final allocation.

ALGORITHM 1: Vertically Layered (VL) Allocation Scheme.

INPUT: A data flow program graph $G(N, A)$, where all $n_i \in N$ has an expected execution time t_i.

OUTPUT: A set of cooperating vertical layers V_m (for $m = 1, 2, ..., p$), where p represents the number of available processors.

Separation Phase
- Perform a cyclic to acyclic transformation by ignoring all backward-pointing arcs that close the loop.
- Partition G into disjoint horizontal layers H_l ($l = 1, 2, ..., k$) such that $H_l <\bullet H_{l+1}$.
- Determine the set of nodes belonging to the approximate critical path and assign it to the vertical layer $m = \lceil p/2 \rceil$.
- Queue the root node in FIFO queue Q.
- Initialize the density parameter D to 1.
- WHILE (Q is not empty) DO
   - CALL VALLOCATE.
- ENDFOR

PROCEDURE VALLOCATE
BEGIN
- Remove the node n_i from the front of the queue Q.
- FOR (All the arcs emanating from n_i) DO
   - Determine the longest directed path V_{LDP}^s from n_i such that

   $$V_{LDP}^s \cap V^{s-1} = \{ \} \text{ and } V_{LDP}^s \cup V^{s-1} = V^s.$$

   - Insert the set of nodes V_{LDP}^s in the queue Q.

   - For each node in V_{LDP}^s, find a corresponding horizontal/vertical intersection which has the number of already assigned nodes less than the density parameter D.
   - If the search fails in the previous step, increment D by 1 and repeat the process.

   - Mark each node in V_{LDP}^s to indicate that these nodes have already been allocated.
- ENDFOR
END

Optimization Phase
DO (if improvement can be made on the new critical path) WHILE
- Determine the new critical path with the effects of inter-PE communication costs.
- If there is an improvement by applying the CRT heuristic, combine the two subsets of nodes into a single vertical layer.
ENDWHILE

I V SIMULATION RESULTS

To evaluate the effectiveness of the Vertically Layered allocation scheme, six data flow graphs were chosen for our simulation studies. The first data flow graph, entitled EX1, is the example utilized throughout this paper (Figure 1). Second is a 16-node data flow graph of a Quicksort algorithm [5]. The final four graphs were obtained from Martin and Estrin with backward-pointing arcs removed [16]. These graphs consist of: (1) 32-node graph entitled NWP 32 representing a numerical weather prediction program, (2) 82-node graph entitled 82V which performs assignment and sequencing, (3) 146-node graph entitled NWP 147 which is a more complex version of the numerical weather prediction problem, and (4) 193-node graph entitled L2 which is a more complex version of the assignment and sequencing program.

Our simulation results are based on the following assumptions:
1. The underlying data flow architecture is a distributed system.
2. The execution time t_i of each node is assigned randomly from a uniform distribution with an average of 5 time units.
3. The inter-PE communication delays are assumed to be constant and the intra-PE delays are assumed to be negligible in comparison to the inter-PE communication delays.
4. The inter-PE communication delays are varied based on a ratio of *communication time to execution time* (C/T).

The major motivation behind the performance analysis is two-fold: (1) to study the effectiveness of the optimization phase in improving the total execution time when inter-PE communication delays are significant in comparison to the execution times of the nodes, and (2) to compare the total execution times of the VL allocation scheme and the Critical Path list schedule, which does not consider the communication delays.

To illustrate the results of the simulation studies, L2 was chosen as a representative data flow graph. Figure 6 depicts the performance improvement versus the number of PEs when the C/T ratio was varied. The comparison was made to see how the VL allocation scheme faired against the critical path method which has been considered *near-optimal* in most cases when communication delays are not considered [13]. The VL allocation scheme showed slight degradation in performance compare to the critical path method when the number of PEs is small and the C/T ratio is low. This is due to the fact that, in such an environment, a number of longest directed paths (LDPs) are forced to be assigned to the same PE. Therefore, our algorithm may not always succeed in reducing the total execution time. As expected, however, when the communication delays are significant, the effectiveness of the VL allocation scheme becomes more apparent. In such cases, the VL allocation scheme significantly reduces the communications overhead involved in sending a token from the predecessor PE to the successor PE.

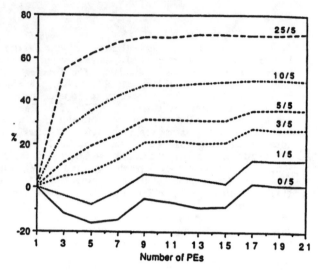

Figure 6: Performance improvement of the VL allocation scheme for various C/T values.

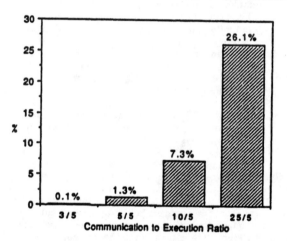

Figure 7: Percentage improvement in performance

by utilizing CTR heuristic.

Figure 7 depicts the effectiveness of the CTR heuristic. The plot shows negligible improvement when the C/T ratio is lower than 5/5. However, as the C/T ratio increases, slight improvement can be observed and for a high C/T ratio (25/5), the improvement becomes more pronounced.

Table 1 represents the performance improvement of the VL allocation scheme in comparison to the CPM for the aforementioned data flow graphs. These results were obtained by considering the average percentage improvement for the various numbers of PEs. As discussed before, when inter-PE communication delays are negligible, a performance degradation generally results by utilizing the VL allocation scheme. However, performance improves as the C/T ratio increases. When the C/T ratio exceeds 1/5, considerable improvement can be noted for all six data flow graphs studied in the simulation.

As mentioned previously, the VL allocation scheme performs poorly when the number of available PEs is much less than the maximum parallelism of the data flow graph. However, in the presence of a sufficient number of PEs (i.e, equal to the maximum parallelism), the performance of the VL allocation scheme is much more promising even when the C/T ratio is low. This is shown in Table 2.

Finally, Table 3 shows the average percentage improvement in performance resulting from the optimization phase. Our findings indicate that the effectiveness of the CTR heuristic is negligible when the C/T ratio is low. On the other hand, as the C/T ratio increases, significant improvement can be noted for all six data flow graphs studied.

V SUMMARY AND CONCLUSIONS

In this paper, the problem of allocating data flow graphs to data flow computers was discussed. The concept of the Vertically Layered allocation scheme which utilizes heuristics to handle the allocation problem was introduced. The basic idea behind the proposed scheme is to arrange the nodes of a data flow graph into vertical layers such that each vertical layer can be allocated to a processor. This is achieved by utilizing CP and LDP heuristics. These heuristics give the highest priority to the critical path for allocation and then recursively determine the vertical layers by finding the longest directed path emanating from the nodes which have already been assigned to vertical layers. The CTR heuristic can then be utilized to further optimize the allocation by considering the inter-PE communication costs.

Performance analysis indicates that the proposed scheme is effective in reducing the communications overhead. On the average, the VL allocation scheme showed promising improvement over the Critical Path list schedule in the presence of inter-PE communication delays. Moreover, given a sufficient number of PEs, the VL allocation scheme showed significant improvement over the Critical Path method.

Although the basic idea behind the VL allocation scheme has been outlined, one major issue concerning the allocation problem still remains unresolved -- the issue of handling dynamic parallelism. As discussed in Section II, dynamic data flow architectures, such as the TTDFM and the MDFM, permit simultaneous firing of multiple instances of a node. In theory, this increases both the asynchrony and parallelism of data flow graphs. For example, consider the implementation of a loop schema. A dynamic architecture unfolds the loop at run-time by generating multiple instances of the loop body and attempts to execute the instances concurrently. However, since a single PE does not allow two simultaneous executions of a node, mapping the source data flow graphs to processors without special

TABLE 1: Performance improvement of the proposed scheme relative to the CPM.

C/T	EXI	Quicksort	NWP32	82V	NWP147	L2
0/5	-3.5	-1.3	-18.6	-2	-17.4	-6.8
1/5	1.8	-2.1	-9.6	8.6	-4.7	4.15
3/5	11.8	6.8	4.9	21.4	7.8	18.9
5/5	11.3	15.5	14.1	26.8	17.7	25.5
10/5	16.5	35.1	23.7	45	29.3	40.1
25/5	32.8	57.4	33	65.4	38.6	67.5

TABLE 2: Percentage improvement when a sufficient number of PEs are available.

C/T	EXI	Quicksort	NWP32	82V	NWP147	L2
0/5	1.1	0.0	1.9	0.2	1.3	1.9
1/5	9.9	0.0	10.7	17.7	10.7	12.7
3/5	16.2	3.6	17.3	30.4	20.3	27.1
5/5	16.4	13.9	25.2	34.9	27.1	35.3
10/5	15.3	41.1	30.3	52.2	33.1	49.2
25/5	30.3	71.6	39.3	72.8	38.2	70.3

TABLE 3: Effect of the CTR heuristic on the performance improvement.

C/T	EXI	Quicksort	NWP32	82V	NWP147	L2
1/5	0.0	0.0	0.0	0.0	0.4	0.0
3/5	0.0	6.8	1.1	0.2	0.8	0.1
5/5	0.6	14.9	2.2	1.7	1.5	1.3
10/5	3.4	33.6	6	7.7	3.1	7.3
25/5	16.2	55.1	10.2	31.2	5.4	26.1

provisions results in the inability to fully exploit the maximum parallelism.

It is therefore necessary to provide a code-copying facility, where an instruction within a code block is duplicated among the available resources. Arvind has proposed a mapping scheme in which the instructions within a code block (called the logical domain) are mapped onto available PEs (called the physical domain) based on a hashing scheme [4]. For example, if a physical domain consists of n PEs, then the destination PE number can be $PE_{base} + i \bmod n$, where i is the iteration number. This will distribute the code uniformly over the physical domain. Since each of the n PEs has a copy of the code, n iterations may be executed simultaneously. A similar approach can be incorporated into the VL allocation scheme by preprocessing the data flow graphs. This is done by duplicating the nodes associated with the body of a loop according to the expected number of iterations. However, the question still remains as to how effectively dynamic parallelism can be exploited at run-time.

VI REFERENCES

[1]   Adam, T. L., Chandy, K. M. and Dickson, J. R., "A Comparison of List Schedules for Parallel Processing Systems," Commun. ACM , Vol. 17, No. 12, Dec. 1974, pp. 685-690.

[2]   Arvind and Culler, D. E, "Dataflow Architectures," Annual Review in Computer Science, 1986, Volume 1, pp. 225-253.

[3]   Arvind, "Decomposing a Program for Multiprocessor System," Proc. Int'l. Conf. on Parallel Processing, 1980, pp. 7-14.

[4]   Dennis, J. B., "Data-Flow Supercomputers," Computer, pp. 48-56, Nov. 1980.

[5]   Eager, D. L., Zahorjan, J., and Lazowska, E. D., "Speedup Versus Efficiency in Parallel Systems," IEEE Transactions on Computer, Vol. 38, No. 3, March 1989, pp. 408-423.

[6]   Gajski, D. D., Padua, D. A., Kuck, D. J. and Kuhn, R. H. "A second opinion on data flow machines and languages," IEEE Computer, Feb 1982, pp. 58-69.

[7]   Ghosal, D. and Bhuyan, L. N., "Analytical Modeling and Architectural Modifications of a Dataflow Computer," Proc. 14th Annual Symposium on Computer Architecture, 1987, pp. 81-89.

[8]   Gostelow, K. P. and Thomas, R. E., "Performance of a simulated data flow computer," IEEE Transactions on Computer, vol. C-29, Oct. 1980, pp. 905-919.

[9]   Granski, M., Koren, I., and Silberman, G. M., "The effect of operation scheduling on the performance of a data flow computer," IEEE Transactions on Computers, Vol. C-36, No. 9, September 1987, pp. 1019-1029.

[10] Gurd, J. R., Kirkham C. C. and Watson, I., "The Manchester Prototype Data-Flow Computer," Commun. ACM, Vol. 28, pp. 34-52, Jan. 1985.

[11] Hurson, A. R., Lee, B., and Shirazi, B., "Hybrid Structure: A Scheme for handling Data Structures in a Data Flow Environment," Lecture Notes in Computer Science, Vol. 365, 1989, pp. 323-340.

[12] Kasahara, H. and Narita, S.,"Practical Multiprocessor Scheduling Algorithms for Efficient Parallel Processing," IEEE Transactions on Computers, Vol. c-33, No. 11, Nov. 1984, pp. 1023-1029.

[13] Kohler, W. H., "A preliminary evaluation of critical path method for scheduling tasks on multiprocessor systems," IEEE Transactions on Computers, Dec. 1975, pp. 1235-1238.

[14] Lee, B., "Data Structuring and Processor Allocation for a Data Flow Environment," Ph.D. Dissertation, in preparation, The Pennsylvania State University, Department of Electrical Engineering, 1990.

[15] Lee, B. and Hurson, A. R., "Hybrid Structure: Data Structuring for Data Flow," Euromicro Journal, Vol. 26, No. 4, 1989, pp. 253-270.

[16] Martin, D. F. and Estrin, G., "Experiments on Model of Computations and Systems," IEEE Transactions on Electronic Computers, Vol. EC-16, No. 1, Feb. 1967.

[17] Patnaik, L. M., Govindarajan, R. and Ramadoss, N. S., "Design and Performance Evaluation of EXMAN: An EXtended MANchester Data flow Computer," IEEE Transactions on Computers, Vol. C-35, No. 3, March 1986, pp. 229-243.

[18] Polychronopoulos, C. D. and Banerjee, U., "Processor Allocation for Horizontal and Vertical Parallelism and Related Speedup Bounds," IEEE Transactions on Computers, Vol. C-36, No. 4, April 1987, pp. 410-420.

[19] Ravi, T. M., Ercegovac, M. D., Lang, T., and Muntz, R. R., "Static Allocation for a Data Flow Multiprocessor System," UCLA Computer Science Department Report No. CSD-860028, Nov. 1986.

[20] Sirini, V. P., "An Architectural Comparison of Data Flow Systems," IEEE Computer, Vol. 19, No.3, March 1986, pp. 68-86.

Chapter 3

Task Granularity and Partitioning

3.1 Introduction

The efficient execution of parallel programs depends on the effective partitioning of the program into modules (or partitions) and the scheduling of those modules for execution on a set of N processors. The size and complexity of the modules can have a great impact on the total execution time of the parallel programs [Gerasoulis 1993a,b]. At peak performance, all N PEs are busy all of the time, executing useful instructions, and thus achieving a factor of N improvement over a uniprocessor. However, reaching peak performance is commonly not attainable, due to the overheads introduced by multiprocessing, such as:

- communication overhead,
- synchronization overhead,
- loss of efficiency when PEs run out of jobs, and
- operating system task management overhead.

Efficient parallel processing consists of finding a good trade-off among several factors, including:

- the number of processors to use,
- the number of modules or partitions to execute (for example, should we combine/cluster several small parallel tasks into a serial task or not), and
- the amount of overhead.

In many cases, for a given program, the addition of more PEs may not improve the performance, since the overhead may be increased at a higher rate as N increases.

Such a trade-off analysis is achieved using a factor called task granularity. The granularity of a task is defined as the ratio of the task computation time over the task communication and overhead. Thus, if R = execution time of a task and C = communication delay generated by the task, $\frac{R}{C}$ is the granularity of the task. A task is said to be a fine-grain task if its $\frac{R}{C}$ ratio is relatively low. Program instructions in dataflow computations are examples of fine-grain tasks. On the other hand, if $\frac{R}{C}$ is relatively high, then the related task is said to be coarse-grain. Examples of coarse-grain tasks are program functions, subprograms, and partitions. In general, finer-grain tasks imply higher degrees of parallelism among the tasks as well as higher amounts of overhead. Conversely, coarser-grain tasks imply less parallelism among the tasks, but less overhead as well.

Thus, system performance is dependent upon the balance between the amount of parallelism among the program modules and the associated overhead. To improve system performance finer-grain tasks can be clustered into coarser-grain partitions. The partitions are then scheduled on the PEs. Therefore, partitioning is a preprocess step to scheduling.

3.2 Partitioning algorithms

The goal of program partitioning is to eliminate as much as possible the overhead caused by intertask communication, while preserving the highest possible degree of parallelism [Cvetanovic 1987]. The algorithms used for the partitioning process vary from method to method. In this section we present three of the more general classes of partitioning algorithms.

3.2.1 Critical path partitioning

As the name indicates, the majority of these algorithms rely on the critical path heuristic to carry out the partitioning step. The idea is that the fine-grain tasks that rely on a critical path of a program graph have to be executed sequentially anyway. Thus, once the nodes on a critical path are identified, they should be clustered into one partition so that they can be assigned to one processor for execution. An example of such a partitioning method is presented in [Lee 1991]. This method, called vertically layered partitioning, consists of two steps:

1. Starting with a fine-grain program DAG, a modified topological sort is performed to transform the DAG into disjoint horizontal layers such that the nodes in each layer can be performed in parallel and the layers are linearly ordered with respect to the precedence constraints among the nodes.
2. A critical path of the transformed DAG is identified and the nodes on this path are clustered into a vertical layer, forming a partition. This partition is temporarily removed from the DAG by marking its nodes as "processed." Step 2 is then iteratively carried out for unprocessed longer paths until there are no nodes left.

Figure 3.1a depicts an example DAG. Figure 3.1b shows the transformed DAG of Figure 3.1a after horizontal layering. Finally, Figure 3.1c presents the vertically layered partitions V1, V2, and V3.

3.2.2 Communication delay elimination partitioning

These methods use the elimination of the communication overhead as the criterion for the clustering of the tasks into partitions. The general approach is to cluster the successors of a node, along with the node itself, into a partition, provided that the overall completion time of these nodes is not prolonged. It should be noted that as a task is put into a cluster, its communication cost with its predecessors becomes negligible. However, at the same time, the concurrence among the successors of a node is lost if they are put into the same partition. Thus, the partitioning algorithms in this class try to cluster the nodes, as long as the benefits of zeroing the communication delays outweigh the serialization of parallel tasks. The methods proposed in [McCreary 1989] and [Yang 1990] are examples of this class of partitioning algorithms.

Figure 3.2 depicts how the dominant sequence clustering algorithm proposed in [Gerasoulis 1990, Gerasoulis 1992, Yang 1990] works. The original DAG is shown in Figure 3.2a, where the numbers in each node represent the $\frac{R}{C}$ ratio. For example, node $n1$ requires 1 time unit to execute, 3 time units to pass a message to task $n2$, and 1 time unit to pass a message to task $n3$. Starting with node $n1$, we need to decide whether $n1$ and $n2$ should be put into the same partition or not. If $n2$ is not put in the same partition as $n1$, then it will take 6.5 time units to complete $n1$ and $n2$. However, by putting $n1$ and $n2$ in the same partition, we can complete the pair of tasks in 3.5 time units. Next, we need to decide whether $n3$ should be put in the $n1$-$n2$ partition or not. If $n3$ joins this partition, then it will take 6 time units to complete the execution of $n1$, $n2$, and $n3$ tasks. If $n3$ is kept independent of the $n1$-$n2$ partition, it will take 4.5 time units to complete the execution of the same three

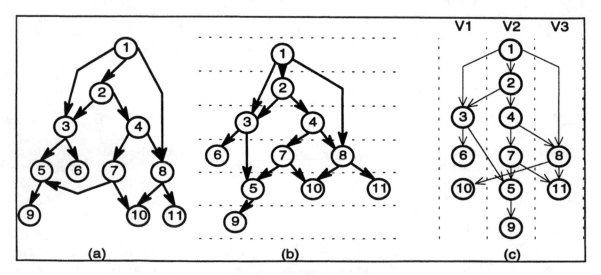

Figure 3.1.   DAG partitioning.

144

tasks. Thus, n3 is not clustered with n1 and n2. Figure 3.2b depicts the final partitioning of the tasks of the DAG of Figure 3.2a. These two partitions should be scheduled on different processors. It should be noted that one of the advantages of the partitioning is that it provides an upper bound on the number of allocated processors. In this example, only two processors are sufficient for the efficient execution of the program.

3.2.3 Task duplication

Task duplication is an alternative method of partitioning process. The idea is to eliminate the communication cost among the tasks by duplicating the tasks among the PEs. The advantage of task duplication is that it not only eliminates the communication costs, it also preserves the original program parallelism. The disadvantages of the method are, of course, increased space requirements and increased synchronization overhead for data accesses among the duplicated tasks. [Kruatrachue 1988], covered in this chapter, presents an example of the task duplication method. Figure 3.3 depicts the scheduling of a DAG on three processing elements. Each numbered node of the DAG represents a task with a 1-time-unit execution delay. The communication costs are marked on the corresponding arcs of the DAG. In this example, task 1 is duplicated in all three processors. This effectively eliminates the communication cost between node 1 and nodes 2, 3, and 4.

3.3 Chapter organization and overview

The body of literature specifically addressing granularity and partitioning issues is rather sparse. This chapter covers four papers, which address different aspects of program partitioning issues. The paper by Gerasoulis and Yang addresses the impact of the granularity on scheduling task graphs. (Readers are referred to [Gerasoulis 1990] and [Gerasoulis 1992] for a comparative study of clustering algorithms.) Two types of clustering—linear and nonlinear—are introduced. It is shown that every nonlinear clustering of a coarse-

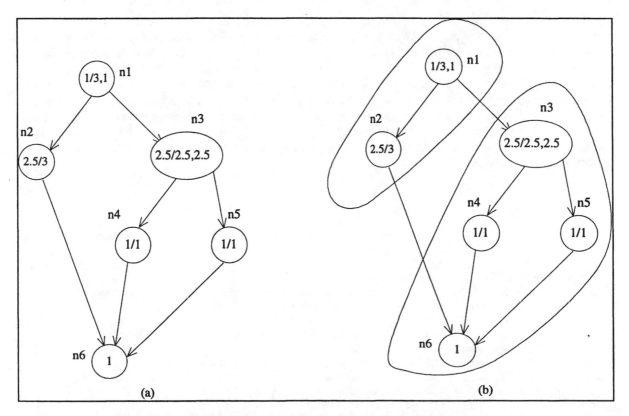

Figure 3.2. Example of communication cost elimination partitioning.

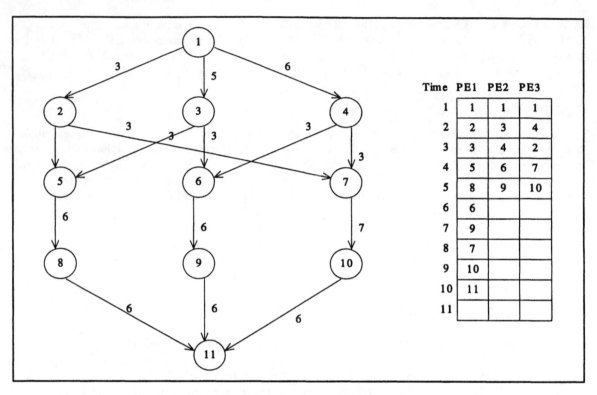

Figure 3.3.   Example of task duplication.

grain DAG can be transformed into a linear clustering which has less or equal parallel time than the non-linear one. The second paper, by Cvetanovic, provides an analysis of the effects program partitioning and grain size have on the performance of multiprocessor systems. It is shown that for algorithms whose computation and communication can be decomposed, the speed-up is an increasing function of the level of granularity, provided that the interconnection bandwidth is greater than unity. If the bandwidth is equal to the unity, then the speed-up converges to $\frac{R}{C}$. As discussed in section 3.2.3, the paper by Kruatrachue and Lewis presents task duplication as an alternative approach to achieve the same goals as program partitioning. Finally, the last paper, by Mohr, Kranz, and Halstead, discusses a totally different approach to the partitioning problem: dynamic task partitioning. In the proposed lazy task creation method, tasks are created retroactively as processing resources become available.

Bibliography

Berger, M. J., and S. H. Bokhari, "A Partitioning Strategy for Nonuniform Problems on Multiprocessors," *IEEE Trans. Computers*, Vol. C-36, No. 5, May 1987, pp. 570–580.

Chen, M.-S., and K. G. Shin, "Subcube Allocation and Task Migration in Hypercube Multiprocessors," *IEEE Trans. Computers*, Vol. C-39, No. 9, Sept. 1990, pp. 1146–1155.

Chuang, P.-J., and N.-F. Tzeng, "A Fast Recognition-Complete Processor Allocation Strategy for Hypercube Computers," *IEEE Trans. Computers*, Vol. C-41, No. 4, Apr. 1992, pp. 467–479.

Cvetanovic, Z., "The Effects of Problem Partitioning, Allocation, and Granularity on the Performance of Multiple-Processor Systems," *IEEE Trans. Computers*, Vol. C-36, No. 4, Apr. 1987, pp. 421–432; reprinted here.

Gerasoulis, A., S. Venugopal, and T. Yang, "Clustering Task Graphs for Message Passing Architectures," *Proc. ACM Int'l Conf. Supercomputing*, ACM Press, New York, N.Y., 1990, pp. 447–456.

Gerasoulis, A., and T. Yang, "A Comparison of Clustering Heuristics for Scheduling Directed Acyclic Graphs on Multiprocessors," *J. Parallel and Distributed Computing*, Vol. 16, 1992, pp. 276–291.

Gerasoulis, A., and T. Yang, "On the Granularity and Clustering of Directed Acyclic Task Graphs," *IEEE Trans. Parallel and Distributed Systems*, Vol. 4, No. 6, June 1993, pp. 686–701; reprinted here.

Gerasoulis, A., and T. Yang, "Scheduling Program Task Graphs on MIMD Architectures," in *Parallel Algorithm Derivation and Program Transformation,* R. Paige, J. Reif, and R. Wachter, eds., Kluwer Academic Publishers, Norwell, Mass., 1993, pp. 153–186.

Kim, J., C. R. Das, and W. Lin, "A Top-Down Processor Allocation Scheme for Hypercube Computers," *IEEE Trans. Parallel and Distributed Systems,* Vol. 2, No. 1, Jan. 1991, pp. 20–30.

Kruatrachue, B., and T. Lewis, "Grain Size Determination for Parallel Processing," *IEEE Software,* Vol. 5, No. 1, Jan. 1988, pp. 23–32; reprinted here.

Lee, B., A. R. Hurson, and T.-Y. Feng, "A Vertically Layered Allocation Scheme for Data Flow Systems," *J. Parallel and Distributed Computing,* Vol. 11, No. 3, 1991, pp. 175–187.

McCreary, C., and H. Gill, "Automatic Determination of Grain Size for Efficient Parallel Processing," *Comm. ACM,* Sept. 1989, pp. 1073–1078.

Middleton, D., "Dynamically Allocating Sets of Fine-Grained Processors to Running Computations," *Proc. 2nd IEEE Symp. Frontiers of Massively Parallel Computations,* IEEE CS Press, Los Alamitos, Calif., 1988, pp. 191–194.

Mohr, E., D. A. Kranz, and R. H. Halstead, Jr., "Lazy Task Creation: A Technique for Increasing the Granularity of Parallel Programs," *IEEE Trans. Parallel and Distributed Systems,* Vol. 2, No. 3, July 1991, pp. 264–280; reprinted here.

Polychronopoulos, C. D., and U. Banerjee, "Processor Allocation for Horizontal and Vertical Parallelism and Related Speedup Bounds," *IEEE Trans. Computers,* Vol. C-36, No. 4, Apr. 1987, pp. 410–420.

Sadayappan, P., and F. Ercal, "Nearest-Neighbor Mapping of Finite Element Graphs onto Processor Meshes," *IEEE Trans. Computers,* Vol. C-36, No. 12, Dec. 1987, pp. 1408–1424.

Yang, T., and A. Gerasoulis, "A Fast Static Scheduling Algorithm for DAGs on an Unbounded Number of Processors," tech. report, Dept. of Computer Science, Rutgers University, 1990.

On the Granularity and Clustering of Directed Acyclic Task Graphs

Apostolos Gerasoulis, *Member, IEEE*, and Tao Yang, *Student Member, IEEE*

Abstract—In this paper we consider the impact of the granularity on scheduling task graphs. Scheduling consists of two parts, the processors assignment of tasks and the ordering of tasks for execution in each processor. The processor assignment part is also known as clustering in the literature when there is no limitation in the number of processors and the architecture is completely connected. We introduce two types of clusterings, the nonlinear and linear clusterings. A clustering is nonlinear if two parallel tasks are mapped in the same cluster otherwise is linear. Linear clustering fully exploits the natural parallelism of a given DAG while nonlinear clustering sequentializes independent tasks to reduce parallelism. We also introduce a new quantification of the granularity of a DAG and define a coarse grain DAG as the one whose granularity is greater than one. We prove the following interesting result: Every nonlinear clustering of a coarse grain DAG can be transformed into a linear clustering which has less or equal parallel time than the nonlinear. We use this result to prove the optimality of some important linear clusterings used in parallel numerical computing. We also present experiments with an actual architecture that verify our theoretical results. These results provide a justification for the popularity of linear clustering in the literature.

Index Terms— Clustering, DAG's, Gauss–Jordan algorithm, granularity, parallel architectures, partitioning, scheduling.

I. INTRODUCTION

IN this paper, we analyze the impact of the granularity on scheduling directed acyclic task graphs (DAG's). Scheduling is a mapping of the nodes of a DAG onto p processors plus the starting time for each task. Clustering is also a mapping of the nodes of a DAG onto m clusters, but the starting time for each task does not have to be given. Every task in a cluster must execute in the same processor. A clustering is called *nonlinear* if at least one cluster contains two independent parallel tasks, otherwise it is called linear. Clustering has been used as a *pre-processing* step in the scheduling of task graphs on parallel architectures. For example, Sarkar [23, p. 124], has proposed a two step approach to compile-time scheduling:

1) Find clusters by scheduling the task graph on an unbounded number of processors on a completely connected *virtual* architecture. Sarkar calls this step the "internalization pre-pass."

2) Schedule the clusters onto p *physical* processors.

Manuscript received August 14, 1990; revised March 1, 1993. This work was supported in part by Grant DMS-8706122 from NSF, by the Air Force Office of Scientific Research and the Office of Naval Research under Grant N00014-90-J-4018, and by Rutgers University Fellowship.

The authors are with the Department of Computer Science, Rutgers University, New Brunswick, NJ 08903.

IEEE Log Number 9209544.

The two step approach above has also been used to schedule DAG's on MIMD architectures and in VLSI processor array design. Examples are the Gaussian-Elimination and Gauss–Jordan algorithms in which the DAG is first clustered by using "data locality" [7] or "owner computes rule" [2], i.e., processors only modify data that they own. Next, clusters are mapped onto the p processors using wrap mapping and scheduled using either the naive or compute-ahead task orderings, e.g., Ortega [17, pp. 88 and 241], Gerasoulis and Nelken [7]. In VLSI array processor design a similar two step approach has been used. The clustering step is called processor assignment using processor projection, S. Y. Kung [15 pp. 133–136, p. 165]. It is interesting to see that in the literature linear clustering is widely chosen. This preference raises the question on what is so special about linear clustering. We provide an explanation in this paper.

We will consider the clustering problem as scheduling a precedence DAG on an unbounded number of fully-connected processors. Sarkar [23] shows that determining the optimal clustering is NP-complete. A similar result has been shown by Chretienne [3] and Papadimitriou and Yannakakis [18]. Assuming that task duplication is permitted, Papadimitriou and Yannakakis [18] have shown that a polynomial time algorithm exists which is within 50% of the optimum. Task duplication, however, could result in considerable increase in the space complexity since data also need to be duplicated. Without task duplication, polynomial time heuristic algorithms [13], [14], [16], [23], [25], [26] for clustering have been proposed and a comparison is given in Gerasoulis and Yang [8].

There are two fundamental scheduling strategies used in clustering: scheduling independent tasks in one cluster (nonlinear clustering) and scheduling tasks that are in a precedence path of the DAG in one cluster (linear clustering). Linear clustering fully exploits the parallelism in the DAG while nonlinear clustering reduces the parallelism by sequentializing independent tasks to avoid high communication. It is important to know when linear or nonlinear clustering strategy should be used. Such knowledge could benefit the design of a scheduling algorithm as well as program partitioning. The tradeoff point of parallelization (corresponding to linear clustering) and sequentialization (corresponding to nonlinear clustering) is closely related to the granularity value: the ratio between the task computation and communication. When communication cost is too high, then the granularity is too fine and parallelization is not suggested. Stone [24] has provided some analysis on the impact of the granularity on tasks that communicate with each other. His analysis, however, does not consider

Reprinted from *IEEE Trans. on Parallel and Distributed Systems*, vol. 4, no. 6, June 1993, pp. 686–701.

task precedence and cannot be extended to the problem of scheduling general DAG's. Gerasoulis and Venugopal [9] have proposed a granularity definition for a DAG. Using this definition, it is shown that the ratio of the parallel time for any linear clustering to that of the optimum parallel time for a DAG is bounded above by one plus the inverse of the granularity. This implies that if the granularity is at least one, the ratio is at most two. However, this granularity definition does not identify the tradeoff point at which linear clustering becomes better than nonlinear clustering.

In Section II, we review some basic definitions and assumptions on the task model, clustering and scheduling. In Section III, we discuss the advantages and some properties of linear clustering strategies. In Section IV, we discuss various granularity definitions and also introduce a new granularity definition. We show how this definition better captures the tradeoff point between parallelization and sequentialization of DAG's. We prove that linear clustering is better than nonlinear clustering for arbitrary coarse grain DAG's and this is the main justification for choosing our granularity definition. In Section V, we show that the performance bound of linear clustering by Gerasoulis and Venugopal [9] can be extended to our granularity definition. These two results provide a theoretical justification for using linear clustering. In Section VI, we apply the results of the paper to the Gauss–Jordan linear algebra algorithm and prove why the ring architecture is the best architecture for clustering the Gauss–Jordan DAG. This is done by showing that the optimum parallel time on a ring is equal to the optimum parallel time on the clique for this case. In Section VII, we present some experiments to examine our theoretical results on a real parallel architectures. Finally, in Section VIII we discuss some open questions and present an example which shows that the results of the paper could be useful even in cases when the DAG is not fully coarse grain, as for example in the case of the Gaussian-Elimination DAG.

II. The Clustering Problem

A weighted DAG is a tuple $G = (V, E, C, T)$, where $V = \{n_j, j = 1 : v\}$ is the set of nodes and $v = |V|$, $E = \{e_{i,j} = <n_i, n_j>\}$ is the set of communication edges and $e = |E|$. The set C is the set of edge communication costs and T is the set of node computation costs. The value $c_{i,j} \in C$ is the communication cost incurred along the edge $e_{i,j} \in E$, which is zero if both nodes are mapped in the same processor. The value $\tau_i \in T$ is the computation cost for node $n_i \in V$. The degree of parallelism in a DAG, also called width of this DAG, is the size of the maximal set of independent tasks. The length of a path is the summation of all node computation and edge communication costs in that path. The critical path is the path with the longest length in the DAG. For example, if we assume that the computation weights are $\tau_i = 1$ for all nodes of the DAG in Fig. 1(a), then $\{n_1, n_3, n_6, n_8\}$ is a critical path with length 9. The width of the DAG is 3.

Clustering is a mapping of the tasks of a DAG onto m clusters. More specifically, the problem is to determine a mapping

$$map(n_j) = i, \quad j = 1 : v, \quad i = 0 : m - 1$$

of the nodes of G onto m clusters $\{M_0, M_1, \cdots, M_{m-1}\}$, so that a certain goal is achieved. Fig. 1(b) and (c) demonstrate two examples of clustering. The goal is to minimize the parallel time on an unbounded number of processors. This is also known as the parallel time minimization or min-max criterion for clustering,

$$\min_S \{ \max_{j=1:v} CT(n_j) \}$$

where S is the set of all possible schedules on an unbounded number of processors and $CT(n_j)$ is the completion time of node n_j. The clustering that attains the minimum parallel time is called the optimum clustering.

To determine clusterings using the min-max model, we need to specify an execution model and the architecture. We make the following assumptions:

- *Duplication* of the execution of tasks in separate clusters is not allowed. This is because duplication results in an increase in the space complexity since data must also be duplicated.

- Each task communicates only before starting and after completing execution. The tasks communicate via asynchronous message passing and they can receive and send *data in parallel*. The task starts execution as soon as all of its input data have arrived in the local message buffer. It sends its output data to successor tasks immediately after completion of its execution. This task model is the same as the compile time macro-dataflow model in which communication may overlap with the computation of each task, e.g., Wu and Gajski [25].

- The architecture is a completely connected *clique* network of processors with local memory and message buffers. The clique has an unbounded number of processors and the communication protocol is via asynchronous message passing.

A schedule is defined by a processor assignment mapping, $PA(n_j)$, of the nodes of G onto the p processors and by the starting times, $ST(n_j)$, of all nodes. In Fig. 2, we show a *Gantt chart* of a schedule for the DAG in Fig. 1(b) on $p = 2$ processors. The Gantt chart completely describes the schedule since it defines both $PA(n_j)$ and $ST(n_j)$. Another way of describing a schedule is through its *scheduled DAG*. The scheduled DAG is a weighted DAG which is derived from the Gantt chart using the execution ordering of the nodes imposed by the schedule within each processor and the communication edges between processors. Communication edges between two nodes mapped in the same processor are assigned zero edge cost. For example, the scheduled graph corresponding to the Gantt chart in Fig. 2(a) is given in Fig. 2(b).

This clustering problem has been shown to be NP-complete [3], [18], [23]. There are two types of fundamental clustering strategies used in heuristic algorithms: *linear* and *nonlinear*, defined in Section I. For example, two nonlinear clusters are depicted in Fig. 1(b) where n_2 and n_3 are independent but scheduled in the same cluster. Three linear clusters are in Fig. 1(c). A clustering is called linear if every cluster is linear otherwise is called nonlinear. If an algorithm only produces a linear clustering for any DAG then we say that it satisfies

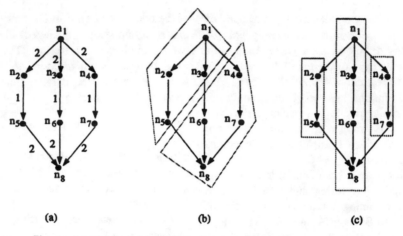

Fig. 1.   (a) Weighted DAG. (b) Nonlinear clustering. (c) Linear clustering.

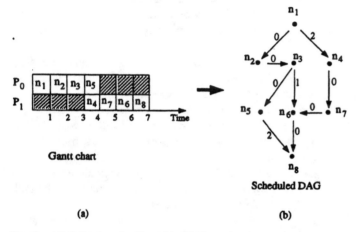

Fig. 2.   (a) Gantt chart for Fig. 1(b). (b) The scheduled graph derived from the Gantt chart.

the *linearity constraint*. Next we will investigate under what conditions linear clustering is a better choice than nonlinear clustering.

III. CLUSTERING ALGORITHMS

In this section, we briefly discuss how a linear clustering strategy could benefit a clustering algorithm by preserving parallelism and at the same time reducing the computational complexity. In [8], we presented a framework of designing and analyzing a clustering algorithm. We have shown that most of previously-developed clustering algorithms can be considered as performing a sequence of clustering refinements. The initial clustering assumes that each task of a DAG is in a separate cluster. Each step of a clustering algorithm tries to refine the previous clustering. A typical refinement is to merge two clusters by zeroing an edge that connects two clusters. By "zeroing," we mean that two end nodes of this edge are mapped into the same cluster and thus the communication cost becomes zero. Let PT_i be the parallel time after the completion of step i, estimated by a scheduling algorithm that assumes that all tasks in a cluster are executed in the same processor. PT_0 is the length of the critical path including

communication delay in the initial graph where no edge has been zeroed. The parallel time value will be used as a cost function to guide the clustering refinement.

As an example of a clustering algorithm we consider Sarkar's [23, pp. 123–131], heuristic "if the parallel time at step i, PT_i, does not increase by zeroing the highest edge cost then zero this edge." In this algorithm, the edges are first sorted using the highest edge cost first principle. Then the algorithm performs e refinement steps by scanning e edges in a descending order of their weights. At each step the algorithm tries to zero the scanned edge if the parallel time does not increase. For example, apply this algorithm to the DAG in Fig. 1 when $\tau_i = 1$. The sorted edges list is

$$\{ <n_1, n_2>, <n_1, n_3>, <n_1, n_4>, <n_5, n_8>,$$
$$<n_6, n_8>, <n_7, n_8>, <n_2, n_5>, <n_3, n_6>,$$
$$<n_4, n_7> \}.$$

In the first step $PT_0 = 9$. Zeroing edge $<n_1, n_2>$ then $PT_1 = 9 \leq PT_0$ and this edge is zeroed. In the next step $<n_1, n_3>$ is zeroed and again $PT_2 = 9$ and so on. Finally all edges will be zeroed which implies that all tasks are mapped in one cluster whose parallel time is $PT_9 = 8$.

Since the merging of two clusters may result in a nonlinear cluster, the sequentialization of independent tasks is necessary to compute the parallel time. Sarkar uses the critical path information from the previous step to order the execution of independent tasks in a nonlinear cluster. Then the parallel time can be estimated by topologically traversing the clustered DAG with a complexity of $O(v+e)$. Thus the total complexity for Sarkar's algorithm is $O(e(v + e))$.

Let us impose the linearity constraint on Sarkar's algorithm and modify the algorithm such that at each step it rejects an edge zeroing if it results in a nonlinear cluster. Then the cost for computing the parallel time at each step is eliminated and the complexity of this algorithm reduces from $O(e(v + e))$ to $O(e \log e)$. We show why this is the case in the next subsection, along with some other fundamental properties of linear clustering.

150

A. Fundamental Properties of Linear Clustering

Property 1 (Monotonicity in parallel time reduction): The parallel time at each clustering step does not increase by zeroing one edge of a given DAG linearly, namely, $PT_i \leq PT_{i-1}$.

Proof: Because of linearity constraint the task ordering in the scheduled graph remains unchanged by the clustering. The parallel time is the length of the critical path of the scheduled graph. If the newly-zeroed edge is in the critical path then the critical path length may be reduced. If the zeroed edge is not in the critical path then the critical path length does not change. ∎

For a nonlinear clustering, the computation of the parallel time requires a sequentialization of independent tasks in a nonlinear cluster. Finding the optimal ordering is NP-complete [12]. But for linear clustering, the problem of computing the parallel time is tractable in a polynomial time complexity.

Property 2 (Simplification of schedule computation): The length of the optimal schedule for a linear clustering on a DAG can be derived in $O(e + v)$ time complexity.

Proof: When m linear clusters are scheduled on exactly m separate processors, task ordering for each processor is uniquely determined by the single dependence chain of each cluster. An optimally scheduled graph is derived by zeroing the edges in each cluster. The edge costs between clusters remain unchanged. The parallel time is the length of the critical path of the scheduled graph. The length of the critical path for a DAG can be determined in $O(v + e)$ time complexity by topologically traversing the DAG. ∎

Property 3 (Preservation of Parallelism): The number of linear clusters for any linear clustering on a DAG is greater or equal to the width of this DAG.

Proof: Assume that the number of linear clusters m is less than w, the width of this DAG. We consider the maximal independent set of this DAG, $MIS = \{n_1, n_2, \cdots, n_w\}$. Because $m < w$, there exist at least two nodes in MIS which are in the same linear cluster. Then there is a path between these two nodes, namely, they are not independent, which is a contradiction. ∎

Next we investigate when linear clustering strategy is a good choice.

IV. THE GRANULARITY OF A TASK GRAPH

Intuitively, the task grain is a local ratio between its computation and communication while the granularity is a global quantity characterizing a DAG based on individual task grains in this DAG, e.g., Golub and VanLoan [10, pp. 270–271], Stone [24, p. 309]. For example, Heath and Romine [11 p. 559] write

"Another important characteristic determining the overall efficiency of parallel algorithms is the relative cost of communication and computation. Thus, for example, if communication is relatively slow, then coarse grain algorithms in which relative large amount of computation is done between communications will be more efficient than fine-grain algorithms."

Stone [24] analyzes the granularity issue by examining a set of tasks where every task computes R units of time and communicates with all other tasks at an overhead cost of C. He defines the ratio R/C as the *task granularity*. His computing model does not consider the precedence between tasks.

We study the granularity issue for general precedence task graphs with arbitrary task and edge sizes. We first show the impact of granularity to clustering by considering a simple precedence DAG in Fig. 3. If we assume that the computation cost w is greater or equal to communication cost c then the parallel time is minimum when n_2 and n_3 are executed in two separate processors as shown in Fig. 3(c). In this case all parallelism in this graph can be fully exploited since it is "useful parallelism." If on the other hand $w < c$, then the parallelism is not "useful" since the minimum parallel time is derived by sequentializing tasks n_2 and n_3 as shown in Fig. 3(b).

Notice that linear clustering preserves the parallelism embedded in the DAG while nonlinear clustering does not. We make the following observation:

If the execution of a DAG uses linear clustering and attains the optimal time, then this indicates that the granularity of the DAG is appropriate for the given architecture; otherwise it is too fine and a scheduling algorithm is needed to execute independent tasks together in the same processor using a nonlinear clustering strategy.

So far we have demonstrated the impact of the granularity on a simple clustering case. An interesting question is if this analysis can be generalized to arbitrary DAG's.

A. A Quantification of the Granularity of a DAG

Gerasoulis and Venugopal [9] have proposed the following definition for an arbitrary DAG:

$$g = \min_{x=1:v} \{\tau_x / \max_j c_{x,j}\}$$

where $c_{x,j}$ are communication costs of the edges going out from node n_x and τ_x is the computation cost of that node. Here we introduce a new granularity definition for a DAG.

A DAG consists of *fork* or/and *join* sets such as the ones shown in Fig. 4. The join set J_x consists of all immediate predecessors of node n_x. The fork set F_x consists of all immediate successors of node n_x. Let $J_x = \{n_1, n_2, \ldots, n_m\}$ and define

$$g(J_x) = \min_{k=1:m} \{\tau_k\} / \max_{k=1:m} \{c_{k,x}\}.$$

Similarly let $F_x = \{n_1, n_2, \ldots, n_m\}$ and define

$$g(F_x) = \min_{k=1:m} \{\tau_k\} / \max_{k=1:m} \{c_{x,k}\}.$$

We define the *grain* of a task as

$$g_x = \min\{g(F_x), g(J_x)\}$$

and the *granularity* of a DAG as

$$g(G) = \min_{x=1:v} \{g_x\}.$$

We call a DAG *coarse grain* if $g(G) \geq 1$. If $\tau_k = R$ and $c_{i,k} = C$ then the grain of every task and the granularity

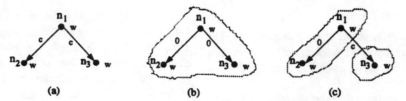

Fig. 3. Sequentialization versus parallelization. (a) A weighted DAG. (b) Sequentialization using nonlinear clustering. (c) Parallelization using a linear clustering.

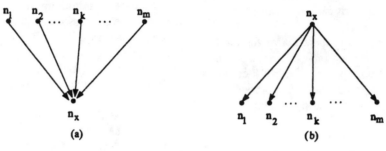

Fig. 4. (a) Join set J_x. (b) Fork set F_x.

of the DAG reduces to the ratio R/C which is the same as Stone's definition. For coarse grain DAG's each task receives or sends a small amount of communication compared to that the computation of its adjacent tasks.

Consider the DAG in Fig. 1(a) and assume that $\tau_i = 1$ for all tasks and the communication cost shown in that figure. The width of this graph is 3. The granularity of the DAG is 1/2 and therefore the DAG is not coarse grain. Fig. 1(b) shows a nonlinear clustering of the DAG in which two parallel nodes n_2 and n_3 are mapped in a cluster and two other parallel nodes n_6 and n_7 in another. This mapping reduces the width from 3 to 2. Scheduling the nonlinear clusters on two processors results in an optimum parallel time of 7, see Fig. 2(a). Notice that linear clustering in Fig. 1(c) does not change the width. Scheduling the linear clusters on three processors results in a schedule of parallel time 8 which is higher than the nonlinear clustering. If on the other hand the task weights were taken to be $\tau_i = 10$ then the DAG becomes coarse grain since the granularity $g(G) = 5$. In this case, linear clustering will have shorter parallel time than the nonlinear one. This example also gives some intuitive feeling on the impact of the granularity on the decision of clustering strategies.

It should be mentioned that our granularity definition, which takes the minimum value among all local task grain values, has its limitation. For example, one task with small local grain value could affect the classification of the entire graph. However, as we will prove in the next section, this granularity definition captures the tradeoff point when linear clustering outperforms nonlinear clustering for arbitrary coarse grain DAG's, which is not the case for other granularity definitions. This is the main justification for choosing our granularity definition. Even with this limitation, our analysis could still be useful when a graph has a large variation in its local grain values. This can be done by partitioning this graph into subgraphs and considering the "local" granularity values

instead. We give an example of such a graph in Section VIII.

Next we will first demonstrate how the above definition captures the tradeoff point between parallelization and sequentialization for a join DAG and then we will generalize it to an arbitrary DAG.

B. Parallelization Versus Sequentialization for a Join DAG

We consider a join DAG J_x with $c_{j,x} = \beta_j$, $j = 1 : m$, see Fig. 5(a), and assume that the nodes and edges are sorted such that $\tau_j + \beta_j \geq \tau_{j+1} + \beta_{j+1}$, $j = 1 : m - 1$.

An algorithm that determines the optimum clustering for this DAG is described in Fig. 6. Initially all tasks are mapped in separate clusters. The result of this algorithm is that tasks $n_x, n_1, n_2, \cdots, n_k$ are in one cluster and the rest of the tasks are mapped in separate clusters as shown in Fig. 5.

Theorem 1: The algorithm in Fig. 6 produces an optimal clustering for a join DAG.

Proof: Assume that the optimum parallel time is PT_{opt}. If $\tau_k + \beta_k + \tau_x > PT_{opt}$ for an optimal algorithm then β_k must be zero otherwise this will not be an optimal algorithm. This result and the fact that the edges are sorted from left to right in Fig. 5, imply that if edge $< n_k, n_x >$ has been zeroed by an optimal algorithm, then every edge to the left of that edge, $j = 1 : k - 1$, must have also been zeroed by this algorithm. On the other hand, if $\tau_k + \beta_k + \tau_x \leq PT_{opt}$ then this edge does not have to be zeroed by an optimal algorithm. Thus, if we assume that $\beta_{m+1} = \tau_{m+1} = 0$, then the optimum value PT_{opt} is

$$PT_{opt} = \tau_x + \min_{k=1}^{m}\{\max(\sum_{j=1}^{k} \tau_j, \beta_{k+1} + \tau_{k+1})\}.$$

We now prove that the algorithm in Fig. 6 produces a clustering with parallel time equal PT_{opt}. Initially all tasks are mapped on a separate cluster, see Fig. 5(a). At iteration

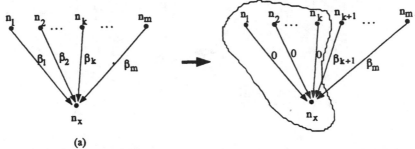

Fig. 5. An optimum clustering algorithm for the join DAG when $\tau_j + \beta_j \geq \tau_{j+1} + \beta_{j+1}$, $j = 1 : m - 1$.

```
k = 1;
WHILE  (∑_{j=1}^{k} τ_j ≤ τ_k + β_k)  DO
          β_k = 0;
          k = k + 1;
ENDWHILE
k = k - 1;
```

Fig. 6. A clustering algorithm for a join DAG.

$k + 1$ of the WHILE loop, edge $< n_{k+1}, n_x >$ is visited. This implies that all tasks n_1, n_2 up to n_k must have been sequentialized within one cluster, see Fig. 5(b) and 7(d). The algorithm zeroes edges from left to right as many as possible up to the point k_{opt} that satisfies

$$\sum_{j=1}^{k} \tau_j \leq \beta_k + \tau_k, \qquad \sum_{j=1}^{k+1} \tau_j \geq \beta_{k+1} + \tau_{k+1}. \qquad (1)$$

Then the parallel time after zeroing k_{opt} edges in the left portion is reduced to the minimum value PT_{opt}. ∎

Each clustering step trades off parallelism with sequentialization depending on whether or not the while loop condition is satisfied. The question is, what role does the granularity play in the sequentialization process? The two inequalities in (1) determine the optimum tradeoff point k_{opt} between sequentialization and parallelization. In Fig. 8(a) and (b) we show two cases of the graphs for $\sum_{j=1}^{k} \tau_j$ and $\beta_k + \tau_k$ along with their tradeoff points k_{opt}.

To explain this result, rewrite the first inequality in (1) as follows

$$(k-1) \min_{l=1:m} \{\tau_l\} \leq \sum_{j=1}^{k-1} \tau_j \leq \beta_k \leq \max_{l=1:m} \{\beta_l\}$$

$$\implies k \leq 1 + \frac{1}{g(G)}.$$

The last inequality intuitively explains why we have included the adjacent nodes of n_x in our granularity definition. The interesting conclusion is that if $g(G) > 1$ then the last inequality implies that $k_{opt} = 1$, since $k < 2$ and k is an integer greater or equal to one, which means that the optimum clustering is a linear clustering. The question that remains to be investigated is that if this result can be extended to general DAG's using our granularity definition. We will do this in the next subsection.

C. Parallelization Versus Sequentialization for a General DAG

Lemma 1: Given a coarse grain DAG, any schedule of the reduced graph, derived by deleting all transitive edges of the DAG, still satisfies all precedence constraints of the given DAG.

Proof: Suppose that there is a path $n_1 \rightarrow n_2 \rightarrow \cdots \rightarrow n_k$ where $k > 2$, and that there is also a transitive edge from n_1 to n_k. Next assume that the transitive edge $< n_1, n_k >$ is deleted. The task n_k still cannot be ready for execution for any schedule until the completion of all tasks $n_1, n_2, \cdots,$ and n_{k-1}, that is,

$$ST(n_k) \geq CT(n_1) + \sum_{i=2}^{k-1} \tau_i.$$

Since the DAG is coarse grain then

$$c_{1,k} \leq \tau_2 \leq \sum_{i=2}^{k-1} \tau_i$$

which implies that

$$ST(n_k) \geq CT(n_1) + c_{1,k}.$$

This indicates that the precedence constraint $< n_1, n_k >$ is automatically satisfied. ∎

Theorem 2: For any nonlinear clustering of a coarse grain DAG, we can always transform this clustering into a linear clustering with less or equal parallel time.

The basic idea of this proof is to show that every nonlinear cluster can be "linearized" without increasing the parallel time. We demonstrate this idea using the example in Fig. 3. We show that for any nonlinear clustering we can extract a linear clustering whose parallel time is less or equal to the nonlinear clustering. If we assume that $w \geq c$, then the parallel time of the nonlinear clustering in Fig. 3(b) is $3w$. By extracting n_3 from the nonlinear clustering and making it a new cluster, we derive a linear clustering shown in Fig. 3(c) whose parallel time is $2w + c \leq 3w$. We can always perform this extraction as long as the task graph is coarse grain. In the proof below, we will give a detailed transformation algorithm for extraction.

Proof: According to Lemma 1, we can assume that the given DAG has no transitive edges. There are two parts in the proof. The first part describes a procedure that extracts linear clusters from nonlinear clusters. The second part shows how to construct a schedule at each step of the extraction whose

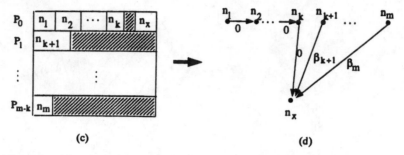

(c)   (d)

Fig. 7. The Gantt chart (c) and scheduled DAG (d) for the optimum join clustering algorithm of Fig. 5(b).

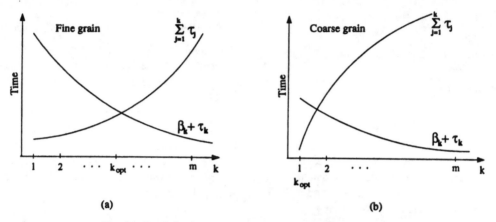

(a)   (b)

Fig. 8. Parallelization versus sequentialization for a join DAG.

parallel time is less or equal to the schedule in the previous step.

Let us assume that $CLUSTER(0)$ is the set of the initial nonlinear clustering and S is its optimum schedule under the assumption that each cluster is executed on a separate processor of a clique architecture. The set $CLUSTER(0)$ consists of nonlinear NLC and linear LC clusters and there exists at least one $NLC \in CLUSTER(0)$. The optimum schedule defines execution sequence, $\{\preceq_i\}$, of the tasks for each processor i. The linearization procedure is given in Fig. 9.

Define

- $PRED(n_k)$ to be the set of all immediate predecessors of n_k in G.
- $pred_l(n_k) = (n_{k_1}, \cdots, n_{k_t}, \cdots, n_{k_q})$ to be the sequence of all immediate predecessors of n_k assigned to the same processor as n_k for schedule S_l. This sequence is derived from the order imposed by S_l.
- $R_l(n_t) = PRED(n_t) - pred_l(n_t)$, the set of all immediate predecessors of n_t that are not in the same processor as n_t for schedule S_l. The "$-$" symbol is the set difference operation.

We first show how to extract a linear cluster from a nonlinear cluster using a bottom-up traversal of the graph and then show that it is possible to construct a schedule for the new clustering with less or equal parallel time. We show both the extraction and the construction inductively. Assume that $NLC = \{n_1, n_2, \cdots, n_m\}$ is the nonlinear cluster in processor i and that the execution order imposed by S_l is $\{\preceq_i\} = (n_1, n_2, \cdots, n_m)$.

```
INPUT: CLUSTER(0)(nonlinear); S;
OUTPUT: CLUSTER(l)(linear); S_l;
l = 0; S_0 = S;
FOR each processor i that contains a nonlinear cluster NLC DO
    WHILE NLC is not linear DO
        Extract a linear cluster from NLC and assign LC to a new processor j;
        NLC = NLC - LC;
        CLUSTER(l + 1) = CLUSTER(l) ∪ {LC};
        Construct a schedule S_{l+1} from S_l with smaller parallel time;
        l = l + 1;
    ENDWHILE
ENDFOR
```

Fig. 9. The linearization procedure.

Extract a linear cluster from a nonlinear cluster:

- Extract n_m first, by removing the node from NLC.
- Assume n_k has been extracted. Then, we show how to extract the next node. There are three cases for performing the extraction:

Case 1: If $pred_l(n_k) = \varnothing$ then stop the extraction. The node n_k is the first node in LC.

Case 2: If $pred_l(n_k) = (n_{k_1}, \cdots, n_{k_q})$ and there exists *no* successor n_{s_q} of n_{k_q} inserted between n_{k_q} and n_k in $\{\preceq_i\}$, then extract n_{k_q} and assign it into LC.

Case 3: If $pred_l(n_k) = (n_{k_1}, \cdots, n_{k_q})$ and there exists a successor n_{s_q} of n_{k_q} such that $n_{k_q} \preceq_i n_{s_q} \preceq_i n_k$, then stop the extraction. The node n_k is the first node of LC.

Notice that the WHILE loop assures that all linear clusters have been extracted from NLC. Also the extracting continues even if NLC becomes linear since checking of linearity of NLC is done after the extraction stops. The term "successor" or "predecessor" of a task always refers to the DAG G and not to the schedule.

154

Define $ST_l(n_p)$ the *starting time* and $RT_l(n_p)$ the *ready time* of node n_p in S_l. The ready time is the time when n_p has received all data from its immediate predecessors and is ready for execution. We have that

$$ST_l(n_p) \geq RT_l(n_p).$$

We also need to define two functions

$$P_l(n_t, X) = \max_{n_p \in X} \{ST_l(n_p) + \tau_p\},$$

$$Q_l(n_t, X) = \max_{n_p \in X} \{ST_l(n_p) + \tau_p + c_{p,t}\}$$

for schedule S_l where X is a subset of $PRED(n_t)$.

Next we construct a schedule S_{l+1} from S_l with the same execution order, i.e., if $n_j \preceq_k n_p$ in S_l then the order will remain the same in S_{l+1} if the nodes are in the same processor. We construct S_{l+1} by topologically examining each task in G and showing that $ST_l(n_p) \geq RT_{l+1}(n_p)$. By *topologically*, we mean that task n_x is visited before n_y if n_x is executed before n_y within the same processor or there is a dependence path from n_x to n_y. Consequently we can define S_{l+1} such that $ST_l(n_p) \geq ST_{l+1}(n_p)$ for all $n_p \in G$, which imply that the parallel times satisfy $PT_{l+1} \leq PT_l$. Assume that for schedule S_l the extracted linear cluster from $NLC = \{n_1, n_2, \cdots, n_m\}$ is $LC = \{n_{c_1}, n_{c_2} \cdots, n_{c_h}\}$ and $n_{c_h} = n_m$. We present the construction inductively in a topological order:

Construct a schedule:

- First set $ST_{l+1}(n_p) = ST_l(n_p)$ for all entry nodes n_p which have no predecessors.
- Assume for a node n_t that $ST_l(n_p) \geq ST_{l+1}(n_p)$ for all $n_p \in PRED(n_t)$ and n_p that is executed before n_t in the same processor. We only consider schedules S_{l+1} with the same execution order as S_l. The starting time of a task n_t in schedule S_{l+1} is assigned as $ST_{l+1}(n_t) = RT_{l+1}(n_t)$ if there is no task executed before task n_t in the processor of n_t of schedule S_{l+1}, or $ST_{l+1}(n_t) = \max\{RT_{l+1}(n_t), ST_{l+1}(n_p)+\tau_p\}$ if a task n_p is executed before n_t. We consider four distinct cases to show that $ST_{l+1}(n_t) \leq ST_l(n_t)$.

1) n_t *is not in* NLC *or* LC: Refer to Fig. 10(1). The node n_t is in some processor $r \neq i$. We have that

$$RT_l(n_t) = \max\{P_l(n_t, pred_l(n_t)), \ Q_l(n_t, R_l(n_t))\}$$

$$RT_{l+1}(n_t) = \max\{P_{l+1}(n_t, pred_{l+1}(n_t)),$$
$$Q_l(n_t, R_{l+1}(n_t))\}.$$

This is because each $n_p \in PRED(n_t)$ sends the *data in parallel* immediately after completion of its execution and since the architecture is a *clique* the arrival time of the data for n_t is not affected if LC becomes a new processor j; see the assumptions on parallel send and clique architecture in Section II.

Because the predecessors of n_t in the same processor are not changed by the extraction we have that

$$pred_{l+1}(n_t) = pred_l(n_t), \quad R_{l+1}(n_t) = R_l(n_t).$$

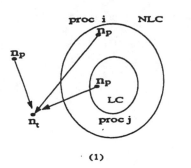 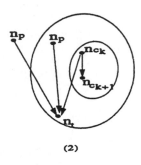

Fig. 10. Case 1 and 2 of **construct** procedure.

The above combined with the induction hypothesis $ST_l(n_p) \geq ST_{l+1}(n_p)$ for all $n_p \in PRED(n_t)$ imply

$$P_{l+1}(n_t, pred_{l+1}(n_t)) \leq P_l(n_t, pred_l(n_t)),$$
$$Q_{l+1}(n_t, R_{l+1}(n_t)) \leq Q_l(n_t, R_l(n_t)).$$

Therefore

$$RT_{l+1}(n_t) \leq RT_l(n_t) \leq ST_l(n_t)$$

and because the execution order in S_{l+1} is chosen to be the same as in S_l, thus

$$ST_l(n_t) \geq ST_{l+1}(n_t).$$

2) n_t *is in* $NLC - LC$: Refer to Fig. 10(2). Since tasks in LC are extracted from processor i, the ready time of n_t is possibly delayed when one of its immediate predecessors, say n_{c_k}, is in LC. This is because n_{c_k} is moved from processor i to processor j and the communication between n_{c_k} and n_t becomes nonzero. According to the extraction procedure, another immediate successor of n_{c_k}, say $n_{c_{k+1}}$, must be in LC and they must satisfy $n_{c_k} \preceq_i n_{c_{k+1}} \preceq_i n_t$. Therefore

$$ST_l(n_t) \geq \max\{P_l(n_t, pred_l(n_t)),$$
$$Q_l(n_t, R_l(n_t)), \ ST_l(n_{c_{k+1}}) + \tau_{c_{k+1}}\}$$

$$RT_{l+1}(n_t) = \max\{P_{l+1}(n_t, pred_{l+1}(n_t)),$$
$$Q_{l+1}(n_t, R_{l+1}(n_t))\}.$$

Because n_{c_k} is on a different processor at schedule S_{l+1} we have that

$$pred_{l+1}(n_t) = pred_l(n_t) - \{n_{c_k}\},$$
$$R_{l+1}(n_t) = R_l(n_t) \cup \{n_{c_k}\}.$$

We can easily see from the definition of P and Q and the induction hypothesis

$$P_{l+1}(n_t, pred_l(n_t) - \{n_{c_k}\}) \leq P_l(n_t, pred_l(n_t)),$$
$$Q_{l+1}(n_t, R_l(n_t)) \leq Q_l(n_t, R_l(n_t))$$

$$Q_{l+1}(n_t, R_l(n_t) \cup \{n_{c_k}\}) =$$
$$\max\{Q_{l+1}(n_t, \ R_l(n_t)), ST_{l+1}(n_{c_k}) + \tau_{c_k} + c_{c_k,t}\}.$$

We also have that

$$ST_l(n_{c_{k+1}}) \geq ST_l(n_{c_k}) + \tau_{c_k}.$$

Since the graph is coarse, then $\tau_{c_{k+1}} \geq c_{c_k,t}$ and

$$ST_l(n_{c_{k+1}}) + \tau_{c_{k+1}} \geq ST_l(n_{c_k}) + \tau_{c_k} + c_{c_k,t}$$
$$\geq ST_{l+1}(n_{c_k}) + \tau_{c_k} + c_{c_k,t}.$$

The above imply that

$$ST_l(n_t) \geq RT_{l+1}(n_t)$$

and thus

$$ST_{l+1}(n_t) \leq ST_l(n_t).$$

3) n_t *is the first task* n_{c_1} *in LC*: Refer to Fig. 11(3). We check the termination condition of **Extract** to determine the start time of n_{c_1}. For case 1 of extraction, n_{c_1} has no predecessor in NLC; thus moving it into processor j will not affect its ready time since the processor architecture is a clique. For case 3 of extraction, $pred_l(n_{c_1}) = (n_{k_1}, \cdots, n_{k_q})$ and there exists a task n_{s_q} in NLC satisfying $n_{k_q} \preceq_i n_{s_q} \preceq_i n_{c_1}$ in S_l. Therefore,

$$ST_l(n_{c_1}) \geq \max\{P_l(n_{c_1}, pred_l(n_{c_1})), Q_l(n_{c_1}, R_l(n_{c_1})),$$
$$ST_l(n_{s_q}) + \tau_{s_q}\}$$

$$RT_{l+1}(n_{c_1}) = Q_{l+1}(n_{c_1}, PRED(n_{c_1}))$$
$$= \max\{Q_{l+1}(n_{c_1}, R_l(n_{c_1})), Q_{l+1}(n_{c_1}, pred_l(n_{c_1}))\}.$$

We now show $ST_l(n_{s_q}) + \tau_{s_q} \geq Q_{l+1}(n_{c_1}, pred_l(n_{c_1}))$. Since $n_{k_q} \in pred_l(n_{c_1})$ and it is executed after all other tasks in $pred_l(n_{c_1})$,

$$ST_l(n_{k_q}) + \tau_{k_q} + c_{k_q,c_1} \geq Q_{l+1}(n_{c_1}, pred_l(n_{c_1})).$$

Because of $n_{k_q} \preceq_i n_{s_q}$ and $\tau_{s_q} \geq c_{k_q,c_1}$,

$$ST_l(n_{s_q}) + \tau_{s_q} \geq ST_l(n_{k_q}) + \tau_{k_q} + c_{k_q,c_1}.$$

Then we have the following

$$ST_l(n_{s_q}) + \tau_{s_q} \geq Q_{l+1}(n_{c_1}, pred_l(n_{c_1})).$$

Also we know

$$Q_{l+1}(n_{c_1}, R_l(n_{c_1})) \leq Q_l(n_{c_1}, R_l(n_{c_1})).$$

Consequently,

$$RT_{l+1}(n_{c_1}) \leq ST_l(n_{c_1}).$$

Since processor j contains a linear cluster,

$$ST_{l+1}(n_{c_1}) = RT_{l+1}(n_{c_1}) \implies ST_{l+1}(n_{c_1}) \leq ST_l(n_{c_1}).$$

4) n_t *is the kth node* n_{c_k} *in LC*: Refer to Fig. 11(4). We examine the relationship between $n_{c_{k-1}}$ and n_{c_k} in case 2 of the extraction procedure. Since $pred_l(n_{c_k}) = (n_{k_1}, \cdots, n_{k_q})$, and $k_q = c_{k-1}$ and there is no successor $n_{s_{k-1}}$ of $n_{c_{k-1}}$ satisfying $n_{c_{k-1}} \preceq_i n_{s_{k-1}} \preceq_i n_{c_k}$ in S_l,

$$ST_l(n_{c_k}) \geq \max\{P_l(n_{c_k}, pred_l(n_{c_k})), Q_l(n_{c_k}, R_l(n_{c_k}))\}$$
$$\geq \max\{ST_l(n_{c_{k-1}}) + \tau_{c_{k-1}}, Q_l(n_{c_k}, R_l(n_{c_k}))\}$$

$$RT_{l+1}(n_{c_k}) = \max\{ST_{l+1}(n_{c_{k-1}}) + \tau_{c_{k-1}},$$
$$Q_{l+1}(n_{c_k}, PRED(n_{c_k}) - \{n_{c_{k-1}}\})\}$$

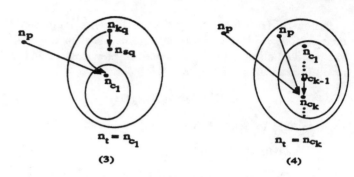

Fig. 11. Case 3 and 4 of **construct** procedure.

$$Q_{l+1}(n_{c_k}, PRED(n_{c_k}) - \{n_{c_{k-1}}\})$$
$$= \max\{Q_{l+1}(n_{c_k}, R_l(n_{c_k})), Q_{l+1}(n_{c_k}, pred_l(n_{c_k})$$
$$- \{n_{c_{k-1}}\})\}.$$

Thus from the induction assumption we have that

$$Q_{l+1}(n_{c_k}, R_l(n_{c_k})) \leq Q_l(n_{c_k}, R_l(n_{c_k})).$$

Since the graph is coarse then $\tau_{k_q} \geq \max_{1 \leq b \leq q-1}\{c_{c_b,c_k}\}$ and since $n_{k_1} \preceq_i, \cdots, \preceq_i n_{k_q}$, we have that

$$ST_l(n_{c_{k-1}}) + \tau_{c_{k-1}} \geq P_{l+1}(n_{c_k}, pred_l(n_{c_k}) - \{n_{c_{k-1}}\})$$
$$+ \max_{1 \leq b \leq q-1}\{c_{c_b,c_k}\}$$
$$\geq Q_{l+1}(n_{c_k}, pred_l(n_{c_k}) - \{n_{c_{k-1}}\}).$$

Therefore, we have shown that

$$RT_{l+1}(n_{c_k}) \leq ST_l(n_{c_k})$$

and since processor j contains a linear cluster,

$$ST_{l+1}(n_{c_1}) = RT_{l+1}(n_{c_1}) \text{ and thus } ST_{l+1}(n_{c_1}) \leq ST_l(n_{c_1}).$$

∎

Example: We explain how the above procedure works for Fig. 12.

Assume that the following nonlinear clustering of the DAG in Fig. 12 is given,

$$CLUSTER(0) = \{ M_1 = \{n_7\}, M_2 = \{n_6\}, M_3 = \{n_5\},$$
$$M_4 = \{n_1, n_2, n_3, n_4\} \}.$$

The optimum schedule S_0 with parallel time $PT_0 = 11$ is shown in Fig. 12(b). The NLC cluster is M_4. The node n_4 is extracted first and $pred_0(n_4) = (n_2, n_3)$ and $LC = \{n_4\}$. Because of case 2, the node n_3 is extracted next and $pred_0(n_3) = (n_1)$ and $LC = \{n_3, n_4\}$. Since $n_1 \preceq_i n_2 \preceq_i n_3$ the extraction stops because of case 3. We rename LC to be M_5, and the linear clustering is,

$$CLUSTER(1) = \{ M_1 = \{n_7\}, M_2 = \{n_6\}, M_3 = \{n_5\},$$
$$M_4 = \{n_1, n_2\}, M_5 = \{n_3, n_4\} \}.$$

In Fig. 12(b) S_0 is the schedule at the beginning of the first step of the linearization procedure. At the end of that step the linear cluster M_5 is extracted. A schedule S_1 is constructed by following **Construct** procedure and shown in Fig. 12(c).

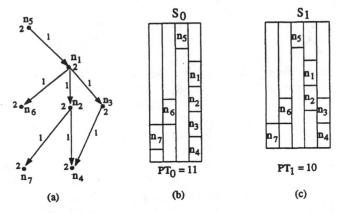

Fig. 12. An example of linearization with $c_{i,j} = 1$ and $\tau_i = 2, i = 1 : 7$. S_0 is the optimum scheduling of a nonlinear clustering. S_1 is a linear clustering with less parallel time.

This schedule satisfies $ST_l(n_t) \geq ST_{l+1}(n_t)$ for all nodes n_t. Notice also that the execution order of S_1 is the same as S_0, i.e., $n_3 \preceq_i n_4$ in S_0 and S_1, and that the parallel time of S_1 is less than the parallel time of S_0.

Since we only need to show the existence of a linear clustering with better parallel time compared with the given nonlinear clustering, the complexity of this transformation algorithm is not of interests in this paper. Also the result of this extraction may not give an optimal linear clustering.

Theorem 2 also shows that the problem of finding an optimal solution for a coarse grain DAG is equivalent to that of finding an optimal linear clustering. Picouleau [19] has shown that the scheduling problem for coarse grain DAG's is NP-complete, therefore optimal linear clustering is NP-complete.

Corollary 1: Determining the optimum linear clustering for a coarse grain DAG is NP-complete.

Thus even though linear clustering has nice properties for scheduling task graphs, determining the optimum linear clustering is still very difficult. Fortunately, for coarse grain DAG's, any linear clustering algorithm guarantees performance within a factor of two of the optimum as the following section demonstrates.

V. Bounds for Linear Clustering

Theorem 3 below shows that the linear clustering performance bound result of Gerasoulis and Venugopal [9] still holds for $g(G) \geq 1$ using our granularity definition. It should be emphasized that the first inequality in Theorem 3 is true for any DAG irrespectively if it is coarse grain or not.

Theorem 3: For any linear clustering algorithm we have

$$PT_{opt} \leq PT_{lc} \leq (1 + \frac{1}{g(G)})PT_{opt}$$

where PT_{opt} is the optimum parallel time and PT_{lc} is the parallel time of the linear clustering. Moreover for a coarse grain DAG we have

$$PT_{lc} \leq 2 \times PT_{opt}.$$

Proof: The proof is identical to Gerasoulis and Venugopal [9]. Assume that the critical path is $CP = \{n_1, n_2, \cdots, n_k\}$. Then for any linear clustering, there could be some edges zeroed in that path but the length of that path L_{cp} satisfies

$$L_{cp} \leq \sum_{i=1}^{k} \tau_i + \sum_{i=1}^{k} c_{i,i+1}.$$

From the definition of the granularity we have that $g(G) \leq \tau_i/c_{i,i+1}$. Then by substituting $c_{i,i+1}$ in the last inequality we get

$$L_{cp} \leq \sum_{i=1}^{k} \tau_i(1 + \frac{1}{g(G)}).$$

Using the fact that

$$\sum_{i=1}^{k} \tau_i \leq PT_{opt} \leq PT_{lc} = L_{cp}$$

the inequality of the theorem is then derived easily. ∎

Recently, Papadimitriou and Yannakakis [18] have proposed a polynomial time clustering algorithm whose performance is within a factor of two of the optimum, but their algorithm requires task duplication. The existence of a polynomial time algorithm for scheduling without duplication which is within a factor of two of the optimal is posed as an open problem by Papadimitriou and Yannakakis. The above result answers this problem for coarse grain DAG's.

Anger, Hwang, and Chow [1] assume: S2) an unbounded number of processors, S3) short communication delays, $c_{i,j} \leq min_{i=1:v}\{\tau_i\}$ for all communication edges, S5) a fully connected architecture. Then they use their bound for their Earliest Task First (ETF) heuristic algorithm

$$PT_{ETF} \leq (2 - \frac{1}{p})PT_{opt} + MaxChainComm$$

where PT_{opt} is the optimum parallel time and $MaxChainComm$ is the longest communication chain in the DAG, to show that

$$PT_{ETF} \leq 3 \times PT_{opt}$$

since $MaxChainComm \leq PT_{opt}$ because of assumption S3). However, assumption S3) implies that $g(G) \geq 1$ and Theorems 2 and 3 provide a sharper upper bound.

VI. Linear Clustering and the Gauss–Jordan Algorithm

In this section, we demonstrate the practicality of the previous results in the area of numerical computing where linear clustering has been widely used. The typical examples are the Gaussian-Elimination (GE) and Gauss-Jordan (GJ) algorithms which have been studied in the literature for a variety of parallel architectures [4], [7], [15], [17], [20]–[22]. Here we consider the kji form without pivoting for the Gauss–Jordan algorithm with interior loop partitioning, see Fig. 13.

```
for k = 1 : n
    for j = k + 1 : n + 1
    T_k^j : {   a_{k,j} = a_{k,j}/a_{k,k}
                for i = 1 : n and  i ≠ k
                a_{i,j} = a_{i,j} - a_{i,k} * a_{k,j}
                end}
    end
end
```

Fig. 13. The kji form for Gauss–Jordan without pivoting and with interior loop task partitioning.

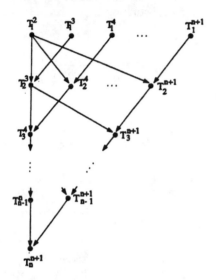

Fig. 14. The Gauss–Jordan DAG. The node computation cost for all nodes is $\tau = n\omega$ and edge communication cost for all edges is $c = \alpha + n\beta$.

The data dependence graph is given in Fig. 14, e.g., [4], [7]. Task T_k^j defined in Fig. 13 uses column k to modify column j of the matrix A. Tasks T_k^{k+1} broadcasts the same column $k + 1$ to all T_{k+1}^j, $j = k + 2 : n + 1$ tasks.

A. Clustering GJ on a Clique Message Passing Architecture

In the GJ DAG, the computation cost τ for each task and the communication cost c for each edge can be taken

$$\tau = n\omega, \quad c = \alpha + n\beta$$

where ω is the time for computing either an addition and multiplication or a division. We have chosen the communication cost model between neighbor processors to be the widely accepted linear model, where α is the start up time and $n\beta$ is the transmission time of a vector of n elements, e.g., Dunigan [6], Heath and Romine [11].

The granularity for the Gauss–Jordan DAG can be easily computed

$$g(GJ) = \frac{n\omega}{\alpha + n\beta} \asymp \frac{\omega}{\beta}$$

where the asymptotic limit "$\asymp$" is taken with respect to $n \rightarrow +\infty$. The *natural linear clustering*

$$M_j = \{T_k^j \mid k = 1 : j - 1\}, \quad j = 2 : n + 1$$

shown in Fig. 15, can be obtained by assuming that each cluster contains all tasks that modify the same column, i.e.,

the locality assumption in Gerasoulis and Nelken [7]. This linear clustering has been used in the literature to schedule the Gauss–Jordan and Gauss-Elimination DAG's on a ring of processors, e.g., [4], [7], [17], [20], [21]. The natural linear clusters are wrapped around (*wrap mapping*) the ring of processors and then the compute-ahead or naive ordering is used to schedule the tasks, Ortega [17, p. 241. Ipsen, Saad, and Schultz [22] have derived lower bounds for the optimum schedule on the ring architecture. Robert, Tourancheau, and Villard [20] have shown the asymptotic optimality of the kij form of the Gauss–Jordan algorithm on a ring of processors, under the assumption that communication does not overlap with computation. This assumption, however, is not practical for message passing architectures where communication usually overlaps with computation to increase performance. As far as we know, there has been no optimality analysis of the natural linear clustering for message-passing architectures.

Applying Theorem 3 on Gauss-Jordan DAG we can derive the following performance upper bound for the natural linear clustering, assuming that $g(GJ) \geq 1$,

$$\frac{PT_{nlc}^{clique}}{PT_{opt}^{clique}} \leq 1 + \frac{\beta}{\omega} + \frac{\alpha}{n\omega} \asymp 1 + \frac{\beta}{\omega}$$

where PT_{nlc}^{clique} is the parallel time of the natural linear clustering and PT_{opt}^{clique} is the optimum parallel time on the clique architecture. However, Theorem 2 could be used to obtain an even stronger result which we present it as a theorem below. We remind the readers that this theorem is true under the macro-dataflow assumptions of asynchronous parallel sends and receives.

Theorem 4 (Gauss–Jordan optimum parallel time on a clique): If the number of processors of the clique is equal to the number of the linear clusters and $g(GJ) \geq 1$, then

$$PT_{nlc}^{clique} = PT_{opt}^{clique} = n^2\omega + (n - 1)(\alpha + n\beta).$$

Proof: We can easily see that for $p = n$ processors, the parallel time for the natural linear clustering is equal to the length of the critical path $\{T_1^2, T_2^3, \cdots, T_n^{n+1}\}$ of the scheduled Gauss–Jordan DAG, see Figs. 14 and 15:

$$PT_{nlc}^{clique} = n^2\omega + (n - 1)c = n^2\omega + (n - 1)(\alpha + n\beta).$$

Since we have assumed that the granularity $g(GJ)$ is greater than one, then Theorem 2 implies that *the optimum parallel time must be achieved by a linear clustering.* We have that

$$PT_{opt}^{clique} \leq PT_{nlc}^{clique} = n^2\omega + (n - 1)(\alpha + n\beta)$$

and PT_{opt}^{clique} must be the parallel time of a linear clustering. We will show that

$$PT_{opt}^{clique} \geq n^2\omega + (n - 1)(\alpha + n\beta).$$

We define a *layer* k of the Gauss–Jordan DAG in Fig. 14 as the set of tasks $\{T_k^{k+1}, \cdots, T_k^{n+1}\}$. We will prove that the completion time of each task T_k^j at layer k satisfies

$$CT(T_k^j) \geq kn\omega + (k - 1)(\alpha + n\beta), \quad j = k + 1 : n + 1.$$

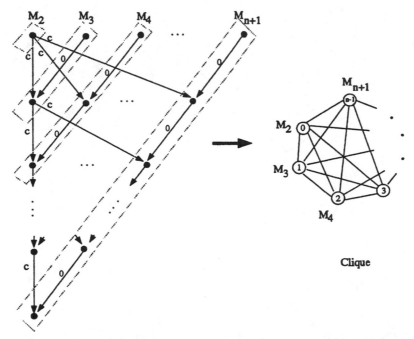

Fig. 15. The natural linear clustering for the Gauss–Jordan DAG executed on a clique with $p = n$ processors.

This is trivial for $k = 1$. Suppose it is true for tasks at layer $k - 1$. We examine the completion time for each task T_k^j at layer k. Since each task has two incoming edges from tasks at layer $k - 1$, and linear clustering zeros at the most only one edge, task T_k^j has to wait at least $\alpha + n\beta$ time to receive the message from one of its two predecessors, say T_{k-1}^r, at layer $k - 1$. Therefore

$$CT(T_k^j) \geq CT(T_{k-1}^r) + \alpha + n\beta + n\omega.$$

From the induction hypothesis we have that

$$CT(T_{k-1}^r) \geq (k-1)n\omega + (k-2)(\alpha + n\beta)$$

which implies

$$CT(T_k^j) \geq kn\omega + (k-1)(\alpha + n\beta).$$

Since the parallel time is the completion time of the last task T_n^{n+1} we have that

$$T_{opt}^{clique} \geq n^2\omega + (n-1)(\alpha + n\beta).$$

∎

Even though a clique architecture is an ideal architecture, its connectivity becomes an obstacle in building such architectures with a large number of processors. On the other hand, architectures with lower connectivity such as ring or hypercubes can be easily built with thousands of processors. Therefore, it is of interest to investigate if the results above can be extended to actual existing architectures.

B. Physical Mapping of the GJ DAG on a Ring Architecture

We choose the ring architecture to extend our results of the previous sections. Ring is one of the simplest architectures with low connectivity and can be easily mapped on several existing architectures such as hypercubes by using the gray code mapping, Saad [21]. Saad [21] observed that using the complete broadcast capabilities of the hypercube for the natural linear clustering will result in worse performance, by a $\log p$ factor, than by simply using the gray code ring broadcast embedded in the hypercube. Saad's result is intuitively surprising since one might expect that an architecture with richer communication capabilities should result in a shorter parallel time. Thus, it is of interest to see if using a ring topology is optimal for solving such a problem. We will show that at least in the case of $p = n$ processors the ring architecture is an optimal architecture for the coarse grain Gauss–Jordan DAG. We define an *optimal architecture* for a DAG as the architecture in which the optimum schedule of the DAG has the same parallel time as the optimum schedule on the clique.

As mentioned in the Introduction, the two step approach to scheduling is: 1) Clustering, 2) Scheduling the clusters. The scheduling problem is equivalent to determining a mapping of the clusters to processors and then determining an ordering of the tasks within each processor. For the second step above, we will show that a schedule of these clusters on $p = n$ processors of a ring architecture is also optimum.

Theorem 5 (Gauss–Jordan optimum parallel time on a ring): Assume that the number of processors of a ring architecture is equal to the number of the natural linear clusters and $g(GJ) \geq 1$. Then the following physical mapping of the clusters to the processors is optimal

$$map(M_j) = j - 2, \quad j = 2 : n + 1.$$

Moreover, the optimum parallel time on the ring is equal to the optimum parallel time on the clique

$$PT_{nlc}^{ring} = PT_{opt}^{clique} = n^2\omega + (n-1)(\alpha + n\beta).$$

159

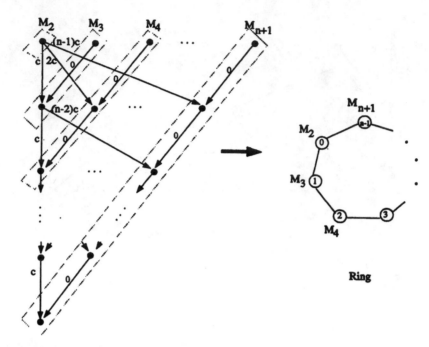

Fig. 16. The natural clustering for the Gauss–Jordan DAG on a ring with $p = n$ processors.

Proof: Due to linear clustering, the execution ordering within a processor in the ring is defined by the dependence chain of the initial DAG. The scheduled DAG on a ring with $p = n$ processors is given in Fig. 16. Notice that the edge communication cost of $< T_k^{k+1}, T_{k+1}^j >$ is

$$(j-k)c = (j-k)(\alpha+n\beta), \quad j = k+2 : n+1, \quad k = 1 : n-1$$

where $(j - k)$ is the maximum distance that column k must travel if we use a *store* and *forward* communication protocol, Saad [21]. However, even if some of the individual communication edge costs in the scheduled DAG have increased for the ring architecture, the edges $< T_k^{k+1}, T_{k+1}^{k+2} >$ remain unchanged and the critical path length of the scheduled DAG is the same as the clique architecture, which implies

$$PT_{nlc}^{ring} = PT_{opt}^{clique} = n^2\omega + (n-1)(\alpha + n\beta). \quad \blacksquare$$

VII. Experiments

In this section we present some experiments to verify the previous theoretical results and also discuss the impact of architectural parameters on the granularity.

Fig. 17 shows the parameters of several commercially available message passing architectures for single precision arithmetic. The granularity of the Gauss–Jordan algorithm for these architectures is also shown. We have taken these parameters from Dunigan [6]. The single precision flop is the sum of an addition and a multiplication. For example for the nCUBE-1 we have $16.6 + 18.5 = 35.1$ which has also been confirmed by Heath and Romine [11].

Performance of linear clustering for different granularity values: If a DAG is produced using statement-level partitioning (i.e., each task performs a simple arithmetic operation and communicates with others a scalar variable), then in general

	iPSC/2	i860	nCUBE-1	nCUBE-2
α (microseconds)	697	136	383.6	200
β (microseconds/word)	1.6	1.6	10.4	2.4
ω (microseconds/flop)	11.4	0.2	35.1	1.6
$\omega/(\alpha+\beta)$	0.016	0.0015	0.089	0.0079
$g(GJ) \geq 1$ when $n \geq$	72		16	
$\lim_{n\to+\infty} g(GJ) = \omega/\beta =$	7.1	0.125	3.4	0.667
$\lim_{n\to+\infty} PT_{lc}/PT_{opt} \leq 1 + \beta/\omega =$	1.14	9.0	1.29	2.5

Fig. 17. Architecture parameters and the granularity values of the GJ DAG.

the granularity value of such a DAG is very small on message-passing architectures because of large startup overhead in interprocessor communication. For example, if we consider the loop body of the GJ program in Fig. 13 as a task instead of the interior loop, we get a three-dimensional task graph with the degree of parallelism equal to n^2, [15]. An estimation of granularity for such a DAG is $\omega/(\alpha+\beta)$. From the above table, we can see this value is too small for exploiting parallelism on these four architectures.

We now consider the interior loop partitioning for the GJ program. The degree of parallelism of the corresponding GJ DAG in Fig. 14 is equal to n. For nCUBE-1 if $n \geq 16$ then the GJ graph is coarse grain implying that the optimum parallel time will be derived by the natural linear clustering. The same is true for iPSC/2 but in this case the size of the problem must be greater than 72. However, for the newest generation of the message passing architectures, the iPSC/860 and nCUBE-2, the GJ DAG based on the interior loop partitioning is fine grain for any size of the matrix. Therefore according to our granularity theory presented in the previous sections, linear clustering is not appropriate in this case and it is expected that its performance will be worse than nonlinear clustering. For the GJ example a simple and successful nonlinear clustering algorithm is based on wrapping the linear clusters around a ring of p processors with $p < n$. Fig. 18 shows the result

p	128	64	32	16	8
PT	855.3	847.8	630.1	780.3	1202.9

Fig. 18. Parallel time of the GJ DAG with $n = 128$ using wrap nonlinear clustering.

$$T_k^j : \{ \begin{array}{l} A_{k,j} = A_{k,k}^{-1} * A_{k,j} \\ \text{for } i = 1 : N \text{ and } i \neq k \\ A_{i,j} = A_{i,j} - A_{i,k} * A_{k,j} \\ \text{end} \} \end{array}$$

Fig. 19. The definition of task T_k^j for the block GJ DAG.

of using wrap nonlinear clustering on nCUBE-2. PT is the parallel time in milliseconds. We see that as p decreases, wrap nonlinear clustering performs well up to the point when $p = 32$. Afterwards the performance becomes worse because parallelism is reduced too much.

We may also use coarser program partitioning to increase the granularity of the GJ algorithm. A popular approach is to use a submatrix data partition known as the BLAS-3 block partition [5]. The matrix of $n \times n$ is divided into $N \times N$ submatrices and each submatrix has size of $r \times r$ where $N = n/r$. Each task T_k^j in the block GJ DAG is operating on a block column composed of N elements and each element is a $r \times r$ submatrix. The task definition of T_k^j is given in Fig. 19.

The dependence structure of the GJ DAG remains the same but the degree of parallelism is reduced from n to $N = n/r$. Also the computation size of T_k^j increases to about $Nr^3\omega$ and a message communicated between tasks is a block column of size Nr^2. Thus the granularity $g(GJ) \asymp r\omega/\beta$ for a sufficiently large matrix, which is increased by a factor of r. To make $g(GJ) \geq 1$ the minimum submatrix size r is $\lceil \beta/\omega \rceil$ which is 2 for nCUBE-2 and 8 for i860. Namely, one must use a partitioning on the iPSC/860 about 4 times coarser than that on nCUBE-2.

To see the actual impact of the granularity on task scheduling and partitioning on a real architecture, we have performed an experiment on the nCUBE-2 with 128 processors using the block GJ algorithm with $n = 128$. Fig. 20 shows the parallel time in milliseconds for two types of broadcasting algorithms: a) the gray-code ring broadcasting b) the hypercube spanning tree. We vary the granularity by varying the size of the submatrix partitioning r. The parallel time for ring broadcasting is slightly smaller than that of tree broadcasting when $\log p \leq 6$, but is much smaller when $\log p = 7$. This result is consistent with Saad [21].

When $r = 1$, GJ has the worst performance for $p = 128$ processors because the granularity is too fine and the parallelism implemented by linear clustering is not useful. When $r \geq 2$, the granularity increases, the GJ DAG becomes coarse grain and linear clustering performs well. Because increasing the granularity has the adverse effect of reducing the parallelism the performance of linear clustering will degrade beyond a certain granularity value as it is the case in Fig. 20 when $r > 4$. Notice the dramatic improvement in performance when when we go from a fine grain DAG ($r = 1$) to a coarse grain DAG ($r = 2$). This example shows that our granularity definition captures the point when parallelism is useful.

Linear clustering versus nonlinear clustering for coarse grain DAG's: Finally, we verify the result that linear clustering outperforms nonlinear clustering for a coarse grain DAG. The theoretical estimation indicates that for $r \geq 2$, BLAS-3 GJ DAG is coarse grain. We compare the natural linear clustering with a nonlinear clustering that wraps N linear clusters into p nonlinear clusters. In Fig. 21, we have the parallel time for block size $r = 2$ and $r = 4$ on the nCUBE-2. We also mark the number of nonlinear and linear clusters (#NLC and #LC) in each case. When $r = 4$, the natural linear clustering always has shorter parallel time. When $r = 2$, the time for the natural clustering (#LC=64) is slightly longer than the nonlinear clustering with #NLC=32 but is shorter than that with #NLC=16 and 8. For this case, some extra communication overhead (e.g., message buffering and physical distance) affects performance and block size $r = 2$ is not large enough to make the actual DAG be coarse grain.

VIII. CONCLUDING REMARKS

In this paper, we considered the question of sequentialization versus parallelization of task graphs. We have shown that the granularity of the task graph affects the optimum tradeoff point and if the granularity is greater than one then linear clustering is optimum. Linear clustering preserves the parallelism and is suitable for coarse grain tasks and nonlinear clustering reduces the parallelism in order to save the communication cost. Our analysis is based on the global quantity of granularity defined as a minimum of the task grains over all tasks in the graph. In a more complicated case, the granularity analysis needs to be conducted at subgraphs of a DAG when some parts of the DAG are fine and others are coarse.

For some cases, the fine grain part of a DAG does not significantly affect the performance, we can still conduct the analysis by ignoring this part. An example is the Gaussian-Elimination DAG described below.

The kji form of Gaussian-Elimination is similar to Gauss–Jordan shown in Fig. 13 and 14 except that the $< i = 1 : n$ and $i \neq k >$ loop is replaced by $< i = k+1 : n >$ instead. The task size becomes $\tau_k = (n-k+1)w$ for every task in layer k which consists of the tasks $\{T_k^{k+1}, \cdots, T_k^{n+1}\}$, see Fig. 14. The communication cost of the edges between layers k and $k+1$ is given by $c_k^{k+1} = \alpha + (n-k+1)\beta$. Therefore, the granularity for Gaussian-Elimination may or may not be greater than one depending on the architecture parameters

$$g(GE) = \frac{(n-k+1)\omega}{\alpha + (n-k+1)\beta} \geq 1 \implies k \leq n+1 - \frac{\alpha}{\omega - \beta}.$$

For the nCUBE-1 parameters the grain of tasks in each layer k gradually changes from coarse to fine when k increases. The grain is coarse for tasks at the top part layers where $1 \leq k \leq n-15$ but becomes fines for the bottom layers where $(n-14) \leq k \leq n$. The results of the paper remain true for the top part of the graph. Since the effect of the bottom part on the parallel time becomes negligible as n increases, by following the same proof as in Theorem 4, we can show that the natural linear clustering is asymptotically optimal with respect to n for Gaussian-Elimination when $p = n$.

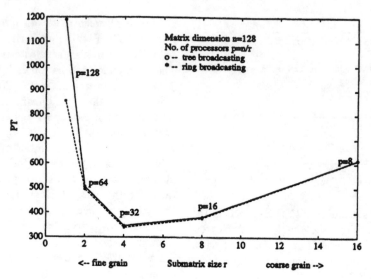

Fig. 20. Performance of linear clustering for fine and coarse grain GJ DAG's on nCUBE-2. $r = 1$ is fine grain and $r \geq 2$ is coarse grain. PT is the parallel time in milliseconds.

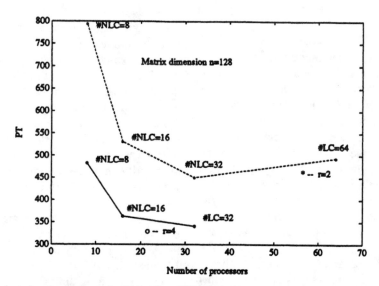

Fig. 21. Linear versus nonlinear clustering for coarse grain GJ DAG on NCUBE-2. PT is the parallel time in milliseconds. #LC is the number of linear clusters. #NLC is the number of nonlinear clusters derived by wrap mapping.

In conclusion, the granularity of a task graph is sensitive to both architecture parameters and program partitioning. Thus architecture-specific optimization techniques must be incorporated in compile-time or run-time scheduling for performance. Clearly for fine grain tasks, nonlinear clustering is necessary and a heuristic algorithm should select an appropriate strategy depending on the size of the local granularity and its impact on the global parallel time. One such clustering algorithm is the DSC algorithm [26]. A preliminary compiler system named PYRROS that incorporates architecture specific parameters in scheduling and code generation and the performance of such a compiler for message passing architectures is described in [27].

ACKNOWLEDGMENT

We would like to thank S. Venugopal for many valuable discussions and suggestions on the initial manuscript. We would also like to thank S. Chakradhar and referees for suggesting improvements on presentation and A. Darte for correcting an error in the proof of Theorem 2.

REFERENCES

[1] F. D. Anger, J. Hwang, and Y. Chow, "Scheduling with sufficient loosely coupled processors," *J. Parallel and Distributed Comput.*, vol. 9, pp. 87–92, 1990.
[2] D. Callahan and K. Kennedy, "Compiling programs for distributed-memory multi-processors, *J. Supercomput.*, vol. 2, pp. 151–169, 1988.
[3] Ph. Chretienne, "Task scheduling over distributed memory machines," in *Proc. Int. Workshop Parallel and Distributed Algorithms*, North Holland, Ed., 1989.
[4] M. Cosnard, M. Marrakchi, Y. Robert, and D. Trystram, "Parallel Gaussian elimination on an MIMD computer," *Parallel Comput.*, vol. 6, pp. 275–296, 1988.
[5] J. J. Dongarra, J. Du Croz, I. Duff, and S. Hammarling, "A set of level 3 basic linear algebra subprograms," *ACM Trans. Math. Software*, vol. 16, no. 1, pp. 1–17, Mar. 1990.
[6] T. H. Dunigan, "Performance of a second generation hypercube," ORNL/TM-10 881, Oak Ridge National Laboratory, TN, Nov. 1988.

[7] A. Gerasoulis and I. Nelken, "Static scheduling for linear algebra DAG's," in *Proc. 4th Conf. Hypercubes*, Monterey, vol. 1, 1989, pp. 671–674.

[8] A. Gerasoulis and T. Yang, "A comparison of clustering heuristics for scheduling DAG's on multiprocessors," *J. Parallel and Distributed Comput.*, Special issues on scheduling and load balancing, vol. 16, no. 4, pp. 276–291, Dec. 1992.

[9] A. Gerasoulis and S. Venugopal, "Linear clustering of linear algebra task graphs for local memory systems," Report, 1990.

[10] G. H. Golub and C. F. Van Loan, *Matrix Computations*. Baltimore, MD: Johns Hopkins, 1989.

[11] M. T. Heath and C. H. Romine, "Parallel solution of triangular systems on distributed memory multiprocessors," *SIAM J. Sci. Statist. Comput.*, vol. 9, pp. 558–588, 1988.

[12] J. A. Hoogeveen, S. L. van de Velde, and B. Veltman, "Complexity of scheduling multiprocessor tasks with prespecified processor allocations," CWI, Rep. BS-R9211 June 1992, Netherlands.

[13] S. J. Kim and J.C Browne, "A general approach to mapping of parallel computation upon multiprocessor architectures," in *Proc. Int. Conf. Parallel Processing*, vol 3, 1988, pp. 1–8.

[14] B. Kruatrachue and T. Lewis, "Grain size determination for parallel processing," *IEEE Software*, pp. 23–32, Jan. 1988.

[15] S. Y. Kung, *VLSI Array Processors*. Englewood Cliffs, NJ: Prentice-Hall, 1988.

[16] C. McCreary and H. Gill, "Automatic determination of grain size for efficient parallel processing," *Commun. ACM*, vol. 32, pp. 1073–1078, Sept., 1989.

[17] J. M. Ortega, *Introduction to Parallel and Vector Solution of Linear Systems*. New York: Plenum, 1988.

[18] C. Papadimitriou and M. Yannakakis, "Toward on an architecture-independent analysis of parallel algorithms," *SIAM J. Comput.*, vol. 19, pp. 322–328, 1990.

[19] C. Picouleau, "New complexity results on the UET-UCT scheduling algorithms," in *Proc. Summer School on Scheduling Theory and its Applications*, Chateau De Bonas, France, 1992, pp. 487–502.

[20] Y. Robert, B. Tourancheu, and G. Villard, "Data allocation strategies for the Gauss and Jordan algorithms on a ring of processors," *Inform. Processing Lett.*, vol. 31, pp. 21–29, 1989.

[21] Y. Saad, "Gaussian elimination on hypercubes," in *Parallel Algorithms and Architectures*, M. Cosnard *et al.*, Eds. Amsterdam: Elsevier Science Publishers, North-Holland, 1986.

[22] I. C. F. Ipsen, Y. Saad, and M. Schultz, "Complexity of dense linear system solution on a multiprocessor ring," *Linear Algebra and Appl.*, vol. 77, pp. 205–239, 1986.

[23] V. Sarkar, *Partitioning and Scheduling Parallel Programs for Execution on Multiprocessors*. Cambridge, MA: M.I.T. Press, 1989.

[24] H. Stone, *High-Performance Computer Architectures*. Reading, MA: Addison-Wesley, 1987.

[25] M. Wu and D. Gajski, "A programming aid for hypercube architectures," *J. Supercomputing*, vol. 2, pp. 349–372, 1988.

[26] T. Yang and A. Gerasoulis, "A fast static scheduling algorithm for DAG's on an unbounded number of processors," in *Proc. IEEE Supercomputing '91*, IEEE, Albuquerque, NM, Nov. 1991, pp. 633–642.

[27] T. Yang and A. Gerasoulis, "PYRROS: Static scheduling and code generation for message passing multiprocessors," in *Proc. 6th ACM Int. Conf. Supercomput.*, Washington DC, July 1992, pp. 428–437.

Apostolos Gerasoulis (M'92) received the B.S. from University of Ioannina, Greece, and the M.S. and Ph.D. degrees from State University of New York at Stony Brook, both in applied mathematics.

He is a Professor of Computer Science at Rutgers University. His research interests are in the areas of numerical computing, parallel algorithms and programming, compilers, parallel languages and environments. He has published extensively in both numerical computing and parallel processing areas. He has participated in the organization of several international conferences and is an editor of the *Parallel Processing Letters Journal* (PPL) and *Computers and Mathematics with Applications and International Journal*.

Tao Yang (S'90) received the B.S. in computer science in 1984 and the M.E. in artificial intelligence in 1987 from Zhejiang University, China, and the M.S. in computer science in 1990 and the Ph.D. degree in computer science in 1993 from Rutgers University, New Brunswick, NJ.

His research interests include algorithms, parallel and distributed computing, programming languages and environments. His dissertation work is on scheduling and code generation for parallel architectures. He will be joining the Department of Computer Science at the University of California at Santa Barbara as an Assistant Professor in the Fall of 1993.

The Effects of Problem Partitioning, Allocation, and Granularity on the Performance of Multiple-Processor Systems

ZARKA CVETANOVIC, MEMBER IEEE

Abstract—In this paper we analyze the effects of the problem decomposition, the allocation of subproblems to processors, and the grain size of subproblems on the performance of a multiple-processor shared-memory architecture. Our results indicate that for algorithms where both the computation and the communication overhead can be fully decomposed among N processors, the speedup is a nondecreasing function of the level of granularity for arbitrary interconnection structure and allocation of subproblems to processors. For these algorithms, the speedup is an increasing function of the level of granularity provided that the interconnection bandwidth is greater than unity. If the bandwidth is equal to unity, then the speedup converges to the value equal to the ratio of processing time to communication time. For algorithms where the computation is decomposable but the communication overhead cannot be decomposed, the speedup is a nondecreasing function of the level of granularity for the best case bandwidth only. If the bandwidth is less than N, the speedup reaches its maximum and then decreases approaching zero as the level of granularity grows. For algorithms where the computation consists of parallel and serial sections of code and the communication overhead is fully decomposable, the speedup converges to a value inversely proportional to the fraction of time spent in the serial code even for the best case interconnection bandwidth.

Index Terms—Allocation, decomposition, granularity, interconnection networks, multiprocessor performance, parallel computing.

I. INTRODUCTION

ANALYZING the performance of multiple-processor systems is a very complex task, since many factors jointly determine system performance and the modification of some factors affects many others. For example, suppose we decide to decrease the grain size of computations executed on processors in order to better exploit the parallelism available in the application. With this modification, processors complete the computation more rapidly, and hence send requests to the interconnection network more frequently, thus increasing the communication overhead and in turn slowing down processors. Since the interaction among various performance factors is very complex and involves many tradeoffs, it is crucial to tune system parameters such that a whole system achieves its peak performance at the minimum cost.

The parameters expected to have the most significant influence on the performance of a multiple-processor system include the following.

1) The amount of parallelism inherent in the application problem.

2) The method for decomposing a problem into smaller subproblems.

3) The method applied to allocate these subproblems to processors.

4) The grain size of a subproblem executed on each processor.

5) The possibility of overlapping processing with communication.

6) The data-access mode where data items are accessed either directly from global memory, or first copied to local memories and then accessed from there.

7) The interconnection structure.

8) The speed of processors, memories, and an interconnection network.

Our goal is to develop a model of a multiple-processor system and evaluate it for a set of parameters listed above in order to understand and analyze their interaction. The results obtained can be used to develop a method for interactively varying some of parameters such that the system design approaches its best cost-effectiveness. We have approached this general problem by developing a model of a shared-memory parallel architecture and evaluating it for some well structured iterative algorithms.

Processing and communication decompositions are used to capture the effect of a parallel algorithm on the performance of a multiple-processor system. By a decomposition group we define a function of N that determines how the processing and the communication overhead can be divided among N processors. We study three different decomposition groups analyzed by Vrsalovic *et al.* [12]. Their analysis was applied to a shared-bus oriented architecture such as Cm*. Our model can be extended to different interconnection structures, provided that the bandwidth of each of them can be defined. It can also capture the effect of applying different methods for allocating data to memory modules and of nonuniform data accesses.

We use the interconnection bandwidth to express the effect of changing the interconnection topology or applying different methods for allocating data to memory modules for a multistage network. In Cvetanovic [1], we show that for a multistage network such as the Omega network proposed by Lawrie [9], the bandwidth is reduced from N provided that

Manuscript received August 22, 1986; revised November 3, 1986. This work was supported in part by the National Science Foundation under Grant MCS-7805298 and by IBM under Contract 462914.

The author is with Digital Equipment Corporation, Acton, MA 01720.

IEEE Log Number 8613054.

Reprinted from *IEEE Trans. on Computers*, vol. C-36, no. 4, April 1987, pp. 421–432.

data are allocated to memories such that all N requests are accepted per network cycle, to unity provided that the allocation causes a serialization of all requests in a single memory module.

For a given problem decomposition and bandwidth of the interconnection structure, our results allow for observing the asymptotic performance of a system as the number of processors increases. For a fixed-size problem, the number of processors is also related to the granularity, since by increasing N the grain size of subproblems executed on each processor decreases. Increasing the level of granularity enhances the exploitation of the parallelism in the algorithm, but at the same time increases the communication overhead. The methods developed here can be used to determine the size of a subproblem executed on each processor yielding the optimum performance.

Our results indicate that for algorithms where the communication overhead can be fully decomposed among N processors, the speedup grows as the number of processors N increases for all values of bandwidth except the worst case value. The worst case bandwidth is equivalent to the bandwidth of a single shared communication resource where only one request can be accepted per cycle time. For the worst case bandwidth, the speedup converges to the value equal to the ratio of processing time to communication time. For algorithms where the communication overhead cannot be decomposed, the speedup approaches its maximum for a value of N which is determined by the ratio of processing to communication, and then it decreases approaching zero. At one point, the performance of such a multiple-processor system becomes worse than the performance of a uniprocessor. This behavior is observed for all values of bandwidth except for the best case where the bandwidth for N requests is proportional to N.

We analyze both cases where processing is overlapped with communication and where processing and communication cannot be overlapped. Our analysis shows that, except for the best case decomposition and bandwidth, the performance can be improved by overlapping processing and communication only for smaller N. As N increases, the speedup for the overlapped case decreases approaching the speedup for the nonoverlapped case. Thus, for large N no performance improvement can be achieved by overlapping processing with communication.

The results obtained here can be used also to compare two different data-access modes: where all data items for one iteration are first copied to local memories of processors and then accessed from there, and where all data items are accessed directly from global memory. If there is no overlap between processing and communication, then the speedup for the case with local/global copying is improved by a factor of $O(\log N)$ comparing to the case with global data access, since copying a block of data can take advantage of pipelining data through stages of the interconnection network. If processing can be overlapped with communication, the performance for both data access modes is the same.

For applications where the computation consists of parallel and serial sections of code, and the communication overhead can be fully decomposed among N processors, the speedup converges to a value inversely proportional to the serial portion of time for the best case bandwidth. As the bandwidth of the interconnection network decreases or the communication decomposition becomes worse, sections of serial code do not affect the complexity of speedup as a function of the level of granularity.

The next section describes the model for computing the speedup and states the assumptions. In Section III, we derive expressions for the speedup for three different decomposition functions and both data-access modes. In Section IV, we analyze the case where the processing consists of parallel and serial portions. Conclusions appear in the final section.

II. MODEL AND ASSUMPTIONS

The analysis that follows is performed for a shared-memory architecture consisting of N processors, an interconnection network, and N memory modules with two levels of memory hierarchy: shared global memories and local memories associated with each processor. We assume that the delay for accessing local data is included in computation time, while each global data access requires traversing the interconnection network. Examples of proposed shared-memory architectures include the NYU Ultracomputer by Gottlieb [7], the more recently announced IBM RP3 prototype by Pfister *et al.* [11], and the University of Illinois CEDAR computer by Gajski *et al.* [5]. Although, due to the limited scope of this paper, we analyze only a shared-memory parallel architecture, a methodology developed here can be applied to other proposed multiple-processor architectures. In Cvetanovic [3], we show how to apply a similar model to a pipelined dataflow architecture, such as a static dataflow computer proposed by Dennis *et al.* [4].

The applications we analyze belong to a class of structured iterative algorithms where computation and communication patterns are well defined during each iteration. Frequently in these applications, the computation can be uniformly distributed among processors resulting in deterministic processing times. Also, the communication pattern is known for each iteration. Therefore, we can apply a deterministic analysis to compute the execution time exactly, instead of estimating an average delay by assuming a certain probability distribution for an arrival process. Furthermore, our model can capture deterministic message transmission times in network switches, and the effect of bursty nature of arrivals at the interconnection network.

We further assume that the problem size M is larger than the number of processors N, which is often a case in computationally intensive applications intended for parallel execution. We consider both cases where processing is not overlapped with communication (*nonoverlapped case*) and where the overlap of processing and communication is possible (*overlapped case*). We compare two data access modes: local/global copying where data are first copied to local memories, and global data access where all data items are accessed directly from global memory.

In some cases, a transformation of a serial algorithm into a parallel form introduces an additional computational overhead. For the purpose of our analysis, we neglect this source of overhead and assume that no additional processing cost is required to execute an algorithm on a parallel computer. However, our model can be extended to include this additional source of overhead.

Using processing and communication decomposition functions we can define the property of a specific parallel algorithm. Similar to the definitions given by Vrsalovic *et al.* [12], we define the *processing decomposition function* $D_p(N)$ as the ratio of processing time for a uniprocessor to processing time for each processor in a multiple-processor system. The *communication decomposition function* $D_c(N)$ is defined as the ratio of data-access time for a uniprocessor to data-access time for each processor in a multiple-processor system.

The bandwidth of the interconnection network reflects the effect of changing an interconnection topology. It can also be influenced by applying different allocations of data to memory modules, as discussed by Cvetanovic [3]. In this paper we consider three different values of bandwidth of the interconnection network.

1) The bandwidth is equal to N, the number of processors. This best case value is obtained for a crossbar switch or a multistage network where data items are allocated to memory modules such that no conflicts are produced in network switches. In both cases, requests arriving at the network simultaneously are routed to different memory modules.

2) The bandwidth is equal to $\sqrt{N}$. This value is obtained as the worst case bandwidth for a multistage network where all requests are routed to different memory modules. Lang [8] has shown that in this case a maximum number of conflicts is proportional to $O(\sqrt{N})$. For the sake of computational simplicity, we assume that $\sqrt{N}$ is an integer and replace $O(\sqrt{N})$ with $\sqrt{N}$.

3) The bandwidth is equal to unity. This worst-case bandwidth is obtained for a communication structure where only one request can be accepted per cycle time. Examples include a single shared bus as well as a multistage network where data items are allocated such that bottlenecks are generated at some memory modules. Such memory bottlenecks are discussed by Pfister and Norton [10] ("hot spots") and Cvetanovic [1].

A. Data Access with Local/Global Copying

In this section, we derive expressions for the speedup for the case where all data items for one iteration are first copied to local memories of processors and then accessed from there.

The serial time for an algorithm of size M is obtained by summing processing times for all iterations

$$\sum_i T_{p_i}(M) t_{p_i} \tag{1}$$

where i is an iteration number, $T_{p_i}(M)$ is the number of computation units per iteration as a function of the problem size, and t_{p_i} is the time to complete one computation.

When executed on a parallel computer, the processing time is obtained as follows:

$$\sum_i \frac{T_{p_i}(M)}{D_{p_i}(N)} t_{p_i} \tag{2}$$

where $D_{p_i}(N)$ is the decomposition function for processing for iteration i.

If we assume that data items are copied to local memories only once per iteration, then the effective communication time for a burst of arrivals at a multistage interconnection network during an iteration is obtained as a sum of the minimum delay proportional to the number of network stages and the queueing delay which is directly proportional to the number of arrivals and inversely proportional to the network bandwidth. The total communication time is obtained as a sum of communication delays for all iterations, according to the following expression.

$$\sum_i \left(\text{Depth } (N) + \frac{T_{c_i}(M)}{D_{c_i}(N)} \frac{N}{BW(N)} - 1 \right) t_c. \tag{3}$$

In the above expression, t_c is the time necessary to transfer a message through a single network stage excluding waiting due to contention, $BW(N)$ is the bandwidth of the network or the number of requests accepted during t_c, Depth (N) is the number of network stages, $T_{c_i}(M)$ is the number of communication steps per processor as a function of the problem size, and $D_{c_i}(N)$ is the decomposition function for communication. The factor $T_{c_i}(M)/D_{c_i}(N)$ accounts for the number of data requests per processor in a burst of arrivals, while the factor $N/BW(N)$ accounts for the network contention which can be influenced by different interconnection network topologies, or by changing allocations of data to memory modules.

If no overlap between processing and communication is possible, then the time to execute an algorithm on an N-processor system is obtained simply by adding the communication overhead to the processing time:

$$\sum_i \left(\frac{T_{p_i}(M)}{D_{p_i}(N)} t_{p_i} \right.$$

$$\left. + \left(\text{Depth } (N) + \frac{T_{c_i}(M)}{D_{c_i}(N)} \frac{N}{BW(N)} - 1 \right) t_c \right). \tag{4}$$

If it is possible to initiate the next iteration during the communication interval, then the total execution time is obtained as a maximum of the processing time and the communication overhead in the bottleneck network stage:

$$\sum_i \max \left\{ \frac{T_{p_i}(M)}{D_{p_i}(N)} t_{p_i}, \frac{T_{c_i}(M)}{D_{c_i}(N)} \frac{N}{BW(N)} t_c \right\}. \tag{5}$$

The speedup of a multiple-processor system is defined as the ratio of the time required to execute an algorithm on a single processor to the time required to execute the same algorithm on an N-processor system. Therefore, the expression for the speedup for the nonoverlapped case is obtained by dividing (1) by (4):

$$S_{\text{nov}} = \frac{\Sigma_i T_{p_i}(M) t_{p_i}}{\Sigma_i \left(\dfrac{T_{p_i}(M)}{D_{p_i}(N)} t_{p_i} + \left(\text{Depth}\,(N) + \dfrac{T_{c_i}(M)}{D_{c_i}(N)} \dfrac{N}{BW(N)} - 1 \right) t_c \right)}. \tag{6}$$

The expression for the speedup for the overlapped case is obtained by dividing (1) by (5):

$$S_{\text{ov}} = \frac{\Sigma_i T_{p_i}(M) t_{p_i}}{\Sigma_i \max \left\{ \dfrac{T_{p_i}(M)}{D_{p_i}(N)} t_{p_i}, \dfrac{T_{c_i}(M)}{D_{c_i}(N)} \dfrac{N}{BW(N)} t_c \right\}}. \tag{7}$$

For homogeneous algorithms where the same computation and communication patterns are repeated during each iteration, the expressions (6) and (7) are simplified to

$$S_{\text{nov}} = \frac{T_p(M) t_p}{\dfrac{T_p(M)}{D_p(N)} t_p + \left(\text{Depth}\,(N) + \dfrac{T_c(M)}{D_c(N)} \dfrac{N}{BW(N)} - 1 \right) t_c} \tag{8}$$

$$S_{\text{ov}} = \min \left\{ D_p(N), T_p(M) \frac{D_c(N)}{T_c(M)} \frac{BW(N)}{N} \frac{t_p}{t_c} \right\}. \tag{9}$$

For the case where the processing and the communication cost are the same function of the problem size, or $T_p(M) = T_c(M)$, the above expressions can be further simplified. If the problem size is much larger than the number of processors ($M \gg N$), then the effect of the depth of the network (Depth (N) − 1) can be neglected and the expressions for the speedup are simplified to

$$S_{\text{nov}} = \frac{t_p}{\dfrac{t_p}{D_p(N)} + \dfrac{N}{D_c(N) BW(N)} t_c} \tag{10}$$

$$S_{\text{ov}} = \min \left\{ D_p(N), D_c(N) \frac{BW(N)}{N} \frac{t_p}{t_c} \right\}. \tag{11}$$

The above expressions allow us to study the influence of various parameters on the speedup: the property of a parallel algorithm characterized by the decomposition functions $D_p(N)$ and $D_c(N)$, the speed of processors and the network expressed through the ratio t_p/t_c, the network topology or the effect of applying different allocations of data to memory modules represented by the network bandwidth $BW(N)$, and the number of processors in the system (N) which is for a fixed-size problem also related to the granularity. Notice that the last approximation results in wrong expressions for the speedup if $N = 1$ is assumed. Hence, in the analysis that follows, we apply these expressions to the systems consisting of more than one processor. In order to obtain more accurate results, the complex expressions given by (6) and (7) should be applied.

B. Global Data Access

In this section, we derive expressions for the speedup for the case where all data items are accessed from global memory such that each data access requires traversing the interconnection network.

For a multistage interconnection network and global data access, the communication overhead per iteration is obtained as a product of the number of memory requests during an iteration and the effective communication delay. The effective communication delay is in this case equal to the sum of the minimum delay which is proportional to the depth of the network and the waiting delay which is inversely proportional to the network bandwidth. The total communication delay of an algorithm is obtained by summing the communication delay per iteration for all iterations, according to the following expression.

$$\sum_i \frac{T_{c_i}(M)}{D_{c_i}(N)} \left(\text{Depth}\,(N) + \frac{N}{BW(N)} - 1 \right) t_c. \tag{12}$$

In the above expression, the factor Depth $(N) t_c$ accounts for the minimum delay proportional to the number of network stages, while the factor $(N/BW(N) - 1) t_c$ accounts for the queueing delay due to conflicts in network switches. The ratio $T_{c_i}(M)/D_{c_i}(N)$ represents the number of data accesses per processor during a single iteration.

If no overlap between processing and communication is possible, then the time to execute an algorithm on an N-processor system is obtained by adding the communication overhead to the processing time

$$\sum_i \left(\frac{T_{p_i}(M)}{D_{p_i}(N)} t_{p_i} + \frac{T_{c_i}(M)}{D_{c_i}(N)} \left(\text{Depth}\,(N) + \frac{N}{BW(N)} - 1 \right) t_c \right). \tag{13}$$

If it is possible to initiate the next computation during the communication interval, then the total execution time is obtained as a maximum of the processing time and the communication delay of the bottleneck network stage

$$\sum_i \max \left\{ \frac{T_{p_i}(M)}{D_{p_i}(N)} t_{p_i}, \frac{T_{c_i}(M)}{D_{c_i}(N)} \frac{N}{BW(N)} t_c \right\}. \tag{14}$$

Note that the execution time above is the same as the execution time from (5) for the case with local/global copying. This is true because for the case with global data access, the global memory is accessed $T_{c_i}(M)/D_{c_i}(N)$ times per iteration, allowing a new initiation every max $\{[T_{p_i}(M)/D_{p_i}(N)]/[T_{c_i}(M)/D_{c_i}(N)] t_{p_i}, [N]/[BW(N)] t_c\}$ cycles. Hence, the initiation time and the speedup for the case with global data access are the same as for the case with local/global copying.

The expression for the speedup for the nonoverlapped case and a multistage network is obtained by dividing (1) by (13) and substituting $\log N$ for $Depth\ (N)$, the depth of the network

$$
S_{nov}
$$

$$
= \frac{\Sigma_l T_{p_l}(M) t_{p_l}}{\Sigma_l \left(\dfrac{T_{p_l}(M)}{D_{p_l}(N)} t_{p_l} + \dfrac{T_{c_l}(M)}{D_{c_l}(N)} \left(\log N + \dfrac{N}{BW(N)} - 1 \right) t_c \right)}.
$$

$$(15)$$

For algorithms where the same computation and communication patterns are repeated during each iteration of an algorithm, the above expression is simplified to

$$
S_{nov} = \frac{T_p(M) t_p}{\dfrac{T_p(M)}{D_p(N)} t_p + \dfrac{T_c(M)}{D_c(N)} \left(\log N + \dfrac{N}{BW(N)} - 1 \right) t_c} \quad (16)
$$

For $T_p(M) = T_c(M)$, the above expression further simplifies to

$$
S_{nov} = \frac{t_p}{\dfrac{1}{D_p(N)} t_p + \dfrac{1}{D_c(N)} \left(\log N + \dfrac{N}{BW(N)} - 1 \right) t_c}. \quad (17)
$$

The expression for the speedup for the overlapped case is the same as for the case with local/global copying and is given by (9).

III. Typical Decomposition Functions

We use expressions for the speedup derived in the previous section to study the influence of various decomposition functions $(D_p(N), D_c(N))$ on the performance.

In this section, we first assume that the computation can be fully decomposed among N processors, therefore $D_p(N) = N$. This decomposition function defines that the processing time at each processor decreases proportionally to the number of processors.

We consider three different decomposition functions for the communication overhead.

1) $D_c(N) = N$ where the communication overhead per processor in an N-processor system is inversely proportional to N. In this case, the total communication requirement of a system does not depend on the number of processors. Application examples of such decomposition function include matrix operations with global data access, matrix-vector operations with global data access, etc.

2) $D_c(N) = \sqrt{N}$ where the communication overhead per processor in an N-processor system is inversely proportional to $\sqrt{N}$. Application examples of such decomposition function include grid computations, weather prediction models, finite element analysis, etc.

3) $D_c(N) = 1$ where the communication overhead per processor in an N-processor system does not depend on the

number of processors. In this case, the total communication requirement of a system grows proportionally to the number of processors. Application examples of such decomposition function include molecular-motion computations, one-dimensional grid problems, matrix-vector operations with local/global copying, etc.

Therefore, we analyze three different decomposition groups: (N, N), $(N, \sqrt{N})$, and $(N, 1)$. Simplified expressions for the speedup for these decomposition groups, two data access modes, and three different values of bandwidth are summarized in Table I. Note that an algorithm can have a communication decomposition function different than those mentioned above; for example, for the parallel FFT algorithm $D_c(N) = O(N/(\log N))$. This however does not reduce generality of our results since the expressions for performance measures allow for substitution of an arbitrary decomposition function.

A. Decomposition Group (N, N)

In this case, both the processing and communication times are inversely proportional to the number of processors, which results in the decomposition $(D_p(N), D_c(N)) = (N, N)$. In this section, we first derive expressions for the speedup for the case with local/global copying, then for the case with global data access, and complete the section with an application example of such decomposition function.

1) Data Access with Local/Global Copying: Expressions for the speedup for the case with local/global copying are obtained by substituting the decomposition functions above into (10) and (11).

$$
S_{nov} = \frac{N t_p}{t_p + \dfrac{N}{BW(N)} t_c} \quad (18)
$$

$$
S_{ov} = \min \left\{ N, BW(N) \frac{t_p}{t_c} \right\}
$$

$$
= \begin{cases} N & \text{if } N \leq BW(N) \dfrac{t_p}{t_c} \\[2ex] BW(N) \dfrac{t_p}{t_c} & \text{if } N > BW(N) \dfrac{t_p}{t_c} \end{cases} \quad (19)
$$

Expressions for the speedup and three different values of bandwidth: $BW(N) = N$, $BW(N) = \sqrt{N}$, and $BW(N) = 1$ are summarized in Table I.

Fig. 1 presents the speedup for the overlapped and nonoverlapped cases as a function of the number of processors for different values of network bandwidth. In this case, increasing N has the same effect as decreasing the size of a subproblem executed on each processor.

From this figure we observe that as the grain size decreases, the speedup increases for all N, provided that $BW(N) > 1$. For $BW(N) = 1$, the speedup converges to a value equal to t_p/t_c for both the nonoverlapped and overlapped cases. For the overlapped case and $BW(N) = 1$, the speedup cannot be improved by increasing the number of processors if N exceeds

TABLE I
SPEEDUP FOR VARIOUS DECOMPOSITION FUNCTIONS

Decomposition function			(N,N)	$(N,\sqrt{N})$	$(N,1)$
Nonoverlapped Case	local	$BW=N$	$\dfrac{N\frac{t_p}{t_c}}{\frac{t_p}{t_c}+1}$	$\dfrac{N\frac{t_p}{t_c}}{\frac{t_p}{t_c}+\sqrt{N}}$	$\dfrac{N\frac{t_p}{t_c}}{\frac{t_p}{t_c}+N}$
		$BW=\sqrt{N}$	$\dfrac{N\frac{t_p}{t_c}}{\frac{t_p}{t_c}+\sqrt{N}}$	$\dfrac{N\frac{t_p}{t_c}}{\frac{t_p}{t_c}+N}$	$\dfrac{N\frac{t_p}{t_c}}{\frac{t_p}{t_c}+N^{3/2}}$
		$BW=1$	$\dfrac{N\frac{t_p}{t_c}}{\frac{t_p}{t_c}+N}$	$\dfrac{N\frac{t_p}{t_c}}{\frac{t_p}{t_c}+N^{3/2}}$	$\dfrac{N\frac{t_p}{t_c}}{\frac{t_p}{t_c}+N^{2}}$
	global	$BW=N$	$\dfrac{N\frac{t_p}{t_c}}{\frac{t_p}{t_c}+\log N}$	$\dfrac{N\frac{t_p}{t_c}}{\frac{t_p}{t_c}+\sqrt{N}\log N}$	$\dfrac{N\frac{t_p}{t_c}}{\frac{t_p}{t_c}+N\log N}$
		$BW=\sqrt{N}$	$\dfrac{N\frac{t_p}{t_c}}{\frac{t_p}{t_c}+\log N+\sqrt{N}-1}$	$\dfrac{N\frac{t_p}{t_c}}{\frac{t_p}{t_c}+\sqrt{N}(\log N+\sqrt{N}-1)}$	$\dfrac{N\frac{t_p}{t_c}}{\frac{t_p}{t_c}+N(\log N+\sqrt{N}-1)}$
		$BW=1$	$\dfrac{N\frac{t_p}{t_c}}{\frac{t_p}{t_c}+\log N+N-1}$	$\dfrac{N\frac{t_p}{t_c}}{\frac{t_p}{t_c}+\sqrt{N}(\log N+N-1)}$	$\dfrac{N\frac{t_p}{t_c}}{\frac{t_p}{t_c}+N(\log N+N-1)}$
Overlapped Case	local	$BW=N$	$\min\{N,N\frac{t_p}{t_c}\}=\begin{cases}N & \text{if }1\le\frac{t_p}{t_c}\\ N\frac{t_p}{t_c} & \text{if }1>\frac{t_p}{t_c}\end{cases}$	$\min\{N,\sqrt{N}\frac{t_p}{t_c}\}=\begin{cases}N & \text{if }N\le(\frac{t_p}{t_c})^2\\ \sqrt{N}\frac{t_p}{t_c} & \text{if }N>(\frac{t_p}{t_c})^2\end{cases}$	$\min\{N,\frac{t_p}{t_c}\}=\begin{cases}N & \text{if }N\le\frac{t_p}{t_c}\\ \frac{t_p}{t_c} & \text{if }N>\frac{t_p}{t_c}\end{cases}$
	and	$BW=\sqrt{N}$	$\min\{N,\sqrt{N}\frac{t_p}{t_c}\}=\begin{cases}N & \text{if }N\le(\frac{t_p}{t_c})^2\\ \sqrt{N}\frac{t_p}{t_c} & \text{if }N>(\frac{t_p}{t_c})^2\end{cases}$	$\min\{N,\frac{t_p}{t_c}\}=\begin{cases}N & \text{if }N\le\frac{t_p}{t_c}\\ \frac{t_p}{t_c} & \text{if }N>\frac{t_p}{t_c}\end{cases}$	$\min\{N,\frac{1}{\sqrt{N}}\frac{t_p}{t_c}\}=\begin{cases}N & \text{if }N\le(\frac{t_p}{t_c})^{2/3}\\ \frac{1}{\sqrt{N}}\frac{t_p}{t_c} & \text{if }N>(\frac{t_p}{t_c})^{2/3}\end{cases}$
	global	$BW=1$	$\min\{N,\frac{t_p}{t_c}\}=\begin{cases}N & \text{if }N\le\frac{t_p}{t_c}\\ \frac{t_p}{t_c} & \text{if }N>\frac{t_p}{t_c}\end{cases}$	$\min\{N,\frac{1}{\sqrt{N}}\frac{t_p}{t_c}\}=\begin{cases}N & \text{if }N\le(\frac{t_p}{t_c})^{2/3}\\ \frac{1}{\sqrt{N}}\frac{t_p}{t_c} & \text{if }N>(\frac{t_p}{t_c})^{2/3}\end{cases}$	$\min\{N,\frac{1}{N}\frac{t_p}{t_c}\}=\begin{cases}N & \text{if }N\le\sqrt{\frac{t_p}{t_c}}\\ \frac{1}{N}\frac{t_p}{t_c} & \text{if }N>\sqrt{\frac{t_p}{t_c}}\end{cases}$

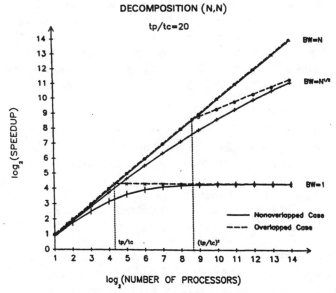

DECOMPOSITION (N,N)

$t_p/t_c = 20$

Fig. 1. Speedup versus N for (N, N) decomposition.

the ratio t_p/t_c. Therefore, for this case, the optimal number of processors is equal to t_p/t_c and the best achievable speedup is equal to the same value. Note that if the optimal number of processors is not an integer, we need to determine an integer which is the closest to this ratio and which results in the maximum speedup.

For the maximum bandwidth ($BW(N) = N$), the speedup for the nonoverlapped case grows as $O(N)$ as N increases. For the overlapped case, the speedup is a linear function of N and it changes in slope from t_p/t_c to one, as the ratio of processing to communication exceeds one. Since the ratio t_p/t_c in Fig. 1 is greater than one, the speedup for the overlapped

case is equal to N and the speedup for the nonoverlapped case is very close to N.

If $BW(N) = \sqrt{N}$, the speedup for the nonoverlapped case grows as $O(\sqrt{N})$ while for the overlapped case its complexity changes from $O(N)$ to $O(\sqrt{N})$ as N exceeds the square of the ratio of processing to communication.

Note that for $BW(N) < N$, the speedup for the overlapped case approaches the speedup for the nonoverlapped case. Therefore, for large N, no performance improvement can be achieved by overlapping communication with processing.

2) Global Data Access: The expression for the speedup for the case where all data items are accessed directly from global memory for the overlapped case is the same as for the overlapped case with local/global copying. The expression for the speedup for the nonoverlapped case and global data access is obtained by substituting decomposition functions $(D_p(N), D_c(N)) = (N, N)$ into (17) as follows:

$$S_{\text{nov}} = \frac{Nt_p}{t_p + \left(\log N + \dfrac{N}{BW(N)} - 1\right)t_c}. \quad (20)$$

Expressions for the speedup for three different values of bandwidth: $BW(N) = N$, $BW(N) = \sqrt{N}$, and $BW(N) = 1$ are summarized in Table I.

Fig. 2 compares the speedup for both data access modes for the (N, N) decomposition group and the nonoverlapped case. The numbers along the curves indicate the number of times the speedup for the case with local/global copying exceeds the speedup for the case with global data access. They are included to clarify the difference in speedup between two data access modes which is covered by the logarithmic function. From this figure we conclude that the speedup for data access

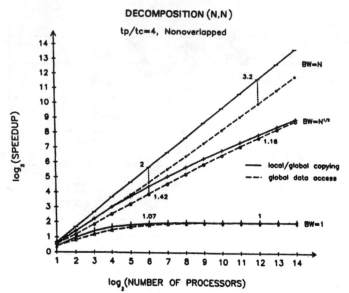

Fig. 2. Speedup versus N for local/global copying and global data access with nonoverlapped case.

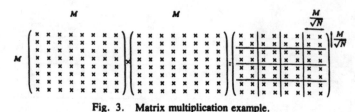

Fig. 3. Matrix multiplication example.

with local/global copying is greater than the speedup for global data access for all N. This is true because the problem size is much larger than the number of processors, and copying a large block of data to local memories can take advantage of pipelining data through stages of the network. Therefore, the communication overhead for the case with local/global copying is reduced by a factor of $O(\log N)$ compared to the case with global data access.

From this figure we further note that the difference in performance between two data access modes becomes more profound as the bandwidth of the interconnection network increases. This is true because for large bandwidth, the influence of a factor of $O(\log N)$ is more significant for the communication delay than for the small values of bandwidth. Note that if $BW(N) = 1$, the values of speedup for both data access modes are very close. Furthermore, as the number of processor increases, the values of speedup for two data access modes diverge if the bandwidth is equal to N, while they converge for the bandwidth less than N, indicating that in this case for large N, no performance improvement can be achieved by local/global copying.

3) Example of (N, N) Decomposition: As an example of the (N, N) decomposition group, we illustrate a parallel algorithm for multiplying two $M \times M$ matrices. We assume that all data items are stored in global memories and are accessed directly from there. Note that the case with local/global data access results in a different decomposition group. The algorithm we illustrate is described by Vrsalovic *et al.* [12]. Fig. 3 shows an example of matrix multiplication where each processor computes elements of a $M/\sqrt{N} \times M/\sqrt{N}$ submatrix.

The total amount of processing at each processor in an N-processor system is determined as follows:

$$\frac{T_p(M)}{D_p(N)} = \frac{M^3}{N} .$$ (21)

The number of data accesses per processor is twice the

processing cost, since data items need to be accessed from both matrices

$$\frac{T_c(M)}{D_c(N)} = 2\frac{M^3}{N} .$$ (22)

By substituting these ratios in (16) and (9), the expressions for the speedup are obtained as follows:

$$S_{nov} = \frac{Nt_p}{t_p + 2\left(\log N + \dfrac{N}{BW(N)} - 1\right)t_c}$$ (23)

$$S_{ov} = \min\left\{N, \frac{BW(N)}{2}\frac{t_p}{t_c}\right\} .$$ (24)

Note that in this example, elements of both matrices can be stored into global memories in a row-major order, but need to be accessed in a skewed pattern in order to prevent contention in either network or memory modules. Therefore, for a multistage network a maximum bandwidth can be achieved by careful allocation of data to memories. However, if data items are allocated in such a way that all processors access the same memory module, then the bandwidth is reduced to one.

B. Decomposition Group $(N, N^{1/2})$

In this subsection, we analyze algorithms for which the processing decomposition function is proportional to the number of processors, while the communication decomposition function is given as $D_c(N) = \sqrt{N}$. We first derive expressions for the speedup for the case with local/global copying, then for the case with global data access and conclude the section with an application example of such decomposition function.

1) Data Access with Local/Global Copying: By substituting processing and communication decomposition functions into (10) and (11) we obtain

$$S_{nov} = \frac{Nt_p}{t_p + \dfrac{N^{3/2}}{BW(N)}t_c}$$ (25)

$$S_{ov} = \min\left\{N, \frac{BW(N)}{\sqrt{N}}\frac{t_p}{t_c}\right\}$$

$$= \begin{cases} N & \text{if } N \le \left(BW(N)\dfrac{t_p}{t_c}\right)^{2/3} \\ \dfrac{BW(N)}{\sqrt{N}}\dfrac{t_p}{t_c} & \text{if } N > \left(BW(N)\dfrac{t_p}{t_c}\right)^{2/3} . \end{cases}$$ (26)

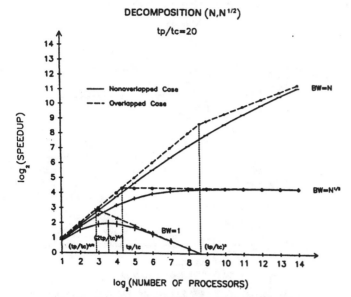

DECOMPOSITION (N,N$^{1/2}$)

tp/tc=20

Fig. 4. Speedup versus N for $(N, N^{1/2})$ decomposition.

Expressions for the speedup for three different values of bandwidth: $BW(N) = N$, $BW(N) = \sqrt{N}$, and $BW(N) = 1$ are summarized in Table I.

Fig. 4 presents the speedup as a function of the number of processors for both the overlapped and nonoverlapped cases. Note that for this decomposition group, no linear speedup can be guaranteed for all N, even for the best case bandwidth of the interconnection network. The curves for $BW(N) = N$ and $BW(N) = \sqrt{N}$ exhibit the same behavior as the curves from the previous decomposition group with $BW(N) = \sqrt{N}$ and $BW(N) = 1$, respectively.

However, if $BW(N) = 1$, then the speedup exhibits a different behavior. For the nonoverlapped case the speedup increases until N approaches $(2t_p/t_c)^{2/3}$. As N exceeds this value, the speedup decreases as $O(\sqrt{N})$. The maximum speedup is equal to $(2t_p/t_c)^{2/3}/3$. For the overlapped case the speedup grows linearly with N until N approaches $(t_p/t_c)^{2/3}$, and then as N increases further the speedup decreases as $O(\sqrt{N})$. Therefore, the optimal number of processors for the nonoverlapped case is equal to $(2t_p/t_c)^{2/3}$ while the optimal number of processors for the overlapped case is $(t_p/t_c)^{2/3}$. Also, from this figure we note that if $BW(N) = 1$, a multiple-processor system performs worse than a uniprocessor provided that the number of processors exceeds a value equal to $(t_p/t_c)^2$.

From this figure we further conclude that by reducing the bandwidth from N to unity, the speedup changes from an increasing function of N to a decreasing function of N as N exceeds $(2t_p/t_c)^{2/3}$ for the nonoverlapped case or $(t_p/t_c)^{2/3}$ for the overlapped case. Therefore the performance can be improved significantly by choosing an appropriate interconnection structure, or by applying different methods for allocating data to memory modules to avoid bottlenecks in memory modules.

2) Global Data Access: The expression for the speedup for the case where all data items are accessed from the global memory for the nonoverlapped case is obtained by substituting

decomposition functions $(D_p(N), D_c(N)) = (N, \sqrt{N})$ into (17) as follows:

$$S_{nov} = \frac{Nt_p}{t_p + \sqrt{N}\left(\log N + \dfrac{N}{BW(N)} - 1\right) t_c}. \tag{27}$$

The performance for the overlapped case with global data access is the same as for the case with local/global copying.

Expressions for the speedup for three different values of bandwidth: $BW(N) = N$, $BW(N) = \sqrt{N}$, and $BW(N) = 1$ are summarized in Table I.

3) Example of $(N, N^{1/2})$ Decomposition Group: As an example of the $(N, \sqrt{N})$ decomposition group, we illustrate grid-type applications where a certain computation is performed at every point of an $M \times M$ grid of data. Let us assume that the matrix *wraps around* so that the Mth row is adjacent to the first row and the Mth column is adjacent to the first column. Examples of such computations include a Poison equation, weather prediction models, and models for solving partial differential equations.

Since the decomposition functions for both data access modes are the same, we analyze only the case with local/global copying. We assume that each processor performs a computation on an $M/\sqrt{N} \times M/\sqrt{N}$ grid of data loaded in its local memory. Fig. 5 illustrates an example of grid computation. As indicated in Fig. 5, during each iteration step a processor needs to load data from local memories of four neighboring processors, requiring $M/\sqrt{N}$ data items from each of them.

In this case, the total amount of processing at each processor is determined to be

$$\frac{T_p(M)}{D_p(N)} = \frac{M^2}{N}. \tag{28}$$

Since each processor needs to copy in its local memory $4M/\sqrt{N}$ data items from its four neighbors and then to copy back to the global memory $4(M/\sqrt{N} - 1)$ data items on the edges of the grid, the total amount of data transferred is obtained as follows:

$$\frac{T_c(M)}{D_c(N)} = 8\frac{M}{\sqrt{N}} - 4 \approx \frac{8M}{\sqrt{N}}. \tag{29}$$

The expressions for the speedup are obtained by substituting these ratios in (8) and (9) as follows:

$$S_{nov} = \frac{Nt_p}{t_p + \dfrac{8}{M}\dfrac{N^{3/2}}{BW(N)}t_c} \tag{30}$$

$$S_{ov} = \min\left\{N, \frac{M}{8}\frac{BW(N)}{\sqrt{N}}\frac{t_p}{t_c}\right\}. \tag{31}$$

Note that the above expressions are the same function of N as the expressions (25) and (26) for the decomposition group $(N, \sqrt{N})$.

As shown by Cvetanovic [2], for some important iterative

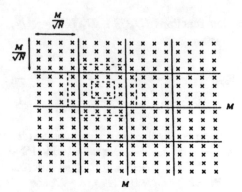

Fig. 5.   Example of grid-type computation.

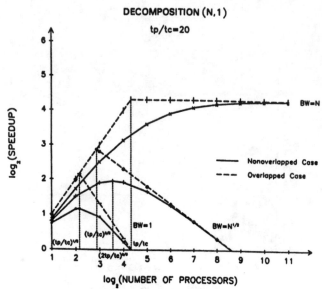

Fig. 6.   Speedup versus N for $(N, 1)$ decomposition.

algorithms an initial allocation of data to global memories determines contention within the multistage interconnection network for all other iterations. For the case of grid-computations and the omega network, if an initial allocation is such that no conflicts are produced with one neighbor, then no conflicts are produced with other three neighbors. Similarly, if a maximum of $O(\sqrt{N})$ conflicts are produced with one neighbor, then the same number of conflicts are produced with all other neighbors. If data items are allocated in a row-major order, then it is possible to avoid contention for a multistage network and achieve a maximum bandwidth. If data items are allocated such that all processors access the same memory module, then the bandwidth is reduced to one.

C. Decomposition Group $(N, 1)$

In this subsection, we analyze application problems where the processing decomposition function is proportional to the number of processors, while the communication overhead does not depend on N; therefore, $(D_p(N), D_c(N)) = (N, 1)$. We first analyze the case with local/global copying, then the case with global data access, and finally give an application example of such decomposition group.

1) Data Access with Local/Global Copying: By substituting these decomposition functions into (10) and (11) we obtain

$$S_{nov} = \frac{Nt_p}{t_p + \dfrac{N^2}{BW(N)} t_c} \qquad (32)$$

$$S_{ov} = \min \left\{ N, \frac{BW(N)}{N} \frac{t_p}{t_c} \right\}$$

$$= \begin{cases} N & \text{if } N \le \sqrt{BW(N) \dfrac{t_p}{t_c}} \\ \dfrac{BW(N)}{N} \dfrac{t_p}{t_c} & \text{if } N > \sqrt{BW(N) \dfrac{t_p}{t_c}}. \end{cases} \qquad (33)$$

Expressions for the speedup for three different values of bandwidth: $BW(N) = N$, $BW(N) = \sqrt{N}$, and $BW(N) = 1$ are summarized in Table I.

Fig. 6 shows the speedup as a function of the number of processors for both overlapped and nonoverlapped cases and for three different values of bandwidth. Note that the curves for $BW(N) = N$ and $BW(N) = \sqrt{N}$ from this figure exhibit the same behavior as the curves for $BW(N) = \sqrt{N}$ and $BW(N) = 1$ for the decomposition group $(N, \sqrt{N})$.

If $BW(N) = 1$, then the speedup for the nonoverlapped case increases until N approaches a value equal to $\sqrt{t_p/t_c}$. Further increase of N causes the speedup to decrease as $O(N)$. The maximum value for speedup is equal to $\sqrt{t_p/t_c}/2$. For the overlapped case, the speedup grows linearly with N until N approaches $\sqrt{t_p/t_c}$ and then the speedup decreases as $O(N)$. Therefore, for both the overlapped and nonoverlapped cases, the optimal number of processors for executing a problem which belongs to the decomposition group $(N, 1)$ is equal to $\sqrt{t_p/t_c}$. A linear speedup in this case can be obtained only for a small number of processors, or if the network is implemented in faster technology than processors ($t_p \gg t_c$). From Fig. 6 we further observe that if $BW(N) = 1$, the speedup becomes less than one provided that the number of processors exceeds t_p/t_c. Therefore, for large N it is essential to achieve bandwidth no less than N in order to prevent reducing the speedup as N increases. As in the previous examples, this bandwidth can be achieved with multistage network and careful allocation of data to memory modules.

2) Global Data Access: The expression for the speedup for the case where all data items are accessed from the global memory are obtained by substituting decomposition functions $(D_p(N), D_c(N)) = (N, 1)$ into (17)

$$S_{nov} = \frac{Nt_p}{t_p + \sqrt{N}\left(\log N + \dfrac{N}{BW(N)} - 1\right) t_c}. \qquad (34)$$

Since the expression for the speedup for the overlapped case is the same as for the case with local/global copying, we derive only expressions for the nonoverlapped case.

Expressions for the speedup for three different values of

172

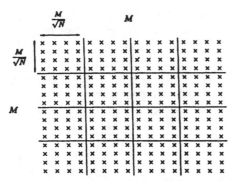

Fig. 7. Example of molecular-motion computation.

bandwidth: $BW(N) = N$, $BW(N) = \sqrt{N}$, and $BW(N) = 1$ are summarized in Table I.

3) Example of $(N, 1)$ Decomposition Group: As an example of the $(N, 1)$ decomposition group, we illustrate an application where a binding energy is computed for a large number of molecules described by an $M \times M$ matrix of data. Various parallel algorithms for computing energetic interactions among the particles are described by Whiteside *et al.* [13].

We analyze the case with local/global copying where during each iteration step a processor needs to load data to its local memory. An example of such computation is illustrated in Fig. 7, where each processor performs a computation on an $M/\sqrt{N} \times M/\sqrt{N}$ submatrix.

In this example, the total processing performed by each processor is

$$\frac{T_p(M)}{D_p(N)} = \frac{M^2}{N} . \tag{35}$$

Since during each iteration step a processor needs M^2 data points, it has to copy in its local memory $M^2 - M^2/N$ data points from global memory. Therefore, the total communication cost per processor obtained is

$$\frac{T_c(M)}{D_c(N)} = \frac{M^2}{N/(N-1)} \approx M^2. \tag{36}$$

Note that the total communication requirement per processor depends only on the problem size, and is not decreasing as the number of processors grows. Expressions for the speedup are obtained by substituting the ratios above in (10) and (11) as follows:

$$S_{\text{nov}} = \frac{Nt_p}{t_p + \frac{N^2}{BW(N)} t_c} \tag{37}$$

$$S_{\text{ov}} = \min \left\{ N, \frac{BW(N)}{N} \frac{t_p}{t_c} \right\}. \tag{38}$$

Note that these expressions are the same as expressions (32) and (33) for the decomposition group $(N, 1)$. As in previous examples, in this case the bandwidth can be improved from unity to N by applying different allocations of data to memory modules.

IV. PROCESSING DECOMPOSITION

In the previous sections we have assumed that for algorithms analyzed, the processing portion of the execution time is fully decomposable. In this section, we study applications where the processing cannot be completely decomposed among N processors. The processing time $T_p(M)t_p$ consists of two components: $T_{pp}(M)t_p$, the portion of time which can be parallelized and $T_{ps}(M)t_p$, the portion of time which is executed solely by only one processor in the system. During serial sections, a processor usually initializes variables, divides the computation among processors in the system, or performs computation on all partial results produced by other processors during the parallel section (as in master–slave structures).

The total processing time on an N-processor system is obtained as a sum of the processing time for the parallel and serial sections

$$\frac{T_{pp}(M)}{D_p(N)} t_p + T_{ps}(M)t_p. \tag{39}$$

In order to simplify the analysis we assume that $T_{pp}(M)$ and $T_{ps}(M)$ are identical functions of M as $T_p(M)$. Then let the fraction of time spent in the parallel section be

$$p = \frac{T_{pp}(M)}{T_p(M)} \tag{40}$$

and hence the fraction of time spent in the serial section is

$$1 - p = \frac{T_{ps}(M)}{T_p(M)} . \tag{41}$$

The new processing decomposition function is obtained by dividing $T_p(M)t_p$, the processing time for a uniprocessor by (39):

$$D_p(N) = \frac{T_p(M)}{\frac{T_{pp}(M)}{N} + T_{ps}(M)} = \frac{1}{\frac{p}{N} + (1-p)} . \tag{42}$$

By substituting (42) for the processing decomposition function in (10) and (11), expressions for the speedup for the case with local/global copying become

$$S_{\text{nov}} = \frac{Nt_p}{(p + (1-p)N)t_p + \frac{1}{D_c(N)} \frac{N^2}{BW(N)} t_c} \tag{43}$$

$$S_{\text{ov}} = \min \left\{ \frac{N}{p + (1-p)N}, D_c(N) \frac{BW(N)}{N} \frac{t_p}{t_c} \right\} . \tag{44}$$

For the best case communication decomposition $D_c(N) = N$ and the best case bandwidth of the interconnection structure $BW(N) = N$, the expression for the speedup for the nonoverlapped case becomes

$$S_{\text{nov}} = \frac{Nt_p}{(p + (1-p)N)t_p + t_c} . \tag{45}$$

173

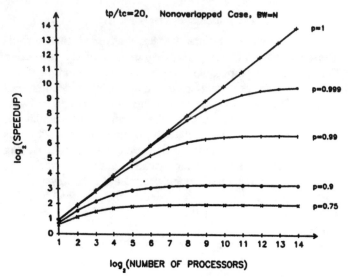

Fig. 8. Speedup versus N for (N, N) decomposition and different values of p, the fraction of time spent in parallel sections.

Fig. 8 plots the speedup for the nonoverlapped case as a function of N for different values of p, the fraction of time spent in parallel sections. The asymptotic speedup is different from the case where the processing can be completely parallelized ($p = 1$) and the speedup is a linear function of N. For $p < 1$, the asymptotic speedup converges to its maximum which is equal to $1/(1 - p)$. Therefore, the maximum speedup is inversely proportional to the fraction of time spent in the serial section. Note from Fig. 8 that for $N \geq 2^9$, the speedup is reduced from linear if the entire problem can be parallelized to a value close to 100 if the serial code presents only one percent of the total code.

However, as the bandwidth of the interconnection network decreases or the communication decomposition becomes worse, the network becomes a bottleneck and portions of serial code cannot change the complexity of the speedup as for the best case bandwidth and the best case communication decomposition function. For example, for $D_c(N) = \sqrt{N}$ and $BW(N) = 1$ the asymptotic speedup exhibits the same complexity as in Section III, only the number of processors for which the speedup reaches its maximum is changed from $(2t_p/t_c)^{2/3}$ to $(2pt_p/t_c)^{2/3}$. If $D_c(N) = 1$ and $BW(N) = 1$, then the number of processors for which the speedup reaches its maximum is changed from $\sqrt{t_p/t_c}$ to $\sqrt{pt_p/t_c}$.

V. Conclusions

In this paper, we have demonstrated the interaction and quantified the influence of several parameters expected to affect the performance of multiple-processor systems. Based on this analysis, we can determine the combination of these parameters such that a multiple-processor system achieves its peak performance. Furthermore, using the methods demonstrated here, we can measure the effect of the bursty nature of arrivals at the interconnection network, as well as the nonuniform access to memory modules which is not achievable by applying a probabilistic analysis.

Our results indicate that if a parallel algorithm allows a full decomposition of both processing and communication, the bandwidth of the interconnection structure can reduce the speedup from $O(N)$ to a constant value. Furthermore, if the communication is not fully decomposable, then the bandwidth can even more seriously limit the performance. For low bandwidth, the speedup approaches a maximum for a very small number of processors and then decreases to zero as the number of processors increases. In order to avoid this undesirable situation where a multiple-processor system performs worse than a uniprocessor, it is essential to have a high-bandwidth network, or to determine a proper allocation of data to memories to eliminate contention within the network. If a high-bandwidth network is not available and a parallel algorithm does not allow for the communication decomposition, then we need to decrease the level of granularity by grouping several computations into larger computational units in order to improve system performance.

The ratio of processing to communication determines both the maximum speedup and the number of processors for which this maximum is obtained. If processors are much faster than the network, the influence of the decomposition strategies and bandwidth on the performance becomes more profound. However if the network is implemented in faster technology then processors, then all other factors analyzed here do not significantly affect the performance.

If the level of granularity is high, then the performance can be improved by overlapping processing and communication only for the best case decomposition and bandwidth. Similarly, processing decomposition reduces the speedup complexity from linear to constant for large N even for the best case communication decomposition and bandwidth.

Note that although the analysis from this paper is limited to a shared-memory oriented architecture, the technique developed here is applicable to any concurrent architecture, including message-passing architectures and dataflow architectures. Further, the importance of the results obtained here is not diminished by the fact that our analysis is limited to simple basic homogeneous problems. Understanding limitations of parallel processing applied to these problems is fundamental for extending the analysis to more sophisticated and complex "real world" applications.

Most of the open questions are concerned with extending the methods demonstrated here so that they can be applied to other parallel architectures and algorithms. If it would be possible to characterize application problems based on the processing and communication decompositions, then our analysis could be applied to these classes of problems. As a result, the performance of various classes of problems rather than specific algorithms could be compared, thus increasing the generality of the methods proposed in this paper. By applying the methods described here to these classes, we can determine the combination of the network bandwidth, the level of granularity, and the data-access mode such that the entire system design approaches its best cost effectiveness.

Acknowledgment

The author would like to thank her adviser, Prof. H. S. Stone, for his numerous comments and suggestions. The

174

author is grateful to Prof. D. F. Towsley for his support during this research.

REFERENCES

[1] Z. Cvetanovic, "Performance analysis of the FFT algorithm on a shared-memory parallel architecture," IBM T. J. Watson Res. Center, Yorktown Heights, NY, RC 11749, May 1986; also submitted to *IBM J. Res. Develop.*

[2] ——, "Best and worst mappings for the omega network," IBM T. J. Watson Res. Center, Yorktown Heights, NY, RC 11748, May 1986; also submitted to *IBM J. Res. Develop.*

[3] ——, "Performance analysis of multiple-processor systems," Ph.D. dissertation, Univ. Massachusetts, Amherst, May 1986.

[4] J. B. Dennis, G-R. Gao, and K. W. Todd, "Modeling the weather with a data flow supercomputer," *IEEE Trans. Comput.*, vol. C-33, pp. 592–603, July 1984.

[5] D. Gajski, D. Kuck, D. Lawrie, and A. Sameh, "Cedar," Dep. Comput. Sci., Univ. Illinois, Urbana, Rep. UIUCDCS-R-83-1123, Feb. 1983.

[6] D. B. Gannon and J. V. Rosendale, "On the impact of communication complexity on design of parallel numerical algorithms," *IEEE Trans. Comput.*, vol. C-33, pp. 1180–1194, Dec. 1984.

[7] A. Gottlieb, R. Grishman, C. P. Kruskal, K. P. McAuliffe, L. Rudolph, and M. Snir, "The NYU Ultracomputer—designing an MIMD shared-memory parallel computer," *IEEE Trans. Comput.*, vol. C-32, pp. 175–189, Feb. 1983.

[8] T. Lang, "Interconnection between processors and memory modules using the shuffle-exchange network," *IEEE Trans. Comput.*, vol. C-25, pp. 496–503, May 1976.

[9] D. H. Lawrie, "Access and alignment of data in an array processor," *IEEE Trans. Comput.*, vol. C-24, pp. 175–189, Dec. 1975.

[10] G. F. Pfister and V. A. Norton, "Hot spot contention and combining in multistage interconnection networks," in *Proc. 1985 Int. Conf. Parallel Processing*, Chicago, IL, IEEE Comput. Soc., Aug. 1985, pp. 790–797.

[11] G. F. Pfister, W. C. Brantley, D. A. George, S. L. Harvey, W. J. Kleinfelder, K. P. McAuliffe, E. A. Melton, V. A. Norton, and J. Weiss, "The IBM research parallel processor prototype (RP3): Introduction and architecture," in *Proc. 1985 Int. Conf. Parallel Processing*, Chicago, IL, IEEE Comput. Soc., Aug. 1985, pp. 764–772.

[12] D. Vrsalovic, E. F. Gehringer, Z. Z. Segall, and D. P. Siewiorek, "The influence of parallel decomposition strategies on the performance of multiprocessor systems," in *Proc. 12th Ann. Int. Symp. Comput. Architect.*, Boston, MA, IEEE Comput. Soc. and ACM, June 1985, pp. 396–405.

[13] R. A. Whiteside, P. G. Hibbard, and N. S. Ostlund, "Conventional and systolic parallel algorithms for Monte Carlo simulations of molecular motions," Dep. Comput. Sci., Carnegie-Mellon Univ., Pittsburgh, PA, 1984.

Zarka Cvetanovic (S'83–M'86) received the B.S. and M.S. degrees in electrical engineering from the University of Sarajevo, Yugoslavia, in 1977 and 1983, respectively, and the Ph.D. degree in electrical and computer engineering from the University of Massachusetts, Amherst, in 1986.

She is presently a member of the Midrange Systems Advanced Development Group, Digital Equipment Corporation, Acton, MA. She was awarded an International Research and Exchanges fellowship in 1982. Her current research interests are in the area of performance analysis of multiple-processor architectures and parallel algorithms.

Grain Size Determination for Parallel Processing

Boontee Kruatrachue and **Ted Lewis**, *Oregon State University*

How does a programmer determine both the number and size of microtasks — grains — in a parallel program? This automatic technique finds the best grain size for a given program.

Optimal execution of parallel programs depends on partitioning the program into modules and scheduling those modules for the shortest execution time possible. This problem has two parts:

• Grain-size problem. How can we partition a program into concurrent modules, called grains, to obtain the shortest possible execution time? What is the best size for each concurrent module?

• Optimal-schedule problem. Assuming we have the best-sized concurrent modules of a program, how can they be scheduled to obtain the shortest possible execution time on a given parallel processor system?

These two problems have been widely studied.[1] But two common techniques — load balancing and writing explicit parallel constructions — can lead to nonoptimal use of parallel processors.

Our solution, called *grain packing*, is a new way to optimize parallel programs. We define a grain as one or more concurrently executing program module. A grain begins executing as soon as all of its inputs are available, and terminates only after all of its outputs have been computed.

Grain packing reduces total execution time by balancing execution time and communication time. Grain packing, used with an optimizing scheduler, gives consistently better results than human-engineered scheduling and packing. Our method is language-independent and is applicable to both extended serial and concurrent programming languages, including Occam, Fortran, and Pascal.

Packing automatically determines grain size for any underlying parallel processing architecture so that each grain is the best size for scheduling. If a grain is too large, parallelism is limited; if a grain is too small, communication delays reduce performance. Small grains are obtained by maximizing parallelism (the max feature) and large grains are constructed by combining (packing) small grains together on a single processor. Packing leads to minimal communication delays (the min feature).

Thus, the best grain size is one which

Reprinted from *IEEE Software*, vol. 5, no. 1, Jan 1988, pp. 23–32.

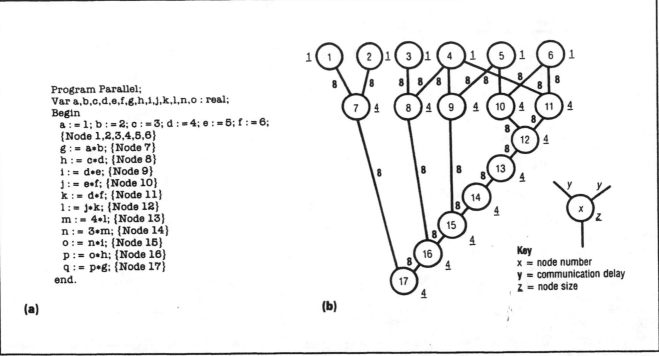

(a)

```
Program Parallel;
Var a,b,c,d,e,f,g,h,i,j,k,l,n,o : real;
Begin
  a : = 1; b : = 2; c : = 3; d : = 4; e : = 5; f : = 6;
  {Node 1,2,3,4,5,6}
  g : = a*b; {Node 7}
  h : = c*d; {Node 8}
  i : = d*e; {Node 9}
  j : = e*f; {Node 10}
  k : = d*f; {Node 11}
  l : = j*k; {Node 12}
  m : = 4*l; {Node 13}
  n : = 3*m; {Node 14}
  o : = n*i; {Node 15}
  p : = o*h; {Node 16}
  q : = p*g; {Node 17}
end.
```

(b)

Key
x = node number
y = communication delay
z = node size

Figure 1. (a) Example code and **(b)** its task graph. Each node in the task graph corresponds to one of the assignment statements in the code; each edge in the graph corresponds to the flow of data from an assignment statement to a dependent assignment state. The value of h in node 16 depends on the assignment of h in node 8, so an edge connects them.

results in the shortest execution time. By "best," we mean the schedule reduces delays caused by communication and execution by carefully trading parallelism for communication time.

Another advantage of this approach is that it can be used as an automatic technique to develop a parallel-processor simulator. Given a program and a target-system specification, a simulator can compute the improvement in execution time without actually running the application. This tells the user if the program has too much communication overhead to take advantage of the parallelism in the target system, saving time and money to find out whether the target system is appropriate. We are developing such a tool; this article describes how it might work for a matrix-multiplication application.

Applicability

Consider a system of fully connected, identical processors and assume that the program submitted to the system can be specified by an acyclic, directed task graph. Figure 1a shows an example parallel program and Figure 1b its task graph.

In the example task graph, $TG(N,E)$, N is a set of numbered nodes. Each node is assigned an integer weight representing its execution time, also called its size (repre-

sented by an underlined number). E is a set of edges representing precedence constraints among nodes. Edges are assigned an integer representing the communication delay between nodes in the form of a message sent from one node to another (represented by a number in boldface). A node must wait for all of its input messages before it can start execution.

More rigorously, our technique applies to task graphs that
• are acyclic;
• are static (they are defined in advance and do not change during execution);
• have heterogeneous labels (message and node sizes are not necessarily identical);
• are nonpreemptive (once a task begins executing, it executes to completion); and
• use static scheduling (once a task has been scheduled on a processor, the schedule is not changed).

In addition, we assume the target parallel processing system has:
• Connectivity. All processors are connected so a message can be sent from any processor to any other processor (for simplicity, we don't take into account the queuing delay that may occur due to congestion on the interconnection network).
• Locality. The transmission time between nodes located on the same processor is zero.

• Identicality. All processors have the same speed and function.

• Coprocessor I/O. A processor can execute tasks and communicate with another processor at the same time. This is typical with I/O (channel) processors and direct memory access. Hence, we use the term *processing element* instead of processor.

• Single application. Only one program is executed at a time on the parallel processing system, to maximize execution speed.

While somewhat idealized, these assumptions are not very restrictive. For example, communication delay in a "multihop" network, such as a hypercube, can be computed to label the edges of the graph. Similarly, node labels can be adjusted to account for different speeds in heterogeneous processor systems. This model would not be appropriate, however, for a parallel processor running a timesharing operating system which maximizes response time at the expense of execution speed.

Related work

Researchers have taken two general approaches to solve grain-size and scheduling problems.

List scheduling. List scheduling[2] assigns the task whose predecessors have been completed to the next available processor. Therefore, if a processor is idle it is because no task can be assigned to it because all predecessor tasks have not been completed.[3]

We know this basic scheduling strategy may not produce the best schedule for a task graph. For example, forcing all processors to remain as active as possible can increase — not decrease — the execution time of some task graphs.[4]

However, a list scheduler does yield near-optimal schedules most of the time.[5] Because of its simplicity and near-optimal performance, it has been used in real parallel-processing systems.

Load balancing. Most parallel programmers believe it is best to take advantage of all parallelism, keep all processors as busy as possible, and start each task as soon as possible. This strategy tends to evenly distribute the load over all processors. This variant of list scheduling is called *load balancing*. We classify load balancing strategies as highest-level-first algorithms. It is generally thought that these provide the best possible execution time.

However, while load balancing works very well in an ideal system, it often yields decreased performance in the presence of unavoidable communication delays in real systems. In fact, in the case of an application with intensive communication, it has been shown that execution time on several processors is greater than execution time on one processor![6] The main reason for this failure is that load balancing tries to use all available parallelism without regard for the corresponding high communication cost.

Max-min problem. List-scheduling algorithms assume zero communication delays. However, when communication delays are considered, the problem is more difficult because the scheduler must examine the start time of each task on each available processor to select the best processor to execute the task.

When there is a communication delay between tasks, scheduling must be based both on the delay and when each processor is ready for execution. Sometimes it is advantageous to assign tasks with large intertask communication delays to the same processor as their immediate predecessors.

Figure 2 shows a small task graph and a form of Gantt chart[7] that shows the scheduling of nodes on processors. Figure 2 shows that it would be a mistake to always increase the amount of parallelism available by scheduling the start of each task as soon as possible (load balancing).

Distributing parallel tasks to as many processors as possible tends to increase the communication delay, which contributes to overall execution time. In short, there is a trade-off between maximizing parallelism and minimizing communication delay. We call this the *max-min* problem.

Figure 3 illustrates the dramatic effect the max-min problem can have on execution time. Figure 3a shows a small task graph. If the communication delays associated with node 4 are larger than the

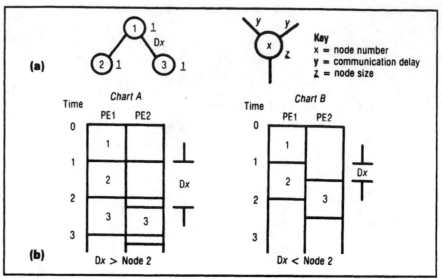

Figure 2. Allocation consideration due to communication delay: **(a)** task graph, **(b)** Gantt charts. Dx is the communication delay. When Dx is greater than the execution time of node 2, the best placement of task 3 is on PE1; when it is less, the best placement is on PE2.

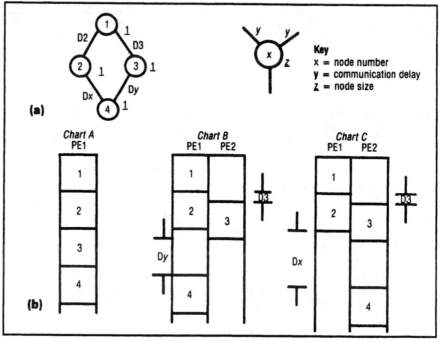

Figure 3. Parallelism versus communication delay: **(a)** task graph, **(b)** Gantt charts. Serial execution of tasks 1,2,3, and 4 results in better performance when both Dx and Dy are considered. Charts B and C show the results of load balancing.

execution time for node 3, then assigning node 3 to PE1 will result in a shorter execution time, as shown in Gantt chart A in Figure 3b. This is true even if node 3 would have executed earlier had it been assigned to PE2, as shown in Gantt charts B and C in Figure 3b.

Our solution. Our solution to the max-min problem is a duplication scheduling heuristic. The DSH duplicates tasks where necessary to reduce the overall communication delay and maximize parallelism at the same time.[6] We don't have the space in this article to repeat the heuristic, but it suffices to say that the DSH trades memory space in favor of reducing communication and enhancing parallelism. It does this by storing duplicate tasks, thus eliminating the need to communicate over the parallel processor interconnection network.

Large-grain dataflow. The second general approach to the problem[1] takes into account communication delays between tasks on different processors. Instead of taking advantage of all available parallelism, it partitions the program so the execution time of each task or group of tasks is much greater than each individual task's communication delay.

While this strategy gives the appearance that communication delays are negligible, it still has problems.

First, it is unclear what is meant by "large grain." According to Babb, "what qualifies as large-grain processing will vary somewhat, depending on the underlying architecture. In general, 'large grain' means that the amount of processing a lowest level program performs during an execution is large compared to the overhead of scheduling its execution."[1] However, Babb offers no method to determine grain size for a particular system. Furthermore, defining grain size manually is time-consuming and error-prone.

Second, this method loses some parallelism because the program runs sequentially inside the large grain. Hence, the application fails to take full advantage of parallelism.

Large-grain dataflow does not solve the max-min problem. Instead, it tries to reduce the communication delay by throwing away the available parallelism in a program.

Grain size

The size of a node can be altered by adding or removing grains from the node. The challenge is to determine the best node size to minimize execution time.

The source code of an application program is represented by a task graph $pg(n,e)$, where each node in n is an atomic operation, as shown in Figure 4. The problem is to find the best task graph $TG(N,E)$ from $pg(n,e)$, where each N_i in N is a module that runs on a processing element in the target parallel-processing system.

The transformation of $pg(n,e)$ into $TG(N,E)$ is done as follows:

1. Each node N_i corresponds to one or more node n_i in n.

2. Mapping n onto N must result in the shortest execution time possible for pg on the target system.

3. Let N_i be formed from a subset of nodes u_i in n. Remove the edges in u_i that connect nodes in u_i to other nodes in u_i. Similarly, form N_i by grouping a subset

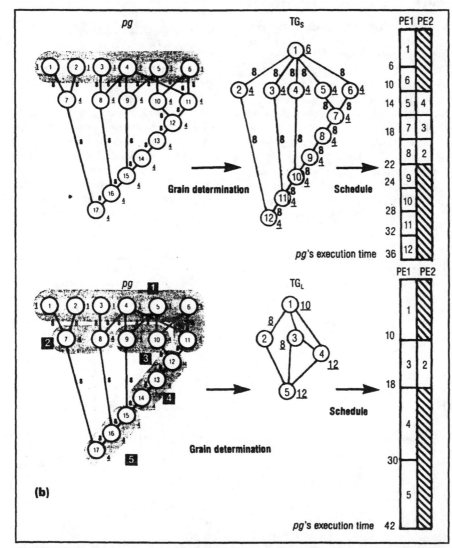

Figure 4. Small-grain versus large-grain scheduling: **(a)** small-grain task graph (TG$_S$), **(b)** large-grain task graph (TG$_L$). It is better to schedule the small-grain task graph first, then pack the grains into larger grains. If the task graph is packed before scheduling, the execution time is not as good.

179

of nodes u_j in n and then removing the edges that connect the nodes in u_j to other nodes in u_j. Finally, collapse the edges connecting u_i and u_j into a single edge E_{ij}, thus connecting N_i with N_j.

4. Let the grain size of a node N_i in $TG(N,E)$ be defined as the number of atomic operations $u_i = \{n_{k1}, n_{k2}, n_{k3}, \ldots, n_{kn}\}$ in $pg(n,e)$ that are mapped into N_i. The best grain size is the grain size that minimizes execution of $pg(n,e)$.

Figure 4 shows two ways to transform the program in Figure 1 — $pg(n,e)$ — into graphs TG_s (Figure 4a) and TG_L (Figure 4b). The average grain size in TG_s is 4.17 units; in TG_L the average grain size is 10 units.

In TG_L, N_1 corresponds to $u_1 = \{n_1, n_2, n_3, n_4, n_5, n_6, n_{11}\}$ of pg. It takes 10 time units to execute. N_2 corresponds to $u_2 = \{n_7, n_8\}$. It takes eight time units to execute, and so on. The edges connecting $\{n_1, n_2, n_3, n_4, n_5, n_6, n_{11}\}$ have been removed and the edges connecting u_1 with u_2 are collapsed into E_{12}, thus connecting N_1 and N_2.

Figure 4a shows the transformation of pg to TG_s. Note the difference in execution time: TG_s takes 36 time units and TG_L takes 42 time units. Figure 4 shows that the small-grain TG_s can take advantage of parallelism better than the large-grain TG_L.

In short, if the grain is too big, parallelism is reduced because potentially concurrent tasks are grouped in a node and executed sequentially. If the grain is too small, the program incurs more overhead in the form of context switching, scheduling time, and communication delay. Solving the grain-size problem means finding the grain size that takes into account all these factors.

Duplication scheduling heuristic

Our DSH duplicates tasks to reduce communication cost. We have published details of this algorithm elsewhere;[6] in this article we illustrate the technique.

Figure 5a shows a task graph with five nodes. The first Gantt chart in Figure 5b shows that node 1 has been duplicated to run on both PE1 and PE2. In this case,

duplication means node 3 can begin executing on PE2 sooner, so parallelism (of nodes 2 and 3) is fully exploited. Nodes 2 and 3 run in parallel on different processing elements so node 5 can start executing sooner than if we had assigned node 2 and node 3 to the same processing element, as the second Gantt chart in Figure 5b shows.

Because node 3 is also running on PE1, there is no communication delay before node 4 can execute, except the time it takes to run the duplicated node 3. But the communication delay is usually greater than the delay caused by executing these duplicate nodes in a small-grain schedule.

Benefits. The benefits of using DSH are:
1. DSH provides up to a 10-fold improvement in performance. In simulated studies reported elsewhere, we found a 420 percent improvement over a highest-level-first algorithm.[6] Figure 6 and 7 compare the performance of HLF algorithms and DSH algorithms.
2. DSH solves the max-min problem.
3. DSH gives monotonic improvements as the number of processors is increased (speedup ratio $> = 1$). That is, as the number of processing elements increases, the improvement in performance either

increases or levels off; it never decreases.
4. DSH is a heuristic — it does not guarantee an optimal schedule in all cases. The optimal scheduling problem is computationally intractable. Yet, comparisons with other near-optimal schedules shows that DSH is very good indeed. DSH time complexity is $O(N^4)$, where N is the total number of nodes in a task graph.[6] Execution time increases proportional to N^4.

Figure 8a shows an 11-node task graph. The three Gantt charts in Figure 8b shows how the DSH is used to schedule the nodes.

Grain packing: An example

Instead of trying to define the best grain size and scheduling those grains, grain packing starts from the smallest grain size, schedules those small grains, and then defines larger grains. Because the final grain sizes are defined after the small grains have been scheduled, grain packing takes into account all parallelism — the only parallelism discarded is the parallelism that leads to decreased performance.

Grain packing has four main steps:

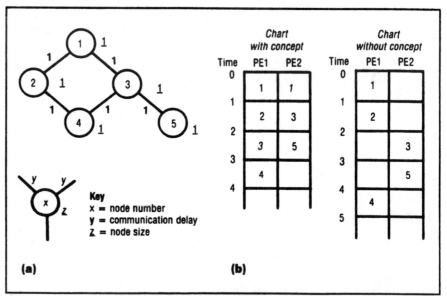

Figure 5. Task-duplication concept: (a) task graph, (b) Gantt charts. Italicized numbers represent duplicated nodes. Duplication may have a dramatic impact on performance: Duplicating tasks 1 and 3 so they run on both processing elements reduces communication delays.

180

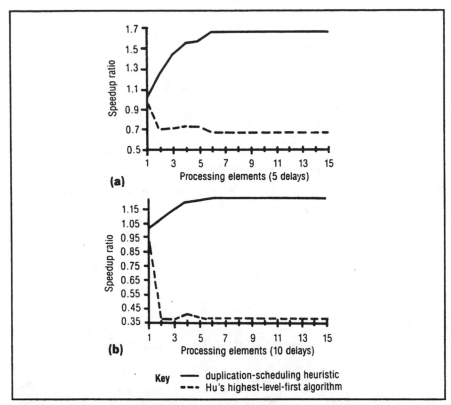

Figure 6. Average speedup-ratio comparison when the task graph has 20 nodes and **(a)** each edge is labeled with five time units of delay and **(b)** each edge is labeled with 10 time units of delay. Pseudorandom task graphs were generated with a certain number of nodes, a fixed communication delay, and an arbitrary — but limited — interconnection structure.

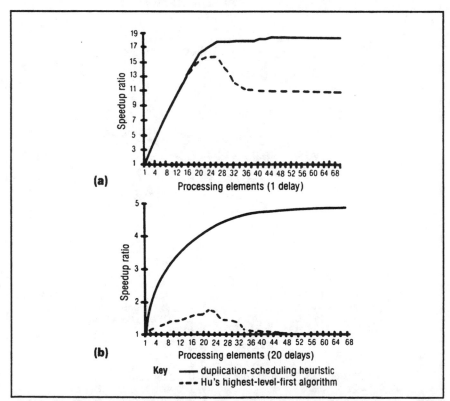

Figure 7. Average speedup comparison (350 nodes) with **(a)** delay = 1 and **(b)** delays = 20. The performance improvement of a more realistic parallel program. Monotonicity of DSH is evident because the relative speedup does not decline beyond a certain point, as is does with the HLF algorithm.

Constructing a small-grain task graph. Figure 9, a matrix-multiplication program in Occam, and Figure 10, an assembly program, show the parallelism extraction[8] involved in this first step.

Also, we must perform some kind of node-size calculation to estimate node running times. Because sizes are measured in units of CPU cycles, the size of each node can be calculated differently for each CPU if they have different speeds. As Figure 10 shows, we only need Move instructions when nodes on different processors must communicate.

We also must make an edge-size calculation. Communication delay is calculated by estimating the time it takes to transmit a message between processors. If each link has a different transmission rate or the distance between two processors in the system is not the same, the communication delay is calculated by adding up all of these effects.

Scheduling small grains. The resulting task graph is scheduled on a parallel processor system using a small-grain scheduler that takes advantage of all available parallelism and reduces communication delay.[6] The application program's execution time is now computed from each node's execution and communication delay times using information from the small-grain task graph and the specific architecture of the target parallel-processing system.

The choice of scheduler is critical because the grain size and the execution time depend on it. It must solve the max-min problem and give monotonic improvement as the number of processors increases.

Figure 11 illustrates how to calculate communication delay. $T1$ and $T5$ represent the Move instructions from Figure 10, $T2$ and $T4$ represent DMA fetch and set-up delay, $T3$ represents a serial-link transmission delay, and $T6$ represents the communication protocol delay. The communication delay is a function of both the application program and the specific architecture of the target system.

Figure 12 shows the task graph from Figure 10 and three possible schedules. The schedule obtained with DSH yields a speedup ratio of 2.39, while load balanc-

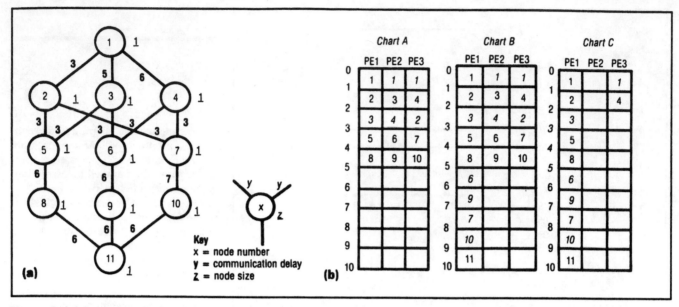

Figure 8. (a) Sample task graph of 11 nodes and **(b)** its intermediate Gantt chart using the duplication-scheduling heuristic. Chart A is an intermediate DSH's scheduling result before node 11's assignment. Chart B is a final result after node 11 is scheduled. Chart C is Chart B after removing redundant tasks. Italicized numbers represent duplicated nodes.

ing yields a speedup ratio of 1.13. This underscores the importance of selecting a scheduler that solves the max-min problem.

Grain packing. After an analysis of Gantt chart A in Figure 12, small grains are packed together to reduce overhead, including all optional move instructions and all communication protocol overhead. Because overhead is system-dependent, how you pack small grains depends on the system. In general, the larger the grain, the smaller the overhead.

Figure 13 shows an example of grain packing. From Gantt chart A, grains are formed by packing nodes located contiguously in the same processing element (node 1,2 and 9 form grain A, node 10, 13, 12, 11, 14, 15 form grain H). Also, some nodes may be duplicated and grouped into more than one large grain to reduce the communication delay and increase the parallelism.

Generating parallel modules. Based on the grain information from step 3, a compiler might construct modules to run in parallel. Alternately, a user program can be restructured to achieve an improved runtime as shown by an Occam[9] program in Figure 14a. Figure 14b shows the steps taken to find the best grain size, starting from a user-defined grain size, transforming to small grain size, and finally to large, packed grain size. The runtime for the user-defined and packed-grain task graph is the same for both DSH and load balanc-

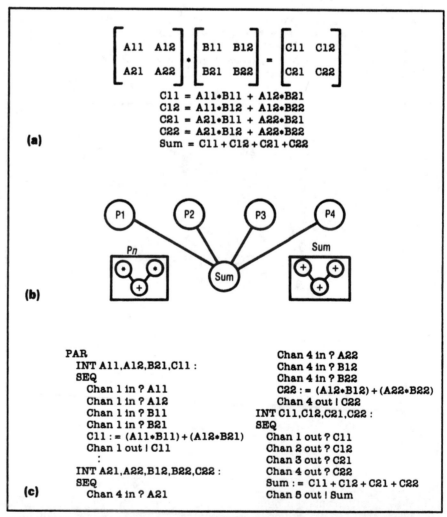

Figure 9. Example matrix-multiplication program: **(a)** matrix multiplication, **(b)** task-graph representation of the Occam program, **(c)** the Occam program.

$$
\begin{bmatrix} A11 & A12 \\ A21 & A22 \end{bmatrix} * \begin{bmatrix} B11 & B12 \\ B21 & B22 \end{bmatrix} = \begin{bmatrix} C11 & C12 \\ C21 & C22 \end{bmatrix}
$$

C11 = A11*B11 + A12*B21
C12 = A11*B12 + A12*B22
C21 = A21*B11 + A22*B21
C22 = A21*B12 + A22*B22
Sum = C11 + C12 + C21 + C22

(a)

(b)

(c)

```
PAR
  INT A11,A12,B21,C11 :
  SEQ
    Chan 1 in ? A11
    Chan 1 in ? A12
    Chan 1 in ? B11
    Chan 1 in ? B21
    C11 := (A11*B11) + (A12*B21)
    Chan 1 out ! C11
    :
  INT A21,A22,B12,B22,C22 :
  SEQ
    Chan 4 in ? A21

    Chan 4 in ? A22
    Chan 4 in ? B12
    Chan 4 in ? B22
    C22 := (A12*B12) + (A22*B22)
    Chan 4 out ! C22
  INT C11,C12,C21,C22 :
  SEQ
    Chan 1 out ? C11
    Chan 2 out ? C12
    Chan 3 out ? C21
    Chan 4 out ? C22
    Sum := C11 + C12 + C21 + C22
    Chan 5 out ! Sum
```

182

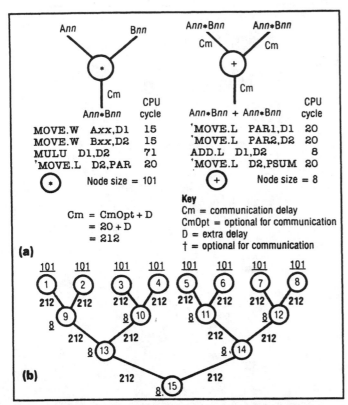

Figure 10. Example of a small-grain node-size calculation in M68000 assembly code: **(a)** delay calculation and **(b)** task graph of small-grain decomposition from user-defined grain. Figure 11 details why Cm=212.

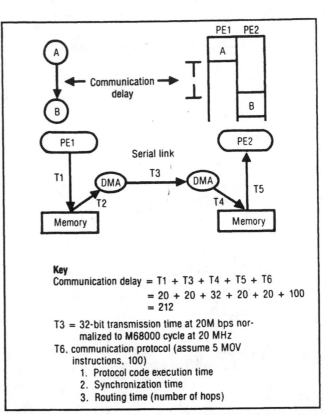

Key
Communication delay = T1 + T3 + T4 + T5 + T6
= 20 + 20 + 32 + 20 + 20 + 100
= 212

T3 = 32-bit transmission time at 20M bps normalized to M68000 cycle at 20 MHz
T6, communication protocol (assume 5 MOV instructions, 100)
1. Protocol code execution time
2. Synchronization time
3. Routing time (number of hops)

Figure 11. Example communication-delay calculation for the M68000 architecture.

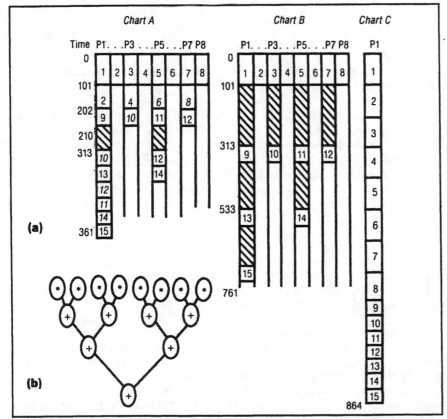

Figure 12. (a) Example of small-grain scheduling using the duplication-scheduling heuristic (Chart A) compared to using load balancing (Chart B) and a single processing element (Chart C). Italicized numbers indicate duplicated nodes. **(b)** Task graph of small grain for scheduling.

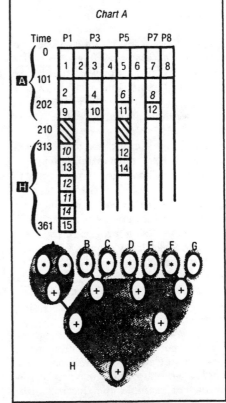

Figure 13. Grain packing. Nodes 1, 2, and 9 form grain A; nodes 10, 13, 12, 11, 14, and 15 form grain H. Italicized numbers indicate duplicated nodes.

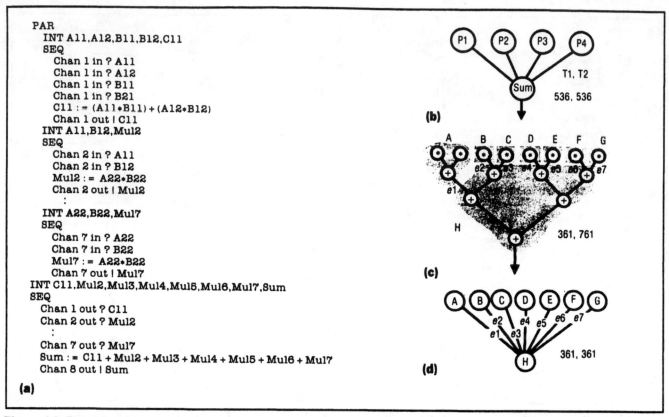

```
PAR
  INT A11,A12,B11,B12,C11
  SEQ
    Chan 1 in ? A11
    Chan 1 in ? A12
    Chan 1 in ? B11
    Chan 1 in ? B21
    C11 := (A11*B11)+(A12*B12)
    Chan 1 out ! C11
  INT A11,B12,Mul2
  SEQ
    Chan 2 in ? A11
    Chan 2 in ? B12
    Mul2 := A22*B22
    Chan 2 out ! Mul2
        :
  INT A22,B22,Mul7
  SEQ
    Chan 7 in ? A22
    Chan 7 in ? B22
    Mul7 := A22*B22
    Chan 7 out ! Mul7
  INT C11,Mul2,Mul3,Mul4,Mul5,Mul6,Mul7,Sum
  SEQ
    Chan 1 out ? C11
    Chan 2 out ? Mul2
        :
    Chan 7 out ? Mul7
    Sum := C11 + Mul2 + Mul3 + Mul4 + Mul5 + Mul6 + Mul7
    Chan 8 out ! Sum

(a)
```

Figure 14. Example of user program reconstruction: **(a)** reconstructed Occam matrix-multiplication program, **(b)** user-defined grain, **(c)** small grain for scheduling, **(d)** grain after grain packing.

ing (536,536 and 361,361 units) because no more duplication is possible.

Once all grains are packed, they can be rescheduled with a simple scheduler for a real system, such as an operating system scheduler that is executed while the user program is running.

By using grain packing, users do not need to learn a parallel-programming language such as Occam. A programmer typically does not know details such as grain-execution time and communication-delay cost, so the grain size and parallelism selected by a programmer is not optimal. Specifically, a programmer who tries to take full advantage of parallelism in matrix multiplication may produce too fine a grain and as a consequence introduce more communication delay than necessary.

The parallelism identified by a programmer using a parallel programming language is not all the information that is needed to produce an optimal parallel program. For example, the Occam matrix-multiplication program in Figure 9 can be restructured to improve performance even though a programmer has written it in parallel form, as Figure 14 shows. We could

have restructured a C or Pascal matrix-multiplication program to execute in parallel with the same improvement in performance.

Therefore, the parallelization done by a programmer using Occam yields no advantage over automated parallelization of a sequential program. This result may seem controversial and counterintuitive, but it is demonstrated in this simple example.

Grain packing automatically defines the best grain size in an application program. While the results from the matrix-multiplication example are tentative, we can conclude that

• load balancing is not the best way to schedule tasks in parallel programs;

• user-defined grains obtained from explicitly parallel programming languages such as Occam are unlikely to be near the optimal grain size;

• the problems of parallel programming, grain-size determination, and module scheduling are related to the max-min problem. The solution to one can be used

to solve the others.

We have shown that an automated solution of the grain-packing problem produces better results than solutions obtained by human programmers. The technique must be studied more carefully on a larger set of problems before generalized conclusions can be made, but early indications are encouraging.

Grain packing provides a new way to develop a program on a particular system.

• It gives an optimal way to partition an extended serial or parallel program on a specific computer architecture.

• It can give a runtime estimate of a particular program on a particular system before running the program. A speedup of less than one means the program is not suitable to run on the specific architecture.

• It gives automatic grain packing, which saves the user time and reduces errors that might occur if grain packing were done by hand.

• It applies to any language such as C, Pascal, Fortran, Modula-2. Grain packing lets more applications take advantage of parallel-processing systems because existing programs need not be rewritten in a new language. ◆

References

1. R.G. Babb, "Parallel Processing with Large-Grain Data Flow Techniques," *Computer*, July 1984, pp. 55-61.

2. R.L. Graham, "Bounds on Multiprocessing Anomalies and Related Packing Algorithms," *AFIPS Conf. Proc., Vol. 40*, AFIPS Press, Montvale, N.J., 1972, pp. 205-217.

3. T.C. Hu, "Parallel Sequencing and Assembly Line Problems," *Operations Research*, June 1961, pp. 841-848.

4. C.V. Ramamoorthy, K.M. Chandy, and M.J. Gonzalez, "Optimal Scheduling Strategies in a Multiprocessor System," *IEEE Trans. Computers*, Feb. 1972, pp 137-146.

5. T.L. Adam, K.M. Chandy, and J.R. Dickson, "A Comparison of List Schedules for Parallel Processing Systems," *Comm. ACM*, Dec. 1974, pp. 685-690.

6. B. Kruatrachue, *Static Task Scheduling and Grain Packing in Parallel Processing Systems*, PhD dissertation, Electrical and Computer Eng. Dept., Oregon State Univ., Corvallis, 1987.

7. W. Clark, *The Gantt Chart, 3rd ed.*, Pittman and Sons, London, 1952.

8. D. Pountain, *A Tutorial Introduction to Occam Programming*, Inmos, Colorado Springs, Colo., 1986.

9. C.V. Ramamoorthy and M.J. Gonzalez, "A Survey of the Techniques for Recognizing Parallel Processable Streams in Computer Programs," *Proc. Fall Joint Comp. Conf.*, CS Press, Los Alamitos, Calif., 1969.

Boontree Kruatrachue is interested in research into parallel processing architectures and their programming development tools.

He received the MS and PhD in electrical and computer engineering from Oregon State University in 1984 and 1987, respectively. He is a member of Phi Kappa Phi.

Ted Lewis is a professor of computer science at Oregon State University and editor-in-chief of *IEEE Software*. He is currently investigating ways to automate the production of both serial and parallel programs. The grain packing technique is being used as a foundation for a parallel programming environment incorporating design, coding, and performance-evaluation tools.

Lewis is cofounder of the OSU/OCATE Workshop on Parallel Processing held annually in Oregon.

Questions about this article can be addressed to Lewis at the Computer Science Dept., Oregon State Univ., Corvallis, OR 97331.

Lazy Task Creation: A Technique for Increasing the Granularity of Parallel Programs

Eric Mohr, David A. Kranz, and Robert H. Halstead, Jr., *Member, IEEE*

Abstract— Many parallel algorithms are naturally expressed at a fine level of granularity, often finer than a MIMD parallel system can exploit efficiently. Most builders of parallel systems have looked to either the programmer or a parallelizing compiler to increase the granularity of such algorithms. In this paper, we explore a third approach to the granularity problem by analyzing two strategies for combining parallel tasks dynamically at run-time. We reject the simpler *load-based inlining* method, where tasks are combined based on dynamic load level, in favor of the safer and more robust *lazy task creation* method, where tasks are created only retroactively as processing resources become available.

These strategies grew out of work on Mul-T [17], an efficient parallel implementation of Scheme, but could be used with other languages as well. We describe our Mul-T implementations of lazy task creation for two contrasting machines, and present performance statistics which show the method's effectiveness. Lazy task creation allows efficient execution of naturally expressed algorithms of a substantially finer grain than possible with previous parallel Lisp systems.

Earlier versions of this paper appeared as [20] and [21].

Index Terms— Load balancing, parallel programming languages, parallel Lisp, process migration, program partitioning, task management.

I. Introduction

THERE have been numerous proposals for implementations of applicative languages on parallel computers. All have in some way come up against a granularity problem—when a parallel algorithm is written naturally, the resulting program often produces tasks of a finer grain than an implementation can exploit efficiently. Some researchers look to hardware specially designed to handle fine-grained tasks [3], [11], while others have looked for ways to increase task granularity by grouping a number of potentially parallel operations together into a single sequential thread. These latter efforts can be classified by the degree of programmer involvement required to specify parallelism, from parallelizing compilers at one end of the spectrum to language constructs giving the programmer a fine degree of control at the other.

In the most attractive world, the programmer leaves the job of identifying parallel tasks to a parallelizing compiler. To achieve good performance, the compiler must create tasks of sufficient size based on estimating the cost of various pieces of code [8], [16], [25]. But when execution paths are highly data-dependent (as for example with recursive symbolic programs), the cost of a piece of code is often unknown at compile time. If only known costs are used, the tasks produced may still be too fine-grained. And for languages that allow mutation of shared variables it can be quite complex to determine where parallel execution is safe, and opportunities for parallelism may be missed.

At the other end of the spectrum a language can leave granularity decisions up to the programmer, possibly providing tools for building tasks of acceptable granularity such as the *propositional parameters* of Qlisp [7], [9], [10]. Such fine control can be necessary in some cases to maximize performance, but there are costs in programmer effort and program clarity. Also, any parameters appearing in the program require experimentation to calibrate; this work may have to be repeated for a different target machine or data set. Or, when the code is run in parallel with other code or on a multiuser machine, a given parameterization may be ineffective because the amount of resources available for that code is unpredictable. Similar problems arise when a parallelizing compiler is parameterized with details of a certain machine.

We have taken an intermediate position in our research on Mul-T [17], a parallel version of Scheme based on the `future` construct of Multilisp [13], [14]. The programmer takes on the burden of identifying *what* can be computed safely in parallel, leaving the decision of exactly *how* the division will take place to the run-time system. In Mul-T that means annotating programs with `future` to identify parallelism without worrying about granularity; the programmer's task is to *expose* parallelism while the system's task is to *limit* parallelism.

In our experience with the mostly functional style common to Scheme programs, a program's parallelism can often be expressed quite easily by adding a small number of `future` forms (which, however, may yield a large number of concurrent tasks at run time). The effort involved is little more than that required for systems with parallelizing compilers, where the programmer must be sure to code in such a way that parallelism is available.

In order to support this programming style we must deal with questions of efficiency. The Encore Multimax[1] implementation of Mul-T [17], based on the T system's Orbit compiler

Manuscript received October 1, 1990; revised March 1, 1990.

E. Mohr is with the Department of Computer Science, Yale University, New Haven, CT 06520.

D. A. Kranz is with the M.I.T. Laboratory for Computer Science, Cambridge, MA 02139.

R. H. Halstead, Jr., is with the DEC Cambridge Research Lab, Cambridge, MA 02139.

IEEE Log Number 9100384.

[1] Multimax is a trademark of Encore Computer Corporation.

Reprinted from *IEEE Trans. on Parallel and Distributed Systems*, vol. 2, no. 3, July 1991, pp. 264–280.

[18], [19], is proof that the underlying parallel Lisp system can be made efficient enough; we must now figure out how to achieve sufficient task granularity. For this we look to dynamic mechanisms in the run-time system, which have the advantage of avoiding the parameterization problems mentioned earlier. The key to our dynamic strategies for controlling granularity is the fact that the `future` construct[2] has several correct operational interpretations. The canonical `future` expression

$$(K \text{ (future } X))$$

declares that a child computation X may proceed in parallel with its parent continuation K. In the most straightforward interpretation, a child task is created to compute X while the parent task computes K. Reversing the task roles is also possible; the parent task can compute X while the child task computes K. Finally, and most importantly for fine-grained programs, it is also usually correct for the parent task to compute first X and then K, ignoring the `future`. This *inlining* of X by the parent task eliminates the overhead of creating and scheduling a separate task and creating a placeholder to hold its value.[3]

Inlining can mean that a program's *run-time granularity* (the size of tasks actually executed at run-time) is significantly greater than its *source granularity* (the size of code within the `future` constructs of the source program). A program will execute efficiently if its average run-time granularity is large compared to the overhead of task creation, providing of course that enough parallelism has been preserved to achieve good load balancing.

The first dynamic strategy we consider is *load-based inlining*. In this strategy, (`future` X) means, "If the system is not loaded, make a separate task to evaluate X; otherwise inline X, evaluating it in the current task." A load threshold T indicates how many tasks must be queued before the system is considered to be loaded. Whenever a call to `future` is encountered, a simple check of task queue length determines whether or not a separate task will be created.

The simple load-based inlining strategy works well on some programs, but its several drawbacks (see Section III) led us to consider another strategy as well: why not inline every task provisionally, but save enough information so that tasks can be selectively "un-inlined" as processing resources become available? In other words, create tasks lazily. With this *lazy task creation* strategy, (K (`future` X)) means "Start evaluating X in the current task, but save enough information so that its continuation K can be moved to a separate task if another processor becomes idle." We say that idle processors *steal* tasks from busy processors; task stealing becomes the primary means of spreading work in the system.

The execution tree of a fine-grained program has an overabundance of potential fork points. Our goal with lazy task creation is to convert a small subset of these to actual forks,

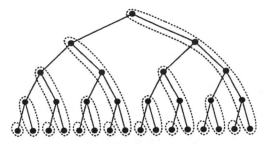

Fig. 1. Direct execution of `psum-tree`.

maximizing run-time task granularity while preserving parallelism and achieving good load balancing. In the subsequent discussion, this is contrasted with *eager task creation*, where all fork points result in a separate task.

An example will help make these ideas more concrete.

II. An Example

As a simple example of the spectrum of possible solutions to the granularity problem, consider the following algorithm (written as a Scheme program) to sum the leaves of a binary tree:

```
(define (sum-tree tree)
  (if (leaf? tree)
      (leaf-value tree)
      (+ (sum-tree (left tree))
         (sum-tree (right tree)))))
```

(where `leaf?`, `leaf-value`, `left`, and `right` define the tree datatype). The natural way to express parallelism in this algorithm is to indicate that the two recursive calls to `sum-tree` can proceed in parallel. In Mul-T we might indicate this by adding one `future`:[4]

```
(define (psum-tree tree)
  (if (leaf? tree)
      (leaf-value tree)
      (+ (future (psum-tree (left tree)))
         (psum-tree (right tree)))))
```

The natural expression of parallelism in this algorithm is rather fine-grained. With eager task creation this program would create 2^d tasks to sum a tree of depth d; the average number of tree nodes handled by a task would be 2. Fig. 1 shows this execution pictorially; each circled subset of tree nodes is handled by a single task. Unless task creation is very cheap, this task breakdown is likely to lead to poor performance.

The ideal task breakdown is one which maximizes the run-time task granularity while maintaining a balanced load. For a divide-and-conquer program like this one, that means expanding the tree breadth-first by spawning tasks until all

---

[2](future X) returns an object called a *future*, a placeholder for the eventual value of X. The placeholder is said to be *unresolved* until X's value becomes available. Any task attempting to use the value of an unresolved future is suspended until the value is available. A *touch* is a use of a value V that will cause a task to be suspended if V is an unresolved future.

[3]Such inlining is not always correct; sometimes it can lead to deadlock as described in Section III-C.

[4]This strategy for adding `future` relies on + evaluating its operands from left to right; if argument evaluation went from right to left, then (`psum-tree (right tree)`) would evaluate to completion before (`future (psum-tree (left tree))`) began, and no parallelism would be realized.

187

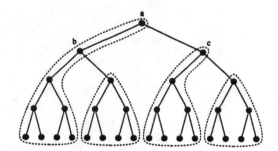

Fig. 2. BUSD execution of psum-tree on four processors.

```
(define (psum-tree-2 tree cutoff-depth)
  (if (leaf? tree)
      (leaf-value tree)
      (+ (spawn (> cutoff-depth 0)
           (psum-tree-2 (left tree)
                        (- cutoff-depth 1)))
         (psum-tree-2 (right tree)
                      (- cutoff-depth 1)))))
```

Fig. 3. Code for psum-tree-2.

processors are busy, and then expanding the tree depth-first within the task on each processor. We will refer to this ideal task breakdown as BUSD (breadth-first until saturation, then depth-first). Fig. 2 shows this execution pictorially for a system with four processors.

How can we achieve this ideal task breakdown? A parallelizing compiler might be able to increase granularity by unrolling the recursion and eliminating some futures, but in this example we *want* fine-grained tasks at the beginning so as to spread work as quickly as possible (breadth-first). The compiler might possibly produce code to do this as well if supplied with information about available processing resources, but making such a transformation general is a difficult task and would still have the parameterization drawbacks noted earlier.

What if we control task creation explicitly as in Qlisp? In many of Qlisp's parallel constructs the programmer may supply a predicate which, when evaluated at run-time, will determine whether or not a separate task is created. (One such predicate, (qemptyp) [10], tests the length of the work queue, achieving the same effect as our load-based inlining.) We might use Qlisp's spawn construct (equivalent to future with an additional predicate argument) to rewrite psum-tree as in Fig. 3; the style of this program psum-tree-2 is very similar to an example in [7].

In this example, cutoff-depth specifies a depth beyond which no tasks should be created. The predicate (> cutoff-depth 0) tells spawn whether or not to inline the recursive call. A cutoff-depth value of 2 would achieve BUSD execution similar to that shown in Fig. 2 (actually its mirror image); below level 2 all futures are inlined.

This solution has two problems. First, the code has become more complex by the addition of cutoff-depth—it is no longer completely straightforward to tell what this program is doing. Second, the program is now parameterized by the cutoff-depth argument, with the associated calibration issues noted previously.

Load-based inlining and lazy task creation are both attempts to approximate the BUSD performance of psum-tree-2 without sacrificing the clarity of psum-tree. In an ideal run of psum-tree on a four-processor system with load-based inlining, the first three occurrences of future (at nodes a, b, and c of Fig. 2) find that processors are free, and separate tasks are created (breadth-first). Depending on the value of the load threshold parameter T, a few more tasks may be created before the backlog is high enough to cause inlining. But since there is a large surplus of work, most tasks are able to defray the cost of their creation by inlining a substantial subtree (depth-first).

In an ideal run of psum-tree with lazy task creation, the future at a (representing the subtree rooted at b) is provisionally inlined, but its continuation (representing the subtree rooted at c) is immediately stolen by an idle processor. Likewise, the futures at b and c are inlined, but their continuations are stolen by the two remaining idle processors. Now all processors are busy; subsequent futures are all provisionally inlined but no further stealing takes place and each processor winds up executing one of the circled subtrees of Fig. 2.

This execution pattern depends on an *oldest-first* stealing policy: when an idle processor steals a task, the oldest available fork point is chosen. In this example, the oldest fork point represents the largest available subtree and hence a task of maximal run-time granularity.

We now consider how these idealized execution patterns match up with real-life execution patterns for these methods.

III. COMPARISON OF DYNAMIC METHODS

Load-based inlining has an appealing simplicity and does in fact produce good results for some programs [17], but we have noted several factors which decrease its effectiveness. A major factor is that inlining decisions are irrevocable—once the decision to inline a task has been made there is no way to revoke the decision at a later time, even if it becomes clear at that time that doing so would be beneficial.

The following list summarizes the drawbacks of load-based inlining; the following sections discuss each in turn as a basis for comparing the two dynamic strategies.

1) The programmer must decide when to apply load-based inlining, and at what load threshold T.
2) Inlined tasks are not accessible; processors can starve even though many inlined tasks are pending.
3) Deadlock can result if inlining is used on some types of programs.
4) In an implementation with one task queue per processor, load-based inlining creates many more tasks than would be created with an optimal BUSD division.
5) Load-based inlining is ineffective in programs where fine-grained parallelism is expressed through iteration.

A. Programmer Involvement

Even though load-based inlining is an automatic mechanism it still requires programmer input. Some programs run significantly faster with eager task creation than they do with load-based inlining, so the programmer must identify where load-based inlining should be applied. For example, load balancing is crucial in a coarse-grained program creating relatively few tasks—inlining even a few large tasks can hurt load balancing by lengthening the "tail-off" period when processors are finishing their last tasks. With lazy task creation however, load balancing cannot suffer because all inlining decisions are revocable. At worst, all lazily-inlined tasks will have their continuations stolen. But because the cost of stealing a task is comparable to that of creating an eager task,[5] performance will not be significantly worse than with eager task creation. Thus, lazy task creation can be used safely on such programs without the danger of degrading performance.

With load-based inlining, the programmer must also get involved by supplying a value for the load threshold T. Experience has shown that choosing the right value for T is crucial for good performance, but is difficult to do except by experimentation [29]. Since lazy task creation requires no parameterization the programmer is freed of this burden as well.

B. Irrevocability

The irrevocability of load-based inlining can mean that processors become idle even though the continuations of many inlined tasks have not yet begun to execute. Such problems can be caused by *bursty task creation* and *parent–child welding*. *Bursty task creation* refers to the fact that opportunities to create tasks may be distributed unevenly across a program. At the moment when a task is inlined, it may appear that there are plenty of other tasks available to execute, but by the time these tasks finish executing there may be too few opportunities to create more tasks. Consequently, processors may go idle because the continuations of the inlined tasks are not available for execution. This problem never arises with lazy task creation because these continuations are always available for stealing.

Parent–child welding refers to the fact that inlining effectively "welds" together a parent and child task. If an inlined child becomes blocked waiting for a future to resolve (or for some other event), the parent is blocked as well and is not available for execution. With lazy task creation, the information kept for each inlined child allows the child to be decoupled if it becomes blocked, allowing the parent to continue.

C. Deadlock

Perhaps the most serious problem with load-based inlining is that, for some programs, *irrevocable inlining is not a correct optimization*. Irrevocable inlining can lead to deadlock because it imposes a specific sequential evaluation order on tasks whose data dependencies might require a different evaluation order. A simple example appears in [17], where an inlined task waits for a semaphore which its "welded-on" parent will never be able to release. But deadlock is possible even without explicit intertask synchronization, as shown by the prime-finding program of [21] and [20] (omitted here because of space considerations). If the wrong tasks are inlined, a task testing the primality of a number could deadlock trying to

---

[5] An exceptional case is discussed in Section IV-D.

access divisor primes which have not yet been computed by its welded-on parents.

This type of deadlock is not possible with lazy task creation because of the decoupling of blocked tasks mentioned above. Any inlined task can be separated from its parent, so programs that are deadlock-free with eager task creation are also deadlock-free with lazy task creation.

Selective load-based inlining (as is possible in Qlisp) could be used by a sophisticated programmer to ensure that inlining is never performed where it might cause deadlock. However, this solution requires the programmer to accurately recognize all situations where the potential for deadlock exists, and still does not offer the other advantages of lazy task creation.

D. Too Many Tasks

The behavior of load-based inlining for programs like `psum-tree` has been analyzed by Weening [29], [30]. He assumes, as we do, that each processor maintains its own local task queue and that inlining decisions are based only on the local queue's length. He shows two ways in which the need to maintain at least one task on the local queue leads to non-BUSD execution. First, a lone processor P executing a subtree of height h creates h tasks instead of just one; second, removing a task from P's queue at an inopportune moment (a "transfer") can lead to the creation of $O(h^2)$ tasks. He derives an upper bound of $O(p^2 h^4)$ tasks using p processors, and points out that this bound guarantees asymptotically minimal task creation overhead as the problem size grows exponentially in h. In our experience, however (see Section V-C), the overhead of task creation with load-based inlining is significant for problems of substantial size.

The bottom line is that load-based inlining with distributed task queues is unable to achieve oldest-first scheduling; many of the tasks created represent small subtrees. For example, consider what happens when a transfer removes a task from the queue of a processor P. The next time P encounters a future call, P will find that its queue is empty and so will create a new task to evaluate the call. But the position of T in the program's call tree is really a matter of chance, determined only by the timing of the transfer operation. Since the majority of potential fork points lie toward the leaves of the tree, T is likely to represent only a small subtree.

It is possible that using one central queue instead of several distributed queues would decrease the number of tasks, but the contention introduced by this alternative would probably be unacceptable and would certainly not be scalable. A much better alternative is the oldest-first scheduling policy of lazy task creation; as can be seen by the task counts in Section V, lazy task creation results in many fewer tasks than load-based inlining. Tasks created by oldest-first scheduling are able to inline larger subtrees, giving a much better approximation to BUSD execution.

E. Fine-Grained Iteration

Not all parallel programs have bushy call trees; for example, some programs contain data-level parallelism expressed by iteration over a linear data structure. Unfortunately, neither load-based inlining nor lazy task creation is particularly effective in increasing the run-time granularity of such programs, so poor performance can result when tasks are fine-grained.

With both methods, granularity can only be increased when tasks are able to inline many other tasks. But because the "call tree" of a fine-grained iteration is long and spindly, granularity can be increased only by grouping together adjacent iterations. The simple task stealing methods used in both load-based inlining and lazy task creation are unable to perform this type of grouping (see [20] for further details), resulting in many small tasks.

We have considered several alternatives for handling such programs, involving more complex dynamic methods and/or compiler support. The best solution is not clear at this point, but we will present some ideas at the end of the paper.

IV. IMPLEMENTATION

We have seen that lazy task creation has several strong advantages over load-based inlining. We now explore the implementation issues to determine whether the overhead of lazy task creation can be acceptably minimized.

Both of our dynamic methods increase efficiency by ignoring selected instances of `future`. But lazy task creation requires maintaining enough information when a `future` is provisionally inlined to allow another processor to steal the `future`'s continuation cleanly. The cost of maintaining this information is *the* critical factor in determining the finest source granularity that can be handled efficiently. The cost is incurred whether a new task is created or not, so a large overhead would overwhelm a fine-grained program. By comparison the cost of actually stealing a task is somewhat less critical; if enough inlining occurs the cost of stealing a task will be small compared to the total amount of work the task ultimately performs.

Still, the cost of stealing a continuation must be kept in the ballpark of the cost of creating an eager future. Stealing a continuation requires splitting an existing stack, which in a conventional stack-based implementation requires the copying of frames from one stack to another. Alternatively, we could use a linked-frame implementation where splitting a stack requires only pointer manipulations. However, care must be taken with such an implementation to ensure that the normal operations of pushing and popping a stack frame have comparable cost with conventional stack operations.

We have pursued both avenues of implementation: a conventional stack-based implementation for the Encore Multimax version of Mul-T as well as a linked-frame implementation for the ALEWIFE multiprocessor. The basic data structures and operations for lazy task creation are common to both implementations, however, and are discussed next.

A. The Lazy Task Queue

Each task maintains a queue of stealable continuations called the *lazy task queue*, shown abstractly in Fig. 4. When making a *lazy future call* corresponding to an instance of `future` in the source code, a task T first pushes a pointer to the `future`'s continuation onto the lazy task queue. If

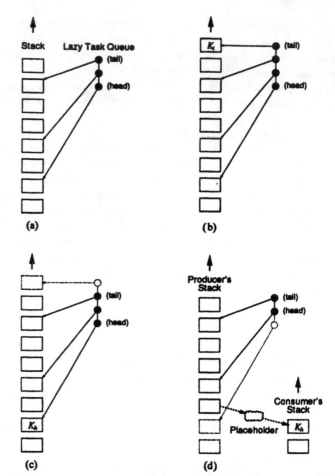

Fig. 4. Lazy task queue data structures and operations. (a) Data structures for lazy task creation. (b) A lazy future call causes a continuation to be queued. (c) Returning from a lazy future call causes a continuation to be dequeued. (d) A continuation is stolen.

upon return the continuation has not been stolen by another processor, T dequeues it. We refer to T as the *producer* of lazy tasks; another processor stealing them is called a *consumer*. Consumers remove frames from the head of the lazy task queue while the producer pushes and pops frames from the tail.

Fig. 4 tells a lazy task creation story for a producer task P. Fig. 4(a) shows P's stack (growing upward), which contains eight frames. Three of these frames represent continuations to lazy future calls; pointers to these frames have been placed on the lazy task queue. Note that the oldest continuation is at the head (bottom) of the queue while the newest continuation is at the tail (top) of the queue.

At this point a lazy future call occurs, corresponding to the code (`future X`), where X denotes an expression to be evaluated. The continuation K_t to this call represents all remaining computation, embodied in Fig. 4(b) by the frame labeled K_t and all those below it. As shown, a frame representing K_t has been pushed onto the stack and a pointer to this frame has been added to the tail of the lazy task queue.

As a result of the lazy future call, P begins evaluating X in-line. Fig. 4(c) shows what happens if P finishes evaluating X before any stealing occurs—P simply returns to K_t after first popping the lazy task queue (removing the pointer to K_t's top frame from the tail of the queue).

Now an idle consumer C decides to steal a continuation from the head of P's lazy task queue. This continuation K_h was originally created by a lazy future call, say (future Y). When P made this lazy future call it began evaluating Y in-line, and has not finished doing so at the time of the steal. In order to steal K_h, C must change P's stack to appear as though an eager future had been created to compute Y. C does this by creating a placeholder and modifying P's stack so that the eventual value of Y will resolve (i.e., supply a value for) the placeholder rather than being passed directly to the continuation K_h. C initializes its own stack to contain the frames of the continuation K_h and then "returns" to K_h, passing the unresolved placeholder as a value.

Fig. 4(d) shows the completed steal operation; it now looks as though an eager future had been created originally, with one processor (the producer P) evaluating the child Y and another (the consumer C) evaluating the parent K_h. Note an important feature of the stealing operation: *the consumer never interrupts the producer.*

Implementations must take care to guard against two kinds of race conditions to ensure correctness of the stealing operation. First, two consumers may race to steal the same continuation; second, a producer trying to return to a continuation may race with a consumer trying to steal it.

B. Encore Implementation

We have implemented lazy task creation in the version of Mul-T running on the Encore Multimax system, a bus-based shared-memory multiprocessor. Our Multimax system has 18 processors; the National Semiconductor 32332 processors used have relatively few general-purpose registers (8) but fairly powerful memory addressing modes. An atomic test-and-set operation provides the fundamental means of interprocessor synchronization.

In this implementation stacks are represented conventionally, in contiguous sections of the heap. As seen in Fig. 5, the lazy task queue is kept in contiguous memory in the "top" part of a stack. As the producer pushes lazy continuations the queue grows downward while the stack frames grow upward. Stealing continuations effectively shrinks the stack by removing information from both ends (the head of the lazy task queue and the bottom frames of the stack). When a stack overflows (i.e., when the gap between stack frames and lazy task queue gets too small), it may either be repacked to reclaim space created by steal operations or its contents may be copied to a new stack of twice the original size.

To steal from the stack pictured, a consumer first locates the oldest continuation by following the `ltq-head` pointer, through the `lazy cont 1` pointer, to `frame 1`. The consumer then replaces `frame 1` in the stack with a continuation directing the producer to resolve a placeholder. Next the consumer copies frames from `frame 1` down to the bottom of the live area of the stack (indicated by `base`) to a new stack, updating `base` and `ltq-head` appropriately.

To guard against the race conditions mentioned earlier is a lock for the entire stack plus a lock for each continuation

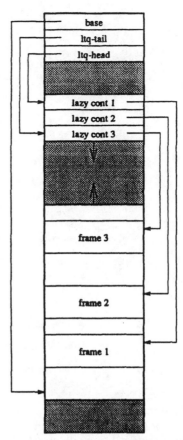

Fig. 5. Lazy task queue implemented in conjunction with a conventional stack.

on the lazy task queue. Only the producer modifies `ltq-tail`, and only consumers modify `ltq-head` and `base`.

1) Lazy Future Call and Return: We now present the lazy task queue operations in somewhat more detail. Fig. 6 gives assembler pseudo-code showing how the expression

$$\text{(g (future (f x)))}$$

would be compiled in Encore Mul-T with lazy task creation. The lazy future call and return in this example show the crucial lazy task queue operations of enqueueing and dequeueing a lazy continuation.

The first block (`entry` and `call-g`) shows the compiled code for the lazy future call to `f` and its continuation, containing the standard call to `g`. `stack` is a pointer to the current stack; lazy task queue pointers such as `ltq-tail` are referenced via an offset to this pointer.[6]

The code shows that two longwords (4 bytes each) are allocated in the lazy task queue area of the stack for each lazy continuation—one for the continuation itself and one for a lock. After storing the continuation pointer `call-g` and initializing the lock to 0 we increment the `ltq-tail` pointer, which makes the lazy continuation available for stealing. There is no need to test explicitly for overflow of the lazy task queue; the stack overflow check on entry simply tests the size of the

---

[6]This is a slight simplification; in actuality, the current stack is stored in a block of data kept locally by each processor; `ltq-tail` is referenced using the double indirection capability of the NS 32332 processor.

```
(lambda (x)
    (g (future (f x))))


entry:
    Standard stack overflow test (3 instructions).
    push-addr    call-g                  # push return address (a.k.a. current
                                         #   continuation) on stack
    move         ltq-tail(stack),r1      # get pointer to tail of lazy task queue
    move         sp,8(r1)                # store pointer to stack continuation
                                         #   in lazy task queue
    move         $0,12(r1)               # initialize lazy task queue item lock
    add          $8,ltq-tail(stack)      # lazy continuation officially enqueued
    push-addr    return-from-lf-call     # call to f will return to
                                         #   return-from-lf-call
    Standard call to unknown procedure f (5 instructions).
call-g:
    Standard continuation code, including call to unknown procedure g
        (6 instructions).

return-from-lf-call:
    move         ltq-tail(stack),r1      # get pointer to lazy task queue tail
    test&set     4(r1)                   # try to lock tail item of lazy task queue
    br-if-clr    pop-ltq                 # if successful, go pop it
    Busy-wait loop to lock tail item of lazy task queue.
pop-ltq:
    sub          $8,ltq-tail(stack)      # lazy continuation officially dequeued
    adjust-sp    $-4                     # remove return-from-lf-call address
                                         #   from stack
    Standard return (2 instructions).
```

Fig. 6. Assembler pseudo-code showing lazy future call and return in the Encore implementation.

empty region between the actual stack (growing upwards) and the lazy task queue (growing downwards).

Before calling f we push `return-from-lf-call` on the stack as the return address. This is a shared, out-of-line routine that serves as the continuation to all lazy future calls. It is shown in the second block of code. Here we see synchronization to guard against interference by a consumer trying to steal the same lazy continuation the producer is trying to return to. The returning producer first acquires the lazy task queue item lock (using the Encore's interlocked test and set instruction), busy-waiting if the lock is currently held by a consumer. Once the lock is acquired the return address on top of the stack is guaranteed to be valid; in this case it will be either the original value `call-g` or else `resolve-placeholder` if the continuation has been stolen. After dequeueing the tail entry of the lazy task queue we return normally.

If, as is usually the case, the continuation to a lazy future call is known (i.e., unless `future` appears in tail-call position), the code shown in Fig. 6 can be streamlined by generating the `return-from-lf-call` code in line. This optimization, which saves four instructions (and increases the code size slightly), has not yet been implemented in the current system.

2) Steal Operation: Fig. 7 gives the algorithm for stealing a lazy continuation from another processor's lazy task queue. The task to be stolen is chosen by a round-robin search of other processors' lazy task queues. Two locks must be acquired before a continuation is stolen—the producer's stack is locked to avoid races with other consumers and the continuation itself is locked to avoid a race with the producer trying to return to it.

Once a stealable continuation has been chosen and the necessary locks obtained, we replace it in the producer's stack with a continuation to resolve the newly created placeholder,

- Allocate and initialize data structures: a placeholder P, a new task object T_2, and a new stack S_2.
- Look for a continuation to steal.
    - Poll other processors to find one whose current stack S_1 has a non-empty lazy task queue (i.e. `ltq-tail` $\geq$ `ltq-head`).
    - Try to lock stack S_1; if it's already locked, skip to next processor.
    - Try to lock head item of S_1's lazy task queue Q; if it's already locked, skip to next processor.
- Steal the continuation. In the head item (now locked) of Q is a pointer CP into the stack S_1. CP points to a stack frame C representing a stealable continuation. The bottom of the stack (the portion between CP and S_1's base pointer) must be copied to the new stack S_2.
    - Replace C in S_1 with the continuation (`resolve-placeholder` P).
    - Update base and `ltq-head` pointers in S_1.
    - S_1 is now in a consistent state; unlock head item of Q.
    - Copy bottom portion of S_1 into S_2.
    - Unlock stack S_1.
    - "Return" to top continuation in new stack S_2, passing placeholder P as the argument.

Fig. 7. Algorithm for steal operation in Encore implementation.

and we update the producer's `base` and `ltq-head` pointers. At this point the producer's stack is in a consistent state, so we unlock the head item of the lazy task queue.[7] Then the bottom of the producer's stack is copied to the consumer's stack (taking care to use the old continuation rather than the newly swapped-in one!) and the consumer can begin executing the stolen continuation, passing the placeholder as an argument. The producer (or another processor if further

---

[7]The producer's stack is not unlocked at this point because of the possibility of stack overflow—the repacking operation discussed earlier would conflict mightily with a stealer's copying operation.

192

stealing occurs!) will eventually return to our swapped-in continuation, providing a value for the placeholder.

3) Blocking: There is one remaining loose end in this discussion: what happens to the lazy task queue when a task T blocks by touching an unresolved future? It is not sufficient to save the lazy task queue as part of T's state because the queued lazy tasks would become inaccessible. We would then have the same potential deadlock problem that arises with load-based inlining.

The simple solution adopted here is for T to "bite its tail." T's stack is split above the most recent lazy continuation (at the tail of the lazy task queue), and only the top piece is blocked along with T. As with a steal operation, a placeholder is created to communicate a value between the two pieces of the split stack. The executing processor P can continue using the bottom piece of the stack, which contains all of the continuations on the lazy task queue. No queued continuations are inaccessible to potential consumers. P dequeues the tail lazy continuation and returns to it, passing the placeholder as an argument.

In essence, P has stolen a task from the *tail* of T's lazy task queue. One problem with this solution is that it goes against our preference for oldest-first scheduling, since we have effectively created a task at the newest potential fork point. Performance can suffer because this task is more likely to have small granularity. And further blocking may result, possibly leading to the dismantling of the entire lazy task queue. An improved solution which avoids these problems has been implemented for ALEWIFE, and is discussed in the next section.

C. ALEWIFE Implementation

The Encore implementation of lazy task creation performs reasonably well by lowering the overhead of using the `future` construct, but it still has several other sources of overhead. Compiler support for future and stack checking is costly (see Section V-A), and locking operations can be costly because a global resource (the bus) is used.

The ALEWIFE machine [1]—a cache-coherent machine being developed at M.I.T. with distributed, globally shared memory—is designed to address these problems. Its processing elements are modified SPARC[8] chips [2]; the modifications of interest here are fast traps for strict operations on futures and support for full/empty bits in each memory word. If a strict arithmetic operation or memory reference operates on a future a trap occurs; thus, explicit checks are not needed. The full/empty bits allow fine-grained locking: ALEWIFE includes memory-referencing instructions that trap when the full/empty state of the referenced location is not as expected. It should be noted that this modified SPARC is not "special purpose" hardware for Mul-T programs. The modifications do not affect the cycle time of the processor and would be useful for the implementation of lazy task creation in the context of any language.

For the ALEWIFE implementation of lazy task creation, a stack is represented as a doubly linked list of stack frames

---

[8]SPARC is a trademark of Sun Microsystems, Inc.

(inspired by [22]) in order to minimize copying in the stealing operation. In this scheme, each frame has a link to the previously allocated frame and another link to the next frame to be allocated. Thus, push-frame and pop-frame operations are simply load instructions. An important feature of this scheme is that stack frames are not deallocated when popped. A subsequent push will reuse the frame, meaning that in the average case the cost of stack operations associated with procedure call and return is very close to the cost of such operations with conventional stacks. The "next frame" link is set to empty when no next frame has been allocated. This strategy avoids the need to check explicitly for stack overflow when doing a push-frame operation: in the (uncommon) case where no next frame is available the push-frame operation will trap and the trap handler will allocate a new frame.

An earlier version of this paper [20] described an initial ALEWIFE implementation. In that version, stealing a lazy task involved copying the topmost stack frame. The version described here avoids this copying and also fixes a subtle bug in the original version.

Each frame is divided into two separate data structures, referred to as the *stack frame* and the *frame stub*. The stack frames form a doubly linked list as described at the beginning of this section. Each stack frame contains local and temporary variables as in an ordinary stack frame; in addition, each stack frame contains a pointer to its associated frame stub. Each frame stub also has a pointer back to its associated stack frame. Separating these two structures is important in allowing a noncopying steal operation.

In this implementation the lazy task queue is threaded through the frame stubs. Figs. 8–11 show the lazy future call and stealing operations graphically. In these figures we use the following register names:

`FP`—Frame pointer register. Points to the current stack frame (not frame stub).

`LTQT`—Lazy task queue tail register. Modified only by the producer. Points to the current frame stub.

`LTQH`—Head of the lazy task queue. This must be in memory so that consumers on other processors can steal frames from the head of the queue. Its full/empty bit serves as the lock limiting access to one potential consumer at a time.

Each stack frame has the following slots:

`next`—This slot points to the "next" frame, which will become current if a stack-frame push operation is performed. The push-frame operation is thus performed simply by loading `next[FP]` into `FP`. If the next frame has not yet been allocated, `next[FP]` is marked as empty.

`cont`—This slot points to the "continuation" frame, which will become current if a stack-frame pop operation is performed. The pop-frame operation is thus a load of `cont[FP]` into `FP`.

`data`—Some number of slots for local variable bindings and temporary results.

`lf-frame`—This slot points to the associated frame stub.
Each frame stub has the following slots:

`ltq-next`—This slot points to the next frame stub on the lazy task queue (toward the tail of the queue). This location's full/empty bit is the lock arbitrating between a consumer stealing a continuation and the producer trying to invoke that continuation.

`ltq-prev`—This slot points to the previous frame stub on the lazy task queue (toward the head of the queue).

`ltq-link`—The lazy future call code stores in this slot the return address that the consumer should use if it steals this frame's continuation. If the continuation is stolen, the consumer reads out this return address and replaces it with the placeholder object it creates.

`ltq-frame`—This slot points to the associated stack frame.

In this implementation, every call—whether a lazy future call or an ordinary procedure call—is preceded by a push-frame operation and followed by a pop-frame operation; this contrasts with the more common approach of pushing a frame upon procedure entry and deallocating it at procedure exit. (The details motivating this choice and a discussion of its cost may be found in [21].)

Fig. 8 shows how the stack frames and relevant registers might look just before a lazy future call (but after that call's push-frame operation has already occurred). Note that each stack frame's `next` pointer points to the next frame toward the top of the stack and each `cont` pointer points to the next stack frame toward the bottom of the stack. If a memory location's contents are left blank in the figure, its contents are either unimportant (they will never be used) or indeterminate: for example, the `next` slot of the leftmost frame in Fig. 8 could either be empty or point to another, currently unused frame. An "X" in the left-hand part of a frame slot (see, for example, the `ltq-next` slots in Fig. 8) indicates that the full/empty bit of the corresponding memory word is set to "empty."

The lazy task queue in Fig. 8 has no frames in it. A consumer would discover this by seeing that the `ltq-next` slot of the frame stub pointed to by LTQH is empty—if this task had stealable frames, this slot would point to the first such frame.

Fig. 9 shows the situation just after the lazy future call. The frame stub associated with the current stack frame (pointed to by FP) has joined the lazy task queue. Accordingly, LTQT has changed to point to that frame stub, and the `ltq-next` and `ltq-prev` links have been updated as needed to maintain the doubly linked lazy task queue. Note that the rightmost frame stub in Fig. 9 is not logically part of the lazy task queue—it is serving as a convenient header object for the doubly linked queue. The middle frame is also not part of the lazy task queue; it is simply part of the stack. The current frame stub's `ltq-link` field contains the address for the lazy future call's continuation, as required.

If no consumer steals this continuation, then this lazy future call will eventually return. The code for the return will restore the state of affairs depicted in Fig. 8, after which the pop-frame operation associated with the lazy future call can be performed.

Fig. 10 shows the state of the producer and consumer tasks if instead a consumer steals the continuation from the task shown in Fig. 9. The consumer task's state variables are shown with a c appended, as in LTQHc. The shaded areas and shaded arrows show structures that have been created by

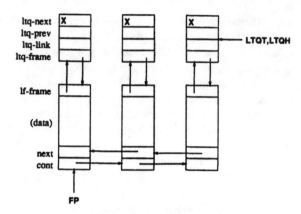

Fig. 8.   Just before lazy future call.

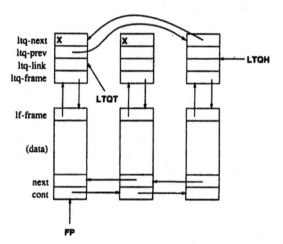

Fig. 9.   Just after lazy future call.

the consumer. An alternate view of this situation is shown in Fig. 11. Note that the consumer's stack (the part that is not blacked out in Fig. 11) now looks just like the producer's stack did in Fig. 8 just before the original lazy future call (and just like the producer's stack would have looked in the case of a normal return from the lazy future call). Effectively, the consumer has "taken over" the continuation, created a placeholder to stand for the value of the called computation (which is still being performed by the producer), and forced an early return from the lazy future call, supplying the placeholder as the call's returned value. (No arrow is shown from any of the consumer's data structures to the placeholder because that value is returned in one of the consumer's registers.)

The consumer has also made the producer's `ltq-link` field point to the newly created placeholder. When the producer completes its computation and finds that its continuation has been stolen, it looks here to find the placeholder that should resolve to this computation's value. The synchronization here is unusual in that `ltq-link` is marked "empty" even though it contains useful data. This technique handles close races between a returning producer and a stealing consumer. By inspecting `ltq-next` and `ltq-prev` pointers, a returning producer can discover that its continuation has been stolen before the consumer has actually stored the placeholder in the `ltq-link` field. Correct operation is ensured by having

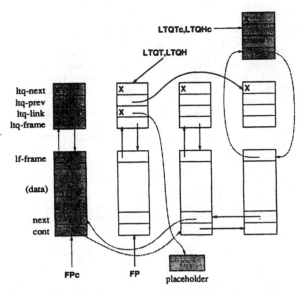

Fig. 10. After steal; new structures shaded.

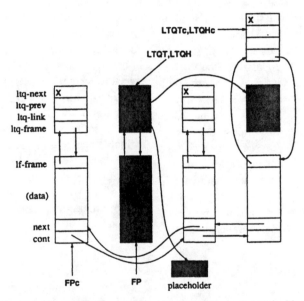

Fig. 11. After steal; frames belonging to producer shown in black.

the consumer set the `ltq-link` field's "empty" flag when the placeholder is installed, and having the producer wait for this "empty" flag before attempting to read out the placeholder.

A producer returning from a lazy future call distinguishes between the situations shown in Figs. 9 and 10 by locating the frame stub F pointed to by the `ltq-prev` field of the frame stub pointed to by LTQT and looking at the `ltq-next` field of F. In Fig. 10, where the continuation has been stolen, this field in F is empty; in Fig. 9, where the continuation has not been stolen, it is not.

The algorithm for lazy future calls is spelled out in more detail in the pseudo-code shown in Fig. 12. The in-line code for a lazy future call starts at the label `lf-call`; the code at `stolen` is out-of-line code shared by all lazy future calls. (Details of the algorithm for a consumer to find and steal a continuation may be found in [21].)

Finally, we return to the issue of what to do with the lazy task queue when a task blocks on an unresolved future. To preserve both oldest-first scheduling and laziness in task creation we would like to make the lazy task queue accessible for normal stealing by consumers. This is accomplished by placing the entire blocked task, lazy task queue and all, on the task queue of an appropriate processor.[9] Consumers may steal either from a task that is actually running or from a queued blocked task; a processor may steal from the lazy task queue of one of its own blocked tasks if it runs out of other useful work. This solution addresses the problems raised in Section IV-B3.

D. Discussion

What are the advantages and disadvantages of these im-

[9] Of course, the task is marked as blocked, so the processor will not attempt to run it.

195

```
lf-call:
    load      next[FP],FP                      # Push stack frame.
    load      lf-frame[FP],temp                # Address of new frame stub.
    store     $continue,ltq-link[temp]         # PC for consumer's return.
    store     LTQT,ltq-prev[temp]              # Make lazy task queue backward ...
    store     temp,ltq-next[LTQT]              # ... and forward links.
    move      temp,LTQT                        # Advance lazy task queue tail pointer.
    Call the procedure.
    load      ltq-prev[LTQT],temp              # Dequeue from lazy task queue tail,
    empty     ltq-next[temp]                   # trap to stolen if continuation stolen.
    move      temp,LTQT                        # Reset lazy task queue tail pointer.
continue:
    load      cont[FP],FP                      # Pop stack frame.

stolen:
    Wait for ltq-link[LTQT] to be empty.
    load-e    ltq-link[LTQT],temp              # Get placeholder to resolve.
    Resolve the placeholder in temp to the value returned by the procedure.
    Terminate the current task and find new work to do.
```

Fig. 12.   Assembler pseudo-code showing lazy future call and return in the ALEWIFE implementation.

plementations? The main disadvantage of the conventional stack implementation is the copying it performs. It would appear that the amount of copying required for a stealing operation is potentially unlimited, so that the cost of stealing a lazy task is also unlimited. While this is technically true it is somewhat misleading; the overhead of copying when stealing a continuation should be viewed against the cost of creating the continuation in the first place. A program with fine source granularity does little work between lazy future calls, and so is not able to push enough items onto the stack to require significant copying. A program which creates large continuations (requiring stealers to do lots of copying) must do a fair amount of work to push all that information on the stack, and the cost of copying is unlikely to be significant in comparison.

One exception to this argument is a program that builds up a lot of stack and then enters a loop that generates futures:

```
(define (example)
  (build-up-stack-and-then-call loop))
(define (loop)
  (future ... )
  (loop))
```

Stealing the first lazy task's continuation requires copying the built-up stack. As argued, that cost is unlikely to be significant compared to the cost of building up the stack in the first place. But in this example the stolen continuation immediately creates another lazy task, so the next steal must copy the same information again. In fact, spreading work to n processors in this example via lazy tasks requires the built-up stack information to be copied n times.

There are two easy solutions to this problem. First, loop can be rewritten so that future appears around the recursive call to loop, resulting in a program where the built-up stack is never copied. Or, future could be inserted around the original call to loop, resulting in a program where the built-up stack is copied only once.

It appears then that the effects of copying in a conventional stack implementation can be minimized. But it is still attractive to eliminate copying altogether using the linked-frame imple-

mentation described for ALEWIFE. Such an implementation is certainly more efficient on lazy task operations. It is somewhat more difficult to gauge exactly the overhead introduced in sequential sections of code. One ramification of reusing stack frames is that all frames have a fixed size; choosing the correct frame size involves a tradeoff. If a small frame size is chosen, frames needing more space will need to create an overflow vector, increasing costs for accessing frame elements and for memory allocation. If a large frame size is chosen, most frames will contain a lot of unused slots. This could lead to more frequent garbage collection and might use up valuable space in cache and/or virtual memory, although these latter factors could well be minimal in today's memory-rich systems. The current ALEWIFE implementation uses a frame size of 17 slots. We must accumulate more experience with this promising implementation technique before making a final evaluation.

V. Performance

In this section, we present performance figures for both Mul-T implementations. Measurements of Encore Mul-T used Yale's Encore Multimax system, configured with 18 NS-32332 processors and 64 megabytes of memory.

Figures for ALEWIFE Mul-T were obtained using a detailed simulator of the ALEWIFE machine. Both the Mul-T run-time system and code for the benchmarks are compiled to SPARC instructions that are interpreted by the simulator. Overheads due to future creation, blocking, scheduling, etc., are accurately reflected in the statistics. Memory-referencing delays were not simulated in these experiments.[10]

When assessing the performance of a multiprocessor system it is important to make comparisons with the "best" sequential implementation. To compare a parallel Mul-T program to, say, a sequential C program, four categories of overhead must be considered:

---

[10] Minimizing memory-referencing delays is crucial to good performance in a distributed-memory machine. ALEWIFE's distributed caching scheme [5] reduces the need for remote references; preliminary results of current research at M.I.T. show that ALEWIFE Mul-T also performs well when network delays are simulated.

1) The cost of using Lisp instead of a language like C, e.g., automatic storage reclamation, manipulation of run-time tags, dynamic linking.
2) The cost of using sequential Mul-T instead of T, e.g., run-time checks for futures and stack overflow.
3) The cost of using a parallel algorithm instead of a sequential algorithm, e.g., using recursive divide and conquer instead of an iterative loop.
4) The run-time costs of multiprocessing, e.g., task creation, idle processors, contention for shared resources.

To ensure that measurements of our task creation strategies are meaningful we must distinguish overhead due to task creation from overhead due to these other sources—it is important to be sure that the overhead of task creation really *is* low, rather than just *looking* low because it is masked by overhead in the rest of the system.

The first two categories of overhead are addressed in Section V-A while the last two are considered in the context of specific benchmarks in Section V-C. Section V-B deals specifically with the overhead of lazy task creation.

A. Overhead in Sequential Code

Despite its reputation for inefficiency, overhead due to Lisp is not a major factor in the benchmarks to be presented. First, we note that code produced by T's Orbit compiler is comparable in quality to code produced by other compilers for the same hardware [19]. Second, we have minimized run-time overhead in our benchmarks by using type-specific arithmetic, avoiding run-time storage allocation, and excluding garbage-collection time from performance statistics. The programs were carefully written for maximum efficiency. As a direct comparison, the "best" version of `tridiag` (see Section V-C) was coded in C (3.33 s) as well as T (3.92 s).

The second category of overhead is significant for Encore Mul-T but insignificant for ALEWIFE Mul-T. Overhead is introduced in sequential Mul-T code by the Encore implementation because compiler support is provided for futures and multiple stacks. The compiler inserts `future?` checks on arguments to strict operations, and inserts tests for stack overflow. Although the Encore implementation is engineered to minimize these sources of overhead [17], the cost can be nontrivial. (We note, however, that compiler support for future checking is orthogonal to support for lazy task creation—lazy task creation also performs well in the Encore implementation when the overhead of future checking is eliminated by using explicit `touch` operations instead of implicit compiler checks.)

Table I compares running times of several sequential programs[11] in T3.1 with the same programs run in Mul-T on one processor. Because of future and stack checking overhead, the Mul-T programs run between 1.4 and 2.2 times as long as their T3.1 counterparts.

The ALEWIFE implementation of Mul-T does not incur these overheads, as hardware traps eliminate the need for

[11] Some of these programs are described in Section V-C, the rest are described in [17].

TABLE I
COMPARISON OF RUNNING TIMES FOR ENCORE MUL-T AND T3.1

Program	Time (seconds)		
	Mul-T	T	ratio
abisort	12.67	6.98	1.62
compiler	159	98	1.62
fib	0.24	0.12	2.00
mergesort	1.82	0.99	1.84
permute	11,600	8,500	1.36
queens	3.95	2.44	1.62
speech	95.9	43.4	2.21
tridiag (best)	6.01	3.92	1.53

explicit checks.[12] The analog of Table I for ALEWIFE would show identical "parallel" and "sequential" times for these programs.

All measurements of Encore Mul-T in Section V-C include the overhead of future and stack checking; this means that the relative granularity of tasks is somewhat larger for Encore than for ALEWIFE.

B. Cost of Lazy Task Queue Operations

As mentioned earlier, it is crucial to minimize the overhead of lazy future calls. Below are statistics for both implementations on the additional cost of a lazy future call over that of a conventional call, namely pushing a continuation onto the lazy task queue and popping it off.

Encore	12 instructions, 12.6 μs
ALEWIFE	9 instructions, 15 SPARC cycles

For the Encore, 4 instructions could be eliminated by using the compiler optimization mentioned in Section VI, saving roughly 3 μs. Still, the ALEWIFE sequence is probably the cheaper of the two, since the RISC instructions of the SPARC processor are simpler than NS-32332 instructions.

The cost of stealing a continuation from another processor's task queue is not as critical, since steals are relatively rare. Still, as seen below, stealing a task in the Encore implementation has comparable cost to creating an eager future. Stealing a task in the ALEWIFE implementation is noticeably cheaper; the linked-frame stack implementation allows a much cleaner steal.

Machine/Operation	Number of Instructions
Encore/Eager Future	118
Encore/Steal	150 + 4 per word copied
ALEWIFE/Steal	100

These instruction counts include all aspects of creating and executing a task, e.g., allocating and initializing placeholder, task, and stack objects, queueing and dequeueing the task, and resolving the placeholder.

[12] It is interesting to note that the presence of hardware tag checking may be more significant in machines supporting parallel Lisp than in machines supporting sequential Lisp.

TABLE II

EFFICIENCY OF THE grain BENCHMARK ON 16 PROCESSORS

Machine / Strategy	Leaf task granularity (number of NS-32332 instructions)									
	6	12	24	48	96	192	384	768	1536	3072
Encore / Eager	.06	.07	.09	.12	.17	.27	.44	.62	.77	.87
Encore / LBI ($T = 2$)	.51	.52	.54	.63	.69	.80	.88	.93	.96	.98
Encore / Lazy	.56	.59	.62	.71	.81	.84	.92	.95	.97	.99
ALEWIFE / Lazy	.74	.78	.82	.86	.91	.95	.97	.98	.99	1.00

C. Benchmarks

We begin our discussion of actual Mul-T programs with the synthetic benchmark grain, designed to measure the effectiveness of the various task-creation strategies over a range of task granularities. grain adds up a perfect binary tree of 1's using a parallel divide and conquer structure very similar to psum-tree, but before returning 1 at any leaf it executes a delay loop of a specified length, allowing granularity control. By timing trials using a range of granularities we can get an "efficiency profile" for each task-creation strategy. The efficiency E for a given trial is calculated using the formula

$$E = \frac{t_{\text{seq}}}{n t_{\text{par}}}$$

where in this case the sequential time t_{seq} is for a Mul-T program without futures and the parallel time t_{par} was measured using $n = 16$ processors. Efficiency of 1.0 means perfect speedup. The tree depth of 16 (65,536 1's) used in these trials ensures that processor idle time at start-up and tail-off is minimal, so close-to-perfect speedup should be achievable.

The granularity figures across the top of Table II tell how many NS-32332 instructions were used at the leaves to execute the delay loop and return 1; they do not include the instructions which implement the basic divide and conquer loop. The average source granularity is actually half of the given figure because internal nodes of the tree (where no delay loop is executed) account for half of the futures in this program. The instruction counts would be different for ALEWIFE due to its RISC instruction set, but because the source code is the same the efficiency figures are roughly comparable.

As expected, the high cost of eager task creation leads to poor efficiency at fine granularities. With load-based inlining, 90–95% of the 2^{16} tasks are eliminated, improving efficiency substantially. Lazy task creation makes an additional improvement by eliminating more than 99% of the tasks. Still, the overhead of lazy future calls is significant, hurting efficiency at the finest granularities. The lower overhead of lazy future calls in ALEWIFE leads to yet higher efficiency.

Table III shows performance statistics for several Mul-T programs. For each task creation strategy, the column marked t shows the elapsed time (in seconds for Encore and in millions of simulated SPARC cycles for ALEWIFE) as well as the relative speedup in parentheses. The column marked f shows the number of tasks (futures) created. Statistics are given for 1, 2, 4, 8, and 16 processors; in addition, the row marked "seq" gives the Mul-T time on one processor when future is ignored, and the row marked "best" gives the Mul-T time for running the best sequential version of the benchmark.

In our experience, Encore timings vary somewhat between trials even when each process acting as a virtual Mul-T processor is given exclusive control of an actual Multimax processor. It appears that changes in program and data locations from trial to trial substantially affect the miss ratio in the Multimax's direct-mapped, physically-addressed cache. Each figure shown here is the average of several trials; code was reloaded between each trial.

Knowing the source granularity of a benchmark (see Section I) is important in interpreting the performance results. To get a measure of source granularity we can divide the sequential execution time of a benchmark by its total number of calls to future:

$$g = \frac{t_{\text{seq}}}{f_{\text{ETC}}}.$$

g estimates average task execution time, excluding task creation overhead. For these benchmarks our Encore runs at about 1 MIPS, so g is roughly comparable to the average number of NS32332 instructions per task as well.

queens ($g = 113$) finds all solutions to the n queens problem, with $n = 10$ in this case.[13] A queen is placed on one row of the board at a time; each time a queen is legally placed, future appears around a recursive call to find all solutions stemming from the current configuration.

abisort ($g = 119$) performs an adaptive bitonic sort [4] of $n = 16,384$ numbers. The "adaptive" algorithm has complexity $O(n \log n)$ rather than the $O(n \log^2 n)$ of the standard bitonic sort algorithm. For comparison, the "best sequential time" shown in Table III is for an optimized merge sort. Adaptive bitonic sort performs about twice as many comparisons as merge sort, and has somewhat greater bookkeeping costs. However, its merge operation has substantial parallelism which allows close to linear speedup; such speedup is not possible with straightforward implementations (on hardware like ours) of other divide-and-conquer sorts such as merge sort or quicksort.

tridiag ($g = 314$) solves a tridiagonal system of $n = 65,535$ equations using cyclic reduction [15] and backsubstitution. "best" measures the standard Gaussian elimination algorithm, which performs fewer operations per equation than cyclic reduction (8 as opposed to 17) but is inherently sequential. The "seq" time reflects this difference, as well as some overhead due to the use of recursion in cyclic reduction. The large value of n simply shows our preference for nontrivial problems; good performance was also achieved for smaller values of n.

---

[13] This version of queens is different from the ones measured in [20] and [21].

TABLE III
PERFORMANCE OF MUL-T BENCHMARKS (ABSOLUTE TIMES ARE IN SECONDS FOR ENCORE AND IN MILLIONS OF SIMULATED SPARC CYCLES FOR ALEWIFE)

queens

| | Encore | | | | | | ALEWIFE | |
| | Eager | | LBI ($T = 2$) | | Lazy | | Lazy | |
n	t	f	t	f	t	f	t	f
seq	3.95		3.95		4.28		6.47	
1	11.69 (1.00)	34814	4.06 (1.00)	30	4.75 (1.00)	0	7.20 (1.00)	1
2	5.91 (1.98)	34814	2.09 (1.94)	528	2.38 (2.00)	11	3.60 (2.00)	11
4	3.05 (3.83)	34814	1.15 (3.53)	2135	1.20 (3.96)	45	1.84 (3.91)	104
8	1.63 (7.17)	34814	.67 (6.06)	4771	.61 (7.79)	98	.94 (7.66)	229
16	1.08 (10.82)	34814	.43 (9.44)	6826	.34 (13.97)	377	.50 (14.40)	554

abisort

| | Encore | | | | | | ALEWIFE | |
| | Eager | | LBI ($T = 2$) | | Lazy | | Lazy | |
n	t	f	t	f	t	f	t	f
best	3.67		3.67		3.56		6.03	
seq	12.67		12.67		12.63		20.27	
1	37.99 (1.00)	106K	15.29 (1.00)	910	14.15 (1.00)	0	23.64 (1.00)	1
2	19.29 (1.97)	106K	7.84 (1.95)	2449	7.13 (1.98)	8	11.82 (2.00)	13
4	9.85 (3.86)	106K	4.19 (3.65)	6309	3.61 (3.92)	55	5.93 (3.99)	55
8	5.17 (7.35)	106K	2.31 (6.62)	12627	1.84 (7.69)	263	3.02 (7.83)	388
16	3.36 (11.31)	106K	1.37 (11.16)	19248	1.00 (14.15)	894	1.57 (15.06)	1018

tridiag

| | Encore | | | | | | ALEWIFE | |
| | Eager | | LBI ($T = 2$) | | Lazy | | Lazy | |
n	t	f	t	f	t	f	t	f
best	6.01		6.01		6.02		4.78	
seq	15.43		15.43		15.40		14.20	
1	26.58 (1.00)	49150	16.04 (1.00)	225	17.18 (1.00)	0	15.35 (1.00)	1
2	13.56 (1.96)	49150	8.10 (1.98)	792	8.61 (2.00)	5	7.68 (2.00)	4
4	6.87 (3.87)	49150	4.18 (3.84)	2524	4.29 (4.00)	13	3.84 (4.00)	9
8	3.54 (7.51)	49150	2.17 (7.39)	4157	2.18 (7.88)	133	1.97 (7.79)	190
16	2.01 (13.22)	49150	1.16 (13.83)	6637	1.14 (15.07)	550	1.02 (15.05)	461

speech

| | Encore | | | | | | ALEWIFE | |
| | Eager | | LBI ($T = 2$) | | Lazy | | Lazy | |
n	t	f	t	f	t	f	t	f
seq	96.0		96.0		97.2		85.3	
1	106.1 (1.00)	39856	97.7 (1.00)	6254	96.8 (1.00)	0	85.6 (1.00)	0
2	53.9 (1.97)	39856	50.8 (1.92)	13562	49.8 (1.94)	632	44.0 (1.95)	613
4	27.8 (3.82)	39856	26.6 (3.67)	19481	26.1 (3.71)	1917	23.3 (3.67)	1946
8	15.1 (7.03)	39856	14.6 (6.70)	24150	14.2 (6.81)	4414	13.0 (6.58)	4807
16	8.9 (11.95)	39856	8.7 (11.19)	29324	8.3 (11.65)	7911	7.8 (10.97)	9930

The performance figures show fairly consistent results for these first three finer-grained benchmarks. Comparing the "seq" and 1-processor rows for these programs gives an indication of the overhead of task creation for each strategy; in queens for example, creating tasks eagerly nearly triples the running time. Load-based inlining greatly reduces this impact (to only 3%) because there is very little overhead when no task is created. Lazy task creation has somewhat higher overhead, though not overwhelmingly so (11%).

Load-based inlining improves running times substantially over the eager task creation times, but it consistently suffers significant task-creation overhead due to the mechanism discussed in Section III-D. For these programs, LBI eliminates only 80–87% of the possible tasks when 16 processors are used. Lazy task creation performs much better, eliminating 98–99% of the possible tasks. Despite its higher overhead, lazy task creation consistently has the best time on 16 processors. In addition, lazy task creation shows better

relative speedup than LBI, suggesting that it will scale better to larger systems.

speech ($g = 2410$) is part of a multistage speech understanding system under development at MIT. This stage is essentially a graph-matching problem, finding the closest dictionary entry to a spoken utterance. The program contains about 150 steps separated by barrier synchronizations; each step contains 200–300 parallel tasks of rather coarse average granularity. The coarse granularity means that eager task creation does not perform too badly, so the improvement with lazy task creation is modest. The barrier synchronizations cause significant idleness, hurting speedup for all strategies.

The statistics we have gathered do not allow precise conclusions about the extent of multiprocessing overhead from sources such as cache turbulence and contention for shared resources. However, because speedup for the finer-grained benchmarks is close to linear with lazy task creation, we can conclude that the effect of these other sources of overhead is fairly small for that strategy.

VI. Related Work

Load-based inlining has been studied previously in the Mul-T parallel Lisp system [17], and is also available in Qlisp by using (deque-size) or (qemptyp) to sense the current load [10], [29]. An analytical model of load-based inlining for programs like psum-tree has been developed by Weening [29], [30]. His analytical results generally agree with empirical observations of load-based inlining in both Mul-T and Qlisp; however, neither the prior Mul-T work nor the prior Qlisp work have explored the alternative of lazy task creation.

Pehoushek and Weening [29] also present a strategy which reduces task creation overhead when a queued task is executed by the processor that created it. This strategy takes advantage of the same phenomenon that lazy task creation leverages: that when parallelism is abundant most tasks are executed locally. Executing such tasks with lazy task creation appears to be cheaper than with their scheme; furthermore, their scheme only works in programs with a fork/join style of parallelism. Lazy task creation has no such restriction, interacting well with the unlimited lifetime of futures in Mul-T.

WorkCrews [27] is a package that does perform lazy task creation, intended for use with a fork-join or cobegin style of programming. It is implemented on top of Modula-2+ (an extension of Modula-2). For every task that is to be created lazily, a WorkCrews program calls RequestHelp(*proc*, *data*) and then proceeds with other work. A free processor looks for unanswered help requests, "steals" one, and applies its *proc* to its *data*. When the requester finishes its other work, it calls GotHelp to see whether the RequestHelp task was stolen. If not, it proceeds to do the work itself; if so, it looks for other work to do. The performance of WorkCrews was evaluated on several parallel Quicksort programs and on MultiGrep, a program that searches for occurrences of a given string in a group of files [27].

The principal difference between WorkCrews-style lazy task creation and Mul-T's lazy futures is that invoking lazy task creation in WorkCrews requires a significantly larger amount of source code to be written—the work performed by *proc* must be broken out into a separate procedure, the argument block to be passed as *data* must be explicitly allocated and filled in, and finally the RequestHelp and GotHelp procedures must be called. Moreover, synchronization with and value retrieval from the lazily created task are explicit responsibilities of the programmer. By contrast, in Mul-T it is only necessary to insert the keyword future to begin enjoying the benefits of lazy task creation.

These stylistic differences lead to some implementation differences: our lazy future implementations directly manipulate implementation objects such as stack frames and are thus more "built in" to the implementation than in the case of WorkCrews. We think some efficiency improvements result from our approach, but the systems are different enough that it is hard to make a conclusive comparison. In any case, although the mechanics of the two systems are rather different, there is a very close relationship between their underlying philosophies.

Motivated by the idea of lazy futures presented in [17], Feeley has independently implemented lazy task creation in a parallel version of Scheme which runs on the BBN Butterfly [12]. His implementation is roughly similar to our Encore implementation, and contains some innovative features.

Our philosophy of encouraging programmers to expose parallelism while relying on the implementation to curb excess parallelism resembles that of data-flow researchers who have been concerned with *throttling* [6], [23]. However, the main purpose of throttling is to reduce the memory requirements of parallel computations, not to increase granularity (which is generally fixed at a very fine level by data-flow architectures [3], [11]). Throttling thus serves the same purpose as our preference for depth-first scheduling and is not directly related to lazy task creation.

VII. Conclusions and Future Work

We are encouraged that our performance statistics support the theoretical benefits of lazy task creation. For programs with bushy call trees the programmer can use future to identify parallelism, effectively ignoring granularity considerations.

A remaining challenge is fine-grained programs without bushy call trees, such as those with data-level parallelism expressed iteratively (see Section III-E). For example, consider a program fragment which performs a fine-grained operation on all elements of an array using an iterative loop, creating one task per element. This program will not execute efficiently in parallel unless its granularity is increased so that tasks handle several array elements instead of just one, but dynamic methods alone are unlikely to partition this program effectively because they are unable to change program structure. If the iterative structure of the program is obeyed, parallelism is inherently limited.

If instead of using iteration this program were restructured to perform a divide-and-conquer division of the array's index set, we know that lazy task creation would achieve the desired partition. But such a restructuring has two problems: it raises program complexity and it lowers program efficiency. To address the complexity problem we envision expressing such parallel operations on data aggregates at a higher level, converting the high-level expressions to appropriate divide-and-conquer divisions at compile time. Ideas for how to express such high-level operations appear in the work of Waters [28], Steele and Hillis [26], and Sabot [24].

The efficiency problem arises because the execution overhead of a divide-and-conquer division is large compared to the low overhead of an iterative loop. This overhead can be reduced substantially by smart compilation, but it will still be significant if the inner loop code is fine-grained. We observe though that a fine-grained inner loop is very likely to contain straight-line code rather than additional loops or calls to unknown procedures, so estimating its cost should be straightforward. Knowing the inner loop cost allows the compiler to unroll enough iterations to balance out the overhead of a divide-and-conquer division.

There is also the important issue of scalability. In both the Encore machine and the ALEWIFE simulator (with memory delays turned off), all memory references are of approximately equal cost, an unreasonable assumption for a large-scale multiprocessor. We are investigating how our lazy task creation strategy can be augmented to take advantage of locality in shared address-space systems where the physical memory is distributed, such as the ALEWIFE machine.

Because of their extra record-keeping burden, lazy future calls are unlikely ever to be as cheap as the cheapest implementation of normal calls, but the incremental cost of a lazy future call can be strongly influenced by a multiprocessor's hardware architecture. For example, the linked-frame implementation shown in Section IV-C benefits greatly from the ALEWIFE architecture's support for full/empty bits in memory that can be accessed efficiently as a side effect of a load or store instruction.

Nevertheless, the linked-frame implementation still requires some memory operations for every call, and even a few more memory operations for every lazy future call. For architectures whose processors have register windows we have contemplated another approach with the potential of eliminating most memory operations: each register window could have an associated bit in a processor register indicating whether it is logically part of the lazy task queue, but only when a register window was unloaded due to a window overflow trap would the frame actually be linked into the in-memory data structure representing the queue. This would further reduce the cost of lazy future calls, since one might expect a large fraction of lazy future calls to return without their associated register window ever having been unloaded. However, some mechanism would have to be provided for querying a processor to see if it contains any stealable continuations (in the event that none are found in memory) and for interrupting a processor to request it to unload stealable continuations needed by other processors. The costs and benefits of this idea are not currently known.

The larger quest in which we have been engaged is to provide the expressive power and elegance of future at the lowest possible cost. Complete success in this endeavor would make it unnecessary for programmers ever to shun future in favor of lower-level, but more efficient, constructs. Success would also encourage programmers to express the parallelism in programs at all levels of granularity, rather than forcing them to hand-tune the granularity (at the source-code level) for the best performance. Lazy task creation moves us closer to this ideal, producing very acceptable performance and greatly reducing the number of tasks created for all of the benchmark programs in Section V. And while the ideal may never be achieved completely, every step in the direction of making future cheaper increases the number of situations in which the cost of future is no bar to its use.

ACKNOWLEDGMENT

Special thanks to D. Nussbaum for his contributions to the ALEWIFE implementation. Thanks to R. Osborne, R. Kelsey, and the anonymous referees for helpful comments on drafts of the paper, to K. Johnson for the speech application, to M. Feeley for the elegant bit-vector version of n queens, and to the Sloan foundation, IBM, Digital Equipment Corporation, the Department of Energy (FG02-86ER25012) and DARPA (N00014-87-K-0825) for their support.

REFERENCES

[1] A. Agarwal et al., "The MIT Alewife machine: A large-scale distributed-memory multiprocessor," in Scalable Shared Memory Multiprocessors, M. DuBois and S. Thakkar, Eds. Boston, MA: Kluwer Academic, 1991.

[2] A. Agarwal, B.H. Lim, D. Kranz, and J. Kubiatowicz, "APRIL: A processor architecture for multiprocessing," in Proc. 17th Annu. Int. Symp. Comput. Architecture, Seattle, WA, May 1990, pp. 104–114.

[3] Arvind and D. Culler, "Dataflow architectures," in Annual Reviews in Computer Science. Palo Alto, CA: Annual Reviews, 1986, pp. 225–253.

[4] G. Bilardi and A. Nicolau, "Adaptive bitonic sorting: An optimal parallel algorithm for shared-memory machines," SIAM J. Comput., vol. 18, no. 2, pp. 216–228, Apr. 1989.

[5] D. Chaiken, J. Kubiatowicz, and A. Agarwal, "LimitLESS Directories: A scalable cache coherence scheme," in Proc. 4th Int. Conf. Architectural Support Programming Languages Oper. Syst., Santa Clara, CA, Apr. 1991.

[6] D.E. Culler, "Managing parallelism and resources in scientific dataflow programs," Ph.D. dissertation, M.I.T. Dep. Elec. Eng. Comput. Sci., Cambridge, MA, June 1989.

[7] R.P. Gabriel and J. McCarthy, "Queue-based multi-processing Lisp," in Proc. 1984 ACM Symp. Lisp and Functional Programming, Austin, TX, Aug. 1984, pp. 25–44.

[8] B. Goldberg, "Multiprocessor execution of functional programs," Int. J. Parallel Programming, vol. 17, no. 5, pp. 425–473, Oct. 1988.

[9] R. Goldman and R.P. Gabriel, "Preliminary results with the initial implementation of Qlisp," in Proc. 1988 ACM Symp. Lisp and Functional Programming, Snowbird, UT, July 1988, pp. 143–152.

[10] R. Goldman, R. Gabriel, and C. Sexton, "Qlisp: An interim report," in Proc. U.S./Japan Workshop Parallel Lisp, (Springer-Verlag Lecture Notes in Computer Science 441), T. Ito and R. Halstead, Eds., Sendai, Japan, June 1989, pp. 161–181.

[11] J. Gurd, C. Kirkham, and I. Watson, "The Manchester prototype dataflow computer," Commun. ACM, vol. 28, no. 1, pp. 34–52, Jan. 1985.

[12] M. Feeley, "Fine grain parallelism in Multilisp on a shared memory MIMD computer," Ph.D. dissertation, Brandeis Univ., in preparation.

[13] R. Halstead, "Multilisp: A language for concurrent symbolic computation," ACM Trans. Programming Languages Syst., vol. 7, no. 4, pp. 501–538, Oct. 1985.

[14] ——, "An assessment of Multilisp: Lessons from experience," Int. J. Parallel Programming, vol. 15, no. 6, pp. 459–501, Dec. 1986.

[15] R.W. Hockney and C.R. Jesshope, Parallel Computers 2. Bristol, England: Adam Hilger, 1988, pp. 475–483.

[16] P. Hudak and B. Goldberg, "Serial combinators: 'Optimal' grains of parallelism," in Functional Programming Languages and Computer Architecture, Springer-Verlag LNCS 201, Sept. 1985, pp. 382–388.

[17] D. Kranz, R. Halstead, and E. Mohr, "Mul-T, A high-performance Parallel Lisp," in Proc. ACM SIGPLAN '89 Conf. Programming Language Design Implementation, Portland, OR, June 1989, pp. 81–90.

[18] D. Kranz, R. Kelsey, J. Rees, P. Hudak, J. Philbin, and N. Adams, "Orbit: An optimizing compiler for scheme," in Proc. SIGPLAN '86 Symp. Compiler Construction, June 1986, pp. 219–233.

[19] D. Kranz, "ORBIT: An optimizing compiler for scheme," Ph.D. dissertation, Yale Univ. Tech. Rep. YALEU/DCS/RR-632, Feb. 1988.

[20] E. Mohr, D. Kranz, and R. Halstead, "Lazy task creation: A technique for increasing the granularity of parallel programs," in Proc. ACM Symp. Lisp and Functional Programming, June 1990, pp. 185–197.

[21] ——, "Lazy task creation: A technique for increasing the granularity of parallel programs," DEC Cambridge Research Lab Tech. Rep. CRL 90/7, Nov. 1990.

[22] J.E.B. Moss, "Managing stack frames in Smalltalk," in Proc. SIGPLAN '87 Symp. Interpreters and Interpretive Techniques, June 1987, pp. 229–240.

[23] C.A. Ruggiero and J. Sargeant, "Control of parallelism in the Manchester dataflow machine," in Functional Programming Languages and Computer Architecture, Springer-Verlag LNCS 274, Portland, OR, Sept. 1987, pp. 1–15.

[24] G. Sabot, The Paralation Model. Cambridge, MA: M.I.T. Press, 1988.

[25] V. Sarkar and J. Hennessy, "Compile-time partitioning and scheduling of parallel programs," in Proc. SIGPLAN '86 Symp. Compiler Construction, July 1986, pp. 17–26.

[26] G.L. Steele, Jr. and W.D. Hillis, "Connection Machine Lisp: Fine-grained parallel symbolic processing," in Proc. 1986 ACM Symp.

201

Lisp and Functional Programming, Cambridge, MA, Aug. 1986, pp. 279–297.

[27] M. Vandevoorde and E. Roberts, "WorkCrews: An abstraction for controlling parallelism," *Int. J. Parallel Programming,* vol. 17, no. 4, pp. 347–366, Aug. 1988.

[28] R. C. Waters, "Series," in *Common Lisp: the Language,* Second Ed., G. Steele, Jr., ed. Bedford, MA: Digital, pp. 923–955.

[29] J. D. Pehoushek and J. S. Weening, "Low-cost process creation and dynamic partitioning in Qlisp," in *Proc. U.S./Japan Workshop Parallel Lisp,* Springer-Verlag Lecture Notes in Computer Science 441, T. Ito and R. Halstead, Eds., Sendai, Japan, June 1989, pp. 182–199.

[30] J. Weening, "Parallel execution of Lisp programs," Stanford Comput. Sci. Rep. STANCS-89-1265, June 1989.

Eric Mohr received the B.A. degree from Macalester College in 1980 and the M.S. degree from Yale University in 1986, where he is currently finishing his Ph.D.

His research interests include parallel computing, design and implementation of programming languages, and computer graphics.

David A. Kranz received the B.A. degree from Swarthmore College and in 1988 received the Ph.D. degree from Yale University where he worked on high-performance compilers for Scheme and applicative languages.

He is a Research Associate in the M.I.T. Laboratory for Computer Science.

His interests are in programming language design and implementation for parallel processing. He has been at M.I.T. since 1987.

Robert H. Halstead, Jr. (M'80) received the S.B., S.M., and Ph.D. degrees from the Massachuesetts Institute of Technology, graduating with the Ph.D. in 1979.

He is a research staff member at the Digital Equipment Corporation Cambridge Research Lab. His research interests include languages, algorithms, architectures, and software engineering tools for general-purpose parallel processing, with an emphasis on symbolic computing. From 1979 to 1989, he served on the computer science faculty of the Massachusetts Institute of Technology, where he developed the Multilisp parallel programming language, which pioneered the use of futures in parallel Lisp programming.

Dr. Halstead is a member of the editorial boards of the *International Journal of Parallel Processing* and the journal *Future Generation Computer Systems.*

Chapter 4

Scheduling Tools

4.1 Introduction

To make the power of parallel processing systems more accessible, it is necessary to provide programming environments that permit the programmers to focus on algorithm development. Even though there are a large number of proposed scheduling methods in the literature, the development of comprehensive scheduling environments (tools) has only recently received the proper attention. By a scheduling tool we refer to a parallel program software development environment that helps the users partition and schedule their programs on a given parallel architecture. These tools are intended to be highly visual and user-friendly. A scheduling tool typically consists of the subtools described below.

4.1.1 Application specification tool

Such a tool is used to generate the graphical equivalent of an application specified in a given programming language. This graphical form, either a DAG or an STG, is then used for the purposes of partitioning and scheduling. Different scheduling tools vary in the way they specify the input program graphs:

- Some tools, for example, PARSA [Shirazi 1994], use a functional language such as SISAL [LLNL 1985] for the coding of parallel programs. The advantage of this approach is that compilers already exist that can translate these programs to a graphical form. For example, the SISAL compiler translates SISAL code to an intermediate form, called IF1, which is the dataflow graphical equivalent of the original code. IF1 can then easily be used to generate an equivalent DAG.
- Some tools, such as Prep-P [Berman 1987] and OREGAMI [Lo 1991], use either specialized code or extensions of existing languages to have the programmer specify the input program structure.
- Finally, many of the existing tools simply expect the user to provide the graph equivalent of the program as input to the scheduling tool [Lewis 1993].

A graph generator tool should also augment the program graph with estimates of the execution times of the tasks and communication delays.

4.1.2 Partitioner tool

As discussed in Chapter 3, this tool is used to reduce interprocess communication while retaining parallelism. Some scheduling environments use a separate partitioning tool, as a precursor step to the scheduling process, and others combine the partitioning and scheduling steps into one subtool [Shirazi 1994, Yang 1992].

4.1.3 Scheduler tool

This tool performs the initial mapping or placement of program partitions on the given underlying architecture. Some tools use a specific scheduling method, while others incorporate a suite of placement algorithms, giving the user the option of experimenting with different methods [Lewis 1993, Shirazi 1994, Yang 1992].

4.1.4 Performance profiler tool

The majority of the scheduling tools contain a tool to display visually the expected performance of the scheduled program. Typical metrics include processor utilization, make-span (completion time) of the program, and speed-up factors. Many tools also include animation windows showing when processors are busy and when communication takes place during program execution [Bailey 1990, Lewis 1993, Shirazi 1994].

4.1.5 Other tools

Most of the existing scheduling environments embody the above four tools. However, there are also some other tools supported by some of the scheduling environments. Examples of such tools include architecture specification [Pease 1991], data distribution [Boppana 1991, Pingali 1990], and debugging tools [Appelbe 1985, 1989]. While some scheduling tools may only address the problem of program scheduling on a particular multiprocessor architecture, others may provide an architecture specification tool, allowing users to select their choice of the underlying architecture. Some environments may augment their partitioning and scheduling tools with a data distribution tool that attempts to reduce remote data memory access delays by efficiently distributing the data among the processing elements. Finally, some tools aid the programmers by providing a debugging tool as part of their scheduling environment.

4.2 Chapter organization and overview

This chapter presents the current parallel software development tools that specifically address the task scheduling problem. [Cheng 1991] presents a survey of parallel programming tools, covering a wider spectrum. The tools included in this chapter are PARSA, TOPSYS, Parallax, Parafrase-2, Prep-P, and OREGAMI. There are several other tools, indirectly related to the topic of this chapter, which could not be included due to space limitation. They can be found in the bibliography section.

PARSA: The objective of this environment is to address the issues and algorithms for the efficient partitioning and scheduling of parallel programs in distributed-memory multiprocessor systems. To achieve this goal, the first paper, by Shirazi et al. shows how the authors have developed a visual, interactive environment to assist the users in the scheduling of their parallel programs on a target architecture. The interactive nature of PARSA allows the choice of many scheduling methods. In addition, PARSA provides an environment that allows the users to play "what if" scenarios in order to evaluate or fine-tune their parallel programs and choose a suitable architecture for the execution of their application. PARSA is developed in C, on a SUN workstation, under Unix, using X-window and Motif interfaces.

TOPSYS: Presented in the second paper, by Bemmerl, TOPSYS is a set of tools, developed at the Technical University of Munich, that can be used for programming and monitoring programs on parallel processing systems. The programmer can specify parallel programs using conventional programming languages, and by inserting calls to multitasking kernel (MMK) calls. MMK permits the specification of parallel objects including tasks, mailboxes, and semaphores. The tasks are mapped onto a 32-node iPSC/2 Hypercube architecture. The debugging tool DETOP can be used for debugging the program, while the performance of the parallel system can be monitored using the PATOP (performance monitoring and tuning tool). Program execution can be animated using the visualization tool (VISTOP). The debugging, performance monitoring, and visualization tools are hosted on an X-window environment.

Parallax: Discussed by Lewis and El-Rewini in the third paper, Parallax incorporates seven scheduling heuristics, providing an environment for parallel program developers to find out how the schedulers affect program performance on various parallel architectures [Currey 1990]. Users must provide the input program as a task graph and estimate task execution times. They also must express the target machine as an interconnection topology graph. Parallax then provides Gantt charts, speed-up curves, processor and communication use/efficiency charts, and an animated display of the simulated running program to help developers evaluate the differences among the heuristics.

Parafrase-2: Discussed in the fourth paper, by Polychronopoulos et al., Parafrase-2 is a multilingual vectorizing/parallelizing compiler implemented as a source-to-source code restructuring tool. It has a convenient user interface and provides a means for user interaction at several levels during the transformation process. Although the partitioning phase is carried out at compile-time, task scheduling is considered to be a dynamic process. Tasks that are ready to execute are queued in a ready-task queue. Each idle processor tries to dispatch the next available task from the queue.

Prep-P: In the fifth paper, Berman shows how this tool aims at addressing all phases of mapping, that is, partitioning, placement, and code-generation. The input algorithm is an undirected graph (known as a communication graph). Each node of the graph describes a computation and is written as a process in a language called XX. The output of the Prep-P tool is assembly language code (for Intel 8051) for execution on a parallel architecture. The parallel architecture is described using a computation graph, where the nodes are processors and the arcs designate the communication network between the processing nodes. Currently, the code is targeted for a fixed-size CHiP machine (and at present runs on a CHiP simulator). The researchers hope to extend the tool to produce code for other types of architecture.

OREGAMI: Discussed by Lo et al. in the last paper, OREGAMI is a set of tools that includes a LaRCS compiler to compile user-task descriptions into specialized task graphs (known as temporal communication graphs), a MAPPER tool for mapping tasks on a variety of target configurations, and a METRICS tool for analyzing and display performance. These tools are being developed at the University of Oregon and are being implemented in C for SUN Workstations with X-window interface.

Bibliography

Appelbe, W. F., and C. McDowell, "Anomaly Detection in Parallel FORTRAN Programs," *Proc. Workshop on Parallel Processing Using the HEP*, 1985.

Appelbe, W. F., K. Smith, and C. McDowell, "Start/Pat: A Parallel Programming Toolkit," *IEEE Software*, Vol. 6, No. 4, July 1989, pp. 29–38.

Bailey, D. A., J. E. Cuny, and C. P. Loomis, "ParaGraph: Graph Editor Support for Parallel Programming Environments," *Int'l J. Parallel Programming*, Vol. 19, No. 2, 1990, pp. 75–110.

Beguelin, A., et al., "Graphical Development Tools for Network-Based Concurrent Supercomputing," *Proc. Supercomputing Conf.*, IEEE CS Press, Los Alamitos, Calif., 1991, pp. 435–444.

Bemmerl, T., "The TOPSYS Architecture," *CONPAR '90, VAPP IV*, LNCS, Vol. 457, Springer-Verlag, New York, N.Y., 1990, pp. 732–743; reprinted here.

Berman, F., "Experience with an Automatic Solution to the Mapping Problem," in *The Characteristics of Parallel Algorithms*, L. H. Jamieson, D. Gannon, and R. Douglass, eds., MIT Press, Cambridge, Mass., 1987, Chapter 12, pp. 307–334.

Boppana, R. V., and C. S. Raghavendra, "Generalized Schemes for Access and Alignment of Data in Parallel Processors with Self-Routing Interconnection Networks," *J. Parallel and Distributed Computing*, Vol. 11, 1991, pp. 97–111.

Chandy, K. M., and C. Kesselman, "Parallel Programming in 2001," *IEEE Software*, Vol. 8, No. 6, Nov. 1991, pp. 11–20.

Cheng, D., "A Survey of Parallel Programming Tools," Report RND-91-005, NASA Ames Research Center, Moffett Field, Calif., May 1991.

Currey, R. W., "The Parallel Programming Support Environment," user manual, Oregon State University, Mar. 1990.

Dongarra, J. J., and D. C. Sorensen, "SCHEDULE: Tools for Developing and Analyzing Parallel Fortran Programs," in *The Characteristics of Parallel Algorithms*, L. H. Jamieson, D. Gannon, and R. Douglass, eds., MIT Press, Cambridge, Mass., 1987, Chapter 15, pp. 363–394.

El-Rewini, H., and T. G. Lewis, "Scheduling Parallel Program Tasks onto Arbitrary Target Machines," *J. Parallel and Distributed Computing*, Vol. 9, 1990, pp. 138–153.

Lewis, T., and H. El-Rewini, "Parallax: A Tool for Parallel Program Scheduling," *IEEE Parallel and Distributed Technology*, Vol. 1, No. 2, May 1993, pp. 62–72; reprinted here.

Lawrence Livermore National Laboratory, "An Intermediate Form Language IF1," reference manual, Lawrence Livermore National Laboratory, 1985.

Lo, V. M., et al., "OREGAMI: Tools for Mapping Parallel Computations to Parallel Architectures," *Int'l J. Parallel Programming*, Vol. 20, No. 3, 1991, pp. 237–270; reprinted here.

Miller, B. P., et al., "IPS-2: The Second Generation of a Parallel Program Measurement System," *IEEE Trans. Parallel and Distributed Systems*, Vol. 1, No. 2, Apr. 1990, pp. 206–217.

Notkin, D., et al., "Experiences with Poker," *ACM/SIGPLAN Parallel Programming: Experience with Applications, Languages and Systems*, ACM Press, New York, N.Y., 1988, pp. 10–20.

Pease, D., et al., "PAWS: A Performance Evaluation Tool for Parallel Computing Systems," *Computer*, Vol. 24, No. 12, Jan. 1991, pp. 18–28.

Pingali, K., and A. Rogers, "Compiling for Locality," *Proc. Int'l Conf. Parallel Processing*, Vol. II, Pennsylvania State Univ., University Park, Penn., 1990, pp. II-142—II-146.

Polychronopoulos, C. D., et al., "Parafrase-2: An Environment for Parallelizing, Partitioning, Synchronizing, and Scheduling Programs on Multiprocessors," *Proc. Int'l Conf. Parallel Processing*, Vol. 2, Pennsylvania State Univ., University Park, Penn., 1989, pp. II-39—II-48; reprinted here.

Shirazi, B., et al., "PARSA: a PARallel Program Scheduling and Assessment Tool," *Proc. 1994 Symp. Assessment of Quality Software Development Tools*, IEEE CS Press, Los Alamitos, Calif., 1994; reprinted here.

Wu, M.-Y., and D. D. Gajski, "Hypertool: A Programming Aid for Multicomputers," *Proc. Int'l Conf. Parallel Processing,* Vol. 2, Pennsylvania State Univ., University Park, Penn., 1989, pp. II–15—II–18.

Wu, M.-Y. and D. D. Gajski, "Computer-Aided Programming for Message-Passing Systems: Problems and a Solution," *Proc. IEEE,* Vol. 77, No. 12, Dec. 1989, pp. 1983–1991.

Yang, T., and A. Gerasoulis, "PYRROS: Static Task Scheduling and Code Generation for Message Passing Multiprocessors," *Proc. 6th ACM Int'l Conf. Supercomputing* (ICS92), ACM Press, New York, N.Y., 1992, pp. 428–437.

PARSA: A Parallel Program Software Development Tool[1]

B. Shirazi, H.B. Chen, K. Kavi

Jeff Marquis

A.R. Hurson

University of Texas-Arlington
Dept. of CSE
Arlington, TX 76109

E-Systems Inc.
Greenville Division
Greenville, TX 75403-6056

Penn State University
Dept. of E.E.
University Park, PA 16802

ABSTRACT

This paper introduces the PARSA (PARallel program Scheduling and Assessment) parallel software development tool to address the efficient partitioning and scheduling of parallel programs on multiprocessor systems. The PARSA environment consists of a user-friendly (visual), interactive, compile-time environment for partitioning, scheduling, and performance evaluation/tuning of parallel programs on different parallel computer architectures.

Keywords: Parallel program partitioning, Static scheduling, Parallel processing, Performance assessment, and Visualization.

1. INTRODUCTION AND BACKGROUND

Efficient partitioning and static scheduling of parallel programs among processing elements of parallel and distributed computer systems are difficult and important issues . The process consists of partitioning a parallel program's tasks into clusters and efficiently scheduling those clusters among the processing elements of a parallel machine for execution. The goals of the static scheduling process are to efficiently utilize resources and to achieve performance objectives of the application (e.g., to minimize program execution time).

The Static scheduling methods [Casav88, Shir92, Shir93a,d] attempt to predict the program execution behavior (task execution times and communication delays) at compile-time. They often partition fine-grain program tasks into coarser-grain processes and schedule (map/allocate) these processes to the processors for execution. The process is static in the sense that a mapped partition will only execute on the processor to which it is allocated at compile-time, with no possibility of migration to another processor at run-time. Static scheduling methods suffer from a number of shortcomings as discussed below.

It has been proven that the general optimal scheduling problem is NP-complete [Geras92, Veltm90]. This implies that there is not a "best" scheduling method that is applicable to all applications. Therefore, except for optimal solutions derived for special-case situations, the research in this area has been focused on sub-optimal solutions during the past two decades. The existing static (compile-time) scheduling methods can be classified as: graph-theoretic methods [Stone77], simulated annealing and genetic algorithm methods [Lee92, Talbi93], mathematical programming methods [Anton93, Praka92], state-space search methods [Green87, Kasah84], and heuristic methods [Casav88, McCre89, Sarka86, Shir90]. It should be noted that there is a very rich body of literature addressing the partitioning and scheduling problems. However, due to space limitations, it is impractical to provide a comprehensive list of references. Interested readers are referred to [Casav88, Shir92, Shir93a,d].

Existing scheduling algorithms have in general been theoretical in that they focus on the scheduling method itself and ignore other important aspects of the process which makes the method

[1]This work is in part supported by the Texas Advanced Technology program (Contract No. 0003656-080) and NSF (Contract no. CDA-9300252).

Reprinted from *Proc. 1994 Symp. on Assessment of Quality Software Development Tools,* IEEE CS Press, Los Alamitos, Calif., 1994, pp. 96–111.

applicable in the real world. For example, almost all of the existing methods assume that a parallel program is specified in a graphical representation and that the execution times of the task and the communication delays are known at compile time. What is not discussed is how the graphical representation of the program is generated from parallel/sequential programs and how the execution times of the tasks and the communication delays are estimated. Furthermore, the existing methods do not provide a way for measuring the effectiveness of the generated schedule, nor do they give the users an opportunity to experiment with different scheduling methods and different architectures in order to meet their performance goals.

These shortcomings led to the advent of *scheduling tools* [Cheng93], which augment scheduling methods with a set of supporting tools to make them applicable and practical in real world applications. This paper introduces the PARSA (PARallel program Scheduling and Assessment) parallel software development tool which is designed to address the efficient partitioning and scheduling of parallel programs on multiprocessor systems [Shir93c]. *The PARSA environment consists of a user-friendly (visual), interactive, compile-time environment for partitioning, scheduling, and performance evaluation/tuning of parallel programs on different parallel computer architectures.* Before presenting PARSA, some of the existing scheduling tools and PARSA's distinguishing features are briefly described below:

TOPSYS: TOPSYS is a set of tools that can be used for programming and monitoring programs on parallel processing systems [Bemme90]. The programmer can specify parallel programs using conventional programming languages and by inserting calls to the Multitasking Kernel (MMK). MMK permits the specification of parallel objects including tasks, mailboxes, and semaphores. The tasks are mapped onto a 32 node iPSC/2 Hypercube architecture. The Debugging Tool (DETOP) can be used for debugging the program and the performance of the parallel system can be monitored using the Performance Monitoring and Tuning tool (PATOP). The program execution can be animated using the Visualization Tool (VISTOP).

Prep-P: This tool aims at addressing all phases of mapping, i.e., partitioning, placement, and code-generation [Berma87]. The input algorithm is an undirected graph (known as a Communication Graph), where each node describes a computation. The output of the Prep-P tool is the assembly language code for execution on a parallel architecture. The parallel architecture is described using a Computation Graph where the nodes are processors and the arcs designate the communication network between the processing nodes. Currently, the code is targeted for a fixed-size CHiP machine (and at present runs on a CHiP simulator). The researchers hope to extend the tool to produce code for other types of architecture.

Parallax: Parallax incorporates seven scheduling heuristics, providing an environment for parallel program developers to find out how the schedulers affect program performance on various parallel architectures [Lewis93]. Users must provide the input program as a task graph and estimate task execution times. They also must express the target machine as an interconnection topology graph. Parallax then provides Gantt charts, speed up curves, processor and communication use/efficiency charts, and an animated display of the simulated running program to help developers evaluate the differences among the heuristics.

OREGAMI: OREGAMI [Lo91] is a set of tools that includes a LaRCS compiler to compile user task descriptions into specialized task graphs (known as Temporal Communication Graphs), a MAPPER tool for mapping tasks on a variety of target configurations, and a METRICS tools for analyzing and displaying the performance. These tools were developed at the Oregon Advanced Computing Institute, and are implemented in C for SUN Workstations with an X- Windows interface.

Parafrase-2: Parafrase-2 is a multilingual vectorizing/parallelizing compiler implemented as a source to source code restructuring tool [Polyc89]. It has a convenient user interface and provides a way for user interaction at several levels during the transformation process. Although the partitioning phase is carried out at compile time, task scheduling is considered to be a dynamic process. Tasks which are ready to execute are queued in a ready-task queue. Each idle processor tries to dispatch the next available task from the queue.

The features of PARSA that distinguish it from similar tools include: (1) accurate communication and execution time estimations at compile time; (2) availability of a suite of scheduling methods; (3) a built-in performance assessment tool; and. (4) a hardware specification tool which facilitates the development of PARSA for different parallel system configurations.

It should be noted that the goal of this manuscript is to present an overview of the PARSA environment and introduce the tool to the parallel processing community. The technical aspects related to different parts of PARSA are briefly presented here. More detailed information are available through the technical reports referenced through-out this manuscript.

Section 2 describes the PARSA environment and its associated tools. Section 3 contains a series of illustrative examples that show how the PARSA approach to parallel programming eliminates many of the problems faced by parallel application developers. Section 4 presents the concluding remarks.

2. THE PARSA PROTOTYPE

The objective of the PARSA environment is to eliminate the need for system architecture and scheduling considerations during the programming phase of a parallel application development [Shir93c]. This is achieved by development of a tool that allows the user to specify an application without regard to scheduling and system architectural considerations. Architectural characteristics of a target parallel machine are specified in a separate tool. A host of partitioning and scheduling methods have been developed and integrated into a tool for mapping the application onto a target architecture. A tool for performance assessment has been developed to assist the user in selection of the most appropriate mapping of an application onto a target architecture. These tools are integrated into an interactive software environment that would allow the user to perform "what-if" scenarios with different scheduling methods and parallel architectures to achieve the performance criteria of the application.

The PARSA prototype has 4 tools (an Application Specification Tool, an Architecture Specification Tool, a Partitioner and Scheduler Tool and a Performance Assessment Tool) integrated into an interactive environment that is portable to any Unix workstation that supports Motif and X Windows. Figure 1 shows the organization of the PARSA

environment and depicts the interaction between its four tools.

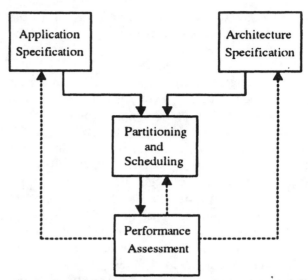

Figure 1: Interaction between PARSA prototype tools.

When using PARSA, a typical flow of activities consists of the following steps: i) the application is specified using the Application Specification Tool, ii) the target architecture is selected using the Architecture Specification Tool, iii) using the Partitioning and Scheduling Tool, the application is mapped on the target architecture, and iv) the expected performance of the application is displayed using the Performance Assessment Tool. The dashed lines in Figure 1 show feedback paths that the user can follow to fine-tune the application, investigate a different scheduling method, or experiment with a different architecture after observing the predicted performance of the application. Each PARSA tool is briefly described below:

2.1. Application Specification Tool:

This tool converts an application program into its equivalent Directed Acyclic Graph (DAG) representation. The DAG nodes represent fine-grain program instructions. The graphical form is used to facilitate the partitioning and scheduling processes and allows the user to graphically observe the application structure (see Figure 2). This tool also attaches execution delays to each application task and inter-task link, using delay information from the Architecture Specification Tool. Currently, this tool accepts programs written in SISAL language [LLN85]. The SISAL programs are then compiled into IF1 - Intermediate Form 1, which is an acyclic graphical language (in textual form) developed by the Lawrence Livermore National Lab as an intermediate form for SISAL language [Har89, LLN85]. The major advantage of using SISAL and IF1 is that their functional, hierarchical structure makes them suitable for data flow analysis, partitioning, and merging of the program tasks for the purpose of scheduling. In IF1, primitive instructions, such as add or multiply, are represented by simple nodes. Compound nodes represent complex constructs, such as while loops, forall loops, and conditionals, in a hierarchical fashion. The application specification tool generates the DAG equivalent of the IF1 code and displays it visually. Figure 2 shows an example of how this tool works. The bottom-left window represents the SISAL source code for the Livermore Kernel Loop 1 (the Hydro Fragment problem). Note that the syntax of the SISAL language is very similar to PASCAL or structured FORTRAN. However, it has a functional programming semantics. The Loop1 Kernel returns a one dimensional array of size n. A **forall** expression (lines 9-14) computes the values in parallel, gathers them into an array, and returns it to main procedure (line 19). The top-middle window of Figure 2 shows the first-level DAG representation of the IF1 code. By clicking on a compound node in each level, the tool pops up a window to show the internal structure of that node. For example, the top-right window of Figure 2 displays the second level structure of the **forall** compound node and the bottom-right window of Figure 2 displays the third level structure of the **forall** compound node. A detailed discussion of this tool can be found in [Chen93] technical report.

2.2. Architecture Specification Tool:

This is a graphical interactive tool for building a database of detailed hardware specifications for the underlying parallel target architectures. Different system parameters, such as instruction timings, memory access timings, communication delays, and interconnection topology, will be stored in a database. The users will have the option of using the database built-in architectures (such as a hypercube, mesh, ring, etc.), modifying the built-in systems, or defining their own architectures. Naturally, the users have the option of specifying many of the system parameters such as the number of processors, the interconnection topology, etc.

Currently, only a fully connected parallel architecture is supported. Other hypothetical topologies, as well as the architectural characteristics of the existing commercial parallel machines, are currently under development.

2.3. Partitioning and Scheduling Tool:

The purpose of this tool is to partition fine-grain program instructions into coarse grain tasks and schedule (or map) those tasks on the target architecture. The goal of this tool is to achieve a minimal execution time with as small of a communication delay overhead as possible. In the current PARSA prototype, the user can select from 3 partitioning and scheduling techniques: Heavy Node First (HNF), Linear Clustering (LC), and Linear Clustering with Task Duplication (LCTD). The LC method is the same as the traditional heuristic-based critical path method of static scheduling. An overview and a brief discussion of the performance capabilities of HNF and LCTD (the two novel methods developed for PARSA) are presented next. For background information and technical details, the reader is referred to the following technical reports: [Shir90 and Shir91] for HNF and [Shir93b] for LCTD.

2.3.1. Heavy Node First Scheduling (HNF):

The existing static schedulers often assume that the time needed to send a message from one Processing Element (PE) to another is either (i) a constant amount, (ii) a constant times the message size, or (iii) the distance between the two PEs times the message size. In all three cases, the communication delay is under-estimated since it not only depends on the distance between the PEs and the message size, but also on the current load, or contention, on the network links. As a result, the schedules based the above assumptions render unpredictable program execution times. In the proposed scheduling method this problem is alleviated through a novel list scheduling method which features accurate estimation of the communication delays, taking into account the load on the network links. The proposed algorithm not only allocates processes to the processors, it also assigns or reserves messages on communication links during the scheduling process. The effect is that if a future message requires use of a link which has been assigned to a previously live (not completed) message, then the future message will be

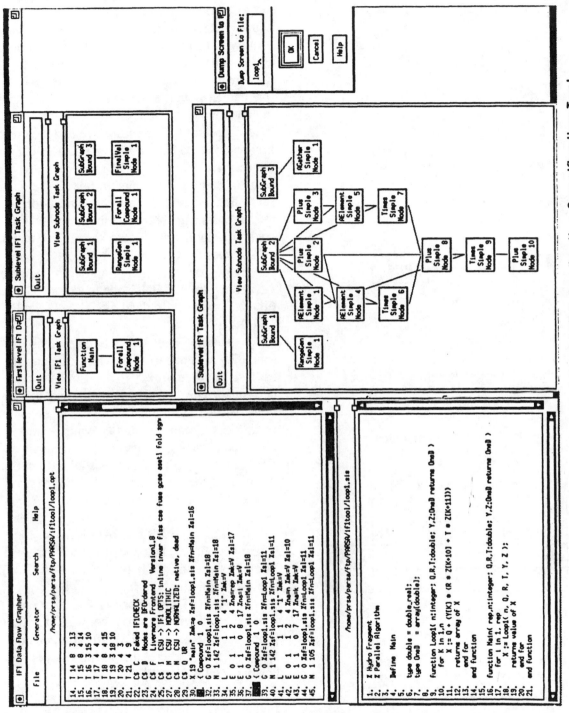

Figure 2: Run-time view of the PARSA Application Specification Tool.

scheduled with additional delays due to the contention on that link.

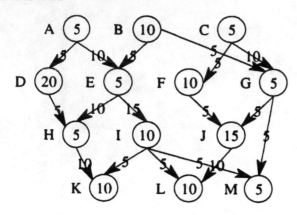

Figure 3a: The DAG for scheduling.

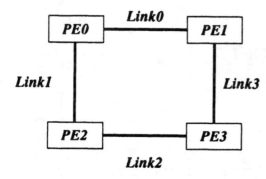

Figure 3b: The target machine.

	0	5	10	15	20	25	30	35	40	45	50
PE0	B	B		E	I	I	H	K	K		
PE1	A	D	D	D	D			M			
PE2	C	F	F	G	J	J	J	L	L		
PE3											

Figure 3c: The scheduling task Gantt chart.

	0	5	10	15	20	25	30	35	40
Link0		A-E				D-H	I-M		
Link1						G-M			
Link2					G-M				
Link3			B-G					I-L	

Figure 3d: The Link scheduling Gantt chart.

The proposed list scheduling method begins by prioritizing the program DAG nodes level by level, beginning with the starting nodes and going towards the exit nodes, and at each level, the node with the highest execution time (heaviest) is given a higher priority. The nodes with the same execution delay and at the same level are randomly prioritized. Then, the node with the highest priority is assigned to the PE that can execute it at the earliest possible time, taking the communication delays into account. This process is repeated until all the tasks are assigned to the PEs. Figure 3(a) depicts a sample DAG in which the number inside each node represents the execution delay of that node (in units of time) and the number on each link represent the communication delay for message-passing between the two nodes on one communication link. Note that this communication delay does not include the delays due to link contention or for going through multiple links. According to the HNF, the nodes of the DAG of Figure 3(a) are prioritized as: B, A, C, D, F, E, G, J, I, H, K, L, and M.

During the scheduling process, a task T should be assigned to a PE which can execute it at the earliest possible time. This time depends on the current load assigned to the PEs and the amount of time needed for this task to receive its input parameters from its predecessors. Let $DSM_{i,T}$, Desirable Starting Moment for executing task T on PE_i, be the time that T receives all its input messages when assigned to PE_i. Then, the Actual Starting Moment (ASM) of a task T assigned to PE_i is defined as:

$$ASM_{i,T} = MAX(LOAD(PE_i), DSM_{i,T}),$$

where $LOAD(PE_i)$ is the load already assigned to PE_i. For n PEs, the most suitable PE for Task T will be the one with minimum ASM:

$$MIN(ASM_{i,T}), \text{ for } i=1,2, ..., n.$$

If n is too large, one may consider a subset of the processors (e.g., m PEs) in computation of the $MIN(ASM_{i,T})$, where the m processors are the m nearest neighbors of PE_i.

For example, consider scheduling DAG of Figure 3(a) on the multiprocessor of Figure 3(b). Assume that nodes A, B, C, D, and F are already assigned to the PEs, as shown in Figure 3(c). According to HNF, we select E for assignment next and must determine the suitable PE for its assignment. We need to compute all possible ASM's for E and select the PE which results in the least ASM. We have: $ASM_{0,E}=15$, $ASM_{1,E}=25$, $ASM_{2,E}=25$, and $ASM_{3,E}=20$. Thus, PE_0 is the most suitable PE for task E since it can begin its execution at the earliest possible time according to the current schedule. However, note that if we assign E to PE_0, then there will be a message communication between tasks A and E from time 5 to time 15 on Link 0. Thus, this message is scheduled in the Gantt chart of Figure 3(d). If sometimes between the times 5 and 15, there is another message which requires use of Link 0, it should be delayed by 10 time units due this link contention. The link schedules; e.g., Figure 3(d), will become the basis of the routing tables which will be used at run-time for message routing.

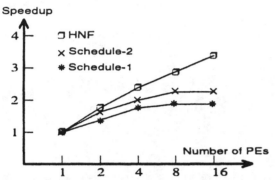

Figure4: Comparison of the proposed scheduler against existing methods.

Figure 4 depicts the effectiveness of the HNF in handling of accurate communication delays. In this Figure, HNF is compared against two other methods which do not take the link contention into account during the scheduling process. These methods (schedule-1 and schedule-2) are the same as the HNF but during the scheduling process, schedule-1 assumes there is no network delay for communication and schedule-2 assumes the communication delay is the message size times the distance between the PEs. This Figure shows the average speedup behavior of a set of benchmark programs. The detailed explanation of this comparison is out of the scope of this paper, but can be found in [Shir91]. The Figure clearly shows that accurate communication delay estimations can have a profound impact on performance of the applications for larger systems.

2.3.2. Linear Clustering with Task Duplication (LCTD):

The proposed LCTD algorithm consists of several steps: task partitioning, task duplication, task merging, and task scheduling. In the first step, task nodes of a DAG are grouped into different linear clusters based on their linear execution order. The task-clustering process is based on the critical path analysis. The tasks in the same cluster will be assigned to the same processor. A Critical Path (CP) is one of the longest paths through a DAG from an entry node to an exit node. In this step, first a CP is found and its nodes are marked and assigned to a linear cluster. While marking the CP nodes, all the incoming and outgoing edges of the CP nodes are marked as "discounted". This process is then repeated for the remaining unmarked nodes and edges until there is no more unmarked task node in the DAG. From the first step, a set of linear task clusters are generated. The edges between the clusters are then marked as "connected" and represent Inter-Process Communication (IPC). The IPC edges represent the precedence and dependency relationship among the task clusters. Figure 5(a) shows an example DAG in which t_i $(i = 1,2,...,11)$ is the task ID and the numbers on the edges indicate the message communication delay between two directly connected task nodes. The underlined numbers next to the nodes specify the computation delay of the corresponding task nodes. Figure 5(b) depicts the result of the linear clustering step; i.e., linear clusters LC0-3 with corresponding IPC's.

In the second step, the IPC delays are minimized by duplicating some tasks among the clusters. In this step the tasks are scanned according to their execution order and IPC with other tasks in other clusters. The goal of the duplication is to reduce IPC delays and attempt to lower the tasks' starting execution times. At the end of the task duplication step, the maximum execution time of the parallel program is identified by the cluster which requires the maximum execution time for its completion. Figure 5(c) shows the contents of the clusters after the task duplication step. In this particular example, all the IPC delays are eliminated by this duplication process. However, it should be noted that, in general, the IPC's cannot always be eliminated; i.e., a point may be reached at which any task duplication will increase the completion time of the program, even though it may eliminate one or more IPC's.

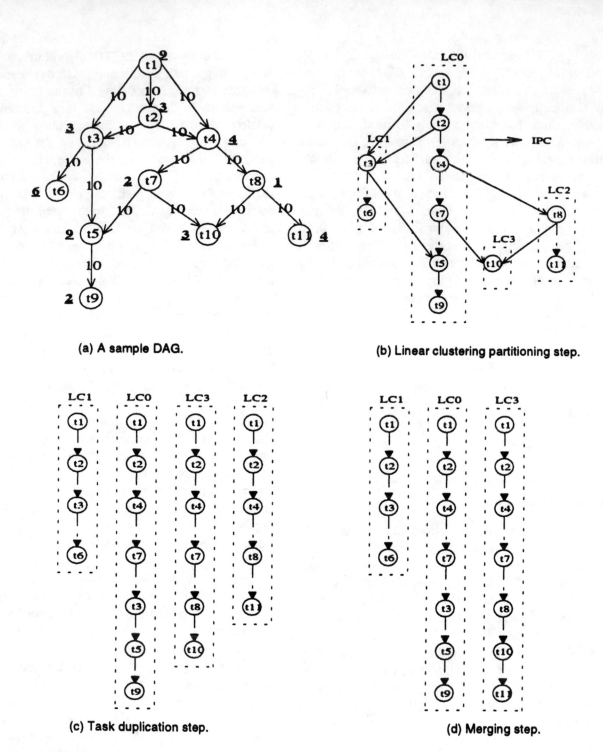

(a) A sample DAG.

(b) Linear clustering partitioning step.

(c) Task duplication step.

(d) Merging step.

Figure 5: An example of the LCTD partitioning and scheduling method.

The novelty of the LCTD method lies in the third step; i.e., task merging. Note from Figure 5(c) that many clusters may contain the same subsets of the tasks, due to the duplication process. For example, clusters LC2 and LC3 share task nodes t1, t2, t4, and t8. The proposed merging heuristic merges the clusters with the maximum number of shared task nodes as long as the overall completion time of the program, established in step 2, is not increased. In the example of Figure 5(d), cluster LC2 is merged into cluster LC3. The major advantage of the merging step is that it provides a better utilization of the resources; i.e., typically fewer processors will be needed and the storage needs are reduced by elimination of some of the duplicated tasks.

Finally, in the fourth step, the partitions or clusters are scheduled on the processing elements, using the HNF method discussed in Section 2.3.1. Naturally, if all the IPC delays are eliminated by the above 3 steps, then the scheduling process will be greatly simplified.

In the following paragraphs, the performance evaluation of the LCTD method is briefly addressed. A simulation study was conducted to compare the HNF, LC, and LCTD scheduling methods [Shir93b]. These methods were compared by their application to randomly generated DAG's to be scheduled on a fully connected multiprocessor system with an unlimited number of processors; i.e., the required number of processors is decided by each scheduling algorithm. In this study, a randomly generated DAG can have from 20 to 100 task nodes. Eleven different ratios of computation and communication delays (RCC) are used to characterize the execution and communication times. The RCC values used are 1:1, 1:2, 1:3, 1:4, 1:5, 1:10, 2:1, 3:1, 4:1, 5:1, and 10:1. For each RCC ratio, ten sample DAG's are randomly generated and fed to the simulator. The simulation results presented here represent the average values over the 10 sample DAG's.

To compare the performance of the LCTD method with those of the LC and HNF, a normalized performance index called $MSL_{x/y}$ (x and y are the scheduling methods) is defined, where MSL stands for Maximum Scheduling Length (or program completion time). For example, MSL_{hnf} represents the completion time of the parallel program when scheduled using the HNF method, and $MSL_{lctd/hnf}$ represents the normalized completion time of the

program, when using the LCTD method, with respect to that of the HNF method (i.e., $MSL_{lctd/hnf}$

$$= \frac{MSL_{lctd}}{MSL_{hnf}}).$$

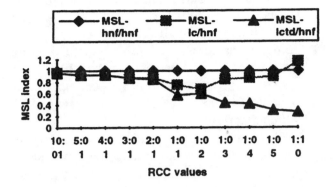

Figure 6: MSL index for the HNF, LCTD and LC methods.

Figure 6 depicts the MSL index for the HNF, LC, and LCTD methods. When the ratio of the computation to communication delay is high (10:1 to 2:1), the three methods perform similarly. This is because even though the LC and LCTD methods reduce the communication delays, the effect of the communication delay on the overall MSL is minimized. However, as the communication delay becomes more significant, the performance of LCTD and LC methods are improved. Nevertheless, while LCTD method shows an almost linear performance improvement, the performance of the LC method degrades when the communication delay is significantly increased. This is due to the fact that the LC method fails to minimize the IPC delays since it lacks the task duplication capability.

2.4. Performance Assessment Tool:

The purpose of this tool is to display the expected run-time behavior of the scheduled program at *compile-time*. Instead of the time-consuming emulation of the program execution, this tool displays the expected performance by analysis of the scheduled program trace file (output of the Partitioning and Scheduling Tool). This file contains the information on where each task is assigned for execution and exactly when each task is expected to start execution, stop execution, or send a message to another task. The output of the performance assessment tool consists of the:

(i) *space and time* related visual information such as the task Gantt chart, the parallelism profile, the IPC traffic, the global IPC, the critical path, and the system load status,

(ii) *animation* related visual information such as the IPC matrix, resource utilization chart, processor status, message queue length, resource utilization meter, and IPC meter, and

(iii) *statistic* related visual information such as the distribution of parallelism, the IPC data, resource utilization summary, speed-up, system overall efficiency, and general summary of the simulating result.

The tool contains a display control panel which provides a flexible and interactive environment to let the user control the display options such as the display speed factor, a simulated clock, a screen dump option, the display cycles, and the scaling width. This information is presented in a visual hierarchical manner, giving the programmer the option of requesting more detailed information from level to level.

Figure 7 depicts a sample of the performance assessment tool output. All these graphs are updated continually as the simulated execution advances. For example, in the PE status display, the colors of the processing nodes change according to their status: busy, sending a message, receiving a message, or idle. The Task Scheduling Gantt Chart window shows the assignment of the tasks to 6 fully connected PE's between the 368 and 466 simulated time units. In this chart, the X axis depicts time and the Y axis shows the processing element ID numbers. For example, at the simulated time 370, PE's 0 and 2 are each executing a task while the other processors are idle. The Utilization Summary window shows the statistic information regarding the PE utilization. For example, PE0 is utilized 78% of the time. The speed-up window depicts a speed-up of 2.12 compared to sequential execution of the program. The Parallelism Profile window indicates the percentage of the time that n processors were busy. For example, 33% of the time either one or two processors were busy.

3. ILLUSTRATIVE EXAMPLES

There are currently many problems associated with parallel application development, including: high parallel application development costs, a lack of portability of parallel applications to different parallel systems, inefficient utilization of parallel system resources, and an inability to efficiently modify and/or enhance (i.e. maintain) existing parallel applications. The following descriptive and illustrative examples demonstrate how the PARSA approach to parallel programming solves many of these problems:

3.1. Example 1:

This example describes how PARSA will reduce development costs associated with parallel programming. This is accomplished by relieving the programmer of scheduling and target architecture characteristics considerations during the application development phase of a project. The PARSA Application Specification Tool allows the developer to specify, i.e., program an application without regard to either scheduling considerations or the target architecture characteristics. The architectural characteristics of the target system are specified in the Architecture Specification Tool and introduced to the application in the Partitioning and Scheduling Tool. The partitioning and scheduling process is introduced to the application after it has been fully specified. This process will reduce the complexity of the application development, and hence, reduce costs. Additionally, because there are a variety of partitioning and scheduling algorithms for the developer to choose from, the partitioning and scheduling algorithm that best fits the application can be chosen.

3.2. Example 2:

This example describes how PARSA will make applications portable among parallel systems. Applications are specified in PARSA independent of architectural characteristics of the target system. The architectural characteristics are specified in the Architecture Specification Tool. This implies that an application specified in PARSA can be scheduled on different architectures *unmodified*. It should be noted that the output from the Application Specification Tool is in a graphical format called IF1, and an IF1 to C compiler will be need for each target architecture.

3.3. Example 3:

This example illustrates how PARSA allows the user to select the scheduling algorithm that utilizes processor resources most efficiently. Figure 8 shows an application scheduled 2 different ways, using HNF and LC methods. The "IPC Traffic" charts depict the application schedule on the target system. The dark

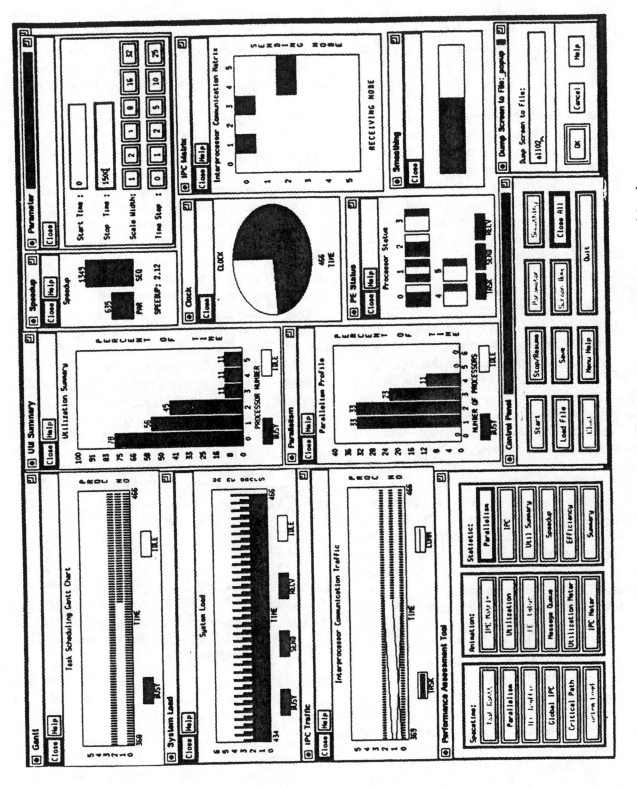

Figure 7: A sample output of the performance assessment tool.

horizontal lines are application tasks on the respective processors (shown on the Y-axis). The diagonal lines show the inter-processor communications among the tasks.

Assuming an unlimited supply of fully-connected processing elements, the first schedule (HNF) of Figure 8 allows the application to execute in 660 time units on 4 processors. The second schedule (LC) allows the same application to execute in 705 time units on 8 processors. The application using the second scheduling algorithm actually takes longer to execute with twice the number of processors. This is not to say that the second scheduling method is a poor algorithm; it is simply not the best scheduling algorithm for this particular application.

3.4. Example 4:

This example illustrates how PARSA facilitates the maintenance of and modifications to an application. Figure 9 shows 3 schedules of an application as it receives enhancements. All 3 schedules are generated using the HNF method.

The first schedule in Figure 9 is the original application. The application is shown to have equal execution time (1 time unit) for each task. The first "Task Gantt Chart" shows the application scheduled on 4 processors. Notice that the application takes 9 time units to execute.

The second schedule in Figure 9 is the same application with the computational weights assigned to task nodes 2, 5 and 8 doubled. The enhanced application has been rescheduled. Notice that the enhanced application executes in exactly the same amount of time, 9 time units, as the original application. Through a simple rescheduling process, using PARSA, it was possible to maintain the original program execution time even though some tasks' run-times were doubled. If the application had been modified but not rescheduled, the performance of the application would have surely suffered.

The application is modified even further in the third schedule in Figure 9. This time the execution times associated with task nodes 7, 9 and 13 have been increased significantly. This modified and rescheduled application takes longer to execute (11 time units) and requires more processors (6), but making relatively large modifications to the application only increased its execution time minimally.

While the application in Figure 9 is rather simple, it does demonstrate an important point: PARSA makes application modifications and enhancements efficient and affordable. Having this capability will extend the life cycle of the application.

4. CONCLUSION

This paper introduced PARSA as a software tool for parallel program partitioning and scheduling in distributed memory multiprocessor systems. The distinguishing features of PARSA include accurate communication and execution time estimations, choice of many partitioning and scheduling tools, and a built-in graphical assessment tool for evaluation and tuning of parallel programs before execution. The novel scheduling methods implemented in PARSA attempt to improve processor utilization (LCTD) and take into account the contention on links due to message communication (HNF). This results in more accurate and predictable schedules. Future extensions of PARSA include: incorporation of several other scheduling methods, coverage of real-time scheduling methods, and verifying the correctness and accuracy of PARSA by comparison of the assessment tool output with the results obtained by running the program on an actual system.

We would like to acknowledge the NSF REU participants (Susan Thrane, Robert McPeak, and Dan Doyle) contributions to the PARSA project.

5. REFERENCES

[Anton93] J. Antonio and R. Metzger, "Hypersphere Mapper: A Nonlinear Programming Approach to the Hypercube Embedding Problem," *The 7th Int'l Parallel Processing Symposium*, April 1993, pp. 538-547.

[Bemme90] T. Bemmerl, "The TOPSYS Architecture," *CONPAR '90*, VAPP IV, Vol. 457, Springer-Verlag, 1990.

[Berma87] F. Berman, "Experience with an Automatic Solution to the Mapping Problem," in The Characteristics of Parallel Algorithms, ed. L. H. Jamieson, D. Gannon and R. Douglass, MIT Press, 1987, Ch. 12, pp. 307-334.

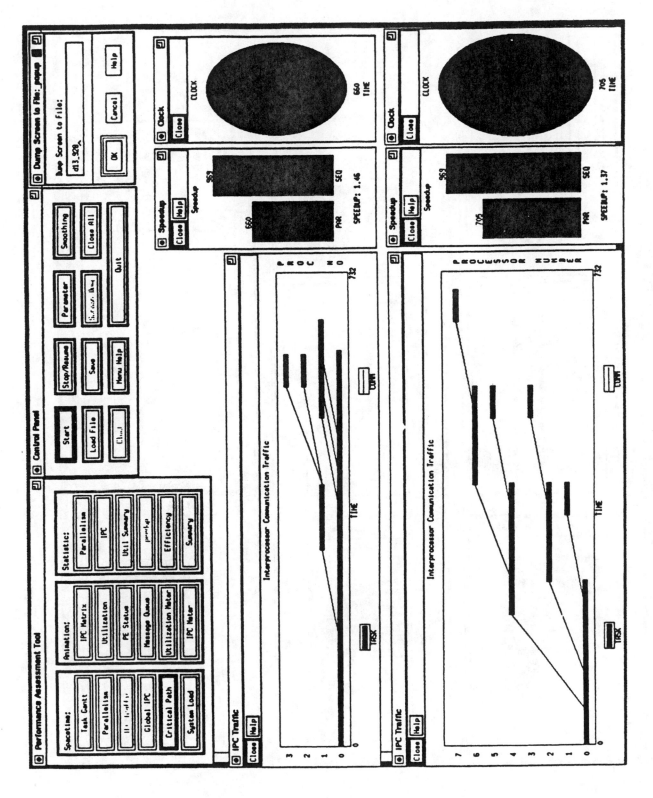

Figure 8: Run-time view of an application scheduled 2 different ways in PARSA.

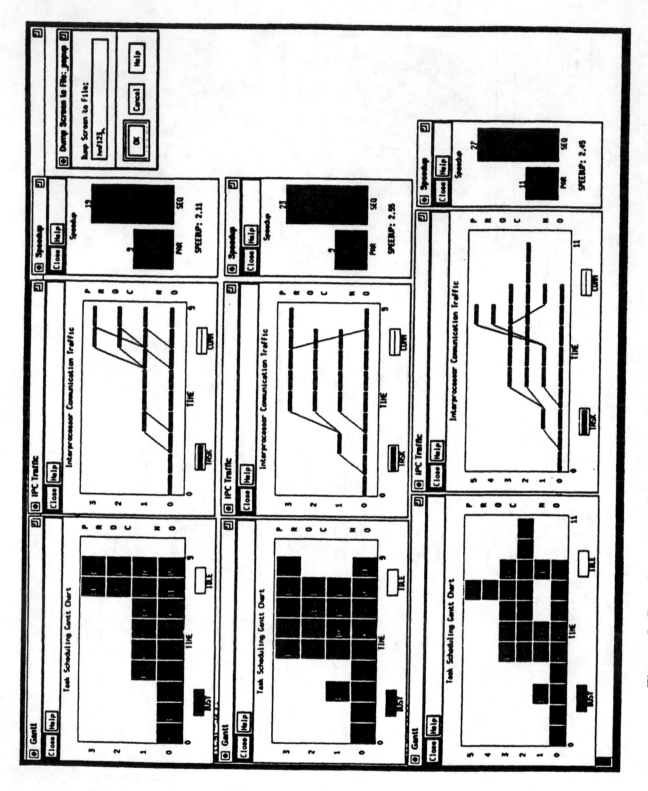

Figure 9: Run-time view of an application rescheduled after enhancements.

[Casav88] Thomas L. Casavant and Jon G. Kuhl, "A Taxonomy of Scheduling in General-Purpose Distributed Computing Systems," *IEEE Transactions on Software Engineering*, Vol. 14, No. 2, Feb. 1988, pp. 141-154.

[Chen93] H.B. Chen, B. Shirazi, and Susan Thrane, "IF1-Viewer: A Visual Tool for Graphical Display and Execution of SISAL Programs," Technical Report, CSE Department, University of Texas-Arlington, Aug. 1993.

[Cheng93] D. Cheng, "A Survey of Parallel Programming Languages and Tools," Report RND-93-005, NASA Ames Center, March 1993.

[Geras92] A. Gerasoulis and T. Yang, "A Comparison of Clustering Heuristics for Scheduling DAGs on Multiprocessors," *J. of Parallel and Distributed Computing*, Dec. 92, pp. 276-291.

[Green87] Bruce Greenblatt and Cathy Jo Linn, "Branch and Bound Style Algorithms for Scheduling Communicating Tasks in a Distributed System," *IEEE Spring CompCon Conference*, 1987, pp. 12-17.

[Har89] S. Harikrishnan, "A Type Inferencing Linkage Editor For Data Flow Graphs Generated From SISAL," Technical report CS-89-110, Department of Computer Science, Colorado State University, June, 1989.

[Kasah84] Hironori Kasahara and Seinosuke Narita, "Practical Multiprocessor Scheduling Algorithms for Efficient Parallel Processing," *IEEE Transactions on Computers*, Vol. C-33, No. 11, November 1984, pp. 1023-1029.

[Lee92] Kyung-Geun Lee and Soo-Young Lee, "Efficient Parallelization of Simulated Annealing using Multiple Markov Chains: An Application to Graph Partitioning," *Int'l Conference on Parallel Processing*, Vol. III, 1992, pp. 177-180.

[Lewis93] T. Lewis, H. El-Rewini, "Parallax: A Tool for Parallel Program Scheduling," IEEE Parallel & Distributed Technology, May 1993, pp. 62-72.

[LLN85] "An Intermediate Form Language IF1," Lawrence Livermore National Laboratory reference manual, 1985.

[Lo91] V.M. Lo, et al, "OREGAMI: Tools for Mapping Parallel Computations to Parallel Architectures," *In'l Journal of Parallel Programming*, Vol. 20, no. 3, 1991, pp. 237-270.

[McCre89] Carolyn McCreary and Helen Gill, "Automatic Determination of Grain Size for Efficient Parallel Processing," *Communications of the ACM*, Sept. 1989, pp. 1073-1078.

[Parka92] Shiv Prakash and Alice Parker, "SOS: Synthesis of Application-Specific Heterogeneous Multiprocessor Systems," *Journal of Parallel and Distributed Computing*, Vol. 16, No. 4, December 1992, pp. 338-351.

[Polyc89] C.D. Polychronopoulos, et al, "Parafrase-2: An Environment for Parallelizing, Partitioning, Synchronizing, and Scheduling Programs on Multiprocessors," *Int'l Conference on Parallel Processing*, 1989, Vol. II, pp. 39-48.

[Sarka86] Vivek Sarkar and John Hennessy, "Compile-Time Partitioning and Scheduling of Parallel Programs," *Symposium on Compiler Construction*, 1986, pp. 17-26.

[Shir90] B. Shirazi, M.F. Wang, G. Pathak, "Analysis and Evaluation of Heuristic Methods for Static Task Scheduling," *Journal of Parallel and Distributed Computing*, Vol. 10, No. 3, 1990, pp. 222-232.

[Shir91] B. Shirazi, K. Kavi, B. Lee, A.R. Hurson, "Accurate Communication Cost Estimation in Static Task Scheduling," Technical Report, CSE Dept., Univ. of Texas-Arlington, Dec. 1991.

[Shir92] B. Shirazi, A.R. Hurson, "Scheduling and Load Balancing: Guest Editors' Introduction," *Journal of Parallel and Distributed Computing*, Dec. 1992, pp. 271-275.

[Shir93a] B. Shirazi, A.R. Hurson, K. Kavi, "Scheduling & Load Balancing," IEEE-Computer Society Tutorial, under contract, *IEEE Press*, 1993.

[Shir93b] B. Shirazi, H.B. Chen, K. Kavi, A.R. Hurson, "Linear Clustering with Task Duplication: A Novel Static Scheduling Method for Distributed Memory Systems," Technical

Report, CSE Department, University of Texas-Arlington, April 1993.

[Shir93c] B. Shirazi, K. Kavi, A.R. Hurson, P. Biswas, "PARSA: a PARallel program Scheduling and Assessment environment," *1993 Int'l Conf. on Parallel Processing*, Aug. 1993.

[Shir93d] B. Shirazi, A.R. Hurson, "A Mini-track on Scheduling and Load Balancing: Track Coordinator's Introduction," *Hawaii Int'l Conf. on System Sciences (HICSS-26)*, January 1993, pp. 484-486.

[Stone77] Harold S. Stone, "Multiprocessor Scheduling with the Aid of Network Flow Algorithms," *IEEE Trans. on Software Engineering*, Vol. SE-3, no. 1, Jan. 1977, pp. 85-93.

[Talbi93] E.G. Talbi and T. Muntean, "Hill-climbing, Simulated Annealing and Genetic Algorithms: A Comparative Study and Application to the Mapping Problem," *The 26th Hawaii International Conference on System Sciences*, Vol. 2, 1993, pp. 565-573.

[Veltm90] B. Veltman, B.J. Lageweg, and J.K. Lenstra, "Multiprocessor Scheduling with Communication Delays," *Parallel Computing*, Vol. 16, 1990, pp. 173-182.

The TOPSYS Architecture

Thomas Bemmerl

Institut für Informatik der TU München
Lehrstuhl für Rechnertechnik und Rechnerorganisation
Arcisstr. 21, D-8000 München 2
Tel.: +49-89-2105-8247 or -2382
e-mail: bemmerl@lan.informatik.tu-muenchen.dbp.de

A survey on the TOPSYS (TOols for Parallel SYStems) project at the Department of Computer Science at Technical University of Munich is presented. Within this project, an integrated tool environment for increasing programmer productivity when using and programming parallel computers is developed. The TOPSYS tool environment offers tools for specification, mapping, debugging, testing, performance analysis, graphical program animation and dynamic loadbalancing of parallel programs. In addition to these tools a distributed operating system kernel and a synthetic workload generator has been developed. Apart from the integrated hierarchical architecture, the major features of the TOPSYS environment are the support of different monitoring techniques, easy adaptability, high portability and a common graphic user interface for all tools. After the description of the project goals, the major design concepts and the state of the project we describe a first application of the TOPSYS tools.

1. Motivation

Massively parallel systems promise to be the only possibility to increase computing performance in the future by several orders of magnitude. The recognition of this fact has lead in recent years to intensified research in the field of parallel and distributed systems [Jes89],[Mae86], [Gib88]. Most of the research projects were concentrated on hardware aspects. The results of these projects have shown that parallel machines are adequate for increasing computing performance. An industrial outcome of this research work are massively parallel computer systems based on various architectures. At the moment, most available parallel computers are used for specific types of applications like numerics or artificial intelligence. A reason for this limited use is the difficult useability and programmability of parallel systems. Most of the parallelization of applications on these machines has to be done by hand from computer science specialists. G. Papadopoulos from MIT comments this fact with the sentence: "It appears to be easier to build parallel machines than to use them" [Pap87]. To open a wider market for parallel computers, it is necessary to simplify their useability and programmability.

Therefore it's time to increase not only performance of parallel systems but also to do research on programmability and useability of these types of computers. In the long run, parallel systems will be successful if they are as easy to use and to program as sequential computers. A first step toward this direction is to increase programmer productivity with adequate tools for configuration, specification, programming, validation and analysis of parallel applications. Adequate tools for all phases of the "software life cycle" for parallel systems have to be taken into account. From our point of view, tools for the first phases of the

Partly funded by the German Science Foundation under contract number SFB 0342, project A1.

design cycle will not be very different from tools for sequential systems. The differences will increase more and more, when you think toward tools for the late phases of the design cycle like validation and analysis. Available parallel machines especially lack in tools for observing the dynamic behaviour of the parallel execution run. Parallel debuggers [Hil89], test systems, performance analyzers[Bur88], [Hof87], [Lek89] and graphical animation tools belong to this type of tools.

Apart form these monitoring and analysis tools, the programmer of a parallel computer needs in particular support for the mapping of the logical program structure onto the physical parallel architecture. This class of tools is represented by static or interactive specification, configuration and mapping tools [Gua89]. For the long term future a remapping and dynamic loadbalancing component has to be integrated into distributed operating systems to balance the load of the parallel machine during execution [Lik89], [Art89]. In order to simplify program creation, the process model offered by the operating system must be easy to use by the programmer. This requires a flexible and dynamic creation of processes as well as transparent and global operations on all processes, regardless on which processor node they are located.

Tools and system software mentioned in the last paragraphs are only partly available on existing parallel systems. In particular an integrated methodology for using the different tools during parallelization of applications is still missing. This fact gave us the major motivation to develope and implement an integrated tool environment for using and programming parallel computers within the TOPSYS project [Bem88]. The actual implementation of the TOPSYS environment was done on an iPSC/2 Hypercube with 32 processor nodes. The following chapters of this paper describe the major goals and design concepts of the project as well as the implementation state and the first experiences in using the TOPSYS tool environment.

2. Major Goals of the TOPSYS Project

In general, the major intention of the TOPSYS project is to simplify the usage and the programming of parallel systems for widening the range of applications for these types of machines. Massively parallel computers should become as easy to use as todays conventional (sequential) workstations. Therefore the first goal of TOPSYS is to work out a general methodology for using and programming parallel architectures and applications. Within the project we try to support the application of this methodology by the implementation of an integrated tool environment for all the phases of the "parallel software developement cycle".

In particular, we develop all the tools mentioned in the previous chapter as there are the distributed operating system kernel MMK [BeL90] with integrated dynamic load balancing, the specification and mapping tool SAMTOP, the parallel debugger DETOP, the performance analyzer PATOP [BHL90] and the graphical animation tool VISTOP. Figure 1 explains the interactive usage of the TOPSYS tools for programming parallel systems.

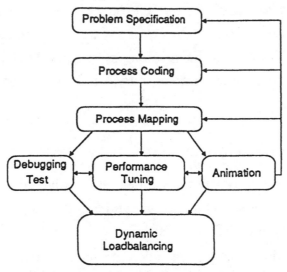

Fig. 1: Interactive TOPSYS methodology

The second goal of the TOPSYS project is motivated by the large number of different available parallel architectures. The range of parallel architectures varies from tightly coupled systems with shared memory and fine grain parallelism to loosely coupled distributed memory machines with coarse grain parallelism based on message passing. None of these proposed architectures became the "industry standard" during the previous decade. In contrary a lot of different architectures are in use and they differ with respect to the node processor, the node architecture (board) and the communication network. This fact gives the motivation to design the TOPSYS environment very portable, flexible and adaptable with respect to:

- the processor architecture of the node processor,
- the communication network and topology of the parallel machine,
- the programming language, the process model and the compiler to be supported,
- the operating system of different host workstations,
- and the tools, monitoring techniques and abstraction levels to be supported.

It is obvious, that the previous goal of the TOPSYS project can not be satisfied completely. But within the design of the tool environment, we strictly have tried to use a very hierarchical and modular design concept for supporting flexibility and adaptability. In addition, the extensive use of industry standards simplifies the portability of the TOPSYS environment to various different parallel architectures.

The last goal of TOPSYS concerns the implementation complexity and the interaction with other subsystems of a parallel architecture. The implementation complexity of the tool environment can be decreased by a strong integration with the other subsystems of a parallel computer without influencing the functionality and the performance of these subsystems.

Within the TOPSYS project we take into account the integration with the parallel architecture and the distributed operating system. This project goal will be reached by integration of monitoring and tool support into the parallel machine at different levels of abstraction; at the node processor level, the node architecture level, the topology (communication network) level and the operating system level. This integrated concept leads to a balance between implementation complexity, functionality and performance of all the subsystems of a parallel computer.

3. The Ideas and Design Concepts

The TOPSYS project is driven by some basic ideas and design concepts which will be explained in this chapter. It is obvious, that these ideas and design concepts have strong influence on the methodology of using the TOPSYS tools.

The first design decision was the selection of the granularity of parallelism and the corresponding process model. Although we concentrated during the implementation of the tool environment on coarse grain parallelism, we also made the overall conceptual design of TOPSYS appropriate for fine grain parallelism. The reason for the selection of coarse grain parallelism was the concentration on distributed memory machines within the project. Coarse grained programming concepts are at the actual state of technology more suitable and powerful for these types of parallel machines. To express the selected type of parallelism we decided to have a process model which is as close to sequential programming languages as possible. This design concept supports a programmer of sequential programs to upgrade with less efforts to the programming of parallel machines.

The implementation of this process model is the distributed operating system kernel MMK (Multiprocessor Multitasking Kernel) which offers dynamically created and deleted global objects and operations. The basics of the process model are communicating sequential processes where communication is done via mailboxes and synchronization via semaphores. The global objects and operations allow to create parallel programs without having in mind the physical topology of the parallel target computer.

The architecture of the TOPSYS tool environment was influenced mostly by the following design concepts. The first of them results from the experience that all tools for validation and analysis of parallel systems mentioned in the first chapter have one requirement in common; they need runtime information on the dynamic behaviour of the parallel execution. As everybody knows, this runtime information can be gathered by monitors. Therefore, one idea of the TOPSYS project is to implement all tools on top of a common distributed monitoring system [BLT90]. The advantage of this integrated design concept is, that the monitoring system has not to be changed when the functionality of the tools is extended. In addition, all tools will be used with a common monitoring environment. The second idea toward an integrated tool environment concerns the monitoring and instrumentation techniques itself. Different monitoring techniques can be used for collecting runtime information. The most famous monitoring techniques are simulation, software monitoring by source code instrumentation or object code instrumentation, hardware monitoring and hybrid monitoring. A well known problem in literature are the different influences on the parallel execution which are introduced by different instrumentation techniques. A still open question in the parallel world deals with the appropriate monitoring technique. Until now it is very hard to qualify and quantify the retardation and therefore the modification of the parallel execution introduced by different monitoring techniques. This fact gave the motivation for the integration and implementation of different monitoring techniques within the TOPSYS environment.

In the actual phase of the project we deal with object code instrumentation, hardware monitoring and hybrid monitoring. An important feature of our approach is, that the tools of the developement environment are independant of the type of monitor they actually use. Therefore the different monitor types offer the same functionality and can be replaced easily without modifying the tools. This also implies the usage of different monitor types across the several nodes of the parallel computer - a heterogeneous monitoring environment. This feature allows a flexible adaption of the TOPSYS tool environment to all application requirements with respect to program retardation. In addition, measurements of the program slow down when using different monitors within the TOPSYS project allow to qualify and quantify the appropriateness of the different instrumentation techniques. Figure 2 shows the integration concept explained in this paragraph.

All tools developed within the project allow to analyse the parallel execution at different levels of abstraction depending on the necessary level of detail and granularity. At the highest level (the system level) the programmer looks at the parallel system as a whole; he abstracts from the distinction into several processor nodes. The next view, the node level, focusses on single processor nodes and their interaction. Finally, at the finest level the programmer can analyse parallel constructs (MMK objects, C constructs) and the interaction and

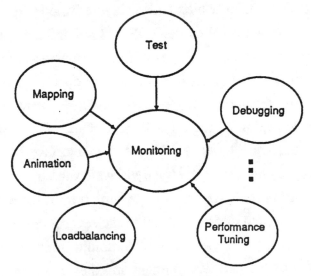

Fig. 2: Integration idea

communication of them. All objects, no matter whether they are MMK objects or C objects, are referred to at the source code level. This means the user of the tools refers all program objects by their names in the source program and the tool environment knows respectively checks the type and the location of these objects.

To support the interactive parallel design cycle illustrated in figure 1, all tools and monitors are running concurrently with the parallel application. In contrast to most other parallel development environments known in the field, the TOPSYS tools are used on-line and not in batch mode. Therefore the collection of the monitoring data on the dynamic behaviour of the parallel execution and the representation of these collected monitoring values is done during runtime of the parallel target system. This implies that all tools and monitors represent processes or tasks with respect to the terminology used within the MMK process model.

The last design decision mentioned here should be the support of so called network based host/target environments using industry standards. Most of the available parallel computers today are programmed in host/target environments where program developement (compilation etc.) is carried out on a sequential host workstation and the parallel program is executed on the target machine connected to the host via a local area network. TOPSYS was designed to support these kinds of host/target environments and different parts of the tool environment are distributed between the host and the target. The portability and adaptability of TOPSYS to different network based host/target environments is simplyfied by the use of the following industry standards: within the project we use C and C++ as implementation language, UNIX as host operating system, X-windows as graphics interface, TCP/IP as network protocol and COFF as symbol table format.

4. The TOPSYS Hierarchical Tool Model

A major result of the research work on the design concepts described in the previous chapter of this paper was the definition of a hierarchical layered model for tool environments like TOPSYS. This layered approach is called the TOPSYS hierarchical tool model and is illustrated in figure 3. The figure shows the interfaces defined between the several subsystems of the development environment. The hierarchical model results mainly from the idea to use all tools together with all monitoring techniques, regardless of the implementation of the corresponding partner. Apart from the definition of some smaller interfaces, the integration idea has lead to the definition of two important interfaces - the monitor interface and the tool interface. The monitor interface is a command driven interface via which the upper layers of the tool model request the different monitors to deliver runtime information of the processor nodes. The monitors are duplicated and adapted or downloaded to the several processor nodes of the parallel target machine. All monitor types of this distributed monitoring system offer the same functionality to the upper layers of the tool environment and they are therefore replaceable by each

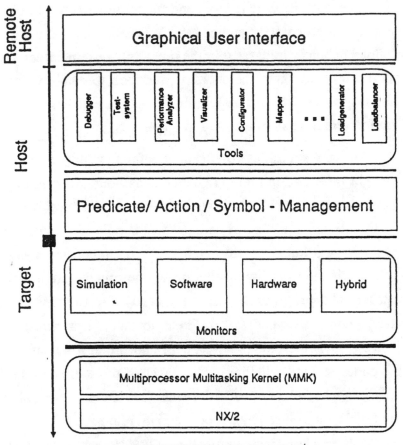

Fig. 3: TOPSYS hierarchical tool model

other. The monitor interface is based on virtual addresses and internal process identifiers of the MMK kernel, i.e. all objects within the commands of the monitor interface are referred to by their virtual address or process identifier.

In contrary to this, the tool interface offers the abstraction level of the source program. All objects of this interface are referred to by their names in the source program, e.g. variable names, task names, etc. The tool interface is a procedural interface. Via this interface all tools can request runtime information about the dynamic behaviour of the parallel execution at the abstraction level of the source program. The advantage of the definition of this interface is the extendability of the tools functionality without a modification of the lower layers. Within the actual phase of the TOPSYS project we have developed several tools with the following functionality based on the tool interface:

- The parallel debugging and test system DETOP for validating parallel programs at the source level.
- A performance analyzer called PATOP for performance tuning and performance measurement of parallel systems.
- The visualization tool VISTOP for dynamic graphical animation of parallel executions.

229

- Interactive configurators, load generators and mapping tools for quick experimentations with different process/processor mappings (SAMTOP).
- The dynamic load balancer integrated in the operating system kernel MMK uses the runtime information collected via the monitor interface to establish more efficinet process/processor mappings. The remapping during runtime is based on a paging oriented process migration scheme explained in [Tri90].

The mentioned tools are examples for using the functionality of the monitor and tool interfaces to get insight information on the dynamic behaviour of a running parallel program. It is relatively easy to create new tools with new functionalities based on the runtime information offerd by the tool interface system calls. Examples are more application oriented animation tools, as they are known from batch mode oriented development environments. Another important issue is the usability of all tools at one time based on one program state of the parallel execution. The programmer can very easily (by moving the mouse from one window to another) switch between the different tools. The transformation between the abstraction level of the tool interface (source code) and the abstraction level of the monitor interface (machine code) is done within a central layer of the tool environment. This layer is responsible for the management of specified events, actions and symbol table objects. The services offered by this layer are used by all tools and monitors.

As most of the tools implemented within the TOPSYS project are interactive tools, an important part of the project is the development of appropriate and easy to use user interfaces. All tools of the tool environment have a graphic and menue driven user interface with the same look and feel, i.e. with the same philosopy of usage. For the implementation of this common graphic user interface a specific graphics library on top of X-windows was developed, which is used by all tools of the TOPSYS project. As already mentioned, we have tried to integrate the tool environment into well known network based host/target environments. Therefore the several layers of the tool model run on different machines. The distributed monitor system MONICA and the operating system kernel MMK are implemented on each processor node of the parallel target system. The central transformation layer and the tools are implemented on the host which is at least logically connected to each processor node of the target system. The graphic interfaces can run on each X-window based workstation connected via a local area network to the host computer. This network based approach makes the TOPSYS functionality available to each programmer within the local area network.

5. State of the TOPSYS project

The TOPSYS project started in 1986 after some evaluations and preliminary experiments in the field of development tools for sequential programs. Till the end of 1989 we have invested about 15 man years into the TOPSYS project. The project was subdivided into four phases. Apart from the integration of more and more tools (we started with the parallel debugger) the four phases of this project are mainly characterized by implementations for different target systems and host computers. The four phases are illustrated together with the different host/target configurations in figure 4.

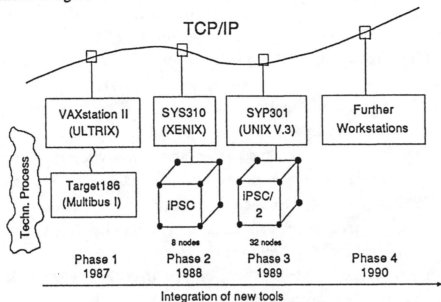

Fig. 4: Phases of the TOPSYS project

In phase one of the project starting from the hierarchical tool model, we implemented a tool environment for bus based (Multibus I, Multibus II) microcomputer systems. The parallel programs were executed in this phase in a single processor multitasking environment which was implemented on top of a single processor version of MMK, the so called RMK (Realtime Multitasking Kernel) [Bem87]. The target system during this phase was a Multibus based 80186 microcomputer system which was used mainly for realtime applications. The first tool developed in this phase was the high level debugger REALBUG based on optional software and hardware monitors [Bem86].

In phase two the tool environment was ported and adapted to the first generation hypercube system iPSC/1 [Bem89]. The parallel computer used for this implementation consists of 8 processor nodes based on the 16-bit processor 80286. The hypercube communication network used a conventional store-and-foreward communication protocol. A typical feature of the environment developed in phase two was the static processor view. The tools focussed at one time only on one processor and the user has to keep in mind the number of physical processor nodes. For getting information from another processor the programmer has to switch between processor nodes.

In phase three we extended the static view to a more dynamic and global one. The tools offer a global view on all objects available in the parallel target machine. Apart from this new feature we integrated in phase 3 the process migration component for the dynamic load balancer into the MMK operating system kernel. The target system in phase 3 is a second generation hypercube iPSC/2 with 32 processor nodes and 2 I/O nodes based on the 32-bit processor family iAPX386/387. The communication protocol between the processor nodes of this machine is no longer the store-and-forward scheme. A new modification of the the wormhole routing protocol, the so called direct connect technology is used in this type of parallel machine. A first integration of all the subsystems of the TOPSYS tool environment on the iPSC/2 shown in figure 3 was finished in late 1989. The schedule of phases one and two can be found in figure 4.

Altough we tried to use the several subsystems of the TOPSYS environment as early as possible for application programming, until now only a few experiences in using the tool environment are available. Most of the experiences in using the system result from the test and integration phase. In phase four, which is scheduled for 1990, we will extensively study the adequacy of TOPSYS for the parallelization of different application programs. The usage of the tools is done in cooperation with application people from industry and university. This kind of cooperation is supported at Technical University Munich since January 1990 by the special research grant SFB 342 "Methods and Tools for Using Parallel Architectures" funded by the German Science Foundation. Within this research grant, applications in the fields of VLSI design tools, data bases and numerical algorithms are parallelized, using the TOPSYS environment.

The application of the TOPSYS environment within these cooperations is the best way for further validation of the tools. Apart from the application of the TOPSYS tools, in phase four, we investigate some effort in performance tuning of the tool environment and porting on other architectures. An already ongoing work is the performance measurement of the different monitor implementations (hardware, software, hybrid) with respect to program retardation.

6. A First Application of the TOPSYS Environment

A first attempt of using TOPSYS for parallelization of a complex application program already has been commenced in mid 1989 [BKL90]. The application program parallelized is called GORDIAN and represents an automatic placement algorithm for VLSI designs. The base of the GORDIAN package is a very large sparse linear equations system. The order of the matrices produced by the placement algorithm is around 200000. Therefore the parallelization of this application is a realistic example and a good real world test for the TOPSYS tools. The parallelization of GORDIAN was done in cooperation with the Department of Electrical Engineering at Technical University of Munich. The solving of the linear equations system is done using a conjugent gradient algorithm. The matrix is partitioned by columns. Each node holds a block of subsequent columns. Only nonzero elements do consume memory. For each nonzero element its value and its row index are stored. The parallel programming of the solver was done using the system calls and the parallel constructs offered by the operating system kernel MMK.

For performance tuning the parallel version of the conjugent gradient linear equation solver was analyzed using the performance analyzer PATOP. Performance parameters measured by PATOP include CPU idle times on each node and the times processes spent waiting for messages. We also observed the dynamic behaviour of communication. Results measured for the computation of the inner product are shown on the PATOP screen dump displayed in figure 5. The PATOP measurements show a high CPU utilization (see upper window in the screen dump). The CPU idle time is below 5% (see lower window). This discussion shows how the TOPSYS tools can be used to get more usefull insights into the dynamic behaviour of parallel programs.

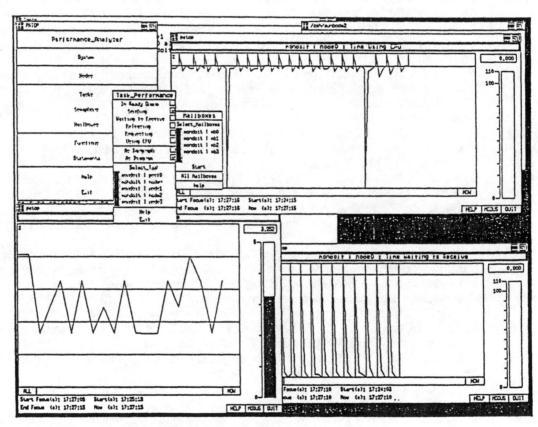

Fig. 5: PATOP screen dump

7. Conclusions

In conclusion we believe that the first experiences in using the tool environment have demonstrated the adequacy of integrated approaches like TOPSYS. An enormous increase in programmer productivity can be the consequence of using the tools within the proposed methodology framework. Future evaluation research on using TOPSYS for large real world problems has to confirm this statement.

Bibliography

[Art89]   Y. Artsy, R. Finkel: Designing a Process Migration Facility: The Charlotte Experience; IEEE Computer, Sept. 1989, p. 47 - 56

[Bai83]   F. Baiardi, N. De Francesco: Development of a Debugger for a Concurrent Language; Proc. SIG-PLAN Symp. on HLL-Deb.; Aug. 1983; p. 81 - 90

[Bem86]   T. Bemmerl: Realtime High Level Debugging in Host/ Target Environments; Proceedings of EURO-MICRO Symp. 1986, Venice, p. 387-400

[Bem87]   T. Bemmerl, G. Schöder: A portable Realtime Multitasking Kernel for Embedded Microprocessor Systems; Proceedings of EUROMICRO Symp. 1987, Porths-mouth, p. 181 - 188

[Bem88]   T. Bemmerl: An Integrated and Portable Tool Environment for Parallel Computers; Proc. of IEEE Int. Conf. on Parallel Processing, St. Charles, USA, Aug. 1988, p. 50-53

[Bem89]   T. Bemmerl, R. Gebhart, P. Ginzinger, T. Ludwig: A Parallel Development Environment for the iPSC Hypercube; 1st European Hypercube Workshop, Oct. 1989, Rennes, France

[BeL90]   T. Bemmerl, T. Ludwig: MMK - A Distributed Operating System Kernel with Integrated Dynamic Loadbalancing; CONPAR 90 - VAPP IV, Sept. 1990, Zürich, Switzerland

[BLT90]   T. Bemmerl, R. Lindhof, T. Treml: The Distributed Monitor System of TOPSYS; CONPAR 90 - VAPP IV, Sept. 1990, Zürich, Switzerland

[BHL90]   T. Bemmerl, O. Hansen, T. Ludwig: PATOP for Performance Tuning of Parallel Programs; CON-PAR 90 - VAPP IV, Sept. 1990, Zürich, Switzerland

[BKL90]   T. Bemmerl, J. Kremenek, P. Luksch: Parallelisierung eines Plazierungsverfahrens für den VLSI-Entwurf auf einem Multiprozessorsystem mit verteiltem Speicher; ITG/GI-Workshop, Jan. 1990, Arnoldsheim, FRG

[Bur88]   H. Burkhart, R. Millen: Techniken und Werkzeuge der Programmbeobachtung am Beispiel eines Modula-2 Monitorsystems; Informatik Forschung und Entwicklung, 3, 1988, p. 6 - 21

[Gar84] Garcia-Molina: Debugging a Distributed Computing System; IEEE Trans. on SWE, Vol SE-10, No. 2, p. 210 - 219, 1984

[Gil88]   W.K. Giloi: The Suprenum Architecture; CONPAR 88, Sept. 88, Manchester, UK

[Gre86]   F. Gregoretti, F. Maddaleno, M. Zamboni: Monitoring Tools for Multimicroprocessors; EUROMI-CRO 86, p. 409 - 416, Venice, Italy

[Gua89]   V.A. Guarna, D. Gannon, D. Jablonowski, A.D. Malony, Y. Gaur: Faust: An Integrated Environment for Parallel Programming; IEEE Software, July 1989, p. 20 - 26

[Hab88]   D. Haban, D. Wybranietz: A Tool for Measuring and Monitoring Distributed Systems during Operation; GI/ITG Tagung, Organisation und Betrieb von Rechensystemen, Paderborn, März 1988, p. 308 - 323

[Hof87]   R. Hofmann, R. Klar, N. Luttenberger, B. Mohr: ZÄHLMONITOR 4: Ein Monitorsystem für das Hardware- und Hybrid-Monitoring von Multiprozessor- und Multicomputer-Systemen; Messung und Modellierung von Rechensystemen, Erlangen, IFB, 1987, p. 79 - 99

[Jes89]   C. Jesshope: Large Scale Concurrent Computations: Systems and Software; University of Southampton, Techn. Report, 1989

[Laz86]   B. Lazzerini, C.A. Prete: DISEB: An Interactive High-Level Debugging System for a Multi-Microprocessor System; EUROMICRO 86, p. 401 - 408

[Leh89]   T. Lehr, Z. Segall, D.F. Vrsalowic, E. Caplan, A.L. Chung, C.E. Fineman: Visualizing Performance Debugging; IEEE Computer, Oct. 1989, p. 38 - 51

[Lik89]   K. Li, R. Schäfer: A Hypercube Shared Virtual Memory System; IEEE Parallel Processing Conf., Aug. 1989, St. Charles, USA, p. I/125 - 132

[Mae86]   E. Maehle, K. Moritzen, K. Wirl: Fault-Tolerant Hardware Configuration Management on the Multi-proces- sor System DIRMU 25; CONPAR 86, Lecture Notes on Computer Science, 1986, p. 190 - 197

[Mil89]   B. Miller, T. LeBlanc: Workshop on Parallel and Distributed Debugging; Univ. of Wisconsin, May 1989

[Nie81]   J. Nievergelt, B. Plattner: Monitoring Program Execution: A Survey; IEEE Computer, Nov. 1981, p. 105 - 114

[Pap87]   Papadopoulos: The New Dataflow Architecture Beeing Built at MIT; Proceedings of MIT-ZTI-Symp. on "Very High Parallel Architectures", Now. 1987

[Tri90]   S. Tritscher: Dynamischer Lastausgleich auf dem iPSC/2 mittels Prozeßmigration; Diplomarbeit, TU-München, 15. Jan. 1990

234

Parallax:
A Tool for Parallel
Program Scheduling

Ted Lewis
Oregon Advanced Computing Institute, Oregon State University
Hesham El-Rewini
University of Nebraska at Omaha

//// Parallax incorporates seven scheduling heuristics, providing an effective way for developers to find out how the schedulers affect program performance on various parallel architectures.

The lack of good programming tools and techniques is the most significant problem facing parallel computing. Programmers especially need a way to allocate parallel tasks to the processors of a particular machine and to order them in time so that the program completes as quickly as possible. This so-called scheduling problem is computationally intensive, and its complexity rises even further given such real-world factors as process initiation time, message initiation time, transmission delay time, and time-complexity of the problem being solved.[1-4]

Traditional scheduling heuristics reduce a problem's complexity by making simplifying assumptions that ignore most of the critical features needed to model modern parallel systems.[3] More recent heuristics handle real-world factors such as link contention, network transmission speeds, and processor topology (some communication delays no longer depend on the distance between source and destination nodes, but some do).[2] But although there have been many scheduling heuristics, there have been few comparisons of their quality and speed.

Our scheduling tool, called Parallax, incorporates seven traditional and nontraditional scheduling heuristics and lets developers compare their performance for real applications on real parallel machines.[2] Of the seven heuristics, two simple ones consider only task execution time, two consider both task execution and message-passing delay times, two use task duplication to reduce communication delay, and one considers communication delays, task execution time, and target machine characteristics such as interconnection network topology and overhead due to message-passing and process creation.

Reprinted from *IEEE Parallel & Distributed Technology*, vol. 1, no. 2, May 1993, pp. 62–72.

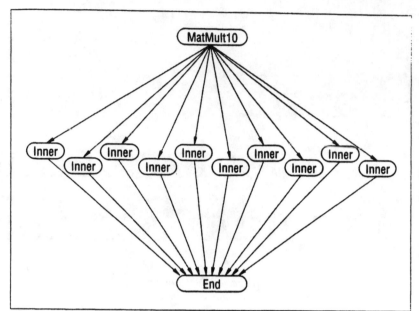

Figure 1. Task graph for SIMD matrix multiply *Ax*.

Parallax's ability to help answer "what if" questions makes it a valuable design tool, but it is not a programming environment. Developers must provide the input program as a task graph and estimate the tasks' execution times (or obtain them by running the program). They also must express the target machine as an interconnection topology graph (with annotations for processing and message speeds). Parallax then provides Gantt chart schedules, speedup graphs, processor and communication use/efficiency charts, and an animated display of the simulated running program to help developers evaluate the differences among the heuristics.

The scheduling problem

A parallel program is a collection of separate cooperating and communicating modules called *tasks*. A task is a locus of control through a sequential segment of code. Tasks can execute in sequence or at the same time on two or more separate processors.

The program is represented by an acyclic directed graph called a *task graph*. There is a directed edge *(i,j)* between tasks *i* and *j* if *j* cannot execute until *i* completes. Such dependencies are due to data or control. In either case, the task graph establishes a precedence relation among all tasks.

Figure 1 shows a task graph for a program that multiplies a 10-element column vector *x* by a square 10×10 matrix using parallel inner products. First, the rows of the square matrix are sent along with the column vector to each inner product process. All 10 inner products are then computed simultaneously, and the results are returned.

Each node of the task graph is named and given an instruction count, which is converted into an estimated execution time. Each arc is labeled with the size of data to be passed between tasks. Once the target machine is known, this size estimate is converted into a communication delay: If two communicating tasks are scheduled onto the same processor, the communication delay is zero; otherwise, the delay equals the message startup time, plus the data size divided by the transfer rate. These estimates are unknown at design time. So what is the effect of communication delay versus execution time

on the program's overall execution time? Parallax was designed to answer this and similar questions.

Even though the task graph in Figure 1 is for an extremely simple program, it is not clear how to arrange the tasks so that the program will run in the shortest time. When ten processors are available we might be tempted to allocate one task to each, but this does not account for communication overhead. Can the program run faster if we place two rows on each processor?

And what do we do when we have fewer processors than tasks? The number of processors is limited, yet even simple problems such as matrix multiplication tend to grow beyond the bounds of processor space. What is an optimal schedule for the task graph in Figure 1 when only eight processors are available?

The Gantt chart in Figure 2a shows a schedule for an eight-processor system arranged as a hypercube; time is on the horizontal axis, and processor space is on the vertical axis. A horizontal bar indicates the allocation and ordering of tasks (when and where each task should execute). The figure shows an elapsed time of 670 μsec to perform the multiplication, assuming that the root and ending nodes each take 100 μsec, and that each inner product node takes 200 μsec. The size of the input arcs is 100 characters, and the size of the output arcs is four characters. The scheduler computes these numbers based on user-supplied characteristics of the target machine (flops ratings, transmission times, and startup times for both processes and messages).

The automatic scheduler that produced Figure 2a placed inner product tasks on different processors until all were allocated, and then placed two tasks each on processors 0 and 1. The shaded areas show communi-

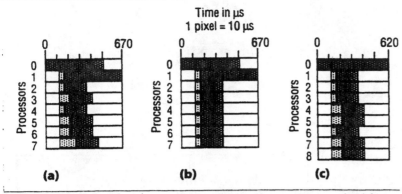

Time in µs
1 pixel = 10 µs

(a) (b) (c)

Figure 2. Schedule for Figure 1 on an eight-processor hypercube (a), on a fully connected eight-processor system (b), and on a nine-processor mesh system (c).

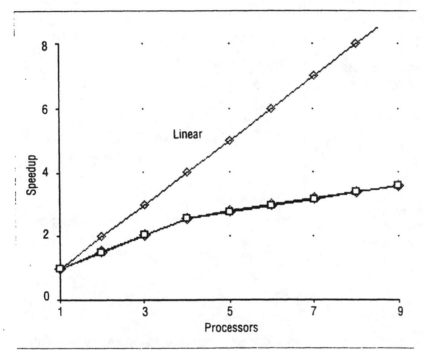

Figure 3. Speedup graph for Figure 1 and nine-processor mesh system.

cation delays, while the white areas indicate idle processors. A process' start time is dictated by the communication delay, which is a function of the number of hops from one processor to another along the hypercube interconnection.

Now consider two different machines: One is identical to the eight-processor hypercube, except that each processor is linked to all other processors; the other is a 3×3 mesh. If we schedule the program from Figure 1 onto these two machines, we get two different schedules (see Figure 2b and c). The fully connected machine has no hop delays, but its elapsed time is the same as the hypercube's. In this limited case, a fully connected system is no faster than a hypercube.

The schedule for the 3×3 mesh runs slightly faster because it uses one more processor (to establish the

mesh), but we gain little if any speed if we add still more processors (see Figure 3). Ten processors might further reduce elapsed time, but the next mesh size is 16 processors (4×4). So the target machine's interconnection network affects the schedule (and, in turn, the running program): A hypercube interconnection can lead to a different Gantt schedule than a fully connected machine, a mesh, or even another hypercube (because of overhead differences). Thus, the scheduling heuristic needs to include the target machine's characteristics.

We model the target machine as a graph whose nodes represent an arbitrary number of processors and whose edges represent an interconnection topology. A processor can execute a task and communicate with another processor at the same time, a feature used by the insertion scheduling heuristic (discussed later) to overlap task execution with message-sending. All processors are similar; that is, they all take the same time to execute an instruction (processor speed), transfer data, start a message, and start a process. These characteristics, along with the graph's topology, are used to shape a schedule. Figure 4 shows Parallax's diagram of a hypercube, and the dialog box used to specify its characteristics; Parallax used these numbers to build the schedules in Figure 2.

OPTIMAL SCHEDULING ALGORITHMS

The general problem of scheduling parallel program tasks on multiprocessor systems is NP-complete, and there are few polynomial-time scheduling algorithms, even when we severely restrict the program task graph and the target machine model. Polynomial algorithms are possible in three cases: when the task graph is a tree, when the task graph is an interval order, and when only two processors are available. All tasks are assumed to have the same execution time, and communication between tasks is not considered. (All the polynomial algorithms and NP-completeness proofs in this section are well-established results.[5])

When the task graph is a tree and all tasks execute in one time unit, Hu's linear algorithm uses a level number — the length of the longest path from the task node to the ending node — as a priority number.[6] Also, Papadimitriou and Yannakakis have shown that interval-ordered tasks can be scheduled in linear time on an arbitrary number of processors; Coffman and Graham have given a polynomial algorithm for developing an optimal-length schedule for an arbitrary task graph on a two-processor system; and Sethi has proposed a more efficient algorithm that provides the same schedule.[2, 7]

Linear speedup generally does not occur in a multiprocessor system because adding processors increases interprocessor communication. Prastein proved that by accounting for communication — even when the execution time for all tasks is identical and equal to the communication cost between any pair of processors — the problem of scheduling an arbitrary precedence program graph on two processors is NP-complete, as is scheduling a tree-structured program onto arbitrarily many processors.[7]

NEAR-OPTIMAL SCHEDULING SOLUTIONS

The scheduling problem is NP-complete even when the target machine is fully connected and no communication is considered among tasks in the task graph (see Table 1). Its complexity rises further when we consider the real world, in which

- tasks can have different execution times,
- communication links between tasks can consume variable amounts of communication time,
- communication links can be shared, giving rise to contention for the links, and
- the network topology might influence the schedule due to multiple-hop links or missing links.

The computational complexity of optimal solutions has created a need for a simplified suboptimal approach. Recent research has emphasized heuristic approaches, which produce a "near-optimal" solution in less than exponential time.[2, 7, 8] One heuristic is considered better than another if its solutions are closer to optimal more often, or if it takes less time to obtain a near-optimal solution. Parallax incorporates seven heuristics, so a developer can quickly determine the "best" from among several near-optimal schedules.

LIST SCHEDULING

List scheduling is the dominant method of scheduling static task graphs.[2,7,8] (Other recent approximation

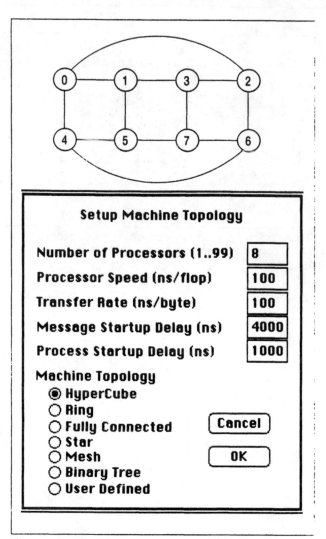

Figure 4. Hypercube target machine and its characteristics.

Table 1. Scheduling problem complexity for a fully connected target machine with no task communication.

TASK GRAPH	TASK EXECUTION TIME	NO. OF PROCESSORS	COMPLEXITY
Tree	Identical	Arbitrary	$O(n)$
Arbitrary	Identical	2	$O(n^2)$
Arbitrary	Identical	Arbitrary	NP-complete
Arbitrary	1 or 2 time units	≥ 2	NP-complete
Arbitrary	Arbitrary	Arbitrary	NP-complete

approaches have not yet been compared to list scheduling.) In list scheduling, each task graph node is assigned a priority, and a list of nodes is constructed in order of decreasing priority. Whenever a processor is available, a ready node with the highest priority is selected from the

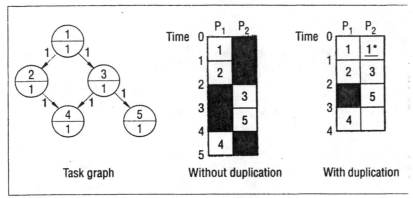

Figure 5. Task duplication versus nonduplication.

list and assigned to the processor. If more than one node has the same priority, a node is selected randomly.

List schedulers differ only in how they assign priorities, but this results in different schedules because nodes are selected in a different order. Adam, Chandy, and Dickson suggest that using a level number as node priority is the nearest solution to optimal.[9] More recent work by Lee and colleagues has added earliest-task-first and earliest-ready-task variants to the family of list heuristics. Yang and Gerasoulis have simplified list scheduling further by scheduling the critical path through the graph.[10] This reduces the heuristic's time complexity, but with some decrease in schedule quality. The basic list scheduling heuristic is

```
begin
    Assign priorities to tasks
    repeat
        Select a task
        Select a processor to run the task
        Assign the task to the processor
    until all tasks are scheduled
end
```

In all cases, the developer must examine the results and determine the best schedule. Parallax helps developers do just that by rapidly generating schedules and letting developers ask "what if" questions such as, "What if the target machine or the communication delays change?"

Heuristics in Parallax

Although Parallax's heuristics all schedule the highest priority task first, they use different techniques to assign priorities to tasks and tasks to processors. They also use different assumptions regarding the task graph parameters or the target machine interconnection. Only the mapping heuristic (discussed below) considers processor interconnection topology; all others assume a fully connected network. All the heuristics produce a Gantt chart schedule, speedup graph, use/efficiency graphs, and so on.

The Parallax heuristics represent the broad spectrum of schedulers proposed over the past 20 years, and a cross section of current parallel programming schedulers. The heuristics range from simple to polynomial complexity in terms of the number of tasks to schedule. The simple heuristics find a schedule in time $O(n)$, while the most complex ones take $O(n^4)$. Early schedulers ignore communication delays.[6, 11] Later heuristics consider communication delays, but not processor topology or link contention.[3] The mapping heuristic minimizes elapsed runtime while considering network interconnection topology and link contention. Although faster heuristics have since been proposed, the schedule quality has not changed significantly.

Hu's heuristic
This heuristic assumes no communication delay. It uses a level number (again, the longest path from the task node to the ending node) to set task priorities. Tasks are executed highest level first, then level by level. Only the task execution times, not the communication delays, are counted in the longest path.

Modified Hu's heuristic
Task selection remains the same, but the communication delay is included in computing a task's start time when selecting a processor. The modified heuristic tries to reduce communication delay by considering the processors containing the node's immediate predecessors, and then trying to place the message source and destination tasks in the same processor.

Yu's heuristic
This heuristic assumes that tasks have equal execution time, and it selects the best one of the processors that will be ready within the next execution time unit. The average node size in the graph is a substitute for all node sizes.

Kruatrachue's insertion scheduling heuristic
This heuristic tries to fill in idle slots created by communication delays. It assumes that a processor can execute a task while it receives a message, which complicates the scheduling problem but offers a more realistic result. Since the longest path through the task graph reflects both execution and communication delay times, adding processors can increase the time needed to com-

Related work

Parallax was inspired by early work on Poker, Prep-P, Hypertool, and Polylith, among others.[1-3] Parallax and Hypertool are especially similar, although they grew out of different investigations. Like Parallax, Hypertool uses list scheduling techniques based on critical path analysis. Hypertool takes as its input a C program and constructs a task graph that is analyzed and then scheduled onto a hypercube. Parallax takes as its input a design in the form of a hierarchical dataflow graph, and schedules a flattened equivalent of the graph onto an arbitrary interconnected target machine. Hypertool requires that the program be written before it can be analyzed, while Parallax does not.

More recently, Pyrros improved the time complexity of heuristics based on critical path scheduling.[4] The Pyrros schedules require considerably less time to compute than Parallax's, but Parallax does not incorporate these newer heuristics because they do not differ largely in quality. We are mainly concerned with qualitative differences: We want to know which heuristics work best for restricted classes of applications.

Our work is predominantly aimed at static scheduling. That is, we assume that the task graph is known beforehand and does not change during computation. This limits our results to graphs without branches and loops, but such graphs are adequate to model large-grain dataflow programs.[5] Thus, this work is not related to the vast literature on dynamic load balancing in parallel and distributed computing.[6]

Our work also has little to do with mapping algorithms.[7,8] Pure mapping ignores the ordering of tasks, which increases the complexity of the scheduling heuristics. A schedule gives a mapping, but it also gives an ordering that minimizes the execution time of the entire task graph.

Finally, although we can characterize Parallax's heuristics by time-complexity analysis, our main goal is to find what works in practice rather than to advance the state of theory of scheduling heuristics. We leave the analysis of these heuristics to others.

REFERENCES

1. M.Y. Wu and D.D. Gajski, "Hypertool: A Programming Aid for Message-Passing Systems," *IEEE Trans. Parallel and Distributed Systems*, Vol. 1, No. 3, July 1990, pp. 101-119.

2. J. Purtilo, D. Reed, and D. Grunwald, "Environments for Prototyping Parallel Algorithms," *Proc. 1987 Int'l Conf. Parallel Processing*, Pennsylvania State Univ. Press, University Park, Penn., 1987.

3. L. Snyder and D. Socha, "Poker on the Cosmic Cube: The First Retargetable Parallel Programming Language and Environment," *Proc. 1986 Int'l Conf. Parallel Processing*, IEEE Computer Society Press, Los Alamitos, Calif., 1986, pp. 628-635.

4. T. Yang and A. Gersoulis, "Pyrros: Static Task Scheduling and Code Generation for Message-Passing Multiprocessors," *Proc. 6th ACM Int'l Conf. Supercomputing*, ACM Press, New York, 1992, pp. 428-443.

5. R.G. Babb, "Parallel Processing with Large-Grain Dataflow Techniques," *Computer*, Vol. 17, No. 7, July 1984, pp. 55-61.

6. T. Casavant and J.A. Kuhl, "Taxonomy of Scheduling in General-Purpose Distributed-Computing Systems," *IEEE Trans. Software Engineering*, Vol. SE-14, No. 2, Feb. 1988.

7. F. Berman and L. Snyder, "On Mapping Parallel Algorithms to Parallel Architectures," *J. Parallel and Distributed Computing*, Vol. 4, 1987, pp. 439.

8. V.M. Lo et al., "Oregami: Software Tools for Mapping Parallel Computations to Parallel Architectures," *Proc. 1990 Int'l Conf. Parallel Processing*, Aug 1990, pp. 77-88.

plete all tasks, often resulting in a system that is even slower than a sequential processor.[3]

Duplication scheduling heuristics

Instead of transmitting results from one processor to others, this heuristic duplicates the calculation on all processors that need the result. Some processors do exactly the same thing on exactly the same data, but in a different location, essentially trading communication delay time for memory space.

Consider the task graph and two Gantt charts in Figure 5. Task 1 is duplicated to run on both P_1 and P_2, which decreases the starting time of task 3 on P_2 and lets tasks 4 and 5 start sooner. This is the slowest heuristic, with $O(n^4)$ time complexity, but the schedule quality is usually good. Another version of this algorithm restricts the duplication process to the immediate predecessors causing the communication delay, which lowers the time complexity to $O(n^2)$ but can also lower the schedule quality. Parallax incorporates both versions.[3]

Mapping heuristic

This is a modified list-scheduling technique that accounts for communication delays due to network topology. It tries to minimize delays in multiple-hop networks by placing communicating tasks as close to one another as possible. The heuristic uses each node's level in the task graph as its priority. If two nodes have the same priority, the heuristic selects the node with the most immediate successors; if this does not break the tie, it selects a node at random. When a task is ready, the heuristic selects a processor for it such that the task could not finish earlier on any other processor; in making this selection, the heuristic considers processor speed, interconnection topology, and contention. The algorithm then allocates the task to the processor. When the task is done, the heuristic modifies the status of the task's immediate successors, decreasing by one the number of conditions preventing the successors from running. A successor node can be scheduled when it has no more conditions.

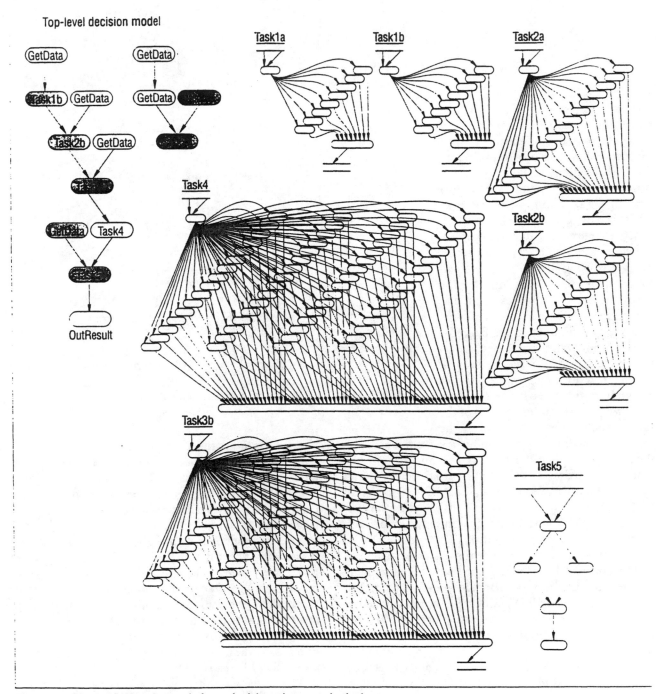

Figure 6. Hierarchical task graph for a decision-theory calculation.

Two delays contribute to the communication delay: the time delay incurred in transmitting data over an empty route, and the queuing delay (contention) due to multiple messages sent through the same route. The heuristic computes the contention delay for each processor via a routing table that has contention information indexed by, and containing one entry for, each other processor. Each entry has three parts: the number of hops, the preferred outgoing line to use for that destination, and the queuing delay due to contention.[2]

Some parallel applications

Let's look at the impact of heuristic quality and speed on a large application. Figure 6 shows the task graph of a decision-theory model for a manufacturing application; the ovals are tasks, and the double bars are storage elements. The task graph is hierarchical because some of the top-level tasks (the shaded tasks: 1a, 1b, 2a, 2b, 3b, and 4) are decomposed into data-parallel graphs. The decomposed graphs show data parallelism of 8, 16, and 64 processes, for a total of 176 tasks.

This application appears to have enormous parallelism, but can this parallelism be exploited on a certain machine? Because of the problem's 64-way parallelism, let's use a 64-processor iWarp machine (see Figure 7) with the same timing characteristics as the hypercube in Figure 4.

We encounter the first limitation of list scheduling when we analyze the task graph using all of Parallax's scheduling heuristics. The duplication heuristics are too complex in time to complete a schedule in less than eight hours, so we eliminate them from the comparison, even though they generally produce the shortest elapsed time.

We next evaluate the effects of scheduling with and without accounting for the mesh connectedness of the target machine; that is, we apply the insertion scheduling and mapping heuristics, which give different results (see Figures 8 and 9). Surprisingly, the simpler insertion scheduling heuristic gives better speedup than the mapping heuristic (2,120 µs versus 4,654 µs), but since it does not consider the interconnection topology, it is essentially limited to modeling a fully connected target machine. Thus, the mapping heuristic result is more realistic for this target machine.

The bottlenecks in both Gantt charts suggest opportunities to tune the application code even further. For example, in the schedule built by the insertion scheduling heuristic, the delay in processor 1 at time 750-1600 µs is due to communication prior to task 3b. In the mapping heuristic schedule, there is a similar communication bottleneck prior to task 4 on processor 1 (processor 0 is scheduled to run task 3b). The program might be redesigned to reduce waiting on communication, but Parallax does not suggest the remedy; it only shows the bottleneck.

The Gantt charts reveal a large degree of parallelism as expected, but the idle regions indicate that processor use is very low. In fact, in its eagerness to reduce communication, the mapping heuristic does not use all the processors, since they are too far apart in terms of communication hops across the mesh. So, what if we used a different machine? Running the task graph on a 64-processor hypercube with the same timing characteristics yields 3,725 ms using the mapping heuristic, and still yields 2,120 ms using the insertion scheduling

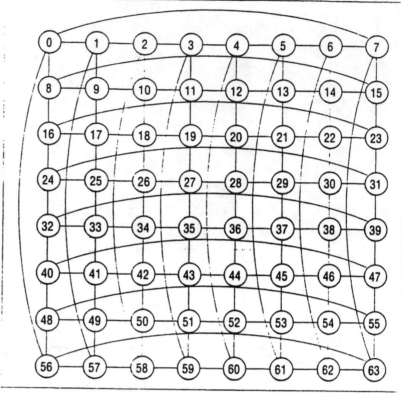

Figure 7. The Intel iWarp's 64-processor mesh topology.

heuristic, which ignores interconnection topology. A hypercube improves the speedup, but not above that of a fully connected machine. The reason: The mapping heuristic doubles-up processes on processors because communication delays become too expensive when multiple hops are considered.

The communication timing parameters for the 64-processor hypercube are very high compared with processor speeds; a machine with a higher ratio of processor speed to communication bandwidth might yield a different result. If we reduce the process startup and message startup times to zero and set the transmission rate to 1 ns/character, the mapping heuristic yields an elapsed time of 310 µs, versus 271 µs for the insertion scheduling heuristic.

This leads to another question: Can we compare the effects of changing the number of processors with the effects of these two scheduling heuristics? As it turns out, the speedup for the solutions in Figures 8 and 9 are far from linear, but the two schedules give comparable speedups versus the number of processors when the overhead for communication and process creation is negligible (see Figure 10). If we ignore communication overhead altogether, these two schedules merge into identical speedup graphs.

ANOTHER EXAMPLE

One goal of a good scheduling heuristic is to minimize the task graph's elapsed execution time. Another is to

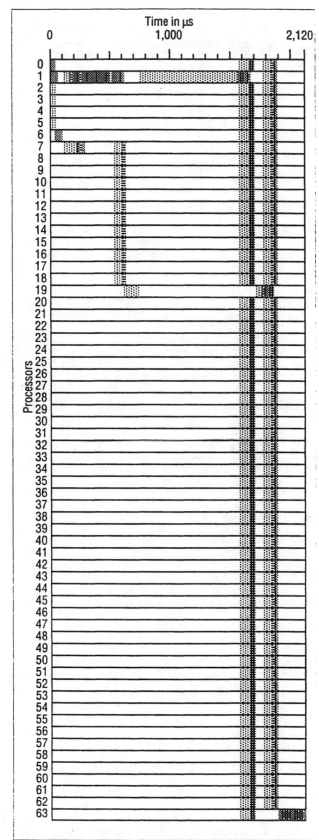

Figure 8. Schedule from the insertion scheduling heuristic for the task graph in Figure 6.

minimize the number of processors used. (Parallax is useful for such resource scheduling, but additional research is needed to combine the two goals.)

Let's consider the behavior of list scheduling heuristics on regular task graphs, such as those in signal processing applications. Figure 11 shows the task graph for a small systolic array calculation. Mapping this task graph's regular pattern onto a similar processor topology seems straightforward, but what if the graph is much larger than the number of processors? What if the target machine topology does not match?

Simulation of this task graph shows a wavefront moving from upper left to lower right tasks, as might be expected. The maximum number of concurrent tasks is three (because the diagonal wavefront moves down and across), so we can run the array on a three-processor system. However, all of Parallax's heuristics give a solution for four processors, except Yu's heuristic, which ignores communication delays and assumes that all tasks take identical time. In this application, all tasks take 500 operations, and communication overhead is negligible. Figure 12 shows the resulting schedule and compares it with a schedule from the insertion scheduling heuristic for a target machine with a 1-µs processor speed, 0.1-µs process and communication startup delays, and a 0.1-µs transfer rate. All target machine topologies show the same speedup for this application — 3,501 µs — because the overhead for communication and process creation is negligible.

Parallax is unique as far as we know. Pyrros and Hypertool are similar, but they do not allow "what if" analysis: They implement only one heuristic and do not provide the same variety of output reports.[4,10]

Simulations on ring, star, mesh, hypercube, and fully connected networks have shown that different scheduling heuristics give different results when the characteristics of the target machine are changed.[2] Applying Parallax to real-world problems has confirmed this intuitive result. Although we discussed only two examples here, the differences in schedulers are vast across many applications. Exploring these differences requires a tool like Parallax.

Our experience has also confirmed some simulation experiments:

- Communication-intensive applications call for scheduling heuristics that include communication delays (such as the insertion scheduling and mapping heuristics).

- Computation-intensive applications call for priority-scheduling heuristics that are insensitive to communication delays (such as the Yu and Hu heuristics).
- Performance is inversely proportional to the ratio of average communication to average task execution time,
- The effect of increasing the task graph's average arc degree increases as the number of processing elements increases.
- The average degree parameter is a good indicator of the amount of communication in the task graph.

Future research directions are clearly indicated: Most "real-world" parallel programs have loops and branches. But task graphs are acyclic, so they do not model loops and branches, which introduce indeterminism that static schedules cannot handle. Another research area is the modeling and representation of data parallelism (although the work reported here does not consider data parallelism at all). ▨

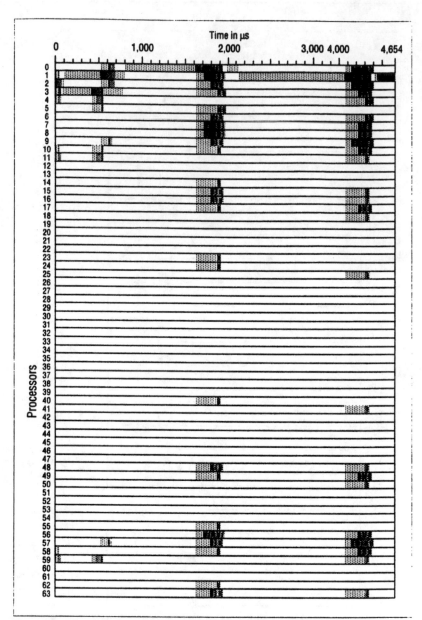

Figure 9. Schedule from the mapping heuristic for the task graph in Figure 6.

ACKNOWLEDGMENTS
Parallax is available from Oregon State University without charge to researchers via ftp at lynx.cs.orst.edu under directory /pub/almanac/ parallax. It was written by Rob Currey, with assistance from Inkyu Kim, Wan-Ju Su, Pat Fortner, Juli Chu, and Hesham El-Rewini. This work was partially supported by the Oregon Advanced Computing Institute.

REFERENCES

1. T. Casavant and J.A. Kuhl, "Taxonomy of Scheduling in General-Purpose Distributed-Computing Systems," *IEEE Trans. Software Engineering*, Vol. SE-14, No. 2, Feb. 1988.

2. H. El-Rewini and T.G. Lewis, "Scheduling Parallel Program Tasks onto Arbitrary Target Machines," *J. Parallel and Distributed Computing*, Vol. 9, No. 2, June 1990, pp. 138-153.

3. B. Kruatrachue, *Static Task Scheduling and Grain Packing in Parallel Processing Systems*, doctoral dissertation, Dept. of Computer Science, Oregon State Univ., 1987.

4. M.Y. Wu and D.D. Gajski, "Hypertool: A Programming Aid for Message-Passing Systems," *IEEE Trans. Parallel and Distributed Systems*, Vol. 1, No. 3, July 1990, pp. 101-119.

5. J. Purtilo, D. Reed, and D. Grunwald, "Environments for Prototyping Parallel Algorithms," *Proc. 1987 Int'l Conf. Parallel Processing*, Pennsylvania State Univ. Press, University Park, Penn., 1987.

6. T. Hu, "Parallel Sequencing and Assembly Line Problems," *Operations Research*, Vol. 9, 1961, pp. 841-848.

7. T.G. Lewis and H. El-Rewini, *Introduction to Parallel Computing*, Prentice-Hall, New York, 1992.

8. L. Snyder and D. Socha, "Poker on the Cosmic Cube: The First Retargetable Parallel-Programming Language and Environment," *Proc. 1986 Int'l Conf. Parallel Processing*, IEEE Computer Society Press, Los Alamitos, Calif., 1986, pp. 628-635.

9. T.L. Adam, K.M. Chandy, and J.R. Dickson, "A Comparison of List Schedules for Parallel-Processing Systems," *Comm. ACM*, Vol. 17, Dec. 1974, pp. 685-690.

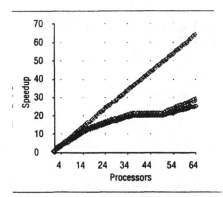

Figure 10. Speedup for the insertion scheduling and mapping heuristics, ignoring communication and process startup costs.

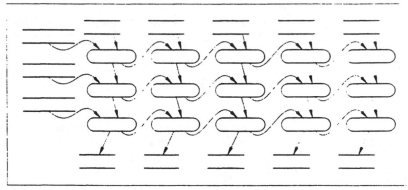

Figure 11. Task graph for a systolic array application.

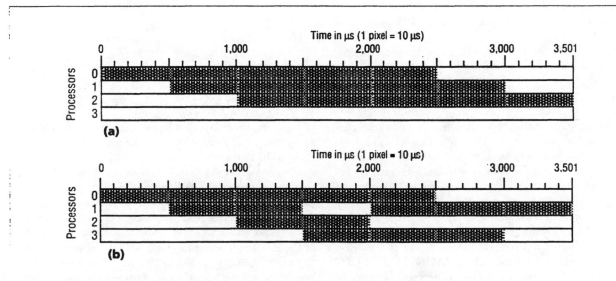

(a)

(b)

Figure 12. Schedules from the Yu (a) and insertion scheduling (b) heuristics for the task graph in Figure 11.

10. T. Yang and A. Gersoulis, "Pyrros: Static Task Scheduling and Code Generation for Message-Passing Multiprocessors," *Proc. 6th ACM Int'l Conf. Supercomputing*, ACM Press, New York, 1992, pp. 428-443.

11. W.H. Yu, *LU Decomposition on a Multiprocessing System with Communication Delay*, doctoral dissertation, Dept. of Electrical Eng. and Computer Sciences, Univ. of California at Berkeley, 1984.

Parafrase-2 : An Environment for Parallelizing, Partitioning, Synchronizing, and Scheduling Programs on Multiprocessors *

Constantine D. Polychronopoulos   Milind Girkar

Mohammad Reza Haghighat   Chia Ling Lee   Bruce Leung

Dale Schouten

Center for Supercomputing Research and Development
University of Illinois at Urbana-Champaign
Urbana, IL 61801/USA

ABSTRACT

Parafrase-2 is a multilingual vectorizing/parallelizing compiler implemented as a source to source code restructurer. This paper discusses the organization of Parafrase-2 and goals of the project. Specific topics discussed are : dependence analysis, timing and overhead analysis, interprocedural analysis, automatic scheduling and the graphical user interface.

Keywords: compilers, data dependences, timing analysis, interprocedural analysis, scheduling.

1 Introduction and Overview

Recent advances in supercomputer architectures in general, and parallel processor architectures in particular, have not been met with corresponding (and necessary) advances in software techniques. This is particularly true of supercomputer compilers. For example, little is known on program restructuring and compiling for message-passing multiprocessors. Most existing compilers use approaches which are direct analogs (or extensions) of schemes used by vectorizing compilers. Program vectorization is a well researched and well understood subject [AC72] [AK82] [AK87] [Kuc78] [KKLW80]. The same cannot be said for program

parallelization (or concurrentization) especially for hierarchical architectures [KDLS86]. Recent (and long overdue) efforts in this direction are underway in a few research centers; PTRAN at IBM and PTOOL at Rice [All88] [Cyt86] [MP86] [Nic84] [PKL80] [Pei86] [PK87] [Pol88a].

This paper describes the Parafrase-2 project which is aimed at developing a source to source multilingual restructuring compiler. It provides a reliable, portable and efficient research tool for experimentation with program transformations and other compiler techniques for parallel supercomputers. It also has a convenient user interface and provides a means for user interaction at several levels during the transformation process. Parafrase-2 also uses a more aggressive approach for dependence testing including traditional tests as well as symbolic dependence analysis techniques. Dependence testing in the presence

*This work was supported in part by the National Science Foundation under Grant No. US NSF MIP-8410110, the U. S. Department of Energy under Grant No. US DOE-DE-FG02-85ER25001, IBM Parafrase Contract No. 632613, Control Data Corporation, and Digital Equipment Corporation.

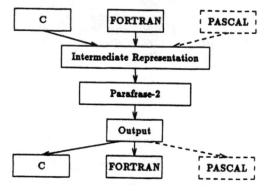

Figure 1: Parafrase-2 Overview

of pointers, records and other structures has not been implemented, but remains one of the priority features to be realized in the near future.

Figure 1 gives the overall view of the system. One of the major features is the ability to allow different source languages as input to the compiler. This is accomplished by means of an intermediate representation used by the *core* of Parafrase-2 and hence transparent to the user. A property of the intermediate representation is the ability to recreate the source program. While this may not be possible (or desirable) at the lexical level, it must be possible at the semantic level. In order to make this intermediate representation transparent to the user, a preprocessor is used to transform each input language to the intermediate representation. This means only having to write a preprocessor for each language desired as input and a postprocessor (or code generator) for each language desired as output.

The pre- and post-processors for C and Fortran (including the Cedar Fortran extensions [Guz87]) have been completed. Our data structures are also able to accept Pascal constructs though a Pascal preprocessor has not been implemented.

The input to Parafrase-2 is a set of data structures. This set of data structures is constructed from the input program by the preprocessor associated with the corresponding language. A *pass* of Parafrase-2 operates on the data structures to transform the program to a form suitable for parallel execution. Passes can be executed in any sensible order. This is achieved by insisting that the form of the data structures is left invariant by each pass. The output of Parafrase-2 is the modified intermediate form, which is

Reprinted from *Proc. of the 1989 Int'l Conf. on Parallel Processing*, Vol. II, IEEE Press, Piscataway, N.J., 1989, pp. II-39–II-48.

acted on by a post-processor to produce the requisite output language.

All modules of the system have been implemented in C except for the C parser which uses yacc. This has resulted in portable code. Parafrase-2 has been designed to make the coding of new passes as "painless" as possible and a fair amount of effort has been put into using data abstraction to code the various data structures. Various debugging facilities have been included to print pass-specific information and allow the traversal of the various internal data structures.

The rest of the paper is organized as follows. Section 2 discusses data dependence testing, including symbolic dependence tests. Static program analysis is covered in Section 3 along with its application to program transformations. The focus of Section 4 is interprocedural analysis to determine alias and summary information. Various program transformations are presented in Section 5. Section 6 examines auto-scheduling by the compiler and Section 7 deals with the user interface.

2 Data Dependences

Data dependence testing has been extensively studied in the context of automatic parallelization of sequential programs [Ban88]. Data dependences give information about the flow of data in a program. This can be used to restructure the program and find blocks of code which do not reference the same data and hence can be executed in parallel. Optimizations are done with the constraint of retaining the correctness of the program (as the programmer intended) and thus conservative estimates for dependences are the norm in compiler writing in the absence of accurate data dependence information.

Data dependences are normally defined with respect to the set of variables which are used and modified by a statement; denoted by the IN set and the OUT set respectively [ASU86]. Detecting scalar dependences among statements is straightforward: it involves taking the intersection of the corresponding IN and OUT sets [ASU86]. The same strategy also works for arrays, but gives coarse dependence results. For more accurate information, subscript analysis of array variables needs to be performed. Testing for dependences then involves checking whether two subscript expressions could take on identical values during the execution of the program. When the subscript expressions are simple linear expressions, two of the most common data dependence tests employed are the *gcd* and *bounds* tests [Ban88]. Data dependence directions were shown to be useful in carrying out many loop transformations[PW86]. Data dependence distances can be seen as logical extensions of dependence direction vectors.

2.1 Symbolic Dependence Tests

Banerjee's gcd and bounds tests are sufficient for a large number of cases and they can be adapted to handle cases where subscript expressions or loop bounds contain symbolic terms. For instance, consider the following code which has been extracted from a block tridiagonal solver:

```
DO J = 1, M
    DO K = 1, M
        F((P-1)*Q+J) = F((P-1)*Q+J) - V(K,J,P-1)
            * F((P-1)*Q-M+K)
    END DO
END DO
```

A simple symbolic manipulation of subscripts of array F shows that the inner loop forms a recurrence and the outer loop can be executed in parallel. That is because in different iterations of the outer loop, say J and J', there can be no dependence due to the index expressions $(P-1)*Q+J$ and $(P-1)*Q-M+K$ because the latter is always less than or equal to $(P-1)*Q$, (since $K \leq M$), while the former is greater than $(P-1)*Q$, (since $J \geq 1$).

Some of the subscripted subscript expressions have the same property as the above example. The following code has also been extracted from the same block tridiagonal solver:

```
LBEG = M + 1
DO J = LBEG, QMM(I)
    DO K = 1, M
        F(QSUM(I)+J) = F(QSUM(I)+J) - V(K,J,I-1)
            * F(QSUM(I)-M+K)
    END DO
END DO
```

Note that I is constant during the execution of the loop, therefore $QSUM(I)$ is also constant. Thus, a similar analysis shows that the outer loop can be executed in parallel, and the inner loop forms a recurrence.

Besides using information about loop bounds, global analysis may also help to eliminate some of the dependences which may be assumed otherwise. For instance, consider the following loop [PW86]:

```
IF (M > 0) THEN
    DO I = LOW, HIGH
        A(I) = B(I) + A(I+M)
    END DO
END IF
```

The loop cannot be executed unless $M > 0$; therefore, it can be vectorized. The compiler can discover this by examining the condition in the IF statement.

247

In Parafrase-2, quick and inexpensive heuristics which capture most of the cases are used instead of doing an extensive symbolic data dependence analysis, which will usually give more information but may be cost-prohibitive [LT88]. First, the set of *loop invariant* variables is found, that is, those variables whose value do not change as long as control stays within the loop. All symbolic expressions are then evaluated in terms of the loop invariant variables. Expressions are represented in *disjunctive normal form*, a sum of terms in which each term is the product of an integer constant and the loop invariant variables.

After this is done, the process of dependence analysis can continue as in the normal case. For instance, in the gcd test we need to know whether a constant divides an expression involving the loop invariant variables. If the remainder of all terms involved in the expression can be found, the gcd test can be completed.

To apply Banerjee's bounds test, the consistency of a set of inequalities should be verified [Ban88]. This is done by keeping the maximum and minimum values of the loop invariant variables wherever possible. In the first example of this section, M is the upper bound of the first and second

loop and M, P and Q are loop invariant variables. Banerjee's inequality would simplify to $-M + 1 \leq M \leq M - 2$. It is easily verified that this can never hold, because M can never be less than or equal to $M - 2$. Hence, there is no dependence due to these expressions. In the second example of this section, M and $LBEG$ are loop invariant variables. Banerjee's inequality would simplify to $M - QMM(I) + 1 \leq 2M \leq M - 2$. The right inequality reduces to $M \leq -2$. In such a case the second loop would not be executed.

3 Static Program Analysis

The Static Program Analyzer (SPA) is the main timing/performance module in Parafrase-2. SPA is used to obtain compile-time estimates of a program's execution time which may then be used in various ways. For the user, an estimate of program execution time can be provided, or a theoretical maximum speedup calculated. From the compiler's point of view, the timing statistics can be used as an aid in program transformations.

3.1 Models

In order to obtain a reasonable timing estimate, certain details about the particular machine architecture must be considered. However, one of our goals is to obtain a general, parameterized timing estimate of the program that can be adapted to a variety of vector/parallel architectures.

There are several timing models that we are considering. In order to determine the accuracy and usefulness of these models, some evaluation and experimentation on actual machines will be performed. Our initial implementation

and evaluation is restricted to shared memory multiprocessors.

The first is an idealized machine model with an unlimited number of processors and without memory access overheads or synchronization delays. By determining the maximum parallelism possible [ABC*88], timing with this model will give the theoretical best time for execution of a program. This can be used as a basis for comparison with other models.

The next simplified model is based on the hypothesis that memory access is the overriding factor in the execution of a program. By counting the various types of memory references, we can achieve a close approximation (within some constant factor) to the actual execution time [GGJ*88].

Another model assumes that all memory references take unit time and we parameterize the execution time by the operations performed. This has limited usefulness. However, if actual timing experiments are performed on the target architecture, this model can provide some measure of how much time is involved with memory conflicts.

Finally, we need a model to determine serial execution time. We assume a sequential execution of the program and consider the longest execution path in the case of multiple execution paths; a variation of this uses the average time over all execution paths.

3.2 Timing Applied to Program Transformations

One immediate use for the timing estimates is within the compiler itself. The primary reason for having a compiler that automatically performs vectorisation and parallelization is to obtain highly optimized parallel code and thus faster execution time. However, most vector/parallel operations have a certain amount of overhead involved that must be overcome before a performance gain is realized. Hence it is possible for some of these "optimizations" to actually slow down the program. By using timing information, the compiler can decide when to do certain transformations and when vectorization is better than parallelization or vice versa. At least one commercial compiler features some level of cost/performance analysis [CGMW88].

In the following loop, each iteration of the outer loop requires a fork and join for the doall. This could involve a fair amount of overhead.

```
DO I = 1, N
  DOALL J = 1, M
    A(I, J) = A(I - 1, J) * X(J)
  END DOALL
END DO
```

However, if we perform a loop interchange, only one fork and join is needed, thus reducing the amount of overhead involved.

```
DOALL J = 1,M
  DO I = 1, N
    A(I, J) = A(I - 1, J) * X(J)
  END DO
END DOALL
```

4 Interprocedural Analysis

Optimizations are often limited by lack of information. This is particularly true in the presence of procedure calls.

By their very nature, they tend to hide information, much of which may be necessary to safely perform transformations on the code. Figure 2 gives an example in which lack of information would lead to serializing a loop that can actually be executed in parallel. Since the subprograms SUMVECTOR and CLEAR reference only one row of array A, there are no cross iteration dependences. Without this detailed information, the compiler would have to assume that the entire array could be referenced and thus the loop could not be parallelized.

Interprocedural data flow analysis seeks to solve the same problems as normal data flow analysis, except that it involves flow problems across procedure boundaries. There are three main objectives :

- Reference Information — knowing when and how an object is referenced. For complex objects such as arrays this includes information about what part of the object is referenced.

- Aliasing Information — knowing when two or more apparently different objects may or must refer to the same physical object. This can happen when the two names indicate identical objects or if they overlap, as with two arrays with different offsets from a common location.

- Constant Propagation — propagating constants across procedure boundaries which can be used for more accurate dependence analysis within the procedure[CCKT86].

A variable is *referenced* in a procedure if it is used or defined as a result of a call to that procedure. A *call graph* is a multi-graph representing the structure of the calls within a program. The vertices (nodes) of the graph represent procedures (subroutines or functions) and the edges represent the procedure calls. Hence if procedure P calls procedure Q, then there is an edge $P \rightarrow Q$ in the call graph. Formal parameters and non-local variables that are referenced by a procedure are uniformly referred to as *parameters*.

4.1 Aliasing

When there is no information about the calling environment for a procedure, conservative assumptions must be made about any aliasing due to duplicate parameters. In order to collect accurate dependence information, it is vital to know which variables may be aliases for other variables.

In Fortran, aliasing problems arise in three cases, COMMON blocks, EQUIVALENCE statements and parameter aliasing.

EQUIVALENCE statements are relatively straightforward, because they specify exactly which aliases exist. COMMON statements are similar to global variables and again aliases are explicitly specified. Parameter aliasing is somewhat more elusive. Parameter aliases are created at call sites and therefore are not always present in a given procedure. A procedure would ideally have different sets of aliases for each call site, but in practice these are all combined resulting in information about aliases that may exist at any time. Since these aliases may propagate all the way through the call graph, flow analysis is required and each instance of a procedure must be analyzed.

In C the situation is even worse, since aliasing problems may arise from the use of pointers as well as unions in structured data types. This requires some form of constant propagation which may not be complete enough to obtain reasonable results. These problems have yet to be investigated in Parafrase-2, though some work has been done in this area [Wei80].

4.1.1 Aliasing Due to Duplicate Parameters

Parameter aliasing in Parafrase-2 determines which parameters may be aliased due to aliasing of reference parameters. Alias information is stored as pairs of symbol table entries. A set of pairs of symbol table entries is associated with each entry. Two objects a and b are aliased if and only if there exists a pair $\langle a, b \rangle$ in the set of alias pairs for their symbol table entries.

The simplest method for deriving aliasing information is to traverse the call graph from the top down and propagate aliasing information down the graph. While this would be sufficient when the call graph is acyclic, it does not work when there are cycles in the graph due to runtime recursion. Instead, this information is gathered by an iterative analysis of the callgraph, according to Banning's algorithm[Ban78] which is shown in Figure 3. Note that this algorithm is limited by the number of possible aliasing pairs, and runs with time complexity O(number of aliases).

This information (the aliasing pairs) may be augmented with offset information, in the case of arrays and more complex data structures. If different sections of two objects are aliased together, then there may be no intersection between some of the references to the two variables.

4.2 Interprocedural Summary Information

A major thrust in interprocedural analysis is the parallelization of call statements[TIF86] [CK87]. This problem is complex in general, but dependences can be eliminated in many common situations.

In the absence of interprocedural analysis, one must make the conservative assumption that any objects in the scope of the called procedure may be modified. In many

```
DO I = 1,N
  V(I) = SUMVECTOR(A(I,1),N)
  CALL CLEAR(A(I,1),N)
ENDDO


FUNCTION SUMVECTOR(B,M)

SUM = 0
DO J = 1,M
  SUM = SUM + B(J)
ENDDO
RETURN SUM


SUBROUTINE CLEAR(B,M)

DO J = 1,M
  B(J) = 0
ENDDO
```

Figure 2: Example program.

languages this means all of the pass-by-reference parameters, global variables and objects accessible by some pointer passed to the procedure. This is generally too conservative for most uses, in particular for detailed dependence analysis.

A first improvement to this is to analyze the procedure to determine which parameters may be referenced. With this approach one may obtain simple reference information about the procedure which can be easily summarized so that reanalysis of the routine is not necessary at every call site. This is easy and often useful, but it is conservative. For the program in Figure 2, this information would not be sufficient to eliminate dependences.

The next step is to improve the granularity of this summary information. Several approaches have been used to solve this problem[TIF86] [CK87]. Naturally there is a trade-off between efficiency of the algorithm and exactness of the information.

The most complete approach is to perform in-line expansion of procedure calls. It allows for complete analysis of the procedure, taking into account the complete calling environment, and is thus as close to ideal as possible. This has two main drawbacks. First, it is time and space inefficient, potentially increasing each exponentially[Sch77]. Second, it fails in the presence of recursion. However, it is useful in many cases and is useful as a test against which other methods may be compared.

Another approach is to summarize reference information for a procedure in terms of the formal parameters at a call site[CK87]. The goal is to collect a set of all the objects that may be defined or used as a result of a call to

Input : a call graph
Output : aliasing pairs

P and *Q* are procedures
W is a worklist of procedures
a_i is the ith actual parameter at a call site
f_{Q_i} is the ith formal parameter of procedure *Q*

Initialize *W* to contain all procedures.
while $W \neq \emptyset$
   begin
   remove procedure *P* from *W*
   for each procedure call, *P* calls *Q*
     if actual parameters, a_i and a_j, may be aliased
       then add $\langle f_{Q_i}, f_{Q_j} \rangle$ to set of aliases
     if any actual parameter, a_i, is aliased to global *g*,
       then add $\langle f_{Q_i}, g \rangle$ to set of aliases
     if this introduces any new alias information to *Q*
       then add *Q* to worklist.
   end

Figure 3: Banning's Algorithm for detection of aliasing pairs

a given procedure. The main advantage of this approach is that it minimizes the analysis required, each routine needs to be analyzed only once rather than reanalyzing it at each call site. At the same time, useful detailed reference information can be determined.

This is the chosen approach on in the case of Parafrase-2 will concentrate. Interprocedural analysis will be performed prior to the dependence analysis phase to gather reference information for each call site. Dependence analysis can then treat procedure calls in the same way it handles other statements.

4.3 Library Summary Information

Summary information for library routines is stored in a separate database. This information can be easily entered by hand, if need be, so that functions for which the source is not available or analysis is conservative can be specified. This is also useful for intrinsic functions. The information consists of a function/subroutine name, number of parameters and reference information for each parameter. This reference information is simple for scalar parameters, either *read* or *write*. For more complex data structures, particularly arrays, information will be stored in a format compatible with the approach used for reference information as mentioned in Section 4.2.

5 Transformations

Once the data dependence graph is computed there are several well known loop transformations which can be used to extract parallelism from the program, a few of which are listed below.

- *Loop parallelization* — If there are no loop carried dependences then all iterations can be executed in parallel. Even if there are loop carried dependences the loop can be parallelized with appropriate synchronization instructions.

- *Loop vectorization* — If all dependences are to lexically forward statements then the loop can be vectorized. Sometimes statement reordering is required to achieve this.

- *Loop distribution* — This is done to isolate parts of the loop which cause dependence cycles and hence inhibit parallelism.

- *Loop interchanging* — Loop interchanging can be done to make better use of machine resources (e.g. to reduce memory access time).

- *Cycle shrinking* — This transformation can be used to restructure certain types of serial loops for parallel execution. It uses dependence distance information.

- *Loop Spreading* — Using this transformation, the execution of loops in sequence can be overlapped to gain limited parallelism.

6 Auto-Scheduling in Parafrase-2

Our approach to the parallelism packaging and scheduling problem is a blend of compiler and run-time schemes. Figure 4 shows the different components of our framework as parts of an auto-scheduling compiler [Pol88b]. Below we briefly discuss the main components of an auto-scheduling compiler.

Partitioning (or packaging of parallelism): This phase is responsible for partitioning the code (and/or data structures) of a program into identifiable modules which are treated as units. For example, compiling vector or VLIW instructions, or grouping a set of instructions into a unit is part of partitioning. Program partitioning can be done statically by the compiler. In a fully dynamic environment (e.g. dataflow) partitioning is implicit and, depending on the execution model, an allocatable unit can range from a single instruction to a set of instructions. Static (explicit) partitioning is desirable because it exploits readily available information of program parallelism and can consider overhead and other performance factors. In our case we use a semi-static partitioner: the formation of tasks is based on the syntax of the language and other program information, but a task is allowed to be decomposed into subtasks dynamically during program execution. The result of the partitioner is a program task graph with nodes corresponding to tasks (instruction modules) and arcs representing data and control dependences.

Pre-scheduling: After a program is partitioned into a set of identifiable tasks, the compiler can insert certain

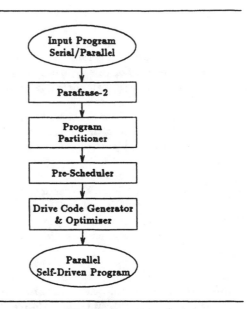

Figure 4: The major modules of an auto-scheduling compiler.

scheduling suggestions based on its knowledge about the program.

Dynamic task scheduling (nested parallel tasks): Scheduling at the task level is then performed dynamically during execution. At this level tasks are treated as units of execution. Tasks which are ready to execute are queued in a ready-task queue. Each idle processor tries to dispatch the next available task from the queue (if any). Also, tasks are queued and thus are qualified for execution as soon as they become "ready". This environment can be realized through an auto-scheduling compiler which generates control code to implement the above procedure [Pol88a].

Loop (or parallel task) scheduling: Upon queueing, a serial task is dispatched at once as soon as a processor becomes idle. However, a parallel task can draw several processors to execute it and thus it remains queued until exhausted. In our case it is safe to assume that the only type of parallel tasks are parallel loops. In Section 6.3 we discuss three main approaches to dynamic scheduling of parallel loops.

6.1 Partitioning and Task Formation

Traditionally, partitioning has been studied in a context which is almost identical to scheduling. Our approach is different in the sense that grouping of tasks and allocating groups to processors is not considered except in special cases. Also, for certain cases (e.g. loops) partitioning of tasks into allocatable units is postponed until run-time.

On a practical basis the partitioning problem can be considered from two different angles: the data and the instruction stream viewpoint. In the first case, partitioning is based on the decomposition of data objects upon which computation is performed. Each processor is assigned the work corresponding to a specific data domain. This form of partitioning is often called *data partitioning* or *horizontal partitioning*. Data partitioning is feasible when the same type of computation is performed on all data domains. Typical computations of this type include loops and other repetitive computations, i.e. the same instruction stream is executed for each data domain.

The second type of partitioning called *functional* or *vertical partitioning* results in the formation of tasks from syntactically identifiable pieces of code. Thus different partitions operate on different data objects or on the same data object but in some specific order. For example, forming two tasks out of two disjoint outer loops or two different subroutine calls is a case of functional partitioning. Another common term for functional partitioning is *high-level spreading*. Partitioning must be done such that the following guidelines are met.

- The tasks formed by partitioning a program should be as independent as possible, i.e. sharability of data objects between tasks should be minimal. Notice that both data and functional partitioning conform to this requirement.

- Tasks should be of approximately equal size. As will be shown later, this helps in balancing the load across processors by using simple and fast scheduling heuristics. Data partitioning tends to satisfy this requirement while functional partitioning does not.

- The size of the tasks formed should be a function of the overhead incurred during task scheduling and the synchronization overhead. In other words, tasks should be large enough compared to the overhead involved in order to achieve any speedup.

- A balance must be achieved between communication and scheduling overhead and degree of parallelism in a task graph. These two objectives are inconsistent since minimizing overhead tends to merge all tasks into fewer large tasks, while increasing the degree of parallelism tends to decompose large tasks into their smallest constituents. The degree of parallelism should be considered in conjunction with the number of available processors.

- Finally, partitioning should be based on realistic assumptions about the program. For example, the type of a task is readily available to the compiler but the execution time of a task is not. If exact algorithms are used for partitioning, e.g. critical path, they should be adapted to compensate for inaccuracies.

Our approach to task formation is based entirely on the syntax of the underlying language. If we consider imperative languages such as C, Fortran, and Pascal, then we choose to use the "natural" boundaries in defining tasks. Thus an *outer loop* is considered to be a single task, as are *subroutine calls* and *basic blocks*. Nodes in the task graph correspond to tasks. An arc implies the existence of one or more data dependences between the two tasks. During execution, a task cannot start unless all preceding tasks on which it depends have completed execution.

The next step of our partitioner is to traverse the call graph bottom-up and check the size of each task against the *critical process size* or CPS. Intuitively, the CPS is the minimum size of a process whose execution time is equal to the overhead that it incurs during scheduling (dispatching) at run-time. The compiler can roughly estimate the CPS for each task in the program as shown in [Pol88a]. The effect of this pass is to merge small tasks into larger ones and serialize certain loops.

6.2 Self-Drive Code Generation

An auto-scheduling compiler would eliminate most (if not all) of the functions of the operating system pertaining to task creation, scheduling, execution, and deletion. At the same time an auto-scheduling compiler will generate *drive code* as part of the object code. Thus, a program will not only perform its intended calculations but it will distribute and drive itself during execution. The function of the drive-code generator and optimizer (DCGO) module is to generate custom drive code for each task based on the type of the task and its position in the task graph. All program information necessary to perform this is readily

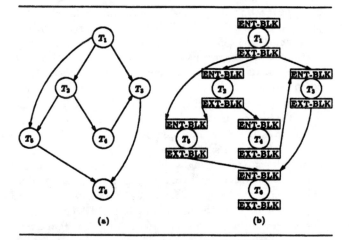

Figure 5: (a) A task graph. (b) The graph with entry and exit blocks.

available to the DCGO module. Optimization of the drive code is also based on available program information. We assume that the hardware supports synchronization primitives such as FETCH & ADD or FETCH & DECR.

Two blocks of code are generated by the DCGO for each task, an *entry-block* (ENT-BLK) and an *exit-block* (EXT-BLK) (Figure 5). The entry block allocates local and shared task variables (in the case of parallel tasks), and performs other implementation-specific functions such as the binding of user to virtual tasks. The entry-block of a parallel task is executed only by the first processor to work on that task.

A task exit-block performs the following three functions, *task deallocation*, *dependence elimination*, and *new task creation*. Task deallocation involves the elimination of the corresponding entry from the queue (and depending on the implementation, the deallocation of virtual tasks). Dependence elimination updates precedence relations of depending tasks. Finally, new task creation activates new tasks by queueing them to the ready-task queue.

Another activity of the ENT-BLK module is to compute the number of iterations which must be allocated to the next processor, and update the loop index(es) accordingly. Consider for example a DOALL with N iterations. If it is executed under self-scheduling, the compiler will generate the following code

```
X = FETCH_&_ADD(loop_index, 1);
IF (X+1 > N) THEN EXIT;

        . . . .

    loop body

        . . . .
```

where FETCH_&_ADD is assumed to update the shared variable after it is read. The compiler also allocates and initializes a *counter* for each task in the program. Each counter is initialized to a value which is equal to the number of predecessors of the corresponding node. Precedence enforcing code is generated as follows. For each task T_i in the program the compiler generates exit-block code which decrements the value of the counter for each task T_j which is dependent on T_i. This decrement operation is performed in a synchronized way. After each decrement operation in an exit-block, code is generated to check whether that counter has become zero. If so, the corresponding task is queued in the ready-task queue. More specifically, for each precedence arc $e = (T_i, T_j)$ in the task graph, the following code is generated for the exit-block of T_j.

```
    temp = FETCH_&_DECR(C_j);
    IF (temp=1) QUEUE(Q, T_j);
```

Thus order of execution is enforced through explicit synchronization generated by the compiler as part of the exit-blocks.

6.3 Loop Scheduling

Since tasks are scheduled in a fully dynamic fashion, the next question of interest is what happens within a task. Serial tasks are treated as units of allocation and upon dispatching they are executed to completion. Hence the only type of tasks that allow for more manipulation are parallel tasks. In this section we consider specific aspects of scheduling the components of a parallel task. Even though task scheduling is performed dynamically, there are several ways of scheduling the iterations of a parallel loop, including static and dynamic approaches. In a static scheme the user or the compiler decides which iterations are allocated to a given processor. The only advantage offered by static allocation is the elimination of the run-time overhead associated with dynamic dispatching of iterations. However, the drawbacks of static scheduling are too many to consider it as a practical and general solution.

Loops in numerical programs can be fairly complex with conditional statements and subroutine calls. A general solution should distribute iterations to processors at run-time based on the availability of processors and other factors. However, the overhead associated with run-time distribution must be kept very low for dynamic scheduling to be practical. We consider here three possible schemes for scheduling of loops.

The first scheme is commonly referred to as *self-scheduling*. An idle processor picks a single iteration of a parallel loop by incrementing the loop indices in a synchronized way [KS88] [TY86]. Thus if N is the total number of iterations of a loop, self-scheduling involves N dispatch operations. Let B be the average iteration execution time and σ the overhead involved with each dispatch. Then self-scheduling is appropriate if $B >> \sigma$ and there is a large variation of the execution time of different iterations. Because self-scheduling assigns one iteration at a time, it is the best dynamic scheme as far as load balancing is concerned (but the worst with respect to overhead). However, a perfectly balanced load is meaningless if the overhead used to achieve it exceeds a certain threshold.

In *chunk-scheduling* a fixed number of iterations (chunk) is allocated to each idle processor (as opposed to a single iteration). By doing so one can reduce the overhead by compromising load balancing. There is a clear tradeoff between load balancing and overhead. At one extreme, the chunk size is roughly N/p and each processor performs only one dispatch per loop. The variation of finish time is also the highest in this case. At the other extreme, the chunk size is one and we have self-scheduling with perfect load balancing and maximum overhead. Intermediate values of the chunk size in the range $[1 \ldots \lceil N/p \rceil]$ will produce results that are better or worse than either of the extreme cases. The main drawback of chunk-scheduling is the dependence of chunk size on the characteristics of each loop which are unknown even at run-time.

Self-scheduling achieves a perfect load balancing but it also incurs maximum overhead. On the other hand chunk-scheduling is an (unsuccessful) attempt to reach a compromise between load balancing and overhead, and the result maybe quite unexpectable. The third scheme, *guided self-scheduling* (or GSS)[PK87], is in general, a much better and more stable approach to reach this compromise. The idea is to start the execution of a loop by allocating chunks of iterations whose size starts from $\lceil N/p \rceil$ and keeps decreasing until all the iterations are exhausted. The last $p - 1$ chunks of iterations are of size one. Thus, chunk sizes vary between the two extremes.

GSS's property of decreasing chunk size is built-in and no extra computation is required to enforce this policy. This simplicity allows for easy and efficient implementation. Second, the two main objectives of perfectly balanced load and small overhead are achieved simultaneously. By allocating large chunks at the beginning of the loop we keep the overhead low. At the same time, the small chunks at the end of the loop serve to "patch holes" and balance the load across all processors.

7   Graphic Interface

Parafrase-2 encompasses a graphical interface for the display of some of the internal data structures. Data structures important to the user include the dependence graph, flow graph, call graph and task graph. This serves two purposes.

First, it allows for the possibility of interaction with the user. Frequently, a compiler generates serial code that is actually parallelizable simply because it lacks information that is not available at compile-time. For example, the compiler might need to know the range of a loop to determine dependence. In the absence of such information, the compiler must assume data dependence and either generate serial code, or generate code that tests the range of the loop and skip to the parallel code if the test is satisfied. In most existing compilers, the user can force the compiler to parallelize certain parts of the source code by inserting compiler directives manually. Parafrase-2 takes a different approach: the dependence graph is displayed graphically, so that the user can see where the data dependences are and request information about the cause of the data dependence. If desired, data dependences can be removed by invoking a menu function.

Second, although there are many known loop transformations that can result in better speedup, there is no known optimal order in which these transformations should be applied. Hence the user should be able to apply transformations manually and transform the code into a form more suitable for parallelization by Parafrase-2.

The graphical interface of Parafrase-2 uses the *Faust* library routines [GGGJ88]. Faust provides a programming environment for parallel computing and has utilities to display general purpose graphs in a convenient form under X windows.

Figure 6 shows a sample program and·its associated flow graph. Each node of the flow graph is essentially a block of assignment statements. If the user wants to know which block of statements a node in the flow graph corresponds to, he can invoke the *Zoom* menu option after selecting the node of interest. In Figure 6, node 3 has been selected and the *Zoom* menu option is just about to be invoked.

8   Conclusion

Automatic parallelism detection in programs has seen significant advances in recent years. Improvements have been made in computing data dependences within and across procedure calls. New loop transformations have been suggested. Parafrase-2 incorporates many existing techniques

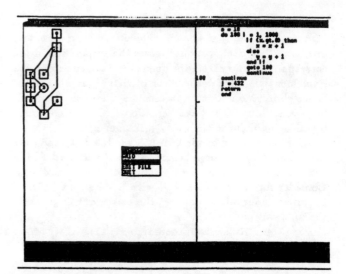

Figure 6: graph 1 : The source code is displayed in the text window on the right and the corresponding flow graph is displayed in the graphics window on the left. The user has selected node 3 and the *Zoom* menu option is about to be invoked. The *Edit* menu option invokes an editor on the source file. The *Quit* menu option allows the user to exit from the flow graph displaying pass immediately.

while providing a tool for implementing new research results.

However, exploiting the resulting parallelism in a useful manner has traditionally been viewed to be beyond the realm of compilers. This issue is addressed in Parafrase-2 through the technique of auto-scheduling. This results in a self-driven program where the code for the scheduling of tasks is generated by the compiler.

The interface between the parallelizing compiler and the user is also of considerable importance. Parafrase-2 provides a graphical interface which is currently used only for displaying compiler information to the user, but will eventually provide the user with the necessary tools for experimenting with the compiler.

References

[ABC*88] F. E. Allen, M. Burke, R. Cytron, J. Ferrante, W. Hsieh, and V. Sarkar. A framework for determining useful parallelism. In *International Conference on Supercomputing*, 1988.

[AC72] F. E. Allen and J. Cocke. *A Catalogue of Optimizing Transformations*, pages 1–30. Prentice-Hall, Englewood Cliffs, New Jersey, 1972.

[AK82] J. R. Allen and K. Kennedy. *PFC: A Program to Convert Fortran to Parallel Form*. Technical Report MASC-TR82-6, Rice University, Houston, Texas, March 1982.

[AK87] R. Allen and K. Kennedy. Automatic translation of fortran programs to vector form. *ACM Transactions on Programming Languages and Systems*, 9(4), October 1987.

[All88] Allen, F. E., et. al. An overview of the PTRAN analysis system. In *Proceedings of the 1987 International Conference on Supercomputing*, Springer-Verlag, LNCS, February 1988.

[ASU86] A. V. Aho, R. Sethi, and J. D. Ullman. *Compilers : Principles, Techniques and Tools*. Addison Wesley, march 1986.

[Ban78] J. Banning. *A Method for Determining the Side Effects of Procedure Calls*. PhD thesis, Stanford University, August 1978.

[Ban88] U. Banerjee. *Dependence Analysis for Supercomputing*. Kluwer Academic Publishers, 1988.

[CCKT86] D. Callahan, K. D. Cooper, K. Kennedy, and L. Torczon. Interprocedural constant propagation. *Journal of the ACM*, :152–161, 1986.

[CGMW88] M. Chastain, G. Gostin, J. Mankovich, and S. Wallach. The Convex C240 architecture. In *Supercomputing 88*, IEEE Computer Society Press, 1988.

[CK87] D. Callahan and K. Kennedy. Analysis of interprocedural side effects in a parallel programming environment. In E. N. Houstis, T. S. Papatheodorou, and C. D. Polychronopoulos, editors, *Lecture Notes in Computer Science Vol. 297 : 1st International Conference on Supercomputing*, pages 138–171, Springer-Verlag, June 1987.

[Cyt86] R. G. Cytron. Doacross: beyond vectorisation for multiprocessors (extended abstract). In *Proceedings of the 1986 International Conference on Parallel Processing*, pages 836–844, August 1986.

[GGGJ88] V. A. Guarna, D. Gannon, Y. Gaur, and D. Jablonowski. Faust : an environment for programming parallel scientific applications. In *Supercomputing 88*, IEEE Computer Society Press, November 1988.

[GGJ*88] K. Gallivan, D. Gannon, W. Jalby, A. Malony, and H. Wijshoff. Behavioral characterisation of multiprocessor memory systems: a case study. 1988.

[Gus87] M. D. Gussi. *CEDAR Fortran Programmers Handbook*. June 1987.

[KDLS86] D. J. Kuck, E. S. Davidson, D. H. Lawrie, and A. H. Sameh. Parallel supercomputing today and the cedar approach. *Science*, 231(4740):967–974, February 28 1986.

[KKLW80] D. J. Kuck, R. H. Kuhn, B. Leasure, and M. Wolfe. The structure of an advanced vectoriser for pipelined processors. In *Fourth International Computer Software and Applications Conference*, October 1980.

[KS88] J. T. Kuehn and B. J. Smith. The horizon supercomputing system: architecture and software. In *Supercomputing 88*, pages 28–34, nov 1988.

[Kuc78] D. J. Kuck. *The Structure of Computers and Computations, Volume I*. John Wiley and Sons, New York, 1978.

[LT88] A. Lichnewsky and F. Thomasset. Introducing symbolic problem solving techniques in the dependence testing phases of a vectoriser. In *Proceedings of the 1988 International Conference on Supercomputing*, 1988.

[MP86] S. P. Midkiff and D. A. Padua. Compiler generated synchronisation for do loops. In *Proc. of the 1986 International Conference on Parallel Processing*, pages 544–551, August 1986.

[Nic84] A. Nicolau. *Parallelism, Memory Anti-Aliasing and Correctness for Trace Scheduling Compilers*. PhD thesis, Yale University, June 1984.

[Pei86] J. K. Peir. *Program Partitioning and Synchronization on Multiprocessor Systems*. Technical Report UIUCCDCS-R-86-1259, Department of Computer Science, University of Illinois at Urbana-Champaign, March 1986.

[PK87] C. D. Polychronopoulos and D. J. Kuck. Guided self-scheduling: a practical scheduling scheme for parallel supercomputers. *IEEE Trans. on Computers*, 36(12), December 1987.

[PKL80] D. A. Padua, D. J. Kuck, and D. H. Lawrie. High-speed multiprocessors and compilation techniques. *IEEE Transactions on Computers*, C-29(9), September 1980.

[Pol88a] C. D. Polychronopoulos. *Parallel Programming and Compilers*. Kluwer Academic Publishers, 1988.

[Pol88b] C. D. Polychronopoulos. Toward auto-scheduling compilers. *The Journal of Supercomputing*, :297–330, 1988.

[PW86] D. A. Padua and M. Wolfe. Advanced compiler optimisations for supercomputers. *Communications of the ACM*, 29(12):1184–1201, December 1986.

[Sch77] R. W. Scheifler. An analysis of inline substitution for a structured programming language. *Communications of the ACM*, 1977.

[TIF86] R. Triolet, F. Irigoin, and P. Feautrier. Direct parallelisation of call statements. *ACM SIGPLAN 86 Symposium on Compiler Construction*, :176–185, 1986.

[TY86] P. Tang and P. C. Yew. Processor self-scheduling for multiple-nested parallel loops. In *Proceedings of the 1986 International Conference on Parallel Processing*, August 1986.

[Wei80] E. W. Weihl. Interprocedural data flow analysis in the presence of pointers, procedure variables and label variables. *Seventh Annual ACM Symposium on Principles of Programming Languages*, :83–94, 1980.

Mapping Function-Parallel Programs with the Prep-P Automatic Mapping Preprocessor*

Francine Berman
Bernd Stramm
Department of Computer Science and Engineering
University of California, San Diego

January 7, 1994

Abstract

In the last decade, there has been a great deal literature in the area of mapping program communication graphs to message-passing multicomputers. As part of this research, there have been important efforts in developing tools to assist the programmer in mapping function-parallel programs to MIMD multicomputers. The Prep-P mapping preprocessor was one of the first tools to accomplish this task and influenced several subsequent tool efforts. In this paper, we describe the Prep-P mapping preprocessor and use it as a test-bed for comparing a set of popular static mapping algorithms on a diverse group of common parallel benchmarks.

1 Introduction

There is little argument that parallelism provides a paradigm for faster and more efficient computation. Over the last decade, this paradigm has been utilized in the development of algorithms and the design of machines to solve many problems more efficiently and expediently.

An important aspect of developing efficient parallel programs for message-passing parallel machines is the mapping of processes or tasks in an algorithm to processors of the target machine. The mapping of processes to processors can promote efficiency by assigning independent processes to distinct PEs so that they can be executed concurrently, and can promote expediency by distributing the computation and communication load among PEs in a balanced fashion.

There have been a number of mapping efforts in the last decade – from the development of mapping algorithms and embedding results to the development of software tools to aid in targeting parallel programs to parallel machines. One of the first efforts to define a mapping tool for automatic mapping of function-parallel programs was the Prep-P mapping preprocessor. The Prep-P approach has influenced

*This research was supported in part by the Office of Naval Research Contract No. N00014-86-K-0218 and NSF Grant No. ASC-9106465.

the development of other mapping tools and models [LRG+], [Gol91], [Str93] and together with the Poker system, provides a prototype integrated parallel programming environment.

The Prep-P mapping preprocessor is a software tool which automatically maps a large, static, function-parallel program to a general message-passing MIMD multicomputer model represented by the Poker simulator. Prep-P "completes" the Poker Parallel Programming Environment [Sny84] by providing a mechanism in which large programs can be specified, mapped and multiplexed on the simulated multicomputer. The mapping portion of Prep-P is modular so that different heuristics for program partitioning can be tried. (The mapping problem is NP-complete [GJ79] so performance-efficient heuristics must be used).

In this paper, we describe the Prep-P mapping preprocessor and use the software as a testbed for several popular static mapping algorithms. Prep-P and Poker provide a concrete metric by which to compare the performance of mapping algorithms, and demonstrate the role mapping software can play in a parallel programming environment.

This paper is organized as follows. In Section 2, we describe the Prep-P and the Poker Parallel Programming Environment and review related projects. We will use Prep-P and Poker to compare common static mapping algorithms with respect to popular non-numeric parallel benchmarks. We review the algorithms and benchmarks used for the comparisons in Section 3. In Section 4, we give performance results for our experiments.

2　The Prep-P/Poker Environment

Prep-P is a software tool which automatically maps and multiplexes a static parallel algorithm, producing code which can be loaded and run on the Poker simulator. To provide context for this discussion, we give a short review of the Poker system before describing the Prep-P software.

2.1　CHiP, Poker and Pringle

The CHiP model is a reconfigurable, message-passing MIMD multicomputer architecture designed and developed by Lawrence Snyder [Sny82]. The CHiP consists of a PE lattice interleaved with rows and columns of switches, and a controller which loads the intended interconnection structures into the PE and switch lattices. CHiP programs are represented by a set of communicating sequential process codes and the mapping of the program graph into the PE lattice (Figure 1). The machine is then intended to execute the process codes assigned to each PE synchronously, passing messages along the communication paths specified by the mapping. One main benefit of this design is that PEs are never used for the forwarding of messages from one site to another; they are used solely for processing, and special-purpose switches are used for the relay of messages.

The Poker system [Sny84] provides a parallel programming environment for the CHiP and also serves as a simulator. The programmer inputs the program graph-

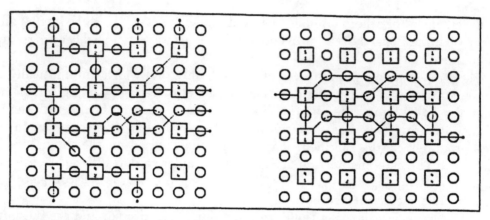

Figure 1: CHiP machine configured as a binary tree (left) and as a hypercube (right).

ically – associating process codes to PEs, connecting communicating PEs through the switch lattice, assigning I/O streams to pads on the periphery of the PE lattice, etc. – using a series of "modes". The Poker simulator is then loaded and provides a visual trace of the program during execution. Note that the Poker system actually simulates the Pringle emulator [KWG+84] of the CHiP rather than the CHiP model itself.

The Pringle machine is a hardware emulator of the CHiP computer which differs from the original model in that it is asynchronous and all messages from one PE to another take the same amount of time in transit. (This is because PEs are polled for messages in Pringle in a round-robin fashion rather than propagating messages on a wafer using VLSI as in the CHiP design). Because of this, Pringle does not distinguish between distinct placements of processes to processors or routings, since all messages take the same time to travel between PEs. Otherwise, differences between CHiP and Pringle are generally transparent to the programmer. The Pringle message-passing protocols do provide an excellent opportunity to compare different partitionings since it is the way in which processes are mapped to PEs which determines the execution performance of the program. In this paper, we focus on the Prep-P mapping software as a testbed for evaluating partitioning strategies.

Figure 10 shows the Poker input for a parallel tournament-method program which finds the maximum of data placed in the leaves of a complete binary tree. Shown are the switch-settings and code names modes; not shown are the port names and chip parameters modes. The process code files (not shown) utilize the XX programming language [Sny84] (basically a pared-down version of C) and are input external to the Poker environment.

The Poker system is a pioneering programming environment and one of the first which allowed the user to implement a general domain of parallel programs in a high-level graphical fashion. Prep-P attempts to address a weakness in the Poker system whereby only programs which can be decomposed into at most 64 parallel processes and which have already been laid out on the CHiP lattice can be executed. In this context, we now describe the Prep-P automatic mapping preprocessor.

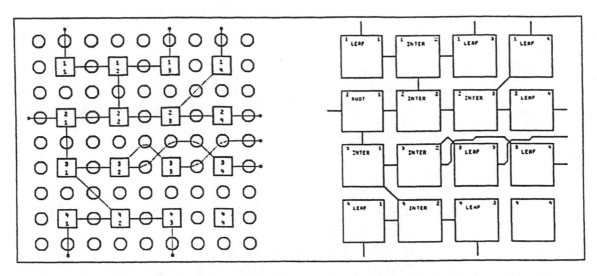

Figure 2: Poker representations of the Tournament Method Max-finding algorithm. Switch-setting mode is on the left; Codenames mode is on the right.

2.2 Prep-P

The Prep-P mapping preprocessor [BGK⁺85, Ber87] takes as input a static function-parallel program represented as a communication graph and a set of associated process codes. The software then *contracts* (partitions the process set), *places* (assigns process partitions to PEs in the PE lattice), *routes* (connects communicating PEs along the switch lattice) and *multiplexes* the program on an 8x8 CHiP lattice. Output from Prep-P is binary code which can be run directly on a modified version of the Poker system (PPoker).

The Prep-P strategy seeks to promote good mappings by optimizing contraction, placement and routing separately. In addition, the Prep-P software includes a graph description language and compiler (*GraphCom*), to facilitate the representation of the input graph in a layout-independent form, and a multiplexing module to oversee the execution of multiple processes by a single PE. In the following subsections, we briefly describe each of these modules.

2.2.1 A Graph Description Language

The task of the user interface in Prep-P is to represent the input program graph, and to create a number of files which describe its attributes and represent its structure internally to the Contraction, Placement and Routing, and Multiplexing modules. Since programs are composed of static function-parallel processes in the Prep-P world, the user interface accepts as input a program communication graph with associated process codes. The program graph is given by a *graph description file* (GDF) which consists of a header and a collection of procedure declarations specifying process interconnections. The header part of the GDF specifies the type of graph and some of its attributes. The procedure declarations enable the programmer to represent patterns in communication dependencies as well as individual communica-

```
tree
{
        k = 4;
        nodemin = 1;
        nodecount = @k − 1;
        lastrow = (nodecount + nodemin)/2;
        side = 4;
        internal = 1;
        external = 1;
}
procedure ROOT
        nodetype: {i == nodemin}
        port LCHILD: {2 * i}
        port RCHILD: {2 * i + 1}
        port DATAOUT: output dataout
procedure INTERNAL
        nodetype: {i > nodemin&&i < lastrow}
        port PARENT: {i/2}
        port LCHILD: {2 * i}
        port RCHILD: {2 * i + 1}
procedure LEAF
        nodetype: {i >= lastrow}
        port PARENT: {i/2}
        port DATAIN: input datain
```

Figure 3: Binary Tree GDF

tion dependencies between processes. Figure 3 gives the GDF for a complete binary tree whose processes are associated with the ROOT, INTERNAL or LEAF process codes.

The graph description language also allows the user to define composite graphs whose subgraphs have been previously defined by a "graph description library", i.e. a template for graph specification. This facility is useful in defining any large-size parallel communication structure which exhibits some modularity. Of course, any graph can be described in Prep-P by listing its adjacencies as well.

When given a GDF and a set of externally defined process codes, the user interface generates a set of internal files. Some of these files are used by the Contraction, Placement and Multiplexing modules of Prep-P and some will not be used until PPoker is finally invoked. A detailed description of these files can be found in [NB88].

2.2.2 The Prep-P Contraction Module

The Contraction Module of Prep-P takes as input an internal representation of the communication graph and produces a partitioning of the vertices such that the number of nonempty partitions does not exceed the number of PEs in the CHiP lattice. (Generally, this number is 64 but Prep-P provides facilities whereby the side dimension of the target PE lattice can be specified as input. See line 5 within the brackets in Figure 3 for an example). The graph whose nodes are the partitions and whose edges are induced from the edges of the communication graph is called the *contracted graph*.

The default contraction algorithm in Prep-P (LNS) is sensitive to the communication load of the program graph. To obtain estimates of the load, the communication graph is preprocessed to estimate the the number of messages passed on each edge between processes. If k messages are passed between processes A and B, then the edge (A,B) is weighted as k. If an unbounded or indeterminable number of messages is to be passed, then we weight the edges as ∞. (For example, if A communicates with B within a loop with a data-dependent index bound, the edge between A and B may be weighted ∞). The weighted communication graph is then partitioned to become the contracted graph.

The algorithm used for contraction in Prep-P is a variation of the Local Neighborhood Search (LNS) algorithm [AHU83]. An initial partitioning is derived and the algorithm iteratively tries to improve the current partitioning by temporarily moving a node of the communication graph from one partition to another and evaluating a cost function. The move is kept if the value of the cost function after the move is an improvement over the value of the cost function before the move. In determining which contraction algorithm to include as the default in Prep-P, we compared a number of different algorithms (including Simulated Annealing) to LNS but in a preliminary model of the system, LNS performed at least as well (i.e. minimized cost functions reflecting communication time for the contracted graph in reasonable time) as its competitors [HB88].

The cost function used for LNS in Prep-P is actually a prioritized list of three cost functions. The first cost function is minimized when processes incident to edges with unbounded (infinite) communications are mapped into the same partition, and infinite edges are distributed roughly evenly among the partitions. The idea is that since intra-partition (intra-PE) communication will likely be faster than inter-partition (inter-PE) communication, the execution time of the contracted graph should be optimized when the edges with the heaviest communication are executed within as many PEs as possible. The cost function which measures the distribution of infinite edges is the *heavy edge cost function*

$$H = \sum_{i=1}^{N} \frac{(H_i - H_{tot})^2}{N^2}$$

where H_i is the number of infinite edges assigned to the ith partition, H_{tot} is the total number of infinite edges, and N is the number of PEs in the target lattice.

The second cost function is similar to the first but applies to edges with finite

261

weights. The *light edge cost function* is minimized when communicating processes are mapped to the same partition and each partition performs roughly the same total amount of internal communication between its processes. A function which reflects this is

$$L = \sum_{i=1}^{N} \frac{(L_i - L_{tot})^2}{N^2}$$

where L_i is the sum of the weights of the edges between processes assigned to the *ith* partition, L_{tot} is the sum of all the finite edge weights in the communication graph, and N is the number of PEs in the target lattice. Note that this cost function is minimized when the number of messages – and not the number of process pairs – is distributed evenly among partitions.

The third cost function is minimized when communication between partitions is balanced. The *distributed I/O cost function*, defined by

$$D = \sum_{i=1}^{N} D_i{}^2$$

reflects the distribution of the message load between partitions. We define D_i to be the sum of the weights of all finite edges from processes in partition i to processes assigned to another partition.

The LNS contraction algorithm implemented in Prep-P starts with an initial assignment of processes to partitions using Breadth-First-Search (BFS). (A random partitioning was tried but the BFS initialization consistently produced better final contractions). The LNS algorithm given configuration C' moves a process and computes the H value of the new configuration C''. If $H(C') > H(C'')$, the move is accepted. If $H(C') < H(C'')$, the move is rejected. If $H(C') = H(C'')$, $L(C)$ and $L(C'')$ are computed. If $L(C') > L(C'')$, the move is accepted; if If $L(C') < L(C'')$, the move is rejected. If If $L(C') = L(C'')$, $D(C')$ and $D(C'')$ are computed and evaluated in similar fashion. An outline of the algorithm is given in Figure 4. For a detailed discussion of the LNS algorithm and other contraction algorithms, see [SB88].

In addition to the default contraction algorithm, user-defined contractions and library contractions are also available. In the first, the programmer may define and input any contraction by specifying the partitions. For known regular parallel communication topologies, there is a library of contractions available. These are generally coalescing or "cut-and-pile" contractions and are specified in the Prep-P documentation.

2.2.3 The Prep-P Placement and Routing Module

The Placement and Routing module of Prep-P takes as input the internal representation of the contracted graph and determines an assignment of its nodes (process partitions) to PEs and an assignment of its edges to paths between PEs in the switch lattice. The placement algorithm used by Prep-P is a modified version of the Kernighan and Lin circuit placement algorithm [KL70].

Kernighan and Lin is a divide-and-conquer algorithm which we use to recursively place a graph G (the contracted graph) on a $k x k$ subgrid of the PE lattice.

```
while consecutive_failures < max_failures do
        save state (contraction $C_0$)
        try a move (to get contraction $C_1$)
        $\delta \leftarrow H(C_1) - H(C_0)$
        if $\delta = 0$
            $\delta \leftarrow L(C_1) - L(C_0)$
            if $\delta = 0$
                $\delta \leftarrow D(C_1) - D(C_0)$
        end if
        if $\delta < 0$
            accept the move
            consecutive_failures $\leftarrow 0$
        else
            restore state
            increment consecutive_failures
        end if
    end while
```

Figure 4: LNS Contraction Algorithm.

The nodes of the contracted graph are initially placed randomly on the PEs of an $8x8$ lattice. Each recursive iteration first determines the four subgraphs of G for which there is a minimum total number of edges between distinct subgraphs. The resulting 4 subgraphs must then be placed in quadrants of the grid. To determine which subgraph is assigned to which quadrant, all $4! = 24$ candidate assignments of subgraphs to quadrants are evaluated by comparing the distance between adjacent vertices assigned to distinct quadrants. (Since the nodes have not yet been placed within the quadrants, the distance between adjacent nodes is defined to be the manhattan distance between the centers of their assigned quadrants). The subgraphs are then placed in the quadrants in which the total external communication distance is minimal, and the algorithm then recurses on each of the four subgraphs, denoting each subgraph as G and its assigned quadrant as the kxk grid.

At the conclusion of the recursive Kernighan and Lin algorithm, the nodes of the contracted graph have now been placed on the $8x8$ PE lattice. To route adjacent partitions[1], we use a simple modification of the classic breadth-first-search Shortest Path algorithm [AHU74] where the paths traverse nodes in the switch lattice. If the algorithm "runs out of room" on the switch lattice, the corridor width (number of switches between adjacent PEs in the lattice) can be increased.

Note that because the Poker simulator models the Pringle machine rather than the CHiP architecture, no empirical data on the efficiency of the placement and

---

[1]Two partitions are adjacent if there is an edge between the processes from the communication subgraphs assigned to them.

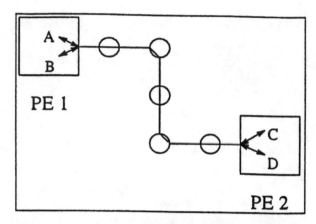

Figure 5: Communication on the lattice between multiplexed processes.

routing algorithms can be obtained. The efficiency of different contractions, however, can be optimally evaluated by directly measuring execution times of mapped programs.

2.2.4 The Prep-P Multiplexing Module

Once a program is contracted, placed and routed on the PE lattice, each PE may have many processes assigned to it. The Prep-P Multiplexing module derives code for each PE so that each of the processes assigned to a PE may be executed, and the source and destination of messages to and from other PEs and off-chip will be identified with its correct process ID. The need for this is illustrated by the following example (Figure 5): Consider a mapping in which processes A and B are assigned to PE1 and processes C and D are assigned to PE2, and there is a path in the lattice from PE1 to PE2 (i.e. they communicate). The same path will be used whether process A wants to communicate with process C or process D, and similarly, if process C or D wants to return a message, A must be distinguished from B as its destination. The management of process execution and message identification is performed in Prep-P by the Support Routines [Mat] which essentially form a local multitasking system at each PE.

The multiplexing of processes at each PE is accomplished by scheduling each process in a round-robin fashion. Processes relinquish control of the PE (context-switch) at each I/O operation to allow other processes to execute. Messages between processes are sent with the job ID of the destination process and are buffered in output queues of the sending PE and input queues of the receiving PE until the appropriate request-to-send and acknowledge messages have been exchanged. The multiplexing strategy is straightforward and robust. For a more detailed explanation, see [BS89].

2.2.5 Prep-P and Poker Together

Poker had already been developed when we began to design and implement Prep-P so Prep-P was designed to serve as a front-end for Poker. Still, several modifications were required so that Prep-P and Poker could be fully integrated. Most importantly, the Poker software had to be modified so that it could simulate execution on the CHiP model (Pringle) for contracted programs *with contracted external I/O*. This was a difficult problem which could not be solved effectively without modifying Poker. In addition, the Prep-P software had to support Poker *phases*. We describe both extensions briefly below.

"External I/O" in the CHiP model is represented by connections between the PEs in the CHiP lattice and I/O "pads" which surround the periphery of the lattice. Paths to and from I/O pads are read-only or write-only and cannot be multiplexed. Prep-P handles external I/O by contracting pads when the PEs they are connected to are contracted and when *all* pads in the same partition are read-only or write-only.

In Poker, each pad is associated with a data substream. These substreams are represented by individual fields in a file of records. The number of fields per record corresponds to the number of substreams each file represents (i.e. each file represents data substreams for some number of pads). There will be as many records in the file as there are data values to be read. One consequence of this approach is that if one PE is reading from or writing to the kth value in its substream, all PEs connected to the pad represented by that file will have to be reading from or writing to the kth value in their substreams. This does not support multiplexed I/O where one process assigned to a PE may be reading from its kth value and another may be reading from its k+jth value. We therefore needed to expand Poker to accommodate multiplexed I/O so that several substreams at different indices could be accessed from the same PE.

The Poker extension required changes to the buffering facilities, IONames format, message-passing facilities and several other parts of the Poker code. We "widened" the I/O buffer to support an array of buffers for each pad, with the size depending upon the number of actual pads mapped to that site (the "virtual pad"). Instead of reading or writing from a specific pad in the Poker lattice, the PEs send messages to the virtual pad mapped to that site. Different data streams can then advance asynchronously simulating multiplexed I/O.

To avoid confusion with the original Poker code, we call the extended code *PPoker*. PPoker (rather than Poker) must be called at the conclusion of Prep-P to execute the mapped, multiplexed program graph and produces the same result as Poker would have given an appropriately-sized PE lattice with external I/O. Note that PPoker is not meant to be used as a stand-alone system. For more information on PPoker, see [RB87]

Another modification that needed to be made to integrate the two systems together was the extension of Prep-P to include Poker *phases*. The Poker software provides a feature called phases which facilitates the description of algorithms that can be decomposed into a linear sequence of parallel subalgorithms. Each subalgorithm has its own interconnection structure and associated process codes that requires a separate user description. To execute an algorithm with multiple phases, the code for all phases in each PE is linked together with a small section of code which enables the PE to switch code from one phase to another. During execution, each phase can be selected and executed by the user in any order.

The Prep-P phase routines utilize the ^d command which allows Poker to dump and save the current state of the emulator to a file. Utilizing this capability, the Prep-P phase routines load and execute each phase separately. This is orchestrated by a special script which contracts, places, routes and calls routines from the multiplexing module for each program graph of each phase. The final program run by the Prep-P script before invoking PPoker is used to generate a PPoker script file to control execution of the individual phases. For more detailed information on the Prep-P treatment of phases, see [CB87].

2.3 Related Work

A number of tools have been developed for mapping static message-passing function-parallel programs into multicomputers. We briefly review a representative group of these tools.

The Oregami system, designed and developed by Lo and Rajopadhye et al. [LRG+], is a set of software tools for automatic and guided mapping of a parallel program into a message-passing parallel architecture. Programs used by Oregami are represented by temporal communication graphs specified in the LaRCS graph description language [LRM+]. The MAPPER tool performs contraction and layout based on user-provided information on the type and regularity of the program graph. The METRICS tool provides a high-level analysis and evaluation display of the mapped program. The approaches taken by Prep-P and Oregami are similar with some major differences. Oregami includes in its language representation temporal information which is used along with programmer directives by the mapping software to determine the assignment. Prep-P's language does not include temporal information and its mapping algorithms are strictly general-purpose. Oregami generates symbolic mapping information targeted to a regular multicomputer model. Prep-P is integrated with the Poker system and produces code ready to run on the Poker simulator.

The *MUPPET* programming environment uses process splitting and merging to foster parallel process execution [MSS88], [KM87]. Programs in this environment are scientific computations represented by process graphs. Processes in these graphs may spawn other processes and may terminate. In the MUPPET system, programs are first transformed into LAM (local memory abstract machine) networks with fixed topologies and next mapped onto the target machine automatically. Mapping is performed on the process level (by splitting and merging processes), the communication level (by shortening or eliminating communication paths) and on the sequential level (by positioning communication statements so that multicast communications may be utilized). The MUPPET environment was targeted towards the SUPRENUM architecture (torus topology) [BGM86] and a Transputer network.

The Parallel Programming Support Environment [LR90] integrates a number of tools which promote architecture-independent program development targeted to a message-passing multicomputer model. The program domain includes both sequential and parallel programs. The system includes TaskGrapher [ERL90], an automatic system which utilizes a set of heuristics to generate and display a mapping and scheduling of tasks into processors. Input to TaskGrapher is a program graph annotated with estimated weights for communication and computation loads. The PPSE environment also includes a number of other tools including a graph editor, a graphical target machine description editor, a parallel code generator (for sequential programs) and performance analysis tools.

The Millipede Project, a programming environment targeted to Transputers, was developed by Aspnas and Back [AB89]. The target machine is Hathi-2, a loosely coupled, MIMD reconfigurable collection of 100 transputers connected by 25 crossbar switches. Programs consist of sequential OCCAM processes which communicate by synchronous message-passing. The program graph is displayed by a hierarchical graph editor as a process graph. The process graph is then condensed by the user into a task graph (the "contracted" graph) – no automatic contraction is available. Automatic placement is available however, and the task graph is mapped to the Hathi-2 model using a tool which utilizes a simulated annealing algorithm for the embedding. The Millipede project combines commercial Transputer software tools with research tools to facilitate the specification, animation, placement, debugging and monitoring of parallel programs.

The TIPS project (Transputer-based interactive parallelizing system) uses a tool called TMAP [Gol91] for automatic mapping of the program graph to an asynchronous MIMD network of 74 Transputers. TMAP integrates the contraction module of Prep-P with the Trollius operating system [SGWC91]. Prep-P provides the mechanism for program specification and mapping while Trollius is used to boot the machine, load programs and perform the high-level message-passing. Additional tools (e.g. Tmon, a performance-monitoring and debugging tool [Jia91]) have been developed making this a relatively complete programming environment for the target machine.

The E-Kernel [MS91] is an embedding kernel for program mapping and network reconfiguration targeted to the IBM Victor Multiprocessor. The software supports the embedding of a task graph onto a system network which has been embedded into Victor's 2-D mesh network. The E-kernel assumes that the program graph has the same number of nodes as the number of processors in the embedded system and uses heuristics to minimize the maximum distance between any two communicating processes.

The PYRROS tool [YG] is an automatic scheduling and code generation tool which targets the NCube2. Pyrros takes as input a static macro-dataflow graph and uses a dominant sequence clustering (DSC) algorithm. The algorithm improves on Sarkar and Hennessy's [Sar87] clustering and merging heuristics and produces theoretically optimal scheduling for several restricted classes of algorithms.

These tools, like Prep-P, provide software which assists in the implementation of large static function-parallel programs on fixed-sized message-passing multicomputers. In the next section, we use the Prep-P/Poker environment to take a closer look at the mapping heuristics themselves, and to assist in comparing and evaluating these approaches for mapped function-parallel programs.

3 Benchmarks and Mapping Algorithms Used for the Experiments

Prep-P was developed as a mapping tool which provides the programmer with the option of using of automatically-derived contractions, library contractions or user-defined contractions. The contraction algorithm has been implemented in a separate module which allows Prep-P to easily be used as a testbed for other mapping techniques. Since the effect of placement and routing in the Pringle model on program execution time is negligible, we can use the execution times of programs executed on Poker (as the Pringle simulator) as a measure of the performance of mapped programs. We describe a study of partitioning algorithms using the Prep-P/Poker environment in this section.

Our strategy for studying mapping algorithms is as follows:

- Identify a set of commonly used mapping algorithms whose performance we would like to compare in the Prep-P/Poker environment.

- Define a diverse set of commonly used parallel programs on which to test the mapping algorithms.

- For each benchmark program, compare the execution time performance in Poker under different mapping algorithms for different contraction ratios (processes/processors). Compare the performance of the mapping algorithms over all programs in the benchmark set.

- Analyze the performance results to compare mapping techniques over different programs and contraction ratios.

We give the results of this study in Section 4. We first describe the mappings and benchmark programs chosen for this study.

3.1 Mapping Algorithms

In selecting the mapping algorithms, we wanted to include popular mapping strategies and heuristics used in existing mapping software for static mapping of function-parallel programs. The popular mapping strategies we use include the cyclic, block and simulated annealing algorithms, a prioritized Local Neighborhood Search Algorithm (used in Prep-P and TMap), and a general Maximum Matching algorithm (used in Oregami for programs which cannot use the special-purpose mapping algorithms).

Note that other mapping strategies, such as those used by Lewis et al. in PPSE [LR90] and the DSC algorithm used in PYRROS [YG] are combined with scheduling. In the Prep-P setting, scheduling for all contracted graphs is done by the Prep-P multiplexer which executes processes in a round-robin fashion, context-switching at each I/O call. Therefore, inclusion of strategies which do both partitioning and scheduling do not provide an appropriate comparison.

It is useful to classify mapping algorithms by the amount of information concerning the communication and computation behavior of the program which is utilized to determine the mapping. If no information is used, the mapping strategy can be called *oblivious*. If only communication or computation information is used, the contraction algorithm can be called *communication-sensitive* or *computation-sensitive* respectively. If information about both the communication and computation behavior is used, the contraction algorithm can be called *program-sensitive* [SB88].

Static mapping strategies in practice are generally oblivious, communication-sensitive or program-sensitive. The contraction algorithms used for our study include representatives from each of these three groups. Assume that we are partitioning a program graph with n processes into a multicomputer with N processors. The mapping algorithms we tested are:

1. An oblivious *block* mapping algorithm (BLOCK) based purely on node labels which contracts each group of $\lceil n/N \rceil$ consecutive nodes in the program graph to the same PE.

2. An oblivious *cyclic* mapping algorithm (CYCLIC) based purely on node labels which assigns node label i in the program graph to PE $i \bmod N$.

3. The communication-sensitive *LNS* mapping strategy (LNS) described in Section 2.2.2 (starting from an initial configuration determined by partitioning the processes using a communication-sensitive Breadth-First Search). This is the default contraction algorithm used by Prep-P.

4. An oblivious *random* mapping (RANDOM) of processes to PEs. Processes are assigned processor index i where i is chosen randomly from 1 to N.

5. A communication-sensitive prioritized *simulated annealing* mapping (SA) of processes to PEs. The algorithm uses estimates of communication load and the heavy edge, light edge and distributed I/O functions given in Section 2.2.2 to determine whether a move is accepted. An outline of the algorithm is given in the Appendix.

6. The communication-sensitive Maximum Matching algorithm (MM) used in Oregami [LRG+]. The algorithm reduces the program graph to an intermediate contracted graph with at most $2N$ nodes and uses an optimal assignment for the intermediate graph using a maximum weighted matching technique. See the Appendix for more details.

Each mapping algorithm was used with each of the benchmark programs for at least two different contraction ratios (n/N). For each program, the contracted graph was multiplexed using Prep-P and executed using PPoker. Execution time was determined by counting the PPoker "ticks", each of which is intended to represent 1 microsecond on Pringle. The non-randomized algorithms were executed once each for each mapping algorithm, program and contraction ratio. The methods which use randomized steps (LNS, SA, and RANDOM) were applied ten times to each benchmark and the average result was reported. The target PE lattice for each of the tests ranged between 4 and 64 PEs. For each of these tests, the running time (the number of simulated clock ticks) on PPoker were recorded. The results are given in Section 4.

3.2 Benchmark Programs

To benchmark the performance of the contraction algorithms in Prep-P/Poker, we used a diverse group of non-numeric XX programs which used distinct communication graphs. (Numeric programs are generally ill-suited to the Poker environment). All programs were taken from the literature and modified to fit the Prep-P/Poker environment. A listing of these programs is given below. For more specific information on the individual programs, see [Pal].

Benchmarks

1. Guibas, Kung and Thompson's Connected Component algorithm (CONNECT) on a torus communication graph ([Ull84]).

2. Kung and Leiserson's Lower Triangular System Solver algorithm (LOWER) on a linear communication graph ([MC80]).

3. A parallel version of Knuth's Odd-Even Transposition Sort (LSORT) on a linear communication graph ([Knu]).

4. A parallel Tournament Method Max-Finding algorithm (MAX) on a binary tree communication graph ([AHU74]).

5. Guibas, Kung and Thompson's Shortest Path algorithm (PATH) for a positively weighted graph on a torus communication graph ([Ull84]).

6. A Matrix Transpose (TRANSPOSE) algorithm on a hexagonal mesh communication graph [Pal].

4 Performance Results

Figures 6 - 12 show the performance of the 6 mapping algorithms (BLOCK, CYCLIC, RANDOM, LNS, SA, MM) for each of the benchmarks (CONNECT, CLOSURE, LOWER, TRANSPOSE, MAX, PATH, LSORT).[2] For each of the figures, the y-axis represents the total number of "ticks" on the Poker system (Pringle emulator) while the x-axis shows the performance of each of the algorithm for a given contraction ratio. Note that the numbers of processes which could be contracted are somewhat small since the Poker system had at most 8K memory per processor to store both the code and the multiplexing software. If the Poker code were modified to accommodate more memory per processor, it would be useful to run additional experiments with larger contraction ratios.

The most clear result from our experiments is that there is no obvious "winner" among the mapping techniques. We considered the experimental data from two viewpoints: we grouped mapping algorithms with respect to the way they balanced

---

[2]Note that a small number of data points are missing. The simulated Poker executions did not terminate in reasonable time for these programs.

270

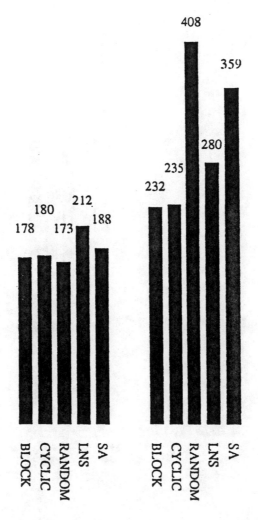

Figure 6: Connect, contraction ratios 2.25 and 1.56. Running time is in thousands of clock ticks.

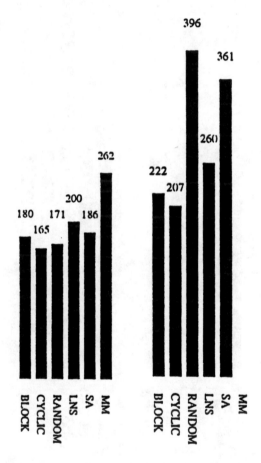

Figure 7: Closure, contraction ratios 2.25 and 1.56. Running time is in thousands of clock ticks.

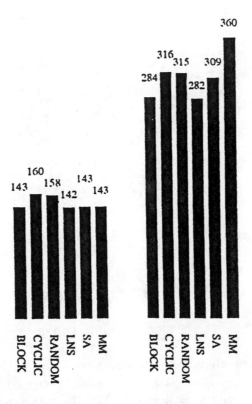

Figure 8: Lower, contraction ratios 2 and 3. Running time is in thousands of clock ticks.

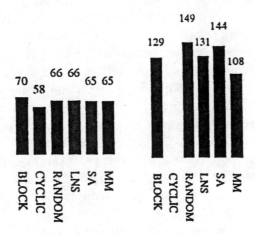

Figure 9: Transpose, contraction ratios 2.25 and 1.56. Running time is in thousands of clock ticks.

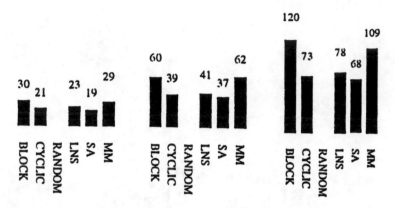

Figure 10: Max, contraction ratios 2, 4 and 8. Running time is in thousands of clock ticks.

communication, and we looked at the performance of each mapping algorithm over the set of benchmarks. We discuss the data with respect to these viewpoints below.

The mapping algorithms can be separated into two groups. One group attempts to balance the total computation load across the available PEs; the other group seeks to preserve and exploit locality of communication. The RANDOM and CYCLIC algorithms would fall within the first group[3], whereas the BLOCK, MM, LNS and SA algorithms fall within the second group. For the benchmarks and sizes tested, it does not seem that either group performs better on average than the other. For contraction ratios greater than two, the RANDOM and CYCLIC algorithms seem to perform consistently well or poorly for most benchmarks. For contraction ratio 1.56, RANDOM performs uniformly poorly. Within the second group (locality-preserving algorithms), no mapping algorithm performed consistently better than the others. For example for the PATH benchmark, contraction ratio 1.56, BLOCK performed well while LNS and SA did poorly, whereas for the MAX benchmark, contraction ratio 8, BLOCK gave the worst performance while SA gave the best.

With respect to individual mapping algorithms over the set of benchmarks, the results are equally inconclusive – no mapping algorithm seems to be a clear "winner" (i.e. consistently gives lower execution times). Moreover, the "winners" at one contraction ratio for a given benchmark are often different from the "winners" at a different contraction ratio. For some of the benchmarks (LOWER/contraction ratio 2, TRANSPOSE/contraction ratio 2.25), the performance of different algorithms seems very closely clustered and it would not seem to matter which algorithm was chosen. For some of the benchmarks (PATH/contraction ratio 1.56), the choice of the mapping algorithm seems to make a real difference.

A surprising result for these benchmarks and sizes is that the sensitivity of the mapping algorithm to the communication load does not seem to provide uniformly better mappings. MM and BLOCK are both generally good for LOWER and LSORT at contraction ratio 2 while RANDOM is the best mapping algorithm for

---

[3]If adjacent node numbers represent processes considered local by the programmer, then CYCLIC randomizes the placement of these processes and breaks locality.

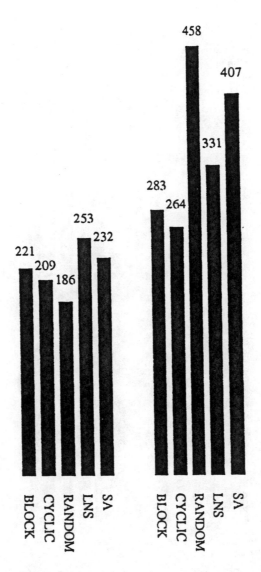

Figure 11: Path, contraction ratios 2.25 and 1.56. Running time is in thousands of clock ticks.

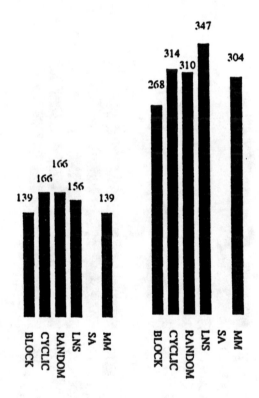

Figure 12: Lsort, contraction ratios 2 and 3. Running time is in thousands of clock ticks.

PATH at contraction ratio 2.25 and the worst for CLOSURE at contraction ratio 1.56.

The data provided in Figures 6 - 12 can be put somewhat in perspective by comparing the performance of the algorithms over different benchmarks for fixed contraction ratios. For most ratios, the BLOCK algorithm seems to be among the best performing algorithms. We conjecture that this may be due to the fact that the programmer will typically logically order the nodes in some way that represents perceived locality (e.g. row major order). By preserving the adjacency of the node numbers, the BLOCK algorithm may also be preserving the locality of the nodes as well as balancing total communication.

Another surprising result is that the probabilistic algorithms LNS and SA perform quite differently over the space of benchmarks. For some benchmarks (LOWER/contraction ratio 2, MAX/contraction ratios 2 and 4), they are quite similar, however for others (CONNECT/contraction ratio 1.56, CLOSURE/contraction ratio 1.56), they are substantially different. In the cases where they are different, LNS typically does better than SA.

The results of these experiments seem to provide both good news and bad news. The good news is that mapping can make a dramatic difference in the performance of programs, in our experiments cutting execution time almost 50% for some cases. The bad news is that no one algorithm seems to do the job for most benchmarks or even across contraction ratios. This means that the programmer must experiment to find a good algorithm – a procedure that is worth doing for code which will run a long time or be reused, but possibly not worth doing for code which will be run only once and will execute in a relatively short time. The use of a performance prediction model [Str93] to simulate the code and compare mapping algorithms would be helpful in the former case.

Acknowledgements

We are grateful to the students at Purdue and UCSD who participated in the design and implementation of the Prep-P mapping preprocessor, and to Jonathon Shade who helped run the experiments. Many thanks to Rich Wolski and Ginnie Lo for their help with DSC and Oregami respectively. We are especially grateful to Larry Snyder for his suggestions, encouragement, and support throughout the duration of the Prep-P project.

References

[AB89]   M. Aspnäs and R.J.R. Back. A programming environment for a transputer-based multiprocessor system (extended abstract). unpublished manuscript, 1989.

[AHU74]   A. Aho, J. Hopcroft, and J. Ullman. *The Design and Analysis of Computer Algorithms.* Addison-Wesley, 1974.

[AHU83]   A. Aho, J. Hopcroft, and J. Ullman. *Data Structures and Algorithms.* Addison-Wesley, 1983.

[Ber87]   F.D. Berman. Experience with an automatic solution to the mapping problem. In L. Jamieson, D. Gannon, and R. Douglas, editors, *The Characteristics of Parallel Algorithms.* M.I.T. Press, 1987.

[BGK+85]   F.D. Berman, M. Goodrich, C. Koelbel, C. Robison, and K. Showell. Prep-P: A mapping preprocessor for CHiP computers. In *Proceedings of the International Conference on Parallel Processing*, 1985.

[BGM86]   P. Behr, W. Giloi, and H. Muhlenbein. Suprenum: The german supercomputer project – rationale and concepts. In *Proceedings of the International Conference on Parallel Processing*, 1986.

[BS89]   F. Berman and B. Stramm. Prep-p: Evolution and overview. Technical Report CS89-158, University of California, San Diego, September 1989.

[CB87]   J. Conroy and F. Berman. Implementation of Phases in prep-p. Technical Report CS87-101, University of California, San Diego, July 1987.

[ERL90]   H. El-Rewini and T. Lewis. Scheduling parallel program tasks into arbitrary target machines. *Journal of Parallel and Distributed Computing*, June 1990.

[GJ79]   M. R. Garey and D. S. Johnson. *Computers and Intractability: A Guide to the Theory of NP-Completeness.* W.H. Freeman and Company, New York, 1979.

[Gol91]   N. Goldstein. A topology-independent parallel development environment. Masters Thesis, 1991.

[HB88]   P. Haden and F. Berman. A comparative study of mapping algorithms for an automated parallel programming environment. Technical Report CS-088, University of California, San Diego, 1988.

[Jia91]   J. Jiang. Performance monitoring in transputer-based multicomputer networks. Master's Thesis, 1991.

[KL70]   B.W. Kernighan and S. Lin. An efficient heuristic procedure for partitioning graphs. *Bell System Technical Journal*, 49(2):291–307, February 1970.

[KM87]   O. Krämer and H. Mühlenbein. Mapping strategies in message based multiprocessor systems. In *Parallel Architectures and Languages Europe, Volume 1: Lecture Notes in Computer Science # 258*, pages 213–225. Springer-Verlag, 1987.

[Knu]   D. Knuth. *The Art of Computer Programming, Sorting and Searching, Volume 3*. Addison-Wesley, Reading, Massachussetts.

[KWG+84]   A. Kapauan, K. Wang, D. Gannon, J. Cuny, and L. Snyder. The pringle: An experimental system for parallel algorithm and software testing. In *Proceedings of the International Conference on Parallel Processing*, 1984.

[LA87]   P.J.M. van Laarhoven and E.H.L. Aarts. *Simulated Annealing: Theory and Applications*. D. Reidel Publishing Company, Boston, 1987.

[LR90]   T. Lewis and W. Rudd. Architecture of the parallel programming support environment. Technical Report 90-80-2, Oregon Statue University, 1990.

[LRG+]   V. Lo, S. Rajopadhye, S. Gupta, D. Keldsen, M. Mohamed, B. Nitzberg, J. Telle, and X. Zhong. Oregami: Tools for mapping parallel computations to parallel architectures. Technical Report CIS-TR-89-18a, Revised 8-1-91, Department of Computer and Information Science, University of Oregon.

[LRM+]   V. Lo, S. Rajopadhye, M. Mohamed, S. Gupta, B. Nitzberg, J. Telle, and X. Zhong. Larcs: A language for describing parallel computations for the purpose of mapping. Technical Report CIS-TR-90-16a, Department of Computer and Information Science, University of Oregon.

[Mat]   J. Mattson. Prep-P support routines overview. Internal Project Report, available from F. Berman, CSE Dept. C-014, UCSD.

[MC80]   C. Mead and L. Conway. *Introduction to VLSI Systems*. Addison-Wesley, 1980.

[MS91]   E. Ma and D. Shea. E-kernel, an embedding kernel on the ibm victor multiprocessor for program mapping and network reconfiguration. *IBM Research Report*, (RC 16771), 1991.

[MSS88]   H. Muhlenbein, T. Schneider, and S. Streitz. Network programming with muppet. *Journal of Parallel and Distributed Computing*, 5:641–653, 1988.

[NB88]   D. Newton and F. Berman. A child's garden of GraphCom. Technical Report CS88-114, University of California, San Diego, January 1988.

[Pal]   M. Palandri. Realtests. Technical report, Prep-P Internal Documentation.

[RB87]   D. Rose and F. Berman. Mapping with external I/O: A case study. In *International Conference on Parallel Processing*, 1987.

[Sar87]   V. Sarkar. *Partitioning and Scheduling Parallel Programs for Execution on Multiprocessors*. PhD thesis, Stanford University, Stanford, Ca. 94305-2192, 1987.

[SB88]   B. Stramm and F. Berman. Communication-sensitive heuristics and algorithms for mapping compilers. *SIGPLAN Notices*, 23(9):222–234, September 1988.

[SGWC91] H. Sreekantaswamy, N. Goldstein, A. Wagner, and S. Chanson. Resource management in a large reconfigurable transputer-based system. In *Proceedings of the 6th Distributed Memory Computing Conference*, 1991.

[Sny82]   L. Snyder. Introduction to the configurable, highly parallel computer. *Computer*, pages 47–56, January 1982.

[Sny84]   L. Snyder. Parallel programming and the Poker programming environment. *Computer*, pages 27–36, July 1984.

[Str93]   B. Stramm. Performance prediction for mapped parallel programs. Technical Report TR CS93-294, Ph.D. Thesis, University of California, San Diego, 1993.

[Ull84]   J. D. Ullman. *Computational Aspects of VLSI*. Computer Science Press, Rockville, Maryland, 1984.

[YG]   T. Yang and A. Gerasoulis. A fast static scheduling algorithm for dags on an unbounded number of processors. In *Proceedings of Supercomputing 91*.

Appendix

We provide more details for some of the contraction algorithms used in these studies and briefly described in Section 3.

Prioritized Simulated Annealing

The *simulated annealing* (SA) algorithm [LA87] is a probabalistic version of the LNS algorithm. It is motivated by analogy to physical systems, in particular the cooling of solids which lead to minimum-energy crystalline structures. There is a large amount of literature on this topic, and the basic algorithm allows for considerable variation and tuning to improve performance. [LA87] provides a good overview of simulated annealing.

The principal difference between LNS and SA is that SA does not necessarily reject moves which are judged to be detrimental by the cost function. Rather, they are accepted with a probability which is computed from the cost function difference

δ and the current value of the control parameter t called the *temperature*. The probability p of acceptance is given by

$$p = e^{\frac{-\delta}{t}} \tag{1}$$

Initially, the temperature is set high, so that "bad" moves are accepted with a fairly high probability. As the execution proceeds, the temperature is gradually lowered so that this probability decreases, until in the final stages the algorithm functions essentially as a local neighborhood search. Our cooling scheme and termination criteria follow the literature: : after the inside loop, we reduce the temperature to a fixed fraction $\alpha = .95$ of its current value. The termination condition is also used for LNS: the algorithm terminates after a fixed number of successive moves without improvement.

For our studies, we considered a version of simulated annealing with three prioritized communication-sensitive functions. To compare the algorithm fairly to LNS, we use H, L and D to compute the heavy edge, light edge and distributed I/O costs associated with each potential move. Since the magnitude of each function is different, we cannot use the same control parameter to calculate the probability of accepting a bad move. Instead, we maintain three different temperatures t_H, t_L and t_D, and use the temperature that corresponds to the cost function which would cause us to reject a move. The prioritized simulated annealing algorithm is outlined in Fig. 13 and discussed in [SB88].

Maximum Matching Algorithm

The general-purpose Maximum Matching algorithm (MM) used in Oregami [LRG$^+$] contracts in two stages. During the first stage, the input program graph is reduced so that the number of partitions is at most twice the number of processors. The second part of the algorithm continues contracting partitions and assigns at most two partitions to each processor. Let $\lceil n/N \rceil \leq B \leq n$ be a bound on the maximum number of processes per processor. The algorithm can be described as follows:

- Input is a program graph in which the edges between each pair of processes is weighted with a cost.

- If n (the number of processes) exceeds $2N$ (twice the number of processors, then group the processes into clusters using the Sort Greedy algorithm. The Sort Greedy algorithm sorts the edges between processes by weight (nonincreasing order). Initially, each node is in its own partiton. The algorithm proceeds through the sorted edge list and clusters together any two partitions whose aggregate number does not exceed $\lceil B/2 \rceil$.

- Sort Greedy is used iteratively until the number of clusters does not exceed $2N$.

- Let the intermediate graph whose nodes are the partitions and whose edges are induced from the edges between nodes in each partition be G'. Let the

```
t_H ← initial_temperature(δ̄_H, p_0)
t_L ← initial_temperature(δ̄_L, p_0)
t_D ← initial_temperature(δ̄_D, p_0)
while consecutive_failures < max_failures and outer_loops < min_outer do
        for i ← 1 to max_inner do
                save state
                try a move
                δ_H ← heavy edge cost difference
                if δ_H < 0 or (δ_H > 0 and accept_badmove(δ_H,t_H)
                        accept the move
                        if δ_H < 0
                                consecutive_failures ← 0
                else if δ_H = 0
                        δ_L ← light edge cost difference
                        if δ_L < 0 or (δ_L > 0 and accept_badmove(δ_L,t_L)
                                accept the move
                                if δ_L < 0
                                        consecutive_failures ← 0
                        else if δ_L = 0
                                δ_D ← distributed edge cost difference
                                if δ_D < 0 or (δ_D >= 0 and accept_badmove(δ_D,t_D)
                                        accept the move
                                        if δ_D < 0
                                                consecutive_failures ← 0
                else
                        restore state
                        increment consecutive_failures
                end if
        end for
        t_H ← α × t_H;  t_L ← α × t_L; t_D ← α × t_D
end while
```

Figure 13: Prioritized Simulated Annealing Algorithm

weight of an edge between partition p_i and partition p_j in G' be the sum of the weights of each of the edges connecting nodes in p_i with a node in p_j.

- Use a maximum weight matching algorithm on G' to find a contraction of G in which each partition has no more than B processes. (The algorithm produces a set of edges which have no vertices in common, and such that the sum of the weights on the edges is maximal.)

For cases in which the number of clusters is less than $2N$, we pad with unconnected clusters which do no computation to achieve $2N$ clusters.

OREGAMI: Tools for Mapping Parallel Computations to Parallel Architectures[1]

Virginia M. Lo,[2] Sanjay Rajopadhye,[3] Samik Gupta,
David Keldsen, Moataz A. Mohamed, Bill Nitzberg,
Jan Arne Telle, and Xiaoxiong Zhong

Received April 1990; Revised March 1992

The OREGAMI project involves the design, implementation, and testing of algorithms for mapping parallel computations to message-passing parallel architectures. OREGAMI addresses the mapping problem by exploiting regularity and by allowing the user to guide and evaluate mapping decisions made by OREGAMI's efficient combinatorial mapping algorithms. OREGAMI's approach to mapping is based on a new graph theoretic model of parallel computation called the Temporal Communication Graph. The OREGAMI software tools include three components: (1) LaRCS is a graph description language which allows the user to describe regularity in the communication topology as well as the temporal communication behavior (the pattern of message-passing over time). (2) MAPPER is our library of mapping algorithms which utilize information provided by LaRCS to perform contraction, embedding, and routing. (3) METRICS is an interactive graphics tool for display and analysis of mappings. This paper gives an overview of the OREGAMI project, the software tools, and OREGAMI's mapping algorithms.

KEY WORDS: Mapping; routing; embedding; task assignment; regular parallel computations; parallel programming environments.

1. INTRODUCTION

The *mapping problem* in message-passing parallel processors involves the assignment of tasks in a parallel computation to processors and the routing of inter-task messages along the links of the interconnection network. Most commercial parallel processing systems today rely on manual task assignment by the programmer and message routing that does not utilize information about the communication patterns of the computation. The goal of our research is *automatic* and *guided* mapping of parallel computations to parallel architectures in order to achieve portability and to improve performance.

The OREGAMI[4] project involves the design, implementation, and testing of mapping algorithms. OREGAMI's approach to mapping is based on (1) its use of a new graph theoretic model of parallel computation which we call the *T*emporal *C*ommunication *G*raph, and (2) its exploitation of regularity found in the structure of parallel computations and of the target architecture.

We are concerned with the mapping of parallel computations which are designed by the programmer as a collection of communicating parallel processes. We note that many practical parallel computations are characterized by regular communication patterns. This regularity occurs both in the topological communication structure of the computation (which tasks send messages to whom) and in the temporal communication behavior exhibited by the computation (the patterns of message-passing phases over

[1] This research is sponsored by NSF grant MIP91-08528 and the Oregon Advanced Computing Institute.

[2] Department of Computer and Information Science, University of Oregon, Eugene, Oregon 97403–1202. lo@cs.uoregon.edu. Partially supported by NSF Grant CCR-8808532.

[3] Partially supported by NSF Grant MIP-8802454.

[4] For University of *OREG*on's techniques for elegant symmetric contractions which resemble the art of ori*GAMI* paper folding.

Reprinted with permission from *Int'l J. of Parallel Programming,* vol. 20, no. 3, 1991, pp. 237–270.

time). Furthermore, the programmer has explicit knowledge of this regularity because it forms the basis of the logical design of her/his computation. While the general mapping problem in its many formulations is known to be *NP*-hard, it has been shown that restriction of the problem to regular structures can yield optimal solutions or good suboptimal heuristics for mapping.

OREGAMI addresses the mapping problem by exploiting regularity whenever possible, and by allowing the user to guide and evaluate mapping decisions made by OREGAMI's mapping algorithms. Our mapping system balances the user's knowledge and intuition with the computational power of efficient combinatorial mapping algorithms.

The contributions of the OREGAMI project include:

- *The TCG model of parallel computation and the LaRCS graph description language.* The TCG model is a new graph theoretic model of parallel computation designed for the purpose of mapping. The TCG can be seen as an augmented version of Lamport's process-time graphs. The TCG integrates the two dominant models currently in use in the areas of mapping and scheduling: the static task graph and the DAG. LaRCS (*L*anguage for *R*egular *C*ommunication *S*tructures) is a graph description language which provides the user with the ability to describe the parallel computation's TCG in a natural and compact representation. LaRCS provides the capability to identify logically synchronous *phases* of communication, and to describe the temporal behavior of a parallel computation in terms of these phases in a notation called *phase expressions*.

- *Mapping algorithms which exploit regularity to yield high performance mappings.* Our mapping algorithms utilize the information provided by LaRCS to achieve mappings that are an improvement over uninformed mappings in two ways: the mapping algorithms themselves are efficient and the resultant mappings are optimal or near optimal based on a variety of standard performance metrics.

- *The OREGAMI software tools.* The OREGAMI tools include the LaRCS compiler; MAPPER, a library of mapping algorithms; and METRICS an interactive graphics tool for display and analysis of OREGAMI mappings. OREGAMI is designed for use as a front-end mapping tool in conjunction with parallel programming languages that support explicit message-passing, such as OCCAM, C*, Dino,[1] Par,[2] and C or Fortran with communication extensions. The underlying architecture is assumed to consist of homogeneous processors connected by some regular network topology, with current focus on the hypercube, mesh, and deBruijn topologies. Routing technologies supported by OREGAMI include store-and-forward, virtual cut-through, and wormhole routing. Systems such as the Intel iWarp, Intel iPSC machines, NCUBE hypercubes, and INMOS Transputer are candidates for use with OREGAMI. Note, however, that OREGAMI is a front-end mapping interface and generates symbolic mapping directives only. Development of back-end software to transform OREGAMI mapping directives to architecture dependent code is beyond the current scope of our work.

This paper provides an overview of the OREGAMI project and software tools. Section 2 discusses the formal foundations underlying OREGAMI's approach to mapping and related research. Section 3 describes the components of OREGAMI: LaRCS, MAPPER, and METRICS, and traces its operation with an illustrative example. Section 4

285

briefly illustrates how the individual mapping algorithms that we have developed for OREGAMI exploit regularity. Section 5 discusses areas of on-going and future work on this project.

2. FORMAL FOUNDATIONS AND RELATED RESEARCH

2.1. Formal Foundations: the Temporal Communication Graph

The foundations for the OREGAMI system lie in a new graph theoretic model of parallel computation we have developed called the *Temporal Communication Graph* and its ability to capture regularity for purposes of mapping. Both the TCG and its forerunner, the classic static task graph of Stone,[3] are designed for systems in which the programmer designs his or her program as a set of parallel processes that communicate through explicit message-passing. The identity of all of the processes is known at compile time, and all processes exist throughout the lifetime of the parallel computation.

The TCG was designed to enrich the static task graph model and to provide a means for describing regularity in the structure of the parallel computation for the purpose of mapping. Specifically,

- *The TCG integrates three important graph theoretic models of parallel computation: Lamport's process-time graphs, the static task graph, and the DAG.* The TCG combines the two predominant models currently in use in the areas of mapping, task assignment, partitioning, and scheduling: the static task graph and the precedence-constrained DAG. The integration of these two models enables a wide spectrum of algorithms to be used for mapping and scheduling which could not otherwise be invoked because of incompatibilities in the underlying graph theoretic models. In addition, the compatibility of the TCG with Lamport's process-time graphs makes it useful as a unified abstraction in parallel programming environments for program development, debugging, and performance evaluation as well as for mapping and scheduling.

- *The ability of the TCG and the LaRCS graph description language to describe* regularity *facilitates the development and use of specialized mapping algorithms which exploit regularity to yield improved performance.* The TCG and LaRCS are capable of representing regularity both in the communication topology and in the temporal patterns of message-passing over time.

2.1.1. Informal Description of the TCG

In this section, we give an intuitive description of the TCG. A formal definition of the TCG is given in Ref. 4 which also defines the formal semantics of LaRCS in terms of the TCG. Consider each individual process comprising the parallel computation. The activity of a given process p_i can be seen as a sequence of atomic events, where each event is either a computation event or a communication event (sending a message/receiving a message). The TCG is a DAG in which each atomic event (compute, send, or receive) is represented as a node. The sequence of atomic events on p_i is represented as a linear chain of nodes, with directed edges indicating the precedence relationship between the events. A message-passing event from process p_i to process p_j is represented with a directed edge from the send-event node on p_i to the corresponding receive-event node on p_j.

The TCG can thus be seen as an unrolling of the static task graph over time. Conversely, the projection of the TCG along the time axis yields the static task graph model. Weights associated with the nodes and edges can be used to represent computation and communication costs, respectively. Note that the TCG also can be viewed as a graph theoretic representation of Lamport's process-time diagrams[5] augmented with weights and colors. The coloring of the Lamport process-time graph is described in Ref. 4 and involves the identification of logically synchronous communication and computation phases as described in the next section.

Figure 1 shows the TCG for a parallel algorithm for the *n-body* problem which was designed for the Cosmic Cube.[6] This algorithm will be used as an example later in the paper to illustrate the use of the OREGAMI mapping tools.

As discussed earlier, the TCG can be seen as a hybrid of the two predominant models of parallel computation: the static task graph model of Stone,[3] and the precedence-constrained (DAG) model[7] used in multiprocessor scheduling and in the parallelization of sequential code. Task assignment and scheduling research utilizing these two models has more or less followed disjoint paths over the past two decades, in that techniques and algorithms developed for one model have not been applicable to the other. The TCG model is compatible with both of these existing models. Thus algorithms for static task assignment such as Refs. 8–11 and scheduling algorithms for precedence-constrained graphs such as in Refs. 7 and 12 can be applied to the TCG model. The contribution of the TCG is that it augments these two models with the ability to explicitly capture regularity, allowing the development of specialized mapping and scheduling algorithms to exploit this regularity.

The TCG is also capable of modeling computations of arbitrary granularity, characterized by irregular and asynchronous communication. We note that the TCG does not model nondeterministic computations and dynamically spawned tasks. More information about the TCG model and its use in parallel programming environments can be found in Ref. 4.

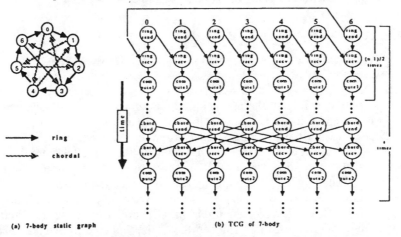

(a) 7-body static graph   (b) TCG of 7-body

The *n-body problem* requires determining the equilibrium of *n* bodies in space (where *n* is odd) under the action of a gravitational or electrostatic, etc. field. This is done iteratively by computing the net force exerted on each body by the others, given their "current" position, updating its location based on this force, and repeating this until the forces are as close to zero as desired. The parallel algorithm presented by Seitz uses Newton's third law of motion to avoid duplication of effort in the force computation. It consists of *n* identical tasks, each one responsible for one body. The tasks are arranged in a ring and pass information about their accumulated forces to its neighbor around the ring. After (*n* − 1)/2 steps, each task will have received information from half of its predecessors around the ring. Each task then acquires information about the remaining bodies by receiving a message from its chordal neighbor halfway around the ring. This is repeated to the desired degree of accuracy.

Fig. 1. Temporal communication graph for the *n-body algorithm*.

287

2.1.2. Describing Regularity in the TCG

We note that many practical parallel algorithms involve one or more *phases* of communication. These phases are often characterized by regularity in the communication topology, i.e., the static task graph is a known graph structure such as a mesh, a tree, etc. In addition, these algorithms also exhibit regularity in the temporal communication behavior (the patterns of message-passing phases that are active over time).

A *compute phase* corresponds to a set of nodes in the TCG (compute events) that are involved in *logically synchronous* computation. A *communication phase* corresponds to a set of edges (sender/receiver pairs) in the TCG that are involved in *logically synchronous* communication. By *logically synchronous* we mean that at run time the activities occur simultaneously from the viewpoint of the programmer, i.e. from the logical structural design of the algorithm. [In reality, when the program executes, the timing of logically synchronous activities may not be synchronous with respect to real time, due to effects such as the hardware characteristics of the execution environment and the multiplexing of processes on the processors.]

These phases are identified using a node labeling scheme for each process. Each communication phase can then be described by a *communication function* whose domain and range are process node labels. For example, a ring of communicating processes can be described as *ring: forall* i *in* $0..n - 1 i \Rightarrow i + 1 \mod n$ where we assume the processes are labeled sequentially from 0 to $n - 1$. In LaRCS, a notation called *phase expressions* is used to describe the temporal behavior of the parallel computation in terms of its compute phases and communication phases. In addition, LaRCS allows the user to describe families of regular graphs in a parameterized notation whose size is independent of the size of the task graph. The LaRCS description of the *n-body algorithm* and further details about LaRCS are described in the next section.

2.2. Related Research

As an integrated set of tools for mapping, OREGAMI is similar in many respects to Francine Berman's Prep-P System.[9,13] Both Prep-P and OREGAMI provide a graph description language for describing the communication structure of the parallel computation. Prep-P's GDL language is based on the static task graph model of parallel computation and is embedded within the system's parallel programming language XX. LaRCS is based on our TCG model, which augments the static task graph with temporal information. The LaRCS specification is independent of any specific parallel programming language and is coded separately by the programmer. Prep-P is a fully integrated system: Prep-P mappings are targeted for the CHiP reconfigurable parallel architecture[14] and Prep-P currently generates code that runs on the CHiP simulator known as Poker. OREGAMI is also related to the TMAP mapping tool, a component of the TIPS transputer-based interactive parallelizing system.[15] TMAP is an adaptation of Prep-P for the transputer architecture. As discussed in the introduction, OREGAMI is currently a front-end mapping tool and only generates symbolic mapping directives.

OREGAMI is also related to a number of mapping and scheduling systems that utilize the classic DAG model of parallel computation such as CODE/ROPE,[16] TaskGrapher,[17] Polychronopoulos[18] and Sakar.[19] These systems differ from OREGAMI, Prep-P, and TMAP because they are designed for the purpose of parallelizing sequential code.

The OREGAMI mapping algorithms take the approach of many researchers who have attacked the mapping problem by exploiting the regularity found in the computation graph and/or the interconnection network. A large body of theoretical work on graph embeddings has yielded 1:1 mappings tailored for specific regular graphs; some of the more recent results are given in Ref. 20. Many of these algorithms have or will be included in the OREGAMI library. Edge grammars[21] use formal language techniques to address the contraction of families of task graphs. Stone[31] and Bokhari[8] use a variety of graph theoretic algorithms to address task assignment for structures including trees, chains, and arbitrary task graphs. Work in the area of systolic arrays has yielded elegant mapping techniques for computations whose data dependencies can be expressed as affine recurrences.[22,23] Related work in the area of application-dependent routing includes Refs. 24 and 25. Our mapping algorithms build on these foundations and utilize techniques from group theory, graph theory, coding theory, and linear algebra. Other approaches to the mapping problem include search algorithms, linear programming, and clustering algorithms. These latter techniques typically do not exploit the regularity of the task graph.

The LaRCS language bears similarities to a number of graph description languages or configuration languages which have been developed for a variety of purposes in the area of parallel and distributed computing. These include formal approaches such as edge grammers[21] and graph grammars,[26,27] as well as more practical languages such as GDL,[13] CONIC,[28] GARP,[26] and ParaGraph.[29] Of these, LaRCS, edge grammars, and GDL were designed specifically to address the mapping problem. LaRCS is unique in its ability to describe the temporal behavior of parallel computations. A primitive form of phase expressions was introduced by Nelson and Snyder.[30]

From the viewpoint of support environments for parallel programming, OREGAMI belongs to the family of systems which take a process-oriented view of parallel computation based on explicit message-passing. Examples of such systems include Prep-P,[9,13] Poker,[14,31] ORCA,[32,33] the Parallel Programming Environments Project,[29] and TIPS.[15] OREGAMI and Prep-P focus on the mapping problem. The other projects address the broader issues of program design and development.

3. OREGAMI SYSTEM OVERVIEW

This section describes the OREGAMI software tools and traces the use of these tools using the *n-body algorithm* as an example. Figure 2 illustrates the three components of the OREGAMI system.

The user first describes his/her parallel computation in LaRCS, by specifying (a) the static structure of the parallel computation graph using a node labeling scheme and simple communication functions, and (b) the temporal communication behavior of the computation using *phase expressions* (notationally similar to regular expressions). The LaRCS specification is program-independent, i.e., it can be used in conjunction with a variety of parallel programming languages to provide information about regularity to be found in the communication structure of the computation.

The LaRCS compiler translates the LaRCS code into an intermediate representation (an abstract syntax tree). The intermediate code is translated into the form needed for specific mapping algorithms, using OREGAMI utility functions to generate the desired data structures for each algorithm, such as the TCG, the static task graph, static task graphs corresponding to each communication phase, the individual communica-

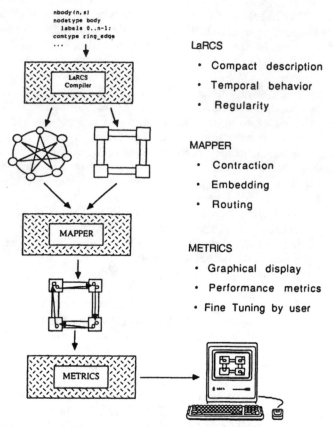

```
nbody(n, s)
nodetype body
    labels 0..n-1;
comtype ring_edge
    ...
```

LaRCS

- Compact description
- Temporal behavior
- Regularity

MAPPER

- Contraction
- Embedding
- Routing

METRICS

- Graphical display
- Performance metrics
- Fine Tuning by user

Fig. 2. OREGAMI System Overview.

tion functions, etc. The information is used by the MAPPER and METRICS software to perform mapping and to display and analyze the mapping, respectively.

The input to MAPPER includes the LaRCS description of the computation and a description of the target architecture which consists of the name plus parameters (e.g. hypercube of dimension 4). MAPPER examines any regular properties specified in the LaRCS code and uses one or more algorithms to do the mapping. These algorithms can be invoked automatically or through user selection. Many parallel computations have well known communication structures (such as trees, meshes, etc.) and the programmer may simply state this. OREGAMI has a library of "canned" mappings for such computations, and generating one simply involves a lookup in a library. Other algorithms may have a regular structure of a particular kind (such as node-symmetric). For such computations OREGAMI uses specialized algorithms which are often extremely efficient. If no regularity can be exploited, efficient polynomial time algorithms are used to perform the mapping in three steps—contraction, embedding, and routing.

Finally, the user may inspect the mapping using METRICS. METRICS is an interactive graphics tool which displays the mapping along with a range of performance metrics reflecting load balancing, communication contention, and communication overhead. METRICS also allows the user to focus on specific processors or links and provides the opportunity for manual modification of the mapping.

The OREGAMI software tools are implemented in C for SUN workstations using Xlib, XtIntrinsic and the MIT Athena widget set. A new *topology* widget has been defined to display and manipulate various architecture types and mappings to them.

290

OREGAMI has been tested with a wide variety of parallel algorithms including several algorithms for matrix multiplication, fast Fourier transform, topological sort, divide and conquer using binary tree, divide and conquer using binomial tree, simulated annealing, Jacobi iterative method for solving Laplace equations on a rectangle, successive-over-relaxation iterative method, perfect broadcast distributed voting, numeric integration, distributed dot product, five point difference operation, Gaussian elimination with partial pivoting, matrix row rotation, and the simplex algorithm.

The performance of the OREGAMI mapping algorithms was evaluated through analytic proofs and through simulations. Simulations were performed using a library of C programs we have developed which generate task graphs derived from actual parallel programs as well as random task graphs. A non-backtracking branch and bound program was used to compute optimal mappings.

3.1. LaRCS

A LaRCS program consists of the following major components: (a) the LaRCS *nodetype* declaration which describes the processes, (b) the LaRCS *comtype* and *comphase* declarations which are used as templates to describe the communication structure of the parallel program, and (c) the LaRCS *phase expression* which describes the entire parallel program in terms of its temporal computation and communication behavior. A *comtype* declaration describes a single communication edge; a *comphase* describes a set of synchronous communication edges. A *phase expression* instantiates all the edges of a parallel computation using the *comtype* and *comphase* declarations, and describes the message-passing behavior of the computation over time. We note that there is a distinction between "temporal communication behavior" (as used here) and dynamically evolving task graphs. In our model the entire graph is known statically. We describe temporal behavior by identifying collections of edges that are "active" simultaneously, and by the pattern of this activity.

Figure 3 gives the LaRCS code for the *n-body* algorithm. The line numbers in the LaRCS code are used for reference purposes only in the following commentary:

1. *Name of algorithm and parameters.* The parameters specify the size of this instance of the parallel algorithm. The parameters for the *n-body algorithm* are n, the number of bodies, and s, the number of iterations. [Since LaRCS is intended for static mapping, we require an estimate of the runtime parameter, s]

```
# LaRCS code for the n-body algorithm

1.    nbody(n,s)
2.    attributes nodesymmetric;
3.    nodetype body
          labels 0..(n-1);
4.    comtype ring_edge(i) body(i) => body((i+1) mod n);
          volume = MSGSIZE;
      comtype chordal_edge(i) body(i) => body((i+(n+1)/2) mod n);
          volume = MSGSIZE;
5.    comphase ring
          forall i in 0..(n-1) {ring_edge(i)};
      comphase chordal
          forall i in 0..(n-1) {chordal_edge(i)};
6.    phase_expr
          {{ring |> compute}**(n-1)/2 |> chordal |> compute}**s;
```

Fig. 3. LaRCS code for the *n-body algorithm*

2. *Attributes.* The programmer may specify global characteristics of the task graph, such as *nodesymmetric* or *planar*.

3. *Nodetype declaration.* A *nodetype* is defined by giving it a name, specifying the number of nodes, and specifying the node labeling. Node labels can be multi-dimensional and parameterized. For the *n-body algorithm* there is one *nodetype* declaration of type *body*. The nodes are labeled from 0 to $n-1$. If there is only one *nodetype*, the explicit declaration may be omitted.

4. *Comtype declaration.* A *comtype* specifies a single potential edge and can be parameterized. In both *comtype* and *comphase* declarations the symbol $\Rightarrow$ denotes unidirectional message passing and $\Leftrightarrow$ denotes bidirectional message passing. In Fig. 3, there are two *comtype* declarations: *ring_edge* and *chordal_edge*. The *volume* field of the *comtype* declaration is an expression which specifies the message volume (typically in bytes) of a single message transfer.

5. *Comphase declaration.* A *comphase* identifies a potential set of edges involved in synchronous message passing, usually by specifying a set of values for the parameter(s) of one or more *comtypes*. The *comphase* declaration may itself be parameterized and these parameters are later instantiated within the phase expression. In the *n-body algorithm* there are two *comphase* declarations: *ring* and *chordal*.

6. *Phase expression.* The phase expression describes the temporal behavior of the computation in terms of its communication phases. Phase expressions are defined recursively below where r and s are phase expressions.

- *compute* is a keyword phase expression denoting a computational phase of activity.

- a single *comphase* is a phase expression.

- sequence: $r \,|\!> s$ is a phase expression which denotes sequential execution of the phases.

- sequential repetition: $r ** expr$ is a phase expression denoting repeated execution of r a number of times specified by arithmetic expression *expr*.

- sequential loop: *for* $var = range\{r\}$ is a phase expression denoting repeated execution of r a number of times specified by *range*, where *var* is a formal parameter in r.

- parallelism: $r \,||\, s$ is a phase expression denoting parallel execution of phases r and s.

- parameterized parallelism: *forall* var *in* $range\{r\}$ is a phase expression denoting parallel execution of phases in r, where *var* appears as a parameter in r.

Only expressions derived by a finite application of these rules are phase expressions. A precise definition of the semantics of phase expressions is given in Ref. 4.

3.1.1. The Benefits of LaRCS for Mapping

LaRCS plays a critical role in OREGAMI by (1) providing information about the regular structure of the parallel computation through the *comphase* declarations and the *phase expression*; and (2) by serving as an efficient representation of *families* of regular computation graphs whose size is independent of the size of the actual instantiated graph. The LaRCS compiler translates the LaRCS code into intermediate code (an abstract syntax tree) representation of the computation to be mapped. This intermediate representation can then be translated into the form needed for specific OREGAMI mapping algorithms such as the TCG, the static task graph for the whole computation, or the static task graph for a single *comphase*. OREGAMI provides a set of utility functions to generate specific data structures for these graphs such as an adjacency matrix, given the parameters that instantiate the size of the problem instance.

An example of the use of the LaRCS *phase expression* in mapping is described next. Further examples of the benefits of LaRCS for mapping are described in Section 4.

Most existing mapping algorithms, including several in OREGAMI, utilize the *static task graph* and require an estimate of communication volume (edge weights.) Current techniques for computation of edge weights include profiling, user estimates, and compiler analysis of the program code. In OREGAMI, the phase expression can be used to derive an arithmetic formula for calculation of communication volumes given the unit volume associated with a single message.

The LaRCS *comtype*-declaration's *volume* field is typically initialized to the number of bytes sent in a single message of that *comtype*. For example, based on the code for the *n-body algorithm*, the volume for the *comtype* *ring* is 108 bytes. This value would be specified by the user in the LaRCS code. The *phase expression* can be used to compute the total communication volume for each communication edge in the static task graph by multiplying the unit volume times the number of iterations derived from the *phase expression*. Thus, the total communication overhead for a *ring* edge of the *n-body algorithm* is equal to $108 \times n \times s$, where n and s are parameters instantiated at compile time.

At this stage in OREGAMI's development, the unit volume and all parameters must be expressed as integer constants; the phase expression then drives the calculation of the total communication volume for each *comphase* and for the complete static task graph. In the future, we will be expanding our system to accept volume declarations in terms of imported variables from the host language. This extension relieves the programmer of the burden of counting up the number of bytes in a message involving complex data structures and/or multiple data structures. In addition, we will examine the feasibility of mapping which utilizes *volume expressions* with uninstantiated variables.

3.2. MAPPER

In OREGAMI, mapping is usually achieved in three steps: *contraction* of the task graph to a smaller graph (in cases where the number of tasks exceeds the number of processors), *embedding*, assignment of the contracted clusters of tasks to processors, and *routing* of the messages through the interconnection network in order to minimize contention. Our mapping algorithms fall into three groups.

- Class I: Canned mapping algorithms for computations whose communication topology matches well-known graph families such as binary tres, binomial trees, rings, etc. Mappings for these computation structures for the hypercube, mesh, and deBruijn networks have been developed *a priori* using human ingenuity. Canned mappings are stored in a library and retrieved given the name and parameters of the computation graph and the network graph.

- Class II: Mapping algorithms for computations for which the regularity is captured by LaRCS code. The mapping algorithms use techniques tailored for the specific regular properties captured by LaRCS.

- Class III: Mapping algorithms for arbitrary computations. Heuristic algorithms are used to compute the mapping in cases when no regularity can be exploited.

Figure 4 shows the organization of MAPPER and Table II summarizes the mapping algorithms we have developed, giving the general approach used, the performance results, and references to the relevant papers. These algorithms are described in more detail in Section 4. OREGAMI is periodically updated with new mapping algorithms, including those developed by other researchers as well.

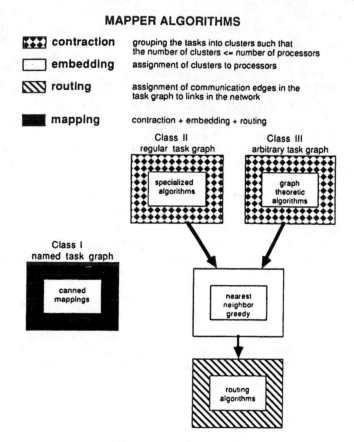

Fig. 4. MAPPER contraction, embedding, routing.

3.3. METRICS

The METRICS software allows the user to view and modify the mapping and routing produced by OREGAMI, while computing a wide range of performance metrics (see table below). METRICS is designed to display the mapping in a clear, logical, and intuitive format so that the user can evaluate it quantitatively (through well-known empirical performance metrics) as well as visually (through the use of colors and spatial layout, particularly when the computation graph exhibits regularity). METRICS is also designed to be interactive to allow the user to manually modify the mapping produced by the OREGAMI software. The target architectures currently supported by METRICS include the mesh and hypercube. METRICS supports analysis for three routing schemes: store-and-forward, virtual cut-through, and wormhole routing.

3.3.1. METRICS Displays

METRICS uses multiple windows to organize information into three selectable objects: the *computation object*, the *architecture object*, and the *mapping object*. Additionally, three subviews of the *mapping object* allow the user to focus on a specific processor, a specific link, or a single communication phase. Information from each of these objects and subviews is presented through three windows: *text window*, *graphics window*, and *metrics window*. (See Fig. 5.)

The *computation object* corresponds to the parallel computation before mapping. The LaRCS program code is displayed in the *text window*. If the user selects the *spatial perspective*, the *graphics window* displays the computation's TCG as a static task graph. By default, the processes of the static task graph are laid out as a ring, but if a predefined computational

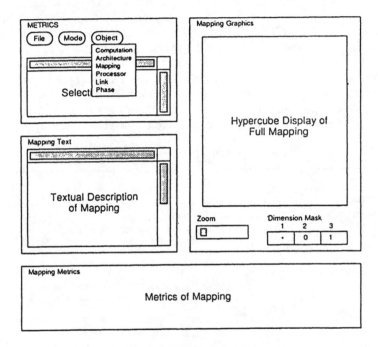

Fig. 5.   METRICS overview.

structure, such as a tree, was specified by the LaRCS code, the graph will be displayed using the display semantics specific to that structure. The user may also view the computation as a DAG by selecting the *temporal perspective*. Communication phases are distinguished by color. The *metrics window* displays performance metrics such as the number of processes, the number of phases, the communication matrix with estimated message volume between processes (per phase and for the entire computation), and the execution matrix with estimated execution time of the processes.

The *architecture object* corresponds to the target machine topology. The *text window* shows the name of the architecture, size parameters, routing scheme (store-and-forward, virtual cut-through, or wormhole), including values for channel bandwidth, message startup time, and message switching time. The *graphics window* displays a graphic representation of the bare machine. The *metrics window* shows an adjacency matrix representation of the network topology, network metrics such as diameter and degree, and architecture characteristics such as channel bandwidth and message-startup time.

The *mapping object* corresponds to the full computation as it is mapped onto the complete architecture. The *text window* identifies which processor each process is assigned to and enumerates each message routing as a list of processor elements. The *graphics window* displays the network topology, with each process displayed in the appropriate processor element and messages rendered as edges, color-coded by phase. This view allows the user to rearrange the mapping by clicking on and dragging processes onto other processor elements. Selectable mapping metrics include processor task load, processor execution load, message dilation, link contention, and link communication volume, and latest finishing time (see Table I). Metrics are displayed as bar graphs, color-coded communication matrices, and color-coded topology views (see Fig. 6).

The *processor subview* allows the user to examine a single processor and the set of processes mapped to it in detail. These windows show a graphic representation of the processor element, as well as the following metrics: task load, execution load, and comparisons to the global average.

The *link subview* focuses on a single architecture link connecting two adjacent processors, displaying the messages routed over that link. The link metrics include the total contention in messages and in communication volume, and a comparison to global averages.

The *phase subview* allows the user to examine a single communication phase in detail. The *text window* displays the LaRCS code for the communication phase, while the *graphics window* shows the topology and the mapped computation for the specified phase. Performance metrics for phases include those displayed for a complete *mapping object*.

Table I. METRICS Performance Metrics

Metric	Description
Processor Task Load	Number of tasks per processor nonzero-avg. avg, max, nonzero-min, min
Processor Execution Load	Sum of execution costs (node weights) per processor nonzero-avg. avg, max, nonzero-min, min
Dilation	Number of hops spanned by a communication edge nonzero-avg. avg, max, nonzero-min, min
Contention	Sum of communication costs (edge weights) per link nonzero-avg. avg, max, nonzero-min, min
Kandlur/Shin metric	Weighted sum combining dilation and contention $T(R) = \sum_{e \in E} (\sum_{m \in M, e \in R(m)} W(m))^2$ where, $T(R)$ is the cost of the routing function R, E is the set of links in the architecture, M is the set of messages, and $W(x)$ is the weight of a message x, $R(x)$ represents the set of edges on which R routes the message x
Total IPC	Sum of communication costs (edge weights) for all inter-processor communication
Total Completion Time	$\sum_{p \in phases} max\{c_p^1, c_p^2, ..., c_p^m\}$ where *phases* includes all instances of both *compute* phases and *comphases*. m is the number of processors, c_p^j is the completion time of phase p on processor j

The phase expression drives the calculation of completion time in a manner similar to the calculation of communication volume described earlier. Our current definition of completion time presumes barrier synchronization between phases *in order to simplify the calculation of this metric*. However, neither the architecture nor the parallel computation are constrained to execute with global synchronization between phases. The calculation of completion time of each phase on each processor takes into account the multiplexing of processes and the overhead of message passing including dilation, and contention. The computation of dilation and contention are based on the specific communication technology used for message-passing, taking into account message startup and switching times. METRICS currently models store-and-forward and wormhole routing.

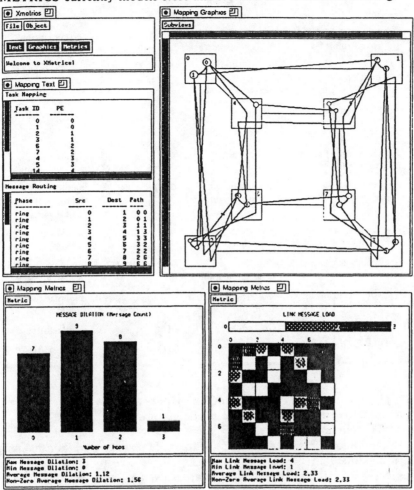

Fig. 6. METRICS windows displaying the 15 body algorithm mapped to the 3-dim hypercube.

4. OREGAMI MAPPING ALGORITHMS

In this section we describe the mapping algorithms we have developed for OREGAMI. These algorithms are summarized in Table II. Our algorithms perform contraction, embedding, and routing for both regular and arbitrary task graphs, utilizing a variety of mathematical techniques. The purpose of this discussion is to give the general flavor behind each of the algorithms and to show how information provided by LaRCS is utilized. A formal treatment of these algorithms and extensive performance evaluation is found in the referenced papers.

4.1. Canned Mapping of Binomial Tree Divide and Conquer Algorithms

Our contribution to the library of canned mappings is a set of mappings of the binomial tree[34] to the mesh and the deBruijn networks. As stated earlier, the input to OREGAMI for these canned mappings is

297

Table II. OREGAMI Mapping Algorithms

Class	Mapping	Technique	Complexity	Performance
I	binomial tree to hypercube[35,46]	Gray code labeling	$O(1)$	no contention avg dilation $\leqslant 1$
I	binomial tree to mesh[35]	Gray code reflection	$O(1)$	no contention avg. dilation $\leqslant 1.2$
I	binomial tree to deBruijn[36]	combinatorial, shift register sequences	$O(1)$	no contention avg. dilation $\leqslant 2$
I	ring to deBruijn[49]	enumeration of necklaces/shift register sequences	$O(1)$	gives precise no. necklaces
II	algorithms expressible as affine recurrences[22] (work in progress)	recurrences theory	$O(1)$	optimal
II	Cayley/node symm. contraction[48]	group theory (Cayley graphs)	$O(VE)$	optimal load balancing
III	arbitrary contraction[40]	maximum weight matching algorithm	$O(EV \log V)$	minimizes IPC subject to load balancing
III	store-and-forward routing	maximal matching algorithm	$O(HDM^3)$	minimizes contention
III	wormhole routing[41]	iteratively reduce contention:	$O(|E| M^2 W^2 d)$	minimize contention: deadlock-free
III	wormhole routing[42]	shortest path algorithm	$O(M(nN + \log M))$	minimize contention: deadlock-free
III	ecube routing	Gray code	$O(1)$	deadlock-free
III	X–Y routing	x then y	$O(1)$	deadlock-free

simply the name of the computation graph and the architecture, plus parameters to instantiate the size of the graphs.

The binomial tree is a highly efficient structure for parallel divide and conquer algorithms, as an alternative to the full binary tree. Our mappings are illustrated in Fig. 7. These mappings have constant time complexity because they are precomputed. They are proven to be optimal with respect to contention and we prove bounds on the average dilation (see Table II.) Space limitations prevents us from discussing the mappings in this paper; a formal treatment can be found in Refs. 35 and 36.

4.2. Contraction of Cayley Node Symmetric Task Graphs

We have developed a contraction algorithm for a subset of node symmetric task graphs called Cayley graphs which is made feasible by the information contained in the LaRCS *comphase* declarations. The algorithm is rooted in group theory[37] and yields a *symmetric contraction* in which there is an identical number of nodes per cluster and with each cluster having exactly one incoming and one outgoing 'contracted edge' for each communication phase. Each contracted edge represents an identical number of messages, thus the contraction is perfectly load balanced with respect to both computation and communication.

Our strategy requires that we detect whether the task graph T is a Cayley graph where the communication phases are in 1-1 correspondence with edge colors, defined as follows: For G a finite group and S a set of generators for G, $Cayley(G, S)$ is a graph where the nodes are the elements of G, and there is an edge with 'color' c from a to b if and only if there is

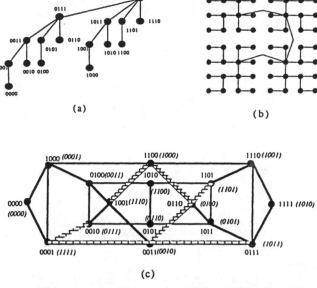

Fig. 7. (a) Binomial tree and its canonical labeling (b) Mapping of 64 node binomial tree to 8 × 8 mesh (c) Mapping of 16 node binomial tree to 16 node deBruijn.

a generator $c \in S$ such that under the group operation $ac = b$. No polynomial-time algorithm is known that recognizes Cayley graphs based on an adjacency matrix representation.[38] However, with the aid of the LaRCS communication phases, for a task graph T with n nodes and m edges, in time $\mathcal{O}(nm)$, our algorithm either reports that T does not satisfy the criteria or produces a contraction as described above while trying to match the number of clusters with the number of processors. The contraction algorithm is thus efficient only with the added information given by the LaRCS code. The algorithm is based on the fact that under certain conditions, the LaRCS communication phases of T can be used to directly derive the generators S of the underlying group G.

We note that this approach to contraction will be especially useful for data parallel algorithms which are inherently node symmetric. In addition, many interesting interconnection networks, such as the butterfly, hypercube, cube-connected cycles, are themselves based on Cayley graphs that have an underlying group structure.[39] Hopefully, this will also be an aid in the embedding and routing steps of the mapping.

Example. We will use the *8-node perfect broadcast algorithm* to illustrate the operation of *Algorithm Cayley-Contract.* (See Fig. 8). In the *perfect broadcast algorithm*, 2^k processes with successive integer labels each disseminate information to all other processes in k steps by sending messages to neighbors whose distance from each sender represents successive powers of 2. In our example there are thus 3 communication phases, and process 0 will send to processes 1, 2 and 4, in that order.

- The first requirement is that each communication phase is a bijection on the set of nodes $X = \{0, 1, ..., 7\}$. In that case, we calculate the value of each communication phase on the points of X and write the associated permutations in cycle notation as

$comm1 = (0\ 1\ 2\ 3\ 4\ 5\ 6\ 7)$

$comm2 = (0\ 2\ 4\ 6)(1\ 3\ 5\ 7)$

$comm3 = (0\ 4)(1\ 5)(2\ 6)(3\ 7)$

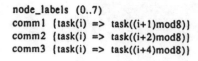

```
node_labels (0..7)
comm1 (task(i) => task((i+1)mod8))
comm2 (task(i) => task((i+2)mod8))
comm3 (task(i) => task((i+4)mod8))
```

(a)

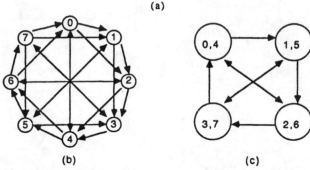

(b)   (c)

Fig. 8. Group theoretic contraction: (a) Fragment of LaRCS code showing the communication types; (b) Task graph; (c) Contracted task graph.

- The crucial point is that the communication phases can also be viewed as the set of generators of a permutation group G acting on X. This generator set gives rise to a unique Cayley graph CG. We can make use of the group G in the contraction of the task graph T when CG is isomorphic to T with the colors of CG and the communication phases in 1-1 correspondence. This is the case precisely when the action of G is *regular* on X. Detecting whether this is the case involves finding a spanning tree of T and thereby expressing elements of G in terms of products of generators. For our example the group G is indeed regular and the correspondence between elements of the group generated and the nodes of the task graph is given as

$E0$: $(0)(1)(2)(3)(4)(5)(6)(7)$ $\Rightarrow$ task 0

$E1$: $(0\ 1\ 2\ 3\ 4\ 5\ 6\ 7)$ $\Rightarrow$ task 1

$E2$: $(0\ 2\ 4\ 6)(1\ 3\ 5\ 7)$ $\Rightarrow$ task 2

$E3$: $(0\ 3\ 6\ 1\ 4\ 7\ 2\ 5)$ $\Rightarrow$ task 3

$E4$: $(0\ 4)(1\ 5)(2\ 6)(3\ 7)$ $\Rightarrow$ task 4

$E5$: $(0\ 5\ 2\ 7\ 4\ 1\ 6\ 3)$ $\Rightarrow$ task 5

$E6$: $(0\ 6\ 4\ 2)(1\ 7\ 5\ 3)$ $\Rightarrow$ task 6

$E7$: $(0\ 7\ 6\ 5\ 4\ 3\ 2\ 1)$ $\Rightarrow$ task 7

- It can be shown that a quotient Cayley graph arising from a subgroup of G is a contraction of T preserving the symmetry of the parallel algorithm. We are interested in contractions where the number of clusters is close to the number of nodes in the graph of our target architecture, and where communication between tasks is internalized in a cluster. In our example, the target architecture has 4 processors and since the subgroup $\{E0, E4\}$ arises from the generator $comm3 = (04)(15)(26)(37)$ it yields a contraction where 2 messages are internalized in each cluster and we can map one cluster to each of the processors. Note that given this contraction, the lockstep symmetry in the execution of the algorithm is preserved by alternately multiplexing tasks in the order $\{0, 1, 2, 3\}$ followed by $\{4, 5, 6, 7\}$ on the four processors. This may be the most desirable property of these group theoretic contractions, which we hope to exploit further in the later stages of mapping and scheduling.

300

4.3. Contraction of Arbitrary Task Graphs

Algorithm MWM-Contract performs contraction of arbitrary task graphs based on the static task graph representation of the parallel computation which is obtained from the LaRCS code. *MWM-Contract* utilizes an $O(EV \log V)$ maximum weighted matching algorithm, where E is the number of edges and V the number of vertices in the static task graph. This contraction merges tasks into clusters such that the total interprocessor communication is minimized while satisfying the load balancing constraint that the total number of tasks per processor be bounded by some constant B. Typically B is set to the number of tasks divided by the number of processors.

If the number of tasks is less than or equal to twice the number of processors, the algorithm yields an optimal symmetric contraction. If the number of tasks is greater than twice the number of processors, a greedy heuristic is used in conjunction with the maximum weight matching algorithm to find suboptimal task clusters. The greedy heuristic converts the original task graph into a smaller graph which satisfies the property that the number of new nodes is less than twice the number of processors. Then an optimal symmetric contraction can be found for this smaller graph, yielding a suboptimal contraction of the original task graph.

Preliminary testing of the performance of *MWM-Contract* involved simulations on a wide range of task graphs. The data used includes four types of task graphs, with the best performance exhibited by graphs characterized by regular communication topologies (90.0% of the contractions found were optimal). Details of Algorithm MWM-Contract, proofs of optimality, and simulation results can be found in Ref. 40.

Example. Figure 9 illustrates the operation of Algorithm *MWM-Contract* on an (irregular) computation in which 12 tasks must be assigned to 3 processors under the load balancing constraint of at most $B = 4$ tasks per processor.

- First, the greedy heuristic merges tasks into clusters until the number of clusters is less than or equal to two times the number of processors. In order to satisfy the load balancing constraint of $B = 4$ tasks per processor, the greedy heuristic ensures that no cluster size exceeds $B/2 = 2$ tasks. This is achieved by examining edges in the task graph in non-increasing order based on the edge weights. Initially, each edge connects individual tasks. After several passes of the heuristic, however, an edge connects clusters of tasks which have been merged in previous passes. When an edge is examined, the two clusters are merged if the total number of tasks in the resulting combined cluster does not exceed $B/2$. For example in Fig. 9, the edge with weight 15 does not result in merging because the combined cluster would have 4 tasks.
  The outcome of the greedy heuristic is a new graph in which each node is a cluster of tasks from the original task graph. A single edge between two clusters will represent the total communication between all the tasks in the two clusters and will thus have a weight equal to the sum of the weights on the corresponding edges from the original task graph. In addition, the new graph will satisfy two conditions: (a) the number of nodes will be less than two times the number of processors and (b) the number of tasks within a cluster will be less than or equal to $B/2$.
- The maximum weight matching algorithm is then invoked on the new graph to produce an optimal contraction of clusters to processors which minimizes the total IPC and satisfies the load balancing constraint B. Figure 9b illustrates the contraction of the

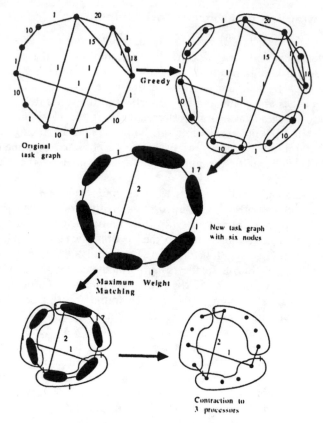

Fig. 9. Algorithm *MWM-Contract.*

6 clusters to 3 processors and the corresponding contraction of the original 12 tasks. The total IPC = 6 and happens to be optimal in this case.

4.4. Embedding of Arbitrary Task Graphs

After contraction, embedding is achieved by *Algorithm NN-Embed* which uses a greedy approach to place highly communicating clusters on adjacent neighbors in the network graph.

NN-Embed is used by OREGAMI to assign process clusters to processors in the target architecture. Currently the mesh and the hypercube are supported. Its input is a contracted task graph which has no more clusters than the number of processors. The edge weights are assumed to represent communication volumes of a single dominant phase. We use a greedy heuristic that attempts to minimize the total weighted dilation of the embedding.

Given a contracted task graph, *NN-Embed* first constructs a list of all the edges in the graph sorted by weight. Ties are resolved by comparing the total weights on *all other* edges adjacent to the two edges. Then the algorithm traverses this list in linear time and for each edge, assigns its endpoints as follows:

- If both nodes have already been assigned, do nothing.
- If only one node has been assigned, then assign the other node to the closest free processor (this may not be unique, but the algorithm scans the processor list in a particular order—increasing integer labels for the hypercube and row major order for the mesh).

302

- If neither node has been assigned, randomly choose a free processor and assign one node to it and the other to its closest free neighbor.

Apart from the sorting step which took $O(V \log V)$ time, the rest of the algorithm runs linearly in the number of edges. In the future, we plan to develop embedding algorithms which exploit regularity.

4.5. Routing in OREGAMI

OREGAMI performs routing after the computation graph has been contracted and the tasks have been assigned to processors. Thus, the input to each of OREGAMI's routing algorithms specifies the set of messages to be routed by giving the source and destination processors corresponding to the sender and receiver processes, respectively. Our algorithms use the information provided by the LaRCS *comphase* declarations to achieve low contention routing. Routing directives are represented symbolically as a list of source processor, intermediate processors, and destination processor. Currently, OREGAMI does not translate these directives into system-specific routing control headers.

To date, we have developed three heuristic routing algorithms, one for systems which utilize store-and-forward routing *MM/SF-Route* and two for systems which utilize wormhole-like routing *WORM1-Route* and *WORM2-Route*. OREGAMI's routing library also includes the fixed *ecube* routing algorithm for the hypercube and the fixed *X-Y* routing algorithm for the mesh.

OREGAMI's routing algorithms perform routing on a phase by phase basis. Recall that the *comphase* declaration identifies logically synchronous communication, i.e. message passing that can occur simultaneously at runtime. This information enables the routing software to focus on only those messages that are capable of actual contention at runtime. There are several advantages to be gained by this approach:

- The likelihood of finding a routing with low contention is greater because fewer communication edges are considered.
- The use of contention as a performance metric for mapping and embedding is more accurate, since we avoid measuring *false contention*, i.e., when two edges are mapped to the same link which are not active simultaneously at runtime.

In this paper, we briefly describe Algorithm *MM/SF-Route* which uses an $O(HDM^3)$ bipartite matching algorithm to evenly distribute the edges of a single communication phase to the links of the interconnection network, where H is the diameter of the network, D is the max degree of a processor node, and M is the number of messages in the phase. *MM/SF-Route* is designed to minimize contention on a hop-by-hop basis and thus is suitable for architectures that use store-and-forward routing. However, we note that this algorithm can be used for systems which utilize wormhole routing schemes by including deadlock avoidance techniques such as virtual network partitioning. Algorithms *WORM1-Route* and *WORM2-Route* are described in Refs. 41 and 42.

Algorithm MM/SF-Route was tested for the hypercube by comparing its performance with random routing and the ecube routing algorithm.[43] The performance metric used in these experiments was *maximum* contention, i.e. maximum number of communication edges assigned to a single link. The experiments were performed on parallel computations from the OREGAMI test suite. Altogether 68 configurations were tested with the number of processors ranging from 8 to 32 and the number of tasks from 16 to 96. In 88.2% of the cases, the optimal routing was found. In 8.8%

of the cases the routing was within 33% of optimal, and in the remaining 3% of the cases the routing was within 50% of the optimal value. We are currently performing additional experiments to test the performance of our routing algorithms using additional metrics for contention.

Example. Suppose the *15-body problem* is embedded on an 8-processor hypercube as shown in Fig. 10. We discuss the operation of *MM/SF-Route* for the chordal edges only; the same procedure would be invoked for the ring edges. In the bipartite graph that is constructed by our routing algorithm, one partition consists of the communication edges in a single *comphase* and the other partition consists of the available (shortest) routes in the network that could potentially service these communication edges.

- In Fig. 10a, nodes in the task graph are labeled with the LaRCS task numbers, and links in the network are numbered arbitrarily from 1 to 12.

- In the chordal communication phase, task 0 sends to task 8, task 1 sends to task 9, etc. From a table of routing information for the 8-processor hypercube, we can determine the possible choices for the shortest routes: e.g., for messages from task 0 to task 8, possible routes are links 4 then 12, or links 9 then 8.

- From this information, we construct a bipartite graph $G = (X, Y, E)$ where nodes in X represent chordal edges in the task graph, nodes in Y represent links in the hypercube, and edges in E connect each edge node to the links that can serve as the *first hop* (or only hop) in the possible routes from sender to receiver. Thus, in Fig. 10b, there is an edge from the node labeled (0–8) to the nodes labeled link 4 and link 9.

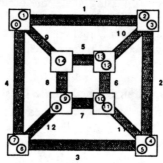

(a)

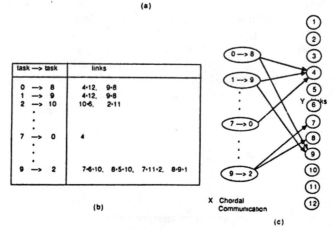

task → task	links
0 → 8	4·12, 9·8
1 → 9	4·12, 9·8
2 → 10	10·6, 2·11
⋮	
7 → 0	4
⋮	
9 → 2	7·6·10, 8·5·10, 7·11·2, 8·9·1

(b)

X Chordal
   Communication

(c)

Fig. 10. Algorithm *MM/SF-Route*: (a) 15-body algorithm mapped to 3 dim hypercube; (b) table of possible shortest routes; (c) bi-partite graph.

- A maximal matching of size M in graph G selects a maximal set of M distinct links in the hypercube and assigns M distinct chordal edges to those links. If $M \neq |X|$ then some nodes in X are unassigned. G is then reconfigured by removing all nodes of X covered by the matching and all edges incident to those nodes, and repeating the call to the maximal matching algorithm. Since each call to the maximal matching algorithm selects a given link at most once, we have achieved a low level of link contention.

- When all nodes in X are covered, a new graph is constructed for those chordal communication edges that have a choice of routes for the second hop. Note that in many cases, selection of the link for the first hop determines the second hop link.

5. ONGOING AND FUTURE WORK

Areas for continuing work on the OREGAMI project include extensions to LaRCS to support dynamically spawned tasks and processor constraints on mapping: new and improved mapping algorithms, and scheduling directives. In addition, we plan to do additional performance testing both through simulation and empirical experiments using the new SUN/X-Windows OREGAMI tools.

LaRCS extensions: OREGAMI currently is designed only for computations in which the number of tasks is static. We plan to extend our software to handle computations with dynamically spawned tasks when the spawning pattern is regular and predictable. For example, parallel divide and conquer algorithms dynamically spawn tasks based on the size of the problem instance; however, it is known *a priori* that the spawning pattern will produce a full binary tree. We plan to augment LaRCS with the capacity to describe regular spawning patterns, and to design task assignment and routing algorithms to accomodate dynamically growing parallel computations. In addition, we will extend LaRCS to include language constructs that specify certain types of mapping constraints, such as the assignment of specific tasks to specialized processors (I/O processors, processors with floating point hardware, etc.).

Mapping algorithms: We will continue to augment the MAPPER library with new and improved algorithms for contraction, embedding, and routing. Some of the new approaches to mapping that we are investigating include algorithms for mapping computations expressible as affine recurrences; algorithms that perform two or more of the mapping steps simultaneously; algorithms that consider migrating processes at run time in order to accommodate phase shifts (as opposed to our current approach of finding one mapping that accommodates all the phases); and algorithms that avoid overspecification of communication topologies for common parallel paradigms such as aggregate and broadcast. For example, many parallel algorithms use a specific tree topology to aggregate results when a variety of alternate communication topologies will suffice (any spanning tree or the perfect broadcast ring[44]). We would like to automatically select the aggregate topology that is 'compatible' with the topologies of other phases in the computation. Finally, we will continue to add to the library of canned mappings for nameable task graphs.

Scheduling: Many parallel algorithms can be characterized as synchronous in nature, i.e., they are designed to run lockstep through their execution and communication phases. Therefore, it is advantageous to be able to coordinate the scheduling of tasks across processors after they have been assigned by MAPPER. We plan to extend OREGAMI to include a means for specifying task *synchrony sets* across processors. A task synchrony set is a set of tasks, one on each processor, that should be executing at the same time. This approach appears to be promising for computations whose task graph fulfills certain Cayley conditions as discussed in Section 4.2. Identification of these synchrony sets can be used to refine the routing algorithm and to produce local scheduling directives for each processor that ensure synchronous execution of the tasks in each set. The scheduling directives can be expressed in a notation similar to path expressions[45] that specify the allowable ways to multiplex the tasks assigned to a given processor.

Testing: Our experiments thus far have focused on testing the performance of individual mapping algorithms. Our plans also include careful testing of the performance of the whole OREGAMI system by comparing OREGAMI mappings to random mapping, user manual mapping, and mapping produced by Berman's Prep-P system. These mappings will be evaluated using METRICS and through empirical experiments on the Intel iPSC/860.

Two key goals of our research are to provide tools that ensure portability of parallel software and to achieve the performance potential of parallel processing. OREGAMI was designed to achieve these goals by offering efficient algorithms for contraction, embedding, and routing, and by utilizing the user's knowledge through LaRCS and METRICS. The OREGAMI project is currently beginning its third year of development in which we hope to continue to contribute towards the development of an effective and practical tool for the mapping of parallel algorithms to parallel architectures.

REFERENCES

1. M. Rosing, R. B. Schnabel, and R. P. Weaver, The Dino Parallel Programming Language, Technical Report CU-CS-457-90, Department of Computer Science, University of Colorado at Boulder (April 1990).
2. M. H. Coffin, Par: An Approach to Architecture-independent Parallel Programming, Technical Report TR90-28, Department of Computer Science, University of Arizona (August 1990).
3. H. S. Stone, Multiprocessor Scheduling with the Aid of Network Flow Algorithms, *IEEE Trans. on Software Engineering* SE-3(1):85–93 (January 1977).
4. V. M. Lo, Temporal Communication Graphs: Lamport's Process-time Graphs Augmented for the Purpose of Mapping and Scheduling, Technical Report CIS-TR-92-04, University of Oregon (1992) (To appear *J. Parallel and Distrib. Computing.*)
5. L. Lamport, Time, Clocks, and the Ordering of Events in a Distributed System, *Comm. of the ACM* 21(7):558–565 (July 1978).
6. C. L. Seitz, The Cosmic Cube, *Comm. of the ACM* 28(1):22–33 (January 1985).
7. C. D. Polychronopoulos, *Parallel Programming and Compilers*, Kluwer Academic Publishers (1988).
8. S. H. Bokhari, *Assignment Problems in Parallel and Distributed Computing*, Kluwer Academic Publishers (1987).
9. F. Berman and B. Stramm, Prep-P: Evolution and Overview, Technical Report CS89-158, Department of Computer Science, University of California at San Diego (1989).
10. V. M. Lo, Heuristic Algorithms for Task Assignment in Distributed Systems, *IEEE Trans. on Comput.* 37(11):1384–1397 (1988).
11. P. Sadayappan, F. Ercal, and J. Ramanujam, Clustering Partitioning Approaches to Mapping Parallel Programs onto a Hypercube, *Parallel Computing* 13:1–16 (1990).
12. J. C. Browne, Framework for Formulation and Analysis of Parallel Computation Structures, *Parallel Computing* 3:1–9 (1986).
13. F. Berman, Experience with an Automatic Solution to the Mapping Problem, *The Characteristics of Parallel Algorithms*, The MIT Press, pp. 307–334 (1987).
14. L. Snyder, Introduction to the Configurable, Highly Parallel Computer, *Computer* 15(1):47–56 (January 1982).
15. A. Wagner, S. Chanson, N. Goldstein, J. Jiang, H. Larsen, and H. Sreekantaswamy, TIPS: Transputer-based Interactive Parallelizing System, Technical Report, Department of Computer Science, University of British Columbia (1990).

16. J. C. Browne, Code: A Unified Approach to Parallel Programming, *IEEE Software* 6(4):10–19 (July 1989).
17. H. El-Rewini and T. G. Lewis, Scheduling Parallel Program Tasks onto Arbitrary Target Machines, *J. of Parallel and Distrib. Computing* 9:138–153 (1990).
18. C. D. Polychronopoulos, *Parallel Programming and Compilers*, Kluwer Academic Publishers (1988).
19. V. Sakar, Partitioning and Scheduling Parallel Programs for Execution on Multiprocessors, Technical Report, Ph.D. Thesis, Department of Computer Science, Stanford University (1987).
20. A. L. Rosenberg, Graph Embeddings 1988: Recent Breakthroughs New Directions, Technical Report 88-28, University of Massachusetts at Amherst (March 1988).
21. F. Berman and L. Snyder, On Mapping Parallel Algorithms into Parallel Architectures, *J. of Parallel and Distrib. Computing* 4(5):439–458 (October 1987).
22. S. V. Rajopadhye and R. M. Fujimoto, Synthesizing Systolic Arrays from Recurrence Equations, *Parallel Computing* 14:163–189 (June 1990).
23. Marina C. Chen, A Design Methodology for Synthesizing Parallel Algorithms and Architectures, *J. of Parallel and Distrib. Computing* 3(6):461–491 (December 1986).
24. D. D. Kandlur and K. G. Shin, Traffic Routing for Multi-computer Networks with Virtual Cut-through Capability, *Proc. of the 10th Int'l Conf. on Distrib. Comput. Syst.*, pp. 398–405 (May 1990).
25. B. P. Bianchini and J. P. Shen, Interprocessor Traffic Scheduling Algorithm for Multiprocessor Network, *IEEE Trans. on Comput.* C-36(4):396–409 (April 1987).
26. Simon M. Kaplan and Gail E. Kaiser, Garp: Graph Abstractions for Concurrent Programming, H. Ganzinger (ed.), *European Symposium on Programming*, Vol. 300 of *Lecture Notes in Comput. Sci.*, Heidelberg, Springer-Verlag, pp. 191–205 (March 1988).
27. D. A. Bailey and J. E. Cuny, Graph Grammar Based Specification of Interconnection Structures for Massively Parallel Computation, *Proc. of the Third Int'l Workshop on Graph Grammars*, pp. 73–85 (1987).
28. J. Magee, J. Kramer, and M. Sloman, Constructing Distributed Systems in Conic, *IEEE Trans. on Software Engineering*, SE-15(6):663–675 (June 1989).
29. D. A. Bailey and J. E. Cuny, *Visual Extensions to Parallel Programming Languages*, MIT Press, pp. 17–36 (August 1989).
30. P. A. Nelson and L. Snyder, Programming Paradigms for Nonshared Memory Parallel Computers, *The Characteristics of Parallel Algorithms*, The MIT Press, pp. 3–20 (1987).
31. L. Snyder and D. Socha, Poker on the Cosmic Cube: the First Retargetable Parallel Programming Language and Environment, *Proc. Int'l Conf. on Parallel Proc.*, pp. 628–635 (August 1986).
32. L. Snyder, *The XYZ Abstraction Levels of Poker-like Languages*, MIT Press, pp. 470–489 (August 1989).
33. W. G. Griswold, G. A. Harrison, D. Notkin, and L. Snyder, Part Ensembles: A Communication Abstraction for Nonshared Memory Parallel Programming, Technical Report, Department of Computer Science, University of Washington (1989).
34. J. Vuillemin, A Data Structure for Manipulating Priority Queues, *Commun. of the ACM* 21(4):309–315 (April 1987).
35. V. M. Lo, S. Rajopadhy, S. Gupta, D. Keldsen, M. A. Mohamed, and J. Telle, Mapping Divide-and-conquer Algorithms to Parallel Architectures, *Proc. IEEE Int'l Conf. on Parallel Proc.*, Vol. III, pp. 128–135 (August 1990). (Also available as University of Oregon Technical Report CIS-TR-89-19.)
36. X. X. Zhong, S. Rajopadhye, and V. M. Lo, Parallel Implementation of Divide-and-conquer Algorithms on Biniary Debruijn Networks, Technical Report CIS-TR-91-21, University of Oregon (1991). (To appear in *Sixth Int'l Parallel Processing Symp.*)
37. H. Wielandt, *Finite Permutation Groups*, Academic Press (1964).
38. M. Fellows, Problem Corner, *Contemporary Mathematics* 89:187–188 (1989).
39. S. B. Akers and B. Krishnamurthy, A Group-theoretic Model for Symmetric Interconnection Network, *IEEE Trans. on Comput.* C-38(4):555–566 (April 1989).
40. V. M. Lo, Algorithms for Static Assignment and Symmetric Contraction in Distributed Computing Systems, *Proc. IEEE Int'l Conf. on Parallel Proc.*, pp. 239–244 (August 1988).
41. X. X. Zhong and V. M. Lo, Application Specific Deadlock Free Wormhole Routing on Multicomputers, Technical Report CIS-TR-92-03, University of Oregon (1992). To appear in *PARLE 92*.
42. X. X. Zhong and V. M. Lo, An Efficient Heuristic for Applications Specific Routing on Mesh Connected Multiprocessors, Technical Report CIS-TR-92-04, University of Oregon (1992). (To appear in 1992 *Int'l Conf. on Parallel Processing*.)
43. C. L. Seitz and W. J. Dally, Deadlock-free Message Routing in Multiprocessor Interconnection Networks, *IEEE Trans. on Comput.* 36(5):547–553 (May 1987).
44. Y. Han and R. Finkel, An Optimal Scheme for Disseminating Information, *Proc. of the Int'l Conf. on Parallel Proc.*, pp. 198–203 (August 1988).
45. R. H. Campbell and A. N. Habermann, *The Specification of Process Synchronization by Path Expressions*, Springer-Verlag 16:89–102 (1974).

46. S. L. Johnsson, Communication in Network Architectures. *VLSI and Parallel Computation*, Morgan Kaufmann Publishers, Inc., p. 290 (1990).

47. V. M. Lo, S. Rajopadhye, S. Gupta, D. Keldsen, M. A. Mohamed, and J. Telle, OREGAMI: Software Tools for Mapping Parallel Algorithms to Parallel Architectures, *Proc. Int'l Conf. on Parallel Proc.*, Vol. II, pp. 88–92 (August 1990). Updated version available as University of Oregon Technical Report CIS-TR-89-18a.

48. V. M. Lo, S. Rajopadhye, M. A. Mohamed, S. Gupta, B. Nitzberg, J. A. Telle, and X. X. Zhong, LaRCS: A Language for Describing Parallel Computations for the Purpose of Mapping, Technical Report CIS-TR-90-16. University of Oregon Department of Computer Science (1990). (To appear in *IEEE Trans. on Parallel and Distrib. Syst.*)

49. R. Rowley and B. Bose, On Necklaces in Shuffle-exchange and DeBruijn Networks, *Proc. Int'l Conf. on Parallel Proc.*, Vol. I, pp. 347–350 (August 1990).

Chapter 5

Load Balancing

5.1 Introduction

Contrary to static scheduling, load balancing/sharing techniques assume little or no compile-time knowledge about the runtime parameters of an application, such as task execution times or communication delays. Instead, these techniques rely on the runtime redistribution of processes among the PEs to achieve defined performance goals [Baumgartner 1989, Casavant 1988, Eager 1986a, Krueger 1987, Litzkow 1988, Wang 1985]. It should be noted that most of the work in this area is to address the problem in distributed systems. In this context a "PE" refers to a node of a network of loosely coupled workstations. The process of redistribution follows a simple heuristic that dynamically redistributes work among PEs in an effort to balance their loads. The performance goal of a load balancing algorithm can be to minimize the execution time of an application, to maximize the system throughput, or to maximize the system's PE utilization. Load balancing and load sharing are used as interchangeable terms in the literature. While load balancing views the redistribution as the assigning of the processes among the PEs, load sharing defines the redistribution as the sharing of the system's processing power among the tasks.

A load balancing algorithm is based on three policies: [Zhou 1988]

1. *The information policy* specifies the amount of load information made available to, and the way this information is distributed among, the job placement decision-makers. Typically the information policy decides whether:

   - the load information of all or a subset of the PEs is made available to the job placement decision-makers,
   - the load information is distributed periodically or on-demand at load balancing time, and
   - the load information is collected at a central PE or distributed among the participating job placement decision-makers.

2. *The transfer policy* determines the suitability of a process for task relocation; that is, the policy identifies whether or not a task is eligible to be transferred to another PE. In this context, the size of a task is measured by its expected execution time. Thus, a small task will require a shorter execution time as compared to a large task. With this notation of size in mind, the transfer policy is based on several factors, including:

   - host load—a process is eligible for transfer only if the load of its host PE is above some threshold value;
   - process size—a process is eligible for transfer only if its size is above a threshold value; that is, the advantage of the load distribution must be greater than the overhead of the process transfer; and
   - process resource needs—in a heterogeneous distributed processing system, a process may not be executable on a subset of the PEs or its execution time may vary considerably on different PEs.

3. *The placement policy* determines the PE to which a process should be transferred. The job placement decision-maker selects the target PE for a transfer based on two general policies:

   - minimum load—select the PE with the minimum current load; and
   - low load—select the first PE whose load is below some threshold value.

The majority of load balancing algorithms use "threshold scheduling" as a general policy for implementing different decisions during the redistribution process. For example, if the local host's load and the size of a process are above some predetermined threshold values, then that process is transferred to another PE. Exactly what parameters are used to define a threshold value varies among different load balancing algorithms.

309

The issue of load indices, that is, the measurement of a PE's load, is discussed in detail in Chapter 7. A typical load index is the size of the ready queue of a PE. The exact estimation of the size of a process is impractical, since the execution time of the job is not known until the job is actually executed. However, it seems that a rough classification of jobs into *small/light* and *large/heavy* workloads works rather well for load balancing purposes. Of course, while large processes are eligible for load distribution, small jobs are not suitable to be transferred. Examples of lightweight jobs in a Unix environment include *cat, ls,* and *cp* commands; examples of heavyweight processes include *cc, eqn,* and *grep* operations.

Another issue in load balancing involves task migration; that is, should an executing task be suspended, migrated to another PE, and have its execution resumed on the target machine? Several factors impact the viability of the migration process, including the task size, process state transfer policy, and system virtual memory organization. The task migration issue is addressed in detail in Chapter 6.

Finally, thrashing, or instability, is a problem that needs to be addressed in any load balancing scheme. The problem arises from the possibility of several overloaded PEs transferring their tasks to an underloaded PE, causing it to overload. That overloaded PE will then transfer some of the tasks to another PE, causing a thrashing effect. A few simple steps can resolve the thrashing problem [Zhou 1988], including:

- the placement decision-maker randomly selecting one of several of the lightly loaded PEs for the job transfer, instead of choosing a PE with the minimum load; and
- randomized searching for a target PE, in order to allow some time for the load information to propagate to the decision-makers.

5.2 Classification of load balancing methods

Load balancing methods can be classified in several different ways, depending on different criteria. For example, [Wang 1985] proposes a taxonomy of load balancing algorithms and introduces a metric for the performance comparison of these methods. Below we present three different criteria for classifying load balancing methods:

1. *Sender- or receiver-initiated* [Eager 1986b]: A load balancing algorithm is said to be sender- or source-initiated, if a local host (or source node) makes a determination as to where a generated task or an arriving task is to be executed. The queues of ready jobs tend to form at the target or server PEs. Job transfer decisions are usually made at task arrival time. In a receiver- or server-initiated load balancing algorithm, a server determines which jobs at different sources it will process. In this case, the ready jobs tend to be queued at the source PEs. Job transfer decisions are made either at job completion times or whenever the load of the server goes below a threshold value. Hybrid methods, combinations of these two methods, have also been proposed [Ni 1985].
2. *Static or adaptive*: In a static load balancing method, the transfer and placement policies are based only on information about the average behavior of the system. Static load balancing algorithms do not rely on the current state of the system at the time of decision-making. Random and round-robin placement policies are examples of static decision-making processes. Adaptive load balancing schemes [Eager 1986b, Kremien 1992, Kumar 1989, Lin 1987, Mirchandaney 1989a,b], on the other hand, react to changes in the system state. Thus, compared to static methods, adaptive load balancing algorithms are better able to respond to system changes and avoid those states that result in poor performance. Obviously, the disadvantage of adaptive load balancing is that these methods are more complex than their static counterparts, in the sense that they require runtime load information and state collection activities. Different forms of threshold scheduling are examples of adaptive load balancing.
3. *Central or distributed information and placement decisions*: Load balancing algorithms can be classified into one of the following three categories, depending upon how load information is distributed and how processes are assigned to PEs.

    - *Centralized policies*—In terms of the load information distribution policy, a PE designated as the central scheduler receives updated load information from all the other hosts and assembles them into a load vector. For the placement policy, when a host decides to transfer a job, it sends a request to the central scheduler who then selects a target host, using the load vector, and informs the source host of this choice. Centralized policies reduce the system overhead due to the load information distribution, but may create a bottleneck at the central scheduler.

- *Distributed policies*—Unlike the centralized policies, each host autonomously constructs its own local load vector by collecting the load information for other PEs. The placement decisions are made locally using the internal load vectors. Distributed policies can significantly speed up the decision-making process, but they will generate an enormous amount of communication overhead due to the load information distribution among the hosts.

- *Mixed policies*—Many of the existing load balancing methods use a combination of central/distributed information and placement policies in order to take advantage of the benefits of each policy [Zhou 1988]. For example, one can use a centralized load information policy along with a distributed placement policy. In that case, the central scheduler needs to periodically distribute the load vector to the other hosts so that each host can make a local placement decision.

It should be noted that the load balancing algorithms can be further subclassified based on the completeness of the amount of load information and the time when the load information is updated. Placement and transfer policies may be based on complete or partial load information. If the load vectors are constructed based on load information from all of the hosts, then complete load information is used. On the other hand, a host may be aware of the load information of only a subset of the hosts, for example, its nearest neighbors. The load information may be updated periodically or on-demand, for example, when there is a need for a job transfer.

5.3 Prognosis and future directions in load balancing

The major disadvantage of dynamic load balancing is its runtime overhead for load information distribution, making placement decisions, and transferring a job to a target host. Therefore, it is reasonable to assume that future research in this area will emphasize simpler but more effective methods that will reduce such overhead. To achieve this goal, effective load index measures and efficient load distribution methods need to be identified. From an architectural point of view, hierarchical system organizations with local load information distribution and local load balancing policies seem to be more amenable to efficient load balancing techniques. Finally, the incorporation of a set of primitive tools at the distributed operating system level can help in the implementation of different load balancing policies, depending on the system architecture and application requirements. Another future direction involves application and extension of the work in this area to message-passing multiprocessor systems.

5.4 Chapter organization and overview

The papers in this chapter are grouped into three classes: those addressing general issues in load balancing (Wang and Morris; Rommel; and Eager, Lazowska, and Zahorjan); those discussing performance issues in this area (Pulidas, Towsley, and Stankovic; Krueger, and Livny; and Casavant and Kuhl); and those describing practical load balancing methods (Litzkow, Livny, and Mutka; Baumgartner and Wah; and Krueger and Chawla).

The paper by Wang and Morris presents a taxonomy of load balancing algorithms. It also introduces a metric for the performance comparison of these methods, which summarizes the overall efficiency and fairness of a given load balancing scheme. In the second paper Rommel proposes a general formula for the probability that any one site in a homogeneous distributed system is underloaded while some other site in the system is overloaded. This probability is then used to define the likelihood of load balancing success in such a system. In the third paper, Eager, Lazowska, and Zahorjan outline the advantages of adaptive load balancing schemes and address the fundamental question of the appropriate level of complexity for load balancing policies. It is shown that simple load balancing policies can be as effective as their more complex counterparts.

In the fourth paper, Pulidas, Towsky, and Stankovic discuss the issue of efficiently determining the optimum threshold parameter values in a decentralized load balancing algorithm. The behavior of a gradient-based decentralized optimization algorithm is studied through simulations to obtain good threshold values. In the fifth paper, Krueger and Livny address the issue of performance comparison among load balancing methods; that is, are some dynamic scheduling policies better than others, or do they have different objectives? It is shown that the choice of an appropriate policy requires the consideration of the performance expectations of the users, together with the system workload characteristics. In the sixth paper, Casavant and Kuhl quantify the effects of response and stability on scheduling algorithms for general-purpose distributed computing systems. It is shown that absolute stability is not always necessary in dynamic systems, and that response is an important first-order metric of dynamic scheduling behavior.

In the seventh paper, Litzkow, Livny, and Mutka present the design, implementation, and performance of the Condor scheduling system. The system operates on a network of workstations. It identifies idle workstations, and schedules background jobs on them with minimal effect on local host operations. In the eighth paper, Baumgartner and Wah discuss an efficient load balancing strategy, called GAMMON, for distributed computing systems connected by multi-access local area networks. The broadcast capability of these networks is used to implement an identification procedure at the applications level for the maximally and the minimally loaded PEs. In the last paper, Krueger and Chawla describe the Stealth Distributed Scheduler, which is implemented on an environment composed of a set of computer workstations. The Stealth Distributed Scheduler relies on a priority resource allocation mechanism to insulate a workstation owner from the effects of any foreign processes that may also be executing at the workstation.

Bibliography

Ahmad, I., and A. Ghafoor, "Semi-Distributed Load Balancing For Massively Parallel Multicomputer Systems," *IEEE Trans. Software Eng.*, Vol. SE-17, No. 10, Oct. 1991, pp. 987–1004.

Barak, A., and A. Shiloh, "A Distributed Load-Balancing Policy for a Multicomputer," *Software-Practice and Experience*, Vol. 15, No. 9, Sept. 1985, pp. 901–913.

Baumgartner, K. M., and B. W. Wah, "GAMMON: A Load Balancing Strategy for Local Computer Systems with Multi-Access Networks," *IEEE Trans. Computers*, Vol. C-38, No. 8, Aug. 1989, pp. 1098–1109; reprinted here.

Boel, R. K., and J. H. van Schuppen, "Distributed Routing for Load Balancing," *Proc. IEEE*, Vol. 77, No. 1, Jan. 1989, pp. 210–221.

Bonomi, F., and A. Kumar, "Adaptive Optimal Load Balancing in A Nonhomogeneous Multiserver System with a Central Job Scheduler," *IEEE Trans. Computers*, Vol. C-39, No. 10, Oct. 1990, pp. 1232–1250.

Bryant, R. M., and R. A. Finkel, "A Stable Distributed Scheduling Algorithm," *Proc. 2nd IEEE Int'l Conf. Distributed Computing Systems*, IEEE CS Press, Los Alamitos, Calif., 1981, pp. 314–323.

Casavant, T. L., and J. G. Kuhl, "Effects of Response and Stability on Scheduling in Distributed Computing Systems," *IEEE Trans. Software Eng.*, Vol. SE-14, No. 11, Nov. 1988, pp. 1578–1588; reprinted here.

Chou, T. C. K., and J. A. Abraham, "Load Balancing in Distributed Systems," *IEEE Trans. Software Eng.*, Vol. SE-8, No. 4, July 1982, pp. 401–412.

Chowdhury, S., "The Greedy Load Sharing Algorithm," *J. Parallel and Distributed Computing*, Vol. 9, 1990, pp. 93–99.

Chu, W. W., et al., "Task Allocation in Distributed Data Processing," *Computer*, Nov. 1980, pp. 57–69.

Deng, X., H.-N. Liu, and B. Xiao, "Deterministic Load Balancing in Computer Networks," *Proc. 2nd IEEE Symp. Parallel and Distributed Processing*, IEEE CS Press, Los Alamitos, Calif., 1990, pp. 50–57.

Eager, D. L., E. D. Lazowska, and J. Zahorjan, "Adaptive Load Sharing in Homogeneous Distributed Systems," *IEEE Trans. Software Eng.*, Vol. SE-12, No. 5, May 1986, pp. 662–675; reprinted here.

Eager, D. L., E. D. Lazowska, and J. Zahorjan, "A Comparison of Receiver-Initiated and Sender-Initiated Adaptive Load Sharing," *Performance Evaluation*, Vol. 6, 1986, pp. 53–68.

Efe, K., and B. Groselj, "Minimizing Control Overheads in Adaptive Load Sharing," *Proc. 9th IEEE Int'l Conf. Distributed Computing Systems*, IEEE CS Press, Los Alamitos, Calif., 1989, pp. 307–315.

Ferguson, D., Y. Yemini, and C. Nikolaou, "Microeconomic Algorithms for Load Balancing in Distributed Computer Systems," *Proc. 8th IEEE Int'l Conf. Distributed Computing Systems*, IEEE CS Press, Los Alamitos, Calif., 1988, pp. 491–499.

Gait, J., "A Distributed Process Manager with Transparent Continuation," *Proc. 5th IEEE Int'l Conf. Distributed Computing Systems*, IEEE CS Press, Los Alamitos, Calif., 1985, pp. 422–429.

Hac, A., and X. Jin, "Dynamic Load Balancing in a Distributed System Using Sender-Initiated Algorithm," *J. Systems Software*, Vol. 11, 1990, pp. 79–94.

Hagmann, R., "Process Server: Sharing Processing Power in a Workstation Environment," *Proc. 6th IEEE Int'l Conf. Distributed Computing Systems*, IEEE CS Press, Los Alamitos, Calif., 1986, pp. 260–267.

Iqbal, M. A., J. H. Saltz, and S. H. Bokhari, "A Comparative Analysis of Static and Dynamic Load Balancing Strategies," *Proc. 6th IEEE Int'l Conf. Distributed Computing Systems*, IEEE CS Press, Los Alamitos, Calif., 1986, pp. 1040–1047.

Kremien, O., and J. Kramer, "Methodical Analysis of Adaptive Load Sharing Algorithms," *IEEE Trans. Parallel and Distributed Systems*, Vol. 3, No. 6, Nov. 1992, pp. 747–760.

Krueger, P., and M. Livny, "The Diverse Objectives of Distributed Scheduling Policies," *Proc. 7th IEEE Int'l Conf. Distributed Computing Systems*, IEEE CS Press, Los Alamitos, Calif., 1987, pp. 242–249; reprinted here.

Krueger, P., and R. Chawla, "The Stealth Distributed Scheduler," *Proc. 11th IEEE Int'l Conf. Distributed Computing Systems*, IEEE CS Press, Los Alamitos, Calif., 1991, pp. 336–343; reprinted here.

Kumar, A., "Adaptive Load Control of the Central Processor in a Distributed System with a Star Topology," *IEEE Trans. Computers*, Vol. C-38, No. 11, Nov. 1989, pp. 1502–1512.

Lin, F. C. H., and R. M. Keller, "The Gradient Model Load Balancing Method," *IEEE Trans. Software Eng.*, Vol. SE-13, No. 1, Jan. 1987, pp. 32–38.

Litzkow, M. J., M. Livny, and M. W. Mutka, "Condor—A Hunter of Idle Workstations," *Proc. 8th IEEE Int'l Conf. Distributed Computing Systems*, IEEE CS Press, Los Alamitos, Calif., 1988, pp. 104–111; reprinted here.

Mirchandaney, R., D. Towsley, and J.A. Stankovic, "Adaptive Load Sharing in Heterogeneous Systems," *Proc. 9th IEEE Int'l Conf. Distributed Computing Systems*, IEEE CS Press, Los Alamitos, Calif., 1989a, pp. 298–306.

Mirchandaney, R., D. Towsley, and J. A. Stankovic, "Analysis of the Effects of Delays on Load Sharing," *IEEE Trans. Computers*, Vol. C-38, No. 11, Nov. 1989b, pp. 1513–1525.

Ni, L. M., and K. Hwang, "Optimal Load Balancing in a Multiple Processor System with Many Job Classes," *IEEE Trans. Software Eng.*, Vol. SE-11, No. 5, May 1985, pp. 491–496.

Nicol, D. M., and P. F. Reynolds, Jr., "Optimal Dynamic Remapping of Data Parallel Computations," *IEEE Trans. Computers*, Vol. C-39, No. 2, Feb. 1990, pp. 206–219.

Pulidas, S., D. Towsley, and J. A. Stankovic, "Imbedding Gradient Estimators in Load Balancing Algorithms," *Proc. 8th IEEE Int'l Conf. Distributed Computing Systems*, IEEE CS Press, Los Alamitos, Calif., 1988, pp. 482–490; reprinted here.

Rommel, C. G., "The Probability of Load Balancing Success in a Homogeneous Network," *IEEE Trans. Software Eng.*, Vol. SE-17, No. 9, Sept. 1991, pp. 922–933; reprinted here.

Rotithor, H. G., and S. S. Pyo, "Decentralized Decision Making in Adaptive Task Sharing," *Proc. 2nd IEEE Symp. Parallel and Distributed Processing*, IEEE CS Press, Los Alamitos, Calif., 1990, pp. 34–41.

Ryon, J.-C., and J. S. K. Wong, "A Task Migration Algorithm for Load Balancing in a Distributed System," *Proc. 22nd Ann. Hawaii Int'l Conf. System Sciences*, Vol. 2: Software Track, IEEE CS Press, Los Alamitos, Calif., 1989, pp. 1041–1047.

Schaar, M., et al., "Load Balancing with Network Cooperation," *Proc. 11th IEEE Int'l Conf. Distributed Computing Systems*, IEEE CS Press, Los Alamitos, Calif., 1991, pp. 328–335.

Shenker, S., and A. Weinrib, "The Optimal Control of Heterogeneous Queuing Systems: A Paradigm for Load-Sharing and Routing," *IEEE Trans. Computers*, Vol. C-38, No. 12, Dec. 1989, pp. 1724–1735.

Shivaratri, N. G., and P. Krueger, "Two Adaptive Location Policies for Global Scheduling Algorithms," *Proc. 10th IEEE Int'l Conference Distributed Computing Systems*, IEEE CS Press, Los Alamitos, Calif., 1990, pp. 502–509.

Tantawi, A. N., and D. Towsley, "Optimal Static Load Balancing in Distributed Computer Systems," *J. ACM*, Vol. 32, No. 2, Apr. 1985, pp. 445–465.

Theimer, M. M., and K. A. Lantz, "Finding Idle Machines in a Workstation-Based Distributed System," *IEEE Trans. Software Eng.*, Vol. SE-15, No. 11, Nov. 1989, pp. 1444–1457.

Wang, Y.-T., and R. J. T. Morris, "Load Sharing in Distributed Systems," *IEEE Trans. Computers*, Vol. C-34, No. 3, Mar. 1985, pp. 204–217; reprinted here.

Zhou, S., "A Trace-Driven Simulation Study of Dynamic Load Balancing," *IEEE Trans. Software Eng.*, Vol. 14, No. 11, Nov. 1988, pp. 1327–1341.

313

Load Sharing in Distributed Systems

YUNG-TERNG WANG, MEMBER, IEEE, AND ROBERT J. T. MORRIS, MEMBER, IEEE

Abstract — An important part of a distributed system design is the choice of a load sharing or global scheduling strategy. A comprehensive literature survey on this topic is presented. We propose a taxonomy of load sharing algorithms that draws a basic dichotomy between source-initiative and server-initiative approaches. The taxonomy enables ten representative algorithms to be selected for performance evaluation. A performance metric called the Q-factor (quality of load sharing) is defined which summarizes both overall efficiency and fairness of an algorithm and allows algorithms to be ranked by performance. We then evaluate the algorithms using both mathematical and simulation techniques. The results of the study show that: i) the choice of load sharing algorithm is a critical design decision; ii) for the same level of scheduling information exchange, server-initiative has the potential of outperforming source-initiative algorithms (whether this potential is realized depends on factors such as communication overhead); iii) the Q-factor is a useful yardstick; iv) some algorithms, which have previously received little attention, e.g., multiserver cyclic service, may provide effective solutions.

Index Terms — Distributed scheduling, distributed systems, load sharing, performance analysis, queueing analysis.

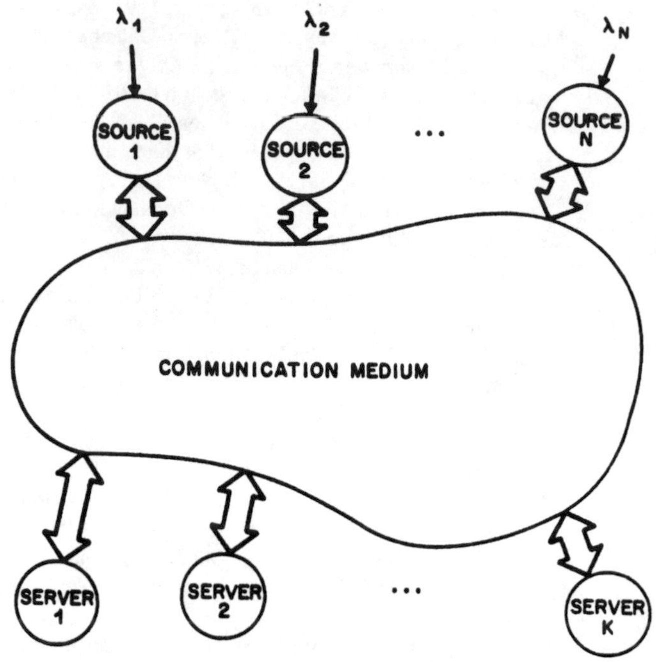

Fig. 1. A locally distributed computer system.

I. INTRODUCTION

THE confluence of low-cost processor (e.g., microprocessor) and interconnect (e.g., local area network) technologies has spurred a great interest in locally distributed computer architectures. The often cited advantages of these architectures include high performance, availability, and extensibility at low cost. But it is also being recognized that to realize this potential, crucial design decisions have to be made for which the performance implications are not intuitively obvious.

To set the stage, we consider a locally distributed computer system with configuration shown in Fig. 1. Jobs enter the system via nodes called *sources* and are processed by nodes called *servers*. This configuration represents a logical view of the system — a single physical processor might be both a source and a server node. This study is concerned with one important design issue: the choice of a *load sharing strategy* by which the multiple servers are made to cooperate and share the system workload.

The load sharing problem can be considered as part of the larger *distributed scheduling problem*.[1] Distributed sched-

uling can be thought of as comprising two coupled subproblems. The *local scheduling* subproblem addresses the allocation of processing resources to jobs within one node, either source or server. The local scheduling problem has been extensively studied; see, e.g., [13], [16], [20], [28]. The *global scheduling* subproblem addresses the determination of which jobs are processed by which server [1], [27]. A global scheduling strategy manifests itself as a collection of algorithms performed by the sources, servers, and possibly the communication medium. One of the key functions[2] of a global scheduling strategy is load sharing: the appropriate sharing and allocation of system processing resources. Load sharing has also been referred to as *load balancing*. This terminology arises from the intuition that to obtain good performance it would appear to be desirable to balance load between servers, i.e., to prevent the situation that one server is congested while another is lightly loaded.

Desirable properties of a load sharing strategy include:

i) *optimal overall system performance* — total processing capacity maximized while retaining acceptable delays;

ii) *fairness of service* — uniformly acceptable performance provided to jobs regardless of the source on which the job arrives;

Manuscript received November 28, 1983; revised March 15, 1984.

The authors are with AT&T Bell Laboratories, Holmdel, NJ 07733.

[1] We will focus on distributed scheduling as opposed to centralized scheduling.

[2] Other functions include data synchronization, concurrency control, etc.

Reprinted from IEEE *Trans. on Computers*, vol. c-34, no. 3, Mar. 1985, pp. 204–217.

iii) *failure tolerance*—robustness of performance maintained in the presence of partial failures in the system.

Other factors that need to be considered are performance of the system under contingent conditions such as overload, and the degree to which the strategy accommodates reconfiguration and extension.

An examination of the literature reveals a plethora of proposed approaches to the load sharing problem. A comprehensive literature survey based on a literature database search is presented in Appendix A. Despite this large body of literature, designers are left with only a collection of seemingly unrelated schemes to choose from, or else they must create their own. Unfortunately, a lack of uniformity of assumptions in different studies and idiosyncratic features of different schemes makes it unclear what performance gains are potentially achievable when more complex load sharing strategies are employed. The purpose of this paper is to begin the process of systematically describing and categorizing load sharing schemes and comparing their performance under a uniform set of assumptions.

II. Approach

To make a reasonably comprehensive study tractable within the space of this paper, we will make further limiting but simplifying assumptions about the system shown in Fig. 1. We assume that the jobs are individually executable, are logically independent of one another, and can be processed by any server. Such a situation might correspond to, for example, a query-intensive database system with replicated data at each server, or a system of "diskless processor" servers to which both program and data are downloaded from the sources. It may also correspond to the projection of a system onto a subsystem containing those servers that can process a class of jobs. We will only be considering load sharing strategies that distribute jobs to servers irrevocably, i.e., a job will not be assigned to one server and later reassigned to a different server. For simplicity, we assume that all servers have the same processing rate.

The load sharing strategy must cause the jobs to be shared among the servers so that concurrent processing is enabled and bottlenecks are avoided whenever possible. To demonstrate to the reader that there are many possible approaches to this problem, we might ask whether it might be better for the sources to "take the initiative" and forward jobs to a selected server or whether the sources should await the removal of the job by an available server. We could also ask what the minimal amount of information sharing is that must take place between nodes to obtain effective resource sharing.

While our model is somewhat idealized, it is general enough to allow numerous load sharing strategies to be discussed and compared. To expose some fundamental differences, in Section III we will present a taxonomy of load sharing strategies. By selecting representative algorithms of each class in the taxonomy, we will be able to conduct a performance comparison on an equal basis.

In comparing the performance of different schemes, there are a number of different and conflicting measures that could

be proposed. But rather than dismiss a performance ranking of different schemes as being unattainable, we will propose in Section IV a single figure of merit for a load sharing strategy which captures some first order effects a designer should consider in selecting an algorithm.

It will be seen that this approach provides a unified framework within which we will be able to expose some fundamental distinctions between various strategies and to explore the inherent tradeoff between performance and communication overhead and complexity.

III. A Taxonomy of Load Sharing

In examining the many possible approaches to load sharing (for some examples, see the literature survey in Appendix A), we find that there are fundamentally distinguishing features of different strategies.

The first distinction we draw demarcates the type of node that takes the initiative in the global searching. If the source node makes a determination as to where to route a job we call this a *source-initiative* strategy. On the other hand, if the server "goes looking for work," i.e., determines which jobs at different sources it will process, we refer to this as *server-initiative*. In a source-initiative algorithm, queues tend to form at the server, whereas in a server-initiative algorithm queues tend to form at the sources. Another difference is that in source-initiative algorithms, scheduling decisions are usually made at job arrival epochs (or a subset thereof), whereas in server-initiative algorithms, scheduling decisions are usually made at job departure epochs (or a subset thereof).

The other axis of classification we propose refers to the level of *information dependency* that is embodied in a strategy. By this is meant the degree to which a source node knows the status of servers or a server knows the status of sources. Naturally, as the level of information available increases we expect to be able to obtain strategies with improved performance. But as more information is exchanged, communication cost may increase and more sophisticated software or hardware mechanisms may become necessary. For two strategies with the same level of information dependency, we will notice a subjective duality at play when considering a source-initiative versus server-initiative strategy. One of the outcomes of our performance analysis in later sections is that provided communication costs are not a dominating effect, server-initiative tends to outperform source-initiative strategies for the same level of information dependency.

In presenting our taxonomy we describe a source-initiative algorithm according to a function

$$\text{server} = f(\cdots)$$

by which we mean that the server selected by the source to process a job is a function of the arguments of f exhibited. Similarly, server-initiative algorithms are described by a function

$$\text{source} = f(\cdots)$$

the source at which a server seeks its next job. The taxonomy is presented in Table I. There are seven levels of information dependency which range from "blind" fixed scheduling where no information is required, to strategies where extensive information is required and algorithms such as global first come first served (FCFS)—one ideal of multiserver behavior—are attained.

Several explanations of Table I are in order. First, the number of levels of information is somewhat arbitrary and could have been aggregated into fewer or expanded into a finer classification. Note that the information levels are arranged so that the information of a higher level subsumes that of the lower levels. The parameter ω plays the role of randomization which can be viewed as providing additional information dependency.

Also shown in Table I are canonical examples of algorithms in each category. For example, a "cyclic splitting" algorithm assigns jobs to servers in a cyclic manner, remembering only where it sent a previous job (the sequence state). Its dual, a "cyclic service" algorithm, serves sources in a cyclic manner, remembering where it picked up the previous job. An algorithm such as FCFS requires much more information. Some of these example algorithms of Table I will be

ing different strategies in our taxonomy, we will point out some fundamental differences in their performance. We find it useful to develop a yardstick based on a metric called the *Q-factor (quality of load sharing factor)* that captures to first-order some important aspects of load sharing performance.

For the system we are considering, a good load sharing algorithm will tend not to allow any server to be idle while there are jobs awaiting processing in the system. It will also not discriminate against a job based on the particular source by which that job arrives. In this sense, one ideal of a global scheduler, as defined above, is one that behaves like a multiserver first come first served (FCFS) queue. Since jobs originated by a specified user may always arrive to a particular source, they may be subject to systematic discrimination, either favorable or unfavorable. Moreover, if the aim of a distributed system design is to provide effective resource pooling, a job's performance cannot be excused by pointing to the particular source from which it originates. Thus, we can view an overall level of performance as being attained only if this level or better is attained by jobs at every source.

This leads to our definition of the Q-factor of an algorithm A:

$$Q_A(\rho) = \frac{\text{mean response time over all jobs under FCFS}}{\displaystyle\sup_{\frac{1}{K\mu}\sum_{i=1}^{N}\lambda_i = \rho} \max_i \{\text{mean response time at }i\text{th source under algorithm }A\}}$$

defined more carefully in Section V.

We will make extensive use of the canonical examples of Table I since they are "pure and simple" representatives of the basic strategy of each category. We maintain that many of the algorithms that have been proposed in the literature can be viewed as variations on or hybrids of members of the taxonomy. In view of some of the simplifying assumptions we have made in Section II, the taxonomy cannot be regarded as exhaustive. Nevertheless, as well as being a useful conceptual tool, in the process of setting up this table we have obtained some attractive simple algorithms that have not received attention in the past. For example, a version of a multiserver cyclic service discipline will be seen to exhibit performance almost as good as FCFS but with much reduced communication and coordination overhead. It should be noted that previous researchers (see, e.g., [5]–[8]) have considered relative performance of a few of these algorithms, although almost all attention has been confined to source-initiative schemes. To relate nomenclature, Level 1 has been referred to as *static*, Level 5 as *dynamic*, and Level 3 as *semidynamic*.

IV. A PERFORMANCE METRIC

We have already indicated some properties we would like a load sharing strategy to possess. Because of a multiplicity of possible performance measures, it is difficult to rank algorithms on any absolute basis. Nevertheless, in compar-

where the response time of a job is defined to be the length of time from when the job arrives at the system until it departs from the system (via a source),

N = number of sources,
K = number of servers,
μ^{-1} = mean service time,
λ_i = arrival rate at the ith source,
ρ = aggregated utilization of system.

This measure provides a factor usually[3] between zero and unity which describes how closely the system comes to a multiserver FCFS system, as seen by every job stream. The larger the Q-factor, the better the performance. Of course, this measure does not take into account conditional (on service time requirement) or delay distributional information but instead attempts to expose the overall load sharing behavior of the system. In particular, it will detect inefficiencies such as servers being idle when there is work to be done and any bias in performance due to arrival on a particular source. We will also see that it is sometimes possible to evaluate the Q-factor for an algorithm even though that algorithm defies a complete queueing analysis. Although we will only consider systems in which all servers are identical, the definition and the evaluation of the Q-factor can easily be extended to include the case of heterogeneous servers. In Section VI we will make use of the Q-factor, as well as

[3]An algorithm can have a Q-factor larger than unity. One example is the well-known "shortest job first" algorithm.

TABLE I
A Taxonomy for Load Sharing Algorithms

Level of Information Dependency in Scheduling	Source-Initiative	Server-Initiative
1	server = f (source) e.g. source partition	source = f(server) e.g. server partition
2	server = f(source, ω)[†] e.g. random splitting	source = f(server, ω) e.g. random service
3	server = f(source, ω, sequence state) e.g. cyclic splitting	source = f(server, ω, sequence state) e.g. cyclic service
4	server = f(source, ω, sequence state, server busy/idle status) e.g. join idle before busy queue (cyclic offer)	source = f(server, ω, sequence state, source queue emptiness) e.g. cyclic service without polling empty sources.
5	server = f(source, ω, sequence state, server queue lengths) e.g. join the shortest queue (JSQ)	source = f(server, ω, sequence state, source queue lengths) e.g. serve the longest queue (SLQ)
6	server = f(source, ω, sequence state, server queue lengths, departure epochs of completed jobs at servers) e.g. JSQ with ties broken by last departure epochs at each server	source = f(server, ω, sequence state, arrival epochs of jobs at sources) e.g. FCFS
7	server = f(source, ω, sequence state, departure epochs of completed and remaining jobs at servers) e.g. FCFS	source = f(server, ω, sequence state, arrival epochs and execution times of jobs at sources) e.g. shortest job first

[†] ω is a randomly generated parameter

other measures to compare the performance of different algorithms.

V. Canonical Algorithms and Performance Analysis

In this section we will define and analyze the performance of some of the canonical scheduling algorithms that were cited as examples in the taxonomy of Table I. We consider the following algorithms, using the earlier defined notation N for the number of sources, and K for the number of servers. The local scheduling policies, i.e., the service disciplines at the sources and servers, are FCFS.

1) Source Partition ($N \geq K$): Level 1, Source-Initiative — The sources are partitioned into groups and each group is served by one server. Each source in a group sends its jobs to the assigned server.

2) Server Partition ($N \leq K$): Level 1, Server-Initiative — The servers are partitioned into groups and each group of servers serves one source. A FCFS queue is formed at each source and jobs are removed one at a time by one of the available assigned servers. This can be considered to be a dual of source partition.

3) Random Splitting: Level 2, Source-Initiative — Each source distributes jobs randomly and uniformly to each server, i.e., it sends a job to one of the K servers with probability $1/K$.

4) Random Service: Level 2, Server-Initiative — Each server visits sources at random and on each visit removes and serves a single job. After each visit it selects the next source to be visited randomly and uniformly. This can be considered a dual to random splitting. A simple variation on this algorithm which may reduce communication overhead would have the server remove a batch of up to B jobs on each visit.

5) Cyclic Splitting: Level 3, Source-Initiative — Each source assigns its ith arriving job to the $i \pmod K$th server.

6) Cyclic Service: Level 3, Server-Initiative — Each server visits the sources in a cyclic manner. When a server visits the ith source it removes and serves a batch of up to B jobs and may then return to revisit the ith source for up to a total of V visits or until the source queue becomes empty. It then moves to the next source queue in a predetermined sequence. The algorithm has two parameters B and V and a visit sequence which may be different for each server.[4] The main cases we will consider have $B = \infty, V = 1$; $B = 1, V = \infty$ (often called exhaustive cyclic service), and $B = 1, V = 1$ (a case of limited cyclic service). Another variation we will consider will be referred to as "$B = 1$, gated" — this means the server revisits a source queue until the queue empties or the server finds a job next in queue that arrived to the source after the server first arrived to that source in a given cycle. This class of algorithms can be considered as dual to cycle splitting.

7) Join the Shortest Queue (JSQ): Level 5, Source-Initiative — Each source independently sends an arriving job to the server that has the least number of jobs (including the one in service). Ties are broken randomly and uniformly over tied servers.

8) Serve the Longest Queue (SLQ): Level 5, Server-Initiative — A dual to JSQ is the algorithm in which whenever a server becomes available it serves a job from the longest source queue. Again ties are broken randomly and uniformly.

9) First Come First Served (FCFS): Level 6, Server-Initiative or Level 7, Source-Initiative — All servers are applied to form an overall multiserver FCFS system. As shown in Table I, it can be considered server-initiative or, alternatively, source-initiative if more information is made available.

10) Shortest Job First: Level 7, Server-Initiative — Servers select the currently waiting job that has the smallest service time requirement.

The performance analysis of the algorithms we have defined leads to many unsolved problems in queueing theory. Some previous work does exist. References [2]–[4] considered the static (Level 1) algorithms and optimized chosen performance indices using mathematical programming or network flow techniques. Random and cyclic splitting algorithms and their variations have been considered in [5]–[9].

---

[4]The advantage in using a different schedule sequence for each server is discussed in [25].

TABLE II
POISSON ARRIVALS, EXPONENTIAL SERVICE TIME DISTRIBUTION, $h_o = h_e = 0$, N SOURCES, K SERVERS

Algorithm	Queueing Model	Solution Techniques
Source Partition	$M/M/1$	exact analysis (see, e.g., [13])
Server Partition	$M/M/C$	exact analysis (see, e.g., [13])
Random splitting	$M/M/1$	exact analysis (see, e.g., [13])
Cyclic Splitting	$\sum_{i=1}^{N} E_K(\lambda_i)/M/1$	simulation, approximate analysis (Appendix B-1)
Cyclic service ($B = 1, V = \infty$)	cyclic service queue	exact analysis for Q-factor (Appendix B-3)
Cyclic service ($B = 1, V = 1$)	cyclic service queue	simulation, heavy traffic analysis for Q-factor (Appendix B-4), exact analysis if $K = 1$, $N = 2$ [14]*
Cyclic service ($B = 1$, gated)	cyclic service queue	simulation, exact analysis if $K = 1$ [15]*
Join the shortest queue		simulation, approximate analysis (Appendix B-2), exact analysis if $K = 2$ [11]*
Serve the longest queue		exact analysis for Q-factor (Appendix B-3)
FCFS	$M/M/K$	exact analysis (see, e.g., [13])
shortest job first		simulation, exact analysis if $K = 1$ [16]*

TABLE III
POISSON ARRIVALS, DETERMINISTIC SERVICE TIME, $h_o = h_e = 0$, N SOURCES, K SERVERS

Algorithm	Queueing Model	Solution Techniques
Source Partition	$M/D/1$	exact analysis (see e.g. [13])
Server Partition	$M/D/C$	exact analysis (see e.g. [17])
Random Splitting	$M/D/1$	exact analysis (see e.g. [13])
Cyclic Splitting	$\sum_{i=1}^{N} E_K(\lambda_i)/D/1$	simulation, approximate analysis (Appendix C-1 and -5), exact analysis if $N = 1$ (Appendix C-5)
Cyclic service ($B=1$, $V=\infty$)	Cyclic service queue	simulation
Cyclic service ($B=1$, $V=1$)	•	simulation, heavy traffic analysis for Q-factor (Appendix C-4)
Cyclic service ($B=1$, gated)	•	simulation, exact analysis if $K=1$ [15]*
Join-the-shortest-queue		simulation
Serve-the-longest-queue		simulation
FCFS	$M/D/K$	exact analysis [17]
shortest-job-first		•

TABLE IV
POISSON ARRIVALS, DETERMINISTIC SERVICE TIME, $h_o = h_e = 0$, N SOURCES, $K \to \infty$ SERVERS

Algorithm	Queueing Model	Solution Techniques
Random Splitting	$M/D/1$	exact analysis (see e.g. [13])
Cyclic Splitting	$\sum_{i=1}^{N} D_i/D/1$	exact analysis [19]
Cyclic service ($B=1$, $V=\infty$)	Cyclic service queue	exact analysis for Q-factor (see Appendix C-6)
Cyclic service ($B=1$, $V=1$)	•	•
Cyclic service ($B=1$, gated)	•	•
Serve-the-longest-queue		•
FCFS	$M/D/\infty$	•

Dynamic algorithms have been found much more difficult to analyze, and in many cases simulation has been necessary. For example, [5], [11] have considered JSQ and [10] studies a "diffusion" algorithm (see Appendix A). Most prior analysis has concentrated on source-initiative algorithms and mainly considered average performance over all jobs excluding any fairness or uniform acceptability measures.

Before describing our analysis, we state assumptions about the transport delay of the communication medium and node processor overhead involved in interprocessor communication (IPC). The transport delay of the communication medium will be assumed to be zero. This is reasonable for many applications and current local area interconnect technology which usually has ample bandwidth and provides rapid message passing between processors. The IPC overhead is assumed to consist of a per message processing time of h_o and h_e at the source and server nodes, respectively. These burdens are supposed to take into account system call, context switch, and communication medium management. Values of h_o and h_e observed in practice are on the order of one or several milliseconds for typical microprocessor technology and are often relatively independent of message length. Thus, the overhead of transferring a bit of scheduling information might well be comparable to the overhead of moving a job. We will consider separately the cases where IPC overhead is negligible and nonnegligible.

The performance of the ten canonical algorithms described above will be analyzed under various assumptions.

1) Poisson arrivals, exponential service time distribution, $h_o = h_e = 0$, N sources, K servers.

2) Poisson arrivals, deterministic service time distribution, $h_o = h_e = 0$, N sources, K servers.

3) Poisson arrivals, deterministic service time distribution, $h_o = h_e = 0$, N sources, $K \to \infty$ servers.

4) Poisson arrivals, hyperexponential service time distribution, $h_o = h_e = 0$, N sources, K servers.

5) Batched Poisson arrivals (batch size a multiple of K), exponential service time distribution, $h_o = h_e = 0$, N sources, K servers.

6) Poisson arrivals, exponential service time distribution, $h_o = h_e > 0$, N sources, K servers.

In each case we will assume that each of the servers has a mean job processing rate of μ and the processing time at sources is negligible. For cases 1)–6), see Tables II–VII which summarize, respectively, the cases considered and the analysis methods used to obtain the results. For completeness, we also include in Tables II–VII some other relevant analysis methods (marked with *). These tables refer extensively to the literature and to Appendix B which contains details of further queueing analysis.

TABLE V
POISSON ARRIVALS, HYPEREXPONENTIAL SERVICE TIME DISTRIBUTION, $h_o = h_e = 0$, N SOURCES, K SERVERS

Algorithm	Queueing Model	Solution Techniques
Source Partition	$M/H_2/1$	exact analysis [13]
Server Partition	$M/H_2/C$	simulation, exact analysis [18]*
Random Splitting	$M/H_2/1$	exact analysis [13]
Cyclic Splitting	$\sum_{i=1}^{N} E_k(\lambda_i)/H_2/1$	simulation, exact analysis, if $N=1$ [18]*
Cyclic service ($B=1$, $V=\infty$)	Cyclic service queue	simulation
Cyclic service ($B=1$, $V=1$)	"	simulation, heavy traffic analysis for Q-factor (Appendix C-4)
Cyclic service ($B=1$, gated)	"	simulation, exact analysis if $K=1$ [15]*
Join-the-shortest-queue		simulation
Serve-the-longest-queue		simulation
FCFS	$M/H_2/K$	simulation, approximate analysis [46], exact analysis [18]*.

TABLE VI
BATCHED POISSON ARRIVALS, BATCH SIZES ARE MULTIPLES OF K (THE NUMBER OF SERVERS), EXPONENTIAL SERVICE TIME DISTRIBUTION, $h_o = h_e = 0$, N SOURCES

Algorithm	Queueing Model	Solution Techniques
Cyclic Splitting	$M^{[x]}/M/1$	exact analysis (Appendix C-7)
Cyclic service ($B=1$, gated)	cyclic service queue	simulation
FCFS	$M^{[x]}/M/K$	exact analysis [47]

TABLE VII
POISSON ARRIVALS, EXPONENTIAL SERVICE TIME DISTRIBUTION, N SOURCES, K SERVERS, $h_o = h_e > 0$

Algorithm	Queueing Model	Solution Techniques
Cyclic Splitting		simulation
Cyclic service ($B=\infty$, $V=1$)		simulation, approximate analysis [25]*

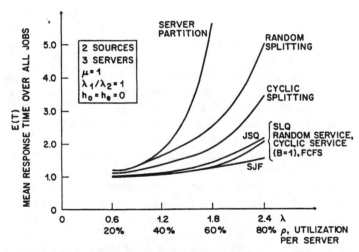

Fig. 2. Mean response time (over all jobs) as a function of utilization of service — balanced loading.

VI. PERFORMANCE ANALYSIS RESULTS AND COMPARISONS

We begin with the case where there is no IPC overhead (i.e., $h_o = h_e = 0$). This case, while idealized, is of considerable importance for several reasons. It approximates the case where IPC overheads are negligible in comparison to the work required to execute the job. More importantly, it gives insight as to what performance gains are, in principle, achievable with different algorithms. If, and only if, a significant performance gain is indicated, the cost of implementing the algorithm (development and execution) needs to be considered. In some cases, special measures (e.g., more efficient operating system procedures, hardware assists such as front ends) may be justified to make the algorithm implementable so that performance gains are achieved.

A. Performance Averaged Over All Jobs

We find that server-initiative algorithms outperform source-initiative algorithms using the same level of informa-tion. The main reason for this is that most server-initiative algorithms do not allow a server to become idle when there are jobs waiting in the system — at the very least a server-initiative algorithm will utilize server idle time to search for new work.

Fig. 2 shows the mean response time over all jobs for various algorithms as a function of utilization for the case $N = 2, K = 3, \lambda_1 = \lambda_2$. First note that the cyclic service ($B = 1$), random service, and SLQ algorithms produce the same mean response time as FCFS. This is because these algorithms simply result in an interchange of order of processing from FCFS and thus (by Little's Law [13], [20], [28]) do not change the mean delay averaged over all jobs. Of the other algorithms shown, SJF gives the best mean delay, as expected, being the only algorithm considered that has knowledge of jobs' service times. The poorer performance of JSQ compared to FCFS is, of course, attributable to the inadequacy of using number in queue as a load indicator. That results in the possibility that a job can wait at a server while

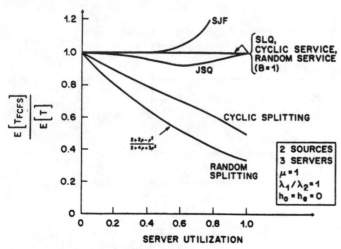

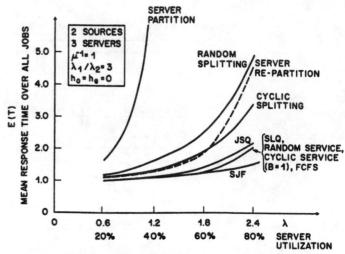

Fig. 3. Fig. 2 redrawn normalized with respect to FCFS.

Fig. 4. Mean response time over all jobs when the load on the sources is unbalanced.

another server is idle. It is interesting to note that, as shown in Table I, if we allow the sources to know which server has the least backlog of work (although this is seldom a practical proposition), we can implement FCFS as a source-initiative algorithm. The phenomenon of jobs waiting while a server is idle and the resulting degraded performance is even more pronounced in the random and cyclic splitting algorithms, which have no knowledge of the server states. The cyclic splitting algorithm outperforms the random splitting algorithm because of the increased regularity of the job stream at the server induced by the cyclic splitting. If we normalize the mean response time of jobs under various algorithms with respect to FCFS, we obtain Fig. 3.

In Fig. 4 we unbalance the load between the two sources and reexamine performance. This imbalance does not affect overall performance of the server-initiative and JSQ algorithms and has only a small effect on the random and cyclic splitting algorithms. It has a major effect on the server partition algorithm which is unable to adapt to the imbalance and one server quickly becomes saturated. This effect can be reduced by repartitioning the servers as shown, but the repartitioning does not happen automatically.

Another interesting aspect of the failure of source-initiative algorithms to reflect actual processing times is the effect of service time distribution on overall performance. Fig. 5 illustrates the effect on mean overall response time relative to FCFS as service time distribution varies from deterministic through exponential to hyperexponential. The overall performance of SLQ and cyclic service ($B = 1$) are not affected (when normalized to FCFS) by service time distribution, but the performance of the random and cyclic splitting algorithms degrade rapidly as more variability is introduced into the service time distribution.

B. Load Sharing Performance

We now evaluate the ability of the algorithms to share load over servers regardless of the distribution of work over sources. We find that server-initiative algorithms usually have a higher Q-factor than the source-initiative algorithms using the same level of information.

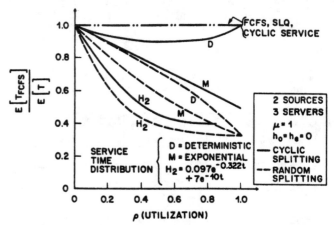

Fig. 5. The effect of service time distribution on the overall mean response time.

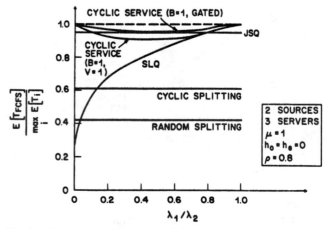

Fig. 6. The effect of load distribution on mean response time at the worst performing source — $\rho = 0.8$.

Figs. 6 and 7 show the delay at the worst performing source as the load distribution varies between two sources for a fixed total load. While server-initiative algorithms are seen to be superior, they are more sensitive to load distribution than source-initiative algorithms. An interesting result is that the cyclic splitting curve is almost flat — this is consistent

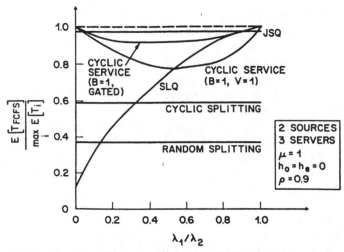

Fig. 7. The effect of load distribution on mean response time at the worst performing source — $\rho = 0.9$.

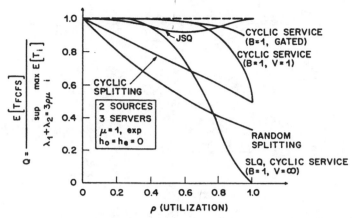

Fig. 8. Q-factors of algorithms as a function of ρ when service time distribution is exponential.

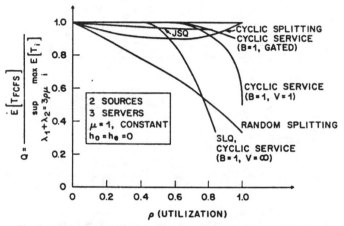

Fig. 9. Q-factors of algorithms as a function of ρ when service time distribution is deterministic.

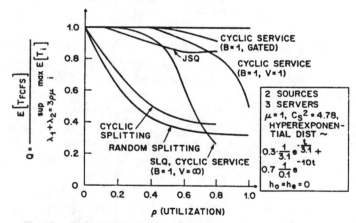

Fig. 10. Q-factors of algorithms as a function of ρ when service time distribution is hyperexponential.

with the observations of [21]. Note that SLQ degrades rapidly when load is unbalanced. This is because the lightly loaded queue receives low priority in gaining service. In the limit, a rare arrival at the lightly loaded queue must wait until the heavily loaded queue has less than K jobs present (i.e., one of the K servers becomes free) before receiving service.

In Figs. 8–10 we use the Q-factor figure of merit introduced earlier to allow a performance summary to be plotted as a function of ρ.[5] Note that in computing the Q-factor we must find the combination of loadings (λ_i's) which cause the worst performance. For most algorithms the Q-factors degrade rapidly as $\rho \rightarrow 1$. The only source-initiative algorithm that holds up adequately well is JSQ. The cyclic service algorithms show reasonable Q-factors except at very high utilization, with the "$B = 1$, gated" version showing the best performance. The reader should note that algorithms that have identical performance when viewed over all jobs have now been delineated by the Q-factor (compare Fig. 3 to Fig. 8). Figs. 9 and 10 treat the deterministic and hyperexponential service time distributions, respectively, and show that load sharing performance of all algorithms degrades as service time variability increases. But the performance of the server-initiative algorithms is less sensitive to the service time variability.

The performance of source-initiative algorithms such as random and cyclic splitting also degrade as the number of servers becomes large (Fig. 11). On the other hand, server-initiative algorithms such as cyclic service approach the ideal of load balancing.

To investigate the effect of "bursty" arrivals on the performance of these algorithms, we consider batch arrivals at sources. The results are shown in Fig. 12. We observe that both cyclic splitting and cyclic service ($B = 1$, gated) are relatively unaffected by batches, with cyclic service showing slightly superior performance.

---

[5]Recall that the Q-factor is designed to compare performance of algorithms over a range of system loadings. It does not necessarily assert, for example, one algorithm is uniformly better than another under all conditions.

C. Effect of IPC Overhead on Algorithms

It was argued at the beginning of this section that performance analysis with assumptions of negligible IPC overhead can still offer considerable insight into design issues. In the remainder of this paper we will limit ourselves to demonstrating a few effects when IPC overhead is not negligible. It is rather difficult to conduct an unbiased and complete performance evaluation when IPC overhead is taken into ac-

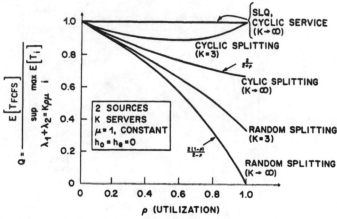

Fig. 11. Q-factors of algorithms as a function of ρ when the number of servers increases.

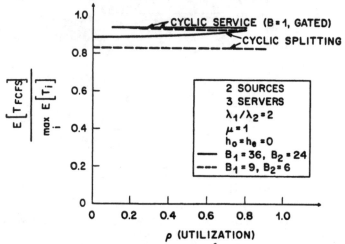

Fig. 12. The effect of batch size of arrivals on the mean response time of jobs at the worst performing source.

count. The amount of overhead introduced by an algorithm is implementation dependent and therefore highly subjective. For example, while JSQ outperforms other source-initiative algorithms it would seem to involve a large IPC overhead. For this reason we select for illustration the cyclic splitting and cyclic service algorithms which have been shown, from the results above, to be promising representatives of the source- and server-initiative approaches. The assumptions on the IPC overhead for these two are as follows.

For the cyclic splitting algorithm, the ith job arriving to a source is sent to the i(mod K)th server. This requires a write per job at the source and a read at the server. On completing service, a server must write each job back to the originating source and that source has to read the result. Thus, the IPC overheads per job are $2h_o$ at the source and $2h_e$ at the server. These overheads are assumed to be deterministic.

For the cyclic service ($B = \infty$, $V = 1$) algorithm, the server polls a source by writing a message to that source. The source receives (by reading) the message and writes back a "batch" of all accumulated jobs ($B = \infty$) to the polling server which receives them with a single read. If the batch is nonempty, the server executes the batch of jobs and writes them with a single write back to the originating source which has

to read the results; otherwise, it polls the next source, etc. Thus, to process a batch, the server has done two writes and a read while the source has done two reads and one write. The IPC overheads are thus $3h_o$ at the source and $3h_e$ at the server per (nonempty) batch of jobs. For this example we are assuming that the IPC overhead of "polling" equals that of moving a job, as discussed in Section V.

When IPC overhead is zero, cyclic service has better performance. But as overhead increases, Fig. 13 shows that cyclic splitting can be advantageous because it has no polling latency and may have smaller per job overhead. Although it is not shown in Fig. 13, as overhead increases even further, cyclic service eventually becomes preferable as a consequence of its batching effect. Fig. 14 shows a similar effect. For a fixed value of overhead, as the arrival rate increases, cyclic splitting shows some initial advantage which is eventually overridden by the decreasing per job overhead of cyclic service.

It could be argued that batching effects can also be incorporated to advantage in a cyclic splitting algorithm using, for example, a time-out mechanism at the sources. But then latency effects also appear in the cyclic splitting algorithm and performance comparisons become ambiguous. This example illustrates some of the difficulties of carrying out an objective comparison of algorithms in the presence of IPC overhead.

VII. CONCLUSIONS

With the enormous scope and complexity of the distributed scheduling problem, we have only been able to touch on a subset of important issues. We have concentrated on what is obviously a crucial component — the load sharing strategy — but we remind the reader that there are also other important components of this problem including data synchronization and concurrency control, maintenance, fault detection/recovery, etc. One issue that we did cite in Section I was that of failure tolerance. It should be noted that of the algorithms we have considered, the server-initiative varieties degrade more gracefully under passive failures since a failed server will cease to request work.

In our analysis of load sharing performance we have only been able to consider a simple class of distributed systems and a small subset of all possible parameter ranges. Much further work needs to be done. But we have demonstrated some basic properties of different approaches. Some of our conclusions are as follows.

i) Widely varying performance, both from an overall and individual sources' viewpoint, is obtained with different strategies — the load sharing algorithm is a critical design decision.

ii) With the same level of information available, server-initiative algorithms have the potential of outperforming source-initiative algorithms. This superiority is demonstrated for the case of negligible IPC overhead but whether this holds true in another situation requires examination of

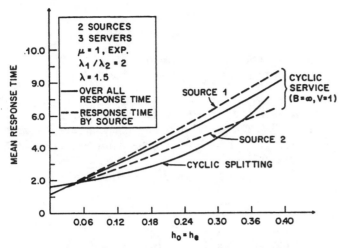

Fig. 13. The mean response of jobs as a function of the interprocessor communication overhead.

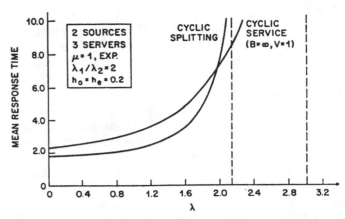

Fig. 14. The mean response time of jobs as a function of load where the interprocessor communication overhead is nonnegligible.

the communication cost involved.

iii) The use of the Q-factor provides a useful yardstick for comparing load sharing performance of different algorithms.

iv) Algorithms that have previously received little attention in the literature, e.g., multiserver cyclic service, can in some circumstances provide effective load sharing at fairly low communication cost.

Of course, these observations cannot be applied out of context. For example, two algorithms, one source-initiative and one server-initiative, may use the same "level of information" but involve considerably different amounts of communication if N is much larger than K or vice versa. And in applications where IPC overhead is significant, implementation options such as batching jobs at nodes need to be pursued.

Throughout this paper we have concentrated on scheduling strategies based on a communication medium that provides only rudimentary message passing. But if we were instead to construct a communication medium with capabilities such as broadcasting, virtual addressing, conditional addressing, and selective or conditional reception, we open up a much wider spectrum of scheduling options.

Appendix A
Literature Survey

Load sharing algorithms have frequently been classified as either *static* or *dynamic*. The static algorithms distribute the load according to some rules that are set *a priori*.

Static algorithms that allocate servers permanently or semipermanently to arriving job streams can be found in [2]–[4] where load sharing is formulated as a mathematical programming or network flow problem. Solutions are obtained by performing optimization against some chosen performance index that assumes a known constant workload. This approach may require an update of server allocations if arrival rates change. A *random splitting* algorithm that distributes jobs among all servers according to a given prob-

ability distribution can be found in [5]. *Cyclic splitting* algorithms in which jobs are distributed among all servers according to some cyclic schedule can be found in [7], [8].

The major drawback of static algorithms is that they do not respond to short-term fluctuations of the workload. Dynamic schedules attempt to correct this drawback but are more difficult to implement and to analyze. There are at least six types of these schedules found in the literature (for other detailed surveys, see [27], [49]).

1) Hierarchical: This type of algorithm can be found in the resource management of the Stony Brook Multicomputer [30], the MicroNet [31], [32], and the X-tree system [33] where schedulers are organized into a logical control hierarchy. Each scheduler is responsible for either some lower level schedulers or servers (sometimes called "workers"). Load distribution is done by requesting and reserving resources up and down the hierarchy until sufficient resources are obtained. The scheduling decisions are usually carried out unilaterally with one scheduler at the root of the hierarchy. The load sharing problem has not been specifically addressed.

2) Sequential: Examples of systems include the ARAMIS [34] and the Delta [26] where the nodes of the system form a virtual ring. Each node has its own scheduler that is responsible for accessing shared resources in the system for the users attached to that node. A control token is passed around the virtual ring to enforce a serial operation of the schedulers in allocating or deallocating shared resources. The emphasis of the scheme is to provide some concurrency control rather than load sharing. It may be viewed as a dynamic centralized scheduling algorithm since at any given time there is only one view of the system state — the view of the scheduler that holds the token. Note that some reliable mechanism has to be provided so that the token will not be lost indefinitely nor be duplicated.

3) Diffusion: Examples of this class of algorithms can be found in MuNet [35], CHoPP [36], and the most recent version of Roscoe [10]. The load sharing effort is accomplished in these systems by having the neighboring nodes communicate and cooperate with each other so that the load migrates from heavily to lightly loaded nodes. One advantage of this algorithm is that the communication cost can remain relatively low even when the size of the system increases. However, the rate of diffusion and the stability of the system are not fully understood. Some simulation results that demonstrate the superiority of the scheme over static scheduling were documented in [10].

4) Contract Bidding: This popular algorithm can be found in DCS [37] and CNET [38]. There can,be two procedures: *normal* and *reversed*. In the normal contract bidding procedure, sources that distribute the load will broadcast a "request for bids" to all servers. On receiving the request for bids, a server may submit a bid for the work according to some criteria, e.g., its work queue length, availability of its resources, etc. Later the requesting source will choose one server (typically the lowest bidder) to process the work based on the bids it has received. In the reversed contract bidding procedure, idle servers will send messages to sources to indicate their willingness to take on work rather than waiting for "request for bids." The multiple cyclic server system analyzed in [25] can be considered as a case of the reversed contract bidding scheme. The performance of this class of algorithm depends on the appropriateness of the choice of the bid and communication overhead.

5) Dipstick: Examples of this type of algorithm may be found in the ADAPT [39] and an earlier version of Roscoe [40]. Similar mechanisms may also be found in ICNS [41] and the POGOS [27]. Under this algorithm, a node always tries to execute a job locally before it sends that job to other nodes. The criterion used by a node to decide whether to accept and execute a job is typically based on some indicator of its load. Often, some minimum and maximum values of the indicator are prespecified. If a node's load is below the minimum, it may broadcast to others that it is willing to take additional load. If a node's load exceeds the maximum, it will attempt to send incoming jobs to other nodes. Provisions have to be made for those jobs that have been given a "run-around." It appears to be difficult to choose an appropriate criterion for accepting or rejecting work by a node so that the system is stable [27]. Note also that the communication overhead can be severe, especially when the system is heavily loaded.

6) State feedback: Examples include DFMP [42], the Purdue University ECN [43], and the classical "Join the Shortest Queue" method and its variants [5], [6], [44]. A scheme based on Bayesian decision theory has also been proposed and analyzed [45]. In this approach an estimate of a system state such as processor queue lengths is maintained and is periodically updated. The algorithm simply routes the work to the currently "least congested" server. One problem with this approach is the potentially high cost of obtaining the required state information (delay and communication overhead, etc.). It is known that excessive delays in updating the information can cause instability of the system. Another problem is that a chosen load indicator, such as queue length, is often inadequate especially when the servers possess a multiplicity of resources. Note that the join the shortest queue method may also be considered as a form of normal contract bidding where the bid is in terms of the queue length.

APPENDIX B
QUEUEING ANALYSIS

1. Approximating the Superposition of Renewal Processes [21]

The superposition of N renewal processes ($\Sigma_{i=1}^{N} GI_i$) may be approximated by a renewal process as follows.

Step 1: Let the approximating mean interevent time be $1/\lambda = 1/\Sigma_{i=1}^{N} \lambda_i$ where λ_i^{-1} is the mean interevent time of the ith component process.

Step 2: Let the approximating coefficient of variation be either Approximation I:

$$c_I^2 = \omega_1 c_a^2 + (1 - \omega_1)c_s^2,$$

$$\omega_1 = \frac{1}{1 + 6(1 - \rho)^{2.2}N}$$

or Approximation II:

$$c_{II}^2 = \omega_2 c_a^2 + (1 - \omega_2)c_m^2,$$

$$\omega_2 = \frac{1}{1 + 2.1(1 - \rho)^{1.8}N}$$

where

$$c_a^2 = \frac{1}{\lambda} \sum_{i=1}^{N} \lambda_i c_i^2 \quad \text{(the asymptotic approximation method)},$$

$$c_m^2 = 1 \quad \text{(the Markov approximation method)},$$

and c_s is the coefficient of variation of the stationary interval distribution of the superposed process which is given by

$$G(t) = 1 - \frac{1}{\lambda} \sum_{i=1}^{N} \lambda_i [1 - F_i(t)] \left\{ \prod_{\substack{j=1 \\ j \neq i}}^{N} \lambda_j \int_t^{\infty} (1 - F_j(x)) \, dx \right\}$$

where $F_j(\cdot)$ is the probability distribution function of the interevent time of the jth component process.

Step 3: Depending on whether $c_I(c_{II})$ is greater or less than one, fit a "convenient" distribution to the approximating renewal process. In [21], Albin has chosen to fit an M^d-distribution (shifted Exponential) if $c_I(c_{II}) \leq 1$ and an H_2^b-distribution (balanced mean hyperexponential) if $c_I(c_{II}) > 1$.

Remarks: a) Both approximations have been tested [21] for queues with exponential service time distributions by comparing the approximating mean waiting time against the simulated results. Good accuracies were reported for both approximations. Further discussions and improvements of these approximations can be found in [50].

b) Suppose the component processes are $E_K(\lambda_i)$ (i.e., of same number of phases with possibly different rate λ_i), $\Sigma_{i=1}^{N} \lambda_i = \lambda$. Then Approximation II (that is based on the asymptotic approximation and the Markov approximation) will produce a coefficient of variation independent of the ratios of λ_i/λ for the approximating renewal stream. This is due to the fact that the coefficient of variation of $E_k(\lambda_i)$ is $1/\sqrt{K}$ and is independent of λ_i. Therefore, the good accuracy of Approximation II implies that the overall mean delay in a $\Sigma_{i=1}^{N} E_K(\lambda_i)/M/1$ would be insensitive to the ratios λ_i/λ

for a given $\sum_{i=1}^{N} \lambda_i = \lambda$. We do observe such an insensitivity in our simulation results when we study the cyclic splitting algorithm.

2. Approximate Analysis of JSQ Discipline

Let the arrival process be Poisson of rate λ. Let the number of queues (servers) be K. Let the service time distribution of jobs be exponential of mean $\mu^{-1} = 1$. It is known that (see, e.g., [13]) the mean waiting time in an $M/M/K$ FCFS system is given by

$$\overline{W}_{\text{FCFS}} = \frac{\lambda^K}{d(\lambda)}$$

where $d(\lambda) = (K - \lambda)\{K!(1 - \lambda/K)\sum_{k=0}^{K-1} \lambda^k/k! + \lambda^K\}$.

We now approximate the mean waiting time in an $M/M/K$ JSQ system by

$$\overline{W}(\lambda) = \frac{n(\lambda)}{d(\lambda)}$$

where $n(\lambda) = \sum_{i=0}^{K+1} a_i \lambda^i$ is to be determined by the jth order derivatives

$$\overline{W}_{\text{JSQ}}^{(j)}(0), \qquad j = 0, 1, 2, \cdots, K$$

and

$$\overline{W}_{\text{JSQ}}(\lambda), \qquad \lambda \to K.$$

a) Light Traffic Analysis of JSQ:[6] Consider the JSQ system with $\lambda \to 0$. The probability of waiting is of the order of the probability that an arriving customer finds K in the system in service. This latter probability is given by the probability that an arrival occurred before any of K jobs in service could depart and the previous job arrived before any of $K - 1$ jobs in service could depart, etc. Thus, the probability of waiting is

$$\frac{\lambda}{\lambda + \mu K} \cdot \frac{\lambda}{\lambda + \mu(K - 1)} \cdot \cdots \cdot \frac{\lambda}{\lambda + \mu} + o(\lambda^K)$$

and

$$\overline{W}_{\text{JSQ}}(\lambda) = \frac{1}{\mu} \prod_{j=1}^{K} \frac{\lambda}{\lambda + j\mu} + o(\lambda^K).$$

Thus,

$$\overline{W}_{\text{JSQ}}^{(n)}(0) = \begin{cases} 0, & n < K \\ \dfrac{1}{\mu^{K+1}}, & n = K. \end{cases}$$

b) Heavy-Traffic Analysis: It has been shown (see, e.g., [23]) by diffusion analysis that for the $M/M/K$ queueing system

$$\frac{\overline{W}_{\text{JSQ}}(\lambda)}{\overline{W}_{\text{FCFS}}(\lambda)} \to 1, \qquad \text{as } \lambda \to K.$$

[6]This is based on the ideas of [22].

From the light traffic result, we have that

$$a_i = 0, \qquad i = 0, 1, \cdots, K - 1$$

$$a_K = K.$$

From the heavy traffic result, we have

$$a_{K+1} = \frac{1}{K} - 1.$$

Hence, the approximate mean waiting time in a $M/M/K$ JSQ system is

$$\overline{W}_{\text{JSQ}}(\lambda) \approx \frac{\lambda^K \left[K - \left(1 - \dfrac{1}{K}\right)\lambda \right]}{d(\lambda)}.$$

Remark: This approximation has been compared to simulation results for $K = 2, 3, 5$. The maximum error (as a function of $\rho = \lambda/K\mu$) for the case where $K = 2$ was about 8 percent (at $\rho \approx 0.7$). The maximum error seems to increase as the number of servers increases. For the case where $K = 5$, we have seen an error of 25 percent. It appears that additional derivative information at $\rho \to 1$ would help to improve the approximation but we do not know of any such results. We have tried requiring that $\overline{W}_{\text{JSQ}}^{(1)}(\lambda)/\overline{W}_{\text{FCFS}}^{(1)}(\lambda)$ also tends to 1 as $\lambda \to K$ and obtained a $K + 2$ degree polynomial $n(\lambda)$ in our approximation. For the case $K = 5$, the approximation errors were reduced significantly (to about 7 percent at $\rho = 0.8$ and 3 percent at $\rho = 0.7$).

3. Derivation of Q-Factors for SLQ and Cyclic Service $(B = 1, V = \infty)$

For the SLQ ($K \geq 2$) and cyclic service ($B = 1, V = \infty$) algorithms, it can be argued that the Q-factor is attained when the ith source has an arrival rate $\lambda_i \to 0$ while all the rest of the jobs go to one of the remaining sources—the system behaves like a nonpreemptive priority queue. Under this condition, a tagged arriving job at the ith source waits if and only if all servers are busy. The mean waiting time given that the tagged job waits is the mean forward recurrence time of the K-server busy period where the latter is defined as the time between when all K servers become busy and the first time one of the servers becomes free. Under the assumption that the arrivals form a Poisson process and that the service time distribution is exponential, the K-server busy period is the same as the busy period of a $M/M/1$ system with a service rate K times that of the servers of the original system. Thus, the mean waiting time of jobs at the ith source is given by

$$Q_{\text{SLQ}}' = Q_{\text{cyclic service }(B=1, V=\infty)}$$

$$= \frac{\dfrac{C(K, \lambda)}{K\mu(1 - \rho)} + \mu^{-1}}{\dfrac{C(K, \lambda)}{K\mu(1 - \rho)^2} + \mu^{-1}}$$

$$= (1 - \rho) \cdot \frac{C(K, \lambda) + K(1 - \rho)}{C(K, \lambda) + K(1 - \rho)^2}$$

325

where $C(K, \lambda)$ is the well-known Erlang-C formula [13], the probability that all K servers are busy in an $M/M/K$ system, and $\rho = \lambda/K\mu$.

4. Derivation of Q-Factor as $\rho \to 1$ for Cyclic Service $(B = 1, V = 1)$

First let

$$\lambda_1(\rho) \doteq \frac{K\mu\rho}{N} + (N - 1)\epsilon,$$

$$\lambda_i(\rho) = \frac{K\mu\rho}{N} - \epsilon, \qquad i \neq 1,$$

and $\lambda(\rho) = \sum_{i=1}^{N} \lambda_i(\rho)$. Assume $Q(\rho) \to Q$ as $\rho \to 1$. Now queues $2, \cdots, N$ see servers which, before each service, take vacations that are dominated by the sum of $N - 1$ service times of mean μ^{-1}. Thus, queues $2, \cdots, N$ each have effective service rates $\geq \mu/N$ for each of the K servers but $\lambda_i(\rho) \to K\mu/N - \epsilon$ as $\rho \to 1$. Thus, each of these queues is stable as $\rho \to 1$ (having queue length dominated by a stable $M/G/K$ queue), and queue 1 alone is unstable. Denote the mean sojourn time of queue i as $\overline{T}_i$ and the overall mean sojourn time as $\overline{T}$, i.e., $\lambda\overline{T} = \sum_{i=1}^{N} \lambda_i\overline{T}_i$. Then as $\rho \to 1$,

$$Q(\rho) \leq \frac{\overline{T}}{\overline{T}_1} = \frac{\lambda_1(\rho)}{\lambda(\rho) - \sum_{i=2}^{N} \lambda_i(\rho)\overline{T}_i/\overline{T}}$$

$$\to \frac{1}{N} + \frac{(N - 1)\epsilon}{K\mu}.$$

Thus, since $\epsilon > 0$ is arbitrary, we have that $Q \leq 1/N$.

Now Q could not be less than $1/N$. For assume the contrary and let $Q(\rho) \to Q = g/N, g < 1$ where $\lambda_1(\rho), \lambda_2(\rho), \cdots, \lambda_N(\rho)$ are now chosen so that

$$\frac{\lambda_j(\rho)}{\lambda(\rho) - \sum_{i \neq j} \lambda_i(\rho)\overline{T}_i(\rho)/\overline{T}(\rho)} < Q(\rho) + 1 - \rho$$

and

$$j = \left\{ j: \max_i \overline{T}_i = \overline{T}_j \right\}.$$

Then

$$\frac{\lambda_j(\rho)}{\lambda(\rho)} < \frac{\lambda_j(\rho)}{\lambda(\rho) - \sum_{i \neq j} \lambda_i(\rho)\overline{T}_i/\overline{T}_i} < Q(\rho) + 1 - \rho$$

so

$$\lim_{\rho \to 1} \frac{\lambda_j(\rho)}{\lambda(\rho)} \leq \frac{g}{N}$$

or

$$\lim_{\rho \to 1} \lambda_j(\rho) \leq \frac{gK\mu}{N}.$$

But the latter result would imply that the queue with the largest delay is stable, and this is a contradiction. Thus, $Q = \lim_{\rho \to 1} Q(\rho) = 1/N$.

5. Equivalence of the Queues $GI/D/c$ and $GI_c/D/1$

Consider a $GI/D/c$ queue with the discipline that the ith arriving job is assigned to a separate queue for the $i(\mod c)$th server. Because of the deterministic service times, this algorithm will always assign a job to a queue with the least backlog of work. It follows that jobs see a system equivalent to $GI/D/c$ FCFS. Thus, we have that the $GI/D/c$ FCFS queue has a sojourn time equivalent to that of a $GI_c/D/1$ FCFS queue where GI_c denotes the renewal stream with inter-arrival time given by the sum of c interarrival times from the renewal stream GI. Similar observations have been made in [24], [48]. In particular, it has been noted in [24] that the waiting time distribution of an $M/D/c$ system is the same as that of an $E_c/D/1$ system.

6. Analysis of Q-Factors for Some ∞-Server Cases

First note that for $M/D/K$ systems, the queue length process (i.e., the number of jobs in the system) is independent of the queueing discipline provided that every server selects a job for processing independently of the job's service requirement and serves it to completion. For these disciplines and a given ρ, as $K \to \infty$ the number of busy servers is distributed as

$$\frac{\rho^i}{i!} e^{-\rho}.$$

In particular, this is true for FCFS as well as cyclic service $(B = 1)$ and SLQ. Thus, with probability 1, the number of idle servers is greater than 0 and consequently jobs do not wait. It then follows that

$$Q_{\text{SLQ}}(\rho) = Q_{\text{cyclic service } (B=1)}(\rho) = 1.$$

7. Mean Waiting Time in a $GI^{[X]}/G/1$ Queue

Let the batch interarrival time have distribution $A(\cdot)$. Let the batch size $X = n$, with probability $p_n, n = 1, 2 \cdots$. Let the service time distribution of each job be $S(\cdot)$. Then the mean waiting time of a tagged job can be written as

$$\overline{W} = \overline{W}_{\text{BATCH}} + \overline{W}_{\text{FB}}$$

where $\overline{W}_{\text{BATCH}}$ is the mean waiting time of the first job in a batch, and $\overline{W}_{\text{FB}}$ is the total mean service times of the jobs in front of the tagged job in the same batch.

$\overline{W}_{\text{BATCH}}$ can easily be obtained by considering the batch as one single job (whose service time distribution has a Laplace–Stieltjes transform $\sum_{n=1}^{\infty} p_n \hat{S}^n$) and solving the corresponding $GI/G/1$ queue. Since the mean number of jobs in front of a randomly chosen job in a batch is given by $(E[X^2]/E[X] - 1)/2$, we have

$$\overline{W}_{\text{FB}} = \frac{1}{2} \left(\frac{E[X^2]}{E[X]} - 1 \right) \mu^{-1}$$

where μ^{-1} is the mean service time of a job.

REFERENCES

[1] G. R. Andrews, D. P. Dobkin, and P. J. Downey, "Distributed allocation with pools of servers," in *Proc. ACM SIGACT-SIGOPS Symp. Princ. Distrib. Comput.*, 1982, pp. 73–83.

[2] H. S. Stone and S. H. Bokhari, "Control of distributed processes," *IEEE Computer*, vol. 11, pp. 97–106, July 1978.

[3] W. Chu, L. J. Holloway, M. T. Lan, and K. Efe, "Task allocation in distributed data processing," *IEEE Computer*, vol. 13, pp. 57–69, Nov. 1980.

[4] T. C. K. Chou and J. A. Abraham, "Load balancing in distributed systems," *IEEE Trans. Software Eng.*, vol. SE-8, pp. 401–412, July 1982.

[5] L. M. Ni and K. Abani, "Nonpreemptive load balancing in a class of local area networks," in *Proc. Comput. Networking Symp.*, Dec. 1981.

[6] Y. C. Chow and W. H. Kohler, "Models for dynamic load balancing in a heterogeneous multiple processor system," *IEEE Trans. Comput.*, vol. C-28, pp. 354–361, May 1979.

[7] T. Yum, "The design and analysis of a semidynamic deterministic routing rule," *IEEE Trans. Commun.*, vol. COM-29, pp. 498–504, Apr. 1981.

[8] A. K. Agrawala and S. K. Tripathi, "On the optimality of semidynamic routing schemes," *Inform. Processing Lett.*, vol. 13, no. 1, pp. 20–22, Oct. 1981.

[9] L. M. Ni and K. Hwang, "Optimal load balancing for a multiple processor system," in *Proc. Int. Conf. Parallel Processing*, 1981, pp. 352–357.

[10] R. M. Bryant and R. A. Finkel, "A stable distributed scheduling algorithm," in *Proc. 2nd Int. Conf. Distrib. Comput. Syst.*, 1981.

[11] Y. C. Chow and W. H. Kohler, "Dynamic load balancing in homogeneous two processor distributed systems," in *Computer Performance*, K. M. Chandy and M. Reiser, Eds. Amsterdam, The Netherlands: North-Holland, 1977.

[12] S. W. Furhman, "Performance analysis of a class of cyclic schedules," unpublished.

[13] R. B. Cooper, *Introduction to Queueing Theory, 2nd ed.* London: E. Arnold, 1981.

[14] M. Eisenberg, "Two queues with alternating service," *SIAM J. Math*, vol. 36, pp. 287–303, 1979.

[15] O. Hashida, "Gating multiqueues served in a cyclic order," *Systems-Computers-Controls*, vol. 1, no. 1, pp. 1–8, 1970.

[16] R. W. Conway, W. L. Maxwell, and L. W. Miller, *Theory of Scheduling*. New York: Addison-Wesley, 1967.

[17] C. D. Crommelin, "Delay probability formula when the holding times are constant," *P. O. Elec. Eng. J.*, vol. 25, pp. 41–50, 1932.

[18] J. H. A. de'Smit, "The queue *GI/M/S* with customers of different types or the queue *GI/H_m/S*," *Adv. Appl. Prob.*, vol. 15, pp. 392–419, 1983.

[19] A. E. Eckberg, Jr., "Response time analysis for pipelining jobs in a tree network of processors," *Applied Probability—Computer Science, The Interface*. Birkhauser, 1982.

[20] D. Gross and C. M. Harris, *Fundamentals of Queueing Theory*. New York: Wiley, 1974.

[21] S. Albin, "Approximating superposition arrival processes of queues," unpublished.

[22] M. I. Reiman and B. Simon, "Queues in light traffic," to be published.

[23] G. J. Foschini, "On heavy traffic diffusion analysis and dynamic routing in packet switched networks," *Computer Performance*, K. M. Chandy and M. Reiser, Eds. Amsterdam, The Netherlands: North-Holland, 1977.

[24] N. U. Prabhu, *Queues and Inventories*. New York: Wiley, 1965.

[25] R. J. T. Morris and Y. T. Wang, "Some results for multi-queue systems with multiple cyclic servers," in *Proc. 2nd Symp. Perform. Comput. Commun. Syst.*, Zurich, Switzerland, Mar. 21–23, 1984.

[26] G. Le Lann, "A distributed system for real-time transaction processing," *IEEE Computer*, vol. 14, pp. 43–48, Feb. 1981.

[27] L. M. Casey, "Decentralized scheduling," *Australian Comput. J.*, vol. 13, pp. 58–63, May 1981.

[28] L. Kleinrock, *Queueing Systems, Vol. 2: Computer Applications*. New York: Wiley, 1976.

[29] H. Aiso, Y. Matsushita, *et al.*, "A minicomputer complex-KOCOS," in *Proc. IEEE/ACM 4th Data Commun. Symp.*, Oct. 1975.

[30] R. G. Kieburtz, "A distributed operating system for the Stony Brook Multicomputer," in *Proc. 2nd Int. Conf. Distrib. Comput. Syst.*, Apr. 1981.

[31] L. D. Wittie and A. M. van Tilborg, "MICROS, A distributed operating system for MICRONET, A reconfigurable network computer," *IEEE Trans. Comput.*, vol. C-29, pp. 1133–1144, Dec. 1980.

[32] A. M. van Tilborg and L. D. Wittie, "Distributed task force scheduling in multi-microcomputer networks," in *Proc. AFIPS*, 1981.

[33] B. Miller and D. Presotto, "XOS: An operating system for the X-tree architecture," *Oper. Syst. Rev.*, vol. 15, pp. 21–32, 1981.

[34] J. P. Cabanel, M. N. Marouane, R. Besbes, R. D. Sazbon, and A. K. Diarra, "A decentralized OS model for ARAMIS distributed computer system," in *Proc. 1st Int. Conf. Distrib. Comput. Syst.*, Oct. 1979.

[35] R. H. Halstead and S. A. Ward, "MuNet: A scalable decentralized architecture for parallel computation," in *Proc. IEEE 7th Annu. Symp. Comput. Arch.*, 1980.

[36] H. Sullivan, T. R. Bashkow, and D. Klappholz, "A large scale homogeneous, fully distributed parallel machine II," in *Proc. 4th Annu. IEEE Symp. Comput. Arch.*, 1977.

[37] D. C. Farber and K. C. Larson, "The distributed computer system," in *Proc. Symp. Comput. Commun. Networks and Teletraffic*, 1972.

[38] R. G. Smith, "The contract net protocol: High level communication and control in a distributed problem solver," *IEEE Trans. Comput.*, vol. C-29, pp. 1104–1113, 1980.

[39] R. Peebles and T. Dopirak, "ADAPT: A query system," in *Proc. COMPCON*, Spring 1980.

[40] M. H. Solomon and R. A. Finkel, "The ROSCOE distributed operating system," in *Proc. 7th Symp. Oper. Syst. Princ.*, 1980.

[41] R. H. Howell, "The integrated computer network system," in *Proc. 1st Int. Conf. Comput. Commun.*, 1972.

[42] F. C. Colon, R. M. Glorioso, W. H. Kohler, and D. C. Li, "Coupling small computers for performance enhancement," in *Proc. AFIPS*, 1976.

[43] K. Hwang, W. J. Croft, G. H. Goble, B. W. Wah, F. A. Briggs, W. R. Simmons, and C. L. Coates, "A UNIX-based local computer network with load balancing," *IEEE Computer*, vol. 15, pp. 55–66, Apr. 1982.

[44] S. Majumdar and M. L. Green, "A distributed real time resource manager," in *Proc. IEEE Symp. Distrib. Data Acquisition, Comput. Control*, 1980.

[45] J. A. Stankovic, "The analysis of a decentralized control algorithm for job scheduling utilizing Bayesian decision theory," in *Proc. IEEE Int. Conf. Parallel Processing*, 1981.

[46] R. Hokstad, "The steady-state solution of $M/K_2/m$ queue," *Adv. Appl. Prob.*, vol. 12, pp. 799–823, 1980.

[47] M. F. Neuts, *Matrix-Geometric Solutions in Stochastic Models*. The Johns Hopkins Univ. Press, 1981.

[48] V. B. Iversen, "Decomposition of an $M/D/r.k$ queue with FIFO into k $E_k/D/r$ queues with FIFO," *Oper. Res. Lett.*, vol. 2, no. 1, pp. 20–21, Apr. 1983.

[49] H. L. Applewhite *et al.*, "Decentralized resource management in distributed computer systems," Carnegie-Mellon Univ., Pittsburgh, PA, Tech. Rep., Feb. 1982.

[50] W. Whitt, "The queueing network analyzer," *Bell Syst. Tech. J.*, vol. 62, no. 9, pp. 2779–2815, Nov. 1983.

Yung-Terng Wang (S'76–M'79) was born in Taiwan, China, on December 27, 1949. He received the B.S. degree in electrical engineering from National Taiwan University in 1972 and the M.S. and Ph.D. degrees in electrical engineering and computer sciences from the University of California, Berkeley, in 1977 and 1978, respectively.

From 1972 to 1974, he served in the Chinese Army. In 1979, before he hoined the AT&T Bell Laboratories, he was a Lecturer in the Department of Electrical Engineering and Computer Sciences, University of California, Berkeley. He is currently a Supervisor of the Department of Performance Analysis, AT&T Bell Laboratories, Holmdel, NJ. His current interests are in the areas of modeling, analysis, and engineering of computer and communications systems.

Robert J.T. Morris (S'75–M'78) received the combined B.Sc.B.E. degree in computer science, mathematics, and electrical engineering from the University of New South Wales, Sydney, Australia, in 1974, and the M.S. degree in system science and the Ph.D. degree in computer science from the University of California, Los Angeles, in 1976 and 1978, respectively.

Since 1978, he has been with AT&T Bell Laboratories, Holmdel, NJ, working on a variety of computer and communication system projects. He is currently Supervisor of the Performance Analysis Studies Group.

The Probability of Load Balancing Success in a Homogeneous Network

C. Gary Rommel, *Member, IEEE*

Abstract—In this paper we examine the problem of load balancing in distributed systems composed of several homogeneous sites connected by a subnet. We determine a general formula for the probability that any one site in the system is underloaded while some other site in the system is overloaded. This probability can be used to define the likelihood of load balancing success in a distributed operating system. This probability gives insight into the utilization of the system and is a useful aid in determining a measure of effectiveness [26] of the system. From our formula we are able to determine this probability when the workload is composed of processes typical to distributed systems such as those given in [15], [20], and [12]. Finally, we demonstrate the influence of variants in the load balancing algorithm on this probability.

Index Terms—Load balancing, distributed systems, queueing theory, performance evaluation, process scheduling, networks.

I. INTRODUCTION

WITH the advent of high-speed local area networks [3], [4], the introduction of massively parallel multicomputer systems [24], [27], and the availability of parallel programming software [17], [2], [14], a fundamental consideration in distributed processing systems is the maximization of system performance through load balancing. Load balancing algorithms on local area network systems such as V [3], [4], NEST [8], and XNOS [22] transfer work from overloaded sites to underloaded sites. Studies in both local area networks [15] and massively parallel multicomputer systems [10] have shown that such simple load balancing algorithms greatly improve performance. We consider two important issues in this paper. The first issue is the workload influence on the probability of load balancing success (PLBS). The second issue is the load balancing algorithm variants on this probability.

Before starting let us integrate the terminology between local area networks and very massively parallel multicomputer systems by defining *process*, *job*, *site*, and *subnet*. A *process* is an executable entity. *Jobs* are composed of one or more processes. Workstations in a local area network or computing nodes in a very massively parallel multicomputer system are defined as *sites*. The ring or bus of the local area network as well as the interconnection subsystem of the massively parallel multicomputer system are defined as the system *subnet*.

Manuscript received April 9, 1990; revised April 19, 1991. Recommended by E. Gelenbe. This work was partially supported by the United Technologies Research Center and the Naval Underwater Systems Center.

The author is with the Department of Mathematics and Computer Science, Eastern Connecticut State University, Willimantic, CT 06226. He is on sabbatic leave at the Naval Underwater Systems Center, New London, CT 06320.

IEEE Log Number 9102385.

The workload of a distributed processing system may be characterized by the process service time distribution, the distribution of number of processes per job placed at a given site, the number of distributed processing sites, and the system traffic intensity. The performance of load balancing algorithms are strongly related to the number of sites which constitute the system. We now proceed to examine each of these issues.

A. Service Time Distribution

Unlike uniprocessor applications, distributed processing applications include two distinct but very important classes of jobs: the traditional sequential job, and the parallel job. A sequential job must be executed as only one process, while the parallel job typifies an application which can be decomposed into numerous processes. Sequential processes have been shown to exhibit very interesting features. The nature of the sequential process in a commercial research facility was explored on a loosely coupled homogeneous system [15] by Leland and Ott. After examining nearly 9.5 million processes, the process behavior was characterized by a very thick tail as the service time approaches ∞. Moreover, service times could largely be grouped into CPU *hogs*, Disk *hogs*, and *ordinary* processes.

The *ordinary* processes required little CPU or disk processing time. In related research by Rommel [20] in which nearly 200 000 processes were considered from an academic environment, the process service time split into short processes and long processes. While not displaying the thick tail found in [15], the ratio of service times was approximately one order of magnitude. Short processes, *ordinary processes*, appeared to have nearly equal service times, while long processes *hogs*, appeared to have exponential service times. Processes derived from parallel programs usually result in either equal service times or extremely different service times [12]. Among applications which can be decomposed are acoustic detection, image processing, fluid dynamics analysis, and weather forecasting. Because acoustic detection and image processing rely on matrix operations and Fourier transforms, these problems may be easily decomposed into virtually equal processes. Fluid dynamics and weather forecasting depend on numerical solutions of partial differential equations and are often divided into processes using a three-dimensional grid method. Processes from these applications are generally computationally unequal. For example, near the blade of a jet engine or at the eye of a storm the computation requirements are most demanding.

Reprinted from IEEE *Trans. on Software Eng.*, vol. 17, no. 9, Sept. 1991, pp. 922–933.

B. Number of Processes Per Job Placed

In many systems [17], [2], the decomposition of a parallel program as well as the assignment of the processes to sites is at the discretion of the user and not the operating system. Since the process assignment is performed by the user, there is no guarantee that the system is load balanced. Such user-dependent assignments may result in an uneven number of processes from one job being located at a given site.

C. Number of Distributed Processing Sites

The state of the art of distributed processing systems suggests an increasing number of processing sites. The commonly available local area networks connect 16, 32, and 256 nodes, while the very massively parallel multicomputer systems may incorporate as many or more processing elements. For example, the Touchstone's Delta system now supports 128 processing elements with predications of 2048 processing elements for the final system.

D. System Traffic Intensity

The system traffic intensity has been shown to strongly influence the performance of load balancing algorithms [16]. This research suggested that load balancing algorithms performed poorly at both low and high system traffic intensity.

Today's load balancing algorithms have several variants. The simplest sends work from sites with two or more processes to sites with no processes; i.e., idle sites. Another variant sends processes to sites with less than a fixed number of processes. Yet another variant removes processes from sites only if the number of processes exceeds some number. Our interest in this paper is to determine exactly how these variants would influence the PLBS.

Although load balancing does generally assist in performance, if it is poorly incorporated into the system load balancing can reduce performance. Let us now explain three ways this can occur:

1) First, load balancing usually requires some local processing. If this requirement is large, then the systems degrades. This is especially evident at high-traffic intensities
2) Another cause of poor performance is process thrashing. Process thrashing is a needless movement of processes from site to site
3) Finally, large subnet delays may result in a performance degradation. Transferring processes through the subnet may take longer than executing the process locally.

Since algorithm overhead, process thrashing, and subnet degradation may occur during the execution of a load balancing algorithm, the proper control of the algorithm activation would result in performance benefits. By knowing which workload characteristics make the load balancing algorithm feasible, the activation of the algorithm may be controlled as a function of workload. Consequently, if the PLBS can be constructed for a loading algorithm, then PLBS itself can be used as the activation control.

Considering both the importance of distributed processing systems and the information regarding process requirements, we define in this paper a measure which provides the PLBS in homogeneous sites. Our definition has the following important properties:

1) Our definition is very robust in the way it considers the process service time distribution, the distribution of number of processes per job placed at a given site, the number of distributed processing sites, and the system traffic intensity.
2) The definition can easily be used in implementing activation control of load balancing algorithms. This would result in lower overheads, less thrashing process, and better system performance.
3) Although queuing theoretic models may be used in conjunction with our definition, the definition itself is independent of any queuing theoretic models. Thus it can be easily implemented in real distributed processing systems.

A major result of the paper is the determination of when load balancing based on an overloaded/underloaded site policy would be likely to facilitate system performance. From our definition and some analysis with queuing theoretic models:

1) We observe that the distribution of the service time does play an important role in determining the PLBS,
2) We demonstrate that the distribution of number of processes per job placed at a given site has a major impact on the PLBS,
3) We establish that the PLBS is strongly related to system traffic intensity,
4) We find that generally increasing the number of sites increases the PLBS.

We have organized the paper as follows. First, Section II defines the basic theory for our analysis. Section III defines our model, while Section IV gives our analysis. Section V presents some closed form results, while Section VI discusses some graphical results. Finally, Section VII concludes the paper with some summary remarks.

II. BACKGROUND

Our paper is related to the problem of heuristic distributed scheduling. This approach is generally formulated into an overloaded/underloaded paradigm. In the heuristic approach an attempt is made to formulate the process assignment problem in a suboptimal fashion. The heuristic approach is taken due to the fact that an optimal approach is too complex to solve, too complex to implement on the actual system, or simply cannot be formulated.

There is a vast amount of work done in this field. We now briefly discuss a representative set of past approaches. Our discussion is divided into one regarding information passing, and a second regarding actual distributed scheduling algorithms.

We examine four approaches to information passing: *sender directed, receiver directed, bidding,* and *focused addressing*.

In *sender directed* control, when a site has more processes than it can handle it becomes a source of work. To reduce its workload it may randomly select a site to send work, or perhaps sequentially select a site to send work. The key idea behind this approach is the lack of interaction between the source and system. In *receiver directed* control, the server, when idle, solicits work from the system. There are many variants of this approach [6], [5], [16], [18]. For example, Eager *et al.* [6] considered sending work to an underloaded site rather than a strictly idle site. They found that using large thresholds resulted in poor performance. The work in [18] studied the effects of nonzero subnet delays.

In *bidding* a local site determines if processes should become candidates for movement. At the local site, a request for bids is sent out to remote sites. These remote sites bid on the candidate and return the bid to the requesting site. The bid is evaluated and the candidate process is either kept or transferred based on the evaluation. Bidding has long been an issue of research in decentralized scheduling. An example of this technique in load balancing may be found in [9].

Another technique which is used in load balancing is *focused addressing* [19]. In this approach, each site keeps state information about other sites. When a newly arriving process enters the system at a local site, the local site queries its information and may immediately select a site for transferring the process.

We now proceed to examine a sample of distributed scheduling algorithms: 1) Efe's two-phase method, 2) a Bayesian Decision Theory method, 3) Bryant and Finkel's time remaining method, and 4) Livny and Melman's probability approach.

Efe [7] considers a simple method of process assignment with interprocess communication by breaking the states of the algorithm into *two phases*. In the first phase Efe has communicating processes clustered at the same site. This phase is designed to reduce communication costs. The second phase simply reassigns clusters from overloaded sites to underloaded sites. The algorithm repeats until the system state reaches an acceptable level.

Stankovic [25] has proposed a heuristic scheduling algorithm based on *Bayesian Decision Theory*. The work is interesting in that it was an initial attempt to use a decentralized and distributed algorithm for load balancing under uncertainty. The approach is based on a fixed number of actions, a discrete state space, utility function, and an adaptive observation procedure. The observations were based on a Bayesian evaluation procedure and prove to be effective when state information is somewhat out of date.

Bryant and Finkel [1] explore an interesting heuristic based on estimating the *remaining time to complete* for a process. They assume no system overhead and homogeneity of all servers. Their algorithm starts by randomly pairing sites for process scheduling. Once the sites are paired they maintain that state until a fixed time has passed. The algorithm then uses the estimated time to complete to balance the site loads. The authors reported that many of the pairings were fruitless and did not result in any process migration.

The work of Livny and Melman [16] considers heuristics centered around the concept of minimizing the probability of at least one process waiting while at least one server is idle. These results were extended by Rommel [21] to consider a

TABLE I

STATE SPACE IN A SIMPLE THREE-SITE SYSTEM

AAA AAB AAC	ABA ABB ABC	ACA ACB ACC
BAA BAB BAC	BBA BBB BBC	BCA BCB BCC
CAA CAB CAC	CBA CBB CBC	CCA CCB CCC

generalized server. In this paper, by considering a generalized notion of underloaded as well as overloaded, we expand both the work of Livny and Melman [16] and Rommel [21].

We use sensitivity to obtain a measure of the importance of utilization on p_n^m. Our definition of sensitivity is drawn from control theory.

Definition 1: Sensitivity is given for a parameter x and a function $f(x)$ as:

$$S_x^f = \frac{x}{f(x)} \frac{\delta f(x)}{\delta x}. \tag{1}$$

III. MODEL

As we stated in the introduction, we are interested in finding the PLBS in a system of homogeneous sites. We base this success on two events occurring in the system. The first event occurs when at least one site is underloaded. The second event occurs when at least one site is overloaded. When these two events occur together, transferring work from the overloaded site to the underloaded one generally results in a performance improvement. Consequently, the load balancing is successful in this situation.

For a systems composed of homogeneous sites, we define the PLBS in Definition 2.

Definition 2: The homogeneous system PLBS, p_n^m, is defined as the probability that at least one site is underloaded with n or less processes, while at least one site is overloaded with m or more processes present. The subscript defines the number of processes associated with the underloaded state, and the superscript defines the number of processes associated with the overloaded state.

We assume that our system is composed of N independent and identical sites. We define A as the event that a site is underloaded, B as the event that a site is executing satisfactorily, and C as the event that the site is overloaded.

For example, if we consider a simple three-site system the state space looks like that shown in Table I.

The total number of states is given as 3^N, where N is defined as the number of sites within the system. In our three site system example the states: AAC, ABC, ACA, ACB, ACC, BAC, BCA, CAA, CAB, CAC, CBA, and CCA represent situations where load balancing could improve performance. In fact, the number c_N of these situations in a system of N sites can be shown to be:

$$c_N = 3^N - 2^{N+1} + 1, \quad N \geq 2. \tag{2}$$

The ratio of c_N to the total number of states is

$$r_N = 1 - 2(\tfrac{2}{3})^N + (\tfrac{1}{3})^N, \quad N \geq 2 \tag{3}$$

where r_N is the ratio. We know r_N tends to 1 as N is increased. For example, at $N = 10$, the value of $r_N = 0.965$.

The conclusion that we can draw from this observation is that the PLBS is greatly enhanced when N is large.

IV. ANALYSIS

As we also referred to in the introduction, we are concerned with the PLBS as a function of the workload and the system parameters. While (3) demonstrates the influence of the number of sites on the system, it does not capture the affect of the process service distribution, the distribution of number of processes per job placed at a given site, and the system traffic intensity. We establish our definition of the PLBS such that these parameters are included.

Before proceeding into the detailed analysis, let us informally describe the influence of the workload and some simple algorithm variants on the PLBS.

- *Service Time Distribution*: Consider a two-site system in which both hog and ordinary processes are present. Perhaps there are three ordinary processes at one site, and three hog processes at the other site. Since the number of processes at each site is identical, the PLBS initially is remote. However, after the ordinary processes complete, the system is left in a state with one free site and one busy site. We can conjecture that mixing CPU hogs with ordinary processes results in a high PLBS. Now suppose the processes were derived from an acoustic detection program. Since the processes are virtually equal, we might expect each site to become free at the same time. Thus we expect a very low PLBS. The exact opposite would be true for a fluid dynamic and weather forecasting program. We see that the service time distribution is very dependent on the application.

- *Number of Processes Per Job Placed*: Suppose that a system is composed of two idle sites. Then a parallel program arrives at a particular site. A system such as Trollius would allow the user to decompose the program into processes. If the processes are initially assigned to the arriving site, the PLBS would be high. We expect that the probability would be determined in part by the number of processes and number of sites.

- *Number of Distributed Processing Sites*: Suppose that there existed a very large number of sites in a system. The chances of any site being idle might be given as $1 - \rho$. If there are N sites, then the chances of at least one free site is $1 - \rho^N$. For example, if $\rho = 0.9$ and $N = 25$, the probability of a free site is 0.928. Thus we would expect that some site would nearly always be free.

- *System Traffic Intensity*: The influence of traffic intensity on the PLBS is a complex relationship. We can speculate that if nearly all sites are busy, then there is little chance of load balancing success. Suppose that there exists a very large number of sites in system. We have seen that this increases the chances of an idle site. At this time we cannot say for certain what the PLBS might be for the system. In this paper we do delineate the affects of traffic intensity on the PLBS.

Two simple algorithm variants arise from different system needs. The first variant occurs when a fixed number of

processes nearly always exists at all sites. For example, the load balancing algorithm and operating system normally are in execution at every site. Thus we see that no site is idle. Let us define that number as n. Rather than sending processes to an idle site, the load balancing algorithm would now send processes to sites with n or less processes. In the introduction we pointed out that load balancing and subnet delays may result in degradation in performance. To avoid such situations a simple variant of the load balancing algorithm would require that a certain number of processes exist at sites before load balancing can take place. Let us define that number as m. Thus the load balancing algorithm would transfer processes from sites with more than m processes to sites with less than n. We see now that an important measure in our system is the difference between m and n. We let this difference Δ be given as:

$$\Delta = m - n.$$

Δ may be used as a parameter to measure the effectiveness in load balancing in which the subnet costs are nonzero. A large Δ reflects that process migration would be costly. Δ may also be used to model a simple threshold policy discussed in [5] or the effects of nonzero subnet delays studied in [18].

With this informal discussion we see that workloads and algorithm variants influence the PLBS in a complex manner. We now proceed in this section to derive the PLBS in a system composed of identical and independent sites. In Section IV-A we first derive the PLBS for a birth–death process. In this analysis an underloaded site is an idle site, while an overloaded site has two or more processes present. Next, in Section IV-B we consider the general case in which an underloaded site has n or less processes, while an overloaded site has m or more processes present.

Since all sites are assumed to be independent and identical, the system traffic intensity is divided equally among the sites. Thus each site has the same site utilization ρ. To derive these results we use three other event probabilities: we let $P(D)$ be the probability that no site is overloaded, while $P(E)$ is the probability that every site is performing satisfactorily. Let $P(F)$ be the probability that every site is either performing satisfactorily or is overloaded. Now, we may express the probability p_n^m in terms of the event probabilities as:

$$p_n^m = 1 - P(D) - [P(F) - P(E)]. \tag{4}$$

A. Idle Workstation Analysis

This section focuses on the important load balancing variant in which an underloaded site is an idle site, while an overloaded site has two or more processes present. Here we extend the work of Livny and Melman [16].

To begin the analysis we make the assumption that the site loading may be modeled as a birth–death process. In Lemma 1 we give the analysis of the PLBS.

Lemma 1: Assume that having two or more processes represents an overloaded site. Let a system be composed of N independent and identical sites. Further postulate that $p_{i=1} = \beta(1 - \rho)$, then $p_0^2 = 1 - \rho^N - (1 - \rho)^N[(1 + \beta)^N - \beta^N]$.

331

Proof: The probability $P(D)$ can be given by a binomial sum and $p = p_{i \geq 2}$:

$$P(D) = 1 - \sum_{i=1}^{N} \binom{n}{k} p^k (1-p)^{n-k}$$
$$= 1 - (1 - (1-p)^N)$$
$$= (1 - p_{i \geq 2})^N.$$

Likewise, the probability $P(E)$ can be represented by a binomial sum and $p = p_{i=1}$:

$$P(E) = \sum_{i=N} \binom{n}{k} p^k (1-p)^{n-k} = p^N = p_{i=1}^N.$$

The last probability $P(F)$ can be defined using the binomial sum with $p = p_{i=1} + p_{i \geq 2}$:

$$P(F) = \sum_{i=N} \binom{n}{k} p^k (1-p)^{n-k} = p^N = (p_{i=1} + p_{i \geq 2})^N.$$

Thus we have:

$$p_0^2 = 1 - (1 - p_{i \geq 2})^N - [(p_{i=1} + p_{i \geq 2})^N - p_{i=1}^N]. \quad (5)$$

This equation can be written as:

$$p_0^2 = 1 - (1 - p_0)^N - (p_0 + p_1)^N + p_1^N. \quad (6)$$

From (5) and with substitution, we have: $p_0^2 = 1 - (1 - \rho + (1-\rho)\beta)^N - [\rho^N - ((1-\rho)\beta)^N]$. By grouping and factoring terms, we have: $p_0^2 = 1 - \rho^N - (1-\rho)^N [(1+\beta)^N - \beta^N]$. $\qquad \square$

Lemma 1 is a generalization of the results found in the work of Livny and Melman [16].

In cases where it is important to determine p_0^2 for a lightly loaded system, an approximation may be desirable. For $\rho \to 0, \beta \to 0$, Lemma 1 may be used to obtain the approximation:

$$\lim_{\rho \to 0, \beta \to 0} p_0^2 \approx 1 - (1 - \rho)^N (1 + \beta)^N.$$

B. Underloaded Workstation Analysis

The objective in this section is to extend the work in Section IV-B to consider some wider variants of the load balancing problem and a more general site model. The results here are an expansion of the work in [21].

To consider these situations we generalize the result of Lemma 1 in Theorem 1.

Theorem 1: Assume that a system is composed of N independent and identical sites. Define an overloaded site as having at least m processes present, while an underloaded site is defined as having not more than n processes present. We presuppose that $n < m$. Let the probability of a site having $0, 1, 2 \cdots, m-1$ processes be $p_{i=0}, p_{i=1}, p_{i=2} \cdots, p_{i=m-1}$, respectively. Let the overloaded site probability be given as $p_{i \geq m}$, while the underloaded site probability be given as $p_{i \leq n}$. Then the probability that a site is overloaded while another site is underloaded is given by $p_n^m = 1 - (p_{i=0} + p_{i=1} + p_{i=2} + \cdots p_{i=m-1})^N - [(1 - (p_{i=0} + p_{i=1} + p_{i=2} + \cdots p_{i=n}))^N - (p_{i=n+1} + p_{i=n+2} + \cdots p_{i=m-1})^N]$.

Proof: Let $P(D)$ be the probability that no site has m or more processes. Let $P(E)$ be the probability that every site has exactly $n+1, n+2, \cdots, m-1$ processes present. Let $P(F)$ be the probability that every site is busy with $n+1, n+2, \cdots$ processes present. The probability p_n^m is given by:

$$p_n^m = 1 - P(D) - [P(F) - P(E)].$$

The probability $P(D)$ can be presented with a binomial sum and $p = p_{i \geq m}$:

$$P(D) = 1 - \sum_{i=1}^{N} \binom{n}{k} p^k (1-p)^{n-k}$$
$$= 1 - (1 - (1-p)^N)$$
$$= (1 - p_{i \geq m})^N.$$

The probability $P(E)$ can be presented with a binomial sum and $p = p_{i=n+1} + p_{i=n+2} + \cdots p_{i=m-1}$:

$$P(E) = \sum_{i=N} \binom{n}{k} p^k (1-p)^{n-k} = p^N$$
$$= (p_{i=n+1} + p_{i=n+2} + \cdots p_{i=m-1})^N.$$

The last probability $P(F)$ can be defined using the binomial sum with $p = p_{i=n+1} + p_{i=n+2} + \cdots p_{i=m-1} + p_{i \geq m}$:

$$P(F) = \sum_{i=N} \binom{n}{k} p^k (1-p)^{n-k} = p^N$$
$$= (p_{i=n+1} + p_{i=n+2} + \cdots p_{i=m-1} + p_{i \geq m})^N.$$

Thus we have $p_n^m = 1 - (1 - p_{i \geq m})^N - [(p_{i=n+1} + p_{i=n+2} + \cdots p_{i=m-1} + p_{i \geq m})^N - (p_{i=n+1} + p_{i=n+2} + \cdots p_{i=m-1})^N]$. By applying the Law of Total Probability, $p_n^m = 1 - (p_{i=0} + p_{i=1} + p_{i=2} + \cdots p_{i=m-1})^N - [(1 - (p_{i=0} + p_{i=1} + p_{i=2} + \cdots p_{i=n}))^N - (p_{i=n+1} + p_{i=n+2} + \cdots p_{i=m-1})^N]$. $\qquad \square$

Remark 1: We see from Theorem 1 that p_n^m may be determined from probabilities $p_{i=0}, p_{i=1}, p_{i=2}, \ldots, p_{i=m-1}$. This makes the computation of p_n^m very simple.

Since p_n^m may be determined from probabilities $p_{i=0}, p_{i=1}, p_{i=2}, \ldots, p_{i=m-1}$, we conclude that the definition can be easily incorporated into load balancing algorithms. Because no explicit queuing models were assumed, the definition is independent of any queuing theoretic models.

Theorem 1 is a generalization of the result given in [21]. Theorem 1 yields close form solutions for p_n^m when the site loading can be modeled as simple birth–death processes. For example, consider a system composed of N sites, each modeled as a $M/M/1$ birth–death process. Let $p_i = \rho p_{i-1}$ and $p_0 = (1 - \rho)$. Again, we hypothesize that a site is overloaded when m or more processes are present, while a station is underloaded when n or less processes are present. We also require that $n < m$. Then the PLBS is simply:

$$p_n^m = 1 - \rho^{(n+1)N} - [(1 - \rho^m)^N - \rho^{(n+1)N}(1 - \rho^{m-n-1})^N]. \quad (7)$$

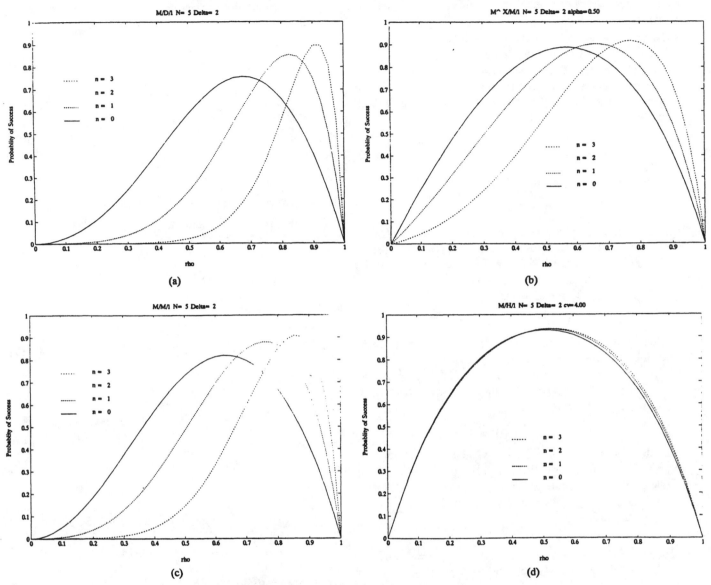

Fig. 1. Probability of load balancing success varying n for $N = 5$.

V. RESULTS

In this section we consider analytical site models. The object of this section is to extend the work of Livny and Melman [16] and Rommel [21] by using realistic process models such as those given in [15] and [20] and by assuming processes derived from parallel programs [12]. In this context we study the PLBS influenced by the workload and number of distributed processing sites.

We use the $M/M/1$ system as a reference site model. This model is useful in comparing the results of other models. To model a system composed of computationally equal processes such as those found in acoustic detection or image processing we use the $M/D/1$ model. With a geometrically distributed bulk arrival, the $M^X/M/1$ model characterizes situations in which parallel programs have been locally divided at a site. Processes which have large variations in service times, such as those in fluid dynamics and weather forecasting, are modeled using $M/H_2/1$ with a hypergeometrically distributed service time. The CPU *hogs* and *ordinary processes* found in [15]

and [20] may also be described as a $M/H_2/1$ model. For ease of computation, we make the following assumption for decomposed parallel jobs. If the job processes are placed at different sites, the processes are assumed to start execution at different points in time. The points in time are assumed to be exponentially distributed. This assumption allows us to view each site's workload as independent.

Now we begin the queuing theoretic analysis. Let X and A denote the random variables defining the service and interarrival times, respectively. Let $E(Z)$ and $Var(Z)$ denote the mean and variance of the random variable Z, respectively. Let $c_v(Z) = \frac{Var(Z)^{1/2}}{E(Z)}$ denote the coefficient of variation of Z. Then the job expected service time is $E(X)$, the job mean interarrival time is $\lambda = E(A)$, and the job service time coefficient of variation $c_v(X)$. The c_v of the $M/D/1$ and $M/M/1$ models are 0 and 1, respectively, while the c_v of the $M/H_2/1$ model is greater than or equal to 1. The c_v of the $M^X/M/1$ model depends on the service time distribution, but in our paper it is strictly greater than 1.

We now give the steady-state probability distributions for the site models:

1) To approximate workloads in which most jobs are expected to run for an equal amount of time, we use a $M/D/1$ model. This model assumes that the service time is constant at $\frac{1}{\mu}$, while the arrival process is Poisson with mean λ. The state probability distribution [11] is given as:

$$p_i = \begin{cases} (1-\rho) & i = 0, \\ (1-\rho)(e^\rho - 1) & i = 1, \text{ and} \\ (1-\rho)(e^{i\rho} + \\ \sum_{k=1}^{i-1}(-1)^{i-k}e^{k\rho}\left[\frac{(k\rho)^{i-k}}{(i-k)!} + \frac{(k\rho)^{i-k-1}}{(i-k-1)!}\right]) & (i \geq 2) \end{cases}$$

where $\rho = \frac{\lambda}{\mu}$.

2) The second workload postulates the classical $M/M/1$ characteristics. We assume exponential service times and Poisson arrivals. The service rate per process is μ, while the process arrival rate is λ. The steady-state probabilities [13] are given as

$$p_i = (1-\rho)\rho^i$$

where $\rho = \frac{\lambda}{\mu}$. This model is similar to a system in which no job is allowed to split into processes.

3) The next workload assumes the $M^X/M/1$ characteristics with the bulk arrival distributed geometrically with parameter, α such that

$$c_x = (1-\alpha)\alpha^{x-1} \quad (0 < \alpha < 1).$$

Each process is assumed to have exponential service time. We again assume Poisson job arrivals with arrival rate λ. The service rate per process is μ while the process arrival rate is $\frac{\lambda}{1-\alpha}$. The state probability distribution [11] is given as:

$$p_i = \begin{cases} (1-\rho) & i = 0, \\ (1-\rho)(1-\alpha)\rho & i = 1, \text{ and} \\ (1-\rho)[\alpha(1-\alpha)\rho]^{i-1}(1-\alpha)\rho & (i \geq 2). \end{cases}$$

where $\rho = \frac{\lambda}{\mu(1-\alpha)}$. This model approximates a parallel program arrival at a particular site which then is decomposed into processes.

4) To approximate workloads composed of both short and long processes we use a $M/H/1$ model. We make the assumption that short processes have zero service time. The nonzero service rate is μ_1. This gives us a simple $M/H_2/1$ model with a coefficient of variation $c_v > 1$. The mean service time $E(X) = \frac{1}{\alpha_1\mu_1}$, where α_1 is the probability of selecting the nonzero service time and $(1 - \alpha_1)$ is the probability of selecting the zero service time. We assume Poisson job arrivals with arrival rate λ. We may use the Pollaczek–Khintchine equation to represent the generating function:

$$P(z) = \frac{B^*(\lambda(1-z))(1-\rho)(1-z)}{B^*(\lambda(1-z)) - z}$$

where B^* is the service time transform. The service time transform is:

$$B^*(s) = \frac{\alpha_1\mu_1}{s + \mu_1} + (1 - \alpha_1).$$

The probability generating function for the state probability distribution reduces to:

$$P(z) = \frac{1 - \frac{(1-\alpha_1)\lambda}{(1-\alpha_1)\lambda+\mu_1}z}{1 - \frac{\lambda}{(1-\alpha_1)\lambda+\mu_1}z}(1 - \rho)$$

where $\rho = \frac{\lambda}{\alpha_1\mu_1}$ and $\alpha_1 = \frac{2}{c_v^2+1}$. The steady-state probabilities are given as:

$$p_i = \begin{cases} (1-\rho) & i = 0, \\ (1-\rho)(\phi - \theta) & i = 1, \text{ and} \\ (1-\rho)(\phi^i - \theta\phi^{i-1}) & (i \geq 2) \end{cases}$$

where $\rho = \frac{\lambda}{\mu}$, $\theta = \frac{(1-\alpha_1)\rho}{(1-\alpha_1)\rho+1}$, and $\phi = \frac{\rho}{(1-\alpha_1)\rho+1}$.

We now give p_0^2 for standard queuing models:

$M/D/1$:

$$p_0^2 = 1 - \rho^N - (1 - \rho)^N\left[e^{\rho N} - (1 - e^\rho)^N\right], \quad (8)$$

$M/M/1$:

$$p_0^2 = 1 - \rho^N - (1 - \rho)^N\left[(1 + \rho)^N - \rho^N\right], \quad (9)$$

$M^X/M/1$:

$$p_0^2 = 1 - \rho^N - (1 - \rho)^N\left[(1 + \rho\alpha)^N - (\rho\alpha)^N\right], \text{ and} \quad (10)$$

$M/H_2/1$:

$$p_0^2 = 1 - \rho^N$$
$$- (1 - \rho)^N\left[(1 + \rho(\frac{2}{c_v^2 + 1})^2(\frac{2}{c_v^2 + 1})^2 - \frac{2}{c_v^2 + 1})\rho - 1)^N\right.$$
$$\left. - (\rho(\frac{2}{c_v^2 + 1})^2(\frac{2}{c_v^2 + 1})^2 - \frac{2}{c_v^2 + 1})\rho - 1)^N\right]. \quad (11)$$

From (8)–(11) we know that PLBS is highest for $M/H_2/1$ and $M/M/1$, and lowest for $M/D/1$ models. We conclude that in general, load balancing should be performed if the processes can be characterized by $M/H_2/1$ and $M/M/1$ models.

VI. DISCUSSION

Although the queuing theoretic approach can give us an understanding into the PLBS, graphical results can extend our insights. In this section we discuss some observations from five sets of plots. Before proceeding, let us summarize the conditions which define our five figures:

1) With $N = 5$: Fig. 1 plots the PLBS in small networks. The figure displays the $M/D/1$, $M/M/1$, $M^X/M/1(\alpha = 0.5)$, and $M/H_2/1(c_v = 4)$ results, while varying n from 0 to 3 with Δ at 2.

2) Setting $N = 25$: Fig. 2 models large local area networks or very massively parallel multicomputer systems. The figure gives the PLBS for $M/D/1$, $M/M/1$, $M^X/M/1(\alpha = 0.5)$, and $M/H_2/1(c_v = 4)$ model by varying n from 0 to 3 with Δ at 2.

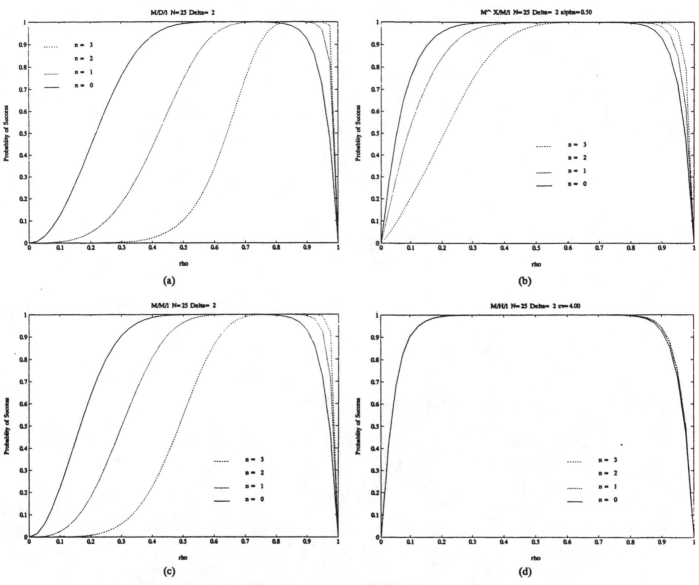

Fig. 2. Probability of load balancing success varying n for $N = 25$.

3) Fig. 3 illustrates the influence of Δ on small networks. This figure presents plots of the PLBS for the $M/D/1$, $M/M/1$, $M^X/M/1(\alpha = 0.5)$, and $M/H_2/1(c_v = 4)$ model results for $N = 5$ by varying Δ from 2 to 5 with $n = 0$.

4) The influence of Δ on large local area networks or a very massively parallel multicomputer system is displayed in Fig. 4. This figure shows plots of the PLBS for the $M/D/1$, $M/M/1$, $M^X/M/1(\alpha = 0.5)$, and $M/H_2/1(c_v = 4)$ models with $N = 25$, and varying Δ from 2 to 5 with $n = 0$.

5) Finally, Fig. 5 contrasts the sensitivity results with $N = 5$, $n = 0$, $\Delta=2$, and $n = 0$; with $N = 5$, $n = 0$, $\Delta=4$, and $n = 0$; with $N = 25$, $n = 0$, $\Delta=2$, and $n = 0$; and with $N = 25$, $n = 0$, $\Delta=4$, and $n = 0$.

We now give out observations:

1) It is evident in Fig. 1 that varying n from 0 to 3 with a fixed Δ causes two outcomes:

a. First, for small values of ρ, p_n^m is reduced as we increase n. This is due to the fact that as we increase n when ρ is small, we reduce the chances of either an underloaded site existing or an overloaded site existing.

b. Second, for large values of ρ and small values of c_v, p_n^m increases as we increase n. This phenomena is explained by the fact that $(p_{i=0} + p_{i=1} + p_{i=2} + \ldots p_{i=m-1})^N$ approaches $(1 - (p_{i=0} + p_{i=1} + p_{i=2} + \ldots p_{i=n}))^N$ as we increase n for large ρ with small c_v. Consequently, we increase the PLBS when ρ is near 1.

The general conclusion from these observations is that the PLBS depends on both ρ and c_v. One practical conclusion from observing these figures is that load balancing algorithms need to explicitly consider the workload characteristics as well as the system state. In particular, we expect that a mixture of *hog* and *ordinary*

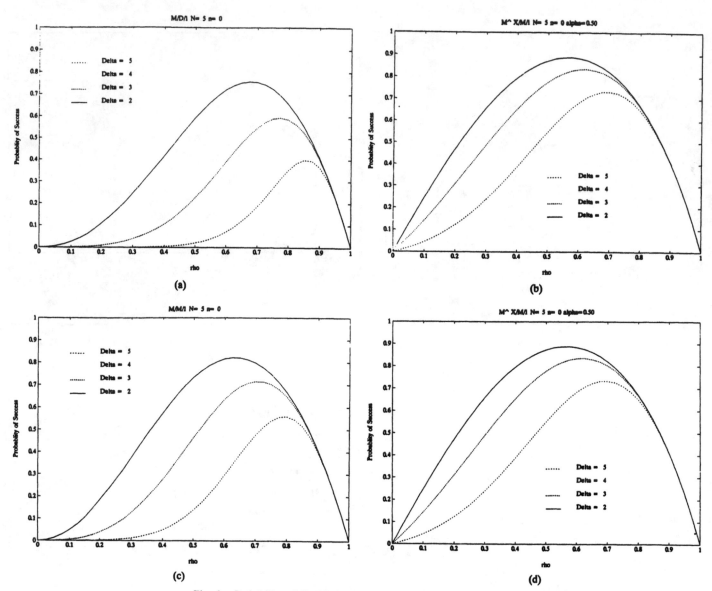

Fig. 3. Probability of load balancing success varying Δ for $N = 5$.

processes as defined in [15] and [20] would increase the chances of load balancing success, while processes from an acoustic detection program would decrease the chances of load balancing success.

2) If we compare the graphs of Fig. 1 to those of Fig. 2, we observe two phenomena:

   a. First, we can see that increasing N generally increases p_n^m. Consequently, reducing N reduces the chances of load balancing success. If we consider the case of $N = 2$, we have a situation similar to that of Bryant and Finkel's [1] randomly pairing algorithm. Our results concerning p_0^2 would suggest the poor performance reported by the authors when studying random pairing.

   b. Second, if we consider the $M/D/1$ graphs, the $M/M/1$ graphs, and the $M/H_2/1_{c_v=4}$ graphs in Figs. 1 and 2, we can see that the values for p_n^m increase as values for c_v increase for small ρ.

A major conclusion from these results is that load balancing algorithms become independent of workload characteristics when the number of system sites is very large. A second conclusion is that load balancing algorithms using partitioning of sites should employ large partition sizes.

3) Now if we consider the graphs in Fig. 4 we see that varying Δ from 2 to 5 with $n = 0$ decreases the value of p_n^m for small c_v models. This is due to the fact that increasing Δ affects both the underloaded and overloaded sites. Given large values of Δ for load balancing to be successful requires that there be a significant difference in the number of processes between the unloaded and overloaded sites. Consequently, the PLBS is reduced as we increase Δ.

4) If we consider the graphs in Figs. 4 and 3 we see that increasing N increases the value of p_n^m for models. This is especially true for small ρ with process service times

336

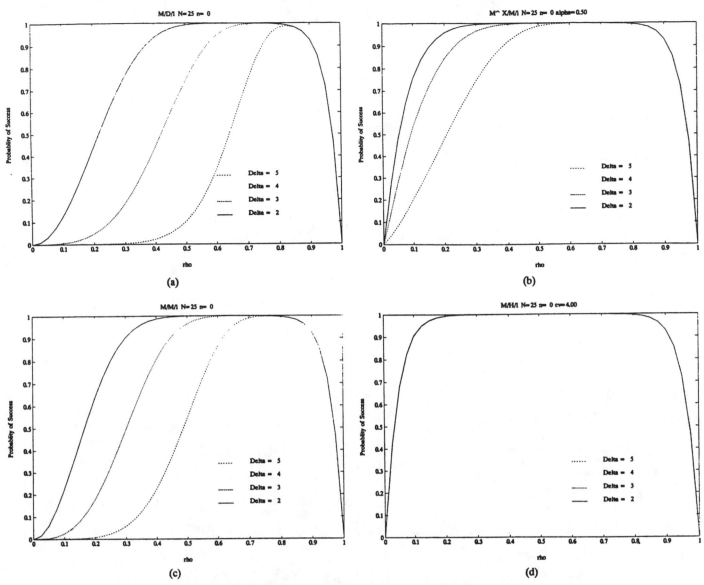

Fig. 4. Probability of load balancing success varying Δ for $N = 25$.

with large c_v. We conclude that increasing N increases the PLBS, even when c_v is allowed to change. Our work supports the general conclusions by Eager *et al.* [6] that large thresholds result in poor performance. However, we do see in these plots that if N is very large, the threshold effects are greatly reduced.

5) We can make a few observations concerning the sensitivity measures from Fig. 5.

    a. First, as we increase N, p_n^m becomes less sensitive to changes in ρ except when $\rho \to 1$. The conclusion from this observation is that for large N, the PLBS is nearly independent of ρ. From this conclusion we conjecture that distributed load balancing algorithms should not use ρ as a method of balancing. Subsequently, a policy which sends a process to the site with the lowest utilization may be a poor algorithm as N is increased. For large values of N $\rho \to 1$, the simple random

assignment algorithm discussed in [5] may work very well.

    b. Our last observation deals with the coefficient of variation of the service time distribution. As we increase the coefficient of variation for the service time, p_n^m becomes less sensitive to changes in ρ. Again, this suggests that for large c_v, robust algorithms need not use ρ in implementing load balancing. Finally, since the PLBS does depend on c_v, c_v should be included in the load balancing algorithm.

VII. SUMMARY

In summary, we have given a general definition for load balancing success in a distributed processing system.

Our definition was shown to have the following properties:

1) Our definition is very robust in the way it considers the process service time distribution, the distribution of

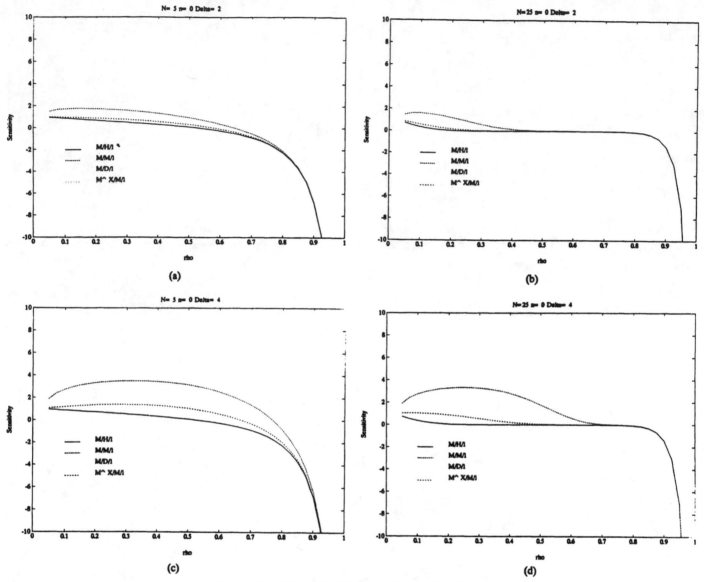

Fig. 5. Sensitivity with different service time distributions

number of processes per job placed at a given site, the number of distributed processing sites, and the system traffic intensity.

2) The definition can easily be used in implementing the activation control of load balancing algorithms.

3) Although queuing theoretic models may be used in conjunction with our definition, the definition itself is independent of any queuing theoretic models.

We have shown the influence of the workload and load balancing variants on the PLBS:

1) We observe that the distribution of the service time does play an important role in determining the PLBS. We found that when the workload is composed of CPU *hogs* and *ordinary* processes as found in research [15], [20], the PLBS is high. When the work is composed of virtually equal processes, the PLBS is low.

2) We demonstrated that the distribution of the number of processes per job placed at a given site has a major impact on the PLBS. From our observation we would

conclude that systems such as Trollius may perform better if load balancing were done at the operating system level.

3) We established that the PLBS is related in a complex way to system traffic intensity.

4) We find that, in general, increasing the number of sites increases the PLBS.

5) We have shown, as in [6], that using an underloaded loaded site rather than a strictly idle site does effect the PLBS.

6) We have demonstrated the influence of Δ on algorithm variants.

Finally, using our results, we believe that activation control of load balancing algorithms can be based on PLBS.

REFERENCES

[1] R. Byrant and R. Finkel, "A stable distributed scheduling algorithm," in *Proc. IEEE Int. Conf. Distributed Comput. Syst.*, 1981, pp. 314–324.

[2] G. Burns and R. Daoud, "The performance / functionality dilemma of multicomputer message passing," in *Proc. IEEE DMCC5 Conf.* (Charleston, SC), 1990, to be published.

[3] D. R. Cheriton, "The V kernel distributed operating system," *Commun. ACM*, vol. 1, pp. 105–115, Feb. 1985.

[4] D. R. Cheriton and W. Zwaenepoel, "Distributed V kernel and its performance for diskless workstations," in*Proc. 9th ACM Symp. Oper. Sys. Principles*, 1983, vol. 5, pp. 128–140.

[5] D. L. Eager, E. Lazowska, and J. Zahorjan, "Adaptive load sharing in homogeneous distributed systems," *IEEE Trans. Software Eng.*, vol. SE-12, pp. 662–675, May 1986.

[6] D. L. Eager, E. Lazowska, and J. Zahorjan, "A comparison of receiver-initiated and sender-initiated adaptive loading," *Perform. Eval.*, vol. 6, 1986.

[7] K. Efe, "Heuristic models of task assignment scheduling in distributed systems," *IEEE Computers*, vol. C-15, pp. 50–56, June 1982.

[8] A. Ezzat, "Load balancing in nest: a network of workstations," in *Proc. IEEE Fall Joint Computer Conf.*, 1986, pp. 1138–1148.

[9] D. Farber *et al.*, "The distributed computer system," in *Proc. 7th Ann. IEEE Computer Soc. Int.*, 1973, pp. 31–34.

[10] D. Grunwald, B. Nazief, and D. Reed, "Empirical comparison of heuristic load distributions in point-to-point multicomputer networks," in *IEEE DMCC5 Conf.* (Charleston, SC), Apr. 8–12, 1990, pp. 984–993.

[11] M. Gross and C. Harris, *Introduction to Queueing Theory*. New York: Wiley, 1976.

[12] D. Hinz, "A run-time load balancing strategy for highly parallel systems," *IEEE DMCC5 Conf.* (Charleston, SC), Apr. 8–12, 1990, pp. 951–961.

[13] L. Kleinrock, *Queueing Systems,* vol. 1. New York: Wiley, 1976.

[14] B. A. Kingsbury, "The network queueing system," NASA Ames, Moffett Field, CA, Rep. 11786, 1986.

[15] W. Leland and T. Ott, "Load balancing heuristics and process behavior," *ACM Perform. Eval. Rev.*, vol. 14, pp. 54–69, 1986.

[16] M. Livny and M. Melmen, "Load balancing in homogeneous broadcast distributed systems," in *Proc. Computer Network Perform. Symp.*, 1982, pp. 47–55.

[17] D. May, "Occam," *ACM SIGPLAN Notices*, vol. 18, 1983.

[18] R. Mirchandaney, D. Towsley, and J. Stankovic, "Analysis of the effects of delays on load sharing," Univ. Massachusetts, Amherst, COINS Tech. Rep. 87–100, 1987.

[19] K. Ramamritham and J. Stankovic, "Dynamic task scheduling in hard real-time distributed systems," *IEEE Computers*, vol. C-1, pp. 96–107, Jan. 1984.

[20] C. G. Rommel, "Scheduling parallel programs in distributed systems," Ph.D. thesis, Univ. Massachusetts, Amherst, Sept. 1988.

[21] C. G. Rommel, "The probability of load balancing success," in *Proc. ISMM Conf.* (Fort Lauderdale, FL), Dec. 13–15, 1989, pp. 18–22.

[22] C. G. Rommel and R. Rossow, *XNOS Users Reference Manual.* Hartford, CT: United Technol. Res. Ctr., 1989.

[23] T. Saaty, *Elements to Queueing Theory.* New York: McGraw-Hill, 1961.

[24] C. Seitz, "The cosmic cube," *Commun. ACM*, vol. 28, 1985.

[25] J. Stankovic, "An application of Bayesian decision theory to decentral control of scheduling," *IEEE Trans. Computers*, vol. C-3, pp. 117–130, Feb. 1985.

[26] D. Sweetman and J Munoz, "Measures of effectiveness and the performance of parallel architectures," presented at the Systems, Man, Cybern. Conf., 1989.

[27] *Parallel Systems User's Guide.*, Topologix, Inc., Denver, CO, 1989.

C. Gary Rommel (S'70–M'71) received the B.Sc. degree in physics–engineering from Loyola College, Baltimore, MD, the M.S.E.E. degree from the University of Virginia, and the Ph.D. degree in computer and electrical engineering from the University of Massachusetts in 1969, 1972, and 1988, respectively.

Currently, he is an Associate Professor of Computer Science at Eastern Connecticut State University, Willimantic. He has been a Consultant at the UTRC Advanced Computing Laboratory, where he designed the XNOS distributed operating system. During his sabbatic leave he did research in distributed computing at the Naval Underwater Systems Center, New London, CT. His interests include computer engineering, distributed computing, operating system, and performance evaluation.

Dr. Rommel is a member of the Association for Computing Machinery, Tau Beta Pi, Eta Kappa Nu, and Upsilon Pi Epsilon.

Adaptive Load Sharing in Homogeneous Distributed Systems

DEREK L. EAGER, EDWARD D. LAZOWSKA, AND JOHN ZAHORJAN

Abstract—In most current locally distributed systems, the work generated at a node is processed there; little sharing of computational resources is provided. In such systems it is possible for some nodes to be heavily loaded while others are lightly loaded, resulting in poor overall system performance. The purpose of *load sharing* is to improve performance by redistributing the workload among the nodes.

The load sharing policies with the greatest potential benefit are *adaptive* in the sense that they react to changes in the system state. Adaptive policies can range from simple to complex in their acquisition and use of system state information. The potential advantage of a complex policy is the possibility that such a scheme can take full advantage of the processing power of the system. The potential disadvantages are the overhead cost, and the possibility that a highly tuned policy will behave in an unpredictable manner in the face of the inaccurate information with which it inevitably will be confronted.

The goal of this paper is not to propose a specific load sharing policy for implementation, but rather to address the more fundamental question of the appropriate level of complexity for load sharing policies. We show that extremely simple adaptive load sharing policies, which collect very small amounts of system state information and which use this information in very simple ways, yield dramatic performance improvements. These policies in fact yield performance close to that expected from more complex policies whose viability is questionable. We conclude that simple policies offer the greatest promise in practice, because of their combination of nearly optimal performance and inherent stabil' y.

Index Terms—Design, load sharing, local area networks, performance, queueing models, threshold policies.

I. INTRODUCTION

LOAD SHARING attempts to improve the performance of a distributed system by using the processing power of the entire system to "smooth out" periods of high congestion at individual nodes. This is done by transferring some of the workload of a congested node to other nodes for processing. The potential attractiveness of load sharing is enhanced by factors such as the increasing size of locally distributed systems, the use of shared file servers, the presence of pools of computation servers, and the development of streamlined communication protocols.

Manuscript received October 31, 1984; revised June 28, 1985. This work was supported by the National Science Foundation under Grants MCS-8302383 and DCR-8352098, and by the Natural Sciences and Engineering Research Council of Canada. Part of this work was conducted while E. D. Lazowska was on leave at Digital Equipment Corporation's Systems Research Center.

D. L. Eager is with the Department of Computational Science, University of Saskatchewan, Sask. S7N 0W0, Canada.

E. D. Lazowska and J. Zahorjan are with the Department of Computer Science, University of Washington, Seattle, WA 98195.

IEEE Log Number 8607941.

Two important components of a load sharing policy are the *transfer* policy, which determines whether to process a task locally or remotely, and the *location* policy, which determines to which node a task selected for transfer should be sent. Policies that use only information about the average behavior of the system, ignoring the current state, are termed *static* policies. Static policies may be either *deterministic* or *probabilistic*. Policies that react to the system state are termed *adaptive* policies.

Numerous static load sharing policies have been proposed. In the earliest formulations of the problem it was assumed that information about the average execution times and intercommunication requirements of all tasks were known. Typically the goal was to find a technique to deterministically allocate tasks to nodes so that the total time to process all tasks was minimized; for example [2], [13], [14]. More recently, Tantawi and Towsley [15] developed a technique to find the optimal probabilistic assignment.

Adaptive load sharing policies have received less attention. Livny and Melman [11] showed that in a network of autonomous nodes there is a large probability that at least one node is idle while tasks are queued at some other node, over a wide range of network sizes and average node utilizations. This is a key result because it clearly indicates the potential benefit of adaptive load sharing. Livny and Melman also developed a taxonomy of load sharing policies, and used simulation to evaluate a number of them. Bryant and Finkel [3] proposed a specific adaptive load sharing policy, and analyzed its performance using simulation. They also explored techniques for estimating the remaining service time of a task already being processed, a quantity of interest in deciding which task to transfer from a congested node. Krueger and Finkel [7] also used simulation to evaluate the performance of a specific policy. Barak and Shiloh [1] used limited experimentation with synthetic workloads to investigate a policy distinguished by the technique used to maintain system state information. They showed that if the workload remained constant, their policy converged to a load distribution that was near optimal.

Static load sharing policies are attractive because of their simplicity: "transfer all compilations originating at node X to computation server Y" or " $\cdots$ to computation servers Y and Z with probabilities 0.8 and 0.2, respectively." It is clear, though, that the potential of static policies is limited by the fact that they do not react to the

Reprinted from IEEE *Trans. on Software Eng.*, vol. SE-12, no. 5, May 1986, pp. 662–675.

current system state: at the time a particular compilation originates at node X, computation server Y may be so heavily loaded that Z is a much superior choice, or both Y and Z may be so congested that processing the task locally is preferable, even considering the impact of this decision on other tasks originating at node X. The attraction of adaptive policies is that they do respond to system state, and so are better able to avoid those states with unnecessarily poor performance. However, since adaptive policies must collect and react to system state information, they are necessarily more complex than static policies. The adaptive policies that have been examined in the literature collect considerable state information and attempt to make the "best" choice possible based on that information. For example, the policy proposed by Krueger and Finkel [7] attempts to keep the queue length at each node near the system average queue length.[1]

From a practical point of view, such complexity raises a number of concerns. The first concern is the effect of overhead. The value of a policy depends critically on the overhead required to administer it, which may vary considerably depending on system characteristics. Excessive overhead may negate the benefits of an improved workload distribution.

The second concern is the effect of the occasional poor decisions that inevitably will be made. Complex policies rely on detailed information about the system state and the behavior of the workload. Not only is this information expensive to gather, but some quantities, such as the expected congestion at nodes in the near future or the amount of processing that a particular task requires to complete, cannot be known precisely regardless of the effort expended. Because of this, a decision that a complex load sharing policy expects to be near optimal may in fact be quite poor.

The final concern is the potential for instability. In attempting to fully exploit system processing power, a complex load sharing policy must make decisions based on subtle apparent misallocations of load. This requirement to react to small distinctions means that the inherent inaccuracy and rapidly changing nature of system state information may cause the policy to react in an unstable manner [6]. At the extreme, a form of *processor thrashing* can occur, in which all of the nodes are spending all of their time transferring tasks. Less complex policies, because they tend to react more slowly to changes in the system state, are inherently less susceptible to such instability.

Motivated by these concerns, in this paper we ask a fundamental question concerning adaptive load sharing policies in general: what is an appropriate level of complexity for such policies? We show that:

- Extremely simple adaptive load sharing policies—policies that collect a very small amount of state information and that use this information in very simple ways—yield dramatic performance improvements relative to the no load sharing case.

- These extremely simple policies in fact yield performance close to that which can be expected from complex policies that collect large amounts of information and that attempt to make the "best" choice given this information—policies whose viability is questionable.

- These results are valid over a wide range of system parameters.

We conclude that simple adaptive load sharing is of considerable practical value, and that there is no firm evidence that the potential costs of collecting and using extensive state information are justified by the potential benefits.

II. POLICIES AND MODELS

In studying the appropriate level of complexity for adaptive load sharing policies, we consider a set of abstract policies that represent only the essential aspects of load sharing, and we investigate these policies using simple analytic models. Our objective is not to determine the absolute performance of particular load sharing policies, but rather to assess the relative advantages of varying degrees of sophistication. By representing only the essential aspects of load sharing and eliminating secondary details, we are better able to interpret the results of our comparative analysis and so build our intuition.

An obvious concern is that this approach may ignore "details" with significant practical implications—the issues noted in Section I, such as the actual cost of collecting and reacting to state information, the behavior of policies when this information is unavailable or out-of-date, etc. If the conclusion of our study were that increasing sophistication yielded substantial benefit, then these concerns would have to be addressed, because failure to properly account for these characteristics will tend to overstate the performance of complex policies relative to the performance of simple ones. However, the conclusion of our study is quite the opposite, despite giving the "benefit of the doubt" to complex policies.

A. System Model

We represent distributed systems as collections of identical nodes, each consisting of a single processor. The nodes are connected by a local area broadcast channel (e.g., an Ethernet). All nodes are subjected to the same average arrival rate of tasks, which are of a single type.

In contrast to previous papers on load sharing, we represent the cost of task transfer as a processor cost rather than as a communication network cost. It is clear from measurement and analysis [9] that the processor costs of packaging data for transmission and unpackaging it upon reception far outweigh the communication network costs of transmitting the data. Further, network delays are small, and are almost entirely overlapped with processing

---

[1] An implicit assumption of most proposed schemes is that it is desirable to attempt to balance the queue lengths at the processors. In fact, such balancing is not required. All that is necessary for optimal performance (in the standard homogeneous model) is that all processors be busy if any task is waiting. Thus in this paper we purposefully adopt the terminology "load *sharing*" rather than "load *balancing*."

related to use of the network. Representing the network cost in addition to the processor cost would not affect the tractability of our models, but nor would it affect our results. Thus, for simplicity, it is omitted. (In Section III-E we will show that, under reasonable assumptions, the total communication network load imposed by adaptive load sharing is negligible.)

Our homogeneity assumptions—that nodes are identical and are subjected to the same average arrival rate of tasks—also are made principally to simplify the presentation, and do not undermine the applicability of the results. Node homogeneity is a reasonable assumption when considering load sharing among clusters of workstations or clusters of computation servers. Arrival homogeneity merely implies that *over the long term* the external load imposed on each node is the same. Over the short term, these loads may vary considerably. The entire objective of adaptive load sharing is to respond to such variations. Even if homogeneity does not hold (the system consists of a mix of nodes of different types, or there are differences in external loads), models that consider this case (but that are not considered here) indicate the suitability of simple policies. These simple policies are similar to those for homogeneous systems, but they additionally utilize the relatively static information specifying the system inhomogeneities.

B. Load Sharing Policies

We will study three abstract load sharing policies, comparing their performance to each other and to two "bounding" cases: no load sharing, and perfect load sharing at zero cost. As noted in Section I, a load sharing policy has two components: a *transfer* policy that determines whether to process a task locally or remotely, and a *location* policy that determines to which node a task selected for transfer should be sent. Each of these subpolicies might be expected to employ system state information. The three load sharing policies that we consider have identical transfer policies, but differ in their location policies.

The transfer policy that we have selected is a *threshold* policy: a distributed, adaptive policy in which each node uses only local state information. *No exchange of state information among the nodes is required in deciding whether to transfer a task.* A task originating at a node is accepted for processing there if and only if the number of tasks already in service or waiting for service (the node *queue length*) is less than some threshold T. Otherwise, an attempt is made to transfer that task to another node. Note that only newly received tasks are eligible for transfer. Transferring an executing task poses considerable difficulties in most systems [12].

The three location policies that we examine for use in conjunction with this extremely simple transfer policy are referred to as *Random*, *Threshold*, and *Shortest*. They are discussed in the subsections that follow.

1) Random: The simplest location policy is one that uses no information at all. With the Random policy a destination node is selected at random and the task is transferred to that node. *No exchange of state information among the nodes is required in deciding where to transfer a task.*

A question that arises in considering the behavior of the random policy is how the destination node should treat an arriving transferred task. The obvious answer is that it should treat it just as a task originating at the node: if the local queue length is below threshold the task is accepted for processing; otherwise it is transferred to some other node selected at random. As shown in Appendix A, this choice has the unfortunate property of causing instability: no matter what the average load, it is guaranteed that eventually the system will enter a state in which the nodes are devoting all of their time to transferring tasks and none of their time to processing them. This instability is analogous to that arising in the infinite population ALOHA system [5]; repeated task transfers in load sharing systems play a similar role with respect to stability as do message collisions in ALOHA.

Instability can be overcome by the use of an appropriate control policy. Such control policies have been developed for a number of multiple access systems [8], [16]. The simple control policy that we adopt here is to restrict the number of times that a task can be transferred using a static *transfer limit*, L_t. The destination node of the L_tth transfer of a task must process that task regardless of its state.

A key result of this paper is that, in many situations, this extremely simple combination of a threshold transfer policy and a random location policy with a static transfer limit dramatically improves system response time relative to no load sharing. Since this policy uses no system state information at all, this is an indication that very simple schemes can yield significant benefits.

2) Threshold: Threshold is a location policy that acquires and uses a small amount of information about potential destination nodes. Under this policy a node is selected at random and *probed* to determine whether the transfer of a task to that node would place it above threshold. If not, then the task is transferred; the destination node must process the task regardless of its state when the task actually arrives. If so, then another node is selected at random and probed in the same manner. This continues until either a suitable destination node is found, or the number of probes exceeds a static *probe limit*, L_p. In the latter case, the originating node must process the task.

The objective of the Threshold policy is to avoid "useless" task transfers (those to nodes already at or above their threshold), although, like Random, it makes no attempt to choose the "best" destination node for a task. The use of probing with a fixed limit, rather than broadcast, ensures that the cost of executing the load sharing policy will not be prohibitive even in large networks. As will be discussed in Section III-D, the performance of this policy is surprisingly insensitive to the choice of probe limit. In other words, the performance with a small (and

342

economical) probe limit, e.g., 3 or 5, is almost as good as the performance with a large probe limit, e.g., 20.

A key result of this paper is that the Threshold policy provides substantial performance improvement relative to the Random policy for a wide range of system parameters. This indicates that the use of a small amount of state information in a simple (and computationally inexpensive) way is likely to more than compensate for the additional cost.

3) Shortest: This location policy acquires additional system state information and attempts to make the "best" choice given this information. L_p distinct nodes are chosen at random, and each is polled in turn to determine its queue length. The task is transferred to a node with the shortest queue length, unless that queue length is greater than or equal to the threshold, in which case the originating node must process the task. The destination node must process the task regardless of its state at the time the task actually arrives. (A simple improvement to Shortest is to discontinue probing whenever a node with queue length of zero is encountered, since that node is guaranteed to be an acceptable destination.)

The Shortest policy uses more state information, in a more complex manner, than does the Threshold policy. A key result of this paper is that the performance of Shortest is not significantly better than that of the simpler Threshold policy. This suggests that state information beyond that used by Threshold, or a more complex usage of state information, is of little benefit.

C. Analytic Model Structure and Solution

The three policies introduced in the previous section have similar analytic models.

Each node is modeled as a queueing center [4]. New tasks arrive at each node at average rate λ. The average task service time (processing cost) is S. We define the *load factor* ρ of each node to be the ratio of offered load to service capacity (i.e., $\rho = \lambda S$). Because of the cost of task transfer, the average utilization of the nodes may be significantly greater than ρ.

The cost of transferring a task from one node to another is represented by a processing cost at the sending node whose average value is denoted by C. This cost is a key parameter. (The processing cost of receiving a task is included in the service time of the task, S.) As discussed earlier, communication network costs are assumed to be negligible (relative to other costs). In addition, the cost of probing a node is assumed to be negligible. These assumptions are examined in Section III-E.

At each node, the transferring of tasks is given preemptive priority over the processing of tasks. In the processing of tasks, any service discipline that selects tasks in a way that is independent of their actual service time (e.g., First-Come-First-Served, Processor Sharing) is allowed. All of the performance measures that will be considered here are independent of the actual discipline used.

Under the assumptions stated above, a Markov model of a distributed system under each of the load sharing policies can be constructed. The model has a very large state space, with complex structure. To simplify the analysis we decompose the model, by assuming that the state of each node is stochastically independent of the state of any other node. Each node can then be analyzed in isolation. The effect of the remainder of the system on an individual node is represented by an arrival process of transferred tasks. Because the network is homogeneous, system performance measures can be obtained by analyzing a model of any individual node.

This decomposition approach is asymptotically exact as the number of nodes in the system increases, since the queue lengths of the nodes are asymptotically independent. For systems of finite size the analysis is an approximation. Results obtained from simulation indicate that this approximation, which also has been used in modeling multiple access protocols such as ALOHA, introduces negligible errors even for relatively small numbers of nodes. In particular, the major numerical results used in our study have been validated through simulation for networks of 20 nodes (and thus certainly for greater numbers of nodes, although not necessarily for smaller numbers). A sample of our simulation results is contained in Appendix C.

All of the quantities needed to determine the state transition rates of the model of an individual node are input parameters, with the exception of a description of the arrival process of transferred tasks. The nature of this arrival process depends on the load sharing policy. For the Random policy, the arrival rate of transferred tasks is independent of the current queue length (i.e., state) of the node, since Random utilizes no information about the state of potential destination nodes. For the Threshold policy, arrivals of transferred tasks are constrained to those states in which the node is below its threshold. For the Shortest policy, the arrival rate of transferred tasks decreases as the queue length at the node increases.

The assumption of homogeneous nodes makes it possible to determine the arrival rate of transferred tasks: the overall arrival rate must equal the overall rate at which the node transfers tasks to other nodes, and the equilibrium state probabilities of potential destination nodes, as "observed" when probing, for example, are identical to those of the node itself. These quantities are model outputs. For the Random and Threshold policies this dependence of model inputs on outputs yields a single equation in a single unknown, which is solved numerically. For the Shortest policy, the dependence is sufficiently complex that an iterative numerical technique is required.

Equations relating the variables of the model are developed by considering the node to be in one of two phases: "processing" (when the node queue length is less than or equal to the threshold value), or "transferring" (when the node queue length is greater than the threshold value). During a processing phase the node is either idle or is processing tasks. During a transferring phase the node is busy, either transferring tasks or processing tasks

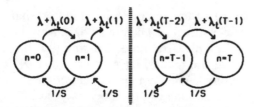

Fig. 1. Processing phase birth–death model.

that could not be transferred because of a restriction imposed by the location policy.

Fig. 1 shows the birth–death model corresponding to the processing phase. In each state the arrival rate of tasks is the sum of the rate of arrival of new tasks (λ) and the rate of arrival of tasks transferred to this node by the remainder of the system ($\lambda_t(n)$). This latter term is in general dependent on the queue length n at the node and the load sharing policy being modelled. This submodel can be analyzed using standard methods.

A transferring phase is identical in behavior to a busy period of a two class, preemptive priority HOL M/M/1 queue [4], where the classes are tasks that are processed and tasks that are transferred. The total arrival rate at the node is ($\lambda + \lambda_t(T^+)$), where $\lambda_t(T^+)$ denotes the arrival rate of tasks transferred to the node conditioned on the node being in a transferring phase. The proportion of this total arrival rate consisting of tasks that will be processed and the proportion consisting of tasks that will be transferred depends on the probability of a task not being transferred because of a location policy restriction.

The analyses of the birth–death model corresponding to the processing phase and of the HOL priority model corresponding to the transferring phase yield conditional state probabilities and performance measures. These are combined using weights representing the proportion of time the system spends in each phase to determine overall performance. The performance measures that can be obtained include average response times, utilizations, queue lengths, transfer rates, and probe rates. Details on the analyses of the two phases and the calculation of performance measures are given in Appendix B.

III. Performance Comparisons

Our objective is to compare the performance of three abstract load sharing policies—Random, Threshold, and Shortest—to each other and to two "bounding" cases: no load sharing (represented by K independent M/M/1 queues, where K is the number of nodes), and perfect load sharing at zero cost (represented by an M/M/K queue). Our measure of performance is mean response time as a function of system load.

This comparison is potentially difficult because of the large number of parameters involved: the average task service time S, the average cost of task transfer C, the threshold T, the probe limit for the Threshold and Shortest policies L_p, the transfer limit for the Random policy L_t, and the number of nodes K. Fortunately, the results are robust in the sense that the intuition gained from studying

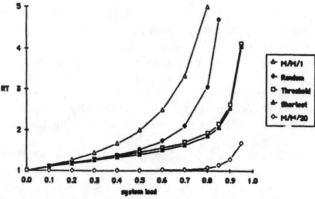

Fig. 2. Principal performance comparison: response time versus load ρ. S(task service time) = 1. C(cost of task transfer) = 0.1. T(threshold) = 2. L_p(probe limit for Threshold and Shortest) = 3. L_t(transfer limit for Random) = 1.

performance for a "representative" set of parameter values is valid over a wide range of parameter values. The structure of our presentation exploits this fact: Section III-A contains a thorough discussion of response time versus system load for a particular choice of parameter values, while Sections III-B–III-F explore the sensitivity of these results to the various parameters.

A. Principal Performance Comparison

Fig. 2 is a graph of average response time versus load for each of the five policies under consideration. For convenience, S is fixed at 1 throughout our analysis so that response times may be considered to be reported in units of the task service time.

We will first discuss the figure, and then the choice of parameter values indicated in the text accompanying the figure. The key observations concerning the figure are as follows.

• The Random policy yields substantial performance improvement over no load sharing. The degree of the improvement is surprising since the Random policy is so simple.

• The Threshold policy yields substantial further performance improvement for system loads greater than 0.5. This shows the value of the small amount of additional information utilized by Threshold.

• The Shortest policy yields negligible further performance improvement over the Threshold policy. Again this is somewhat surprising, since Shortest acquires considerably more information than Threshold, and attempts to make the "best" decision based on that information.

If factors such as the actual cost of collecting and reacting to state information, the behavior of policies when this information is unavailable or out-of-date, etc., are ignored, then intuitively Shortest should have the best performance among all load sharing policies that employ threshold transfer policies. Thus, based on the comparison of Threshold and Shortest, we can conclude (subject to verification that our results are robust with respect to the choice of parameter values) that relatively simple information concerning potential destination nodes is sufficient to obtain essentially all of the benefit available through this class of policies. This conclusion is reinforced by the fact that our analysis indeed gives the "benefit of the doubt" to complex policies by ignoring the issues just noted, which clearly are more significant for complex policies such as Shortest than for simpler policies such as Threshold.

In Fig. 2 there is significant room for improvement between the performance of the Shortest policy and the bound established by the M/M/K analysis. This might suggest that our conclusion with respect to the information required by location policies does not hold for transfer policies: perhaps significantly improved performance can be obtained by using a transfer policy that employs more than local threshold information. However, there are reasons (in addition to the obvious pragmatic ones) to believe that simple transfer policies are as relatively advantageous as simple location policies. The M/M/K analysis does not provide a tight bound: it assumes perfect load sharing at zero cost, when in fact an "optimal" policy would require a significant rate of task transfers, each of which has a nonnegligible cost. Further, the parameter values used in Fig. 2 are conservative, rather than being advantageous to the policies under consideration. We will discuss these parameter values now, and return to the question of an appropriate optimistic bound on achievable performance in Section III-F.

In Fig. 2, the average cost of task transfer C was 0.1, that is, 10 percent of the average task service time. We believe this to be a conservative (overly high) choice; our reasoning, as well as the sensitivity of the results to the cost of task transfer, is explored in Section III-B.

The threshold T was 2. That is, a node would attempt to transfer a task that arrived when two (or more) tasks already were present. The sensitivity of the results to the choice of threshold is explored in Section III-C.

The probe limit for the Threshold and Shortest policies L_p was 3. The sensitivity of the results to the choice of probe limit is explored in Section III-D. The rates of probing in the Threshold and Shortest policies are compared in Section III-E.

The transfer limit for the Random policy L_t is set to 1. The implications of this will be discussed in Section III-B. The rate of task transfers for all policies, and its impact on network congestion, is discussed in Section III-E.

As noted in Section II, the number of nodes K is not a parameter of our analysis of Random, Threshold, and Shortest. The analysis is asymptotically exact as the number of nodes increases. Our major results have been validated through simulation for networks of 20 nodes, implying that the performance of the policies quickly becomes insensitive to the number of nodes as the number of nodes increases.

B. Sensitivity to Transfer Cost

We believe that the average cost of task transfer C, although nonnegligible, can be expected to be quite low relative to the average cost of task processing S; the range

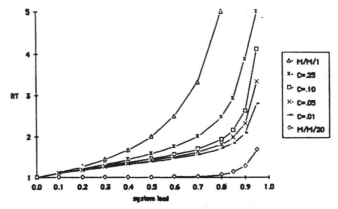

Fig. 3. Response time versus load ρ for various transfer costs C(Threshold policy). S(task service time) = 1. T(threshold) = 2. L_p(probe limit) = 3.

1–10 percent seems to include the cases of greatest interest. (We mean this to be interpreted as an average across many tasks; we are not asserting a relationship between processing cost and transfer cost.)

Transfer costs higher than 10 percent, although certainly possible, would likely be infrequent. On current systems not designed to facilitate load sharing (e.g., 4.2 BSD Unix running on Vaxes connected by Ethernet, using FTP on top of TCP/IP for task transfer), the transfer costs for relatively small compilations and formatting runs are a few percent of the processing costs. We would expect that any practical implementation of load sharing would attempt to select tasks such as these for migration—tasks with a relatively high ratio of processing cost to transfer cost. One also can easily imagine more efficient protocols. The advent of systems based on file servers and database servers will further decrease the cost of task transfer: only a descriptor will be shipped.

At the other end of the spectrum, performance is insensitive to transfer cost for costs of 1 percent or less.

Fig. 3 shows average response time versus system load for the Threshold policy for four different average transfer costs C: 0.01 (1 percent of the processing cost), 0.05 (5 percent), 0.10 (10 percent as shown in Fig. 2) and 0.25 (25 percent). The other parameters (e.g., threshold, probe limit) are fixed as in Fig. 2. Note that in practice the average transfer cost would be a factor considered in selecting the value of the threshold, whereas a fixed threshold of 2 was used for each transfer cost in Fig. 3.

Fig. 4 shows average response time versus average transfer cost C for all policies, for a fixed system load of 0.7. (Note that a log scale is used for the transfer cost axis.) Again, the other parameters (e.g., threshold, probe limit) are fixed as in Fig. 2. The performance of Threshold and Shortest relative to one another is insensitive to transfer cost. Their performance relative to the extremes of the M/M/1 and M/M/K analyses is insensitive to transfer cost for values below 0.05 (5 percent of processing cost), but degrades rapidly as transfer costs exceed 0.25 (25 percent). The Random policy performs relatively better at low transfer costs than at high ones. In fact, our

345

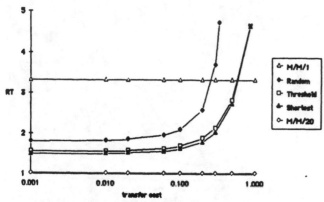

Fig. 4. Response time versus transfer cost C at fixed load ρ. S(task service time) = 1. ρ(system load, λS) = 0.7. T(threshold) = 2. L_p(probe limit for Threshold and Shortest) = 3. L_t(transfer limit for Random) = 1.

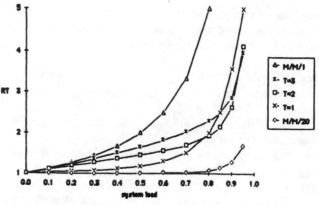

Fig. 5. Response time versus load ρ for three thresholds T (Threshold policy). S(task service time) = 1. C(cost of task transfer) = 0.1. L_p(probe limit) = 3.

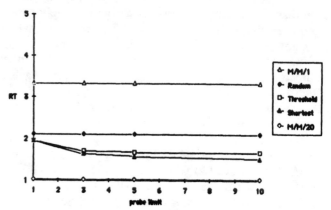

Fig. 6. Response time versus probe limit L_p at fixed load ρ. S(task service time) = 1. C(cost of task transfer) = 0.1. ρ(system load, λS) = 0.7. T(threshold) = 2. L_t(transfer limit for Random) = 1.

analysis does not do justice to Random at low transfer costs. Reasonable performance at relatively high transfer costs requires a transmission limit L_t of 1, the value used throughout our analysis. However, at relatively low transfer costs a higher transmission limit yields substantially better performance, since tasks can be transferred multiple times (at low cost) in search of a suitable node. This yields behavior similar to that of the Threshold policy, except that the task itself is sent, rather than a probe.

C. Choice of Threshold

The threshold T is a fundamental parameter: for each of the three load sharing policies it determines when a task transfer will be attempted (through the transfer policy); for the Threshold and Shortest policies it determines whether the transfer will be allowed (through the location policy).

Clearly the "best" threshold depends on the system load and the transfer cost. At low loads a low threshold is appropriate because many nodes are idle, whereas at high loads a high threshold is appropriate because most nodes have significant queue lengths. Low thresholds are appropriate for low transfer costs, since smaller differences in node queue lengths can be exploited; high costs demand higher thresholds.

One might imagine that a complex adaptive threshold selection strategy would be required to obtain reasonable performance. Figs. 2–4, which used a fixed threshold of 2, indicate that this is not the case. To explore this point further, Fig. 5 shows average response time versus system load for the Threshold policy for three thresholds: 1, 2 (as shown in Fig. 2) and 3. (The corresponding graph for Shortest is essentially indistinguishable.) The other parameters are fixed as in Fig. 2. We see that 1 is the optimal threshold for system loads below 0.8, 2 is the optimal threshold for loads between 0.8 and 0.9, and thresholds greater than 2 are advantageous at (unreasonably high) system loads above 0.95. (The Random policy exhibits greater sensitivity to choice of threshold, but the optimal threshold still is 1 over a wide range of system load.)

These results suggest that the optimal threshold is not very sensitive to system load. Thus, a simple adaptive policy that selects among two or three threshold values, perhaps based on information acquired while probing, offers potential benefit at low cost and risk. Such policies are an area of current research.

D. Choice of Probe Limit

Fig. 6 shows average response time versus probe limit for all policies, for a fixed system load of 0.7. (Random has no probe limit; it is included along with M/M/1 and M/M/K for comparison purposes.)

In the case of Threshold, the rapid decrease in the marginal benefit of increasing the probe limit is easy to explain. The purpose of probing in this policy is to locate a node that is below threshold. If p is the probability that a particular node is below threshold, then (because the nodes are assumed to be independent) the probability that a node below threshold is first encountered on the ith probe is $p(1 - p)^{i - 1}$. For large p, this quantity decreases rapidly: the probability of succeeding on the first few probes is high. For small p, the quantity decreases more slowly. However, since most nodes are busy, the improvement in system-wide response time that will result from locating a node below threshold is small, so abandoning the search after the first few probes does not carry a substantial penalty. It is clear that small probe limits are appropriate.

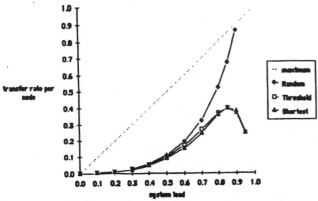

Fig. 7. Task transfer rate per node versus load ρ. S(task service time) = 1. C(cost of task transfer) = 0.1. T(threshold) = 2. L_p(probe limit for Threshold and Shortest) = 3. L_t(transfer limit for Random) = 1.

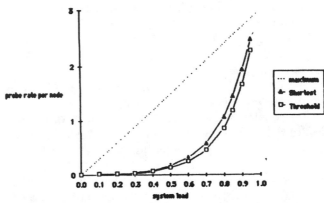

Fig. 8. Rate of probes per node versus load ρ. S(task service time) = 1. C(cost of task transfer) = 0.1. T(threshold) = 2. L_p(probe limit) = 3.

In the case of Shortest, the situation is somewhat more complex. There may be some marginal benefit even to very large probe limits. Fig. 6 shows this, but understates the effect for two reasons. First, this benefit is greatest at high system loads; the load of 0.7, selected for consistency with other figures and a "reasonable" high load for illustrative purposes, is not high enough to fully display the effect. Second, at a threshold value of 2, Shortest cannot find a node with a queue length more than one task shorter than that of the first acceptable destination found, since the maximum acceptable destination queue length is 1. If the threshold were higher (because of a higher system load, for example), there would be more room for improvement. However, it still is the case that relatively small probe limits are appropriate for Shortest. The marginal benefit of increasing the probe limit does decrease (although this decrease is not as rapid as for Threshold), and, as the probe limit increases, the rate and hence the cost of probing increases (this increase is actually greater for Shortest than for Threshold). (The latter effect is not shown in the figures, since the cost of probing is omitted from our analysis.)

E. Transfer and Probing Traffic

Here we consider the network traffic due to task transfers (for all three policies) and probes (for Threshold and Shortest).

Threshold and Shortest each will transfer an individual task at most one time. This also is true of Random with the transfer limit of 1 that we have been using in our examples. This implies that the transfer rate *per node* can be no greater than λ, and that the task transfer rate over the entire system can be no greater than $K\lambda$.

As illustrated in Fig. 7, the actual task transfer rates for Threshold and Shortest are extremely similar and are considerably less than this maximum value, while the rate for Random approaches this maximum only for relatively high system loads. (The unit of time in the figure is the task processing time S, which is equal to 1.) It is impossible to translate these results into network utilization without making rather arbitrary assumptions, but for the sake of illustration, suppose that the processing cost of tasks is

related to their size in the ratio of 1 second per 1 kbytes (e.g., a 100K task would process for 100 seconds), and that we are considering a 10 Mbit network (i.e., each 1K transferred requires 0.0008 seconds of network time). Then, an upper bound network utilization due to task transfers under the Threshold or Shortest policies would be $0.4 \times 0.0008 \times K$ (since these policies never exceed a transfer rate of 0.4), yielding a network utilization of 3 percent in a system of 100 nodes. If we envision a system based on file servers, then the network cost of load sharing over and above the inherent cost of remote file access is insignificant regardless of the particular assumptions that are made.

Note, incidentally, that the decrease in transfer rate at high loads for Threshold and Shortest is exactly what one should expect: in this situation many nodes are over threshold, so there is an increasing probability that a transfer attempt will fail, i.e., that no suitable destination node will be found during the probe phase.

Fig. 8 shows the rate of probes per node for Threshold and Shortest. Because the probe limit is 3, the maximum probe rate per node can be no greater than 3λ. The figure shows that the two policies behave similarly, with Threshold requiring marginally fewer probes than Shortest. The difference is maximized at approximately the point corresponding to the maximum transfer rate. (The difference between the two policies can be much larger or larger probe limits and/or thresholds.) As the system load increases beyond 0.7, the probe rate for each policy begins to increase substantially. Still, given the maximum rate per node of $L_p\lambda$, the network load and processor load due to probing will be negligible. (Note that at most L_p probes can be performed per processed task.) Probing could be implemented, for example, using a single remote procedure cell with a return value that is binary (in the case of Threshold) or integer (in the case of Shortest).

F. An Optimistic Evaluation

We noted in Section III-A that our evaluation was conservative in two respects: the M/M/K analysis does not provide a tight bound, and the choice of parameter values is not advantageous to the policies under consideration.

In this section we briefly consider the Threshold scheme from a more optimistic point of view:

- The threshold T, rather than being fixed, is set to either 1 or 2 depending on the system load. Fig. 5 suggests the improvement that this offers.
- The probe limit is increased from 3 to 5. Fig. 6 suggests the improvement that this offers.
- We consider an average transfer cost of 0.01, in addition to 0.10. (The average task processing time remains fixed at 1.) Fig. 3 suggests the improvement that this offers.
- We compare performance to a plausible lower bound that includes the average transfer cost, obtained as follows:

An M/M/K queueing system can be viewed as a model of perfect load sharing among K nodes: no node will ever be idle when more than a single task is present at some other node. The results of an M/M/K analysis are "too optimistic," though, because the cost of the task transfers required to achieve this perfect load sharing is ignored.

Livny and Melman [11] calculate a lower bound on the number of task transfers required to ensure that no node will ever be idle when another node has a queue length greater than 1. They note that a task must be transferred when one of the following events occurs: an arrival occurs at a busy node when there are less than K tasks in the system, or a completion occurs at a node with only one task present when there are more than K tasks in the system. Thus, the minimum rate of task transfers $\tilde{\lambda}_T$ can be expressed as

$$\tilde{\lambda}_T = \sum_{i=1}^{K-1} \left\{ \lambda i P[i] + \frac{1}{S}(K-i)P[K+i] \right\}$$

where $P[j]$ is the probability that there are j tasks in an M/M/K queueing system with arrival rate $K\lambda$ and service rate per server $1/S$.

This expression can be used to increase the average task service time S by the transfer cost C multiplied by the probability that a task requires a transfer, $\tilde{\lambda}_T/\lambda$. Since the use of these increased service times in the M/M/K analysis results in a new set of state probabilities (implying a new rate of task transfers), an iteration is used.

Fig. 9 shows a comparison of M/M/1, Threshold with transfer costs of 0.1 and 0.01, the modified M/M/K analysis just described (labeled "Mod. M/M/20") with a transfer cost of 0.1, and the traditional M/M/20 analysis. The important observations are:

- With a variable threshold and a probe limit of 5, the performance of Threshold with a transfer cost of 0.1 is noticeably improved over that shown in Fig. 2, i.e., noticeably further from the performance of the M/M/1 system, and noticeably closer to the performance of the M/M/20 system.
- Viewing the modified M/M/K analysis as a plausible lower bound, there is little room for improvement beyond the performance of Threshold.

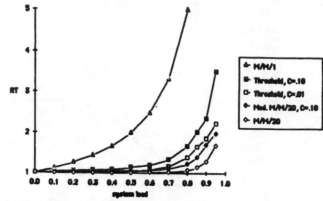

Fig. 9. Optimistic evaluation of the Threshold policy. S(task service time) = 1. T(threshold) = *variable*. L_p(probe limit) = 5.

- When the transfer cost drops to 0.01, the performance of Threshold is such that there is very little room for improvement relative to the absolute bound established by the M/M/20 analysis. (The performance of the modified M/M/20 system with a transfer cost of 0.01 is indistinguishable from the performance of the traditional M/M/20 system.)

IV. Summary

We have explored the use of system state information in adaptive load sharing policies for locally distributed systems, with the goal of determining an appropriate level of policy complexity. Our investigations have been based on the use of simple analytic models of load sharing policies. Simulation results have indicated the validity of these models.

Our results suggest that extremely simple load sharing policies using small amounts of information perform quite well—dramatically better than when no load sharing is performed, and nearly as well as more complex policies that utilize more information. This provides convincing evidence that the potential benefits of adaptive load sharing can in fact be realized in practice.

Our original intent in considering the class of threshold policies in general, and the Threshold policy in particular, was to establish a plausible bound on the performance of realistic load sharing schemes by considering a policy so simple that one expects to be able to do better in practice. However, the results of our analysis indicate that fairly direct derivatives of Threshold are plausible candidates for implementation. In particular, our results have shown the benefit of "threshold-type" information, as opposed to no information at one extreme or to "complete" information at the other.

Appendix A
Instability of Random with No Transmission Limit

This Appendix considers a variation of the Random policy in which there is no transfer limit ($L_t = \infty$): transferred tasks are treated exactly as new tasks when applying the transfer policy. We refer to this policy as *Uncontrolled Random*. Uncontrolled Random is *unstable* for a

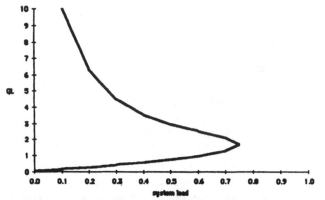

Fig. 10. Uncontrolled Random: queue length equilibrium contour. S(task service time) = 1. C(cost of task transfer) = 0.1. T(threshold) = 2.

nonzero transfer cost. No matter what the average load ρ, the system does not approach an equilibrium behavior: the expected backlog of work increases monotonically with time. Intuitively, this behavior occurs since there is a positive probability that all nodes will be in a transferring phase simultaneously. In Uncontrolled Random, each node would then begin to receive transferred tasks at rate $1/C$, and would try to retransfer these tasks at the same rate. Since no useful work is being done, the queue size at each node would increase at rate λ.

The instability of Uncontrolled Random is analogous to that of the infinite population ALOHA system [5]. Much of the terminology regarding stability that has been developed for use in the ALOHA context will be used here.

Fig. 10 is a result of the analysis that follows in this Appendix. The figure shows the mean node queue length *equilibrium contour* as a function of the system load, for Uncontrolled Random with a threshold of 2 and a transfer cost of 0.1. The average task service time is fixed at one. The equilibrium contour is composed of *system equilibrium points*, at which the output traffic intensity of the system (defined as the throughput multiplied by the average task service time) equals the input traffic intensity (or loading factor). A *load line* is defined as a vertical line corresponding to a particular value of input traffic intensity. There may be none, one, or two points of intersection of an equilibrium contour with a particular load line. At the input traffic intensity ρ_{max} equal to the maximum possible output traffic intensity, there is only one intersection point. For values of ρ greater than ρ_{max}, the system is overloaded and queue lengths grow without bound; in this case there are no intersection points. For values of ρ less then ρ_{max}, there are two intersection points; the lower is termed the *system operating point* and the upper the *system saturation point*. Below the system saturation point, the tendency of the system is to return to the system operating point. However, once the system saturation point is exceeded (which occurs eventually due to random fluctuations), the performance of the system degrades rapidly.

The remainder of this Appendix consists of the analysis of the Uncontrolled Random policy for system equilib-

rium points. Here $p_n (0 \le n \le T)$ and $\bar{n}_p$ denote the conditional probability of queue length n, and the mean queue length, respectively, given that the node is in a processing phase. λ_t and $\lambda_t(n)$ denote unconditioned and conditioned arrival rates of transferred tasks, respectively.

In Uncontrolled Random, the arrival rate of transferred tasks is independent of the node state. Therefore, for all n:

$$\lambda_t(n) = \lambda_t. \qquad \text{(UR1)}$$

The arrival rate of transferred tasks must equal the rate of task transfers. Also, since no tasks are processed in the transferring phase, the probability of being in this phase is equal to that portion of the node utilization that is due to transferring tasks, or $C\lambda_t$. Since only those tasks that arrive while the queue length is greater than or equal to T are transferred,

$$\lambda_t = [p_T(1 - C\lambda_t) + C\lambda_t](\lambda + \lambda_t).$$

Solving for p_T yields

$$p_T = \frac{\dfrac{\lambda_t}{\lambda + \lambda_t} - C\lambda_t}{1 - C\lambda_t}. \qquad \text{(UR2)}$$

Consider now the birth–death model of Fig. 1. The conditional probability p_0 is given by

$$p_0 = \frac{1 - \rho - C\lambda_t}{1 - C\lambda_t}.$$

Using this expression, (UR1), and the formula for the solution of a birth–death model [4] yields, for $0 \le n \le T$,

$$p_n = \frac{1 - \rho - C\lambda_t}{1 - C\lambda_t} [S(\lambda + \lambda_t)]^n. \qquad \text{(UR3)}$$

Equating the right-hand side of (UR3) for $n = T$ with the right-hand side of (UR2) gives

$$\frac{\lambda_t}{\lambda + \lambda_t} - C\lambda_t = (1 - \rho - C\lambda_t)[S(\lambda + \lambda_t)]^T. \qquad \text{(UR4)}$$

Equation (UR4) has the solution $\lambda_t = (1/S) - \lambda$ for all $C \ge 0$. However, for each S in the region of interest ($C < S < (1/\lambda)$), this solution does not result in conditional state probabilities that sum to one, except for a special case value of λ that depends on S. This special value can be found by substituting this solution for λ_t into equation (UR3). Noting that the right-hand side is then independent of n, and that all of the conditional probabilities must therefore be equal, the conditional probabilities sum to one if and only if $p_n = 1/(T + 1)$. Making this substitution and solving for λ yields as the special case value:

$$\lambda = \frac{1 - \dfrac{C}{S}}{\dfrac{T + 1}{T} S - C}.$$

If $C = 0$ (and $\rho < 1$), (UR4) has exactly one valid so-

349

lution. Therefore, there is only one equilibrium point, and the system is stable. If $C > 0$, (UR4) has exactly two valid solutions for all positive values of ρ less than some value $\rho_{max} < 1$, one valid solution for $\rho = \rho_{max}$, and no valid solutions for $\rho > \rho_{max}$. The value ρ_{max} defines the maximum possible throughput of the system. For $\rho \geq \rho_{max}$ the system is overloaded. For $0 < \rho < \rho_{max}$ the system is unstable.

The solutions of equation (UR4) may be found numerically by any appropriate method. (The method used to obtain the numerical results of Fig. 10 is based on the bisection method of finding roots.) For each valid solution, the conditional state probabilities p_n are given by (UR3). The conditional mean queue length $\bar{n}_p$ is given by

$$\bar{n}_p = S(\lambda + \lambda_t) \left[\frac{1 - \rho - C\lambda_t}{1 - C\lambda_t} \right] \left[\frac{1 - [S(\lambda + \lambda_t)]^T}{[1 - S(\lambda + \lambda_t)]^2} \right.$$
$$\left. - \frac{T[S(\lambda + \lambda_t)]^T}{1 - S(\lambda + \lambda_t)} \right]. \tag{UR5}$$

From this solution all of the performance measures of interest can be derived. For example, the mean response time R of tasks is given by

$$R = \frac{\bar{n}_p(1 - C\lambda_t) + TC\lambda_t}{\lambda} + \frac{\lambda_t}{\lambda} \left[\frac{C}{1 - C(\lambda + \lambda_t)} \right]. \tag{UR6}$$

The first term in (UR6) is derived by applying Little's equation [10], using expressions for the throughput and mean queue length of locally processed tasks. The throughput of processed tasks is given by λ. The mean queue length of tasks to be processed at the node is given by the mean queue length during a processing phase, multiplied by the probability of being in a processing phase, plus the queue length during a transferring phase, multiplied by the probability of being in a transferring phase. The second term in (UR6) is just the mean number of times a task must be transferred, multiplied by the mean delay experienced each time.

APPENDIX B
SOLUTION OF MODELS

This Appendix completes the analysis of the load sharing models introduced in Section II. As in Appendix A, $p_n(0 \leq n \leq T)$ and $\bar{n}_p$ denote the conditional probability of queue length n and the mean queue length, respectively, given that the node is in a processing phase; λ_t and $\lambda_t(n)$ denote unconditioned and conditioned arrival rates of transferred tasks, respectively. In addition, p_{T+}^a denotes the absolute probability of being in a transferring phase.

A. Random Policy

In the Random policy, the arrival rate of transferred tasks is independent of the node state. Therefore, for all n,

$$\lambda_t(n) = \lambda_t. \tag{R1}$$

The arrival rate of transferred tasks must equal the rate of task transfers. Since only those tasks that arrive while the queue length is greater than or equal to T are transferred, under the constraint of the transfer limit L_t,

$$\lambda_t = \lambda \left[\sum_{l=1}^{L_t} [p_T(1 - p_{T+}^a) + p_{T+}^a]^l \right].$$

Note, in the above equation, that λ multiplied by the lth term in the summation gives the rate at which tasks that have already been transferred $l - 1$ times are transferred once more. Performing the summation yields

$$\lambda_t = [p_T(1 - p_{T+}^a)$$
$$+ p_{T+}^a] \lambda \left[\frac{1 - [p_T(1 - p_{T+}^a) + p_{T+}^a]^{L_t}}{1 - [p_T(1 - p_{T+}^a) + p_{T+}^a]} \right]. \tag{R2}$$

The probability of being in a transferring phase is just that portion of the node utilization due to performing task transfers and processing tasks that could not be transferred because of the transfer limit. Therefore,

$$p_{T+}^a = C\lambda_t + S\lambda[p_T(1 - p_{T+}^a) + p_{T+}^a]^{L_t+1}.$$

Using (R2) to substitute for the exponentiated term and solving for p_{T+}^a yields

$$p_{T+}^a = \frac{p_T S(\lambda + \lambda_t) - (S - C)\lambda_t}{1 - (1 - p_T) S(\lambda + \lambda_t)}. \tag{R3}$$

Consider now the birth-death model of Fig. 1. Using the formula for the solution of a birth-death model along with equation (R1) yields

$$p_T = \frac{[S(\lambda + \lambda_t)]^T [1 - S(\lambda + \lambda_t)]}{1 - [S(\lambda + \lambda_t)]^{T+1}}. \tag{R4}$$

Equation (R4) can be used to substitute for p_T in (R2) and (R3). Equation (R3) can then be used to substitute for p_{T+}^a in (R2), yielding a nonlinear equation in the single unknown λ_t. The solution of this equation may be found numerically by any appropriate method. (The method used to obtain numerical results is based on the bisection method of finding roots.) Once λ_t has been found, p_T is given by (R4), and p_{T+}^a is then given by (R3). From the formula for the solution of a birth-death model, the conditional mean queue length $\bar{n}_p$ is given by

$$\bar{n}_p = S(\lambda + \lambda_t) \left[\frac{1 - \rho - C\lambda_t}{1 - p_{T+}^a} \right] \left[\frac{1 - [S(\lambda + \lambda_t)]^T}{[1 - S(\lambda + \lambda_t)]^2} \right.$$
$$\left. - \frac{T[S(\lambda + \lambda_t)]^T}{1 - S(\lambda + \lambda_t)} \right]. \tag{R5}$$

All of the performance measures of interest can now be computed. In particular, the mean response time R of tasks is given by:

$$R = \frac{\bar{n}_p(1 - p^a_{T+}) + Tp^a_{T+} + \lambda[p_T(1 - p^a_{T+}) + p^a_{T+}]^{L_t + 1} R_{T+p}}{\lambda} + \frac{\lambda_t}{\lambda} R_{T+t} \qquad \text{(R6)}$$

where R_{T+t} denotes the mean delay experienced in being transferred, and R_{T+p} denotes the processing delay for a task that arrives at the node when the node is at or over threshold, and yet is not transferred due to the transfer limit. The first term in (R6) is derived by applying Little's equation, using expressions for the throughput and mean queue length of locally processed tasks. The throughput of processed tasks is given by λ. The mean queue length of tasks to be processed at the node is given by the mean queue length during a processing phase, multiplied by the probability of being in a processing phase, plus the threshold multiplied by the probability of being in a transferring phase, plus the mean queue length of tasks that are processed locally only because of the transfer limit (which is given by the arrival rate of such tasks multiplied by their mean delay). The second term in (R6) is just the mean number of times a task must be transferred, multiplied by the mean delay experienced each time.

Expressions for R_{T+t} and R_{T+p} are derived from the solution of a preemptive priority HOL M/M/1 queue [4]. R_{T+t} is given by

$$R_{T+t} = \frac{C}{1 - C\dfrac{\lambda_t}{p_T(1 - p^a_{T+}) + p^a_{T+}}}. \qquad \text{(R7)}$$

R_{T+p} is given by

$$R_{T+p} = \frac{S - (S - C)\, C\, \dfrac{\lambda_t}{p_T(1 - p^a_{T+}) + p^a_{T+}}}{\left[1 - C\dfrac{\lambda_t}{p_T(1 - p^a_{T+}) + p^a_{T+}}\right]\left[1 - C\dfrac{\lambda_t}{p_T(1 - p^a_{T+}) + p^a_{T+}} - S\lambda[p_T(1 - p^a_{T+}) + p^a_{T+}]^{L_t}\right]}. \qquad \text{(R8)}$$

B. Threshold Policy

In the model of the Threshold policy, all transferred tasks arrive when the node queue length is less than the threshold T. Therefore, $\lambda_t(T)$ and $\lambda_t(T^+)$ are both zero. When the node queue length is less than T, the arrival rate of transferred tasks is independent of the node state. Since the probability that the node queue length is less than T is $(1 - p_T)(1 - p^a_{T+})$, it must be the case that, for $0 \le n \le T - 1$,

$$\lambda_t(n) = \lambda^*_t \qquad \text{(T1)}$$

where λ^*_t is defined by

$$\lambda^*_t = \frac{\lambda_t}{(1 - p_T)(1 - p^a_{T+})}. \qquad \text{(T2)}$$

The arrival rate of transferred tasks must equal the rate of task transfers. Since only those tasks that arrive while the queue length is greater than or equal to the threshold T are transferred, under the constraint of a probe limit of L_p,

$$\lambda_t = [p_T(1 - p^a_{T+}) + p^a_{T+}]\,\lambda$$
$$\cdot [1 - [p_T(1 - p^a_{T+}) + p^a_{T+}]^{L_p}].$$

This gives

$$\lambda^*_t = \frac{[p_T(1 - p^a_{T+}) + p^a_{T+}]}{(1 - p_T)(1 - p^a_{T+})}\,\lambda$$
$$\cdot [1 - [p_T(1 - p^a_{T+}) + p^a_{T+}]^{L_p}]. \qquad \text{(T3)}$$

The probability of being in a transferring phase is just that portion of the node utilization due to performing task transfers and processing tasks that could not be transferred because of a failure to find a suitable destination. Therefore,

$$p^a_{T+} = C\lambda_t + S\lambda[p_T(1 - p^a_{T+}) + p^a_{T+}]^{L_p + 1}.$$

Using (T3) to substitute for the exponentiated term and solving for p^a_{T+} yields

$$p^a_{T+} = \frac{p_T S\lambda - (1 - p_T)(S - C)\,\lambda^*_t}{1 - (1 - p_T)(S\lambda + (S - C)\,\lambda^*_t)}. \qquad \text{(T4)}$$

Consider now the birth–death model of Fig. 1. Using the formula for the solution of a birth–death model along with (T1) yields

$$p_T = \frac{[S(\lambda + \lambda^*_t)]^T (1 - S(\lambda + \lambda^*_t))}{1 - [S(\lambda + \lambda^*_t)]^{T+1}}. \qquad \text{(T5)}$$

Equation (T5) can be used to substitute for p_T in (T3) and (T4). Equation (T4) then can be used to substitute for p^a_{T+} in (T3), yielding a nonlinear equation in the single unknown λ^*_t. The solution of this equation may be found numerically by any appropriate method. (The method used to obtain numerical results is based on the bisection method of finding roots.) Once λ^*_t has been found, p_T is given by (T5), p^a_{T+} is then given by (T4), and λ_t is then given by (T2).

From the formula for the solution of a birth–death model, the conditional mean queue length $\bar{n}_p$ is given by

$$\bar{n}_p = S(\lambda + \lambda^*_t)\left[\frac{1 - \rho - C\lambda_t}{1 - p^a_{T+}}\right]\left[\frac{1 - [S(\lambda + \lambda^*_t)]^T}{[1 - S(\lambda + \lambda^*_t)]^2}\right.$$
$$\left. - \frac{T[S(\lambda + \lambda^*_t)]^T}{1 - S(\lambda + \lambda^*_t)}\right]. \qquad \text{(T6)}$$

The mean response time R of tasks is given by

$$R = \frac{\bar{n}_p(1 - p_{T+}^a) + Tp_{T+}^a + \lambda[p_T(1 - p_{T+}^a) + p_{T+}^a]^{L_p+1} R_{T+p}}{\lambda} + \frac{\lambda_t}{\lambda} R_{T+t} \quad (T7)$$

where R_{T+t} denotes the mean delay experienced in being transferred, and R_{T+p} denotes the processing delay for a task that arrives at the node when the node is at or over threshold, and yet is not transferred since a suitable destination has not been found after the maximum number of probes. This equation is quite similar to that for the Random policy, and is derived in a similar manner.

Expressions for R_{T+t} and R_{T+p} are derived from the solution of a preemptive priority HOL M/M/1 queue. R_{T+t} is given by exactly the same equation as for the Random policy

$$R_{T+t} = \frac{C}{1 - C \dfrac{\lambda_t}{p_T(1 - p_{T+}^a) + p_{T+}^a}}. \quad (T8)$$

R_{T+p} is given by

$$R_{T+p} = \frac{S - (S - C) C \dfrac{\lambda_t}{p_T(1 - p_{T+}^a) + p_{T+}^a}}{\left[1 - C \dfrac{\lambda_t}{p_T(1 - p_{T+}^a) + p_{T+}^a}\right]\left[1 - C \dfrac{\lambda_t}{p_T(1 - p_{T+}^a) + p_{T+}^a} - S\lambda[p_T(1 - p_{T+}^a) + p_{T+}^a]^{L_p}\right]}. \quad (T9)$$

C. Shortest Policy

Iteration is used to evaluate the model of the Shortest policy. In a typical step, a model solution is used to derive new values for the arrival rates of transferred tasks, and a new solution is computed. In the following description of the iteration equations, $pshort_n$ denotes the probability that a node with queue length n is selected when attempting to find a suitable node to which to transfer a task. The following equation gives $pshort_n$, $0 \leq n \leq T - 1$, in terms of the probe limit L_p, the conditional state probabilities p_n, and the probability of being in a transferring phase p_{T+}^a:

$$pshort_n = \left[1 - \left(\sum_{m=0}^{n-1} p_m\right)(1 - p_{T+}^a)\right]^{L_p}$$

$$- \left[1 - \left(\sum_{m=0}^{n} p_m\right)(1 - p_{T+}^a)\right]^{L_p}. \quad (S1)$$

The first term in (S1) gives the probability that all of the L_p randomly chosen nodes have queue length greater than or equal to n; the second term gives the probability that all of the L_p randomly chosen nodes have queue length greater than or equal to $n + 1$. The difference of the two terms provides the required probability. Noting that only those tasks that arrive when a node is at or over threshold can be transferred, under the constraint of a probe limit of L_p, and that the arrival rate of transferred tasks must equal the rate of task transfers,

$$\lambda_t = [p_T(1 - p_{T+}^a) + p_{T+}^a] \lambda$$

$$\cdot [1 - [p_T(1 - p_{T+}^a) + p_{T+}^a]^{L_p}]. \quad (S2)$$

The probability of being in a transferring phase is just that portion of the node utilization due to performing task transfers and processing tasks that could not be transferred because of a failure to find a suitable destination. Therefore:

$$p_{T+}^a = C\lambda_t + S\lambda[p_T(1 - p_{T+}^a) + p_{T+}^a]^{L_p+1}. \quad (S3)$$

The arrival rates $\lambda_t(n)$, for $0 \leq n \leq T - 1$, are then given by

$$\lambda_t(n) = \frac{\lambda_t}{p_n(1 - p_{T+}^a)} \frac{pshort_n}{1 - [p_T(1 - p_{T+}^a) + p_{T+}^a]^{L_p+1}}. \quad (S4)$$

The formula for the solution of a birth–death model yields, for $1 \leq n \leq T$,

$$p_n = p_{n-1}\left[1 + \frac{\lambda_t(n - 1)}{\lambda}\right] \rho. \quad (S5)$$

Finally, p_0 is given by

$$p_0 = \frac{1 - \rho - C\lambda_t}{1 - p_{T+}^a}. \quad (S6)$$

In one iteration of the method used to compute numerical results, (S1)–(S6) are applied to a model solution in order, yielding a new model solution. The conditional state probabilities of the new solution then are normalized to sum to one by scaling the probabilities p_k for $k > 0$. The iteration stopping criterion is based on comparing old and new conditional mean queue length values, as obtained from the conditional state probabilities. Empirically, the iteration is insensitive to the initializations used. Once the solutions of (S1)–(S6) have been obtained, the mean response time R of tasks is given by the same equations as in the analysis of the Threshold policy.

APPENDIX C
SIMULATION RESULTS

Experimentation with an event-driven simulation program has provided validation of the decomposition approximation utilized in our analytic models. The simulation program uses the same system model as do the analytic models, but does not make the decomposition approximation.

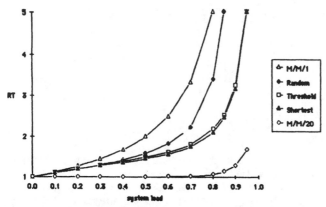

Fig. 11. Simulation results: response time versus load ρ. S(task service time) = 1. C(cost of task transfer) = 0.1. T(threshold) = 2. L_p(probe limit for Threshold and Shortest) = 3. L_t(transfer limit for Random) = 1.

In Fig. 11 we present a small sample of the results of our simulation experiments. A system with 20 nodes has been simulated. Fig. 11 should be compared to Fig. 2; for the Random, Threshold, and Shortest policies the former figure shows the simulation results that correspond to the analytic results of the latter figure. (Fig. 11 also includes the analytic results for M/M/1 and M/M/20 for comparison purposes.) Note the close correspondence between the two figures, both with respect to the absolute values of the performance measures (particularly at low to moderate loadings), and with respect to the indicated relative performance of the three load sharing policies.

Acknowledgment

D. Towsley of the University of Massachusetts discussed these issues extensively with us. K. Sevcik of the University of Toronto provided comments on an earlier draft.

References

[1] A. Barak and A. Shiloh, "A distributed load balancing policy for a multicomputer," Dep. Comput. Sci., Hebrew Univ. of Jerusalem, Jerusalem, Israel, 1984.
[2] S. H. Bokhari, "Dual processor scheduling with dynamic reassignment," IEEE Trans. Software Eng., vol. SE-5, pp. 341–349, July 1979.
[3] R. Bryant and R. A. Finkel, "A stable distributed scheduling algorithm," in Proc. 2nd Int. Conf. Distributed Comput. Syst., 1981, pp. 314–323.
[4] L. Kleinrock, Queueing Systems: Volume I—Theory. New York: Wiley, 1976.
[5] L. Kleinrock and S. S. Lam, "Packet switching in a multiaccess broadcast channel: Performance evaluation," IEEE Trans. Commun., vol. COM-23, pp. 410–423, Apr. 1975.
[6] A. Kratzer and D. Hammerstrom, "A study of load levelling," in Proc. IEEE Fall COMPCON, 1980, pp. 647–654.
[7] P. Krueger and R. A. Finkel, "An adaptive load balancing algorithm for a multicomputer," Dep. Comput. Sci., Univ. Wisconsin, Madison, Tech. Rep. 539, Apr. 1984.
[8] S. S. Lam and L. Kleinrock, "Packet switching in a multiaccess broadcast channel: Dynamic control procedures," IEEE Trans. Commun., vol. COM-23, pp. 891–904, Sept. 1975.
[9] E. D. Lazowska, J. Zahorjan, D. R. Cheriton, and W. Zwaenepoel, "File access performance of diskless workstations," Dep. Comput. Sci., Univ. Washington, Seattle, Tech. Rep. 84-06-01, June 1984.
[10] J. D. C. Little, "A proof of the queueing formula $L = \lambda W$," Oper. Res., vol. 9, pp. 383–387, May 1961.
[11] M. Livny and M. Melman, "Load balancing in homogeneous broadcast distributed systems," in Proc. ACM Comput. Network Performance Symp., 1982, pp. 47–55.
[12] M. L. Powell and B. P. Miller, "Process migration in DEMOS/MP," in Proc. 9th ACM Symp. Operat. Syst. Principles, 1983, pp. 110–119.
[13] H. S. Stone, "Multiprocessor scheduling with the aid of network flow algorithms," IEEE Trans. Software Eng., vol. SE-3, pp, 85–93, Jan. 1977.
[14] ——, "Critical load factors in two processor distributed systems," IEEE Trans. Software Eng., vol. SE-4, pp. 254–258, May 1978.
[15] A. N. Tantawi and D. Towsley, "Optimal static load balancing in distributed computer systems," J. ACM, vol. 32, pp. 445–465, Apr. 1985.
[16] F. A. Tobagi and L. Kleinrock, "Packet switching in radio channels: Part IV—Stability considerations and dynamic control in carrier sense multiple access," IEEE Trans. Commun., vol. COM-25, pp. 1103–1119, Oct. 1977.

Derek L. Eager received the B.Sc. degree in computer science from the University of Regina, Regina, Sask., Canada, in 1979, and the M.Sc. and Ph.D. degrees in computer science from the University of Toronto, Toronto, Ont., Canada, in 1981 and 1984, respectively.

He is currently an Assistant Professor in the Department of Computational Science at the University of Saskatchewan, Saskatoon. His research interests are in the areas of performance modeling and distributed systems.

Edward D. Lazowska received the A.B. degree from Brown University, Providence, RI, in 1972 and the Ph.D. degree in computer science from the University of Toronto, Toronto, Ont., Canada, in 1977.

Since 1977 he has been on the faculty of the Department of Computer Science at the University of Washington, Seattle, where he recently returned after a sabbatical leave at Digital Equipment Corporation's Systems Research Center. His research interests fall within the general area of computer systems: modeling and analysis, design and implementation, and distributed systems.

Dr. Lazowska is the Chairman of SIGMETRICS, the Association for Computing Machinery's Special Interest Group concerned with computer system performance.

John Zahorjan received the Sc.B. degree in applied mathematics from Brown University, Providence, RI, in 1975, and the M.Sc. and Ph.D. degrees in computer science from the University of Toronto, Toronto, Ont., Canada, in 1976 and 1980, respectively.

Presently, he is an Associate Professor of Computer Science at the University of Washington, Seattle. His active research interests include performance modeling of computer systems, load sharing policies in distributed systems, and issues in naming in distributed systems. He is an author of papers in these areas, and is coauthor of a recent book on performance modeling of computer systems using queueing network models.

IMBEDDING GRADIENT ESTIMATORS IN LOAD BALANCING ALGORITHMS[1]

Spiridon Pulidas
Don Towsley
John A. Stankovic

University of Massachusetts
Amherst, MA 01003

Abstract

Simple threshold policies for load balancing algorithms have been shown to provide improved performance over no load balancing. However, in order to achieve this improvement, the threshold values must be chosen to provide the best performance. In this paper we study the problem of efficiently determining the optimum threshold parameter values for a decentralized load balancing algorithm. Through simulation we study the behavior of a gradient based decentralized optimization algorithm for obtaining good values for these thresholds. The algorithm computes the incremental job delay as a function of changes in both the local and remote job arrival rate. This paper describes estimators for these two quantities that are imbedded in the our optimization algorithm. We describe several experiments designed to evaluate the performance of this algorithm in an stationary environment and in an environment where there are changes in the workload. The results of these experiments indicate that the estimators are accurate, the algorithm chooses good thresholds, and the resultant response time of jobs is near optimal. Although the decentralized optimization approach (with imbedded gradient estimators) is presented in the context of a specific load balancing policy based on thresholds, it should also be possible to use it with other load balancing policies.

1 Introduction

In distributed computing systems, *load balancing* algorithms have been developed to improve the performance of the system (e.g. to minimize the mean response time of a job) by efficiently utilizing the processing power of the entire system. This is done by transferring jobs from heavily loaded nodes to lightly loaded nodes. Although a communication delay is typically incurred by transferring a job from one node to another, the performance of a distributed computer system can generally be improved by an effective load balancing policy [2,15,16,20,21,23].

In this paper we consider a class of *threshold* load balancing policies, that have been shown to be useful when jobs are completely independent and consist of single threads of control. This situation is fairly common in networks of workstations. The reader is referred to the following papers for work on threshold policies [2,11,12,13,16,23]. Such threshold policies contain control parameters (e.g. threshold values and transfer probabilities for every host), that require fine-tuning in order to yield optimal or near-optimal performance. An efficient distributed algorithm for determining the optimum values of parameters for such threshold policies has been proposed in [11]. The algorithm is iterative in nature and at each iteration the load balancing parameters at each host are updated. The algorithm requires that each host estimate the incremental delay as a function of changes in both the local and remote arrival rates. The hosts exchange this gradient information with each other and use these quantities to update the load balancing parameters for the next iteration of the algorithm. In [11] the distributed optimization algorithm for quasi-static load balancing was studied analytically under the assumptions that the required gradient information is available.

In this paper, we relax the assumption that gradient information is available and perform a simulation study to determine the effectiveness of the distributed optimization algorithm. Specifically, we describe estimators for all of the required gradient information and imbed them in the optimization algorithm. We study the effectiveness of the distributed optimization algorithm with these estimators in environments where the workload is stationary and in environments where the workload changes in time. The conclusion is that in both cases, the optimization algorithm with the imbedded estimators yields *optimal* or *near optimal* values for the thresholds.

To make our ideas concrete, we adopt a threshold policy first studied in [2], where jobs at each host are divided into two classes; local and remote jobs. *Local jobs* are those processed at the site of origination and *remote jobs* are those transferred for processing to another node. A job arriving at a host from the external world is processed locally only if the current queue length is less than the threshold. Otherwise, the job is sent for remote processing to another randomly selected host. Remote jobs are always accepted by the destination hosts and therefore jobs can move at most once. Both local and remote jobs are processed according to a first-come-first-served (FCFS) discipline at a given host.

A number of techniques exist for estimating gradient information from real sample paths. One class of estimators is based on the technique of perturbation analysis; see, e.g., Ho

---

[1]This work was supported by RADC under contract RI-448896X.

Reprinted from *Proc. IEEE 8th Int'l Conf. on Distributed Computing Systems,* IEEE CS Press, Los Alamitos, Calif., 1988, pp. 482–490.

and Cassandras [7] for an introduction to the subject and Heidelberger, Cao, Zazanis and Suri [5] (and the references therein) for a discussion of the convergence properties of Infinitesimal Perturbation Analysis gradient estimates. A second class of estimators is based on the derivative of the logarithm of the likelihood [4,18,19,6]. These estimators have been shown to produce valid derivative estimates for a large class of systems. We adopt one of the second class of estimators because the estimators based on perturbation analysis cannot handle thresholds without a large computational cost.

All of the above techniques apply to continuous valued parameters. Cassandras [1] describes an estimator for system performance when the threshold is increased by one. This technique requires storage of potentially an infinite amount of state information. Instead, we present a technique that assumes that the arrival process is Poisson and relies on the memoryless property of the exponential distribution to reduce the storage requirements to three counters. A similar technique has also been proposed in [22].

It is also worthwhile mentioning that a number of theoretical studies of distributed optimization algorithms applied to specific problems have been reported in the literature. These include applications to routing [3], static load balancing [10], and file allocation, [8,9]. However, none of these studies consider the problem of imbedding gradient estimators in the algorithm and evaluating the resulting performance.

In Section 2, we describe the system model, the load balancing policy, and discuss the gradient information required. In Section 3, we briefly describe the estimation techniques which provide the necessary gradient information. For a more detailed description of the estimation techniques see [17]. In Section 4, we describe how the two estimators are imbedded in the decentralized threshold scheduling algorithm discussed in Section 2. Simulation results are presented for a system with five hosts modeled as single server queueing systems. The results show that after a fairly small number of algorithm iterations, the behavior of the system in a static environment is confined in a neighborhood of the optimal performance. We also present simulation results showing that the algorithm adapts well to a changing system environment and that the adaptivity improves performance over a simpler static approach. Further, as was expected, a great improvement in the performance measure (average response time of a job) has been observed in the system executing the load balancing policy, compared to a system with no load balancing at all. Finally, we summarize our work in Section 5.

2 A Decentralized Load Balancing Scheme

2.1 System Model

We model a distributed system as N autonomous hosts interconnected through a communication network. Jobs arrive at each host from the external world according to some arrival process with rate λ_i, $i = 1, 2, ..., N$. Jobs originating at host i can be processed either locally or at any other host $j \neq i$. If a job is chosen for remote processing, it is transferred to a remote node and the results are returned to the origin node. Commu-

nication delays are incurred during both transfers. We assume that each node has a communication server that handles job transfers between computers.

2.2 The Load Balancing Policy

Jobs at each host are divided into two classes; namely *local* and *remote* jobs. Local jobs are those processed at the site of origination, while remote jobs are those transferred from other hosts for remote processing. Let L_i denote the total number of jobs at host i.

- If a job arriving at host i from the external world finds that $L_i < T_i$, where T_i is a threshold parameter associated with host i, it is processed locally.

- If an external job arriving at host i finds $L_i \geq T_i$, then this job is transferred for remote service to a host $j \neq i$ chosen randomly from all other hosts.

- Remote jobs arriving at host i from other hosts are always accepted.

- Jobs arriving at each host are processed in a first-come-first-served (FCFS) basis.

The above threshold policy uses only local state information for making job transfer decisions. However, since these decisions are independent of the state of the other nodes, a job sent for remote service may find a busy destination node. As a potential solution to this problem, the origin node may probe possible destination nodes to see whether they are busy or not. The resulting system performance improvement, if any, has been studied in [2,16]. Performance can also be improved by choosing remote hosts according to some distribution. However, our experience, [16] indicates that when the hosts do not deviate significantly from each other in processing speed, the improvement in performance is slight. Consequently, we shall study the above algorithm.

2.3 Optimal Load Balancing Problem

The described threshold policy contains thresholds which require fine-tuning in a changing system environment. We wish to choose threshold values so as to reduce the mean response time of a job in the system. We model each node as a single-server queueing system with two classes of jobs. Let $\lambda_i^{(l)}$ and $\lambda_i^{(r)}$ be the throughput of local and remote jobs respectively at host i. Let $f_i(\lambda_i^{(l)}, \lambda_i^{(r)})$ and $g(\Lambda^{(r)})$ denote the mean queue length at node i and the communication network respectively, where $\Lambda^{(r)} = \sum_{i=1}^{N} \lambda_i^{(r)}$. The mean response time $E[R]$ of a job in the system is given by the following formula:

$$E[R] = \frac{\sum_{i=1}^{N} f_i(\lambda_i^{(l)}, \lambda_i^{(r)}) + g(\Lambda^{(r)})}{\Lambda}. \tag{1}$$

where $\Lambda = \sum_{i=1}^{N} \lambda_i$. Our purpose is to minimize $E[R]$ with respect to T_i's under the constraints that T_i's are non-negative integers ($i = 1, 2, ..., N$). This is an intractable problem because of the integer constraints. In the remainder of this section we describe a distributed algorithm proposed in [11] for solving this problem where each node performs a portion of the whole computation and collaborates with each other to solve the problem by exchanging information in an iterative fashion.

Let $x_{i,j}$ denote the flow of jobs originating at host i and processed at host j. Obviously, $x_{i,i} = \lambda_i^{(l)}$ and $\sum_{i \neq j} x_{i,j} = \lambda_j^{(r)}$. In addition, $x_{i,j} = (\lambda_i - \lambda_i^{(l)})/N$, $j = 1, 2, \cdots, N$; $j \neq i$ according to the description of the policy. Although we wish to minimize $E[R]$ through proper choice of the T_i's, we have found it easier to formulate the problem with the $x_{i,j}$'s as the control variables. There exists a mapping between the $x_{i,j}$'s and the T_i's. However most values for the $x_{i,j}$'s map onto noninteger values for the T_i's. For the moment we ignore this problem. The optimisation problem is [12]:

MINIMIZE $\quad F(x) = \Lambda E[R]$

under the constraints

$$\sum_{j=1}^{N} x_{i,j} = \lambda_i, \quad i = 1, 2, ..., N,$$

$$x_{i,j} \geq 0, \quad i = 1, 2, ..., N.$$

where $x = [x_{i,j}]$. The following conditions are necessary for the optimal solution of the above problem (see [11] for details).

For all $i, j = 1, \cdots, N$,

$$\frac{df_j}{dx_{i,j}} + (1 - \delta_{ij})\frac{dg}{dx_{i,j}} \begin{cases} = C_i, & \text{for } x_{i,j} > 0 \\ \geq C_i, & \text{for } x_{i,j} = 0 \end{cases} \quad (2)$$

where C_i is some constant (Langrange multiplier), and δ_{ij} denotes the Kronecker delta function. Here $df_j/dx_{i,j}$ is the change in delay incurred for jobs processed at host j due to a change in job flow from host i to host j and $dg/dx_{i,j}$ is the change in delay at the communication server for jobs originating at host i and transferred to host j. Using relation (2) Lee and Towsley [11] developed a distributed algorithm for decentralized load balancing. In this algorithm each host compares its own incremental delay to the minimum incremental delay of the other hosts to determine whether to increase or decrease its threshold parameter. The algorithm is iterative in nature and the threshold at each host is updated at each iteration. Initially, each host i sets T_i to some arbitrary value. At each iteration of the algorithm, host i executes the following algorithm.

Algorithm

- Host i computes the incremental delay information $df_i/dx_{i,i}$ and $df_i/dx_{j,i}$ for $j = 1, 2, ..., N$ and $j \neq i$. It reports the incremental delay information, due to jobs originating at a host $j \neq i$ but transferred for remote service at host i, to every host j, $j = 1, 2, ..., N$.

- Using the incremental delay information

$$df_j/dx_{i,j} + dg/dx_{i,j} \quad (3)$$

reported by every host $j \neq i$, host i computes the quantity

$$A(i) = \min_{j \neq i}\{df_j/dx_{i,j} + dg/dx_{i,j}\}. \quad (4)$$

- Host i compares its own incremental delay to the minimum incremental delay reported by the other hosts:

If $df_i/dx_{i,i} > A(i) + \theta$ then $\quad T_i := T_i - 1$,

If $df_i/dx_{i,i} < A(i) - \theta$ then $\quad T_i := T_i + 1$,

else $\quad T_i := T_i$,

where θ is a non-negative constant, which can be added to prevent a change in threshold due to a slight imbalance to the incremental delays. It has been shown [11] for conditions similar to those tested in this paper that $\theta = 0$ is acceptable.

The reader should observe that this algorithm produces integer valued T_i's. Consequently, the optimality conditions (equation (2)) may not be satisfied.

The algorithm described in [11] also included a mechanism for determining the optimum distribution for selecting hosts for remote processing rather than just choosing sites randomly.

In order to implement the above algorithm, the incremental delay information at each host must be computed. We shall assume that the delay incurred due to the transfer of jobs through the communication network does not depend on the job transfer rate and that is has mean $1/\mu_c$. Therefore, the incremental delay due to the job transfer is $dg/dx_{j,i} = 1/\mu_c$. Consequently, there are two types of incremental delays; namely, those which are due to local job flow (i.e. $df_i/dx_{i,i}$) and those which are due to remote job flow (i.e. $df_j/dx_{i,j}$). Incremental delays of the former category are affected by the integer threshold constraints, since local job flow is directly controlled by the threshold parameter. On the other hand, we assume that incremental delays of the latter category are not affected by the integer threshold constraints.

The following backward difference formula is proposed in [11] to approximate the incremental delay due to local job flow:

$$\frac{df_i}{dx_{i,i}} \approx \frac{E[L_i]_{T_i} - E[L_i]_{T_i-1}}{[\lambda_i^{(l)}]_{T_i} - [\lambda_i^{(l)}]_{T_i-1}} \quad (5)$$

where $E[L_i]_{T_i}$ and $[\lambda_i^{(l)}]_{T_i}$ denote the mean queue length and the local job throughput at host i when the threshold is T_i.

We describe two techniques for on-line estimation of the above gradient information in the next section.

3 Gradient Estimation Techniques

In this section we briefly describe the estimation techniques which are required to provide the gradient information used by the distributed threshold update algorithm. The major advantage of these estimators is the fact that they effectively provide performance sensitivity information while the actual system is running (on-line estimation) and at a low cost.

3.1 Incremental delay with respect to local arrival rates

We introduce the notation $M/G/1/T$ with $T = (T_l, T_r)$ to be a two class $M/G/1$ system where class i jobs can enter the system if the queue length is less than T_i, $i = l, r$. We assume that each host can be modeled as a $M/G/1/(T, \infty)$ system where the local and remote jobs correspond to the class l and class r jobs. If the local job arrival process is Poisson, then this assumption is not unreasonable for large systems (see [12] for a discussion of this point). Let $E[L]$ be the average queue length, and $\lambda^{(l)}$ the throughput of local jobs. In the following discussion we shall add the subscript T when referring to a system with the conditions that $T_l = T$ and $T_r = \infty$. The physical system will be referred to as the *nominal system*. What we actually want is to estimate the derivative $dE[L]/d\beta^{(l)}$ while the nominal system is running, using the backward difference formula:

$$\frac{dE[L]}{d\lambda^{(l)} TPUT^{(l)}} \approx \frac{E[L]_T - E[L]_{T-1}}{\lambda^{(l)}_T - \lambda^{(l)}_{T-1}}. \tag{6}$$

We shall refer to the system with threshold value $T - 1$ as the *perturbed system*. The nominal system observes itself and after an observation interval estimates the average queue length and the local job throughput as if it had a threshold value equal to $T - 1$.

Fig. 1a illustrates the portion of a nominal sample path for a two class $M/G/1/(T, \infty)$ system. Let a_i be the time of the $i - th$ arrival and d_j be the time of the $j - th$ departure. Figure 1b represents the corresponding portion of the perturbed system with threshold parameter $T = 2$. We assume that the service time s_k of the $k - th$ customer ($k = 1, 2, ...$) depends only on k. Arrivals a_1 and a_2 are accepted by both the nominal and the perturbed system. Arrival a_3 is also accepted by the nominal system. However, if it is a local job, it is shipped out by the perturbed system. In general, whenever the nominal system reaches or exceeds its threshold T, local arrivals are shipped out by the perturbed system with threshold value $T - 1$. Obviously, every local arrival rejected by the nominal system is also rejected by the perturbed one. As soon as a local arrival accepted by the nominal system is rejected by the perturbed one, the latter system has one less customer than the former one. The two systems will continue to differ by one customer until an idle period appears in the nominal path. This is the case with the idle period just before the arrival a_5 in Figures 1a and 1b assuming that a_3 is a local job.

The first two departures in both the nominal and the perturbed paths of Figure 1a and 1b occur at times d_1 and d_2 ($d_1 = d'_1$, $d_2 = d'_2$). Departure d_2 leaves the nominal system with just one customer. Since the perturbed system has one less customer than the nominal one (due to the rejection of arrival a_3), a new *idle period* will appear in the perturbed path. This idle period is terminated by arrival a_4. Therefore, the major effect of the threshold change on the perturbed path is the generation of new idle periods due to the rejection of local arrivals which are accepted by the nominal system. Since all the jobs rejected by the nominal system are also rejected by the perturbed one, it is not possible that an idle period that appeared in the nominal path be eliminated in the perturbed path.

The nominal system observes itself and keeps track of when the nominal and perturbed paths are out of phase (i.e. their queue lengths differ by one). When a departure leaves the nominal system with only one job and the two systems are out of phase, then the nominal system knows that the perturbed one

starts an idle period waiting for the next customer. Instead of waiting for that next arrival, an *idle period* is generated, terminated by a *ficticious customer*. The currently available service time is assigned to that customer. This new idle period is derived from an exponential distribution with parameter λ (where λ is the arrival rate of local and remote jobs); this is permissible because of the *memoryless property* of the Poisson arrival process. All the subsequent events in the perturbed path are shifted in time by the introduced idle period. The above situation is illustrated in Figure 1b, where a'_4 is the ficticious arrival terminating the introduced idle period.

Although the sample path shows a specific length of inserted idle periods, the estimation algorithm need not maintain a cumulative count of this length. The algorithm need only maintain a count of the number of idle periods introduced in the perturbed system during the observation interval. During that interval the nominal system estimates the rate λ_{est} of its arrival process (local and remote jobs). At the end of the observation interval, it can use this value to estimate the *total idle time* introduced in the perturbed system, using the formula:

$$idle\ time = \frac{(\#\ idle\ periods)}{\lambda_{est}}. \tag{7}$$

Let $IDLE$ be the total number of idle periods introduced in the perturbed path during the observation interval and $TLESS$ be the total time during the observation interval that the perturbed and nominal system queue lengths are out of phase. The nominal system observes itself for an observation interval τ. At the end of that interval, knowing the statistics $E[L]_T$ and $\lambda^{(l)}_T$, it is able to estimate the corresponding statistics for the perturbed system using the following formulas:

$$\lambda^{(l)}_{T-1} = \frac{\tau \lambda^{(l)}_T}{\tau + (IDLE/\lambda_{est})} \tag{8}$$

$$E[L]_{T-1} = E[L]_T - \frac{TLESS + (IDLE/\lambda_{est})}{\tau + (IDLE/\lambda_{est})}. \tag{9}$$

The minimum length of the observation interval τ necessary to obtain a good estimate for $E[L]_{T-1}$ and $\lambda^{(l)}_{T-1}$ depends on the specific application and can be determined empirically. A formal algorithmic description, simulation results, and a discussion of the convergence properties of the above estimator can be found in [17]. Tables 1 and 2 contain simulation results from a representative experiment. The above estimator is applied in an $M/M/1/(3, \infty)$ system with two classes of jobs, where only jobs belonging to the first class are governed by the threshold parameter. The arrival rate of the first class (local jobs) is $\lambda^{(l)} = 0.5$ *jobs/sec*, the arrival rate of the second class is $\lambda^{(r)} = 0.25$ *jobs/sec* and the service rate is $\mu = 1.0$ *jobs/sec*. The estimated parameters are the local throughput $\lambda^{(l)}_2$ and the average queue length $E[L]_2$ of the perturbed system averaged over 10 independent simulations each containing N_c service completions.

3.2 Gradients with respect to the remote arrival rate

We use a method for estimating the derivative of the average queue length with respect to the remote arrival rate that is

N_c	exact $\lambda_2^{(l)}$	estimated $\lambda_2^{(l)}$	% error	σ_s
100	0.350	0.365	4.28	0.167
500	0.350	0.365	4.28	0.017
1000	0.350	0.365	4.28	0.010
5000	0.350	0.360	2.86	0.004
10000	0.350	0.356	1.71	0.004

Table 1: Estimation of $\lambda_2^{(l)}$ for a 2-class $M/M/1/(3,\infty)$ system.

N_c	$E[L]_2^{act}$	$E[L]_2^{est}$	% error	σ_s
100	1.000	0.670	33.00	0.121
500	1.000	1.055	5.50	0.110
1000	1.000	1.041	4.10	0.041
5000	1.000	1.016	1.60	0.023
10000	1.000	1.015	1.50	0.019

Table 2: Estimation of $E[L]_{T=2}$ for a 2-class $M/M/1/(3,\infty)$ system.

based on the derivative of the logarithm of the likelihood. This method was introduced in [4,18,19]. As described initially, these estimators require apriori knowledge of the arrival rate. Consequently, we have modified the estimator described in [18] to use an estimate of the arrival rate. This produces a strongly consistent, unbiased estimate of the derivative. The reader is referred to [6] for details on the convergence properties of this estimator. We describe this last estimator in the remainder of this subsection.

To make things concrete, consider our $M/G/1/T$ system. Let Y_k denote the sum of waiting times over the k'th busy period when the arrival rate of the remote class jobs is $\lambda^{(r)}$, let τ_k denote the length of the k'th busy period, and let N_k denote the number of class r customers that are served during the k'th busy period. By regenerative process theory, the expected stationary queue length $E[L]$ is given by the ratio

$$E[L] = \frac{E[Y_k]}{E[\tau_k]}. \tag{10}$$

Consider the problem of estimating $dE[L]/d\lambda^{(r)}$. This can be expressed as

$$\frac{dE[L]}{d\lambda^{(r)}} = \frac{dE[Y_k]/d\lambda^{(r)}E[\tau_k] - E[Y_k]dE[\tau_k]/d\lambda^{(r)}}{E[\tau_k]^2}. \tag{11}$$

If $\lambda^{(r)}$ is known, then the following expressions are estimates of $dE[Y_k]/d\lambda^{(r)}$ and $dE[\tau_k]/d\lambda^{(r)}$ at the end of n busy periods,

$$\hat{Y}_n = \sum_{k=1}^{n} \left(\frac{N_k}{\lambda^{(r)}} - \tau_k \right) Y_k, \tag{12}$$

$$\hat{\tau}_n = \sum_{k=1}^{n} \left(\frac{N_k}{\lambda^{(r)}} - \tau_k \right) \tau_k. \tag{13}$$

When used in equation, 11, the result is an asymptotically unbiased, strongly consistent estimate of $dE[L]/d\lambda^{(r)}$ [18]. The following expression provides an estimate of $\lambda^{(r)}$ after n busy periods,

$$\hat{\lambda}_n^{(r)} = \frac{\sum_{k=1}^{n} N_k}{\sum_{k=1}^{n} \tau_k}. \tag{14}$$

If we replace $\lambda^{(r)}$ with $\hat{\lambda}_n^{(r)}$ in equations 12 and 13, then we still obtain an asymptotically unbiased, strongly consistent estimate of $dE[L]/d\lambda^{(r)}$ [6].

We use this method to estimate the incremental delay due to remote job flow at host i of the distributed system considered throughout this work. Simulation results reported in [17] suggest that the number of busy periods in the observation period must be large enough in order for the estimator to give accurate estimates of the desired gradient. However, estimates after a small number of busy periods apparently are sufficiently accurate for our purposes as will be shown by the results in Section 4. The reason is that we only need to compare derivatives without worrying about their absolute value. Therefore, the estimate derived even over a small number of busy cycles is good enough for that purpose.

Table 3 contains simulation results for an $M/M/1/(3,\infty)$ system with two classes of jobs, where only jobs belonging to the first class are governed by the threshold parameter. In our experiment the arrival rate of the first class (jobs arriving from the external world) is $\lambda = 0.5$ jobs/sec, the arrival rate

N_b	exact $dE[L]/d\lambda^{(r)}$	estimated $dE[L]/d\lambda^{(r)}$	% error	σ_s
1000	2.700	2.446	9.40	0.277
5000	2.700	2.748	1.77	0.200
10000	2.700	2.690	0.37	0.157
20000	2.700	2.693	0.26	0.134

Table 3: Estimation of $dE[L]/d\lambda^{(r)}$ for a 2-class $M/M/1/(3,\infty)$ system.

of the second class (remote jobs) is $\lambda^{(r)} = 0.25$ jobs/sec and the service rate is $\mu = 1.0$ jobs/sec. The likelihood estimator is used to estimate the derivative of the average queue length with respect to the arrival rate of remote jobs. The estimate of the derivative is given for five runs with N_b busy cycles in each run. Analysis provides us with the exact gradient for this system. For this example, the value of the above derivative is $dE[L]/d\lambda^{(r)} = 2.70$.

4 An Example

In this section we consider a simple example where hosts are interconnected through a communication network and execute the *distributed load balancing* algorithm described in section 2. The estimation techniques described in section 3 are imbedded in the decentralized threshold updating algorithm to provide the necessary gradient information. Each host computer is modeled as a single-server queueing system with two classes of arrivals; namely local and remote jobs. In such a system we study the behavior of the algorithm in a static as well as in a changing environment.

The service time at host i is exponentially distributed with mean $1/\mu_i$ for $i = 1, 2, ..., N$. The times between arrivals of jobs to a host from the external world are exponentially distributed with mean $1/\lambda_i$ for $i = 1, 2, ..., N$. The communication delay of a job due to its transfer for remote service is assumed to be an exponentially distributed random variable with mean $1/\mu_c$. Recall that jobs can move only once through the communication network, since remote jobs are always accepted. Whenever a host rejects a job because it reaches its threshold, it sends this job randomly to any one of the other hosts for remote service.

We have simulated a distributed system with five hosts which can be easily expanded to a system with N hosts. Each host executes the threshold updating algorithm independently of each other. All of them begin execution of the algorithm at time 0 using some initial thresholds. Each host observes itself for a number of busy cycles and at the end of the observation period computes the derivatives of its average queue length with respect to the local and remote job flow. Then, it sends the necessary gradient information to the other nodes and uses the currently available gradients reported by the other nodes, as well as its own gradient information to update its local threshold. Threshold updating completes an iteration of the algorithm at that node. Another observation period can start immediately and the host will execute the load balancing policy with the new threshold value until the next iteration. Note that the algorithm operates in an asynchronous mode. Nodes complete their iterations at different times and possbly at different rates.

We make the following interesting observation regarding the application of the gradient estimation techniques. If the initial threshold value at a particular node is large enough, so that this host never reaches its threshold during the observation period, then the incremental delay with respect to the local job flow cannot be determined using formula (8). If this derivative is assumed to be 0, due to the lack of information, this will lead to an unnecessary increase in the threshold value during the next iteration. Therefore, a heuristic modification must be made; namely, if a host does not hit its threshold during the observation interval, then it automatically decrements its threshold value by one.

We present 5 numerical examples for particular sets of system parameters. However, we have observed similar results for a wide range of system parameters. In all cases, we take the observation interval to consist of 50 busy periods. We first consider the following experiment:

- Experiment 1: The distributed system consists of five nodes with the same utilization $u_1 = u_2 = u_3 = u_4 = u_5 = 0.5$. All the processors have the same job processing rate ($\mu_1 = ... = \mu_5 = 1.0$). The average communication delay of a job is assumed to be 10% of the mean job service time.

We initalize the thresholds at 10, $T_1^{init} = .. = T_5^{init} = 10$.

Figure 2 shows the threshold value at host 1 of the simulated distributed system as a function of the number of iterations of the algorithm at that host. We observed similar behavior of the algorithm for all the hosts of the system. In this experiment the algorithm converges very quickly to the optimal (or near-optimal) threshold value. Figure 3 shows the average response time of a job in the system of the five hosts as a function of time. Two curves are presented corresponding to different initial threshold values. The solid curve is derived for initial values $T_1^{init} = ... = T_5^{init} = 10$ while the dotted curve is derived for initial threshold values $T_1^{init} = ... = T_5^{init} = 15$. The algorithm yields the same solution regardless of the initial threshold value. However, the system with the larger initial threshold values converges more slowly. A comparison is made with a system with no load balancing at all (NLB), where all the hosts are modeled as M/M/1 systems with utilization 0.5.

- Experiment 2: Hosts have the same job processing rate ($\mu_1 = ... = \mu_5 = 1.0$) but different utilizations. Namely $u_1 = u_2 = u_3 = 0.9$ and $u_4 = u_5 = 0.5$.

- Experiment 3: The same as experiment 2 except that $u_1 = u_2 = u_3 = 1.2$.

The average response time of a job in the system is shown as a function of time in Figures 4 and 5. Curves for different initial threshold values are presented and a comparison is made with a system with no load- balancing at all (NLB). In experiment 3, hosts 1, 2 and 3 are saturated without load balancing (Figure 5). Since these three nodes are overloaded, busy cycles are extremely long and consequently threshold updates occur infrequently. Therefore, convergence is very slow when the intial thresholds are large (Figure 5).

The three experiments described so far are for a static system environment. In these environments, after a finite (and small) number of algorithm iterations, the behavior of the system is confined in a neighborhood of the optimal performance. A great improvement in the performance measure (average response time of a job) has been observed in the system executing the distributed load balancing algorithm when compared to a system with no load balancing. Although we used short observation periods (e.g. 50 busy cycles), the performance of the algorithm is not affected. It appears that the accuracy of the gradient information is not crucial, since it is the *relative* values of the gradients, not their *absolute* values, that are important.

We next study the *adaptivity* of the threshold updating algorithm in a dynamically changing system environment. When the change in the environment produces an imbalance in the incremental delays environment, we expect that the algorithm will correct the imbalance properly so that the system performance will improve. Figures 6 and 7 show the results for 2 representative experiments:

- Experiment 4: Hosts in the system have the same processing power ($\mu_1 = ... = \mu_5 = 1.0$). Initially all five hosts have the same utilization 0.5. Immediately after the 2500-th time unit (simulation time) the utilizations of hosts 1, 2 and 3 change to 0.9 (Figure 6). Immediately after the 5000-th time unit (simulation time) the utilizations of hosts 1, 2 and 3 return to 0.5.

- **Experiment 5:** This is identical to experiment 1, except that the utilizations at nodes 1, 2 and 3 change from 0.5 to 1.2.

As it turns out from the simulation results as exemplified by experiments 4 and 5, the algorithm adapts smoothly to a change of increasing or decreasing workload. After a short transient time the average response time converges to the value we had observed for the corresponding system in a static environment (Figures 3, 4 and 5). In Figure 7 the solid curve indicates the behavior of the algorithm in a system changing environment when the initial threshold values are 10 for all the nodes. The dotted curve represents its behavior in the same environment but in this case threshold value is kept constant $T = 2$ for all the nodes. Note that in Figure 7, the difference between the dotted and solid curves during time units 10 to 20 represent the advantage of adapting the threshold over a static approach where the threshold is set to the optimal value for the steady state behavior.

5 Conclusions

In this paper we considered the problem of improving the performance of a distributed system by using balancing techniques to smooth-out periods of high congestion at individual nodes. For distributed systems running independent jobs it had been previously shown that threshold policies work well. We have extended this idea, by developing a distributed optimization algorithm based on a threshold policy and two gradient estimation techniques. The algorithm is shown to be efficient, and can be run on-line. The algorithm is iterative in nature and threshold parameters are updated at each iteration. Between updates, each host computes and exchanges with other hosts gradient information which is used to update load balancing parameters in the next iteration. Two different methods towards estimating the required gradients have been imbedded in the above distributed optimization algorithm. Both of them effectively provide sensitivity information estimates while the actual system is running (on-line estimation), by using real data gathered during an observation period. Simulation results have been produced for a system with five nodes. It turns out that after a small number of algorithm iterations the behavior of the system, in a static environment stabilizes in a neighborhood of the optimal performance. The adaptivity of the algorithm has also been studied in a dynamically changing system environment. Simulation results pointed out that the algorithm adapts smoothly to a change of the workload. It is interesting to notice that the overhead of exchanging gradients between the hosts of the distributed system is small, since the gradients are not instantaneous information such as queue lengths. When the system environment changes over time the algorithm can run in the background so that it can track the system variation in a quasi-static manner. Finally, although our approach is presented in the context of a specific threshold policy, it should be possible to use it with other policies.

Acknowledgments: The authors would like to thank C. Cassandras and S. Strickland for extensive discussions on the design of gradient estimators.

References

[1] C.G. CASSANDRAS, "On-Line Optimization of a Flow Control Strategy," to appear in *IEEE Trans. on Automatic Control*.

[2] D. EAGER, E. LAZOWSKA, J. ZAHORJAN, "Adaptive Load Sharing in Homogeneous Distributed Systems", *IEEE Trans. on Software Eng.*, SE-12, pp. 662-675, May 1986.

[3] R.G. GALLAGER, "A Minimum Delay Routing Algorithm Using Distributed Computation," *IEEE Trans. of Communications.*25, pp. 73-85, Jan. 1977.

[4] P.W. GLYNN, "Stochastic Approximation for Monte Carlo Optimization," *Proc. 1986 Winter Simulation Conf.*, J. Wilson, J.Henriksen, S. Roberts (eds.) IEEE Press, pp. 356-365, 1986.

[5] P. HEIDELBERGER, X.R. CAO, M.A. ZAZANIS, and R. SURI, "Convergence Properties of Infinitesimal Perturbation Estimates," IBM Research Report, Yorktown Heights, NY, 1987.

[6] P. HEIDELBERGER and D. TOWSLEY, "Sensitivity Analysis from Sample Paths Using Likelihoods," Tech Report 87-131, Dept. Comp. & Info. Science, Univ. Massachusetts, 1987.

[7] Y.C. HO and C.G. CASSANDRAS, "A New Approach to the Analysis of Discrete Event Dynamic Systems," *Automatica*, Vol. 19, pp. 149-167, 1983.

[8] J.F. KUROSE and R. SIMHA, "A Microeconomic Approach to Optimal File Allocation," *Proc. 6th International Conf. on Distr. Comp. Systems*, May 1986.

[9] J.F. KUROSE, R. SIMHA, Second Derivative Algorithms for Optimal Resource Allocation in Distributed Computer Systems, *Proc. 7th Int. Conf. on Distributed Computer Systems*, Sept. 1987.

[10] J.F. KUROSE and S. SINGH, "A Distributed Algorithm for Optimal Static Load Balancing in Distributed Computer Systems," *Proc. INFOCOM'86*, 1986.

[11] K. J. LEE, D. TOWSLEY, "Distributed Optimization Algorithms for Quasi-static Threshold Load Balancing," COINS Technical Report 87-113, U. Massachusetts, Oct. 1987.

[12] K. J. LEE, Load Balancing in Distributed Computer Systems, Ph.D. Thesis, Dept. of Elect. & Comp. Eng., Univ. of Massachusetts, 1987.

[13] K. J. LEE, D. TOWSLEY, "A Comparison of Priority-based Decentralized Load Balancing Policies", *Proc. of PERFORMANCE'86 and ACM Sigmetrics Conf.*, pp. 70-77, 1986.

[14] D. LUENBERGER, Introduction to Linear and Nonlinear Programming, Addison-Wesley, 1973.

[15] R. MIRCHANDANEY, J. STANKOVIC, "Using Stochastic Learning Automata for Job Scheduling in Distributed Processing Systems", *Journal of Parallel and Distributed Computing*, Vol. 3, pp.527-552, 1986.

[16] R. MIRCHANDANEY, D. TOWSLEY, J. STANKOVIC, "Analysis of the Effects of Delays on Load Sharing", to appear in *IEEE Trans. on Computers*.

[17] S. PULIDAS, D. TOWSLEY, J.A. STANKOVIC, "Design of Efficient Parameter Estimators for Decentralized Load Balancing Policies", Tech. Report 87-79, Dept. Comp. & Info. Science, Univ. of Massachusetts, 1987.

[18] M. REIMAN, A. WEISS, "Sensitivity Analysis for Simulations via Likelihood Ratios", *Proc. Winter Simulation Conf.*, 1986.

[19] R.Y. RUBINSTEIN, "On the Score Function Approach for Sensitivity Analysis of Computer Simulation Models," *Mathematics and Computers in Simulation*, Vol. 28, pp. 351-379, 1986.

[20] J. STANKOVIC, "Simulations of Three Adaptive, Decentralized Controlled, Job Scheduling Algorithms", *Computer Networks*, Vol. 8, pp. 199-217, 1984

[21] J. STANKOVIC, "An Application of Bayesian Decision Theory to Decentralized Control of Job Scheduling," *IEEE Trans. on Computers*, Vol. C-34, No. 2, pp. 117-130, Feb. 1985.

[22] S.G. STRICKLAND and C.G. CASSANDRAS, "Augmented Chain Analysis of Markov and Semi-Markov Processes," to appear in *Proc. 25th Allerton Conf.*.

[23] Y. WANG, R. MORRIS, "Load Sharing in Distributed Systems", *IEEE Trans. on Computers*, vol. 34, pp. 204-217, March 1985.

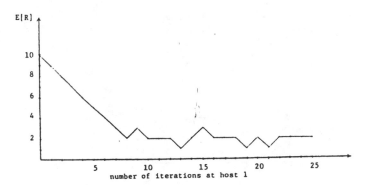

Fig. 2 - Behavior of the threshold updating algorithm at host-1 of a distributed system with 5 hosts
($T_1^{init} = ... = T_5^{init} = 10$ and $u_1 = ... = u_5 = 0.5$).

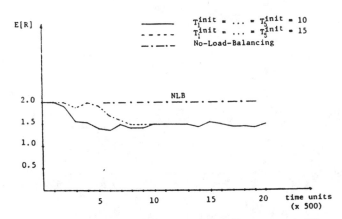

Fig. 3 - Average response time of a job in the system of five hosts
as a function of time ($u_1 = ... = u_5 = 0.5$).

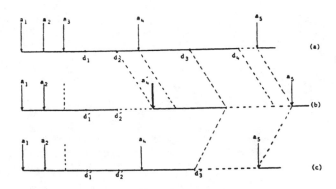

Fig. 1 - Estimation of gradients with respect to the threshold.

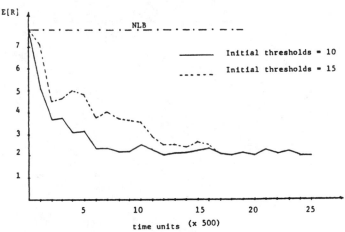

Fig. 4 - Average response time of a job in the system of five hosts as a function of time
($u_1 = u_2 = u_3 = 0.9$ and $u_4 = u_5 = 0.5$).

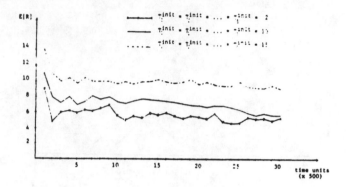

Fig. 5 - Average response time of a job in the system of
five hosts as a function of time
$(u_1 = u_2 = u_3 = 1.2$ and $u_4 = u_5 = 0.5)$.

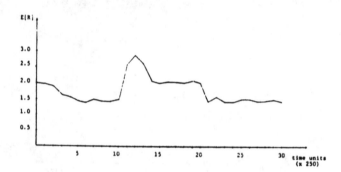

Fig. 6 - Behavior of the threshold updating algorithm in a
changing system
environment (utilization at nodes 1, 2 and 3 changes from
50% to 90% and back to 50%).

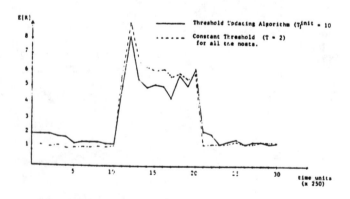

Fig. 7 - Behavior of the threshold updating algorithm in a
changing system
environment (utilization at nodes 1, 2 and 3 changes from
50% to 120% and back to 50%).

362

The Diverse Objectives of Distributed Scheduling Policies

Phillip Krueger and Miron Livny

Computer Sciences Department
University of Wisconsin - Madison
Madison, WI 53706

Abstract

A distributed scheduling policy for a general-purpose distributed system can be divided into two components: a *local scheduling discipline* determines how the CPU resource at a single node is allocated among its resident processes, while a *load distributing strategy* distributes the system workload among the nodes through process migration. Since several choices exist for each of these components, we are faced with a wide variety of distributed scheduling policies. In this paper, we address the question: Are some distributed scheduling policies better than others, or do they have different objectives? We find that there is significant diversity in objective and that the choice of an appropriate policy requires consideration of the performance expectations of the users together with the system workload characteristics.

1. Introduction

Scheduling for distributed systems is significantly more complex than for single-processor systems. A distributed scheduling policy for a general-purpose system can be divided into two components: a *local scheduling discipline* determines how the CPU resource at a single node is allocated among its resident processes, while a *load distributing strategy* distributes the system workload among the nodes through process migration. Eager, Lazowska and Zahorjan [Eager86] have noted that within the myriad load distributing algorithms proposed in the literature lie two distinct strategies for improving performance. *Load balancing* algorithms strive to equalize the workload among nodes, while *load sharing* algorithms simply attempt to assure that no node is idle while processes wait for service. Similarly, many choices exist for local scheduling disciplines, ranging from simple non-preemptive disciplines to those that are complex and preemptive. As a result, we are faced with a wide variety of distributed scheduling policies. In this paper, we address the question: Are some of these policies better than others, or do they have different performance objectives? In addition to identifying, comparing and evaluating the applicability of the objectives of distributed scheduling policies, this paper provides a unique perspective of the interaction between load distributing strategies and local scheduling disciplines in forming these objectives.

The users of a computer system have certain performance expectations. The goal of a scheduling policy is to allocate resources in such a way that these expectations are most nearly met. It is important, then, that the performance objectives of the scheduling policy match the expectations of the users as nearly as possible. However, just as there is no universal set of user expectations, no single performance objective is applicable to every system.

User performance expectations generally center on the quality of service provided to the processes they initiate. In addition to the average quality of service received, fairness is an important concern. Two users simultaneously initiating equivalent processes expect to receive about the same quality of service. Similarly, a user submitting the same job several times, under equivalent workloads, expects each to receive about the same quality of service. To ensure fairness, the variance in quality of service under a given workload should be acceptably low.

A second aspect of fairness relates to the way in which quality of service is measured. Both wait time and wait ratio are accepted measures of the quality of service received by a process. Wait time is the total amount of time a process spends waiting for resources, while wait ratio is the wait time per unit of service. Which measure is used carries an implied assumption about the importance of fairness. The use of wait time implies that the important factor in assessing quality of service is the absolute amount of time one waits for a resource, *regardless* of one's service demand. A person wanting to check out a book from a library and a person requesting a complete library tour would be considered to have received equal service if each waited the same amount of time for the attention of the librarian. The use of wait ratio implies that the important factor is the amount of time one waits for a resource *relative* to one's service demand. In providing equal quality of service, the person requesting an exhaustive library tour would be expected to wait longer for that service than the person wanting to borrow a book. The use of wait ratio, in preference to wait time, allows a more fair comparison of quality of service received.

Finally, fairness may imply that scheduling is *non-discriminatory*: variation in quality of service received by processes should be strictly random. The correlation between the quality-of-service metric and service demand can be used to measure an important aspect of discrimination in scheduling.

While previous performance studies have often been limited to mean wait time, we examine a broad range of performance indices, including the means and standard deviations of process wait times and wait ratios, and the correlations between wait ratio and service demand and between wait time and service demand. To identify the performance objectives of distributed scheduling policies, we examine performance in the absence of scheduling overhead. This idealized framework allows a scheduling policy to achieve its best-case performance bound, which defines its performance objective. How nearly this objective can be met under more realistic assumptions is dependent on the efficiency with which primitive scheduling operations, such as context switching and message handling for migration, are implemented and on system workload characteristics. The effects of these factors are examined in [Krueg87]. In the following pages, we show that:

- Some performance objectives are better met by load balancing than load sharing. Which strategy best meets a given objective may depend on workload characteristics.

Reprinted from *Proceedings IEEE 7th International Conference on Distributed Computing Systems,* 1987, pp. 242–249.

- The choice of local scheduling discipline may be more important than the choice of load distributing strategy in determining performance.

- Optimization of some performance indices is mutually exclusive.

- Migrations between nodes with queue lengths differing by one can be productive.

We conclude that the choice of an appropriate distributed scheduling policy requires consideration of the performance expectations of the users together with the system workload characteristics. No single policy is best for all systems.

2. Distributed System Model

The models used in this study are an extension of the m*(M/M/1) family of distributed system models proposed by Livny [Livny82, Livny83], augmented to allow the processor queuing discipline, or *local scheduling discipline*, to be specified as a parameter and to allow hyperexponentially, as well as exponentially, distributed task service demands. It is important that hyperexponential service demand distributions be considered, as those that have been observed [Rosin65, Trive82, Zhou86] are poorly approximated by exponential distributions. We categorize service demand distributions according to C_X (see table 2.1 for notation), with exponential distributions having $C_X = 1$ and hyperexponential distributions having $C_X > 1$.

The resulting m*(M/H/1) system, illustrated in figure 2.1, consists of m nodes, connected by a communication device. A load distributing algorithm allows processes to migrate between nodes at any time during their execution. Each of the m processing elements provides identical functional capabilities. Tasks arrive independently at each node and join the queue. The distribution of interarrival times is exponential, so the task arrival process of the system consists of m independent Poisson processes.

In this study, we assume that nodes have equal processing bandwidths and that the service demands of processes arriving at different nodes are identically distributed. The rates at which processes initially arrive (as opposed to arriving as the result of migration), however, may be different at different nodes. We refer to such a workload as having *inhomogeneous initiation rates*. Studying load distributing under such a workload is important. Mutka and Livny [Mutka87] have observed that, on a collection of workstations, user processes had executed within the previous 7 minutes on an average of only 30% of the nodes, varying with time of day from 18% to 53% of the nodes. Based on this data, we expect process initiation rates in some distributed systems to be generally inhomogene-ous, with wide variability in the degree of inhomogeneity. Since we are interested in scheduling for general-purpose computer systems, we assume that the scheduler has no deterministic a priori information about process service demands. In addition, we assume that processes do not leave the system before completing service.

With one final assumption, we arrive at the M/H/m-like system, on which this study is based. We assume that no work is associated with scheduling; both context switches and process migrations are instantaneous and without cost. The M/H/m-like system is the distributed-queue analogue of the M/H/m queue, from which it derives its name. As such, it provides a vantage-point for identifying the performance objectives of distributed scheduling policies. Within this idealized framework, a scheduling policy is able to achieve its best-case performance bound for a given workload. This best-case bound defines the performance objective of the scheduling policy.

To allow an M/H/m-like system to be *work-conserving* [Klein76], its local scheduling discipline must not allow its server to lie idle while processes wait in the queue. Correspondingly, its load distributing strategy must guarantee that no node is idle while processes wait for service. Such a system assures that "no work (service requirement) is created or destroyed within the system." [Klein76] If scheduling is non-preemptive and $C_X = 1$, $\overline{WT}$ in a work-conserving system is [Laven83]:

$$\overline{WT} = \overline{X} \left[(\overline{N} / m\rho) - 1 \right] \qquad \text{for } \rho < 1 \qquad (2.1)$$

Simulation results indicate that this equation also holds for all preemptive disciplines studied in this paper. Kleinrock sums up the lack of discriminatory power inherent in this performance index ([Klein76] page 171): "One may therefore conclude that the average response time by itself is not a very good indicator of system performance."

3. Performance Objectives

Our approach to identifying the objectives of distributed scheduling policies is to separately identify the objectives of load distributing strategies and those of local scheduling disciplines. We then examine the performance of scheduling policies using combinations of these components. To simplify analysis, Round Robin scheduling is approximated by Processor Sharing (PS) [Klein67]. For a description of the remaining local scheduling disciplines studied, the reader is referred to [Klein76].

To begin, we note that in an M/H/m-like system, both the LB and LS strategies are work-conserving. None of the work potential of the system is wasted by leaving nodes idle while processes wait.

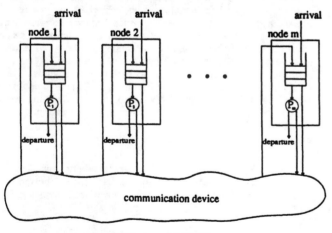

Figure 2.1 An m*(M/H/1) system

m	number of nodes
n	total number of resident processes
$\overline{N}$	mean number of resident processes
ρ	system load
x	service demand of a process
$\overline{X}$	mean process service demand
σ_X	standard deviation of service demand
C_X	coefficient of variation $= \sigma_X / \overline{X}$
$\overline{WT}$	mean process wait time
$\overline{WR}$	mean process wait ratio
σ_{WT}	standard deviation of wait time
σ_{WR}	standard deviation of wait ratio
$r(wait\ time, X)$	correlation between wait time and service demand
$r(wait\ ratio, X)$	correlation between wait ratio and service demand

Table 2.1 Notation

However, unlike LS, LB goes beyond conservation of work. By balancing the workload among nodes, each process residing in the system perceives approximately the same level of contention. If the local scheduling discipline is PS, each resident process receives service at approximately the same rate. Thus, LB in an M/H/m-like system emulates PS in an M/H/m system, with the goal of achieving similar performance. Essentially, LB is the distributed analogue of PS. LS, on the other hand, is the distributed analogue of any work-conserving M/H/m scheduling discipline.

This perspective of load distributing strategies allows us to predict the differences in performance between the LB and LS strategies in M/H/m-like systems through a less complicated study of performance in M/H/m queues, where many analytical results are available. In effect, the search for the performance objectives of these strategies is greatly simplified. These performance objectives are then validated through a study of performance in M/H/m-like systems. A second benefit of this perspective is that it allows us to identify a new load distributing strategy.

Unfortunately, identifying the objectives of local scheduling disciplines is more complicated than identifying those of load distributing strategies. Even when the system arrival process is Poisson, load distributing results in non-Poisson arrival processes for individual queues. Local scheduling disciplines, then, operate on G/G/1 queues. Since some of our results for M/H/m queues also apply to G/G/1, we are able to identify some local scheduling objectives. The remaining predictions are validated through a study of performance in M/H/m-like systems. Performance is studied both analytically and through simulation, with simulation results having less than 3% error at the 95% confidence level. Unless otherwise noted, results are from simulation.

3.1. Performance of Single-Queue Scheduling Disciplines

Since both LB and LS are concerned with conservation of work, with this being the sole goal of LS, we begin by considering work-conserving M/H/m scheduling disciplines. As analogues for LS, we consider non-preemptive M/H/m scheduling disciplines, since preemption gives no advantage in conserving work. When necessary, we specifically consider First-Come-First-Served (FCFS), since it is perhaps the simplest M/H/m scheduling discipline and has few goals beyond conservation of work. Simulation results displayed in figure 3.1 show that $\overline{WT}$ for FCFS, increases with C_X, as does σ_{WT}. In this plot, as well as all other plots of these indices, $\overline{WT}$ and σ_{WT} are normalized by $\overline{X}$. In their favor, work-conserving non-preemptive scheduling disciplines are non-discriminatory with respect to wait time; process wait times are independent of their service demands. However, non-preemptive scheduling has disastrous consequences for $\overline{WR}$ and σ_{WR}. In [Krueg87a], it is proven that all such disciplines result in infinite $\overline{WR}$ and σ_{WR} for G/H/m or G/H/m-like systems. These statistics become finite only when the processes having the highest wait ratios, those having the shortest service demands, are ignored.

PS is the single-queue analogue of LB. Similar to FCFS, PS is a non-discriminatory scheduling discipline, but with respect to wait *ratio*, rather than wait time. Since, when random variables Y and Z are independent, $E[g(Y)h(Z)] = E[g(Y)]E[h(Z)]$, this property allows $\overline{WR}$ for PS to be easily derived from eq. 2.1:

$$\overline{WT} = E((\text{wait time } / x)(x)) = E((\text{wait ratio})(x)) = \overline{WR}\,\overline{X}$$

$$\overline{WR} = \overline{WT} / \overline{X} = (\overline{N} / m\rho) - 1 \qquad \text{for } \rho < 1 \quad (3.1)$$

---

1. When $C_X > 1$, we assume a 2-phase hyperexponential distribution, with 70% of service demands drawn from the phase having the smaller mean.

An important property of PS is that $\overline{WR}$ and σ_{WR} are finite for stable ($\rho < 1$) M/H/m and G/G/1 queues (see [Krueg87a]). Another advantage of PS over non-preemptive disciplines is that $\overline{WT}$ is independent of C_X [Laven83]. Regardless of C_X, $\overline{WT}$ for PS is given by eq. 2.1. Thus, as shown in figure 3.1, PS results in lower $\overline{WT}$ than FCFS when $C_X > 1$, as well as lower σ_{WT} for high C_X. Since $\overline{WT}$ is independent of C_X, eq. 3.1 shows that $\overline{WR}$ is also independent of C_X. Simulation results displayed in figure 3.2 validate that $\overline{WR}$ is independent of C_X and show that the same is true for σ_{WR}.

Unlike FCFS and PS, simulations show Last-Come-First-Served-Preemptive-Resume (LCFSPR) to be a discriminatory scheduling policy, giving better quality of service, both in terms of wait time and wait ratio, to processes having short service demands. Figure 3.2 shows that $\overline{WR}$ and σ_{WR} *decrease* with increasing C_X, though σ_{WT} increases (figure 3.1). Based on these results, we can predict that load distributing algorithms in M/H/m-like systems that discriminate by providing better service to processes having short service demands will reduce $\overline{WR}$ with respect to those that are non-discriminatory. However, this reduction may come at the cost of increased σ_{WT}.

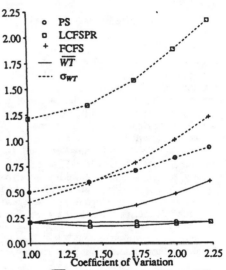

Figure 3.1 $\overline{WT}$ and σ_{WT} vs. C_X ($m = 10$, $\rho = 0.8$)

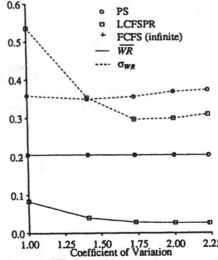

Figure 3.2 $\overline{WR}$ and σ_{WR} vs. C_X ($m = 10$, $\rho = 0.8$)

To summarize, conservation of work is not sufficient to provide finite $\overline{WR}$ or σ_{WR}. Even when the 1% of processes having the highest wait ratios are trimmed from the sample, simulations show that FCFS results in considerably higher $\overline{WR}$ and σ_{WR} than PS or LCFSPR. For example, when $C_X = 1$, $\overline{WR}$ for FCFS is over 400% that for PS, while σ_{WR} is over 1300%. These values increase rapidly with C_X, to over 12000% for $\overline{WR}$ and 40000% for σ_{WR} at $C_X = 2.24$. Additionally, conservation of work is not sufficient to minimize $\overline{WT}$ when $C_X > 1$. Figure 3.1 shows that both PS and LCFSPR result in lower $\overline{WT}$ than FCFS under such a workload. In addition, PS results in lower σ_{WT} than FCFS for high C_X. Applying these results to distributed scheduling policies, the use of PS as a local scheduling discipline will result in finite $\overline{WR}$ and σ_{WR}, while the use of FCFS or any other non-preemptive discipline will result in infinite $\overline{WR}$ and σ_{WR}. We can predict that the use of PS will result in lower $\overline{WT}$ than any non-preemptive discipline when $C_X > 1$ and lower σ_{WT} for high C_X. Using the perspective of LB as the distributed analogue of PS and LS as the analogue of FCFS, we can predict that LB will result in lower $\overline{WT}$ than LS when $C_X > 1$, lower σ_{WT} for high C_X and, when LB is allied with PS as a local scheduling discipline, lower $\overline{WR}$ and σ_{WR} than LS under all conditions.

3.2. Performance of Distributed-Queue Scheduling Policies

3.2.1. Load Sharing (LS)

Under LS, simulations show that $\overline{WR}$, σ_{WR}, $r(wait\ ratio, X)$ and $r(wait\ time, X)$ are dependent on the level of inhomogeneity in the rates at which processes initiate at individual nodes. Performance in terms of these indices is generally best when initiation rates are homogeneous, and worst when all processes initiate at a single node. An additional complication of LS is that all of the performance indices studied are dependent on the criteria used to select a process to migrate. We will consider the two bounding criteria: First-Come-First-Migrate (FCFM) selects the process that has least recently arrived at the node, either through initiation or migration, while Last-Come-First-Migrate (LCFM) selects the most recent arrival. By giving an advantage to processes having short service demands, LCFM captures some of the properties of LCFSPR, reducing $\overline{WR}$ with respect to that of FCFM but increasing σ_{WT}, while FCFM retains the properties of FCFS. These differences are accentuated when process initiation rates are inhomogeneous.

Since LS is concerned solely with conserving work, it is naturally allied with a local scheduling discipline that shares this narrow perspective, such as FCFS. This partnership, which we refer to as LS_FCFS, results in a simple distributed scheduling policy that, in an M/H/m-like system, minimizes $\overline{WT}$ for workloads having $C_X = 1$. In addition, when $C_X = 1$, LS_FCFS generally results in lower σ_{WT} than policies using PS for small numbers of nodes or high system loads. However, as predicted in the previous section, $\overline{WT}$ increases with increasing C_X (figures 3.3 and 3.4) as does σ_{WT}. Also as predicted, the single-minded concern of LS_FCFS with conserving work is an insufficient perspective from which to improve $\overline{WR}$ and σ_{WR}. As shown in [Krueg87a], these statistics are infinite, becoming finite only if the processes having the highest wait ratios, which are those having the shortest service demands, are ignored. Simulations show that, even when the shortest processes are removed from the sample, $\overline{WR}$ and σ_{WR} are considerably higher for LS_FCFS than for distributed scheduling policies using PS as a local scheduling discipline.

Pairing LS with PS appears inconsistent, since LS is solely concerned with conservation of work, while PS has broader goals. However, studying this hybrid distributed scheduling policy provides insight into the relative effects on performance of the local scheduling discipline and the load distributing strategy. LS_PS corrects many of the weaknesses of LS_FCFS. One of the most important consequences of merging LS with PS is that $\overline{WR}$ and σ_{WR} are finite [Krueg87a]. In addition, LS_PS reduces the degrading effect of increasing C_X on $\overline{WT}$ (figures 3.3 and 3.4) and on σ_{WT}. However, inhomogeneity in initiation rates continues to have a degrading effect on performance, as can be seen in figures 3.3 through 3.10. Simulations show that this degradation in performance is continuous with increasing inhomogeneity, rather than occurring suddenly at high levels of inhomogeneity. Like LS_FCFS, performance under LS_PS is also dependent on the migration selection criterion, with LCFM providing lower $\overline{WR}$ and σ_{WR}, while FCFM results in lower σ_{WT}.

3.2.2. Load Balancing (LB)

True PS scheduling in a multiple-queue system, such as an M/H/m-like system, is not feasible, since it requires an infinite migration rate. Such a migration rate is necessary to provide service at the same rate to all resident processes when there are more processes than nodes and $n\ mod\ m \neq 0$. The goal of the LB strategy is to approximate PS scheduling, achieving similar performance, but with a finite migration rate.

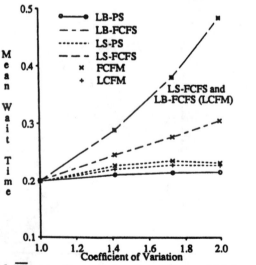

Figure 3.3 $\overline{WT}$ vs. C_X assuming homogeneous initiation rates ($m = 10$, $\rho = 0.8$)

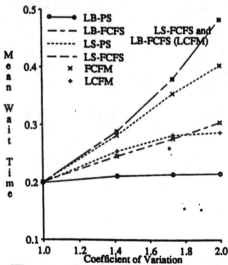

Figure 3.4 $\overline{WT}$ vs. C_X assuming all process initiations at a single node ($m = 10$, $\rho = 0.8$)

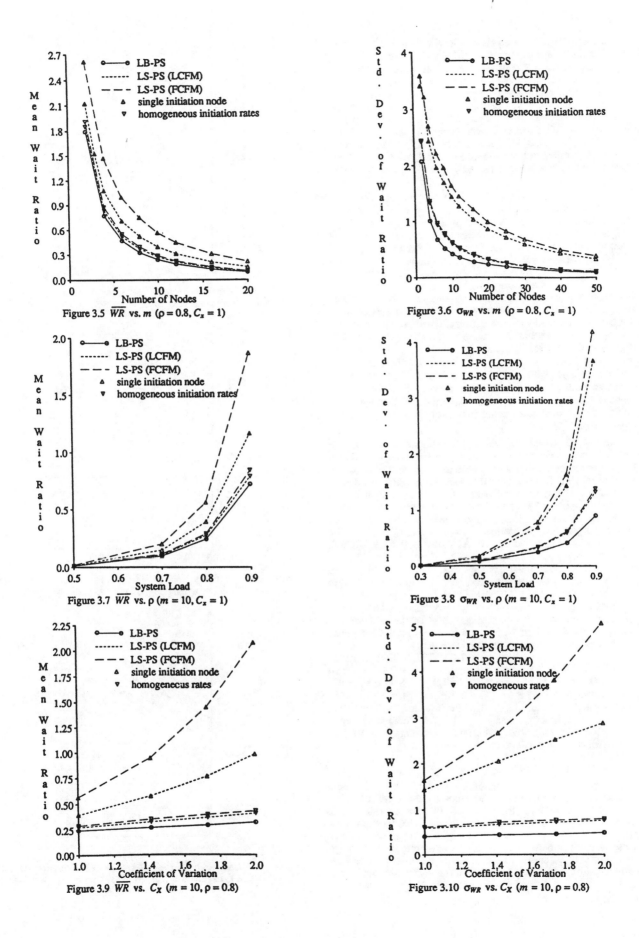

Figure 3.5 $\overline{WR}$ vs. m ($\rho = 0.8$, $C_x = 1$)

Figure 3.6 σ_{WR} vs. m ($\rho = 0.8$, $C_x = 1$)

Figure 3.7 $\overline{WR}$ vs. ρ ($m = 10$, $C_x = 1$)

Figure 3.8 σ_{WR} vs. ρ ($m = 10$, $C_x = 1$)

Figure 3.9 $\overline{WR}$ vs. C_X ($m = 10$, $\rho = 0.8$)

Figure 3.10 σ_{WR} vs. C_X ($m = 10$, $\rho = 0.8$)

LB is naturally allied with PS as a local scheduling discipline. In [Krueg87a], $\overline{WR}$ and an upper bound for σ_{WR} are derived for LB_PS. In contrast to LS, neither of these performance indices is dependent on the homogeneity of process initiation rates or the criteria used to select a process to migrate. Through simulation, we have shown that the remaining performance indices are independent of these factors, as well. How closely LB_PS achieves its goal of emulating PS scheduling can be seen in figures 3.11 through 3.13. In terms of $\overline{WT}$ and σ_{WT}, LB_PS is identical to PS scheduling under all conditions. For other performance indices, LB_PS best approximates PS at high system loads, for small numbers of nodes or for low C_X.

As shown in figures 3.5 through 3.10, LB_PS achieves lower $\overline{WR}$ and σ_{WR}, under all conditions, than any other distributed scheduling policy examined. When all processes initiate at a single node, figures 3.14 through 3.16 show that LB_PS results in considerable improvement in these indices over its nearest competitor, LS_PS(*LCFM*). However, when process initiation rates are homogeneous, improvement is large only for σ_{WR}. In addition, as predicted, LB_PS results in lower $\overline{WT}$ than any other policy when $C_X > 1$ (figures 3.3 and 3.4) and lower σ_{WT} when C_X is high. These advantages of LB_PS over LS_PS(*LCFM*) are even greater when inhomogeneous initiation rates are coupled with service demands having $C_X > 1$. For a system having 16 nodes, a system load of 0.8, C_X=2.24 and all processes initiating at a single node, the difference in performance between LB_PS and LS_PS(*LCFM*) is 280% for $\overline{WR}$, 575% for σ_{WR}, 30% for $\overline{WT}$ and 90% for σ_{WT}. Improvement under such conditions is important, since, as noted in chapter 2, inhomogeneous initiation rates and hyperexponentially distributed service demands are likely to be common in many general-purpose distributed systems.

Like LS_PS, pairing LB with FCFS as a local scheduling discipline results in a distributed scheduling policy with inconsistent goals. However, since FCFS is simple to implement and can be expected to result in less overhead than most local scheduling disciplines, it is interesting to examine how nearly the performance of LB_FCFS approaches that of LB_PS. In addition, studying such a hybrid policy allows us to gauge the relative effects on performance of its two components. Unfortunately, the influence of FCFS on WR and σ_{WR} is greater than that of LB. As shown in [Krueg87a], both $\overline{WR}$ and σ_{WR} are infinite under LB_FCFS. Even when the shortest processes are ignored, simulations show that, while not as high as for LS_FCFS, $\overline{WR}$ and σ_{WR} are much higher than for LB_PS. Also showing similarity to LS_FCFS rather than LB_PS, performance is dependent on C_X, the level of inhomogeneity in initiation rates and the process selection criterion. Using FCFM as the selection criterion generally results in better performance than LCFM, since LCFM causes the same processes to be repeatedly migrated. Showing the influence of the LB strategy LB_FCFS(*FCFM*) results in lower $\overline{WT}$ than LS_FCFS for $C_X > 1$ (figures 3.3 and 3.4). When all processes initiate at a single node, $\overline{WT}$ for LB_FCFS(*FCFM*) is also generally lower than LS_PS for $C_X > 1$. LB_FCFS(*FCFM*) exhibits another characteristic trait of LB: it is discriminatory with respect to wait time. This trait arises because LB_FCFS(*FCFM*) is a preemptive discipline; processes that have begun service may not continue to receive service immediately after migrating.

3.2.3. Load Shuffling (LSh)

LB_PS differs from PS scheduling in that not all processes receive service at the same rate when there are more processes than nodes and $n \bmod m \neq 0$. However, LB_PS can be extended to approximate PS scheduling arbitrarily closely by periodically varying the set of processes that receive service at a faster rate. We refer to these migrations between nodes differing by one in queue length as *shuffling* and to the resultant load distributing strategy as Load Shuffling (LSh). As the length of the *inter-shuffle time* approaches

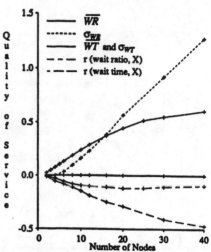

Figure 3.11 Comparison of LB_PS with PS. All indices except r(*wait ratio*, X) are plotted as (LB_PS - PS) / PS. ($\rho = 0.8$, $C_x = 1$)

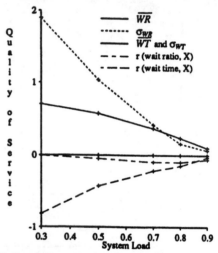

Figure 3.12 Comparison of LB_PS with PS. All indices except r(*wait ratio*, X) are plotted as (LB_PS - PS) / PS. ($m = 10$, $C_x = 1$)

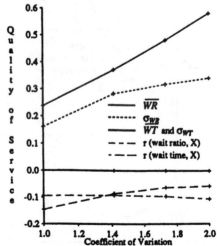

Figure 3.13 Comparison of LB_PS with PS. All indices except r(*wait ratio*, X) are plotted as (LB_PS - PS) / PS. ($m = 10$, $\rho = 0.8$)

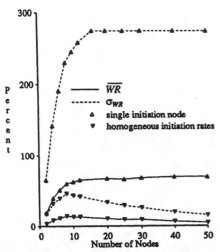

Figure 3.14 Comparison of LB_PS with LS_PS(*LCFM*): Percent difference in $\overline{WR}$ and σ_{WR} ($100(LS - LB) / LB$) vs. m ($\rho = 0.8, C_x = 1$)

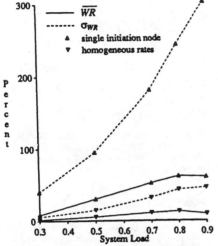

Figure 3.15 Comparison of LB_PS with LS_PS(*LCFM*): Percent difference in $\overline{WR}$ and σ_{WR} ($100(LS - LB) / LB$) vs. ρ ($m = 10, C_x = 1$)

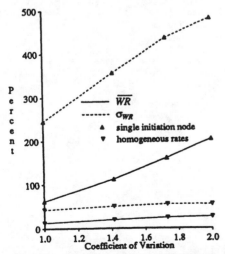

Figure 3.16 Comparison of LB_PS with LS_PS(*LCFM*): Percent difference in $\overline{WR}$ and σ_{WR} ($100(LS - LB) / LB$) vs. C_X ($m = 10, \rho = 0.8$)

zero, the performance of LSh_PS more closely approximates that of PS. LCFM is not a suitable process selection criterion for LSh, since it results in the same process being repeatedly migrated. This property undermines the goal of LSh, which is to give equal service to all resident processes. The difference in performance between LB_PS in an M/H/m-like system and PS in in M/H/m queue is the potential improvement in performance that can result from LSh_PS. Figure 3.17 plots the percentage of this potential improvement that is achieved by LSh_PS against inter-shuffle time. Surprisingly, migrations between nodes that differ in load by one can significantly reduce $\overline{WR}$, σ_{WR} and r (*wait ratio*, X). This improvement may be large under conditions in which LB_PS poorly approximates PS scheduling: low system load, high C_X or a large number of nodes.

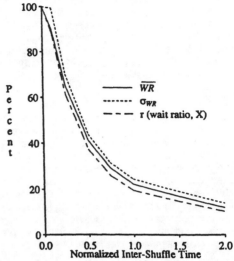

Figure 3.17 Percentage of potential improvement achieved through shuffling (100 (LB_PS - PS) / (LSh_PS - PS)) vs. normalized intershuffle time (intershuffle time / $\overline{X}$) ($m = 10, \rho = 0.8, C_x = 1$)

3.3. Conclusions: Distributed Scheduling Objectives

From our study, we can identify the performance objectives of each of the components of a distributed scheduling policy in terms of a broad range of performance indices.

Among local scheduling disciplines, any work-conserving discipline, such as FCFS, minimizes $\overline{WT}$ when $C_X = 1$. However, conservation of work does not address the wait ratio perspective of quality-of-service. $\overline{WR}$ and σ_{WR} are infinite for many work-conserving disciplines, including all non-preemptive disciplines, such as FCFS. Alternatively, PS has the broader goal of providing finite $\overline{WR}$ and σ_{WR} and minimizing r (*wait ratio*, X). In addition, PS results in lower $\overline{WT}$ than non-preemptive disciplines when $C_X > 1$ and lower σ_{WT} when C_X is high.

Among load distributing strategies, the objective of LS is to reduce $\overline{WT}$ with respect to no load distributing, minimizing it when $C_X = 1$. Like non-preemptive local scheduling disciplines, LS does not address the wait ratio perspective of quality-of-service. The broader objective of LB is to reduce $\overline{WR}$ and σ_{WR} with respect to LS under all conditions, and to reduce $\overline{WT}$ relative to LS when $C_X \geq 1$. Finally, the performance objective of LSh is to further reduce $\overline{WR}$ and σ_{WR} with respect to LB, and to minimize r (*wait ratio*, X).

369

When a load distributing strategy and local scheduling discipline are chosen to have matching performance characteristics, the resultant distributed scheduling policy mirrors those characteristics. However, when a distributed scheduling policy has components with inconsistent objectives, its performance is a hybrid of the objective of each component. For such distributed scheduling policies, while the load distributing strategy has a significant effect on $\overline{WR}$ and σ_{WR}, the effect of the local scheduling discipline on these indices is more fundamental, since it determines whether they are finite. In contrast, figures 3.3 and 3.4 show that the relative effect of the load distributing strategy and local scheduling discipline on $\overline{WT}$ is dependent on the workload. The local scheduling discipline has greater effect when process initiation rates are homogeneous, while the load distributing strategy is more influential when all processes initiate at a single node.

In certain situations, these hybrid policies may be useful. If $\overline{WR}$ is considered important, but σ_{WR} is not, and if $C_X \approx 1$ and process initiation rates are generally homogeneous, LS_PS may be a suitable replacement for LB_PS. Alternatively, if only $\overline{WT}$ is considered important, but $C_X > 1$ or process initiation rates are often inhomogeneous, LB_FCFS may provide significantly lower $\overline{WT}$ than LS_FCFS, though not as low as results from LB_PS.

4. Summary

Much insight can be gained into the performance objectives of distributed scheduling policies by examining performance from a broader perspective than mean wait time. By considering a relatively large set of performance indices, we have shown that different scheduling policies have considerably different objectives and result in significantly different performance. However, since each index has significance only in terms of the performance expectations of the users, no single policy can be identified as being best for all systems. To choose the components of a policy suitable to a particular system, the performance expectations of the users together with the system workload characteristics must be considered.

As a load distributing strategy, LS is suitable only for those systems having narrow performance objectives and tightly constrained workloads: $C_X \approx 1$ and generally homogeneous process initiation rates. More typical workloads or broader performance objectives necessitate the use of LB. Among local scheduling disciplines, a non-preemptive discipline, such as FCFS, may be used when $\overline{WR}$ and σ_{WR} can be ignored. When the performance objective of the system includes $\overline{WR}$ and σ_{WR}, a preemptive discipline that gives immediate service to newly arriving processes, such as PS, is necessary.

With consideration for the humanistic appeal of a performance metric that includes $\overline{WR}$ and σ_{WR}, together with the likelihood of workloads having inhomogeneous initiation rates and $C_X > 1$, we believe that LB_PS has broad applicability to general-purpose distributed systems. However, this observation is incomplete without considering the relative resource overheads of LB and LS. In [Krueg87], we compare these overheads and their effects on the performance resulting from each of these strategies. We find that the distinction between the LB and LS strategies is obscured. The best strategy to meet a given objective is dependent on the overheads of individual load distributing operations, as well as on dynamic characteristics of the workload and resource availability. To be effective at meeting either the LB or the LS objective over the wide range of conditions occurring within a distributed system, a load distributing algorithm must be adaptive.

References

[Eager86] D. L. Eager, E. D. Lazowska, and J. Zahorjan, "Adaptive Load Sharing in Homogeneous Distributed Systems," *IEEE Transactions on Software Engineering SE-12, 5*, pp. 662-675 (May 1986).

[Klein67] L. Kleinrock, "Time-Shared Systems: A Theoretical Treatment," *Journal of the ACM 14*, pp. 242-261 (1967).

[Klein76] L. Kleinrock, *Queuing Systems: Volume 2, Computer Applications*, John Wiley & Sons (1976).

[Krueg87a] P. Krueger and M. Livny, "Load Balancing, Load Sharing and Performance in Distributed Systems," Technical Report 700, University of Wisconsin–Madison, Dept. of Computer Sciences (July 1987).

[Krueg87] P. Krueger and M. Livny, "When is the Best Load Sharing Algorithm a Load Balancing Algorithm?," Technical Report 694, University of Wisconsin–Madison, Dept. of Computer Sciences (April 1987).

[Laven83] S. S. Lavenberg, *Computer Performance Modeling Handbook*, Academic Press (1983).

[Livny82] M. Livny and M. Melman, "Load balancing in homogeneous broadcast distributed systems," *Computer Network Performance Symposium*, pp. 47-55 (April 1982).

[Livny83] M. Livny, The Study of Load Balancing Algorithms for Decentralized Distributed Processing Systems, PhD Thesis, Weizmann Institute of Science, Rehovot, Israel (available as Technical Report 570, University of Wisconsin–Madison Computer Sciences) (August 1983).

[Mutka87] M. Mutka and M. Livny, "Profiling Workstation's Available Capacity for Remote Execution," Technical Report 697, University of Wisconsin–Madison, Dept. of Computer Sciences (May 1987).

[Rosin65] R. F. Rosin, "Determining a Computing Center Environment," *CACM 8*, 7, (July 1965).

[Trive82] K. S. Trivedi, *Probability & Statistics with Reliability, Queuing and Computer Science Applications*, Prentice-Hall (1982).

[Zhou86] S. Zhou, "A Trace-Driven Simulation Study of Dynamic Load Balancing," Technical Report, UCB/CSD 87/305, Computer Science Division, University of California, Berkeley (September 1986).

Effects of Response and Stability on Scheduling in Distributed Computing Systems

THOMAS L. CASAVANT, MEMBER, IEEE, AND JON G. KUHL, MEMBER, IEEE

Abstract—This paper quantitatively examines the effects of response and stability on scheduling algorithms for general-purpose distributed computing systems. Response characterizes the time required, following a perturbation in the system state, to reach a new equilibrium state. Stability is a measure of the ability of a mechanism to detect when the effects of further actions (which potentially consume the resource being scheduled) will not improve the system state as defined by a user-defined objective. These results have implications for distributed computations in general. Analysis is performed through the exercise of formal communicating finite automata models of two distinct approaches to the scheduling problem, each employing the objective of global optimal load balancing. The results indicate that absolute stability, as defined here, is not always necessary in dynamic systems for the same reasons that relatively small amounts of instability are tolerated in the design of analog control systems. It is also shown that response is a very important first-order metric of dynamic scheduling behavior, and that response and stability are related. As a paradigm for distributed computations in general, the schedulers examined reveal much about algorithm behavior.

Index Terms—Communicating finite automata, distributed algorithm modeling and analysis, distributed systems, load balancing, response, scheduling, stability.

I. INTRODUCTION

SCHEDULING algorithms for computer systems are the operating system components which function continuously to manage the processing resource (among others) in the system. Proper design of such mechanisms has a great impact on overall system behavior. This design problem becomes two-dimensional in the domain of distributed computing systems since not only the question of *when* to execute, but also *where* to execute a particular task must be addressed. Towards this goal, many approaches to the problem have been tried, with variously reported results [3].

The design and analysis of distributed scheduling algorithms (DSA's) for large dynamic systems is complicated because there are a number of related factors which influence the aggregate behavior of the system and its scheduler. Two such factors are *response* and *stability*. While these are not the only factors influencing aggregate behavior, they are of particular interest since they are

commonly discussed in the literature as either absolute requirements (stability) [1] or as strongly influential (response) in terms of their effect upon overall system behavior. The modeling technique given in [2] provides precise definitions of these terms as they apply to decision-making in distributed systems. Intuitively, response is a measure of how rapidly a scheduler reacts to restore the system to an equilibrium state following a perturbation from equilibrium. Stability relates to the amount of schedulable resource being consumed while the system state is changing, but not moving toward a more optimal state.

This paper addresses the relationship between the particular characteristics of response and stability and the aggregate characteristics of performance and efficiency. We define performance to be the degree to which an algorithm achieves its global objective, and efficiency to be a measure of the costs (e.g., resources consumed) associated with this level of goal achievement.

This paper describes experiments which measure the performance and efficiency of a class of distributed algorithms. Each of the chosen algorithms is in the category of global, dynamic, physically distributed, cooperative, optimal or suboptimal, approximate or heuristic techniques. Furthermore, the algorithms have the (globally defined) objective of load balancing, may be either adaptive or nonadaptive, and may involve one-time assignment or dynamic reassignment of tasks. The two strategies are based on the following philosophies.

1) Bidirectional Multilateral (BDML): This is a simple heuristic approach based on limited assumptions regarding the amount and type of information available to each node[1] of the scheduling algorithm. This information consists of a scalar value describing the desirability of the neighboring node accepting load from the node receiving the (scalar) information. Furthermore, each node may either choose to transfer a fraction of its own load to one or more of its own neighbors or request a fraction of the load from one or more of its neighbors.

2) Bidding: This is an application of the three-step contract net protocol [12]. In the first step, a request for bids is broadcast. In the second step, bids are received by the node which requested the bids, and in the third step, contracts are awarded and broadcast to the bidders.

Each algorithm variation has been completely and for-

Manuscript received June 23, 1986; revised June 6, 1988.

T. L. Casavant was with the Department of Electrical and Computer Engineering, University of Iowa, Iowa City, IA 52242. He is now with the School of Electrical Engineering, Purdue University, West Lafayette, IN 47907.

J. G. Kuhl is with the Department of Electrical and Computer Engineering, University of Iowa, Iowa City, IA 52242.

IEEE Log Number 8823660.

[1]Node refers to the computation on a local processor which executes to carry out the global scheduling policy.

Reprinted from *IEEE Trans. on Software Eng.*, vol. 14, no. 11, Nov. 1988, pp. 1578–1588.

mally specified using a communicating finite automata (CFA) modeling technique, as briefly described in the next section. These models were then automatically analyzed using a simulation-like method of model *exercising* to derive quantitative results.

Section II is an overview of the essential components of the model and provides definitions of the metrics of behavior used. Section III presents the analysis methods, specifies the algorithms, and discusses results of the analyses. Section IV makes some concluding remarks.

II. Quantitative Model Overview and Definitions

This section provides a brief overview of the CFA modeling technique [2] for the analysis of distributed decision-making (DDM) algorithms. This technique allows different mechanisms to be described uniformly under a set of standard terms and notation and permits characterization of the algorithm characteristics of information flow, the degree of global information sharing, the costs associated with a decision-making policy in terms of message passing events, and the performance of the policy in terms of satisfying a desired objective. Finally, these models provide a framework for quantitative evaluation and comparison among different approaches to a given problem.

Distributed algorithms have two types of characteristics: *structure* and *semantics*. Structure includes the topology of interconnection of decision-making entities, the static components of state, and some representation of static global knowledge at each node. Semantic characteristics are those which describe the actions of the algorithm at each node during execution.

The structural description of DSA's[2] employs the notation of directed graphs where the vertices represent the nodes of the scheduling algorithm and the edges represent the *neighbor relation*. Multiple message exchanges are required for communication between a pair of scheduling components not defined in the neighbor relation. The semantics of a DSA are specified by defining finite automata (FA) for each node of the graph. Communication of state information between nodes is implied by the input and output components of the FA. The portion of the model which conveys the semantics of the policy at a node is the FA transition function.

We define a component of node state (*phase*) which changes only when messages are passed. Using the value of this component to define equivalence classes of states, we greatly reduce the number of transitions which must be defined. This is done by collapsing large sets of states based only on the current information exchange phase of the node of the algorithm. The phase component also models the characterization of the degree of information sharing required by the algorithm and the passage of time in the system (i.e., we use message passing events as the basic quanta of *virtual time*).

The following definitions will be used in Section III to

discuss the analysis of the two examples chosen. An important aspect affecting the performance of any dynamic scheduling function is the stability of the system resulting from a sequence of scheduling decisions. Formally, we define stability as follows.

Definitions: A *stable* scheduling algorithm, following a perturbation of the system state from equilibrium, will return the system to a state of equilibrium and *additionally* will cease continuing to take actions which cause changes in system state in finite time.

Here, *equilibrium* is defined as the condition in which the sequence of states visited by the system forms a cycle in the absence of further input changes. "Absence of further input" refers to the condition in which there are no externally-induced perturbations to system state. This is represented in a model by permitting the definition of functions which may change the internal state of a node of the algorithm without utilization of one of the algorithm's transition functions. From the algorithm's "point of view," these functions appear as stochastic processes.

Stability, as defined here, is not concerned with the rate of convergence to an equilibrium state. This rate of convergence is an efficiency attribute and is discussed next.

Definitions: Response is defined by the number of phase changes required, following a perturbation of the system state from equilibrium and in the absence of input, to return the system to an equilibrium condition.

Here, *equilibrium* is defined as the condition in which the sequence of global states visited by the system forms a cycle in the absence of further input changes. This is represented in the model by permitting the definition of functions which may change the internal state of a node of the algorithm without utilization of one of the algorithm's transition functions. From the algorithm's "point of view," these functions appear as stochastic processes.

Although optimality is not one of the metrics with which we are explicitly concerned here, it is the desired equilibrium state. Therefore, we include this definition as well.

Definition: An *optimal* DSA is one which, following a perturbation of the system state from an optimal state, will return the system to an optimal state in a finite period of time in the absence of further input.

III. Analysis Methods, Algorithms, and Experimental Results

DSA's which utilize widely varying approaches and structural frameworks present a difficulty to the task of objective quantitative comparison. Whereas the existence of static global knowledge assumptions may always produce a problem of subjectivity, the use of the model described earlier allows quantification of the cost of maintaining dynamic global knowledge in the form of measuring the amount of state information maintained internally and externally, and hence represents the density of communication load on the interconnection medium and ultimately provides the standard mechanism for objective evaluation of efficiency. In addition, fixed costs such as node complexity and cost per communication link

---

[2]DSA's are the subset of DDM's in which we are interested.

may be calculated using this model since the formal framework provides a way to quantify each. The neighbor relation provides a way to count numbers of communication links, and sequential algorithm analysis techniques may be used to evaluate nodal complexity.

A. Analysis Methods

The CFA modeling technique provides for *consistent* measures, useful in making comparisons between different approaches to a given problem and, ultimately, in making design choices. This is accomplished by performing two types of analysis: *static* and *dynamic*.

Static analysis is the direct measurement of the performance and efficiency attributes as defined in Section II. In our work, this was done through the application of a single perturbation to the system state, followed by a finite period of observation of the behavior of the modeled system.. This is analogous to step analysis of control systems.[3] This type of measurement has two advantages: ease of measurement and consistency of measurement.

Dynamic analysis is used to measure the behavior of the system for a realistic execution environment for the scheduling algorithm. This type of analysis consists of dynamic application of multiple stochastic inputs for a (relatively) long period of time. In this research, dynamic analyses were performed to verify and correlate measurements made under static analysis to the behavior of the algorithm under simulated-dynamic operating conditions.

B. The Algorithms

Examination of the effects of response and stability will be accomplished by applying the model to two fundamentally different distributed scheduling mechanisms and presenting a number of general conclusions regarding performance and efficiency attributes. To simplify the discussion of performance, the global performance objective of load balancing will be used. This objective was chosen primarily because it is simple to describe and quantify and is also a very common factor contributing to overall system throughput in actual and proposed systems [6]–[11].

1) BDML Algorithms: The first type of algorithms to be considered are the BDML algorithms. BDML algorithms may be intuitively described as having one or more phases of exchange of scalar values describing the current load of neighbors or the current desire of neighbors to change their load. After some fixed number of iterations of this information exchange, simple "give-and-take" decisions are made with respect to neighbors. What follows is a brief description of a representative set of BDML algorithms from those analyzed.

UDI1 (Unidirectional Incremental Transfers): Each node examines the load of itself and that of its neighbors. One unit of load will be given to the neighbor with the

least load if that load is less than its own load. Otherwise, no load is given. Ties are arbitrarily broken in one direction.

UDI2: This is the same as UDI1, except that the observed imbalance must be at least two units prior to making a decision to transfer any load.

UDI3: Each node examines the load of itself and that of its neighbors, beginning with the least heavily loaded neighbor and continuing through each neighbor in order of increasing load values. One unit of load will be given to each neighbor with load less than its own load, where the value of its own load used for purposes of comparison is repeatedly modified to reflect the total number of units committed to other neighbors up to this point.

UDI4: This is the same as UDI3, except that the observed imbalance must be at least two units prior to making a decision to transfer any load.

UDF1 (Unidirectional Fractional Transfers): Each node examines the load of itself and that of its neighbors. For each node which is less heavily loaded, the difference between the perceived mean value of load among all neighbors and the load of the receiving node will be given to each of these neighbors.

UDF2: This algorithm is the same as UDF1, except if after applying this heuristic no change was affected, UDI4 is applied.

BDF1 (Bidirectional Fractional Transfers): This algorithm is a true multilateral and bidirectional version of UDF1. Each node examines the load of itself and that of its neighbors. For each neighboring node, the difference between the load of the neighbor and the perceived mean value of load among all neighbors and itself will be the decision made regarding that neighbor. Note that these decisions may be negative, implying that load is intended to be taken from the neighbor, while UDI1 through UDF2 only allow decisions to take on positive values. In all further information exchanges (i.e., phases), the decision made in the previous phase is used to infer the load of neighbors at a distance 2 from the scheduling node. As more phases are added, the quality of the information upon which these inferences are made increases, but the volume of information describing the global state is not enlarged. A tunable parameter K is also added to this algorithm to control the rate at which decisions grow as a result of seeing a large imbalance towards one neighbor.

Regardless of the number of phases in this type of mechanism, the information passed is a scalar value, and the information stored by each node is a vector of scalars. The dimensionality of this vector is related only to the size of the neighbor set of a node, not the number of phases in the algorithm or the number of nodes in the system.

2) Bidding: The second mechanism evaluated is the bidding approach [12]. Here, each node has a unique identifier known to the node itself. The bidding approach collects predicted load information from only that subset of nodes which responds to bid requests. While this *may* equate to an estimated view of the entire system load dis-

---

[3]The mathematical methods used in quantitatively analyzing control systems, however, are not applicable to distributed computing systems in general due to inherent nonlinear behavior and semantics not easily characterized by mathematical relations such as transfer functions.

tribution, the mechanism itself does not require such an estimate in order to function. The bidding schemes examined are characterized as follows.

BID1: During the first phase, a "request-for-bids" message is broadcast to the system by the bid requester. The requester then "waits" for $N/3$ phases in order to allow all nodes within a distance $N/3$ to receive the bid request. The requester then "waits" for $N/3$ more phases in order to allow all nodes within a distance $N/3$ to respond to the bid request. Bids consist of a single positive-valued integer indicating the amount of load that the bidder is willing to receive. After $2N/3$ phases have occurred, the requester processes all bids and transmits the awards along with the load to be transferred. All decisions to transfer load are positive valued; hence, load is never requested from a bidder. A final $N/3$ phases are allowed to pass before the requester begins a new bidding cycle.

BID2: In this algorithm, the same fundamental mechanism as in BID1 is employed; however, the problem of overcommitment of resources is more intelligently dealt with. In BID1, when a bid is sent, all the load committed by the bid is assumed to be unavailable for commitment to other bid requests. BID2 incorporates a parameter which allows some load to be committed more than once. This is done by using a multiplicative factor to describe the fraction of a bid which is to be considered committed to another bid. Note that this parameter has the value 1.0 by default in BID1.

A formal specification of each algorithm was done in order to conduct extensive simulated[4] examinations of algorithm behavior. The volume of space required, however, for formal specification in this paper is prohibitive. The data supplied as illustrations in this section were obtained using the distributed scheduling simulation and analysis package) (DSSAP) [4], a tool developed to conduct simulation experiments. These experiments varied along many dimensions, including topology, algorithm type, algorithm parameter values, and system loading characteristics. The descriptions presented here are more informal and intuitive in an attempt to relate general properties of algorithms to their behavior.

C. Response

A critical aspect of analysis from control theory is that of measuring the response of a system to a reference input signal. A common reference input is the step. This is also our basis for evaluating distributed scheduling response. With respect to the objective of load balancing, we are primarily concerned with the ability of a system to respond reasonably to externally-induced changes in system load in order to arrive at a favorable load balance. This favorable response has two aspects. The first deals with the degree of optimality with which load is ultimately distributed in the system when equilibrium is reached. The second aspect is the rate of response following a perturbation from equilibrium.

Both aspects of response are measured by applying a reference signal and observing the resulting sequence of states. In our experiments, this is a step input of some number of units of load (positive, which represents arrival, or negative, which represents removal) at one processor of the system and observation of the response of the system over a period of time following the input. The observations made consist of 1) the statistical variance at equilibrium and 2) the number of phase transitions, or subcycles,[5] until equilibrium is reached.

While the actual means of detecting equilibrium varies between algorithms, common measures include the number of subcycles until the variance or range of load is within some tolerance of the equilibrium value or until incremental load movement is within some tolerance of the equilibrium value of movement per subcycle. The former mechanism is used in algorithms which are stable, and the final value of load variance is attained very slowly as equilibrium is approached. The latter mechanism is used in cases of unstable algorithms, but in which the amount of load moved per cycle is a (possibly large) constant.

As a first example, we consider two instances of a BDML load-balancing approach. The potential for instability is apparent in both UDI1 and UDI3 since a node could give load in such a way as to leave itself less heavily loaded than some of its neighbors at the end of the cycle. Then, on the following cycle, that load *could* all be returned. The element of the algorithm which makes this possible is the fact that the imbalance (bias) between nodes which may cause movement is of unit size. Therefore, load may be moved to a node when there is the possibility that the same unit of load may be returned on the next cycle. Analysis of the algorithm under a step input reveals that both UDI1 and UDI3 are unstable at equilibrium (i.e., load continues to move from node to node, even though the system is not tending towards a more optimal load distribution), as is shown in Fig. 1 and discussed in Section III-D. However, the difference between the two approaches is that UDI3 may be able to respond more quickly by being able to give load to *any* neighbor with less load.

As a specific example, we consider 20 nodes arranged under a number of topologies. The first topology is a loop (labeled l), the second and third are chordal rings of chord lengths 3 and 7 (labeled c3 and c7, respectively), the fourth is an irregular interconnection (labeled i) shown in Fig. 2, and the final topology is a full interconnection (labeled f).

The step input is an arrival of 100 units of load to node 0 at time 1 (time being measured in terms of phase transitions or subcycles). The dynamic load arrivals are characterized by two independent stochastic processes. The first describes interarrival times, and the second describes the size of arrivals in units of load. The removal of load models the completion of work and is represented in a

---

[4]The term simulation is used here to refer to the process of exercising an algorithm model and gathering performance and efficiency information.

[5]A cycle is the sequence of subcycles, or phases, over which information is gathered and a decision is carried out by a local scheduling entity.

cycle number	Node number				
	0	1	2	3	4
0	0	0	0	0	0
3	10	0	0	0	0
6	9	0	0	0	1
9	8	1	0	1	0
12	7	0	2	0	1
15	6	2	1	1	0
18	5	1	2	0	2
21	4	2	1	2	1
24	3	1	3	1	2
27	2	3	2	2	1
30	2	2	2	1	3
33	2	2	1	3	2
36	2	1	3	2	2

Fig. 1. Movement of load in a five-node loop under algorithm UDI1.

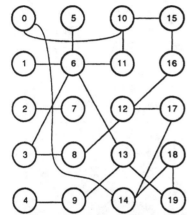

Fig. 2. Irregular topology used in simulations.

TABLE I
STEP-INPUT ANALYSIS COMPARISON OF TWO UNSTABLE BDML SCHEMES

	UDI1		UDI3	
topology	subcycles to equilibrium	final variance	subcycles to equilibrium	final variance
l	320	0.1	203	0.9
c3	287	0.5	149	1.0
c7	287	0.6	107	1.1
i	332	0.8	206	1.6
f	263	22.0	17	0.0

TABLE II
DYNAMIC ANALYSIS COMPARISON OF TWO UNSTABLE BDML SCHEMES

		UDI1		UDI3	
topology	system load	mean range	mean variance	mean range	mean variance
l	dl	7.0	3.22	6.6	3.0
	dm	17.8	22.6	16.5	20.1
	dh	66.4	339.9	58.1	286.0
c3	dl	6.6	2.56	5.9	2.14
	dm	15.6	15.7	13.0	10.3
	dh	61.1	245.9	40.9	123.6
c7	dl	6.4	2.31	5.7	1.94
	dm	16.1	15.7	12.7	9.2
	dh	59.6	221.3	37.0	91.6
i	dl	6.7	2.58	6.3	2.27
	dm	16.9	18.02	14.0	11.79
	dh	72.9	396.87	51.0	191.0
f	dl	17.4	30.8	16.7	14.65
	dm	23.8	46.97	19.3	21.51
	dh	61.0	226.8	25.8	40.7

manner similar to load arrival. Three load conditions are simulated for each algorithm. Light loading (labeled dl) is characterized by geometrically distributed interarrival periods with a mean of 30 subcycles, and the size is described by a Poisson distribution with a mean of 2 units. Moderate dynamic load (labeled dm) is characterized by geometric interarrivals of mean 20 subcycles and Poisson sizes of mean 4 units. Finally, a heavy load (labeled dh) is characterized by the same distribution types, but with respective means of 15 and 8. This is summarized below.

Loading	Period Distribution	Period Mean	Size Distribution	Size Mean
dl	Geometric	30	Poisson	2
dm	Geometric	20	Poisson	4
dh	Geometric	15	Poisson	8

Table I shows the results of the step-input analysis of UDI1 and UDI3. In Table II, the results of the dynamic simulations are shown. Although UDI3 demonstrates generally poorer equilibrium states as indicated by the variance of load, the number of subcycles until equilibrium is smaller for all topologies considered. Note that in the case of a fully interconnected system, UDI3 performs better with respect to variance, but this is not a general characteristic; rather, it is a peculiar characteristic of this extreme case. A discussion of this phenomenon appears in [5] and is related to assumptions regarding static global knowledge. However, the values of range and variance averaged over time, as shown in Table II, show correlation not with improved final variance, but with increased response, as shown in Table I. Hence, the final variance in static step analyses must not be used exclusively to compare algorithms.

As a second example, we consider UDI2 and UDI4. The main difference between these and UDI1 or UDI3 is that both of these algorithms are stable. The same set of simulations was performed for these two algorithms, and the results are given in Tables III and IV. Note that even in the step analysis, a slight improvement or no change in the final variance is observed from UDI2 to UDI4. While this differs from the previous examples, it does not change the previously stated correlation because the magnitude of increase in response is easily identifiable as the change which may account for the improvement in the dynamic analysis.

We now consider the response of UDF1 and UDF2. Here, nodes may make decisions which not only include information regarding the state of their neighbors, but also the state of their neighbors' neighbors. UDF2 is designed to have the ability both to respond quickly and to achieve better equilibrium balances during times of lighter loading. The result, as justified in Tables V and VI, is that the basic mechanism of using averaging as a determining factor for the amount of load transferred works well with increasing response, and that this increase in response corresponds to improved performance over UDI2 and UDI4 in a dynamic environment. Also shown is that the

TABLE III
STEP-INPUT ANALYSIS COMPARISON OF TWO STABLE BDML SCHEMES

topology	UDI2 subcycles to equilibrium	UDI2 final variance	UDI4 subcycles to equilibrium	UDI4 final variance
l	278	8.5	161	8.5
c3	278	2.5	110	1.3
c7	284	0.7	104	0.6
i	284	0.7	110	0.7
f	287	0.0	17	0.0

TABLE IV
DYNAMIC ANALYSIS COMPARISON OF TWO STABLE BDML SCHEMES

topology	system load	UDI2 mean range	UDI2 mean variance	UDI4 mean range	UDI4 mean variance
l	dl	7.7	4.49	7.4	4.31
	dm	18.2	24.11	17.0	21.6
	dh	66.5	343.0	58.2	287.2
c3	dl	6.6	2.64	6.0	2.3
	dm	16.0	16.1	13.3	11.1
	dh	61.1	245.7	41.4	126.2
c7	dl	6.3	2.3	5.7	1.9
	dm	16.0	15.7	13.0	10.0
	dh	59.4	220.4	37.0	92.2
i	dl	6.7	2.67	6.3	2.32
	dm	17.0	18.58	14.4	12.75
	dh	73.1	398.7	51.5	196.0
f	dl	15.5	24.1	12.3	8.3
	dm	23.6	44.0	18.0	17.3
	dh	59.5	217.8	25.3	38.2

TABLE V
RESPONSE AND OPTIMALITY OF UDF1 AND UDF2

topology	UDF1 subcycles to equilibrium	UDF1 final variance	UDF2 subcycles to equilibrium	UDF2 final variance
l	77	5.8	71	6.9
c3	41	0.8	41	0.8
c7	23	0.4	23	0.4
i	38	0.3	26	0.7
f	0	0.0	0	0.0

TABLE VI
DYNAMIC PERFORMANCE OF UDF1 AND UDF2

topology	system load	UDF1 mean range	UDF1 mean variance	UDF2 mean range	UDF2 mean variance
l	dl	4.2	1.7	4.1	1.6
	dm	10.9	11.1	10.8	10.7
	dh	20.9	41.0	20.8	41.0
c3	dl	3.9	1.4	3.6	1.2
	dm	8.9	6.2	8.9	6.1
	dh	19.5	29.5	19.9	30.7
c7	dl	4.0	1.2	3.8	1.1
	dm	8.9	5.8	8.6	5.5
	dh	19.3	29.0	18.8	27.1
i	dl	4.4	1.6	4.3	1.5
	dm	9.2	6.4	9.2	6.4
	dh	20.6	33.2	20.9	33.7
f	dl	5.2	2.0	3.8	1.2
	dm	14.9	30.2	15.6	36.2
	dh	-	-	53.4	512.9

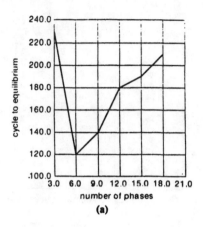

(a)

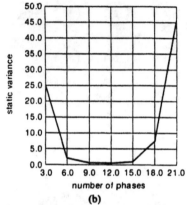

(b)

Fig. 3. Behavior of bidding. (a) Response. (b) Optimality.

and in fact, it may be detrimental. This deficiency is explained by the similarity of the lightly loaded environment to the static environment under which UDI1 displayed a better equilibrium load than UDF1.

We now consider BID1. Here, response is controlled through varying the number of information-exchange phases between decision-making phases. Fig. 3(a) shows a composite graph of the number of phases necessary to reach equilibrium versus the number of information exchanges per decision. Fig. 3(b) shows the relationship between the number of phases and the equilibrium values of variance—the measure of optimality. The curves are a composition of the data values sampled for each of the topologies and were constructed by averaging the values observed from each topology. Finally, Fig. 4 shows the dynamic performance of BID1 by plotting the number of phases for each topology versus the dynamic performance metric—the mean variance. Each part of Fig. 4 shows the dynamic performance under a different dynamic loading condition. A trend similar to those of the BDML algorithms is indicated. The general observation to be made again is that with respect to response in the bidding examples studied, dynamic performance correlates more strongly with response than with the ability to achieve an optimal steady state. If equilibrium optimality were used to select the number of phases to be used, a larger value would be chosen since with a higher ratio of message-passing phases to decision-making phases there is the potential for less movement of load. However, these results

increased algorithm complexity introduced in order to improve the steady-state optimality is capable of producing minor improvements in the lightly loaded cases, but that in a moderate to heavily loaded system there is no benefit,

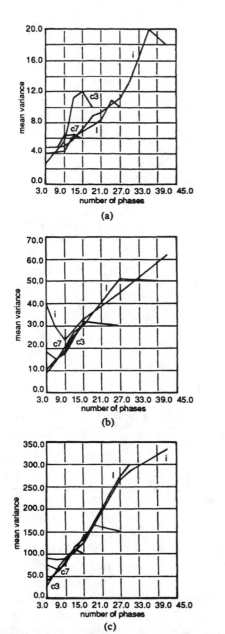

Fig. 4. Simulation of bidding under a dynamic load. (a) Light loading.
(b) Moderate loading. (c) Heavy loading.

illustrate that the choice is not trivial, and that a tradeoff exists between the volume of load moved and dynamic performance.

This is not to say that any mechanism which simply responds faster will perform better in a dynamic setting. There is also a tradeoff between making decisions which make rapid changes in the gross load imbalance and making small variations in load in a region in order to find a completely optimal global load distribution. Response has been shown to have a positive effect on system behavior in this section, but it is obviously possible to create conditions of overresponse in which too high a level of response causes unacceptable levels of instability, and hence poor performance.

Another significant observation made in this portion of the study is that designing an algorithm to respond to local

variations according to rules which allow the exact balancing of load under closely controlled conditions of a step workload arrival may be too simple an approach. The more relevant basis for algorithm design may be to choose algorithm parameters which allow the algorithm to adjust its rate of response to the rate of workload arrival instead of simply working from the assumption that the work which just arrived is the only event to deal with for the near future. In trying to develop distributed algorithms which satisfy an optimization criterion, while operating under a dynamic and noisy environment, it is tempting to focus on fine tuning the equilibrium decisions of the mechanism. However, the actual dynamic environment in which the algorithm is required to operate may differ from this equilibrium state to a great degree. While in some cases a mechanism may be developed which is provably optimal (in the sense of reaching an optimal state) or provably stable in equilibrium, this same mechanism may perform no better than, and possibly not as well as, an algorithm which focuses on achieving a more favorable rate of response. There are two implications of this point.

First, a common mechanism for thinking about the solution to a complex dynamic system problem is to look at localized effects and solve a local or regional subset of the original problem in a static environment. This is a logical approach since it is more difficult to try to develop mechanisms which respond intelligently to stochastic inputs than to do so for (somewhat) restricted static inputs. However, this approach may be invalid. Second, the analysis techniques used here are capable of predicting the relative merits of different factors which may influence a design. However, this is not to say that response is the most critical component in developing successful scheduling algorithms. It is generally difficult to determine which components influencing design are more critical to dynamic performance. Certainly, response is a factor which warrants examination. Finally, abstractions and simplifications made for the sake of design must be used, but the resulting mechanisms ultimately need to be evaluated in terms of dynamic performance.

D. Stability

Stability is an issue which arises in the analysis of any dynamic system, and while it is precisely defined in any particular discipline, the fundamental definition of stability is that a bounded input produces a bounded response. In the study of distributed scheduling, we consider an input to be any externally-induced change (perturbation) in the overall system state.

Without a precise or formal definition, earlier work which studied the notion of stability in distributed scheduling algorithms has implicitly assumed that unstable behavior is generally a detriment to performance [1], [13]–[16]. Using the CFA model described in Section II, we are able to examine carefully the effect of instability on performance.

1) Causes of Instability: As mentioned earlier, the BDML algorithm labeled UDI1 exhibited unstable behavior. Fig. 1 illustrates this. Here, the movement of load among the nodes of a five-node loop, initially with no load present at any node, when a step input of ten units is applied to node 0, is shown. The state of the system is shown only after it changes, and in this case, that is at the end of each cycle (every three subcycles). Since the overall state is not continuing to improve toward the ultimate goal of an optimal load distribution and the sequence of system states visited forms a cycle, this is identified as an unstable algorithm. The cause of the instability is the algorithm's rule for deciding whether to transfer load at a particular point in time. In this case, the rule is based on whether there is *any* perceived load imbalance. In a second example, UDI2, the rule is modified so that a transfer of load will not take place if the transfer itself will cause another imbalance to occur. Hence, if the bias is exactly two, then the result is to move a single unit, thus balancing the load, but if the bias is only one, then no load will be moved. Note that in order to avoid a condition of instability the definition of optimality for this scheduler is being loosened. In general, this is an example of *intolerance* instability since the inability to tolerate any condition other than complete optimality results in instability. The modified algorithm (UDI2) does not exhibit this phenomenon, as shown in Fig. 5.

A second cause of instability is the attempt to respond too quickly to inputs or to local conditions of suboptimality. As an illustration, consider BDF1. In this algorithm, K, a tunable parameter, is used to amplify requests for load when there is a perceived imbalance. In Table VII, observe that the effect of increasing K near and past the threshold value of approximately 1.1 causes the mean number of units moved per cycle to increase dramatically. This condition of increased scheduler activity coupled with a decreased level of dynamic performance represents severe instability. This is categorized as *overresponse* instability.

A third cause of instability is a situation in which the static level of loading in a system directly influences the amount of load moved in the system. This is termed *high static load* instability, and an illustration of this is seen in Table VIII. What is seen here is that as the initial loading of the system (data are drawn from algorithm UDF1 using the c3 topology) increases from 0 through 40 a condition of increasing instability arises. Since the arrival and departure processes are identical in the dynamic simulation of this algorithm, the mean load of the system throughout time is determined by the initial loading. This increase in scheduler activity is not simply linked to a more rapid arrival of larger amounts of load, but to the total amount of load present in the system at a given point in time. Notice that as the mean load increases, the number of units of load transferred per cycle increases roughly proportionally to the increase in mean load. The basic problem is that as the load continues to increase, the opportunity for the algorithm to overreact becomes greater. On a microscopic level, when the combination of aged information and noisy information allows the scheduler to make

cycle number	Node number				
	0	1	2	3	4
0	0	0	0	0	0
3	10	0	0	0	0
6	9	0	0	0	1
9	8	1	0	0	1
12	7	1	0	0	2
15	6	2	0	1	1
18	5	1	1	1	2
21	4	2	1	1	2
24	3	2	1	2	2
27	3	2	1	2	2
30	3	2	1	2	2

Fig. 5. Movement of load in a five-node loop under algorithm UDI2.

TABLE VII
OVER-RESPONSE INSTABILITY

K	load moved per cycle			mean variance		
	dl	dm	dh	dl	dm	dh
1.0	7.7	15.6	42.4	6.35	26.6	162.5
1.075	7.7	27.3	121.0	6.35	50.8	886.0
1.09	8.0	103.7	222.0	6.74	585.2	2117.0
1.1	141.6	19.0	232.0	761.4	32.0	2267.0
1.2	137.1	180.0	240.0	750.0	1242.0	2565.0
1.25	157.0	192.0	273.0	86.0	1383.0	3195.0
1.3	158.0	190.0	174.0	900.0	1373.0	3247.0
no alg.	0	0	0	95	300	1050

TABLE VIII
HIGH STATIC LOADING INSTABILITY

initial load	load moved per cycle		
	dl	dm	dh
0	2	9	20
10	24	33	40
20	50	65	75
30	75	90	100
40	110	120	135

a first decision which causes a very large local imbalance, the algorithm tries to react quickly to rebalance the load. However, this condition is detected as an imbalance from the point of view of all those involved, and thus all parties try to respond to the imbalance in the same manner. Hence, the condition of instability propagates to a point where it is self-perpetuating. In the environment of lower static load, the opportunity to create large imbalances is not present, and therefore the situation is avoided. In the following section, the effect of this behavior pattern will be examined.

A fourth cause of instability is less easily stated in such quantifiable terms as the previous three. This cause is termed *invalid assumption* instability. It results when the operating environment of the scheduler violates certain assumptions made by the designer of the mechanism. Although this may seem quite obvious, the following example shows how the violation of an assumption which anticipates a poor operating environment in favor of a seemingly better one produces a negative impact on stability and performance.

In BDF1, a design assumption is made which presumes that the static cost of rich processor interconnection must be avoided. Hence, it is envisioned that there may be a high mean internode distance and, if a large load imbal-

TABLE IX
INVALID ASSUMPTION INSTABILITY

dynamic load	load moved per cycle			
	l	i	c3	c7
dl	7.7	111.0	142.8	142.1
dm	15.5	122.0	159.0	163.0
dh	46.2	158.0	181.0	200.0

TABLE X
A COMPARISON OF PERFORMANCE AND STABILITY SHOWING A NEGATIVE CORRELATION

topology/ algorithm	dl		dm		dh	
	mean variance	load moved	mean variance	load moved	mean variance	load moved
l/UDI1	3.22	3489	22.6	4151	340.0	4451
/UDI2	4.5	1638	24.1	3305	343.0	4219
c3/UDI1	2.56	3977	15.7	4605	245.9	4882
/UDI2	2.94	1943	16.1	3704	245.7	4633
i/UDI1	3.76	2983	28.9	3524	472.8	3899
/UDI2	4.4	1593	29.0	2995	471.0	3742
l/UDI3	3.0	3971	20.1	5170	286.0	6090
/UDI4	4.3	1739	21.6	3892	287.2	5633
c3/UDI3	2.14	5192	10.3	6646	123.6	8664
/UDI4	2.3	2123	11.1	4940	126.2	7933
i/UDI3	3.5	3680	23.1	4794	382.2	5795
/UDI4	4.1	1643	24.6	3724	388.5	5404

ance is detected locally, that this condition would be best alleviated (on a global basis) by actually predicting that the optimal value of system mean load will be less than the value computed among the scheduling node and its neighbors alone. This results in the transfer of more load than would be transferred under the control of an algorithm which made decisions attempting to create a local balance only. In other words, a new condition of local imbalance is purposely generated in the hope that this will lead to a faster convergence of overall system load balance. However, as is seen in Table IX, the poorly connected topology of the loop produces a more stable response, and as will be shown in the next section, the performance also improves as the topology becomes apparently worse.

2) The Effects of Instability on Dynamic Behavior: In this section, the effects of the various causes or forms of instability which were presented in the previous section will be discussed. We first consider intolerance instability.

This form is unique in that it is easily identifiable. It is simple to identify whether an optimality requirement is the cause of instability since this results in the unceasing movement of a small amount of load with little change in the value of the objective function during step analysis. Naturally, one might consider instability to be an undesirable attribute for a system in all cases. As described earlier, algorithms UDI1 and UDI3 both have the attribute of intolerance instability. Variants of these two algorithms called UDI2 and UDI4, respectively, were developed to be stable in this respect and to be otherwise equivalent to UDI1 and UDI3, respectively. However, interesting results, which did not support this expectation were obtained in the dynamic simulations of these algorithms. The following discussion refers to Table X. The results shown are based on a simulation length of 1000 subcycles, which was adequate for clearing initial conditions. In the presence of a light dynamic load, both UDI2 and UDI4 experience roughly half the load movement experienced by UDI1 and UDI3, respectively. This trend is continued to a somewhat lesser degree in the moderate loading environment, and in the heavily loaded simulation, the difference in load movement is barely noticeable. The explanation for this is that under light loading there are far more situations in which the load varies by a single unit than in the moderate or heavy load situations. More interesting is the fact that the unstable algorithms (UDI1, UDI3) each experienced consistently better dynamic performance than the stable algorithms. Although the reason

for this lies in the fact that the instability causes a situation of more favorable response, this result demonstrates that the existence of instability may not *always* cause poorer performance. Although this example shows that instability does not always imply poor performance, the majority of the simulation results obtained did show a direct relationship between instability and poor performance.

In the example of overresponse instability in the previous section, it was observed that as the response parameter K increased, the system passed out of the domain of stable algorithms into one of extreme instability. As seen in Table VII, the number of units of load moved per cycle takes on about the same degree of increase as does the value of mean variance. In fact, the actual values of mean variance increase to levels near or above the figures for mean variance in the presence of no scheduling algorithm at all. These data show that an increase in load movement is *always* accompanied by an increase in mean variance. This illustrates the more intuitive relationship between instability and poor performance.

In the example of high static load instability presented in the previous section, it was observed that a mechanism exhibited more stable behavior for low values of system mean load than for higher values. As the amount of load increases, a corresponding decrease in system performance might be expected. However, the decrease in performance is not proportional to either the increase in static loading or the value of mean load movement. Here, as shown in Table XI, the value of mean variance under algorithm control eventually overtakes that when no algorithm is being used at all. This statistic supports the belief that under conditions of heavy system load the scheduler may do more harm than good with respect to dynamic performance. This certainly is true when considering only the cost of load movement, but here it is observed that the actual performance is degraded by the scheduler in times of heavy load independently of this cost.

Finally, in the case of invalid assumption instability, it was observed that the level of increase in load movement corresponding to an increase in static global knowledge is reflected in the degradation of performance as well. This

TABLE XI
TABLE XI
THE EFFECT OF AN EXAMPLE OF HIGH STATIC LOAD INSTABILITY ON SYSTEM PERFORMANCE

initial load	mean variance using BDF1/no algorithm		
	dl	dm	dh
0	2/33	15/150	80/750
10	44/70	90/230	250/900
20	180/95	280/300	520/1050
30	430/100	575/380	900/1300
40	800/108	900/430	1408/1400

TABLE XII
POSITIVE RELATIONSHIP BETWEEN INVALID ASSUMPTION INSTABILITY AND DEGRADED DYNAMIC PERFORMANCE

dynamic load	mean variance			
	l	l	c3	c7
dl	6.4	568.0	877.0	767.0
dm	27.4	701.0	1045.0	991.0
dh	183.0	1103.0	1408.0	1614.0

dynamic load	number moved per cycle			
	l	l	c3	c7
dl	7.7	111.0	142.8	142.1
dm	15.5	122.0	159.0	163.0
dh	46.2	158.0	181.0	200.0

result is combined with that of Table IX in Table XII to illustrate this.

3) Summary of Stability Results: In this section, examples of both the causes and effects of instability in distributed scheduling algorithms are illustrated. An underlying goal has been to demonstrate the use of the CFA model in providing insight into the problem of locating instability and then determining whether there is a positive or negative impact on dynamic system performance. It was observed that it is possible for a limited amount of instability actually to have a positive effect on system performance. However, instability in itself is a source of lowered efficiency. This lowered level of efficiency is evident in the form of increased system overhead (message and/or load movement). As previously stated, without a precise or formal definition, earlier work which studied the notion of stability in distributed scheduling algorithms has implicitly assumed that stable behavior generally is an essential component of good performance. Utilizing the CFA model, we defined stability for the balancing of load and carefully examined the effect of instability on performance, thus answering the question of whether or not absolute stability is essential. In fact, we have shown that stability may not always be essential and, in addition, that some amount of instability may actually improve response in a way which improves overall dynamic performance. Finally, we observed that not only does instability carry a cost in terms of system overhead, but that it may also degrade the absolute performance independent of the efficiency penalty.

IV. SUMMARY AND DESIGN IMPLICATIONS

This paper addressed several issues. One of these is the use of a CFA model which allows specification of differ-ent mechanisms under the same framework. Another is the definition of metrics of quantitative behavior within the model. Finally, consistent analysis of two basic structures of scheduling algorithms for distributed systems has been reported.

The following two statements summarize the significant experimental results.

• Stability, as an absolute entity, is not essential to favorable operation of distributed scheduling algorithms. In fact, it was observed that in order to improve response in at least one class of algorithms a certain amount of instability is desirable.

• Designing algorithms for dynamic systems by assuming locally time-invariant conditions may not be a productive approach. While no other simple mechanism for design conceptualization is proposed here, it is acknowledged that the behavior of algorithms designed with static conditions in mind may operate as expected under static conditions, but may exhibit far from predictable behavior under dynamic conditions.

REFERENCES

[1] R. M. Bryant and R. A. Finkel, "A stable distributed scheduling algorithm," in *Proc. 2nd Int. Conf. Distrib. Comput.*, Apr. 1981, pp. 314–323.
[2] T. L. Casavant and J. G. Kuhl, "A formal model of distributed decision-making and its application to distributed load balancing," in *Proc. 6th Int. Conf. Distrib. Comput. Syst.*, May 1986, pp. 232–239.
[3] ——, "A taxonomy of scheduling in general-purpose distributed computing systems," *IEEE Trans. Software Eng.*, vol. SE-14, pp. 141–154, Feb. 1988.
[4] T. L. Casavant, "DSSAP—An automated design aid for algorithms and software development in distributed computing systems," in *Proc. 2nd Int. Conf. Supercomput.*, Santa Clara, CA, May 1987, pp. 123–132.
[5] T. L. Casavant and J. G. Kuhl, "Analysis of three dynamic load-balancing strategies with varying global information requirements," in *Proc. 7th IEEE Int. Conf. Distrib. Comput. Syst.*, Sept. 1987, pp. 185–192.
[6] T. C. K. Chou and J. A. Abraham, "Load balancing in distributed systems," *IEEE Trans. Software Eng.*, vol. SE-8, pp. 401–412, July 1982.
[7] Y. C. Chow and W. H. Kohler, "Models for dynamic load balancing in a heterogeneous multiple processor system," *IEEE Trans. Comput.*, vol. C-28, pp. 354–361, May 1979.
[8] L. M. Ni and K. Hwang, "Optimal load balancing for a multiple processor system," in *Proc. Int. Conf. Parallel Processing*, 1981, pp. 352–357.
[9] L. M. Ni and K. Abani, "Nonpreemptive load balancing in a class of local area networks," in *Proc. Comput. Networking Symp.*, Dec. 1981, pp. 113–118.
[10] L. M. Ni and K. Hwang, "Optimal load balancing in a multiple processor system with many job classes," *IEEE Trans. Software Eng.*, vol. SE-11, pp. 491–496, May 1985.
[11] M. L. Powell and B. P. Miller, "Process migration in DEMOS/MP," in *Proc. 9th Symp. Oper. Syst. Principles, OS Rev.*, vol. 17, no. 5, pp. 110–119, Oct. 1983.
[12] R. G. Smith, "The contract net protocol: High-level communication and control in a distributed problem solver," *IEEE Trans. Comput.*, vol. C-29, pp. 1104–1113, Dec. 1980.
[13] J. A. Stankovic, "The analysis of a decentralized control algorithm for job scheduling utilizing Bayesian decision theory," in *Proc. Int. Conf. Parallel Processing*, 1981.
[14] ——, "Simulations of three adaptive, decentralized controlled, job scheduling algorithms," *Comput. Networks*, vol. 8, no. 3, pp. 199–217, June 1984.
[15] ——, "Stability and distributed scheduling algorithms," *IEEE Trans. Software Eng.*, vol. SE-11, pp. 1141–1152, Oct. 1985.
[16] G. M. Weinberg and D. Weinberg. *On the Design of Stable Systems.* New York: Wiley, 1979.

Thomas L. Casavant (S'85–'86) received the B.S. degree in computer science and the M.S. and Ph.D. degrees in electrical and computer engineering from the University of Iowa, Iowa City, in 1982, 1983, and 1986, respectively.

He is currently an Assistant Professor of Electrical Engineering at Purdue University, West Lafayette, IN. His research interests include computer architecture, operating systems, distributed systems, and performance analysis.

Dr. Casavant is a member of the IEEE Computer Society and the Association for Computing Machinery.

Jon G. Kuhl (S'76–M'79) received the M.S. degree in electrical and computer engineering and the Ph.D. degree in computer science from the University of Iowa, Iowa City, in 1977 and 1980, respectively.

He is an Associate Professor in the Department of Electrical and Computer Engineering at the University of Iowa. His primary research interests are in distributed systems, parallel processing, and fault-tolerant computing. His other research interests include computer architecture, graph theory, and computer communications.

Condor - A Hunter of Idle Workstations

Michael J. Litzkow, Miron Livny, and Matt W. Mutka

Department of Computer Sciences
University of Wisconsin
Madison, WI 53706

ABSTRACT

This paper presents the design, implementation, and performance of the Condor scheduling system. Condor operates in a workstation environment. The system aims to maximize the utilization of workstations with as little interference as possible between the jobs it schedules and the activities of the people who own workstations. It identifies idle workstations and schedules background jobs on them. When the owner of a workstation resumes activity at a station, Condor checkpoints the remote job running on the station and transfers it to another workstation. The system guarantees that the job will eventually complete, and that very little, if any, work will be performed more than once. The system has been operational for more than five months. In this paper we present a performance profile of the system based on data that was accumulated from 23 stations during one month. During the one-month period, nearly 1000 jobs were scheduled by Condor. The system was used by heavy users and light users who consumed approximately 200 CPU days. An analysis of the response times observed by the different users is a clear display of the ability of Condor to protect the rights of light users against heavy users who try to monopolize all free capacity. Since a user of Condor has to devote some local capacity to support the remote execution of his/her jobs, the effectiveness of the remote scheduling system depends on the amount of this capacity. We show that this overhead is very small. On the average, a user has to sacrifice less than one minute of local CPU capacity to acquire a day of remote CPU capacity. Condor has proven to be an extremely effective means to improve the productivity of our computing environment.

1. Introduction

Workstations are powerful machines capable of executing millions of instructions each second. In many environments, individuals are allocated such stations to guarantee fast response to processing demands. In such cases the workstation becomes a private resource of the user who controls access to it. In most cases, the resources of the workstation are under utilized. The processing demands of the owner are much smaller than the capacity of the workstation he/she owns. However, very often some of the users face the problem that the capacity of their workstations is much too small to meet their processing demands. These users would like to take advantage of any available capacity they can access that can support their needs. Modern processing environments that consist of large collections of workstations interconnected by high capacity networks raise the following challenging question: can we satisfy the needs of users who need extra capacity without lowering the quality of service experienced by the owners of under utilized workstations? In other words, can we provide a high quality of service in a highly utilized network of workstations? The Condor scheduling system is our answer to this question. The Condor system schedules long running background jobs at idle workstations. In this paper we present the design and implementation of Condor and portray its performance. A performance profile based on data accumulated from 23 VAXstation II[*] workstations over a one-month period is presented along with an analysis of our experience with the usage of the system over the past five months.

A number of researchers have been exploring ways of effectively utilizing computing capacity in networks of workstations [1-8]. This work has been conducted in three areas, which are the analysis of workstation usage patterns, the design of remote capacity allocation algorithms, and the development of remote execution facilities. In the first area of research, workstation usage patterns and their availability as sources of remote execution have been analyzed [1]. An analysis of a group of workstations over 5 months showed that only 30% of their capacity was utilized. The study showed that not only was a large amount of capacity available during the evenings and on weekends, but also during the busiest times of the day. Available intervals were often very long. This makes workstations good candidates to serve as a source of remote processing cycles.

The second area of research is the exploration of algorithms for the management of idle workstation capacity [2]. In a system where long running background jobs are scheduled on idle workstations, it has been observed that some users try to acquire all the capacity available, while others only acquire capacity occasionally. Those who request large amounts of capacity should be granted as much as possible without inhibiting the access to capacity of other users who want smaller amounts. The *Up-Down* algorithm presented by Mutka and Livny [2] was designed to allow fair access to remote capacity for those who lightly use the system in spite of large demands

---

† This research was supported in part by the National Science Foundation under grants MCS81-05904 and DCR-8512862 and by a Digital Equipment Corporation External Research Grant.

---

[*] VAXstation II is a trademark of Digital Equipment Corporation.

Reprinted from *Proc. IEEE 8th Int'l Conf. on Distributed Computing Systems,* IEEE CS Press, Los Alamitos, Calif., 1988, pp. 104–111.

by heavy users.

The development of remote execution facilities that allow jobs to be executed on idle workstations is the third area of research. A number of papers have reported on the development of systems that allow for remote execution of jobs on idle workstations. These include the NEST project [3], the V-Kernel [4], the Process Server [5], the Remote Unix (RU) facility [6], the process migration facility of Sprite [7], and the Butler [8] system. With the exception of the Remote Unix facility, these systems were not specifically designed to remotely execute long jobs. For example, when a user reclaims a station in the Butler system, the remote job that is currently running on the station is terminated and all intermediate results are lost. The remote execution facilities of NEST, V-Kernel, Process Server, and Sprite enable job movement during its execution but do not save intermediate results if there is no place to move the job. If a user at a remote site terminates a foreign job running on the station, the foreign job loses all the work it accomplished up to this point. In our department, we use the Remote Unix (RU) facility to execute remote jobs. The RU facility is ideally suited for backgrounds jobs that are computationally intensive and run for long periods without any interaction from users. An unique feature of this facility is *checkpointing*. Checkpointing is the saving of the state of a program during its execution so that it can be restarted at any time, and on any machine in the system. This enables successful completions of jobs that consume months of CPU capacity. When a remotely executing program is stopped due to the shutdown of a remote workstation, or when a program is intentionally terminated by the remote workstation's owner, the program is resumed from its most recent checkpoint.

This paper presents results that extend previous work with respect to the exploration of effective means of utilizing idle workstation capacity. Previous research of scheduling algorithm design and remote execution facilities are merged into a system where actual user jobs are profiled and the system is measured. The Condor system combines the RU remote execution facility with the Up-Down algorithm for the fair assignment of remote capacity. Our study covers one month in which users' jobs were profiled and the system utilization was monitored. We show the pattern of service demands of users and the quality of service experienced by the users.

A new performance measure called *leverage* is introduced. It is the ratio of the capacity consumed by a job remotely to the capacity consumed on the "home" station to support remote execution. When little local capacity is needed to support the execution of remote jobs, the leverage of the jobs is large. A job with a small leverage should be executed locally since it consumes a great amount of local capacity to support its remote execution. We observed the leverage of jobs executing on our system to quantify the benefit the Condor system provided to its users.

Section 2 discusses the design issues of the Condor system and the decisions made to resolve the issues. Included in section 2 are some of the implementation details. Section 3 provides a performance profile of the system and the impact remote execution has on local workstations. In section 4, we present a discussion of issues that were brought to light due to our implementation. Plans for future work are presented in section 5 and conclusions are given in section 6.

2. System Design

There are over 100 VAXstation II workstations in our department. Since less than 30% of their capacity is utilized [1], a system has been designed and implemented to execute jobs remotely at idle workstations. Within our department there are many users working on problems that need large amounts of computing capacity. A few example problems include studies of load-balancing algorithms [9], simulation of real-time scheduling algorithms [10], studies of neural network learning models [11], and mathematical combinatorial problems [12]. These jobs typically require several hours of CPU time and little interaction with their users. The Condor system is designed to serve these users by executing their long running background jobs at idle workstations. To make our system attractive to these users, several issues must be addressed. First, the placement of background jobs should be transparent to users. The system should be responsible for knowing when workstations are idle and users should not need to know where their remote jobs execute. Second, if a remote site running a background job fails, the job should be restarted automatically at some other location to guarantee job completion. Third, since a workstation can serve as a source of remote cycles for others when it is not used by its owner, users expect to receive fair access to cycles when remote capacity is wanted. Fourth, the mechanisms implementing the system are expected to consume very little capacity. Otherwise users would not allow their workstations to be part of such a system if it interferes with their local activity.

This paper presents a design and evaluation of a real system that faces these issues. We will describe our remote job execution and recovery facilities, the method of job scheduling, and the system performance. We begin with a description of the structure of the scheduling system.

2.1. Scheduling Structure

The remote job scheduling structure should be transparent to the user. When users have background jobs to run, they should not need to request the remote machines explicitly or know on which machines their jobs are placed. A wide spectrum of scheduling structures could provide this objective. On one end of the spectrum, a centralized, static coordinator would assign background jobs to execute at available remote workstations. The coordinator would gather system information in order to implement the long-term scheduling policy that the system administrator has chosen. It would know which jobs were waiting and which were executing, and the location of idle stations. At the other end of the spectrum is a distributed approach. The assignment of available processors is accomplished by each workstation cooperating to conduct a scheduling policy. This approach requires negotiations among the workstations to resolve contentions for available processors.

Both the centralized and the distributed approaches have well known advantages and disadvantages. The centralized approach can efficiently decide which job is next granted a remote processor because each job submitted is registered with the central coordinator. The central location knows both the number of idle workstations and the number of jobs demanding service. The important duties of this location require that it is protected from users so that they do not have direct access to it. Direct access compromises the security of the scheduling pol-

383

icy. A system with a static central coordinator that keeps all jobs' state and workstation availability information is not easily extendible and is critically subject to failure. If the central coordinator fails, all scheduling in the system would cease. In the distributed scheduling system, each requesting workstation does its own searching for idle workstations. Message exchanges among contending workstations would be required to place jobs at idle workstations. This is less efficient than a centralized scheme when deciding which job should be next allocated a processor. However, the distributed scheduling approach is not subject to failure if a single station quits operating.

We have decided to follow an approach for structuring the background job scheduler that lies between a centralized, static approach and the fully distributed approach. This approach uses the efficiency of scheduling with a central node to avoid the overhead of messages to decide which workstations should be allocated available capacity. Each workstation keeps the state information of its own jobs and has the responsibility of scheduling them. A workstation knows the relative priority of the jobs and schedules them accordingly. The central coordinator merely assigns capacity to workstations which they use to schedule their own jobs.

Figure 1 illustrates our approach to structuring the Condor system. Each workstation has a local scheduler and a background job queue. The jobs that the user submits are placed in the background queue. One workstation holds the central coordinator in addition to a local scheduler and background job queue. In our implementation, every two minutes the central coordinator polls the stations to see which stations are available to serve as sources for remote cycles, and which stations have background jobs waiting. Between successive polls, each local scheduler monitors its station to see if it can serve as a source of remote capacity. If a background job is running on the workstation, the local scheduler checks every ½ minute to see if the background job should be preempted because the local user has resumed using the station. When local activity is detected, the local scheduler will immediately preempt the background job so that the user can have the workstation's capacity under his/her control. The central coordinator allocates capacity from idle workstations to local schedulers on workstations that have background jobs waiting. A local scheduler with more than one background job waiting makes its own decision of which job should be executed next.

Our structure follows the principle that workstations are autonomous computing resources and they should be managed by their own users. This also helps to keep the responsibilities of the coordinator simple. Simplicity is important so that a central site is not required to maintain a large amount of information about each workstation. This allows the system to be extendible to a large number of workstations and eases the required recovery when the centralized coordinator fails. Local schedulers are not affected if a remote site discontinues service. If the site on which the coordinator is executing fails, remotely executing jobs initiated and executing on other machines are not affected. Only the allocation of new capacity to requesting users is affected. Since the coordinator has few duties, its recovery at another site is simplified in relation to a fully centralized strategy. To balance the burden of coordination, the central coordinator can be moved to other locations. However, we have observed that the coordinator contributes

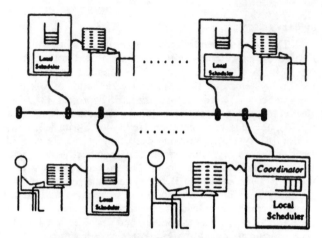

Figure 1: The Condor Scheduling Structure.

less than 1% to the CPU consumption of a workstation so that there is probably little need to move the coordinator.

In order to schedule jobs remotely, a remote execution facility is needed. Since our workstations operate under the Berkeley BSD 4.3 Unix* operating system, we decided to have a remote execution facility that is compatible with our local job execution facility. This led to the development of the *Remote Unix* (RU) facility [6].

2.2. The Remote Unix (RU) Facility

Remote Unix turns idle workstations into cycle servers. When RU is explicitly invoked, a *shadow* process runs locally as the surrogate of the process running on the remote machine. Any Unix system call made by the program on the remote machine invokes a library routine which communicates with the shadow process. A message indicating the type of system call is sent to the shadow process on the local machine and can be viewed as a remote procedure call.

When someone resumes using a workstation that is executing a remote job, the job must be stopped. If the state of the stopped job is not preserved, as is the case in the Butler system [8], all the work accomplished by the job is lost. Because background jobs can require several hours of CPU, it is important that the system restart background jobs without losing all the work accomplished so far. In the Condor system, the intermediate state from which background jobs can be restarted is made possible by the checkpointing feature of RU.

2.3. Checkpointing

When a job is removed from a remote location, RU checkpoints it. The checkpointing of a program is the saving of the state of the program so that its execution can be restarted. The state of an RU program is the text, data, bss, and the stack segments of the program, the registers, the status of open files, and any messages sent by the program to its shadow for which a reply has not been received. In our system, we do not need to save messages since checkpointing is deferred until the shadow's reply has been received. The text of the program contains the executable code, the data segment contains the initialized variables of the program, and the bss segment holds the uninitialized variables. It is assumed that there is no self-

---

* Unix is a trademark of AT&T Bell Laboratories.

384

modifying code in the program, and therefore the text segment is expected not to be essential in a checkpoint file. However, programs can execute for a very long time, perhaps months. A user might want to modify a program that has its executable file running as an RU job. For this reason, we save the text segment. Otherwise, the user would have to make sure that the new program's executable file is given a new name when there is an old version running.

2.4. Fair Access to Remote Cycles

Once a scheduling structure has been established, we need to understand the characteristics of the users in order to design algorithms that meet their needs. We have observed that the user community can be divided into heavy users and light users. Heavy users try to consume all available capacity for long periods, while light users only consume remote cycles occasionally. In order to serve all users fairly, we need to take into account their workload. Otherwise, heavy users might inhibit light users' access to remote cycles.

To provide fair access to resources, we manage available capacity with the Up-Down algorithm [2]. This algorithm enables heavy users to maintain steady access to remote cycles while providing fair access to cycles for light users. The algorithm trades off the remote cycles users have received with the time they have waited to receive them by maintaining a schedule index for each workstation. When remote capacity is allocated to a workstation, the index is increased. When a workstation wants remote capacity, but is denied access to it, the index is decreased. The priority to remote cycles of a workstation is determined by the value of its index. Initially the index for each station is zero. The indexes of the workstations are updated periodically. Every two minutes the coordinator will check if any stations have new jobs to execute. If a station with higher priority has a job to execute, and there are no idle stations, the coordinator preempts a remotely executing job from a station with lower priority. After the preempted job is checkpointed, the newly available capacity will be assigned to the high priority station. Further details of the algorithm and an evaluation of its performance is given in [2].

The implementation of the system has given us an opportunity to measure its performance under a real workload. It enabled us to measure the costs and benefits of providing a background scheduling service. The next section presents the detailed measurements we obtained from the system when it was used by members of our department.

3. Performance

The performance results we report are from preliminary observations of the Condor system. We present details of the way the system was used and analyze the quality of service it provided. This analysis includes the wait ratios users endure when they submit background jobs and the cost suffered by users at their local workstation to support remotely executing jobs. Our results are based on observing 23 workstations for one month. Table 1 summarizes the activity of users during that time period. It presents the number of jobs each user submitted, and the average job service demand per user. User A accounted for most of the consumption of remote capacity. This *heavy* user often tried to execute as many remote jobs as there were workstations in the system. The other users of Condor consumed capacity occasionally and can be classified as

light users.

The service demand of jobs submitted to the system were typically several hours in length. With the exception of User D, all users had an expected demand per job that was greater than 1 hour. Figure 2 shows the cumulative frequency distribution of jobs served by the system. For each hour i, the curve shows the percentage of jobs whose service demand was less than i hours. The average service demand was about 5 hours. The median service demand was less than 3 hours because shorter jobs were submitted more frequently than longer jobs.

Jobs arrived at the system in batches. Figure 3 depicts the queue length of jobs in the system on an hourly basis. The dotted line represents the queue length of light users. Jobs in service are considered part of the queue. The difference between the total and light users' queue lengths is the heavy user's queue length. The figure shows that the heavy user kept more than 30 jobs in the system for long periods.

We evaluated the quality of service users receive for the remote execution of their jobs. One measure of the quality of service is the wait ratio which is the ratio between the amount of time a job waits for service and its service time. The average of observed wait ratios of remotely executed jobs is illustrated in Figure 4. The solid line is the average wait ratio of all jobs, whereas the dashed line is the wait ratio of the light users. Note that in most cases light users did not wait at all. Their wait ratio is very small. The average wait ratio results are dominated by the wait ratio of the heavy user who waited significantly more. This is due to the Up-Down algorithm

User	Number of Jobs	% of Jobs	Demand/Job (in Hours)	Demand (in Hours)	% of Demand
A	690	75	6.2	4278	90
B	138	15	2.5	345	7
C	39	4	2.6	101	2
D	40	4	0.7	28	0.6
E	11	1	1.7	19	0.4
Total	918	100	5.2	4771	100

Table 1: Profile of User Service Requests.

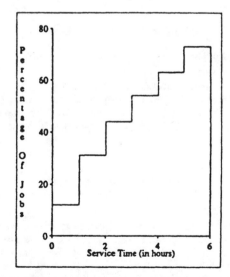

Figure 2: Profile Of Service Demand.

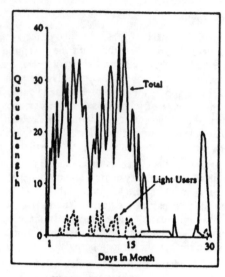

Figure 3: Queue Length.

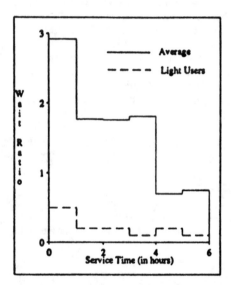

Figure 4: Average Wait Ratio.

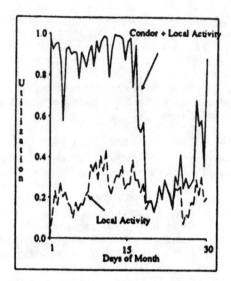

Figure 5: Utilization of Remote Resources.

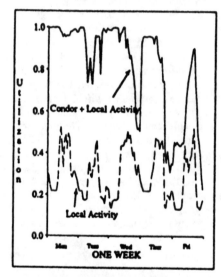

Figure 6: Utilization for One Week.

giving steady access to light users without allowing heavy users to dominate the system. Light users obtained remote resources regardless of whether the heavy users increased or decreased their load. Requests of the light users were typically small enough that available capacity could be immediately allocated to them. The Up-Down algorithm allocated remote capacity to light users and preempted the heavy user. When the light users' jobs were completed, the heavy user's jobs were resumed to consume available capacity. Typically the heavy user was allocated some capacity since the light users' requests were not large enough to consume all available capacity.

We measured the amount of extra capacity the 23 workstations provided to Condor users. During the observed period, 12438 hours were available for remote execution, of which 4771 machine hours of capacity was consumed by the Condor system. Note that almost 200 machine days of capacity that otherwise would have been lost were consumed by the Condor

system! Figure 5 shows how the utilization varied over time. The solid line is the system utilization which is the combination of local activity and remote executions, whereas the dashed line shows the local workstation utilization. Local activity remained low for the month period. On the average, local utilization for the month was 25%. However, due to the Condor system, we observed long periods that all workstations were utilized. The Condor system identified available capacity and allocated it to its users.

Each day of the month the amount of available capacity in the system varied. Figure 6 gives a closer view of the utilization of the system over one working week (Monday through Friday). Notice the peaks of local activity during the day, and how the capacity decreased in the evenings. The range of local utilization generally varied from 20% in the evenings and nights to 50% for short peak periods in the afternoons. Figure 7 presents the queue length of light users and the total queue length for that week. Notice the sharp rises in the queue length

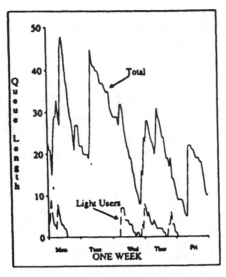

Figure 7: Queue Lengths for One Week.

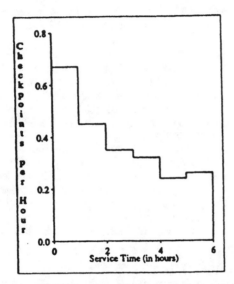

Figure 8: Rate Of Checkpointing.

which represents batch arrival of jobs. Much of the time during the week the queue length of the heavy user was larger than the number of machines available.

3.1. Impact on Local Workstations

The implementation of remote execution facilities should be efficient so that users at workstations need not use much of their local capacity to support remote executions. We studied the impact the remote execution facility has on users at their workstations. A user has to devote some local capacity to support the placement and checkpointing of remote jobs and the execution of system calls. In addition, a local scheduler and the coordinator consume some resources.

It is important to keep the capacity consumed by the coordinator and each local scheduler small since some users might rarely use the remote execution facility. Our observations show that these costs are indeed small. The local scheduler of a station with background jobs running has been observed to consume less than 1% of a station's capacity. This capacity is

independent of the size of the system. The consumption of capacity by the coordinator has been observed to be less than 1% of a workstation's capacity as well. The size of the system is expected to affect the amount of capacity consumed by the coordinator. We have observed a system with as many as 40 workstations. Even with this system size, the coordinator consumes less than 1%. This leads us to believe that a coordinator can manage as many as 100 workstations with only a small impact on the workstation that hosts it.

We measured the costs that remotely executing jobs bring on their home workstations. To support the remote execution of background jobs, the home workstation has to transfer jobs to remote sites, checkpoint them when they are preempted, and execute their system calls. This support can have a significant impact on the local workstation. The costs associated with this support depend on the *costs* and *rates* of these activities.

The capacity required to place and checkpoint a remote job depends on the size of the job. Placing and checkpointing jobs consume approximately 5 seconds per megabyte of the checkpoint file. We observed that the average checkpoint file size was ½ megabyte. Therefore, the average cost of placement and checkpointing was approximately 2½ seconds.

The rate at which jobs were checkpointed after they were initially placed is shown in Figure 8. This rate is the number of times per hour of CPU that a remotely executing job is moved from one location to another. Jobs are checkpointed when the location at which they have been running becomes unavailable for remote execution. In addition, jobs can be checkpointed when the coordinator decides that one user requesting remote cycles has priority over another user. The rate of checkpointing was relatively steady over the range of service demands, with the exception of short jobs. The reason that longer jobs have a lower rate of checkpointing can be explained in terms of the local usage patterns of workstations. When jobs are preempted due to local user activity, they will be placed at another remote location if one is available. Since local workstation activity is not uniform across the system, some workstations tend to be available for short periods, and other workstations tend to be available for much longer periods [1]. Long jobs have a lower checkpoint rate because eventu-

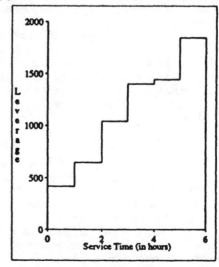

Figure 9: Remote Execution Leverage.

ally they are placed at a workstation that experiences no local activity.

System calls by a remotely executing job can have a significant impact on a local workstation. The average capacity consumed on a VAXstation II to support a remote job executing a system call is approximately 10 msec. This is 20 times the cost of a Unix system call. Programs executing large numbers of system calls, such as reads or writes, in proportion to other instructions would be better off if they were executed locally instead of remotely. For a remotely executing job with an extreme number of system calls, a local workstation supporting the remote system calls would consume more capacity than the amount of useful work accomplished at the remote site.

We define a new performance measure called *leverage* to compare the amount of effort a local workstation must endure to benefit from having useful work conducted remotely. The leverage of a remote job is defined as the amount of remote capacity consumed to execute a job divided by the amount of local capacity consumed to support remote execution. The local capacity is the combination of capacity used to support placement, checkpointing, and system calls. If more capacity is consumed locally to support remote executions than what is actually accomplished remotely, the leverage of the job is less than 1. Figure 9 shows a profile of the leverage of jobs. The average leverage was approximately 1300. This means for every 1 minute of local capacity consumed to support remote execution of jobs, nearly 22 hours of remote capacity was received by the users! Longer jobs had a larger leverage than shorter jobs. This is because the rate of checkpointing for short jobs was higher than for long jobs, and the amount of input/output for the short jobs was relatively the same as that of long jobs. Nevertheless, the leverage for jobs with service demands less than 2 hours averaged approximately 600. This means that even a short job with only a service demand of 1 hour required less than 6 seconds of local capacity to support remote execution.

4. Discussion

The implementation of the Condor system brought a clearer understanding of several issues. Many of these issues relate to the nature of background jobs and the large amount of memory needed for their remote execution. For example, if a job is to be executed remotely, it must be placed on the remote station's disk. Because users of workstations often do little to manage their own disk space, users let their disk become full. When a disk is full, a remote job cannot be placed on the workstation for remote execution. Even if a workstation is idle so that its processor is available for executing remote jobs, the disk might be full so that no remote job can execute there. The coordinator must know not only which workstation's processor is available, but has to keep track of available disk space.

The issue of disk space affects users in another way. Users often like to execute many background jobs at a time. If users do not have much local disk available, they will be restricted on the number of background jobs that they can execute simultaneously. The restriction occurs since checkpoint files of remotely executing background jobs are kept locally. Space can be saved if disk servers from additional hardware are implemented to store checkpoint files. Another solution to the disk space problem is to share text segments of programs. This is effective since users often submit several occurrences of the same job with only different parameters to evaluate. An example is when users submit simulation programs to the system. Only one copy of the text segment might be needed for several job executions.

Because placing and checkpointing remote jobs has an impact on a local workstation and the network, our implementation does not place or checkpoint several jobs simultaneously. We have noticed that if several machines are available, and users have several background jobs waiting for service, the performance of the local machine is severely degraded if all jobs are placed at the same time. Our implementation places one job every two minutes to distribute over time the impact of this activity on local workstations and the network.

Our design philosophy has been to ensure that the Condor system does not interfere with users and their local activity. Remote jobs are only executed when there is no local activity. However, one element of our implementation differs with our design philosophy. When local activity resumes at a workstation where a foreign job is running, the foreign job is stopped on the station and is kept there to see if the workstation will soon be available. If the workstation does not become available within 5 minutes, the job will be checkpointed and moved from the location. The strategy has worked well since many of the workstations' unavailable intervals are short. However, it does not completely follow a model where users reclaim all local resources as soon as they return to their workstations. The CPUs are immediately returned, but disk space consumed by remote jobs is not released until the checkpoint files are moved. If a user has little local available disk space, the checkpoint file might interfere with local activity until the file is moved. We consider a modification to our strategy so that checkpoints of remote executions are periodically taken. When a workstation's owner resumes activity at a location executing a remote job, the new strategy is to kill the job immediately. This minimizes the interference a remote job has with the owner of a workstation. The only work lost is that between the job's most recent checkpoint and the time it was terminated.

5. Further Work

Our work is the first step in exploring design and implementation issues regarding background job scheduling in a network of workstations. There are several performance evaluation and implementation issues which we intend to study further. Some of the example issues are:

(1) Other work [1] has found that workstations with long available intervals tend to have their next available interval long. Workstations with short available intervals tend to have their next available intervals short. This correlation means that the coordinator could choose sources of remote cycles on the basis of the history of workstation availability. We intend to study the impact on the number of preemptions long running jobs suffer when we use knowledge of past available interval lengths.

(2) We are considering an implementation of Condor which will allow the execution of parallel algorithms. The model of interprocess communication will be communicating sequential processes as proposed by Hoare [13]. Depending on the availability of multiple remote machines, multiple cooperating processes may share a

remote site or be placed on multiple sites.

(3) The implementation of a reservation system would improve the computing service available to users. Reservations guarantee computing capacity for users in advance in order to conduct experiments in distributed computations. Many important issues are open on how to manage a reservation system in which workstations become available whenever their owners are not using them.

(4) We are porting our system to the SUN [14] workstations. This system means that a background job compiled into two different binary files could be executed at either a VAXstation II or SUN workstation. This system leads to interesting scheduling questions regarding at which workstation should a job be placed. The decision of placement should take into account the usage patterns of each type of workstation. Once a job has been placed on one type of workstation, the job could not be moved to the other type of workstation without losing all the work done on the first type of workstation.

6. Conclusions

Networks with workstations have increased in great numbers in recent years. These networks represent powerful computing environments that were previously only available to users at institutions with supercomputers. With the implementation of the Condor system, users can expand their capacity to that of the entire computing network. This paper discusses a system that effectively utilizes idle workstation capacity and presents a profile of its performance. The results are from a one-month observation of the system where actual users obtained capacity from workstations that otherwise would have been idle.

Condor has proven to be an extremely effective means of improving the productivity of our computing environment. For a system of 23 workstations, large amounts of capacity were observed to be available for remote execution. About 75% of the time the workstations were available as sources of remote cycles. Our system caused the workstations to be fully utilized over long periods of time. Over a one-month period, users consumed as much as 200 machine days of computing cycles from available workstations. The checkpointing feature of our remote execution facility insured users that their jobs would complete regardless if their jobs were forced by users at remote locations to stop, or if remote locations failed. We showed that users need only to dedicate an extremely small amount of workstation capacity locally to received huge amounts of remote cycles. We report that the leverage of remote execution observed was 1300, which means for every minute of local capacity supplied, almost 1 day of remote CPU capacity was received.

Acknowledgements

We would like to thank Don Nuehengen and Tom Virgilio for their pioneering work on the remote system call implementation.

References

[1] M. W. Mutka and M. Livny, "Profiling Workstations' Available Capacity for Remote Execution," *Performance '87, Proceedings of the 12th IFIP WG 7.3 Symposium on Computer Performance,* Brussels, Belgium, (December 7-9, 1987).

[2] M. W. Mutka and M. Livny, "Scheduling Remote Processing Capacity in a Workstation-Processor Bank Computing System", *Proceedings of the 7th International Conference of Distributed Computing Systems,* Berlin, West Germany, pp. 2-9, (September 21-25, 1987).

[3] R. Agrawal and A. K. Ezzat, "Processor Sharing In Nest: A Network Of Computer Workstations," *Proceedings of 1st International Conference on Computer Workstations,* (November, 1985).

[4] M. M. Theimer, K. A. Lantz, and D. R. Cheriton, "Preemptable Remote Execution Facilities for the V-System," *Proceedings of the 10th Symp. on Operating Systems Principles,* pp. 2-12, (December, 1985).

[5] R. Hagmann, "Processor Server: Sharing Processing Power in a Workstation Environment," *Proceedings of the 6th IEEE Distributed Computing Conference,* Cambridge, MA, pp. 260-267, (May, 1986).

[6] M. Litzkow, "Remote Unix," Proceedings of 1987 Summer Usenix Conferences, Phoenix, Arizona, (June, 1987).

[7] F. Douglis and J. Ousterhout, "Process Migration in the Sprite Operating System," *Proceedings of the 7th International Conference of Distributed Computing Systems,* Berlin, West Germany, pp. 18-25, (September 21-25, 1987).

[8] D. A. Nichols, "Using Idle Workstations in a Shared Computing Environment", *Proceedings of the 11th Symp. on Operating System Principles,* pp.5-12, (November, 1987).

[9] P. Krueger and M. Livny, "The Diverse Objectives of Distributed Scheduling Policies", *Proceedings of the 7th International Conference of Distributed Computing Systems,* Berlin, West Germany, pp. 242-249, (September 21-25, 1987).

[10] H.-Y. Chang and M. Livny, "Priority in Distributed Systems," *Proceedings of the Real-Time Systems Symposium, (December, 1985).*

[11] P. Sandon, "Learning Object-Centered Representations," Ph. D. Thesis, University of Wisconsin, Madison, Wisconsin, (August, 1987).

[12] D. Chavey, *Private Correspondence,* University of Wisconsin, Madison, Wisconsin, (December, 1986).

[13] C. A. R. Hoare, "Communicating Sequential Processes," *Communications of the ACM* 21, No. 8, pp. 666-677, (August, 1978).

[14] A. Bechtolsheim, V. R. Pratt, and F. Baskett, "The SUN Workstation Architecture", Technical Report 229, Computer Systems Laboratory, Stanford University (February, 1982).

GAMMON: A Load Balancing Strategy for Local Computer Systems with Multiaccess Networks

KATHERINE M. BAUMGARTNER, MEMBER, IEEE, AND BENJAMIN W. WAH, SENIOR MEMBER, IEEE

Abstract—This paper investigates an efficient load balancing strategy, GAMMON (global allocation from maximum to minimum in constant time), for distributed computing systems connected by multiaccess local area networks. The broadcast capability of these networks is used to implement an identification procedure at the applications level for the maximally and the minimally loaded processors. The search technique has an average overhead which is independent of the number of participating stations. An implementation of GAMMON on a network of SUN workstations is described. Its performance is found to be better than other known methods.

Index Terms—Broadcast, collision detection, dynamic programming, load balancing, multiaccess networks.

I. INTRODUCTION

LOAD balancing uses communication facilities in a distributed computing system to support remote job execution in a user-transparent fashion in order to improve resource utilization and reduce response time. A decision to load balance a job is made if the job is likely to be finished sooner when executed remotely than when executed locally. Load balancing has been found to be essential because a job will almost always be waiting for service at one processor while another processor is idle in a system with ten or more processors [15].

Load balancing decisions can be made in a centralized or in a distributed manner. A *centralized* decision implies that status information is collected, and decisions to load balance are made at one location. An example would be a system with a job scheduler at one location that collects jobs and dispatches them to stations for processing. Theoretical studies on centralized load balancing have been made by Chow and Kohler [5] and Ni and Hwang [17]. The disadvantage of centralized scheduling is the overhead of collecting processor status information and jobs. When this overhead is large, scheduling decisions are frequently based on inaccurate and outdated status information. In contrast, a *distributed* load balancing scheme does not limit the scheduling intelligence to one processor. It avoids the bottleneck of collecting status information and jobs at a single site and allows the scheduler to react quickly to dynamic changes in the system state.

Load balancing can also be classified as state-dependent or probabilistic [5]. A decision based on the current state of the system is *state-dependent*. A decision is *probabilistic* if an arriving job is dispatched to the processors according to a set of branching probabilities which are collected from previous experience or are based on system characteristics. In the case that the branching probabilities are derived from the service rates of processors, the strategy is called *proportional branching* [5]. It was found that a probabilistic strategy for a single job class performed better than a proportional branching strategy with a single arrival stream [17]. An optimal probabilistic algorithm for multiple job classes was found to be easier to implement than state-dependent strategies. An optimal probabilistic load balancing algorithm with multiple arrival streams has also been shown [19]. Other research on load balancing include studies characterizing state-dependent load balancing, determining appropriate state information [8], proposing efficient algorithms [4], [7], [13], [15], [25], and topology-dependent strategies [6], [10]–[12], [21], [22].

State-dependent load balancing is implemented on the Purdue Engineering Computer Network, which is a system of computers connected by a hybrid of Ethernet and point-to-point links [9]. The load balancing decisions are distributed: each processor decides whether to send its jobs for remote execution. A processor polls other processors for status information about their loads, decides which processor has the lowest load, and sends the job for remote processing if the turnaround time is shorter.

Some results of these previous studies are as follows.

1) A network with load balancing performs better than a network without load balancing.

2) State-dependent load balancing strategies perform better than probabilistic strategies, but have higher overhead.

3) Probabilistic strategies are sometimes insensitive to dynamic changes in system load and may result in suboptimal performance.

4) Load balancing decisions considering the state of the source only do not have the potential for performance improvement that decisions considering the state of the destination do [25].

5) Extensive state information is not needed for effective load balancing and can be detrimental to system performance [7].

6) Status information used in a state-dependent decision

Manuscript received September 21, 1988; revised April 10, 1988. This work was supported by the National Aeronautics and Space Administration under Contract NCC 2-481 and the National Science Foundation under Grant DMC 85-19649.

K. M. Baumgartner is with Digital Equipment Corporation, Maynard, MA 01754.

B. W. Wah is with Department of Electrical and Computer Engineering and the Coordinated Sciences Laboratory, University of Illinois at Urbana-Champaign, Urbana, IL 61801.

IEEE Log Number 8928532.

Reprinted from *IEEE Trans. on Computers*, vol. 38, no. 8, Aug. 1989, pp. 1098–1109.

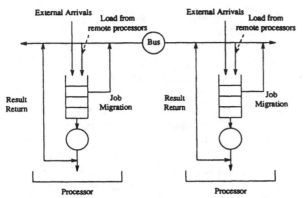

Fig. 1. Queueing diagram of a system of processors connected by a broadcast bus.

must be readily available. Decisions based on outdated or inaccurate status information could degrade performance.

7) Load balancing increases network load which can impede message transmissions.

This study considers load balancing on local computer systems connected by multiaccess networks. These networks have a broadcast bus topology that allows only one job or message to be sent across the network at a time. Response time is the amount of time elapsed from job submission to job completion and is an indication of the processor load. Due to the constraint of sending one job at a time across the bus, an efficient load balancing strategy is to send a job from the processor with the maximum load to the processor with the minimum load when the overhead of sending these jobs and identifying the participating stations is small. This paper proposes a strategy for load balancing that can be implemented at the applications level on *existing* systems. The strategy uses an efficient technique to identify the minimally and the maximally loaded processors with constant average overhead. The strategy is called GAMMON: global allocation from maximum to minimum in constant time.

The organization of this paper is as follows. The section following this introduction gives an overview of GAMMON. Section III shows a window protocol that can be used for distributed extremum search on bus networks and that requires hardware modification to existing network interfaces. Section IV extends this protocol for implementation on existing systems without hardware changes. The implementation of GAMMON is described in Section V, and concluding remarks are drawn in Section VI.

II. GLOBAL SCHEDULING STRATEGY

A model of the system under consideration is shown in Fig. 1. There are multiple identical processors connected by a broadcast bus. Each processor can have arrivals external to the system or from the bus. Jobs are modeled as independent tasks. If jobs are migrated to a processor across the bus, the results must be returned to the originating processor when execution is completed. Moreover, the queue at each processor is finite: only a limited number of jobs may be waiting for execution.

A good load balancing procedure should avoid the occurrence of the idle-while-waiting condition, as well as any state which makes idle-while-waiting more likely. In a batch processing system, idle-while-waiting will not occur when there is at least one job at each processor at any time. Hence, the likelihood of idle-while-waiting can be minimized if jobs are evenly distributed. In a multiprogrammed system, assuring that processors are busy is not sufficient to minimize the occurrence of the idle-while-waiting condition; it is important to distribute all available jobs evenly in order to have a reasonable response time for every job.

The strategy discussed here uses the queue length of active jobs at a processor as a metric to indicate workload. A queue length imbalance will make the idle-while-waiting condition more likely. Hence, load redistribution is needed when there is significant difference between queue lengths, such that the estimated total overhead of migrating a job and queueing delay at a remote processor and later returning results is less than the delay a job would experience at its source processor.

An important point here is that the number of jobs at a processor, while frequently a good reflection of load, is not always adequate. Other factors that may contribute to the workload at a processor include physical differences of processors (such as speed or size of main memory), paging activity, and the ratio of processing activities and input/output activities in jobs. Future work will involve investigating a more inclusive measure of processor load [24].

An ideal redistribution of jobs, given that the metric used is the queue length at each processor, is to have equal number of jobs at each processor. Since a single bus connects all the computers, only one job can be migrated at any one time. The best strategy is to take a job from the maximally loaded processor, and send it to the minimally loaded processor. Such a strategy is both source- and sink-initiated. Furthermore, it requires the minimal amount of status information transferred.

Three basic scheduling operations are required for this redistribution on a bus network: identification of the maximally and the minimally loaded processors, job migration, and result return. Migrating jobs and returning results are straightforward because existing communication facilities can be used. However, identifying processors with the load extremes efficiently is more difficult. Such an operation should have very low complexity, preferably independent of the number of processors connected to the bus. Any centralized scheduling algorithm, such as polling, is not suitable here. Efficient algorithms are studied in Sections IV and V.

The three basic scheduling operations, in addition to regular message transfers, must be prioritized in order to achieve the best performance. Regular message transfer is assigned the highest priority, since it is the original purpose of the network. The priorities of the remaining tasks are determined by considering the relative overheads in terms of the additional total system delay (the sum of the delays of all jobs) incurred.

First, the relative priority of identifying the ith maximally/minimally-loaded-processor pair and migrating the job between the $(i - 1)$th pair is determined. Two cases are considered. The first is when there are idle processors. If job migration is done first, then the migrated job can begin execution immediately upon arrival at the destination processor, so its delay is increased by the time required to send it across the network. In contrast, if the max/min identification is done first, then the same job will incur the delay of that operation as well. Clearly, migrating the job first is better. The second case is when there are no idle processors. The ordering of the tasks is not critical in this case, since migrating the job first does not immediately contribute to reducing the job delay, as the job may not begin execution upon arrival at the destination. This result is true for any job migration and max/min identification, and performing the migration first will result in a total delay equal to or smaller than performing the max/min identification first. Consequently, job migration should have priority over max/min identification.

Next, the relative priority between result return and job migration is considered. When there are no idle processors, delay is added directly to the job waiting for result return. Since the job waiting for job migration will not be able to begin execution immediately upon arrival at the destination, result return should take precedence. When there are idle processors, reducing either the delay for job migration or the delay for result return will reduce the overall delay. In short, performing the result return first always improves the overall performance as much or more than performing job migration first. It is also easy to see that result return should always have precedence over max/min identification by a similar argument.

In summary, the priority ordering for tasks using the bus network is 1) regular message transfer, 2) result return, 3) job migration, and 4) max/min identification.

The scheduling strategy GAMMON consists of two steps that are executed repeatedly. The first is to determine which of the current tasks has the highest priority, and the second step is to execute that task. Due to the ordering of the priorities, only one job will ever be waiting for job migration, but potentially more than one may be waiting for result return.

A consideration with priorities are the overhead of priority resolution among tasks and the overhead of the tasks themselves. The discussion above assumes that each of the steps has similar overhead. If the overheads associated with tasks are considerably different, priority enforcement changes. A specific case is processors sharing a common secondary storage. Job migration and result return have lower overhead in such a system than in one with a shared disk. File transfer is not explicitly needed as all processors have access to the common secondary storage. Furthermore, if the overhead of resolving priorities is large, then it is more efficient not to schedule tasks according to priorities. Such a tradeoff is performed in the implementation of the load balancing algorithm, which is presented in Section V.

III. Window Protocol for Distributed Extremum Searches

Carrier-sense-multiaccess networks with *collision detection* (CSMA/CD) are a type of local-area network with packet switching and a bus topology [18]. CSMA/CD networks evolved from CSMA networks that have *listen-before-talk* protocols to avoid overlapping transmissions. The collision-detection ability of CSMA/CD networks allows processors to additionally *listen-while-talk,* so collisions

resulting from simultaneous transmissions can be detected and stopped immediately.

There are three types of protocols for contention resolution CSMA/CD networks. Collision-free protocols strictly schedule bus accesses, so no collisions occur. Contention protocols function at the other extreme by allowing processors to transmit whenever they find the bus idle. When collisions occur because of simultaneous transmissions, processors stop transmitting, wait for some prescribed amount of time, and try again. The backoff algorithm of Ethernet [16] is an example in this class. The disadvantage of collision-free protocols lies in the overhead of waiting for transmission, while the disadvantage of contention protocols is the time wasted during collisions. A third type of contention-resolution protocol is the limited-contention protocol. This type of protocol chooses a processor for transmission from among those waiting to transmit based on *a priori* information, such as the channel load.

The *virtual-window protocol* (VWP) proposed by Wah and Juang [10], [21]–[23] is an example of a limited-contention protocol. It is based on a three-state collision-detection mechanism. After each attempted broadcast, there are three possible outcomes: *collision* (more than one broadcast), *idle* (no broadcast), and *success* (exactly one broadcast). The protocol can be adapted easily to perform distributed extremum searches in a load balancing strategy. In the remainder of this section, we briefly explain this protocol and discuss its limitations.

Stations wishing to transmit packets participate in a *contention period* that consists of a number of *contention slots*. Each station generates a random number called a *contention parameter* that is used for the entire contention period. The parameter is in an interval with upper and lower bounds U and L, respectively. Without loss of generality, assume that the station with the minimum contention parameter is sought. The results developed apply to the case in which the station with the maximum contention parameter is to be found. Successive choices of smaller intervals in each contention slot attempt to isolate the minimum contention parameter.

For regular message transfers, each station has equal chance of being chosen for transmission, so the contention parameters are random numbers generated from a uniform distribution in the interval (0, 1]. The stations maintain a common window (or interval) for contention. In a contention slot, stations having contention parameters within the window broadcast a short signal to contend for the channel. If a collision or no transmission occurs, the window boundaries are adjusted in parallel for the next contention slot. Stations having contention parameters outside the window stop contending and wait for the next contention period. The above steps are repeated until a single station is isolated in the window. This station is the winner and is allowed to transmit its packet. The distribution of the contention parameters and an estimate of the channel load are used to update the window efficiently, so the number of contention slots is kept to a minimum.

The global window required in the protocol can be maintained by updating an initially identical window with a common algorithm and using the identical information broad-

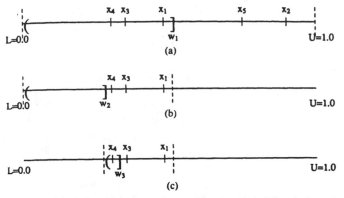

Fig. 2. Example of the virtual-window protocol. The dashed lines indicate the portion of the interval being searched during the current contention slot. The current window, enclosing stations eligible to contend, is delimited by (]. (a) First iteration. (b) Second iteration. (c) Third iteration.

cast on the bus. Assuming that the information broadcast is received correctly by all stations, the global window will be synchronized at all sites.

An example of the VWP is shown in Fig. 2. There are five processors contending, and station i has contention parameter x_i. In this example, $x_1 = 0.48$, $x_2 = 0.90$, $x_3 = 0.35$, $x_4 = 0.30$, and $x_5 = 0.75$. These contention parameters were chosen arbitrarily, but for different purposes they may reflect processor loads or priorities. The windows chosen in these examples are not the optimal windows but are chosen to illustrate the characteristics of the protocols. w_1, the upper bound for the first window chosen, is 0.51. All stations with contention parameters less that or equal to 0.51 are allowed to broadcast; in this case, stations 1, 3, and 4. The result of this contention slot is a collision; the interval to be searched is updated to (0, 0.51]; and stations 2 and 5 are eliminated from further contention. w_2, the upper bound for the next window, is 0.25. The result of the second contention slot is idle (no broadcast), so the interval is updated to (0.25, 0.51]. No stations were eliminated as a result of this contention slot. For the third contention slot, the upper bound of the window is chosen to be 0.32. The result is a successful transmission, so station 4 is isolated and "wins" the contention.

The window-selection process can be formulated as a dynamic programming algorithm, and details have been shown elsewhere [22]. Analyses and simulations have shown that contention can be resolved in an average of 2.4 contention slots, independent of the number of contending stations and the distribution function of the contention parameters, if the parameters are independent and identically distributed [21].

A major limitation of the VWP is that its implementation requires minor hardware modifications of existing Ethernet interfaces [22]. At the applications level, such modifications are not always possible. Many existing networks do not make three-state collision-detection information available to the applications software because a contention slot is a small amount of time (50–100 μs) relative to the time required to propagate information through all levels of software to the applications level (hundreds of microseconds). Consequently, a different protocol must be developed for distributed extremum search at the application level. Several alternatives are discussed in the next section.

IV. Window Protocols with Two-State Collision Detection

At the applications level, each station has an independent *search parameter*, and an iteration is a *broadcast slot* which is a contention resolution at the network interface followed by a broadcast of a message to all stations. A broadcast slot has two possible outcomes, *idle* (no stations attempt to broadcast), or *transmission* (one or more stations attempt to broadcast resulting in contention resolution, and one station broadcasts its search parameter). A broadcast slot may consist of a number of contention slots, and information about each contention slot is not sent to the applications level.

There are a number of differences between searching at the applications level and the network level.

1) The contention parameters are the search parameters for the VWP, which is not the case for the window protocol at the applications level.

2) An iteration of the VWP is a contention slot with three possible outcomes: idle, collision, and success. An iteration of the window protocol at the applications level is a broadcast slot with two possible outcomes: transmission and idle.

3) An iteration of the VWP takes less time than an iteration of the window protocol at the applications level. Normally, a contention slot takes tens of microseconds, while broadcasting a short message takes hundreds of microseconds.

Since the information available for window selection is different at the applications level, the decision process has to be modified. Three possible window-search strategies to identify the minimum are described below. The identification of the maximum is similar and is not described. Further details about these strategies can be found elsewhere [1], [2]. In contrast to the VWP, dynamic programming methods to optimize window choices cannot be used here because the Principle of Optimality is violated. The performance of these strategies is compared using the number of broadcast slots they require to isolate the minimum search parameter. These strategies assume that information about the distribution of search parameters is available. This distribution is characterized experimentally in Section IV-D.

A. One-Broadcast Strategy

The one-broadcast strategy allows a maximum of one broadcast slot per iteration. Starting with an interval $(L, U]$, each station has a search parameter x_i in the interval. The stations maintain a global window in the interval. Stations with parameters within the window attempt to broadcast their search parameters, and if there are one or more parameters in the window, there will be a contention resolution followed by a broadcast of one of the search parameters. The upper bound of the interval will be updated to the value broadcast. If there are no parameters within the window, the lower bound of the interval is updated to the upper bound of the window used, and the protocol continues. The minimum is identified when the lower bound of the interval is equal to the upper bound.

An example of the one-broadcast strategy is shown in Fig. 3. The stations and parameters are the same as those in Fig. 2. In the first iteration [Fig. 3(a)], the upper bound of the window chosen is 0.51. Stations 1, 3, and 4 attempt to broadcast their

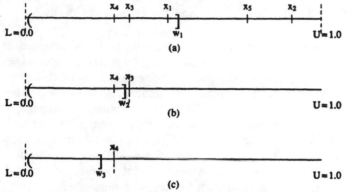

Fig. 3. Example of the window protocol using the one-broadcast strategy. The dashed lines indicate the portion of the interval being searched during the current broadcast slot. The current window is delimited by (]. (a) First iteration. (b) Second iteration. (c) Third iteration.

parameters. Suppose that station 3 is the winner and transmits. The next interval to be searched is $(0, x_3)$. Let the upper bound of the next window chosen be 0.33. Only station 4 tries to transmit its parameter, and x_4 is broadcast. The search has not concluded even though x_4 is the minimum because the fact that it was the only station broadcasting is not available to station 4 or to the other stations. The next window chosen is 0.25. There is, of course, no broadcast. This process will continue until the bounds of the window isolate x_4, and the minimum is globally known.

The choice of the window in each broadcast slot is based on the probabilities of the two states, transmission and idle, which are dependent on previous broadcasts. If a previous broadcast slot resulted in the transmission of a value, say x_{b1}, then any subsequent transmissions must be less than x_{b1}. This implies that any subsequent x_i's broadcast were eligible to broadcast during the iteration that x_{b1} was broadcast, but lost the contention. The probability of the subsequent transmissions must be conditioned on the fact that any x_i's in the current

window did not broadcast when they were eligible during previous iterations. The choice of the window is, thus, dependent on previous broadcasts, and the Principle of Optimality is not satisfied. As a result, the choice cannot be optimized by dynamic programming methods.

Assume that station i has an independent search parameter x_i with distribution $F(x)$ and density $f(x)$. The following definitions are used to formulate the problem of choosing the upper bound of the next window as a recurrence after k broadcasts.

$N_{E1}(a, b, v^k, q^k)$: the minimum expected number of broadcast slots to isolate the minimum x_i in the interval $(a, b]$ using a one-broadcast strategy, given that there have been k previous broadcasts with

values and corresponding upper bounds of windows stored in the k-element arrays v^k and q^k, respectively;

$\phi_E(a, b, w, v^k, q^k)$: the probability of a transmission in the interval $(a, w]$, given that there have been k previous broadcasts with values and corresponding upper bounds of windows stored in the k-element arrays v^k and q^k, respectively;

$\theta_E(a, b, w, v^k, q^k)$: the probability of idle in the interval $(a, w]$, given that there have been k previous broadcasts with values and corresponding upper bounds of windows stored in the k-element arrays v^k and q^k, respectively.

The notation v^k and q^k indicates a set of k values broadcast and the corresponding upper bounds of windows used. v_k and q_k are the kth value and the corresponding upper bound of window used. It follows directly from the above definitions that

$$\phi_E(a, b, w, v^k, q^k) + \theta_E(a, b, w, v^k, q^k) = 1.0. \quad (1)$$

After k successful broadcasts, there are $2(k + 1)$ subintervals in the interval $(a, U]$. They are $(a, w]$, $(w, v_k]$, $(v_k, q_k]$, $(q_k, v_{k-1}]$, $\cdots$, $(v_1, q_1]$, and $(q_1, U]$. For reference, they can be numbered from left to right and from 1 to $2(k + 1)$. Let s be a set of elements $\{s_i\}$, where s_i is the number of x_i's in the ith subinterval. Let S be the set of s that are possible with previous windows and values broadcast, and let I be a subset of S such that $s_1 = 0$. The set I is the subset of S that corresponds to a distribution of x_i's such that there will be no x_i's in $(a, w]$ and that the result of the broadcast slot is idle. Then

$$\theta_E = \frac{\sum_{s \in I} \left(\Pr[\text{arrangement } s] \sum_{i=1}^{k} \Pr[v_i \text{ broadcast with a window upper bound } q_i | s] \right)}{\sum_{s \in S} \left(\Pr[\text{arrangement } s] \sum_{i=1}^{k} \Pr[v_i \text{ broadcast with a window upper bound } q_i | s] \right)}. \quad (2)$$

The probability of a given arrangement is found using the distribution function $F(x)$. Let $b(a, b, i) = [F(b) - F(a)]^i$ then

$$\Pr[\text{arrangement } s] = \binom{n}{s_1} b(a, w, s_1) \binom{n - s_1}{s_2}$$
$$\cdot b(w, v_k, s_2) \cdots \binom{n - \sum_{i=1}^{2k} s_i}{s_{2k+1}}$$
$$\cdot b(v_1, q_1, s_{2k+1}) b(q_1, U, s_{2k+2}). \quad (3)$$

$\Pr[v_k \text{ broadcast with a window upper bound } q_k | s]$ is easily determined because each station in the subinterval search has equal probability of winning and broadcasting in a broadcast slot, so

394

$\Pr(v_i$ broadcast with a window upper bound $q_i | s)$

$$= \frac{1}{2(k-i+1)} \cdot \sum_{j=1}^{w} s_j . \quad (4)$$

Using a conditional density function

$$f_c(a, w, x_b) = \frac{f(x_b)}{\Pr(a < x_b \le w)} = \frac{f(x_b)}{F(w) - F(a)}, \quad (5)$$

the choice of the upper bound of the next window is formulated as a recurrence. Let

$$\gamma(a, w, v^k, q^k) = \int_a^w f_c(a, w, x_b)$$
$$\cdot N_{E1}(a, x_b, v^{k+1}, q^{k+1}) \, dx_b \quad (6)$$

then

$$N_{E1}(a, b, v^k, q^k)$$

$$= \min_{a < w < b} \{1 + \phi_E(a, b, w, v^k, q^k)\gamma(a, w, v^k, q^k)$$

$$+ \theta_E(a, b, w, v^k, q^k)N_{E1}(w, b, v^k, q^k)\} \quad (7)$$

with

$$N_{E1}(a, b, v^k, q^k) = 1 \quad \text{for all } b = a. \quad (8)$$

The first term on the right-hand side of (7) counts the current broadcast. The second term is the expected number of additional broadcast slots to isolate the minimum if the current broadcast slot results in a transmission. γ is the weighted average number of broadcast slots for the value broadcast, x_b, and the probability that this value was broadcast. The third term is the number of additional broadcast slots if the current broadcast slot is idle.

Boundary conditions must be set to terminate the evaluations after a reasonable number of broadcast slots. In practice, the x_i's may represent indistinguishable physical measures when their difference is less than δ. It is assumed that when the window size is smaller than δ, the probability that two stations have generated parameters in this interval is so small that contention can always be resolved in one step. The boundary condition becomes

$$N_{E1}(a, b, v^k, q^k) = 1 \quad \text{for all } (b - a) < \delta. \quad (9)$$

The optimal window choices found in (7) and (9) can be organized by the decision tree shown in Fig. 4. The top of the structure contains the roots of decision trees with different numbers of processors. For a given n_i, there is an initial window $w_{1,1}$, and two pointers to substructures corresponding to the two outcomes: transmission and idle. Note that the substructure for a transmission contains windows for each of the possible values that can be transmitted in the subinterval. Each box in the structure corresponds to a decision point, and the contents of the box, $w_{a,b,c}$, is the window upper bound for the current broadcast slot. The subscripts of the window upper

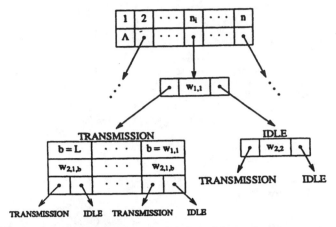

Fig. 4. Data structure for the exact solution of the one-broadcast strategy. The data structure shows a method for storing the windows and indicates the tree-structured progression of window choices.

bound indicate the iteration number, whether the last iteration outcome was transmission or idle (transmission = 1, idle = 2), and the value broadcast if the last iteration was a transmission. There are two branches from each decision point corresponding to the two possible outcomes in each broadcast slot. Starting from the root, if the broadcast slot results in a transmission of b, then the search will terminate if $(b - L) < \delta$; otherwise, the search will continue with a new decision point corresponding to the interval $(L, b]$. If the broadcast slot is idle, then the search will terminate if $(U - w_{1,1}) < \delta$; otherwise, the search continues with the interval $(w_{1,1}, U]$.

The data structure in Fig. 4 shows the final window choices, but during computation of the best window choice for each decision point, all possible choices of windows have to be tried. This evaluation process is extremely complex. For each possible window, there can either be a transmission or no transmission. If there is a transmission, all possible values within the window must be considered as the possible value broadcast. Each level of the tree indicates the outcome of an iteration. For every decision in the exact solution, the entire tree above the current decision point, which is determined by v^k and q^k, must be taken into consideration in computing the next set of branching probabilities. With $\delta = 1/(10n)$, and $n = 5$, there are 69 007 690 decision points, and for $n = 6$, the number increases to 8 501 194 726. The number of decision points increases so rapidly that the problem becomes intractable. Fortunately, reasonable results can be obtained using a heuristic decision based on the current upper and lower bounds only.

In the approximate solution, the probabilities of transmission and idle are assumed to be independent of previous broadcasts and are computed without information from previous broadcasts. The following definitions are used.

$N_{A1}(a, b)$: the minimum expected number of broadcast slots to isolate the minimum x_i in the interval $(a, b]$ using an approximate solution of the one-broadcast strategy, given that all x_i's are in $(a, U]$, and that at least one x_i is in $(a, b]$;

$\phi_A(a, b, w)$: the probability of a transmission in the interval

395

$(a, w]$, given that all x_i's are in $(a, U]$, and that at least one x_i is in $(a, b]$;

$\theta_A(a, b, w)$: the probability of no transmission in the interval $(a, w]$, given that all x_i's are in $(a, U]$, and that at least one x_i is in $(a, b]$.

It is obvious that

$$\phi_A(a, b, w) + \theta_A(a, b, w) = 1.0. \qquad (10)$$

There are two cases to consider when calculating $\theta_A(a, b, w)$, namely, $b = U$ and $b \neq U$. When $b = U$, it is uncertain whether there is an x_i at b, and all arrangements of the n x_i's must be considered, so

$$\theta_A(a, U, w)|_{b=U} = \frac{(F(U) - F(w))^n}{(F(U) - F(a))^n}. \qquad (11a)$$

When $b \neq U$, there must be a station at b, since b is only updated to a value of x_i in the event of a transmission. In this case, we are only concerned with the placement of at most $(n - 1)$ of the x_i's,

$$\theta_A(a, b, w)|_{b=U} = \frac{(F(U) - F(w))^{n-1}}{(F(U) - F(a))^{n-1}}. \qquad (11b)$$

The recurrence for choosing the window is

$$N_{A1}(a, b) = \min_{a < w < b} \left\{ 1 + \phi_A(a, b, w) \right.$$
$$\cdot \left[\int_a^w f_c(a, w, x_b) N_{A1}(a, x_b) \, dx_b \right]$$
$$\left. + \theta_A(a, b, w) N_{A1}(w, b) \right\}. \qquad (12)$$

Again, the three terms on the right-hand side of the above equation count the current broadcast slot, additional broadcast slots in the event of a transmission, and additional broadcast slots if the current broadcast slot is idle.

The assumption that contention can be resolved in one step when the window size is smaller than δ holds, so the following boundary condition is used again.

$$N_{A1}(a, b) = 1 \qquad \text{for all } (b - a) < \delta. \qquad (13)$$

The decision tree is the same as for the exact solution, but there is a savings since many of the nodes at different levels are duplicates. The data structure for storing the windows is simply a two-dimensional array. The number of decision points for the approximate solution is determined by the values of a and b. The total number of unique nodes with $\delta = 1/(10n)$ is $((10n)^2 + 30n)/2$, which is determined by counting the decision points indicated by the above recurrences. For $n = 5$ and $n = 6$, the numbers of decisions points are 1325 and 1890, respectively, and the complexity of the solution is considerably reduced from the exact solution.

The performance results of the one-broadcast strategy will be discussed in Section IV-C.

B. Other Strategies

Other strategies were considered to determine if it were possible to improve the performance of the one-broadcast strategy, particularly in reducing the number of iterations after the station with the minimum search parameter has broadcast. The one-broadcast strategy continues until the interval is so small that it is certain that there were no stations with parameters in that interval. An alternative is a *two-broadcast strategy*, which allows up to two broadcast slots per iteration and uses the second slot to determine whether there are any stations with search parameters smaller than the parameter broadcast in the first slot. Initially, as with previous strategies, the intervals is $(L, U]$, and each station has a search parameter x_i in the interval. A global window is determined, and stations with parameters within the window attempt to broadcast their search parameters. If there are no search parameters in the window, the strategy proceeds as in the one-broadcast strategy: the lower bound of the interval is updated to the window's upper bound, and the protocol continues. The difference between the one- and two-broadcast strategies occurs when there are parameters within the window. In this case, the upper bound is updated to x_{b1}, the value broadcast, and a second broadcast slot is allowed for all stations with $x_i < x_{b1}$. If the second slot is idle, x_{b1} is the minimum, and the algorithm terminates. If there is a broadcast, the next iteration begins with x_{b2}, the second value broadcast, as the upper bound of the interval. Note that x_{b2} is smaller than x_{b1}.

A problem in the two-broadcast strategy is that the window for the second broadcast slot is chosen suboptimally when there are stations with search parameters smaller than the current broadcast value. Therefore, a better solution is a *combined strategy*, which combines the one-broadcast and two-broadcast strategies and makes a decision in each iteration whether one broadcast or two broadcasts will be used. Again, the objective is to minimize the expected number of future broadcasts.

Analyses and complexities of the two-broadcast and the combined strategies are similar to those of the one-broadcast strategy. They are not presented here because of space limitation and of their inferior performance as compared to the one-broadcast strategy. Interested readers can find them in [1] and [2].

C. Simulation Results for the Approximate Distributed Searches

The simulation results for the distributed window search using the three strategies are shown in Fig. 5. The windows were generated using the equations derived in Sections IV-A and in [1] and [2]. The broadcast parameters were generated from a uniform distribution in $(0, 1]$, and sufficient cases were simulated until a confidence interval of 0.95 was reached. The average number of broadcast slots is bounded by 2.7 for the two-broadcast strategy, and by 2.6 for the one-broadcast and combined strategies. The two-broadcast strategy is not as good as the one-broadcast strategy because, although it can reduce the number of broadcast slots after the minimum has been identified, it uses suboptimal window choices for earlier broadcast slots. The combined strategy always chooses the

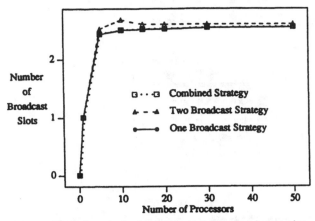

Fig. 5. Simulations results for different window-search strategies.

one-broadcast strategy, so their results are identical. The overhead for the combined strategy is higher than that of the one-broadcast strategy because the strategy for each decision point must be stored in addition to the window choices. For these reasons, the one-broadcast strategy is superior to the other two.

Note that the broadcast parameters are assumed to be independent and uniformly distributed in $(0, U]$ in the simulations. In case that the distribution function is nonuniform but independent and identical for all broadcast parameters, a uniformly distributed broadcast parameter can be obtained from the original broadcast parameter by the following formula:

$$z = F^{-1}(x) \qquad (14)$$

where x is the original broadcast parameter with distribution F, and z is the new broadcast parameter with a uniform distribution.

The proposed scheme is practical as a result of the constant expected number of broadcast slots. The time required for a contention slot is approximately 50 μs, and the time required to broadcast a search parameter may be estimated at approximately 100 μs. It follows that each broadcast slot would require on the order of 220 μs if 2.4 contention slots [22] were required to resolve contention. If it takes 120 μs to resolve contention and 100 μs to transmit a one-kbyte packet, then the overhead of each load balancing decision to identify the maximally and the minimally loaded processors is equivalent to transmitting 5.2 one-kbyte packets.

D. Distribution of Load Averages

The knowledge on the distribution of workload (or load averages) is needed in the distribution search in order to choose the windows. In this section, we present statistics of load averages on a system experiencing a real workload. The study consisted of measuring the load on a system of ten Sun workstations (servers and clients). Every sixty seconds, the one-minute load average was measured and logged. The load data were analyzed using an adjusted Komolgorov–Smirnov test [14], [20]. This goodness-of-fit test can be used to detect differences between a normal distribution and the empirical distribution indicated by the measured data. The agreement was measured over time. The results indicate that the

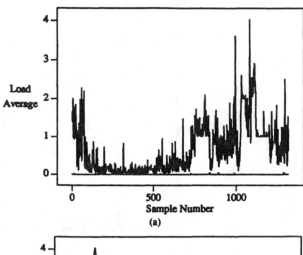

(a)

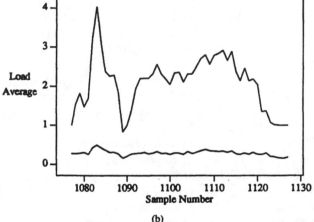

(b)

Fig. 6. Load maximums and minimums. (a) Load maxima and minima for one day. (b) Load maxima and minima for one hour.

distribution of load averages can be estimated using a normal distribution. During 80 percent of the time when the system is active, the distribution is within 0.215 of a normal distribution.

The results of the study are shown in Fig. 6. Fig. 6(a) shows the maximum and minimum load averages over time. The minimum is almost always zero and the maximum varies. The peak utilization is between sample number 700 and 1400 which reflects the load from 1 p.m. until midnight. From 1 a.m. until 11 a.m., the loads measured were uniformly low (≤ 1). Fig. 6(b) shows one hour of the minimum, average, and maximum load averages.

V. IMPLEMENTATION

The Sun system on which GAMMON has been implemented consists of servers and clients connected by Ethernets. The servers have secondary disk storage, and the clients do not. A client can access a server's disk via the network, and is allocated a portion of the server's disk for swap space. Swapping over the network is a part of the regular message transfer. A network file system (NFS) allows transparent access to remote file systems. This mechanism allows uniform access by the clients to the secondary storage.

The Sun system is multiprogrammed; when a process is initiated on a server or a client, a core image of that process containing run-time information exists in the swap space

TABLE I
RESULTS OF SIMULATION FOR THE TRUNCATED SEARCH (RANK OF THE
MINIMUM IS 0)

Number of processors	% of searches unresolved	% resolved searches finding minimum	average rank of result	% difference of result from minimum
3	20.0	78.00	0.194	2.790
4	18.6	76.04	0.224	2.192
5	20.1	73.97	0.268	2.086
6	21.8	73.66	0.252	1.665
7	21.4	72.26	0.279	1.506
8	20.5	70.57	0.292	1.495
9	23.1	72.82	0.256	1.151
10	21.8	74.04	0.256	0.959

associated with that server or client. This core image may be quite large (on the order of several megabytes). Since it is not possible to copy data from one swap space to another, the only way to transfer the core image is over the network. Due to the size of the core image, this transfer would have high overhead (on the order of seconds); consequently, the current implementation migrates jobs only at their entry point. Future enhancements to GAMMON will study preemption strategies.

There are two program modules (daemons) that comprise GAMMON in the current implementation: the searcher and the job migrator. The search daemon periodically participates in a search for the minimum. Job migration is performed by sending the necessary information of a job at entry point to a remote processor; result return is performed when execution of the migrated job is completed. Priorities of the various phases in load balancing, as discussed in Section II, are not enforced because the overhead of explicit priority resolution is very high and is not compensated by the resulting reduction in response time.

A. Implementation of the Distributed Search

The search for the minimum load normally takes 2.6 broadcast slots on the average (see Section III). Table I shows the simulation results of the search truncated at one broadcast slot. This table shows that, under this condition, the absolute minimum is located 70–78 percent of the time and there are 18.6–23.1 percent of the unresolved cases in which all search parameters are in the interval $(w_1, U]$ and no workload information is broadcast. Unresolved searches are not critical here because they reflect a condition in which no processors are lightly loaded enough to accept additional jobs. For cases that are resolved, those that do not find the absolute minimum have a one to two percent difference from the absolute minimum. Since workload information is heuristic in nature, small errors in identifying processors for load balancing are not critical. An important tradeoff we have achieved is that reasonable results are obtained at substantially lower overhead.

The minimum search as implemented on the Sun network is shown in Fig. 7. Execution is initiated, as mentioned above, by an alarm signal, or by a packet arriving from another search module. When an alarm is received, the processor's current load is compared to the lower bound of the window. If the load is smaller than the lower bound, it is broadcast with a time stamp and processor address. If a packet is received, the load is accepted as the minimum and is stored with the current time. If more than one processor sends a load packet due to their both receiving an alarm simultaneously, the minimum load is accepted. If the loads are identical, the processor address is used as a tie breaker. The alarm is set when packets are received, so the process is loosely synchronized. The search daemon obtains load information (in the current implementation the load average) directly from the kernel.

The contents of received packets are written to a file to reflect the current status of the network. As the status (the minimum load, and the location of the processor with the minimum load) is stored, the current time is also stored. When the status information is read from the file, its time stamp is used to determine if the load value is out of date. If the status information is out of date, the processor considers itself ineligible for job migration until it receives another status packet. This time stamping allows an unreliable communication mechanism to be used to communicate load information (broadcast datagrams) and reduces network traffic in the form of acknowledgments. If load information is lost by a processor, that processor does not migrate packets. This has a minimal affect on the overall performance of the scheduling strategy. Moreover, since packet loss is a relatively rare occurrence, acknowledgments are unnecessary.

The search was tested on two Sun systems: one with a server (Aquinas) and two clients (Calvin and Hobbes), and one with a server (Dwarfs) and ten clients. On Aquinas, the search was resolved in 50–80 ms, and on Dwarfs, the searches were resolved in 150–180 ms. The performance on Dwarfs can be considered the worst case because the Ethernet cable the clients are connected with is at the allowable length limit. The results for both Aquinas and Dwarfs were consistent with the simulation results in which the absolute minimum was located 70 percent of the time for resolved searches.

The search for the maximum load is not performed explicitly. It was observed that if a processor's load was above the upper bound of the initial window in the minimum search, its load was the maximum the majority of the time. As a result, processors with loads above the upper bound of the initial

```
/* INTERVAL: constant indicating time interval at which search is performed
 * packet{   information contained in the packets exchanged
 *   load:     processor load
 *   source: processor address
 * }
 * load_status { information contained in load status
 *   timestamp:            timestamp of the load status
 *   minimum_load:         load at the minimally loaded processor
 *   minimum_location:     location of the minimally loaded processor
 * }
 * current_time():    function returning the current time
 * current_load():    function returning the current load at a processor
 * set_alarm():       function to set an alarm signal ARGUMENT seconds from now
 * on_alarm():        function that sets a call to the argument when an alarm occurs
 * reset_alarm():     function to reset the alarm signal to ARGUMENT seconds from now
 * wait_arrival():    function that waits for the arrival of a packet
 * write():           writes to a file
 */

structure load_status load_status;      /* global structure containing load status */

procedure main;
    on_alarm(send_packet());
    set_alarm(INTERVAL);
    while (TRUE)
        receive_packet();
    endwhile
end

procedure send_packet;
    if (current_load() < window) then
        packet.load = current_load();
        packet.source = MY_ADDRESS;
        broadcast(packet);
    endif
    set_alarm(INTERVAL);
end

procedure receive_packet();
    wait_arrival(packet);
    reset_alarm(INTERVAL);
    if (current_time() > load_status.time) then
        load_status.minimum_load = packet_load;
        load_status.minimum_location = packet_source;
        load_status.timestamp = current_time();
        write(load_status);
    endif
end
```

Fig. 7. Procedures for the minimum search.

window can migrate the current job if the minimum load is current, and an explicit search of the maximally loaded processor is not needed.

A potential problem with not explicitly identifying the maximally loaded processor is that a lightly loaded processor may be swamped by jobs from more heavily loaded ones. There are two solutions to resolve this problem. First, a processor may only be allowed to migrate jobs if it has a load higher than the upper bound of the initial window and a new arrival. Second, a processor may be allowed to migrate at most one job between searches. Our performance data indicate that swamping is not a problem for a moderate number of participating processors. However, if preemption were implemented, it would be necessary to identify a unique maximum, as a large fraction of the processors may be preempting jobs at any time.

Another obvious technique for distributing status information is to broadcast it periodically, as is done with the *rwhod* daemon in Unix. To determine the savings of using the proposed method as opposed to using the technique of the *rwhod* daemon, the resource utilization of both was measured for the period of one hour. The overhead is summarized in

TABLE II
COMPARISON OF OVERHEAD FOR STATUS DISTRIBUTION OF THREE COMPUTERS IN ONE HOUR OF OPERATION

Deamon	Cumulative System Time in Seconds	Cumulative User Time in Seconds	Total Number of Broadcasts
search	0.1094	0.0137	65
broadcast	0.2593	0.0316	181
rwho	0.2633	0.0613	181

Table II. For comparison, a daemon that only broadcasts the load average value is studied (as opposed to the *rwho* daemon which broadcasts other information as well). Recall that the daemons perform a search every minute. When a search using GAMMON is performed, it is possible for daemons at two computers to start a broadcast simultaneously; hence, the total number of broadcast is slightly above 60 (first value in the last column of Table II). When the broadcast or *rwho* daemons are used, each computer initiates a broadcast every minute independent of other computers.

TABLE III
PERFORMANCE OF THE GLOBAL SCHEDULING STRATEGY

Name	Job Time w/out Global Scheduling	Job Time with Global Scheduling	% Difference
Aquinas (Sun 3/260 server)	18963	18540	2.23
Calvin (Sun 3/50 client)	12143	10430	14.10
Hobbes (Sun 3/50 client)	7319	5912	19.22
Totals	38425	34882	9.2

The results in Table II indicate that both the *rwhod* and the simple broadcast daemon introduce considerably more communication overhead than the search daemon proposed here.

B. Implementation of Job Migration and Result Return

In the general case, result return and job migration require that input file (and executable files if necessary) be sent over the network from the source processor to the destination process, and that output files be sent back. In the Sun environment, it is not necessary to send files from the source to the destination because all processors and clients have access to the same secondary storage. In this environment, job migration requires sending the command from the source to the destination, and result return requires sending any error information back.

In the procedure for job migration, the current load of the processor is first compared to the upper bound of the initial window for the maximum search. If the load is above this upper bound, then the global minimum location and its time stamp are read from a local file. If the timestamp indicates the minimum is current, the job is executed on the processor with the minimum load using a remote shell. This causes any error messages associated with the remote execution to be send back directly. The remote shell uses the reliable TCP/IP protocol, so execution of the job is guaranteed. Further details of this implementation can be found in [3].

C. Performance of GAMMON

We evaluate GAMMON by comparing the response time of a system with GAMMON to that of a system without global scheduling. The server, Aquinas, with two clients, Calvin and Hobbes, are used. First, workload was generated by processes that either initiated a CPU-bound job or slept for the amount of time the job consumed during its last execution with equal probability. As these processes were executed, the load and the amount of time consumed by executing processes was tabulated. Also, a history of the initiation of jobs was created. Next, the global scheduling strategy was enabled and the jobs were initiated according to this history. Again the load was monitored and the execution time tabulated.

The results summarized in Table III show a small improvement for the server and a much larger improvement for the clients. This is expected as the server is about 2.7 times faster than the clients and has direct access to the secondary storage through the VME bus rather than the Ethernet. As a result, the clients will benefit more by sending jobs to the server.

VI. Concluding Remarks

In this paper, we have presented an efficient technique for a distributed extremum search and a load balancing protocol using this technique. The search technique can be implemented at the applications level on *existing* distributed computing systems connected by multiaccess networks. This is important because it is typically not possible to make hardware modifications to existing networks. The maximum or the minimum of a set of numbers, which reflect the workloads, can be identified in a small bounded number of broadcast slots on the average. Since the search technique has a constant average behavior, the GAMMON strategy using this efficient search technique is feasible. GAMMON was implemented on a network of Sun workstations. Performance measurements indicate that the system with GAMMON allows improvement in overall performance as well as improved individual processor performance.

Acknowledgment

We gratefully acknowledge the help of R. M. Kling, who has participated in developing the implementation on the network of Sun computers.

References

[1] K. M. Baumgartner and B. W. Wah, "Load balancing protocols on a local computer system with a multiaccess bus," in *Proc. Int. Conf. Parallel Processing.* University Park, PA: Pennsylvania State University Press, Aug. 1987, pp. 851–858.

[2] K. M. Baumgartner, "Resource allocation on distributed computer systems," Ph.D. dissertation, School of Electrical Engineering, Purdue University, West Lafayette, IN, May, 1988.

[3] K. M. Baumgartner, R. M. Kling, and B. W. Wah, "Design and implementation of an efficient load balancing strategy for a local computer system," in *Proc. Int. Conf. Parallel Processing.* University Park, PA: Pennsylvania State University Press, 1989.

[4] T. C. K. Chou and J. A. Abraham, "Load Balancing in distributed systems," *IEEE Trans. Software Eng.*, vol. SE-8, pp. 401–412, July 1982.

[5] Y. C. Chow and W. Kohler, "Models for dynamic load balancing in a heterogeneous multiple processor system," *IEEE Trans. Comput.*, vol. C-28, pp. 334–361, May 1979.

[6] W. W. Chu, L. J. Holloway, M. T. Lan, and K. Efe, "Task allocation in distributed data processing," *IEEE Computer*, pp. 57–68, Nov. 1980.

[7] D. L. Eager, E. D. Lazowska, and J. Zahorjan, "Adaptive load sharing in homogeneous distributed systems," *IEEE Trans. Software Eng.*, vol. SE-12, pp. 662–675, May 1986.

[8] D. Ferrari and S. Zhou, "A load index for dynamic load balancing," in *Proc. Fall Joint Comput. Conf.*, Nov. 1986, pp. 684–690.

[9] K. Hwang, W. J. Croft, G. H. Goble, B. W. Wah, F. A. Briggs, W. R. Simmons, and C. L. Coates, "A UNIX-based local computer network with load balancing," *Computer*, vol. 15, no. 4, pp. 55–66, Apr. 1982. Also in *Tutorial: Computer Architecture*, D. D. Gajski, V. M.

Milutinovic, H. J. Siegel, and B. P. Furht, Eds. New York: IEEE Computer Society, 1987, pp. 541–552.

[10] J. Y. Juang and B. W. Wah, "Unified window protocols for contention resolution in local multiaccess networks," in *Proc. INFOCOM*, Apr. 1984, pp. 97–104.

[11] ——, "Optimal scheduling algorithms for multistage resource sharing interconnection networks," in *Proc. Comput. Software Appl. Conf.*, Nov. 1984, pp. 217–225.

[12] ——, "Global state identification for load balancing in a computer system with multiple contention busses," in *Proc. Comput. Software Appl. Conf.*, Oct. 1986, pp. 36–42.

[13] A. Kratzer and D. Hammerstrom, "A study of load leveling," in *Proc. COMPCON*, Fall 1980, pp. 647–654.

[14] A. M. Law and D. W. Kelton, *Simulation Modeling and Analysis*. New York: McGraw-Hill, 1982.

[15] M. Livney and M. Melman, "Load balancing in homogeneous broadcast distributed systems," in *Proc. Modeling Perform. Eval. Comput. Syst.*, ACM SIGMETRICS, 1982, pp. 47–55.

[16] R. Metcalfe and D. Boggs, "Ethernet: Distributed packet switching for local computer networks," *Commun. ACM*, vol. 19, no. 7, pp. 395–404, 1976.

[17] L. M. Ni and K. Hwang, "Optimal load balancing strategies for a multiple processor system," in *Proc. 10th Int. Conf. Parallel Processing*, Aug. 1981, pp. 352–357.

[18] A. S. Tanenbaum, *Computer Networks*. Englewood Cliffs, NJ: Prentice-Hall, 1981.

[19] A. N. Tantawi and D. F. Towsley, "Optimal static load balancing in distributed computer systems," *J. ACM*, vol. 32, pp. 445–465, Apr. 1985.

[20] K. S. Trivedi, *Probability and Statistics with Reliability, Queuing, and Computer Science Applications*. Englewood Cliffs, NJ: Prentice-Hall, 1982.

[21] B. W. Wah and J. Y. Juang, An efficient protocol for load balancing on CSMA/CD networks," in *Proc. 8th Conf. Local Comput. Networks*, Oct. 1983, pp. 55–61.

[22] ——, "Resource scheduling for local computer systems with a multiaccess network," *IEEE Trans. Comput.*, vol. C-34, pp. 1144–1157, Dec. 1985.

[23] ——, "An efficient contention resolution protocol for local multiaccess networks," U.S. Patent 4630264, Filed Sept. 21, 1984, Granted Dec. 16, 1986.

[24] B. W. Wah and P. Mehra, "Learning parallel search in load balancing," in *Proc. Workshop Parallel Algorithms Machine Intel. Pattern Recognition*, AAAI, Minneapolis, MN, Aug. 21, 1988.

[25] Y. T. Wang and J. T. Morris, "Load sharing in distributed systems," *IEEE Trans. Computers*, vol. C-34, pp. 204–217, Mar. 1985.

Katherine M. Baumgartner (S'81–M'89) received the B.S.E.E., M.S.E.E., and Ph.D. in electrical engineering all from Purdue University, West Lafayette, IN, in 1981, 1984, and 1988 respectively.

From 1986 to 1988 she was a Research Assistant at the Coordinated Sciences Laboratory at the University of Illinois, Urbana. Her research interests include architectures for parallel and distributed computer systems and distributed operating systems. She is currently a Senior Engineer at the Digital Equipment Corporation in Maynard, MA.

Benjamin W. Wah (S'74–M-'79–SM'85) received the Ph.D. degree in computer science from the University of California, Berkeley, CA, in 1979.

He was on the faculty of the School of Electrical Engineering at Purdue University, West Lafayette, IN, between 1979 and 1985. He is now a Professor in the Department of Electrical and Computer Engineering and the Coordinated Science Laboratory, University of Illinois at Urbana-Champaign, Urbana. Between 1988 and 1989, he served as a program director of the Microelectronic Systems Architecture Program, National Science Foundation. His areas of research include computer architecture, parallel processing, artificial intelligence, distributed databases, and computer networks.

Dr. Wah is an Associate Editor-in-Chief of the *IEEE Transactions on Knowledge and Data Engineering*, an area editor of the *Journal of Parallel and Distributed Computing*, and an editor of *Information Sciences*. He serves as a member of the Governing Board of the IEEE Computer Society and a program evaluator for ABET (computer engineering) and CSAC (computer science).

The Stealth Distributed Scheduler

Phillip Krueger and Rohit Chawla

Department of Computer and Information Science
Ohio State University
Columbus, OH 43210

ABSTRACT

Over the past several years, distributed systems composed of computer workstations have become increasingly prevalent. To make fullest use of their often enormous aggregate computing capacity, distributed schedulers must be developed that are appropriate to the unique features of these systems. In this paper, we study the features necessary for a distributed scheduler to be effective in this environment and describe an innovative distributed scheduler specifically designed for such systems.

1. Introduction

The Stealth Distributed Scheduler is designed specifically for a class of distributed systems that has recently emerged — those composed of computer workstations. These systems, which we refer to as *Workstation-Based Distributed Systems* (WDS), have increasingly replaced large multi-user computer systems. While many WDS's have the potential to deliver enormous computing capacity, often rivalling that of the most powerful supercomputers, much of their capacity is generally untapped because of the inability of WDS system software to efficiently share computing resources among workstations. The goal of Stealth is to make use of this capacity without undermining the valuable and unique features of a WDS.

The purpose of a distributed scheduler is to allocate the computing resources of a distributed system so that they are used to their fullest advantage. A distributed scheduler can be divided into two components working either independently or in concert: A *local scheduler* determines how the resources at a single node are allocated among its resident processes, while a *global scheduler* distributes the system workload among the nodes through *process transfer*, with the goal of correcting any anomalies that arise in the distribution of work among nodes. Process transfer can be performed either preemptively or non-preemptively. Non-preemptive transfer entails selecting a suitable node as the execution site for a process and initiating the process at that node. Later, if another node should become a better execution site, preemptive transfer entails stopping the process, moving it to the new node and resuming its execution. Because the process state, which must accompany the process to its new node, becomes more complex after execution begins, preemptive transfer is much more costly than non-preemptive transfer in two senses: First, implementing and maintaining the mechanisms necessary to encapsulate, transfer and resume execution from this complex state is expensive. Second, having

This material is based upon work supported by the National Science Foundation under Grant No. CCR-8909072, and by the Ohio State University under a University Seed Grant.

implemented this mechanism, it is not obvious what performance improvement might result beyond what is possible through non-preemptive transfer, since its resource overhead is likely to be much greater than that of non-preemptive transfer [13, 15].

Distributed scheduling is more complicated in a WDS than in many other types of distributed systems, because of a unique feature that distinguishes a WDS from these other systems: the high degree of predictability in quality of service that is provided to individual users. On seating oneself at a workstation, a user can expect to receive about the same level of service as was received when the workstation was last used, regardless of the overall workload of the WDS. In many cases, a user has the right to *insist* on this degree of autonomy because she owns or controls the workstation she is using. Whether or not individual workstations are independently owned, predictability has proved to be a valuable feature that many users, once accustomed to, would be reluctant to give up. Recognizing this value, we interpret 'ownership' loosely, assuming whoever is working at a workstation's console to be its owner.

Preserving predictability imposes special constraints on distributed scheduling. Rather than striving for the common good, scheduling must be done in such a way that no owner receives noticeably poorer service than would be provided by an autonomous workstation, regardless of how much some processes in the system must be delayed. Workstation owners who perceive that their service has been harmed are likely to insist that their workstations be removed from the pool of shared computing resources allocated through distributed scheduling.

Several distributed schedulers have been designed for the WDS environment, including Condor [10] and the Process Server [7]. In addition, several systems, including Butler [4, 11], NEST [1], Sprite [5, 12], and V-SYSTEM [3], have provided mechanisms to support remote execution of processes in the WDS environment, though they have not provided policies to control these mechanisms. All these systems share a common *conservative* approach to preserving predictability of service: *Foreign* processes (those executing at a workstation, but not initiated by the owner of that workstation) are not allowed to execute at a workstation while it is being used by its owner. For example, under Condor, a workstation is considered unavailable for use by foreign processes while any activity initiated by the workstation owner is in progress, and for some period after any such activity has completed. The duration of this period is a parameter of the system, with a default of 17.5 minutes. Any foreign process that is executing when an owner begins using a workstation is preempted automatically and transferred from the workstation to a holding area, from which it is transferred to an idle workstation, when one is located. The other systems mentioned above use similar criteria for

Reprinted from *Proc. IEEE 11th Int'l Conf. on Distributed Computing Systems,* IEEE CS Press, Los Alamitos, Calif., 1991, pp. 336–343.

determining when a workstation is unavailable for use by foreign processes. We will show that, as simple and intuitively reasonable as this conservative approach is, it is unduly costly and fails to make accessible a large portion of the unused capacity of a WDS.

A more *liberal* approach to preserving predictability of service is taken by the Stealth Distributed Scheduler. Instead of relying on preemptive transfer as the fundamental mechanism for preserving predictability, Stealth uses a far cheaper mechanism, priority resource allocation, to insulate an owner's processes from foreign processes. As a result, accessibility is increased by allowing foreign processes to continue executing at a workstation even while it is in use by its owner, and overhead is reduced by avoiding unnecessary preemptive transfers.

The remainder of this paper is organized as follows: We begin by examining the workload of a particular WDS. First, we measure the portion of the WDS computing capacity that is unused, and thus available to be exploited through distributed scheduling. Second, we estimate the improvement in *accessibility* of this capacity that can be achieved by taking a liberal, rather than a conservative, approach to preserving predictability. Chapter 3 discusses the Stealth approach to distributed scheduling, describing a prototype system which is currently being tested. Finally, we summarize our results and present conclusions in chapter 4.

2. Workload Characterization

2.1. The WDS Observed and the Workload Monitor

The WDS observed for this section is composed of 199 Sun-3/50 diskless workstations and 18 Sun fileservers. Workload measurements were collected over a 3-month period (February through April, 1989) from the diskless workstations, only. All the diskless workstations are functionally identical, having identical hardware and having access to the same files (through NFS). The primary characteristic that differs among workstations is location: some are contained in private faculty or staff offices, while others are located in public graduate or undergraduate instructional laboratories. As a result, we were able to gather workload measurements for each of four user populations: faculty, staff, graduate and undergraduate.

The WDS observed has only the primitive means provided by 4.3BSD UNIX[1] for sharing computing resources among workstations. A job can be invoked at a remote workstation (using either a remote procedure call or the remote shell), or a user can login to a remote workstation. In both cases, the remote workstation must be chosen and specified by the user.

Because we are interested in tapping otherwise-unused computing potential, our workload measurements focus on the processor utilizations at workstations composing the WDS. To measure utilization, a monitor was constructed in software. This monitor executes on each workstation composing the WDS, gathering statistics from within the kernel at 5-minute intervals. The influence of this monitor on the workload is negligible, which is not surprising, since it does little work and executes infrequently.

---

1. Sun-3 is a trademark of Sun Microsystems, and UNIX is a registered trademark of AT&T Bell Laboratories.

2.2. Unused Computing Capacity

We have found the WDS observed to be, on the average, 91% idle. The standard deviation of our observations is 2.5%, indicating that the amount of unused capacity is rather constant. The overall range of our observations, however, is from 77% to 96%, which shows that significant variation in unused capacity is possible. Figure 1 shows hourly variation in unused capacity over a period of a week. A given point in this figure represents the average of our observations for that hour over the three months observed. Typical standard deviations for the data plotted range between 1% and 3% utilization. Figure 1 shows that the amount of unused capacity is periodic, being lowest in the afternoons (particularly on weekdays) and highest in the early morning hours. Exceptions to the generally high level of unused capacity in the middle of the night occur in short bursts, and are due to individual users starting groups of jobs on large sets of workstations. Even during the periods that the WDS is most heavily used, unused capacity rarely falls below 87%. Clearly, the WDS has great reserves of computing capacity that are currently untapped.

Based on this low level of WDS utilization, we might correctly assume that considerable improvement in throughput is possible through distributed scheduling. We might also conjecture that average job response time in the WDS is quite good even without distributed scheduling, and that little improvement in this aspect of performance can be gained. A closer look at the WDS workload, however, shows this second conjecture to be false. Figure 2 plots the average distribution of workstation utilizations, ranked from greatest to least, during two representative one-hour periods. The first, beginning at 3:00 PM on weekdays, is generally a period of high utilization (average utilization = 12.1%). In contrast, the second period, beginning at 6:00 AM every day, is generally a time of light utilization (average = 6.5%). We observe that in each period, even though *overall* WDS utilization is low, some workstations are very heavily loaded, and a large number are idle. As a result, significant delays can occur at heavily used workstations at times when other workstations could provide immediate service. Since a large portion of the total number of jobs in the system are executing at these workstations, overall average job response time can be significantly reduced through distributed scheduling.

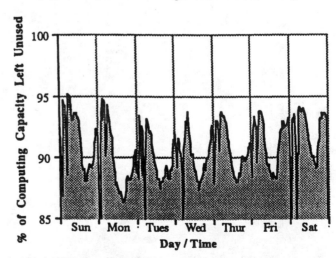

Fig. 1. Hourly variation in unused WDS computing capacity over the course of a week.

2.3. Accessibility of Unused Capacity

Until now, the systems that have supported remote execution of processes in a WDS while preserving predictability of service have done so by disallowing foreign processes from executing at workstations that are in use by their owners. This approach, which we refer to as *Conservative*, fails to make all the unused computing capacity of a WDS available to foreign processes for two reasons: First, it is difficult to determine when a workstation is no longer 'in use'. If a user has processes that are active, but are waiting for user input (such as editors or command line interpreters), after what period of time can the system assume that the user has temporarily left the workstation? A longer *waiting period* allows the system to make this determination with greater confidence, but leaves more unused computing capacity inaccessible for use by foreign processes. Second, even when the workstation *can* be determined to be in use, the workstation is rarely *fully* utilized. For example, many programs block while accessing a disk, either explicitly through reads and writes or implicitly through page faults. As a result, the processor is often left idle, again leaving unused capacity dormant.

Our next goal is to evaluate the effectiveness of the Conservative approach by estimating how much unused capacity it would leave dormant under the WDS workloads we have observed. We compare *actual* unused capacity (the portion of the total computing capacity of the WDS left unused over some period) with *apparent* unused capacity (the portion of actual unused capacity that the Conservative approach makes available to foreign processes). To estimate apparent unused capacity from our data, we filtered the utilization data collected so that whenever activity occurred on a workstation, and for some waiting period after such activity, the workstation appeared fully utilized.

Figure 3 compares actual unused capacity (from figure 1) with apparent unused capacity over a week. We assume a relatively short waiting period of 10 minutes. The most striking feature of this figure is the large difference between actual and apparent unused capacity, *particularly* during periods of peak usage. To focus on this difference, figure 4 plots the percentage of actual unused capacity that is made available by the Conservative approach (100 * (*apparent / actual*)) during weekdays over the 3-month period observed. During the afternoon period

of peak usage, (2:30 - 3:30 PM) only 45% of the actual unused capacity is made available through this approach. If we narrow our focus to a group of workstations that are particularly heavily used, those assigned to the systems programming staff in our department, this value falls to 35%

To increase the accessibility of unused capacity, one might consider reducing the length of the waiting period. Figure 5, however, shows that modifying this parameter does not have a substantial effect. This figure compares the percentages of actual unused capacity made available under several waiting periods, ranging from 5 to 20 minutes. Waiting periods shorter than 5 minutes are not likely to be useful, since they are not likely to provide sufficient confidence that the workstation is no longer in use by its owner. Differences resulting from these waiting periods are relatively small. During the period of peak usage, where the difference is greatest, reducing the waiting period from 10 to 5 minutes only increases the percent of actual unused capacity made available from 45% to 52%. Even with this minimal waiting period, little more than half the used capacity can be used by foreign processes. Increasing the waiting period from 10 to 20 minutes, on the other hand, allows greater confidence but decreases the portion of unused capacity made

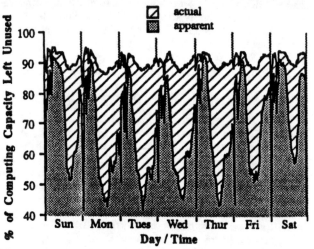

Fig. 3. Comparison of actual unused capacity with apparent unused capacity (waiting period = 10 minutes).

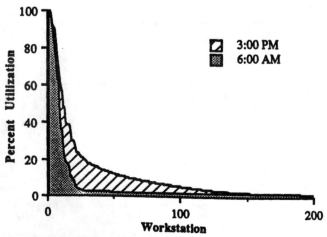

Fig. 2. Average distribution of workstation utilizations, ranked from greatest to least, at two representative times of day.

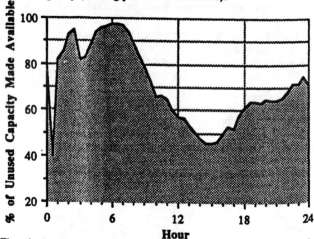

Fig. 4. Apparent unused capacity as a percentage of actual unused capacity (waiting period = 10 minutes).

available from 45% to 35%. Overall, tuning the waiting period is not likely to be effective in substantially improving the ability of the Conservative approach to make unused capacity available. Instead, new approaches to distributed scheduling in a WDS should be explored.

3. The Stealth Approach

By relying on preemptive transfers to preserve predictability of service for workstation owners, the Conservative approach incurs considerable overhead and fails to make a large part of the available capacity of a WDS accessible for use. The goal of the Stealth Distributed Scheduler is to correct both of these faults by relying on a far simpler and cheaper mechanism, priority resource allocation, to preserve predictability. Through preemptive priority allocation of resources for which significant contention is likely to develop, Stealth insulates a workstation owner from the effects of any foreign processes that may also be executing at the workstation. At the same time, foreign processes are allowed to continue executing, making use of whatever resources are not being used by the owner, which the previous section showed to be substantial. Stealth, then, replaces global scheduling mechanisms (preemptive transfer) with local scheduling mechanisms (priority allocation of local resources). Because innovative local scheduling is a key feature of the Stealth Distributed Scheduler, and to conserve space, we focus our discussions on local scheduling, and provide only an overview of global scheduling under Stealth.

Stealth is currently being implemented and tested on a WDS composed of Sun 3/50 and IBM RT workstations, using Mach 2.5 as a base. Mach was chosen in large part due to its architecture-independent virtual memory system. Since Stealth is entirely implemented at the architecture-independent level, it is portable to a wide variety of systems. For example, the Sun 3/50 and IBM RT workstations currently in use bear little resemblance architecturally.

3.1. Local Scheduling

As one of two primary components of a distributed scheduler, the purpose of a local scheduler is to allocate resources local to a node so as to support the overall goals of the

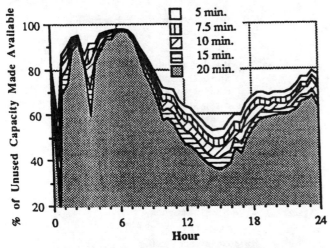

Fig. 5. Comparison of the percentages of actual unused capacity made available by the Conservative approach resulting from several representative waiting periods.

distributed scheduler. In keeping with the goals of Stealth, the goal of the Stealth Local Scheduler (*StealthLS*) is to allocate local resources so that processes belonging to the owner of the workstation get whatever resources they need, and foreign processes get whatever is left.

One of the most obvious resources for which contention between owner and foreign processes is likely to develop is the CPU. Priority CPU scheduling alone, however, can not protect the owner from foreign processes that require enough primary memory to induce thrashing. To insulate the owner from such processes, memory management must also be prioritized. In addition, to insulate the owner from foreign processes that make heavy use of the file system, file accesses must be prioritized. StealthLS prioritizes such accesses at a high level by providing a prioritized file system cache. While prioritized CPU schedulers are common, no previous operating system has included prioritization for virtual memory or the file system cache. We focus our discussion on the novel features of these two subsystems.

Prioritized Virtual Memory System (*StealthPVM*)

To begin, we give a brief overview of the Mach virtual memory system [14]. Under Mach, each page is kept in one of three lists: active, inactive or free. Initially, all pages are in the free list. Later, as memory is accessed by active processes, pages are allocated from the free list and moved to the tail of the active list. To allow these active pages to be considered for freeing, they are moved to the inactive list as follows: If the number of pages in the inactive list falls below its 'target', pages are moved from the head of the active list to the tail of the inactive list until this threshold is reached. Maintenance of the free list is also based on thresholds, though two are used. If the number of pages in the free list falls below its lower threshold, pages at the head of the inactive list are examined, and those that have not been referenced are moved to the free list until it reaches its upper threshold. These pages are then available for replacement. Pages that *have* been referenced while in the inactive list are given a 'second chance' by being moved to the tail of the active list.

To prioritize page replacement, if a page must be replaced due to a shortage of primary memory, we would prefer to choose a page belonging to a low-priority (foreign) process for replacement, rather than one belonging to a high-priority (owner) process. To accomplish this goal, StealthPVM *dynamically* partitions physical pages into two sets: one that is accessible to high-priority processes, while the other is accessible to low-priority processes. The relative sizes of these partitions vary according to the memory requirements of high-priority processes. These sets are implemented by duplicating the active, inactive and free lists. The high-priority lists contain pages that have recently been accessed by high-priority processes, while the low-priority lists contain pages that have not. Page movement among these lists is illustrated by figure 6. This figure shows that several lists have more than one source of pages. The numbers beside the arrows in the figure indicate the order in which the sources are tapped. For example, to fill the high-priority inactive list, pages are removed first from the low-priority active list, with additional pages being removed from the high-priority active list only if necessary. In this way, pages can be 'stolen' from the low-priority level if needed at the high-priority level.

Pages do not normally move from the high to the low-priority level. An exception, referred to as *reverse-flow*, is symbolized by the dotted lines in the figure (labeled 'r'). This exception is made when there is a shortage of low-priority memory, but no shortage of high-priority memory. At such times, the low-priority free list is allowed to replenish itself from the high-priority free list, and in addition, the high-priority free list is refilled from the high-priority inactive list, rather than the low-priority inactive list. In this way, after an extended period of little shortage of high-priority memory, nearly all the pages in the system become available for use by low-priority processes. As a simple heuristic to measure the shortage of high-priority memory, we note the time at which a page was most recently moved from an inactive list to the high-priority free list. If more than *low_activity_indicator* time has passed since such a transfer, page replacement operates in the reverse-flow mode.

Even if page replacement is prioritized, thrashing low-priority processes can hurt the performance of high-priority processes by causing contention at the backing store device. Whenever a page that is not resident in memory is accessed, it must be read from backing store. While this page is being retrieved, the process is blocked. A group of low-priority processes that are thrashing will generate a high rate of page-ins. At any moment, one page for each process may be queued at the backing store device. High-priority page-ins will be slowed, having to wait for earlier low-priority page-ins to complete. To correct this problem, StealthPVM includes prioritized paging. A page-in for a low-priority process is initiated only if no page-ins for high-priority processes are waiting.

Prioritized File System Cache (*StealthPFC*)

Like UNIX, Mach provides a file system cache. This cache includes three lists of available buffers [9]. The first, the *LRU* list, contains buffers whose contents are likely to be used repeatedly. The second, the *AGE* list, contains buffers that are less likely to be accessed in the near future, such as read-ahead blocks. Finally, the *EMPTY* list contains buffers which currently have no physical memory associated with them (so are temporarily useless). Whenever a buffer in the AGE or LRU list is accessed, it is returned to the end of the LRU list, making it less likely to be 'recycled'. Recycling is similar to page

replacement, occurring when a requested block is not found in the cache. At such a time, a buffer is chosen from the front of the AGE list if the AGE list is not empty, or otherwise from the front of the LRU list. This buffer is then used for the pending block request.

To add prioritization to the file system cache, StealthPFC duplicates the LRU and AGE lists. One set of lists contains buffers that are available for recycling by high-priority processes only, while the other set contains buffers that can be recycled by either high or low-priority processes. On a block request, if the block is not found in the cache, a buffer is chosen for recycling as follows: If the request is from a high-priority process, a buffer is chosen from the low-priority AGE or LRU list as described above, if one is available, or from the high-priority AGE or LRU list, if the low-priority lists are empty. If the request is from a low-priority process or is the result of low-priority paging activity by StealthPVM, a buffer is chosen from the low-priority AGE or LRU list, if either of these lists is non-empty. Similar to 'reverse flow', if both lists are are empty, a buffer can be 'stolen' from the high-priority AGE or LRU list only if the buffer has not been accessed within *recent-usage-indicator* time. If no such buffer is available, the request must wait until such a buffer is available.

Performance

While detailed performance measurements of the Stealth Local Scheduler have not yet been completed, we present some preliminary results. Our measurements were performed on a Sun-3/50 workstation, having 4 megabytes of primary memory and a local disk. While this workstation has less memory than would be found on most current workstations, we expect the trends observed will be the same for workstations having more memory. The parameters for StealthPVM and StealthPFC, *low-activity-indicator* and *recent-usage-indicator*, are set to 30 seconds and 60 seconds, respectively. All results reported have less than 5% estimated error at the 90% confidence level.

To measure the performance of StealthLS, we constructed the benchmark program detailed in figure 7. This benchmark is meant to simulate a workstation owner arriving at a workstation that is executing a low-priority (foreign) process, and invoking a series of commands. To test worst-case conditions, the low-

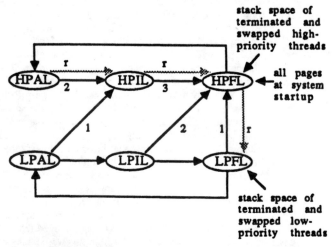

Fig. 6. Flow of pages among high-priority active, inactive and free lists (HPAL, HPIL and HPFL), and low-priority active, inactive and free lists (LPAL, LPIL and LPFL) under StealthPVM.

```
Start low-priority thrasher in background
Wait 2 minutes
loop 15 times

        Run 'ls' at high priority
        Sleep 5 seconds
        Run 'egrep' at high priority
        Sleep 5 seconds
        Compile large C program ('cc') at high priority
        Sleep 5 seconds
        Run 128K byte high-priority thrasher
        Sleep 5 seconds
        Run 256K byte high-priority thrasher
        Sleep 5 seconds
        Run 512K byte high-priority thrasher
        Sleep 5 seconds

end of loop
Kill low-priority thrasher
```

Fig. 7. Benchmark sequence.

406

priority process is an infinite loop that is both CPU and memory intensive (we refer to it as a *thrasher*). This process is composed of a loop that sequentially writes the first field from each 1K record in an array of records. The size of a thrasher is mostly determined by the size of this array. The sequence of memory accesses executed by a thrasher results in the worst case for the page replacement policy. As a result, the load that the thrasher puts on the memory system is far greater than would be expected from other programs of the same size.

The commands executed by the owner are simulated by a loop containing a mix of UNIX commands [2] and thrasher programs, of varying size. These commands were chosen to represent programs ranging from CPU-intensive (thrasher) to I/O-intensive (egrep), as well as varying in memory-intensiveness. These commands are separated by delays, representing 'think time'. Differing from the low-priority thrasher, the high-priority thrashers are finite loops, each requiring one minute of CPU time.

As our first measure of performance, we examine the increase in the mean response time of high-priority processes that results from competing for resources with a low-priority process. Process response time is the time that elapses from the moment a process is invoked until it completes execution. We compare the percent increase that occurs under an unmodified Mach 2.5 kernel including BSD compatibility code, with that occurring under the same operating system modified to include StealthLS. Figure 8 plots percent increase against the size of the concurrently executing low-priority thrasher. This figure shows that StealthLS is very effective at insulating high-priority processes from the effects of degenerate low-priority processes. Without StealthLS, large low-priority processes cause considerable degradation in mean response time. Degradation is noticeable even when the low-priority process is small. In contrast, under StealthLS, the effect on the high-priority process is negligible, regardless of the size of the low-priority thrasher.

Turning our attention to low-priority processes, figure 9 illustrates the ability of StealthLS to provide these processes with access to necessary resources when those resources are available, but to limit access when use of those resources would harm performance for high-priority processes. This figure plots the percentage of the available capacity in our benchmark program (the portion not used by high-priority processes) that is used by the low-priority process against the size of the low-priority process. Small low-priority processes are able to acquire the resources necessary to be able to take advantage of nearly all the available computing capacity. Large low-priority processes, however, are not given sufficient access to resources, since it would cause contention for high-priority processes. Consequently, these low-priority processes perform poorly when high-priority processes are executing.

3.2. Global Scheduling

Since many of the novel features of the Stealth Distributed Scheduler are in its local scheduling component, we give only a brief overview of the Stealth Global Scheduler (*StealthGS*). Several unique features differentiate StealthGS from previous approaches to global scheduling for the WDS environment, including the following:

Minimize use of preemptive transfers: Since the goal of distributed scheduling is to improve performance, efficiency is essential. When designing for efficiency, a key component to consider is the process transfer mechanism, since it is responsible for a large portion of the overhead of distributed scheduling. While preemptive transfers incur considerably more overhead than non-preemptive transfers, earlier studies have shown non-preemptive transfers to be capable of achieving most of the performance benefit of distributed scheduling [6, 8]. The addition of preemptive transfers can improve performance only if the overall system utilization is high [8]. In section 2.2, we noted that average utilization for the WDS observed is only 9%, with peaks of 23%. While distributed scheduling can be expected to increase this level of utilization by increasing the accessibility of remote computing capacity, we do not expect to see utilization levels high enough to allow preemptive transfers to have a significant effect on performance. In addition, unlike distributed schedulers using the Conservative approach, preemptive transfers are unnecessary for preserving predictability of service for workstation owners under Stealth. Consequently, under StealthGS, preemptive transfers are needed only to avoid starvation.

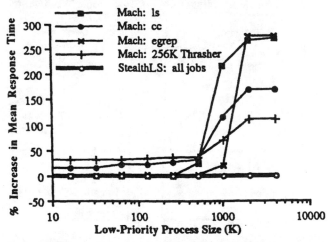

Fig. 8. Percent increase in mean process response time for high-priority processes vs. the size (K bytes) of the low-priority 'thrasher' process.

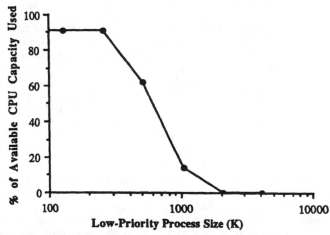

Fig. 9. Percentage of available CPU capacity exploited by a low-priority process during vs. size (K bytes) of the low-priority process.

Maximize pool of transferable processes: Previous distributed schedulers for the WDS environment have considered only certain classes of processes, which must be identified by the user, to be suitable for transfer. These processes may be identified by being specially compiled, by being submitted to a 'batch' scheduler, by being specifically requested for transfer, or through some other means. As a result, backlogs at workstations can persist even when remote computing capacity is available, if the user has not specified any of the backlogged jobs as being transferable. StealthGS is able to increase use of available remote computing capacity by considering all processes to be potentially eligible for transfer. StealthGS then automates the selection of suitable processes to transfer, taking system state into account in determining which can be transferred advantageously. To avoid transferring the small class of programs that are not suitable for transfer under *any* conditions (such as *inetd*), their object files are marked 'non-transferable'. By maximizing the pool of transferable processes and automating process selection, StealthGS both increases its ability to improve performance and provides a higher level of transparency to users.

Fully decentralized global scheduling: We wish to avoid the problems endemic to centralized global schedulers, including emerging bottlenecks and reduced reliability. Departing from many previous approaches to WDS scheduling, we circumvent these problems by focusing our design effort on global scheduling algorithms that are fully decentralized.

3.2.1. Implementation

Our prototype StealthGS implementation is targeted for a class of WDS's that holds particular promise for benefitting from distributed scheduling. A member of this class is characterized by being composed of diskless workstations, with a shared file system that gives every node the same view of the file system. Distributed scheduling is likely to be particularly effective for such a system because the amount of information that must be sent between workstations to complete a process transfer is small relative to other types of WDS's. For example, input and output files need not be transferred, since they reside at a disk server, rather than at the sending workstation. In addition, for non-preemptive transfers, the executable image of the process being transferred does not need to be sent to the receiving workstation. Figure 10 illustrates the three principal components of StealthGS:

Global Scheduling Daemon (GSD): This user-level task, an instance of which executes on every workstation in the system, is responsible for all StealthGS policy decisions. These decisions include choosing which processes to transfer, when to transfer them, and to which workstations to transfer them. Transfer decisions are made through negotiation between the GSD at the workstation at which a process is initiated (the *home* workstation for that process) and GSD's at potential receiving workstations (*remote* workstations) for that process. Each GSD task has several threads, allowing negotiation for several processes to progress concurrently.

Shadow: Residual dependencies that can not be avoided are managed by this user-level task, which executes at the home workstations of a transferred process. One shadow task exists for each transferred task. A shadow task accepts requests to perform location-dependent system calls, performs them, and returns their results. Location-dependent system calls include I/O requests to devices that exist at specific workstations (such

as video screens and mice), time-related system calls (since clocks are not synchronized), and system calls that specify a process ID as an argument (since process IDs are not globally unique). All system calls that are not location-dependent are executed at the remote workstation.

System Calls: For efficiency, all mechanisms to support StealthGS policies are implemented within the kernel, as modified system calls. These system calls include 'execve' and all location-dependent system calls. Execve, which replaces the text of the calling process with the specified file, has been modified to notify the local GSD that a process is available for transfer. The GSD responds by notifying execve whether or not the process has been transferred. If not, execve continues normally; otherwise, it continues with the text for a shadow task substituted for the requested file. The location-dependent system calls have been modified to check whether the caller is a foreign task. If so, a request is forwarded to the shadow for that task to invoke the system call on its home workstation. Finally, a new system call installs a foreign process at a remote workstation, initializing its state to reflect any attributes inherited from its parent. The process is connected to its shadow and marked 'low-priority', so that it receives low-priority access to local resources.

4. Summary and Conclusions

This paper is an overview of the justification, design and performance of the Stealth Distributed Scheduler. The goal of Stealth is to exploit the unused computing capacity of a workstation-based distributed system (WDS) without undermining the predictability in quality of service that a WDS provides to workstation owners.

We began by examining the workload characteristics of a large WDS. We found, first, that the unused computing capacity of the WDS is considerable, averaging 91% and nearly always exceeding 87% of the total capacity. Second, we found that the Conservative approach to preserving predictability of service to workstation owners, disallowing foreign processes from executing at workstations that are in use by their owners, fails to exploit large portions of the unused capacity of the WDS. Often,

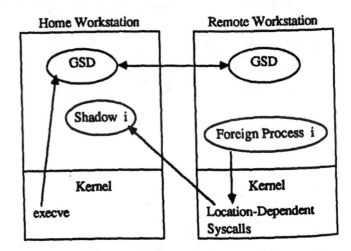

Fig. 10. Communication among the components of StealthGS at the home workstation of a transferred process and the workstation to which it is transferred.

less than half the unused capacity is made available for use by foreign processes. Particularly disturbing is the tendency of this approach to make the least efficient use of unused capacity precisely when it is most needed, during periods of peak usage. In addition, through its use of preemptive transfers to move foreign processes from workstations whose owners have arrived, the Conservative approach incurs considerable overhead. We concluded that more liberal approaches to preserving predictability in a WDS should be considered.

The purpose of the Stealth Distributed Scheduler is to explore a liberal approach to preserving predictability. Stealth seeks to correct the shortcomings of the Conservative approach by replacing an expensive global scheduling mechanism, preemptive transfer, with a far cheaper local scheduling mechanism, priority resource allocation. Through priority allocation of local resources, Stealth insulates a workstation owner from the effects of foreign processes, while allowing foreign processes to continue using whatever resources are left over.

The local scheduling component of Stealth (StealthLS) currently includes priority access to three types of resources: CPU, primary memory and the file system. Priority memory allocation and file system access are accomplished by an innovative prioritized virtual memory system and prioritized disk cache. Preliminary performance measurements show that StealthLS is very effective at insulating owner processes from the effects of foreign processes. In sharp contrast to a system not using StealthLS, increases in mean process response times for owner processes, caused by concurrent execution of foreign processes, are negligible under StealthLS.

The global scheduling component of Stealth (StealthGS) includes several features that differentiate it from other global schedulers designed for the WDS environment. First, because StealthLS makes preemptive transfers unnecessary to preserve predictability, and because performance improvements resulting from preemptive transfers are likely to be small under expected WDS workloads, StealthGS gains efficiency by emphasizing the use of non-preemptive transfers. Preemptive transfers are necessary only to avoid starvation of foreign processes. Second, StealthGS both increases its ability to improve performance and provides a higher level of transparency to users by considering all processes to be eligible for transfer, and by automating the selection of processes to transfer. Third, StealthGS implements fully decentralized global scheduling.

In summary, the liberal approach taken by the Stealth Distributed Scheduler is a promising method of exploiting the vast quantity of unused computing capacity typically present in a WDS, while preserving predictability of service for workstation owners. By increasing the accessibility of unused computing capacity, by reducing the overhead of distributed scheduling in a WDS environment, and by increasing the pool of transferable processes, we believe the Stealth Distributed Scheduler to have the potential to provide significant performance improvement relative to other distributed schedulers in the WDS environment.

Acknowledgments

We are grateful to Terri Watson and Khalid Shcta for implementing the Stealth Global Scheduler, to Davender Babbar for implementing the prioritized disk cache, and to Steve Romig for his help in gathering workload measurements for this study.

References

[1] R. Agrawal and A. K. Ezzat, "Processor Sharing in NEST: A Network of Computer Workstations," *Proceedings of the 1st International Conference on Computer Workstations*, IEEE, pp. 198-208 (November 11-14, 1985).

[2] Anon., *UNIX Programmer's Reference Manual*, Computer Systems Research Group, Computer Science Division, Dept. of Electrical Engineering and Computer Science, University of California, Berkeley, CA (April 1986).

[3] D. R. Cheriton and W. Zwaenepoel, "The Distributed V Kernel and its Performance for Diskless Workstations," *Proceedings of the Ninth ACM Symposium on Operating Systems Principles*, pp. 128-139 (10-13 October 1983) In *ACM Operating Systems Review* 17:5.

[4] R. B. Dannenberg and P. G. Hibbard, "A Butler Process for Resource Sharing on Spice Machines," *ACM Transactions on Office Information Systems 3*, 3, pp. 234-252 (July 1985).

[5] F. Douglis and J. Ousterhout, "Process Migration in the Sprite Operating System," *Proc. 7th International Conference on Distributed Computing Systems*, pp. 18-25 (September 1987).

[6] D. L. Eager, E. D. Lazowska, and J. Zahorjan, "The Limited Performance Benefits of Migrating Active Processes for Load Sharing," Proceedings of ACM SIGMETRICS 1988 (May 1988).

[7] R. Hagmann, "Process Server: Sharing Processing Power in a Workstation Environment," *Proc. 6th International Conference on Distributed Computing Systems*, pp. 260-267 (May 1986).

[8] P. Krueger and M. Livny, "A Comparison of Preemptive and Non-Preemptive Load Distributing," *Proc. 8th International Conference on Distributed Computing Systems*, pp. 123-130 (June 1988).

[9] S. J. Leffler, *The Design and Implementation of the 4.3BSD UNIX Operating System*, Reading, Massachusetts: Addison-Wesley Publishing Company (1989).

[10] M. J. Litzkow, M. Livny, and M. W. Mutka, "Condor - A Hunter of Idle Workstations," *Proc. 8th International Conference on Distributed Computing Systems*, pp. 104-111 (June 1988).

[11] D. Nichols, "Using Idle Workstations in a Shared Computing Environment," *Proc. Eleventh ACM Symposium on Operating Systems Principles*, pp. 5-12 (8-11 November 1987) In *ACM Operating Systems Review 21:5*.

[12] J. K. Ousterhout, A. R. Cherenson, F. Douglis, M. N. Nelson, and B. B. Welch, "The Sprite Network Operating System," *Computer*, pp. 23-36 (February 1988).

[13] M. L. Powell and B. P. Miller, "Process migration in DEMOS/MP," *Proc. Ninth ACM Symposium on Operating Systems Principles*, pp. 110-118 (10-13 October 1983) In *ACM Operating Systems Review* 17:5.

[14] A. Tevanian, "Architecture-Independent Virtual Memory Management for Parallel and Distributed Environments: The Mach Approach," Technical Report CMU-CS-88-106, Carnegie Mellon University (December 1987).

[15] M. Theimer, K. Lantz, and D. Cheriton, "Preemptable Remote Execution Facilities for the V-System," *Proc. Tenth ACM Symposium on Operating Systems Principles*, pp. 2-12 (December 1985).

Chapter 6

Mechanisms for Process Migration

6.1 Introduction

Load balancing schemes can be either nonpreemptive or preemptive. In nonpreemptive dynamic scheduling, called *dynamic task placement,* the tasks are eligible for redistribution only before they have started to execute. Thus, once a task starts executing on a host, it will remain on the host until its execution is complete. In preemptive scheduling, called *process migration,* a task may be relocated after it has started to execute [Eskicioglu 1989, Theimer 1991, Zayas 1987]. The steps involved in process migration consist of:

1. suspending the migrating process on the source host;
2. transferring the process, along with its current state, to the target host; and
3. resuming the execution of the process on the target host.

Process migration policies are similar to those of dynamic task placement. However, in order to avoid thrashing, a migration policy needs to ensure [Krueger 1988] that an eligible task:

- is larger than a threshold value,
- has been executed on the source machine for longer than a threshold value, and
- belongs to the set of processes that have been transferred least often among those residing on the source machine.

Both dynamic task placement and process migration have some basic overhead associated with them, such as load information management, load information distribution, transfer decision-making, and task transfer delays [Krueger 1988]. However, process migration also has the additional overhead of transferring the source machine state to the target machine. The transfer of state information is required, since a process state contains the necessary information for resuming the execution of the suspended process. A typical process state consists of virtual memory information, open files, message buffers, machine state, and environment data such as the process identifier and the current working directory.

A major component of a process state consists of the virtual memory information of the process. There are several ways to transfer the virtual memory information:

- *Entire virtual memory transfer*: This is perhaps the most primitive, straightforward, inefficient technique for process state transformation. Once a process is suspended on the source machine, the entire virtual memory is transferred to the target machine as part of its state.
- *Pre-copy transfer*: The idea is to set up a pipeline so that process execution and state transformation can take place simultaneously. Thus, after a migration decision is made, the source kernel begins the transfer of the process state to the target host while the process still executes on the source host. This transfer is followed by a set of transfers of dirty pages until a threshold is reached, for example, until a number of dirty pages are transferred or a set time period has elapsed. Finally, the process is suspended on the source host and the current dirty pages are transferred.
- *Copy-on-reference transfer*: At migration time, the process and its state, with the exception of the virtual memory, are transferred to the target host. The process then resumes its execution on the target machine. However, individual pages are transferred from the source host on demand, that is, whenever they are referenced by the executing process on the target machine.
- *Enhanced copy-on-reference transfer*: The idea is similar to the copy-on-reference transfer, but it is assumed that the source and target hosts share a file server. Thus, the target machine will demand pages from the file server on missed references. Of course, at the time of migration, the dirty pages in the memory of the source machine must be flushed to the file server.

411

6.2 Is migration worthwhile?

It is obvious that the size of the process state can easily become very large, making process migration a very expensive operation. In addition, the processes spawned by an executing parent process would not know where the parent has migrated. As a result, a name-server or forwarding service would be needed to handle this kind of situation. Therefore, process migration, as the only means of load balancing, is considered to be quite inefficient. However, when process migration is augmented with dynamic task placement (non-preemptive load balancing), it can provide additional performance improvements [Artsy 1989, Powell 1983, Theimer 1985].

[Krueger 1988] shows that most of the performance improvement potentially available through load balancing is gained by using a dynamic task placement policy. However, process migration can improve the performance additionally when the migration's overhead, relative to task placement, is low. For example, in systems with a local file server at each node, the overheads of process migration and dynamic task placement are almost identical, since they both require the transfer of a large amount of information. In such systems, the addition of the process migration to dynamic task placement can provide extra performance improvement over the same system with only a placement policy. On the other hand, in shared file-server systems, the overhead of process migration is much higher than placement. In that case, process migration provides only a small amount of additional performance improvement.

6.3 Chapter organization and overview

The papers of this chapter can be classified into two groups: those addressing general issues in process migration (Eskicioglu, Theimer and Hayes; and Zayas), and those describing specific process migration mechanisms (Artsy and Finkel; Powell and Miller; and Theimer, Lantz, and Cheriton). In the first paper, Eskicioglu discusses the design of the process migration facilities in distributed systems, with respect to such key issues as the system models on which the mechanisms are implemented, hardware platforms they run on, methods used in moving a process from one machine to another, load balancing policies employed, and so on. In the second paper, Theimer and Hayes describe an approach to heterogeneous process migration that involves building a machine-independent migration program that specifies the current code and data state of the process to be migrated. Before a migrated task is compiled and executed, its process state is reconstructed by the target host (pre-copying). In the third paper, Zayas addresses the problems of virtual memory transfer during process migration. It is shown that the copy-on-reference policy can handle the virtual memory transfers successfully in the Accent distributed computing environment.

In the fourth paper, Artsy and Finkel discuss the process migration operations in the Charlotte distributed operating system. Charlotte's migration facility separates policy (when to migrate which process to what destination) from mechanism (how to detach, transfer, and reattach the migrant process). The mechanism allows concurrent multiple migrations and premature cancellation of migration. In the fifth paper, Powell and Miller describe the addition of a process migration facility to the DEMOS/MP operating system. In this environment, a process can be moved during its execution and continued on another PE, with continuous access to all its resources. The system's uniform and location-independent communication interface correctly delivers messages to the new location of the process. In the last paper, Theimer, Lantz, and Cheriton elaborate on the design and performance of the remote execution facility in the V distributed system. In particular, the preemption and migration of remotely executed programs are addressed. It is shown that preemptable remote execution allows idle workstations to be used as a "pool of PEs" without interfering with processes of their owners, and without significant overhead for the normal execution of programs.

Bibliography

Artsy, Y., and R. Finkel, "Designing a Process Migration Facility: The Charlotte Experience," *Computer*, Vol. 22, No. 9, Sept. 1989, pp. 47–56; reprinted here.

Douglis, F., and J. Ousterhout, "Process Migration in the Sprite Operating System," *Proc. 7th IEEE Int'l Conf. Distributed Computing Systems*, IEEE CS Press, Los Alamitos, Calif., 1987, pp. 18–25.

Douglis, F., and J. Ousterhout, "Transparent Process Migration: Design Alternatives and the Sprite Implementation," *Software—Practice and Experience,* Vol. 21, No. 8, Aug. 1991, pp. 757–785.

Eskicioglu, M. R., "Design Issues of Process Migration Facilities in Distributed Systems," *IEEE Technical Committee on Operating Systems Newsletter,* Vol. 4, No. 2, Winter 1989, pp. 3–13; reprinted here.

Hac, A., "A Distributed Algorithm for Performance Improvement Through File Replication, File Migration, and Process Migration," *IEEE Trans. Software Eng.,* Vol. SE-15, No. 11, Nov. 1989, pp. 1459–1470.

Krueger, P., and M. Livny, "A Comparison of Preemptive and Non-Preemptive Load Distributing," tech. report, Dept of Computer Science, University of Wisconsin-Madison, 1988.

Powell, M. L., and B. P. Miller, "Process Migration in DEMOS/MP," *Proc. 9th ACM Symp. Operating Systems Principles,* ACM Press, New York, N.Y., 1983, pp. 110–119; reprinted here.

Suen, T. T. Y., and J. S. K. Wong, "Efficient Task Migration Algorithm for Distributed Systems," *IEEE Trans. Parallel and Distributed Systems,* Vol. 3, No. 4, July 1992, pp. 488–499.

Theimer, M. M., and B. Hayes, "Heterogeneous Process Migration by Recompilation," *Proc. 11th IEEE Int'l Conf. Distributed Computing Systems,* IEEE CS Press, Los Alamitos, Calif., 1991, pp. 18–25; reprinted here.

Theimer, M. M., K. A. Lantz, and D. R. Cheriton, "Preemptable Remote Execution Facilities for the V-System," *Proc. 10th ACM Symp. Operating Systems Principles,* ACM Press, New York, N.Y., 1985, pp. 2–12; reprinted here.

Zayas, E. R., "Attacking the Process Migration Bottleneck," *Proc. 11th ACM Symp. Operating Systems Principles,* ACM Press, New York, N.Y., 1987, pp. 13–24; reprinted here.

Design Issues of Process Migration Facilities in Distributed Systems[†]

M. Raşit Eskicioğlu
Department of Computing Science
University of Alberta
Edmonton, Alberta, CANADA T6G 2H1

Abstract

Distributed systems are composed of several loosely-coupled computers communicating over a high-bandwidth network. To achieve an even distribution of the workload in a distributed system, either preemptive or non-preemptive load distribution strategies are used. Preemptive load distribution involves process migration, while non-preemptive strategies are based on initial placement of processes on the machines. *Process migration* is a mechanism where a process on one machine is moved to another machine in a distributed system. This paper discusses the design of process migration facilities in distributed systems with respect to the key issues, such as: the system models on which the mechanisms are implemented, the hardware platforms they run on, the methods used in moving a process form one machine to another, load distribution policies adopted, network transparency, etc.

1 Introduction

Enhancements to the computer hardware have made "distributed computing systems" more and more available to the user community. Similarly, dramatic changes in operating systems provide users with better view of such systems [1]. *Distributed computing systems* are composed of several loosely-coupled computers communicating over a network [2, 3]. In a distributed computing system it is often desirable to achieve a uniform distribution of the workload among the machines in such a way that, each machine would have the same workload that is, there will be no idle machines, while some machines are overloaded. The problem of load distribution mainly involves reallocating the workload among the nodes of the system. Load distribution is used to obtain better response time and to increase resource utilization, and thus to achieve improved performance [4]. Load distribution can be achieved by using either preemptive or non-preemptive strategies. Preemptive strategies are carried out by moving active[1] processes from one machine to another. This mechanism is called *process migration*. On the other hand, non-preemptive load distribution is referred to as *initial placement*, where a process is assigned to a machine before starting execution and it resides and executes on the same machine until it terminates.

Theoretical and experimental studies have shown that both process migration and initial replacement have their merits. For example, Cabrera [5] and Hać [6] argue in favor of process migration, while Eager et al. [7] argue that only in extreme conditions can process migration offer a performance improvement. Furthermore, Leland and Ott [8] have shown that both strategies can improve performance for the large jobs if applied individually; moreover, further improvements can be achieved if both strategies are applied together. Krueger and Livny's work [9] produced similar results indicating a significant performance improvement when both strategies are used. Kyrimis and Alonso [10] have concluded that if the system load is not heavy, no strategy should be em-

---

[†]This work is supported in part by the Natural Sciences and Engineering Research Council (NSERC) of Canada under grants OGP9110 and OGP9183.

[1]An "active" process is a process that has started execution.

Reprinted from *IEEE Technical Committee on Operating Systems Newsletter,* vol. 4, no. 2, Winter, 1989, pp. 3–13.

ployed; but when the load is heavy, process migration should be used in every possibility. Kyrimis and Alonso have also shown that the use of process migration, even if the load is not heavy, does not degrade the overall system performance.

This paper discusses the design issues of process migration facilities available in various distributed systems[2]. The paper is organized as follows: section 2 introduces some terminology and elaborates on the concept of process migration. Section 3 describes the motivations for process migration in distributed systems and discusses several design issues of process migration. Section 4 reviews the cost of process migration and provides some figures from existing systems. And finally, section 5 concludes the paper commenting on the future of process migration.

2 Terminology

Since a variety of distributed systems exist, it is not easy to introduce terms describing concepts that are common to these systems. Nevertheless, we believe that the following definitions are general enough to describe the basic concepts of process migration that are discussed in this paper.

A *process* is a computation in execution. An instance of a process containing the necessary information required for resuming the process, is called the *process state*. The term "state," which is used loosely, refers to *all* the information needed for resuming a process properly and correctly. Since the resumption of the process may occur on a different machine, the process should be able to continue executing from the instruction where it was suspended and in the proper environment. The components of a process state depend on the machine where the process is running [11] and may show substantial differences on different machines. Nevertheless, a typical process state includes the following [12]:

- *virtual memory*—code, stack and data segments of a process,
- *open files*—file identifier, displacement pointers, I/O buffers, etc.,
- *message buffers*—sender and receiver information and the contents of the messages,
- *machine state*—current condition codes, PSW, PC, SP, registers, etc.,
- *environment data* —process ID, user ID, current working directory, references to children and parent processes, etc.

The virtual memory occupies the largest amount of space. It could be several megabytes, while the other components all together, usually only occupy a few thousand bytes.

Process migration is a mechanism in which a process on one machine is transferred to another machine. It is also referred to as *program migration, job migration, or task migration*. The *source machine* is the machine on which the process resides and executes before the transfer and the *destination machine* is the one where the process is to be transferred. Note that the instruction sets and the architectural differences of processors restrict process migration to be applied among homogeneous computers. On the other hand, distributed computer systems consisting of heterogeneous architectures can still benefit from process migration by migrating processes among a subset of computers in the system with the same processors. Moreover, process migration is still possible among processors that are upward compatible if the executable code is compiled for the oldest architecture. The following discussion of process migration applies to such homogeneous environments.

Process migration is a way to improve resource sharing and to increase resource utilization in distributed systems [13]. Migrating a process from the source machine to the destination machine is done in several steps:

1- suspend the process on the source machine[3],

---

[2]The term "distributed system" refers to the operating system that controls a distributed computing system.

[3]If the process is not in a "ready" state (usually wait-

2- transfer the process state to the destination machine, and

3- resume its execution on the destination machine.

These basic steps can be repeated for different pairs of machines as many times as required, depending on the load distribution policies adopted. In other words, a process may migrate from one machine to another, and then may further migrate to another machine.

3 Design Issues

In general, designing an operating system facility is a complex task because of the many different issues that one has to consider. Designing a process migration facility is equally complex, where the issues to be considered include: *when* and *where* to migrate *which* process, how to transfer the process state from source to destination, how to define failure semantics, how to provide transparency and reliability, etc. Not only are these issues are complex, but also they are closely interrelated to other issues of the operating systems (memory management, process management, secondary storage management, communications management, etc.).

Process migration is difficult to implement in a loosely-coupled system, while it is trivial in a tightly-coupled system. In a loosely-coupled system, the process state has to be transferred from the source machine to the destination machine over the network, whereas in a tightly-coupled system, it is a matter of updating the machine state of the destination processor with the source processor's current machine state and updating the page tables of the destination processor. In addition, in a tightly-coupled system, one has to deal with *other* design issues, such as: memory contention, processor organization, configuration of communication switches, etc. This paper only addresses the design issues of process migration in loosely-coupled systems.

---

ing on I/O) the suspension is delayed until the process becomes ready.

Process migration has been a useful and a desirable feature in distributed systems. Smith [14], Jul et al. [15], and Joosen and Verbaeten [16] summarize the benefits of process migration facilities as follows:

Reconfiguration—long running processes will not face problems of system shutdown or system failures; in such cases they could be migrated to other available machines.

Load balancing—moving processes across the network might increase performance of the distributed system by balancing the load of individual machines.

Communication performance—for an I/O bound process, where data is retrieved through the network, the process could be migrated to the machine where the data resides, decreasing the network traffic.

Resource sharing—not all resources are available to the processes remotely, that is, the hardware configuration may differ from one machine to another, and yet some devices may not be available remotely. By migrating those processes that require special devices to the appropriate machine, the assortment of services provided to the users may increase.

Process migration has been proposed in several systems to improve the overall performance by distributing the workload of these systems. There are some successful implementations. The next section describes the models on which these systems were built, the virtual memory transfer schemes used, and the policies adopted to migrate processes across the network. The residual dependencies on source machines, the transparency issue, and some other issues of process migration implementations are also discussed.

3.1 System models

Distributed systems that have process migration facilities are built on either of two models [17]: a *workstation model* and a *minicomputer model*. ACCENT [18], SPRITE [19] and the

V Distributed System [20] are based on the workstation model where the underlying system is composed of high performance workstations with powerful microprocessors, a high resolution display, large (4-32 megabytes) main memory, an optional secondary storage and a network adapter. Mos [21], Locus [22], Charlotte [23] and Demos/MP [24] are based on the minicomputer model, where the system is composed of several minicomputers (e.g., PDP 11's, VAX 11/750 or 780's) on which several users are logged on. Accent also runs on a cluster of VAX 11/750 and 780 minicomputers and Mosix [25], the workstation version of Mos, also runs on NS32532-based single processor and multiprocessor workstation prototypes.

From the communication mechanisms perspective, these distributed systems are based on either message passing (MP) or remote procedure call (RPC) models. Among them, Accent, Charlotte, Demos/MP, and the V Distributed System use message passing mechanisms and Locus, Mos–Mosix and Sprite use RPC mechanisms.

3.2 Virtual Memory Transfer

The dominant cost of the process migration is the time spent in transferring the virtual memory. The implementations introduced in the previous section use either of the following schemes to transfer the virtual memory from source to destination machines:

(a) *Entire virtual memory transfer.* This scheme is the most primitive and straightforward technique. First, the process on the source machine is suspended, then the *entire* virtual memory is transferred to the destination machine along with the other parts of the process state, and finally, the process is allowed to resume its execution on the destination machine.

(b) *Pre-copying.* In this scheme, after the migration decision has been made and a destination machine has been found, the source kernel starts transferring the process state to the destination machine while

the process still executes. This is followed by repeated transfer of dirty pages until a threshold is reached (e.g., the amount of dirty pages is small or the amount of dirty pages is not changing in time, etc.), and the process is suspended. Then, the current dirty pages are transferred for the last time. Finally, the destination kernel sets up the new environment, and the process resumes its execution on the destination machine.

(c) *Lazy-copying—Copy-on-reference.* The lazy-copying copies basically all the state information except the virtual memory to the destination machine after suspending the process. Once the initial copying is done, the process is allowed to resume its execution on the destination machine. The basic idea of lazy-copying is to copy only the minimum necessary state information initially, and then copy the individual pages on demand when they are referenced by the destination machine.

(d) *Enhanced copy-on-reference.* This scheme is an enhanced version of the copy-on-reference. The difference is that the dirty pages are flushed to a file server before any part of the process state is transferred to the destination machine rather than being kept on the source machine. The rest is the same as the original copy-on-reference scheme. When the migrated process references a page that does not reside on the destination machine's main memory, it is retrieved from the file server, as opposed to requesting the page from the source machine.

The entire virtual memory transfer scheme is used by Demos/MP [26], Locus [27], Mos–Mosix [28], and Charlotte [29]. There are two disadvantages of this scheme. First, the freeze time of a process during a transfer that may take many seconds is not acceptable in many real-time or interactive applications. Second, the bulk transfer of the virtual memory causes wasted work, since some of the pages transferred may not be needed after migration.

The pre-copying scheme, used by the V DISTRIBUTED SYSTEM [30], tries to overcome the disadvantage of prolonged freeze times of the previous scheme by continuing the execution of the process on the source machine while transfer of virtual memory is in progress. Theimer showed that the freeze time can be substantially reduced with this scheme [31]. The disadvantage of this scheme is that some of the pages may be transferred more than once as they are modified on the source machine. Also, like in the previous scheme unneeded pages may be transferred.

The lazy-copying scheme, used by ACCENT [32], allows a process to continue executing on the destination machine with a minimal freeze time. But, since the virtual memory of the process is not transferred, the process will take longer to execute because of the page faults. Another disadvantage is that this scheme leaves residual dependencies on the source machine.

The enhanced lazy-copying scheme, used by SPRITE [33], overcomes the disadvantage of lazy-copying by flushing the dirty pages to a file server (on the swap space of the process); thus, no residual dependencies are left on the source machine after migration. A disadvantage is that a page fault may be more costly than with the previous approach.

3.3 Load Distribution Policies

Load distribution for improving the overall performance of a distributed computing system has been extensively discussed in the literature and many theoretical models and algorithms have been proposed (e.g., [34, 35, 36, 37, 38, 39, 40], to list a few). It has been shown that performance improvements can be achieved by relocating processes in a distributed computing system [5, 7, 8]. Several distributed systems adopt these models as their design goals for process migration [28, 38]. Irrespective of its model, a load distribution policy must answer the following questions:

- *which* process to move,
- *when* to move the process, and

- *where* to move the process.

In workstation model of distributed systems, the problem of load distribution is attacked by sharing the computing power of otherwise idle workstations; that is, part of the workload from heavily loaded workstations is moved to idle workstations.

SPRITE and the V DISTRIBUTED SYSTEM adopt a similar policy to process migration: the users have sole control of the process migration. In other words, users execute special commands explicitly if they wish to migrate local processes to idle workstations[4]. The migration mechanism in these systems is semi-automatic: when a migration request is issued by the user the system finds an idle workstation and performs process migration automatically. Moreover, the user can explicitly specify the destination machine with a special command. On the other hand, eviction is fully automatic. SPRITE uses the information, as a database, to identify idle hosts. A special daemon running on each host monitors the use of the machine and updates the corresponding entry in the database.

In the V DISTRIBUTED SYSTEM, this database is virtual and distributed: a workstation multicasts and gathers the workload information of the other workstations when the special command for migration is issued. Then, the system picks the first available workstation and starts migrating the process.

Both systems implement preemption mechanisms, that is, when the *owner* of the idle workstation returns to work, the foreign processes are forced to move either to their originating workstations or to another idle workstations. This type of preemption is introduced as a mechanism for using otherwise idle workstations which belong to individual users who want exclusive access to their machines.

The scenario is different in distributed systems based on the minicomputer model, where the objective of load distribution is to balance the workload at each node of the system. Nodes are no longer owned by individual users and the

---

[4]In SPRITE, however, *pmake* utility and the *exec* system call make use of the migration facility automatically.

problems of preemption are different from those in the workstation environment.

In LOCUS, the UNIX process control functions *fork* and *exec* are extended to operate over the network, while retaining their formal semantics. One way to balance the load is to run a special daemon that looks for the CPU-bound jobs and migrates them to unloaded sites automatically. Furthermore, the migrate system call permits a process to change its execution site while in the middle of execution. At the user-level, each user of the system can select a group of execution sites by a shell command that establishes a list of preferred execution sites. The decision about where the new process will execute can then be made by examining this list automatically by the shell. Yet another way of distributing the load is achieved with the modified "make" program that automatically distributes intermediate targets to a group of sites.

In CHARLOTTE, the migration policy is dictated by a privileged process, called the Starter. There are several Starter utilities running on the network. Each Starter controls a subset of the machines. The Starters continuously evaluate the statistical information collected by the kernels they control and exchange among themselves a summary of this information. A Starter process executes a policy procedure when it gets the statistical information or a notice of process creation or termination. The policy procedure can then communicate with the other Starters and request some source kernel to undertake migration.

In MOS-MOSIX, the load balancing policy consists of three levels [28]: processor load calculation, information exchange, and the process migration consideration. At the first level, a special process monitors the local load of each processor continuously. At the second level, load information about a subset of processors is gathered by exchanging a load vector between the processors at random. Finally, at the last level, a candidate for migration is selected according to the information provided by the second level. All the internal control algorithms of MOS-MOSIX are distributed to limit the network-related management activities at each node.

Unfortunately, there has been no report describing the load balancing policy of DE-MOS/MP.

3.4 Mechanism–Policy Structure

In some of the distributed systems, the migration mechanism is separated from the policy, i.e., the mechanism is integrated in the kernel with IPC and short-term scheduling, and the policy is a trusted utility associated with long-term scheduling and resource management. Although this separation simplifies the interface between the two, it introduces an extra cost: the latency caused by the communication during the exchange of the statistical information. Such delays are not acceptable in systems with real-time constraints because some deadlines must be met. On the other hand, these delays would not harm the system in the long run, since the policy decisions are usually based on accumulated information that reflects the system status, thus giving better view of the system. ACCENT, CHARLOTTE, and DEMOS/MP fall into this category.

On the other end of the spectrum is the interleaved structure of the mechanism and the policy. SPRITE and the V DISTRIBUTED SYSTEM adopted this policy, because of its implementation simplicity. In both systems, the policy is manual and it is supported by automatic eviction. The major disadvantage of this approach is that it may impose maintenance problems, especially when generalizing and/or expanding the system.

The approach adopted by MOS is between the above solutions: both the mechanism and the policy are in the kernel, but are implemented as two separate layers. The disadvantage of this approach is that it becomes cumbersome to change the policy, since it requires recompilation of the whole kernel. This is unpleasant, especially during implementation and tuning of the system.

Finally, LOCUS adopted yet another approach, where the decision is left to the users at the application level. The users decide where to move their processes. This approach usually degrades the performance, since it is time consuming to acquire the process state and machine load information at this level.

3.5 Residual Dependencies

A *residual dependency* is defined by Douglis and Ousterhout as "an on-going need for a host to maintain data structures or provide functionality for a process even after the process migrates away from the host" [41]. The residual dependency is considered as a major disadvantage in terms of reliability and performance. For example, if a host fails, those processes with the residual dependencies on that host will be affected. Moreover, the overhead of dealing with the residual dependencies (e.g., updating them) affects the performance of the other processes running on that host. On the other hand, for some systems these dependencies are required to maintain transparency, and improve the performance. For example, ACCENT's lazy copying scheme benefits from the residues on the source machine by deferring the memory transfer until it is necessary. The benefit of this approach is that, pages are never copied to the destination unless they are referenced, thus eliminating the overhead of unnecessary transfers.

CHARLOTTE, MOS–MOSIX, SPRITE and the V DISTRIBUTED SYSTEM do not leave any residual dependencies on the source machine. Since the DEMOS/MP message system guarantees message delivery, a "forwarding address" is temporarily kept on the source machine after migration to forward messages to the process at the new location. In LOCUS, the origin site keeps track of the processes when they migrate to assure the delivery of signals.

3.6 Transparency

An important feature of distributed systems is transparency, or more precisely, network transparency. Network transparency is the composition of access transparency, location transparency and naming transparency [42]. The primary goal of network transparency is to hide the underlying network from the users, as well as from the distributed system itself.

Naming transparency ensures that the same name used on different machines will address the same resource. Location transparency means that a resource name does not carry any dependency of the machine it resides, which implies that a resource can be moved without changing its name. Access transparency is two fold: device transparency and process transparency. It means that one can use the same system calls, device names, process IDs, etc. regardless of their locations.

Process migration transparency adds yet another facet to the transparency, which implies that the execution of a process, thus its results do not depend on where it executes on the network. SPRITE assigns a *home machine* to each process. Whenever a migrated process issues a location-dependent system call, the call is forwarded to the home node and executed there. The V DISTRIBUTED SYSTEM maintains a *logical host* for each process, which is mapped to a physical machine. When a message fails to arrive at its destination, the logical host of the recipient of the message is used to obtain the new location of the migrated process. LOCUS identifies each process by their *origin site*, where the current location of the process is always known. Thus, calls are forwarded through the origin site to the new location of the process. ACCENT's ports, CHARLOTTE's and DEMOS/MP's links provide transparency during process migration. The linker and the ambassador process provide transparency in MOS–MOSIX, as well as the universal inodes.

3.7 Other Issues

Efficiency and transparency are among the common and most important design goals in today's distributed systems that implement process migration mechanisms. These characteristics are successfully reflected on the implementation of the process migration mechanisms. However, there are some other issues that are crucial in distributed systems: fault tolerance, concurrency, reliability, to name a few. For example, failure, in terms of software and hardware, is unavoidable in today's computers, thus it should be taken care of. Although these issues are addressed at large in some of the above distributed systems, they are simply ignored in process migration mechanisms of those systems. This is because the designers did not want to add yet another complexity to the already complex structure of the migration mechanisms.

The difficulties in design and implementation of process migration are: to detach the process from its environment efficiently and reliably, to transfer the process to the destination, and to establish the same environment and resume the process at the destination. A failure that may occur between these steps can be controlled in several ways depending on the failure/cost characteristics. When the source machine fails, if the process has been completely detached before the failure, the migrant process will not be affected. Similarly, when the destination machine fails, the migrated process may not be affected, if it could be resumed on the source properly. When the communication medium fails, the worst scenario would be loosing parts of the process that cannot be recovered; therefore, the process is terminated. Usually, the effect of the failure could be hidden from the migrant process. Among the above distributed systems, only CHARLOTTE gives some consideration to the reliability issue. Other systems simply terminate the migrant process when the source or the destination machine, or the communication medium fails.

One other issue was pointed out by Maguire, Jr. and Smith, regarding the effects of process migration in scientific computation [43]. Actually, this issue is more related to *file migration* than process migration. As discussed in their paper, the problem arises only when the data is moved between different architectures, and does not cause any problem in homogeneous environments. Since process migration occur between homogeneous machines, one should not worry about it.

4   Cost of Migration

The cost of moving a process from one machine to another includes the cost of selecting a destination machine, the cost of transferring the process state, and the cost of setting up the environment on the new machine. The dominant cost among them is the cost of transferring the process state. As the size of the process state increases, the cost of process migration increases. Transferring a process from one machine to another, which involves moving large address spaces, is time consuming. All the distributed systems mentioned above consider these costs. In DEMOS/MP, there is an additional cost, namely the cost of updating the links and forwarding messages to the new location of the migrated process.

Every distributed system has been developed with different goals, and usually runs on different hardware platforms. For example, ACCENT runs on PERQ workstations and VAX 11/780's connected with Ethernet, CHARLOTTE runs on VAX 11/750's connected with a token ring network, DEMOS/MP runs on Z8000 processors, etc. Besides, each system dictates different process structure. Therefore, the performance of process migration mechanisms in these systems cannot be compared with each other. Nevertheless, to give an idea, some performance figures of ACCENT, CHARLOTTE, MOSIX, SPRITE and the V DISTRIBUTED SYSTEM are given below. Performance information on the other systems were not available in the literature.

The experiments have shown that the *lazy transfer* technique adopted in copy-on-reference scheme reduces the cost of process migration by exploiting the fact that processes do use only small portions of their address spaces during execution. Zayas [32] claims that the number of bytes exchanged between machines have dropped by 58.2 %, and the cost of message handling has dropped by 47.8 % on average when copy-on-reference strategy was used in ACCENT's process migration facility. On the other hand, the experiments have also shown that because of the complex mappings of the processes into virtual memory, the remote execution times of the processes have shown moderate increases.

Artsy and Finkel reported in [29] that, with a deviation of about five percent, a CHARLOTTE process of 100 kilobytes with six links requires 750 milliseconds to migrate. Each additional link has an overhead of 1.6 to 2.8 milliseconds. Moreover, collecting statistics requires one percent, and delivering this statistics to the Starter requires another two percent of the overall elapsed time.

MOSIX runs on a cluster of experimental multiprocessor workstations connected by an 80 Mbit/sec token-ring based LAN. A 100 kilobytes process requires 55–187 milliseconds to migrate from one processor to another [25].

In SPRITE, running on a Sun-3 workstation, it takes about 600 milliseconds to migrate a 100 kilobytes process with three open files [33].

Unfortunately, there are no published specific measurements of DEMOS/MP and LOCUS.

5 Concluding Remarks

The design issues of process migration mechanisms in distributed systems have been presented. The observation of these systems shows that process migration is expensive and not easy to implement. Douglis [41] discusses the difficulties in implementing process migration mechanisms and the lessons learned in general. Though in message-based systems, such as DEMOS/MP and the V DISTRIBUTED SYSTEM, the implementations have shown to be easier than that of RPC-based systems. This is due to the fact that the small kernels of such systems contain little information about processes, thus the location dependency of a process is minimal. In any case, it is argued that process migration is a useful tool. The systems can more easily adapt to changes in the load and in the requirements of the users [44]. The general trend in workstation-based distributed systems is to leave the decision of migrating processes to the owners of the workstations. In minicomputer-based systems however, the computers are dedicated to service a group of users, thus equity of the service is expected. Therefore, final decision of migrating processes is left to the distributed system itself.

Because the developments in computer technology are growing very fast, problems incurred in today's process migration mechanisms (e.g., the communication costs, the uncertainty of the machine states, etc.) will not be the problems of tomorrow. To be precise, given the availability of very high speed networks ($>$ 1 gigabits/sec), the communication costs would be negligible.

References

[1] Joseph Boykin and Susan J. LoVerso. Recent Developments in Operating Systems. *IEEE Computer Magazine*, 23(5):5–6, May 1990.

[2] J. A. Stankovic. A Perspective on Distributed Computer Systems. *IEEE Transactions on Computers*, C-33(12):1102–1115, December 1984.

[3] Philip H. Enslow, Jr. What is a "Distributed" Data Processing System? *IEEE Computer Magazine*, 11(1):13–21, January 1978.

[4] Luis L. Cova and Rafael Alonso. Distributing Workload Among Independently Owned Processors. Technical Report CS-TR-200-88, Princeton University, December 1988.

[5] Luis-Felipe Cabrera. The Influence of Workload on Load Balancing Strategies. In *Proceedings of the USENIX Summer Conference*, June 1986.

[6] Anna Haḉ. A Distributed Algorithm for Performance Improvement through File Replication, File Migration and Process Migration. *IEEE Transactions on Software Engineering*, SE-15(11):1459–1970, November 1989.

[7] D. L. Eager, E. D. Lazowska, and J. Zahorjan. The Limited Performance Benefits of Migrating Active Processes for Load Sharing. Technical Report 87-12-10, University of Washington, December 1987.

[8] Will E. Leland and Tenuis J. Ott. Load-balancing Heuristics and Process Behavior. In *The PERFORMANCE'86 and ACM SIGMETRICS 1986 Proceedings*, May 1986.

[9] Phillip Krueger and Miron Livny. A Comparison of Preemptive and Non-Preemptive Load Distributing. In *Proceedings of the 8th International Conference on Distributed Computer Systems*, June 1988.

[10] Kriton Kyrimis and Rafael Alonso. An Experimental Comparison of Initial Placement vs. Process Migration for Load Balancing Strategies. Technical Report CS-TR-199-88, Princeton University, December 1988.

[11] Hugh C. Lauer and Roger M. Needham. On the Duality of Operating System Structures. *ACM Operating Systems Review*, 13(2), April 1979.

[12] Fred Douglis and John K. Ousterhout. Transparent Process Migration for Personal Workstations. Technical Report UCB/CSD 89/540, University of California at Berkeley, November 1989.

[13] Chin Lu. *Process Migration in Distributed Systems*. PhD thesis, University of Illinois at Urbana-Champaign, 1989.

[14] Jonathan M. Smith. A Survey of Process Migration Mechanisms. *ACM Operating Systems Review*, 22(3):28–40, July 1988.

[15] Eric Jul, Henry Levy, Norman Hutchinson, and Andrew Black. Fine-grained Mobility in the Emerald System. *ACM Transactions on Computer Systems*, 6(1):109–133, February 1988.

[16] W. Joosen and P. Verbaeten. On the Use of Process Migration in Distributed Systems. Technical Report CW-83, Leuven Catholic University, November 1988.

[17] A. S. Tanenbaum and R. van Renesse. Distributed Operating Systems. *ACM Computing Surveys*, 17(4):419–470, December 1985.

[18] Richard F. Rashid and George G. Robertson. Accent: A Communication Oriented Network Operating System. In *Proceedings of the 8th ACM Symposium on Operating System Principles*, December 1981.

[19] J. K. Ousterhout, A. R. Cherenson, F. Douglis, M. N. Nelson, and B. B. Welch. The Sprite Network Operating System. *IEEE Computer Magazine*, 20(2):23–36, February 1988.

[20] David R. Cheriton. The V Distributed System. *Communications of the ACM*, 31(3):314–333, March 1988.

[21] Amnon Barak and Ami Litman. MOS: A Multicomputer Distributed Operating System. *Software—Practice and Experience*, 15(8):725–737, August 1985.

[22] B. Walker, G. Popek, R. English, C. Kline, and G. Theil. The LOCUS Distributed Operating System. In *Proceedings of the 9th ACM Symposium on Operating System Principles*, November 1983.

[23] R. A. Finkel, M. L. Scott, Y. Artsy, and H.-Y. Chang. Experience with Charlotte: Simplicity and Function in a Distributed Operating System. *IEEE Transactions on Software Engineering*, SE-15(6):676–685, June 1989.

[24] B. T. Miller, D. L. Presotto, and M. L. Powell. DEMOS/MP: The Development of a Distributed Operating System. *Software—Practice and Experience*, 17(4):277–290, April 1987.

[25] Amnon Barak and Richard Wheeler. MOSIX: An Integrated Multiprocessor UNIX. In *Proceedings of the USENIX Winter Conference*, November 1989.

[26] M. L. Powell and B. T. Miller. Process Migration in DEMOS/MP. In *Proceedings of the 9th ACM Symposium on Operating System Principles*, November 1983.

[27] Gerald J. Popek and Bruce J. Walker, editors. *The LOCUS Distributed System Architecture*. MIT Press, Cambridge, Mass., 1985.

[28] Amnon Barak and Amnon Shiloh. A Distributed Load-balancing Policy for a Multicomputer. *Software—Practice and Experience*, 15(9):901–913, September 1985.

[29] Yeshayahu Artsy and Raphael Finkel. Designing a Process Migration Facility. *IEEE Computer Magazine*, 22(9):47–56, September 1989.

[30] Marvin M. Theimer, Keith A. Lantz, and David R. Cheriton. Preemptive Remote Execution Facilities for the V System. In *Proceedings of the 10th ACM Symposium on Operating System Principles*, December 1985.

[31] M. Theimer. *Preemptable Remote Execution Facilities for Loosely-Coupled Distributed Systems*. PhD thesis, Stanford University, 1986.

[32] Edward R. Zayas. Attacking the Process Migration Bottleneck. In *Proceedings of the 11th ACM Symposium on Operating System Principles*, December 1987.

[33] Fred Douglis and John K. Ousterhout. Process Migration in the Sprite Operating System. In *Proceedings of the 7th International Conference on Distributed Computer Systems*, September 1987.

[34] R. K. Arora and S. P. Rana. Heuristic Algorithms for Process Assignment in Distributed Computing Systems. *Information Processing Letters*, 11(4–5):199–203, December 1980.

[35] Harold H. Stone and S. H. Bokhari. Control of Distributed Processes. *IEEE Computer Magazine*, 10(7):97–106, July 1978.

[36] Y. C. Chow and W. H. Kohler. Models for Dynamic Load Balancing on a Heterogeneous Multiprocessor System. *IEEE Transactions on Computers*, C-28(5):354–361, May 1979.

[37] P. E. Krueger. *Distributed Scheduling for a Changing Environment*. PhD thesis, University of Wisconsin—Madison, 1988.

[38] P. Krueger and R. A. Finkel. An Adaptive Load Balancing Algorithm for a Multicomputer. Technical Report 539, University of Wisconsin–Madison, April 1984.

[39] Y.-T. Wang and R. J. T. Morris. Load Sharing in Distributed Systems. *IEEE Transactions on Computers*, C-34(3):204–217, March 1985.

[40] L. M. Ni, C.-W. Xu, and T. B. Gendreau. A Distributed Drafting Algorithm for Load Balancing. *IEEE Transactions on Software Engineering*, SE-11(10):1153–1161, October 1985.

[41] Fred Douglis. Experience with Process Migration in Sprite. In *Proceedings of the Workshop on Experiences with Distributed and Multiprocessor Systems*, October 1989.

[42] Bruce J. Walker and Gerald Popek. A Transparent Environment. *BYTE*, 14(7):225–233, July 1989.

[43] Gerald Q. Maguire, Jr. and Jonathan M. Smith. Process Migration: Effects on Scientific Computation. *ACM SIGPLAN Notices*, 23(2):102–106, March 1988.

[44] Michael Stumm. The Design and Implementation of a Decentralized Scheduling Facility for a Workstation Cluster. In *Proceedings of the 2nd International Conference on Computer Workstations*, March 1988.

Heterogeneous Process Migration
by Recompilation

Marvin M. Theimer

Xerox Palo Alto Research Center
3333 Coyote Hill Rd.
Palo Alto, CA 94304

Barry Hayes

Department of Computer Science
Stanford University
Stanford, CA 94309

Abstract

Heterogeneous process migration involves moving a process between machines that have differing hardware and software configurations, including different processor architectures, machine instruction sets, and operating systems. This paper describes an approach to heterogeneous process migration that involves building a machine-independent "migration program" that specifies the current code and data state of the process to be migrated. When this program is compiled and executed on the target machine, it will first reconstruct the process's state and then continue the normal execution of the now-migrated process. The principal advantage of this approach is that it hides the details of code and data translation in the compilers for each machine.

1 Introduction

In a distributed system supporting transparent remote execution of applications, process migration can be useful for a variety of reasons:

- It can be used to reduce the disruption of activities such as maintenance and repair of hardware.

- It can be used to improve the performance of individual processes and an entire system in the face of changing resource availabilities. For example, Leland and Ott [2] have shown that many systems can be characterized as containing many small jobs and a few "hogs" that consume the vast majority of all computing cycles. These hog processes typically run for extended periods of time and considerable efforts can be justified to ensure that they are properly spread among the available computing nodes.

- It provides a second axis of optimization for a "data browser" class of applications that interact with various large databases, reading and writing data from one database for a while, and then moving on to another. Optimal behavior for these applications involves trading off both data motion and program motion.

Process migration has already received extensive study for the homogeneous case, where both the source and target machine of a migrating process consist of the same kind of hardware and run the same underlying systems software. *Homogeneous process migration* can be done without knowing all the details of the process state being migrated because the code and data elements involved can be copied without being understood.

Heterogeneous process migration involves moving a process between machines that have differing hardware and software configurations. To migrate a process between heterogeneous bases requires sufficient knowledge about a process's state to be able to create an equivalent state on the target machine, so that the migration is transparent to the rest of the world. A prerequisite concern is that the state of a process be sufficiently specified to make such a translation possible.

This paper concerns itself primarily with those issues of heterogeneous process migration that are not already addressed by the requirements of homogeneous process migration. We are concerned with the issue of translating the running state of a process from its representation on one machine to an equivalent representation on another machine. We propose to implement migration by means of recompilation, building a machine-independent *migration program* that specifies the state of the process to be migrated.

When this program is compiled and executed on the target machine, it will first reconstruct all of the global and heap data from the process on the source machine and then execute one chain of calls for each stack to modified versions of the procedures that were on the

Reprinted from *Proc. IEEE 11th Int'l Conf. on Distributed Computing Systems*, IEEE CS Press, Los Alamitos, Calif., 1991, pp. 18–25.

call stacks of the process on the source machine. These modified procedures will first reconstruct the stack data and then resume execution of the now migrated process.

Many programming languages do not specify the semantics of their behavior exactly or in a machine-independent manner. For example, the same floating point operation may yield different results on different machines. Machine-dependent values like the size of data types may be available as part of the language, allowing programs to exhibit machine-dependent behavior. If the behavior of a program depends on the underlying hardware, it is senseless to ask the semantics of transparent migration.

Assuming that the incarnation of a program as a process on one machine can be translated to an equivalent incarnation of the program as a process on another machine, there is still the question of how to actually implement this translation. In general, it will require detailed knowledge of the hardware and systems software of each machine involved. This knowledge already exists in the compilers and debuggers for each machine. We would like to be able to take advantage of that knowledge and avoid recreating it. By specifying the state of a process in terms of a program and compiling that program we achieve this goal. However, specifying a process's state in terms of a high-level programming language is difficult for some languages. If an intermediate language is available, such as one used to communicate between compiler front-ends and back-end code generators, then process state specification may be considerably simplified.

Finally, efficiency is always a concern. The migration program for a process always includes the program that the process is executing. Full recompilation would add substantially to the overhead of migration, but partial recompilation techniques may be employed to reduce this overhead to a more acceptable level.

The rest of this paper addresses these issues in more detail. Section 2 summarizes other approaches to the topic. Section 3 describes our model of computation and the requirements placed on programming languages for which our approach will work. Section 4 presents the approach we propose for heterogeneous process migration, while section 5 examines the costs of our approach. Section 6 finishes with conclusions and suggestions for future work.

2 Related Work

Homogeneous process migration is a fairly well understood operation [5, 8, 9, 4]. When the two hardware platforms are not the same, solutions to date work only in special cases [6] or by interpretation of the source code of a program [1]. The latter approach is in reality a case of homogeneous process migration since the machine—the interpreter—is the same on all hardware. The disadvantage of this approach is that it sacrifices the performance obtainable from running programs that have been compiled to the native instruction set of a physical machine.

We are aware of one effort, by Shub [6], based on the former approach. This effort has focused on a restricted class of C programs and has not specified how translation between source and target program states could be performed in a general, automated fashion. C programs are not allowed to alias pointers, so that the state of a program's data can be determined from its binary object file and from special tables kept by a modified heap storage allocation package. This prohibits all C pointer coercions, including the common case of "narrowing" a generic C pointer to be a pointer to a specific data type. Compiler optimizations involving code motion are also disallowed.

The translation techniques used by Shub are based on a combination of "hand-coded" translation procedures and the availability of a single compiler that can target every machine existing in a system. A common compiler allows for space allocation policies that simplify data element translation. For example, structure packing can be guaranteed to be the same on all machines and the storage size for a data type can be made to be the maximum required by any machine. Identical optimizations are compiled for a program without regard for target machine, so that the states of the process on one machine correspond to the states on any other. The compiler also directs all calls to heap storage management to a modified package that generates runtime symbol tables describing the data layout of the heap. The actual translation of process state is done by means of hand-coded migration procedures that use the symbol tables generated by the compiler and the heap storage management package to find all the data elements of a process. Note that these translation procedures must be coded for every machine type existing in a system and are compiler dependent.

For systems with failure recovery, process migration can be implemented in an entirely different manner. The process to migrate is destroyed on the source machine and then recovered on the target machine. If the information logged for process recovery is written in a machine-independent manner then this approach can handle the heterogeneous process migration case. We know of no system that has actually implemented such an approach, but Argus [3] supplies the necessary facilities to do so in theory. The tradeoff of this approach compared to others—including ours—is that failure recovery facilities typically impose an overhead throughout the execution of a program. State checkpoints are periodically written out to stable storage. Our approach imposes an overhead only at migration time and hence should be the more desirable for migratory processes that don't need failure recovery capabilities.

Our approach is similar to that of Shub in that we deal with compiled binary programs rather than interpretd source programs. However, we avoid the details of machine and compiler-dependent data translation procedures by employing recompilation techniques to keep knowledge of these matters hidden within the compilers and debuggers. Also, by going to this level of abstraction, our approach extends easily to a large class of programming languages rather than being specifically targetted for the implementation idiosyncrasies of a single programming language and compiler. The price we pay for this is an increase in the time to migrate, since migration now involves recompilation and relinking of various parts of a program instead of direct manipulation of memory values at absolute addresses in a program binary image.

3 Model of Computation

3.1 Abstract and physical program states

The key notion of our approach is that a programming language defines an abstract machine on which a program can be run. At many points in the program's execution on physical devices its state can be specified in terms of the current state of this abstract machine. Intuitively, these are the points in the execution of a program where a source-level debugger could make sense of the state. We migrate a process by automatically writing a program that first reconstructs the data, and then continues on with the processing where the source process left off. There are many ways to reconstruct the data, and we will compare some of their efficiencies later.

Some programming languages have the ability to "undo" their execution to a previous state. Two examples of such languages are Prolog and Snobol. The techniques for migrating programs in such languages are substantially different, since execution history is accessible to the program. We exclude languages with such backtracking facilities, and focus only on languages with easily reconstructible state.

Compilers translate a source program for an abstract machine into a binary program for a physical machine that produces the same external behavior as the source program. "Behavior" means externally visible state, such as the values of data elements as they are defined and understood by the world surrounding a program, at the points where the program interacts with the world.

The compiler is free to change the program in any way that does not change its external behavior. Compilers strive to find ways to cut resource use, while maintaining behavior. With an optimizing compiler, the internal states of the source program on the abstract machine and the binary program on the physical machine will correspond only at a subset of the execution points of each program.

At an execution point where the states of the abstract and physical machines correspond we can represent the state of the binary machine program by means of a source program that describes the corresponding abstract machine state. We call such points *migration points*. We can invoke the same primitives used for source-level debugging to reverse-compile the machine-dependent binary program state to a machine-independent source program description.

3.2 Code Optimization

3.2.1 Frequency of Migration Points

To keep the delays in migration small, there should be as many migration points in a program as possible, so that the option to migrate is available as frequently as possible. If the compiler used does not perform any optimizations then the number of migration points available will be maximized. Unfortunately, inhibiting optimizations also imposes a heavy penalty on the program's execution time.

What we really want is a bounds on the time required for a program to reach a migration point from the time that migration is requested. Restating our requirement in this fashion allows any optimizations to occur, including rearranging basic code blocks and optimizing loops, as long as we can guarantee such behavior. Even complex optimizations are allowed if fix-up code invoked at migration brings the physical state in line with an abstract state.

If we assume time bounds for migration on the order of a second, then this leaves room for several million machine instructions to occur before a migration point must be reached. Migration points might have to be inserted into long blocks and loops to meet the requirements.

If a procedure on the stack, but not currently executing, is not in a state corresponding to an abstract state, we cannot migrate easily. We must wait for the procedure it has called to return, and then let it run to a migration point. Some procedures may always execute in a short time, and we can wait for these calls to terminate. For calls to procedures with no such guarantee, we require that the call point also be a migration point, and so at migration time any procedure on a call stack will be at a migration point.

Migration points are also abundant if a program periodically returns to a predetermined migration point. To migrate individual objects in an object-oriented system we can make the "waiting for message" state of each object a migration point. If we can assure that every method invocation terminates within the time bounds we require for reaching a migration point, then the compiler is free to optimize the individual methods without restrictions.

3.2.2 Compiler Intermediate Languages

The abstract language used for the migration program could be a high-level language, but it is more convenient to use a lower-level language such as the language used to communicate between a language-dependent compiler front-end, and a machine-dependent code generator. The machine-specific optimizations available in the code generator are then available to the migrating process, but we can avoid much of the expense of language processing. This approach does not even require all machines to share a retargetable compiler, but each pair of machines must understand a common language, and the migration program must be written in the appropriate language.

3.3 Completeness of the Language Specification

There are several important requirements we make of the abstract machine specification for a programming language in order to support our approach to process migration. These center around the need to specify the current state of a program running on the abstract machine in sufficient detail to be able to translate between it and some equivalent physical machine state. There can be no ambiguity about the meaning of a program's data elements or the operations that may be performed on them. Unfortunately, this is not the case for most programming languages. For example, the specification of floating point numbers and the results of various operations on them is frequently ill-specified. Consequently the results of performing the same operations on the same data on two different machines may differ because the compiler used for each machine is free to implement the ill- or unspecified aspects of the semantics in any fashion it chooses.

I/O operations are also frequently ill-specified. Many programming languages simply do not specify how activities such as I/O are performed. Others specify behavior in terms of a standard "system procedure library". We must wait for any such operations to terminate before we migrate, and rely on the network-transparent nature of the execution environment to allow the process to migrate after the call.

We must also disallow machine-specific variables, such as the storage sizes of data types, and exclude from our consideration programs whose behavior can depend on machine-dependent values. Many programs are *portable* in the sense that they can be started and successfully run on a given machine independent of its hardware configuration, but these programs are not machine-independent—and hence not migratable—since their behavior will differ from machine to machine. Their source specification is in fact the specification for a class of programs. An illustrative example of a portable, machine-dependent program is a program that packages data records into a fixed size byte array buffer to ship across a network. The number of records that will fit into the buffer will depend on the size of the records on the specific physical machine.

Programs are not allowed to have "hidden knowledge" of their abstract state. A program with untagged union data, for example, may be able to remember which branch of the union is appropriate and never access the data through an inappropriate branch, but this knowledge cannot generally be discovered. It is generally difficult to prove that such programs have no type errors, and discovering the data type in the absence of tagged data or tagged pointers is equally difficult.

In general, type-safe languages are more likely to meet our requirements. Even these sometimes do a poor job of specifying how floating point operations or I/O behave. Such languages limit the manufacture and type coercion of data references and hence prevent the hiding of information.

3.4 Problem Definition

At this point we are ready to specify what we mean by the term *process migration*. Our goal is to suspend a running process on one machine, copy its state to a newly created process on a second machine of possibly differing hardware and software configuration, destroy the first process, and set the second process running in a fashion such that the rest of the world remains unaware of the change unless an explicit query for the location of the logical process is made.

This goal requires all the preconditions needed for the well-studied topic of homogeneous process migration, such as network-transparent execution environments and network-transparent IPC [7]. We will not address these aspects of the problem here, other than to assume their solution. We will focus only on the question of copying and translating the state of a process on the source machine to an equivalent process state on the target machine.

We assume that the programs being run by processes contain migration points and that there exists a means of suspending a process at a migration point. This might require, for example, suspending a process, setting a breakpoint at some migration point, and then resuming the process. We assume that the compilers ensure that migration points occur frequently enough to satisfy the time bounds on migration for a system.

Finally, we assume that programs are written in a programming language whose state at any migration point is sufficiently well-specified to allow its complete translation between machine-dependent and machine-independent forms.

4   Migration Through Recompilation

4.1   The Machine-Independent Migration Program

The outline of the approach we propose for process migration can be described as follows:

- Suspend the process to migrate on the source machine.

- Translate the machine dependent state of the process into a machine independent state.

- Create a machine-independent "migration program" that represents this state.

- Compile, link, and load the machine-independent program on the target machine.

- Destroy the source process.

- Run the loaded program on the target machine to recreate the migrated process.

We assume the problems of maintaining consistent external connections, such as IPC, in the face of migration have already been solved, and the only remaining problem is to create the migration program.

The machine-independent migration program must first recreate the current data state of the process to migrate and then return control to the appropriate point of that program. We will use modified versions of each

procedure on the stack to first recreate the stack data, and then resume the execution of the original procedure at an appropriate point.

There are typically three kinds of data space in a program: global data, heap data, and procedure local data. The global and heap data can be recreated by a global initialization procedure that can be run at the beginning of the migration program, before any of the modified stack procedures are called.

In a language where jumps may be made to any point in a procedure, we can construct a modified call stack procedure in a simple and separable manner. Consider a call stack where procedure A calls procedure B, which in turn calls procedure C. The modified version of B, call it B1, will consist of the following parts:

1. Code to initialize all local variables.

2. A call to the modified procedure C1.

3. A jump to the point just past the call to C in a copy of the code from the original procedure B.

4. A copy of the code of B.

More specifically, consider the following pseudo code version of B:

```
procedure B:
    s0;
    for (i=0; i<n; i++) {
        s1;
        C();
        s2;
    }
    s3;
```

If the loop has been executed fully four times, the value of i is now 4, and we are calling C for the fifth time. The transformation to make B1 would be:

```
procedure B1:
    InitLocalVars;
        /* This includes i := 4 */
    C1();
    goto L;

    /* Copy of B, with label */
    s0;
    for  (i=0; i<n; i++) {
        s1;
        C();
    L:
        s2;
    }
    s3;
```

429

This procedure initializes its local variables, and calls other modified routines to initialize the variables of frames further up the stack. When C1 returns, it will have done all the work the second invocation of C was committed to before the migration, and the goto will cause resumption of the work B was committed to. If the code represented by s0 is now dead, the compiler is free to eliminate it. Note that the next time around the loop C, not C1, will be called. Each modified procedure is called only once.

To appreciate the advantage of not using a high-level language for the migration program, consider what would happen if the language disallowed the goto into the loop in the above example. The portions of the loop not yet executed must be completed before the goto is performed, and the target of the goto is moved past the end of the loop.

```
procedure B1:
    InitLocalVars;
        /* This includes i := 4 */
    C1();
    s2;
    for (i=5; i<n; i++) {
        s1;
        C();
        s2;
    }
    goto L;

    /* Copy of B with label */
    s0;
    for (i=0; i<n; i++) {
        s1;
        C();
        s2;
    }
L:
    s3;
```

This rewriting can be arbitrarily complex and lead to code explosion, depending on the restrictions in the language. The code above could be more complicated if s1 or s2 contained break or continue statements, gotos, labels or assignments to the loop variable. The complexities involved in rewriting for a more restrictive high-level language argue for using a less restrictive intermediate language. However, our approach will work for high-level languages, including those similar to Modula-2, type-safe Cedar, and Lisp.

4.2 Translating and Sending the State of a Process

To construct our migration program we need to translate the entire current state of a process from its machine dependent form to a machine independent form. We assume that the compilers generate source-level symbol tables describing the locations at which one can find any global and procedure-local variable. The global and procedure-local state can be evaluated in the same fashion that a source-level debugger can be asked to list the state of any given procedure on a call stack or of all global variables. A procedural interface to such a source-level debugger would be sufficient to gather the information we need.

To find the state of the heap, we must trace it in a fashion similar to that used by tracing garbage collectors. We must follow each pointer variable in the global and call stack state to find the transitive closure of the data elements they point to. Again, we assume that the abstract program state is sufficiently self-describing that we can correctly interpret all pointers encountered. Note that in addition to interpreting the pointers, which is all that garbage collection requires, we must also be able to interpret every field of every heap object.

Once we have the state of a process, we must still send it to the target machine. Since the language of the migration program is determined by the available compilers, it may be inefficient to transmit the migration program between machines in this language. In addition, the migration program is highly idiomatic, containing many elements built from a few simple templates. We can reduce the communication cost associated with migration by employing compaction techniques to obtain a shorter representation of the migration program.

There are even better ways to handle some idiomatic constructions. For example, the initialization of an array in the migration program can be compact, but still explicitly includes each data value in the array, and we would like to avoid making the compiler process these constants. Instead, we may write the array to a file and include in the migration program code to read the file. If the migration program is compiled and run before the source process is destroyed, we can avoid explicitly creating this file and use a network connection to stream the data directly to the running migration program.

4.3 Recompilation

At the conceptual level, we simply recompile a migration program in its entirety for the target machine. If we assume the preexistence of a binary program version of the original source program for the desired target machine, then we can use incremental recompilation techniques to avoid most of the overhead, since the new stack procedures are slightly modified versions of the originals. With the correct choice of intermediate language, each new procedure is just like its doppelganger, except for the addition of a preamble, and only these preambles need to be compiled.

In addition, we should be able to take advantage of incremental linking. The new procedures are called at migration and never from the original code, so the linker only needs to deal with the new procedures and doesn't need to change or add any references in the previously linked code.

If the migration program is specified in an intermediate language then several additional efficiencies should be obtainable. To begin with, recompilation of the various migration procedures will be significantly cheaper if none of the language-specific steps are performed and the machine-independent optimizations have already occurred.

5   Performance Issues

The dominant cost for homogeneous process migration is the cost of copying state between machines. For heterogeneous process migration there are additional costs of comparable size for translation of the data state of a process to the machine-independent form and for recompilation and relinking the migration program.

These three activities can be overlapped. If data are streamed directly from the source machine to the newly created process on the target machine then the extraction, transmission, and insertion of this state can be overlapped. Depending on the hardware parallelism available in the two machines, this overlapping could reduce the cost of migrating this part of the process's state by a factor of 2 or 3.

Since the binary of the original program must be linked with the modified procedures, we shouldn't begin a migration until the binary is present on the target machine. We can continue executing the process on the source machine until the binary is recreated on the target machine or fetched from some central server.

Employing such techniques to reduce our migration time cost is especially important because our approach to state specification prevents any of the VM paging techniques used in homogeneous process migration, such as precopying state or demand-paging state, to reduce the time during which a migrating process is suspended. Fortunately, by "precopying" the target binary, overlapping the processing of the global and heap data, and employing incremental recompilation techniques, we may be able to keep the cost of migration relatively low.

6   Summary and Conclusions

For programs written in a programming language with sufficient semantic clarity we have described a method by which they can be migrated between heterogeneous hardware and software bases. We believe our method should work for several important classes of languages, including those characterized by languages such as Modula-2, type-safe Cedar, and Lisp.

The approach we have taken emphasizes hardware and software independence at the expense of migration time cost. By employing recompilation and source-level debuggers we hide the details of migration within the compilers and debuggers for a language for each machine. This implies that the details of data and code translation need not be addressed by the implementor of migration.

Equally importantly, our approach allows us to migrate between different operating system bases since we rely on the abstract definition of a language's system library interface. Any operating system that correctly implements the semantics of the programming language used will be transparent to our migration activities.

Finally, the approach of recompilation is not tailored to any particular programming language. However, using a compiler intermediate language for migration has several significant benefits. Most important of these is that frequent migration points can be generated in source programs without hindering compiler optimizations. This allows a migration capability that imposes overhead on programs only at the point of migration instead of on the entire execution cost of every program run.

Another interesting capability afforded by the use of a compiler intermediate language is that we can migrate mixed-language programs, and automatically gain migration for programs in a new language when its front end is completed.

Our method entails additional time cost for migration. Migration now includes creation and compilation of state initialization code, in addition to the cost of sending a process's state between machines. Incremental recompilation and relinking techniques help mitigate these costs.

Hardware independence implies that we cannot employ VM paging techniques to precopy or demand-page process state between machines. We must suspend the migrating process for the entire time needed to migrate its state, which is measured in seconds, rather than suspending it for only a brief, subsecond "initialization" period and letting it run in parallel with the migration activity for most of the time.

There is still much work to be done to understand how our approach to heterogeneous process migration would work in practice. Foremost is the need for an implementation and performance evaluation to determine the actual overheads. Despite the additional costs of heterogeneous process migration over homogeneous migration, we feel that many applications will benefit.

Most programming languages do not specify their entire semantics, falling down when it comes to such topics as floating point numbers and I/O operations. We can approach this wall from both sides. Pragmatically, we can explore exactly how far from the formal requirements a real programming language can get and still allow reasonably coherent migration. For example, while different hardware floating-point implementations cause problems a "best effort" at migration would produce reasonable results for many programs. At the same time, it would also be interesting to determine what subsets of some popular languages, such as C or C++, would be suitable for our approach. For example, one could envision a preprocessor for appropriate C and C++ subsets that could be employed to "certify" that a program is suitable for migration.

References

[1] G. Attardi, A. Baldi, U. Boni, F. Carignani, G. Cozzi, A. Pelligrini, E. Durocher, I. Filotti, and W. Qing. Techniques for dynamic software migration. In *Proc. 5th Annual Esprit Conference*, pages 475–491. North Holland, November 1988.

[2] W.E. Leland and T.J. Ott. Load-balancing heuristics and process behavior. In *Proc. of PERFORMANCE 86 and ACM SIGMETRICS 1986*, pages 54–69. ACM, May 1986.

[3] B. Liskov, D. Curtis, P. Johnson, and R. Scheifler. Implementation of argus. In *Proc. 11th Symposium on Operating Systems Principles*, pages 111–122. ACM, November 1987. Proceedings published as *Operating System Review* 21(5).

[4] J.K. Ousterhout, A.R. Cherenson, F. Douglis, M.N. Nelson, and B.B. Welch. The sprite network operating system. *IEEE Computer*, pages 23–45, February 1988.

[5] M.L. Powell and B.P. Miller. Process migration in DEMOS/MP. In *Proc. 9th Symposium on Operating Systems Principles*, pages 110–119. ACM, October 1983. Published as *Operating Systems Review* 17(5).

[6] C. Shub. Native code process-originated migration in a heterogeneous environment. To appear in the February, 1990 ACM 18th Annual Computer Science Conference.

[7] M. M. Theimer. *Preemptable Remote Execution Facilities for Loosely-Coupled Distributed Systems.* PhD thesis, Stanford University, 1986. Technical Report STAN-CS-86-1128, Department of Computer Science.

[8] M.M. Theimer, K.A. Lantz, and D.R. Cheriton. Preemptable remote execution facilities for the V-System. In *Proc. 10th Symposium on Operating Systems Principles*, pages 2–12. ACM, December 1985. Proceedings published as *Operating System Review* 19(5).

[9] E. Zayas. Attacking the process migration bottleneck. In *Proc. 11th Symposium on Operating Systems Principles*, pages 13–24. ACM, November 1987. Proceedings published as *Operating System Review* 21(5).

Attacking the
Process Migration Bottleneck

Edward R. Zayas
Computer Science Department
Carnegie Mellon University
Pittsburgh, PA 15213

(Currently at the Information Technology Center, Carnegie Mellon University)

Abstract

Moving the contents of a large virtual address space stands out as the bottleneck in process migration, dominating all other costs and growing with the size of the program. Copy-on-reference shipment is shown to successfully attack this problem in the Accent distributed computing environment. *Logical* memory transfers at migration time with individual on-demand page fetches during remote execution allows relocations to occur up to one thousand times faster than with standard techniques. While the amount of allocated memory varies by four orders of magnitude across the processes studied, their transfer times are practically constant. The number of bytes exchanged between machines as a result of migration and remote execution drops by an average of 58% in the representative processes studied, and message-handling costs are cut by over 47% on average. The assumption that processes touch a relatively small part of their memory while executing is shown to be correct, helping to account for these figures. Accent's copy-on-reference facility can be used by *any* application wishing to take advantage of lazy shipment of data.

1. Introduction

Process migration is a valuable resource management tool in a distributed computing environment. However, very few migration facilities exist for such systems. Part of the problem lies in providing an efficient method for naming resources that is completely independent of their location. The major difficulty, though, is the cost of transferring a computation's context from one system node to another. This context, which consists primarily of the process virtual address space, is typically large in proportion to the usable bandwidth of the interconnection medium. Moving the contents of a large virtual address space thus stands out as the bottleneck in process migration, dominating all other costs. As programs continue to grow, the cost of migrating them by direct copy will also grow in a linear fashion.

Any attempt to make process migration a more usable and attractive facility in the presence of large address spaces must focus on this basic bottleneck. One approach is to perform a *logical* transfer, which in reality requires only portions of the address space to be *physically* transmitted. Instead of shipping the entire contents at migration time, an *IOU* for all or part of of the data can be sent. As the relocated process executes on the new host, attempts to reference "owed" memory pages will result in the generation of requests to copy in the desired blocks from their remote locations. Context transmission times during migration are greatly reduced with this demand-driven *copy-on-reference* approach, and are virtually independent of the size of the address space. Processes are assumed to touch relatively small portions of their address spaces, justifying the higher cost of accessing each page during remote execution.

This paper describes the process migration facility built for the SPICE [12] environment at Carnegie Mellon University, which demonstrates the validity of using copy-on-reference transfer to attack the migration bottleneck. Section 2 describes the design of the Accent copy-on-reference mechanism, available to *any* application wishing to lazy-evaluate its data transfers. Accent's organization and abstractions not only provide the transparency needed to support migration, but lend themselves to the natural construction of such a mechanism. Section 3 show how the migration system capitalizes on copy-on-reference data delivery. Section 4 presents performance measurements taken on a set of representative processes that were migrated using different transmission strategies. Process relocations occur up to one thousand times faster using copy-on-reference transfers. While the amount of allocated data varies by four orders of magnitude across the processes studied, their transfer times are practically constant. The number of bytes exchanged between machines as a result of migration and remote execution drops by 58.2% on average, and message-handling costs are cut by 47.8%. The assumption that processes touch a relatively small part of their memory while executing is shown to be correct, helping to account for these figures. The detailed measurements are used to assess the effect of such copy-on-reference variations as prefetching in response to remote page requests and migration-time transfer of the address space portions resident in main memory. Section 5 compares the Accent migration work to other activity in the

This research was supported by the AT&T Cooperative Research Fellowship Program. It was also supported by the Defense Advanced Research Projects Agency (DoD), ARPA Order No. 3597, monitored by the Air Force Avionics Laboratory under contract F33615-84-K-1520.

Reprinted with permission from *Proc. of the 22th ACM Symp. on Operating Systems Principles,* ACM Press, New York, N.Y., 1987, pp. 13–24. ©1987 Association for Computing Machinery.

field. Finally, Section 6 summarizes the lessons learned from the Accent migration system and considers future research directions suggested by this work.

2. The Accent Copy-On-Reference Mechanism

Accent's design and organization allows such intelligent virtual memory techniques as copy-on-write to be applied to data passed through the IPC system. It is this feature which aids in the construction of another intelligent strategy, copy-on-reference. This section begins by providing a quick overview of the Accent features that contribute to the natural construction of a transparent, generic copy-on-reference facility. Accent's *imaginary segment* abstraction serves as the basis for lazy data delivery, and is described next. The consequences of permitting imaginary objects to exist are explored, along with the method of shipping imaginary areas between machine boundaries.

2.1. Accent Features

The Accent IPC and virtual memory facilities are closely integrated, operating symbiotically. Unlike most message-based systems, a single Accent IPC message can hold *all* of the memory addressable by a process. Message contents are conceptually copied by value directly from the sender's address space into the receiver's. In reality, a message is first copied into the kernel's memory, buffered there until the recipient decides to accept it, and then copied out again. Accent provides the advantages of double-copy semantics for transferring message data between address spaces while still achieving the performance expected of a system that passes data by reference. This is possible through the use of a *copy-on-write* virtual memory mechanism by the IPC facility. If the amount of message data falls below a certain threshold, it is physically copied to the receiver. However, the kernel uses much faster memory-mapping techniques for messages exceeding this threshold. The receiver's virtual memory map is modified to provide access to the message data, and the region is marked copy-on-write for both parties. The two processes share this single copy of the data until either one tries to modify it. The deferred copy operation is then carried out, but *only* for the 512-byte page(s) affected. Files are accessed through an IPC interface and mapped in their entirety into process memory, allowing these techniques to be applied to their data as well. Since large amounts of data are often transferred through IPC messages and only rarely modified to any degree, this lazy strategy realizes performance that approaches by-reference transfer. Fitzgerald's study [3] reveals that up to 99.98% of data passed between processes in a system-building application did not have to be physically copied.

2.2. Imaginary Segments

Accent's copy-on-reference mechanism is based on a new segment class, the imaginary segment. Imaginary segment data is accessed not by direct reference to physical memory or a hard disk, but rather through the IPC system. Each imaginary segment is associated with a *backing IPC port* which provides memory management services for the object. When a process touches a page mapped to an imaginary segment,

the high-level *Pager/Scheduler* process sends an *Imaginary Read Request* message to the region's backing port. The process with Receive rights for this port interprets the request and returns the required page in an *Imaginary Read Reply* message. The *Pager/Scheduler* completes the handling of the imaginary "fault" by mapping in the page and resuming the process attempting the access. Currently, page-outs for imaginary data are performed to the local disk at the site that touched the page. Any process may create an imaginary segment based on one of its ports, map all or part of it into its address space and pass this memory to another process via an IPC message. In effect, it transmits an "IOU" for the region's data, promising to deliver it as needed. The backing process continues to field page request messages aimed at the imaginary object until all references to it die out. At this point, Accent informs the backer of the object's demise by sending it an *Imaginary Segment Death* message.

2.3. Accessibility Maps

The existence of imaginary objects forces the operating system to provide a facility for determining the accessibility of any given virtual address range. Carelessly touching imaginary regions can result in deadlock. For example, an Accent process executing in the kernel context deadlocks if it touches a page with port-based backing. The faulter is caught holding the system critical section, preventing the backing process from executing the protected *Receive* operation needed to respond to the fault.

Accessibility Maps (or *AMaps*) were created to supply the necessary addressing information in Accent. Four different memory "distances" have been defined for AMaps:

1. **RealZeroMem:** This is a region that has been validated (allocated) by a process but has never been accessed. When memory is validated, it is conceptually filled with zeros. Accent postpones these filling operations until the pages are first touched. A special fault condition, the *FillZero* fault, is realized for this case. The only action the *Pager/Scheduler* process takes is to reserve a page of physical memory, fill it with zeros and create the appropriate virtual memory mappings. The disk is never consulted while handling this type of fault. In practice, Accent processes validate large amounts of virtual memory and only touch a small percentage. Lazy initialization of address space regions and the use of a special inexpensive fault-handling operation combine to make creation and maintenance of large virtual memory regions affordable. These *RealZeroMem* pages are considered immediately accessible to the process.

2. **RealMem:** The data in this type of region is either already present in physical memory or accessible by fetching the corresponding local disk page. The distinction between disk address mappings owned by the kernel and process mappings for the same data allows a disk page image to be resident without being visible to a user process. In this eventuality, the

434

Pager/Scheduler again simply fills in the missing user mapping and promotes the faulted process to a runnable state. If neither the disk nor the process mapping are available for the page, the matching disk block is determined. The page is brought in, and disk and process mappings for it are entered. *RealMem* pages are rated "moderately" accessible, since the system may have to go out to disk to get them.

3. ImagMem: The contents of memory regions mapped to imaginary segments have *ImagMem* accessibility. Touching a page in this accessibility class results in the the generation and processing of an imaginary fault, as described in Section 2.2. *ImagMem* pages are considered distantly accessible, since it may take an arbitrarily long time to complete a page fetch. The network state, the load on the machines involved and the amount of work being performed by the backing process all contribute variables to the service time.

4. BadMem: Attempting to touch a page in a region that hasn't been validated causes a true addressing error. Referencing a *BadMem* page invokes a debugger so the human user can analyze and properly terminate the delinquent process. Since referencing a *BadMem* page is illegal, its accessibility is considered infinitely distant.

2.4. Extending Imaginary Segments

As with the port abstraction, copy-on-reference access via imaginary segments depends on a user-level server for transparent extension across the network. The *NetMsgServer* process, running on each host, provides this service by changing its message fragmentation and reassembly algorithms to account for imaginary subranges. Using an AMap as a guide on both sides, the *RealMem* portions are physically transmitted to the remote location and placed in the corresponding locations in the reassembly buffer. The receiving *NetMsgServer* creates its own local ports and imaginary object(s) to stand in for the originals. Messages generated in response to faults on the remote imaginary objects are automatically channeled to the correct backing site.

On its own initiative, a *NetMsgServer* may cache the *RealMem* portions of a message destined to a remote site and instead pass IOUs for them, becoming the manager for that data. Senders can inhibit this behavior by setting the *NoIOUs* bit in the message header, which is inspected by the *NetMsgServer*. This action guarantees that non-imaginary message data is physically copied to the remote site.

3. Migration Using Copy-On-Reference

The SPICE migration facility is designed to take advantage of the copy-on-reference mechanism described in the previous section. This is done by special migration primitives which automatically separate out the context portions eligible for copy-on-reference shipment. Using these operations, the *MigrationManager* process on each machine has several options for context delivery to the new execution site.

3.1. *ExciseProcess* and *InsertProcess*

The *ExciseProcess* kernel trap allows the complete context of an active process to be removed from its current host. Accent contexts are divided into five components: the state of the Perq[1] microengine, the kernel stack if the process is executing in supervisor mode, the PCB, the set of port rights owned by the process and the virtual address space contents. While the first four parts combined only account for roughly 1 Kbyte, the address space contributes up to 4 gigabytes. Once a context is excised, the process ceases to exist. Since all port rights are passed transparently to the caller, there is no disruption to the set of processes capable of naming these ports.

ExciseProcess delivers a process context in two separate IPC messages, ready for shipment to the new execution site. The *Core* message contains the first four context pieces, which must be physically copied to the remote site. It also carries an AMap describing the entire process address space. The *RIMAS*[2] message contains all of the *RealMem* and *ImagMem* portions of the address space, collapsed into a contiguous area. This allows the caller to fit one or more excised address spaces into its own memory at one time. It also allows the bearer to cache the *RealMem* portions and substitute its own imaginary objects in the *RIMAS* message. If the migration agent doesn't wish to actively manage the excised address space, it simply turns off the *NoIOUs* bit in the *RIMAS* message header as described in Section 2.4, prompting the local *NetMsgServer* to assume backing services for the memory.

The counterpart for *ExciseProcess* is *InsertProcess*, which uses the two context messages to recreate the process. Since the messages are self-contained, they do not have to be preprocessed in any way. The embedded port rights are passed to the new incarnation. Using the AMap for guidance and the *RIMAS* data for ammunition, the process address space mappings are restored. The reconstituted process is finally placed into the kernel queue representing the original execution status.

3.2. The *MigrationManager* Process

Each SPICE machine wishing to participate in process migration runs a simple *MigrationManager* process. This server accepts and executes commands to perform migrations. Given a process name, it uses the *ExciseProcess* primitive to acquire the process context. The two context messages are then simply sent to the *MigrationManager* at the new execution site, which uses *InsertProcess* to reconstruct the target process.

The current *MigrationManager* doesn't attempt sophisticated address space management for the processes it extracts. If asked to use copy-on-reference transfer for process memory, the *MigrationManager* allows the intermediary *NetMsgServers* to cache the data and become its backer.

---

[1]Designed by Perq Systems, Inc., the Perq workstation has a microcoded CPU, 16-bit words and a 150 nanosecond cycle time. It's rated at between 1/5 and 1/2 the speed of a Vax-11/780, depending on the instruction set used. More detailed specs are in [3].

[2]*RIMAS* stands for *Real and Imaginary Memory Address Space*.

4. Evaluation

This section summarizes the results of experiments carried out on the augmented Accent testbed system to determine the effectiveness of the copy-on-reference technique in reducing the dominant cost of migration: transfer of large process address spaces. Representative processes were chosen and monitored as they were migrated with the different strategies of interest. These programs are implemented in a variety of languages, perform widely different tasks and differ greatly in memory requirements and access patterns. Figures on their address space composition and utilization are presented, along with the basic costs of the migration primitives used to extract and insert process contexts on a host. Based on such metrics as the quantity and distribution of byte traffic, message processing costs and end-to-end elapsed times, copy-on-reference is shown to be superior to the brute-force method. Two variations on the basic lazy-transfer theme were simulated using the detailed performance figures and also evaluated. While prefetch of between 1 and 15 nearby pages in response to imaginary faults proved to be a valuable optimization, the shipment of process resident sets (as an approximation to their working sets [2]) was found to be generally detrimental. Overall, the experiments show that this lazy transfer technique significantly reduces the dominant context transmission costs by exploiting the fact that processes tend to use only small portions of their address spaces during execution.

4.1. Representative Processes

Several processes were chosen to undergo relocation, each representing a class of programs sharing similar attributes. The results obtained for these representatives should be characteristic of other programs in their class.

1. Minprog: This program is used to judge the effects of the various transmission strategies on a "minimal" program. Written in Perq Pascal, Minprog prints a message on the standard output, waits for user input and terminates. Measurement of this program is the equivalent of timing the "null trap" when exploring operating system performance.

2. Lisp-T: Accent supports the SPICE Lisp dialect, complete with a customizable screen editor and compiler. The Lisp-T trial resembles Minprog in that the minimum computation is performed. After migration, the Lisp interpreter is simply asked to evaluate T. This process represents simple Lisp programs, or larger Lisp jobs migrated late in life. The primary difference between Lisp-T and Minprog is the amount of address space used. Lisp processes validate their entire 4 gigabyte address spaces at birth, compared to Minprog's use of only 330 Kbytes.

3. Lisp-Del: This Lisp process performs a significant amount of computation and I/O. Immediately after migration, a Delaunay triangulation package written at Carnegie Mellon by Rex Dwyer is loaded. Utilizing a divide-and-conquer algorithm on a random set of points, this package displays its actions graphically on the screen as the triangulation is built.

4. PM-Start: The Pasmac macro processor for Perq Pascal represents the class of programs whose primary duty is to read files from the disk, process them in some way and write the results back out. In this instance, a 164 Kbyte file containing the program with macro references imports five definition files totaling 114 Kbytes. Migration takes place at the point the first definition file is being accessed.

5. PM-Mid: This trial postpones migration of the above macro processor until all of the definition files have been read in. Thus, the file images have become part of the process context and are carried along by the migration. The relocated program doesn't perform any more file accesses until it writes out the expanded program text.

6. PM-End: The final trial involving the Perq Pascal macro processor further postpones migration until the original file has almost been completely expanded. With little computation left to perform, this trial reveals the performance of the various migration strategies on processes near the end of their lifetimes.

7. Chess: A chess program written by Charly Drechsler at Siemens rounds out the group. It performs a large amount of computation to evaluate board positions and generate moves, but doesn't use a lot of its address space. A graphical representation of the chess board is displayed on the screen along with a game clock. The game clock ticks every second, so screen updates occur at least that often. Migration takes place as soon as the program initializes itself and draws the first screen image.

4.2. Address Space Analysis

4.2.1. Composition

Table 4-1 expresses the address space sizes and breakdowns of the representative processes at migration time.

	Real	RealZ	Total	% RealZ
Minprog	142,336	187,904	330,240	56.9
Lisp-T	2,203,136	4,225,926,144	4,228,129,280	99.9
Lisp-Del	2,200,064	4,225,929,216	4,228,129,280	99.9
PM-Start	449,024	501,760	950,784	52.8
PM-Mid	446,464	466,432	912,896	51.1
PM-End	492,032	398,848	890,880	44.8
Chess	195,584	305,152	500,736	60.9

Table 4-1: Representative Address Space Sizes in Bytes

Listed for each representative process is the amount of non-zero data it addresses (*Real*), the allocated but untouched zero-filled memory (*RealZ*), the total memory addressed (*Total*) and the percentage of the overall process memory taken up by allocated, untouched zero-filled regions (% *RealZ*). Memory quantities are in bytes.

There is wide variance in the amount of validated memory in

436

the representative Accent processes. The space utilized by the biggest process is a factor of 12,803 larger than that of the smallest. This is the consequence of the way Lisp processes manage their address spaces. The amount of *RealMem* mapped into processes doesn't vary nearly as much, only by a factor of 15 for these samples. Notice that *RealZeroMem* forms a significant part of all process address spaces, more than half even in most non-Lisp examples.

4.2.2. Resident Set Analysis

The process resident set sizes at migration time and their relationships to their host address spaces are shown in Table 4-2.

	RS Size	% of Real	% of Total
Minprog	71,680	50.4	21.7
Lisp-T	190,464	8.6	0.005
Lisp-Del	190,464	8.7	0.005
PM-Start	132,096	29.4	13.9
PM-Mid	190,976	42.8	20.9
PM-End	302,080	61.4	33.9
Chess	110,080	56.3	22.0

Table 4-2: Representative Resident Sets

Listed is the resident set size in bytes at migration time (column *RS Size*) for each representative, as well as the relative size compared to the process non-zero data (*% of Real*) and total allocated space (*% of Total*).

The range of resident set sizes is even narrower than that of the *RealMem* figures in Section 4.2.1, a factor of only 4. With the unrealistic Minprog process excluded, the factor drops to 2.7. This implies that the transfer of a process resident set will contribute a relatively consistent delay to the migration operation. Because of the amount of memory involved, resident set transfers are a significant expense. Viewing resident set transfer as a middle ground between a pure-copy transfer and a pure-IOU strategy appears reasonable, since the resident sets are roughly half as large as the *RealMem* in most cases. However, Section 4.3.4 demonstrates that this added expense at migration time doesn't translate into better overall performance.

4.2.3. Address Space Utilization

As postulated, Accent processes reference a small portion of their address spaces on average in their lifetimes. Table 4-3 reveals the amount of data transferred between machines during the trials in relation to address space size. Percentages are listed for the pure-IOU and resident set strategies without prefetching (pure-copy transmits 100% of *RealMem* by definition). Pure-IOU figures (the first column) indicate the portions actually touched by the process at the remote site.

	IOU	RS
Minprog	8.6 [3.7]	50.4 [21.7]
Lisp-T	3.0 [0.002]	9.0 [0.005]
Lisp-Del	16.5 [0.009]	17.4 [0.009]
PM-Start	58.0 [27.4]	76.0 [35.9]
PM-Mid	51.5 [25.2]	77.5 [37.9]
PM-End	26.9 [14.8]	72.5 [40.1]
Chess	35.6 [13.9]	66.0 [25.8]

Table 4-3: Percent of Address Space Accessed

For each representative process, the portion of the address space transferred to the new site is given for the pure copy-on-reference (*IOU*) and resident set (*RS*) strategies. The first number in each column represents the percent of the allocated, non-zero (*RealMem*) memory shipped, while the number in square brackets reports the percent of the total allocated address space. By definition, the pure-copy technique transfers 100% of non-zero data.

The Lisp representatives, while they have the largest address spaces, touch the smallest percentage in the course of execution. This applies even when performing a considerable amount of computation and I/O, as in the case of Lisp-Del. The Pasmac macro processor trials showed the highest address space utilization, as their mapped disk files are touched sequentially and in their entirety. In all cases, the resident set transfer method accessed larger portions of the address space, bringing over pages that are never used. This is especially acute for Pasmac. Since physical memory under Accent tends to act as a disk cache, old file pages that have *already* been processed are still sent to the new execution site. This explains why the pure-IOU method references significantly less of the Pasmac process address space the later in life it is migrated while the resident set approach results in nearly constant utilization.

4.3. Migration Phase Timings

Migration under Accent may be broken down into three phases:

1. Packaging and unpackaging the process context at the source and destination hosts.

2. Transferring the context between the sites.

3. Running the program at its new location.

This section examines how the migration strategies and their variations perform in each of these phases, and also presents an end-to-end analysis. Copy-on-reference transfers are shown to greatly reduce the time spent in the transfer phase while only moderately increasing remote execution times, resulting in significant overall performance improvements. While the first phase is insensitive to the migration strategy chosen, the experiments reveal some interesting facts about Accent's virtual memory system.

4.3.1. Process Excision and Insertion

Two operations dominate the removal and packaging of a process context, as revealed by Table 4-4: AMap construction for the target address space and the collapse of process memory into a contiguous chunk.

	AMap	RIMAS	Overall
Minprog	.37	.36	.82
Lisp-T	2.12	.59	2.79
Lisp-Del	2.46	.73	3.38
PM-Start	.98	.63	1.67
PM-Mid	1.01	.68	1.74
PM-End	1.4	.94	2.45
Chess	.37	.43	1.00

Table 4-4: Process Excision Times in Seconds

The rightmost column of this table lists the amount of elapsed time used by the *ExciseProcess* kernel trap on each of the representatives (*Overall*). Also listed are the individual timings for the two dominant activities carried out during extraction: AMap construction (*AMap*) and creation of the IPC message containing the condensed process address space (*RIMAS*).

There are two reasons why AMap construction is an expensive operation under Accent. The complex process map organization chosen to support sparse address spaces and copy-on-write makes it difficult to determine accessibility for *ranges* of addresses. Also, the lazy update algorithm employed for process maps often forces a costly search of system virtual memory tables. The Lisp processes take the longest to service, as might be expected. The Minprog and Chess programs have small, uncomplicated address spaces and hence require the shortest amount of time.

While process memory is rearranged into a compact form and delivered to the migration agent via memory-mapping techniques instead of physical copies, it is still an important part of the excision activity. Address space collapses contribute a much smaller variation to excision times than does AMap construction. Overall, excision times vary only by a factor of 4, compared to the 4 *orders of magnitude* difference in the address space contents.

Process reincarnation given the two context messages involves reestablishing the microcode and port state of the process, along with setting up its address space to correspond to the original structure. The times required to insert the transferred contexts into the new site ranged from 263 milliseconds for Minprog to 853 milliseconds for Lisp-Del. Address space reconstruction is the major factor in the insertion operation, and times are very similar to the *RIMAS* creation times during context extraction. As with other portions of the migration mechanism, this insertion costs grow much more slowly than the address spaces involved, only a factor of 3.3.

4.3.2. Context Transfer Times

Approximately one second is required to transmit the *Core* context message (microstate, PCB, port rights) in all cases. These messages differ by a small number of bytes, since some AMaps are slightly larger than others. The real variation involves the delivery of the *RIMAS* message (valid, non-zero address space) under the different transfer strategies. Table 4-5 provides these timings.

	Pure-IOU	RS	Copy
Minprog	.16	5.0	8.5
Lisp-T	.16	25.8	157.0
Lisp-Del	.17	25.8	168.5
PM-Start	.15	9.0	30.8
PM-Mid	.16	13.0	28.1
PM-End	.19	20.5	31.0
Chess	.21	7.7	11.7

Table 4-5: Address Space Transfer Times in Seconds

Address space transfer times are closely clustered for the copy-on-reference approach (*IOU*), but vary considerably for the resident set (*RS*) and pure-copy (*Copy*) techniques.

Times required to ship process address spaces pure-IOU are nearly independent of the amount of memory involved. Use of pure-copy doesn't fare nearly as well, where *RIMAS* trans-

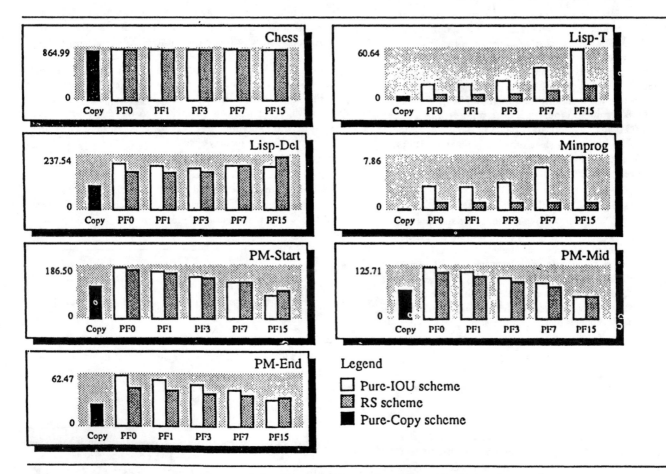

Figure 4-1: Remote Execution Times in Seconds

The measurement interval starts when the relocated program is restarted at its new location and ends when remote execution completes. Column PF*n* describes a trial where *n* pages were prefetched in response to an imaginary fault. Note: each chart is scaled individually.

mission times vary by a factor of 20. Pure-IOU allows the address space transmission to complete in significantly less time. Lisp-Del is the most extreme example, where a physical copy is almost 1,000 times more expensive. Resident set transfers once again display intermediate performance.

4.3.3. Remote Execution Times

Figure 4-1 shows the remote execution times of the representative processes, namely the elapsed time in seconds from the first instruction executed at the new host up to the program's termination. These figures show the effects of the different migration strategies, combined with differing prefetch values for the pure-IOU and resident set approaches.

Part of the effort saved in the lazy transfer of an address space must be expended as the process accesses its memory remotely. Referencing imaginary memory through the intermediary *Scheduler* and *NetMsgServer* processes on both testbed machines is roughly 2.8 times more expensive than accessing data backed by a local disk (115 milliseconds vs. 40.8 milliseconds). The most glaring effect of this cost differential on remote execution time is seen in the Minprog case, which executes 44 times slower under the pure-IOU strategy. The majority of this time is spent collecting its

working set as it attempts to execute the few instructions before it terminates. The long-lived, compute-bound Chess program suffers a much smaller execution penalty, running only about 3% longer.

Dependent on the memory access patterns exhibited, the effect of prefetch varies considerably among the representatives. The Lisp family, which doesn't display memory locality, suffered from increased prefetch. The additional pages were rarely used and did not justify the larger fault-handling time. Hit ratios on these extra Lisp pages dropped from around 40% to 20% as prefetch increased. On the other hand, programs such as Pasmac, which access large tracts of memory in a sequential fashion, benefitted greatly from large prefetch. Pasmac tallied a steady 78% hit ratio across all prefetch values used, and improved its IOU remote execution times by up to a factor of 2 across this range.

Transferring process resident sets to the new execution site only had a significant impact on the extremely short-lived processes (Lisp-T, Minprog). This implies that the underlying working sets change quickly for Accent processes, in turn suggesting that resident set transfers are not a useful optimization in this setting.

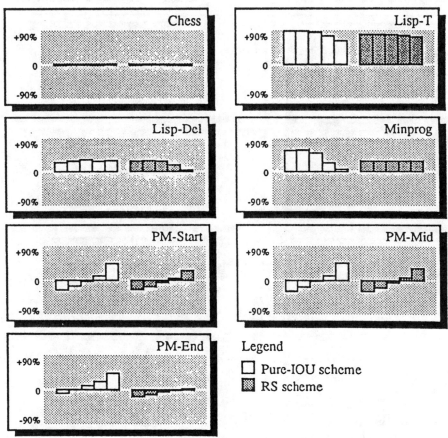

Figure 4-2: Percent Overall Speedup over Pure-Copy

Shown are the end-to-end speedups resulting from use of pure-IOU and RS transmissions. Elapsed times for address space transfer and remote execution are summed for each representative process and prefetch value and compared to the pure-copy results. From left to right in each group, bars indicate percent speedup over pure-copy for prefetch values of 0, 1, 3, 7 and 15 pages. Negative values (bars drawn in the bottom half of each gray area) represent slowdowns in relation to pure-copy.

4.3.4. Overall Migration Speedup

As demonstrated above, the pure-IOU and RS schemes hold a clear advantage in the address space transfer phase of migration yet generally cause processes to execute longer at the remote site. In order to get overall or end-to-end performance figures, elapsed times for context transfer and remote execution are summed for these strategies and compared to the pure-copy results. The percent speedups over the straightforward pure-copy technique are displayed in Figure 4-2 for the pure-IOU and RS approaches as different amounts of prefetch are performed. The pure-IOU results (white bars) are grouped together on the left-hand side of each chart; similarly, the resident set results (dark gray bars) are placed on the right-hand side. From left to right in each group, the bars show the percent speedup for prefetch values of 0, 1, 3, 7 and 15. Negative values indicate slowdowns in relation to pure-copy.

As expected, processes that access the smallest portion of their address spaces at the new site are best suited to use the copy-on-reference technique when overall elapsed time for migration and remote execution is the metric. In the current implementation, the breakeven point is around one-quarter of the process *RealMem*. Once past this percentage, as in the Pasmac family of processes, the higher cost of fetching in-dividual pages during remote execution in the pure-IOU system outweighs the savings achieved during migration itself. The exception to this observation is the Chess program, which is insensitive to the transfer method used. In that case, the differences imposed the various strategies were drowned out by the program's longevity.

With its strong influence on remote execution times, the amount of prefetch performed is a critical factor in end-to-end performance. Pasmac, as a representative for processes past the breakeven point and demonstrating strong sequential access patterns, went from an overall 21% slowdown on average to a 44% *speedup* as prefetch increased. In all cases, the results demonstrate that returning one additional contiguous page per remote fault improves performance. With intelligent use of prefetch, copy-on-reference migration is significantly faster than pure-copy transfer for the representatives (except the long-lived Chess process) when overall timings are considered. On the other hand, process resident sets didn't "pay their way" by cutting remote faulting activity enough to offset their shipment costs.

4.4. Cost Analysis

Section 4.3 reports that copy-on-reference treatment of ad-

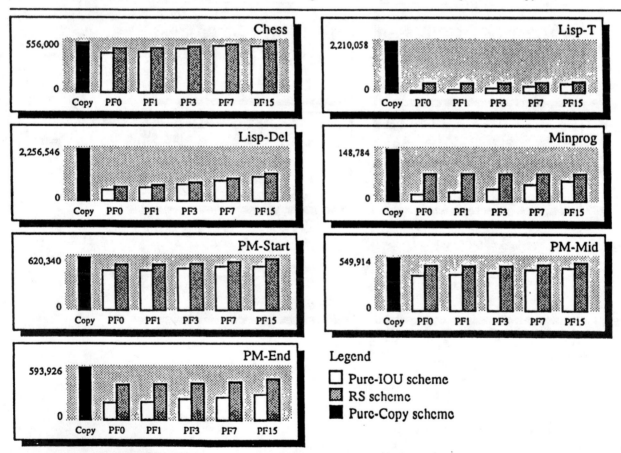

Figure 4-3: Bytes Transferred During Trials

Number of bytes transferred for each program, transmission strategy and page prefetch value during the migration trials. The measurement interval starts when the migration request is received by the *MigrationManager* and ends when the program completes its remote execution. Column PF*n* describes a trial where *n* pages were prefetched in response to an imaginary fault. Note: each chart is scaled individually.

dress space transfers significantly improves the time required to migrate a process to a new site and complete its execution there. This section supports these results by examining the specific costs incurred by the different migration strategies, and how these costs are distributed across the migration phases. Experiments reveal that copy-on-reference reduces the number of bytes transferred between the hosts as well as the cost of handling messages related to migration activities. Not only are the overall costs lowered by this approach, but they are also more evenly distributed across the context transfer and remote execution phases.

4.4.1. Bytes Transferred

Figure 4-3 reports the number of bytes exchanged between machines due to migration and remote execution of the representatives under the different strategies. Note that a single value is reported for each pure-copy trial, since prefetch doesn't apply in these cases.

The pure copy-on-reference strategy was superior to pure-copy across all prefetch settings. This technique reduced byte traffic by an average of 58.2% over pure-copy when no prefetch was used. As a rule, more data was exchanged as the number of contiguous pages prefetched grew. This is reasonable, since not all the extra pages were referenced. Shipping resident sets cut into the savings realized by the IOU strategy,

again implying that very little of this data was actually used at the remote site.

4.4.2. Message Costs

Pure-copy is the clear winner when evaluated by the *number* of messages processed by the test systems. However, it does not fare nearly as well in a more important metric, the amount of time required to process and deliver these messages. Each second of execution time spent by the *NetMsgServer* to handle message traffic is not only a second stolen from the migrated process but from *all* processes in *both* systems. Figure 4-4 displays the amount of time spent by each node in message manipulation.

These figures further confirm the utility of a lazy approach to address space access. By putting off the apparent work that needs to be performed until the last moment, a significant portion does not need to be done at all. Although the bulk transfer of the process context when the pure-copy strategy is employed allows a higher throughput than the page-by-page access imposed by the pure-IOU and resident set approaches, the majority of pages sent by the pure-copy approach are never used. The pure-IOU strategy only performs work that is productive and necessary.

In every case, the IOU and resident set strategies outperform pure-copy. The average savings in message processing is

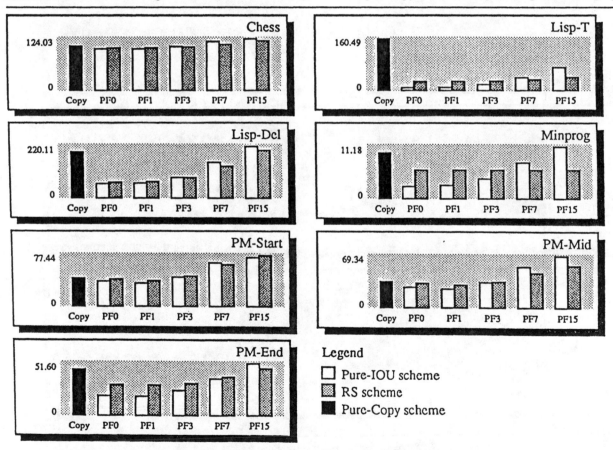

Figure 4-4: Total Message Times in Seconds

Displayed are the elapsed time in seconds required to process the IPC messages generated for each migration trial. Column PF*n* describes a trial where *n* pages were prefetched in response to an imaginary fault. Note: each chart is scaled individually.

441

47.8% for IOU trials without prefetch. The effect of prefetch is an interesting one. When only a single additional page is prefetched in response to an imaginary fault, the time spent processing messages drops slightly. As we increase the number of pages prefetched, the system spends more and more time in message handling. Although the prefetching eliminates many of the imaginary faults, it also transfers some "dead weight" pages that are never used. Also, since each message carries more data, the time to process each imaginary reply message grows.

Combined with the results on end-to-end costs, these figures suggest that one page should be prefetched regardless of the transfer strategy chosen.

4.4.3. Distribution of Costs

The vast majority of migration costs charged to the pure-copy strategy are incurred during the transfer phase of process migration. On the other hand, the copy-on-reference approaches radically reduce the cost of context shipment and

instead incurs its expenses across the remote lifetime of the process involved. Thus, not only are costs reduced overall, but they are also more evenly distributed. Pure IOU transfers don't experience the same magnitudes and bursts of activity required by the pure-copy strategy. Instead, a lower, more constant rate of work is exhibited. The trials demonstrate that sustained network transmission speeds are reduced up to 66%.

Figure 4-5 presents the data transfer rates caused by the migration and remote execution of the Lisp-Del case under the different strategies, starting at the time of migration and ending with the execution of the final remote instruction.

These panels depict the results of a full-IOU transfer of Lisp-Del, a resident set approach and finally the full-copy method. The areas in white represent bytes exchanged in support of imaginary fault activity. Full-copy transfers have a characteristic signature, with a large bulk data transfer early on. The resident set panel illustrates that a sizable amount of data is still physically shipped during the migration phase, but does not improve the overall time significantly from the pure-

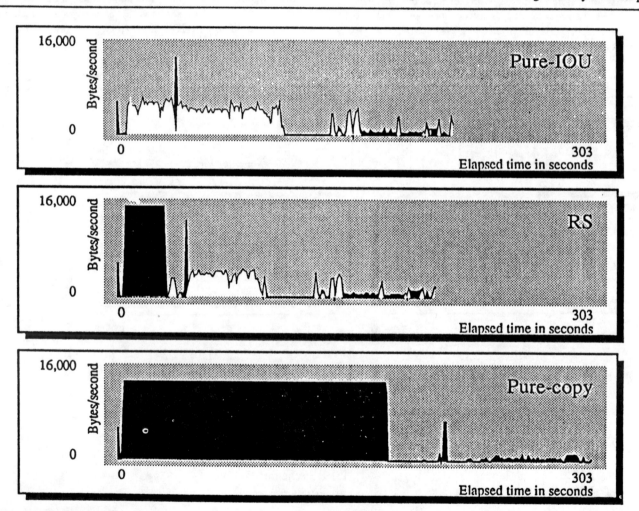

Figure 4-5: Byte Transfer Rates for Lisp-Del

Network data transfer rates during the migration and remote execution of the Lisp-Del (Delaunay triangulation) program. No prefetch is being performed. White areas show data transferred in support of imaginary faults, black areas show all other transfers.

IOU approach. Copy-on-reference allows the process to resume execution very quickly. In this case, Lisp-Del finishes its work shortly after the full-copy trial *begins* its remote execution.

4.5. Summary

The trial data collected for the Accent migration facility reveals several interesting facts about process composition and behavior. While address space size varies by as much as a factor of 12,803 in the representative processes, the amount of *RealMem* only differs by a factor of 15. *RealZeroMem* forms a significant portion of every process address space, more than half in most cases and 99.9% in the Lisp examples. These representatives touched between 0.002% and 27.4% of their validated address spaces, and between 3% and 58% of the *RealMem* portions. This verifies the assumption that processes access relatively small parts of their addressible data.

Process excision and insertion times are also much less variable in this study, factors of 4 and 3.3 respectively across the samples. IOU context transfers take roughly one second in all cases, and thus provide a lower bound for this activity. Pure-copy transfers vary by a factor of 20, and in the most extreme case are 1,000 times more expensive than the corresponding pure-IOU transfer.

Much less data needs to be communicated between machines when copy-on-reference tactics are used. On average, 58% fewer bytes are transferred and message processing times drop by 47%. Touching remote pages via the copy-on-reference mechanism is roughly 2.8 times more expensive than local disk accesses, and this figure can likely be improved through tuning.

The copy-on-reference variations studied in this system produced mixed results. Resident sets were found to be poor predictors of the data required by the process at its remote site. Since Accent uses its physical memory as a disk cache, many resident pages are sometimes guaranteed *not* to be referenced again, especially by the Pasmac class of processes. On the other hand, small amounts of page prefetch were found to always be useful. Prefetching more pages each time degrades performance in some cases, but greatly aids programs performing mostly sequential accesses.

5. Related Work

Investigation into process migration began in the early 1970's. Such efforts as the "Creeper" program [11] by Bob Thomas at BBN and the "Relocatable McRoss" [14] air traffic controller demonstrated migration's feasibility. However, they did little to address the transparency issues. DCN [6] added name transparency by associating resources with processes, but failed to provide location transparency. DCN's resource names specified the supplying host, and were invalidated if the resource was moved. The RIG system [4] is Accent's direct ancestor and shared many of the same concepts. RIG's ports were visibly tied with the process owning them, so it suffered from DCN's problem. The DEMOS/MP operating system [9] was among the first to offer full transparency. Link names contained *hints* to the location of the service, and were not invalidated by resource relocation. The

University of Washington's object-oriented Eden [5] system provided full transparency and migration services, but could not take advantage of a copy-on-reference mechanism. Eden's objects were forced to reside entirely on a single host. Dannenberg's Butler [1] made use of an older version of Accent which did not provide copy-on-reference data shipment, but demonstrated Accent's suitability for transparent migration support.

Various systems have attempted different attacks on the cost of context transfer. The LOCUS [8] remote invocation facility exploits shared code present at the target site, cutting down the amount of data that must flow to the new site. This approach doesn't address the data portions of a process context, including memory-mapped files. Marvin Theimer's migration facility for the V system [13] tried to hide transmission costs from processes by *pre-copying* the context in an iterative fashion before moving the process. Process downtime was thus reduced, but both hosts still paid the transfer costs. Theimer's measurements reveal that this technique suffers from network buffering problems and overruns.

6. Conclusions

The Accent testbed's use of copy-on-reference address space transfer has demonstrated its effectiveness in tackling process migration's dominant cost. Unlike the conventional transmission technique, copy-on-reference avoids the linear growth in costs as processes address more and more data. Any distributed system in the same class can expect similar results in the construction and use of a copy-on-reference facility.

Studying the Accent example also teaches important lessons in operating system design. The simple yet powerful port abstraction and the close integration of IPC and virtual memory facilities give Accent the transparency needed to cleanly support migration without sacrificing performance. These features, along with extensibility through user-level processes, allows a generic copy-on-reference mechanism to be built in a natural way. This mode of data transfer has proven useful in the migration domain, but may be just as easily applied to *any* task requiring sparse access to large tracts of memory.

Copy-on-reference data transmission is inherently more flexible than the conventional method. Only two variations of actual data delivery have been explored here. Tasks with special knowledge of the data requirements they will encounter may apply that knowledge to optimize the physical shipment of data.

This investigation opens many avenues for future research. The creation and evaluation of automatic migration strategies appropriate for such systems have not been addressed here. Good strategies are necessary to capitalize on the inherent advantages of lazy transfers. Part of this activity will involve the development of good load metrics which specifically take into account the fact that a process virtual address space may be physically dispersed among several computational hosts. Copy-on-reference may be proven useful in remote file and database accesses, remote invocation facilities and intelligent RPCs. It would be interesting to attempt to extend this work to systems allowing shared memory, and to evaluate the application of copy-on-reference techniques to a shared centralized file system such as Andrew [7].

Although Accent is no longer actively in use at Carnegie Mellon University, the lessons learned from this work are being applied to the Mach environment [10] currently being developed there. A successor to Accent aimed at supporting a wide range of hardware configurations, Mach allows *external pager* processes which provide copy-on-reference administration of data. Study of copy-on-reference behavior in this new facility will provide further insights on the basic mechanism in a more modern computing system.

References

1. Roger B. Dannenberg. *Resource Sharing in a Network of Personal Computers*. Ph.D. Th., Carnegie Mellon University, December 1982.

2. Peter J. Denning. "The Working Set Model for Program Behavior". *Communications of the ACM 11*, 5 (May 1968), 323-333.

3. Robert P. Fitzgerald. *A Performance Evaluation of the Integration of Virtual Memory Management and Inter-Process Communication in Accent*. Ph.D. Th., Carnegie Mellon University, October 1986. Available as CMU technical report CMU-CS-86-158.

4. Keith A. Lantz, Klaus D. Gradischnig, Jerome A. Feldman and Richard F. Rashid. "Rochester's Intelligent Gateway". *Computer* (October 1982), 54-68.

5. E.D. Lazowska, H.M. Levy, G.T. Almes, M.J. Fischer, R.J. Fowler, S.C. Vestal. The Architecture of the Eden System. Tech. Rept. 81-04-01, Department of Computer Science, University of Washington, April, 1981.

6. David. L. Mills. An Overview of the Distributed Computer Network. National Computer Conference, University of Maryland, 1976, pp. 523-531.

7. James H. Morris, Mahadev Satyanarayanan, Michael E. Conner, John H. Howard, David S. H. Rosenthal and Donelson Smith. "Andrew: A Distributed Personal Computing Environment". *Communications of the ACM 19*, 3 (March 1986), 184-201.

8. G. Popek, B. Walker, J. Chow, D. Edwards, C. Kline, G. Rudisin, G. Thiel. LOCUS: A Network Transparent, High Reliability Distributed System. Joint Conference on Computer Performance Modelling, Measurement and Evaluation, ACM, 1986.

9. Michael L. Powell and Barton P. Miller. Process Migration in DEMOS/MP. Proceedings of the Sixth Symposium of Operating System Principles, ACM, November, 1983, pp. 110-119.

10. Richard F. Rashid. "Threads of a New System". *Unix Review 4*, 8 (August 1986), 37-49.

11. John F. Shoch and Jon A. Hupp. "The 'Worm' Programs - Early Experience with a Distributed Computation". *Communications of the ACM 25*, 3 (March 1982), 172-180.

12. CMU Computer Science Department. Proposal for a Joint Effort in Personal Scientific Computing. Carnegie Mellon University, August, 1979.

13. Marvin M. Theimer, Keith A. Lantz and David R. Cheriton. Preemptable Remote Execution Facilities for the V-System. Proceedings of the Tenth Symposium on Operating System Principles, ACM SIGOPS, 1985, pp. 2-12.

14. Robert H. Thomas and D. Austin Henderson. McRoss - A Multi-Computer Programming System. Proceedings, Spring Joint Conference, 1972.

Designing a Process Migration Facility
The Charlotte Experience

Yeshayahu Artsy, Digital Equipment Corporation*

Raphael Finkel, University of Kentucky*

Process migration is possible, if not always pleasant. The Charlotte migration protocol offers high code modularity and ease of maintenance while minimizing the impact of software and hardware failures.

A preemptive process migration facility in a distributed system dynamically relocates running processes among the component machines. Such relocation can help cope with dynamic fluctuations in loads and service needs,[1] meet real-time scheduling deadlines, bring a process to a special device, or improve the system's fault tolerance. Yet, successful migration facilities are not common in distributed operating systems,[2-7] due largely to the inherent complexity of such facilities and the potential execution penalty if the migration policy and mechanism are not tuned correctly. Not surprisingly, some operating systems terminate remote processes rather than rescue them by migration.[8]

There are several reasons why migration is hard to design and implement. The mechanism for moving processes must reliably and efficiently detach a migrant process from its source environment, transfer it with its context (the per-process data structures held in the kernel), and attach it to a new environment on the destination machine. Migration may fail in case of machine and communication failures, but it should do so completely. That is, the effect should be as if the process were never migrated at all or, at worst, as if the process had terminated due to machine failure.

A wide range of migration policies might be needed, depending on whether the main concern is load sharing (avoiding idle time on one machine when another has a nontrivial work queue), load balancing (such as keeping the work queues similar in length), or application concurrency (mapping application processes to machines to achieve high parallelism). Policies might need elaborate and timely state information, since unnecessary process relocations might otherwise degrade performance of both the migrant process and the entire system.

The mechanisms to support different policies can differ significantly. If several policies are used under different circumstances, the migration mechanism must be flexible enough to allow policy modules to switch policies. We cannot completely separate the migration mechanism from process scheduling, memory management, and interprocess communication. Nevertheless, we prefer to keep mechanisms for these activities as separate as possible to allow more freedom in testing and upgrading them. The fact that a process has moved should be invisible to both it and its peers, while interested users or processes should be able to advise the system about desired process distribution.

This article discusses our experience with process migration in the Charlotte distributed operating system. Charlotte's migration facility is a fairly elaborate addition to the underlying kernel and utility-process base. It separates policy (when to migrate which process to what destination) from mechanism (how to detach, transfer, and reattach the migrant process). While

* Yeshayahu Artsy and Raphael Finkel were at the University of Wisconsin-Madison when the work described in this article was done.

Reprinted from *Computer,* vol. 22, no. 9, Sept. 1989, pp. 47–56.

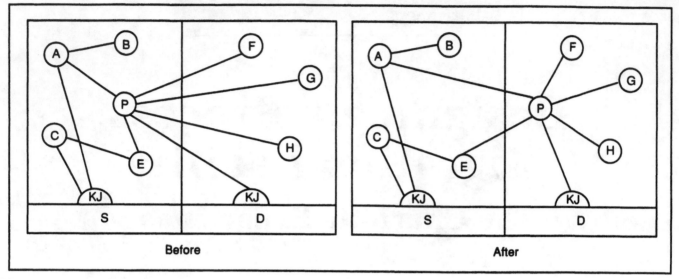

Figure 1. Example of migration.

the mechanism is fixed in the kernel and one of the utilities, the policy is relegated to a utility and can be replaced easily. The kernel provides elaborate state information to that utility. The mechanism allows concurrent multiple migrations and premature cancellation of migration. It leaves no residual dependency on the source machine for the migrant process. The mechanism copes with all conceivable crash and termination scenarios, rescuing the migrant process in most cases.

The following sections present an overview of Charlotte, its process migration facility, and issues we encountered that have general application for any such facility. In discussing each issue, we present alternative design approaches adopted by other process migration facilities. (A discussion of specific migration policies is beyond the scope of this article.) We hope this account will help researchers contemplating the addition of a process migration facility, as well as those designing other operating system facilities that might need to interact later with added process migration facilities.

Charlotte overview

Charlotte is a message-based distributed operating system developed at the University of Wisconsin for a multicomputer composed of 20 VAX-11/750 computers connected by a token ring.[9] Each machine in the multicomputer runs a kernel respon-

sible for simple short-term process scheduling and a message-based interprocess communication (IPC) protocol. Processes are not swapped to a backing store. A battery of privileged processes, called *utilities*, runs at the user level to provide additional operating system services and policies. The kernel and some utilities are multithreaded.

Processes communicate via *links*, which are capabilities for duplex communication channels. (The Lynx[10] high-level language actually hides this low-level mechanism and provides a remote-procedure-call interface.) The processes at the two ends of a link can both send and receive messages using nonblocking service calls. A process can post several such requests and await their completion. It also can cancel a pending request before the request completes. A link can be destroyed or given to another process, even during communication. In particular, a link is automatically destroyed when the process holding its other end terminates or when its machine crashes; the process holding the local link end is so notified by the kernel.

The protocol that implements communication semantics is efficient but quite complex.[11] It depends on full, timely link information in the kernels supporting both ends of each link. Processes are completely unaware of the location of their communicating partners. Instead, they establish links to servers by having other processes (their parents or a name-server utility) provide them.

Utility processes are distributed throughout the multicomputer. They cooperate to allocate resources, provide file and connection services, and set policy. In particular, the KernJob utility runs on each machine to provide a communication path between the local kernel and nonlocal processes. The Starter utility creates processes, allocates memory, and dictates medium-term scheduling policy. Each Starter process controls a subset of the machines, communicating with their kernels (directly or via their KernJobs) to receive state information and specify its decisions.

Process migration

We designed Charlotte as a platform for experimentation with distributed algorithms and load distribution strategies. We added the process migration facility to better support such experiments. Equally important, we wanted to explore design issues raised by process migration in a message-based operating system. Figure 1 shows the effect of process migration. For convenience, we call the kernels on the source and destination machines S and D, respectively. P represents the migrant process, and KJ is the KernJob.

During transfer, P's process identifier changes, and the kernel data structures for it are completely removed from S, but the transfer is invisible to both P and its communication partners. As shown in Figure 1,

446

P's links relocate to the new machine. All processes are unaware that link descriptors have moved and that local communication (performed in shared memory) has become remote communication (sent over the wire) and vice versa. The processes name their links the same after migration as before, and they see no change in message flow.

Policy. Migration policy is dictated by Starter utility processes, which base their decisions on statistical information provided by the kernels they control and on summary information they exchange among themselves. In addition, Starters accept advice from privileged utilities (to allow manual direction of migration and to enable or disable automatic control). A Starter process executes a policy procedure when it receives messages carrying statistics, advice, or notice of process creation or termination. (Introducing migration into the Starter only required writing the policy procedure and invoking it at the right times.) The policy procedure can choose to send messages to other Starters or to request some source kernel to undertake migration. Such requests are sent to the KernJob residing on the source machine to relay to its kernel. As discussed later, this approach adds insignificantly to the cost of migration (a few procedure calls and perhaps a round-trip message), while it allows policies that integrate scheduling and memory allocation as well as local, clustered, or global policies.

Mechanism. The migration mechanism has two independent parts: collecting statistics and transferring processes. Both parts are implemented in the kernel.

Statistics include data on machine load (number of processes, links, and CPU and network loads), individual processes (age, state, CPU utilization, and communication rate), and selected active links (packets sent and received). These statistics are intended to be comprehensive enough to support most conceivable policies. We collect statistics in several ways, as shown in Table 1. To balance accuracy with overhead, we used an interval of 50-80 milliseconds and a period of 100 intervals (5-8 seconds) in our tests. The overhead for collecting statistics was less than one percent of total CPU time.

Process transfer occurs in three phases:

(1) Negotiation. S and D, after being told by their controlling Starter processes to migrate P, agree to the transfer and reserve required resources. If agreement

cannot be reached (for example, because resources are not available), the migration aborts and the Starter processes controlling S and D are notified.

(2) Transfer. P's address space moves from the source to the destination machine. Meanwhile, each kernel controlling a process with a link to P receives separate messages informing it of the link's new address.

(3) Establishment. Kernel data structures pertaining to the migrant process are marshaled, transferred, and demarshaled. (Marshaling involves copying the structure to a byte-stream buffer and converting some data types, particularly pointer types.) No information related to the migrant is retained at the source machine.

Process-kernel interface. We added four kernel calls to the process-kernel interface:

- Statistics(What : action; Where : address). The KernJob invokes this call on behalf of a Starter so that the kernel will start collecting statistics and placing them in the given address (in the KernJob virtual space). The call can also stop statistics collection.
- MigrateOut(Which : process; Where-To : machine). This call enables the Starter (or its KernJob proxy if the Starter resides on another machine) to initiate migration.
- MigrateIn(Which : process; Where-From : machine; Accept : Boolean; Memory : list of physical regions). The Starter or its KernJob proxy uses this call to approve or refuse a migration from the given machine to the machine on which the call is performed. If Starters have negotiated among themselves, the Starter controlling the destination machine can approve a

migration even before the Starter controlling the source machine calls MigrateOut. The Memory parameter tells the kernel where in physical store to place the segments that constitute the new process. (The Starter learns the segment sizes either from negotiation with its peer or from D's request to approve a migration offer received from S.)

- CancelMigration(Which : process; Where : machine). The Starter invokes this call to abort an active MigrateIn or MigrateOut request. This call is rejected if the migration has already reached a commitment point.

None of these calls blocks the caller. The kernel reports the eventual success or failure of the request by a message back to the caller.

Mechanism details. Three new modules in the kernel implement the migration mechanism.

- The migration interface module deals with the new service calls from processes.
- The migration protocol module performs the three phases listed above.
- The statistics module collects and reports statistics.

These modules are invoked by two new kernel threads.

- The statistician thread awakens at each interval to sample, or average and report, statistics to the Starter.
- A process-receiver thread starts in D for each incoming migrant process. It uses a simpler and faster communication protocol than that used by ordinary IPC. However, negotiation and other control messages use the ordinary communication protocol and are funneled through the IPC

Table 1. Statistics collected by migration mechanism.

Condition	Action
Significant event: message sent or received, data structure freed, process created or terminated	Increment associated count
Interval passes	Sample process states and CPU, network loads
Period of *n* intervals passes	Summarize data, send to starter

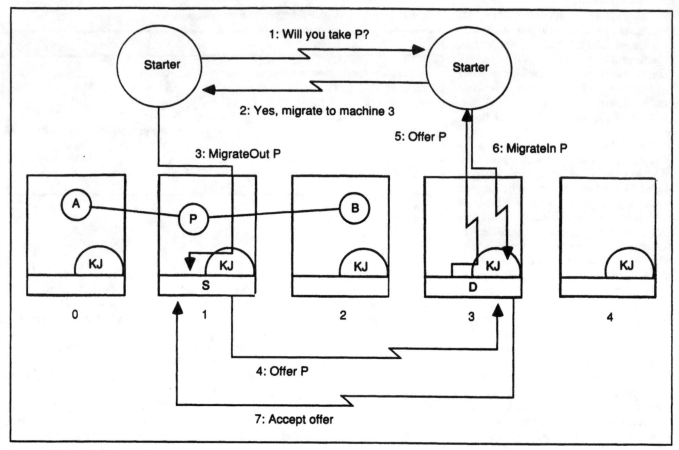

Figure 2. Negotiation phase.

queues to synchronize process and link activities. (The standard protocol must expect extremely complex scenarios that cannot arise in the transfer phase and must employ link data structures that are not germane here. The cost of introducing a streamlined protocol was slight in comparison to the speed it achieved.)

Figure 2 shows both high- and low-level negotiation messages. The left Starter controls machine 1, and its peer controls machine 3. The first two messages represent a Starter-to-Starter negotiation that results in a decision to migrate process P from machine 1 to machine 3. The decision is communicated to S in message 3, which is either a direct service call (if the Starter runs on machine 1) or a message to the KernJob on machine 1 to be translated into a service call.

S then offers to send the process to D. The offer includes P's memory requirements, its age, its recent CPU and network use, and information about its links. If D is short of the resources needed for P, or if too

many migrations are in progress, it can reject the offer. Otherwise, D relays the offer to its controlling Starter (message 5). The relay includes the same information as the offer from S. We relay the offer to let the policy module reject a migrant at this point. Although D's Starter might have agreed to accept P (in message 2), it might need to reject the offer now due to an actual or anticipated increase in load or lack of memory. Furthermore, D must ask its Starter because the kernel cannot know if the latter has even been consulted by its peer Starter, and the Starter must allocate memory for the migrant.

The Starter's decision is communicated to D by a MigrateIn call (message 6). This call can also reject the migration offer (not shown). No relay occurs if the Starter has already called MigrateIn to preapprove the migration. Before responding to S (message 7), D reserves necessary resources to avoid deadlock and flow-control problems. Preallocation is conservative; it guarantees successful completion of multiple migrations at the expense of reducing

the number of concurrent incoming migrations.

D commits itself to the migration when it sends message 7. If P fails to arrive and S has not cancelled the migration (see the next step), then S's machine must be down or unreachable. D discovers this condition through the standard mechanism by which kernels exchange "heart-beat" messages; it then reclaims resources and cleans up its state.

When it receives message 7, S also commits itself to the migration and starts the transfer. Before each kernel commits itself, its Starter can successfully cancel the migration, in which case D replies Rejected to S (in message 7), or S sends Regretted to D (not shown). The latter also occurs if P dies abruptly during negotiation. To separate policy from mechanism, S does not retry a rejected migration unless so ordered by its Starter.

Figure 3 shows the transfer phase. S concurrently sends P's virtual space to D (message 8) and link update messages (message 9) to the kernels controlling all of

448

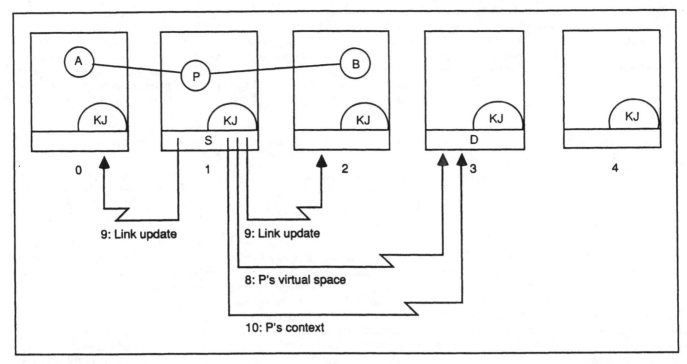

Figure 3. Transfer phase.

P's communication peers. Message 8 is broken into packets as required by the network. D has already reserved physical store for them, so the packets are copied directly to the correct place. Message 9 indicates the new address of the link; it is acknowledged for synchronization purposes (not shown). After this point, messages sent to P will be directed to the new address and buffered there until P is reattached. Kernels that have not yet received message 9 can still send messages for P to S. Failure of either the source or the destination machine during this interval leaves P's state very unclear. Since recovering P's state would require a very complex protocol that would be sensitive to further machine failures, we opted to terminate P if one of the two machines crashes at this stage.

Finally, S collects all of P's context into a single message and sends it to D (message 10). This message includes control information, the state of all of P's links, and details of communication requests that have arrived for P since transfer began. Pointers in S's data structures are tracked down, and all relevant data are marshaled together. D demarshals the message into its own data structures.

Although it is conceptually simple, the transfer stage is actually quite complex

and time-consuming, mainly because Charlotte IPC is rich in context. Luckily, our design saves the migration mechanism from dealing with messages in transit to or from P. Since the kernel provides message caching but no buffering,[9] a message remains in its sender's virtual address space until the receiver is ready to accept it or until the send is cancelled. Hence, S does not need to be concerned with P's outgoing messages; likewise, it can drop from its cache any message received for P that P has not yet requested to receive. Such a message will be requested by D from the sender's kernel when P requests to receive it. The link structures in message 9 clearly indicate which links have pending sent or received messages. Another advantage of our design is that we do not have to alter or transfer P's context as maintained by distributed utilities (such as open files, which are accessed via location-independent links).

The establishment phase is interleaved with transfer. Data structures are deallocated as part of marshaling, and the reserved structures are filled during demarshaling. After transfer, D adjusts P's links and pending events and inserts P in the appropriate scheduling queue. Communication requests that were postponed while P was moving have been buffered by

S and D; they are now directed to the IPC kernel thread in D in their order of arrival (for each link, all requests buffered at S precede those buffered at D). The effect of the messages on P is not influenced by the fact that P has moved. Finally, the Starter and KernJob processes for both the source and destination machines are informed that migration has completed so that they can update their data structures appropriately. A failure of either machine at the transfer phase is detected by the other machine, which aborts the migration, terminates the migrant, and cleans up its state.

Performance. We measured Charlotte's migration performance on VAX/ 11-750 machines connected by a Pronet token ring. The underlying mechanisms have the following costs: It takes 11 milliseconds to send a 2-kilobyte packet to another machine reliably via the transport package we use, 0.4 millisecond to switch context between kernel and process, 10 milliseconds to transfer a single packet between processes residing on the same machine, and 23 milliseconds to transfer a packet between processes residing on different machines.

The average elapsed time to migrate a small (32-kilobyte) linkless process is 242 milliseconds (standard deviation $\sigma = 2$

Table 2. Kernel time spent migrating a linkless 32-kilobyte process.

S action	Kernel time in ms	D action	Kernel time in ms
Handle an offer	5.0	Handle an offer	5.4
Prepare 2-kilobyte image to transfer	2.6	Install 2 kilobytes of image	1.2
Marshal context	1.8	Demarshal context	1.2
Other (mostly kernel context switching)	6.9	Other	4.7

milliseconds), provided D's Starter has preapproved the migration. Each additional 2 kilobytes of image adds 12.2 milliseconds to the migration time. The following formula fits our measurements of the average elapsed time spent in migration:

Charlotte time =
$$45 + 78p + 12.2s + 9.9r + 1.7q$$

where p equals 0 if D's Starter has preapproved migration, 1 if D's Starter is not on the destination machine, or about 0.2 otherwise; s is the size of the virtual space in 2-kilobyte blocks; r equals 0 if all links are local, and 1 otherwise; and q is the number of nonlocal links (1 if none).

These measures deviate by about five percent with different locations of the Starter and the overall load. This formula shows that it takes about 750 milliseconds to migrate a typical process of 100 kilobytes and six links (or 670 milliseconds if D's Starter is local), and about 6 seconds for a large process of 1 megabyte. Actual CPU time spent on the migration effort for a 32-kilobyte process with no links is about 60 milliseconds for S and about 32 milliseconds for D. Table 2 shows how this time is spent.

Each link costs S an additional 1.6-2.8 milliseconds of CPU time to prepare link-update messages and marshal relevant data structures. Collecting statistics requires about one percent of the overall elapsed time, and another two percent is spent delivering the statistics to the Starter. A production version of Charlotte, optimized and stripped of debugging code, could exhibit a significant speed improvement.

Comparing Charlotte's migration performance with results published for other implementations is difficult because each uses a different underlying computer, and each operating system dictates its own

process structure. Nonetheless, to provide some form of comparison, we present formulas for migration speed under Sprite (Sun-3 workstations, about four times faster than our VAX-11/750 machines), V (Sun-2 workstations, about two times faster than our machines), and Accent (Perq workstations, about 2.5 times slower than our machines). These formulas are extrapolations from a few measurement points reported elsewhere.[4,6,7]

$$\text{Sprite time} = 200 + 3.6s + 14f$$
$$\text{V time} = 80 + 6s$$
$$\text{Accent time} = 1180 + 115s$$

where s equals the size of the virtual space in kilobytes and f is the number of open files. In particular, a typical 100-kilobyte process would transfer in about 560 milliseconds in Sprite, 680 milliseconds in V, and perhaps 12.7 seconds in Accent. To migrate a large, 1-megabyte process would take at least 3.8 seconds in Sprite, 6 seconds in V, and 116 seconds in Accent. In Accent, sending the context of a process takes about one second. The virtual space is sent later on demand, so the full cost of transfer is spread over a long period, but part of this cost is saved if not all the pages are referenced. V precopies the address space while the process is still running, so the time lost by the process is quite short.[6]

Design issues

The problem of designing a process migration facility encompasses such complex issues as the separation of policy and mechanism, the interplay between migration and other mechanisms, reliability, concurrency, the nature of context transfer, and the extent to which processes should be independent of their location.

These issues interrelate, so the following discussion will occasionally postpone details until later sections. Moreover, the approaches that we and others take to various problems depend somewhat on the design of other components of the operating system. Due to space limitations, we do not discuss these dependencies in detail.

Structure. The first step in designing a process migration facility is deciding where the policy-making and mechanism modules should reside. This decision is of major importance, since it cannot be easily reversed, unlike most of the migration protocol's design. Communication-kernel operating systems tend to put mechanisms in the kernel and policy in trusted utility processes. In the case of process migration, mechanism is intertwined with both short-term scheduling and IPC, so it fits best in the kernel. Policy, on the other hand, is associated with long-term scheduling and resource management, so it fits well in a utility process. Several considerations affect the success of separation, including the efficiency of the result, how adequately it provides the needed function, and the degree of conceptual simplicity of the interfaces and the implementation.

Efficiency and simplicity. The principal reason one might place policy in the kernel instead of in a utility is to simplify and speed up the interface between policy and mechanism. Any reasonable policy depends on statistics that are maintained primarily in the kernel. High-quality decisions could require large amounts of accurate and comprehensive data. Placing policy outside the kernel incurs execution overhead and latency in passing statistics in one direction and decisions in the other.

Our experience with Charlotte, however, shows that placing the policy in a utility results in a net efficiency gain. Although separation incurs the extra cost of one message for statistics reporting and one kernel call (and perhaps another message round-trip) for decision reporting, it allows reduction of communication and more-global policy, since each Starter process decides policy for a set of machines. Also, concerning the latency in passing statistics and decisions, it is likely that good policies depend mostly on aggregate and medium-term conditions, ignoring short-term conditions or small delays.

A designer who chooses to support only simple policies might well put them in the kernel. For example, the migration policy

450

in V[6] and Sprite[4] is mostly manual, choosing a remote idle workstation for a process or evicting it when the station's owner so requires. In systems where migration is used to meet real-time scheduling deadlines, policy tends to be simple or very sensitive to even small delays, and hence could (or should) be placed in the kernel. Integrating the policy in the kernel, however, might obstruct later expansion or generalization.

We can achieve conceptual separation of policy and mechanism without incurring a large interface cost by assigning them to separate layers that share memory. MOS adopts this approach by dividing the kernel into two layers: one to implement migration mechanism and other low-level functions, and the other to provide policy.[2] These layers share data structures and communicate by procedure calls. Such sharing improves efficiency but makes it harder to modify policy, since changes require kernel recompilation, and inadvertent errors become more serious.

Function and flexibility. Placing policy outside the kernel facilitates testing diverse policies and choosing among policies designed for different goals, such as load sharing, load balancing, improving responsiveness, reducing the communication load, and placing processes close to special devices. The ability to modify policy is especially important in an experimental environment. Our students needed only a few hours to learn the interface and major components of the Starter to begin trying different policies; they did not need to learn peculiarities of the kernel or of the migration mechanism. This flexibility would have been impossible if policy were embedded in the kernel.

In distributed systems such as Demos/MP,[5] Accent,[12] and Charlotte, resource-management policies are often relegated to utilities. Putting migration policy in those same processes can allow more integration and coordination of the policies governing the system.

The designer of process migration should be aware of the danger of separating policy and mechanism too far. Letting policy escape from trusted utility servers into application programs can result in performance degradation or even thrashing. This problem occurs, for example, when applications can decide the initial placement and later relocation of their processes, as in Locus,[3] without assistance from the kernel in the form of timely state and load information.

Rescuing migrating processes under all failure circumstances requires complex recovery protocols and, most likely, large overhead.

Interplay between migration and other mechanisms. The process-migration mechanism can be designed independently of other mechanisms, such as IPC and memory management. The actual implementation is likely to have interactions among these mechanisms. However, design separation means that the migration protocol should not change when the IPC protocol does. In Charlotte, for example, we did not change the IPC to add process migration, nor did migration change when we later modified the semantics of two IPC primitives. In contrast, we had to change the marshaling routines when an IPC data structure changed.

We feel that ease of implementation is a dominant motivation for separating mechanisms when adding process migration to an existing operating system, as was the case in Demos/MP, Charlotte, V, and Accent. A secondary motivation is that the migration code can be deactivated without interfering with other parts of the kernel. In Charlotte, for instance, we can easily remove all the code and structures of process migration at compile time or dynamically turn the mechanism on and off.

In contrast, efficiency arguments favor integrating all mechanisms. Accent, for example, uses a transfer-on-reference approach to transmitting the virtual space of the migrant process, based on its copy-on-write memory management.[7] If process migration is intended from the start, as in MOS and Sprite, integration can reduce redundancy of mechanisms. In retrospect, we would have used a different IPC implementation for Charlotte if the two mechanisms had been integrated from the start. We would have used hints for link addresses, which are inaccurate but can be readily checked and inexpensively maintained, rather than using absolutes, whose complete accuracy is achieved at a high maintenance cost.

Some interactions seem to be necessary. In Charlotte, for instance, we chose to simplify the migration protocol by refusing to migrate a process engaged in multipacket message transfer. We therefore depend slightly on knowledge of the IPC mechanism to avoid complex protocols. Similarly, both MOS and Sprite refuse to migrate a process engaged in a remote procedure call until it reaches a convenient point, which might not happen for a long time. Other interactions make sense for process migration to take advantage of existing facilities. For example, Locus uses existing process-creation code to assist in process migration.

Reliability. Migration failures can occur due to network or machine failure. The migration mechanism can simply ignore these possibilities (as does Demos/MP) to streamline protocols. The Charlotte implementation can rescue the migrant from many failures by several means. First, it transfers responsibility for the migrant as late as possible to survive failure of the destination or the network. Second, it detaches the migrant completely from its source to survive later failures of the source. Third, the migrant is protected from failures of other machines; at worst, some of its links are automatically destroyed if the machine where their other ends reside crashes.

Rescuing migrating processes under all failure circumstances requires complex recovery protocols and, most likely, large overhead for maintaining process replicas, checkpoints, or communication logs. We were unwilling to pay that cost in Charlotte. Instead, we terminate the migrant if either the source or destination machine crashes during the sensitive time of transfer when messages for the migrant might have arrived at either machine, as discussed earlier. Modifying our IPC to use hints for link addresses, as mentioned above, would have made this step less fragile.

Concurrency. Various levels of concurrency are conceivable:

- only one migration in the network at a time;
- only one migration affecting a given machine at a time; or
- no constraints on the number of simultaneous migrations.

The Charlotte mechanism puts no constraint on concurrency. Restricting process migration can make the mechanism simpler, especially in operating systems using a connection-based IPC. The most restrictive alternative guarantees that the peers of the migrant process are stationary, so redirection of messages is straightforward. It also tends to mitigate policy problems of migration thrashing, flooding a lightly loaded machine with immigrants, and completely emptying a loaded machine.

Enforcing such a constraint, on the other hand, requires contention arbitration, which can be expensive. In addition, limiting concurrency constrains policies that otherwise could evacuate a failing machine quickly or react immediately to a severe load imbalance. We therefore believe that the policy problems mentioned above should be solved by policy algorithms, not by a limitation imposed by the mechanism.

Allowing simultaneous migrations introduces the peculiar problem of name and address consistency: ensuring that all processes and kernels have a consistent view of the world. The problem is manifest in operating systems like Charlotte, in which communication is carried out over established channels and kernels require up-to-date location information. If two processes connected by a channel migrate at the same time, their kernels might have a false conception of the remote channel ends.

The problem is not critical in operating systems such as V that treat communication addresses as hints because communication that encounters a hint fault will restore the hint by invoking a process-finding algorithm. This solution incurs execution and latency costs as messages are transmitted. Where absolutes are used, forwarding pointers, such as those used in Demos/MP, can solve the problem, but they introduce long-lived residual dependencies. In Charlotte, we send link-address updates before migration completes, and we buffer notifications for messages arriving during the transfer. The immediate acknowledgment of the updates, even when the other link end is simultaneously given away or migrating, prevents deadlock. When migration completes, D processes the notifications buffered by the two kernels and regains a consistent view of P's links, even if their remote ends have moved in the meantime.

Within a single source or destination, we could restrict concurrency to one migration attempt at a time. This restriction simplifies the kernel state and again reduces the risk of thrashing. However, we reduce complexity by creating a new kernel thread for each migration in progress,

> **Resorting to a home machine makes communication failures more likely and sharply increases the cost of certain kernel calls.**

executing a finite-state protocol independently of other migration efforts. Using these techniques, we found that allowing concurrent migrations in the same machine incurs only a small space overhead and minor execution costs.

Context transfer and residual dependency. The migrating process must be frozen at some point to ensure a consistent transfer.

What and when to freeze. Three activities need to be frozen: process execution, outgoing communication, and incoming communication. The first two activities are trivial to freeze. Incoming communication can be frozen by

- telling all peers to stop sending,
- delaying incoming messages, or
- rejecting incoming messages.

The first option requires a complex protocol if concurrent migrations are supported or if crashes must be tolerated. The third option requires that the IPC be able to resend rejected messages, as in V. We chose the second option because it seems the simplest and does not interfere with other mechanisms.

Very early freezing of the process (for example, when it is considered as a migration candidate) has the advantage that the process does not change state between the decision and migration. Otherwise, the migration decision might be worthless, since the process could terminate or start using resources differently. However, freezing a process hurts its response time, which flies in the face of one of the goals of migration. Less conservatively, we can freeze a process when it is selected as a candidate but before the destination machine has accepted the offer. Even less-conservative alternatives include freezing

when migration is agreed on or only when it is completed. As the choices become less conservative they increase the process' responsiveness at the cost of protocol complexity.

We chose to balance responsiveness and protocol simplicity by freezing both execution and communication only when context is marshaled and transferred. We delay incoming communication until P is established by buffering input notifications at S and D. We verified (by exhaustive enumeration of states in our automata that drive the IPC protocol) that the ensuing delays could not cause deadlock or flow-control problems.[11] In this way, a minimal context is transferred during negotiation (such as how many links P has and where their ends are); the final transfer reflects any change in P's state during migration.

MOS and Locus freeze the migrant earlier, when it is selected for migration. V, in contrast, freezes a process for a minuscule interval near the end of transfer. The migrant continues to execute during the transfer; pages dirtied during this episode are sent again in another transfer pass, and so forth until a final pass. Incoming messages are rejected during the short freeze, with the understanding that the IPC mechanism will time out and retransmit them. The result is that the migrant suffers a delay comparable to that required to load a process into memory.[6]

Redirecting communication. Redirecting communication requires that state information relevant to the communication channels be updated and that peer kernels discover the migrant's new location. In a connectionless IPC mechanism, a process holds the names of its communication peers. For example, V processes use process identifiers as destinations.[13] A kernel can then broadcast the new location, but this can be expensive for large networks with frequent migrations. Alternatively, peers can be left with incorrect data that can be resolved on hint faults. Another alternative assigns a home machine to each process; the home machine always knows where the process is. Locus uses this method to find a signal's target. Sprite is similar; the home machine manages signals and other location-dependent operations on behalf of the migrant. Of course, resorting to a home machine makes communication failures more likely and sharply increases the cost of certain kernel calls.

In a connection-based IPC environment

with simplex connections, such as Accent and Demos/MP, the kernel of a connection's receiving end does not know where the senders are. Thus, S does not know which kernels to inform about P's migration. Instead, a forwarding pointer can be left on S to redirect new messages as they arrive. Demos/MP uses this strategy. Another approach introduces a stationary "middleman" between two or more mobile ends of a connection. In Locus, cross-machine pipes can have several readers and writers, but they have only one fixed storage site. When a reader or writer migrates, the kernel managing the storage site is informed. In Charlotte, the duplex nature of links suggests maintaining information at each end about the other, so S can tell all of P's communication peers that P has moved. Transferring these link data along with P, though, incurs marshaling, transmission, and demarshaling overhead.

Residual dependency. The migrant process can start working on the destination machine faster if it temporarily leaves some of its state on the source machine. When it needs to refer to that state, it can access it with some penalty. To reduce the penalty, state can be gradually transferred during idle moments. State can also be pulled on demand. The choice between moving all or only a part of the address space is reminiscent of the controversy in network file systems about whether entire files or only pages should be transferred for remote file access. Locality of execution suggests transferring at least the working set of P during migration and the rest when needed. On the other hand, the objective of residual independence suggests removing any trace of P from the source machine.

In MOS, virtually the entire state of P could remain in the source machine, since D can make remote calls on S for anything it needs. For efficiency reasons, however, MOS transfers most of P's context and state when it migrates. In Sprite, part of P's context always resides in its home machine, but none is left on the source machine when P is evicted. This approach costs about 15 milliseconds to demand-load a page and perhaps 4 milliseconds to execute some of the kernel calls remotely (about a ninefold increase). In Accent, processes do not make kernel calls directly; rather, they send messages to a kernel port. Therefore, no state needs to move with a process; it can all remain with S and be accessed as needed by kernel calls to the old port. In addition, Accent imple-

Separating the modules that implement mechanism from those responsible for policy allows more efficient and flexible policies and simplifies the design.

ments a lazy transfer of data pages on demand. Similarly, in Sprite, S acts as a paging device for D. These approaches trade efficiency of address-space transfer for risks of machine unavailability, protocol complexity, and later access penalties.

Location transparency. Many distributed operating systems adhere to the principle of location transparency. In particular, process names are independent of their location, processes can request identical kernel services wherever they reside, and they can communicate with their peers equally well (except for speed) wherever they might be.

The principle of location transparency must be followed carefully to enable migration. Migration requires that naming schemes be uniform for local and remote communication and that resource references not depend on the host machine. For example, Charlotte objects are named by the links that connect a client to them. When a process moves, its names for the links are unchanged, even though D remaps them to different internal names.

The fact that local communication is treated differently from remote communication is localized in a few places in the kernel. Processes might have pointers or indices to kernel data structures, but those are maintained by the kernel. The actual data structures, pointers, and indices are remapped invisibly during migration. If such values were buried inside the processes' address spaces, migration would be impossible or extremely complicated. Sprite maintains location transparency throughout multiple migrations by keeping location-dependent information on P's home machine and by directing some of P's kernel calls there.

Transaction management and multithreading also pose transparency problems. A transaction manager must not

depend on the location of its clients. Multithreaded processes must be moved in toto. If threads can cross address spaces, the identity of one thread might be recorded in several address spaces, leading to location dependencies.

Of course, any policy setter, such as the Charlotte Starter, needs to know the location of all processes and perhaps the endpoints of their heavily used links. Making this information available need not compromise the principle of transparency. The policy module does not use this information to send messages, only to inform itself about decisions it needs to make. Likewise, for the sake of openness, a design might allow processes willing to participate in migration decisions to receive location information and contribute migration advice.

O ur experience with Charlotte and others' experience with Sprite, V, MOS, and Demos/MP show that process migration is possible, if not always pleasant. We found that separating the modules that implement mechanism from those responsible for policy allows more efficient and flexible policies and simplifies the design. Migration interacts with other parts of the kernel. In particular, the implementation shares structures and low-level functions with other mechanisms. Nonetheless, we found it possible to keep the mechanisms fairly independent of each other, gaining high code modularity and ease of maintenance.

Software and hardware failures are a fact of life. Our migration protocol can rescue the migrant in most failure situations and restore the state in all of them, despite the fact that the migrant continues its interaction with other processes at early stages of migration. In some cases, though, we opt to kill the migrant even if rescue is dimly conceivable. We postpone committing migration until the transfer itself (to deal with early destination crash), while removing any dependency of the migrant on the source as soon as migration completes (to deal with late source crash).

Except for potential confusion suffered by policy modules, it is not particularly hard to achieve simultaneous migrations, even those involving a single machine. The Charlotte IPC requires absolute state information, so we could not reduce the cost of migration by sacrificing accuracy. IPC mechanisms that use hints or are connectionless can shorten the elapsed time for migration but then probably pay more during communication. Designs that require previous hosts to retain forwarding information for an arbitrary period after migration are overly susceptible to machine failure. Forwarding data structures, although small, tend to build up over time. □

Acknowledgments

Charlotte's process migration design was inspired by discussions with Amnon Barak of the Hebrew University of Jerusalem in 1984. The authors are indebted to Cui-Qing Yang for modifying Charlotte utilities to support process migration, and to Hung-Yang Chang for many fruitful discussions about the design. Andrew Black and Marvin Theimer provided helpful comments on an early draft, and the referees suggested many stylistic improvements. The Charlotte project was supported by NSF grant MCS-8105904 and DARPA contracts N00014-82-C-2087 and N00014-85-K-0788.

References

1. P. Krueger and M. Livny, "When is the Best Load-Sharing Algorithm a Load-Balancing Algorithm?" Computer Sciences Tech. Report No. 694, University of Wisconsin-Madison, Apr. 1987.

2. A.B. Barak and A. Litman, "MOS: A Multicomputer Distributed Operating System," Software Practice and Experience, Aug. 1985, pp. 725-737.

3. D.A. Butterfield and G.J. Popek, "Network Tasking in the Locus Distributed Unix System," Proc. Summer Usenix Conf., 1984, pp. 62-71.

4. F. Douglis and J. Ousterhout, "Process Migration in the Sprite Operating System," Proc. Seventh Int'l Conf. Distributed Computing Systems, CS Press, Los Alamitos, Calif., Order No. 801, 1987, pp. 18-25.

5. M.L. Powell and B.P. Miller, "Process Migration in Demos/MP," Proc. Ninth Symp. Operating Systems Principles in ACM Operating Systems Review, Vol. 17, No. 5, 1983, pp. 110-118.

6. M.M. Theimer, K.A. Lantz, and D.R. Cheriton, "Preemptable Remote Execution Facilities for the V-System," Proc. 10th Symp. Operating Systems Principles in ACM Operating Systems Review, Vol. 19, No. 5, 1985, pp. 2-12.

7. E.R. Zayas, "Attacking the Process Migration Bottleneck," Proc. 11th Symp. Operating Systems Principles in ACM Operating Systems Review, Vol. 21, No. 5, 1987, pp. 13-24.

8. D.A. Nichols, "Using Idle Workstations in a Shared Computing Environment," Proc. 11th Symp. Operating Systems Principles in ACM Operating Systems Review, Vol. 21, No. 5, 1987, pp. 5-12.

9. Y. Artsy, H-Y Chang, and R. Finkel, "Interprocess Communication in Charlotte," IEEE Software, Vol. 4, No. 1, Jan. 1987, pp. 22-28.

10. M.L. Scott, "Language Support for Loosely Coupled Distributed Programs," IEEE Trans. Software Eng., Vol. SE-13, No. 1, Jan. 1987, pp. 88-103.

11. Y. Artsy, H-Y Chang, and R. Finkel, "Charlotte: Design and Implementation of a Distributed Kernel," Computer Sciences Tech. Report No. 554, University of Wisconsin-Madison, Aug. 1984.

12. R.F. Rashid and G.G. Robertson, "Accent: A Communication-Oriented Network Operating System Kernel," Proc. Eighth Symp. Operating Systems Principles in ACM Operating Systems Review, Vol. 15, No. 5, 1981, pp. 64-75.

13. D.R. Cheriton, "The V Kernel: A Software Base for Distributed Systems," IEEE Software, Vol. 1, No. 2, Apr. 1984, pp. 19-42.

Yeshayahu Artsy has been with the Distributed Systems Advanced Development Group at Digital Equipment Corporation since October 1987. From 1983 to 1986, he participated in the design and implementation of the Charlotte distributed system at the University of Wisconsin and was responsible in particular for the IPC and process migration mechanisms. His interests include distributed operating systems and services, open systems, and object-oriented programming.

Artsy received his MS and PhD in computer science from the University of Wisconsin-Madison in 1984 and 1987, respectively, a BA in economics and an MBA in management information systems from Tel-Aviv University in 1979 and 1981, respectively, and a BA in political science and statistics from the Hebrew University of Jerusalem in 1975. He is a member of ACM, the IEEE Computer Society, and the IEEE Communication Society.

Raphael Finkel has been a professor of computer science at the University of Kentucky in Lexington since 1987. From 1976 to 1987, he was a faculty member of the University of Wisconsin-Madison. His research interests include distributed data structures, interconnection networks, distributed algorithms, and distributed operating systems. He has received several teaching awards and has published an introductory text on operating systems.

Finkel received a PhD in robotics from Stanford University in 1976, and an MA in teaching and a BA in mathematics from the University of Chicago. He is a member of ACM and the IEEE Computer Society.

Readers may contact Yeshayahu Artsy at Digital Equipment Corporation, 550 King St., Littleton, MA 01460, and Raphael Finkel at the Computer Science Dept., University of Kentucky, Lexington, KY 40506.

Process Migration in DEMOS/MP

Michael L. Powell
Barton P. Miller

Computer Science Division
Department of Electrical Engineering and Computer Sciences
University of California
Berkeley, CA 94720

Abstract

Process migration has been added to the DEMOS/MP operating system. A process can be moved during its execution, and continue on another processor, with continuous access to all its resources. Messages are correctly delivered to the process's new location, and message paths are quickly updated to take advantage of the process's new location. No centralized algorithms are necessary to move a process.

A number of characteristics of DEMOS/MP allowed process migration to be implemented efficiently and with no changes to system services. Among these characteristics are the uniform and location independent communication interface, and the fact that the kernel can participate in message send and receive operations in the same manner as a normal process.

This research was supported by National Science Foundation grant MCS-8010686, the State of California MICRO program, and the Defense Advance Research Projects Agency (DoD) Arpa Order No. 4031 monitored by Naval Electronic System Command under Contract No. N00039-82-C-0235.

1. Introduction

Process migration has been discussed in the operating system literature, and has been among the design goals for a number of systems [Finkel 80][Rashid & Robertson 81]. Theoretical and modeling studies of distributed systems have suggested that performance gains are achievable using relocation of processes [Stone 77, Stone & Bokhari 78, Bokhari 79, Robinson 79, Arora & Rana 80]. Process migration has also been proposed as a tool for building fault tolerant systems [Rennels 80]. Nonetheless, process migration has proved to be a difficult feature to implement in operating systems.

As described here, *process migration* is the relocation of a process from the processor on which it is executing (the *source* processor) to another processor (the *destination* processor) in a distributed (loosely-coupled) system. A loosely-coupled system is one in which the same copy of a process state cannot directly be executed by both processors. Rather, a copy of the state must be moved to a processor before it can run the process. Process migration is normally an involuntary operation that may be initiated without the knowledge of the running process or any processes interacting with it. Ideally, all processes continue execution with no apparent changes in their computation or communications.

One way to improve the overall performance of a distributed system is to distribute the load as evenly as possible across the set of available resources in order to maximize the parallelism in the system. Such resource load balancing is difficult to achieve with static assignment of processes to processors. A balanced execution mix can be disturbed by a process that suddenly requires larger amounts of some resource, or by the creation of a new process with unexpected resource requirements. If it is possible to assess the system load dynamically and to redistribute processes during their lifetimes, a system has the opportunity to achieve better overall throughput, in spite of the communication and computation involved in moving a process to another processor [Stone 77, Bokhard 79]. A smaller relocation cost means that the system has more opportunities to improve performance.

System performance may also be improved by reducing inter-machine communication costs. Accesses to non-local resources require communication, possibly through intermediate processors. Moving a process closer

Reprinted with permission from *Proc. of the 9th ACM Symp. on Operating Systems Principles,* ACM Press, New York, N.Y., 1983, pp. 110–119.
©1983 Association for Computing Machinery.

to the resource it is using most heavily may reduce system-wide communication traffic, if the decreased cost of accessing its favorite resource offsets the possible increased cost of accessing its less favored ones.

A static assignment to a processor may not be best even from the perspective of a single program. As a process runs, its resource reference pattern may change, making it profitable to move the process in mid-computation.

The mechanisms used in process migration can also be useful in fault recovery. Process migration provides the ability to stop a process, transport its state to another processor, and restart the process, transparently. If the information necessary to transport a process is saved in stable storage, it may be possible to "migrate" a process from a processor that has crashed to a working one. In failure modes that manifest themselves as gradual degradation of the processor or the failure of some but not all of the software, working processes may be migrated from a dying processor (like rats leaving a sinking ship) before it completely fails.

Process migration has been proposed as a feature in a number of systems [Solomon & Finkel 79, Cheriton 79, Feldman 79, Rashid & Robertson 81], but successful implementations are rare. Some of the problems encountered relate to disconnecting the process from its old environment and connecting it with its new one, not only making the new location of the process transparent to other processes, but performing the transition without affecting operations in progress. In many systems, the state of a process is distributed among a number of tables in the system making it hard to extract that information from the source processor and create corresponding entries on the destination processor. In other systems, the presence of a machine identifier as part of the process identifier used in communication makes continuous transparent interaction with other processes impossible. In most systems, the fact that some parts of the system interact with processes in a location-dependent way has meant that the system is not free to move a process at any point in time.

In the next section, we will discuss some of the structure of DEMOS/MP, which eliminates these impediments to process migration. In subsequent sections, we will describe how a process is moved, how the communication system makes the migration transparent, and the costs involved in moving a process.

2. The Environment: DEMOS/MP

Process migration was added to the DEMOS/MP [Powell, Miller, & Presotto 83] operating system. DEMOS/MP is a version of the DEMOS operating system [Baskett, Howard, & Montague 77, Powell 77] the semantics of which have been extended to operate in a distributed environment. DEMOS/MP has all of the facilities of the original uni-processor implementation, allowing users to access the multi-processor system in the same manner as the uni-processor system.

DEMOS/MP is currently in operation on a network of Z8000 microprocessors, as well as in simulation mode on a DEC VAX running UNIX. Though the processor, I/O, and memory hardware of these two implementations are quite different, essentially the same software runs on both systems. Software can be built and tested using UNIX and subsequently compiled and run in native mode on the microprocessors.

2.1. DEMOS/MP Communications

DEMOS/MP is a message-based operating system, with communication as the most basic mechanism. A kernel implements the primitive objects of the system: executing processes, messages, including inter-processor messages, and message paths, called links. Most of the system functions are implemented in server processes, which are accessed through the communication mechanism.

All interactions between one process and another or between a process and the system are via communication-oriented kernel calls. Most system services are provided by system processes that are accessed by message communication. The kernel implements the message operations and a few special services. Messages are sent to the kernel to access all services except message communication itself.

A copy of the kernel resides on each processor. Although each kernel independently maintains its own resources (CPU, real memory, and I/O ports), all kernels cooperate in providing a location-transparent, reliable, interprocess message facility. In fact, different modules of the kernel on the same processor, as well as kernels on different processors, use the message mechanism to communicate with each other.

In DEMOS/MP, messages are sent using *links* to specify the receiver of the message. Links can be thought of as buffered, one-way message channels, but are essentially protected global process addresses accessed via a local name space. Links may be created, duplicated, passed to other processes, or destroyed. Links are manipulated much like capabilities; that is, the kernel participates in all link operations, but the conceptual control of a link is vested in the process that the link addresses (which is always the process that created it). Addresses in links are context-independent; if a link is passed to a different process, it will still point to the same destination process. A link may also point to a kernel. Messages may be sent to or by a kernel in the same manner as a process.

The most important part of a link is the message process address (see Figure 2-1). This is the field that specifies to which process messages sent over that link are delivered. The address has two components. The first is a system-wide, unique, process identifier. It consists of the identifier of the processor on which the process was created, and a unique local identifier generated by that machine. The second is the last known location of the process. During the lifetime of a link, the first component of its address never changes; the second, however, may.

456

Changes with process location	Set on process creation. Does not change	
Last Known Machine	Unique Process ID	
	Creating Machine	Local Unique ID

Structure of a process address
Figure 2-1

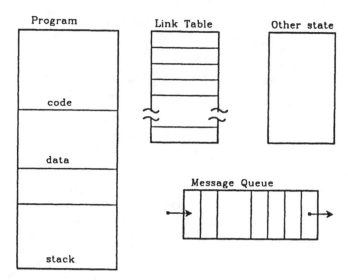

Components of a DEMOS/MP process
Figure 2-2

2.2. Special Kernel Communications

A link attribute, called *DELIVERTOKERNEL*, causes the link to reference the kernel of the processor on which a particular process resides. Except for the DELIVERTOKERNEL flag, a link with this attribute looks the same as a link to the process to which it points. Links with the DELIVERTOKERNEL attribute used to cause the kernel to manipulate the process in ways that system processes cannot do directly.

A message sent over a DELIVERTOKERNEL link follows the normal routing to the process. However, on arrival at the destination process's message queue, the message is received by the kernel on that processor. A link with the DELIVERTOKERNEL attribute allows the system to address control functions to a process without worrying about which processor the process is on (or is moving to).

This mechanism has simplified a number of problems associated with moving a process. It is often the case that some part of the system needs to manipulate the state of a process, for example, the process manager may wish to suspend a process. Using a link with the DELIVERTOKERNEL attribute, the process manager can send a message to the process's kernel asking that the process be stopped. If the process is temporarily unavailable to receive the message (for instance, it is in transit during process migration), the message is held and forwarded for delivery when normal message receiving can continue.

In addition to providing a message path, a link may also provide access to a memory area in another process. When a process creates a link, it may specify in the link read or write access to some part of its address space. The process holding the link may use kernel calls to transfer data to or from the data area defined by the link. This is the mechanism for large data transfers, such as file accesses or data transfer in process migration. The kernel implements the data move operation by sending a sequence of messages containing the data to be transferred. These messages are sent over a DELIVERTOKERNEL link to the kernel of process containing the data area. Using DELIVERTOKERNEL links allows the data to be read from or written to the kernel of the remote process without the kernel that instigated the operation being aware of the process's location.

The inter-machine communication of DEMOS/MP provides reliable delivery of messages. The fundamental guarantee is that any message sent will eventually be delivered.

A DEMOS/MP process is shown in Figure 2-2. A process consists of the program being executed, along with the program's data, stack, and state. The state consists of the execution status, dispatch information, incoming message queue, memory tables, and the process's link table. Links are the only connections a process has to the operating system, system resources, and other processes. Thus, a process's link table provides a complete encapsulation of the execution of the process.

2.3. DEMOS/MP System Processes

DEMOS/MP *system* processes are those processes assumed to be present at all times. *User* processes are created dynamically to perform computation, usually at the request of some user. A system process will often be a *server* process, that is, most other processes will be able to ask it to perform some functions on their behalf. The system processes being used in DEMOS/MP are the switchboard, process manager, memory scheduler, file system (actually, four processes), and command interpreter. The switchboard is a server that distributes links by name. It is used by the system and user processes to connect arbitrary processes together. An example of the system process structure is shown in Figure 2-3.

The process and memory managers handle all the high-level scheduling decisions for processes. These processes allocate and keep track of usage for system resources such as the CPU, real memory, etc. They control processes by sending messages to kernels to manipulate process states. For example, although the kernel implements the mechanisms of migrating a process, the process manager makes the decision of when and to where to migrate a process.

457

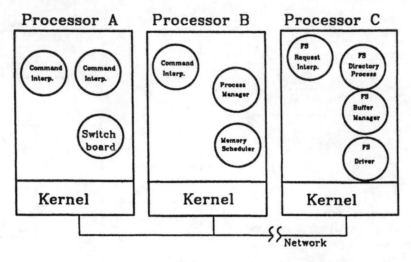

Example of system process lay-out
Figure 2-3

The file system is the same as that implemented for the uni-processor DEMOS [Powell 77], with the added freedom that the file system processes can be located on different processors. The command interpreter allows interactive access to DEMOS/MP programs.

One of our test examples of process migration runs the above processes. It migrates a file system process while several user processes are performing I/O. This is more difficult than moving a user process would be, as we shall see below.

2.4. The Long and Short of Links

It is important to consider all the places where links to a process might be stored when that process is moved, since they contain information specifying the location of the process. Although a link is not useful after the process that it addresses terminates, some links last for relatively long periods of time. For example, a *request* link, which represents a service such as process management, or a *resource* link, which represents an object such as an open file, may exist for as long as the system is up, if they are held by a system process. Other links, such as *reply* links, have short lifetimes, since they are used only once to respond to requests.

Links may be either in some process's link table or in a message that is enroute to a process. Once a link is given out, it may be passed to other processes without the knowledge of the process that created the link (the process to which the link points). There is no way short of a complete system search of finding all links that point to a process. The mechanism for handling messages during and after a process is migrated must provide a way for messages to be directed to the new location, despite out-of-date links. Moreover, for performance reasons, it should eventually bring these links up-to-date.

Moving a *user* process will usually be simple. The only processes likely to have links to a user process are system processes. Such links may be used to send only one message, so the out-of-date link will no longer exist after forwarding the reply message to the new location of the user process.

Moving a *system* process (or, more precisely, a *server* process), is more difficult, since many processes may have links to it, and such links may last a long time, being duplicated and passed to other processes. In fact, the server process may not know how many copies of links there are to it (it is possible, but optional, for a process to keep track of how many, but not where they are). Since such links may be used for many messages, performance considerations will require a method for updating these links.

3. Moving a Process

Most of the low-level mechanisms required to manipulate the process state and move data between kernels were available in the version of DEMOS/MP that existed when this effort began. Process migration was implemented by using those facilities to move the process, and adding the mechanisms for forwarding messages and updating links.

3.1. The Mechanism

A process is moved between two processors called the *source processor* and the *destination processor*. A request to the kernel to move a process is made by the process manager system process. In the absence of an authentic workload for our test cases, the decision to move a particular process and the choice of destination were arbitrary. However, adding a decision rule for when and to where to move a process will be easy. The process manager and memory scheduler already monitor system

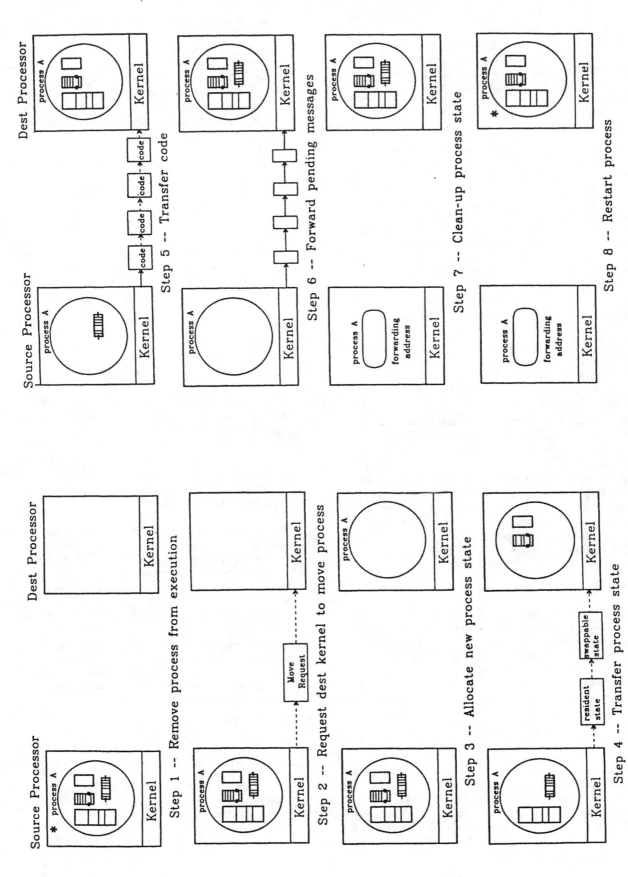

Steps in moving a process

Figure 3-1

activity for memory and cpu scheduling, and can use the same information to make process migration decisions. Information on the communications load is also available. It is of course possible for a process to request its own migration. This request can be thought of as one more piece of information that the process manager can use in making migration decisions. Designing an efficient and effective decision rule is still an open research topic.

There are several features of a decision rule that we have considered in our implementation. The migration scheme depends on the ability to evaluate the resource use patterns of processes. This function is normally available in the accounting or performance monitoring part of the system. There must also be a way to assess the load on individual processors. This function is often available in systems with load-limiting schedulers, which activate or deactivate processes based on overall system load. The three features not usually available are the means to collect the above information in one place, an strategy for improving the operation of the system considering the appropriate costs, and a hysteresis mechanism to keep from incurring the cost of migration more often than justified by the gains.

Information used to determine when and where to move a process involves the state of machine on which the process currently resides, and machines to where the process could move. Processor loading and memory demand for each machine is required.

More difficult is integrating the communications cost incurred by a process. Processes cooperating in a computation may exhibit a great deal of parallelism, and therefore should be on different machines. However, separating them could increase the latency of communication beyond the savings accrued by parallel execution. Collection of the communication data is beyond the ability of most current systems.

Once the decision has been made to migrate a process, the following steps are performed (shown in figure 3-1).

1. Remove the process from execution:

   The process is marked as "in migration". If it had been ready, it is removed from the run queue. No change is made to the recorded state of the process (whether it is suspended, running, waiting for message, etc.), since the process will (at least initially) be in the same state when it reaches its the destination processor. Messages arriving for the migrating process, including DELIVERTOKERNEL messages, will be placed on its message queue.

2. Ask destination kernel to move process:

   A message is sent to the kernel on the destination processor, asking it to migrate the process to its machine. This message contains information about the size and location of the the process's resident state, swappable state, and code. The next part of the migration, up to the forwarding of messages (Step 6), will be controlled by the destination processor kernel.

3. Allocate a process state on the destination processor:

   An empty process state is created on the destination processor. This process state is similar to that allocated during process creation, except that *the newly allocated process state has the same process identifier as the the migrating process*. Resources such as virtual memory swap space are reserved at this time.

4. Transfer the process state:

   Using the move data facility, the destination kernel copies the migrating process's state into the empty process state.

5. Transfer the program:

   Using the move data facility, the destination kernel copies the memory (code, data, and stack) of the process into the destination process. Since the kernel move data operation handles reading or writing of swapped out memory and allocation of new virtual memory, this step will cause definition of memory to take place, if necessary. Control is returned to the source kernel.

6. Forward pending messages:

   Upon being notified that the process is established on the new processor, the source kernel resends all messages that were in the queue when the migration started, or that have arrived since the migration started. Before giving them back to the communication system, the source kernel changes the location part of the process address to reflect the new location of the process.

7. Clean-up process's state:

   On the source processor, all state for the process is removed and space for memory and tables is reclaimed. A *forwarding address* is left on the source processor to forward messages to the process at its new location. The forwarding address is a degenerate process state, whose only contents are the (last known) machine to which the process was migrated. The normal message delivery system tries to find a process when a message arrives for it. When it encounters a forwarding address, it takes the actions described in the next section. The source kernel has completed its work and control is returned to the destination kernel.

8. Restart the process:

   The process is restarted in whatever state it was in before being migrated. Messages may now arrive for the process, although the only part of the system that knows the new location of the process is the source processor kernel. The destination kernel has completed its work.

At this point, the process has been migrated. The links from the migrated process to the rest of the system are all still valid, since links are context-independent. Links created by the process after it has moved will point to the process at its new location. The only problem is what to do with messages sent on links that still point to the old location.

3.2. A Note on Autonomy and Interdomain Migration

The DEMOS/MP kernels trust each other, and thus are not completely autonomous. Moreover, for practical purposes, all DEMOS/MP processors are identical and provide the same services. This makes process migration particularly useful in our environment. However, the process migration mechanism could work even if the kernels were autonomous and had different resources.

The crucial questions for autonomous processors are "Is the process willing to be moved?" and "Will the destination machine accept it?" Any policy to decide which process to migrate could take into account the former question. The second question can be addressed during the migration. Note that the destination machine actually performs most of the steps. In particular, in Step 2, the source machine asks the destination machine to accept the process. If the destination machine refuses, the process cannot be migrated.

It is also possible to migrate processes between domains. By domain, we mean that the destination processor belongs to a collection of machines under a different administrative control than the source processor, and may be suspicious of the source processor and the incoming process. The destination processor may simply refuse to accept any migrations not fitting its criteria. The source processor, once rebuffed, has the option of looking elsewhere.

The source and destination kernels must, of course, be able to communicate with each other in order to accomplish the migration, and the destination machine must be able to handle messages sent over the links held by the process. Since the ability to send and receive messages over links is all a DEMOS process expects of its environment, so long as that continues to be provided, the process can continue to run.

4. Message Forwarding

Since DEMOS/MP guarantees message delivery, in moving a process it must be ensured that all pending, enroute, and future messages arrive at the process's new location. There are three cases to consider: messages sent but not received before the process finished moving, messages sent after the process is moved using an old link, and messages sent using a link created after the process moved.

Messages in the first category were in process's message queue on the source machine, waiting for the process to receive them, when the process restarted on the destination machine. These messages are forwarded immediately as part of the migration procedure.

Messages in the middle category are forwarded as they arrive. After the process has been moved, a forwarding address is left at the source processor pointing toward the destination processor. When a message is received at a given machine, if the receiver is a forwarding address, then the machine address of the message is updated and the message is resubmitted to the message delivery system (see Figure 4-1). As a byproduct of forwarding, an attempt may be made to fix up the link of the sending process (See next section).

The last case, messages sent using links created after the process has moved, is trivial. Links created after the process is moved will contain the same process identifier, and the last known machine identifier in the process address will be that of the new machine.

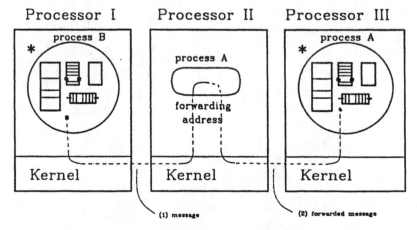

Message sent through a forwarding address
Figure 4-1

461

Simply forwarding messages is a sufficient mechanism to insure correct operation of the process and processes communicating with it after it has moved. However, the motivation for process migration is often to improve message performance. Routing messages through another processor (with the forwarding address) can defeat possible performance gains and, in many cases, degrade performance. The next section discusses methods for updating links to reduce the cost of forwarding.

An alternative to message forwarding is to return messages to their senders as not deliverable. This method does not require any process state to be left behind on the source processor. The kernel sending the message will receive a response that indicates that the process does not exist on the destination machine. Normally this means that the process the link points to has terminated; in this case, it may mean the process has migrated. The sending kernel can attempt to find the new location of the process, perhaps by notifying the process manager or some system-wide name service, or can notify the sending process that the link is no longer usable, forcing it to take recovery action. The disadvantage of this scheme is that, even if the kernel could redirect the message without impacting the sending process, more of the system would be involved in message forwarding and would have to be aware of process migration. This method also violates the transparency of communications fundamental to DEMOS/MP.

When the forwarding address is no longer needed, it would be desirable to remove it. The optimum time to remove it is when all links that point to the migrated process's old location have been updated. This typically would require a mechanism that makes use of reference counts. An alternative is to remove the forwarding address when the process dies. This can be accomplished by means of pointers backwards along the path of migration.

The forwarding address is compact. In the current implementation, it uses 8 bytes of storage. As a result of the negligible impact on system resources, we have not found it necessary to remove forwarding addresses. Given a long running system, however, some form of garbage collection will eventually have to be used.

It is possible for the processor that is holding forwarding address to crash. Since forwarding addresses are (degenerate) processes, the same recovery mechanism that works for processes works for forwarding addresses. Process migration assumes that reliable message delivery is provided by some lower level mechanism, for example, *published communications* [Powell & Presotto 83].

5. Updating Links

By *updating links*, we mean updating the process address of the link. Recall that a process address contains both a unique identifier and a machine location. The unique identifier is not changed, but the machine location is updated to specify the new machine.

As mentioned above, for performance reasons, it is important to update links that address a process that has been migrated. These links may belong to processes that are resident on the same or different processors, and processes may have more than one link to a given process (including to themselves). Links may also be contained in messages in transit. It is therefore impractical to search the whole system for links that may point to a particular process.

Since race conditions might allow some messages to be in transit while the process is being moved, the message forwarding mechanism is required. As long as it is available, it can also be used for forwarding messages that are sent using links that have not yet been updated to reflect the new location of the process.

The following scheme allows links to be updated as they are used, rather than all at once: As it forwards the

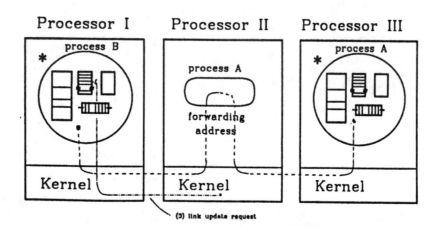

Updating a link after a message forward
Figure 5-1

462

message, the forwarding machine sends another special message to the kernel of the process that sent the original message (see Figure 5-1). This special message contains the process identifier of the sender of the message, the process identifier of the intended receiver (the migrated process), and the new location of the receiver. All links in the sending process's link table that point to the migrated process are then updated to point to the new location.

Movement of a process should cause only a small perturbation to message communication performance. If the process that has moved is a user process, there will usually be few links that point to it. The links will tend to be either reply links, which will generate only one message and thus not need to be fixed up, or links from other user processes with which it is communicating, which will quickly be updated during the first few message exchanges. As a general rule, system processes do not retain non-reply links to user processes.

The worst case will be when the moving process is a server process. In this case, there may be many links to the process that need to be fixed up. Generally, links to servers are used for more than a few message exchanges, so the overhead of fixing up such a link is traded off against the savings of the cost to forward many messages. Moreover, the likelihood of server processes migrating is lower than for user processes. Servers are often tied to unmovable resources and usually present predictable loads that allow them to be properly located, reducing the need to move them.

6. Cost of Migration

The cost of moving a process dictates how frequently we are willing to move the process. These costs manifest themselves in two areas; the actual cost in moving the process and its related state, and the incremental costs incurred in updating message paths.

The cost of the actual transfer of the process and its state can be separated into *state transfer cost* and *administrative cost*. The state transfer cost includes the messages that contain the process's code, data, state, and message queue. DEMOS/MP uses the data move facility to transfer large blocks of data. This facility is designed to minimize network overhead by sending larger packets (and increasing effective network throughput). The packets are sent to the receiving kernel in a continuous stream. The receiving kernel acknowledges each packet (but the sending kernel does not have to wait for the acknowledgement to send the next packet). Three data moves are involved in moving a process. These are for the program (code and data), the non-swappable (resident) state, and the swappable state. The non-swappable state uses about 250 bytes, and the swappable state uses about 600 bytes (depending on the size of the link table). For non-trivial processes, the size of the program and data overshadow the size of the system information.

In addition, each message that is pending in the queue for the migrating process must be forwarded to the destination machine. The cost for each of these messages is the same as for any other inter-machine message.

The administrative cost includes the message exchanges that are used to initiate and orchestrate the task of moving a process. These costs depend on the internal structures of the system on which it is being implemented. The current DEMOS/MP implementation uses 9 such messages, each message being in the 6-12 byte range. These messages use the standard inter-machine message facility.

The incremental costs for process migration are incurred when a link needs to be updated. Each message that goes through a forwarding address generates two additional messages. The first is the actual message being forwarded to its new destination, and the second is the update message back to the sender. This will occur for each message sent on a given link until the update message reaches the sending process. In current examples, the worst case observed was two messages sent over a link before it was updated. Typically, the link is updated after the first message.

The movement of a process involves a small number of short, control messages, and a large number of block data transfers. The cost of migrating a process depends on the efficiency of both of these types of communications.

7. Conclusion

Process migration has proven to be a reasonable facility to implement in a communication-based distributed operating system. Less than one person-month of time was required to implement and test the mechanism in the current version of DEMOS/MP.

A number of DEMOS/MP design features have made the implementation of process migration possible. DEMOS/MP provides a complete encapsulation of a process, with the only method of access to services and resources being through links. There is no uncontrolled sharing of memory and all contact with the operating system, I/O, and other processes is made through a process's links. DEMOS/MP has a concise process state representation. There is no *process* state hidden in the various functional modules of the operating system. On the other hand, the system servers each maintain their own states, thus no *resource* state (except for links) is in the process state. Once a process is taken out of execution, it is a simple matter to copy its state to another processor. The location transparency and context independence of links make it possible for both the moved process and processes communicating with it to be isolated from the change in venue.

The DELIVERTOKERNEL link attribute allows control operations to be performed without concern for where the process is located. Thus control can follow a process through disturbances in its execution.

The mechanism for moving a process has been implemented, but there is not yet a strategy routine that actually decides when to move a process. The literature contains a few studies of metrics to use for processor and message traffic load optimization. Our continuing work involves implementing process load balancing algorithms, and developing facilities for the measurement and analysis of the performance of communications in distributed programs.

References

Arora & Rana 80
>Arora, R.K. & Rana, S.P., "Heuristic Algorithms for Process Assignment in Distributed Computing Systems", *Information Processing Letters* 11, 4-5, December, 1980, pp. 199-203.

Baskett, Howard, & Montague 77
>Baskett, F., Howard, J.H., Montague, J.T., "Task Communication in DEMOS", *Proc. of the Sixth Symp. on Operating Sys. Principles*, Purdue, November 1975, pp. 23-32.

Bokhard 79
>Bokhari, S.H., "Dual Processor Scheduling with Dynamic Reassignment", *IEEE Trans. on Software Engineering* SE-5, 4, July, 1979.

Cheriton 79
>Cheriton, D.R., "Process Identification in Thoth", *Technical Report* 79-10, University of British Columbia, October 1979.

Feldman 79
>Feldman, J.A., "High-level Programming for Distributive Computing", *CACM* 15, 4 (April), 1972, pp. 221-230.

Finkel 80
>Finkel, R., "The Arachne Kernel", *Technical Report* TR-380, University of Wisconsin, April, 1980.

Powell 77
>Powell, M.L., "The DEMOS File System", *Proc. of the Sixth Symp. on Operating Sys. Principles*, Purdue, November 1975, pp. 33-42.

Powell & Presotto 83
>Powell, M.L., Presotto, D.L., "Publishing: A Reliable Broadcast Communication Mechanism", *Proc. of the Ninth Symp. on Operating Sys. Principles*, Bretton Woods N.H., October 1983.

Powell, Miller, & Presotto 83
>Powell, M.L., Miller, B.P., Presotto, D.L., "DEMOS/MP: A Distributed Operating System", *in preparation*.

Rashid & Robertson 81
>Rashid, R.F., Robertson, G.G., "Accent: A Communication Oriented Network Operating System Kernel", *Proc. of the Eighth Symp. on Operating Sys. Principles*, Asilomar, Calif., December 1981, pp. 64-75.

Rennels 80
>Rennels, D.A., "Distributed Fault-Tolerant Computer Systems", *Computer*, 13, 3, March, 1980, pp. 39-46.

Robinson 79
>Robinson, J.T., "Some Analysis Techniques for Asynchronous Multiprocessor Algorithms", *IEEE Trans. on Software Engineering* SE-5, 1, January, 1979.

Solomon & Finkel 79
>Solomon, M.H., Finkel, R.A., "The Roscoe Operating System", *Proc. of the 7th Symp. on Operating Sys. Principles*, Asilomar, Calif., 1979, pp. 108-114.

Stone 77
>Stone, H.S., "Multiprocessor Scheduling with the Aid of Network Flow Algorithms", *IEEE Trans. on Software Engineering* SE-3, 1, January, 1977, pp. 85-93.

Stone & Bokhari 78
>Stone, H.S. & Bokhari, S.H., "Control of Distributed Processes", *Computer*, July, 1978, pp. 97-106.

Preemptable Remote Execution Facilities
for the V-System

Marvin M. Theimer, Keith A. Lantz, and David R. Cheriton
Computer Science Department
Stanford University
Stanford, CA 94305

Abstract

A remote execution facility allows a user of a workstation-based distributed system to offload programs onto idle workstations, thereby providing the user with access to computational resources beyond that provided by his personal workstation. In this paper, we describe the design and performance of the remote execution facility in the V distributed system, as well as several implementation issues of interest. In particular, we focus on network transparency of the execution environment, preemption and migration of remotely executed programs, and avoidance of residual dependencies on the original host. We argue that preemptable remote execution allows idle workstations to be used as a "pool of processors" without interfering with use by their owners and without significant overhead for the normal execution of programs. In general, we conclude that the cost of providing preemption is modest compared to providing a similar amount of computation service by dedicated "computation engines".

1. Introduction

A distributed computer system consisting of a cluster of workstations and server machines represents a large amount of computational power, much of which is frequently idle. For example, our research system consists of about 25 workstations and server machines, providing a total of about 25 MIPS. With a personal workstation per project member, we observe over one third of our workstations idle, even at the busiest times of the day.

There are many circumstances in which the user can make use of this idle processing power. For example, a user may

wish to compile a program and reformat the documentation after fixing a program error, while continuing to read mail. In general, a user may have batch jobs to run concurrently with, but unrelated to, some interactive activity. Although any one of these programs may perform satisfactorily in isolation on a workstation, forcing them to share a single workstation degrades interactive response and increases the running time of non-interactive programs.

Use of idle workstations as computation servers increases the processing power available to users and improves the utilization of the hardware base. However, this use must not compromise a workstation owner's claim to his machine: A user must be able to quickly reclaim his workstation to avoid interference with personal activities, implying removal of remotely executed programs within a few seconds time. In addition, use of workstations as computation servers should not require programs to be written with special provisions for executing remotely. That is, remote execution should be *preemptable* and *transparent*. By preemptable, we mean that a remotely executed program can be migrated elsewhere on demand.

In this paper, we describe the preemptable remote execution facilities of the V-system [4, 2] and examine several issues of interest. We argue that preemptable remote execution allows idle workstations to be used as a "pool of processors" without interfering with use by their owners and without significant overhead for the normal execution of programs. In general, we conclude that the cost of providing preemption is modest compared to providing a similar amount of computation service by dedicated "computation engines". Our facilities also support truly distributed programs in that a program may be decomposed into subprograms, each of which can be run on a separate host.

Reprinted with permission from *Proc. of the 10th ACM Symp. on Operating Systems Principles,* ACM Press, New York, N.Y., 1985, pp. 2–12.
©1985 Association for Computing Machinery.

There are three basic issues we address in our design. First, programs should be provided with a network-transparent execution environment so that execution on a remote machine is the same execution on the local machine. By *execution environment*, we mean the names, operations and data with which the program can interact during execution. As an example of a problem that can arise here, programs that directly access hardware devices, such as a graphics frame buffer, may be inefficient if not impossible to execute remotely.

Second, migration of a program should result in minimal interference with the execution of the program and the rest of the system, even though migration requires atomic transfer of a copy of the program state to another host. Atomic transfer is required so that the rest of the system at no time detects there being other than one copy. However, suspending the execution of the migrating program or the interactions with the program for the entire time required for migration may cause interference with system execution for several seconds and may even result in failure of the program. Such long "freeze times" must be avoided.

Finally, a migrated program should not continue to depend on its previous host once it is executing on a new host, that is, it should have no *residual dependencies* on the previous host. For example, a program either should not create temporary files local to its current computation server or else those files should be migrated along with the program. Otherwise, the migrated program continues to impose a load on its previous host, thus diminishing some of the benefits of migrating the program. Also, a failure or reboot of the previous host causes the program to fail because of these inter-host dependencies.

The paper presents our design with particular focus on how we have addressed these problems. The next section describes the remote execution facility. Section 3 describes migration. Section 4 describes performance and experience to date with the use of these facilities. Section 5 compares this work to that in some other distributed systems. Finally, we close with conclusions and indications of problems for further study.

2. Remote Execution

A V program is executed on another machine at the command interpreter level by typing:

<program> <arguments> @ <machine-name>

Using the meta-machine name *

<program> <arguments> @ *

executes the specified program at a random idle machine on the network. A standard library routine provides a similar facility that can be directly invoked by arbitrary programs. Any program can be executed remotely providing that it does not require low-level access to the hardware devices of the machine from which it originated. Hardware devices include disks, frame buffers, network interfaces, and serial lines.

A suite of programs and library functions are provided for querying and managing program execution on a particular workstation as well as all workstations in the system. Facilities for terminating, suspending and debugging programs work independent of whether the program is executing locally or remotely.

It is often feasible for a user to use his workstation simultaneously with its use as a computation server. Because of priority scheduling for locally invoked programs, a text-editing user need not notice the presence of background jobs providing they are not contending for memory with locally executing programs.

2.1. Implementation

The V-system consists of a distributed kernel and a distributed collection of server processes. A functionally identical copy of the kernel resides on each host and provides address spaces, processes that run within these address spaces, and network-transparent interprocess communication (IPC). Low-level process and memory management functions are provided by a *kernel server* executing inside the kernel. All other services provided by the system are implemented by processes running outside the kernel. In particular, there is a *program manager* on each workstation that provides program management for programs executing on that workstation.

V address spaces and their associated processes are grouped into *logical hosts*. A V process identifier is structured as a *(logical-host-id, local-index)* pair. In the extreme, each program can be run in its own logical host. There may be multiple logical hosts associated with a single workstation, however, a logical host is local to a single workstation.

Initiating local execution of a program involves sending a request to the local program manager to create a new address space and load a specified program image file into this address space. The program manager uses the kernel server to set up the address space and create an initial process that is awaiting reply from its creator. The program manager then turns over control of the newly created process to the requester by forwarding the newly created process to it. The requester initializes the new program space with program arguments, default I/O, and various "environment variables", including a name cache for commonly used global names. Finally, it starts the program in execution by replying to its initial process. The communication paths between programs and servers are illustrated in Figure 2-1.

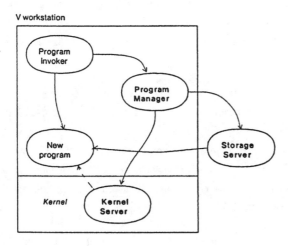

Figure 2-1: Communication paths for program creation.

A program is executed on another workstation by addressing the program creation request to the program manager on the other workstation. The appropriate program manager is selected using the process group mechanism in V, which allows a message to be sent to a group of processes rather than just individual processes [5]. Every program manager belongs to the well-known program manager group. When the user specifies a particular machine, a query is sent to this group with the specified host name, requesting that the associated program manager respond. The response indicates the program manager to which to send the program creation request. When the user specifies "*", a query is sent requesting a response from those hosts with a reasonable amount of processor and memory resources available for remotely executing programs. Typically, the client receives several responses to the request. Currently, it simply selects the program manager that responds first since that is generally the least loaded host. This simple mechanism provides a decentralized implementation of scheduling that

performs well at minimal cost for reasonably small systems.

Beyond selection of a program manager, remote program execution appears the same as local program execution because programs are provided with a network-transparent execution environment, assuming they do not directly access hardware devices. In particular:

- The program address space is initialized the same as when the program is executed locally. For example, arguments and environment variables are passed in the same manner.

- All references by the program outside its address space are performed using network-transparent IPC primitives and globally unique identifiers, with the exceptions of the host-specific kernel server and program manager. For example, standard input and output are specified by global identifiers for the server processes implementing them.

- The kernel server and program manager on a remote workstation provide identical services for remotely executing programs as the local kernel server and program manager provide for locally executing programs.[1] Access to the kernel server and program manager of the workstation on which a program is running is obtained through *well-known local process groups*, which in this case contain only a single process. For example, the kernel server can be accessed by constructing a process-group-id consisting of the program's logical-host-id concatenated with the index value for the kernel server.[2] Thus, host-specific servers can be referenced in a location-independent manner.

- We assume that remotely executed programs do not directly access the device server[3] The limitation on device access is not a problem in V since most programs access physical devices through server processes that remain co-resident with the devices that they manage. In particular, programs perform all "terminal output" via a display server that remains co-resident with the frame buffer it manages [10, 14].

---

[1] It only makes sense to use the kernel server and program manager local to the executing program since their services are intrinsically bound to the machine on which the program is executing, namely management of processor and memory resources.

[2] A process-group-id is identical in format to a process-id.

[3] Actually, references to devices bind to devices on the workstation on which they execute, which is useful in many circumstances. However, we are not able to migrate these programs.

3. Migration

A program is migrated by invoking:

`migrateprog [-n] [<program>]`

to remove the specified program from the workstation. If no other host can be found for the program, the program is not removed unless the "-n" flag is present, in which case it is simply destroyed. If no program is specified, `migrateprog` removes all remotely executed programs.

A program may create sub-programs, all of which typically execute within a single logical host. Migration of a program is actually migration of the logical host containing the program. Thus, typically, all sub-programs of a program are migrated when the program is migrated. One exception is when a sub-program is executed remotely from its parent program.

3.1. Implementation

The simplest approach to migrating a logical host is to freeze its state while the migration is in progress. By *freezing* the state, we mean that execution of processes in the logical host is suspended and all external interactions with those processes are deferred.

The problem with this simple approach is that it may suspend the execution of the programs in the logical host and programs that are executing IPC operations on processes in the logical host for too long. In fact, various operations may abort because their timeout periods are exceeded. Although aborts can be prevented via "operation pending" packets, this effectively suspends the operation until the migration is complete. Suspension implies that operations that normally take a few milliseconds could take several seconds to complete. For example, the time to copy address spaces is roughly 3 seconds per megabyte in V using 10 Mb Ethernet. A 2 megabyte logical host state would therefore be frozen for over 6 seconds. Moreover, significant overhead may be incurred by retransmissions during an extended suspension period. For instance, V routinely transfers 32 kilobytes or more as a unit over the network.

We reduce the effect of these problems by copying the bulk of the logical host state before freezing it, thereby reducing the time during which it is frozen. We refer to this operation as *pre-copying*. Thus, the complete procedure to migrate a logical host is:

1. Locate another workstation (via the program manager group) that is willing and able to accommodate the logical host to be migrated.

2. Initialize the new host to accept the logical host.

3. Pre-copy the state of the logical host.

4. Freeze the logical host and complete the copy of its state.

5. Unfreeze the new copy, delete the old copy, and rebind references.

The first step of migration is accomplished by the same mechanisms employed when the program was executed remotely in the first place. These mechanisms were discussed in Section 2. The remainder of this section discusses the remaining steps.

3.1.1. Initialization on the New Host

Once a new host is located, it is initialized with descriptors for the new copy of the logical host. To allow it to be referenced before the transfer of control, the new copy is created with a different logical-host-id. The identifier is then changed to the original logical-host-id in a subsequent step (Section 3.1.3).

The technique of creating the new copy as a logical host with a different identifier allows both the old copy and the new copy to exist and be accessible at the same time. In particular, this allows the standard interprocess copy operations, *CopyTo* and *CopyFrom*, to be used to copy the bulk of the program state.

3.1.2. Pre-copying the State

Once the new host is initialized, we pre-copy the state of the migrating logical host to the new logical host. Pre-copying is done as an initial copy of the complete address spaces followed by repeated copies of the pages modified during the previous copy until the number of modified pages is relatively small or until no significant reduction in the number of modified pages is achieved.[4] The remaining modified pages are recopied after the logical host is frozen.

The first copy operation moves most of the state and takes the longest time, therefore providing the longest time for modifications to the program state to occur. The second copy moves only that state modified during the first copy, therefore

---

[4] Modified pages are detected using dirty bits.

taking less time and presumably allowing fewer modifications to occur during its execution time. In a non-virtual memory system, a major benefit of this approach is moving the code and initialized data of a logical host, portions that are never modified, while the logical host continues to execute. For example, consider a logical host consisting of 1 megabyte of code, .25 megabytes of initialized (unmodified data) and .75 megabytes of "active" data. The first copy operation takes roughly 6 seconds. If, during those 6 seconds, .1 megabytes of memory were modified, the second copy operation should take roughly .3 seconds. If during those .3 seconds, .01 megabytes of memory were modified, so the third copy operation should take about 0.03 seconds. At this point, we might freeze the logical host state, completing the copy and transferring the logical host to the next machine. Thus, the logical host is frozen for about .03 seconds (assuming no packet loss), rather than about 6 seconds.

The pre-copy operation is executed at a higher priority than all other programs on the originating host to prevent these other programs from interfering with the progress of the pre-copy operation.

3.1.3. Completing the Copy

After the pre-copy, the logical host is frozen and the copy of its state is completed. Freezing the logical host state, even if for a relatively short time, requires some care. Although we can suspend execution of all processes within a logical host, we must still deal with external IPC interactions. In V, interprocess communication primitives can change the state of a process in three basic ways: by sending a request message, by sending a reply message, or by executing a kernel server or program manager operation on the process.[5] When a process or logical host is frozen, the kernel server and program manager defer handling requests that modify this logical host until it is unfrozen. When the logical host is unfrozen, the requests are forwarded to the new program manager or kernel server, assuming the logical host is successfully migrated at this point.

In the case of a request message, the message is queued for the recipient process. (The recipient is modified slightly to indicate that it is not prepared to immediately receive the message.) A "reply-pending" packet is sent to the sender on each retransmission, as is done in the normal case. When the

---

[5] We treat a *CopyTo* operation to a process as a request message.

logical host is deleted after the transfer of logical host has taken place, all queued messages are discarded and the remote senders are prompted to retransmit to the new host running these processes. For local senders, this entails restarting the send operation. The normal Send then maps to a remote Send operation to the new host, given that the recipient process is no longer recorded as local. For remote senders, the next retransmission (or at least a subsequent one) uses the new binding of logical host to host address that is broadcast when a logical host is migrated. Therefore, the retransmission delivers the message to the new copy of the logical host.

Reply messages are handled by discarding them and relying on the retransmission capabilities of the IPC facilities. A process on a frozen logical host that is awaiting reply continues to retransmit to its replier periodically, even if a reply has been received. This basically resets the replier's timeout for retaining the reply message so that the reply message is still be available once the migration is complete.

The last part of copying the original logical host's state consists of copying its state in the kernel server and program manager. Copying the kernel state consists of replacing the kernel state of the newly created logical host with that of the migrating one. This includes changing the logical-host-id of the new logical host to be the same as that of the original logical host.

Once this operation has succeeded, there exist two frozen identical copies of the logical host. The rest of the system cannot detect the existence of two copies because operations on both of them are suspended. The the kernel server on the original machine continues to respond with reply-pending packets to any processes sending to the logical host as well as retransmit Send requests, thereby preventing timeout.

If the copy operation fails due to lack of acknowledgement, we assume that the new host failed and that the logical host has not been transferred. The logical host is unfrozen to avoid timeouts, another host is selected for this logical host and the migration process is retried. Care must be taken in retrying this migration that we do not exceed the amount of time the user is willing to wait. In our current implementation, we simply give up if the first attempt at migration fails.

3.1.4. Unfreezing the New Copy and Rebinding References

Once all state has been transferred, the new copy of the logical host is unfrozen and the old copy is deleted. References to the logical host are rebound as discussed next.

The only way to refer to a process in V is to use its globally unique process identifier. As defined in Section 2, a process identifier is bound to a logical host, which is in turn bound to a physical host via a cache of mappings in each kernel. Rebinding a logical host to a different physical host effectively rebinds the identifiers for all processes on that logical host. When a reference to a process fails to get a response after a small number of retransmissions, the cache entry for the associated logical host is invalidated and the reference is broadcast. A correct cache entry is derived from the response. The cache is also updated based on incoming requests. Thus, when a logical host is migrated, these mechanisms automatically update the logical host cache, thereby rebinding references to the associated process identifiers.

Various optimizations are possible, including broadcasting the new binding at the time the new copy is unfrozen.

3.2. Effect of Virtual Memory

Work is underway to provide demand paged virtual memory in V, such that workstations may page to network file servers. In this configuration, it suffices to flush modified virtual memory pages to the network file server rather than explicitly copy the address space of processes in the migrating logical host between workstations. Then, the new host can fault in the pages from the file server on demand. This is illustrated in Figure 3-1.

Just as with the pre-copy approach described above, one can repeatedly flush dirty pages out without suspending the processes until there are relatively few dirty pages and then suspend the logical host.

This approach to migration takes two network transfers instead of just one for pages that are dirty on the original host and then referenced on the new host. However, we expect this technique to allow us to move programs off of the original host faster, which is an important consideration. Also, the number of pages that require two copies should be small.

Finally, paging to a local disk might be handled by flushing the program state to disk, as above, and then doing a disk-to-disk transfer of program state over the network to the new host or the file server it uses for paging. The same techniques for minimizing freeze time appear to carry over to this case, although we can only speculate at this time.

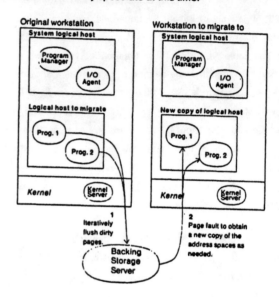

Figure 3-1: Migration with virtual memory.

3.3. Residual Host Dependencies

The design, as described, only deals with migrating programs whose state is contained in the kernel, the program manager and the address space(s) of the program being migrated. However, there are several situations where relevant state is stored elsewhere. This is not a problem if the state is stored in a globally accessible service, such as a network file server. However, extraneous state that is created in the original host workstation may lead to residual dependencies on this host after the program has been migrated. For example, the program may have accessed files on the original host workstation. After the program has been migrated, the program continues to have access to those files, by virtue of V's network-transparent IPC. However, this use imposes a continued load on the original host and results in failure of the program should the original host fail or be rebooted.

To remove this dependency it is necessary to identify and migrate (copies of) all files associated with the program being migrated. These files are effectively extensions of the program state, as considered in the above discussion, and could be moved in a similar fashion. We note, however, a few complications. First, a file may be arbitrarily large, introducing unbounded delay to the program migration. Second, a file that is being read may be a copy of some standard header file that also exists on the machine to which the process is being moved. Recognizing this case would save on file copying as well as reduce the final problem, namely, a program may have the symbolic name of the file stored internally, precluding changing the symbolic name when the file is migrated. However, this name may conflict with an existing file on the machine to which the file is moving. Related to this, a program may have written and closed a temporary file, yet be planning to read the file at some later point. There is no reliable way of detecting such files, so there is no reliable way to ensure they are migrated. With our current use of diskless workstations, file migration is not required and, moreover, file access cost is essentially the same for all workstations (and quite acceptable) [4, 11].

Similar problems can arise with other servers that store state specific to a particular program during its execution. Again, our approach has been to avoid local servers and thereby circumvent the problem of residual host dependencies.

4. Evaluation

At the time of writing, the remote execution facility has been in general use for one year and the migration facility is operational on an experimental basis. This section gives an indication of the cost of remote execution and migration, in both time and space, as well as general remarks about the usage we have observed.

4.1. Time for Remote Execution and Migration

The performance figures presented are for the SUN workstation with a 10 MHz 68010 processor and 2 Mbytes of local memory. Workstations are connected via a 10 Mbit Ethernet local area network.

The cost of remotely executing a program can be split into three parts: Selecting a host to use, setting up and later destroying a new execution environment, and actually loading the program file to run. The latter considerably dominates the first two. The cost of selecting a remote host has been measured to be 23 milliseconds, this being the time required to receive the first response from a multicast request for candidate hosts. Some additional overhead arises from

receiving additional responses. (That is, the response time and the processing overhead are different.) The cost of setting up and later destroying a new execution environment on a specific remote host is 40 milliseconds. For diskless workstations, program files are loaded from network file servers so the cost of program loading is independent of whether a program is executed locally or remotely. This cost is a function of the size of the program to load, and is typically 330 milliseconds per 100 Kbytes of program.

The cost of migration is similar to that of remote execution: A host must be selected, a new copy of the logical host's state in the kernel server and program manager must be made, and the logical host's address spaces must be copied. The time required to create a copy of the logical host's kernel server and program manager state depends on the number of processes and address spaces in the logical host. 14 milliseconds plus an additional 9 milliseconds for each process and address space are required for this operation. The time required to copy 1 Mbyte of an address space between two physical hosts is 3 *seconds*.

Measurements for our C-compiler[6] and *Tex* text formatter programs indicated that usually 2 precopy iterations were useful (i.e. one initial copy of an address space and one copy of subsequently modified pages). The resulting amount of address space that must be copied, on average, while a program is frozen was between 0.5 and 70 Kbytes in size, implying program suspension times between 5 and 210 milliseconds (in addition to the time needed to copy the kernel server and program manager state). Table 4-1 shows the average rates at which dirty pages are generated by the programs measured.

Time interval (secs)	0.2	1	3
make	0.8	1.8	4.2
cc68	0.6	2.2	6.2
preprocessor	25.0	40.2	59.6
parser	50.0	76.8	109.4
optimizer	19.8	32.2	41.0
assembler	21.6	33.4	48.4
linking loader	25.0	39.2	37.8
tex	68.6	111.6	142.8

Table 4-1: Dirty page generation rates (in Kbytes).

---

[6]Which consists of 5 separate subprograms: a preprocessor, a parser front-end, an optimizer, an assembler, a linking loader, and a control program.

The execution time overhead of remote execution and migration facilities on the rest of the system is small:

- The overhead of identifying the team servers and kernel servers by local group identifiers adds about 100 microseconds to every kernel server or team server operation.

- The mechanism for binding logical hosts to network addresses predates the migration facility since it is necessary for mapping 32 bit process-ids to 48 bit physical Ethernet host addresses anyway. Thus, no extra time cost is incurred here for the ability to rebind logical hosts to physical hosts. The actual cost of rebinding a logical host to physical host is only incurred when a logical host is migrated.

- 13 microseconds is added to several kernel operations to test whether a process (as part of a logical host) is frozen.

4.2. Space Cost

There is no space cost in the kernel server and program manager attributable to remote execution since the kernel provides network-transparent operation and the program manager uses the kernel primitives. Migration, however, introduces a non-trivial amount of code. Several new kernel operations, an additional module in the program manager and the new command `migrateprog` had to be added to the standard system. These added 8 Kbytes to the code and data space of the kernel and 4 Kbytes to the permanently resident program manager.

4.3. Observations on Usage

When remote program execution initially became available, it was necessary to specify the exact machine on which to execute the program. In this form, there was limited use of the facility. Subsequently, we added the "@ *" facility, allowing the user to effectively specify "some other lightly loaded machine". With this change, the use increased significantly. Most of the use is for remotely executing compilations. However, there has also been considerable use for running simulations. In general, users tend to remotely execute non-interactive programs with non-trivial running times. Since most of our workstations are over 80% idle even during the peek usage hours of the day (the most common activity is editing files), almost all remote execution requests are honored. In fact, the only users that have complained about the remote execution facilities are those doing experiments in parallel distributed execution where the remotely executed programs want to commandeer 10 or more workstations at a time.

Very limited experience is available with preemption and migration at this time. The ability to preempt has to date proven most useful for allowing very long running simulation jobs to run on the idle workstations in the system and then migrate elsewhere when their users want to use them. There is also the potential of migrating "floating" server processes such as a transaction manager that are not tied to a particular hardware device. We expect that preemption will receive greater use as the amount of remote and distributed execution grows to match or exceed the available machine resources.

5. Related Work

Demos/MP provides preemption and migration for individual processes [15]. However, hosts are assumed to be connected by a reliable network, so Demos-MP does not deal with packet loss when pending messages are forwarded. Moreover, Demos/MP relies on a *forwarding address* remaining on the machine from which the process was migrated, in order to handle the update of outstanding references to the process. Without sophisticated error recovery procedures, this leads to failure when this machine is subsequently rebooted and an old reference is still outstanding. In contrast, our use of logical hosts allows a simple rebinding that works without forwarding addresses.

Locus provides preemptable remote execution as well [3]. However, it emphasizes load balancing across a cluster of multi-user machines rather than on sharing access to idle personal workstations. Perhaps as a consequence, there appear to have been no attempts to reduce the "freeze time" as discussed above. Moreover, in contrast to Locus, virtually all the mechanisms in V have been implemented outside the kernel, thus providing some insight into the requirements for a reduced kernel interface for this type of facility.

The Cambridge distributed system provides remote execution as a simple extension of the way in which processors are allocated to individual users [13]. Specifically, a user can allocate additional processors from the pool of processors from which his initial processor is allocated. Because no user owns a particular processor, there is less need for (and no provision for) preemption and migration, assuming the pool of processors is not exhausted. However, this processor allocation is feasible because the Cambridge user display is coupled to a processor by a byte stream providing conventional terminal service. In contrast, with high-performance bitmap displays, each workstation processor is closely bound to a particular display, for instance, when the frame buffer is part of its addressable memory. With this architecture, personal claim on a display implies claim on the attached processor. Personal claim on a processor that is currently in use for another user's programs requires that these programs are either destroyed or migrated to another processor.

Several problem-specific examples of preemptable remote execution also exist. Limited facilities for remote "down-loading", of ARPANET IMPs, for example, have been available for some time. Early experiments with preemptable execution facilities included the "Creeper" and "relocatable McRoss" programs at BBN and the "Worms" programs at Xerox [17]. Finally, a number of application-specific distributed systems have been built, which support preemptable remote executives (see, for example, [1, 9]). However, in each case, the facilities provided were suitable for only a very narrow range of applications (often only one). In contrast, the facilities presented here are invisible to applications and, therefore, available to all applications.

Our work is complementary to the extant literature on task decomposition, host selection, and load balancing issues (see, for example [6, 7, 8, 12]).

6. Concluding Remarks

We have described the design and performance of the remote execution facilities in the V distributed system. From our experience, transparent preemptable remote program execution is feasible to provide, allowing idle workstations to be used as a "pool of processors" without interfering with personal use by their owners. The facility has reduced our need for dedicated "computation engines" and higher-performance workstations, resulting in considerable economic and administrative savings. However, it does not preclude having such machines for floating point-intensive programs and other specialized computations. Such a dedicated server machine would simply appear as an additional free processor and would not, in general, require the migration mechanism.

The presentation has focused on three major issues, namely: network-transparent execution environment, minimizing interference due to migration and avoiding residual host dependencies. We review below the treatment of each of these issues.

The provision of a network-transparent execution environment was facilitated by several aspects of the V kernel. First, the network-transparency of the V IPC primitives and the use of global naming, both at the process identifier and symbolic name level, provide a means of communication between a program and the operating system (as well as other programs) that is network-transparent. In fact, even the V debugger can debug local and remote programs with no change using the conventional V IPC primitives for interaction with the process being debugged.

Second, a process is encapsulated in an address space so that it is restricted to only using the IPC primitives to access outside of its address space. For example, a process cannot directly examine kernel data structures but must send a message to the kernel to query, for example, its processor utilization, current-time and so on. This prevents uncontrolled sharing of memory, either between applications or between an application and the operating system. In contrast, a so-called *open system* [16] cannot prevent applications from circumventing proper interfaces, thereby rendering remote execution impossible, not to mention migration.

Finally, this encapsulation also provides protection between programs executing on behalf of different (remote) users on the same workstation, as well as protection of the operating system from remotely executed programs. In fact, the V kernel provides most of the facilities of a multi-user operating system kernel. Consequently, remotely executed programs can be prevented from accessing, for example, a local file system, from interfering with other programs and from crashing the local operating system. Without these protection facilities, each idle workstation could only serve one user at a time and might have to reboot after each such use to ensure it is starting in a clean state. In particular, a user returning to his workstation would be safest rebooting if the machine had been used by remote programs.

Thus, we conclude that many aspects of multi-user -timesharing system design should be applied to the design of a workstation operating system if it is to support multi-user resource sharing of the nature provided by the V remote execution facility.

Interference with the execution of the migrating program and the system as a whole is minimized by our use of a technique we call *pre-copying*. With pre-copying, program execution and operations on this program by other processes are suspended only for the last portion of the copying of the program state, rather than for the entire copy time. In particular, critical system servers, such as file servers, are not subjected to inordinate delays when communicating with a migrating program.

The suspension of an operation depends on the reliable communication facilities provided by the kernel. Any packet arriving for the migrating program can be dropped with assurance that either the sender of the packet is storing a copy of the data and is prepared to retransmit or else receipt of the packet is not critical to the execution of the migrating program. Effectively, reliable communication provides time-limited storage of packets, thereby relaxing the real-time constraints of communication.

To avoid residual dependencies arising from migration, we espouse the principle that one should, to the degree possible, place the state of a program's execution environment either in its address space or in global servers. That way, the state is either migrated to the new host as part of copying the address space or else the state does not need to move. For example, name bindings in V are stored in a cache in the program's address space as well in global servers. Similarly, files are typically accessed from network file servers. The exceptions to this principle in V are state information stored in the kernel server and the program manager. These exceptions seem unavoidable in our design, but are handled easily by the migration mechanism.

Violating this principle in V does not prevent a program from migrating but may lead to continued dependence on the previous host after the program has migrated. While by convention we avoid such problems, there is currently no mechanism for detecting or handling these dependencies. Although this deficiency has not been a problem in practice, it is a possible area for future work.

There are several other issues that we have yet to address in our work. One issue is failure recovery. If the system provided full recovery from workstation crashes, a process could be migrated by simply destroying it. The recovery mechanism would presumably recreate it on another workstation, thereby effectively migrating the process. However, it appears to be quite expensive to provide application-independent checkpointing and restart facilities. Even application-specific checkpointing can introduce significant overhead if provided only for migration. Consequently, we are handling migration and recovery as separate facilities, although the two facilities might use some common operations in their implementations.

Second, we have not used the preemption facility to balance the load across multiple workstations. At the current level of workstation utilization and use of remote execution, load balancing has not been a problem. However, increasing use of *distributed execution*, in which one program executes subprograms in parallel on multiple host, may provide motivation to address this issue.

Finally, this remote execution facility is currently only available within a workstation cluster connected by one (logical) local network, as is the V-system in general. Efforts are currently under way to provide a version of the system that *can* run in an internet environment. We expect the internet version to present new issues of scale, protection, reliability and performance.

In conclusion, we view preemptable remote execution as an important facility for workstation-based distributed systems. With the increasing prevalence of powerful personal workstations in the computing environments of many organizations, idle workstations will continue to represent a large source of computing cycles. With system facilities such as we have described, a user has access to computational power far in excess of that provided by his personal workstation. And with this step, traditional timesharing systems lose much of the strength of one of their claimed advantages over workstation-based distributed systems, namely, resource sharing at the processor and memory level.

Acknowledgements

Michael Stumm implemented the decentralized scheduler and exercised many aspects of the remote execution early in its availability. Other members of the Stanford Distributed Systems Group have also contributed to the ideas and their implementation presented in this paper. Comments of the referees inspired a significant revision and improvement to the paper.

This research was supported by the Defense Advanced Research Projects Agency under contracts MDA903-80-C-0102 and N00039-83-K-0431.

References

1. J.-M. Ayache, J.-P. Courtiat, and M. Diaz. "REBUS, a fault-tolerate distributed system for industrial real-time control." *IEEE Transactions on Computers C-31*, 7 (July 1982), 637-647.

2. E.J. Berglund, K.P. Brooks, D.R. Cheriton, D.R. Kaelbling, K.A. Lantz, T.P. Mann, R.J. Nagler, W.I. Nowicki, M. M. Theimer, and W. Zwaenepoel. *V-System Reference Manual.* Distributed Systems Group, Department of Computer Science, Stanford University, 1983.

3. D.A. Butterfield and G.J. Popek. Network tasking in the Locus distributed UNIX system. Proc. Summer USENIX Conference, USENIX, June, 1984, pp. 62-71.

4. D.R. Cheriton. "The V Kernel: A software base for distributed systems." *IEEE Software 1*, 2 (April 1984), 19-42.

5. D.R. Cheriton and W. Zwaenepoel. "Distributed process groups in the V kernel." *ACM Transactions on Computer Systems 3*, 2 (May 1985), 77-107. Presented at the SIGCOMM '84 Symposium on Communications Architectures and Protocols, ACM, June 1984.

6. T.C.K. Chou and J.A. Abraham. "Load balancing in distributed systems." *IEEE Transactions on Software Engineering SE-8*, 4 (July 1982), 401-412.

7. D.H. Craft. Resource management in a decentralized system. Proc. 9th Symposium on Operating Systems Principles, ACM, October, 1983, pp. 11-19. Published as *Operating Systems Review* 17(5).

8. E.J. Gilbert. *Algorithm partitioning tools for a high-performance multiprocessor.* Ph.D. Th., Stanford University, 1983. Technical Report STAN-CS-83-946, Department of Computer Science.

9. H.D. Kirrmann and F. Kaufmann. "Poolpo: A pool of processors for process control applications." *IEEE Transactions on Computers C-33*, 10 (October 1984), 869-878.

10. K.A. Lantz and W.I. Nowicki. "Structured graphics for distributed systems." *ACM Transactions on Graphics 3*, 1 (January 1984), 23-51.

11. E.D. Lazowska, J. Zahorjan, D.R. Cheriton, and W. Zwaenepoel. File access performance of diskless workstations. Tech. Rept. STAN-CS-84-1010, Department of Computer Science, Stanford University, June, 1984.

12. R. Marcogliese and R. Novarese. Module and data allocation methods in distributed systems. Proc. 2nd International Conference on Distributed Computing Systems, INRIA/LRI, April, 1981, pp. 50-59.

13. R.M. Needham and A.J. Herbert. *The Cambridge Distributed Computing System.* Addison-Wesley, 1982.

14. W.I. Nowicki. *Partitioning of Function in a Distributed Graphics System.* Ph.D. Th., Stanford University, 1985.

15. M.L. Powell and B.P. Miller. Process migration in DEMOS/MP. Proc. 9th Symposium on Operating Systems Principles, ACM, October, 1983, pp. 110-119. Published as *Operating Systems Review* 17(5).

16. D.D. Redell, Y.K. Dalal, T.R. Horsley, H.C. Lauer, W.C. Lynch, P.R. McJones, H.G. Murray, and S.C. Purcell. "Pilot: An operating system for a personal computer." *Comm. ACM 23*, 2 (February 1980), 81-92. Presented at the 7th Symposium on Operating Systems Principles, ACM, December 1979.

17. J.F. Shoch and J.A. Hupp. "Worms." *Comm. ACM 25*, 3 (March 1982), .

Chapter 7

Load Indices

7.1 Introduction

As discussed in Chapter 5, the estimation and updating of a PE's load information are among the issues that need to be addressed in dynamic load balancing. These issues are of particular importance because the load information serves as one of the most fundamental elements in the load balancing process. The efficiency of a load balancing scheme can be affected heavily by how the load information is chosen and when that information is updated.

The load information is typically represented by a *load index* which is a quantitative measure of a PE's load. A load index is defined as a nonnegative variable taking a zero value if the resource is idle, and taking increasing positive values as the load increases [Ferrari 1987]. Periodic updating of the load index is necessary, since a PE's load is likely to change over time, making older load indices stale. However, the choice of the length of this period is significant, because the overhead of short update periods may negate the advantages of up-to-date indices, and long update periods may render load indices obsolete. A good load index should have the following characteristics:

- The load index should take into account not only the CPU needs of a process, but also its I/O and memory operation requirements. For example, an I/O-bound task typically requires little CPU time for computations. If the load index is based only on the computational needs of a process, then the load of the PE on which this task is assigned is greatly underestimated.
- The load index must reflect quantitatively the qualitative estimates of the current load on a host. For example, if the size of the ready queue is perceived as a good indication of a PE's load, then the definition of the load index should be a function of either the length of the ready queue or the summation of the expected execution times of the jobs in the queue.
- Since the response time of a job is affected more by the future load of a PE than the present one, the load index should be usable for the prediction of the near future load. For example, it is argued that if a PE has been heavily utilized in the recent past, it will also be heavily utilized in the near future. Thus, based on this argument, one may choose a function of the PE utilization as the load index.
- The load index should be relatively stable; that is, high frequency fluctuations in the load should be discounted or ignored. This is especially important to avoid the thrashing problem discussed in Chapter 5.
- Finally, there needs to be a direct relationship between the load index and the performance of the system. This relationship is important from two points of view: 1) the load index, as an integral part of the load balancing process, is used to improve system performance; 2) the performance index can be used to fine-tune the load index.

A wide variety of load indices have been used in the literature [Devarakonda 1989, Ferrari 1987, Hac 1990, Kunz 1991, Svensson 1990]. A partial list of possible load indices includes:

- *CPU queue length*: The load index is a function of the ready queue length. To determine the load index one can either use an instantaneous CPU queue length or an average queue length over the last T seconds. Some of the most effective load indices are defined as functions of several queue lengths, for example, averaged CPU, I/O, and memory queue lengths.
- *CPU utilization*: As mentioned above, some researchers argue that a PE's utilization is a good indication of its load, and thus can be used as a load index. Again, either instantaneous or averaged over some recent period, processor utilization measures are used as a load index.
- *Response time or processing time*: Several variations or combinations of a task's response time have been suggested as a load index in the literature. Some choices include:

1. normalized response time, as the ratio of the response time of a task on a loaded machine over its response time on the same machine when it is empty;
2. summation of the remaining processing times of the jobs running on a host;
3. summation of the processing times used by all the active processes up to the current time; and
4. summation of the total processing times of all the active processes.

- *Aggregate functions*: One can define the load index as a function of several of the above mentioned indices.

[Ferrari 1987] presents a comparative study of different load indices and reports that load balancing methods, based upon the queue length information, do much better than methods based on CPU utilization. It also recounts that averaged queue length indices do better than instantaneous indices. Finally, it is concluded that a relatively short update interval is needed to reflect the most recent changes in the load.

7.2 Chapter organization and overview

Among the few papers in this area, Chapter 7 presents three of the manuscripts that address different aspects of load indices issues. Although the first paper by Devarakonda and Iyer does not discuss load indices directly, it proposes a statistical approach for predicting the CPU time, the file I/O, and the memory requirements of a program at the beginning of its life. This information can then be used in the definition of a load index. In the second paper, Ferrari and Zhou present an empirical evaluation of several load indices. The evaluation is used to study the effects on performance of the choices of load index, the averaging interval, the load information-exchange period, and the characteristics of the workload. In the last paper, Kunz reports on the implementation of a task scheduler based on the concept of a stochastic learning automaton on a network of Unix workstations. Using a synthetic, executable workload, a number of experiments are conducted to determine the effect of different workload descriptions (load indices). It is shown that by using a simple workload descriptor, such as the number of tasks in the ready queue, one can achieve an equal or better performance as compared to more complex load descriptors.

Bibliography

Devarakonda, M. V., and R. K. Iyer, "Predictability of Process Resource Usage: A Measurement-Based Study on UNIX," *IEEE Trans. Software Eng.*, Vol. SE-15, No. 12, Dec. 1989, pp. 1579–1586; reprinted here.

Ferrari, D., and S. Zhou, "An Empirical Investigation of Load Indices for Load Balancing Applications," *Proc. Performance '87, 12th Int'l Symp. Computer Performance Modeling, Measurement, and Evaluation*, North-Holland, Amsterdam, 1987, pp. 515–528; reprinted here.

Hac, A., and T. J. Johnson, "Sensitivity Study of the Load Balancing Algorithm in a Distributed System," *J. Parallel and Distributed Computing*, Vol. 10, 1990, pp. 85–89.

Kunz, T., "The Influence of Different Workload Descriptions on a Heuristic Load Balancing Scheme," *IEEE Trans. Software Eng.*, Vol. SE-17, No. 7, July 1991, pp. 725–730; reprinted here.

Svensson, A., "History, an Intelligent Load Sharing Filter," *Proc. 11th IEEE Int'l Conf. Distributed Computing Systems*, IEEE CS Press, Los Alamitos, Calif., 1990, pp. 546–553

Predictability of Process Resource Usage: A Measurement-Based Study on UNIX

MURTHY V. DEVARAKONDA AND RAVISHANKAR K. IYER, SENIOR MEMBER, IEEE

Abstract—This paper develops a statistical approach for predicting the CPU time, the file I/O, and the memory requirements of a program at the beginning of its life, given the identity of the program. Initially, statistical clustering is used to identify high-density regions of process resource usage. The identified regions form the states for building a state-transition model to characterize the resource usage of each program in its past executions. The prediction scheme uses the knowledge of the program's resource usage in its last execution together with its state-transition model to predict the resource usage in its next execution. The prediction scheme is shown to work using process resource-usage data collected from a VAX 11/780 running 4.3 BSD UNIX. The results show that the predicted values correlate strongly with the actual; the coefficient of correlation between the predicted and actual values for CPU time is 0.84. The errors in prediction are mostly small and are heavily skewed toward small values.

Index Terms—Measurement-based study, prediction accuracy, resource-usage prediction, state-transition models, statistical cluster analysis, UNIX environment.

I. INTRODUCTION

THE study reported in this paper addresses the following question: is it possible to predict the resource requirements of a process and, if so, how well can these requirements be predicted? Resource-usage prediction can be a sound basis for load balancing in a distributed computer system, since costs associated with frequent exchange of load information and process migration can be avoided. Additionally, in the area of reliable distributed computing, the knowledge of resource commitments can be valuable in reconfiguring a system under failure. To our knowledge, there are no empirical studies which attempt to predict process resource usage in a dynamic sense.

We propose a statistical, pattern-recognition-based approach for predicting the CPU-time, the file-I/O, and the memory usage of a process at the beginning of its life, given the identity of the program being executed. Initially, statistical clustering is used to identify high-density regions of process resource usage for the measured system. The identified regions are used as the states to build

state-transition models to characterize the resource usage of each program in its past executions. The prediction scheme uses the knowledge of a program's resource usage in its last execution and its state-transition model to estimate the resource requirements for the next execution. The scheme is shown to work on process resource-usage data collected from a VAX®11/780 running 4.3 BSD UNIX® [2]. The quality of the prediction is quantified in two ways. First, statistical correlations between the predicted and the actual values are shown. Second, the distributions of the prediction errors are shown and, their characteristics are discussed.

The results of our experiments show that the coefficient of correlation between the predicted CPU-time requirements and the actual values is 0.84. A perfect prediction would give a result of 1.0. The distributions of the prediction errors are heavily skewed towards small values. In other words, even though there are a few large errors, most of the errors are small. For example, over 80 percent of the errors in CPU-time prediction are less than 0.5 standard deviations. In contrast, the variability in CPU-time is large (the difference between 99 and 1 percentiles is about 18 standard deviations).

The remainder of the paper is organized as follows. Section II discusses the motivation for this study and related research; Section III describes the statistics related to process resource usage; Sections IV and V describe the development of the prediction methodology and evaluates its accuracy; Section VI examines the influence of the extent of past knowledge on the prediction error, and Section VII summarizes the paper.

II. BACKGROUND

In this section, the desirability of resource-usage prediction for load-balancing purposes is evaluated. Many load-balancing algorithms have been proposed in the literature (e.g., [6], [3]) and a large number simulation studies have been made (e.g., [5], [1], [11]. Two schemes, which employ actual measurements, are [7] and [12], [13]. In [7], a heuristic algorithm based on an observed linear relationship, between the residual CPU-time of a process and its age, is proposed. The heuristic approximates to a *spiral assignment* of processes, i.e., assuming that the processes are ordered by their age, the

Manuscript received February 12, 1988; revised July 5, 1989. Recommended by W. Royce. This work was supported by the National Aeronautics and Space Administration under NASA Grant NAG-1-613.

M. V. Devarakonda was with the Coordinated Science Laboratory, University of Illinois, Urbana, IL 61801. He is now with the IBM Thomas J. Watson Research Center, Yorktown Heights, NY 10598.

R. K. Iyer is with the Center for Reliable and High Performance Computing, the Coordinated Science Laboratory, and the Department of Electrical and Computer Engineering, University of Illinois, Urbana, IL 61801.

IEEE Log Number 8931157.

®VAX is a registered trademark of Digital Equipment Corporation.
®UNIX is a registered trademark of AT&T Bell Laboratories.

Reprinted from *IEEE Trans. on Software Eng.*, vol. 15, no. 12, Dec. 1989, pp. 1579–1586.

assignment assigns process *i* to processor *i* mod *N*, where *N* is the total number of processors. Although the proposed heuristic (prediction of the CPU-time based on age) holds good on the average, it may not always hold for individual processes.

The load-balancing scheme in [12] is actually a family of algorithms that gathers or propagates load information about a distributed system (depending on whether the algorithm is centralized or decentralized), and uses this information to assign a new job to a processor in a manner that reduces the response time. In a related study [13], it is shown that the process response time strongly depends on the processor load, and that the CPU and I/O queue lengths are good indicators of this load.

Using trace-driven simulations, the above schemes have been shown to reduce process response times. Both algorithms rely on rapid and regular propagation of the global system status to all processors. Since costs associated with such frequent exchanges of load information or process migration can be substantial, proper initial placement of processes based on predicted resource requirements of the processes is particularly attractive. None of the above studies (or any other measurement-based studies) address the question of the predictability of process resource requirements. We propose a statistical approch to predict process resource usage and show that the scheme works on trace-data, collected from a production system.

III. BASIC STATISTICS

The resource-usage data used in this study consists of four resource parameters namely, the CPU-time, the memory used, the logical file-I/O, and the starting (and ending) times, for each UNIX process,[1] collected from a VAX11/780 system running 4.3 BSD UNIX. Data on the CPU-time and the memory usage per process, came from the *rusage* structure maintained by the 4.3 BSD UNIX kernel, and was collected by tracing the *_exit* systemcalls [2]. The process starting and ending times were collected by tracing the *fork* systemcall along with the *_exit*. The file-I/O data, per process, was collected by tracing file-related systemcalls as outlined in [4]. The identity of the program being executed by a process was obtained by tracing *execve* systemcalls. The data was collected for one week and consisted of over 65 000 processes and 2.5 million file *open–close* operations.

Figs. 1–4 show the cumulative distributions of process the CPU-time, the file-I/O, the memory usage and the in-

---

[1] The term process as used in this paper refers to a 4.3BSD UNIX process. In [10], the authors explain how a process is related to an execution of a program.

A process is a program in execution. To execute a new program, a new process is first produced by the *fork* system call, creating two almost identical processes, each with a copy of the original data space. Then the *execve* primitive may be used by one process to replace its virtual memory space with that for a new program (read from a file).

In our measurements, we identified a process with its unique id and time of its creation, and a program by the id of the file (*inode* and device number) that contains its executable code.

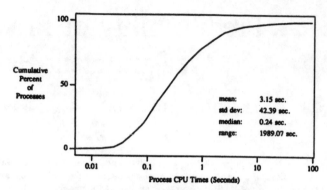

Fig. 1. Distribution of process CPU times.

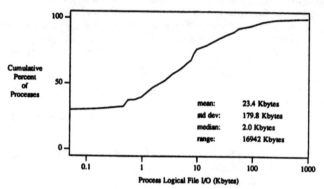

Fig. 2. Distribution of process file I/O.

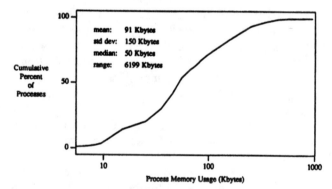

Fig. 3. Distribution of process memory usage.

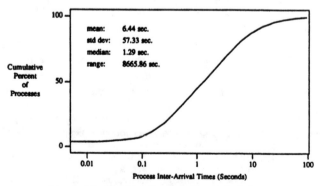

Fig. 4. Distribution of process interarrival times.

terarrival times. The figures show that most processes use only a small amount of CPU-time (median 0.24 seconds), but there are processes that use up to 33 minutes of CPU-time. This large variability in process CPU-times is also apparent from the fact that the standard deviation is over 13 times larger than the mean (the mean is larger than the median by a similar ratio). Figs. 2 and 3 show the file-I/O distribution and memory-usage distributions respectively. Approximately 30 percent of the processes perform no file-I/O at all. Most processes use only a small fraction of the available memory (median memory usage is 50K bytes). The memory-usage distribution also shows the least amount of variability. The mean is less than twice the median, and the ratio of the standard deviation to the mean is also about the same. This characteristic makes the memory usage somewhat easier to predict than the CPU-time.

Even though the process interarrival time (the time between starts of successive processes) is of little consequence to the prediction scheme itself, we discuss its distribution for completeness. As can be seen from Fig. 4, both the mean and median interarrival times are larger than the corresponding statistics for the process CPU-times. This implies that on an average the system utilization is not very high. However, since there are processes with both large CPU-times and small interarrival times, the system is seen to have heavy as well as light usage periods.

IV. RESOURCE USAGE MODELING

In this section, a state-transition model is developed to describe the dynamics of resource usage in a series of processes representing the consecutive executions of a program. The three resource-usage parameters (the CPU-time, the file-I/O, and the memory-used) define a three-dimensional space and the processes that run on the system are represented by points in this three-dimensional space. A statistical clustering algorithm is then employed to identify high-density clusters in this space. The clusters, represented by their centroids, are defined to be the states representing process resource usage, and appropriate transition probabilities from one state to another are determined. The identified state-transition model represents the resource usage of a program in its past executions and is used to predict the program's resource requirements in its future executions.

A. Cluster Analysis

A k-means clustering algorithm is used to partition the three-dimensional population into k clusters. Briefly, the algorithm starts with k clusters, each of which consists of a single random point. New points are added to the cluster with the closest centroid. After all the points are assigned, new centroids are calculated. This process is repeated several times; each time the initial means of the k clusters are set to the means from the previous iteration, until the changes in the cluster-means become negligibly small. More formally, k nonempty clusters, $C_1, C_2, \cdots, C_k$, are sought, such that the sum of the squares of the Euclidean distances of the cluster members, from their centroids, is

minimized [9], i.e.,

$$\text{minimize} \sum_{i=1}^{k} \sum_{j} |x_{ij} - \bar{x}|^2$$

where $x_{ij} \in C_i$ and $\bar{x}_i$ is the centroid of the cluster C_i.

A common problem that arises in calculating the Euclidean distances above is that the measured variables are usually expressed in nonhomogeneous units. To overcome this problem, a standardizing scale change needs to be performed. We use the following standardization in our calculations:

$$z_i = \frac{x_i}{\sigma_d}$$

where z_i is the standardized value of x_i and σ_d is its standard deviation usually calculated after removing the top d percent of the samples (i.e., the outliers). We used $d = 1.5$ for the CPU-time and for file-I/O and $d = 0.5$ for memory usage.[2] The removal of the largest d percent of samples eliminates the influence of the outliers on the standardization, and is helpful in obtaining well-defined clusters. The outliers are however included in the clustering process and in all subsequent uses of the data.

The application of the above algorithm to our data resulted in seven clusters. Table I shows the cluster statistics and the percentage of processes in each cluster. We see from the table that majority of the processes are relatively light resource consumers. Clusters 1 and 7 represent heavy processes, and they account for about 22 percent of the population. Cluster 1 consists of CPU-bound processes, and cluster 7 consists of balanced (CPU as well as I/O) processes. Cluster 2 represents memory-intensive processes.

B. State-Transition Model

Once the clusters are determined, the centroids of the identified clusters form the states for building a state-transition model for program resource usage. For a specific program (e.g., the C-compiler), its past executions are ordered by the terminating times of the processes (where the processes are the executions of the program). Transition probabilities from state i to state j, p_{ij}, are estimating using:

p_{ij}

$$= \frac{\text{observed number of transitions from state } i \text{ to state } j}{\text{observed number of transitions from state } i}.$$

A state-transition model for a program, built using the measured data, is shown in Table II and in Fig. 5. The state-transition model shows a distinct pattern. The transition probabilities from state 5 to itself (0.576) and from state 7 to itself (0.516), are the largest out of states 5 and 7, respectively. Thus, it can be concluded that an execu-

---

[2]The value of d usually depends on the number of outliers in an empirical distribution. They typically range from 1 to 5 percent. We determined the specific values by examining a detailed plot of the empirical distribution for each resource.

TABLE I
CLUSTER STATISTICS

Cluster Number	Cluster Frequency	Cluster Statistics (median values of the resources)		
		CPU (seconds)	File I/O (Kbytes)	Memory (Kbytes)
1	11.26%	4.62	13.870	194.726
2	2.64%	0.25	0.000	446.461
3	6.43%	0.80	8.486	192.444
4	9.42%	0.25	0.732	117.294
5	29.76%	0.07	0.000	16.000
6	29.69%	0.25	2.000	50.238
7	10.77%	1.54	103.804	134.386

TABLE II
STATE-TRANSITION TABLE FOR THE SELECTED PROGRAM

cluster#	1	2	3	4	5	6	7
1	.	.	.	.	.	.	.
2	.	0.250	.	.	0.250	.	0.500
3	.	.	.	.	.	.	.
4	.	.	.	0.410	0.205	0.154	0.231
5	.	0.003	.	0.038	0.576	0.050	0.333
6	.	0.018	.	0.036	0.382	0.109	0.455
7	.	0.003	.	0.031	0.357	0.093	0.516

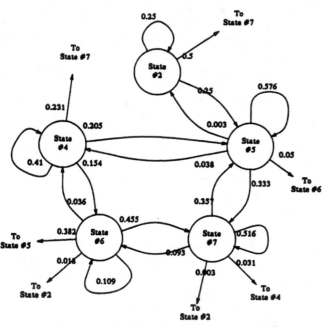

Fig. 5. State-transition diagram for the selected program.

tion of the modeled program is likely to be in state 5 or 7, and in addition, once an execution occurs in one of the states it tends to remain there. Such patterns suggest predictability. Further, states (clusters) 1 and 3 are not used by this program, indicating that not all the defined states are used by all programs.

For some series of processes, the specific transitions into and out of a given state may be too few to be statistically significant. In such cases it is preferable to use visit-ratios. We define the visit-ratio for a given state as the ratio of the number of occurrences of the state to the total number of processes (executions) in the series. Table III shows the visit-ratios for the series of processes represented in Fig. 5. States 5 and 7, visited with probabilities 0.450 and 0.412, are clearly the most frequently visited states.

TABLE III
VISIT RATIOS FOR THE SELECTED PROGRAM

cluster#	1	2	3	4	5	6	7
ratio	-	0.005	-	0.056	0.450	0.077	0.412

V. A PROGRAM-BASED RESOURCE PREDICTION SCHEME

Now that we have a state-transition model for representing the dynamics of resource usage, we describe its use in prediction. The particular scheme described here is a program-based approach; it predicts the resources required by a process, given the identity of the program and the resource usage of the program in its past executions.

In practice, an upper as well as a lower limit on the number of processes is used in building the state-transition model. The upper limit, enforced via a parameter T_1, restricts the number of past executions used, and thus makes the model reflect a desired level of dynamic behavior. The exact number of past executions used is $\min(m, T_1)$, where m is the actual number of past executions of the program. The lower limit on the number of processes guarantees that the resource-usage model is stable enough to make a prediction. A parameter T_2 in the prediction algorithm provides this lower limit. The choice of T_1 and T_2 is discussed in Section VI-B.

If the number of transitions into and out of a state are less than a specified minimum (i.e., too small to be significant), the prediction algorithm uses visit-ratios instead of the transition probabilities to compute resource requirements. A parameter T_3 is used to specify this minimum; it ensures that a state has a statistically significant number of entries and exits for calculating the transition probabilities.

The procedure for computing the predicted process resource requirements can be explained as follows. For each program, its past executions are considered to be subclusters within the defined clusters. The midpoint of each subcluster is calculated from the most recent executions of a program that belongs to a specific cluster. The process resource requirements are then obtained by multiplying the transition probabilities, $p_{lj}, j = 1, 2, \cdots, N$ with the midpoints d_{jk} ($j = 1, \cdots, N, k = $ CPU, or I/O, or MEM), of the subclusters:

$$r_k = \sum_{j=1}^{N} p_{lj} \times d_{jk}, \quad k = \text{CPU, or I/O, or MEM.}$$

Note that d_{jk} are specific to a cluster as well as to a program. A parameter T_4 is used to specify the minimum number of past executions to be used in computing d_{jk}. In our implementation, T_4 was set equal to 1. The overall protection scheme is summarized in Fig. 6. Parameter values used in our implementation of the scheme are shown in parentheses.

1) How Good Is the Prediction? In order to determine prediction quality using the proposed scheme, a trace-driven prediction experiment was conducted. The experiment consisted of predicting process resource require-

Parameters:
T_1 Maximum number of past executions used in building the model (all).
T_2 Minimum number of past executions required to make a prediction (3).
T_3 Minimum number of visits to a state needed, to use the transition probabilities of the state ($max(T_2,\ 5\%\ of\ min(m, T_1))$).
T_4 Number of past executions used in computing subcluster centroids (1).

Constants:
N Number of clusters (7).

Variables:
l Cluster number to which the previous execution belonged.
m Number of completed executions of the program so far.

Data structures:
$[p_{i,j}]$ State-transition matrix. $i = 1, ..., N$, and $j = 1, ..., N$.

$[v_i]$ Visit ratios. $i = 1, ..., N$.

$[z_{i,j,k}]$ Resources used in previous T_4 executions. $i = 1, ..., N$, $j = CPU, I/O,$ or MEM, and $k = 1, ..., T_4$.

$[c_{i,j}]$ Cluster medians. $i = 1, ..., N$, $j = CPU, I/O,$ or MEM.

Computations:

$$d_{i,j} = \begin{cases} \dfrac{1}{T_4}\sum_{k=1}^{T_4} z_{i,j,k} & \text{if } T_4 > 0 \\[2mm] c_{i,j} & \text{if } T_4 = 0 \end{cases} \qquad i = 1, ..., N, \text{ and } j = CPU, I/O, \text{ and } MEM$$

$$r_j = \begin{cases} \sum_{i=1}^{N}[\,p_{l,i} \times d_{i,j}\,] & \text{if } min(m, T_1) \geqslant T_3 \\[2mm] \sum_{i=1}^{N}[\,v_i \times d_{i,j}\,] & \text{if } min(m, T_1) < T_3 \end{cases} \qquad j = CPU, I/O, \text{ or } MEM$$

Fig. 6. Summary of the program-based prediction scheme.

ments just prior to the commencement of the process. The difference between the predicted and the actual resource-usage values was calculated after the process terminated. This section discusses results of this experiment.

For some processes, resource prediction was not possible owing to the lack of sufficient number of past executions. However, both the percentage of such processes and the CPU-time consumed by them were small. For example, with $T_1 = 3$, less than 4 percent of the processes could not be predicted, and these processes consumed only 8 percent of the CPU-time.

The quality of the prediction was measured in two ways. First, the product-moment (Pearson) and the rank (Spearman) correlations [8] between the predicted and the actual values were calculated. The Pearson correlation coefficient measures the strength of the linear relationship between two quantities, and the Spearman rank correlation measures the correlation between the ranks (ordered sets) of the two quantities. In our case Spearman's rank correlation was a better indicator (because we are not necessarily looking for a linear relationship here). Table IV shows that the Pearson correlation coefficient was over 0.84 for both the CPU-time and memory was small (about 0.20) for file-I/O. The Spearman correlation coefficient, however, ranged from 0.81 to 0.89 for all the resources. Thus, we can conclude that not only do the predicted and the actual values generally correlate well, but that the ordered values (i.e., the high and the low) also correlate well.

Next, the distributions of the prediction errors were examined. A standardized value of the prediction error was defined as the ratio of the absolute difference between the

TABLE IV
CORRELATIONS BETWEEN ACTUAL AND PREDICTED RESOURCE USAGE VALUES

Resource	Correlation Coefficients	
	Rank (Spearman) Correlation	Product-Moment (Pearson) Correlation
CPU Time	0.8379	0.8406
File I/O	0.8105	0.1974
Memory	0.8925	0.8834

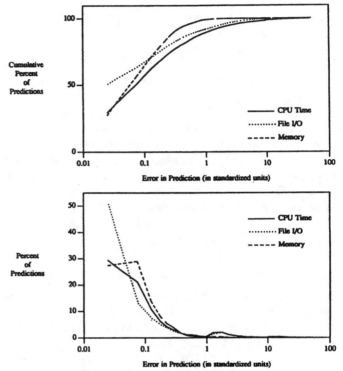

Fig. 7. Distributions of prediction errors.

predicted and the actual resource usage to the standard deviation of the actual resource usage.[3] Fig. 7 shows distributions of prediction errors for the CPU-time, the file-I/O, and the memory usage.[4] It can be seen that error distributions are skewed toward small values. For example, over 80 percent of errors in the predicted CPU-time are less than 0.5 standard deviations. The error in predicting memory usage is the smallest.

[3]In reality, the standard error is given by $(e - \hat{e})/\sigma_R$. In our measurement, $\hat{e}$ was small enough to be set to zero. We also considered other measures of prediction quality but rejected them on the grounds that they are not suited for the domain we are concerned with. For example, it might seem like a good idea to express the errors as percentages of the actual, and show a distribution of the percentages. However, since the smallest amount of resource a process can use is 0, when a predicted value is smaller than actual, prediction error can be 0–100 percent, but when a predicted value is larger than actual, prediction error is potentially unbounded. This distorted view of error can lead to a misleading perception that a scheme that makes a few large over-estimations is worse than a scheme that consistently underestimates.

[4]Since the memory usage is the physical memory allocated by the operating system, a reasonable question is how the prediction is affected by the variations in system load. In our system, although there was some correlation between the allocated memory and the system load but this was not significant enough to affect predictions [4].

TABLE V
PREDICTION ERRORS AND ACTUAL RESOURCE USAGE VALUES

Resource		Statistic (in standardized units)	
		Median	99th Percentile
CPU Time	Error	0.073	16.24
	Actual	0.168	18.23
File I/O	Error	0.024	6.13
	Actual	0.051	7.26
Memory	Error	0.059	0.97
	Actual	0.447	3.61

Table V shows the median values of the standardized errors. It is clear from the table that the error distribution has much less variability in comparison with the distribution of the actual values. For example, the median value of the error is less than one half of the actual (median standardized error in CPU-time prediction = 0.073). Since the variability in the measured CPU-time is large, (approximately 18 standard deviations, as measured by the difference between 99 percentile and 1 percentile), we believe that this error is acceptable. A comparison of the means and variances of the predicted and the actual values also showed a close match. This combined with the fact that 80 percent of errors are less than 0.5 standard deviation shows that the predicted values follow the actual with a reasonable degree of accuracy.

VI. ADDITIONAL IMPLEMENTATION ISSUES

Here, we discuss two issues related to implementation of the prediction scheme:

1) The influence of program execution frequency on accuracy of the prediction;

2) The influence of maximum and minimum past knowledge on prediction quality.

A. The Influence of Program Execution Frequency

In order to measure the impact of the execution frequency of a program, each program was categorized as type 0, 1, 2, or 3 based on the total number of executions of the program during the measured period. Using the trace-driven experiment described in the previous section, the prediction quality was quantified for each program type. The results are shown in Table VI. Type 0 consists of programs that are executed three times or less during the measured period. The remaining three types are defined as shown in the table.

Table VI shows that approximately about 36 percent of all programs belong to type 0, and about 21 percent of the programs belong to each of the remaining types. The processes resulting from type 0 programs, however, constitute only 2.7 percent of total processes. In comparison, processes resulting from type 3 programs are over 92 percent of the total. Programs of type 1 and 2 provide 0.8 and 4.4 percent of the processes, respectively. Clearly, a small fraction of programs are executed very frequently (i.e., 21 percent of the programs are executed 92 percent of the time).

TABLE VI
IMPACT OF PROGRAM EXECUTION FREQUENCY

Item	Type #0 programs	Type #1 programs	Type #2 programs	Type #3 programs
Number of executions	1 thru 3	4 thru 8	9 thru 45	46 or more
Percent programs	36.4%	21.2%	21.0%	21.4%
Percent processes	2.7%	0.8%	4.4%	92.1%
Correlation of predicted and actual CPU times	-	0.803	0.794	0.879
Median CPU time (in std. units)	-	0.488	0.595	0.160
Median pred. error (in std. units)	-	0.099	0.238	0.069

For type 3 programs, the coefficient of correlation between the predicted and the actual CPU-times is 0.879, and for types 1 and 2, the coefficient is about 0.8. The strong observed correlations are an indication of the high quality of prediction for processes generated by programs with more than three executions. Table VI also shows the median values for the process CPU-times and the associated prediction errors for each program type. The CPU-time is the largest for processes resulting from type 2 programs, and the prediction errors follow the CPU-time pattern. In summary, the prediction quality is essentially independent of the execution frequency of a program.

B. The Influence of Maximum and Minimum Past Used

1) Maximum Past Knowledge: To determine the influence of the maximum past information used in prediction (parameter T_1), the trace-driven experiment described in a previous section was repeated several times, each time with a different value for the maximum number of the past executions used in building the resource-usage model. The value of the minimum past used, T_2 was kept fixed at 1. The mean error[5] in the predicted CPU-time, obtained from these experiments, is shown in Fig. 8 for the maximum past ranging from 1 through 300 executions.

The figure shows that the mean error decreases as the maximum past is increased. The rate of improvement saturates around a value of 100. Note, however, that a change in the maximum past from 1 to 300 reduces the error in CPU-time prediction by only 7 percent.

An examination of the error distributions for different values of maximum past shows that when the maximum number of past executions is small (e.g., $T_1 = 1$), the prediction is overly sensitive to local variations in the resource-usage pattern. With $T_1 = 1$, the error distributions are heavily skewed towards small values and have very long tails. In comparison, when a large maximum past (e.g., 200) is used, the errors are more evenly distributed between the large and the small values. The appropriate

---

[5] As before, the error is shown in the same normalized units as the actual process CPU-time, which is obtained using (4.1).

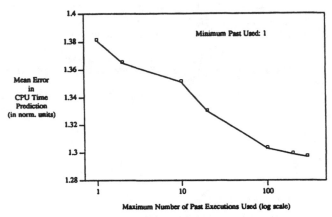

Fig. 8. Effect of maximum-past on prediction error.

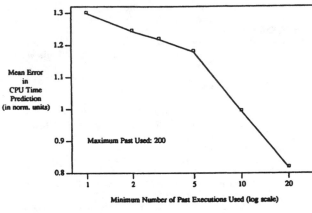

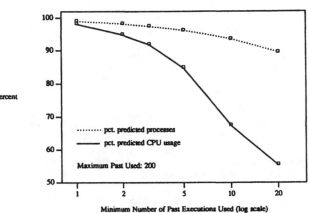

Fig. 9. Effect of minimum-past on prediction error.

value for T_1 should be determined via experimentation and would depend on the relative importance of the outliers vis-a-vis the core distribution. We found that $T_1 = 200$ gave satisfactory results for the measured system.

2) Minimum Past Used: Next, the effect of varying the minimum past used (parameter T_2), on the prediction quality was examined. The trace-driven experiments were repeated, this time with different values for the minimum past, while keeping the maximum past fixed at 200. The results of these experiments are shown in Fig. 9.

The figure shows that the mean error[6] in CPU-time prediction drops dramatically as the minimum past is increased from 1 to 20 executions. However, unlike the changes in the maximum past, increasing the minimum past has undesirable side-effects: it decreases the percentage of processes that can be predicted as well as the percentage of the predicted CPU-usage. For example, as the minimum past is increased from 1 to 20, the percentage of the predicted processes drops by 9 percent, and the percentage of the predicted CPU-usage drops by 43 percent. Our experience shows that a compromise value of 3, for T_2, produces satisfactory results. With $T_2 = 3$, over 90 percent of the CPU-usage and over 95 percent of the processes can be predicted.

VII. Summary

This paper has described a statistical scheme for predicting the CPU-time, the file-I/O, and the memory usage of a process at the beginning of its life, given the identity of the program being executed. The scheme determines the specific state-transitions of each program in its past executions, and then uses the current state information together with the state-transition model to compute the resource requirements for the next execution. The prediction scheme was shown to work on process resource-usage data collected from a VAX11/780 running 4.3BSD UNIX.

The results of the trace-driven experiment show that the predicted values correlate strongly (correlation coefficient of 0.84) with the actual. Further, an investigation of the error distributions showed that the errors in prediction are mostly small and are usually skewed toward small values.

More recently, we have used the prediction scheme proposed in this paper as a basis for developing several centralized load-sharing policies [14]. Performance comparisons to conventional methods show that the use of prediction results in improvements in response times of up to 35 percent for the systems studied. In addition, it makes the load-sharing policies significantly less dependent on the status-update rate and on wide variations in load.

Acknowledgment

The authors would like to thank their colleagues at the Center for Reliable and High Performance Computing for many useful comments and suggestions during the course of this work. Particular thanks are due to R. Llames, S. Peterson, and D. Jabusch for their invaluable assistance in the preparation of this manuscript.

References

[1] A. Barak and A. Litman, "A distributed load balancing policy for a multicomputer," *Software—Practice and Experience*, vol. 15, no. 8, Aug. 1985.
[2] *UNIX Programmer's Manual: Reference Guide*, 4.3 Berkeley Software Distribution, Virtual VAX-11 Version, Dep. Elec. Eng. Comput. Sci., Univ. California, Berkeley, 1986.

---

[6]Once again, the error is shown in the same standardized units as the actual process CPU-times, which is obtained using (4.1).

[3] R. Bryant and R. Finkel, "A stable distributed scheduling algorithm," in *Proc. Second. Int. Conf. Distributed Computing Systems*, IEEE Comput. Soc., Los Alamitos, CA, Apr. 1981.

[4] M. Devarakonda, "File usage analysis and process resource usage prediction: A measurement based study," Univ. Illinois at Urbana-Champaign, Tech. Rep., Dec. 1987.

[5] D. Eager, E. Lazowska, and J. Zahorjan, "Dynamic load sharing in homogeneous distributed systems," *IEEE Trans. Software Eng.*, vol. SE-12, no. 5, May 1986.

[6] K. Hwang, W. Croft, G. Goble, W. Wah, F. Briggs, W. Simmons, and C. Coates, "A UNIX-based local computer network with load balancing," *Computer*, vol. 15, no. 4, Apr. 1982.

[7] W. Leland and T. Ott, "Load-balancing heuristics and process behavior," in *Proc. Performance '86 and ACM SIGMETRICS Conf.*, Raleigh, NC, May 1986.

[8] W. Mendenhall and T. Sincich, *Statistics for the Engineering and Computer Sciences* San Francisco, CA: 1984.

[9] H. Spath, *Cluster Analysis Algorithms*. West Sussex, England: Ellis Horwood, 1980.

[10] J. S. Quarterman, A. Silbershatz, and J. L. Peterson, "4.2BSD and 4.3BSD as examples of the UNIX system," *ACM Comput. Surveys*, vol. 17, no. 4, Dec. 1985.

[11] Y.-T. Wang and R. Morris, "Load sharing in distributed systems," *IEEE Trans. Comput.*, vol. C-34, no. 3, Mar. 1985.

[12] S. Zhou, "A trace-driven simulation study of dynamic load balancing," Univ. California, Berkeley, Tech. Rep. UCB/CSD87/305, Sept. 1986.

[13] ——, "An experimental assessment of resource queue length as load in indices," Univ. California, Berkeley, Tech. Rep. UCB/CSD 86/298, Sept. 1986.

[14] K. K. Goswami, R. K. Iyer, and M. V. Devarakonda, "Load sharing based on task resource prediction," in *Proc. 22nd Annu. Hawaii Int. Conf. System Sciences*, Kona, HI, Jan. 1989.

Murthy V. Devarankonda received the B.E. degree from Osmania University, India, the M.Tech. degree from the Indian Institute of Technology, India, the M.S. degree from the University of Wisconsin–Madison, and the Ph.D. degree in computer science from the University of Illinois at Urbana-Champaign in 1987.

He is a Research Staff Member at IBM Thomas J. Watson Research Center, Yorktown Heights, NY, where he is currently involved in the development of new heuristics for performance improvement in host-connected workstations and in large mainframes. His research interests include file systems, workstation networks, performance measurement, data analysis, UNIX kernel design, and UNIX-based distributed and parallel systems.

Dr. Devarankonda is a member of the Association for Computing Machinery.

Ravishankar K. Iyer (S'76–M'77–SM'89) recived the B.E. and Ph.D. degrees from the University of Queensland, Brisbane, Australia, in 1973 and 1977, respectively.

From 1979 to 1983 he was with the Center for Reliable Computing, Computer Systems Laboratory, Departments of Electrical Engineering and Computer Science, Stanford University. Since the Fall of 1983 he has been at the University of Illinois at Urbana-Champaign, where he is currently Professor of Electrical and Computer Engineering, Computer Science, and Research Professor in the Coordinated Science Laboratory. His is Co-Director of the Illinois Computer Laboratory for Aerospace Systems and Software, a NASA Center of Excellence in Aerospace Computing and Director of the Center for Reliable and High Performance Computing. His research interests are in the area of reliable and fault-tolerant computing, measurement, experimentation, and statistical modeling.

Dr. Iyer is a member of the Association for Computing Machinery, Sigma Xi, and IFIP Working Group (10.4) on fault tolerant computing. He has served on several program committees and was General Chair of the 19th International Symposium on Fault-Tolerant Computing (FTCS-19). He is also a consultant to industry in the area of reliable computing.

AN EMPIRICAL INVESTIGATION OF LOAD INDICES
FOR LOAD BALANCING APPLICATIONS

Domenico Ferrari and Songnian Zhou

Computer Systems Research Group
Computer Science Division
Department of Electrical Engineering and Computer Sciences
University of California, Berkeley 94720
USA†

In this paper, we empirically evaluate the quality of several load indices in the context of dynamic load balancing. We have implemented a load balancer for Sun/UNIX‡ environments. In our experimental setup, six Sun-2 workstations were driven by job scripts, and job response times were measured while loads were being balanced and various load indices used to make job placement decisions. We study the effects on performance of the choice of load index, the averaging interval, the load information exchange period, and the characteristics of the workload. Measurements show that the performance benefits of load balancing are indeed strongly dependent upon the load index. Load indices based on resource queue lengths are found to perform better than those based on resource utilization, and the use of an exponential smoothing method yields further improvement over that of instantaneous queue lengths.

1. INTRODUCTION

In a loosely-coupled distributed system, the potential for resource sharing and its possible rewards are substantial. Two frequently cited advantages of resource sharing are the larger number of accessible resources, in terms of both type and quantity, and the higher reliability that may result from the multiplicity of available resources. In order to share these resources effectively, however, some measure of the loads being imposed on the resources has to be made available to the clients. The information about resource loads is part of the system's state, and is among the most rapidly changing aspects of it. Since the loads are likely to be changing all the time, load information tends to become stale rapidly. To quantify the concept of load, we use a *load index*, which preferably is a non-negative variable taking on a zero value if the resource is idle, and increasing positives values as the load increases. This paper is concerned with the quality of the possible load indices for hosts in a particular but important application of load indices, that of load balancing in distributed systems.

A job arriving at a host will very likely demand services from a number of resources (e.g., CPU and disks). Hence, it is important to define not only the load on a single resource in a host, but also that of the host viewed as a collection of resources. Since the resource consumption patterns of the jobs are likely to be different, it may not be meaningful to talk about "the load" of the host. For example, the CPU may be heavily congested, while the disks are not. In this case, to an incoming CPU-bound job the host's load is very high, whereas to an incoming

---

† This work was partially sponsored by the Defense Advanced Research Projects Agency (DoD), Arpa Order No. 4871, monitored by Space and Naval Warfare Systems Command under Contract No. N00039-84-C-0089, and by the National Science Foundation under grant DMC-8503575. The views and conclusions contained in this document are those of the authors and should not be interpreted as representing official policies, either expressed or implied, of the Defense Research Projects Agency or of the US Government.

‡ UNIX is a trademark of AT&T Bell Laboratories.

I/O-bound job the host's load is low because it will not experience much queueing at the disks. This observation is formalized in [1], where a job type-dependent load index based on the resource queue lengths is proposed and experimentally evaluated.

Load information is important since it can serve as the basis of the efforts to improve the system's performance by redistributing the loads. It is frequently observed that, in a distributed system, the loads of the hosts are not evenly distributed all the time. Livny and Melman pointed out that, for a queueing system consisting of multiple homogeneous service centers with Poisson arrivals of identical rates, the probability of some hosts being idle while some others have more than one job can be very significant; hence, redistributing the workload among the resources has the potential of improving performance [2].

In order to evaluate the quality of a load index for load balancing, we specify a number of criteria, or desirable properties. These criteria, in turn, are dependent on the objective of load balancing, i.e., the *performance index* that is to be optimized by balancing the loads. In this research, we are mostly concerned with interactive computing environments, where the job response time and its predictability are very important measures of system performance. Therefore, we use the mean job response time as our performance index, supplemented by the standard deviation of the response times. A good load index should:

1) be able to reflect our qualitative estimates of the current load on a host;

2) be usable to predict the load in the near future, since the response time of a job will be affected more by the future load than by the present load;

3) be relatively stable; i.e., high-frequency fluctuations in the load should be discounted, or ignored;

4) have a simple (ideally, linear) relationship with the performance index, so that its value can be easily translated into that of the expected performance.

We recognize that it is difficult, perhaps impossible, to find a load index that satisfies all of the above requirements, as they may even turn out to be contradictory. But a load index may be judged by the degree to which it meets the above criteria.

A number of load indices have been proposed in the past, most of them related to the load balancing problem. In this paper, we conduct an empirical comparison study of a number of those indices, and attempt to rationalize and generalize our observations. The experimental environment we use includes a load balancer running on diskless Sun/UNIX workstations. By driving the workstations with job scripts and by using different load indices, we were able to measure the mean response times and compare them. In the next section, we examine the types of load index proposed and used in the past. The load balancer and the workloads we used are described in Section 3. In Section 4, we discuss the design of the experiments and their results. The major results are summarized in Section 5.

2. LOAD INDICES

A wide variety of load indices have been explicitly or implicitly used in the literature, mostly in load balancing schemes. For example, in most of the studies using queueing network analysis, as well as some in other studies, the CPU queue length was used as the load index [2, 3, 4, 5, 6, 7, 8]. Some other authors used the CPU utilization [9, 10]. Other possibilities include the normalized response time [11] (defined as the ratio between the response time of a process on a loaded machine and its response time on the same machine when it is empty), the remaining processing time of all the jobs running on a host, the processing time accumulated by the active processes [12], and the total processing time of the active processes [13]. Functions of the above simple variables have also been used [1, 10, 14]. In a number of studies in which reducing job response time was the objective of load balancing, the estimated response time was used as the load index [15, 16]. Performance improvements were often reported using the indices discussed above. However, since no systematic and comprehensive comparisons between the indices have been made, their relative merits remain unclear. We note with regret that, in most cases, the authors did not even provide a scientific justification for the choice of the load index.

The first systematic attempt to study the load indices to be used in load balancing was made in [1]. Based on mean value analysis, a linear combination of resource queue lengths was proposed as a load index. In that linear combination, the coefficient of a resource queue length is the amount of service time that the particular job being considered requires from that resource. Thus, if an incoming job requires s_j seconds of service from resource r_j, and the queue length of resource r_j is q_j, then the load index li of the host, *as perceived by this job*, is

$$li = \sum_{j=1}^{N} s_j \times q_j$$

where N is the total number of resources for which there is queueing in the host. This index was evaluated with measurement experiments under a production time-sharing workload [17].

The index introduced in [1] is response time oriented, and job dependent. Instead of a unique value at a particular moment in time, the load of a host differs for different jobs because of their varying resource demands, which are assumed to be known upon job arrival. This assumption enables us to predict the response time of a job more accurately, hence to make better load balancing decision. However, while we have found some simple relationships between the arguments of a job and the job's resource demands [18], the assumption that the demands of a job are known in advance may be too strong in many cases. In this study, we investigate versions of the same load index in which the coefficients of the resource queue lengths are *job independent*, and only reflect the relative importance of the resources (with respect to a "basket" of jobs) For example, we can use unity as the coefficients to reduce the linear combination to the sum of the resource queue lengths, that is, in queueing modeling terms, "the number of jobs (or processes) in the system."

Our extensive measurements of production time-sharing workload show that the system load is changing quite rapidly [17]. On top of a low-frequency main component, there are a number of high-frequency load components that may be regarded as "noise" rather than useful information. Using the instantaneous resource queue lengths may give excessive importance to such noise and lead to bad job transfer decisions. We used a smoothing algorithm to compute the time-averaged queue length and compared load balancing performance using smoothed queue lengths to that of the same scheme using instantaneous queue lengths.

3. SYSTEM AND WORKLOAD

In this section, we describe the experimental environment in which the measurements were taken, and the workloads used to drive the system.

3.1. System

We implemented a dynamic load balancer for Sun/UNIX environments. The structure of the system is shown in Figure 1†. The UNIX user interface program, *csh*, is modified so that the commands typed in by the user are intercepted, and some of them are transferred to some remote host for execution when the local host is heavily loaded‡. At startup time, the C-shell reads in a configuration file that specifies a list of job types that are eligible for remote execution*. When an eligible job is submitted by the user to the C-shell, the C-shell contacts the local *Load Information Manager* (LIM), a software module that constantly exchanges load information with its peers on other hosts and performs job placements. If the local host is heavily loaded, while some other hosts are not, one of the remote hosts is selected as the destination for the job. In any case, the placement decision is returned to the C-shell.

---

† To distinguish our modified C shell from the standard one [19], we call it *C-shell*. The *R-shell*, to be described below, shares the same software with the C-shell, but its only function is to receive remote jobs and execute them.

‡ Our system is based on a modified C shell implemented at Berkeley by Harry Rubin and Venkat Rangan for the Berkeley UNIX 4.3 BSD system running on VAX machines [20, 21].

* This list is part of the context of each user, just like command aliases, and may be dynamically modified by the user to suit his or her needs.

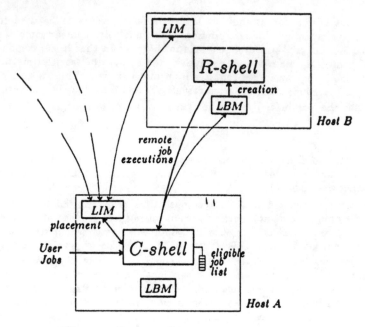

Figure 1. Structure of the load balancer.

For remote execution, the C-shell contacts the *Load Balancing Manager* (LBM) on the destination host, which starts up an R-shell and establishes a stream connection between it and the home C-shell. The command line is transmitted over this connection to the R-shell after the user's identity has been authenticated, and an appropriate user environment set up there. Access control to files and other resources in the system is automatically enforced as the R-shell assumes the same user identity as that of the home C-shell. Since starting an R-shell is an expensive operation (several seconds of real time), we keep such a shell alive after the execution of the first job so that, if a later command from the same user login session is placed on the same host, we do not have to go through the same process described above. The R-shells on remote hosts act as agents for the home C-shell, and are terminated when the home C-shell exits. This scheme has the potential problem of R-shell proliferation. However, the code segments of all C-shells and R-shells on each host are shared, so that, when an R-shell is not active, almost no resources are consumed. Since files are retrieved from file servers, as the workstations are diskless, only the command line needs to be shipped, and the cost of file access is essentially the same from all hosts.

Load balancing algorithms have a strong influence on performance. We implemented and studied a number of algorithms using different methods for load information exchange and job placement [14]. For this study of load indices, however, we just selected one of the best realizable algorithms, that is, the one we called GLOBAL. For every time period P, the LIM on each host extracts load information from the local kernel to compute the local host's load index. If the new value of the load index is significantly different from the previous one, the new value is sent to the *master* LIM, which collects load information from every host and broadcasts the entire load vector in each period P. When a job whose name is on the eligibility list is submitted to a host, the local LIM is contacted for job placement. If the local load is high, the host perceived by the local LIM to have the least load is selected, and the job is sent there.

The implementation described above provides a transparent, low-cost, and general-purpose load balancer whose installation requires no changes to the kernel† or to the application programs. Since the emphasis of this paper is on the measurement experiments we performed on the system, we will not describe the design and implementation issues in more detail. The interested reader is referred to [14].

---

† For our experiments, to obtain accurate values of resource queue lengths and to perform the smoothing operations efficiently, some code had to be added to the kernel. No functional changes were made, however.

3.2. Workload

Workload characterization and selection are crucial to a measurement study. Although artificial workloads considerably increase the repeatability of experiments, they ought to represent natural workloads reasonably well, so as to strengthen our confidence in the results. We traced a production VAX-11/780 machine running under the Berkeley UNIX 4.3BSD system [20, 21] for an extended period of several months, and analyzed the types and frequencies of the commands executed by the system. On the basis of such an analysis, we selected 30 frequently executed commands, listed in Table 1, and used them to construct job scripts, i.e., sequences of commands.

To obtain various levels, or intensities, of a host's load, we ran a variable number of jobs in the background. The artificial workloads were not intended to represent the typical workloads of personal workstations, but rather those of small (i.e., not very powerful) time-sharing systems. Workstations were used because of their being available in our distributed systems laboratory. We simulated user think times by the "sleep" command. The scripts are classified into three levels: light (L), moderate (M), and heavy (H), with a number of distinct scripts constructed for each level, so that hosts subjected to the same level of workload always use different scripts. The ranges of CPU utilization and average CPU queue length values of the three levels of scripts are shown in Table 2. Each script runs for about 30 minutes on a Sun-2 workstation. Job and system performance statistics, such as resource demands, response times, resource utilizations, and resource queue lengths, were measured throughout each run. We used six Sun-2 workstations in our experiments.

As in any measurement experiment, we must consider the variability of the experimental environment, and therefore that of the measurement results. In dynamic load balancing, the placement of each job may vary from one run of the experiment to the next, because of the unavoidable variations in the timings of the events. This problem was further complicated in our experiments by the fact that we had to share the file server and the network with other parts of the research community. We tried to minimize this impact by running the experiments during the night. We repeated each experiment a number of times (typically 6), and computed the mean and the 90% confidence interval (CI) of the values of the performance indices over these replications.

Table 1. Commands used in scripts and their eligibilities for remote execution

command	elig.	function	command	elig.	function
cat	N	view a file	ls	N	directory listing
cc	Y	C compiler	man	Y	manual page viewing
cp	N	file copying	mv	N	move a file
date	N	current time	nroff	Y	text formatter
df	N	file system usage	ps	N	process checking
ditroff	Y	text formatter	pwd	N	current directory
du	N	disk usage	rm	N	delete a file
egrep	Y	text pattern search	sort	N	file sorting
eqn	Y	equation formatter	spell	Y	spelling checker
fgrep	Y	text pattern search	tbl	Y	table formatter
finger	N	user information	troff	Y	text formatter
grep	Y	text pattern search	uptime	N	system uptime
grn	Y	graph printing	users	N	list of current users
lint	Y	C program checker	wc	N	word count in a file
lpq	N	printer queue check	who	N	user information

491

Table 2. Characterization of the workload levels

type	CPU utilization	average load index
light (L)	30-45%	0.3-0.7
moderate (M)	60-70%	1.0-1.8
heavy (H)	70-85%	1.8-3.0

4. DESIGN AND RESULTS OF THE EXPERIMENTS

4.1. Experimental Factors

Four factors were identified to be of interest in the study of load indices:

1) *Load index*. We used as load indices the following quantities: the instantaneous CPU queue length; exponentially averaged CPU queue length; the sum of averaged CPU, file and paging/swapping I/O, and memory queue lengths†; and the average CPU utilization over a recent period. Inside the kernel, we kept variables for the queue length of each resource type. The length of each queue was sampled every 10 ms by the clock interrupt routine, and used to compute the one-second average queue length, q_i. Exponential smoothing was used to compute the average queue length over the last T seconds:

$$Q_i = Q_{i-1}(1-e^{-T}) + q_i e^{-T}, \qquad i \geq 1$$

$$Q_0 = 0$$

2) *Averaging interval T*. For exponentially smoothed values of a resource queue length, and for the average CPU utilization, the interval T over which the average is computed conceivably affects the quality of the index, and hence the system's performance.

3) *Workload*. There may be interactions between the load index chosen and the workload the system is subjected to. Using the three suites of host workloads described in the previous section, we were able to construct several combinations of system workload for the six workstations in our system. The canonical workload consisted of two heavy, two moderate, and two light scripts (2H, 2M, 2L). We also studied the indices under a more balanced workload, with all six workstations driven by moderate scripts (6M).

4) *Exchange interval P*. The GLOBAL algorithm employs periodic updates of load information. If P is too short, the overhead may be too high, but, if P is too long, then job placements are based on stale information, and performance may deteriorate, and system instability may result.

4.1. Measurement Results

We shall first study the indices and the averaging interval T by fixing the workload at its canonical level, and the exchange interval at 10 seconds. We will then use the more balanced workload 6M to examine the interactions between load indices and workload. Finally, we will study the effect of load exchange interval P on performance.

Table 3 shows the performance under various load indices. The numbers following the response time values indicate their 90% confidence intervals.

The indices can be divided into two categories: those based on resource queue length and those based on resource utilization. For each category, we can do the averaging over intervals of varying lengths.

We see in Table 3 that all the indices provide performance improvement, that is, they all contain some amount of *current* load information. The amount of improvement, however, varies quite widely: from 20% to 40%. This means that the performance of load balancing is heavily dependent on the load index used,

---

† For simplicity, we treated the disk queues as a single aggregate queue for I/O operations. For the memory queue, we identified a number of places inside the kernel where processes queue up for various types of memory resources e g, buffer space, page table, and treated all these as a single memory queue.

Table 3. Measured performance with various indices
(Canonical workload, $P = 10$ s)

replication count: 6
total number of jobs per run: 501
total number of eligible jobs per run: 254 (50.7%)
total number of processes per run: 766 (1.53 processes/job)
average process execution time: 7.45 s
approximate average CPU utilization for NoLB case: 60%

Load Index	Resp. Time	Improv.	Std. Dev.	Improv.
NoLB (no load bal.)	53.3 ±0.83	---	90.1	---
inst. CPU ql	35.0 ±0.68	34.4%	46.7	46.7%
1 s avg CPU ql	33.8 ±0.65	36.6%	45.8	49.2%
4 s avg CPU ql	33.1 ±0.39	37.9%	42.3	48.7%
4 s CPU+I/O+Mem ql	32.2 ±0.45	39.6%	44.3	50.9%
20 s avg CPU ql	37.0 ±1.20	30.6%	51.8	42.6%
20s CPU+I/O+Mem ql	35.6 ±0.12	33.3%	49.1	45.6%
60 s avg CPU ql	39.7 ±1.69	25.5%	54.1	40.0%
60s CPU+I/O+Mem ql	40.0 ±0.56	25.0%	56.2	37.6%
60 s UNIX load average	37.2 ±0.85	30.2%	54.9	39.1%
10 s CPU utilization	38.5 ±2.10	27.8%	55.4	38.5%
60 s CPU utilization	42.9 ±1.36	19.5%	67.6	25.0%

and hence studying load indices is important. Comparing the two categories, the indices based on resource queue lengths are able to perform substantially better. This is probably because, when a host is heavily loaded, its CPU utilization is likely to be close to 100%; thus, in that region, the exact load level cannot be reflected by the value of the utilization. In contrast, queue lengths can directly reflect the amount of contention for a resource under heavy load. As an example, both a resource with an average queue length of 3 and one with a queue length of 6 probably have utilizations close to 100%, while they are obviously very differently loaded.

Comparing the queue-length-based indices with each other, we notice that the exponentially smoothed indices can perform best, but, if the averaging period T is too long (e.g., $\geq$ 20 s), performance may even become worse. Earlier in this paper, we have pointed out that, by averaging the queue lengths, the adverse effect of the high-frequency "noise" in the load can be reduced. This is reflected by improved performance. However, since the system load is changing all the time, averaging over too long a period will emphasize too much the past loads, which have little correlation with the future ones. The optimum averaging interval is clearly dependent upon the dynamics of the workload: the faster the load changes, the shorter the interval should be. In a measurement study of production workloads on a VAX-11/780 running Berkeley UNIX 4.2BSD [17], we found that the average *net change* in CPU queue length in 30 seconds was 2.31, when the average CPU queue length itself was 4.12. This suggests that T should be substantially shorter than 30 seconds.

The performance difference between the cases in which indices based on CPU queue alone are used, and those in which indices consider I/O and memory contention also, is not significant, suggesting that the CPU is the predominant resource in our hosts. We found that the I/O and memory queue lengths were generally much shorter than that of CPU; that is, the former are much less contended for. It should be pointed out that our systems support general computing in a research environment; with other types of workload, e.g., database-oriented one, the contention profile of the various resource types may be substantially different. However, to achieve near-optimal performance, we do not have to consider all the resources in the system, but rather only those with significant contention. We also studied more general forms of linear combinations of queue lengths by using coefficients other than unity, but no significant changes in performance were observed. This, again, is probably due to the dominating influence of the CPU queue.

The load average shown in Table 3 is an index provided by a UNIX command; it is the exponentially smoothed number of processes ready to run, or running, or waiting for some high-priority event (e.g., disk I/O completion). A number of load balancers constructed in the past in the UNIX environment have used the load average as their load index (e.g., [22]). This research shows that significant further improvement can be obtained by using indices that more accurately reflect the current queueing at the resources.

The performances produced by the indices under the more balanced workload 6M is shown in Table 4.

Since the workload is now more balanced and moderate, the amount of improvement in response time is not as much as that under the canonical workload; however, the relative rankings of the indices are quite similar. This suggests that the above analyses of the qualities of the indices and the appropriate values for T remain valid under a more balanced, moderate workload. It is worth noting that, in this case, due to the smaller improvement, using a poor load index (e.g., load average or 60 s CPU utilization) may yield little or no performance improvement.

Finally, we study the influence of the load exchange period P. Figure 2 shows the mean job response time as a function of P, and with the other three factors fixed. The brackets around the data points show their 90% confidence intervals. When the exchange period P is very short, the load information used in job placements is generally up to date, but this positive influence is outweighed by high message overhead. Conversely, if P is too long, the information may get stale, the quality of job placements deteriorates, and performance suffers. The optimal exchange rate depends not only on the communication costs, but also on the workload. Specifically, the rate of load information exchanges should be higher if the job arrival rate is high and the average resource demands of the jobs are low. This was the case in our simulation studies of load balancing in multi-user time-sharing systems [8]. It is remarkable, however, that substantial performance gains are still achieved with an exchange period as long as 60 seconds. At that point, it becomes quite possible that multiple jobs are transferred during the period to a host that used to be lightly loaded, and actually make it overloaded. This form of system instability is called *host overloading* [8]. Thus, it seems that a load balancing system can tolerate some host overloading without suffering substantial performance degradation.

Table 4. Measured performance with various indices
(6M workload, $P = 10$ s)

Load Index	Resp. Time	Improv.	Std. Dev.	Improv.
NoLB (no Load bal.)	49.5 ±0.27	---	72.4	---
inst. CPU ql	42.3 ±0.79	14.5%	61.4	15.2%
4 s avg CPU ql	39.9 ±0.63	19.4%	54.0	25.4%
4 s CPU + I/O + Mem ql	36.5 ±0.91	26.3%	51.0	29.6%
20s CPU + I/O + Mem ql	45.2 ±0.89	8.7%	63.8	11.9%
60s CPU + I/O + Mem ql	47.1 ±1.34	4.9%	67.7	6.5%
60 s load average	47.9 ±1.12	3.2%	73.1	-1.0%
10 s CPU utilization	44.0 ±1.97	11.1%	60.9	15.9%
60 s CPU utilization	48.6 ±1.34	1.8%	68.3	5.7%

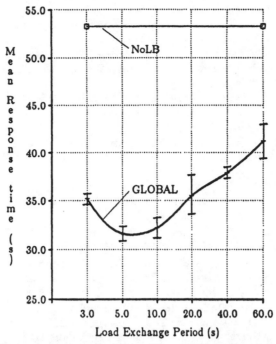

Figure 2. Mean process response time under various load exchange periods P (Canonical workload, load index 4 s CPU+I/O+Mem ql).

5. CONCLUSIONS

The empirical study of load indices described in this paper was motivated by the conjecture that performance improvements due to load balancing are heavily dependent on the quality of the load index used. Measurement results seem to support this conjecture. Two families of load indices based on resource queue length and utilization, respectively, were studied, and the former was found to be able better to represent the load, thereby yielding better performance. Averaging the queue lengths over a short interval (up to about 10 seconds) produced significant improvement over the instantaneous values, but using too long an averaging interval reduced the responsiveness of the index to load changes. Some advantage was found in using a linear combination of queue lengths instead of using the CPU queue length alone, but the improvement was very small due to the dominating role of the CPU in our systems.

In Section 1, we identified four criteria for determining the goodness of a load index. An exponentially smoothed linear combination of resource queue lengths can meet these criteria reasonably well: the queue length is an accurate measure of a resource's load, and smoothing over a short interval into the past gives predictive capabilities to the value of the index, as well as stability against the noise in the load waveform. Queue-length-based load indices also appear to be more adaptable to a heterogeneous environment, but more studies are needed to substantiate this conjecture.

Our results support indices compatible with the one proposed in [1], as they can be seen as degenerate forms of that index. However, the comparisons performed in this study are far from being complete. We decided to use the same load balancing algorithm for all the indices, so that the qualities of the load indices may be directly comparable. On the other hand, the algorithm limited the varieties of load indices that could be studied. We demonstrated, using a particular set of workloads and in a particular computing environment, that linear combinations of resource queue lengths may be good load indices. No proof, however, is offered that they are the best.

REFERENCES

[1] D. Ferrari and S. Zhou, "A Load Index for Dynamic Load Balancing," Proc. 1986 Fall Joint Computer Conference, Dallas, TX, pp. 684-690, November 4-6.

[2] M. Livny and M. Melman, "Load Balancing in Homogeneous Broadcast Distributed Systems," Proc. ACM Computer Network Performance Symposium, pp. 47-55, April 1982.

[3] Y. Chow and W. Kohler, "Models of Dynamic Load Balancing in a Heterogeneous Multiple Processor System," IEEE Trans. Comp. Vol. C-28, No.5, pp. 354-361, May 1979.

[4] D. Eager, E. Lazowska, and J. Zahorjan, "A Comparison of Receiver-Initiated and Sender-Initiated Dynamic Load Sharing," Performance Evaluation, Vol.6, No.1, pp. 53-68, April 1986.

[5] D. Eager, E. Lazowska, and J. Zahorjan\\"Dynamic Load Sharing in Homogeneous Distributed Systems," IEEE Trans. Soft. Eng., Vol.SE-12, No.5, pp. 662-675, May 1986.

[6] K. Lee and D. Towsley, "A Comparison of Decentralized Load Balancing Policies in Distributed Systems Characterized by Bursty Job Arrivals," Proc. 1986 SIGMETRICS Conference, pp. 70-77, May 1986.

[7] Y. Wang and R Morris, "Load Balancing in Distributed Systems," IEEE Trans. Comp. Vol.C-34, No.3, pp. 204-217, March 1985.

[8] S. Zhou, "A Trace-Driven Simulation Study of Dynamic Load Balancing," Tech. Rept No. UCB/CSD 87/305, September 1986, also submitted for publication.

[9] R. Alonso, "Query Optimization in Distributed Databases through Load Balancing," Ph.D thesis, also as Tech Report, UCB/CSD 86/296, Computer Science Division, University of California, Berkeley, June 1986.

[10] A. Ezzat, "Load Balancing in NEST: A Network of Workstations," Proc. 1986 Fall Joint Computer Conference, Dallas, TX, pp. 1138-1149, November 4-6.

[11] K. Hwang, W. Croft, G. Goble, B. Wah, F. Briggs, W. Simmons, and C. Coates, "A UNIX-based Local Computer Network with Load Balancing," IEEE Computer, Vol.15, No.4, pp. 55-66, April 1982.

[12] A. Hac, "Load Balancing Algorithms for Distributed Systems," presentation at the Univ. of Calif., Berkeley, April 3, 1987

[13] W. Leland and T. Ott, "Load-balancing Heuristics and Process Behavior," Proc. Performance '86 and ACM SIGMETRICS Conf on Measurement and Modeling of Computer Systems, pp. 54-69, May 1986.

[14] S. Zhou and D. Ferrari, "An Experimental Study of Load Balancing Performance," To appear, Proc. Inter. Conf. on Distributed Systems Principles, Berlin, September, 1987, also as Tech. Report, UCB/CSD 87/336, Computer Science Division, Univ. of Calif., Berkeley, January 1987.

[15] R. Bryant and R. Finkel, "A Stable Distributed Scheduling Algorithm," Proc. 2nd International Conf. on Distributed Computing Systems, pp. 314-323, 1981.

[16] M. Carey, M. Livny, and H. Lu, "Dynamic task allocation in a distributed database system," Proc. 5th International Conference on Distributed Computing Systems, Denver, May 1985.

[17] S. Zhou, "An Experimental Assessment of Resource Queue Length as Load Indices," Proc. Winter USENIX Conference, Washington, D.C., pp. 73-82, January 21-24, 1987.

[18] S. Zhou, "Predicting Job Resource Demands: a Case Study in Berkeley UNIX," in preparation.

[19] W. Joy, "An Introduction to the C Shell," Computer Science Division, University of California, Berkeley, November 1980.

[20] W. Joy, E. Cooper, R. Fabry, S. Leffler, K. McKusick, and D. Mosher, "4.2BSD System Manual," Computer Systems Research Group, University of California, Berkeley, July 1983.

[21] K. McKusick, M. Karels, and S. Leffler, "Performance Improvements and Functional Enhancements in 4.3 BSD," Proc. Summer USENIX Conference, June 1985, Portland, OR, pp. 519-531.

[22] B. Bershad, "Load Balancing with Maitre d'," Tech Report, UCB/CSD 85/276, Computer Science Division, University of California, Berkeley, December 1985.

The Influence of Different Workload Descriptions on a Heuristic Load Balancing Scheme

Thomas Kunz

Abstract—This paper discusses load balancing heuristics in a general-purpose distributed computer system. To minimize the mean response time of a task, every new task is scheduled to be executed either locally or at a remote host, depending upon the current load distribution. We implemented a task scheduler based on the concept of a stochastic learning automaton on a network of Unix workstations. The used heuristic and our implementation are shortly discussed. Creating an artificial, executable workload, a number of experiments were conducted to determine the effect of different workload descriptions. These workload descriptions characterize the load at one host and determine whether a newly created task is to be executed locally or remotely. Six one-dimensional workload descriptors have been examined. Also, two more complex workload descriptions were considered. The best results were obtained with a relatively simple workload description, the number of tasks in the run queue per host. Using more complex workload descriptions, in contrast, did not improve the mean response time, as compared to the best single workload descriptor.

Index Terms—Distributed systems, heuristics, load balancing, stochastic learning automata, workload descriptions.

I. INTRODUCTION

THE advantages of a distributed computer system over a single powerful general-purpose computing facility are multiple, for example: availability, extensibility, and increased overall performance. In order to make use of these advantages, efficient algorithms for the system-wide control of resource sharing are needed. One especially important resource is processor power. In a general-purpose computing facility, each host (processing unit) has to execute a number of tasks. The scheduling problem consists in determining the host at which a specific task is to be executed such that a system-wide function is optimized. Possible global goals are minimizing the mean response time of all tasks, the costs of executing the tasks, etc. This paper concentrates on heuristic load balancing algorithms, because finding the optimal solution has shown to be NP-complete in general; see Price and Krishnaprasad [7] or Stramm and Berman [14]. Efficient optimal algorithms exist only for special cases, like Stone's algorithm for assigning tasks to a system of two or three processors. This algorithm requires that the complete knowledge of the behavior of a task (e.g., run costs and interprocessor communication costs) is available (see [13]).

Manuscript received September 18, 1990; revised February 6, 1991. Recommended by E. Gelenbe.

The author was with the University of Illinois at Urbana-Champaign, Urbana, IL 61801. He is now with the Institut for Theoretical Computer Science, Technical University Darmstadt, 6100 Darmstadt, Germany.

IEEE Log Number 9100233.

Global task scheduling heuristics have been proposed in a number of articles. These heuristics differ with regard to the characteristics of the underlying network, the information required to make a scheduling decision, considered constraints, used performance criteria, and the design choices as discussed by Casavant and Kuhl [1]. We impose the following requirements upon a scheduler for a general-purpose distributed computer system:

1) no assumptions about the underlying network (e.g., topology, homogeneity, etc.);
2) no *a priori* knowledge about incoming tasks;
3) dynamic, physically distributed, and cooperative scheduling;[1]
4) mean response time of a task as performance criteria.

In any specific case, other requirements may prove to be more important. However, in general, those schedulers with the above-mentioned characteristics are best suited for a general-purpose distributed computer system. Among the reviewed heuristics, those proposed in [5], [9], and [11] come closest in fulfilling these requirements.

One important characteristic of a load-balancing scheme is the workload description used to characterize the load of a single host. Most schedulers reported in the literature use the number of tasks in the run queue as a workload descriptor. This descriptor seems to be an important workload characteristic and one obvious advantage of it is the simplicity of its measurement. However, an ongoing area of research is the impact of more sophisticated workload descriptions.

Although intuitively it may seem obvious that the use of more sophisticated workload descriptions may only improve the overall performance, this is not necessarily the case. More sophisticated descriptions are typically more difficult to measure and to broadcast, thereby increasing the scheduling overhead. Eager *et al.* [2], for example, noticed in their experiments, using different kinds of scheduling algorithms, that extremely simple load-sharing policies using small amounts of information perform nearly as well as more complex policies that utilize more information.

The research reported here examined the effects of experimenting with different ways of characterizing the workload of a single host. The reported results have been collected by running experiments with an implemented scheduler. This scheduler is based on the concept of a stochastic learning automaton, as described in Mirchandaney and Stankovic [5]. The next section describes this heuristic and our implemented scheduler. Section III discusses the general setup of our exper-

---

[1] As defined by Casavant and Kuhl [1].

Reprinted from *IEEE Trans. on Software Eng.*, vol. 17, no. 7, July 1991, pp. 725–730.

iments and Section IV reports the results of these experiments. Six one-dimensional and two more complex workload descriptors have been examined. Our goal was to identify which workload description would result in the lowest mean response time of a task, creating an artificial, executable workload. The paper ends with a summary of our findings and discusses their implication.

II. THE LOAD BALANCING HEURISTIC

A. The Implementation

A scheduler based on the heuristic described in [5] was implemented in C on five Sun 3/50 workstations connected by Ethernet. All Suns are diskless, sharing a common file server. Because all workstations are homogeneous and all files are equally accessible from each host due to the implemented network file system (NFS), executing a task on a remote host only requires transferring the appropriate command to this host.

A copy of the scheduler runs at each workstation. This copy decides where locally created tasks are to be executed. It also receives requests from other copies to execute one of their tasks. No tasks are executed at a remote host as long as the local host is underloaded. If the local host is overloaded, newly arriving tasks are executed at a remote host according to the heuristic described below. If all hosts are overloaded, remote task execution is suppressed because no performance gains are possible. In this case, locally created tasks will be executed locally.

B. The Heuristic

1) An Extended Stochastic Learning Automaton: The algorithm is based upon the concept of a stochastic learning automaton as described in [5], [6], and [12]. Such an automaton serves the purpose of finding optimal actions out of a set of possible actions. Possible actions for our scheduler are of the form "execute a task at host x," where host x is a remote host. A stochastic automaton attempts to solve this problem in the following way. A probability for the selection of an action is attached to all possible actions. Originally, all these probabilities are equal, since nothing is known about the optimality of each action. One action is selected at random and the response of the environment to this action is observed. Based on this response the action probabilities are changed. The way in which the action probabilities are updated is determined by a learning scheme. The next time an action is to be selected, the updated action probabilities are used and the whole procedure is repeated.

This general scheme has been extended in [5], where the notion of automaton states is introduced. The automaton as described above uses only one probability vector (one probability for each action). An automaton with multiple states uses multiple probability vectors for the selection of actions. When a scheduling decision is to be made, one of these vectors is selected and used as described above. Since every automaton state is uniquely associated with a certain probability vector,

we will use the terms "automaton state i" and "probability vector i" as synonyms.

The network-wide state determines in which automaton state the scheduler will work. This network wide state is determined by passing status information of the form "host i is underloaded/overloaded" between all hosts. To determine the appropriate automaton state, a mapping between the status information and the automaton states/probability vectors is defined. In our experiments, a scheduler with 4 states (on a network of five hosts) was used. The mapping between the observed network-wide state and the internal automaton state was defined as follows. Host $i(i = 0, \cdots, 4)$ successively scans the received status information for hosts $i + j + 1 \bmod 5(j = 0, \cdots, 3)$ until an underloaded host is found. If host $i + j + 1 \bmod 5$ is the first underloaded host, the probability vector j will be used in making a placement decision. According to [12], this mapping leads to a stable behavior of the scheduler.

2) The Load Threshold: Each host periodically broadcasts its status (underloaded or overloaded) to all other hosts. To be able to determine this status, the value of a specified workload descriptor is measured and compared to a given threshold. A host is considered overloaded when the measured workload exceeds the threshold. Determining the optimal threshold value is not trivial and depends on the network wide load (see [8]).

3) The Learning Process: The stochastic learning automaton aims to learn the best actions for each automaton state to improve the performance of the scheduler. That is, the action probability for remotely executing a task at an underloaded host is increased and/or the action probability for remotely executing a task at an overloaded host is decreased. The goodness of an action is evaluated at the remote host and is transmitted to the local scheduler copy as a binary measure of goodness (selected action was good/bad). The way in which the action probabilities are updated is defined by the learning scheme used, which can be described by the following high-level description. Let $p_j(n)$ denote the probability for choosing action j at time n. Then $p_j(n + 1)$ denotes the same probability at time $n + 1$. Assume action i was chosen at time n. The probabilities $p_j(n)$ are updated in the following way:

for Reward update :

$$p_j(n + 1) = p_j(n) - f[p_j(n)], \quad j \neq i$$
$$p_i(n + 1) = p_i(n) + \sum f[p_j(n)]$$

for Penalty update :

$$p_j(n + 1) = p_j(n) + g[p_j(n)], , \quad j \neq i$$
$$p_i(n + 1) = p_i(n) + \sum g[p_j(n)]$$

where f and g are reward and penalty functions, respectively. The learning scheme reported in [5] and used in our implementation uses the following reward and penalty functions:

$$f[p_j(n)] = A * p_j(n), \quad 0 < A < 1$$
$$g[p_j(n)] = B/(r - 2) - B * p_j(n), \quad 0 < B < 1$$

where r is the number of hosts in the network and A and B are constants. The functions f and g should be non-negative for the whole range from 0 to 1 to fit the intuitive impressions of reward and penalty. However, non-negativity is not a necessary requirement, as penalty function g demonstrates.

4) Summarized Description of the Scheduler: The scheduler can be summarized as follows. Each copy periodically checks the status (overloaded or underloaded) of its host and broadcasts this status to all other copies. Using this status information, each copy determines the overall network-wide state it is observing and maps this network-wide state to one of its automaton states. Each time a task is to be executed remotely, a remote host is randomly chosen, using the probability vector currently in effect (i.e., the probability vector associated with the current automaton state). The selected remote copy evaluates the goodness of the selection, depending on the status of its local host. This evaluation (called measure of goodness) is sent back to the scheduling copy, which updates the appropriate probability vector. After a while, each copy learns the best actions for different observed network-wide states.

C. Preliminary Tuning Results

The scheduler contains a number of parameters that influence its performance. In a number of tuning runs, values for these parameters have been established and have been used in the subsequently reported experiments. Status information is measured and broadcasted every 8 s. The learning scheme uses a reward constant A of 0.25 and a penalty constant B of 0.3. Other experiments not reported here examine the influence of different numbers of automaton states, the behavior of the scheduler under different network sizes, and the use of different learning schemes.

III. The Test Environment

A. Generating a Workload

The tasks that are scheduled are invocations of a single generic task. Since this task is written especially for our experiments and does not represent a sample of a production workload, we are using an executable artificial workload approach as defined in [3]. We chose this approach because artificial workloads are easier to reproduce and have a greater flexibility than natural workloads. The main disadvantage of artificial executable workloads is that they require the computer network to be totally dedicated to each experiment. This is the main reason why we ran our experiments at nighttime.

Tasks are created in real-time, that is, at the time they are needed, by a driver. The driver is a program which generates task parameters from given distributions. Then it passes these values to a copy of the task and simulates the tasks' arrival.

B. The Artificial Workload Model

To emphasize the differences between workload descriptors, we developed a workload model which characterizes a workload along the following four dimensions:

1) arrival process;
2) processing time requirements;

TABLE I
Workload Model Data

host #	μ	λ	%b	%i	%c	om (Kbytes)
1	0.102	0.224	0.355	0.350	0.295	55.218
2	0.036	0.196	0.053	0.789	0.158	58.066
3	0.020	0.210	0.048	0.952	0.000	58.631
4	0.130	0.176	0.159	0.062	0.779	61.630
5	0.140	0.209	0.097	0.171	0.732	57.832

3) I/O-volume;
4) memory requirements.

The generic task has the following structure. First, the required memory is allocated. Second, a specified amount of data sentences are read from a file. Third, a processing phase is simulated by repeatedly reading/writing 256 consecutive bytes into the allocated memory space for a specified amount of time. The starting position for each of these byte blocks is selected randomly. Fourth, the data sentences are written back into the file and the memory is de-allocated.

A specific probability distribution underlies each of these dimensions. The task arrival process follows a Poisson distribution with arrival rate μ. The processing times are exponentially distributed with processing rate λ. The I/O volume is determined by multiplying the processing time with a constant, depending on the class of the task. We distinguish three different classes: balanced (b), I/O-bound (i), and CPU-bound (c). Balanced tasks read/write 50 data sentences per processing second, I/O-bound tasks 300 sentences and CPU-bound tasks 5 sentences. Tasks are assigned randomly to these classes; the percentage of tasks in each class varies from host to host. The required memory (m) also depends on the processing time. Tasks with a processing time less than 4 s require memory in the range from 0.25 to 50.25 Kbytes. Longer tasks have memory requirements in the range from 0.25 to 200.25 Kbytes. Table I shows the significant values for our new workload model.

Creating a good workload is far from simple. Leland and Ott [4] or Svensson [15] discuss some problems with modeling real workloads. Even though we do not claim that our workload is a typical one, we feel confident that our artificial workload allows us to observe some interesting differences with regard to the used workload descriptor.

C. Conducting a Single Experiment

A single experiment runs for 36 min, leaving enough learning time for the scheduler. Each task writes his response time (measured as the difference between creation time and end of execution time)[2] in a result file. Mean response times for each host and for the experiment as a whole were calculated from these result files. Each run was repeated two more times, varying the random number seed for the selection of a scheduling action. Thus our results are independent from a specific learning sequence. The results reported in this paper are the mean response times over all three runs.

---

[2] For tasks that are created at one host but executed at another host, clock differences between the hosts had to be taken into account.

TABLE II
No Load Balancing

host #	# tasks	φ response time (seconds)
1	220	19.098
2	076	13.980
3	042	12.509
4	276	45.012
5	299	34.402

TABLE III
Using the Number of Tasks in the Run Queue as Workload Descriptor

threshold	φ response time (seconds)
0	15.217
1	13.576
2	14.602

TABLE IV
Using the Size of the Free Memory as Workload Descriptor

threshold	φ response time (seconds)
400	18.255
450	16.710
500	17.993

TABLE V
Using the CPU Context Switch Rate as Workload Descriptor

threshold	φ response time (seconds)
15	25.609
20	17.613
25	16.127
30	14.747
35	15.762
40	17.566

TABLE VI
Using the System Call Rate as Workload Descriptor

threshold	φ response time (seconds)
250	15.242
300	14.702
350	14.423
400	16.307
450	16.514

IV. Experimental Results

First, we examined whether there is any simple workload descriptor which is better suited for the implemented scheduler than the commonly used number of tasks in the run queue. In a second step, we considered more than one descriptor at the same time, describing the workload of a host by using a combination of multiple descriptors.

A. Single Workload Descriptors

The criteria used to evaluate the scheduler versions is the mean response time of all tasks. To obtain a reference point for the performance of different scheduler versions, we generated our artificial workload without trying to balance the load. The mean response time for the whole system of five hosts is 31.215 s. The results for each individual host are presented in Table II.

Unix provides a large amount of statistical information that can be used to describe a workload. We successively used the following descriptors.

- number of tasks in the run queue;
- size of the free available memory;
- rate of CPU context switches;
- rate of system calls;
- 1-min load average;
- the amount of free CPU time.

For every workload descriptor used, we expected the mean response time first to decrease and then to increase with increasing threshold value. For lower threshold values, executing tasks remotely is frequently suppressed because the whole network is characterized as being overloaded. For higher threshold values, the loads at different hosts become more and more imbalanced before an attempt is made to balance the load.

The first workload descriptor examined was the number of tasks in the run queue. Table III shows the obtained results.

Task scheduling improves the performance of the distributed system by as much as 56.5% (13.576 s versus 31.215 s) for our workload model. The performance resulting from the use of the other descriptors will be compared to the lowest observed mean response time of 13.576 s for a threshold value of 1.

The second workload descriptor we examined is the size of the free memory list in Kilobytes. Table IV shows our experimental results as we varied the threshold value.

The results show that this workload descriptor also improves the performance of the distributed system over the "no load balancing" case. The lowest mean response time, however, is with 16.710 s over 3 s or 23% worse than when using the number of tasks in the run queue as workload descriptor.

As a third workload descriptor we selected the CPU context switch rate. This rate is provided by Unix as the average context switch per second over the last 5 s. We obtained the results reported in Table V when using this descriptor to measure a host's load.

The use of the CPU context switch rate as a workload descriptor also improves the performance of the distributed system. The best performance we obtained lies with 14.747 s for a threshold value of 30 between the performances we achieved with the first two workload descriptors.

The fourth workload descriptor we examined is the rate of system calls. This rate, again, is provided by Unix as the average system call rate per second over the last 5 s. Table VI shows our experimental results.

The best obtained performance is 14.423 s for a threshold value of 350. This is clearly better than the "no load balancing" case. Compared to the first three workload descriptors, the use of the system call rate as a workload descriptor resulted in the second best performance so far.

TABLE VII
Using the 1-Min Load Average as Workload Descriptor

threshold	ϕ response time (seconds)
0.8	22.915
1.2	18.988
1.6	17.932
2.0	19.364
2.4	20.288

TABLE VIII
Using the Idle CPU-Time as Workload Descriptor

threshold	ϕ response time (seconds)
0	16.501
2	15.692
5	16.255
10	16.469
15	16.841

TABLE IX
Using a Single Workload Descriptor

workload descriptor	optimal threshold	ϕ response time (seconds)
number of tasks in the run queue	1	13.576
system call rate	350	14.423
CPU context switch rate	30	14.747
percentage of idle CPU-time	2	15.692
size of the free memory (Kbytes)	450	16.710
1-min load average	1.6	17.932

The fifth workload descriptor is the 1-min load average. This descriptor, measuring the average number of tasks in the run queue during the last minute, is similar to our first descriptor, the number of tasks in the run queue. However, the new descriptor measures the load of a host over a period of time rather than at a certain point of time. Also, whereas the number of tasks in the run queue is always an integer value, the new descriptor is a real value, potentially allowing for a finer tuning of our implementation. By varying the threshold value, we obtained the results reported in Table VII.

The use of this workload descriptor results in the worst performance so far, despite its similarity to the best workload descriptor. The load average is calculated over a relatively long time period. The scheduled tasks spend less than 20 s on the average in the distributed system. Our workload descriptor averages the number of tasks in the run queue over the last minute, a period more than three times as long. Therefore the descriptor value is influenced by tasks that are no longer in the system, reflecting the current load in an inaccurate way. Using a load average over a shorter time period may result in a better scheduler performance. However, Unix does not provide such a descriptor. Using the 1-min load average as a workload descriptor may be more appropriate when the tasks run longer.

The last workload descriptor we examined is the amount of idle CPU-time between two successive load measurements. We measured this descriptor as the percentage of idle time compared to the total period length. A host is considered overloaded when this percentage is less than or equal to a given threshold. We obtained the performance results reported in Table VIII.

In contrast to the other workload descriptors, the percentage of idle CPU-time is influenced by the used status update period length. However, experiments varying this period length showed no improvements in the resulting mean response time.

Table IX summarizes our results using a single workload descriptor. For each workload descriptor used, it shows the optimal threshold value and the resulting mean response time

of the distributed computer system. All examined workload descriptors lower the mean response time, compared to the "no load balancing" case. The best workload descriptor in our experiments is the number of tasks in the run queue. Using this descriptor results in a performance of 13.576 s for a threshold value of 1. The worst workload descriptor is the 1-min load average for the reasons discussed above. Its usage resulted in a mean response time of 17.932 s for a threshold value of 1.6. This is over 4 s or 32% worse than the performance resulting from the use of the best descriptor.

B. Combination of Workload Descriptors

So far, we characterized the workload of a host by using a one-dimensional workload descriptor. We also examined the combination of multiple descriptors to measure a host's load. N workload descriptors $d_1, d_2, \cdots, d_n$ can be combined in a number of ways to determine the status of a host. One possibility is to define a function $f(d_1, d_2, \cdots, d_n)$ of the form $f(d_1, d_2, \cdots, d_n) = a_1 * d_1 + a_2 * d_2 + \cdots + a_n * d_n$. A host may then be characterized as being overloaded whenever the value of this function exceeds a given threshold. The coefficients a_i have two different functions. First, they are necessary to equalize the different workload descriptors (the number of tasks in the run queue, for example, is typically less than 10, the size of the free memory list is somewhere in the range between 200 and 1000 Kbytes). Second, they determine the relative impact of different descriptors on the function value.

We pursued two different approaches to combine multiple workload descriptors. In one scheduler version, the status of a host is determined by an "OR combination" of multiple descriptors. A host is considered overloaded whenever at least one of the workload descriptors has a value above its respective threshold. In another scheduler version, a host is considered overloaded only when all descriptors have values above their respective threshold (an "AND combination").

A complete examination of workload descriptor combinations is beyond the scope of this paper. In two experiments, we combined the best two workload descriptors, the number of tasks in the run queue (descriptor 1), and the system call rate (descriptor 2), and observed the resulting performance. The goal of these experiments was to provide a first idea about the relative merits of combining multiple workload descriptors rather than to determine an optimal workload characterization.

Our experimental results indicate that no performance improvements over the scheduler versions using a one-dimensional workload descriptor can be obtained. An "OR combination" of two workload descriptors shows the following characteristic. The lowest measured mean response time of 14.41 s is considerably higher than the one that can be obtained when using descriptor 1 as workload descriptor. 14.41 s is measured when the threshold for descriptor 2 is set to a high value, thereby decreasing its influence on a host's reported workload status. The second scheduler version, using an "AND combination" of workload descriptors, showed better performance results. The lowest mean response time of 13.68 s was obtained when setting the two threshold values to the optimal values reported in Table IX. Still, even this scheduler version is not superior to a scheduler using the best one-dimensional workload descriptor.

V. Conclusions

We implemented a scheduler based upon the concept of a stochastic learning automaton on a network of Unix workstations. Using this implementation, we conducted a number of experiments to examine the influence of workload descriptions on the performance of the implemented scheduler. First, we examined one-dimensional workload descriptors. All examined workload descriptors lower the mean response time of tasks, compared to the "no load balancing" case. We found that the best single workload descriptor is the number of tasks in the run queue. The use of the worst workload descriptor, the 1-min load average, resulted in an increase of the mean response time of over 32%, compared to the best descriptor. Therefore, while the use of all descriptors results in shorter mean response times, the selection of a workload descriptor is nontrivial when minimal mean response times are desired.

In a second step, we combined the best two workload descriptors, the number of tasks in the run queue and the system call rate, to measure a host's load. Our experimental results indicate that no performance improvements over the scheduler versions using a one-dimensional workload descriptor can be obtained. Although these two experiments do not cover the area of combined workload descriptors comprehensively, we conclude that major performance improvements can hardly be expected when more complex workload descriptors are used.

Acknowledgment

The author would like to thank T. P. Ng, who constantly provided valuable support and advice.

References

[1] T. L. Casavant and J. G. Kuhl, "A taxonomy of scheduling in general-purpose distributed computing systems," *IEEE Trans. Software Eng.*, vol. 14, pp. 141–154, Feb. 1988.
[2] D. L. Eager, E. D. Lazowska, and J. Zahorjan, "Adaptive load sharing in homogeneous distributed systems," *IEEE Trans. Software Eng.*, vol. SE-12, pp. 662–675, May 1986.
[3] D. Ferrari, *Computer Systems Performance Evaluation*. Englewood, Cliffs, NJ: Prentice-Hall, 1978.
[4] W. E. Leland and T. J. Ott, "Load-balancing heuristics and process behavior," ACM 0-89791-184-9/86/0500-0054.
[5] R. Mirchandaney and J. A. Stankovic, "Using stochastic learning automata for job scheduling in distributed processing systems," *J. Parallel Distributed Comput.*, pp. 527–551, 1986.
[6] K. S. Narendra and M. A. L. Thathachar, "Learning automata—A survey," *IEEE Trans. Syst., Man, Cybern.*, pp. 323–334, July 1974.
[7] C. C. Price and S. Krishnaprasad, "Software allocation models for distributed systems," in *Proc. 5th Int. Conf. on Distributed Computing*, 1984, pp. 40–47.
[8] S. Pulidas, D. Towsley, and J. Stankovic, "Design of efficient parameter estimators for decentralized load balancing policies," Tech. Rep. 87–79, Univ. of Massachusetts, Amherst, Aug. 1987.
[9] J. A. Stankovic, "The analysis of a decentralized control algorithm for job scheduling utilizing Bayesian decision theory," in *Proc. 1981 Int. Conf. on Parallel Processing*, 1981, pp. 333–340.
[10] ——, "Simulations of three adaptive, decentralized controlled, job scheduling algorithms," *Comput. Networks*, pp. 199–217, June 1984.
[11] ——, "An application of Bayesian decision theory to decentralized control of job scheduling," *IEEE Trans. Comput.*, pp. 117–130, Feb. 1985.
[12] ——, "Stability and distributed scheduling algorithms," *IEEE Trans. Software Eng.*, vol. SE-11, pp. 1141–1152, Oct. 1985.
[13] H. S. Stone, "Multiprocessor scheduling with the aid of network flow algorithms," *IEEE Trans. Software Eng.*, pp. 85–93, Jan. 1977.
[14] B. Stramm and F. Berman, "Communication-sensitive heuristics and algorithms for mapping compilers," in *Proc. ACM SIGPLAN Conf. on Parallel Programming: Experiences with Applications, Languages and Systems*, July 1988, pp. 222–234.
[15] A. Svensson, "History, an intelligent load sharing filter," in *Proc. 10th Int. Conf. on Distributed Computing Syst.*, May 1990, pp. 546–553.

Thomas Kunz received a joint diploma in computer science and business administration from the Technical University of Darmstadt in 1990.

From 1988 to 1989 he was with the University of Illinois at Urbana-Champaign. Currently, he is a Faculty Research Assistant in computer science at the Technical University of Darmstadt, working in the area of distributed systems. His research interests are in load balancing, distributed object-oriented programming languages, and parallel and distributed debugging.

About the Authors

Behrooz Shirazi

Behrooz Shirazi is an associate professor of computer science and engineering at the University of Texas at Arlington (UTA) and was on the faculty of computer science and engineering at Southern Methodist University before joining UTA. His research interests include parallel and distributed systems, dataflow computing, cache designs, task partitioning and scheduling, and computer architecture. His research has been sponsored by grants from NSF, DARPA, AFOSR, Texas Instruments, E-Systems, Mercury Computer Systems, and the State of Texas Advanced Technology Program. Shirazi received his PhD degree in Computer Science from The University of Oklahoma in 1985. He is currently on the editorial board of the Journal of Parallel and Distributed Computing. He is the principal founder of the IEEE Symposium on Parallel and Distributed Processing and has served on the program committee of many international conferences. He is currently an IEEE Distinguished Visitor as well as an ACM Lecturer.

Ali R. Hurson

Ali R. Hurson is on the computer engineering faculty at The Pennsylvania State University. He has published over 140 technical papers in areas including computer architecture, parallel processing, dataflow architectures, database systems and database machines, and VLSI algorithms. He has served as guest coeditor of special issues of *Proceedings of the IEEE* (on supercomputing technology,) *Journal of Parallel and Distributed Computing* (on load balancing and scheduling,) and the *Journal of Integrated Computer-Aided Engineering* (on multidatabase and interoperable systems.) He is the coauthor of the IEEE Computer Society Press tutorials *Parallel Architectures for Database Systems, Multidatabase Systems: An Advanced Solution for Global Information Sharing,* and *Parallel Architectures for Data/Knowledge Base Systems.* His research for the past 14 years has been directed toward the design and analysis of general- and special-purpose computer architectures. Hurson cofounded the IEEE Symposium on Parallel and Distributed Processing and has been active in various IEEE/ACM Conferences by giving tutorials on dataflow processing, database management systems, supercomputer technology, data/knowledge-based systems, scheduling and load balancing, and parallel computing. He served as a member of the IEEE Computer Society Press Editorial Board and is an IEEE Distinguished speaker.

Krishna Kavi

Krishna M. Kavi is a professor of computer science and engineering at the University of Texas at Arlington. He currently serves as the Program Director for the Operating Systems and Systems Software program in the division of Computer and Computation Research at the National Science Foundation. He received the BS in electrical engineering from the Indian Institute of Science and the MS and PhD in computer science from Southern Methodist University. Kavi has published widely on computer architecture, performance and reliability analyses, formal specification and program verification, and real-time systems. He edited the IEEE Computer Society Press tutorial on *Real Time Systems: Abstractions, Languages, and Design Methodologies.* He is on the editorial board of the IEEE Transactions on Computers. He was an IEEE Computer Society Distinguished Visitor and an editor of the Computer Society Press. He is a senior member of the IEEE and a member of the ACM.

503

Printed in the United States
15558LVS00001B/27-120